APPROACHING DEMOCRACY

Larry Berman

University of California at Davis

Bruce Allen Murphy

The Pennsylvania State University

with
Oliver H. Woshinsky

University of Southern Maine

PRENTICE HALL, Upper Saddle River, New Jersey 07458

Library of Congress Cataloging-in-Publication Data

Berman, Larry.
    Approaching democracy/Larry Berman, Bruce Allen Murphy.
        p.   cm.
    Includes bibliographical references and index.
    ISBN 0-13-033457-X
        1. United States—Politics and government.   2. Democracy—United
States.   I. Murphy, Bruce Allen.   II. Title.
    JK274.B524   1996
    320.473—dc20   95-36407
                                                                    CIP

Acquisitions Editor: Michael Bickerstaff
Editor-in-Chief: Nancy Roberts
Editorial Director: Charlyce Jones Owen
Development Editor: Sharon Balbos
Project Manager: Rob DeGeorge
Copy Editor: Carole Brown
Cover Design: Maria Lange
Interior Design: Delgado Design, Inc.
Buyer: Bob Anderson
Photo Researchers: Dallas Chang and Joelle Burrows
Photo Editor: Lorinda Morris-Nantz
Editorial Assistant: Anita Castro
Cover Art: J. W. Stewart

© 1996 by Prentice-Hall, Inc.
Simon & Schuster/A Viacom Company
Upper Saddle River, New Jersey 07458

Printed in the United States of America

10 9 8 7 6 5 4 3 2 1

ISBN 0-13-033457-X

Prentice-Hall International (UK) Limited, *London*
Prentice-Hall of Australia Pty. Limited, *Sydney*
Prentice-Hall Canada Inc., *Toronto*
Prentice-Hall Hispanoamericana, S.A., *Mexico*
Prentice-Hall of India Private Limited, *New Delhi*
Prentice-Hall of Japan, Inc., *Tokyo*
Simon & Schuster Asia Pte. Ltd., *Singapore*
Editora Prentice-Hall do Brasil, Ltda., *Rio de Janeiro*

TO OUR OWN TEACHERS,
AND THEIR EXTENDED LEGACY—
OUR STUDENTS.

BRIEF CONTENTS

PART I FOUNDATIONS OF AMERICAN
DEMOCRACY

1 Approaching Democracy 1
2 The Founding: America's First Approach to
Democracy 24
3 The Constitution 54
4 Federalism 96

PART II INSTITUTIONS OF AMERICAN
DEMOCRACY

5 Congress 134
6 The Presidency 176
7 The Judiciary 216
8 The Bureaucracy 260

PART III PROCESSES OF AMERICAN
DEMOCRACY

9 Public Opinion 296
10 Political Parties 330
11 Participation, Voting, and Elections 364
12 Interest Groups 404
13 The Media 440

PART IV LIBERTIES AND RIGHTS IN
AMERICAN DEMOCRACY

14 Civil Liberties 472
15 Civil Rights and Political Equality 508

PART V POLICYMAKING IN AMERICAN
DEMOCRACY

16 Public Policy: Regulation and Social Welfare 546
17 Economic Policy 580
18 Foreign Policy 612

APPENDICES

CONTENTS

BOXED FEATURES XIV
PREFACE XVI
ABOUT THE AUTHORS XXVII

PART I FOUNDATIONS OF AMERICAN DEMOCRACY

CHAPTER 1 APPROACHING DEMOCRACY 1

CASE STUDY: THE BACK OF THE BUS 1
INTRODUCTION: AMERICA'S APPROACH TO DEMOCRACY 2
    Democracy as an Evolutionary Process 3
    Forming a Picture of Democracy 6
DEMOCRACY DEFINED 6
    Direct and Indirect Democracy 6
THE ROOTS OF DEMOCRACY IN AMERICA 9
THE IDEALS OF DEMOCRACY 10
    Freedom and Equality 10
    Order and Stability 13
    Majority Rule and Protection of Minority Rights 14
    Participation 15
THE ELEMENTS OF DEMOCRACY 18
APPROACHING DEMOCRACY 21

CHAPTER 2 THE FOUNDING: AMERICA'S FIRST APPROACH TO DEMOCRACY 24

CASE STUDY: SHAYS'S REBELLION 25
INTRODUCTION: THE ROAD TO DEMOCRACY 26
THE SEEDS OF AMERICAN DEMOCRACY 27
    Government by Compact 27
    The Massachusetts Bay Colony 30
    Proprietary Colonies and Their Legislatures 30
    Colonial Governors 32
    Social Contract Theorists 32
FIRST MOVES TOWARD A UNION 35
REBELLION: CAUSES AND CONSEQUENCES 36
    The Sugar and Stamp Acts 36
    No Taxation without Representation 37

Colonial Williamsburg

The Townshend Revenue Acts 38
The Boston Massacre 39
Committees of Correspondence 39
The Boston Tea Party 40
REVOLUTION AND THE STIRRINGS OF A NEW
    GOVERNMENT 41
The First Continental Congress 42
"The Shots Heard 'Round the World" 42
Common Sense 43
The Second Continental Congress 45
The Declaration of Independence 45
THE FIRST NEW GOVERNMENT: A CONFEDERATION
    OF STATES 46
The Articles of Confederation (1781–89) 47
THE NEED FOR A MORE PERFECT UNION 50
THE FOUNDERS: PAVING THE WAY FOR AP-
    PROACHING DEMOCRACY 50

CHAPTER 3 THE CONSTITUTION 54

CASE STUDY: THE
    BATTLE OVER
    THE ERA 55
INTRODUCTION:
    THE CON-
    STITUTION
    AND DE-
    MOCRACY 56
THE CONSTITUTIONAL CONVENTION 58
The Task 58
The Participants 59
The Major Players 60
Plans for a New Government 62
Debate and Compromise: The Turning Point
    of the Convention 65
The Issue of Slavery 68
The Nature of the Presidency 69
THE MIRACLE: RESULTS OF THE CONVENTION 71
A Republican Form of Government 71
The Governmental Powers 72
The Articles of the Constitution 75
RATIFICATION: THE BATTLE FOR THE
    CONSTITUTION 78
The Federalist Papers 79

Federalists versus Antifederalists 80
Ratification by Way of Compromise: A Bill of
    Rights 82
Politics the Old-fashioned Way: A Look at the
    Battle for Ratification 82
Adoption of the Bill of Rights 85
APPROACHING DEMOCRACY THROUGH
    CONSTITUTIONAL CHANGE 86
The Amendment Process 86
Updating the Constitution by Judicial
    Interpretation 90
Updating the Constitution in Response to Political
    and Social Change 90
THE CONSTITUTION: TWO HUNDRED YEARS OF
    APPROACHING DEMOCRACY 92
The Constitution of the United States of America

CHAPTER 4 FEDERALISM 96

CASE STUDY: SPEED LIMITS: WHO DECIDES? 97
INTRODUCTION: FEDERALISM AND
    DEMOCRACY 98
FEDERALISM DEFINED 99
Federalism: Advantages and Disadvantages 100
FEDERALISM IN THE CONSTITUTION 102
The Triad of Powers 103
How the Triad Works 106
The Resulting Division of Powers 106
THE DEVELOPMENT OF FEDERALISM 110
Debating the National Role: Hamilton versus
    Jefferson 110
Asserting National Power: *McCulloch* v.
    Maryland 111
Expanding National Power Further: *Gibbons* v.
    Ogden 111
Asserting State Power: Nullification 112
Developing a System of Separation: Dual
    Federalism 112
Creating a Cooperative System: The New Deal
    Era 113
Seeking Uniformity: Federalism in the Post–New
    Deal Era 115
USING FEDERAL GRANTS TO CHANGE SOCIETY:
    FEDERALISM SINCE 1930 117

Jasper Johns, *Three Flags*, 1958; Whitney Museum of American Art

Types of Federal Grants 117

Meeting National Needs During the Era of Cooperative Federalism (1930–63) 120

The Era of Creative Federalism (1963–68) 120

Richard Nixon's New Federalism (1969–74) 124

Creative Federalism Returns under Jimmy Carter (1977–80) 125

Ronald Reagan's "New New Federalism" (1981–88) 125

The Bush Years (1988–92) 128

Bill Clinton and the Future of Federalism (1992–?) 128

CONTEMPORARY FEDERALISM AND APPROACHING DEMOCRACY 130

PART II INSTITUTIONS OF AMERICAN DEMOCRACY

CHAPTER 5 CONGRESS 134

CASE STUDY: CREATING AMERICORPS 135

INTRODUCTION: CONGRESS AND DEMOCRACY 136

THE STRUCTURE AND POWERS OF CONGRESS 137

What the Framers Had in Mind 138

Limits on Congress's Power 140

THE MEMBERS OF CONGRESS 141

Who Are the Members? 141

Congressional Districts 143

Delegates versus Trustees 145

The Incumbency Factor 148

The Public's View of Congress 149

THE CONGRESSIONAL ODYSSEY: HOW A BILL BECOMES A LAW 151

HOW CONGRESS ORGANIZES ITSELF 155

Congressional Leadership 155

Congressional Committees: The Laboratories of Congress 158

Why Does Congress Use Committees? 159

The Rise of Subcommittees 161

CONGRESS IN SESSION 163

The Rules and Norms of Congress 163

How Members Make Voting Decisions 167

Obstacles to Passage of a Bill 170

THE FUNCTIONS OF CONGRESS: OVERSIGHT AND BUDGET CONTROL 171

THE '94 ELECTIONS AND THE FUTURE OF CONGRESS 172

CONGRESS AND APPROACHING DEMOCRACY 172

CHAPTER 6 THE PRESIDENCY 176

CASE STUDY: WATERGATE AND THE PRESIDENCY 177

INTRODUCTION: THE PRESIDENCY AND DEMOCRACY 178

THE CONSTITUTIONAL DESIGN 180

Who Is Eligible to Be President? 181

The Presidential Powers 181

THE FUNCTIONAL ROLES OF THE PRESIDENT 186

TWO VIEWS OF THE EXECUTIVE POWER 189

EXPANDING PRESIDENTIAL POWER: MOVING BEYOND THE CONSTITUTION 193

The Doctrine of Inherent Powers and Presidential Character 193

Congress Delegates Power to the President 195

Conducting Foreign Policy and Making War 196

Going Public 199

THE INSTITUTIONALIZED PRESIDENCY 202

The White House Office 203

The Executive Office of the President 206

The Cabinet 207

The Vice Presidency 208

THE CHALLENGES OF PRESIDENTIAL LEADERSHIP 209

THE PRESIDENCY AND APPROACHING DEMOCRACY 212

CHAPTER 7 THE JUDICIARY 216

CASE STUDY: THE COP AND THE BARTENDER 217

INTRODUCTION: THE COURTS AND DEMOCRACY 218

THE ORIGINS AND DEVELOPMENT OF JUDICIAL POWER 219

Creating the "Least Dangerous Branch" 219

Marbury v. *Madison:* The Source of Judicial Power 220

Judicial Review: The Court's Ultimate Power 221

Other Powers of the Supreme Court 221

Independence of the Judiciary 223

HOW THE AMERICAN COURT SYSTEM IS
    ORGANIZED 224
    Types of Courts 224
    Organization of the Federal Courts 226
COURT APPOINTMENTS: THE PROCESS AND THE
    POLITICS 227
    The Supreme Court Appointment Process 227
    The Impact of Presidential Appointments on the
        Supreme Court 234
    Staffing the Lower Federal Courts 235
HOW THE SUPREME COURT OPERATES 238
    Selecting Cases 238
    The Solicitor General: The "Tenth Justice" 240
    The Process of Deciding Cases 240
    Marshaling the Court: The Opinion-Drafting
        Process 243
    The Role of Law Clerks 244
    The Announcement of Opinions 244
    The Chief Justice's Role 246
ANALYZING SUPREME COURT DECISIONS 246
    The Use of Precedent and Other Legal
        Factors 246
    The Mindset of Individual Justices 247
    Judicial Character 250
    Looking at the Whole Court and Voting
        Blocs 251
    Limitations of Court Analysis 251
THE RESULTS OF SUPREME COURT
    DECISIONS 251
    Implementing Supreme Court Decisions 252
    Public Opinion and the Supreme Court 254
THE COURTS AND APPROACHING
    DEMOCRACY 256

CHAPTER 8 THE BUREAUCRACY 260

CASE STUDY: ENGINEERING
    A DISASTER 261
INTRODUCTION: BUREAU-
    CRACY AND DEMOC-
    RACY 262
SOME BACKGROUND ON
    THE BUREAUCRACY 263
    Bureaucracy Defined 263
    Growth of the Federal Bureaucracy 265
    Evolution of the Bureaucracy: Creating a Civil
        Service 269
MEETING THE BUREAUCRACY 272
    What the Bureaucracy Does 272
    The Structure of the Federal Bureaucracy 277

Constraints on the Bureaucracy and Bureaucratic
    Culture 278
BUREAUCRATIC ACCOUNTABILITY 280
    Presidential Control 281
    Congressional Oversight 283
    The National-Security Bureaucracy 284
WHAT THE PUBLIC THINKS OF THE
    BUREAUCRACY 286
    Are the Criticisms Justified? 288
REFORMING THE BUREAUCRACY 289
BUREAUCRACY AND APPROACHING
    DEMOCRACY 293

PART III PROCESSES OF AMERICAN
DEMOCRACY

CHAPTER 9 PUBLIC OPINION 296

CASE STUDY: LANDON DEFEATS
    ROOSEVELT? 297
INTRODUCTION: PUBLIC OPINION AND
    DEMOCRACY 298
WHAT IS PUBLIC OPINION? 299
MEASURING PUBLIC OPINION 301
POLITICAL SOCIALIZATION 304
    The Role of Family 304
    Schooling 306
    Peers 307
    Television 307
    Political Socialization: A Lifelong
        Experience 308
SOCIAL VARIABLES THAT INFLUENCE OPINION
    FORMATION 308
    Class and Income 309
    Race and Ethnicity 309
    Religion 310
    Region 311
    Gender 311
AMERICAN POLITICAL CULTURE 313
    Core Values 313
    Political Ideology 315
    Culture and Lifestyle 318
THE STATE OF AMERICAN PUBLIC OPINION 318
    Political Awareness and Involvement 318
    How Are Political Opinions Formed? 321
STABILITY AND CHANGE IN PUBLIC
    OPINION 322
FROM PUBLIC OPINION TO PUBLIC POLICY 325

PUBLIC OPINION AND APPROACHING
    DEMOCRACY 326

CHAPTER 10 POLITICAL PARTIES 330

CASE STUDY: THE FREE-
    DOM DEMOCRATS 331
INTRODUCTION:
    POLITICAL PARTIES
    AND DEMOC-
    RACY 332
DEFINING PARTY BY
    FUNCTION 333
A BRIEF HISTORY OF THE AMERICAN PARTY
    SYSTEM 336
    The First Party System (1790s–1820s) 337
    The Second Party System (1820s–1850s) 338
    The Third Party System (1850s–1890s) 339
    The Fourth Party System (1896–1932) 339
    The Fifth Party System (1932–present) 340
    A Sixth Party System? 341
WHY A TWO-PARTY SYSTEM? 343
    Institutional Factors 343
    Cultural Factors 344
    Party Identification 345
MINOR PARTIES 345
PARTY ORGANIZATION 349
    Parties at the Grassroots 349
    National Party Organization 351
NOMINATING A PRESIDENT: PARTIES AND
    ELECTIONS 353
    Nominating Candidates 353
    Reforming the Nominating Process 356
THE PARTY IN GOVERNMENT 358
    The Importance of Party Ideology 359
POLITICAL PARTIES AND APPROACHING
    DEMOCRACY 361

CHAPTER 11 PARTICIPATION, VOTING, AND
    ELECTIONS 364

CASE STUDY: THE MOTOR-VOTER LAW 365
INTRODUCTION: POLITICAL PARTICIPATION AND
    DEMOCRACY 366
WHO PARTICIPATES 367
VOTING 369
    A Brief History of the Vote in the
        United States 369
    Voter Turnout 371
    Who Votes? 375

A Voting Trend: Direct Democracy 377
EXAMINING VOTING CHOICE 378
    Party 378
    Candidate Appeal 379
    Policies and Issues 379
    Campaigns 381
OTHER FORMS OF POLITICAL
    PARTICIPATION 381
    Campaign and Election Activities 381
    Information Seeking 382
    Protest, Civil Disobedience, and Violence 383
ELECTIONS AND CAMPAIGNS 385
    Congressional Elections 386
    Presidential Elections 387
    Campaigning for President 392
    Voters and Presidential Elections 395
    Money and Elections 397
PARTICIPATION, VOTING, ELECTIONS, AND
    APPROACHING DEMOCRACY 400

CHAPTER 12 INTEREST GROUPS 404

CASE STUDY: REFORMING HEALTH CARE? 405
INTRODUCTION: INTEREST GROUPS AND
    DEMOCRACY 406
INTEREST GROUPS: A TRADITION IN AMERICAN
    POLITICS 407
    What Is an Interest Group? 408
    A Long History of Association 409
    Interest Group Functions 412
TYPES OF INTEREST GROUPS 414
    Economic Interest Groups 416
    Public Interest Groups 418
    Government Interest Groups 420
    Other Interest Groups 421
CHARACTERISTICS OF INTEREST GROUPS 422
    Interest Group Membership 423
    Other Characteristics of Interest Groups 424
INTEREST GROUP STRATEGY 425
    Lobbying 425
    Lobbying Tactics 426
    Grassroots Activity 427
    Using the Courts and the Executive Branch 431
POLITICAL ACTION COMMITTEES 432
REGULATION OF INTEREST GROUPS 434
ASSESSING THE IMPACT OF INTEREST
    GROUPS 435
INTEREST GROUPS AND APPROACHING
    DEMOCRACY 437

CHAPTER 13 THE MEDIA 440

CASE STUDY: "THE VOICE
OF BAGHDAD" 441
INTRODUCTION: THE
MEDIA AND
DEMOCRACY 442
THE EMERGENCE OF
THE MEDIA 444
Newspapers 444
Magazines 447
Radio 448
Television 450
New Media Technologies 450
FUNCTIONS OF THE MEDIA 451
Surveillance 452
Interpretation 452
Socialization 454
LIMITS ON MEDIA FREEDOM 455
Regulating the Media 455
Prior Restraint versus the Right to Know 457
IDEOLOGICAL BIAS AND MEDIA CONTROL 458
Media Pluralism 459
A Liberal "Media Elite"? 460
Media Ownership and Control 461
Media–Government Symbiosis 461
THE MEDIA AND ELECTIONS 462
Press Coverage 462
Polling 462
Talk Shows 465
Television and Presidential Elections 465
Political Advertising 467
Infomercials 469
THE MEDIA AND APPROACHING
DEMOCRACY 469

PART IV LIBERTIES AND RIGHTS IN
AMERICAN DEMOCRACY

CHAPTER 14 CIVIL LIBERTIES 472

CASE STUDY: FLAG BURNING AND THE FIRST
AMENDMENT 473
INTRODUCTION: CIVIL LIBERTIES AND
DEMOCRACY 474
Civil Liberties and Civil Rights 475
Studying Civil Liberties 475
A HISTORY OF THE APPLICATION OF CIVIL LIBER-
TIES TO THE STATES 476

The Fourteenth Amendment 477
The "Clear and Present Danger" Test 480
The Beginnings of Incorporation 481
Selective Incorporation of the Bill of
Rights 481
FREEDOM OF RELIGION 482
Establishment of Religion 483
Free Exercise of Religion 486
FREEDOM OF SPEECH 487
Political Speech 488
Public Speech 488
Symbolic Speech 489
FREEDOM OF THE PRESS 489
Prior Restraint 490
Libel 491
Obscenity 491
THE RIGHTS OF DEFENDANTS 492
The Fourth Amendment 494
The Fifth and Sixth Amendments 498
IMPLIED RIGHTS 500
Privacy 501
Abortion 502
The Right to Die 504
CIVIL LIBERTIES AND APPROACHING
DEMOCRACY 505

CHAPTER 15 CIVIL RIGHTS AND POLITICAL
EQUALITY 508

CASE STUDY: INTEGRATING YONKERS 509
INTRODUCTION: CIVIL RIGHTS AND DEMOCRACY
510
Defining Civil Rights 511
ESTABLISHING CONSTITUTIONAL
EQUALITY 512
The Dred Scott Case 512
The Civil War and Reconstruction 513
CREATING LEGAL SEGREGATION 514
Separate but Equal? 515
The Disenfranchisement of Black Voters 515
ESTABLISHING LEGAL EQUALITY 516
The White House and Desegregation 516
Seeking Equality in the Schools 518
State and Federal Responses 519
THE CIVIL RIGHTS MOVEMENT 520
The Civil Rights Acts 522
The Supreme Court and Civil Rights 523
De Jure versus De Facto Discrimination 524
AFFIRMATIVE ACTION 527

Nam June Paik, *Fin de Siecle II*, 1989; Whitney Museum of American Art.

Seeking Full Equality: Opportunity or
Result? 527
Affirmative Action in the Reagan/Bush Era 531
Whither Civil Rights? 532
WOMEN'S RIGHTS 533
Two Steps Forward, One Step Back 534
The Struggle for Suffrage 535
The Road to Equality 535
Seeking Equality through the Courts 536
CIVIL RIGHTS AND OTHER MINORITIES 540
Hispanic Americans 540
Native Americans 541
Americans with Disabilities 542
CIVIL RIGHTS AND APPROACHING
DEMOCRACY 542

PART V POLICYMAKING IN AMERICAN
DEMOCRACY

CHAPTER 16 PUBLIC POLICY: REGULATION
AND SOCIAL WELFARE 546

CASE STUDY: POLITICS AND AIDS 547
INTRODUCTION: PUBLIC POLICY AND
DEMOCRACY 548
WHAT IS PUBLIC POLICY? 549
TYPES OF POLICIES 549
Reflexive Policies 550
Original Policies 550
Symbolic-reflexive Policies 551
Symbolic-original Policies 551
THE POLICYMAKING PROCESS 552
Getting onto the Public Agenda 553
Getting onto the Formal Agenda 556
Implementing the Policy 557
Evaluating a Policy's Impact 558
Terminating a Policy 559
Mature Policies: Continuation, Refinement, and
Feedback 560
THE POLITICS OF POLICYMAKING 560
Federalism: Fragmentation and Multiple
Actors 561
Logrolling and Pork Barrel Policies 561
Iron Triangles and Issue Networks 561
POLICYMAKING IN ACTION 562
Regulatory Policy 563
Social-Welfare Policy 568
PUBLIC POLICY AND APPROACHING
DEMOCRACY 575

CHAPTER 17 ECONOMIC POLICY 580

CASE STUDY: THE 1994
BUDGET 581
INTRODUCTION:
ECONOMIC POLICY
MAKING AND
DEMOCRACY 582
THE GOALS OF ECONOMIC
POLICY 583
THEORIES OF DOMESTIC ECONOMIC POLICY 586
Laissez-faire Economics 586
Keynesian Economics and Active Fiscal
Policy 586
Monetarism 588
Supply-side Economics and the Shrinking Role of
Government 590
THE POLITICS OF THE FEDERAL BUDGET 592
Preparing the Budget: The President Proposes,
Congress Disposes 592
How the Budget Is Prepared 592
Balancing the Budget 594
Taxing and Spending Policies 597
TAXATION 597
Sources of Tax Dollars 598
Tax Reform 600
GOVERNMENT SPENDING 601
Balancing the Books: The Deficit and the National
Debt 603
THE POLITICS OF INTERNATIONAL ECONOMIC
POLICY 606
The GATT Uruguay Round 607
The NAFTA Treaty 607
U.S.–Japanese Trade Negotiations 608
THE NEED FOR INTERNATIONAL POLICY
COORDINATION 608
ECONOMIC POLICY AND APPROACHING
DEMOCRACY 610

CHAPTER 18 FOREIGN POLICY 612

CASE STUDY: THE "JUST CAUSE" 613
INTRODUCTION: FOREIGN POLICY AND
DEMOCRACY 614
A HISTORY OF AMERICAN FOREIGN POLICY 615
Isolation and Regionalism 616
World War I 617
World War II 618
Globalism and the Cold War 620
The Post–Cold War Era and into the Future 625

THE CONSTITUTION AND FOREIGN POLICY 628
THE PRESIDENT IN FOREIGN POLICY
    MAKING 629
CONGRESS AND THE FOREIGN-POLICY
    PROCESS 630
    Constraints on Congress 631
    Congressional Oversight of Foreign
        Policy 631
THE EXECUTIVE BUREAUCRACY IN FOREIGN POLI-
    CY MAKING 634
    The Department of State 635
    The Department of Defense 635
    The National Security Council 636
    The CIA and Intelligence Gathering 638
    The Agencies behind Economic Policy
        Making 639
    The Agents behind Policy Making 640

DEMOCRATIC CHECKS ON FOREIGN POLICY 641
FOREIGN POLICY AND APPROACHING
    DEMOCRACY 644

APPENDICES A-1
THE DECLARATION OF INDEPENDENCE A-1
FEDERALIST NO. 10 (1787), JAMES MADISON A-3
FEDERALIST NO. 51 (1788), JAMES MADISON A-5
PRESIDENTS AND CONGRESSES, 1789–1995 A-8
JUSTICES OF THE U.S. SUPREME COURT, 1789–1995
    A-11

GLOSSARY G
REFERENCES R-1
PHOTO CREDITS P-1
INDEX TO REFERENCES IR-1
INDEX I-1

BOXED FEATURES

Thinking Critically

What Would You Do If You Were in King George's Shoes?	44
The Nation's Founders—Were They Really Demigods?	63
Cleaning Up the Environment: Who Pays?	126
The President versus the Court	184
You Be the Judge	245
Cutting Government Spending	290
Should the Whole World Watch?	445
Immigrants and Public Policy	554
Balancing the Budget: Who Wins, Who Loses?	595

The Struggle for Equality

"Slavery Was Once a Tradition"	13
Abigail Adams—the First Feminist?	51
Are Women's Rights Protected by the Constitution?	79
Old Enough to Fight, Old Enough to Vote	116
Race-Based Redistricting	146
From First Lady to First Woman	204
Thurgood Marshall and the Fight for Integration	230
Diversity in the Federal Bureaucracy	274
Forty Years after Brown	525
Racial Harmony in the Military	619

Global View

Freedom and Democracy	4
The U.S. Constitution: A Gift to All Nations	93
Federalism under Fire: Will Canada Survive?	104
Democracy and Judicial Independence	222
The French Bureaucracy	286
Generational Change in Israel	305
Go, Italy!	347
Approaching Democracy in Mexico	396
The Case of Japanese Rice Farmers	418
The Meaning of Silence	500
Achieving Racial Equality in South Africa	517
Inequality in an Egalitarian Society	569
Coping with Taxes	598

Political Participation in the Electronic Age   **17**
Congress on TV   **162**
president@white-house.gov   **200**
Judicial Politics and the Media   **232**
Participation via E-mail   **383**
From Grassroots to Astroturf   **430**
Talk Radio   **449**
Spreading Hate   **539**
Patrolling the Information Superhighway   **639**

OTHER FEATURES

A Few Minutes with a Minuteman   **48**
The Setting: Life at the Convention   **60**
Some Metaphors for Studying Federalism   **100**
House Speaker Newt Gingrich: A Man with a Vision   **156**
Life of a Legislator   **169**
The People's Court?   **255**
Bureaucratic Doublespeak   **280**
The Presidential Pollster   **303**
The Political Spectrum: Left, Right, and Center   **316**
The Major American Parties   **340**
Realignment versus Dealignment   **342**
The Drive for Congressional Term Limits   **388**
Media Masters   **464**
Does Freedom of Religion Include the Right to Pray in School?   **485**
Inconsistencies in the Death Penalty   **493**
Chipping Away at Affirmative Action   **530**
Reforming Health Care   **576**
The "Political Business Cycle"   **585**
Other Recent Tax Reform Alternatives   **602**
McNamara's War   **624**

PREFACE

Our deep commitment to undergraduate teaching led us to write this textbook; our abiding respect for democracy led us to our theme. In *Approaching Democracy* we join you in an exploration of the American experiment in self-government. As your guides we know that democracy has evolved over time in America and that the United States today has become a beacon for those seeking freedom and democratic government.

As teachers we have taken our title and theme from Vaclav Havel, a former dissident Czechoslovakian playwright once imprisoned by that country's Communist government and later elected its president. Addressing a joint session of the U.S. Congress on February 21, 1990, Havel noted that with the collapse of the Soviet Union, millions of people from Eastern Europe were involved in a "historically irreversible process," beginning their quest for freedom and democracy. And it was the United States of America that represented the model, "the way to democracy and independence," for these newly freed peoples. But Havel put his own spin on the notion of American democracy as a model. "As long as people are people," Havel explained, "democracy, in the full sense of the word, will always be no more than an ideal. In this sense, you too are merely approaching democracy. But you have one great advantage: you have been approaching democracy uninterruptedly for more than 200 years, and your journey toward the horizon has never been disrupted by a totalitarian system."

This image of an America "approaching democracy" inspired the theme for our textbook. We write about American democracy as a work still in progress. Democracy as a system has become increasingly popular. The number of democracies worldwide, while just a handful of nations a century ago, increased from three or four dozen in the 1950s to 114 by the end of 1995. Clearly, we live in an age of democratic aspiration, and for many who seek to achieve democracy the United States represents a model of the democratic process. The United States has been making efforts to approach democracy for over two hundred years. In spite of its astonishing diversity and the consequent potential for hostility and violence, the United States has moved closer to the democratic ideal than nearly any other country, certainly more than any other country of comparable heterogeneity and size. But the process of approaching democracy is a continual one.

We believe in the linkage between democracy and education. Indeed, everything about democracy is educational; it's about ideas, history, and politics. From civil rights to civil liberties; from the powers of Congress to the *Contract With America;* from judicial review to presidential vetoes; from motor voter to campaign finance reform; from affirmative action to immigration; from national health care to balanced budgets; from talk radio to C-SPAN—democracy is educational because it involves discussion, be it speaking from wooden soap boxes or on the Internet. Ideas drive democracy!

We also believe the world in which we live has validated the democratic experiment in self-government. The triumph of democratic ideas in Eastern Europe was inspired by America's example of freedom and democracy. We are the laboratory for those who have broken from their totalitarian pasts and for those who dream of doing so. Nevertheless, democracy did not come easy to

Americans. Like Vaclav Havel, we believe that the United States is still approaching democracy. America's 200-year experience with government has been a lesson in the gradual expansion (and occasional restriction) of liberty, justice, and freedom. The chapters in this textbook examine the American approach to democracy, sorting out the ideals, studying the institutions, processes, and policies, and analyzing the dilemmas and paradoxes of freedom.

In this text we examine the elements and ideals of democracy in detail to help students understand how American government works. These democratic institutions and traditions—free elections, competitive political parties, a free press, interest groups, an independent judiciary, civilian control of the military, and a commitment among citizens to a set of democratic ideals—are indispensable for the preservation of democracy.

We also believe in the future. As teachers and parents we believe your generation can shape the future. In his memorable Gettysburg Address, Abraham Lincoln observed that in the "new birth of freedom," ours was "government of the people, by the people, for the people" and that it "shall not perish from the earth." This is your greatest challenge as a citizen and student. People need not be a consequence of their past; *Approaching Democracy* may help shape your future. We can all work to safeguard democratic accomplishments by understanding our government and participating in it. By being informed American citizens, you can help American democracy continue to flourish.

THE ORGANIZATION OF THIS TEXT

Part I presents the foundations of American Government. Our theme is introduced in Chapter One, where we identify the goals and elements which can be used to evaluate America's approach to democracy. Throughout this book we ask that you think about how closely modern Americans have approached the ideals of true democracy. Political scientists are constantly trying to define and categorize democracy, using one or another set of objective indicators. While there is still healthy debate about the nature of these indicators, in Chapter One we introduce you to a few widely-accepted "elements of democracy." These institutional elements will serve as markers to identify progress toward the democratic ideals discussed earlier. Only political systems that meet or at least approach those ideals can be considered democratic; by using these elements, you can discuss the strength and robustness of American democracy or any democracy.

In Chapter 2, "The Founding," we offer a unique look over the decades of experimentation leading to the creation of the world's oldest continuous constitutional system. You will see that democracy took root early in America. Drawing on shared commitment to individual security and the rule of law, the frontier governments provided models on which the constitutional structure of American government was eventually built. To trace the development of American democracy from the early settlements to an independent United States, this chapter explores the ideas that inspired the American Revolution, including the impact of European political thinking on the founding and the struggle for independence from England.

From the Revolution sprang not just a declaration but a national identity rooted in the embodiment of the words "life, liberty, and the pursuit of happiness." The Founders shared a commitment to classical democratic ideals. From this they built a foundation from which the country could approach democracy. In Chapter 3, "The Constitution," we look at the participants and their discussions in that remarkable gathering which produced the Constitution of the United States. We will see how, not unlike the discussions that raged over the proposed Equal Rights Amendment to the Constitution, the debates raged in the states over the ratification of the Constitution itself. Finally, we examine how the Constitution has changed over the last two hundred years and take a look at the debates over what the Constitution has come to mean to Americans. The Framers made it possible for the government they created to approach democracy. The Constitution was an imperfect document but a highly elastic one that over the years and in response to the times would become more democratic. The paradox of this foundation of American democracy, then, is that a Constitution written in secret by representatives of less than 5 percent of the population established processes that have led to the most openly democratic nation in the world.

Chapter 4 explores federalism and the relationship between the power of the national government and the needs and powers of the state governments. Federalism is one of America's unique contributions to democratic theory and republican government. Only by understanding how the system works can you come to understand how it has helped the United States to approach democracy. But, as you will learn, the precise nature of this governmental relationship has been a matter for ongoing debate, most recently during the 1995 attempts to implement the terms of the Republican *Contract With America*.

Part II explores the institutions of American Democracy. Chapter 5 on Congress proved to be one of most challenging to write because of the historic changes resulting from the 1994 election and the actions of the 104th Republican Congress involving the *Contract With America*.

Although most members of Congress are sincere, honest, hard-working, and dedicated to doing a difficult job under trying circumstances, the institution in which they serve continually faces criticism. When Congress works in a deliberative fashion, as it was meant to, it is labeled as obstructionist; when it approves most of the president's programs, it is accused of being a rubber stamp. And if it takes strong actions on its own, it is accused of overreaching its powers. Clearly the truth lies somewhere among these extremes. Above all, we need to recognize that Congress was designed as a consensus-building institution in a nation where public preferences are frequently contradictory.

Chapter 6 on the presidency illustrates one of the greatest challenges facing the Constitutional Framers—a strong leader was needed to energize the government but this powerful president can simultaneously represent a significant threat to the democratic nature of the government. The great paradox of the presidency is that nowhere in America is there an office that unites power as well as purpose to help Americans approach their democratic potential, yet also poses the most serious potential threats to democracy.

The Supreme Court becomes the focus of Chapter 7. The most procedurally undemocratic institution in the system (its members are unelected, serve unlimited terms, and work in secrecy) actually increases the democratic nature of human rights and balances the powers of the other institutions through judicial review. In this chapter we examine the developing powers of the Supreme Court, the organization of the American court system, judicial appointments, and how cases are appealed to and then decided by the Supreme Court. We also look at how judges arrive at decisions and, perhaps most important, how those decisions affect both public policy and democracy.

Over the years, the willingness of the Supreme Court and the lower federal courts to use the full extent of their power has varied based on the nature of the legal issues, the number of cases heard, the political situation, and who the justices are. In recent years, the federal courts have been more willing to defer to Congress and the states. Will this continue, or will the courts seek out a new direction and role? The actions of the judiciary in America's democracy have powerful implications for both government and individual rights.

Finally, Chapter 8 examines the Bureaucracy. Part of the suspicion Americans feel about their bureaucracy comes from the realization that most government agencies function, most of the time, with little or no restraint from the American people. Indeed, the bureaucracy has been called the "fourth branch of the government," as powerful as Congress, the president, and the Supreme Court, but operating without the regular elections that keep at least the first two institutions responsive to public opinion.

Despite their problems, bureaucracies are necessary and have come to characterize modern industrialized societies. Large-scale bureaucratic organizations allow for high levels of productivity and the coordination of government programs such as road building, air traffic control, environmental management, the postal system, and telecommunications. Nevertheless, bureaucracies can pose serious problems in terms of accountability and power.

Part III focuses on the processes of American Government and Democracy. Chapter 9 on public opinion illustrates the means by which the desires, needs, and demands of the American people are translated into action by their government. Public opinion is the keystone of democracy. No government can claim to be the legitimate voice of a people, unless public opinion plays an integral role in the choice of political leaders and the development of public policy. Thus, the gathering of information about public opinion becomes a vital task for a democracy.

Chapter 10 studies the political parties that lie at the heart of democracy. They represent the crucial link between what citizens want and what government does. That's why parties are continually changing, adapting, and adjusting to the new popular forces of their time. They want to stay in touch with the voters—those people from whom they derive support and power—so that they can gain control of government and the policymaking process.

In Chapter 11 we study participation, voting, and elections. For the framers, republican government represented a balance between popular input and deliberative statesmanship. Most government officials would be elected and ultimately accountable to the people. On the other hand, they would be somewhat removed from the immediate expression of popular will. Hence, they could use discretion and deliberation in making public policy. Since the framer's day, the spirit of democratic equality has gained ascendancy over the view that officials should be removed from the immediate winds of public opinion. This development has not been a revolutionary one. It has evolved, often with painful slowness, over the entire course of American history, so that today it is fully ingrained in American political life. And the American people have evolved with it.

It is true that even today millions of Americans forego their democratic rights by failing to take advantage of the many opportunities to participate in the politics of their free society. Nevertheless, it is also true that tens of millions of Americans, regardless of class, race, gender, or ethnic background, do express their political viewpoints and engage in civic activity to protect their interests. The American system presents no legal barriers to full participation by all; it also goes a long way toward maintaining the economic and psychological barriers that still hamper involvement for some. The people's relatively unrestricted ability to participate in political life stands as the best possible evidence that Americans have made enormous progress toward the ideal of a truly democratic society.

In Chapter 12 we examine the subject of interest groups and discover one of the paradoxes of democracy. Interest groups provide a vital link between citizens and public officials. They convey substantive information and public sentiment to policymakers and they provide knowledge about government programs to citizens and assist them in gaining access to these programs. Interest groups even provide the inspiration necessary to stimulate citizen involvement in politics. It remains true that the most powerful, most influential, and most resourceful interests have advantages. Politics is rarely played on a level field. Business and corporate interests far outweigh public interest groups in most power struggles. And, small but powerful interests often gain their ends from government, seemingly at the expense of the public good.

Chapter 13 examines the media, especially the evolution of media technologies and electronic telecommunications as well as the media's coverage of politics. We also explore the process by which members of the media determine what is newsworthy and the ways in which government officials manipulate the media. Throughout the chapter it will be evident that freedom of the press and other media is of fundamental importance in approaching democracy.

Part IV provides a detailed analysis of various issues of civil rights and liberties in American Democracy. Civil liberties are the individual rights that are guaranteed to every citizen by the Bill of Rights and the due process clause of the Fourteenth Amendment. They include the most fundamental rights of Americans, such as freedom of speech and religion. Civil rights are concerned with protection of citizens against discrimination because of characteristics such as gender, race, ethnicity, or disability; they are derived largely from the equal protection clause of the Fourteenth Amendment. Chapter 14 examines the subject of civil liberties, illustrating both how America has approached democracy by extending the Bill of Rights to the states and through the process of Supreme Court interpretations of these rights. Chapter 15 then addresses civil rights and political equality, where we explore how the rights of African Americans, Women, Hispanics, and Native Americans have developed over the years, including groups of people in the political process who were not a part of the Framers' political era.

Part V provides three chapters which address the policymaking process and its consequences. Chapter 16 focuses on public policies of regulation and social welfare. Social welfare policymaking, like regulatory policymaking, has a long political history and faces tremendous challenges. There is no easy formula for providing equal resources for all, a fair chance for all to succeed, and the opportunity for all to flourish financially and personally. How well national policymakers respond to these challenges—and how democratic the policies are—will remain crucial questions as American government continues the process of approaching democracy. Chapter 17 examines federal economic policies and the philosophies which guide these policies. Politicians know very well that they will be rewarded for good economic times and punished for economic downturns. Politics and economics are thus fundamentally intertwined, and it is this linkage, with all of its different variations, that provides the economic signposts on the road that we follow in our continuing approach to democracy. Decisions about taxes, the budget, currency, and government intervention into the economy pose fundamental questions about the fairness of democracy. How can we talk about democracy not merely in political but in economic terms? How fair is our tax system? How democratic is the process through which economic policy is created?

Finally, Chapter 18 addresses the evolution of U.S. foreign policy and the role of the United States in the post-Cold War world, with special attention given to President Clinton's first two years in office. There are really two related challenges for U.S. foreign policy today. First, the U.S. must try to determine a foreign policy course in a complicated and changing international environment, one that involves an appropriate balance of commitments and resources. Second, it must do so within the democratic limits established in the Constitution. Ultimately then, the paramount challenge is how to balance the interests of security and the requirements of democracy.

FEATURES OF THE TEXT

We hope that readers will take advantage of the unique features which are designed to illustrate our theme, approaching democracy. Each chapter begins with a full length chapter opening case study that integrates our theme and lays the groundwork for the material that follows. We have taken special care in selecting cases that provide anchors for the material covered in each chapter.

A series of other boxed features appearing periodically throughout the book will highlight different aspects of the book's theme. The ***Global View*** boxes examine politics from a comparative perspective by looking at the approach to democracy around the world. Here we compare the different features of the American political system to those of other countries around the world. The ***Struggle for Equality*** boxes examine the struggle that many groups have endured, and the people who have served as torches on the road to democracy leading them in their effort to be included in the American democratic experiment. The ***Cutting Edge*** boxes will show how the constantly changing technological and media advances have changed the process of American government as well as student and citizen involvement. At any time you may visit our own ***Approaching Democracy Home Page on the WorldWideWeb.*** Here you will be brought up to date on the week's current events with a special narrative linking these events to our theme and then be directed to a myriad of internet resources on American government. You may also leave us a message or even a question about the book or an assignment. We promise to "reply." You may also utilize our multimedia CD-ROM which includes an interactive study guide, videos, simulations, and text. Despite all of these technological changes, you will be surprised at how many of the issues and the balancing of interests remains the same as in the era when the Framers wrote by the light of a candle. In the ***Thinking Critically*** boxes, we seek to develop the critical analysis powers of students by presenting a series of key incidents or decisions in history and placing you in the position of a decision-maker charged with directing the government at *that* point. A series of other ***General Interest*** boxes discuss numerous valuable political issues that have occupied the country's attention in its present location on the road to democracy. Here we also learn about some of the most intriguing people on the American political scene.

SUPPLEMENTS

Supplements for the Instructor

INSTRUCTOR'S MANUAL   This exceptional resource provides learning objectives, chapter outlines, questions for discussion, activities, and a detailed description of the supplements available for each chapter. The instructor's manual is also available on computer disk in ASCII.
- **3.5" Electronic Instructor's Resource Manual**

STRATEGIES FOR TEACHING AMERICAN GOVERNMENT: A GUIDE FOR THE NEW INSTRUCTOR BY FRED WHITFORD, MONTANA STATE UNIVERSITY This unique guide offers a wealth of practical advice and information to help new instructors face the challenges of teaching American government.

TEST ITEM FILE   This test bank contains over 1,600 multiple choice, true-false, and essay questions including answers and page references to the text.

PRENTICE HALL CUSTOM TEST   This new testing system, a computerized version of the test item file, offers a two-track design for constructing tests: EasyTest for novice users and FullTest for more advanced users. In addition, Prentice Hall Custom Test offers a rich selection of features such as On-Line Testing and an Electronic Gradebook.
- **Windows®**
- **3.5" IBM®**
- **Macintosh®**

PRENTICE HALL TELEPHONE TEST PREPARATION   With this free service, you can select up to 200 questions from the test item file and with one toll-free call, we will mail a master test within 48 hours. Ask your local Prentice Hall representative for details.

AMERICAN GOVERNMENT TRANSPARENCIES, SERIES III AND IV   Two different sets of four-color acetates, reproducing illustrations, charts, and maps taken from the text and outside sources, for a total of over 175 transparencies. Designed in a large type format for lecture settings.
- **Series III**
- **Series IV**

**INSTRUCTOR'S GUIDE TO AMERICAN GOVERNMENT TRANSPARENCIES, SE-
RIES III AND IV**   These manuals provide a description of each transparency,
ideas for incorporating the transparencies into lectures and approximately two
to five questions with each transparency for stimulating class discussion.
- **Series III Instructor's Guide**
- **Series IV Instructor's Guide**

 ABC NEWS/PRENTICE HALL VIDEO LIBRARY   Prentice Hall and
ABC News bring this innovative video collection to your American
government classroom. This video library brings chapter concepts to
life by illustrating them with newsworthy topics and pressing issues.
- **1992 Primaries**
- **1992 Elections**
- **Images in American Government**
- **Issues in American Government**
- **1994 Elections**

**INSTRUCTOR'S GUIDE TO ABC NEWS/PRENTICE HALL VIDEO LIBRARIES:
AMERICAN GOVERNMENT**   This guide provides a brief synopsis and discussion questions for each segment in the video library.

PRENTICE HALL LASERDISCS   The story of American government is vividly illustrated with this exciting technology. This five-disc series contains approximately 500 still images and over four hours of moving images to support the
concepts in the text. Accompanying manuals are provided.
- **1992 Primaries and 1992 Elections**
- **Images in American Government**
- **Issues in American Government**
- **1994 Elections**

Supplements for the Student

STUDY GUIDE   Learning objectives, chapter outlines, a glossary, and practice
tests reinforce information in the text and help students develop a greater understanding of American government and politics.

INTERACTIVE STUDY GUIDE   This interactive software program allows students to test themselves on concepts presented in the text. Multiple choice,
true/false, and fill-in-the-blank questions integrate graphics from the text in a
colorful, visually appealing format. Students receive immediate feedback, including hints and page references to the text as well as chapter objectives and
an on-line glossary.
- **3.5" IBM®**
- **5.25" IBM®**
- **Windows®**
- **Macintosh®**

PRENTICE HALL CRITICAL THINKING AUDIO CASSETTE   A 60-minute cassette
teaches students how to develop their critical thinking and study skills.

THE WRITE STUFF: WRITING AS A PERFORMING AND POLITICAL ART, SECOND EDITION, BY THOMAS E. CRONIN   This brief booklet provides ideas and suggestions on writing in political science.

A GUIDE TO CIVIC LITERACY BY JAMES CHESNEY AND OTTO FEINSTEIN, WAYNE STATE UNIVERSITY   This brief booklet provides ideas and suggestions for students to get involved in politics. It includes nine political activities on topics such as agenda building; coalition building; registering, educating, and mobilizing voters; and increasing accountability.

"THEMES OF THE TIMES" READER FROM *THE NEW YORK TIMES*   Prentice Hall and *The New York Times* have joined forces to bring students a complimentary newspaper supplement containing recent articles pertinent to American government. These articles augment the text material and provide real-world examples. Updated twice a year.

AMERICAN GOVERNMENT SIMULATION GAMES, SERIES III, BY G. DAVID GARSON, NORTH CAROLINA STATE UNIVERSITY   Eight simulations that engage students in various role-playing situations: Bill of Rights; House of Representatives; Presidential Budget; Secretary of State; Supreme Court; Washington Ethics; Crime and Social Policy; and a new simulation for 1996.
- **3.5" DOS**®
- **Windows**®
- **Macintosh**®

***APPROACHING DEMOCRACY* INTERACTIVE CD-ROM**   This CD-ROM version of the text provides students with an interactive American government experience including video, images, simulation, and sound, in addition to the text. The CD-ROM also includes excerpts from Professor Berman's interactive satellite interviews with prominent policy makers who include Speaker of the House Newt Gingrich, Congresswoman Maxine Waters, and Chairman of the Republican National Committee Haley Barbour.
- **Windows**®
- **Macintosh**®

ACKNOWLEDGMENTS

At Prentice Hall we remember with gratitude the early support of Karen Horton, Julie Berrisford, and Maria DeVincenzo. We want to thank our current political science editor, Mike Bickerstaff, for his efforts in bringing the book to completion and for his commitment to the CD-ROM.

We are especially indebted to Rob DeGeorge for all his hard work, understanding, and common sense when it came to moving the book through production.

Rochelle Diogenes, Sharon Balbos, Carolyn Smith, and Susanna Lesan were all involved in development of the book. We especially thank Susanna for being there at the beginning and the end.

Charlyce Jones Owen, Editorial Director, never lost faith in her two authors (or never let us know) and always provided the best motivational talks. Nancy Roberts, Editor in Chief, proved to be a pillar of support and promised us that there really would be a light at the end of the tunnel. She is now correct!

We also wish to thank the following reviewers for their valuable suggestions:

Danny Adkison, Oklahoma State University

John Bloomquist, Lanson Junior College

Christopher J. Bosso, Northeastern University

William Coogan, University of Southern Maine

Douglas Costain, University of Colorado, Boulder

Douglas L. Crane, Dekalb College, South

Frank Davis, Lehigh University

Larry Elowitz, Georgia College

John Ferejohn, Stanford University

Stefan Haag, Austin Community College

Scott J. Hammond, James Madison University

Michael Horan, University of Wyoming

Michael Johnston, Colgate University

William E. Kelly, Auburn University

Dwight Kiel, University of Central Florida

Fred A. Kramer, University of Massachusetts at Amherst

Susan Leeson, Willamette University

Joel Lieske, Cleveland State University

James Meader, Augustance College

J.A. Myers, Marist College

Max Neiman, University of California, Riverside

Richard Pacelle, University of Missouri, St. Louis

Leonard Ritt, North Arizona University

Ron Romine, University of South Carolina, Spartenburg

Denise Scheberle, University of Wisconsin, Green Bay

Robert W. Small, Massasoit Community College

Mary Stuckey, The University of Mississippi

We would also like to thank the following people for their work on specific chapters: David Balaam and Michael Veseth, University of Puget Sound (Ch. 17, Economic Policy); Bob Brown, University of Mississippi (Ch. 16, Public Policy); William Coogan, University of Southern Maine (Ch. 8, Bureaucracy); Patrick Haney, Miami University of Ohio (Ch. 18, Foreign Policy); and Robert J. Waste, California State University at Chico (Ch. 17, Economic Policy). We are especially grateful to Oliver Woshinsky, University of Southern Maine, who contributed greatly to Chapters 9–12.

Larry Berman thanks his colleagues at Davis who were especially helpful for reading early chapter drafts of this book: Edmond Costantini, John Drew Froeliger, John Gates, Emily Goldman, Alexander Groth, Stuart Hill, Scott James, Bruce Jentleson, Miroslav Nincic, Gary Segura, Andrew Skalaban, Jim Spriggs, and Geoffrey Wandesforde-Smith. He also thanks his hard-working research assistants Scott Hill and Nicole Sherbert. He especially acknowledges the substantive contributions of Bill Hughes and Linda Valenty; both provided indispensable support to the project. Larry Berman is indebted to the extraordinary staff at U.C., Davis, especially production word processors Linda Potoski and Kelly Ramos.

Bruce Murphy thanks his colleagues in the Institute for the Arts and Humanistic Studies at Penn State, its directors, George Mauner and Stanley Weintraub, and its amazing staff, Shirley Rader and Sue Reighard, for providing an oasis of continual encouragement, interest in and support of, his work. He would also like to thank the following people for their assistance on various chapters: graduate student and now academic colleague Ken Mash, for his help on the Civil Rights chapter; Professor Bob Harkavy for his help on the foreign policy chapter; research assistants Amy Wilson, Ken Martin, Donna Schilling, Blaine Rummet, and Stefan Tillander, for their help on various chapters. He would also like to thank best-selling Western Civilization textbook author and valued colleague Jackson Spielvogel, as well as the students of the International Cultures Interest House, for their periodic pep talks that this book would finally be done and it would all be worth it. Thanks, also, to the amazing staff of Pattee Library, especially the government documents and reference sections, who never failed to provide immediate answers to countless perplexing problems.

Since no two scholars can know all of the fields in the discipline of political science, we would both like to thank all of our colleagues for their many academic contributions upon which we drew for the writing of this book.

We would both like to thank the generation of students at University of California, Davis, and Penn State, for their constant flow of unique questions and ideas, their continual interest in this subject, and their constant complaints about the other books we assigned them, all of which helped to spur us initially to write this book and improved the outcome.

Finally, but most importantly, we would both like to thank our wives, Nicole Berman and Carol Lynn Wright, and our children Scott and Lindsay (for Larry) and Emily and Geoffrey (for Bruce) for their patience in waiting for two besieged authors to surface and for the return of their houses from the sea of papers lying around. Finally, we can say "we are done. . . . until the next edition!" See you then.

Larry Berman   *Bruce Allen Murphy*
Davis, California   *Port Matilda, PA*

ABOUT THE AUTHORS

Larry Berman is a nationally recognized specialist on the American presidency. He is currently Professor and Chairman of the Department of Political Science at the University of California, Davis.

Berman's observations on the presidency and politics are frequently reported in national publications. He is the author of several books and articles that include *The New American Presidency; Looking Back on the Reagan Presidency; The Office of Management and Budget and the Presidency; Lyndon Johnson's War: The Road to Stalemate in Vietnam;* and *Planning a Tragedy: The Americanization of War in Vietnam.*

Berman has been featured on Bill Moyers's public television series, "Moyers: The Public Mind," and the national Public Broadcasting System documentary, "LBJ." His class on the American presidency is cited in Lisa Birnbach's *New and Improved College Guide* as the most recommended class for undergraduates at U.C., Davis. He has just completed a series of live satellite interactive television interviews for his American government class, including an interview with Speaker of the House Newt Gingrich.

Bruce Allen Murphy is a nationally recognized scholar on the American Supreme Court and judicial behavior. He is currently a Professor of American History and Politics, and a Fellow of the Institute of the Arts and Humanistic Studies at The Pennsylvania State University.

Murphy is the author of many publications, including the best-selling *The Brandeis/Frankfurter Connection: The Secret Political Activities of Two Supreme Court Justices,* which received the American Bar Association's Certificate of Merit, was listed among *The New York Times* "Best Books" for 1983, and was serialized by *The Washington Post*. He also wrote *Fortas: The Rise and Ruin of a Supreme Court Justice,* which was nominated for both the Pulitzer Prize and the National Book Award, and edited *Portraits of American Politics: A Reader.*

Murphy has received numerous teaching awards for his courses in Constitutional Law and American Politics. He has been a finalist in the Council for the Advancement and Support of Education's national "Professor of the Year" competition, and was cited as one of Penn State's "Best Professors" in Lisa Birnbach's *New and Improved College Guide.*

CHAPTER 1

APPROACHING DEMOCRACY

CHAPTER OUTLINE

CASE STUDY: THE BACK OF THE BUS
INTRODUCTION: AMERICA'S
    APPROACH TO DEMOCRACY
DEMOCRACY DEFINED

THE ROOTS OF DEMOCRACY IN AMERICA
THE IDEALS OF DEMOCRACY
THE ELEMENTS OF DEMOCRACY
APPROACHING DEMOCRACY

Rosa Parks, a forty-two-year-old African American seamstress with a pleasant face and rimless glasses, rode the bus every day to and from work in Montgomery, Alabama. The white majority in the city, abiding by the 1896 Supreme Court decision Plessy v. Ferguson, *which held that state facilities could be*

The Back of the Bus

"separate" for white and black citizens as long they were "equal" in quality, had constructed a complicated system for riding the bus. White citizens always rode in front (if there were no whites on the bus, those seats were left vacant). Black citizens sat or stood in the back of the bus. The middle of the bus was not assigned to either race. If there was no demand from the white customers, black customers could ride there. But if a black rider was seated in the middle and a white rider demanded the seat, the black rider was required by Alabama law to move to the back of the bus.

On December 1, 1955, Rosa Parks was on the way home from her job. She sat in the middle of the bus, but as the bus filled up, a white patron demanded her seat. Three other black riders vacated their seats, but Parks refused to leave. The bus driver told Parks that she had to move to the back of the bus. When she did not move, he arrested her.

Parks later explained: "I simply decided that I would not get up. I was tired, but I was usually tired at the end of the day, and I was not feeling well, but then there had been many days when I had not felt well. I had felt for a long time, that if I was ever told to get up so a white person could sit, that I would refuse to do so."

Parks had decided that Alabama's bus segregation law was unfair, but the courts offered her no justice. Although the American Constitution guarantees citizens a trial by a jury of their peers, before an impartial judge, such was not the case for

blacks in the South in 1955. The state judges were all local white lawyers who, like the white majority, supported the "separate but equal" doctrine. They implemented the laws and regulations of the white state legislatures and the white city councils. Through unfair election laws, blacks were almost entirely excluded from voting. Thus, they had little say in who passed or administered the laws they had to live under. Since juries were chosen from the voting rolls, jurors were almost all white. No wonder that Parks was quickly convicted of violating the Alabama ordinance requiring the segregation of buses and sentenced to pay a fourteen-dollar fine. As a result of this case, Parks lost her job and eventually had to leave the South.

But while Rosa Parks lost in the courts, civil rights activists were determined that she and others like her would not lose in the court of public opinion. These activists decided to use this incident to seek change and justice for African Americans. They asked the twenty-six-year-old son of a Baptist minister, Martin Luther King, Jr., with his compelling voice and hypnotizing command of the spoken word, to speak at a rally of the newly formed protest group known as the Montgomery Improvement Association. Turnout for the rally was impressive. The Baptist church on Holt Street was full to overflowing, several city blocks around the church were packed with as many as fifteen thousand protesters, and loudspeakers were set up to accommodate the crowd. "You know something," King told a friend as he prepared to thread through the crowd to the church, "this could turn into something big."

Speaking from a few notes hastily scribbled on a piece of paper, King observed, "We are here in a general sense because first and foremost—we are American citizens—and we are determined to apply our citizenship—to the fullness of its means. But we are here in a specific sense—because of the bus situation in Montgomery." As he spoke about the injustices suffered by African Americans, the

1

crowd was visibly moved. Finally, King boomed out: "And you know, my friends, there comes a time when people get tired of being trampled over by the iron feet of oppression."

Though African Americans were dependent on the buses for transportation, they decided to boycott the service until the policy of segregation was abolished. They walked or car-pooled, and though they were arrested and harassed by the local police, they persevered. After boycotting for more than a year, their hopes were realized—the bus segregation policy was overturned by a panel of federal judges who found it unconstitutional. This ruling was affirmed without opinion by the U.S. Supreme Court in 1956. Though Rosa Parks lost her case, her willingness to stand up for human justice won her the title of "Mother of the Civil Rights Movement."[1] ❧

After refusing to give up her seat to a white passenger, Rosa Parks was arrested, fingerprinted, booked, and convicted for violating Alabama's segregation ordinance.

INTRODUCTION: AMERICA'S APPROACH TO DEMOCRACY

By refusing to obey what she knew to be an unjust law, Rosa Parks had exercised her rights within a democratic society. Nearly one hundred years earlier the Thirteenth Amendment to the Constitution had guaranteed African Americans the right of full citizenship. As recently as 1954 the Supreme Court had guaranteed African Americans the right of equality in public schools. Why, then, did Parks and the members of the movement she helped ignite need to fight for the rights they were already supposedly guaranteed? Clearly, for African Americans, as for many other minorities in American society, democracy had not yet arrived.

This case tells us much about America's approach to democracy. Most of us associate democracy with an expansion of the range of freedoms enjoyed by citizens. Rosa Parks knew, however, that while democracies expand certain freedoms, they do not always protect basic human rights, political rights, and civil liberties. American citizens have sometimes been denied the right to vote, to obtain an education, to choose where to live, or to decide which occupations to pursue, simply because of their race, ethnicity, religion, gender, or sexual orientation. Rosa Parks's case is just one example of a group of American citizens being denied their basic freedoms.

Other examples are all too easy to find. One thinks, for instance, of the forced relocation—in some cases the actual extermination—of Native Americans during much of this country's history. In addition, 110,000 Japanese American citizens were interned during World War II for fear that they might commit treason merely because of their ancestry. For many Americans, democracy has not been a guarantee of rights but an outright denial of them—or at best, an invitation to struggle for rights.

In an emotional address to a joint session of the U.S. Congress in February 1990, Vaclav Havel told his audience that the United States' great advantage over the world's newly emerging democracies is that it has been approaching democracy for over two hundred years.

On the positive side, American democracy has been remarkably open, over the long run, to expanding rights and liberties for all its citizens—even if those rights and liberties have been achieved only with struggle, sacrifice, and occasional failure.

Democracy as an Evolutionary Process

Democracy has evolved over time in America. Today the United States stands as a beacon for those seeking freedom and democratic government. One of the most eloquent statements on the evolutionary nature of American democracy was made by Vaclav Havel, a former dissident Czechoslovakian playwright once imprisoned by that country's Communist government and later elected president. Addressing a joint session of the U.S. Congress on February 21, 1990, Havel noted that with the collapse of the Soviet Union, millions of people from Eastern Europe were involved in a "historically irreversible process," beginning their quest for freedom and democracy. And it was the United States of America that represented the model, "the way to democracy and independence," for these newly freed peoples. But Havel put his own spin on the notion of American democracy as a model. "As long as people are people," Havel explained,

> democracy, in the full sense of the word, will always be no more than an ideal. In this sense, you too are merely approaching democracy. But you have one great advantage: you have been approaching democracy uninterruptedly for more than 200 years, and your journey toward the horizon has never been disrupted by a totalitarian system.

This image of an America "approaching democracy" inspired the theme for this textbook. Democracy as a system has become increasingly popular. The number of democracies worldwide, while just a handful of nations a century ago, increased from three or four dozen in the 1950s to 114 by the end of 1994. Clearly, we live in an age of democratic aspiration, and for many who seek to achieve democracy the United States represents a model of the democratic process.[2]

The plight of Rosa Parks in 1955, however, is a reminder that even the United States can fall far short of the democratic ideal. Similarly, many countries that today claim to be democratic nevertheless place significant constraints on the freedom of their citizens. For example, India, Pakistan, and Turkey are often considered democracies because they hold regular, competitive, free, and open elections. But in Pakistan and Turkey, the intrusive power of the military limits the power of democratically elected officials. In India and Turkey high levels of political violence accompany elections. And all three countries have governments either unwilling or unable to protect the rights of religious and ethnic minorities. These countries, like the United States, provide ample evidence that the formal institutions of a democracy—campaigns, elections, legislatures—do not alone guarantee the protection of individual liberties associated with democratic systems.

We believe that the theme of "approaching democracy" is particularly exciting because, in the universal struggle for freedom, the United States is often the world's model. The ideal of American democracy certainly influenced the

As part of prodemocracy demonstrations in Beijing's Tiananmen Square, student activists erected a thirty-foot replica of the Statue of Liberty. This "goddess of democracy" faced the portrait of Communist leader Mao Tse-tung at the center of the square. Less than a week after this photograph was taken, the statue was destroyed by government troops, and many of the prodemocracy demonstrators were arrested.

Freedom and Democracy

Freedom House, a research institute, conducts an annual survey of the rights and freedoms of citizens in all of the world's countries and territories. Nations are ranked on a seven-point scale, from 1 (free) to 7 (not free). The degree of freedom within a nation is judged by two criteria: political rights (the right to vote, free and fair elections, participation of minorities, etc.) and civil liberties (freedom of speech, religion, press, assembly, etc.). Thus, a very free, open society with strong democratic institutions is ranked 1 for civil liberties and 1 for political rights; a society that represses individuals and forbids the free interplay of competitive political forces would receive scores of 7 and 7.

Niger, for example, is ranked as partly free, and it is making progress toward free expression and democratic elections. Pakistan also is partly free; despite its democratic electoral processes, the powers of elected leaders are limited by the influence of the military.

Turkmenistan is ranked as not free. Its president, Saparmurat Niyazov, exercises almost total control and requires official worship of his person. China is not free; neither are Cuba and Iraq. In these nations, government control over the daily lives of citizens is pervasive, and independent organizations are banned.

Canada, the United Kingdom, and Switzerland are among the nations ranked as free.

In 1995 the Freedom House survey revealed that the overall gains in freedom made during the past decade had been reversed. About one billion people were "free," compared with more than two billion in 1990 and 1991. The number living in "not free" societies was higher than ever, at about two and a quarter billion. The worst-rated countries included Afghanistan, Burma (now Myanmar), Cuba, North Korea, Somalia, and Vietnam. Australia, Belgium, Canada, Denmark, Sweden, and Switzerland were among the highest-ranked nations.

Is a democratic society necessarily free? No. Although all countries ranked as free are democracies, in a number of democratic societies, citizens' political rights and civil liberties are limited. For example, in India and Turkey, regional and ethnic conflicts have led to political violence, which has undermined the level of freedom enjoyed by their citizens. While a democratic form of government provides a framework for a free society, it is not by itself a guarantee of freedom.

In the early 1990s many nations, especially in Central and Eastern Europe, made successful transitions from totalitarianism to democracy and, thus, to greater freedom for their citizens. Many others, mostly in sub-Saharan Africa, became increasingly democratic, opening up the political process to multiparty competition and reducing state control over economic and civil life. For many other nations, however, freedom is threatened by violence, repression, and state control. This can be seen most clearly in the cases of Bosnia and Somalia, where tyrannical leaders and warlords have flouted international law and made a mockery of human rights.

The United States is, of course, a democracy, and its citizens (as well as those of other nations) call it "the land of the free." How would you rank it on the Freedom House scale?

The United States is ranked as free, but the Freedom House analysts point out that it is not entirely free from undemocratic political and social conditions. American political rights are generally free,

hundreds of thousands of Chinese students who demonstrated in Tiananmen Square during the spring of 1989, with hopes of reforming their totalitarian government. These so-called dissidents identified their movement as "pro-democracy." They carried a statue similar to the Statue of Liberty through the square, calling it the "goddess of democracy," and proclaimed their inalienable

but it is difficult for candidates from parties other than the Democratic and Republican parties to gain political office, and voter registration procedures are less effective than in some other democracies. In the area of civil liberties, ethnic minorities and women have made great strides in recent decades, but still face discrimination in employment. In addition, racial intolerance has increased in recent years. So while America has come a long way in its approach to democracy, it still has some distance to travel.

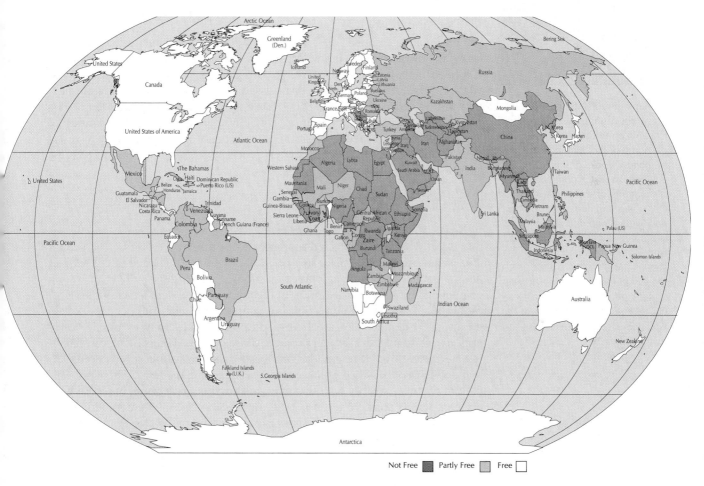

The Freedom House Map of Freedom
Source: *Freedom Review,* January–February 1995. © 1995 by Freedom House.

rights to life, liberty, and the pursuit of happiness. These demonstrations revealed something other than the desire to achieve democratic ideals; they showed also the difficulty of doing so under a repressive system. The student movement was crushed by the state, though for many in China the dream of democracy endures.

Perhaps the most memorable scene confirming the end of the Cold War and the victory of freedom and democracy over communism was the dramatic celebration that accompanied the dismantling of the Berlin Wall in 1989. The wall had separated East and West Berlin and stood as a symbol of communist power and oppression. The celebration, shown here, was broadcast worldwide to millions of viewers and included singing, dancing, cheers, and tears, with parts of the wall collected as souvenirs of the historic occasion.

Forming a Picture of Democracy

The most astute observer of the original American experiment in self-government was the Frenchman Alexis de Tocqueville. In 1835 he published a book of observations, *Democracy in America,* based on his journey throughout this new nation. "In America I sought more than America," he wrote. "I sought there the image of democracy itself, with its inclinations, its character, its prejudice, its passions, in order to learn what we have to fear or to hope from its progress." The eminent writer wanted to do more than just describe one nation. "America was only the frame," Tocqueville later told the English philosopher John Stuart Mill. "My picture was Democracy."[3]

Our goal is a similar one. We wish to portray democracy as a system by showing how it works in the world's oldest democratic state. The United States has been making efforts to move toward democracy for over two hundred years. In spite of its astonishing diversity and the consequent potential for hostility and violence, the United States has approached closer to the democratic ideal than nearly any other country, certainly more than any other country of comparable heterogeneity and size. But the process of approaching democracy is a continual one. Understanding that process in America begins with a discussion of the term *democracy* itself.

DEMOCRACY DEFINED

Webster's Dictionary defines **democracy** as "a government by the people, either directly or through elected representatives; rule by the ruled." The central idea is that democracies place key political powers in the hands of the people. At a minimum, citizens in a democracy choose their leaders freely from among competing groups and individuals. In highly developed democracies, the rights of the people extend well beyond this simple act of choosing leaders. Voters in advanced democracies are free to propose a wide array of public-policy options and to join groups that promote those options. Voters may even directly determine, through referenda (proposed policy measures submitted for direct popular vote), which policy options will become the law of the land. This pattern contrasts sharply with that of an **authoritarian regime,** in which government stands apart from the people, oppressing citizens by depriving them of their basic freedom to speak, associate, write, and participate in political life without fear of punishment.

Although political power in a democracy is in the hands of the people, not all democracies are alike. Let us look at two types of democracy: direct and indirect democracy.

Direct and Indirect Democracy

Some democratic systems give their citizens direct political control; others allow them only indirect power. **Direct democracy** assumes that people can govern themselves. The people as a whole make policy decisions rather than acting through elected representatives. In an **indirect democracy,** voters designate a relatively small number of people to represent their interests; those people, or representatives, then meet in a legislative body and make decisions on behalf of the entire citizenry.

DIRECT DEMOCRACY   The political system of Athens and similar Greek city-states of the time can be thought of as an elite-based, direct democracy. Even though most people in Athens were not considered citizens, the small fraction of the population that was eligible to participate in political life met regularly, debated policy, and voted directly on the issues of the day. They needed no intermediaries and made all political decisions themselves. In contrast, the later Roman republic was an indirect, representative democracy—closer to the structures we have become used to in the United States.[4]

The closest American approximation of direct democracy is the New England **town meeting,** a form of governance dating back to the early 1700s. In these meetings, town business has traditionally been transacted by the consent of a majority of eligible citizens, all of whom have an equal opportunity to express their views and cast their votes at an annual gathering. In this system the people directly affected by the issues of the day are the ones who decide how to resolve those issues. When it came into being, this method of direct participation represented a startling change from the undemocratic dictates of King George III of England and the authoritarian traditions of European politics in general. The town-meeting system proved durable, even today representing the primary form of government in over 80 percent of the townships in New England.

The town meeting instituted two of the indispensable features of effective democracy—equality and majority rule. **Equality** in this case means that all participants have equal access to the decision-making process, equal opportunity to influence the decisions made, and equal responsibility for those decisions. Under **majority rule,** when more than half of the voters agree on an issue, the entire group accepts the decision, even those in the minority who voted against it. This can happen because of group consensus on a key procedural norm: majorities make the rules. Acceptance of this norm allows the government to operate. If minorities failed to abide by the law as determined by the majority, the result would be anarchy or even civil war.

Note that minorities accept majority rule for the same reason that majorities accept minority rights. Those in the minority hope to become the majority some day, and when they do, they will want that day's minority to obey the laws they pass. At a minimum then, obedience to any majority-approved law represents a crude calculation of future self-interest. But for many in a democracy, this constant shifting between majority and minority positions broadens one's perspective. It produces an understanding of, even an empathy for, the positions of people in the opposite political camp. The result is a degree of tolerance for different political points of view, an openness to the others' opinions that lies at the heart of the democratic ideal.

Direct democracy (like the system prevailing in New England town meetings) works well for small, homogeneous groups of people. Once a population grows and diversifies, however, direct democracy can become cumbersome, even impossible to operate. One form of direct democracy—statewide balloting—is still used in states such as California. This procedure allows everyone in the state to vote on policy matters (through referenda) or on changes in the state constitution or to state statutes (via initiatives).[5] However, individuals in a large community cannot realistically all gather in the same place at the same time to discuss policy matters, as citizens in smaller communities can at town

Direct democracy in California led to passage of Proposition 187, a measure approved by California voters, barring illegal aliens from most public social services (soon after it was passed, federal courts put the measure on hold). Despite the United States' history as a nation of immigrants, economic and other concerns influenced public opinion in California, leading to a tidal wave of anti-immigrant sentiment and the popularity of Proposition 187. Here, California residents opposed to Proposition 187 march in protest before the November 1994 vote on the measure.

meetings. Approximately 260 million people live in America; over 100 million will vote in the next presidential election. Bringing all these Americans together to meet and make collective decisions would be impossible. As one political scientist observed:

> Merely to shake hands with that many people would take a century. . . . A single round of five-minute speeches would require five thousand years. If only 1 percent of those present spoke, the assembly would be forced to listen to two million speeches. People could be born, grow old, and die while they waited for the assembly to make one decision.[6]

With large numbers of people and a varied population, an indirect form of democracy makes more sense.

INDIRECT DEMOCRACY   As the size of the country grew, then, democracy became less pure and direct. The town meeting gave way to *representative town meetings,* a form of indirect democracy in which voters designate a few people to attend town meetings and vote on issues for the entire community. But even this system was ineffective. A myriad of decisions needed to be made on a daily or weekly basis, and towns would come to a standstill if they had to call daily or weekly town meetings. The business of government was too complex and demanding even for this approach. To expedite matters, towns voted for "selectmen" who would conduct routine town business in the periods between full town meetings.

This new system of **representative democracy** became the means by which a larger and more diverse group of people could govern themselves. Under this system, voters select representatives to make the decisions of government for them. Citizens still retain the ultimate decision-making power, in theory, since periodic elections allow them to eject representatives who don't carry out their wishes. Still, the day-to-day operations of government and the workaday flow of policy decisions no longer rest directly in the people's hands. Immediate power to run government now resides with elected officials, delegates of the people. The resulting system is related to, but still something different from, the framework of direct citizen rule.

Given the choice between direct versus representative democracy, the framers of the Constitution chose the latter, fearing that direct rule by the people—pure democracy—would mean rule by the mob. As John Adams once wrote: "Remember, democracy never lasts long. It soon wastes, exhausts, and murders itself. There never was a democracy yet that did not commit suicide."[7] Seeking to keep their new democratic system from committing suicide, the framers decided to create a **republic,** a governing structure that places political decision makers at least one step away from the citizens they are governing. For instance, the members of the U.S. House of Representatives are elected by citizens grouped into several dozen districts. Each district is allowed to vote for one individual to represent their wishes and interests in an assembly at the nation's capital.

To further dilute the political influence of the American people, the framers placed other units of government even further from their direct control. The Senate would not be chosen directly by the people but by state legislators. The people would not directly vote for president, but for members of an electoral college who would then name the president. The Supreme Court would be even further removed from the people's will, and chosen for life terms by the indirectly elected president and confirmed by the indirectly elected Senate. Thus, the highest court in the land would be three times removed from the popular will.

Although the framers clearly opted for an indirect and representative form of democratic governance, over the years, the system they devised has developed in ways that make it much closer to the Athenian ideal of direct democracy than it was originally. Still, one must marvel at how well the original structures, set up over two hundred years ago, have held up. Everywhere in the country today, we see the system of representative democracy at work: in local, state, and national governments. Yet something in the original scheme seems to have met with the ideals and goals of the American democratic spirit: equality, freedom for all, a representative democracy based on majority rule and minority rights, a system of total participation. Precisely why American democracy has endured and advanced is one of the most interesting and complex questions of our time.

To begin to answer this question, it helps to understand the origins of democracy and how it took root in America.

THE ROOTS OF DEMOCRACY IN AMERICA

Democracy did not begin in America; rather, it was the logical progression of a movement with a long history. Its seeds were first sown in the fertile soil of the ancient Greek city-state of Athens. The term *democracy* is derived from the Greek words *demos* and *kratia,* meaning literally "rule by the people." In Athenian democracy, roughly five centuries before Christ, the people were expected to participate actively in political life. To facilitate this participation, Athens organized government around the Assembly *(Ekklesia)*. This body, composed of all native-born adult male property owners, met forty times a year to discuss the pressing issues of the day. From Plato and Aristotle we know that Athenian democracy involved such characteristics as citizen participation, rule of law, and free and open political discussion. It thus provided the world's first model of what a democratic political system might look like.[8]

Athenian democracy was far from perfect, however. It was based on two conditions, one of which is virtually impossible, the other undesirable, in modern democracies. First, this city-state was small, comprising no more than fifty thousand people, with perhaps six thousand of them eligible to participate in the political process. Thus, democracy in Athens emphasized face-to-face political discussion and decision making. Most modern states contain millions of citizens, so, as we've seen, an Athenian town-meeting style of government is simply out of the question. Second, Greek democracy was highly exclusive. Women, slaves, and immigrants—who together formed the majority of residents—were barred from participating in the *Ekklesia*. Modern democracies guarantee equal political rights to nearly every adult citizen, thus ensuring a boisterous political life and a much more complex set of institutions than was needed by a simple, small republic like Athens.

What is the American conception of democracy? Some of its ideals clearly derive from the Athenian model. One example can be found in Thomas Jefferson's famous phrase from the Declaration of Independence, that America is a "government by the consent of the governed." Also borrowed from Athens is the

Here, popularly elected president Jean-Bertrand Aristide returns to Haiti in October 1994 after three years in exile. Aristide had been deposed by a **military** junta and forced to flee his country after only a few months in office. Today, with its democratically elected president in office, Haiti faces many of the challenges that all fledgling democracies encounter, which include creating a loyal police force and army, maintaining a free press, and allowing participation by interest groups and opposition political parties. In its move toward democracy, Haiti also faces unique challenges that arise from its history of corrupt military rule, its lack of an infrastructure, and its sharp class divisions.

"Fourscore and seven years ago our fathers brought forth on this continent a new nation, conceived in liberty and dedicated to the proposition that all men are created equal."

—Abraham Lincoln

idea of freely conducted debates and, following those debates, elections, with majority rule forming the basis for determining actual public policy.

Despite the influence of the Athenian model of democracy, however, when America's early leaders met to draft the American Constitution, they clearly hoped to avoid some of its weaker elements. James Madison, for instance, spoke out strongly against the kind of pure democracy represented by Athens. He insisted that it was inherently unstable and prone to self-destruct:

> Such democracies have ever been spectacles of turbulence and contention; have ever been found incompatible with personal security or the rights of property; and have in general been as short in their lives as they have been violent in their deaths.[9]

It is true that Athenian democracy was short-lived. Its death has often been attributed to a series of citizen decisions that led to disastrous consequences, even though those decisions were made in a perfectly democratic manner. In America, the framers wished to avoid a system in which the immediate desires of average citizens had an instant impact on the policies of the state. The democratic model they chose was less inclusive, but turned out to be more durable, than the Athenian ideal of populist decision making.

The system of democracy that the framers created is built upon certain core values, or ideals, that we will now examine.

THE IDEALS OF DEMOCRACY

America's commitment to democracy rests on its profound belief in an idealistic set of core values. These include freedom, equality, order, stability, majority rule, protection of minority rights, and participation. If the United States could uphold these values at all times, it might be regarded as the "perfect democratic system." It doesn't however, even today, and has fallen short of them even more frequently in the past. Still, it was these worthy ideals—and the country's long and continuing efforts to move toward them—that led Vaclav Havel to see America as "approaching democracy." This text explores in detail the degree to which the American political system, as presently constituted, realizes these democratic ideals. But right now we'll look closely at each of the ideals.

Freedom and Equality

Two of the key values that American democracy claims to safeguard often lead in contradictory directions. Frequently, the more freedom citizens have, the less equality they are likely to achieve—and vice versa. Beyond that, each of these admirable ideals, when applied to real-world circumstances, can produce contradictory results, depending on how one interprets their meaning. The dilemmas that arise when pursuing these two goals, both individually and together, are many.

To begin, take that quintessential American value, **freedom.** This value suggests that no individual should be within the power or under the control of another. We often take this to mean that we should have freedom from government interference in our lives. But to complicate matters, the notion of freedom means different things to different people. As the noted historian

As these photos clearly show, the notion of freedom means different things to different people, particularly regarding divisive social issues. On the left, gays protest an antigay amendment, citing the equal-protection provisions of the Fourteenth Amendment to support their position that gays are entitled to the same rights as all Americans. These protesters also seek freedom from government intervention in their personal lives. On the right, an opposing camp parades in Cobb County, Georgia, where the county commission has passed a resolution condemning "the gay lifestyle." The float, shown here, addresses the various topics taken up by the county commission in this southern community.

Isaiah Berlin has argued, freedom can be understood in two ways, either negative or positive.[10] Negative freedom implies *freedom from* government intervention. People have a right to certain liberties, such as freedom of speech, and government cannot violate or interfere with that right. For this reason, the First Amendment begins with the famous words, "Congress shall make no law . . ." and goes on to list several key citizen rights that government cannot restrict: notably, the rights to speak, write, assemble, and worship freely.

Contrast that approach with positive freedom, or *freedom to*—such as the freedom to exercise certain rights guaranteed to all U.S. citizens under the Constitution. Some examples might be the right to vote, the right to counsel, and the right to equal protection under the law.

Note how these two views of freedom lead to different roles for government. To ensure negative freedom, freedom *from* restrictions, government is expected to do nothing, to keep its hands off. For instance, a person can say and write practically anything he or she wants about any political official, and government agencies in a democracy will do nothing—or at least, they are supposed to do nothing.

On the other hand, to secure rights involving freedom *to,* government is often expected, and even required, to take positive action to protect citizens and ensure that those rights can be exercised. In the 1960s, for instance, the federal government had to intervene with a heavy hand in the South to ensure that African Americans could exercise one of the basic freedoms of a democratic citizen: the right to vote. Thus, some elements of freedom require a weak or even nonexistent government, while others require a strong and interventionist one.

Similar contradictions arise in attempting to maximize the key democratic value of *equality*. This ideal suggests that all citizens, regardless of circumstance, should be treated the same way by government. What equal treatment means in practice, however, is not always easy to say. Does it mean equality of opportunity or equality of result? Underlying the goal of **equality of opportunity** is the idea that "people should have equal rights and opportunities to develop their talents."[11] This implies that all people should have the chance to begin at the same starting point. But what if life's circumstances make that impossible, placing people from different situations at different starting points, some much farther behind than others? For example, the person born into a poor family in which no one has ever graduated from high school will be less prepared for college than the son or daughter of generations of college professors. Even more dramatic is the difference in life opportunities available to the children of poor black families, compared with the children of wealthy white families. Equalizing opportunities for all Americans would clearly take an enormous effort.

The difficulty of achieving equal opportunity for all has led some people to advocate another kind of equality. They promote **equality of result,** the idea that all forms of inequality, including economic disparities, should be eradicated. Policies aimed at maximizing this goal place less stress on helping people compete and more stress on redistributing benefits after the competition has taken place. Equality of result would produce a redistribution of goods, services, and income from those who have more to those who have less. These two forms of equality—equality of opportunity and equality of result—are often in conflict and represent different notions of what a democratic society would look like.

Besides these internal contradictions, freedom and equality conflict with each other in a number of ways. For instance, if your view of freedom is freedom *from* government intervention—a belief that government should have as little power to control citizens as necessary—then equality of any kind will be an extremely difficult goal to achieve. If government stays out of all citizen affairs, then some people will become extremely wealthy, others will fall through the cracks, and economic inequalities will multiply. On the other hand, if you wish to promote equality, especially equality of *result,* then you will have to restrict some people's freedoms—the freedom to earn an unlimited amount of money, for example.

What values should a democratic society promote? There are no easy answers to this theoretical dilemma. In practice, a democracy like ours works continuously toward some kind of middle ground, promoting each of these values to the extent possible while always making difficult choices and tradeoffs when conflicts arise over different values or different interpretations of the same value.[12]

"Slavery Was Once a Tradition"

For African Americans, the Confederate flag—the official flag of the states that seceded from the Union at the beginning of the Civil War—stands for a way of life that had slavery at its very core, a society in which African Americans were treated like a subhuman species with no legal rights. They could not vote, own property, get an education, or run their own affairs. To African Americans, therefore, the Confederate flag symbolizes the exact opposite of liberty and equality.

The flag also produces strong emotions in some white Americans. Many white southerners, for example, see it not as a racist emblem but as a symbol of regional pride. Still, anyone with any knowledge of American history can understand why African Americans feel that displaying the Confederate flag amounts to a statement that slavery was and should be a legitimate social enterprise.

In July 1993 these conflicting views reached the floor of the U.S. Senate. As the national-service bill was being debated in a nearly empty Senate chamber, southern conservative senators Jesse Helms and Strom Thurmond managed to attach an amendment to the bill that would allow the Confederate flag to remain on a patent design held by the United Daughters of the Confederacy. Renewal of patent designs by Congress bestows prestige, honor, and legitimacy on patriotic groups. The proposal had already been rejected by the Senate Judiciary Committee, but with most of the senators unaware of the amendment to the national-service bill, it won approval by 52 to 48 in a test vote.

Upon learning the results of the vote, Carol Moseley-Braun of Illinois, the Senate's only African American member, rushed to the Senate floor and stated that she would not leave until the amendment had been rescinded. In a powerful speech focusing on the symbolism of the Confederate flag for the descendants of slaves, she declared that "the issue is whether or not Americans such as myself who believe in the promise of this country . . . will have to suffer the indignity of being reminded time and time again that at one point in this country's history we were human chattel. We were property. We could be bought and sold." When Senator Helms defended the amendment as showing respect for tradition, Ben Nighthorse Campbell, the Senate's only Native American member, took the floor. "I would point out that slavery was once a tradition," he said.

Perhaps the most poignant speech was given by Senator Howell Heflin of Alabama. One of Heflin's grandfathers had signed the Ordinance of Secession in 1861 and another had served as a surgeon in the Confederate Army. Although his family was "rooted in the Confederacy," Heflin said that he would vote with Senator Moseley-Braun because "we live today in a different world . . . trying to heal the scars that occurred in the past. We must get racism behind us. We must move forward. We must realize we live in America today."

The Senate defeated the Helms amendment by 75 to 25. During a three-hour period, twenty-seven senators had changed their votes. It was just one of many battles in the struggle for equality that began hundreds of years ago and continues today.

Source: Congressional Record, July 22, 1993, S. 9257; and *New York Times,* July 23, 1993, p. B6.

Order and Stability

The values of freedom and equality, central to a democracy, often stand in tension with the power of the state to control its citizens. Every society, to be successful, must maintain **order** and provide social **stability,** so that citizens can go about their business in a secure and predictable manner. Governments make use of laws, regulations, courts, the police, and the military to prevent societal chaos. This need for order does, however, place limits on individual freedom, and it frequently violates certain notions of equality.

Think, for example, about one of the more obvious controls that government places on us to prevent social disorder: the need for a state-approved driver's license before an individual is allowed to operate a motor vehicle. Americans who wish to drive a car cannot simply get into a car and start driving. They must first fill out a number of forms, write a hefty check to a government agency, pass a written examination created by government officials, and then prove to other government officials through a driving test that they actually know how to drive a car. There are perfectly valid reasons for each of these steps, springing from the desire to make society orderly and safe, but government policies that derive from these goals do have the effect of limiting (very modestly, of course) the values of both freedom and equality.

The limit on personal freedom is obvious: We can't do what we want (drive a car) without satisfying certain government requirements. The limit on equality is perhaps less severe but is still there: Not everyone is allowed to drive a car (those under a certain age, those who fail the various tests, those whose eyesight is weak, those who have violated certain laws, and so forth). This modest example suggests dozens of additional cases in which state powers aimed at ensuring order stand in conflict with some individual desires for freedom and equality. The constant tension between individual rights and state power creates a great deal of controversy in a democracy and gives rise to numerous policy disputes, many of which we examine in this text.[13]

Majority Rule and Protection of Minority Rights

Just as democracies must balance freedom and equality with order and stability, so must they also strike a balance between the rule of the majority (*majoritarianism*) and the protection of minority rights. Whenever disagreement arises in a democracy, each party to the dispute seeks to persuade more than half of the populace in its favor. To accomplish this end, supporters of each position must agree among themselves on the desired goal; they must achieve some kind of internal consensus. In successful democracies, political scientist E. E. Schattschneider argues, consensus develops out of debate and persuasion, campaigning and voting, rather than being imposed by dictate. The majority becomes the majority, in other words, only through open procedures that encourage popular input and rational argument, not from some small group's authoritarian decision to impose its policy preferences on everyone else.[14]

Furthermore, policy questions in a democracy are rarely settled "once and for all." The majority remains the majority only as long as it can keep persuading all its members of the rightness of its positions. Those in the minority are constantly trying to influence the majority to change its mind. Free to express their views without fear of harm, proponents of the minority opinion will speak out persuasively, hoping to see their ideas become the majority perspective. Hence, majorities in a vibrant democracy can never feel secure for long. They must always defend themselves from the continuing arguments of the minority; they must always imagine that that same minority will replace them some day in the majority position.

To make matters more complicated still, note that few people ever find themselves in the majority on all issues. One may hold the majority viewpoint on prayer in public schools and on nuclear power but find oneself in the minority on the minimum-wage issue. Democracy is never static; it's an elusive, dynamic, and constantly shifting process. For that reason everyone in a democracy will at times be part of the majority, but just as surely everyone at many other times will take an unpopular, minority position.

Knowing that majority status must inevitably be temporary, members of any majority must be careful. They must be reasonable in their demands and programs, seeking not to antagonize the minority excessively, since they would have to expect retribution when leaders of an oppressed minority become part of next week's or next year's majority. The knowledge that one might become the minority any day has a profound effect, leading the current majority in a democratic system to treat minorities fairly.

The idea of **minority rights** springs from this perspective. We give rights to the minority because when we end up in the minority, as inevitably we must, we want to enjoy those rights ourselves rather than endure the repression that is the usual fate of minorities in nondemocratic systems. Thomas Jefferson understood this idea well. When in the minority, his Republican party had been victimized by the Alien and Sedition Acts, passed by the majority Federalist party in 1798 specifically to outlaw the Republicans' views. When Jefferson himself entered the majority as president in 1801, he stressed the importance of majority restraint, referring in his first inaugural address to the "sacred principle, that though the will of the majority is in all cases to prevail, that will to be rightful must be reasonable."[15]

When those in the minority band together into groups based on particular interests and seek to influence policy by allying with other groups, we have a system of **pluralism.** Continual competition among groups in a democracy ensures that power moves around in a shifting alliance of interests. One year it might be the religious and education groups that unite on the question of governmental assistance to schools, while the next year those groups might split on the issue of teachers' wages, with the labor unions and taxpayer interest groups weighing in with their own views.

In a system of democratic pluralism, maintaining a cohesive majority becomes more and more difficult. Coalitions constantly shift, and new majorities appear on every issue. In these circumstances the ephemeral majorities of the day are bound to respect minority rights and pay close attention to unpopular opinions. The large number of groups and the strong likelihood that everyone will frequently be in the minority diminishes the chance that one dominant, oppressive group will form. The framers of the American Constitution worried a good deal about "the tyranny of the majority," but in a modern, complex democracy this problem seems relatively minor. Indeed, the excessive power of minorities, including special-interest groups, seems more of a worry to many observers today—an issue we examine carefully in a later chapter.

Participation

Since democracy is rule by the governed, all citizens must have an opportunity to influence the activities of government. That opportunity is best expressed by the institution of **universal suffrage,** the requirement that everyone must have

Women continue to struggle for the right to participate equally in all aspects of life. Denied the right to vote by the Constitution, women struggled for over a century for that inalienable right, which was secured in 1920 with the passage of the Nineteenth Amendment. On the left is one of the suffragists who called attention to the cause by picketing the White House in 1917. On the right is Shannon Faulkner, who more recently waged a struggle for gender equality in education. Faulkner sought admission to the Citadel, a state-sponsored, all-male military college in South Carolina. The Citadel admitted Faulkner in 1993 based on an impressive application that omitted any reference to gender. Admission was withdrawn once the college learned that Faulkner is a woman. In response, Faulkner filed suit and won, explaining: "If you believe in something go for it."

the right to vote. Democracy also requires that this vote be meaningful; that is, voters must have real choices at the polls, and their choices must be reflected in governmental policies. Beyond voting, democracies must provide citizens with ample opportunities to participate in and influence the direction of their government. Such participation may involve serving in the government, lobbying for governmental action, or simply reading and talking about government actions.

Participation is a central democratic ideal, and the United States has approached it over the years by continually expanding opportunities for Americans to participate in and influence their government. Only a minority of people—white, landowning males over the age of twenty-one—could exercise full citizenship rights in 1787. The expansion of citizenship rights toward inclusiveness has continued for two centuries. The amendment structure of the

Political Participation in the Electronic Age

In ancient Greek cities citizens met regularly in the *agora,* a public square or marketplace, to discuss the issues and problems of the day. The *agora* was part of a tradition of face-to-face democracy and political discussion, a place where all citizens were free to participate in the political process.

Today, many democratic theorists claim that such direct political discussion is impossible in large industrialized nations like the United States. However, some public-spirited innovators have begun to exploit rapidly developing technology to bring American citizens together in surprisingly effective ways.

In 1992, Oregon governor Barbara Roberts used existing telephone lines and video technology to set up an "electronic town hall meeting." With two-way voice communication and one-way video, Governor Roberts took questions from a group of voters and discussed at length the various options available for modifying state tax policies. She emerged from the process with a much clearer picture of what her constituents really want.

Also in 1992, breakthroughs in computer technology made possible the first interactive political discussion between citizens and presidential candidates. President George Bush, Democratic challenger Bill Clinton, and Libertarian Andre Marrou each logged onto a personal computer linked to a commercial computer network and fielded a wide range of questions from interested citizens also linked to the network.

Another innovation was introduced by Vote Smart, a nonpartisan, nonprofit, tax-exempt organization established to encourage broad-based participation in political discussion. This group set up a toll-free 800 number; callers could talk with Vote Smart representatives, who would pro-

Cutting Edge

vide them with information on the various presidential candidates. Vote Smart received approximately 209,000 calls between mid March and the election. On election day alone the organization answered 34,000 calls.

New electronic devices that increase the availability of political information appear almost daily. In October 1994 the White House went on-line, making thousands of executive branch documents available to anyone with access to a computer and a modem. Within three months, over 1.25 million people had taken advantage of the service. Congress entered the cyberspace era in January 1995. Every bill introduced in Congress, and every word uttered there, is now available to Internet users around the world through a service known as "Thomas" (short for "Thomas Jefferson").

Technological innovations like the electronic town hall meeting, interactive computer networking, and call-in information lines may not reproduce the intimacy and familiarity of the ancient *agora,* and some of them are available only to those who can afford the necessary computer equipment. But such developments do bring people more fully into the political process, provide them with valuable information, and stimulate interest in the issues and actors that determine the way we all live. In these respects, they can be considered a step forward in the nation's approach to democracy.

House Speaker Newt Gingrich introduces "Thomas," the on-line public-access system of congressional information, in January 1995. Government information is now widely available in cyberspace, and Thomas provides citizens with another opportunity to become better informed on policy matters and to communicate with their elected leaders in Washington.

Constitution, in particular, facilitated this expansion. The Thirteenth and Fifteenth Amendments freed the slaves and gave them the right to vote (though as you will learn, it was years before state laws were changed to ensure this goal), the Seventeenth Amendment gave the people the right to vote for their senators directly, the Nineteenth Amendment gave women the right to vote, the Twenty-fourth Amendment ended the practice of charging people a "poll tax" before they could vote, and the Twenty-sixth Amendment lowered the minimum voting age from twenty-one to eighteen. Today, the opportunity exists for nearly every adult American to participate in the political life of American society. Many, it is true, do not take advantage of the opportunities available, but no one can any longer point to serious barriers that prevent the exercise of the crucial democratic right of participation.[16]

Beyond participation and the other core ideals that we've just examined are certain institutions and traditions that help sustain those ideals—we refer to these as the elements of democracy.

THE ELEMENTS OF DEMOCRACY

Following the struggle for democracy in Poland, Adam Michnik, an early leader in the Solidarity movement, noted that "dictatorship has been defeated and freedom has been won, yet the victory of freedom has not yet meant the triumph of democracy. Democracy is something more than freedom. Democracy is freedom institutionalized."[17] Throughout this text we examine those characteristics of American democracy that have helped to "institutionalize freedom." The institutions and traditions of the American system have allowed it to develop toward democracy, a democracy that has not yet "committed suicide," as John Adams feared it would.

How closely have modern Americans approached the ideals of true democracy? Political scientists are constantly trying to define and categorize democracy, using one or another set of objective indicators. While there is still healthy debate about the nature of these indicators, we have chosen to stress five widely accepted "elements of democracy." These institutional elements will serve as markers to identify progress toward the democratic ideals discussed earlier. Only political systems that meet or at least approach those ideals can be considered democratic; using the following elements, you can measure the strength and robustness of American democracy or any democracy.

"For there is nothing mysterious about the foundations of a healthy and strong democracy. The basic things expected by our people of their political and economic systems are simple. They are: Equality of opportunity for youth and for others; Jobs for those who can work; Security for those who need it; The ending of special privilege for the few; The preservation of civil liberties for all; The enjoyment of the fruits of scientific progress in a wider and constantly rising standard of living."

—Franklin D. Roosevelt

A SYSTEM FOR POPULAR PARTICIPATION   The United States provides numerous opportunities for citizen involvement in politics. With the unfolding of American history, an increasing number of people gained the opportunity to participate in public life. The institutions that most clearly allow people to influence government are **elections.** The entire population now has the chance to participate in regularly scheduled elections, where at least two opposing groups have some likelihood of winning. By voting in these elections, citizens can convey their desires to government and can expect government to act with those desires in mind.

This right to vote has been expanded over the years through constitutional amendments and court rulings, as you've seen, so that it now includes nearly everyone over the age of eighteen. Voting itself would not be sufficient to

America's approach to democracy suffered a setback in the 1950s when Senator Joseph McCarthy led a witch hunt against supposed Communist sympathizers, who, he claimed, were sweeping the nation. McCarthy's anti-Communist campaign ruined the lives and reputations of many Americans but turned up few actual Communists. McCarthyism eventually came to an end, but it demonstrates how vulnerable the American system of democracy is.

influence government, however, if voters could not make meaningful choices at the polling booth. The institution of free, competing **political parties** enables this element of choice to be exercised. Stable, representative political parties exist and, once elected to office, seek to impose their will on policymakers. Parties allow like-minded members of the population to group together and magnify their individual voices into a focus for government action.

Important as they are, political parties are never the only outlet for citizen participation in a developed democracy. Citizens must be free to join a wide array of groups that promote their particular interests. That situation has long been true in the United States, where a vigorous civil society allows public and private **interest groups** to thrive. These groups allow citizens to meet, organize, plan strategy, and lobby government for action. They even allow people to protest government policies, without fear that government will punish them.

A COMMITMENT TO PRESERVE FREEDOM AND EQUALITY FOR ALL   For democracy to flourish, the government must work to safeguard democratic ideals for all its citizens. That goal implies several kinds of action. First, it means that government stays out of the personal lives of its citizens, who have an inherent **right to privacy.** Furthermore, citizens must have access to a vigorous **free press** and other means of open exchange of information. Debate must be encouraged and fueled by freedom of speech and thought, not to mention freedom of information.

In a secure democracy, people must be free to think for themselves, inform themselves about governmental policies, and exchange information. A totalitarian government, using the state to maintain total authority over all citizens, suppresses open communication so as to maintain an iron grip over the minds of its populace.

AN INDEPENDENT JUDICIARY   Central to functioning democracies are the rule of law and the protection of civil liberties. Only an independent judiciary, free of political influence, can safeguard citizen rights, protecting both the majority and minorities at the same time. Like other federal courts, the Supreme

Court in America possesses a unique power, **judicial review,** that makes it the final interpreter of the Constitution. The federal judiciary has often used this power to strike down government actions to protect individual freedoms. Independent state courts have also acted to preserve the rights of individuals. Courts have also used their authority to make a powerful statement about equality and the rule of law: *All are equal under the law,* and no one, not even the president of the United States, is above it.

CIVILIAN CONTROL OF THE MILITARY AND THE POLICE   In dictatorships, political parties come and go, but the group that controls the military and the police is the real power. The nation's nominal leader may be irrelevant. Although Jean-Bertrand Aristide was democratically elected to the presidency of Haiti in September 1991, he was soon ousted from power by military leaders who took a dislike to him. This kind of arbitrary military action does not happen in the United States or in any advanced democracy. Thanks in part to the example of George Washington, the American military is controlled by the civilian government. Military leaders take no policy actions other than those they are directed to take by civilian political leaders, in particular the elected American president. Furthermore, they never intervene in civilian political affairs. Since 1800 every losing political party has simply left power and turned control over to its winning competitors. Never have civilian leaders, rejected by the voters, called on the military or police to keep them in office. Never have the military or police intervened to keep in office a candidate or party that has come up short at the polls. Both occurrences are common in countries such as Haiti, where democratic institutions are weak.

> "The orderly transfer of authority as called for in the Constitution routinely takes place, as it has for almost two centuries, and few of us stop to think how unique we really are. In the eyes of many in the world, this every-four-year-ceremony we accept as normal is nothing less than a miracle."
>
> —Ronald Reagan

As a result of this tradition of civilian control of the military, Americans did not have to worry that the same George Bush who commanded the American armed forces in the Persian Gulf War of 1991 would, following his electoral defeat in November 1992, use his powers as commander in chief to call off the election and surround the White House with an army. Nor did we have to worry that Generals Schwartzkopf or Powell, both of whom emerged from the Gulf War as heroes, would use their new-found popularity to oust Bush from the Oval Office and establish themselves therein. Indeed, these hypothetical examples of military misconduct, common enough in many nations, seem so outrageously unlikely in the American setting as to be laughable. Yet we must understand why they are so unlikely. They seem farfetched precisely because Americans deeply believe in the norm of civilian control over the military and the police, a norm that is vital to the democratic process. After all, how democratic could a society be if the people's decisions could be arbitrarily set aside by the whims of a powerful few?

A CULTURAL COMMITMENT TO DEMOCRATIC IDEALS AMONG ALL LEVELS OF SOCIETY   Democracy doesn't just happen. People in general and leaders in particular must believe in it, understand how it works, and abide by its norms. All levels of society must agree on a set of common governmental ideals. In the United States, those ideals include reverence for the Constitution, the pursuit of freedom and equality, the value of minority rights, and the rule of law. This commitment to democratic ideas is indispensable for maintaining stability. It produces a remarkable result, one found only in a democratic society:

The responsibility for preserving and advancing democracy falls to the people who enjoy the benefits of living in a free society, a principle understood by these student protesters at Carnegie Mellon University in Pittsburgh, Pennsylvania. Participating in a protest for freedom in cyberspace, these students charged that their university had "decided, 'to hell with the First Amendment'" in attempting to censor sexual content on the campus computer network. On their sign is Thomas Jefferson's warning that liberty depends on the vigilance of an attentive and active citizenry.

Americans unhappy with their government complain but with rare exceptions do not take up arms. They simply wait for the next election and then vote the ruling party out of power.

APPROACHING DEMOCRACY

All of the democratic institutions and traditions just discussed—free elections, competitive political parties, a free press, interest groups, an independent judiciary, civilian control of the military, and a commitment among citizens to a set of democratic ideals—are indispensable for the preservation of democracy. In this text, we examine the elements and ideals of democracy in detail to help you to understand how American government works. As you read, keep in mind that democracy is a *process* whereby conflict is resolved and consensus achieved between a ruling majority and a minority that accepts the legitimacy of majority rule.

This text also looks at American democracy as an evolving process. Like Vaclav Havel, we believe that the United States is still approaching democracy. America's two-hundred-year experiment with government has been a lesson in the gradual expansion (and occasional restriction) of liberty, justice, and freedom. The chapters that follow examine the American approach to democracy, sorting out the ideals; studying the institutions, processes, and policies; and analyzing the dilemmas and paradoxes of freedom. After observing American government, we want to ask, and be able to answer, these basic questions: Is America closer to or further away from democracy? To what degree does the United States currently meet the standards of a truly democratic society?

Rosa Parks's brave stand took us much closer to the democratic ideal of equality for all. But such gains do not come easily, and each advance must be zealously safeguarded. Forty years after Rosa Parks helped ignite the civil rights movement, women, African Americans, and all Americans continue to struggle with the ideal of equality. The continuing debate over civil rights laws and

"No one pretends that democracy is perfect or all-wise. Indeed, it has been said that democracy is the worst form of government except all those other forms that have been tried from time to time."

—Winston Churchill

affirmative action, for example, shows that no advance toward democracy is without unintended consequences; no democratic victory can ever be taken for granted. We can all work to safeguard democratic accomplishments by understanding the government and participating in it. We hope that you come to appreciate what Justice Felix Frankfurter meant when he observed: "Democracy is always a beckoning goal, not a safe harbor. For freedom is an unremitting endeavor, not a final achievement." By being informed American citizens and vigorously seeking to protect freedom, you can help American democracy continue to flourish.

SUMMARY

1. Throughout the world democracy has become increasingly popular; by 1995 the number of democratic nations had reached 114. The United States is often viewed as a model of the democratic process. However, the formal institutions of a democracy do not by themselves guarantee the protection of individual liberties.

2. The term *democracy* means government by the people, either directly or through elected representatives. Citizens in a democracy choose their leaders freely from among competing groups and individuals. In highly developed democracies, voters are free to propose public-policy options and join groups that promote those options. In contrast, in an authoritarian regime, government deprives citizens of the freedom to participate in political life.

3. In a direct democracy, the people as a whole make policy decisions. In an indirect democracy, voters designate a few people to represent their interests; those people meet in a legislative body and make decisions on behalf of the entire citizenry. Such a system of representative democracy makes it possible for a larger and more diverse group of people to govern themselves.

4. Freedom and equality are core values of American democracy, but they often pull in contradictory directions. The more freedom citizens have, the less equality they are likely to achieve, and vice versa. Both of these ideals can be seen as requiring that government take no action. Conversely, they can be viewed as requiring governmental intervention to protect individual freedom or guarantee equal treatment. The desire for order and stability places limits on freedom and equality.

5. A democracy must strike a balance between majoritarianism (the rule of the majority) and minority rights. In successful democracies a consensus is reached through debate, persuasion, campaigning, and voting. In a pluralist system those in the minority band together based on particular interests and seek to influence policy by allying with other groups.

6. In a democracy all citizens must have an opportunity to influence the activities of government. This is achieved through universal suffrage and other opportunities for political participation, such as serving in the government or lobbying for governmental action.

7. A republic places political decision makers at least one step away from the citizens they are governing. Thus, in the United States voters originally chose electors and state legislators, who in turn chose the president and senators, who then chose the justices of the Supreme Court. Over the years this system has been modified in ways that bring it closer to direct democracy.

8. Among the basic elements of American democracy is a system for popular participation consisting of regularly scheduled elections; free, competing political parties; and public and private interest groups. Another basic element is the commitment to preserve freedom and equality, which implies a right to privacy, a free press, and freedom of speech. Additional elements are an independent judiciary (including the power of judicial review), civilian control of the military and the police, and a cultural commitment to democratic ideals.

9. Democracy is a process whereby conflict is resolved and consensus achieved between a ruling majority and a minority that accepts the legitimacy of majority rule. The United States has been approaching democracy for over two hundred years and continues to do so today.

KEY TERMS

democracy	republic	universal suffrage
authoritarian regime	freedom	elections
direct democracy	equality of opportunity	political parties
indirect democracy	equality of result	interest groups
town meeting	order	right to privacy
equality	stability	free press
majority rule	minority rights	judicial review
representative democracy	pluralism	

SUGGESTED READINGS

- Burnheim, John. *Is Democracy Possible?* Berkeley: University of California Press, 1985. A thoughtful contribution that explores the basis of genuine democracy while critiquing the procedures, results, and underlying assumptions of democracies worldwide.

- Cronin, Thomas E. *Direct Democracy: The Politics of Initiative, Referendum, and Recall.* Cambridge, Mass.: Harvard University Press, 1989. An informative account of how ballot measures affect democratic politics. Cronin examines the strengths and weaknesses of these measures.

- Dahl, Robert A. *Democracy and Its Critics.* New Haven, Conn.: Yale University Press, 1989. One of the most prominent political theorists of our era examines the assumptions of democratic theory. The book provides a justification for democracy as a political ideal by tracing modern democracy's evolution from the early nineteenth century to the present.

- Diamond, Larry. *The Democratic Revolution.* Latham, Md.: Freedom House, 1992. The first organized presentation of the stories of key participants in struggles for a democracy that are now taking place throughout the developing world.

- Inkeles, Alex, ed. *On Measuring Democracy.* New Brunswick, N.J.: Transaction Publishers, 1991. These articles written by social scientists reveal that political democracy is not only conceptually but also empirically distinct from various social and economic patterns and outcomes.

- Ravitch, Diane, and Abigail Thernstrom, eds. *The Democracy Reader.* New York: HarperCollins, 1992. This reader distills all of the enduring issues of democracy in a collection of documents, essays, poems, declarations, and speeches.

- Schattschneider, E. E. *Two Hundred Million Americans in Search of a Government.* Hillsdale, Ill.: Dryden Press, 1969. An original and thought-provoking exploration into the game of government, how it is played, and what it is good for.

- Tismanednu, Vladimir. *Reinventing Politics: Eastern Europe from Stalin to Havel.* New York: Free Press, 1992. A well-balanced account of the factors leading to the revolutions of 1989 and the evolution of democratic institutions in Eastern Europe.

CHAPTER 2

THE FOUNDING:
AMERICA'S FIRST APPROACH
TO DEMOCRACY

Colonial Williamsburg

CHAPTER OUTLINE

CASE STUDY: SHAYS'S REBELLION

INTRODUCTION: THE ROAD TO DEMOCRACY

THE SEEDS OF AMERICAN DEMOCRACY

FIRST MOVES TOWARD A UNION

REBELLION: CAUSES AND CONSEQUENCES

REVOLUTION AND THE STIRRINGS OF A

NEW GOVERNMENT

THE FIRST NEW GOVERNMENT: A
CONFEDERATION OF STATES

THE NEED FOR A MORE PERFECT UNION

THE FOUNDERS: PAVING THE WAY FOR
APPROACHING DEMOCRACY

WE HOLD THESE TRUTHS TO BE SELF-EVIDENT, THAT ALL MEN ARE CREATED EQUAL, THAT THEY ARE ENDOWED BY THEIR CREATOR WITH CERTAIN UNALIENABLE RIGHTS, THAT AMONG THESE ARE LIFE, LIBERTY AND THE PURSUIT OF HAPPINESS. THAT TO SECURE THESE RIGHTS, GOVERNMENTS ARE INSTITUTED AMONG MEN, DERIVING THEIR JUST POWERS FROM THE CONSENT OF THE GOVERNED. THAT WHENEVER ANY FORM OF GOVERNMENT BECOMES DESTRUCTIVE OF THESE ENDS, IT IS THE RIGHT OF THE PEOPLE TO ALTER OR TO ABOLISH IT, AND TO INSTITUTE NEW GOVERNMENT, LAYING ITS FOUNDATION ON SUCH PRINCIPLES AND ORGANIZING ITS POWERS IN SUCH FORM, AS TO THEM SHALL SEEM MOST LIKELY TO EFFECT THEIR SAFETY AND HAPPINESS. ■

These words from the Declaration of Independence, drafted by Thomas Jefferson in 1776, would come to represent America's commitment to the principle that all people possess a natural right to be free and the power to make themselves free. These ideals had inspired the American colonists to fight the first significant and bloodiest battle of the American Revolution on June 17, 1775, at Bunker Hill, near Boston. One of the militia captains at this battle was a farmer from western Massachusetts, Daniel Shays.

Shays's Rebellion

Shays fought in two revolutions in his lifetime. The first was the Revolutionary War, ending with the Treaty of Paris in 1783, which freed the colonists from English rule and recognized American independence. The second, between 1786 and 1787, was a protest against the new American government. Both times Shays fought for change, for "a new order of the ages," as inscribed on the seal of the United States.

This second revolution took root as economic conditions in America deteriorated, particularly for farmers, who lacked markets and could not pay off their debts. They were often forced to pay exorbitantly high interest rates, and those who could not pay faced prison or indentured servitude. Between 1784 and 1786 in Hampshire County, Massachusetts, about a third of all males over sixteen were involved in debt cases, a figure typical for the entire country. During the same period, seventy-three men in Hampshire County were thrown into debtors' prisons.[1] Making matters worse, the farmers lacked government representation for their interests because the Massachusetts state legislature was dominated by merchants from the eastern part of the state (most farmers were from the western part).

The spirit that led the farmers to revolt against the British a decade earlier inspired them to organize and protest once again, in a populist uprising now remembered as **Shays's Rebellion.** Now the "tyrant" was not a distant monarch, but other Americans of a different socio-economic class. The farmers succeeded in shutting down several local courts, sometimes setting them ablaze. (A court closed or burned could not foreclose.) They also demanded that the Massachusetts legislature print cheap paper money—as Rhode Island had done—that would be acceptable to creditors. The legislature refused and instead legislated new taxes.

Shays, like many farmers, was desperate. After unsuccessful protests and petitioning against taxation, the farmers rebelled. Shays led a force of 2,500 men against the state militia. Ironically, members of the militia included men who had fought with Shays at Bunker Hill. After a series of confrontations, the Shaysites were finally repelled by General Benjamin Lincoln, a hero of the Revolution. Massachusetts governor James Bowdoin described the farmers as engaging in "riot, anarchy, and confusion."

The populist rebellion horrified most of the new nation's political leaders, who were also of the wealthy, propertied class. To them, Shays's Rebellion symbolized lawlessness as a mob of wild men took the law into their own hands. Had revolution failed to produce anything but democracy run amuck? Many believed that America was on the brink of anarchy.

Fear stemming from the rebellion pushed some antidemocratic sentiments to the center of political debate. On October 27, 1786, John Jay wrote to Thomas Jefferson that "a spirit of licentiousness has infected Massachusetts. . . . I feel for the cause of liberty, and for the honour of my countrymen who have so nobly asserted it, and who, at present, so abuse its blessings." George Washington was equally distressed and expressed his uneasiness to James Madison: "There are combustibles in every state which a spark might set fire to. . . . If government cannot check these disorders, what security has a man for life, liberty, or property?" Not all leaders agreed with the perspective of Jay and Washington. From Paris, Thomas Jefferson wrote to a friend back home, "The tree of liberty must be refreshed from time to time with the blood of patriots and tyrants."

Although most Americans wondered whether their new nation could survive the unrest, it is clear that Shays's Rebellion served an important purpose: It helped strengthen the position of those advocating stronger centralized government. To these people, the Shaysites were living proof that tyranny had many sources. Most citizens of the day linked liberty with security of property. By threatening the institutions created to protect property (the banks and courts), the Shaysites appeared to threaten liberty and replace it with anarchy.[2] The revolt was put down, but it would have an impact on the construction of American democracy. ⚔

Daniel Shays's rebels take control of a courthouse in western Massachusetts in 1786 to prevent farm foreclosures by creditors.

INTRODUCTION: THE ROAD TO DEMOCRACY

Despite the fears and concerns raised by Shays's Rebellion, democratic government survived and gained strength in the new nation. But how? To help answer that question this chapter focuses on the foundations of the American constitutional system. You will see that democracy took root early in America. Because of the tremendous distance from the British Empire and the rough-and-tumble character of frontier existence, early colonial settlers were forced to devise some form of self-government. Drawing on a shared commitment to individual security and the rule of law, the frontier governments provided models on which the constitutional structure of American government was eventually built. To trace the development of American democracy from the early settlements to an independent United States, this chapter explores the ideas that inspired the American Revolution, including the impact of European political thinking on the founding and the struggle for independence from England.

To understand democracy in America, it also helps to understand where the idea of democracy got started. Although the colonists began their fight for independence in 1776, the idea of democracy that inspired them originated much earlier. As we discussed in Chapter 1, democracy in America resulted from the logical progression of an idea over time. Democracy first emerged in 508 B.C. in the Greek city-state of Athens. The Athenians devised a political system called *demokratia,* meaning "rule of the people." But it was the Roman **republic,** allowing indirect representation of the popular will, that attracted the founders. In fact, the framers of the American constitution looked to the Roman republic (rather than to Greece, because Athens appeared to be ruled by mobs) as a model of democracy. In the *Federalist Papers,* Alexander Hamilton and James Madison argued that "had every Athenian citizen been a Socrates, every Athenian assembly would still have been a mob." Indeed, the Shaysites reminded many of the Founders of the dangers of passion over reason, which they attributed to such "mob rule." In the next chapter, you will see how this fear of democracy led the Founders to create a system of government that limited direct popular participation.

Characteristics of British government also strongly influenced America's political arrangement. Britain's Magna Carta, formulated in 1215, limited the exercise of power by the monarch; the notion of limited government accompanied the early colonists to North America. Its impact is visible on the Mayflower Compact, the Declaration of Independence, and the Articles of Confederation.[3]

THE SEEDS OF AMERICAN DEMOCRACY

While the colonists drew extensively on the historic forms of democracy, America's political system was as much "homegrown" as it was imported. The actions and experiences of the early settlers established a foundation for the emergence of a peculiarly American form of democracy, one that is still developing. In this section we examine some of the early attempts to establish a society under law in the early days of the American colonies. It is during this period that the first and most enduring seeds of democracy were sown, germinating in the fertile soil of a rugged frontier existence far from the British homeland.

Government by Compact

Most of the New England colonies (including Plymouth, the Providence plantations, the Connecticut River towns, and New Haven) based their first governments on the idea of a **compact,** a type of agreement that legally binds two or more parties to enforceable rules (see Figure 2.1). Compacts developed directly

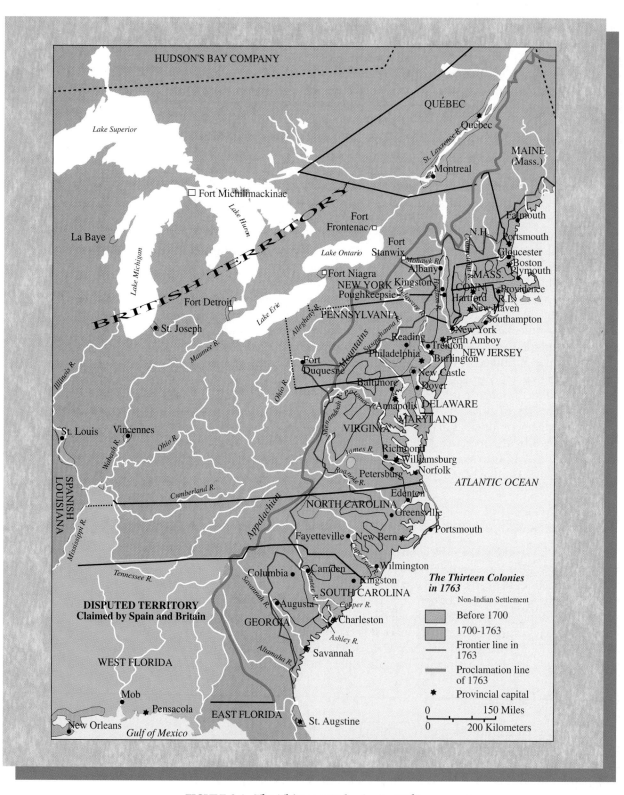

FIGURE 2.1   The Thirteen Colonies in 1763

from Puritan church theory. Pilgrims, like those who would settle Plymouth Colony, felt that just as they had entered into a covenant with God to found a church and secure their own salvation, so, too, they could forge a covenant or compact among themselves to protect those "natural" liberties provided by God.[4]

The Pilgrim families aboard the *Mayflower* on its voyage from England to Plymouth Colony in the summer of 1620 had cut all ties with the Church of England and were seeking the freedom to practice their own religion. They hoped to create a protected community from which they could spread "the gospel of the Kingdom of Christ in those remote parts of the world." Indeed, the king gave assurances to those aboard that he would "not molest them, provided they carried themselves peacefully."[5] After a long voyage, the Pilgrims sighted land; however, it was the shore of what is now Cape Cod—well beyond the London Company's territory. Once they set foot on American soil, they would be without any recognized political authority. Moreover, not everyone aboard the *Mayflower* was a Pilgrim. Thirty-five were Puritan separatists, but sixty-seven others were "strangers" (not part of the congregation), beggars and thieves who had been exiled from Britain and joined the religious separatists. William Bradford, the Pilgrim leader, was concerned that these settlers wanted "to use their own libertie" once ashore.

Thus, before coming ashore at Plymouth Rock, the Pilgrims drew up the **Mayflower Compact,** signed on November 21, 1620, by the forty-one adult males aboard the *Mayflower* (women and children were excluded). This compact provided the basis for **civil government,** meaning that all citizens agree to abide by the laws made by leaders of their choosing. Civil government as we know it evolved from the Mayflower Compact. In the compact's words, "We whose names are underwritten . . . do by these Presents, solemnly and mutually in the presences of God and one another, covenant and combine ourselves together into a civil Body Politick." For the next seventy-one years (until absorbed into the Massachusetts Bay Colony) Plymouth was ruled by this compact, which, as the first democratic constitution written in North America, provided the foundation for American constitutional thinking.

The Mayflower Compact inspired other early settlers to put pen to paper and create a framework for self-government. By 1640, English settlers in Virginia, Massachusetts, Maryland, Connecticut, Rhode Island, and New Hampshire had established a framework for state governments in six of the thirteen original states of the American republic. Another early New England compact was the Fundamental Orders of Connecticut, drawn up in 1639 between the three towns of Hartford, Windsor, and Wethersfield. The orders established a colonial government with rules for calling general assemblies, qualifying voters, organizing courts, and levying taxes.

Clearly, the early colonists recognized the importance of written rules as the basis for political authority. The compacts provided a means to describe and limit the powers of government as well as to state the **natural rights** that belong to all people no matter what type of government they live under. These rights—security from harm, liberty from oppression, and protection of private possessions—are derived from the natural state of human beings; they are rights that government cannot alter. Thus, well over a century before the constitutional convention, the ideas of compact, consent of the governed, rule of law, and natural rights had taken root.

The Massachusetts Bay Colony

Several of the original American colonies were created by charters granted to trading companies for the purpose of exploiting the resources of the New World. In 1629, the Massachusetts Bay Company, a private business venture, was chartered by King Charles I. The charter provided for the creation of a governing council that would include a governor, a deputy governor, and eighteen assistants, as well as a general court system composed of the "freemen" of the company, those with property and wealth. In the Cambridge Agreement of 1629, the stockholders in the venture transferred all governing authority from the trading company in England to the Massachusetts Bay Company in the colonies. Thus, Massachusetts Bay became de facto independent of the authority of any British corporation, and the new council became the exclusive government. The stockholders voted John Winthrop, a lawyer, to be their first governor. In March 1630, the flagship *Arbella* carried Winthrop and the first of what would soon be a great migration of forty thousand to fifty thousand English men and women to the New World. Seventeen ships and 1,000 people joined the expedition. Winthrop saw Massachusetts Bay as a refuge for persecuted Puritans. In his sermon written and delivered aboard the *Arbella,* "The Model of Christian Charity," Winthrop told his fellow Puritans, "Wee shall bee as a city upon a hill, the eyes of all people . . . upon us.[6] (The image of America as a unique focus of human endeavor would remain a staple of American political rhetoric, invoked by American presidents as recent as Ronald Reagan.)

Once established in the New World, however, Winthrop and the other members of the council attempted to run the settlement without including the more representative General Court. Disgusted by their exclusion from political power, the freemen of the company finally demonstrated to the council that, under the original terms of the charter, the real lawmaking powers of the company were vested not in the council—as was then the practice—but in the more democratic General Court. Winthrop and the council reluctantly conceded to regular sessions of the General Court, which acted as a legislative body.

This was the first instance of an English trading company evolving into a more broadly inclusive government (the General Court) rather than a small ruling group such as the more elite council. The victory of the freeholders over the tight hold of the council members broadened the base of participation (although still narrow by today's standards) and secured a greater place for the legislature as a governing authority, providing one of many precedents upon which the constitutional framers would draw when founding a national government after independence.

Proprietary Colonies and Their Legislatures

Not all of the colonies were based on a compact or evolved from an English trading company. Maryland, New York, New Jersey, Pennsylvania, Delaware, the Carolinas, and Georgia developed from royal grants. In these cases, as a way of discharging the Crown's debts, the king issued a warrant, granting land and full governing rights to a lord or baron. The recipient of the grant became sole proprietor of the grant of land, enjoying virtually absolute authority over its jurisdiction. Any settlement established there became known as a proprietary colony, and the original proprietor determined the nature of the local

THE
OATH
OF A
FREE-MAN

I A.B. being by Gods Providence an Inhabitant and FREEMAN within the Iurifdiction of this Common wealth; doe freely acknowledge myfelfe to be fubject to the Government thereof.
AND therefore doe here fweare by the Great and Dreadful NAME of the Everliving GOD, that I will be true and faithfull to the fame, and will accordingly yield affiftance & fupport thereunto with my perfon and eftate as in equity I am bound; and will alfo truly endeavour to maintaine & preferve all the liberties & priviledges thereof, fubmitting myfelfe to the wholefome Lawes & Orders made and eftablifhed by the fame. +++ AND further that I will not Plot or practife any evill againft it, or confent to any that fhall fo doe: but will timely difcover and reveal the fame to lawfull authority now here eftablifhed, for the fpeedy preventing thereof.

MOREOVER I doe folemnly bind myfelfe in the fight of GOD, that when I fhall be called to give my voyce touching any fuch matter of this State in which FREEMEN are to deale +++ I will give my vote and fuffrage as I fhall judge in mine own confcience may beft conduce and tend to the publicke weale of the body without refpect of perfon or favour of any man.
So help me GOD in the LORD IESVS CHRIST.

Printed at Cambridge in New England:
by Order of the Generall Courte:
Moneth the Firft - 1639

The right to elect a governor and deputies came with the establishment of provincial government in Massachusetts Bay. Here, in the "Oath of a Free-man," the "free men" (all shareholders) pledge themselves to their right of franchise.

government of the colony. Thus, in 1632 Lord Baltimore was granted territory in Maryland, and in 1664 the Duke of York was granted the territory of New York.

Given that the proprietors of these territories enjoyed the power and authority of kings, the proprietary colonies made an unlikely but important contribution to emerging American democracy by importing parliamentary systems. The legislatures of the proprietary colonies borrowed their form from England's Parliament, with its bicameral houses of Lords and Commons, its committee system, and its procedures. *A bicameral legislature* is a representative lawmaking body consisting of two chambers or two houses. In the United States, the Senate and the House of Representatives are the two legislative chambers.

The bicameral colonial legislatures had an upper house, whose members were appointed by the Crown (or by the proprietor on recommendation of the royal governor), and a lower house, whose members were elected based on the traditional English suffrage requirement of a "forty-shilling freehold," meaning that to vote one had to own at least forty shillings' worth of land. Thus, only men who owned land or other property were viewed as sufficiently responsible to vote (and women were not allowed to vote). Many of the colonies prohibited certain religious groups, such as Catholics and Jews, from voting, and the southern colonies barred "Negroes and mulattoes" from voting, as well as Native Americans and indentured servants.

The colonial legislatures claimed the right to control local legislation, taxes, and expenditures as well as to fix the qualifications for and judge the eligibility of house members. They also desired freedom of debate, immunity from unrest, and the right to choose their own assembly speakers. To the colonists, these were their rights as English citizens living under British domain in America. However, the British Parliament claimed these rights for itself as the only representative body of a sovereign nation, viewing the colonies as subordinate entities with no inherent sovereignty. In Britain's eyes, the colonial legislatures were entitled only to the privileges the king or Parliament chose to give them. It was this fundamental clash between colonial legislatures and the power of the British Parliament and Crown that was to erupt into the war that would tear the fledgling colonies out of the grasp of the British Empire forever.

Colonial Governors

Every colony had a governor, the principal executive authority acting as the representative of the Crown. Colonial governors were traditionally appointed by the Crown, although Rhode Island and Connecticut chose their own. The governors wielded an absolute veto, had the power of appointment, and commanded the colony's military forces. They were assisted by a council whose members they nominated for life. Almost all judicial authority rested in this council. The governor also had the power to call the legislative assembly into session and dismiss it, to create courts, and to name and remove judges. The roots of the modern American presidency can be found here.

But confrontations between the colonial assemblies and the governor over various issues occurred frequently. Because the colonial governor was the symbol of royal authority within the colonies and represented Britain's interests, such tension was inevitable, particularly since the colonists developed an extreme suspicion of executive power. In addition, the colonists saw advantages to spreading governmental responsibilities among separate compartments of government rather than concentrating power in the hands of one potentially despotic ruler. The thinking of the French philosopher Charles de Montesquieu (1689–1755), was influential. Montesquieu viewed the separation of powers as the best way to counteract tendencies toward despotism. He felt that freedom could be best preserved in a system of checks and balances through which the powers of government are balanced against and checked by one another. Montesquieu's writings, particularly *The Spirit of the Laws* (1734), helped the Founders formalize a three-part government divided into executive, legislative, and judicial functions.

Social Contract Theorists

Democracy developed and flourished in America because of the new settlers but also because of the emergence of influential new theories of governing. Just as religious leaders of the day derived a notion of social compact from the natural order of life under God, a group of European philosophers known as **social contract theorists** reasoned that individuals existed in a state of nature before the creation of a society or an organized government. Social contracts provide the philosophical foundation for the obligations that individuals and states have toward each other. If a citizen violates the social contract, the state is legally empowered to enforce appropriate punishment in the name of the people. If the state breaks the social contract, the citizens have a right to revolt against its excessive authority and even to form another government in its stead. This theory provided a philosophical foundation for the Declaration of Independence, for Shays's Rebellion, and for the 1989 student uprising in Tiananmen Square in China.

Thomas Hobbes (1588–1679) was the first of the major social contract theorists. In *Leviathan* (1651) Hobbes described the early state of nature as "nasty, brutish and short." People needed the authority of the state as protection from one another. Hobbes described people's relationships with each other as "war of all against all . . . a general inclination of all mankind, a perpetual and restless desire of power after power, that ceaseth only in death." In Hobbes's view, life without authority brings no security or liberty; he reasoned that human beings require a Leviathan, or authoritarian leader, to produce harmony and safety.

Hobbes also proposed a comprehensive theory of government. Since life in the state of nature was so threatening, individuals surrendered freedom in return for a government that provided protection and order in the form of a supreme authority, the *sovereign,* to whom all were subject. This embrace of absolute power in the form of a sovereign has led many to dismiss Hobbes as a legitimate founding thinker of modern democratic thought. Yet Hobbes clearly stated that even the authority of the sovereign must be carefully codified into a body of laws and that those laws must be applied to all with absolute equality. It was this notion of equality under the law, even in the harsh frontier world of the colonial era, that was Hobbes's most significant contribution to social contract theory.

The most influential social contract theorist, though, was John Locke (1632–1704). Locke published extensively on a number of subjects, but his most significant political works are his *Two Treatises on Government,* published in

Social contract theory has inspired a long history of political protest in America. Here, protestors show their opposition to the Vietnam War by taunting the military police in front of the Pentagon in October 1967. Many Americans believed the war in Vietnam was a horrible mistake that claimed innocent lives; at the time, those Americans took to the streets to vent their rage at a flawed policy and to let their government know they disapproved.

1690. Here, Locke rejected the notion of a Hobbesian Leviathan or even a divine right to rule. In the *Second Treatise,* Locke enumerated his theory of a social contract among citizens to create government and protect property, and for the right to revolt against an unjust government. Locke believed that governments exist to preserve the rights already present in society under nature; specifically, the protection of life, the enjoyment of personal liberty, and the possession and pursuit of private property. For Locke, these rights were inalienable, emanating from God's natural law. To deny any individual life, liberty, or property was to take away that which had been granted by God, either through birth, social status, or individual effort and ability.

Above all, and in support of the growing merchant class in England, Locke insisted that government was necessary to protect property. (In the case study on Shays's Rebellion, the framers' concern for this same obligation was clear.) According to Locke, "The great chief end of Men's uniting into Commonwealths, and putting themselves under government, is the Preservation of their Property," for property represented all that was noble in the human embodiment of God, the talents and energy that are the tools of divine will on earth. Because Locke recognized property as a result of individual ability and energy, he also accepted inequality in the distribution of that property. However, as with Hobbes, Locke believed that all individuals must be equally subject to the laws constituting the social contract between all citizens under government.

Along with the principle of an inalienable right to life, liberty, and property, Locke asserted the importance of **limited government** based on popular consent. By *limited government,* Locke meant that the powers of the government should be clearly defined and bounded, so that governmental authority could not intrude in the lives of private citizens. Unlike Hobbes, Locke did not see the necessity for an absolute sovereign but argued instead for a strong legislature. His model was, of course, the British Parliament, whereas Hobbes's sovereign bore more resemblance to the British Crown. But, like Hobbes, Locke insisted that whenever government oversteps its role, the people have a right to react. According to Locke, "Whenever the legislators endeavor to take away and destroy the property of the people, or to reduce them to slavery under arbitrary power, they put themselves onto a state of war with the people, who are thereupon absolved from any further obedience, and are left to the common refuge which God hath provided for all men against force and violence." Locke's limited government is strong enough to provide protection for all citizens and their property but not so strong that it infringes on individual liberty.

Locke's *Second Treatise of Civil Government* was such a clear statement of the themes just outlined that much of the Declaration of Independence draws from his rationale to justify severing ties with a tyrannical king. Locke's idea of limited government is also embedded in the Constitution. The separation of governing powers and the numerous guarantees of individual liberties found in the Bill of Rights are derived from the Lockean notion of limited government based on popular consent.

For the government of Britain, under which both Hobbes (for most of his life) and Locke lived, the theory of the social contract was just a theory. In the American colonies of the 17th century, however, each colonial territory was in part a miniature experiment in social contract theory. Coming to a land that indeed often rendered life "nasty, brutish, and short," with little real governmental authority reaching directly into their lives, the colonists did live in something like the "state of nature." And, just as both Hobbes and Locke theorized they must, the colonists entered into binding contracts, established laws and ruling bodies, and formed governments. The Mayflower Compact, the Fundamental Orders of Connecticut, and even the rather Hobbesian regimes established in the proprietary colonies all required the willing entry of individuals into a legally ordered arrangement of power, a society under law.

FIRST MOVES TOWARD A UNION

By 1753, over a century after the signing of the Mayflower Compact, the American colonists recognized the need for greater union and cooperation among themselves. On September 18, 1753, the Board of Trade in London requested that the colonies "enter into articles of union and confederation with each other for the mutual defense of His Majesty's subjects and interests in North America, as well in time of peace as war." The goal was to protect the economic interests of the empire.

French expansionism in the backwoods of America led to increasing conflict and to the French and Indian War (1756–1763), as it was known in America (in Europe it was known as the Seven Years' War). A congress was scheduled to be held from June 19 to July 10, 1754, in Albany, New York, to draft an agreement calling for a union of the colonies. On May 9, 1754, *The Pennsylvania Gazette* published a lead article and cartoon authored by Ben Franklin. Originally, the cartoon was published in an attempt to unify the colonists against the French, but here, Franklin sought to illustrate the peril of disunity in opposing the repressive policies of the British Crown. At the meeting in Albany, Franklin proposed the Albany Plan, a plan of union calling for a self-governing confederation for the colonies. A **confederation** is a league of sovereign states that delegates powers on selected issues to a central government. The plan created the 48-member Grand Legislative Council in which all colonies would be represented; its responsibilities would include raising an army and navy, making war, and regulating trade and taxation. The plan also called for a chief executive, to be called president–general of the United Colonies, appointed by the Crown.

Franklin's plan was endorsed unanimously by the Albany delegates, but it was soon rejected by individual colonial assemblies because it appeared to give too much power to the Crown, and by the British Crown, which claimed it gave too much power to the colonists. Franklin later wrote, "If the foregoing

Franklin's 1754 "Join or Die" woodcut was originally designed to symbolize the need for the colonies to unite for their common defense against the French. The symbol became popular again during the revolutionary period when the colonies faced the British threat.

plan, or something like it, had been adopted and carried into execution, the subsequent separation of the colonies from the mother country might not so soon have happened."[7] Some twenty years later Franklin's design would resurface in an early draft of the Articles of Confederation.

REBELLION: CAUSES AND CONSEQUENCES

With the end of the French and Indian War in 1763, France's claim to power and territory came to an end in North America, and the British Empire had established its control. But Britain was heavily in debt from financing the war. To alleviate this debt, it turned to the colonies with a program of direct taxation. Prior to 1763 the British were interested in the colonies primarily as new markets and sources of raw materials. Now undertaking a new policy of imperialism, Britain sought more efficient political and military control in the New World. To this end, several units of British soldiers were dispatched to protect the colonial frontier, at great annual expense to the Crown.

To generate revenues sufficient to defray the considerable expense of British occupation and control, the "first lord of the Treasurey," George Grenville, elected to raise taxes, first on the already burdened British and then on the American colonists, whose taxes had been relatively modest to this point. Such direct taxation of the colonists without their consent and without representation in Parliament had grave consequences: Resistance to British control and to what the colonists perceived as unjust taxation led to revolution and then to independence.

The Sugar and Stamp Acts

The British viewed taxation as part of the sovereign's inherent authority and sought to extend its influence and extract revenue from the colonists through a series of acts, most notably the Sugar Act of 1764 and the Stamp Act of 1765. The **Sugar Act** levied a three-penny-per-gallon tax on molasses and other goods imported into the colonies. The tax threatened to cut deeply into the profits of several northern colonies, whose thriving rum industries were dependent on imported molasses. The preamble of the Sugar Act stated that the tax was to be used for "defraying the expenses of defending and securing the colonies." This was how the British saw it. The colonists, however, viewed the act as a revenue measure imposed on them by the sovereign, without their consent.

On February 13, 1765, Lord George Grenville proposed before Parliament another measure to raise money from the colonies—this time to pay the cost of stationing British troops in America. The **Stamp Act** was quickly passed by Parliament in March; the act required that revenue stamps be placed on all printed matter and legal documents including newspapers, almanacs, bonds, leases, college diplomas, bills of sale, liquor licenses, insurance policies, playing cards, and dice. The tax was felt in every aspect of commercial life in the colonies, its influence extending well beyond that of the sugar tax by affecting more people directly. The act was scheduled to go into effect on November 1, 1765.

Most colonists opposed the Stamp Act, and public protest against it raged throughout the spring and summer of 1765. Some protestors, calling themselves the "Sons of Liberty," often assembled under "liberty trees" and erected "liberty poles," actions that helped unify the colonists. Patrick Henry, one of the great, fiery radical figures of the revolutionary period, standing before the Virginia House of Burgesses in May 1765, summed up the prevailing sentiment against the Stamp Act: "Taxation of the people by themselves . . . is . . . the distinguishing characteristic of British freedom, without which the ancient constitution cannot exist. . . . The General Assembly of this Colony have the only and sole exclusive right and power to lay taxes and impositions upon the inhabitants of this colony." Henry ended his dramatic speech by predicting that if present policies were not revised, George III might lose his head. "Caesar had his Brutus, Charles I had his Cromwell, and George III . . ." Henry reportedly exclaimed. At that moment some delegates rose to shout "treason!" to which Henry replied, "If this be treason, make the most of it."

No Taxation without Representation

In October 1765 nine colonies sent delegates to a hastily called Stamp Act congress in New York. Called by James Otis, a lawyer from Boston, this congress issued a series of resolutions (written by Philadelphia lawyer John Dickinson) maintaining that the king's subjects in America were entitled to be free of taxation imposed without their consent; they were "entitled to all the inherent rights and liberties of his natural born subjects within the Kingdom of Great Britain . . . . [It was] the undoubted right of Englishmen, that no taxes be imposed on them but with their own consent, given personally or by their representatives."

Since the American colonists had no representative in Parliament, they reasoned that Parliament had no right to tax them. To counter the colonists' demand of "no taxation without representation," Parliament offered the idea of

British control was met with increasing hostility in the American colonies. "If this be treason, make the most of it," Patrick Henry replied defiantly on May 1, 1775 to defenders of King George III. On July 9, 1776, King George's detractors, of whom there were many, toppled the king's statue in Bowling Green, New York. The Sons of Liberty orchestrated the downing of the statue, which was then melted down and used to make bullets.

"You know, the idea of taxation *with* representation doesn't appeal to me very much either."

Drawing by Handelsman; © 1970 The New Yorker Magazine, Inc.

"virtual representation," upholding that members of Parliament represent the interests of the whole empire, whether the whole of Ireland or American colonies. In addition, many new and old boroughs and cities in England did not yet have representation in Parliament. Thus, there was no practical difference between Charleston, South Carolina, and Manchester, England—both had no voice in Parliament but were still represented by virtue of Parliament's role in the British Empire.

The colonists' experiences with their town meetings and colonial assemblies led them to reject the idea of virtual representation. "A mere cobweb, spread to catch the unwary, and entangle the weak," argued Maryland legislator Daniel Dulany. If Manchester was not represented in Parliament, "it ought to be," said Otis. Ideas about compacts, natural rights, and social contracts informed colonial reaction. The colonists, by virtue of written constitutions and documents, expected to be granted the rights of freeborn Englishmen. They believed instead in actual representation, a system in which legislators were freely chosen by the people. By rejecting the theory of virtual representation, the colonists accepted the idea that a legislature should be "an actual representation of all classes of the people by persons of each class" to be a "true picture of the people." And although they accepted the supremacy of Parliament, they embraced the doctrine of limited government—that Parliament had no claim to a power that would violate the natural rights and laws to which all free people hold claim.

The colonists had some support in Parliament. Edmund Burke argued, "The British Empire must be governed on a plan of freedom, for it will be governed by no other." In the House of Commons William Pitt argued, "Taxation is no part of the governing or legislating power"; the idea of virtual representation is one of "the most contemptible ideas that ever entered the head of man."[8]

By March 1766 Lord Grenville had been removed over a falling out with the king (their failing relationship was not a result of the volatile colonial reaction to Grenville's tax policies). His replacement, the marquis of Rockingham, was part of a faction more sympathetic to the colonists. In a delicate political compromise, Parliament repealed Grenville's Stamp Act but, so as not to offend Grenville's considerable parliamentary support, it passed the Declaratory Act, granting the king and Parliament complete legislative authority to make laws binding to the colonies "in all cases whatsoever."

The Townshend Revenue Acts

In 1767 Parliament sought to impose yet another series of taxes on glass, lead, tea, and paper imported into the colonies. The preamble of the **Townshend Revenue Acts** stated that these acts were intended for "the support of civil government, in such provinces as it shall be found necessary." Revenues would also be used to pay salaries for governors and other officers, thereby diluting the strength of colonial assemblies, which until then had controlled governors' salaries.

Few colonists protested Parliament's authority to regulate trade among the colonies of its empire, but most felt that only the colonial assemblies had the authority to directly tax the colonies. The Townshend Acts provoked numerous boycotts and mob action as well as the twelve "Letters of a Pennsylvania Farmer," an eloquent and moderate interpretation of the colonial position, written by John Dickinson, a Philadelphia lawyer. "The cause of Liberty is a cause of too much dignity to be sullied by turbulence and tumult," he cautioned. Appearing in the *Pennsylvania Chronicle,* the letters challenged British authority. "For who are a free people? Not those over whom government is reasonably and equitably exercised, but those, who live under a government so constitutionally checked and controlled, that proper provision is made against its being otherwise exercised."

Dickinson's pamphlet was followed by the "Massachusetts Circular Letter," written by the Sons of Liberty organizers Samuel Adams and James Otis. Massachusetts was the center of revolutionary activity, and in this letter to the colonial legislatures on February 11, 1768, Adams espoused the themes of constitutional supremacy and limited government, helping to widen the division between the colonies and England. "In all free states the constitution is fixed; and as the supreme Legislat[ure] derives its power and authority from the constitution, it cannot overleap the bounds of it, without destroying its own foundation."

Echoing John Locke, Adams reasoned that the Townshend Acts violated the sacred right to preserve one's property. "That is an essential unalterable right in nature, engrafted into the British Constitution, as a fundamental law and ever held sacred and irrevocable by the subjects within the realm, that what a man has honestly acquired is absolutely his own, which he may freely give, but cannot be taken from him without his consent."

With arguments like these, a crossroads in relations with the Crown had been reached.

The Boston Massacre

When words failed, the colonists resorted to more extreme measures, and the cause of revolution was soon to have its first martyrs. On March 5, 1770, British soldiers fired a volley of shots into a crowd of hecklers who had been throwing snowballs at the redcoats to protest enforcement of the Townshend Acts. Five colonists were killed, including their leader, Crispus Attucks. The first colonists had now lost their lives protesting taxation without representation. The **Boston Massacre** aroused intense public protest and led to the removal of troops from Boston and the repeal of virtually all of the import duties. The massacre also alerted the colonists to a dramatic truth—organized local resistance revealed the impotence of imperial power in the colonies.

Committees of Correspondence

The fact that the colonists were able to publicize Parliament's encroachment on their rights helped fuel revolutionary fervor. In 1772 Samuel Adams emerged as a major agitator for colonial independence and formed the Boston **Committee of Correspondence,** which published a statement of rights and grievances warning colonists that Britain could disband colonial legislatures and take away individual rights. Similar committees quickly sprang up throughout Massachusetts and the other colonies. Committees of correspondence thus became the first institutionalized mechanism for communication among the colonies. One Loyalist (a person loyal to Britain) called the committees (no

In 1839, on the occasion of the 50th anniversary of George Washington's inaugural as president, former president John Quincy Adams described the British Empire on the eve of revolution: "She had established an uncontested monopoly of the commerce of all her colonies. But forgetting all the warnings of preceding ages—the lessons written in the blood of her own children, through centuries of departed time, she undertook to tax the people of the colonies without their consent. Resistance, instantaneous, unconcerned, sympathetic, inflexible resistance like electric shock startled and roused the people of all the English colonies on this continent."

—John Quincy Adams

Paul Revere's dramatic engraving of the Boston Massacre depicts the initial bloody conflict between British troops (redcoats) and Boston laborers. The engraving was used effectively as propaganda by patriots who wished to fuel emotions against the British in the 1770s. Among those killed in the massacre was Crispus Attucks, the leader of the laborers and the first African American man to die in the American struggle for independence.

doubt a tribute to their effectiveness) "the foulest, subtlest, and most venomous serpent ever issued from the egg of sedition." Indeed, the continuing cooperation among the colonies was aided by intercolonial committees of correspondence.

The Boston Tea Party

The East India Company had fallen on hard business times. Before the Townshend Acts, the company had been the chief supplier of tea to the colonists. In an effort to avoid paying the Townshend duty, colonists started smuggling in tea from the Netherlands, thus cutting deeply into the East India Company's profits. With seventeen million pounds of tea in its warehouses, the company asked Parliament for help. Parliament allowed the company to sell tea to the colonies at a price below market value.

The colonists were in an uproar over this, realizing that colonial tea merchants would be undercut. Even worse, no one knew which commodity might be next. Parliament's actions provoked a most famous incident of civil disobedience, the **Boston Tea Party.** At midnight on December 16, 1773, colonists dumped 342 chests of tea into Boston Harbor.

Colonial women were among the principal consumers of tea and led the boycott against it. An organization of colonial women known as the Daughters of Liberty committed itself to agitation against British policies, proclaiming that "rather than Freedom, we'll part with our Tea."

To punish Massachusetts for the tea party and send a message to the other colonies, the king and his ministers legislated the Coercive Acts. This series of punitive measures, passed by Parliament in the spring of 1774, proved so loathsome to the colonists that the acts were dubbed the **Intolerable Acts.** In addition to closing Boston Harbor until the tea was paid for and requiring the quartering of British soldiers in private homes, the acts created the position of military governor. General Thomas Gage, commander in chief of British forces

This scene from the Boston Tea Party depicts the tarring and feathering of an unpopular customs agent while, in the background, tea is dumped into Boston Harbor. As the tea was thrown overboard, a crowd cheered from the shore. This protest was a result of the colonists' resentment over oppressive taxation and the denial of liberty. Note the liberty tree in the background.

in North America, was named to the post. Gage's consent was necessary for convening most town meetings, making him all but a dictator. In addition, he could use writs of assistance to search every part of a house for evidence of a crime, whether real or perceived.

Rather than forcing the colonists to submit to the will of King George III, the Intolerable Acts helped to unify the colonies against the Crown. Massachusetts's plight inspired other colonies to defend its cause. A young member of Virginia's Committee on Correspondence, Thomas Jefferson, proposed setting aside June 1, the date of the closing of Boston Harbor, as a day of fasting and prayer in Virginia, hundreds of miles to the south. With this first instance of one colony's empathy for another's plight, a new nation was beginning to emerge. On learning of Jefferson's proposal, the Virginia governor immediately dissolved the assembly, whose members went down the road to the Raleigh Tavern and drew up a resolution for a continental congress with representation for all the colonies.[9]

REVOLUTION AND THE STIRRINGS OF A NEW GOVERNMENT

In the wake of the Boston Tea Party, the colonists's differences with the Crown moved far beyond the taxation question. While the tax policies of Lord Grenville served to ignite the first intense clash between Britain and America, the heavy-handed response of the Intolerable Acts symbolized the real basis of the schism between Crown and colonies. Whereas the British wanted order and obedience, the colonists wanted greater liberty. "Although Liberty was not the only goal for Americans in the 1770s and 1780s," writes political scientist James MacGregor Burns, "they believed also in Independence, Order, Equality, the

Pursuit of Happiness—none had the evocative power and sweep of Liberty, or Freedom—two terms for the same thing. To preserve liberty was the supreme end of government."[10] In Boston, this sentiment had taken the form of dumping tea into the harbor and standing up to the hated British troops stationed there. At the First Continental Congress, the signs of both revolution and American democracy were visible. In a speech before the Virginia House of Burgesses on March 23, 1775, Patrick Henry cried out, "Is life so dear, or peace so sweet, as to be purchased at the price of chains and slavery? Forbid it, Almighty God! I know not what course others may take; but as for me, give me liberty, or give me death!"

The First Continental Congress

On September 5, 1774, 55 elected members (from provincial congresses or irregular conventions) of the **First Continental Congress** met in Philadelphia's Carpenter's Hall to devise a plan to unify the colonies in an attempt to reestablish more cordial relations with the British Crown, although the colonists still insisted on the restoration of their rights as English citizens. Twelve colonies except Georgia and Florida were represented at the congress, which ran through October 26, 1774. Assembled was an extraordinarily prominent group of Americans, among them Samuel and John Adams of Massachusetts; John Jay of New York; John Dickinson of Pennsylvania; and Patrick Henry and George Washington of Virginia. Before leaving for Philadelphia, Washington wrote to a friend, expressing the intensity of feelings common to those attending the Congress: "The crisis is arrived when we must assert our rights, or submit to every imposition, that can be heaped upon us, till custom and use shall make us as tame and abject [as] slaves, as the blacks we rule over with such arbitrary sway."[11]

The First Continental Congress issued The Declaration of American Rights, claiming in the name of the colonies exclusive legislative power over taxation and "all the rights, liberties, and communities of free and natural-born subjects within the realm of England." By taking responsibility for taxes, operating a court system, and raising militias, the colonies began to assume the character of states; they also laid the institutional groundwork for the later Constitution.

The Congress also rejected a plan of union introduced by George Galloway of Pennsylvania. Galloway's plan closely resembled Franklin's Albany Plan of twenty years earlier. The Congress did endorse the plan of a silversmith from Boston. Paul Revere's radical Suffolk Resolves, which declared the Intolerable Acts null and void, supported arming Massachusetts to defend itself against Britain and urged economic sanctions on all British products. The delegates agreed to meet again in May 1775 if Britain did not restore the rights it had taken away. Most delegates hoped to avoid war with Britain; few were ready to publicly declare a war for American independence.[12]

"The Shots Heard 'Round the World"

Following the Boston Tea Party, Parliament had declared the state of Massachusetts to be in open rebellion, giving British troops the right to shoot rebels on sight. General Gage was determined to put down this rebellion, so in the spring of 1775 he marched on Concord, near Boston, to destroy ammunition

A woodcut depicting the British retreat from Concord on April 19, 1775.

and gunpowder being stored by patriots. On April 19, 1775, his troops reached Lexington and were met by seventy Minutemen, whom Gage ordered to disperse. Minutemen were farmers and townspeople who had been training to fight on a minute's notice. A stray shot was fired, the British opened fire, and eight Minutemen were dead. Seven hundred British troops continued their march on Concord as Paul Revere, Samuel Prescott, and William Dawes spread word that the British were approaching. The British then clashed with Minutemen at Concord's North Bridge. At Lexington there had been no return fire, but at Concord, in Longfellow's words, was fired "the shot heard 'round the world," the first armed resistance by Americans. By day's end, 250 British troops and 90 Americans were dead or wounded. The colonies were now at war with the powerful British Empire; the American War of Independence was under way.

Common Sense

Although many colonists were reluctant to fight a war with England, Thomas Paine's pamphlet of January 1776, ***Common Sense*** (published anonymously to avoid charges of treason), helped crystallize the idea of revolution for them. Paine, who would later serve with General Washington during the war, changed the terms of revolutionary rhetoric. He moved beyond merely stating the colonists' claims against Parliament to questioning the very institution of monarchy. He also concluded that the colonies needed to separate from England immediately. Paine wrote:

> A government of our own is our natural right; and when a man seriously reflects on the precariousness of human affairs, he will become convinced, that it is infinitely wiser and safer to form a constitution of our own in a cool deliberate manner, while we have it in our power, than to trust such an interesting event to time and chance. . . .

What Would You Do If You Were in King George's Shoes?

Imagine yourself in King George's shoes. You are faced with rebellion in the colonies. You can seek reconciliation with the colonists by compromising on the taxation issue, or you can go to war to keep that part of your empire in line in the hope of maintaining it as a source of revenue.

The colonists seem eager for a peaceful settlement. In July 1775, their continental congress issues the Declaration of Causes and Necessity of Taking Up Arms, which denounces the unprovoked British assault at Lexington and reaffirms colonial resolve to fight for the rights due them as Englishmen. The congress also issues the Olive Branch Petition, which disavows any intention of independence but "pledge[s] resistance until Parliament abandon[s] its unconstitutional rule in America."

There is support for reconciliation in Parliament as well. In a speech to the House of Commons on March 22, 1775, Edmund Burke takes note of the colonists' "fierce spirit of liberty" and recognizes the justness of

Thinking Critically

their claims to the rights and liberties enjoyed by all English citizens.

You review the history of the colonies in your mind's eye and assess your actions, starting with the Sugar Act and ending with the skirmishes at Lexington and Concord. You evaluate colonial reaction over time to arrive at a decision. As king, what would you do?

What Happened

As anyone familiar with American history knows, the king chose war. He ignored the Olive Branch Petition, refused to meet with the colonial representatives to arrive at a settlement on taxation without representation, and would not allow himself to be swayed by parliamentary debates, particularly Burke's speech on liberty. He ordered his army to regard the colonists as "open and avowed enemies." He then issued the Proclamation of Rebellion on August 23, 1775, setting the stage for war.

Ye that tell us of harmony and reconciliation, can ye restore to us the time that is passed? Can ye give to prostitution its former innocence? Neither can ye reconcile Britain and America. The last cord now is broken.

In addition, *Common Sense* enumerated the advantages of republican government over monarchy. In this form of government, as described earlier in the discussion of the Roman republic, instead of participating directly in the decision making of government, citizens elect representatives who make decisions on their behalf. Thus, a republic is one step removed from a direct democracy, in which the citizens, not their representatives, form the decision-making body of government. According to Paine, America would be a laboratory for such a political experiment, a struggle for full representation and equality of rights.

Common Sense profoundly influenced thinking in the colonies. George Washington testified to the impact of this revolutionary pamphlet when he declared, "*Common Sense* is working a powerful change in the minds of men." Over 150,000 copies of the pamphlet were sold within three months of its first printing. Virtually every colonist had access to it, and the demand for independence moved rapidly.

The Second Continental Congress

Three weeks after the clashes at Lexington and Concord, the **Second Continental Congress** convened, on May 10, 1775, with all thirteen colonies represented. The purpose of the congress was to decide whether or not to sever the bonds with England and declare independence. The brief but dramatic skirmishes at Lexington and Concord were still fresh in the minds of the delegates. In the absence of any other single legislative body, without any legal authority to speak of, and in the midst of growing hostility toward the British, the congress had little choice but to assume the role of a revolutionary government. It took control of the militiamen gathered around Boston and named George Washington general and commander in chief of this rather ragtag army. Then, on June 17, the first major confrontation between the colonials and British forces occurred—the battle of Bunker Hill, in which Daniel Shays fought.

The Declaration of Independence

On June 7, 1776, a resolution for independence was introduced by Richard Henry Lee, a Virginia delegate to the Continental Congress, which was meeting at Philadelphia's State House: "Resolved, that these United Colonies are, and of right ought to be, free and independent States, and that they are absolved from all allegiance to the British Crown, and that all connection between them and the State of Great Britain is, and ought to be, totally dissolved."

No longer was the reestablishment of their "rights as Englishmen" sufficient for the colonial leaders attending the congress; it was to be independence or nothing. Lee's resolution for independence was considered and finally passed when the Congress reconvened on July 2. Writing to his wife Abigail, John Adams predicted that July 2 "will be the most memorable epoch in the history of

On July 2, 1776, the Continental Congress voted on Richard Henry Lee's resolution, "That these United Colonies are, and of right ought to be, free and independent states." After the vote for independence, John Adams wrote to his wife, Abigail, that the day "will be the most memorable epoch in the history of America."

America." In the meantime a committee had already been formed to draft a formal proclamation declaring independence. This committee included such notables as John Adams, Ben Franklin, and Thomas Jefferson. It was the thirty-three-year-old Virginian, Jefferson, who drafted the final document on which the Congress voted. On July 4, after three days of vigorous debate, the Declaration of Independence was approved and signed. According to legend, John Hancock, the first to sign, used large letters so that King George would be able to read Hancock's signature without putting on his glasses.

The **Declaration of Independence** detailed the colonists' reasons for breaking with England, justified the revolution, and provided a philosophical basis for limited government based on popular consent. We have already touched on the origins of these themes in the discussion of social contract theory on pp. 8–11.

In declaring independence from England, the colonists renounced their allegiance to the British Crown and their chartered rights as English citizens. Clearly echoing social contract theorist John Locke, the declaration proclaimed that the colonists were "created equal" and were endowed, by God, with certain natural rights—the inalienable right to life, liberty, and the pursuit of happiness. The declaration also proclaimed that government was instituted to secure these rights and derived its just powers from the consent of the governed. When governments become destructive of these ends, the people have the right to reconstitute it. The declaration listed the colonists' many grievances against King George III and concluded that he had become a "tyrannical King" who was "unfit to be the ruler of a free people." Thus, the colonies "are, and of right ought to be, free and independent States."

By instituting government based on popular consent, in which power is exercised by representatives chosen by and responsive to the populace, the 18th-century revolutionaries sought "to become republican." Political power would come from the people, not a supreme authority such as a king. The ultimate success of a government would be dependent on the character or civic virtue of its citizenry. The key assumption was that "if the population consisted of sturdy, independent property owners imbued with civic virtue, then the republic could survive."[13] As Madison later wrote, "No other form would be reconcilable with the genius of the people of America; with the fundamental principles of the revolution; or with the honorable determination, which animates every votary of freedom, to rest all our political experiments on the capacity of mankind for self-government."

By signing the declaration, these revolutionaries were risking their liberty and even their lives. The declaration itself was an act of treason against the Crown, punishable by death. Following the signing of the declaration, Ben Franklin is alleged to have summed up the gravity of the occasion with the words, "We must, indeed, all hang together, or most assuredly we shall hang separately."

THE FIRST NEW GOVERNMENT: A CONFEDERATION OF STATES

Even before the War of Independence was won, Americans faced the challenge of devising a new government. To do this, they drew from their experiences with compacts, social contract theory, separation of governmental powers, and natural rights. Between 1776 and 1780, all states except Rhode Island and

The Founding:
Key Events

1620	Mayflower Compact signed. Plymouth Colony founded.
1630	Massachusetts Bay Colony founded.
1760	King George III assumes the throne of England.
1764	Sugar Act passed by Parliament.
1765	Stamp Act passed by Parliament. Delegates to Stamp Act Congress draft declaration of rights and liberties
1766	Stamp Act repealed, Declaratory Act issued.
1767	Townshend Acts passed.
1770	Boston Massacre.
1772	First committees of correspondence formed by Samuel Adams.
1773	Boston Tea Party.
1774	Coercive Acts against Massachusetts passed. First Continental Congress convened.
1775	Skirmish at Lexington and Concord officially begins the War of Independence. Second Continental Congress convened .
1776	*Common Sense* published. Declaration of Independence signed.
1781	Articles of Confederation adopted.
1783	Peace of Versailles. Great Britain formally recognizes the independence of the United States.
1786	Shays's Rebellion.

Connecticut adopted new constitutions (these two states simply struck from their original governing charters any mention of colonial obligation to the Crown) reflecting the idea of **sovereignty,** the total independence and self-government of the people. Seven of the state constitutions even contained a separate bill of rights guaranteeing citizens certain natural rights and protection from their government. The Virginia Bill of Rights, for example, provided for the right of revolution, freedom of the press, religious liberty, separation of powers, free elections, prohibition against taxation without consent, and fair legal procedures such as the right to trial by jury and moderate bail.

None of these state constitutions contained any provision for a central governmental authority that would help define the thirteen states as a nation. Thus, a few days after the Declaration of Independence was signed, a committee was called to draft a plan to bring the colonies together as a confederation. Fighting a war for independence necessitated a central direction, a plan for union.

The Articles of Confederation (1781–89)

After one year and six drafts, on July 12, 1777, the **Articles of Confederation** were presented to the Continental Congress. Following several months of debate, on November 15, 1777, the plan was adopted by the congress and

A Few Minutes with a Minuteman

Levi Preston was a Minuteman at Danvers, Massachusetts. When asked about British oppression sixty-seven years after Lexington and Concord, the following dialogue resulted:

A: What were they? Oppression? I didn't feel them.

Q: What, were you not oppressed by the Stamp Act?

A: I never saw one of those stamps, and always understood that Governor Bernard put them all in Castle William. I am certain I never paid a penny for one of them.

Q: Well, what then about the tea-tax?

A: Tea-tax! I never drank a drop of the stuff; the boys threw it all overboard.

Q: Then I suppose you had been reading Harrington or Sidney and Locke about the eternal principles of liberty.

A: Never heard of 'em. We read only the Bible, the Catechism, Watts's Psalms and Hymns, and the Almanac.

Q: Well, then, what was the matter? And what did you mean in going to the fight?

A: Young man, what we meant in going for those redcoats was this: we always had governed ourselves, and we always meant to. They didn't mean we should.

Source: George Brown Tindall, *America* (New York: W. W. Norton, 1988) p. 218.

submitted to the individual states for ratification. The Articles formally took effect on March 1, 1781, after being ratified by all of the states.

The colonists were not about to jeopardize the power and freedom they had won, so the Articles sought to limit the powers of the government. The confederation they created was a loosely knit league or alliance of thirteen independent states agreeing to cooperate in certain instances. The central government was extremely weak. All of the national power—executive, legislative, and judicial—was housed in a single house of Congress, in which each state had one vote. Fearing a new king, no separate executive branch was created.

Under the Articles, the states reigned supreme in a "league of friendship." They retained almost total sovereignty over their affairs, with the Congress strictly limited in its powers. Congress was not given the power to tax, though it could coin its own money. And though it could declare war, it could not raise its own army. Without an army, it was unable to act when the British refused to decamp from their forts on the Great Lakes after signing the Treaty of Paris in 1783; it was also powerless when the Spanish closed off the Mississippi River and the port of New Orleans to United States trade and when both Spain and Britain began arming Native Americans in the hope that they would attack frontier settlements. When Shays's Rebellion flared up, Congress was unable to raise or finance an army. The Congress had no power over interstate or international commerce, no power to make treaties with foreign governments (instead, each state could make its own foreign policy), and no power over state citizens. Congress could not even make laws; it was limited to passing

The revolution was fought on the two principles of liberty and equality, but slavery became the practice of the land in all of the original colonies. George Washington, Thomas Jefferson, and Patrick Henry were slaveholders (although both Washington and Jefferson would later release their slaves). Shown here, a slave auction in Virginia where human beings of all ages were sold to the highest bidder. Only Rhode Island, Connecticut, and Pennsylvania had restricted the import of slaves prior to the revolution.

resolutions or regulations. It took the agreement of nine states to pass any legislation, and a unanimous vote of all thirteen states was required to amend the Articles. Unable to raise funds, the Congress was forced to borrow vast sums of money from France and Holland to pay for the war with Britain. Unable to defend itself without the voluntary support of state militias and powerless to legislate, the new central government was simply too weak to govern effectively.

The problems of the confederation of states seemed to grow, ranging from financial and commercial difficulties to civil disorder. The political chaos that inevitably resulted made the nation appear not so much a country as an organization of thirteen little kingdoms, each directed by a state legislature. The irony here, of course, is that in this respect, the Articles did what they were devised to do. However, without any central-governmental oversight, the dominant governing institutions, the state legislatures, often acted against democratic principles, while state executive authority steadily weakened. James Madison summed up the problem: "Experience had proved a tendency in our governments to throw all power into the Legislative vortex. The Executives of the State are in general little more than Cyphers: the legislatures omnipotent. If no effectual check be devised for restraining the instability and encroachments of the latter, a revolution of some kind or other would be inevitable."

With the "omnipotent" state legislatures operating to the advantage of their individual interests, in many ways certain states flourished economically. Agricultural exports had doubled, and the national debt was so low that states were paying back principal as well as interest. The states were cooperating in their trade policies to keep out British goods and were working together to raise money for capital improvements.

But when a crisis arose, the central government proved incapable of handling it, revealing the glaring weaknesses of the Articles. This was clearly demonstrated in the case of Shays's Rebellion—when skyrocketing interest rates and taxes forced many farmers into bankruptcy and ultimately revolt, the central government could not respond when asked by Massachusetts to do so.

Instead, private citizens hired soldiers to put down the insurrection. The Articles, then, were destined to fail.

THE NEED FOR A MORE PERFECT UNION

After six years of confederation, it became clear that a stronger, more centralized government was needed. Shays's Rebellion led the colonists and Founding Fathers alike to fear anarchy and desire order. Even George Washington recognized that the Articles were founded on a too-trusting view of human nature. The states seemed incapable of promoting a common good; the "intervention of a coercive power" would be required.

In September 1786, spurred on by Alexander Hamilton, delegations of twelve "commissioners" from five states (all states had been invited to attend) met at the Annapolis Convention in Annapolis, Maryland, ostensibly to create a uniform system of commerce. Hamilton's real purpose, however, was to try to foster a stronger centralized national government. In the end, though, the commissioners could agree only to have another meeting in Philadelphia, in May of 1787.

On February 21, 1787, a resolution was approved stating the goal of that meeting: "For the sole and express purpose of revising the Articles of Confederation." But as the delegates arrived in May, James Madison, the first to arrive, shared Hamilton's view that a mere revision of the Articles would not be enough. The complex mix of economic, political, and other problems plaguing the confederation required not a loose arrangement of individual states struggling to sink or swim on their own but a centralized authority for the common protection and prosperity of all.

The convention was held in the East Room of the State House, the same room in which the Second Continental Congress had met in May 1775 and the Declaration of Independence had been signed in 1776. The convention opened on May 14, although nothing could be done for lack of a quorum, and delegates continued straggling in until well into the summer. Four months later the participants would accomplish what is frequently described as "the Miracle of Philadelphia." In Chapter 3 we look at what was accomplished in Philadelphia.

THE FOUNDERS: PAVING THE WAY FOR APPROACHING DEMOCRACY

Most of the American revolutionaries would not pass a modern test of democratic standards. As we have seen, their eighteenth-century world excluded many people from participating in politics—women, blacks, Native Americans, poor whites, and members of certain religions. Yet their revolution helped pave the way for America to approach democracy. How can this be? Essentially, the Revolution united Americans by teaching them to think as a nation. At the First Continental Congress, Patrick Henry declared that "the distinctions between Virginians, Pennsylvanians, New Yorkers, and New Englanders are no more. I am not a Virginian but an American."[14]

From the Revolution sprang not just a declaration but a national identity rooted in the embodiment of the words "life, liberty, and the pursuit of happiness." The Founders shared a commitment to classical democratic ideals. From this they

Abigail Adams—the First Feminist?

In the early decades of America's history the voices of women were largely unheard. No women attended the Continental Congress, nor were any involved in the drafting of the Declaration of Independence. Women did however play an essential role in campaigns to boycott British goods in protest against the taxes imposed by Parliament. They were also active behind the scenes during the Revolution: They plowed fields, managed shops, and melted down pots to make shot. Yet they played virtually no part in political affairs; they could not vote, nor could they hold elective office. The only route open to them was to persuade their husbands to act on their behalf in Congress and the state assemblies.

The Struggle for Equality

The situation of women in the late eighteenth century is illustrated in a letter from Abigail Adams to her husband John, who was attending the Continental Congress. "I desire you would remember the Ladies," she wrote, "and be more generous and favourable to them than your ancestors." Although she conceded the traditional dominance of men—women were "beings placed by providence under [male] protection"—she issued a challenge, if only half seriously: "If perticuliar care and attention is not paid to the Ladies we are determined to foment a Rebelion, and will not hold ourselves bound by any laws in which we have no voice, or Representation."

John Adams was amused by his wife's remarks on behalf of "another Tribe more numerous and powerfull than all the rest. . . After stirring up Tories, Landjobbers, Trimmers, Bigots, Canadians, Indians, Negroes, Hanoverians, Hessians, Irish Catholicks, Scotch Renegadoes, at last [the members of the Congress] have stimulated the ladies to demand new Priviledges and threaten to rebell." But he was quick to point out that such a rebellion would lead nowhere: "Depend upon it, We know better than to repeal our Masculine systems" and submit to "the Despotism of the Peticoat."

In part, Abigail appears to have been teasing her husband; she did not directly challenge the prevailing notion of male superiority. But one may see in her correspondence a faint glimmer of what would ultimately emerge as modern feminism. Although more than a century would pass before the beginning of the "Rebelion" she warned of, in her gentle way she sounded a chord that has reverberated through the years and moved many other women to assert themselves in a male-dominated world.

built a foundation from which the country could approach democracy. This commitment is visible in the early colonial governing systems, emphasizing the willing entry of individuals into a social contract. This same commitment to democratic ideals led Daniel Shays to fight at Bunker Hill and later to rebel against the new government he had fought to create. The same commitment would inspire those who fought against slavery and many others, including Rosa Parks, whose story was told in the case study at the beginning of Chapter 1.

Two hundred years later, at the Lincoln Memorial in Washington, D.C., Martin Luther King, Jr., echoed these self-evident truths: "I have a dream that one day this nation will rise up and live out the true meaning of its creed: 'We hold these truths to be self-evident; that all men are created equal.'" This pursuit of liberty and equality has characterized America's approach to democracy.

As you will see, with time and experience, the American experiment in self-government has become more democratic. Free elections, competitive political parties, a free press, interest group participation broadening political involvement, an independent judiciary, civilian control of the military, and a commitment to democratic ideals would evolve in a manner that reflects the character of the American people. Let us continue our look at America's approaching democracy. We begin the next chapter with the framing of a constitution that opens with the words "We the people."

SUMMARY

1. The governments of some American colonies were based on the idea of a compact, an agreement legally binding two or more parties to enforceable rules. Other colonies evolved from royal grants of land and governing rights to a lord or baron, who became the colony's proprietor.

2. Frequent conflicts between the governors and the colonial legislatures made the colonists highly suspicious of executive power. The colonists were also influenced by the ideas of Charles de Montesquieu, who saw the separation of executive, legislative, and judicial powers as the best way to counteract any tendency toward despotism, and by the ideas of social contract theorists such as Thomas Hobbes and John Locke—especially the latter, who asserted the importance of limited government based on popular consent.

3. By 1753 the American colonists had recognized the need for greater union and cooperation. Benjamin Franklin proposed the Albany Plan, which called for a self-governing confederation, a league of sovereign states that would delegate specific powers to a central government. However, Franklin's plan was rejected by both the Crown and the colonial assemblies.

4. After 1763 Britain imposed a series of direct taxes on the American colonies. The Sugar Act levied a tax on molasses and other goods imported into the colonies; the Stamp Act required that revenue be placed on all printed matter and legal documents. The Townshend Revenue Acts imposed taxes on glass, lead, tea, and paper imported into the colonies.

5. The tax on tea especially irritated the colonists. The most famous protest against this tax was the Boston Tea Party of December 16, 1773, in which colonists dumped chests of tea into Boston Harbor. Parliament responded by passing the Coercive Acts, which closed Boston Harbor and required the quartering of British soldiers in private homes. In September 1774 representatives of twelve colonies met in Philadelphia at the First Continental Congress to devise a plan to unify the colonies.

6. In the spring of 1775 an attempt by British troops to destroy ammunition stored by colonists led to the battles of Lexington and Concord. Within three weeks the Second Continental Congress convened, becoming in effect a revolutionary government. The congress approved and signed the Declaration of Independence.

7. On November 15, 1777, the congress adopted the Articles of Confederation and Perpetual Union. Under the Articles the central government lacked the power to impose taxes or raise an army and hence was unable to protect the states or regulate commerce among them.

KEY TERMS

Shays's Rebellion
republic
compact
Mayflower Compact
civil government
natural rights
social contract theorists
limited government

confederation
Sugar Act
Stamp Act
Townshend Revenue Acts
Boston Massacre
Committees of Correspondence
Boston Tea Party

Intolerable Acts
First Continental Congress
Common Sense
Second Continental Congress
Declaration of Independence
sovereignty
Articles of Confederation

SUGGESTED READINGS

- Bailyn, Bernard. *The Ideological Origins of the American Revolution*. Cambridge, Mass: Harvard University Press, 1967. An excellent study of the ideas that forged the revolution.

- Burns, James MacGregor. *The Vineyard of Liberty*. New York: Random House, 1982. A brilliant interpretation of the American attempt to preserve liberty during the founding.

- Jensen, Merrill. *The Articles of Confederation*. Madison, Wis.: University of Wisconsin Press, 1940. The best treatment of the Articles and their shortcomings.

- Lipset, Seymour Martin. *The First New Nation*. New York: Basic Books, 1963. An interesting analysis of nation building by a political sociologist.

- McDonald, Forrest. *Novus Ordo Seclorum: The Intellectual Origins of the Constitution*. Lawrence, Kan. University of Kansas Press, 1985. One of the country's most distinguished historians covers the creation of the new republic.

- Wills, Gary. *Inventing America: Jefferson's Declaration of Independence*. New York: Random House, 1978. An original and provocative account of the Declaration of Independence.

- Wood, Gordon S. *The Creation of the American Republic*. Chapel Hill, N.C.: University of North Carolina Press, 1969. An excellent study of the political ideology of the constitutional convention and the revolutionary and founding periods.

CHAPTER 3

THE CONSTITUTION

Jasper Johns, *Three Flags*, 1958. Collection of Whitney Museum of American Art, New York.

CHAPTER OUTLINE

CASE STUDY: THE BATTLE OVER THE ERA

INTRODUCTION: THE CONSTITUTION AND DEMOCRACY

THE CONSTITUTIONAL CONVENTION

THE MIRACLE: RESULTS OF THE CONVENTION

RATIFICATION: THE BATTLE FOR THE CONSTITUTION

APPROACHING DEMOCRACY THROUGH CONSTITUTIONAL CHANGE

THE CONSTITUTION: TWO HUNDRED YEARS OF APPROACHING DEMOCRACY

In the late 1970s, Donna Schilling of Harrisburg, Pennsylvania, was shocked when a boy ran through the girls' bathroom at her high school screaming "ERA! ERA!" at the top of his lungs. Confused about why her sanctuary was invaded, Donna asked the school principal, "Why was that boy in our bathroom?" "If the

The Battle over the ERA

ERA is passed," the principal announced firmly, "then all we will have is unisex bathrooms." Donna's mother, a longtime supporter of the proposed amendment, was stunned at the principal's claim and said, "With all of these misconceptions, it's no wonder this amendment hasn't been passed yet!"

The Equal Rights Amendment (ERA) sought to protect the rights of women. It was first introduced in Congress in 1923 by the National Women's party and was finally passed on March 22, 1972, then sent to the states for ratification. The amendment stated simply: "Equality of rights under the law shall not be denied or abridged by the United States or by any state on account of sex." It also granted Congress the power to enforce by appropriate legislation its provisions and stated that it would take effect two years after the ratification date. ERA advocates argued that including this amendment in the Constitution would further guarantee women their rights. Opponents maintained that these rights were already guaranteed by laws, state constitutions, the federal and state judiciary, and the U.S. Constitution itself.

The debate over this proposed amendment illustrates the politically charged nature of modern battles over both the meaning of, and possible changes to, the Constitution. Underlying these battles are questions about whether the Constitution needs updating to fit modern circumstances.

Initially, the ERA ratification process was a suc-

cess: Within one year, thirty of the thirty-eight states needed for passage had given their assent. Five years later, however, with only three more states needed for ratification, the effort failed. Why?

The pro-ERA movement ran into political difficulty when it was unable to articulate how the amendment would improve women's lives. The claims of "ending sex discrimination" and "equality of rights" were considered vague. In an attempt to redefine the goals of the amendment, advocates tried the slogan Fifty-nine Cents, meaning that women were being paid fifty-nine cents for every dollar earned by a man for comparable work. But this approach also fell flat because past experience showed that equal pay could not be legislated. The Equal Pay Act of 1963 and Title VII of the Civil Rights Act of 1964, both more sweeping than the ERA on the issue of pay equality, failed to close the gap. When some women realized that the ERA would not benefit them financially, their interest waned. Advocates also tried the argument that the ERA would be a symbol of the need for equality between the sexes. But this explanation of the purpose of the amendment proved to be ineffective as well.

By 1973, divisions within the ranks of the National Organization for Women (NOW) made ratification less likely. The split occurred between the moderate followers of feminist Betty Friedan, whose book The Feminine Mystique had helped to revive the feminist movement in the 1960s, and a more radical fringe group, which believed the ERA did not go far enough to protect women's rights. When these radical members of the movement began to belittle mainstream ERA supporters, many of whom were housewives and mothers, many people began to question their association with the movement. By late 1973 the movement's political momentum was lost; very few pro-ERA state coalitions were being organized to pressure state legislatures for ratification.

The "Stop-ERA" movement, under the leadership of attorney Phyllis Schlafly, geared up to defeat the amendment. This movement united conservatives and fundamentalist churchgoers, who opposed the amendment anyway, with those disaffected homemakers who had split from NOW. This movement raised the fear that the ERA would lead to unisex bathrooms, a compulsory draft for women, and the breakup of the family unit. (While these issues would have been left up to the Supreme Court to decide, it seems clear that all grew out of unfounded fears.) Some opponents even twisted the arguments around to say that equality would mean that men's pay would be lowered to equal some women's. In time, these fears influenced the thinking of state legislators, despite the fact that public support for the amendment never fell below 54 percent.

Since there was a seven-year time limit on the ratification process, by late 1978 time was running out for the ERA. Leaders of the movement were able to persuade Congress to pass a thirty-nine-month extension on the ratification deadline (making the final deadline June 30, 1982), but this wasn't enough to save the amendment. Stalled out at thirty-five states, the movement suffered one defeat after another. Ratification was eventually voted down by a substantial margin in Virginia, Illinois, and Georgia. The movement was so debilitated that Idaho, Kentucky, Nebraska, and Tennessee later voted to rescind their ratification. With the election of conservative Ronald Reagan to the presidency in 1980, the ERA was dead.

For a time Donna Schilling and her mother despaired about the nature of their rights as women in America. But they also realized that the approach to democracy and the struggle for equality and women's rights never end. Although the Constitution does not contain an amendment guaranteeing women equal rights, women have made inroads, and many of the goals of ERA advocates have been achieved anyway. In the 1990s there are few barriers to women. Women serve on naval ships and fly military aircraft; two women sit on the Supreme Court, with over a dozen more in Congress; sexual harassment is an important social issue; and 50 percent of the students in medical school as well as 40 percent of the students in law school are female. Despite these successes, women have not yet achieved complete equality. Some women still call for an equal rights amendment to protect recent gains and to ensure future opportunities for women. ❖

INTRODUCTION: THE CONSTITUTION AND DEMOCRACY

America's Constitution was born of revolution and altered by evolution. In 1787, the approach to constitutional democracy was made possible by a revolutionary process unlike any other in world history. Up to that time, governmental change resulted from violence and bloodshed. This time, in this country, representatives gathered to mend a failing governmental system through discussion and voting. That was revolutionary.

Imagine the task confronting delegates sent by the states to the "Foederal Convention," as it was called. They came to, in their words, "form a more perfect Union," meeting "for the sole and express purpose of revising the Articles of Confederation." How different life was in 1787. People traveled on horseback or in buggies and drank only well water. Doctors frequently prescribed leeches to cure ailments. The free press, which did not exist under the Crown, now flourished with broadsides, large sheets of paper with print on one side, regularly handed out on the streets. Free speech was exercised by those standing on soap boxes and was limited only by the power of one's voice. Punishments for certain criminal acts included public brandings or nostril puncturing. The delegates to the Constitutional Convention were all white, male landowners over the age of twenty-one—the only people permitted to participate in the American political system at that time. If they were typical of anything it was of each other. Yet they designed a model of democratic government that has endured for over two hundred years and has been used as a model for the constitutions of 160 of the 170 countries in the world today.

The democratic process that began in 1787 has been shaped by evolution. Even though the ERA failed, its course illustrates one stage in that evolution. By the time it was proposed, attitudes about women, who were not present at the Constitutional Convention and were never mentioned in the final document, had evolved to the point that a national debate ensued about whether to include them by the amendment process. Such discussions over the expansion of the base of the body politic and of the notions of freedom, equality, and human rights have moved us farther on the road to democracy.

Two hundred years later, the world we know is very different from that of the framers. We regularly travel hundreds of miles by car or airplane, fly into space on a shuttle, and communicate instantaneously by computer, and can even create life in a petri dish. Free speech can now be conveyed to millions through television. A free press can instantly report events to the world, whether they be wars half a world away or the spectacle of a fugitive fleeing from

In the framers' time, the news was often delivered orally by a town crier. This method of conveying the news was revived in 1992 during a strike at the *Pittsburgh Post–Gazette.* The modern day town crier shown here in wig and colonial dress uses news summaries prepared by the paper's reporters to keep the lunchtime crowd in downtown Pittsburgh informed.

The original handwritten version of the Constitution is preserved in a helium-filled case and is on display at the National Archives in Washington, D.C. Every year, a million people stand in line to view a document revered as the soul of a nation.

justice on a Los Angeles highway. The framers "could not have imagined," Justice Thurgood Marshall noted in 1987, "nor would they have accepted, that the document they were drafting would one day be construed by a Supreme Court to which had been appointed a woman and the descendant of an African slave."[1]

Most fascinating of all is the fact that a document written two hundred years ago, with very few amendments, is used to govern today. How is this possible? The answer, as you will learn in this chapter and in Chapter 7, on the Supreme Court, lies in the unique brilliance of the framers in creating a document that could be constantly updated to meet future needs and a judicial branch capable of helping with that task.

In this chapter we examine what historian Catherine Drinker Bowen called the "Miracle at Philadelphia," the Constitutional Convention and its results.[2] First we look at the participants and discussions in that remarkable gathering. Then we analyze the constitutional document that resulted. We will see how, not unlike the discussions that raged over the proposed Equal Rights Amendment to the Constitution, the debates raged in the states over the ratification of the Constitution itself. Finally, we examine how the Constitution has changed over the last two hundred years and take a look at the debates over what the Constitution has come to mean to Americans.

THE CONSTITUTIONAL CONVENTION

The unique nature of the American Constitution, and its success both in forging together a nation that was becoming fragmented under the Articles of Confederation and in guiding the nation for centuries to come, can be explained in many ways. Part of the answer lies in the democratic political theory of the time, theory that was applied to the problems facing the government. However, theory does not govern a nation—people do. So, the actual framing of the Constitution in 1787 is better understood by examining the circumstances under which various theories were advanced in debate and the people who were debating and making the compromises that made success possible.

The Task

As we saw in the last chapter, the problems of governing under the Articles of Confederation made it clear that a stronger central government was needed. But the mission of the Constitutional Convention was not quite so clear. The explicit goal, according to a resolution adopted on February 21, 1787, was to revise the Articles of Confederation. It was hoped that this group could solve the problems of governmental gridlock created by the dominance of the states and the government's inability to tax, form a military, or regulate commerce. But some, like James Madison, wondered whether revision of the Articles would be enough. Several states had already authorized their delegates "to render the constitution of government adequate to the exigencies of the Union." Some of the delegates came to the convention with an understanding that the Articles needed to be scrapped altogether, and they were prepared to propose a new form of government from the outset.[3] Their success in doing so would be decided by whichever of the fifty-five men attending the convention happened to be present during those debates. But it was not a success that was preordained, as Congressman William Grayson of Virginia wrote: "What will be the result of their meeting I cannot with any certainty determine, but I hardly think much good can come of it: the people of America don't appear to me to be ripe for any great innovations."[4]

The Participants

While many have come to see the participants of the Constitutional Convention as legends, the delegates to the convention are better understood as skilled politicians. What resulted came about not from a singular theoretical vision of a government but from a series of brilliant political compromises and fortuitous events.

The delegates came from a very narrow band of American society, the elite aristocracy. This should not be surprising, since less than 5 percent of the total population (150,000 of 3.9 million people) possessed the right to vote. Many rich men were present, and a variety of professions were represented. Over half were lawyers, another quarter were large-plantation owners, eight were judges, and the rest were doctors, merchants, bankers, clergymen, and soldiers. All of the delegates owned property, and several owned slaves. Although it was a young group, with over three-fourths under the age of fifty, what really distinguished this group was its experience in politics. There were several former members of the Continental Congress, forty-two former congressmen, and seven former governors.

From their efforts at drafting earlier political documents, these experienced statesmen brought with them an understanding of the issues and the need for compromise. Six delegates had signed the Declaration of Independence, while nine more, including George Mason of Virginia, Alexander Hamilton of New York, and John Rutledge of South Carolina, had drafted their states' constitutions. Both Roger Sherman of Connecticut and John Dickinson of Delaware had played a major role in drafting the Articles of Confederation, while three other members—Elbridge Gerry of Massachusetts, and Gouverneur Morris and Robert Morris of Pennsylvania—had been among its signers.

Although elite and experienced, the delegates were far from representative of the general population. Only two delegates were farmers even though 85 percent of the population came from small farms. There were no members of the working class, artisans, businessmen, or tradesmen among the delegates.

African Americans, Native Americans, non-Protestants, and women were nowhere to be found in the meeting either. Over 600,000, or about 20 percent of the total population, was African American, about 520,000 of which were slaves living in the South, while most of the rest were poor, working-class laborers in the northern cities.[5] Native Americans did not participate because they were not citizens. Viewed as foreigners, they were specifically excluded from the Constitution, except in the "interstate commerce" power of Article I, Section 8, where they were lumped with the foreign nations as possible trading partners. Non-Protestants were excluded because they were in the minority. The few Catholics and Jews living in this country at the time would not have been in the political elite from which the delegates were drawn.[6] For all practical purposes, women in American society had no political rights. Since they

FYI

Was there a spy at the convention? Scholars disagree whether total and absolute adherence to the secrecy rule was maintained. With so many of the delegates in financial distress, there is speculation that one of the delegates tried to sell information on the proceedings to a British agent. Whether this happened cannot be proved conclusively, but it is possible.

Little-known Fact

Not all of the delegates were rich. By 1787 Robert Morris, who had speculated so successfully in land and stocks that he became one of the richest men in America, was well on the way to bankruptcy. George Mason attended the convention only after borrowing sixty pounds from fellow delegate Edmund Randolph. Participation in the convention was no guarantee of future success either, as six delegates eventually went bankrupt (Morris would spend over three years in debtors' prison), two went crazy, two died in gun duels (including Alexander Hamilton, at the hand of Aaron Burr), and two were charged with treason.

The Setting: Life at the Convention

Life was tough at the convention, as participants made clear in their letters and journal entries. "We move slowly in our business," North Carolina's William R. Davie wrote to a friend. "It is indeed a work of great delicacy and difficulty, impeded at every step by jealousies and jarring interests."*

Seventy-four delegates, many of them among the best-educated men in the country, were chosen by their states to attend, but only fifty-five arrived. The other nineteen failed to attend for a variety of reasons ranging from a lack of funds and the difficulty of travel, to a lack of interest in, or support for, the enterprise. One state—Rhode Island (or "Rogues Island," as it was called by a less-than-appreciative convention prepared to divide up the state among the other states in attendance)—never sent any delegates because the heavily indebted agrarian party that controlled the state feared that a new government would force them to pay off their debts. The participants met in complete secrecy for between five and seven hours a day; five, often six, and sometimes even seven days a week; over a four-month period, in the gray-walled East Room on the first floor of the Philadelphia State House, now called Independence Hall, where the Declaration of Independence was debated. The delegates were arranged at long tables in concentric half-circles surrounding the ornate chair in which sat General George Washington, who was made president of the convention. Washington said very little, which was his practice during debates, but it is generally agreed that his mere presence kept the delegates on track.

The convention was scheduled to begin on May 14, 1787, but did not officially begin until May 25, because delegates from seven states, needed for a quorum, were eleven days late. During the convention, attendance was sporadic. One never knew from day to day who would be present, with no more than thirty delegates making it to any one meeting. Only James Madison, who kept the most complete set of records of the proceedings, was present all of the time.

Two early actions helped to promote the success of the proceedings. First, the delegates invoked a secrecy rule for the debate. This was done to keep the nature of the discussions from the public until the final product was crafted. Opponents of the proceeding could not object if they were kept in the dark and delegates were permitted complete freedom to express their views without fear of reprisal. During the four months of debate, not one word of it appeared in the local Philadelphia newspaper. Delegates also agreed that any issue could be raised for debate a second time. While this *reconsideration rule* meant that careful compromises were frequently undone, the spirit of open discussion kept the delegates talking rather than leaving in anger.

While summer was a bit cooler than normal in Philadelphia that year, the weather was hot and sticky nonetheless.† Since it was agreed that the proceedings were to be held in secret, the windows

did not have the vote, participation in politics, much less the convention, was inconceivable. Thus, no woman attended a single state ratifying convention or voted for a state convention delegate. Despite this lack of diversity at the convention, however, the framers crafted a constitution capable of including women and other groups over time.

The Major Players

The proponents of a strong national government, also called *nationalists*, were led by James Madison, the so-called Father of the Constitution. A short, thin, painfully shy, thirty-six-year-old bachelor from Virginia, Madison was one of

A Philadelphia street scene in the late 1700s. At center is Christ Church, which was open to those Founders who wished to pray for the success of the Constitutional Convention.

phia's hot season is the innumerable flies which constantly light on the face and hands, stinging everywhere and turning everything black because of the filth they leave wherever they light."[**] Sport for the participants consisted of chasing the many flies in the room, or betting on how long the eighty-two-year-old Ben Franklin would stay awake. Franklin needed his sleep, because he would stay up late at night drinking in the local tavern or private homes, always attended by another delegate to ensure that he would not reveal any secrets.

By the end of August, eleven of the fifty-five participants had invented some excuse to leave permanently, citing ill health, family business, or disagreement with the proceedings. But those who remained fashioned, through debate and compromise, a remarkable document that continues to govern a population far greater than they could ever have imagined.

were kept shut. The cooler summer air that greeted the participants at ten in the morning would be stale and lifeless by noon and completely stifling by mid-afternoon. When the setting got too oppressive, the men moved to a similarly furnished room upstairs so they could open the windows without fear of being overheard. Dirt had been poured on the cobblestones outside the windows to keep down the noise from the wooden wagon wheels. The flies were so thick in the summer heat that a French visitor at the time wrote: "A veritable torture during Philadel-

[*]Hutson, (ed.) *Farrand Supplement*, p. 97.

[†]*Ibid.*, pp. 325—37.

[**]Bowen, *Miracle at Philadelphia*, p. 97.

Source: This account of life at the convention is based on Catherine Dinker Bowen, *Miracle at Philadelphia,* (Boston: Little, Brown, 1966), Chapters 1, 2, and 8; Christopher Collier and James Lincoln Collier, *Decision in Philadelphia* (New York: Random House, 1986), Chapter 8; Clinton Rossiter, *1787: The Grand Convention* (New York: W. W. Norton & Co., 1966), Chapter 8; and Richard B. Morris, *Witnesses at the Creation.* (New York: New American Library, 1985), Chapter 9.

the best political theorists of his day. He spent months preparing for the convention, studying and developing a new plan for a strong, central national government to counteract the problems of the Articles of Confederation.

Opposing Madison were the states'-rights proponents, also called the *antinationalists,* who were led by New Jersey's William Paterson. The son of a shopkeeper and a lawyer by trade, Paterson believed that as a representative of the state of New Jersey, all of his actions should take into consideration the needs of small states. He argued that the power and position of individual states needed to be protected from the proposed central government. Joining Paterson was his old friend Luther Martin. The most prominent lawyer in his

James Madison (1751 – 1836), the Father of the Constitution and one of the brightest political theorists of his day, was also the best note taker at the convention. He went on to become a member of the U.S. House, secretary of state, and the nation's fourth president.

native Maryland, Martin's characteristic heavy drinking, leading to his nickname of "Lawyer Brandy Bottle," had a negative effect on his persuasiveness at the convention. For Martin, states were sovereign entities deserving greater protection than people.

The wide gulf between the nationalists and the antinationalists made Roger Sherman of Connecticut a major player in the discussions. The third-oldest delegate to the convention at 66, Sherman had spent nearly all of his life in public service. As the only man to have signed all of the basic formative documents in early American history, Sherman was a cautious, careful politician who bargained for the common ground that would secure a negotiated compromise.

These major players would seek to arrive at some kind of consensus on the various plans presented for the new government.

Plans for a New Government

Governor Edmund Randolph of Virginia opened the formal debate on May 29, 1787, with a four-hour speech containing fifteen resolves, or resolutions, for a "strong consolidated union" rather than a federal one with continued state power. When the delegates agreed the next day to debate these resolves, the convention was no longer a debate about improving the Articles of Confederation; it was about creating an entirely new form of government. Once it was decided that the Articles of Confederation would be replaced, two central questions guided debate:

- How powerful would the new national government be?
- How powerful would the states be?

Of five plans submitted to the delegates for consideration, debate centered mainly around two of them: the Virginia Plan and the New Jersey Plan. The differences between these two proposals show clearly the divisions among the large-state and the small-state advocates.

THE VIRGINIA PLAN   The **Virginia Plan** was presented by Governor Randolph and was so named because he and its author, James Madison, came from Virginia. This proposal was favored by the delegates from the bigger states. It was based on the following propositions designed to remedy the perceived defects in the Articles of Confederation:

1. It called for three branches of government consisting of a **legislative branch** that makes laws, an **executive branch** that executes the laws, and a **judiciary** that interprets the laws. Since Madison feared the negative effects of power, his plan championed a system of **checks and balances**. For every power in government there would be an equal and opposite power placed in a separate branch to restrain that force. This idea presumed another feature of the new government, the **separation of powers**, meaning that the powers of government are divided among the three branches, thus preventing the accumulation of too much power in any one branch.

2. Operating from a belief that the ultimate power to govern resides in the people, Randolph proposed a system of **proportional representation**, meaning that the size of each state's delegation in both houses of Congress would be based on the size of its population, rather than the one-state, one-vote rule in the

The Nation's Founders—Were They Really Demigods?

Thomas Jefferson described the delegates to the Constitutional Convention as "an assembly of demigods," and before 1913 this was the prevailing opinion among constitutional scholars. The framers were assumed to have been guided by only the highest and purest of motives in fashioning a governing document for a new nation.

In an influential book published in 1913, however, the historian Charles Beard questioned this view of the nation's Founders, suggesting that the Constitution had been drafted by a group of wealthy landowners seeking to preserve their property and economic position. He pointed out that many of the delegates held securities that were worthless and that their financial position was becoming increasingly shaky under the Articles of Confederation. Perhaps, he argued, they believed that a newer, stronger government would be better able to protect them against the far more numerous and increasingly vocal class of debt-ridden farmers.

What were the delegates' true motives? Were the delegates patriots seeking to protect the rights of all citizens and to establish stability and order in a new nation? Or were they interested in forming a government that would preserve and enhance their own wealth?

A close look at the Constitution seems to support Beard's view. To protect the sanctity of private property, Article I, Section 10, barred the states from establishing their own monetary systems or passing laws "impairing the Obligation of Contracts." Article VI states that "all debts contracted and engagements entered in-

Thinking Critically

to, before the Adoption of this Constitution" would continue to be valid under the new government.

It is also important, however, to consider the condition of the country under the Articles of Confederation. The nation's Founders could well have been motivated by fear of another uprising like Shays's Rebellion, which the central government had been powerless to quell; they might also have been concerned about the potential for economic chaos stemming from the government's inability to regulate interstate commerce.

What do you think was the primary motive underlying the drafting of the Constitution?

What Happened

At first Beard's thesis was widely accepted, but later generations of scholars tested it by examining the financial records of the framers. They discovered that support for the new Constitution did not follow class lines. Seven of the delegates who refused to sign the document (or left the convention before it was completed) had twice as much wealth as the thirty-nine men who did sign it. On the other hand, several of the most influential delegates, including James Madison and Alexander Hamilton, were deeply in debt.

It appears, therefore, that the framers' motives were more complex than Beard's thesis suggests. While some of the delegates did benefit financially under the Constitution, and others may have had economic motives, most of the framers seem to have been more concerned with the need to bring order and stability to their troubled young nation.

Articles of Confederation. The size of Virginia's population (691,737), then, would give it more than ten times as many members in Congress as Delaware (population 59,096).

3. The legislature of Congress would be **bicameral**, consisting of two houses, both apportioned on the basis of population. A state would send members to the lower house, elected directly by the people. The lower house would elect the upper house from nominees provided by the state legislatures.

4. The executive, whose size was yet to be determined, would be elected for a maximum of one term by the Congress.

5. The judiciary, which would consist of one or more supreme courts and other national courts, would be staffed by life-tenured judges.

6. There was also to be a **council of revision**, a combined body of judges and members of the executive branch, having a limited veto over national legislation and an absolute veto over state legislation.

7. The legislature would have the power to override state laws.

It is not hard to see the impact of the Virginia Plan. It centered much more power in the national government, giving it authority over the states. And by placing so much of the governing and appointment powers in a legislature chosen by proportional representation, states with the largest population would dominate that branch. Since the executive branch was put in place by the Congress, the big states would dominate there as well, thus giving them control over the central government.

THE NEW JERSEY PLAN   For the representatives of the small states, the Madisonian notion of proportional representation was unacceptable because it gave populous states the ability to force their will on the smaller states. "New Jersey will never confederate on the plan," William Paterson said. "She would be swallowed up.... Myself or my state will never submit to tyranny or despotism." This reaction infuriated Pennsylvania's James Wilson, who asked, "Does it require 150 [voters of my state] to balance 50 [of yours]?" So, the small-state delegates countered with a series of resolutions advanced by Paterson and called it the **New Jersey Plan**. This plan was designed to refine and strengthen the Articles of Confederation rather than to replace it, and in so doing protected the interests of the smaller, less populous states. The New Jersey Plan proposed the following:

1. The power of the national government would be centered in a *unicameral,* or one-house, legislature, and, to minimize the impact of population, each state would have one vote.

2. An executive board would be elected by the legislature, for one term only, and authorized to enforce national laws even in the face of opposition from the states. The executive could be removed by a majority of state governors.

3. A supreme court would be appointed by the executive board and be empowered to deal with impeachment of national officers, foreign-policy questions, and tax and trade problems.

4. The power to tax imports would be taken away from the states and given to the national government.

5. The legislature would be empowered to tax state governments on the basis of population and collect the money by force if an unspecified number of states agreed.

6. All congressional acts would become "the supreme law of the respective states," with the executive board being authorized to use force to "compel an obedience to such acts" if necessary.

As you can see from these provisions, while this plan increased the power of the central government, a great deal more power was left in the hands of the states. In this way, the plan was much closer to what the delegates were originally sent to do at the convention. And with each state having an equal voice in many government actions, the small states would continue to play a prominent role. In spite of the state-centered philosophy of this plan, its final provision making congressional acts "supreme law" and compelling obedience to national acts (not found in the Virginia Plan), became an early version of what is known as the **supremacy clause** of the Constitution. This clause holds that in any conflict between federal laws and treaties and state laws, the will of the national government always prevails. Provisions like this one, along with granting the central government the power to tax, made it possible for compromise to be reached with the strong-central-government advocates of the Virginia Plan.

Whether the New Jersey Plan could have successfully governed America, or whether, as some think, it was a proposal designed specifically to thwart the notion of proportional representation at the convention remains a matter of some debate.[7] Table 3.1 provides a quick overview of the differences between the Virginia and New Jersey Plans.

Swayed by an impassioned speech by James Madison, the delegates chose the Virginia Plan over the New Jersey Plan by a seven-to-three vote. The representatives of the small states then turned their attention to achieving some influence for their states in the new government. Only by securing a compromise on the "proportional-representation" aspects of the Virginia Plan, they reasoned, would their states have any voice in the government. Thus, it was over this issue that the convention's success would turn.

Debate and Compromise: The Turning Point of the Convention

The Articles of Confederation failed because the prospect of a veto by each state over the actions of the central government resulted in a powerless Continental Congress. Thus, the composition of the new Congress and its means of selection were critical issues at the convention. Would it be one house (unicameral), as

FYI

In 1790 the population of New Jersey was only 184,139, making it the fifth-least-populous state of the original thirteen. Two hundred years later, New Jersey's population was 7,730,188, making it the ninth-*most*-populous state of fifty. Do you think the representatives from that state would be proposing the small-state plan now?

Table 3.1
Differences between the Virginia and New Jersey Plans

ISSUE	VIRGINIA PLAN	NEW JERSEY PLAN
Source of Legislative Power	Derived from the people and based on popular representation	Derived from the states and based on equal votes for each state
Legislative Structure	Bicameral	Unicameral
Executive	Size undetermined, elected and removable by Congress	More than one person, removable by state majority
Judiciary	Life-tenured, able to veto state legislation in council of revision	No power over states
State Laws	Legislature can override	Government can compel obedience to national laws
Ratification	By the people	By the states

before; or two houses (bicameral), as some delegates now preferred? Would the members be apportioned by the population of each state (proportional representation), as in the Virginia Plan; or would each state have the same number of representatives (one-state, one-vote), as in the New Jersey Plan? By the middle of June the convention had split into two opposing groups: the "big states" composed of Massachusetts, Pennsylvania, Virginia, the Carolinas, and Georgia (the southern states sided with the big states, believing that given their large size, proportional representation would eventually be in their interest), against the rest of the states, whose only hope for influence lay in the equal-representation scheme.

Repeatedly in the early debates the small states failed to pass the New Jersey Plan, partly because Maryland's Luther Martin had alienated his colleagues by giving a virulent, two-day speech against proportional representation. Martin's effort backfired when the delegates quickly approved proportional representation of the House. However, when the delegates also voted to establish a bicameral legislative branch to seek some sort of balance of power, the issue now became how the upper house of Congress, known as the Senate, would be apportioned. During this debate, Georgia delegate Abraham Baldwin later recalled, "The convention was more than once upon the point of dissolving without agreeing upon any system."[8]

At this turning point in the debate, it was the selfless action of Baldwin and several other delegates that narrowly averted the complete failure of the convention. The large-state delegates sought proportional representation in both the Senate and in the House of Representatives, giving them total control over the Congress, while the small-state delegates pressed for the old Articles of Confederation system of equality of votes in the legislature. Because of their numbers, the large states expected to win the issue by a narrow margin. But well-timed absences and changes of heart ended the big states' chances for dominance in the Senate and in the process saved the convention from failure.

This painting by Junius Brutus Stearns shows the framers of the Constitution at work in Philadelphia in 1787. George Washington, who played a central role in the convention, presides over the proceedings.

When the vote was taken on the question of Senate representation, Maryland's Daniel of St. Thomas Jenifer, who otherwise had an exemplary record of attendance for the convention, deliberately stayed away, keeping Maryland allied with the small states. Then, the three Georgia delegates conspired to switch their state's vote from the big-state position to the small-state position. Two of them suddenly left the convention, and the third delegate, Abraham Baldwin, voted for the small-state position. Thus, proportional representation in the Senate had failed.

With compromise now possible, a committee of compromise consisting of one member from each state was formed to prepare suggestions for resolving the question of representation in the Senate. When the selection process for the committee was finished, it turned out that every member favored the small states' position, so the result was preordained. What would emerge was a plan acceptable to the small states but capable of being passed by the large states as well.

This plan has become known as the **Great Compromise** (also called the **Connecticut Compromise**), based on a plan advanced by Roger Sherman of Connecticut. This compromise upheld the large-state position for the House, its membership based on proportional representation, and balanced that decision by upholding the small-state posture of equal representation in the Senate, where each state would have two votes. Since all legislation would have to pass through both houses, neither large nor small states could dominate. The compromise also stated that *money bills,* or measures that raise revenue, must begin in the House, to keep the power to tax with the people. This arrangement would prevent an alliance of small states in the Senate voting for programs that had to be paid for by the large states.

The composition and purpose of the two houses of Congress, then, would be very different. Members of the House would be chosen based on a state's population; there would be one representative for every 40,000 people, as determined by periodic census (at the request of George Washington this number was changed to 30,000 on the last day of the convention). The House was constructed to be closest to the people and to reflect their desires. The Senate, with its equal representation and indirect method of selection by state legislatures, was intended as a more deliberative council of the political and economic elite. This body would serve as an advisory council to the president and would eventually be entrusted with reviewing presidential appointments and treaties.

This compromise did not come easily. Debate got so heated that at one point an exasperated James Wilson of Pennsylvania asked why the small states were so unwilling to accept the compromise. In response, Gunning Bedford of Delaware stated simply: "I do not, gentlemen, trust you."

Delegates voted in favor of the Connecticut Compromise by the narrowest of margins—five states to four, with one state delegation tied. The compromise effectively ended the debate between the large and small states by giving each a balanced stake in the legislature of the new centralized national government. Acceptance of the compromise meant that the states would never again be seen as sovereign entities but would be part of one national government.

The Constitution was on its way to being realized, but there were still two vexing questions to resolve—one dealing with the issue of slavery and the other with the nature of the new executive.

The Issue of Slavery

While the word *slavery* was never mentioned in the Constitution, it was very much on the minds of each of the framers. Since the 1600s, Africans had been brought over to this country and sold as slaves to southern plantation owners. Without slave labor, southern plantations could not operate. While the northern delegates wanted to abolish slavery, citing the inalienable human rights of freedom and equality, they understood that such a call would lose southern support and doom the convention to failure. So the institution of slavery was not debated directly. Instead, it was discussed indirectly through the question of how to distribute the 65 seats in the First Congress.

Since membership in the Congress was based on population, just how to count the slaves, who constituted almost 18 percent of the population, became a point of contention. If the slaves were not included in the count, as the North wanted, then the slave states would have had only 41 percent of the House seats; including all of the slaves, as the South wanted, would have given the southern states 50 percent of the seats.

After much debate, the convention delegates arrived at the **three-fifths compromise**, which stated that the apportionment of representatives by state should be determined "by adding to the whole number of free persons…three-fifths of all other persons" (Article I, Section 2). Since the phrase "all other persons" was a euphemism for slaves, this meant that it would take five slaves to equal three free people when counting the population for representation and taxation purposes. While convention delegates understood the political compromise being effected here, the stated rationale for this partial counting of slaves was that they produced less wealth.

This compromise represented a victory of political expediency over morality. Since slaves could not vote, their numbers were simply being used to add to the South's political power. Some have argued that even though the compromise kept the Constitutional Convention on track, it was immoral because it denigrated blacks by suggesting that they were only three-fifths as valuable and productive as whites. Others, though, have pointed out that while it did increase southern influence in the Congress and thus the presidential electoral count, this unique political compromise actually weakened the power of the southern states while also ensuring the Constitution's passage: As a result of the compromise, the slave states ended up with only 47 percent of the seats in Congress, thus keeping them in the minority and making it possible to outvote them on slavery issues.[9] As part of the compromise, Congress was barred from legislating on the institution of slavery until 1808, thus allowing the South to import as many slaves as it could in the next twenty years (Article I, Section 9), and slavery continued to thrive. Finally, a provision was added without much discussion that allowed the return of fugitive slaves to their masters (Article IV, Section 2).

In leaving it to later generations to address the practice of slavery and put an end to it, were the framers condoning slavery? Were they hypocrites for protecting slavery while discussing the high principles of freedom and equality? One response is that while they were hypocritical, their thinking reflected the vast majority of public opinion at the time; most people were indifferent to slavery. However, we must also realize that just as Thomas Jefferson discovered when he was forced to strike his criticism of slavery from the draft of the

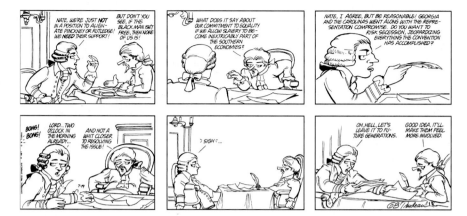

Declaration of Independence, a successful outcome for the Constitutional Convention would not have been possible without compromise on the slavery issue. Had the southern states walked out, which they surely would have if slavery were banned, the nation would have been doomed to continue operating under the defective Articles of Confederation or perhaps to falter entirely. However, the horrible human losses of the Civil War, fought over slavery and other issues over seventy years later, led to considerable debate about the value of such compromises.

The Nature of the Presidency

One of the most original contributions made by the framers of the American Constitution was their blueprint for the presidency, including the means for filling the job. (The presidency is described more fully in Chapter 6.)

The framers were ambivalent about the nature of the position they were creating, fearing that it would lead to a return of a new monarchy in democratic clothing. This same fear was reflected in the weak executive branches proposed in the Virginia and New Jersey plans, which consisted of boards subservient to the legislature. To correct this approach, Charles Pinckney of South Carolina called for the creation of a "vigorous executive," because, in his words, "our government is despised because of the loss of public order." However, Edmund Randolph of Virginia, who favored instead a board of executives, expressed his fear that Pinckney's call for a single executive represented the "foetus of monarchy," or the beginnings of the reinstatement of a British Crown in America.

It was James Wilson of Pennsylvania, fearing an all-powerful legislature similar to those in some of the states during the Articles of Confederation, who proposed a plan creating a national executive much like the powerful governor of New York—a single-person executive with substantial powers such as a veto over legislation. This plan was not debated by the delegates but was instead submitted to the Committee on Detail, which was charged with organizing the resolutions passed by the convention into a coherent document. Since Wilson and three other strong-national-government advocates sat on this five-person committee, the matter was settled in his favor. The powerful single executive that came out of that committee was adopted by the convention three months later.

Although the delegates agreed on a one-person executive, they disagreed over the length of the term of office for the new president and how to select that powerful person. Some delegates proposed a three-year term with reelections possible, while others sought a single term of seven years. Originally, the convention narrowly voted for a single seven-year term. This was eventually revised to a four-year term, with reelection possible. Nothing was said about the number of terms a president could serve.

The vital question of how to select the right person for the office of president led to yet another compromise in the form of the **electoral college system.** In an attempt to ensure the selection of statesmen like George Washington, whom everyone in the Convention expected to become the first president, the framers took the selection away from the voters. Instead, they designed a selection system of "electors" chosen by state legislatures in numbers equal to the total number of senators and representatives of their states. The electors of this *electoral college* would vote for two people, at least one of whom could not be from their own state, with the highest overall vote-getter becoming the president, and the runner-up, the vice president. The intention here was that the best-known and most-qualified person for president would appear somewhere on the ballots of the most electors from around the country. A tie vote would be sent to the House of Representatives for selection, with each state delegation having one vote.

Such a system struck a compromise between the large and small states. The president would not be chosen by direct popular vote or by the legislature because those methods would have favored the large states. Still, the large states would have some advantage, because the proportional-representation feature of Congress would affect the number of electors from each state. On the other hand, if the matter was sent to the House because of the lack of a majority vote in the electoral college, as the delegates fully expected, the small states would get the one-state, one-vote system that favored them. (More will be said about the electoral college system in Chapter 11.)

After nearly four months of debate, on September 17, 1787, the new constitution was drafted. The eldest delegate, eighty-two-year-old Benjamin Franklin, moved that the draft be approved, saying, "I consent to this constitution because I expect no better, and because I am not sure that it is not the best." To encourage even those who disagreed with the results to sign it, those who affixed their names became "witnesses" to the document. Even so, several of the delegates refused to sign, and only thirty-nine names were penned. Perhaps the best blessing on the whole enterprise was Franklin's, when the weeping old man told his fellow delegates that he had long puzzled over the half-sun design on the back of the convention president's chair. Was the design of a rising or setting sun, he often wondered. "Now at length I have the happiness to know that it is a rising and not a setting sun," he told the delegates.[10] With that, George Washington penned in his journal: "The business being closed, the members adjourned to the City Tavern, dined together and took a cordial leave of each other."[11] But, they would soon discover, the battle had just begun.

THE MIRACLE: RESULTS OF THE CONVENTION

The purpose of the Constitution is laid out in the eloquent preamble:

> We the People of the United States, in Order to form a more perfect Union, establish Justice, insure domestic Tranquility, provide for the common defence, promote the general Welfare, and secure the Blessings of Liberty to ourselves and our Posterity, do ordain and establish this Constitution for the United States of America.

The goals of the framers' exercise in democracy are outlined in this one-sentence paragraph. America was now one people rather than thirteen individual states. This people had certain hopes—for justice, tranquility, and liberty. They were placing their sovereign power in a new constitution that would guide a new national government, a union more perfect than the one that existed under the Articles of Confederation.

The new constitution was unlike any seen before. It created a **republican** form of government, granting indirect power to the voting public, whose desires would be served by a representative government. Until that time, such a system seemed possible only for small countries like Greece or Switzerland.

To fully understand the magnitude of what the framers accomplished, let's look at the nature of this new government, its specific powers, and the articles of the constitution.

A Republican Form of Government

At the end of the convention, a woman asked Ben Franklin what kind of government the delegates had created, a republic or a monarchy? "A republic, Madam," responded Franklin, "if you can keep it."

Believing that the people are more interested in their own welfare than the good of the whole, and realizing that the size of the new nation prevented implementing a pure democracy, the framers created a republican form of government with built-in checks and balances, in which the people hold an indirect voting power over their elected officials. Table 3.2 outlines the distinctions between a republican system and a pure democracy. Instead of governing themselves, the people elect representatives to protect their interests. These representatives could, however, vote against the desires of their constituents if it was for the good of the whole nation. Because the framers feared the instincts of the people, they devised a series of filters to minimize the effects of the popular vote. Only the House of Representatives would be elected directly by the people, with voting qualifications being determined by individual states. The people were given an indirect voice in the choice of the Senate, which would be chosen by the state legislatures, and their say in the choice of a president would be even more indirect because of the electoral college system. Finally, the people would have only the most indirect voice in the selection of the judiciary, which would be chosen by the already indirectly selected president and Senate. Since the framers did not fully trust the instincts of the representatives in the republican government either, they further limited this indirect power through the systems of separation of powers and checks and balances.

Table 3.2

Comparing a Republican System and Pure Democracy

PURE REPUBLICAN SYSTEM	PURE DEMOCRACY
1. Government based on popular consent	**1.** Government based on popular consent
2. Only a select number are able to vote	**2.** Everyone votes
3. Majority acts indirectly through chosen representatives in government	**3.** Majority acts directly as the government
4. Representatives act as "trustees," following their own instincts even if sometimes against the public will	**4.** Representatives act as "delegates", following the will of the voting populace.
5. Some chance exists for minority rights to be protected from the majority	**5.** The minority is much more at risk of being forced to adhere to majority will

One of the main constitutional changes in the American system of government over the years has been a shift from a purely republican system of government, created by the framers, to a system that is much more democratic. The voting base has been extended, giving more people a direct voice in their government. For instance, the Seventeenth Amendment provided for the direct popular election of the Senate, the Nineteenth Amendment extended the right to vote to women, and the Twenty-sixth Amendment extended the vote to citizens age eighteen and over. Finally, fewer representatives now act as independent "trustees," choosing instead to serve as "delegates" instructed by the voters through public-opinion polls, mail counts, and the media. In these ways, the American republic has indeed approached democracy.

In moving closer to a system of pure democracy, is the republican system designed by the framers to protect liberty in danger? Not at all. The Constitution's mechanisms for limiting power provide an adequate check on the actions of the leaders and the demands of the people. A judiciary more powerful than the framers could ever have imagined, using the Constitution and its amendments to preserve liberty, also keeps the republic strong. In the end, just how far the country actually goes toward direct democracy depends on how much confidence the people have in the motives and wisdom of their leaders.

We look more closely at how the Constitution has evolved later in this chapter, in the section on amendments to the Constitution.

The Governmental Powers

You can better understand the results of the framers' efforts by taking two different approaches to studying the Constitution and the distribution of power: a horizontal view and a vertical view.

HORIZONTAL POWERS Governmental powers are apportioned horizontally among the branches of the national government—the executive, legislative, and judicial branches—according to the system of *separation of powers* (see Figure 3.1). Each of the major branches of government was given a separate set of powers so that no one branch could become too powerful. The first three articles of the Constitution are concerned solely with the powers, responsibilities, and selection processes for each separate branch and include specific prohibitions against a person becoming a member of two branches at the same time.

But James Madison understood that separating the powers among three distinct branches would not be sufficient unless each branch was given the power to "check" the other, preventing encroachment into its own sphere. For this reason, a system of *checks and balances* was incorporated into the structure, giving each branch the power to approve, disapprove, or alter what the other branches do. "Ambition must be made to counteract ambition," Madison counseled in *Federalist* no. 51 on checks and balances. "If men were angels," he explained, "no government would be necessary. If angels were to govern men, neither external nor internal controls on government would be necessary. In framing a government which is to be administered by men over men, the great difficulty lies in this: you must first enable the government to control the governed; and in the next place oblige it to control itself."[12] With the checking powers outlined in Figure 3.1, no one branch can take control and run the government.

While the president nominates ambassadors, cabinet officials, and justices, the Senate can reject those choices by refusing to give the majority vote required for its "advice and consent." Congress passes laws, but the president can then veto those efforts. Congress can react by overriding a presidential veto with a two-thirds vote of both houses. Theoretically, the president can then refuse to execute the new law, but the president is kept in check by the fact that Congress has an impeachment power if "high crimes or misdemeanors" are committed. The judiciary has the power to interpret laws or use the power of *judicial review* to judge the constitutionality of, and thereby check the actions of, the other branches. Meanwhile, the judiciary itself is checked by the president's prerogative of nominating justices (with the advice and consent of the Senate) and Congress's power to create lower federal courts or change the Supreme Court's appellate jurisdiction.

Because the framers deliberately allowed for elasticity in each branch's powers, the government that resulted was destined to become one in which powers overlap. As Justice Robert Jackson described it: "While the Constitution diffuses power the better to secure liberty, it also contemplates that practice will integrate the dispersed powers into a workable government."[13] The result over the years has not been a strict separation of powers but, as political scientist Richard Neustadt has said, a "government of separated institutions *sharing* powers." By this, he means that each institution frequently exercises the powers of the others—judges can make law, Congress can interpret law, and presidents can do both.[14]

VERTICAL POWERS Vertical powers refer to the relationship between the centralized national government and the individual state governments. This distribution of power is known as **federalism**. We cover the subject of federalism more extensively in the next chapter.

©1985 by Sidney Harris.

BRANCHES OF GOVERNMENT

	Legislative	**Executive**	**Judiciary**
POWERS OF GOVERNMENT — Legislative	• Makes federal laws • Institutes and collects taxes, duties, imposts, and excises to pay debts and provide for the common defense • Coins and borrows money • Regulates commerce with foreign nations and among the states • Establishes post offices and promotes the progress of science • Creates lower federal courts • Declares war and calls up the militia	• Can veto Congressional legislation • Recommends laws	• Interprets laws or invalidates them as unconstitutional
POWERS OF GOVERNMENT — Executive	• Can override the veto of the President • Can refuse to confirm presidential appointments • Can impeach the Executive • Can refuse to ratify presidential treaties	• Responsible for implementing federal laws • Can call Congress into special session • Submits legislation to Congress • Makes treaties with foreign nations • Is commander-in-chief of the armed forces	• Interprets presidential actions or invalidates them as unconstitutional
POWERS OF GOVERNMENT — Judicial	• Can eliminate or refuse to create lower federal courts • Can refuse to implement judicial decisions • Can change jurisdiction of federal courts • Can impeach judges • Confirms federal judges	• Can appoint federal judges • Can pardon people	• Can interpret laws or actions of the executive • Can invalidate as unconstitutional acts of either Congress or the Executive

FIGURE 3.1 Constitutional Powers in a Nutshell

The diagonal blue portion of this figure displays the powers allotted to each of the branches and shows the separation of powers. The remainder of the diagram indicates the powers that each of the branches holds as a check on the other branches. A careful examination of these constitutional powers reveals the truth of political scientist Richard Neustadt's description of a "government of separated institutions sharing powers." While each of the branches has primary responsibility in either the executive, legislative, or judicial realms, each also shares powers with the other two branches.

During the framing, the delegates tried to create the right balance of power between the national government and the state governments. Having seen that the confederation of states did not work, they wanted to give the national government sufficient authority to govern while leaving the state governments enough power to accomplish what they needed at the local level. The framers created a national government of **delegated powers**, meaning powers that are expressly granted or enumerated, and limited in nature, while leaving the state governments with general **reserved powers**, or the remainder of the authority not specifically delegated to the national government. For example, to avoid the problem of various states under the Articles of Confederation conducting their own foreign policy, that power was delegated to the national government. However, if state governments wish to go to a foreign government seeking business investment, they may do so using the power to improve the economic welfare of their citizens, a power reserved for the states.

By viewing the Constitution from a vertical perspective, a number of other features become apparent. For instance, to remedy the lack of central control over the economy under the Articles of Confederation, Congress has the power over commerce *among* the states, while the states individually are left to govern commerce *within* their own boundaries. To handle a case in which a state militia does not respond to an emergency such as Shays's Rebellion, the president was made commander in chief, and Congress was given power both to raise and support an army and to send it into battle. States, however, retained their own powers over a police force to keep order at home. The most important element of the vertical power is the so-called *supremacy clause,* in Article VI, which states that in any controversy between the states and the federal government, federal dictates will always prevail. With the acceptance of this provision came the guarantee that sovereign states would never again be the dominating power that they were under the Articles of Confederation.

The success of this reordering of governmental priorities between the national and state governments depends on one's point of view. Many of these powers have been interpreted to expand the national power to such a great degree that individual states have much less power than many of the framers ever imagined. Some praise the uniformity and comprehensive nature of such a government, while others express concerns about the burgeoning size and remoteness of the national government and the need for policy innovation by the individual state governments.

The Articles of the Constitution

All the national powers, including those we have already looked at, are outlined in the individual articles of the Constitution. The Constitution is divided into seven Articles, each with a unique purpose. The first three apportion power among the three branches of national government, two others (Articles IV and VI) apportion power between the national and state governments, and the remaining two articles (Articles V and VII) lay out the procedures for amending and ratifying the Constitution. Gaps were deliberately left in each of these articles, and the language was given a certain elasticity to allow the Constitution to expand and evolve as the nation needed.

ARTICLE I   Article I sets forth the powers of the legislative branch. For the framers, this was the most important article (and therefore the first) because it sought to expand the powers of the old Continental Congress while still preventing it from achieving the omnipotent power of the state legislatures under the Articles of Confederation. This intent is clear from the limiting nature of the first words of the article: "All legislative powers *herein granted* shall be vested in a Congress of the United States." The article then contains a long list of specific and narrowly drawn powers. Those powers include the power to declare war, borrow and coin money, regulate interstate commerce, and raise and support an army. But the list is not as restrictive as it seems at first; the article also mandates that Congress can "make all Laws which shall be *necessary and proper* for carrying into Execution the foregoing Powers." As we will see in the next chapter, this **necessary and proper clause**, with its vague grant of power, has allowed a broad interpretation of Congress's powers under the Constitution. It is such built-in flexibility that makes the Constitution just as viable today as it was in 1787.

From the vertical perspective, Article I, Section 9 denies Congress the power to place a tax or duty on articles exported from any state. Moreover, under Section 10 states are denied the power to execute treaties, coin money, impair the obligation of contracts, and lay any imposts or duties on imports or exports without the consent of Congress.

ARTICLE II   Article II outlines the powers of the executive. At first glance, it seems to limit the president's power to simply granting pardons, making treaties, nominating certain officials, and commanding the army and navy. But, as with the legislative branch, the executive was granted an elastic clause in the ambiguous first sentence of the article: "The executive Power shall be vested in a President of the United States of America." As you will see in Chapter 6 on the presidency, a broad interpretation of the words *executive power* provides a president with considerable power. For example, should the life of a Supreme Court justice or a member of Congress be threatened, it is within the "inherent powers" of the president to provide protection using a United States marshal. It is the executive power that allows presidents to send troops to foreign countries even in the absence of a formal declaration of war by Congress.

This article also gives the president powers including the veto and the power to make judicial appointments. These powers enable the president to check the powers of the other two branches. Article II has additional elasticity built into it in Section 3, which states: "[The President] shall take Care that the Laws be faithfully executed." A president who disagrees with congressional legislation can "faithfully" execute the law by reinterpreting it or by devising a new law. For instance, if Congress appropriates too much money for a program, the president can "take Care" by *impounding,* that is, either delaying or refusing to spend, the full appropriation. Thomas Jefferson did this in 1803, when he withheld money for gunboats on the Mississippi. However, Richard Nixon expanded this power, not to save money, but to derail programs with which he disagreed.

ARTICLE III   Article III outlines the powers of the judicial branch. As we will see in more detail in Chapter 7, the framers provided the vaguest grant of powers to the judiciary because they could not agree on the role of this branch. This article establishes only a Supreme Court and grants Congress the power

A president who agrees with congressional legislation will sign a bill into law. Exercising his Article II powers, President Bill Clinton signs the North American Free Trade Agreement (NAFTA) into law on September 14, 1993. The agreement lowers tariffs between the United States, Mexico, and Canada and aims to create jobs and spur economic growth. Joining in the signing ceremony and perhaps preparing to receive their commemorative pens are NAFTA supporters, including three former presidents (Ford, Carter, and Bush).

to "ordain and establish" inferior federal courts. Federal judges are to serve for life, as long as they maintain good behavior, and are removable only by impeachment. They have the power to decide "Cases, in Law and Equity" arising under the Constitution and also to interpret federal laws and federal treaties. As you will learn later on, the power of the judiciary would expand dramatically because of the 1803 case of *Marbury* v. *Madison*. In this case Chief Justice John Marshall established the power of the Supreme Court as the final interpreter of the Constitution with the authority to judge whether the actions of other political branches were constitutional.

ARTICLE IV   Article IV establishes guidelines for interstate relations. Under the Articles of Confederation, no such guidelines existed. A state could disregard the laws of other states; it could also treat its own citizens one way and citizens of other states another way. This article establishes uniformity by guaranteeing that "full faith and credit" must be granted by all states to the various laws, debts, and judgments of other states. In addition, citizens of all states must receive the same "privileges and immunities." Because of this amendment, a decision to avoid repaying a state-financed college loan or even parking fine by crossing state boundaries is ill advised. Those obligations are in force in all states of the union, as individuals who try to avoid paying child support by moving out of state are discovering.

Once again, some central vertical powers are found here. Section 3 states that Congress can decide what states to admit to the union, while Section 4 establishes that the national government "shall guarantee to every State in this Union a Republican form of government, and shall protect each of them against Invasion; and on application of the legislature, or of the executive (when the legislature cannot be convened), against domestic violence." This power to preserve and protect the state governments, and thus the union, can be expanded further than one might think. It is to this power that Pete Wilson, the governor of California, turned when seeking federal assistance after the Los Angeles riots in 1992. Florida governor Lawton Chiles did the same after the damage from Hurricane Andrew later that year raised fears of extensive looting. A declaration that these states could not handle the disasters enabled the president to send in federal troops to help maintain order. Using this authority then, the national government is able to support state governments in a way that was impossible under the Articles of Confederation.

ARTICLE V   Article V outlines the procedure for amending the Constitution. The framers understood that changes in their original document might be necessary to correct imperfections in their work or to update it for use by future generations, as, for example, with the Equal Rights Amendment, discussed in the case study.

ARTICLE VI   Article VI deals with federal–state relations, and the financial obligations of the new government. This article not only contains the supremacy clause, affirming the predominance of the national government, but also ensures that all debts entered into before the Constitution shall be valid against the United States. Moreover, it states that all national officers must swear an oath of office supporting the Constitution and cannot be subjected to a religious test.

ARTICLE VII   Article VII explains the process for ratifying the Constitution. We now turn to a discussion of the battle for ratification.

RATIFICATION: THE BATTLE FOR THE CONSTITUTION

Drafting the Constitution was just the first step toward creating a new government. The vote for or against the new document was now in the hands of the various state conventions. According to Article VII, nine of the thirteen states had to ratify the Constitution for it to take effect. Realistically, though, everyone understood that unless the most populous states—Pennsylvania, Massachusetts, New York, and Virginia—signed it, the Constitution would never succeed.

Ratifying the Constitution involved hardball politics. This reality is often surprising for those who believe that creating the Constitution was a nonpartisan and academic process of debating the philosophical issues concerning a new government. A close look at this first political crisis in the American government's history is instructive both for seeing how the nation was formed and understanding how the arguments over constitutional issues continue to rage today.

As in every good political fight, the side that was best organized at the beginning had the advantage. Those in favor of the Constitution, many of whom were nationalists at the convention, took the lead by calling themselves the **Federalists**. Thus, they stole the semantic high ground by taking the name of supporters of the federal form of government under the Articles of Confederation. The true supporters of the federal form of government, the states'-rights advocates, had to call themselves the **Antifederalists**. Among the members of this group were most but not all of the convention's antinationalists.

Are Women's Rights Protected by the Constitution?

"Equality of rights under the law shall not be denied or abridged by the United States or by any State on account of sex." So begins the Equal Rights Amendment (ERA), whose supporters claim that the rights of women are not protected by the U.S. Constitution. Women are not even mentioned in the Constitution, and therefore, according to advocates of the ERA, their rights are not safeguarded from arbitrary legislative or executive action. Instead, whatever rights women are granted under the law are dependent on the support of the legislature or the actions of judges who are willing to expand existing law to fit the needs of women in particular cases. For many women's organizations this is not enough; they argue that only a constitutional amendment guarantee women equality under the law would assure full protection of their rights.

It can be argued, however, that the Constitution does in fact protect women's rights, albeit implicitly. Philosopher Robert Goldwin acknowledges that women are not mentioned in the Constitution, but he goes on to point out several clauses that have the effect of protecting both sexes equally. For example, Article I, Section 2, Clause 3 seems to include women by not excluding them. It deals with the number of people who will be counted to determine a state's representation in Congress: "The whole number of free persons" and "those bound to service for a term of years" and "all other persons." According to Goldwin, by speaking of "persons" and not differentiating between males and females, the Constitution seems to extend protection to both sexes.

Goldwin also notes the utter lack of "a single noun or adjective that denotes sex" in the Constitution. The framers instead relied on nonsexist terms such as *electors, citizens, members, inhabitants, officers, representatives,* and *persons.* It appears, therefore, that the Constitution poses no barriers to women's rights, including the right to be elected to national office—even the presidency. Goldwin concludes his argument by noting that women are not mentioned in the Constitution because "the Framers designed a better way to make sure that no one was left out." They used general language to protect the rights of all free persons.

Over the years, advocates of women's rights have found the language of the Constitution inadequate on several occasions. Women won the right to vote in 1920, but only after a long, sometimes violent struggle. Decades later they lobbied unsuccessfully for the Equal Rights Amendment (see the case study at the beginning of the chapter). In the future, the ERA may be reintroduced in Congress, and perhaps it will succeed in gaining ratification by the required number of states. Until then, the rights of women will continue to be determined by judicial rulings and congressional legislation, both of which are based largely on the implicit protections embedded in existing constitutional language.

Source: Robert Goldwin, "Why Blacks, Women and Jews Are Not Mentioned in the Constitution," *Commentary* (May 1987): 31–33.

The Federalist Papers

The debate over the Constitution raged in newspapers and hand-distributed pamphlets, the only source of communication in that period. Federalists Alexander Hamilton, James Madison, and John Jay wrote eighty-five essays in New York newspapers under the pen name of *Publius,* a Latin term meaning "public man," seeking to influence the debate in the New York state convention in favor of ratification. All of these articles were intended to answer the arguments of the states'-rights advocates that the new central government would be too powerful and too inclined to expand further, and thus likely destroy liberty. Hamilton, Madison, and Jay argued instead that without this new Constitution the states would break apart and the nation would fail. With it, they reasoned, the government would act in the national interest while also preserving liberty. Later collected under the title of *The Federalist Papers: A Commentary on the Constitution of the United States,* these pieces offer us what historian Henry Steele Commager calls a handbook on how the Constitution should operate. While these essays had little effect on the ratification debate, generations of judges, politicians, and scholars have considered them, together with Madison's notes of the convention, to indicate "the intent of the Framers" in creating the Constitution. (See, for example, *Federalist* nos. 10 and 51 in the Appendix.) For this reason, many scholars believe the *Federalist Papers* to be the most important work of political theory written in U.S. history.

In opposition, the Antifederalists made their case in scores of articles such as those authored by Robert Yates, who wrote the *Letters of Brutus;* Luther Martin, who wrote *Genuine Information;* and Mercy Otis Warren, who wrote *Observations on the New Constitution...by a Columbian Patriot.* While these men understood that the central government needed more power than it had under the Articles of Confederation, they feared that the structure established in the convention would supersede the state governments, rendering them obsolete. By placing too much power in the hands of a government so removed from the people, they argued, the new government would likely expand its power and have to rule by force rather than the consent of the governed. They sought ways to establish a better balance between the power of the central government and the states by placing further checks on the newly established central government.

By looking at the issues, the debate between the Federalists and Antifederalists, the compromises, and the political battle over ratification, we can get a clear sense of the framers' intentions and begin to understand what the Constitution means.

Federalists versus Antifederalists

The difference between the Federalists and the Antifederalists can be found on the most fundamental theoretical level. Since the Federalists, led by Hamilton and Madison, believed that *the people* had created the Constitution, and not *the states,* they argued that a strong central government was the best representation of the sovereignty of the people. The Federalists sought energy and leadership from a centralized government that would unite the entire nation, thus safeguarding the interests of the people. They also argued that the powers of the central government should be expandable to meet the needs of the people and to enable the government to respond to any emergencies that arise.

The Antifederalists, led by Thomas Jefferson, believed that the Constitution was created by the states, meaning that the national government's power was carved out of the states' power. Accordingly, they argued that the states should remain independent and distinct rather than be led by a supreme national government. The Antifederalists sought to preserve the liberty and rights of the minorities, those people not in the majority, by bolstering individual state governments that would be closer to the people.

In addition to the theoretical differences between Federalist and Antifederalist views, the groups differed over who would have the authority for solving practical, real-world problems. The Federalists, supporters of a strong central government, realized that some problems spill over state boundaries and need to be resolved by a neutral, national arbiter. These problems include control of interstate waterways and economic matters. Federalists believed that a single solution to these problems would be more sensible and cost-effective than having each state devise and pay for its own program. They reasoned that the states would place their economies at a competitive disadvantage by attempting to resolve problems by themselves. While the Federalists were thinking of slavery and interstate commerce here, such problems as organized crime and pollution would arise later to prove them correct about the need for a centralized source of authority.

Not surprisingly, the Antifederalists disagreed with the Federalists. To them, the government that was closer to the people, and thus more accountable to them, should solve problems among states. Antifederalists reasoned that it is best to have solutions tailored to the talents of and conditions in each state rather than to have a single compromise solution imposed on everyone from some distant national government.

Out of these two opposing groups, two political parties would emerge. George Washington's Federalist party, supporting a strong nationalist government, was an outgrowth of the Federalist position. This party evolved into the Whig party and then the Republican party. The Democratic-Republican party of Thomas Jefferson supported states' rights (like the Antifederalists) and later became the Democratic party.

It is clear from their arguments that the Federalists and Antifederalists were motivated by different fears. In one of the most famous of the *Federalist Papers,* the tenth *Federalist,* James Madison tried to explain how the new democratic government would overcome political differences that are "sown in the nature of man." The nation, he argued, is divided into **factions,** "a number of citizens, whether amounting to a majority or a minority of the whole, who are united and actuated by some common impulse or passion or...interest."[15] These groups of people, much like interest groups today, were united largely along the lines of property classifications—for example, farmers versus the manufacturing class—and would seek to have the government protect their own interests to the exclusion of all others.

Madison then sought to explain in this article, and later in *Federalist* no. 51, how the new government was designed to prevent a "tyranny of the majority," or 50 percent plus 1 of the citizens taking away the liberty of those in the minority. Since there was no way to eliminate the divisive *causes* of factions (there will always be rich and poor and differences in employment), Madison explained how the new system of representative government was designed to control the harmful *effects* of factions. The key was to increase the size of the political unit, or "expand the sphere" from the smaller states, in which minorities could easily be outnumbered and oppressed, to the larger central government, where they had a better chance for political protection.

In *Federalist* no. 51 Madison expanded his argument to show how the separation of powers system would protect liberty by allowing each of the parts of the government to "be the means of keeping each other in their proper places." Because of the two-year term of the popularly elected House of Representatives, the six-year term of the state legislature–elected Senate, and the four-year term of the electoral college–elected president, each branch of government would represent different groups. The common people's voice in the House would turn over quickly and be restrained by the long-term elite aristocratic view of the Senate and the national perspective of the president. Moreover, the powers of each branch would check the others. When combined with the system of federalism, in which national and state government checked each other, it was hoped that no one majority faction could dominate American politics, because every group would have effective representation somewhere. Those in a minority in one branch of the national government or in one state might find a representative in another branch of government or in another state.

At the other end of the spectrum, the Antifederalists argued that the central government was not to be trusted; they feared that the Constitution had traded English tyranny for tyranny from the central government at home. Worried that the central government would overrun the states and the rights of those in the minority, they asked what guarantees the Constitution contains to protect and preserve the rights of all Americans.

As far apart as these two groups were at the time of the drafting of the Constitution, some means had to be found to secure an agreement between them if the new document was to be ratified. The answer was the addition of a protective list of rights to the new constitution.

Ratification by Way of Compromise: A Bill of Rights

Though the convention delegates had repeatedly refused to place in the new constitution a long list of rights to be protected, the issue did not end with its signing. Led by Thomas Jefferson, the Antifederalists insisted during the ratification debate that a list of amendments be included, guaranteeing that the new central government could not restrict certain rights. The Federalists argued that a constitutional guarantee of rights was unnecessary since citizens were already adequately protected by the Constitution or by the constitutions of the individual states.

The debate over adding amendments to the Constitution presented an interesting philosophical dilemma. If the new government did not in fact already protect these rights, then many felt that it should not have been created in the first place. If it did in fact protect them, then why was it necessary to repeat those rights in a series of amendments? In the end, philosophy gave way to politics. Following the tradition of the Magna Carta, compacts, social contracts, and state bills of rights, it was agreed that the people would get to see their rights guaranteed in writing, in the Constitution. In fact, the expectation of such amendments helped sell the Constitution.

Politics the Old-fashioned Way: A Look at the Battle for Ratification

You might be surprised by the tactics used once the ratification debates moved from being a secret discussion among aristocratic political elites into the public arena. The debates were hardly genteel.

Initially, ratification seemed inevitable. After all, the Federalists had the dual advantages of an existing document that defined the terms of the debate, and an opposition movement that was disorganized. Within eight months after the Constitution had been signed, eight states had ratified the document. However, the difficult battles in two of them—Pennsylvania and Massachusetts—indicated just how difficult it would be to get the critical ninth state, not to mention the two large-state holdouts, Virginia and New York.

The lengths that proponents of the Constitution were willing to go to achieve success was made clear in Pennsylvania. Ben Franklin forced the State Assembly, which was about to adjourn, to appoint a ratifying convention even before enough copies of the Constitution arrived for everyone to read. Seeking to derail this effort, the Antifederalists hid, thinking they might deny Franklin a voting quorum. The sergeant at arms was directed to take the necessary action to make a vote possible. A mob of angry Federalists volunteered to help him, roaming the streets of Philadelphia looking for any missing assemblymen they could find. They eventually found two assemblymen hiding in their rooms over a local tavern and, after dragging them through the streets of Philadelphia, threw them into the assembly hall while a mob of Constitution supporters blocked their escape. Not surprisingly, these two men cast their votes against a ratifying convention, but the measure passed by a vote of forty-four to two.

Protests against such strong-arm tactics were ignored. Mobs of Federalists used similar tactics to ensure that the final ratifying vote favored the Constitution by a two to one margin. The damage to the Federalists' prestige in Philadelphia was so great that James Wilson, a leading Federalist, was nearly beaten to death by a mob of angry Antifederalists weeks later.

In Massachusetts, clever political strategy rather than strong-arm tactics turned the tide. Three hundred and fifty delegates, many of them from the less populous western part of the state, where the Antifederalists dominated, met in Boston on January 8, 1788. The opponents of the Constitution held a slight numerical advantage. Governor John Hancock, a Federalist but also a cagey politician, was so unsure of how the vote would go that he decided to stay away, complaining of the gout. But to convince Hancock to join them, the Federalists dangled the possibility that if Virginia failed to ratify the Constitution, leaving George Washington outside the new nation, then Hancock was the most likely prospect for the presidency of the country. With that, Hancock's gout miraculously abated, and he was carried to the convention as a hero, with his legs wrapped in flannel. There he proposed a series of amendments protecting such local concerns as taxation and merchants' rights. These amendments, an early version of what would later become the Bill of Rights, changed the terms of the debate. Now those who supported the Constitution could vote for it, and those who opposed it could vote for the document as amended. On February 6, 1788, Massachusetts ratified the Constitution by only nineteen votes (187 to 168). Hancock's amendment strategy was later used by other states to smooth the way to ratification.

By June 2, 1788, with only one state needed to ratify the Constitution and put it into effect, the eyes of the nation turned to Virginia, where some found the notion of "the people" running a democratic government preposterous. Patrick Henry, the leader of the Antifederalists, argued that even the first three words of the document were wrong: "Who authorized them to speak the

How do you celebrate the birth of a nation? This rare 1789 woodcut depicts New York City's celebration of the Constitution's ratification. At center is a float honoring Alexander Hamilton, one of the leaders of the convention. At left is the fort at Bowling Green, where members of Congress stood to greet the procession.

language of *We the people,* instead of, *We the states?* States are the characteristics and the soul of a confederation."[16] But James Madison, thoroughly convinced of the need for a national government, saw no danger to the states, saying that the national government's "delegated powers" would keep it within limits. This sentiment could not persuade George Mason, who had refused to sign the Constitution: "Where is the barrier drawn between the government, and the rights of the citizens?"

The key to success was Edmund Randolph, the politically ambitious thirty-four-year-old governor of Virginia, who had proposed the Virginia Plan in the convention and then, unhappy with the outcome of the debates, refused to sign the final version of the Constitution. He switched to Madison's side in the ratification debate, arguing that he would "assent to the lopping [of his right arm] before I assent to the dissolution of the union." Randolph urged the acceptance of subsequent amendments to the document just as Hancock had done in Massachusetts. Randolph's argument proved decisive. On June 25, 1788, by a narrow margin of ten votes, the Constitution was ratified in Virginia. New Hampshire had moved more quickly, becoming the ninth state to ratify, but although tenth, Virginia's size made its action important in securing the success of the new government.

A week after Virginia's vote, New York State ratified the Constitution by a razor-thin thirty-to-twenty-seven margin. North Carolina waited until after the Bill of Rights had been sent to the states for ratification before adding its assent in November 1789. And Rhode Island continued to take its time, waiting until May 29, 1790, to ratify the Constitution by a narrow thirty-four-to-thirty-two vote.

This highly political debate over the Constitution was proof that the new system would work because democracy had worked. The American people had freely and peacefully debated and chosen their new form of government. They had put aside their individual needs and local interests for the common good. As Benjamin Rush, a Philadelphia physician who had lived to sign the

Declaration of Independence and see the Constitution ratified, said, "'Tis done, we have become a nation."[17]

Adoption of the Bill of Rights

When the First Congress convened, James Madison sifted through 200 amendments proposed in state debates and chose 17 to be debated by Congress. Of these, twelve amendments were passed and sent to the states for ratification. Ten were ratified in 1791, becoming known as the **Bill of Rights**. As you can see from Figure 3.2, the first 8 amendments drafted by the First Congress guaranteed a variety of rights against government control and provided procedural safeguards in criminal trials and against arbitrary governmental action. The Ninth and Tenth amendments were intended to describe the new constitutional structure, assuring that rights not listed in the Constitution, or powers not delegated to the national government, would be retained by the people or the states. The amendments placed limits on government power by prohibiting the

Safeguards of Personal and Political Freedoms

1. Freedom of speech, press, and religion, and right to assemble peaceably and to petition government to redress grievances

Outmoded protections against British occupation

2. Right to keep and bear arms
3. Protection against quartering troops in private homes

Safeguards in the Judicial Process and against Arbitrary Government Action

4. Protection against "unreasonable" searches and seizures by the government
5. Guarantees of a Grand Jury for capital crimes, against double jeopardy, against being forced to testify against oneself, against being deprived of life or property without "due process of law," and against the taking of property without just compensation
6. Guarantees of Rights in criminal trials including right to speedy and public trial, to be informed of the nature of the charges, to confront witnesses, to compel witnesses to appear in one's defense, and to the assistance of counsel
7. Guarantee of right of trial by jury of one's peers
8. Guarantee against excessive bail, and the imposition of cruel and unusual punishment

Description of Unenumerated Rights, and Reserved Powers

9. Assurance that rights not listed for protection against the power of the central government in the Constitution are still retained by the people
10. Assurance that the powers not delegated to the central government are reserved by the states, or by the people

FIGURE 3.2 The Bill of Rights
The first ten amendments to the Constitution, known as the Bill of Rights, were ratified on December 15, 1791. These amendments were crucial for the ratification of the Constitution and provide the most visible evidence of the importance of civil rights and civil liberties in American democracy.

national government from intruding on fundamental rights and liberties. However, the rights of the people against *state* intrusion would be left to the individual state constitutions and legislatures. As we will see in Chapter 7, though, over time America would further approach democracy as the Supreme Court applied all but a few of the provisions of the Bill of Rights to the states as well.

APPROACHING DEMOCRACY THROUGH CONSTITUTIONAL CHANGE

The framers viewed the Constitution as a lasting document, one that would be viable long after the debates and ratification. They did not believe as Thomas Jefferson and George Washington did that a new constitution should be written every 20 years or so. To create a lasting document, the framers drafted a constitution that included an amendment process that would allow for adjustments to their handiwork. In addition, the Supreme Court would play a role, along with the pressures of social and political change, to alter a flexible and responsive constitution. This way, the Constitution could be kept timely and current. But as we saw in the ERA case at the beginning of the chapter, the Constitution is not easy to alter—no matter how strong, compelling, or passionate the need.

As former Supreme Court justice Thurgood Marshall noted in 1987, the Constitution was "defective from the start." As a result, the document required "several amendments, a civil war and momentous social transformation to attain the system of constitutional government, and its respect for the individual freedoms and human rights, we hold as fundamental today."[18] Many of the most important changes to the Constitution have been the result of the amendment process.

The Amendment Process

The framers deliberately made the amendment process difficult, thus placing the Constitution beyond the temporary passions of the people, but they did not require unanimity, which had already failed in the Articles of Confederation. Clearly, the amendment process was designed to be used only for the most serious issues.

The framers established a two-stage amendment process, resembling the one used to approve the Constitution. First, there must be a **proposal** for a change that the states must then **ratify**. The framers wanted to ensure that each new amendment would be considered carefully. Thus, they required a vast consensus of political and social support for amendments, known as a **supermajority**. This means that each stage of the process has to be approved by more than the simple majority of 50 percent plus one. The proposal stage requires either a two-thirds vote of both houses of Congress or an application from two-thirds of the states for a constitutional convention. Ratification is accomplished by a vote of three-quarters of the state legislatures or a three-quarters vote of specially created state ratifying conventions. While the framers reserved this extraordinary voting requirement for other important tasks, such as overriding a presidential veto and ratifying a treaty, here alone the supermajority has to be mustered twice on the same issue. The amendment process is illustrated in Figure 3.3.

Little Known Fact

Thomas Jefferson and John Adams both died on July 4, 1826, the 50th anniversary of the Declaration of Independence. This coincidence was taken by many to be a sign that America was blessed.

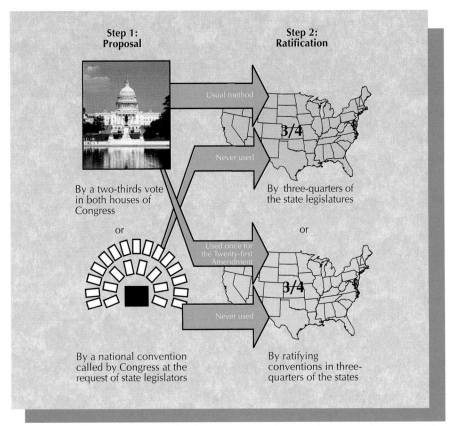

**Step 1:
Proposal**

**Step 2:
Ratification**

Usual method

Never used

Used once for
the Twenty-first
Amendment

Never used

3/4

3/4

By a two-thirds vote
in both houses of
Congress

By three-quarters of
the state legislatures

or

or

By a national convention
called by Congress at the
request of state legislators

By ratifying
conventions in three-
quarters of the states

**FIGURE 3.3 Procedures for
Amending the Constitution**
Although the framers provided
four ways to amend the Constitution, only one method is usually
used: proposal of an amendment
by two-thirds of each house of
Congress and ratification by three-
quarters of the state legislatures.
The sole exception was the Twenty-first Amendment repealing prohibition. Ratification of this
amendment took place in special
state conventions.

No formal time limit was placed on the amendment, but a limit can be included in the body of the amendment, as it was in the ERA, and Congress can
extend the limit if it wishes. While the Supreme Court has been reluctant to rule
on the constitutionality of such time limits, in 1921 it did rule that the seven-
year limit placed in the Eighteenth Amendment was "reasonable."[19]

While a new convention has been proposed several times, to date no
amendment has been approved by constitutional convention. All have been
proposed in Congress, and all except the Twenty-first Amendment, repealing
Prohibition, have been ratified using state legislatures. Since there has been
only one constitutional convention, a variety of interesting questions remain
about the prospects for another such event. How would the delegates be selected? How would the votes be apportioned among the fifty states? Is there a
need to ensure that all social groups are represented, and is there a way of doing so? And even if a convention is called to consider a specific proposal, is
there a chance of a runaway convention resulting in reconsideration of the entire Constitution, as was done with the Articles of Confederation in 1787? The
answers to these questions are unknown, and since the one example in this
country was a runaway convention, few are willing to risk having another one.

Between 1974 and 1988 it looked as if a constitutional convention would
be called to draft a balanced-budget amendment, requiring the national government to spend no more than it had collected in taxes. Of the necessary thirty-four states, thirty-two passed petitions calling for the convention, but

uncertainty about how the amendment would operate and about its necessity, as well as the constantly changing political climate, prevented the effort from succeeding. With the increasing budget deficit, though, there are renewed calls for such an amendment. In early 1995, Congress tried but failed to pass just such a proposal. However, should we come close to another constitutional convention, Congress would very likely pass such an amendment quickly and send it on to the states. This happened in 1911, when thirty-one states called for a convention to consider the direct election of the Senate. A fearful Congress quickly proposed such an amendment in 1912, and after ratification by the states in 1913, it became the Seventeenth Amendment.

The success of the process for screening changes to the Constitution is illustrated by the fact that around 10,000 amendments have been proposed over the years, but only thirty-four have passed the proposal stage. Of these, only twenty-seven have survived ratification. Some of the rejected amendments include proposals for abolishing the Senate, prohibiting drunkenness in the United States and its territories, changing the name of the country from "The United States of America" to "The United States of the Earth," and making the marigold the national flower. Five hundred amendments have been proposed to revise the presidential selection process (one of which sought to have the president chosen by lot).

At times, the amendment proposal process can be used in an attempt to reverse Supreme Court decisions. In recent years, as you will learn in Chapter 14, after the Supreme Court struck down state and federal laws designed to outlaw burning the American flag, an amendment that would accomplish the same thing was proposed.

Much can happen between the proposal and ratification stages to doom an amendment. The opening case study on the ERA shows the consequences of a shift in political sentiment. Initially, it looked as if that amendment would pass readily; then the tide turned. Similarly, the proposal in 1978 to give the District of Columbia the same representation in Congress as a state passed by a substantial margin. But with its effect of diluting the representation of all the other states in Congress, only sixteen states voted for ratification within the set seven-year time limit.

If you look at the ratified amendments you will see how remarkably few changes have been made in the Constitution, with all of them grouped around four purposes: to expand rights and equality, to correct flaws in, or revise, the original constitutional plan for government, to make public policy, and to overturn Supreme Court decisions. The amendments and their effects are outlined in Table 3.3.

The history of the disastrous Eighteenth Amendment and the Twenty-First Amendment repealing it best illustrates the problems that result when a special-interest group takes over a process designed to express the wishes of the vast majority. The Prohibition era of the 1920s began when temperance, or antiliquor, groups around the country forced Congress to pass in 1917, and the states to ratify two years later, an amendment banning the manufacture, sale, and transportation of liquor. Through a quirk of the process, most of the ratification support came from the less populous western states, meaning that the amendment was ratified by thirty-six states having a total of nine million fewer people than the other twelve states. The result was a conflict between those seeking

Table 3.3
The Constitutional Amendments: 11 to 27

NO.	PROPOSED	RATIFIED	SUBJECT	PURPOSE
11	1794	1795	To sue a state in federal court individuals need state consent	Overruled a Supreme Court decision
12	1803	1804	Requires separate electoral college votes for president and vice president	Corrected a government flaw
13	1865	1865	Prohibits slavery	Expanded rights
14	1866	1868	Gives citizenship to freed slaves, guarantees them due process and equal protection of the laws, and protects their privileges and immunities	Expanded rights
15	1869	1870	Grants freed slaves the right to vote	Expanded rights
16	1909	1913	Grants Congress power to collect income tax	Overruled a Supreme Court decision
17	1912	1913	Provides for direct election of the Senate (formerly elected by state legislatures)	Expanded rights
18	1917	1919	Prohibited the sale or production of liquor	Public policy
19	1919	1920	Grants women the right to vote	Expanded rights
20	1932	1933	Changes presidential inauguration date from March 4 to January 20, and opening date of Congress to January 3	Revised a government plan
21	1933	1933	Repeals the Eighteenth Amendment	Public policy
22	1947	1951	Limits the president to two terms in office	Revised a government plan
23	1960	1961	Grants citizens of Washington, D.C., status in electoral college to vote for president	Expanded rights
24	1962	1964	Prohibits charging a poll tax to vote	Expanded rights
25	1965	1967	Provides for succession of president or vice president in the event of death, removal from office, incapacity, or resignation	Revised a government plan
26	1971	1971	Grants the right to vote to eighteen- to twenty-year-olds	Expanded rights
27	1789	1992	Prohibits a pay raise voted by Congress from going into effect until the following session	Public policy

Prohibition commenced in 1919 with the passage of the Eighteenth Amendment, banning the manufacture, sale, and transportation of alcoholic beverages. Throughout the 1920s, federal agents sought to seize contraband alcohol, often destroying kegs in full public view to drive home the point of the law. Nonetheless, illegal imbibing in "speakeasies" and at home continued along with the manufacture and transportation of "moonshine." Disobedience of the ban on alcohol was so commonplace that fourteen years later the Eighteenth Amendment was repealed.

virtue through abstinence and the majority, who still wanted to drink. So drink they did. By 1929, thirty amendments repealing the Eighteenth had been proposed in Congress, with one finally being passed on February 20, 1933. In December of that year, the amendment was ratified by state conventions—the only time in American history that that particular route was taken to pass an amendment.[20]

There have been other efforts by special-interest groups and political parties to amend the Constitution in an attempt to either shape the morality of the nation or further their political agenda. For example, the amendment process has been used in an attempt to ban abortions and to reestablish prayer in public schools. But the double super-majority feature of the amendment process usually prevents such uses by special-interest and political groups, reserving amendments for the expression of the overwhelming desires of the vast majority.

Updating the Constitution by Judicial Interpretation

How has the Constitution managed to remain vibrant and current even though it has been amended only twenty-seven times? The answer to this question has to do both with the brilliant ambiguity built into the Constitution and the power of the Supreme Court to interpret it.

But where did the Court get such power? As you will learn in Chapter 7 on the judiciary, in the 1803 case of *Marbury* v. *Madison,* the Court, under Chief Justice John Marshall, ruled that since the Court interprets laws and the Constitution is a law, then the Court has the power to be the final interpreter of the Constitution. This power, **judicial review,** enables the Court to overturn acts of the other two branches of government if those acts are in violation of the Constitution. In doing so, the court interprets the Constitution, giving new meaning to the phrases and provisions from 1787. Since overturning a constitutional ruling by the Supreme Court can only be done by the Court itself, or through a constitutional amendment, these rulings, in effect, change the meaning of the Constitution.

The powers of the federal government have expanded and contracted in accord with these and other Supreme Court interpretations of the vague provisions of the Constitution. In exercising this power, the justices take on the role of modern constitutional framers, trying to define what the document should mean in the modern age. Throughout American history, scholars have debated the Court's role, with some believing that the justices should uphold the framers' original meaning of the Constitution and others maintaining that they should continue to update the document using a modern perspective.

Since changes to the Constitution are never made in a political and social vacuum, we now turn to the third source of constitutional change.

Updating the Constitution in Response to Political and Social Change

The most remarkable feature of the Constitution is how it has adapted to the times, changing along with an ever-changing nation. The world has changed dramatically from that of 1787, when it took four days for German immigrant Jacob Shallus to write the Constitution by hand on four pieces of stretched vellum with a quill pen and ink made from oak galls and dyes. Now we can create a version of the same document in just a few minutes using computer software.

We have gone from a nation of a little more than the population of Los Angeles to one of 250 million people; from a geographic base of thirteen seashore colonies to fifty states spread across more than three thousand miles. In 1787, wars took months to develop as ships crossed vast oceans; now, one press of a button could mean instant annihilation. According to former Supreme Court justice Byron White, "From the summer of 1787 to the present the government of the United States has become an endeavor far beyond the contemplation of the Framers. But the wisdom of the Framers was to anticipate that the nation would grow and new problems of governance would require different solutions."[21] Essentially, the Constitution was devised to allow the government to evolve as the nation did.

Over time, actions taken by the different branches of government have changed the nature of the government's structure without changing the Constitution. The framers originally gave Congress the power to declare war, but the speed of modern warfare has created the need for quicker responses. Now the president has the power to make war. The Korean and Vietnam wars, along with a host of other conflicts, were presidential wars. The framers also intended, despite the creation of a system of checks and balances, for Congress to be the predominant branch. But certain presidents have enlarged the powers of the executive. Thomas Jefferson directed the purchase of the Louisiana Territory, Abraham Lincoln imposed martial law and freed the slaves, Woodrow Wilson and Franklin D. Roosevelt became virtual dictators during world wars, and a host of other presidents exercised powers well beyond those delegated to them by Congress. While it is doubtful that Madison and Franklin would recognize much of the government today, they would appreciate the fact that their handiwork allowed this evolution to take place.

Also, as you will learn in later chapters, changes in the meaning of the Constitution, and thus its ability to direct the government, can result from social pressure. As new groups of people find their voices, or as established groups perceive new needs, the open-ended nature of the Constitution enables them to press for reforms. Many changes have been made in response to the demands of interest groups and could not have been imagined by the framers. As Harvard professor Laurence Tribe puts it:

> The framing of the Constitution has been a continuous process rather than a purely episodic one. I think the real framers were not only the gentlemen who met in Philadelphia and those who drafted and ratified the crucial amendments…but also the many people who often in the roles of dissent and rebellion, sat in, or marched and sang, or sometimes gave their lives, in order to translate their vision of what the Constitution might be and how it should be understood into political and legal reality.[22]

Indeed, the efforts of social reformers like Rosa Parks and the Reverend Martin Luther King, along with the efforts of many others, resulted in changes, not just in government, but also in the way Americans perceive their democracy. The movement seeking rights for women is one illustration of this building-block process of approaching democracy. The efforts of Susan B. Anthony to secure rights for married women in the 1850s started to change perceptions and expectations about women. Those altered perceptions led Elizabeth Cady Stanton in the 1870s to seek changes in laws dealing with divorce and reproduc-

It appears to me, then, little short of a miracle, that the Delegates from so many different States (which States you know are also different from each other), in their manners, circumstances, and prejudices, should unite in forming a system of national Government, so little liable to well founded objections.

—George Washington, 1788

Although the Equal Rights Amendment was never ratified, women have made great strides in eliminating barriers to "equality of rights" in their professional lives, some even becoming successful fighter pilots in the U.S. armed services. Despite such successes, however, many would argue that the battle for true equality has not yet been won.

tive rights. Then the two of them labored for women's suffrage in the 1890s. The establishment of women's suffrage by the Nineteenth Amendment in 1920 gave women a means for expressing their demands for other rights. This evolutionary process was continued by Ruth Bader Ginsburg's efforts in the 1970s to convince the Supreme Court to extend constitutional protection for women under the Fourteenth Amendment. (For more on all of these efforts, see Chapter 15.) Without the efforts of each of these women in the chain pushing for constitutional change—and in the process, changing the way women are viewed—we might never have heard of the ERA or seen the strides that women have made toward equality. Thus, the words of the Constitution might remain the same, but their *meaning* changes in response to the demands of each new generation.

THE CONSTITUTION: TWO HUNDRED YEARS OF APPROACHING DEMOCRACY

"More than any other society," journalist Anthony Lewis has written, "we have a rights culture. Prick an American, and he reaches for his constitutional rights."[23] Like a mirror, the Constitution reflects for everyone what they see, or want to see, in it. For each of us, this remarkable document written two hundred years ago is just as alive now as it was in those heated debates in Philadelphia.

As you have seen, the original Constitution was hardly a testament to full participatory democracy. It begins with the words, "We the People," but in the beginning the "we" who drafted the document were the fifty-five delegates to the Constitutional Convention in Philadelphia and the elite landowners they represented. The Constitution did not fully protect the rights of all citizens, and the framers did not seek to use their 4,400-word document to advance social or political equality. Slavery was not banned; in fact, it seemed to be condoned. The feminine pronoun never appeared in the document, and women had no more rights than they had under the Articles of Confederation. Most Americans could not vote and had essentially no voice in the operation of their government. The government was designed for a coastal nation of only thirteen states, one in which the geographical center of the population was actually several dozen miles *east* of Baltimore, Maryland. Perhaps for this reason some of the framers anticipated that this document would have to be revised within a couple of decades as the nation expanded. In that sense, as Vaclav Havel has said so eloquently, democracy in America only began in 1787, and the experiment would have to continue.

But the framers made it possible for the government they created to approach democracy. The Constitution they created was an imperfect document but a highly elastic one that over the years and in response to the times would become more democratic. The paradox of this foundation of American democracy, then, is that a Constitution written in secret by representatives of less than 5 percent of the population established processes that have led to the most openly democratic nation in the world. The Bill of Rights included in the document protects the rights of most citizens. When a super-majority of the public demands change in the Constitution, change can occur through the amendment process. The Constitution can also evolve through judicial decisions and political action. In short, as new generations press for their rights and a greater voice in their government, the Constitution can change to fit the time and circumstances, thus allowing the nation to approach democracy. Even

The U.S. Constitution: A Gift to All Nations

"America has been and remains the great constitutional laboratory for the entire world," says Joseph Magnet, a professor of law at the University of Ottawa in Canada. He is referring to the fact that the constitutions of more than 160 nations have been modeled on the U.S. Constitution.

The trend began after Germany, Japan, and Italy were defeated in World War II. The American Constitution was used as a model for those nations' postwar constitutions, but with some unique additions. The Japanese charter guarantees that the country will never again engage in military conflict and prohibits the maintenance of an army. In Germany, an "anti-Hitler" provision limits the powers of the executive branch. Italy's constitution places a large number of controls on executive power.

Three-fourths of the world's nations have written constitutions since 1965, and a great many of them have used the U.S. Constitution as a model, often with the assistance of American legal scholars. But the results have differed greatly, both because of the traditions of particular regions and the nature of the leadership in power at any given time. For example, China's constitutional declaration of human rights, which protects "freedom of speech, of the press, of assembly, of association, of procession and of demonstration," meant nothing to the Communist party leaders who sent tanks into Tiananmen Square to halt student-led demonstrations calling for democratic government. Similarly, leaders of many African nations, fearful of military coups and tribal wars, have simply outlawed opposing political parties, thereby creating one-party states.

Many Latin American countries have constitutions that enumerate human rights similar to those set forth in the U.S. Constitution. Yet those nations have experienced a cycle of military dictatorships and coups d'état that have resulted in one-party rule. Mexico, for example, has a constitution that makes it possible for political parties to share power, yet one party, the Institutional Revolutionary party, has controlled all branches of the government almost continuously since 1929.

India, the world's largest democracy, has been the most faithful in observing the principles contained in the U.S. Constitution. The Indian constitution, drafted in 1949, includes a declaration of "fundamental rights" and a system of judicial reform to enforce them. As a result, when repressive laws have been passed by political parties attempting to destroy the opposition, those laws have quickly been overturned by the courts.

Perhaps the most significant effort to import the principles of the U.S. Constitution occurred in the late 1980s and early 1990s, when the Eastern European nations broke away from the Soviet Union. Many of these nations turned to American legal scholars for help in drafting their new constitutions. One of those scholars, the late Professor Albert P. Blaustein of Rutgers University Law School, helped draft more than forty constitutions. After drafting the constitutions of Liberia, Fiji, Zimbabwe, Bangladesh, and Peru, Blaustein journeyed to Poland and Romania. Other scholars went to Czechoslovakia and Hungary.

The Eastern European nations did not simply copy the American model. Because their history of dictatorship had created a strong fear of powerful executive leaders, many of those nations chose not to create a presidential system like that of the United States. Instead, they opted for a parliamentary system, in which leadership of the government is divided between two executives. Moreover, wishing to safeguard human rights such as free speech, most of the Eastern European countries inserted very specific guarantees in their constitutions. "Our own document is too general," said Blaustein, "so we've had to fill in the blanks over the years with case law. We can save others the trouble of all that by encouraging them to make explicit choices at the beginning and putting those choices into their constitutions."

Sources: Lis Wiehl, "Constitution, Anyone? A New Cottage Industry," *New York Times,* Feb. 2, 1990, sec. B; "A Gift to All Nations," *Time,* July 6, 1987, pp. 64–65.

when these mechanisms do not work as they should, for example, when African Americans were not able to secure their promise of a right to vote and full equality, the legislative and judicial institutions created in the Constitution provide a way to seek redress.

The framers hoped that their constitution would lead to a stable republic, an improvement over the Articles of Confederation. They did not seek to establish a system of pure democracy, relying instead on the notion of a representative government. Yet the convention was truly the "Miracle" described by Catherine Drinker Bowen not only because these men were able to reach some sort of compromise on the shape of a new government but also because the compromise they reached would create a system of government that continues to govern in ways that the framers could not fully anticipate.

SUMMARY

1. Although the stated goal of the Constitutional Convention was to revise the Articles of Confederation, some delegates believed that the Articles needed to be scrapped altogether and replaced by an entirely new document. Debate at the convention centered on two major proposals. The Virginia Plan called for a system of proportional representation in which the legislature would consist of two chambers, or "houses," and each state's representation in both houses would depend on its population. The New Jersey Plan proposed a unicameral (one-house) legislature in which each state would have one vote. The delegates voted to use the Virginia Plan as the basis for further discussion.

2. A key debate at the convention dealt with representation in the two houses of Congress. States with large populations sought proportional representation in both houses, while those with smaller populations called for an equal number of votes for each state. In the Great (or Connecticut) Compromise the delegates decided that representation in the House of Representatives would be based on each state's population, while each state would have two votes in the Senate.

3. Another important debate was over slavery. The southern states wanted slaves to be counted as part of the population when determining representation in Congress; the northern states wanted slaves to be excluded from the count. The outcome of the debate was the three-fifths compromise: Each state's representation would be determined by adding three-fifths of the number of slaves to the number of free citizens in that state.

4. The delegates were also divided over the nature of the presidency. Some favored a single national executive with the power to veto legislative acts, while others were concerned that a single executive would hold too much power and called instead for a board of executives. Eventually they agreed on a single executive.

5. The new Constitution created a republican form of government, in which the people hold an indirect voting power over elected officials. Originally, only members of the House of Representatives would be elected directly by the people; senators would be chosen by the state legislatures, and the president by an electoral college. Over the years the people have gained a more direct voice in the government through a series of constitutional changes such as popular election of senators and extension of the right to vote to all people over the age of eighteen.

6. The Constitution established a system of separation of powers in which different powers are granted to the three major branches of government. In addition, it set up checks and balances, giving each branch the power to approve, disapprove, or alter what the other branches do. It also distributed powers between the central government and the state governments. The powers of the central government are delegated—expressly granted and limited in nature—while all remaining powers are reserved to the states. The supremacy clause states that the dictates of the national government take precedence over those of any state government.

7. Supporters of the Constitution called themselves *Federalists;* opponents took the name *Antifederalists.* The Federalists claimed that the new government was designed to represent the sovereignty of the people, while the Antifederalists believed that the states should remain independent of the central government. The Constitution was finally ratified after the Federalists agreed to the addition of the Bill of Rights.

8. The Constitution can be amended through a two-stage process. First, there must be a proposal for a change, which requires either a two-thirds vote of both houses of Congress or a request by two-thirds of the states for a constitutional convention. Then the amendment must be ratified by a vote of three-quarters of the state legislatures or a three-quarters vote of specially created state ratifying conventions. The primary source of constitutional change, however, is judicial interpretation in response to political and social changes.

KEY TERMS

Virginia Plan
legislative branch
executive branch
judiciary
checks and balances
separation of powers
proportional representation
bicameral legislature
council of revision

New Jersey Plan
supremacy clause
Great or (Connecticut) Compromise
three-fifths compromise
electoral college system
republican government
federalism
delegated powers
reserved powers

necessary and proper clause
Federalists
Antifederalists
factions
Bill of Rights
proposal
ratify
super-majority
judicial review

SUGGESTED READINGS

- Bailyn, Bernard, ed. *The Debate on the Constitution*. 2 vols. New York: Library of America, 1993. The complete primary documentary record of all of the arguments that occurred among the general public and various legislatures in the states during the ratification process.

- Beard, Charles A., *Economic Interpretation of the Constitution of the United States*. New York: Macmillan, 1913. Beard argues that the framers acted out of economic self-interest in drafting the Constitution.

- Brooks, 1993. A complete history of the many attempts to amend the Constitution.

- Bowen, Catherine Drinker. *Miracle at Philadelphia: The Story of the Constitutional Convention, May to September 1787*. Boston: Little, Brown, 1966. A highly readable account of the Constitutional Convention.

- Collier, Christopher, and James Lincoln Collier. *Decision in Philadelphia: The Constitutional Convention of 1787*. New York: Random House, Reader's Digest Press, 1986. A popular account of the Constitutional Convention using all of the latest scholarship to bring it to life.

- Farrand, Max, ed. *The Records of the Federal Convention of 1787*. 4 vols. New Haven, Conn.: Yale University Press, 1931–37. The definitive set of primary documents recording the events of the Constitutional Convention.

- Hamilton, Alexander, James Madison, and John Jay. *The Federalist Papers*. New York: New American Library, 1961. The compelling arguments by three framers on behalf of the Constitution, the starting point for our understanding of the meaning of that document.

- Hutson, James H., ed. *Supplement to Max Farrand's "The Records of the Federal Convention of 1787."* New Haven, Conn.: Yale University Press, 1987. An update of the Farrand volume, containing many useful letters and documents from the framers in the Constitutional Convention period.

- Kammen, Michael. *A Machine That Would Go of Itself: The Constitution in American Culture*. New York: Knopf, 1986. A lively and highly informative cultural history of the Constitution.

- McDonald, Forrest. *Novus Ordo Seclorum: The Intellectual Origins of the Constitution*. Lawrence: University Press of Kansas, 1985. The definitive analysis of the intellectual roots of the Constitution.

- Mee, Charles L., Jr., *The Genius of the People*. New York: Harper and Row, 1987. A fascinating account of the Constitutional Convention supplemented by the riveting story of the ratification process.

- Rossiter, Clinton. *1787: The Grand Convention*. New York: Norton, 1966. The classic account of the Constitutional Convention by one of the great scholars of presidential power.

- Wood, Gordon S. *The Creation of the American Republic, 1776–1787*. Chapel Hill: University of North Carolina Press, 1969. A fascinating study of the political thought in this country during the time of the framing.

The Constitution
of the
United States of America

THE PREAMBLE

We the People of the United States, in Order to form a more perfect Union, establish Justice, insure domestic Tranquility, provide for the common defense, promote the general Welfare, and secure the Blessings of Liberty to ourselves and our Posterity, do ordain and establish this Constitution for the United States of America.

ARTICLE I—THE LEGISLATIVE ARTICLE

Legislative Power

Section 1 All legislative Powers herein granted shall be vested in a Congress of the United States, which shall consist of a Senate and House of Representatives.

House of Representatives: Composition; Qualifications; Apportionment; Impeachment Power

Section 2 The House of Representatives shall be composed of Members chosen every second Year by the People of the several States, and the Electors in each State shall have the Qualifications requisite for Electors of the most numerous Branch of the State Legislature.

No Person shall be a Representative who shall not have attained to the Age of twenty five Years, and been seven Years a Citizen of the United States, and who shall not, when elected, be an Inhabitant of that State in which he shall be chosen.

Representatives and direct Taxes[1] shall be apportioned among the several States which may be included within this Union, according to their respective Numbers, *which shall be determined by adding to the whole Number of free Persons, including those bound to Service for a Term of Years, and excluding Indians not taxed, three fifths of all other Persons.*[2] The actual Enumeration shall be made within three Years after the first Meeting of the Congress of the United States, and within every subsequent Term of ten Years, in such Manner as they shall by Law direct. The Number of Representatives shall not exceed one for every thirty Thousand, but each State shall have at least one Representative; and until each enumeration shall be made, the State of New Hampshire shall be entitled to chuse three, Massachusetts eight, Rhode-Island and Providence Plantations one, Connecticut five, New-York six, New Jersey four, Pennsylvania eight, Delaware one, Maryland six, Virginia ten, North Carolina five, South Carolina five, and Georgia three.

When vacancies happen in the Representation from any State, the Executive Authority thereof shall issue Writs of Election to fill such Vacancies.

The House of Representatives shall chuse their Speaker and other Officers; and shall have the sole Power of Impeachment.

Senate Composition: Qualifications, Impeachment Trials

Section 3 The Senate of the United States shall be composed of two Senators from each State, *chosen by the Legislature thereof,*[3] for six Years; and each Senator shall have one Vote.

Immediately after they shall be assembled in Consequence of the first Election, they shall be divided as equally as may be into three Classes. The Seats of the Senators of the first Class shall be vacated at the Expiration of the second Year, of the second Class at the Expiration of the fourth Year, and of the third Class at the Expiration of the sixth Year, so that one third may be chosen every second Year; *and if Vacancies happen by Resignation, or otherwise, during the Recess of the Legislature of any State, the Executive thereof may make temporary Appointments until the next Meeting of the Legislature, which shall then fill such Vacancies.*[4]

No person shall be a Senator who shall not have attained to the Age of thirty Years, and been nine Years a Citizen of the United States, and who shall not, when elected, be an inhabitant of that State for which he shall be chosen.

The Vice President of the United States shall be President of the Senate, but shall have no Vote, unless they be equally divided.

The Senate shall chuse their other Officers, and also a President pro tempore, in the Absence of the Vice President, or when he shall exercise the Office of President of the United States.

The Senate shall have the sole Power to try all Impeachments. When sitting for that Purpose, they shall be on Oath or Affirmation. When the President of the United States is tried, the Chief Justice shall preside: And no Person shall be convicted without the Concurrence of two thirds of the Members present.

Judgment in Cases of Impeachment shall not extend further than to removal from Office, and disqualification to hold and enjoy any Office of honor, Trust or Profit under the United States; but the Party convicted shall nevertheless be liable and subject to Indictment, Trial, Judgment and Punishment, according to law.

---

[1]Modified by the 16th Amendment
[2]Replaced by Section 2, 14th Amendment

[3]Repealed by the 17th Amendment
[4]Modified by the 17th Amendment

Congressional Elections: Times, Places, Manner

Section 4 The Times, Places and Manner of holding Elections for Senators and Representatives, shall be prescribed in each State by the Legislature thereof; but the Congress may at any time by Law make or alter such Regulations, except as to the Places of chusing Senators.

The Congress shall assemble at least once in every Year, *and such Meeting shall be on the first Monday in December, unless they shall by Law appoint a different Day.*[5]

Powers and Duties of the Houses

Section 5 Each House shall be the Judge of the Elections, Returns and Qualifications of its own Members, and a Majority of each shall constitute a Quorum to do Business; but a smaller Number may adjourn from day to day, and may be authorized to compel the Attendance of absent Members, in such Manner, and under the Penalties as each House may provide.

Each House may determine the Rules of its Proceedings, punish its Members for disorderly Behaviour, and, with the Concurrence of two thirds, expel a Member.

Each House shall keep a Journal of its Proceedings, and from time to time publish the same, excepting such Parts as may in their Judgment require Secrecy; and the yeas and Nays of the Members of either House on any question shall, at the Desire of one fifth of those Present, be entered on the Journal.

Neither House, during the Session of Congress, shall, without the Consent of the other, adjourn for more than three days, nor to any other place than that in which the two Houses shall be sitting.

Rights of Members

Section 6 The Senators and Representatives shall receive a Compensation for their Services, to be ascertained by Law, and paid out of the Treasury of the United States. They shall in all Cases, except Treason, Felony and Breach of the Peace, be privileged from Arrest during their Attendance at the Session of their respective Houses, and in going to and returning from the same; and for any Speech or Debate in either House, they shall not be questioned in any other Place.

No Senator or Representative, shall, during the time for which he was elected, be appointed to any civil Office under the authority of the United States, which shall have been created, or the Emoluments whereof shall have been encreased during such time; and no Person holding any Office under the United States, shall be a Member of either House during his Continuance in Office.

Legislative Powers: Bills and Resolutions

Section 7 All Bills for raising Revenue shall originate in the House of Representatives; but the Senate may propose or concur with Amendments as on other Bills.

Every Bill which shall have passed the House of Representatives and the Senate, shall, before it becomes a Law, be presented to the President of the United States; if he approve he shall sign it, but if not he shall return it, with his Objections to that House in which it shall have originated, who shall enter the Objections at large on their Journal, and proceed to reconsider it. If after such

Reconsideration two thirds of that House shall agree to pass the Bill, it shall be sent, together with the Objections, to the other House, by which it shall likewise be reconsidered, and if approved by two thirds of that House, it shall become a Law. But in all such Cases the Votes of both Houses shall be determined by yeas and Nays, and the Names of the Persons voting for and against the Bill shall be entered on the Journal of each House respectively. If any Bill shall not be returned by the President within ten Days (Sundays excepted) after it shall have been presented to him, the Same shall be a Law, in like Manner as if he had signed it, unless the Congress by their Adjournment prevent its Return, in which Case it shall not be a Law.

Every Order, Resolution, or Vote to which the Concurrence of the Senate and House of Representatives may be necessary (except on a question of Adjournment) shall be presented to the President of the United States; and before the Same shall take Effect, shall be approved by him, or being disapproved by him, shall be repassed by two thirds of the Senate and House of Representatives, according to the Rules and Limitations prescribed in the Case of a Bill.

Powers of Congress

Section 8 The Congress shall have Power To lay and collect Taxes, Duties, Imposts and Excises, to pay the Debts and provide for the common Defence and general Welfare of the United States; but all Duties, Imposts and Excises shall be uniform throughout the United States.

To borrow Money on the Credit of the United States;

To regulate Commerce with foreign Nations, and among the several States, and with the Indian Tribes;

To establish an uniform Rule of Naturalization, and uniform Laws on the subject of Bankruptcies throughout the United States;

To coin Money, regulate the Value thereof, and of foreign Coin, and fix the Standard of Weights and Measures;

To provide for the Punishment of counterfeiting the Securities and current Coin of the United States;

To establish Post Offices and post Roads;

To promote the Progress of Science and useful Arts, by securing for limited Times to Authors and Inventors the exclusive Right to their respective Writings and Discoveries,

To constitute Tribunals inferior to the supreme Court,

To define and punish Piracies and Felonies committed on the high Seas, and Offences against the Law of Nations;

To declare War, grant Letters of Marque and Reprisal, and make Rules concerning Captures on Land and Water;

To raise and support Armies, but no Appropriation of Money to that Use shall be for a longer Term than two Years;

To provide and maintain a Navy;

To make Rules for the Government and Regulation of the land and naval Forces;

To provide for calling for the Militia to execute the Laws of the Union, suppress Insurrections and repel Invasions;

To provide for organizing, arming, and disciplining, the Militia, and for governing such Part of them as may be employed in the Service of the United States, reserving to the States respectively, the Appointment of the Officers, and the Authority of training the Militia according to the discipline prescribed by Congress;

To exercise exclusive Legislation in all Cases whatsoever,

---

[5]Changed by the 20th Amendment

over such District (not exceeding ten Miles square) as may, by Cession of particular States, and the Acceptance of Congress, become the Seat of the Government of the United States, and to exercise like Authority over all Places purchased by the Consent of the Legislature of the State in which the Same shall be, for the Erection of Forts, Magazines, Arsenals, dock-Yards, and other needful Buildings;—And

To make all Laws which shall be necessary and proper for carrying into Execution the foregoing Powers, and all other Powers vested by this Constitution in the Government of the United States, or in any Department or Officer thereof.

Powers Denied to Congress

Section 9 The Migration of Importation of such Persons as any of the States now existing shall think proper to admit, shall not be prohibited by the Congress prior to the Year one thousand eight hundred and eight, but a Tax or Duty may be imposed on such Importation, not exceeding ten dollars for each Person.

The privilege of the Writ of Habeas Corpus shall not be suspended, unless when in Cases of Rebellion or Invasion the public Safety may require it.

No Bill of Attainder or ex post facto Laws shall be passed.

No Capitation, or other direct, Tax shall be laid, unless in Proportion to the Census or Enumeration herein before directed to be taken.[6]

No Tax or Duty shall be laid on Articles exported from any State.

No Preference shall be given by any Regulation of Commerce or Revenue to the Ports of one State over those of another; nor shall Vessels bound to, or from, one State, be obliged to enter, clear, or pay Duties in another.

No Money shall be drawn from the Treasury, but in Consequence of Appropriations made by Law; and a regular Statement and Account of the Receipts and Expenditures of all public Money shall be published from time to time.

No Title of Nobility shall be granted by the United States; And no Person holding any Office of Profit or Trust under them, shall, without the Consent of Congress, accept of any present, Emolument, Office, or Title, of any kind whatever, from any King, Prince, or foreign State.

Powers Denied to the States

Section 10 No State shall enter into any Treaty, Alliance, or Confederation; grant Letters of Marque and Reprisal; coin Money; emit Bills of Credit; make any Thing but gold and silver Coin a Tender in Payment of Debts; pass any Bill of Attainder, ex post facto Law, or Law impairing the Obligation of Contracts, or grant any Title of Nobility.

No State shall, without the Consent of the Congress, lay any Imposts or Duties on Imports or Exports, except what may be absolutely necessary for executing its inspection Laws: and the net Produce of all Duties and Imposts, laid by any State on Imports or Exports, shall be for the Use of the Treasury of the United States; and all such Laws shall be subject to the Revision and Controul of the Congress.

No State shall, without the Consent of Congress, lay any Duty of Tonnage, keep Troops, or Ships of War in time of Peace, enter into any Agreement or Compact with another State, or with a foreign Power, or engage in War, unless actually invaded, or in such imminent Danger as will not admit of Delay.

ARTICLE II—THE EXECUTIVE ARTICLE

Nature and Scope of Presidential Power

Section 1 The executive Power shall be vested in a President of the United States of America. He shall hold his Office during the Term of four Years and, together with the Vice President, chosen for the same Term, be elected as follows:

Each State shall appoint, in such Manner as the Legislature thereof may direct, a Number of Electors, equal to the whole Number of Senators and Representatives to which the State may be entitled in the Congress: but no Senator or Representative, or Person holding an Office of Trust or Profit under the United States, shall be appointed an Elector.

The Electors shall meet in their respective States, and vote by Ballot for two Persons, of whom one at least shall not be an Inhabitant of the same State with themselves. And they shall make a List of all the Persons voted for, and of the Number of Votes for each; which List they shall sign and certify, and transmit sealed to the Seat of the Government of the United States, directed to the President of the Senate. The President of the Senate shall, in the Presence of the Senate and House of Representatives, open all the Certificates, and the Votes shall then be counted. The Person having the greatest Number of Votes shall be the President, if such Number be a Majority of the whole Number of Electors appointed; and if there be more than one who have such Majority and have an equal Number of Votes, then the House of Representatives shall immediately chuse by Ballot one of them for President; and if no person have a Majority, then from the five highest on the List the said House shall in like Manner chuse the President. But in chusing the President, the Votes shall be taken by States, the Representation from each State having one Vote; A quorum for this Purpose shall consist of a Member or Members from two thirds of the States, and a Majority of all the States shall be necessary to a Choice. In every Case, after the Choice of the President, the person having the greatest Number of Votes of the Electors shall be the Vice President. But if there should remain two or more who have equal Vote, the Senate shall chuse from them by Ballot the Vice President.[7]

The Congress may determine the Time of chusing the Electors, and the Day on which they shall give their Votes; which Day shall be the same throughout the United States.

No Person except a natural born Citizen, or a Citizen of the United States, at the time of the Adoption of this Constitution, shall be eligible to the Office of President; neither shall any Person be eligible to that Office who shall not have attained to the Age of thirty five Years, and been fourteen Years a Resident within the United States.

In Case of the Removal of the President from Office, or of his Death, Resignation, or Inability to discharge the Powers and Duties of the said Office, the same shall devolve on the Vice President, and the Congress may by Law provide for the Case of Removal, Death, Resignation, or Inability, both of the President and Vice President, declaring what Officer shall then act as President, and such Officer shall act accordingly, until the Disability be removed, or a President shall be elected.[8]

The President shall, at stated Times, receive for his Services, a Compensation, which shall neither be encreased nor diminished during the Period of which he shall have been elected, and he shall not receive within that Period any other Emolument from the United States, or any of them.

---

[6]Modified by the 16th Amendment

[7]Changed by the 12th and the 20th Amendments
[8]Modified by the 25th Amendment

Before he enter on the Execution of his Office, he shall take the following Oath or Affirmation:—"I do solemnly swear (or affirm) that I will faithfully execute the Office of President of the United States, and will to the best of my Ability, preserve, protect and defend the Constitution of the United States."

Powers and Duties of the President

Section 2 The President shall be the Commander in Chief of the Army and Navy of the United States, and of the Militia of the several States, when called into the actual Service of the United States, he may require the Opinion, in writing, of the principal Officer in each of the executive Departments, upon any Subject relating to the Duties of their respective Offices, and he shall have the Power to grant Reprieves and Pardons for Offences against the United States, except in Cases of Impeachment.

He shall have Power, by and with the Advice and Consent of the Senate to make Treaties, provided two thirds of the Senators present concur; and he shall nominate, and by and with the Advice and Consent of the Senate, shall appoint Ambassadors, other public Ministers and Consuls, Judges of the supreme Court, and all other Officers of the United States, whose Appointments are not herein otherwise provided for, and which shall be established by Law: but the Congress may by Law vest the Appointment of such inferior Officers, as they think proper, in the President alone, in the Courts of Law, or in the Heads of Departments.

The President shall have Power to fill up all Vacancies that may happen during the Recess of the Senate, by granting Commissions which shall expire at the End of their next Session.

Section 3 He shall from time to time give to the Congress Information of the State of the Union, and recommend to their Consideration such Measures as he shall judge necessary and expedient; he may, on extraordinary Occasions, convene both Houses, or either of them, and in Case of Disagreement between them, with Respect to the Time of Adjournment, he may adjourn them to such Time as he shall think proper; he shall receive Ambassadors and other public Ministers; he shall take Care that the Laws be faithfully executed, and shall Commission all the Officers of the United States.

Section 4 The President, Vice President and all civil Officers of the United States, shall be removed from Office on Impeachment for, and Conviction of, Treason, Bribery, or other High Crimes and Misdemeanors.

ARTICLE III—THE JUDICIAL ARTICLE

Judicial Power, Courts, Judges

Section 1 The judicial Power of the United States, shall be vested in one supreme Court, and in such inferior Courts as the Congress may from time to time ordain and establish. The Judges, both the supreme and inferior Courts, shall hold their Offices during good Behaviour, and shall, at stated Times, receive for their Services, a Compensation, which shall not be diminished during their Continuance in Office.

Jurisdiction

Section 2 The judicial Power shall extend to all Cases, in Law and Equity, arising under this Constitution, the Laws of the United

States, and Treaties made, or which shall be made, under their Authority;—to all Cases affecting Ambassadors, other public Ministers and Consuls;—to all Cases of admiralty and maritime Jurisdiction;—to Controversies to which the United States shall be a Party;—to Controversies between two or more States; *between a State and Citizens of another State;*[9]—between Citizens of different States;—between Citizens of the same State claiming Lands under Grants of different States, and between a State, or the Citizens thereof, and foreign States, Citizens, or Subjects.

In all Cases affecting Ambassadors, other public Ministers and Consuls, and those in which a State shall be Party, the supreme Court shall have original Jurisdiction. In all the other Cases before mentioned, the supreme Court shall have appellate Jurisdiction, both as to Law and Fact, with such Exceptions, and under such Regulations as Congress shall make.

The Trial of all Crimes, except in Cases of Impeachment, shall be by Jury; and such Trial shall be held in the State where the said Crimes shall have been committed; but when not committed within any State, the Trial shall be at such Place or Places as the Congress may by Law have directed.

Treason

Section 3 Treason against the United States, shall consist only in levying War against them, or in adhering to their Enemies, giving them Aid and Comfort. No Persons shall be convicted of Treason unless on the Testimony of two Witnesses to the same overt Act, or on Confession in open Court.

The Congress shall have Power to declare the Punishment of Treason, but no Attainder of Treason shall work Corruption of Blood, or Forfeiture except during the Life of the Person attainted.

ARTICLE IV—INTERSTATE RELATIONS

Full Faith and Credit Clause

Section 1 Full Faith and Credit shall be given in each State to the public Acts, Records, and judicial Proceedings of every other State. And the Congress may by general Laws prescribe the Manner in which such Acts, Records and Proceedings shall be proved, and the Effect thereof.

Privileges and Immunities; Interstate Extradition

Section 2 The Citizens of each State shall be entitled to all Privileges and Immunities of Citizens in the several States.

A person charged in any State with Treason, Felony or other Crime, who shall flee from Justice, and be found in another State, shall on Demand of the executive Authority of the State from which he fled, be delivered up to be removed to the State having jurisdiction of the Crime.

No person held to Service or Labour in one State, under the Laws thereof, escaping into another, shall, in Consequence of any Law or Regulation therein, be discharged from such Service or Labour, but shall be delivered up on Claim of the Party to whom such Service or Labour may be due.[10]

---

[9]Modified by the 11th Amendment
[10]Repealed by the 13th Amendment

Admission of States

Section 3 New States may be admitted by the Congress into this Union; but no new State shall be formed or erected within the Jurisdiction of any other State; nor any State to be formed by the Junction of two or more States, or Parts of States, without the Consent of the Legislatures of the States concerned as well as of the Congress.

The Congress shall have Power to dispose of and make all needful Rules and Regulations respecting the Territory or other Property belonging to the United States; and nothing in this Constitution shall be so construed as to Prejudice any Claims of the United States, or of any particular State.

Republican Form of Government

Section 4 The United States shall guarantee to every State in this Union a Republican Form of Government, and shall protect each of them against Invasion; and on Application of the Legislature, or of the Executive (when the Legislature cannot be convened) against domestic Violence.

ARTICLE V—THE AMENDING POWER

The Congress, whenever two thirds of both Houses shall deem it necessary, shall propose Amendments to this Constitution, or, on the Application of the Legislatures of two thirds of several States, shall call a Convention for proposing Amendments, which, in either Case, shall be valid to all Intents and Purposes, as Part of this Constitution, when ratified by the Legislatures of three fourths of the several States, or by Conventions in three fourths thereof, as the one or the other Mode of Ratification may be proposed by the Congress; Provided that no Amendment which may be made prior to the Year One thousand eight hundred and eight shall in any Manner affect the first and fourth Clauses in the Ninth Section of the first Article; and that no State, without its Consent, shall be deprived of its equal Suffrage in the Senate.

ARTICLE VI—THE SUPREMACY ACT

All Debts contracted and Engagements entered into, before the Adoption of this Constitution, shall be as valid against the United States under the Constitution, as under the Confederation.

This Constitution, and the Laws of the United States which shall be made in Pursuance thereof; and all Treaties made, or which shall be made, under the Authority of the United States, shall be the supreme Law of the Land; and the Judges in every State shall be bound thereby, any Thing in the Constitution or Laws of any State to the Contrary notwithstanding.

The Senators and Representative before mentioned, and the Members of the several State Legislatures, and all executive and judicial Officers, both of the United States and of the several States, shall be bound by Oath or Affirmation, to support this Constitution; but no religious Test shall ever be required as a Qualification to any Office or public Trust under the United States.

ARTICLE VII—RATIFICATION

The Ratification of the Conventions of nine States, shall be sufficient for the Establishment of this Constitution between the States so ratifying the Same.

Done in Convention by the Unanimous Consent of the States present the Seventeenth Day of September in the Year of our Lord one thousand seven hundred and Eighty seven and of the Independence of the United States of America the Twelfth. *In Witness whereof We have hereunto subscribed our Names.*

AMENDMENTS

[The first ten amendments were ratified on December 15, 1791, and form what is known as the "Bill of Rights."]

AMENDMENT 1—RELIGION, SPEECH, ASSEMBLY, AND POLITICS

Congress shall make no law respecting an establishment of religion, or prohibiting the free exercise thereof; or abridging the freedom of speech, or of the press; or the right of the people peaceably to assemble, and to petition the government for a redress of grievances.

AMENDMENT 2—MILITIA AND THE RIGHT TO BEAR ARMS

A well regulated Milita, being necessary to the security of a free State, the right of the people to keep and bear Arms, shall not be infringed.

AMENDMENT 3—QUARTERING OF SOLDIERS

No Soldier shall, in time of peace be quartered in any house, without the consent of the Owner, nor in time of war, but in manner to be prescribed by law.

AMENDMENT 4—SEARCHES AND SEIZURES

The right of the people to be secure in their persons, houses, papers, and effects, against unreasonable searches and seizures, shall not be violated, and no Warrants shall issue, but upon probable cause, supported by Oath or affirmation, and particularly describing the place to be searched, and the persons or things to be seized.

AMENDMENT 5—GRAND JURIES, SELF-INCRIMINATION, DOUBLE JEOPARDY, DUE PROCESS, AND EMINENT DOMAIN

No person shall be held to answer for a capital, or otherwise infamous crime, unless on a presentment or indictment of a Grand jury, except in cases arising in the land or naval forces, or in the Milita, when in actual service in time of War or public danger; nor shall any person be subject for the same offence to be twice put in jeopardy of life or limb; nor shall be compelled in any criminal case to be a witness against himself, nor be deprived of life, liberty, or property, without due process of law; nor shall private property be taken for public use, without just compensation.

AMENDMENT 6—CRIMINAL COURT PROCEDURES

In all criminal prosecutions, the accused shall enjoy the right to a speedy and public trial, by an impartial jury of the State and district wherein the crime shall have been committed, which district shall have been previously ascertained by law, and to be informed of the nature and cause of the accusation; to be confronted with the witnesses against him; to have compulsory process for obtaining Witnesses in his favor, and to have the Assistance of Counsel for his defense.

AMENDMENT 7—TRIAL BY JURY IN COMMON LAW CASES

In Suits at common law, where the value in controversy shall exceed twenty dollars, the right of trial by jury shall be preserved, and no fact tried by a jury shall be otherwise re-examined in any Court of the United States, than according to the rules of the common law.

AMENDMENT 8—BAIL, CRUEL AND UNUSUAL PUNISHMENT

Excessive bail shall not be required, nor excessive fines imposed, nor cruel and unusual punishments inflicted.

AMENDMENT 9—RIGHTS RETAINED BY THE PEOPLE

The enumeration in the Constitution, of certain rights, shall not be construed to deny or disparage others retained by the people.

AMENDMENT 10—RESERVED POWERS OF THE STATES

The powers not delegated to the United States by the Constitution, nor prohibited by it to the States, are reserved to the States respectively, or to the people.

AMENDMENT 11—SUITS AGAINST THE STATES

[Ratified February 7, 1795]

The Judicial power of the United States shall not be construed to extend to any suit in law or equity, commenced or prosecuted against one of the United States by Citizens of another State, or by Citizens or Subjects of any Foreign State.

AMENDMENT 12—ELECTION OF THE PRESIDENT

[Ratified July 27, 1804]

The Electors shall meet in their respective states, and vote by ballot for President and Vice-President, one of whom, at least, shall not be an inhabitant of the same state with themselves; they shall name in their ballots the person voted for as President, and in distinct ballots the person voted for as Vice-President, and they shall make distinct lists of all persons voted for as President, and of all persons voted for as Vice-President, and of the number of votes for each, which lists they shall sign and certify, and transmit sealed to the seat of the government of the United States, directed to the President of the Senate;—The President of the Senate shall, in presence of the Senate and House of Representatives, open all the certificates and the votes shall then be counted;—The person having the greatest number of votes for President, shall be the President, if such number be a majority of the whole number of Electors appointed; and if no person have such majority, then from the persons having the highest numbers not exceeding three on the list of those voted for as President, the House of Representatives shall choose immediately, by ballot, the President. But in choosing the President, the votes shall be taken by states, the representation from each state having one vote; a quorum for this purpose shall consist of a member or members from two-thirds of the states, and a majority of all states shall be necessary to a choice. And if the House of Representatives shall not choose a President whenever the right of choice shall devolve upon them, *before the fourth day of March next following,* then the Vice-President shall act as President, as in the case of the death or other constitutional disability of the President.[11] The person having the greatest number of votes as Vice-President, shall be the Vice-President, if such a number be a majority of the whole numbers of Electors appointed, and if no person have a majority, then from the two highest numbers on the list, the Senate shall choose the Vice-President; a quorum for the purpose shall consist of two-thirds of the whole number of Senators, and a majority of the whole number shall be necessary to a choice. But no person constitutionally ineligible to the office of President shall be eligible to that of Vice-President of the United States.

AMENDMENT 13—PROHIBITION OF SLAVERY

[Ratified December 6, 1865]

Section 1   Neither slavery nor involuntary servitude, except as a punishment for crime whereof the party shall have been duly convicted, shall exist within the United States, or any place subject to their jurisdiction.

Section 2   Congress shall have power to enforce this article by appropriate legislation.

AMENDMENT 14—CITIZENSHIP, DUE PROCESS, AND EQUAL PROTECTION OF THE LAWS

[Ratified July 9, 1868]

Section 1   All persons born or naturalized in the United States, and subject to the jurisdiction thereof, are citizens of the United States and of the State wherein they reside. No State shall make or enforce any law which shall abridge the privileges or immunities of citizens of the United States; nor shall any State deprive any person of life, liberty, or property, without due process of law; nor deny to any person within its jurisdiction the equal protection of the laws.

---

[11]Changed by the 20th Amendment

Section 2 Representatives shall be apportioned among the several States according to their respective numbers, counting the whole number of persons in each State, excluding Indians not taxed. But when the right to vote at any election for the choice of electors for President and Vice President of the United States, Representatives in Congress, the Executive and Judicial officers of a State, or the members of the Legislature thereof, is denied to any of the male inhabitants of such State, being twenty-one[12] years of age, and citizens of the United States, or in any way abridged, except for participation in rebellion, or other crime, the basis of representation therein shall be reduced in the proportion which the number of such male citizens shall bear to the whole number of male citizens twenty-one years of age in such State.

Section 3 No person shall be a Senator or Representative in Congress, or elector of President and Vice President, or hold any office, civil or military, under the United States, or under any State, who, having previously taken an oath, as a member of Congress, or as an officer of the United States, or as a member of any State legislature, or as an executive or judicial officer of any State, to support the Constitution of the United States, shall have engaged in insurrection or rebellion against the same, or given aid or comfort to the enemies thereof. But Congress may by a vote of two-thirds of each House, remove such disability.

Section 4 The validity of the public debt of the United States, authorized by law, including debts incurred for payment of pensions and bounties for services in suppressing insurrection or rebellion, shall not be questioned. But neither the United States nor any State shall assume or pay any debt or obligation incurred in aid of insurrection or rebellion against the United States, or any claim for the loss or emancipation of any slave; but all such debts, obligations and claims shall be held illegal and void.

Section 5 The Congress shall have power to enforce, by appropriate legislation, the provisions of this article.

AMENDMENT 15—THE RIGHT TO VOTE

[Ratified February 3, 1870]

Section 1 The right of citizens of the United States to vote shall not be denied or abridged by the United States or by any State on account of race, color, or previous condition of servitude.

Section 2 The Congress shall have power to enforce this article by appropriate legislation.

AMENDMENT 16—INCOME TAXES

[Ratified February 3, 1913]

The Congress shall have power to lay and collect taxes on incomes, from whatever source derived, without apportionment among the several States, and without regard to any census or enumeration.

AMENDMENT 17—DIRECT ELECTION OF SENATORS

[Ratified April 8, 1913]

The Senate of the United States shall be composed of two Senators from each State, elected by the people thereof, for six years; and each Senator shall have one vote. The electors in each State shall have the qualifications requisite for electors of the most numerous branch of the State legislatures.

When vacancies happen in the representation of any State in the Senate, the executive authority of such State shall issue writs of election to fill such vacancies: *Provided,* That the Legislature of any State may empower the executive thereof to make temporary appointment until the people fill the vacancies by election as the legislature may direct.

This amendment shall not be so construed as to affect the election or term of any Senator chosen before it becomes valid as part of the Constitution.

AMENDMENT 18—PROHIBITION

[Ratified January 16, 1919   Repealed December 5, 1933 by Amendment 21]

Section 1 After one year from the ratification of this article the manufacture, sale, or transportation of intoxicating liquors within, the importation thereof into, or the exportation thereof from the United States and all territory subject to the jurisdiction thereof for beverage purposes is hereby prohibited.

Section 2 The Congress and the several states shall have concurrent power to enforce this article by appropriate legislation.

Section 3 This article shall be inoperative unless it shall have been ratified as an amendment to the Constitution by the legislatures of the several states, as provided in the Constitution, within seven years from the date of the submission hereof to the States by the Congress. [13]

AMENDMENT 19—FOR WOMEN'S SUFFRAGE

[Ratified August 18, 1920]

The right of the citizens of the United States to vote shall not be denied or abridged by the United States or by any State on account of sex.

Congress shall have power, by appropriate legislation, to enforce the provision of this article.

AMENDMENT 20—THE LAME DUCK AMENDMENT

[Ratified January 23, 1933]

Section 1 The terms of the President and Vice President shall end at noon on the 20th day of January, and the terms of the Senators and Representatives at noon on the 3rd day of January, of the years in which such terms would have ended if this article had not been ratified; and the terms of their successors shall then begin.

---

[12]Changed by the 26th Amendment

[13]Repealed by the 21st Amendment

Section 2 The Congress shall assemble at least once in every year, and such meeting shall begin at noon on the 3rd day of January, unless they shall by law appoint a different day.

Section 3 If, at the time fixed for the beginning of the term of the President, the President elect shall have died, the Vice President elect shall become President. If a President shall not have been chosen before the time fixed for the beginning of his term, or if the President elect shall have failed to qualify, then the Vice President elect shall act as President until a President shall have qualified; and the Congress may by law provide for the case wherein neither a President elect nor a Vice President elect shall have qualified, declaring who shall then act as President, or the manner in which one who is to act shall be selected, and such person shall act accordingly until a President or Vice President shall have qualified.

Section 4 The Congress may by law provide for the case of the death of any of the persons from whom the House of Representatives may choose a President whenever the right of choice shall have developed upon them, and for the case of the death of any of the persons from whom the Senate may choose a Vice President whenever the right of choice shall have devolved upon them.

Section 5 Sections 1 and 2 shall take effect on the 15th day of October following the ratification of this article.

Section 6 This article shall be inoperative unless it shall have been ratified as an amendment to the Constitution by the legislatures of three-fourths of the several States within seven years from the date of its submission.

AMENDMENT 21—REPEAL OF PROHIBITION

[Ratified December 5, 1933]

Section 1 The eighteenth article of amendment to the Constitution of the United States is hereby repealed.

Section 2 The transportation or importation into any State, Territory, or Possession of the United States for delivery or use therein of intoxicating liquors, in violation of the laws thereof, is hereby prohibited.

Section 3 This article shall be inoperative unless it shall have been ratified as an amendment to the Constitution by conventions in the several States, as provided in the Constitution, within seven years from the date of the submission hereof to the States by the Congress.

AMENDMENT 22—NUMBER OF PRESIDENTIAL TERMS

[Ratified February 27, 1951]

Section 1 No person shall be elected to the office of the President more than twice, and no person who has held the office of President, or acted as President, for more than two years of a term to which some other person was elected President shall be elected to the Office of the President more than once. But this Article shall not apply to any person holding the office of President when this article was proposed by the Congress, and shall not prevent any person who may be holding the office of President, or acting as President, during the term within which this Article becomes operative from holding the office of President or acting as President during the remainder of such term.

Section 2 This Article shall be inoperative unless it shall have been ratified as an amendment to the Constitution by the legislatures of three-fourths of the several states within seven years from the date of its submission to the States by the Congress.

AMENDMENT 23—PRESIDENTIAL ELECTORS FOR THE DISTRICT OF COLUMBIA

[Ratified March 29, 1961]

Section 1 The District constituting the seat of Government of the United States shall appoint in such manner as the Congress may direct:

A number of electors of President and Vice President equal to the whole number of Senators and Representatives in Congress to which the District would be entitled if it were a State, but in no event more than the least populous State; they shall be in addition to those appointed by the States, but they shall be considered, for the purposes of the election of President and Vice President, to be electors appointed by a State; and they shall meet in the District and perform such duties as provided by the twelfth article of amendment.

Section 2 The Congress shall have power to enforce this article by appropriate legislation.

AMENDMENT 24—THE ANTI-POLL TAX AMENDMENT

[Ratified January 23, 1964]

Section 1 The right of citizens of the United States to vote in any primary or other election for President or Vice President, for electors for President or Vice President, or for Senator or Representative in Congress, shall not be denied or abridged by the United States or any State by reason of failure to pay any poll tax or other tax.

Section 2 The Congress shall have power to enforce this article by appropriate legislation.

AMENDMENT 25—PRESIDENTIAL DISABILITY, VICE PRESIDENTIAL VACANCIES

[Ratified February 10, 1967]

Section 1 In case of the removal of the President from office or his death or resignation, the Vice President shall become President.

Section 2 Whenever there is a vacancy in the office of the Vice President, the President shall nominate a Vice President who shall take the office upon confirmation by a majority vote of both houses of Congress.

Section 3 Whenever the President transmits to the President pro tempore of the Senate and the Speaker of the House of Representatives his written declaration that he is unable to discharge the powers and duties of his office, and until he transmits to them a written declaration to the contrary, such powers and duties shall be discharged by the Vice President as Acting President.

Section 4 Whenever the Vice-President and a majority of either the principal officers of the executive departments, or of such other body as Congress may by law provide, transmit to the President pro tempore of the Senate and the Speaker of the House of Representatives their written declaration that the President is unable to discharge the powers and duties of his office, the Vice President shall immediately assume the powers and duties of the office as Acting President.

Thereafter, when the President transmits to the President pro tempore of the Senate and the Speaker of the House of Representatives his written declaration that no inability exists, he shall resume the powers and duties of his office unless the Vice President and a majority of either the principal officers of the executive departments, or of such other body as Congress may by law provide, transmit within four days to the President pro tempore of the Senate and the Speaker of the House of Representatives their written declaration that the President is unable to discharge the powers and duties of his office. Thereupon Congress shall decide the issue, assembling within 48 hours for that purpose if not in session. If the Congress, within 21 days after receipt of the latter written declaration, or, if Congress is not in session, within 21 days after Congress is required to assemble, determines by two-thirds vote of both houses that the President is unable to discharge the powers and duties of his office, the Vice President shall continue to discharge the same as Acting President; otherwise, the President shall resume the powers and duties of his office.

AMENDMENT 26—EIGHTEEN-YEAR-OLD VOTE

[Ratified July 1, 1971]

Section 1 The right of citizens of the United States, who are eighteen years of age, or older, to vote shall not be denied or abridged by the United States or by any State on account of age.

Section 2 The Congress shall have power to enforce this article by appropriate legislation.

AMENDMENT 27—CONGRESSIONAL SALARIES

[Ratified May 7, 1992]

No law, varying the compensation for the services of the Senators and Representatives, shall take effect, until an election of Representative shall be intervened.

CHAPTER 4

FEDERALISM

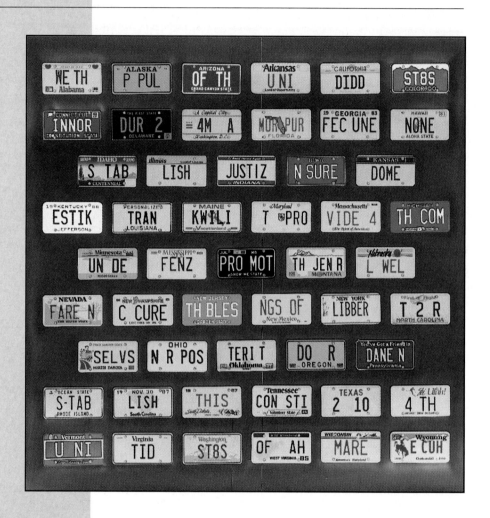

CHAPTER OUTLINE

CASE STUDY: SPEED LIMITS: WHO
    DECIDES?
INTRODUCTION: FEDERALISM AND
    DEMOCRACY
FEDERALISM DEFINED
FEDERALISM IN THE CONSTITUTION

THE DEVELOPMENT OF FEDERALISM
USING FEDERAL GRANTS TO CHANGE
    SOCIETY: FEDERALISM SINCE
    1930
CONTEMPORARY FEDERALISM AND
    APPROACHING DEMOCRACY

In 1974, during the height of the energy crisis caused by a Middle Eastern oil embargo, the powerful chairman of the House Public Works and Transportation Committee, James Howard of New Jersey, proposed a law mandating a national speed limit of fifty-five miles an hour. Such a law, he argued, would conserve fuel and save lives. But there was a problem: Congress had no authority to dictate highway speed limits. That authority was reserved for the states by the Tenth Amendment, which enables them to protect the safety of their citizens.

Speed Limits:
Who Decides?

But Howard found a way around this. He knew that federal money pays for the building and upkeep of state highways. Why, he reasoned, couldn't the national government establish highway speed limits when it finances those highways? To pass his speed limit law, Howard made abiding by the speed limit a precondition for federal funding. States would need to limit maximum speeds on their highways to fifty-five miles an hour to receive funding. Congress approved this plan, and on January 2, 1974, President Richard Nixon signed it into law.

From a policy standpoint, the law was a success: Annual fuel consumption dropped by twenty-five million barrels, and highway deaths fell by four thousand. Politically, however, the law was not popular. "This is one stupid, idiotic Federal provision," said Senator Max Baucus of Montana. "Washington D.C. is on the East Coast. I don't think folks have a conception of the sense of space and distance we have in the West."

Because the states found the law intrusive, compliance was spotty. Although the posted speed limit was fifty-five, in many rural states the law was rarely enforced. One study found that in Nebraska the average speed on interstate highways varied from sixty-three to seventy-five miles an hour. Even if the law was enforced, the penalties for exceeding the speed limit were nominal. To force compliance, the national government selected Vermont and Arizona as examples of flagrant violators of the law and threatened them with the loss of 10 percent of their federal highway money if they did not comply immediately (which they did). For a decade this issue continued to simmer in the states. Then, in 1984, many western members of Congress, led by Representative James Hansen of Utah, banded together in an effort to allow the states to choose whether to raise the speed limit once again to seventy miles an hour. However, Chairman Howard defeated them.

Two years later, in August 1986, President Reagan announced his support for lifting the national speed limit as part of his "new New Federalism" plan; he wished to return power to the states. The year ended before the measure could be passed, but in 1987 a new ninety-billion-dollar highway-funding bill finally passed in the House without an amendment lifting the speed limit. After moderate debate, the Senate approved a smaller sixty-five-billion-dollar funding bill by a substantial margin, and their version of the bill included a provision allowing states to raise the speed limit on interstate highways to sixty-five miles an hour. Because the House and Senate versions of the bill differed, the highway bill ended up in a conference committee. Made up of members of both houses, the committee was charged with crafting a compromise measure. After prolonged negotiations, and a threat by President Reagan to veto any proposal that was too expensive, an agreement was reached to separate the sixty-five-mile-an-hour limit from the funding package for its own vote.

Finally, on March 18, 1987, the House passed both the ninety-billion-dollar highway bill and the companion speed limit repeal amendment by a 217 to 206 margin. Two days later, the Senate did the same by a vote of 60 to 21. President Reagan vetoed the highway bill, however, saying that its expense made it a "budget buster." But within days, both houses of Congress overrode his veto, and the money flowed to the states.

According to this new law, it was up to the discretion of the individual states to raise their speed limits by ten miles an hour on rural highways. Governor Garrey Carruthers of New Mexico rushed out to change the old signs himself. However, people traveling Interstate 80 from Ohio to Pennsylvania were surprised to find that they could go sixty-five miles an hour in Ohio but only fifty-five in Pennsylvania. The reason was that Pennsylvania governor William Casey refused to raise that state's speed limit. Once more in America, how fast you drive depends on what state you are in. ✖

New Mexico governor Garrey Carruthers, left, changing the speed limit sign on Interstate 25 near Santa Fe.

INTRODUCTION: FEDERALISM AND DEMOCRACY

The chapter-opening case illustrates the classic battle between Washington, seeking national control, and the states, seeking to protect **states' rights,** those rights that have neither been granted to the national government nor forbidden to the states by the U.S. Constitution. In conflict, then, were two arenas of power over one particular policy area—the highway system. At the heart of this battle is the notion of federalism.

Few subjects in American government are as likely to serve as a cure for insomnia as federalism. Yet few subjects are more important. If you doubt this, glance at the daily paper and see how many articles deal with the relations between the national, state, and local governments. A typical front page of a local newspaper might discuss a new national crime bill that would provide funding for state and local police; a state road that won't be funded because of changes in a bill dealing with the national highway system; and a flood hitting a local town and leading to a request for national assistance.[1] All of these are examples of federalism in action.

This chapter begins with a definition of *federalism*. It then looks at federalism as outlined in the Constitution and how it has developed through the years. Finally, it examines the dynamic and changing nature of the federal structure. As you will see, as a result of a series of Supreme Court decisions and public policies, the government system we have now is far different from that envisioned by the framers.

Federalism is one of America's unique contributions to democratic theory and republican government. Only by understanding how the system works can you come to understand how it has helped the United States to approach democracy. But, as you will learn, the precise nature of this governmental relationship has been a matter for ongoing debate.

FEDERALISM DEFINED

Federalism is a political system in which two or more distinct levels of government share and exercise power over the same body of citizens. The American system consists of an overarching national government sharing power with governmental subdivisions such as state and local governments. To understand the nature of the federal system in America, it is important to know the framers' intentions in constructing it. The framers rejected the *unitary* system of government, one in which all of the power is vested in a central authority, that could compel the state governments to respond. This was the relationship between the English monarchy and the American colonies. The framers also rejected the *confederation* system of government, in which the power to govern is decentralized among sovereign states, and the national government has such limited powers that it must respond to state dictates. This was the system of government under the Articles of Confederation. Instead, the framers sought to create a structure that combined the best features of both systems—a uniform central government with the ability to deal with the larger national problems, and a more decentralized government at the state level, able to address the needs of the people at the state and local level.

In the case study, you saw an example of this structure in operation. Using its power to spend for the general welfare, the national government tried to impose its goal of saving fuel and lives on the states by implementing a uniform speed limit of fifty-five miles an hour. But the states claimed that establishing speed limits is a power best reserved to them. Different states requested flexibility in applying the speed limit to take into account the differing conditions in each region. In time, a compromise was reached that enabled the national government to maintain a national system of roads while taking into account the individual interests of the state governments. It is the constant tension between the different levels of government, and the resulting compromise policies, that the framers believed would serve the interests of everyone.

As you can see from this example, the allocation of powers between the two levels of government is not simple and clear-cut. If the national government should once again decide that it is in the interests of the entire nation to impose the fifty-five-mile-an-hour speed limit, it would have the power to do so under its spending authority.

Building flexibility into the federal structure was also the intent of the framers. They wanted to delegate enough powers to the central government to allow it to govern the entire nation, thus correcting the weaknesses inherent in the Articles of Confederation. But they also saw functional reasons for maintaining powerful states within that system. As James Madison explained in *Federalist* no. 10: "The federal Constitution forms a happy combination in this

State and national governments often work together. When Iowa governor Terry Branstad was faced with massive flooding in his state in July 1993, he called on the president for federal disaster relief (as any governor would do in a similar situation). Here, President Bill Clinton joins Governor Branstad to survey the damage to Des Moines.

Some Metaphors for Studying Federalism

Over the years, scholars have searched for an image to best explain the relationship between federal and state governments. One researcher discovered that there have been 497 such images: a bamboo fence, a stream, a piece of spaghetti, a piece of flypaper, a kaleidoscope, a flower, a gelatinous mass, and even a kamikaze pilot. President Ronald Reagan saw it as a brick wall, with the states being the bricks and the national government the mortar. Some of these images were designed to capture changes in the system of federalism over the years, while others were designed just to give the same old subject a slightly different spin.

The most common federalism metaphor employs the image of a cake. Numerous versions of this analogy have been developed over time to describe each new variety of federalism that has appeared on the scene. When federal and state governments were viewed as separate entities, the image of a layer cake was used to illustrate how each government's programs, functions, and responsibilities remained separate from each other, like individual layers in a cake.

When the relationship between the two layers of government evolved into a more cooperative and intermingled system, as it did as a result of the emergency legislation of the New Deal and World War II, the federal system was described as "marble-cake federalism." Just as the flavors of this cake are inextricably mixed, so too are the cooperative programs of the national and state governments. To exemplify this concept, political scientist Morton Grodzins pointed to rural county health officials, whom he called sanitarians. These officials were appointed by the state government using merit standards that had been created by the national government, their salaries were provided by a combination of state and federal monies, and the county provided them with offices and paid their expenses.

In addition, when programs seemed to result in more power residing in the state and local governments than in the national government, the "upside-down cake" seemed a fitting description. When policy programs made it almost impossible to decipher the relationship between layers of government, the metaphor of a "fruitcake" was used to describe the lack of definition and clarity (since no one ever seems to know what is really in a fruitcake).

Whatever the metaphor, the task is always the same—to portray in an arresting, visual way the varying relationships between the national and state governments in the federal system.

respect; the great and aggregate interests being referred to the national, the local and particular to the State legislatures."[2] In other words, the federal system was designed to consist of a national government limited to areas of common concern, while the power to make particular policy would remain with the states. Over the years, though, the gaps deliberately left in the Constitution regarding allocation of powers between the two levels of government have been filled by the experience of dealing with political problems. As a result, a new relationship was forged, leaving the national government as the controlling partner in the structure.

Federalism: Advantages and Disadvantages

Although your first instinct may be to envision three layers of government—national, state, and local—there are, in fact, well over eighty-six thousand governments of all types in this country. Among these are numerous layers of government at the local level, as Table 4.1 indicates.

National policy is the same for everyone, but state and local policy varies widely by region. Variations are found in tax policy, in public programs, and in services such as police and education. What are the advantages and disadvantages of such a federal system? It is to that question that we now turn.

ADVANTAGES There are many advantages to federalism. Rather than one uniform policy for everyone, a great deal of diversity among policies and programs is ensured by this large number of different governments. Diverse policies are needed to accommodate such a diverse populace across the country. We saw this benefit of federalism at work in the opening case study. It was the states, with their greater proximity and awareness of local needs, who pressured for a more appropriate speed limit policy.

Policy diversity also minimizes policy conflict. If groups are unsuccessful in passing their programs at the national level, they can try at the state or local level, thus minimizing pressure on the national government for action. But should action fail at the state level, then the focus of attention can shift back to the national government. The greater the number of centers of power for implementing policy, the greater the opportunity for government to respond to the needs and desires of the people. An example of this comes from the field of health-care reform. When successive efforts to pass a national health-insurance program covering everyone failed in the 1960s and 1970s, states such as Vermont, Massachusetts, and Oregon passed their own programs. However, these programs failed because of lack of financial resources and various political problems. Other states failed even to address health-care reform despite the skyrocketing cost of health care and health insurance, shifting pressure for action back to the national government. As a result, President Bill Clinton pushed for national health-care reform in 1994.[3] After Clinton's proposal failed to pass, several states attempted again to establish their own health-care programs (see Figure 4.1).

Federalism also results in a healthy dispersal of power. The framers were highly concerned by the possibility of establishing a national government with too much power. In the Constitution they reserved certain powers for the states to protect against this possibility. This dispersal of political power creates more opportunity for political participation: Individuals or political parties that cannot take power nationally have the opportunity in the federal structure to establish bases of power at state and local levels. Thus, the Republican party, which had no foothold in the national government in the early 1960s, was able to build a base of power at the state level and retake the White House in 1968.

America's system of federalism also enhances the prospects for governmental experimentation and innovation. Justice Louis D. Brandeis described this possibility when he wrote: "It is one of the happy incidents of the federal system that a single courageous state may, if its citizens choose, serve as a laboratory and try novel social and economic experiments without risk to the rest of the country."[4] Thus, the national government can observe which of the experimental programs undertaken by various states are working and perhaps adopt the best of those ideas for the rest of the nation. The Social Security Act, for example, was passed in 1935 to provide economic security for those over age sixty-five and unemployment insurance for the millions thrown out of work by the depression. It was based on an unemployment program being used at the time in Wisconsin.

Table 4.1
The Number of American Governments

National	1
States	50
Counties	3,043
Municipalities	19,296
Towns	16,666
School Districts	14,556
Special Districts	33,131
Total	86,744

Source: U.S. Department of Commerce, Bureau of the Census, Census of Government, 1992.

State government at work in Texas. Depicted here is the Texas state senate.

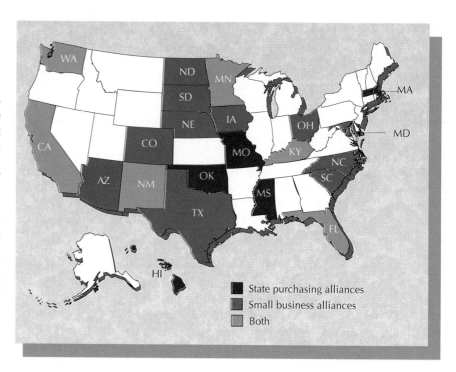

FIGURE 4.1 The States' Approach to Health Care

States have been the leading source of innovation in health care policy for almost ten years. California, Florida, and Texas, for example, have used health-insurance alliances to pool the purchasing power of small businesses, allowing them to get health coverage at a low rate. Over twenty states, as you can see from this map, are experimenting with such alliances. Other states are working with reforms to expand health-insurance coverage.

Source: From the *New York Times*, Friday, Sept. 16, 1994, p. A22.

In 1963, Alabama governor George Wallace stood in the doorway of the all-white University of Alabama in an unsuccessful attempt to prevent two African American students from enrolling. He did this despite the 1954 Supreme Court ruling in *Brown* v. *Board of Education* outlawing segregation in public schools.

DISADVANTAGES   But federalism has its disadvantages. The dispersal of power and opportunities for participation within America's federal structure allow groups in certain regions to protect their interests, sometimes with the undemocratic result of obstructing and even ignoring national mandates. For example, in the 1960s, the southern states were able to perpetuate a policy of racism by citing states' rights and resisting the desegregation movement.

There are also inequities in a federal system. Poor regions are unable to provide the same services as wealthier ones. Thus, governmental programs at the local level vary dramatically based on region. The schools in the rich suburb of Scarsdale, New York, will be very different from those in the poorer sections of south central Los Angeles.

It takes a proper balance of national and state powers to realize the benefits of federalism and minimize its drawbacks. What, then, constitutes this proper balance? That question has been debated since the framers' day.

FEDERALISM IN THE CONSTITUTION

Let us now look at the vertical powers the framers outlined in the Constitution and the effect of those powers on the relationship between the national and state governments. Three constitutional provisions are particularly important—the interstate commerce clause, the general welfare clause, and the Tenth Amendment—because they help to continually shift the balance of power between the national and state governments. We refer to these three provisions as the **triad of powers.**

The Triad of Powers

Each power in the triad has a specific function. Two of them—the interstate commerce clause and the general welfare clause—have been used to expand the powers of the national government. The third—the Tenth Amendment—has been used to protect state powers.

THE INTERSTATE COMMERCE CLAUSE In Article I, Section 8, the framers gave Congress the power "to regulate Commerce with foreign Nations, and among the several States." This clause sought to rectify the inability of the national government, under the Articles of Confederation, to control the movement of goods across the state lines. But it really did much more. Using the interstate commerce clause, the framers designed a national government with the power to provide some uniformity of policy among the states. A broad interpretation of this clause, and the change from individual industrial states to a series of linked commercial enterprises across state lines, would ultimately provide the means for expanding national power even within state borders.

Using the Commerce Clause To demonstrate how the national government can use the commerce clause to achieve uniform policy, let's look at an example. Let's say that the restaurateur Joe Bigot is determined to discriminate against minorities in his world-famous, national, fast-food hamburger business. "Joe's Best Burgers" franchises are sold everywhere. One franchise is started on a train club car that travels between New York and Connecticut, another is located on an interstate highway between Texas and Oklahoma. Clearly, the national government would be able to bar discrimination here because the restaurants serve interstate travelers, and thus affect commerce.

Thoroughly dismayed, Joe is so determined to do business his way that he sells his franchise, goes to his hometown high in the Rocky Mountains, and opens a single restaurant in an area that hasn't seen an interstate customer since the wagon trains brought the gold rush settlers to California. Can the federal government bar discrimination here, too? The answer is yes, because the meat Joe serves, all of the kitchen machinery, and the eating implements were imported from out of state. Since those purchases affect interstate commerce, federal regulations apply.

This example is based on a pair of Supreme Court cases upholding Congress's use of its interstate commerce power as the basis for the 1964 Civil Rights Act, which expanded the rights of African-Americans and barred discrimination in public accommodations.[5] As you can see from this example, a broad interpretation of the interstate commerce clause can give the national government tremendous power to reach policy areas previously reserved to the states. Using the interstate commerce clause the national government can, if it so desires (and it invariably does), regulate the wages and work hours on your campus; the admissions and scholarship rules, including the apportionment of scholarships between men and women on college sports teams; campus housing regulations; and campus codes of conduct. Off campus, the food you eat in a restaurant, the operations of the local government, and the operations of the businesses you patronize can all be regulated by the national government's use of its interstate commerce power.

In 1972, using the immense authority derived from the interstate commerce clause, the national government passed Title IX, an education amendment, barring federal funding to educational institutions that discriminate against women. Equity in spending for men's and women's programs in colleges, including sports teams, was usually the result. Title IX was one of many civil rights laws passed by the national government with the aim of combating discrimination.

Federalism under Fire: Will Canada Survive?

As early as 1839 Lord Durham, the British governor general, described Canada as "two nations warring in the bosom of a single state." Durham was referring to the conflict between the French-speaking people of Quebec and the English-speaking people dispersed throughout all the provinces of Canada. His words were prophetic: Today some scholars believe that Quebec may vote to separate from Canada, an action that would split the midwestern and western provinces from the Atlantic provinces and could result in the breakup of the entire nation.

Quebec is a province of Canada in much the same way that each American state is part of the United States. But Quebec never signed the Canadian Constitution; instead, in the 127 years since the formation of the dominion it has sought to preserve a separate identity based on its unique culture. The primary language of Quebec is French, and its institutions and legal system are derived from those of France.

"When I see the maple leaf flag," says Charles Dion, a chemical engineer from Quebec, "I see the emblem of an occupying power. . . . My country is Quebec, not Canada." Many of his fellow Québécois

feel the same way. As a result, Québécois politicians, legislators, and voters have repeatedly debated the idea of separating or seceding from Canada. They claim that Quebec was forced into the dominion and has no constitutional obligation to remain part of Canada.

In November 1992 all the provinces of Canada voted on the Charlottetown Accord. Under this accord, which would take effect only if the Canadian Parliament and the legislatures of all the provinces agreed to it, Quebec would be given the status of a "distinct society" and would control one-quarter of the seats in the House of Commons. The accord was overwhelmingly rejected, however; it won the approval of only four of the ten provinces, and even Quebec voted against it by a margin of 56.6 to 43.4 percent.

The defeat of the Charlottetown Accord did not daunt the separatists. In 1993 a separatist party, the Bloc Québécois, won fifty-four of the seventy-five seats allocated to Quebec in the Canadian Parliament, thereby gaining the second-largest bloc of seats in Parliament after those held by the governing Liberal party. The separatists thus became the offi-

---

While the interstate commerce power is an important power for the national government, not every issue can be linked to it. Thus, the national government turned to another of the framers' grants of authority, the "power of the purse," or the ability to "tax and spend for the General Welfare" to encourage or even force state governments to do what was deemed to be in the national interest.

THE GENERAL WELFARE CLAUSE In the same Article I, Section 8 of the Constitution, the framers granted Congress the power to "lay and collect Taxes, Duties, Imposts and Excises, to pay the Debts and provide for the common Defense and general Welfare of the United States." The combination of this spending power with the "necessary and proper" clause, known as the **elastic clause,** in Article I, Section 8 has enabled the national government to legislate indirectly, influencing state policy through the power of the pocketbook. This power has expanded the national government's reach into formerly state-controlled areas via "carrot-and-stick" programs. The "carrot" is the money that the federal government provides for states that abide by national programs,

cial opposition in Parliament. And in 1994 another provincial party, the Parti Québécois, won a majority of the seats in the Quebec National Assembly. The latter victory is widely viewed as a mandate for independence, and it is anticipated that in 1995 Quebec will hold a referendum for complete independence from Canada.

What would happen if Quebec voted to secede from Canada? Some scholars predict a nightmare scenario. Lansing Lamont believes that the English-speaking residents of Quebec would flee the province to escape discrimination by the new government. The western provinces (British Columbia and Alberta) and the Atlantic prov-inces (Newfoundland, Prince Edward Island, Nova Scotia, and New Brunswick) would apply for statehood in the United States rather than remain part of a fragmented nation. This would leave the poorer middle provinces to try to cope with the task of paying for the nation's social programs while feuding with Quebec.

Coming on the heels of the breakup of the Soviet Union into its component republics in the 1990s, the potential breakup of Canada raises serious questions about the concept of federalism. It is clear that the forces that hold a country together in a federal structure can easily reverse themselves, creating a centrifugal force that eventually fragments the nation into its component parts.

Sources: Tom Masland and Molly Colin, "Oy, Canada: Another 'No,'" *Newsweek,* Nov. 9, 1992, p. 36; Clyde H. Farnsworth, "Canadians Reject Charter Changes," *New York Times,* Oct. 27, 1992, pp. 1, 10; Clyde H. Farnsworth, "The Canadian Impasse," *New York Times,* Oct. 28, 1992, pp. 1, 12; Mordecai Richler, "O Quebec," *New Yorker,* May 30, 1994, pp. 50–57; Colin Nickerson, "In Quebec, Separatism Enjoys a Renaissance," *Boston Globe,* July 5, 1994, p. 9; Lansing Lamont, *Breakup: The Coming End of Canada and the Stakes for America* (New York: Norton, 1994).

Demonstrators calling for Quebec's secession, June 1990.

while the "stick" is the threatened loss of money if they do not. This sort of approach to spending was evident in the opening case study, where national-highway funds could be received by the state only if it abided by the fifty-five-mile-an-hour speed limit.

Using the General Welfare Clause   The most visible evidence of the carrot-and-stick approach to policymaking is the manner in which the legal drinking age was changed around the country. Before 1984, the drinking age varied from state to state, and sometimes even from county to county. In 1984, however, Mothers Against Drunk Driving (MADD) demanded that the drinking age be raised nationally to twenty-one. MADD pointed out that ninety-five hundred Americans under the age of twenty-five were dying annually in alcohol-related driving accidents. Only by imposing a national drinking age of twenty-one, they argued, could drinking and driving be discouraged among young people. But liquor sales meant big business in various states, a formidable obstacle to a policy change. Congress used the carrot-and-stick approach to prevail. If states did not raise their drinking age to twenty-one, they would lose

5 percent of their 1986 federal highway funds and 10 percent of the 1987 total. Not surprisingly, near uniformity on the new legal drinking age was achieved almost immediately.[6]

What was it that kept the national government from dominating the federal structure from the beginning? The answer can be found in the Tenth Amendment.

THE TENTH AMENDMENT   The Tenth Amendment states: "The powers not delegated to the United States by the Constitution, nor prohibited by it to the States, are reserved to the States, or to the people respectively." In reserving certain powers for the states, the Tenth Amendment is seen by some as a power and by others as a mere description of the constitutional system. With this amendment, the framers intended to preserve the individuality of the states and restrict the national government to its delegated powers. It was through this power that the western states sought to take back control of the highway speed limits in their region. In the early years of this nation the Tenth Amendment was used by state-centered-federalism advocates as a barrier to national intrusion into their powers.

How the Triad Works

The beauty of the federal system is the balance of power built into it. While the national government is most effective in designing broad, uniform policy goals for the entire country, these programs work best when implemented by the states. Thus, overarching national programs created using the interstate commerce and general welfare powers can be tailored to fit the individual needs of specific areas.

With two of the three powers in the triad appearing to favor the national government, for a long time it was Congress's unwillingness to use those powers fully, the Supreme Court's lack of acceptance when Congress did, and the Tenth Amendment that prevented the national government from predominating. But as you will soon see, the Tenth Amendment was stripped of its power to limit the national government, resulting in a federal system in which the national government became the dominant partner. While states still have a very important role to play in this structure, they are far less powerful than many of the framers envisioned.

While these three constitutional provisions help to establish a balance of power between the national and state governments, a variety of other provisions in the Constitution divide the powers between the two governments.

The Resulting Division of Powers

Beyond the triad of powers, the framers were careful to express in the Constitution a series of other powers that preserve the independent power of each of the two levels of government. You will recall from Chapter 3 that the **supremacy clause** upholds national laws and treaties as the "supreme law of the land." This clause sketches the broad outlines of the federal structure by establishing the predominance of national laws whenever national and state legislation overlap. There are also powers granted to, and limits placed on, the states. Those provisions are outlined in Table 4.2.

"The power surrendered by the people, is first divided between two distinct governments, and then the portion allotted to each, subdivided among distinct and separate departments. Hence a double security arises to the rights of the people. The different governments will control each other; at the same time that each will be controlled by itself."

—James Madison, *Federalist* no. 51

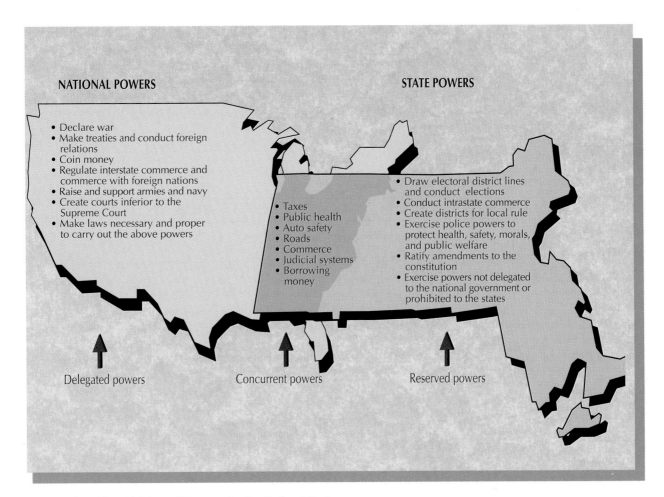

NATIONAL POWERS

- Declare war
- Make treaties and conduct foreign relations
- Coin money
- Regulate interstate commerce and commerce with foreign nations
- Raise and support armies and navy
- Create courts inferior to the Supreme Court
- Make laws necessary and proper to carry out the above powers

- Taxes
- Public health
- Auto safety
- Roads
- Commerce
- Judicial systems
- Borrowing money

STATE POWERS

- Draw electoral district lines and conduct elections
- Conduct intrastate commerce
- Create districts for local rule
- Exercise police powers to protect health, safety, morals, and public welfare
- Ratify amendments to the constitution
- Exercise powers not delegated to the national government or prohibited to the states

Delegated powers   Concurrent powers   Reserved powers

FIGURE 4.2   The Division of Powers in the Federal System

Carefully detailed are the powers delegated to the national government, the powers reserved to the states, and the powers that apply to the two governments concurrently (see Figure 4.2).

First are the **express powers,** those delegated specifically to the national government. Generally, these are the powers that the framers saw were lacking in the old Articles of Confederation. The framers reasoned that a nation must speak with one voice when declaring war and negotiating with foreign countries; it also needs a uniform monetary system for its economy to function. Thus, only the national government can declare war, raise and support an army, make treaties with other nations, and coin money. You should not think, though, that these delegated powers limit national authority. Another category of powers comprises the **implied powers,** those not specifically enumerated in the Constitution but that can be inferred from the delegated powers. Many can be justified through the elastic clause. Thus, as you saw in the case study, the national government's power to tax and spend can be extended by the necessary and proper power to cover construction of a national system of roads. In addition, there are **inherent powers,** which do not appear in the Constitution but are assumed because of the nature of government. Thus, only the national government has the power to conduct foreign relations, make war even in the absence of a formal declaration, and protect its officials against bodily harm or threats.

Those powers not assigned to the national government are left with the states. These **reserved powers** are guaranteed in the Tenth Amendment and protect the role of the states in the federal system. Among the reserved powers

Table 4.2
Constitutional Guarantees of and Limits on State Power

GUARANTEES	LIMITS
1. STATE INTEGRITY AND SOVEREIGNTY	
No division of states or consolidation of parts of two or more states without state legislative consent (Art. IV, Sec. 2)	States cannot enter into treaties, alliances, or confederations (Art. I, Sec. 10)
Guarantee of republican form of state government (Art. IV, Sec. 2)	No interstate or foreign compacts without consent of Congress (Art. I, Sec. 10)
Protection against invasion and against domestic violence (Art. IV, Sec. 2)	No separate coinage (Art. 1, Sec. 10)
Powers not delegated to national government reserved for states (10th Amend.)	National constitution, laws, and treaties are supreme (Art. VI)
State equality in Senate cannot be denied (Art. V)	All state officials bound by national Constitution (Art. VI)
	No denial of privileges and immunity of citizens (14th Amend.)
	No abridgment of right to vote on basis of race (15th Amend.)
	No abridgment of right to vote on basis of sex (19th Amend.)
2. MILITARY AFFAIRS AND DEFENSE	
Power to maintain militia and appoint militia officials (Art. I, Sec. 8, 2nd Amend.)	No maintenance of standing military in peacetime without congressional consent (Art. I, Sec. 10)
	No engagement in war without congressional consent, except in emergency (Art. I, Sec. 10)
3. COMMERCE AND TAXATION	
Equal apportionment of direct federal taxes (Art. I, Secs. 2, 9)	No levying of duties on vessels of sister states (Art. I, Sec. 9)
No federal export duties imposed on any state (Art. I, Sec. 9)	No legal tender other than gold or silver (Art. I, Sec. 10)
No preferential treatment for ports of one state (Art. I, Sec. 9)	No impairment of the obligations of contract (Art. I, Sec. 10)
Reciprocal full faith and credit among states for public acts, records, and judicial proceedings (Art. IV, Sec. 1)	No levying of import or export duties without Congressional consent, except the levying of reasonable inspection fees (Art. I, Sec. 10)
Reciprocal privileges and immunities for citizens of different states (Art. IV, Sec. 2)	No tonnage duties without Congressional consent (Art. I, Sec. 10)
Intoxicating liquor may not be imported into states where its sale or use is prohibited (21st Amend.)	

Table 4.2

Constitutional Guarantees of and Limits on State Power (continued)

GUARANTEES	LIMITS
4. ADMINISTRATION OF JUSTICE	
Federal criminal trials to be held in state where crime was committed (Art. III, Sec. 2)	No bills of attainder (Art. I, Sec. 10)
Extradition for crimes (Art. IV, Sec. 2)	No ex post facto laws. (Art. I, Sec. 10)
Federal criminal juries to be chosen from state and district where crime was committed (6th Amend.)	Supreme Court has original jurisdiction over all cases in which state is a party (Art. III, Sec. 2)
Federal judicial power extends to controversies between two or more states, between a state and citizens of another state, and between a state or its citizens and a foreign nation or its citizens (Art. III, Sec. 2)	No denial of life, liberty, or property without due process of law (14th Amend.)
	No denial of equal protection of state laws to persons within its limits (14th Amend.)

Source: Adapted from Daniel Elazar, *American Federalism: A View from the States,* 3d ed. (New York: Harper and Row, 1984), pp. 42–43.

are the so-called *police powers,* or the ability to regulate the health, morals, public safety, and welfare of state citizens. You have already seen that such regulations include speed limits on highways, but they also involve such areas as education, marriage, criminal law, zoning regulations, and contracts. Over time, it has been necessary to shift some of these powers to the national government. For example, some of the state criminal-law powers have been supplemented by congressional acts and Supreme Court decisions to provide more uniformity among the states and prevent criminals from escaping punishment simply by crossing state boundaries. The Lindbergh Law, for example, gave the national government power to investigate and prosecute kidnapping cases that involve the crossing of state lines.

There are also powers that are shared by both levels of government; these are known as **concurrent powers.** Both levels can regulate commerce, levy taxes, run a road system, establish their own elections, and maintain their own judicial structure. Sometimes these overlapping powers give citizens an additional forum in which to seek support or to secure their rights. For instance, when a California court acquitted two of the four Los Angeles police officers who were accused of using excessive force in the beating of African American Rodney King, the officers were successfully prosecuted in federal court under federal civil rights laws.

Despite the existence of concurrent powers, the national government can, if it chooses, use the authority in the supremacy clause to *preempt,* or supersede, state action in areas where both governments have legislative authority.[7] Over the years, the federal government, looking to impose uniform policies over the entire country, has devised laws that have superseded state action in

FYI

If you're planning to relocate to earn your fortune after graduation, consider that per capita state and local taxes can vary dramatically from state to state. Alaska, New York, and Connecticut have the highest taxes (in the three-thousand- to thirty-eight-hundred-dollar range). Tennessee, Alabama, and Mississippi have the lowest taxes (in the thirteen-hundred- to fourteen-hundred-dollar range). The national average is about twenty-two hundred dollars (these figures are for 1992).

areas such as pollution control, transportation, nutrition labeling, taxation, and civil rights.

In addition to granting powers, the framers *denied* certain powers to both levels of government. Fearful of creating an all-powerful central government that would override the rights of the states and the people, the framers withheld from the national government powers that might have that result. For example, Article I, Section 9 denies the national government, among other things, the right to place an export tax on products from the states and the power to impose a direct tax on the people unless it was levied proportionally to each state's population (a provision that was overridden by the Sixteenth Amendment, allowing for the creation of a national income tax). The Bill of Rights, beginning with the words "Congress shall make no law . . ." can also be seen as a long list of powers denied to the national government in areas such as freedom of speech, freedom of religion, freedom of the press, and defendants' rights.

The powers denied to the states were designed to keep their functions separate from those of the newly established national government. These limits to state powers, some of which can be overridden by Congress, are outlined in Article I, Section 10 of the Constitution. Among these prohibited powers are those delegated exclusively to the national government; they include the power to declare war, make treaties, and coin money. In addition, states are denied the power to impair the obligations of contracts, thus preventing them from wiping out any debts including those that existed prior to the formation of the Constitution.

Finally, the framers denied to both the national and state governments certain powers deemed offensive based on their British experience. These include the power to grant titles of nobility; pass bills of attainder, which legislate the guilt of an individual without the benefit of a trial; and pass ex post facto laws, which declare an action to be a crime after it has been done.

THE DEVELOPMENT OF FEDERALISM

Despite this enumeration of powers in the Constitution, the framers left much undiscussed in mapping out the relationship between the national and state governments. That relationship had to be developed over time by policymakers at both levels, and by the judicial system. Many of these decisions were made in response to crises faced by the nation.

How much leeway would Congress have to legislate beyond its enumerated constitutional powers, thereby increasing the national government's power over the states? The debate began in the Washington administration over the creation of a national bank.

Debating the National Role: Hamilton versus Jefferson

At issue here was Article I, Section 8, Clause 18 of the Constitution, known as the elastic clause, which grants Congress the power "to make all laws which shall be necessary and proper for carrying into execution" its enumerated powers. Thus, Secretary of the Treasury Alexander Hamilton argued in 1791 that the national government could build on its power to coin money, operate a uniform currency system, and regulate commerce by chartering a national bank. Secretary of State Thomas Jefferson, however, opposed this idea, arguing that since no explicit power to charter banks was written into the Constitution, that power was reserved to the states.

This debate over the constitutionality of creating a bank represented two very different visions of federalism. Hamilton's argument favoring a national bank suggested the prospect of a whole new series of implied powers for the national government. Jefferson's argument that such a broad interpretation of the clause would give Congress unlimited power to, in his words, "do whatever evil they please," with the result that the national government would "swallow up all the delegated powers" and overwhelm the states. In the end, President Washington was more persuaded by the expansive national-powers position of Hamilton, and the bank was chartered in 1791. But was the bank constitutional?

Asserting National Power: <u>McCulloch</u> v. <u>Maryland</u>

After a second national bank was chartered in 1816, the state of Maryland challenged the bank's operation by placing a state tax on it. When the bank refused to comply, the Supreme Court was asked in 1819 to rule in **McCulloch v. Maryland** on both the constitutionality of Congress's chartering the national bank and the constitutionality of a state's tax on that bank.

Chief Justice John Marshall, an advocate of strong, centralized national power, wrote a resounding unanimous opinion supporting the power of Congress to charter the bank. Marshall turned to the necessary and proper clause of the Constitution and found there the implied power for the national government to do what was convenient to carry out the powers delegated to it in Article I, Section 8. According to Marshall, the powers of the national government would now be broadened considerably: "Let the end be legitimate, let it be within the scope of the Constitution, and all means which are appropriate, which are plainly adapted to that end, which are not prohibited, but consistent with the letter and spirit of the Constitution, are constitutional."

This was indeed the broadest possible definition of national power. Now Congress could justify any legislation simply by tying it to one of the delegated national powers in the Constitution. This created the potential for the national government to expand its powers into many areas that had previously been thought to be reserved to the states.

Having established the constitutionality of the national bank, the Court also declared Maryland's tax on the bank unconstitutional, reasoning that states have no power to impede or retard congressional laws. In this case, Marshall argued, "the power to tax involves the power to destroy" the bank, and thus congressional power. The Court's reading of the supremacy clause made the national government "supreme within its sphere of action," meaning that it was the dominant power in areas where its power overlaps with that of the states. It seemed that Jefferson was right in fearing that the national government was well on the way to "swallowing up" the states.

Expanding National Power Further: <u>Gibbons</u> v. <u>Ogden</u>

The Constitution states quite clearly that Congress has the power "to regulate Commerce . . . among the several States." But does the power to control commerce "among the several States" extend to control of commerce entirely within a state? And, if so, how extensive would that power be? In the 1824 case **Gibbons v. Ogden,** John Marshall once again interpreted the Constitution broadly, ruling in favor of expanding national power.

This case involved a license to operate steamboats in the waters between New York and New Jersey. One man, Aaron Ogden, had purchased a state-issued license to do so in New York waters, while his former partner, Thomas Gibbons, had gone to the national government for a federal coasting license. It was left to the Supreme Court to decide whether the central government's power over *interstate* commerce, or commerce among states, predominated over an individual state's power to regulate *intrastate* commerce, or commerce within a state boundary. Marshall used this opportunity to give the interstate commerce clause the broadest possible definition, holding that the national government had the power to regulate any "commercial intercourse" having an effect in two or more states. This meant that the national government could now reach activities that affect interstate commerce, even within state boundaries. All that was left to the states, then, was the power to regulate commerce that was wholly within one state. But with the growth of industries such as mining and food production, it would soon be hard to find such enterprises.[8] This made states'-rights advocates unhappy. Slaveholders in the South, for example, feared national incursion into their peculiar form of labor "commerce."

Asserting State Power: Nullification

Inevitably, there was an organized response to Marshall's strong-central-power position in the *McCulloch* and *Gibbons* cases. In the 1830s, southerners such as John Calhoun of South Carolina objected to the national government raising tariffs on cotton, thereby restricting the South's ability to export cotton to England. Lacking the numbers in Congress to reverse this direction, Calhoun adopted the theory of **nullification** (initially proposed by Jefferson and Madison in 1798), which upheld that states faced with unacceptable national legislation could declare such laws null and void and refuse to observe them. South Carolina, for example, declared the national tariffs null and void in 1832 and threatened to *secede* from, or leave, the union over the issue. A crisis was averted when President Jackson lowered the tariff, while also threatening to use military force to prevent secession.

However, nullification reared its head again over attempts by the national government to restrict slavery. This time the South did secede, and the Civil War was the result. This war was a turning point in American federalism, because the North's victory ensured that the union and its federal structure would survive. No longer could states declare national laws unconstitutional or threaten to secede.

Developing a System of Separation: Dual Federalism

After the Civil War, the prevailing view of federalism was one of **dual federalism,** in which each level of power remains supreme in its own jurisdiction, thus keeping the states separate and distinct from the national government. Using the cake metaphor, the federal system under dual federalism resembles a layer cake, with neither the national nor state powers, or layers, spreading into the other.

Little-known Fact

After the decision in the *Gibbons* v. *Ogden* case, Ogden, who had lost his license, died a pauper, and Gibbons, who had succeeded in wresting it from him, died a millionaire.

Dual federalism prevailed during this period as a result of two factors. Supreme Court rulings between 1887 and 1937 fueled a state-centered view of federalism. In addition, industrial expansion created an economic environment opposed to government interference and regulation, thereby limiting the national government's power over industry and giving states the upper hand in the federal structure. For instance, in 1895 the Court ruled that the national government had no power to regulate the monopoly of the sugar-refining industry, which, while national in scope, had factories located in the state of Pennsylvania. The Court ruled in *United States* v. *E. C. Knight* that while the national government had the power to regulate the *shipment* of sugar, which constituted interstate commerce, it did not have the power to regulate the *manufacture* of sugar, because that was local in nature and thus wholly within the supreme power of the states.[9]

In another ruling in 1918, the Court placed additional limits on national power. With the 1916 Keating Owen Child Labor Act, Congress sought to regulate child labor. But in overturning this act in *Hammer* v. *Dagenhart,* Justice William R. Day indicated just how state-centered the Court had become. He wrote: "The grant of authority over a purely federal matter was not intended to destroy the local power always existing and carefully reserved to the States in the Tenth Amendment to the Constitution."[10] In this classic statement of dual federalism, the states' reserved powers now represented a limitation upon the national government.

Creating a Cooperative System: The New Deal Era

The Great Depression of the 1930s and President Franklin D. Roosevelt's New Deal eventually put an end to dual federalism. In 1932, the country was in the throes of the worst economic depression in its history. To relieve the suffering, Roosevelt promised Americans a "New Deal," which involved taking immediate steps to get the economy moving and create jobs. At Roosevelt's behest, Congress passed programs involving tremendous new powers for the national government, such as creating large, national administrative agencies to supervise manufacturing and farming. These programs also involved an increase in spending by the national government, a large number of regulations, and even larger numbers of bureaucrats to administer the regulations.

Initially, the Supreme Court used the rulings of the dual-federalism era to restrict these programs, arguing that the problems they addressed were local in nature and not in the province of the national government. The first of these Court-tested programs involved the National Recovery Administration (NRA), which developed codes of fair competition, covering wages, hours, working conditions, and competitive practices for entire industries. The highly conservative Supreme Court overturned this and other programs, arguing that the regulations of manufacturing, production, and agriculture were reserved to the states. As a result, the national government was hampered in its effort to end the suffering and economic stagnation of the depression.[11]

But the nation's needs were so great that the Supreme Court's position could not endure. A highly critical President Roosevelt proposed his "Court-packing plan," whereby he sought to add one new justice for each one over the age of seventy (up to a total of fifteen). While the plan was before

Child laborers at a Massachusetts textile factory in 1912, a common sight at the time. In 1918, the Supreme Court refused to allow Congress to regulate child labor, ruling that the power to do so belonged to the states. Fearing that businesses would simply move to another state without labor restrictions, the states were unwilling to ban cheap child labor. Reforms of the New Deal Era put an end to child labor along with the Depression, by leading unemployed adults to seek out the jobs held by children.

Congress, the Supreme Court, in what became known as "the switch in time that saved nine," suddenly began ruling in favor of the New Deal programs. (For more on this switch, see Chapter 6.) In a 1937 case, *National Labor Relations Board (NLRB)* v. *Jones and Laughlin Steel,* the Court upheld the national government's right to impose collective bargaining by unions and ban certain unfair labor practices. The Court was now willing to support the use of national power and allow the national government to control manufacturing, production, and agricultural activities through the interstate commerce powers. (As a result, the Court-packing plan failed.)[12]

But what of the Tenth Amendment, which reserves to the states powers not delegated to the national government? A Supreme Court that was in the process of being completely remade by eight new Roosevelt appointees put an end to dual federalism in 1941. In *United States* v. *Darby,* which upheld the national government's power to regulate the wages and hours of the lumber industry under the interstate commerce power, the Court ruled that the Tenth Amendment "states but a truism that all is retained which has not been surrendered." In short, this amendment was no longer seen as a limitation on the national government, or a bar to the exercise of its power even wholly within state boundaries.[13]

A new era in the federal relationship had been ushered in by the New Deal, one of cooperation between the national and state governments rather than the separation of governments and functions. This system known as **cooperative federalism.** Solutions for various state and local problems were directed and sometimes funded by the national government and in turn were administered by the state governments according to national guidelines. Federalism had changed from a separated layer cake to a marble cake of interwoven funding and programs.[14]

What were the results of this partnership between the national and state governments? States came to look to the national government for help and funding to deal with problems viewed as beyond their means. Similarly, citizens began to look to Washington for solutions to their problems rather than to their state and local governments. The result was an increase in the power of the national government and a drive to achieve uniformity of programs throughout the country, often at the expense of state power and innovation. As a result of the New Deal, the national government has been supreme in the federalism partnership despite the fleeting return of dual federalism in response to a Court challenge in 1976 that was overturned nine years later.[15]

Seeking Uniformity: Federalism in the Post–New Deal Era

Another major judicial movement in the 1950s and 1960s created a new role for the national government in the federal system, that of protector of personal rights as guaranteed by the Constitution. Prior to the 1930s, defendants rights had been a power reserved to the states. This resulted in variations in policy, particularly with regard to minorities, who were often denied personal liberties and legal protection in certain states. As you will learn in greater detail in Chapters 14 and 15, the Court ruled to extend most of the protections of the Bill of Rights to the states (the Bill of Rights originally applied to the national government only) to ensure uniformity and help combat racism and inequality nationally. The Court did this by ruling that certain guarantees in the Bill of Rights are part of the *due process* right guaranteed by the Fourteenth Amendment against state government intrusion. This process was called the *incorporation of the Bill of Rights.*

Uniformity of the judicial process was thus established around the country. For instance, in the 1932 *Scottsboro* case, in which a group of young African Americans had been convicted of rape and sentenced to death without a fair trial, the Supreme Court ruled that the Sixth Amendment right to counsel should be extended to all future state trials like this one to ensure fairness. States could still operate their judicial systems, or guarantee personal rights, but in doing so they had to adhere to national standards regarding constitutional protections.

The national government also sought to impose national standards regarding equality. Social equality was promoted through a series of Court decisions, such as *Brown* v. *Board of Education* in 1954, which called for the end of segregation in public schools, and later cases that promoted racial integration in the nation.[16] Political equality was sought through a series of cases such as *Reynolds* v. *Sims* in 1964. This case established the "one-person, one-vote" standard in which the number of voters in each district was made roughly the same, thus giving people an equal say in the operation of their government.[17] Personal equality was guaranteed by a series of First Amendment cases granting citizens the same rights of speech, press, assembly, religion, and thought no matter where they live. On the political-action front, economic equality was the goal of a series of welfare, educational, and social programs adopted by Congress as part of the "War on Poverty" program of the Johnson administration in the 1960s. In many respects, these judicial decisions and political actions establishing uniformity of rights have helped America approach democracy as

Old Enough to Fight, Old Enough to Vote

"Never trust anyone over thirty" was the rallying cry of college students protesting the Vietnam War in the 1960s and 1970s. In the era of the "generation gap," many young people felt that a government led by older people was unresponsive to their needs. At the time, citizens of college age (eighteen to twenty) could not vote. The voting age was twenty-one, based on the age of majority established in the Middle Ages. The theory behind this is that a man must be twenty-one before he could comfortably carry armor into battle.

But times change. As Senator Birch Bayh of Indiana pointed out, eighteen- to twenty-year-olds were considered old enough to fight and die in Vietnam yet were not considered old enough to vote for the national leaders who were sending them to war. Senator Bayh was not the only champion of a lower voting age. Throughout the nation increasingly vocal demands for legislation that would lower the voting age from twenty-one to eighteen were being made. However, the proposal faced some intriguing problems arising from the nature of the federal system.

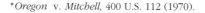

The Struggle for Equality

Making the change at the national level was easy; Congress simply included a provision in the Voting Rights Act that lowered the voting age to eighteen. However, while Article I, Section 4 of the Constitution gives Congress the power to "make or alter" voting regulations, it grants the states the power to determine the "times, places, and manner of holding elections." This overlap in the electoral powers of the two levels of government created obstacles to the effort to extend the vote to eighteen- to twenty-year-olds.

In the case of *Oregon* v. *Mitchell* the Supreme Court upheld Congress's right to set voter qualifications for federal elections, but it overturned the provisions for state elections.* Thus, the voting age of eighteen remained in force for federal elections, while the age of twenty-one was the law at the state level. The Court's ruling meant that the states would have to hold two sets of elections, which would entail maintaining two sets of voter regulation books, buying new voting machines, and hiring more workers to oversee elections. And the states had only one year to make these arrangements before the 1972 elections.

There were other complications. In some states, candidates for Congress would be nominated at state conventions from which citizens under twenty-one were barred. Yet those same citizens could vote in the general election for the candidates selected at the conventions. In addition, four states—Alaska, Hawaii, Kentucky, and Georgia—had already enfranchised eighteen- to twenty-year-old voters. Young voters in those states could vote for candidates for national office, while their peers in the forty-six other states could not.

The only solution to this dilemma was for Congress to propose an amendment to the Constitution overturning the Supreme Court's decision. In March 1971 both houses of Congress overwhelmingly passed the Twenty-sixth Amendment, which enfranchised eighteen- to twenty-year-olds for all elections, both federal and state. Thirty-eight states ratified the amendment within thirteen weeks, by far the shortest ratification period in the nation's history.

Oregon v. *Mitchell,* 400 U.S. 112 (1970).

people grew to understand that within the federal system, final recourse for seeking constitutional rights exists beyond one's own state.

Once the partnership between the national government and the state governments was established, the question of how the two levels of government would interact remained. This leads us into the practical study of federalism as the fiscal relationship between the two levels of government.

USING FEDERAL GRANTS TO CHANGE SOCIETY: FEDERALISM SINCE 1930

To understand the development of federalism since 1930, you need to be aware of two key ingredients: money and the national government's ability, as a result of its general welfare powers, to spend.

Federal spending and power began to grow during the 1930s and 1940s in response to the Depression. When the New Deal Court ruled that the national power to spend was not limited to the enumerated grants of power in the Constitution, further growth was inevitable.[18] Since then, national power has continued to grow, particularly in the last three decades, helping to shape the U.S. political system. At issue in this federal system is how much money will be spent by the national government and under what conditions it may be used by the states (with the answers usually being "lots" and "according to specific guidelines"). We now look at the different types of federal grants and then at how various administrations have worked with the grant-in-aid system.

Types of Federal Grants

There are a variety of national spending programs. The most frequently used is the **grant-in-aid,** money paid to states and localities to induce them to implement policies in accordance with federally mandated guidelines. Money is made available through an intergovernmental transfer, but only if it is spent by the states in certain policy areas. If the states do not wish to abide by federal mandates, they can refuse federal funds. But, of course, with the deep pockets of the national government, and states being forever short of funds, that rarely happens.

The number of such grants are vast and have been rising steadily for the last decade. National grants to states and localities have risen from 557 to 593 in the years from 1991 to 1993. Simultaneously, the size of grant outlays rose to $206.4 billion, an increase of 36 percent from the $152 billion in 1991. While some of these increases occurred in education, employment retraining, and the environment, escalating health-care costs accounted for over one-half of the total increase.[19] Some of the health-care grants came in the areas of AIDS/HIV, drug abuse, Alzheimer's disease, tuberculosis, rural health services, and emergency medical care, reflecting the nature of problems confronted by the government.[20] The increase in health-care costs, compared to other costs, is illustrated in Figure 4.3.

Grants-in-aid come in a wide variety of types. **Categorical grants** are the most common and are given for specific purposes, usually with strict rules attached. We saw an example of this kind of grant with the highway funds in the case study. Categorical grants usually require the state or local government,

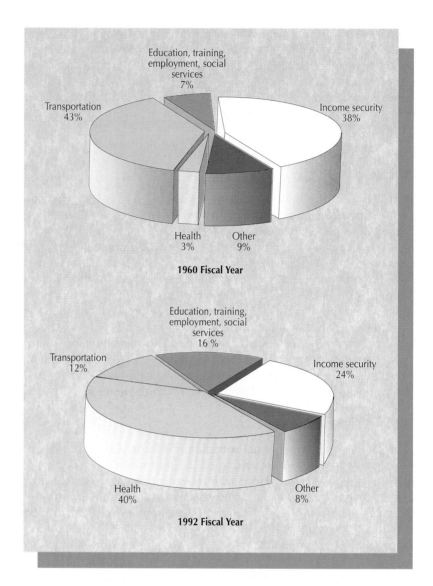

FIGURE 4.3 The Changing Functions of National Grants to States and Localities

Over the last thirty years, there has been a dramatic shift in the purposes for national grants. In short, national funding for transportation and "safety net" welfare programs has been replaced by a system of "safety net" health-care programs and funding for job training.

Source: U.S. Advisory Commission on Intergovernmental Relations, Characteristics of Federal Grant-in-Aid Programs to state and local governments, 1993, Jan. 1994, p. 16.

or a nonprofit organization, to come up with matching funds, say of 10 percent, since the grant is supposed to cover only a part of the costs. In this way, the grants induce increased spending by states for a desired program area and encourage cooperation. Approximately 75 percent of the national aid to the states and localities comes in the form of categorical grants. This is such a fast-growing form of national assistance that in the four years of the Bush administration, the number of categorical grants rose by 21 percent, from 478 to 578. In 1992–93 alone, 74 new categorical grants were created.[21]

Categorical grants come in three types: formula grants, project grants, and combined formula/project grants. **Formula grants** are based on a prescribed legislative formula to determine how the money will be distributed to eligible governmental units (states or big cities). A recent listing of these grants shows that depending on their policy aim, they can take into account a wide variety of factors such as total population, median family income, miles of coastline, total enrollment in education, miles of highways and railways, total level of governmental expenditures, and age of housing stock in the area. Governmental units meeting the strict rules for distribution automatically qualify for the grant. For example, part of the highway bill you read about in the case study was a typical formula grant distributed on the basis of the number of miles of highway in a state.[22]

The **project grant** is not based on a formula but is distributed for specific purposes after a fairly competitive application and approval process. These are sometimes called "discretionary grants" because they are distributed at the discretion of a designated legislator or administrator. In 1993 project grants were awarded for constructing military bases, improving nuclear waste management, increasing forestry research, establishing mortgage credit for farmers, requiring the use of seat belts and motorcycle helmets, developing bilingual education, and providing interpreters for the deaf. The vast majority of the categorical grants, 72.5 percent in 1993, are project grants, with 419 in existence (representing an increase of 35 from two years earlier).[23]

In recent years a combined **formula/project grant** has been developed in which competitive grants are awarded, but they are also restricted by the use of a formula. For example, limits may be placed by Congress on the amount of grant money that can be awarded to a state or region of a state.

As grants proliferated and became more complex, a new type of grant was created in the 1960s to simplify the process. **Block grants** provide money for general program funding without any strings attached. For example, the Partnership for Health Act of 1966 and the Safe Streets Act of 1968 provided unrestricted money for health care and crime control. It was left to the state or locality to decide what specific health and crime-control programs would be funded. Compared with the vast number of categorical grants, in 1993 only fifteen block grants were awarded, covering such diverse areas as maternal and child health services, low-income energy assistance, job training for disadvantaged youths, treatment for substance abuse, and assistance for surface transportation programs.

As you can see, grants-in-aid provide a means for this country to approach democracy. Faced with the prospect that certain regions of the country are not spending in a manner that reflects the needs of their citizens, the national government can take tax money from one region of the country and redistribute it to another region. While dictating the spending of governmental resources in this way has helped to remove some inequalities, it has come with political costs for the states. Because all national money carries with it certain strings, the national government is able to dominate the federal-system partnership once more by dictating the way state governments must act to receive the money they need. More than that, states very quickly grew to depend on national money, thus further impelling them to allow the national government to dictate their policy direction.

FEDERAL MANDATES   Congress can exercise considerable control over the states by attaching to federal money certain **federal mandates,** or national requirements, that must be observed. For example, sometimes states are asked to create certain programs, such as bans against discrimination or regulations affecting personal behavior. A program to increase employment might have a provision setting aside 10 percent of the grants for minority hirings, or a national health grant may place restrictions on the availability of abortions.

Since these mandates are uniformly imposed by the national government, they lead to some very unusual policy choices in different regions. In 1994, to receive federal funding for its water supply the city of Chicago continued to observe a federal mandate to test its water for two pesticides present only in the Hawaiian water supply, where they are used on the pineapple crops.

Some of these federal mandates are underfunded or unfunded, thus shifting the financial burden to the states. In 1993, for example, ten federal mandates, including the Clean Air Act and the Americans with Disabilities Act, cost states and localities over $6.5 billion.[24] In 1994, local governments were spending between 25 and 30 percent of their budgets to meet certain federal mandates. Federal laws passed in 1994 called for even greater state and local spending on unfunded mandates, for example, to reduce the emission of hydrocarbons into the atmosphere. However, in response to state and local officials' complaints that the national government restrict the use of unfunded mandates, the Republican Congress in 1995 passed, as part of its "Contract With America," a bill restricting the creation of new federal mandates unless companion legislation considers providing funding for them.

Because of the continual demand by the states for national funding, the willingness of the national government to provide it, and the growing presence of complicated restrictions on the spending of that money, the grant-in-aid system has spiraled out of control. An examination of the history of this system will illustrate how presidents in the last sixty years initially used federal grants to change the relationship between the national and state governments and then sought, beginning in the 1970s, to bring that system under control.

Meeting National Needs During the Era of Cooperative Federalism (1930–63)

As you have learned, the system of cooperative federalism began during the depression in the 1930s. Congress authorized a large number of new grants-in-aid beyond the fifteen that already existed for state support.[25] By 1939, total federal outlays were fifteen times greater than they had been in 1933.[26]

As public demands for greater government action increased following the New Deal, the national grant-in-aid became the major tool for responding. The Truman administration created a number of new programs involving areas such as education, health, and transportation. By 1952 there were 71 separately authorized grant programs. The increase in grants-in-aid even continued through the conservative Eisenhower administration. By 1960, 132 grants were consuming $6.8 billion—a 250 percent increase in federal outlays. As the number and size of national grants grew, so did the conditions attached to these grants.

The Era of Creative Federalism (1963–68)

In the 1960s President Lyndon B. Johnson launched his Great Society program, which involved using federal programs to create a smoother-functioning social-welfare system. Johnson used what is called **creative federalism,** an initiative that expanded the concept of the partnership between the national government and the states. The national government would now work with cities,

Little-known Fact

In 1957, President Dwight Eisenhower dedicated the national interstate highway system, which offered, for the very first time, a direct link between the East and West Coasts. Eisenhower recognized the need for such a highway in 1919, when as an army private it took him sixty-two days to lead a military convoy across the country. With the new stretch of linked interstate highways (designated the Dwight D. Eisenhower Highway in 1973), the trip could be made in less than a week.

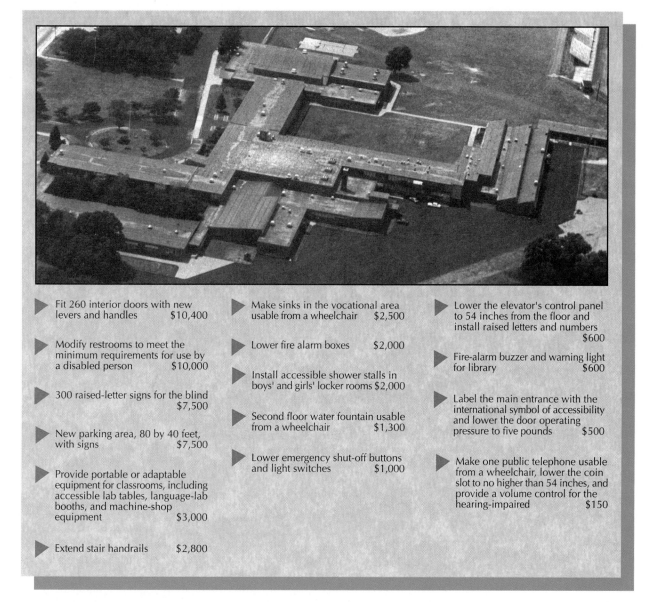

▶ Fit 260 interior doors with new levers and handles $10,400

▶ Modify restrooms to meet the minimum requirements for use by a disabled person $10,000

▶ 300 raised-letter signs for the blind $7,500

▶ New parking area, 80 by 40 feet, with signs $7,500

▶ Provide portable or adaptable equipment for classrooms, including accessible lab tables, language-lab booths, and machine-shop equipment $3,000

▶ Extend stair handrails $2,800

▶ Make sinks in the vocational area usable from a wheelchair $2,500

▶ Lower fire alarm boxes $2,000

▶ Install accessible shower stalls in boys' and girls' locker rooms $2,000

▶ Second floor water fountain usable from a wheelchair $1,300

▶ Lower emergency shut-off buttons and light switches $1,000

▶ Lower the elevator's control panel to 54 inches from the floor and install raised letters and numbers $600

▶ Fire-alarm buzzer and warning light for library $600

▶ Label the main entrance with the international symbol of accessibility and lower the door operating pressure to five pounds $500

▶ Make one public telephone usable from a wheelchair, lower the coin slot to no higher than 54 inches, and provide a volume control for the hearing-impaired $150

There are hidden costs in unfunded mandates. When Congress passed the Americans with Disabilities Act in 1993, it was left to state and local agencies to provide funding to make public buildings accessible to the physically challenged. Here is what Warwick, Rhode Island's, Veterans Memorial High School needed to do to modify its building at a total cost of $51,850.
Source: The New York Times, July 28, 1993, p. A15.

counties, school districts, and even nonprofit organizations to provide social services.

With creative federalism the central government was now stepping into a number of areas that had been neglected by the states. Johnson directed his administration to attack poverty, promote equal opportunity in education, solve the "urban crisis" through direct aid to the big cities (thereby bypassing the states), and guarantee equal rights for minority groups. The Great Society initiative led to a rapid increase in new programs, most significantly Medicare and Medicaid, which provided national health-care assistance for the aged and the impoverished; the Elementary and Secondary Education Act (ESEA), which provided national funding for public education; and Model Cities, which was aimed at rejuvenating the inner cities. Broad national guidelines were attached to these programs, but it was left to the states and localities to implement the programs. For instance, the Medicaid program included national guidelines such as the level of income that would qualify a person for assistance, but it was left to the states to implement the program by determining who would be eligible, how broad health coverage would be, and how health-care providers would be reimbursed.

In the 1960s, the focus of the grants-in-aid program shifted from needs that were perceived by the states and pressed on the national government to needs perceived by the national government and pressed on the states. In addition, national spending increased dramatically. Between 1960 and 1967, the number of grants increased from 132 to 379. In one year alone, 1965, 109 new grant programs were created. Public as well as private resources were mobilized and pooled in an effort to meet a variety of goals, including improving farming, combating drug abuse, securing disaster relief after a flood or a storm, and improving education. As a result of these programs the national government became bloated and overloaded. Bureaucracies to administer the spending programs were enlarged at both the national and state level. States engaged in the "grantsmanship game," tailoring their applications to fit national requirements rather than their own policy needs. More than that, the American people grew more and more accustomed to looking toward the national government for solutions to their problems.

This effort to use federalism creatively helped the nation to approach democracy by empowering groups that had been voiceless for years. Grants were given for programs aimed at improving the quality of life for the handicapped, migrant workers, and neglected children. Other programs promoted bilingual education and desegregation. States that had previously ignored the needs of certain groups in their region found that they could attract additional national funds by being attentive to those groups' needs. In short, it was now in the states' financial interest to promote democracy.

As you will learn in Chapter 16, while the goals of creative federalism were laudable, the very nature of the American federal structure served to thwart these goals. The size of the programs, the sharp disagreements among groups about their goals, and the lack of proper governmental oversight doomed them to failure. For instance, the Model Cities program was originally designed for twelve major cities, but it could not be passed until members of Congress from around the country got a piece of the pie for their own region, thus expanding the program to an unmanageable 150 cities.

By the end of the 1960s there was widespread disenchantment with the Great Society and the national government's efforts to make sweeping social changes. While the number of grant programs had multiplied and progress had been made in addressing some of America's problems, such as poverty and inequity in education, the full promise of the Great Society had not been fulfilled.[27] An example of the frustration and lack of tangible results was detailed by political scientists Jeffrey Pressman and Aaron Wildavsky in their examination of the national government's attempt to promote economic development in Oakland, California. The Business Loans program was designed to encourage the private sector to provide beneficial loan terms for small businesses in inner cities as a means of battling poverty. The actual implementation of the program, however, led to problems, as diverse groups with widely divergent and sometimes conflicting goals, such as different minority groups, businesses, and labor organizations, attempted to cooperate in the decision-making process. In the end, after several years and the expenditure of one million dollars, the program created only forty-three new jobs. Interestingly, it was the highly democratic nature of this program that contributed to its lack of effectiveness.[28]

However, many of the programs from that era still exist, such as the Head Start program, which provides preschool instruction for poor children; the Legal Services program, which provides legal assistance for the indigent; and food stamps, which provides national funding to feed the poor. But with poverty still an enduring problem in America, the question of whether the benefits of the Great Society exceeded its administrative costs continues to be debated.[29]

The increased involvement of the federal government in the business of states and localities during the 1960s led to a shift in the way federalism was viewed by scholars.

INTERGOVERNMENTAL RELATIONS   During this time, federalism, for some, became a study of the way in which local, state, and national governments actually interrelated on various policy questions. This approach to the study of federalism is called **intergovernmental relations,** or IGR, and it examines the pattern of interaction among the levels of government and government officials as a result of the aid sent from one level to another. This study downplays the idea of federalism as a system of perpetual competition and conflict. Instead, it focuses on the interdependent system of meetings, negotiations, cooperation, and bargaining between the levels of government. IGR, then, looks at federalism as dynamic, with ongoing changes in response to new demands.

This new focus for the study of federalism led to the creation of a new metaphor to portray the federal system. Since no type of cake adequately described the increased interdependence among the levels of government, the notion of **picket fence federalism** emerged (see Figure 4.4). As political scientist and former North Carolina governor Terry Sanford, who is credited with inventing the concept, explained it, the horizontal crosspieces of the fence represent each level of the government—national, state, and local. The vertical pickets of the fence each represent a particular government policy area such as health, education, or transportation. The notion then is that the bureaucrats, interest groups, lobbying organizations, and members of the general public interested in each of these policy areas work together to lobby the different levels of government simultaneously on their issue. For example, those who want better sex education to prevent teenage pregnancies will unite and lobby the national, state, and local governments for their goals. Although serving to bring the actors in those governments on each individual policy question together, the potential always exists for members of opposing policy groups to battle each other for governmental attention.[30] At the same time, governmental actors such as members of Congress, governors, and mayors work intensely among all of

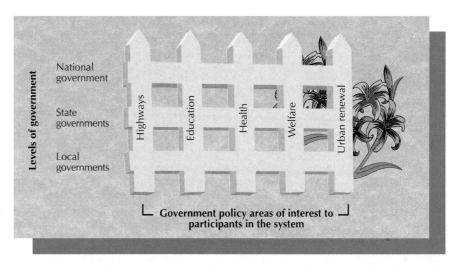

FIGURE 4.4 A New Metaphor: Picket Fence Federalism
This figure shows how policy interests can unite to work simultaneously on every level of government and how government officials can "ride across the cross-rails" to explore a wide variety of policy areas to complete the work of government.

the different policy areas to build a consensus for change. Because the various policy groups are fragmented and their interests differ, political actors on the picket fence might undertake parallel campaigns in each of the policy sectors. Thus, a state governor concerned with coordinating a set of programs to meet the needs of children would consult with the education sector for better teaching programs, the health sector for better medical care, the housing sector for better shelter, and the welfare sector for better financial support, all the while seeking to stay within budgetary constraints.

Richard Nixon's New Federalism (1969–74)

President Nixon's **New Federalism** program, so labeled because it was designed to return fiscal power to the states and localities, was, in essence, a reaction to the excesses of Johnson's creative federalism. The cornerstone of this policy was **general revenue sharing** (GRS), in which money would be given to the states with no restrictions on how it could be spent. Also important was **special revenue sharing,** in which groups of categorical grants-in-aid in related policy areas such as crime control or health care would be consolidated into a single block grant.

After the passage of revenue sharing in 1972, thirty billion dollars was distributed among the states and local governments, but the program was not a complete success. One-third of the funds was given to the states according to a complicated formula taking into account poverty levels and city size. The remaining two-thirds were paid directly to local governments, such as the cities of New York, Dallas, and San Francisco. The list of allowed expenditures was so general that rather than using the revenue-sharing money to replace old grant-in-aid programs, many states and localities began using it to cover basic governmental operating expenses, such as the salaries of public officials. As a result, many program areas that were once funded by categorical grants-in-aid now went unfunded.

Paradoxically, while it was intended to return power to the states, the GRS in fact further extended the influence of the national government. Even though GRS money had few funding restrictions, since the money went into the

Members of one of this nation's largest and most powerful interest groups, senior citizens, meet California senator Dianne Feinstein, showing picket fence federalism in action. With powerful organizations such as the American Association of Retired Persons (AARP) representing their interests in Congress, senior citizens, who are also the most likely to vote come election day, cannot be easily ignored by legislators at any level of government.

general treasury of each jurisdiction, states were now subject to national regulations in such areas as civil rights, affirmative action, and fair wages.

The movement toward increased dominance of the national government in the federal structure could not be reversed. Although Presidents Nixon and Ford attempted through consolidation to slow the growth of national grants, by 1976 the total number of national-aid programs actually increased by 250 percent. Because there was a layer of unrestricted revenue-sharing money in addition to an increasing number of categorical-grant programs, national spending expanded. Unhappy with its lack of control over both the amount and nature of this spending, Congress abolished revenue sharing to the states in 1981 and then did the same for revenue sharing to the localities in 1986.

With more time in the White House, the state-oriented Republican party might have been able to carry out its plan to reform and reduce the categorical-grants program. But the Democrats returned to the White House in 1976.

Creative Federalism Returns under Jimmy Carter (1977–80)

President Carter tried to combine the best aspects of Johnson's creative federalism and Nixon's New Federalism to more precisely target national aid to the most hard-pressed communities. He also sought to use public funds to encourage private investment for certain problems. With these two goals, Carter hoped to mount a full-fledged attack on governmental red tape. As a result of these efforts, federal aid to the states and localities leveled out and, in the last years of Carter's term, even began to decrease. But while Carter had begun to reverse the trend toward increased national involvement in the American federal system, once more the failure to win reelection cut short a reform effort.

Ronald Reagan's "New New Federalism" (1981–88)

When Ronald Reagan ran for president in 1980 he promised to restore the power and authority of the state governments. In his first inaugural address on January 20, 1981, Reagan vowed "to curb the size and influence of the federal establishment and to demand recognition of the distinction between the powers granted to the federal government and those reserved to the States or to the people."[31] Reagan's logic was simple: Why should the national government tax the people and then ship the money back to the states? Why not simply let the states do the taxing and administer the programs?

Reagan's crusade against big government was approached from several different angles. In his February 18, 1981, speech to Congress, Reagan presented his economic-recovery strategy in an Omnibus Budget Reconciliation Act, which consisted of tax cuts, vast budget cuts, and cuts in federal regulations, all of which were designed to give "local government entities and states more flexibility and control."[32]

The president faced stiff opposition from those who would be affected by the cuts. State governors began to balk when the cuts proved to be deeper than anticipated. Interest groups speaking for the recipients of grant money also pressed for continued funding. Nevertheless, Congress consolidated seventy-seven categorical programs into nine block grants. While funding for the national programs was cut by less than half of what the administration had requested, Reagan's first year in

Cleaning Up the Environment: Who Pays?

In the early 1960s it became evident that environmental pollution in the United States had reached intolerable levels. The Great Lakes, the Mississippi River, and other interstate waterways were polluted. Acid rain caused by smoke emitted by factories in the Midwest made lakes in New England uninhabitable for fish. The carbon dioxide contained in automobile exhaust polluted the air, cancer-causing chemicals were being dumped into rivers, and barrels of radioactive waste were being buried underground or dumped into the ocean.

What could be done to reverse these trends and clean up the mess? There were several options, each with its drawbacks. Industries could regulate themselves, but the costs of doing so would cut into their profits and weaken their competitive position. Individual states could try to limit pollution, but they feared that job-creating industries would move across state lines to avoid regulation. Besides, nothing could be done about pollution that is carried across state lines by wind or water. Groups of states could band together, but they could not agree on the cause of a given environmental problem and assign responsibility for the cleanup on a state-by-state basis. Another option was for the national government to impose environmental regulations on states and industries.

Which of these options was most likely to be effective?

Thinking Critically

What Happened

In 1963 Congress passed the Clean Air Act, which was designed to encourage states and private industry to clean up the environment voluntarily. In 1970, after none of the states had implemented the plan, Congress amended the act; two years later it passed the Water Pollution Control Act. These measures established national standards for environmental action and set deadlines for the states to meet them. The Environmental Protection Agency (EPA) was created to monitor those actions. If the states failed to comply with the new laws, the EPA would draw up pollution control plans for them.

The initial results were positive. By 1979 the levels of soot, dust, sulfur dioxide, and carbon monoxide in the air had declined dramatically. Air pollution in the nation's inner cities had decreased by more than 30 percent. Pickerel and pike were once again thriving in Lake Erie. And approximately 90 percent of the major polluters in the nation were meeting their cleanup deadlines.

But there was still a long way to go before the pollution problem could be said to have been solved. In 1990, therefore, Congress rewrote the Clean Air Act, setting new and stricter timetables for states to reduce air pollution. According to the new act, they must do so by 2010. In 1993 the EPA began warning states that they would face sanctions if they did not comply with the law. It is still too early to judge the effectiveness of the new policies; although air quality improved somewhat in the early 1990s, about half of the states are lagging in meeting the timetable established by the 1990 law.

In sum, while the federal system has had some success in dealing with environmental pollution, continued efforts are needed at both levels of government. However, in 1995 the Republican Congress considered measures designed to weaken the environmental pollution controls on industry. What this means for the future of environmental regulation remains to be seen.

Sources: John E. Schwarz, *America's Hidden Success* (New York: Norton, 1983); "Authority, Money at Issue: EPA, States Differ in Views of Environmental Federalism," *Congressional Quarterly,* Nov. 27, 1982, pp. 2915–20; John H. Cushman, "States and Government Lag in Meeting Clean Air Law," *New York Times,* Nov. 16, 1993, Sec. A; Denise Goodman, "Drivers Fuming over Business Break," *Boston Globe,* July 10, 1994. p. 29.

---

office marked a significant break with the past. Figure 4.5 illustrates the drop in national funding of state and local budgets in the 1980s.

To further his reforms, in January 1982 Reagan proposed a complete reordering of the national spending priorities. First, there would be a swap or turn-back program, in which the national government would take over Medicaid, while the states,

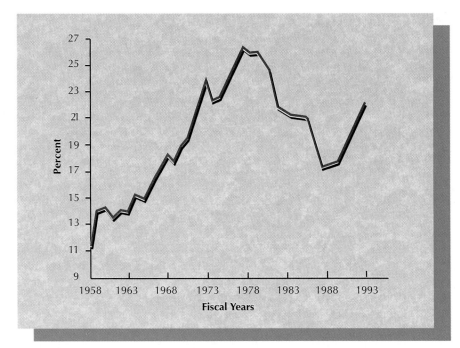

FIGURE 4.5 National Aid to States, 1958–93
We can see here how national spending rose and fell over the past thirty-five years. Note how national aid rose from 1958–1978, then dropped during Reagan's early years in office. A sharp rise began during the Bush years, increasing from about 17 percent in 1988 and 1989 to 22 percent by 1993 (Bush was less successful at downsizing than his predecessor). In early 1995 the figure remained at about 21 percent.
Sources: "Giving Power to Fifty Little Washingtons," *Newsweek,* Feb. 6, 1995, pp. 18–19; *The Book of the States, 1994–1995 Edition,* Vol. 30, Lexington, KY: Council of State Governments, 1989, pp. 580–581; Norman Beckman, "Developments in Federal–State Relations," *The Book of the States, 1988–1989 Edition,* Vol. 24, Lexington, KY: Council of State Governments, 1989, p. 439; U.S. Advisory Commission on Intergovernmental Relations, *Intergovernmental Perspective,* Vol. 14, Winter 1988, p. 13.

in turn, would take over sixty programs, such as Aid to Families with Dependent Children (AFDC) and food stamps. Relying on budget estimates, the White House promised that the swap would not result in increased expenditures for the states, and since the health costs taken over by the national government were destined to rise sharply, the result would likely represent future savings for the states.

Stiff resistance quickly developed over these new reforms. While states wanted greater control over spending for programs, they also wanted the security of guaranteed national funding. And while the national government wanted to reduce its level of spending, a transfer of program responsibilities to the states would mean a loss of control over tax revenues. In short, this attempt to move away from national dominance in the federal partnership threatened to send a hesitant government into uncharted waters.

As a result, Reagan's new brand of New Federalism achieved mixed results. Immediately following the program swap, an eight-billion-dollar absolute reduction in national spending was realized, and 140 national grant programs were cut or consolidated. However, after 1982, the number of federal grants began rising again, from 400 in 1982 to 492 in 1988.

Reagan's new New Federalism created challenges and dilemmas for states now faced with doing more with less.[33] National-grant funding dropped from 25 percent of state budgets in the late 1970s to less than 17 percent in the late 1980s.[34] States such as New Jersey, California, Massachusetts, New York, and Pennsylvania found that the combination of increased program responsibilities and declining national-grant funding led to rapidly escalating budget deficits. In response, governors argued that large tax increases had to be adopted or important programs, such as funding for college education, had to be cut significantly. But the general public, which had grown so accustomed to national funding programs that it didn't care *where* the programs originated, only that they continue to exist, decided to vote some governors out of office. Despite these problems, the potential for greater state innovation as a result of funding cuts did offer some hope for the future of policy reform.

The Bush Years (1989–92)

President George Bush sought to continue the Reagan downsizing of government. He called for personal volunteerism to address social ills and encouraged state and local governments to pick up the costs of certain national programs such as wastewater treatment plants and mass transit. In addition, Bush tried to lower welfare spending and find other ways to pay for environmental protection and education programs. Despite these funding cuts, however, the sharp increases in the cost of Medicaid, now the responsibility of the national government after the Reagan reform, led to national grant outlay increases from $101.2 billion to $166.9 billion, or an average increase of 9.2 percent per year.[35]

Because of these escalating costs and the huge budget deficits, the Bush administration was unable to carry out its plans to refocus domestic initiatives.[36] In 1992 and 1993 Bush tried to consolidate $20 billion in categorical-grant programs into a single block grant and turn it back to the states, but the proposal was not enacted.

The experience of the Bush administration, like that of the previous Reagan administration, reveals the difficulty of reversing heavy national financial involvement in the federal structure. Rising budget deficits, the public's demands for increased services and lower taxes, and the inability of financially strapped states to meet policy expectations make successful implementation of reforms difficult. With the budget deficit out of control (see Chapter 17) and Medicaid expenses continuing to add to the deficit, choices will have to be made about which grant programs to fund. These choices will not be easy to make, as various interest groups remain ready to do battle over any cuts or reforms.

Bill Clinton and the Future of Federalism (1993–?)

Bill Clinton took office facing an escalating national budget and the dilemma that the vast majority of Americans wish to retain the national programs they have come to expect over the years but have become less willing to pay for them. He also knew from his experience as governor of Arkansas of the states' ability to devise new programs if given a chance.

Clinton was elected based on his campaign promise to be a "New Democrat"—a conservative Democrat who supports states' rights and a less activist national government that provides people with tools to help themselves, such as job training, rather than with an array of expensive social services. But Clinton's first two years in office left him looking more like an "Old Democrat" from the liberal wing of the party which upholds that the national government should provide people with a safety net, even if it means that government will grow. Clinton's 1994 health-care reform package, although aimed at reducing escalating health costs, failed largely because of the perception that it would foster big government.

The overwhelming victory in both houses of Congress by the states'-rights–oriented Republicans in the 1994 elections clearly indicated popular discontent and put pressure on the President to reformulate his position.

It remains to be seen whether a Democratic president and a Republican-controlled House and Senate will be able to work together or whether they will be at odds with one another in their attempts to shape the nature of the federal–state partnership as America moves into the twenty-first century. But there can be little doubt that a much greater role for the states will be an important topic of discussion in political circles and among the general population. Figure 4.6, for example, indicates that Americans are concerned about the size of their government and also about how it functions.

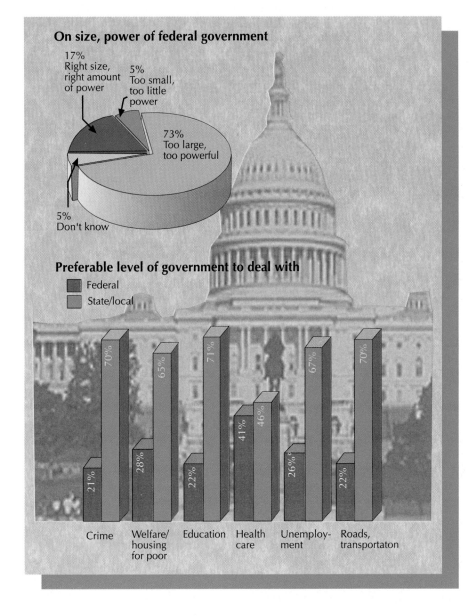

On size, power of federal government

17%
Right size, right amount of power

5%
Too small, too little power

73%
Too large, too powerful

5%
Don't know

Preferable level of government to deal with

Federal
State/local

	Crime	Welfare/ housing for poor	Education	Health care	Unemployment	Roads, transportaton
State/local	70%	65%	71%	46%	67%	70%
Federal	21%	28%	22%	41%	26%	22%

FIGURE 4.6 What Americans Think about Government
Although torn between a desire for retaining certain national programs and an unwillingness to pay for them, judging from this poll taken soon after the 1994 election, Americans are also concerned about the size and policy functions of the national government. Americans seem to want less national government and more state and local government involvement. By tapping into this sentiment and pledging to make it a reality, the Republicans positioned their candidates perfectly for electoral success in the 1994 elections.
Note: 1994 telephone survey of 1,300 adult Americans; margin of error 2.7%.
Source: Luntz Research Companies.

THE COURTS AND THE FUTURE OF FEDERALISM   What does the future hold for our federal system? In addition to presidential and congressional policies, Supreme Court and lower-court rulings will continue to define the direction of federalism. In its 1994–95 term, the Supreme Court, ruling in the case of *United States* v. *Lopez* overturned a section of the 1990 federal law making it a crime to possess firearms within one thousand feet of a school zone. The case was important and closely watched because the justices were considering whether to rein in Congress by restricting its ability to use its interstate commerce power to pass laws on crime and education, both traditionally in the domain of states. During oral arguments, several justices expressed concern about the potentially unlimited nature of congressional power: "Presumably there is nothing left if Congress can do this, no recognizable limit," said Justice David Souter. In overturning the law, the Court appeared ready to establish new limits on congressional authority by requiring Congress, for the first time in fifty years, to justify the link between a law and the commerce clause. This decision may represent a change in the expansive interpretation of the interstate commerce clause typical of most rulings since the New Deal. Shortly after this decision, the Court ruled to overturn term limits and support states' rights under the Tenth Amendment, indicating yet again that the Court's direction may be changing.[37] We will have to watch the Court to see if these cases lead to others exploring the extent of federal power in areas that were once traditionally the responsibility of the states. But at the heart of this Supreme Court case is the question of who decides—the national government or the states. The case study at the start of this chapter explored this question, which will likely continue to be asked about the American federal system in the future.[38]

CONTEMPORARY FEDERALISM AND APPROACHING DEMOCRACY

The debate over federalism and the proper balance of power between national and state governments, then, is ongoing. Consider this comment, heard on a television news program: "That's the difference between us," moderate political commentator Cokie Roberts said to her ultraconservative colleague George Will about the pending health-care legislation in 1994. "You think that *any* government is too much government, while I would like some more bipartisan action at the national level in this area."[39] That has been the nature of the debate for over two centuries. There's usually agreement that problems involving crime, the economy, health care, toxic waste, and the environment exist and need to be dealt with. The disagreement, however, comes over which level of government, or whether any government at all, should address such matters.

Where one stands in the federalism debate reveals a lot about one's political ideology. In this century, Franklin D. Roosevelt's New Deal put the liberal Democrats firmly in the position of the nation-centered party, upholding that only the national government can provide a basic standard of living and uniform democratic rights for all citizens. Lyndon Johnson's Great Society is a classic example of this position. The powers of the national government were used to create a welfare state aimed at helping the underprivileged, solving civil rights problems, improving education, and so forth. Conservative Republicans, on the other hand, advocate a state-centered approach, arguing that

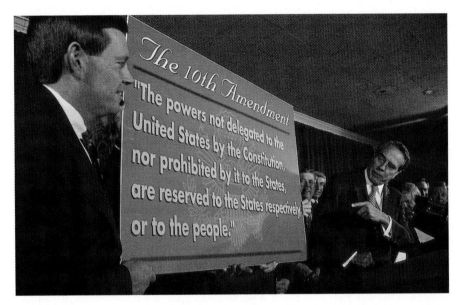

The Tenth Amendment enjoyed a dramatic resurgence after the 1994 elections, which gave Republicans a majority in both Houses of Congress. The amendment was an important component of Republican House Speaker Newt Gingrich's "Contract With America," which, among other things, sought to return to the states power exercised by the national government for over a half century. The intent: to cut back the bloated national government and ultimately make government more responsive to the needs of Americans.

solutions are best left either to the state governments or to the private sector. These conservatives were understandably overjoyed with Ronald Reagan's election in 1980, whose platform opposing big government and advocating the return of power to the states was more to their tastes. Reagan sought to dismantle the welfare state and to cut national spending. At the same time, Democrats and liberals were left to worry about the potential consequences of a shrunken national role. To some, then, a stronger national government means more democracy, while to others it means less.

Although federalism is not a precondition for democracy (democracies such as Great Britain do not have a federal structure), the federal structure is central to American government and its ability to approach democracy. You've seen how this system, consisting of an overarching national government tempered by innovation at the state level, has enabled regions and groups of citizens to seek out the policies that best suit them. Through the workings of federalism, a variety of legal and political rights have been guaranteed uniformly throughout the nation when states were either unable or unwilling to protect the rights of their citizens, usually minorities. In addition, the spending power of the national government has allowed it to redistribute resources to promote equality and fairness. Overall, federalism has helped empower various groups of people as they pressed for new rights or financial support. In this way, the federal structure designed by the framers initially to preserve the rights of states has served to provide a necessary fail-safe system for the rights of people.

America's experience with federalism has involved a continual shifting of power from the states to the federal government and back again. And the nature of the federal structure continues to change. Although the national government predominates, today there is less money in its coffers, meaning less leverage over the states and a new role for the states as they try to figure out ways to make more efficient use of whatever federal monies come their way. It is likely that federal spending will continue to decline and that the American public will remain unreceptive to the idea of higher taxes to pay for government programs. The result will likely be even more responsibility shifting to the states and perhaps a return to the days when government policies and programs varied from state to state. Will the states find innovative and cost-efficient ways to provide services that the public has come to expect? Or, will states follow the example of the national government and reduce their spending? And what repercussions will such shifts have for democracy in America?

Through it all, though, in exercising its political role, each level of government plays an important part in ensuring that our federal structure, the result of a careful compromise forged by the framers in Philadelphia, continues to function and thrive.

SUMMARY

1. The term *federalism* refers to a political system in which two or more distinct levels of government exercise power over the same body of citizens. Federalism differs from a confederation, in which the power to govern is decentralized among sovereign states.

2. Among the advantages of federalism are the ability to accommodate a diverse population, a tendency to minimize policy conflict, dispersal of power, and enhanced prospects for governmental innovation. Such a system also has disadvantages: Groups that wish to protect their interests may obstruct national mandates, and the system may produce inequities in different regions.

3. The most important powers shared by federal and state government are the ability to regulate commerce and the right to collect taxes to provide for the general welfare. Also important are the powers reserved to the states by the Tenth Amendment to the Constitution; these help create a balance of power between the two levels of government.

4. The Constitution delegates certain powers exclusively to the national government; these include the power to declare war, raise and support an army, negotiate with foreign countries, and coin money. The powers reserved to the states include the ability to regulate the health, morals, public safety, and welfare of state citizens. Concurrent powers are shared by the two levels of government; in addition to the power to regulate commerce and impose taxes, they include the power to regulate elections and maintain a judicial structure.

5. A few powers are denied both to the national government and to the states. These include the power to grant titles of nobility and to pass bills of attainder and ex post facto laws.

6. Efforts in the early 1800s to expand the power of the national government were hotly debated, leading to a Su-preme Court decision upholding the dominance of the national government in areas where its powers overlapped with those of the states. One response was the theory of nullification, which held that states could refuse to observe national legislation that they considered unacceptable. After the Civil War the concept of dual federalism prevailed; each level of power was viewed as separate and supreme within its own jurisdiction. During the Great Depression the national government regained its dominance despite numerous Supreme Court rulings setting limits on its activities. Eventually a new approach, known as cooperative federalism, emerged. Since the 1930s Supreme Court decisions have sought to ensure uniformity in policies involving the rights of individuals and to impose national standards to reduce inequality.

7. A grant-in-aid gives money to states and localities to induce them to implement policies favored by the national government. Categorical grants are given for specific purposes and are usually accompanied by strict rules. Federal mandates are national requirements that must be observed by the states.

8. In the 1960s creative federalism was used to address problems in areas that had been neglected by the states. One result was rapid growth in the size and cost of the federal bureaucracy. Another result was a shift in the way scholars view federalism, with the notion of "picket fence federalism" gaining widespread support.

9. President Nixon's New Federalism included the policy of general revenue sharing, by which money was given to the states with no restrictions on how it could be spent; and special revenue sharing, by which categorical grants in related policy areas were consolidated into a single block grant. President Carter attempted to combine this approach with creative federalism, while President Reagan attempted to do away with revenue sharing and

restore power to the state governments, a policy that was continued by President Bush. At present, federalism is caught in a dilemma resulting from conflicting desires—to reduce spending by the national government on the one hand, and to maintain national assistance to the states on the other.

KEY TERMS

states' rights
federalism
triad of powers
elastic clause
supremacy clause
express powers
implied powers
inherent powers
reserved powers
concurrent powers

McCulloch v. *Maryland*
Gibbons v. *Ogden*
nullification
dual federalism
cooperative federalism
grant-in-aid
categorical grant
formula grant
project grant
formula/project grant

block grant
federal mandate
creative federalism
intergovernmental relations
picket fence federalism
New Federalism
general revenue sharing
special revenue sharing

SUGGESTED READINGS

- Banfield, Edward. "Federalism and the Dilemma of Popular Government." In Edward Banfield, ed., *Here the People Rule: Selected Essays,* 2d ed. Washington D.C.: American Enterprise Institute 1991. An intriguing explanation of how the nation-centered view of federalism originated and developed.

- Beer, Samuel H. *To Make a Nation: The Rediscovery of American Federalism.* Cambridge, Mass.: Harvard University Press, 1993. A highly readable account tracing the philosophical origins of federalism from the British experience, through the constitutional founding, to the use of federalism today.

- Berger, Raoul. *Federalism: The Founder's Design.* Norman: University of Oklahoma Press, 1987. An interesting depiction of the philosophical basis for the state-centered federalism position, arguing that since the states preceded the national government they still have sovereign power.

- Dye, Thomas R. *American Federalism: Competition Among Governments.* Lexington, Mass.: Lexington Books, 1990. An intriguing picture of American federalism as a system of competition among the national and state governments.

- Elazar, Daniel J. *American Federalism: A View from the States.* 3d ed. New York: Harper and Row, 1984. A very helpful and comprehensive examination of American federalism from the perspective of state governments.

- Goldwin, Robert, ed. *A Nation of States.* Chicago: Rand McNally, 1961. Contains a series of classic essays by experts on federalism.

- Grodzins, Morton. *The American System.* Chicago: Rand McNally, 1966. The classic account of the "marble-cake" image of cooperative federalism.

- Osborne, David. *Laboratories of Democracy.* Boston, Mass.: Harvard Business School, 1988. A highly readable series of case studies on state governors and governments operating to solve public-policy problems.

- Pressman, Jeffrey, and Aaron Wildavsky. *Implementation.* Berkeley: University of California Press, 1973. An excellent account of how the democratic processes in federalism thwarted the implementation of one of Johnson's economic-development projects in Oakland, California.

- Reagan, Michael D., and John G. Sanzone. *The New Federalism,* 2d ed. New York: Oxford University Press, 1981. A comprehensive and classic analysis of fiscal federalism outlining both the grant-in-aid and revenue-sharing systems.

- Riker, William H. *The Development of American Federalism.* Boston, Mass.: Kluwer Academic Publishers, 1987. Essays on the continuity of American federalism, written over a thirty-year period by Riker and his colleagues.

- Stewart, William H. *Concepts of Federalism.* Lanham, Md.: University Press of America, 1984. A comprehensive dictionary on the meanings of, and metaphors for, federalism.

- Walker, David B. *Toward a Functioning Federalism.* Cambridge, Mass.: Winthrop, 1981. An in-depth examination of the intergovernmental-relations system, offering a series of suggestions for reform.

CHAPTER 5

CONGRESS

CHAPTER OUTLINE

CASE STUDY: CREATING AMERICORPS

INTRODUCTION: CONGRESS AND
 DEMOCRACY

THE STRUCTURE AND POWERS OF
 CONGRESS

THE MEMBERS OF CONGRESS

THE CONGRESSIONAL ODYSSEY: HOW A
 BILL BECOMES A LAW

HOW CONGRESS ORGANIZES ITSELF

CONGRESS IN SESSION

CONGRESSIONAL FUNCTIONS:
 OVERSIGHT AND BUDGET CONTROL

THE '94 ELECTIONS AND THE FUTURE OF
 CONGRESS

CONGRESS AND APPROACHING
 DEMOCRACY

B ill Clinton's vision of an army of young people helping to rebuild the inner cities, assisting the poor and the sick, and teaching others in return for college tuition assistance became a key element of his 1992 presidential campaign. Voters responded favorably, but the main problem was the cost: In its proposed form, this volunteer national service program would cost seventeen billion dollars—an impossible amount in a time of soaring federal budget deficits. To have any hope of acceptance, the program had to be scaled back.

In addition to the critics who worried about its cost, banks wanted to protect the existing college loan program; veterans' groups were afraid that national service would be paid for by cuts in their programs; representatives of the education community were afraid that other educational programs would be scaled back; administrators, worried about their community service programs, felt threatened; and leaders of some minority groups worried that the volunteer corps would be composed entirely of poor minorities.

To neutralize opposition, the White House searched for Republican co-sponsors for the national-service bill. By the time it was introduced in Congress on April 30, 1993, the bill had more than two hundred co-sponsors in the House. However, there were only fifty-six Democrats in the Senate; sixty votes would be needed to prevent a Republican filibuster. To gain Republican support, deals would have to be made. Republican Senator Nancy Kassebaum of Kansas was promised that the national-service bill would be separated from reform of the student loan program; Senator David Durenberger of Minnesota was assured that community service as well as national service would be included. Once these and other deals

had been arranged, the president felt confident that the bill would easily pass in both houses of Congress. But the ordeal was just beginning.

In early June the House Education and Labor Committee and the Senate Labor and Human Resources Committee began holding hearings, and in mid June both committees began "marking up," or modifying, the language of the bill. Republican members of the House committee proposed thirty-three amendments, most of which were defeated. However, these members were able to make some significant changes, such as reducing the duration of the program from five years to three.

The legislation reached the floor of the House and Senate in mid July. It was now going to face an even more difficult time. In the House, Republican Dick Armey of Texas called the national-service program "a welfare program for the aspiring yuppies of America." During floor debate, Republican representatives offered one amendment after another. Each of those amendments was defeated by the Democratic majority. Late in the debate, however, veterans' organizations joined conservative Republicans to force the Democrats to reduce the yearly benefit to 90 percent of veterans' college benefits (i.e., from $5,000 to $4,725). With that, the House passed the bill by a margin of 275 to 152.

In the Senate, Senator Kassebaum introduced a substitute bill that would cut the number of volunteers to five thousand and their yearly benefit to only $1,500, thereby reducing the cost of the program by 75 percent. When the Senate voted down this attempt, she broke the bill up into twenty-seven separate amendments to be proposed from the floor; and her Republican colleagues added another fifteen for consideration.

Floor debate in the Senate continued for eleven days. After their numerous proposed amendments were defeated, the Republicans began calling national service a $10.8 billion boondoggle. When Democrat Bob Kerrey of Nebraska, a veteran,

135

began to waver, fellow Democrat Harris Wofford of Pennsylvania, a former Peace Corps organizer, pleaded with him: "This is my flesh and guts. This is my blood and soul. You let me know when you have a flesh-and-blood issue like this, and I'll be there." Then word leaked out that the Republicans were planning to filibuster. "This bill is a turkey, an absolute turkey . . . that we should shoot," charged Alphonse D'Amato of New York. "Kill it now!" As if that weren't enough, Jesse Helms of North Carolina succeeded in adding an amendment that would give patent protection to the Confederate flag. Whereupon Carol Moseley-Braun, an African American from Illinois, threatened to "stand here until this room freezes" unless the Senate reconsidered the Helms amendment immediately and voted it down. (It did.)

When the filibuster began, a frustrated presidential staff adopted a dual strategy: make a deal with Senator Kassebaum to reduce the size of the national-service program and put pressure on moderate Republicans to end the stalling. Senators from the two parties eventually negotiated an agreement in which the program would be funded at "three, five, seven"—that is, $300 million in the first year, $500 million in the second, and $700 million in the third. With that, the Republicans agreed to end the filibuster, and on August 3 the Senate passed the bill by a vote of 58 to 41.

The House and the Senate had passed different versions of the bill, resulting in another obstacle.

The bill went to a conference committee, which produced a compromise version in which the House accepted lower spending limits while the Senate agreed to a provision under which members of the state commissions distributing the money for the program would be covered by the civil service. President Clinton signed the National and Community Service Trust Act on September 21, 1993, and announced that the program would be called Americorps. By early 1995 the president could point with pride to a corps of twenty thousand volunteers involved in more than three hundred projects around the country.[1] Among the projects undertaken by this domestic Peace Corps were disaster relief efforts in flooded California, a housing rehabilitation program in Houston, employment-retraining programs throughout the nation, and a program to assist homeless veterans.[2] ❧

INTRODUCTION: CONGRESS AND DEMOCRACY

The legislative journey of Americorps illustrates the complex route bills must follow to become law. Each newly introduced bill faces a daunting set of obstacles. One is the sheer volume of proposed legislation. Community service was one of 14,508 bills introduced in the 103rd Congress; it was also one of only 675 laws to be passed.[3] Small wonder that most legislative proposals fail—they simply get lost in the frenzy of competing demands for members' attention.

Suppose a bill does get serious consideration in Congress. To move forward, it needs strategically placed supporters on key committees in both houses. As we have seen in this case, these advocates must work to overcome all obstacles by building and reinforcing successive majority coalitions (at different stages of the legislative process).

Even when a bill has strong backing, it can be derailed by partisan politics. Conservatives opposed the community service idea because of its cost and its

The 1994 elections resulted in a Republican majority in both houses and ended forty-two years of Democratic control of Congress. The freshman class of the 104th Congress poses in front of the Capitol. The members of this class will play an important role in legislating the items in the Republican party's manifesto: the Contract With America.

negative impact on allies in banking. Some Senate Democrats opposed the bill for fear of having it labeled "another Democratic tax-and-spend boondoggle." Opponents of big government opposed any new program on principle. As if all that weren't enough, for most bills the possibility of a presidential veto looms large.

There are many stages in the legislative process. Countless actors play a role in the drama of lawmaking, and enemies of any proposal lurk in a dozen or more places. It often seems amazing that *any* bill ever passes. Occasionally, however, a "breakthrough moment" arrives in American politics when Congress finds the political will to work like a well-oiled machine. The first one hundred days of the New Deal Congress (1933) was one of those moments. Opening day of the 104th Congress (1995), and the ninety-nine days that followed, was another.

This chapter will help you understand Congress—its structure and powers, its members and their roles, and the dynamics of legislation. It also looks at how Congress has helped, and at times thwarted, America's approach to democracy as it transforms public demands into governmental action.

THE STRUCTURE AND POWERS OF CONGRESS

The tortuous process of lawmaking derives from one simple fact: Congress is extremely powerful. In fact, it can probably be considered the world's most powerful legislature. If the dominant congressional faction is large and determined enough, it can override presidential vetoes and make national policy entirely on its own. Presidents cannot force Congress to do their bidding. Neither can they simply ignore it, and they cannot get rid of Congress by dissolving it and calling for new elections. In most non-democratic nations executives *can* do all these things: legislatures are little more than puppets for the nation's authoritarian leadership.

The U.S. Congress then, is a major power within the American constitutional system, but it is also a democratic body: Its members are elected by the American people. These two facts—that Congress is powerful *and* democratic—may seem obvious, but they are worth stressing for their significant political implications. If Congress is powerful, then it makes sense for citizens to focus on this body if they wish to influence national-policy outcomes.

Congress is pluralistic and decentralized.[4] Each of its 535 members has real power in the sense that each of them has one vote. That means, in essence, 535 power points. The result is that the decision-making process is much more complex than it would be if power were concentrated in the hands of a few people or just one group. Those wishing to influence Congress must persuade a large number of people who have different outlooks, who are found at different points in a complex structure, and whose impact on policy outcomes can vary dramatically.

What the Framers Had in Mind

Knowing that Congress would be powerful, the framers took steps to prevent it from becoming the tyrannical force the state legislatures had been under the Articles of Confederation. We have already seen in Chapter 3 the constitutional limits on Congress's power (through the Bill of Rights, for example) and the way other institutions (the president, the Supreme Court) can check its actions.

But the framers went further. Through the Connecticut Compromise, the Constitutional Convention devised a way to make Congress check itself. They divided Congress into a **bicameral,** or two-chambered legislature, and gave each the power to inhibit the other's actions. Each house was to have a very different structure and purpose. James Madison referred to the House of Representatives as "the great repository of the democratic principle of government," that is, the one most sensitive to public opinion. The House would be made up of popularly elected representatives serving two-year terms; the entire body would have to face the electorate every other year. This requirement was supposed to ensure that representatives would reflect the popular will.

The Senate, in contrast, was designed as a brake on the public's momentary passions, or as Madison put it, a "necessary fence" against the "fickleness and passion" of the people. It would be an advisory council to the president, a judicious group of wise elder statesmen, one step removed from the passions and demands of the people. This distinction was based on the British tradition, in which the House of Commons represents the masses and the House of Lords the aristocracy. Until 1913 most members of the Senate were chosen by their respective state legislatures (some western states had direct elections), ensuring that they were, in fact, somewhat removed from the mass electorate. In our more democratic age, senators, like House members, are now directly elected

- To lay and collect taxes, duties, imposts, and excises
- To borrow money
- To regulate commerce with foreign nations and among the states
- To establish rules for naturalization and bankruptcy
- To coin money, set its value, and punish counterfeiting
- To fix the standard of weights and measures
- To establish a post office and post roads
- To issue patents and copyrights to inventors and authors
- To create courts inferior to the Supreme Court
- To define and punish piracies, felonies on the high seas, and crimes against the law of nations
- To declare war
- To raise and support an army and navy and make rules for their governance
- To provide for a militia
- To exercise exclusive legislative powers over the District of Columbia and over places purchased to be federal facilities
- To "make all laws which shall be necessary and proper for carrying into execution the foregoing powers, and all other powers vested by this Constitution in the government of the United States"

FIGURE 5.1 The Key Powers of Congress

by their state's residents. Still, they remain more removed than representatives from day-to-day popular desires since they serve for six years, not two. Furthermore, their terms are staggered so that only one-third of the Senate is subject to election every two years. This staggering of terms also makes Senate membership more stable than that of the House. After any given election, two-thirds of the Senate—those whose terms did not expire that year—automatically remain in place.[5]

With this two-chambered legislature, the framers deliberately created obstacles to the passage of legislation. They intended these difficulties to ensure that lawmaking would take into account the many and varied voices of the public. Forced to consider all relevant interests, Congress in theory would become the foundation of representative democracy but never be dominated by just one of the many competing factions.

In allocating legislative powers, the framers went to great lengths to specify the powers of Congress in the Constitution in order to avoid the chaos of the state legislatures under the Articles of Confederation. In Article I, Section 8, they gave Congress authority in three broad areas: economic affairs, domestic affairs, and foreign affairs. The grants of power, as detailed in Figure 5.1, are sizable. In the economic area, Congress can lay and collect taxes, borrow and coin money, impose import duties, and deal with problems of indebtedness and bankruptcy. In the domestic area, Congress is empowered to regulate

Table 5.1
Differences between the House and Senate

HOUSE	SENATE
435 members	100 members
Two-year term	Six-year term
Smaller constituencies	Larger constituencies
Fewer personal staff	More personal staff
Equal populations represented	States represented
Less flexible rules	More flexible rules
Limited debate	Virtually unlimited debate
More policy specialists	Policy generalists
Less media coverage	More media coverage
Less prestige	More prestige
Less reliance on staff	More reliance on staff
More powerful committee leaders	More equal distribution of power
Very important committees	Less important committees
More partisan	Less partisan
Nongermane amendments (riders) not allowed	Nongermane amendments (riders) allowed

interstate commerce and the judiciary. And in the foreign-affairs realm, Congress is given the power to declare war, raise and regulate the armed forces, and regulate commerce with other countries.

In delegating these powers to Congress as a whole, the framers allotted certain distinct responsibilities to each house. The Senate has the power to ratify treaties and confirm appointments of federal judges, ambassadors, and cabinet members. The House has the power to initiate all revenue-raising legislation. The power to impeach is divided between the two chambers, with the House drafting and voting on articles that are then tried in the Senate. Additional differences between the two houses of Congress are outlined in Table 5.1.

Although the framers wished to limit the powers of Congress, they realized that it was impossible to foresee all the issues and emergencies that were likely to arise in the future. Therefore, they included in Article I, Section 8 the so-called necessary and proper clause, also called the **elastic clause,** which grants Congress the power to "make all Laws which shall be necessary and proper" to carry out all the other powers specified in Article I. This sweeping grant of power has enabled Congress to interpret its role broadly with regard to regulating commerce, borrowing money, and collecting taxes.[6]

Limits on Congress's Power

Although extensive, Congress's powers are limited in many ways. As with every agency of the U.S. government, Congress is checked at the most essential level by what the public will tolerate. Voters can ignore hated laws (the fifty-five-mile-an-hour speed limit) or even force Congress to rescind them (Prohibition). Congress is also limited by important elements of the Constitution. It cannot infringe on a number of state powers, for instance, beginning with an essential one: It cannot abolish or change the boundaries of any state without that state's consent. Congress is also subject to the judicial-review powers of the Supreme Court; that body can declare null and void almost any congressional action.

Beyond these checks, perhaps the most important day-to-day limit on Congress's power is the president. No matter what the party line-up, Congress and the president are continually playing complex games of power politics involving both competition and cooperation. Both institutions must work together if government is going to operate, yet each can check the other quite dramatically. The president has an array of powers that can stymie the will of Congress, including his role as commander in chief of the military, his appointment powers, his control of the national bureaucracy, and his veto powers.

THE MEMBERS OF CONGRESS

Now that we've looked at the structure and powers of Congress, we turn to the members. Senators and representatives take popular demands and transform them into laws. Who are the people with this power and where do they come from?

Who Are the Members?

When the First Congress met in 1789 there were only sixty-five representatives and twenty-six senators, all of them from the most elite families in America. They were rich, white, and male. Superficially, members of Congress today differ little from that first group: They are still disproportionately rich, white, and male, and they come overwhelmingly from the fields of law, banking, and big business. Over the last two decades, millionaires have become at least thirty times more common on Capitol Hill than in American society in general.[7] Some ask, how can such a group claim to be a representative body? While others respond, does it matter whether the country's representatives are rich or poor, white or black, male or female—as long as they support the policies its citizens like and oppose those they don't?[8]

Many of the wealthiest members of Congress, such as Ted Kennedy and Jay Rockefeller, represent the interests of the poor. And many male members of Congress work diligently to promote the welfare of women. Still, it seems reasonable to conclude that a healthy democracy would include leaders from all social groups. How does Congress shape up in this regard?

One measure of Congress's approach to democracy in the twentieth century is the increasing ethnic diversity of its members. When we compare the present makeup of Congress with its composition a few decades ago, we can see how the institution has approached democracy by becoming far more diverse. In 1952, the House included only two African Americans and ten women; the Senate had no African Americans and only one woman. In 1995 eight women are in the Senate, including the first female African American senator, Carol Moseley-Braun; two Asian Americans, Daniel K. Inouye and Daniel K.

Little-known Fact

There have been only twenty-two female senators in U.S. history. In addition, only six states have ever had two female senators (Maine, Alabama, California, Louisiana, Nebraska, and South Dakota).

Although the number of women in Congress has increased recently, women have been serving for decades. On the left is Republican Jeannette Rankin of Montana (shown here in Washington, D.C., in 1918), the first woman elected to the U.S. Congress as well as the first woman elected to a national legislative body in any of the world's democracies. An ardent suffragist, Rankin served two separate terms: in the 65th Congress of 1916–18 and in the 77th Congress of 1941–43. On the right are Rankin's modern-day counterparts, members of a much more diverse Congress. From the left are Representatives Cynthia McKinney of Georgia, Carrie Meek of Florida, and Eva Clayton of North Carolina. These African American women are three of forty-eight female members currently serving in the House. There are now eight women serving in the Senate.

Akaka; and the first native American senator, Ben Nighthorse Campbell. The 1995 membership of the House includes thirty-nine blacks, eighteen Hispanics, forty-nine women, and six Asian Americans, as well as immigrants from Cuba, Kenya, and Korea. Thus, in the past four decades African Americans have increased their numbers on Capitol Hill by 2,000 percent. The eighteen Hispanic Americans elected in 1994 bring the number of Hispanics in Congress to its highest level ever.[9] Although the 104th Congress is far more diverse than its predecessors, it still falls short of reflecting the population as a whole. Table 5.2 suggests what Congress would look like if its members represented a true cross-section of the nation.

Table 5.2
To What Extent Does the House Mirror Society?

SOCIAL GROUP	NUMBER IN THE U.S. HOUSE OF THE 104TH CONGRESS (OF 435)	NUMBER IN THE HOUSE IF IT WERE REPRESENTATIVE OF AMERICAN SOCIETY AT LARGE
White Men	386	184
Women	49	226
African Americans	39	52
Hispanics	18	30
Holders of Advanced College Degrees	275	31
People in Poverty	0	65
Lawyers	170	2
Americans under Age 45	124	300

Source: All of the information calculated from *Congressional Quarterly* and *Statistical Abstract of the United States.*

Congressional Districts

The racial and ethnic makeup of Congress is strongly influenced by the nature of the districts from which its members are elected. The way the boundaries of these districts are drawn can determine a candidate's chances of election, making determining the size and the geographic shape of any legislative district a political act.

Article I, Section 2 of the Constitution arbitrarily set the size of the first U.S. House of Representatives at 65 and apportioned those seats roughly by population: Bigger states got more seats. Later, after the 1790 census, the size of the House was set at 105 seats, with each state given 1 seat for each 33,000 inhabitants. As the nation's population grew, so did the number of representatives. By the early twentieth century the House had expanded to 435 members, each with a constituency of approximately 200,000 people. At that point members agreed that the House had reached an optimum size. The Reapportionment Act of 1929 formalized this sentiment; it placed total House membership at 435, a number that has remained stable to this day. Because the nation's population has almost tripled since then, each congressional district now contains about 570,000 citizens.

Population growth and shifts *within* each of these 435 districts vary dramatically over time. To keep the numerical size of districts relatively equal, it becomes necessary to redraw district lines from time to time, and even to adjust the number of representatives allotted each state. This process is known as **reapportionment.** Each reapportionment of House seats reflects the nation's

Ben Nighthorse Campbell of Colorado, the only Native American in the U.S. Senate, startled politicians and constituents when he announced in March 1995 that he was leaving the Democratic party and becoming a Republican. "I can no longer represent the agenda that is put forth by the party," he explained.

population shifts since the last census.[10] Thus, reapportionment in the United States occurs every ten years, always producing "winners" and "losers." Because of population growth in the South and Southwest, such states as California, Texas, and Florida picked up seats after the 1990 census, while population loss in the industrial North and Northeast led to a reduction in the number of representatives from such states as New York, Pennsylvania, and Ohio.

Within these 435 districts, one finds every imaginable variation. Each has its own character; none is an exact replica of the larger society. Because of their particular social composition, some districts view Democrats more favorably than others, while others lean toward Republicans. An enormous political struggle ensues when a new census changes the number of seats a state will receive. The state legislature must then redraw the boundaries of its congressional districts. This process is not simply a matter of counting voters and redrawing boundaries to make the districts equal. There are, after all, a large number of ways to carve out numerically equal congressional districts. Some of those ways help Democrats get elected, while others help Republicans. Boundary lines can be drawn to make a large ethnic group the majority within a single district or to dilute that group's influence by dispersing its members into two, three, or more districts where they can be outvoted by the majority in each area. Redistricting, as the process is called, therefore becomes very political. State legislators naturally seek to establish district boundaries that will favor candidates from their own party.

The term **gerrymander** is used to describe the often bizarre district boundaries set up to favor the party in power. This word was coined in the early nineteenth century after Republican governor Elbridge Gerry of Massachusetts signed a redistricting bill that created a weirdly shaped district to encompass most of the voters who supported his party. One critic looked at the new district and said, "Why, that looks like a salamander!" Another said, "That's not a salamander, that's a gerrymander." The term is now used to describe any attempt to create a "safe" seat for one party, that is, a district in which the number of registered voters of one party is large enough to guarantee a victory for that party's candidate. Figure 5.2 illustrates the gerrymander and its modern-day equivalent.

Sometimes the redistricting process has been used to further social as well as political goals. After the 1990 census, states with histories of racial discrimination were required by law to draw new district boundaries that would give minority candidates a better chance of election. The mandated redistricting was meant to ensure representation for nonwhites living in white-dominated areas. As a result of the redistricting, nineteen new black and Hispanic members were added to Congress in 1992. Proponents point to these gains as evidence that the new districts have made Congress more representative of the general population. Critics claim that they constitute "racial gerrymandering."[11]

North Carolina's Twelfth Congressional District was one of those created to strengthen the voting power of African Americans. However, it was so narrow in some places that it spanned only one lane of Interstate Highway 85 (leading one local legislator to say that half the voters in the district would be killed if someone drove down the highway with one car door open). This district was challenged in the case of *Shaw* v. *Reno* and disallowed by the Supreme Court in 1993. Although the Court sidestepped the general question of racial gerrymandering, it did prohibit racially based redistricting in the case of "those rare districts [like

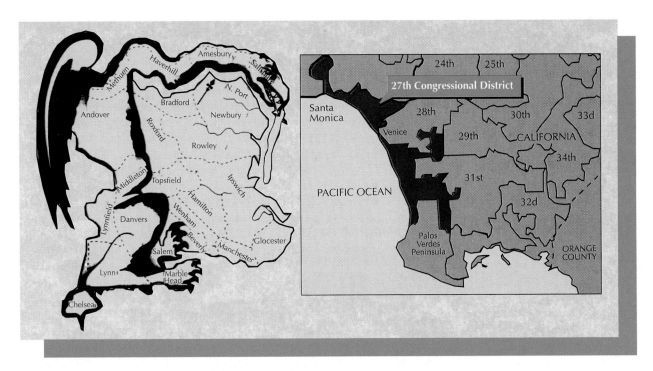

FIGURE 5.2   The Gerrymander and the Burton, 1981
An 1812 cartoon lampooning the original "Gerry-Mander" of a Massachusetts district (left). This district was redrawn to guarantee a Republican victory. The term *gerrymander* soon became a standard political term. Gerrymanders are used by political parties to draw favorable congressional districts. After the 1980 census, California Democratic Representative Phillip Burton led his state's legislators in creating district boundaries that Burton described as "my contribution to modern art." An example was the state's 27th Congressional district, redrawn to defeat incumbent Republican Robert Dornan and elect a Democrat. In 1982, Democratic assemblyman Mel Levine was elected to represent the 27th Congressional district.
Source: Map of 27th Congressional District based on *Congressional Quarterly Weekly Report*, September, 1990, p. 2787; and Robert Reinhold, "Surgery on G.O.P. Was Deft, Not Painless," *New York Times*, March 3, 1991, p. 28.

North Carolina's Twelfth] that are especially bizarre." It added acidly that the district "bears an uncomfortable resemblance to political apartheid.

Since this ruling, a number of other states, mostly in the South, have challenged redistricting plans, but the standards for determining which districts are "bizarre" have been inconsistent. Redistricting laws will continue to be tested in the courts, as minorities seek to maximize their electoral power and white voters try to protect theirs.

Delegates versus Trustees

If Congress is to function as a representative institution, individual members must want to represent their constituents. In theory, legislators may view themselves as either delegates or trustees.[12] **Delegates** feel bound to follow the

Race-Based Redistricting

In 1992 Cynthia McKinney, an African American, was elected to the House of Representatives from Georgia's Eleventh District. Along with about a dozen other African American legislators, she owed her election to the 1965 Voting Rights Act and its 1982 amendments, which have been interpreted as requiring states to redraw the boundaries of legislative districts so that they maximize the voting strength of black, Hispanic, and other minority populations. Numerous such districts were created after the 1990 census, especially in areas where voting discrimination has occurred in the past. The resulting "majority minority districts" produced a dramatic increase in African American and Hispanic representation in Congress, but they have been subjected to a great deal of criticism and several legal challenges.

Since 1982 the Justice Department has used the Voting Rights Act to prod the states into creating districts designed to give minority voters representation in proportion to their numbers in the population. In 1992, in the first election held after the new district lines were drawn, thirteen new African American representatives and six Hispanic members were elected to the House; none of them was defeated in the 1994 election. But as cases like *Shaw* v. *Reno* reach the courts, their positions are in jeopardy. If the districts from which they were elected are ruled unconstitutional, they will have little chance of retaining their seats in future elections.

Opponents of majority minority districts argue that they are unconstitutional because they amount to reverse discrimination against white voters—that they constitute a "racial quota system" or "political apartheid." Advocates of such districts counter that they are necessary if states are to elect members of Congress who are truly representative of the state's population. They also point out that gerrymandering has been tolerated in the past as a way of favoring candidates from particular parties; thus, drawing district boundaries to favor candidates from particular population groups should also be considered acceptable.

Underlying the controversy are some deeper issues. One of those issues might be described as "political segregation." According to Justice Sandra Day O'Connor, racially based districting "can be viewed only as an effort to segregate the races for purposes of voting."

---

wishes of a majority of their constituents; they make frequent efforts to learn the opinions of voters in their state or district.[13]

But how does a legislator represent minority groups in the district or raise issues of national importance that are not a high priority for constituents? For example, should a representative with only a few African American constituents vote for an affirmative action program that is opposed by an overwhelming majority of voters in the district?

In these situations many legislators see themselves not as delegates but as **trustees** authorized to use their best judgment in considering legislation. The trustee role was most famously expressed by the English philosopher Edmund Burke (1729–97), who as a member of Parliament explained to his constituents that representatives should never sacrifice their own judgment to voter opinion. In Congress, the role of trustee, which often leads to policy innovations, is more likely to be favored by representatives from "safe" districts, where a wide margin of victory in the past assures future reelection. Legislators from marginal districts tend to be delegates, keeping their eyes firmly fixed on the

The effect of such districts may be to separate voters into competing racial factions, isolating blacks from the white majority and from other blacks who live in different districts.

One can also ask whether such an approach is truly democratic. American democracy is based on the idea of equal representation—legislators are elected to represent all the citizens of a district, not a particular ethnic group, faction, or social class. From this perspective, the requirement that district boundaries be drawn to favor minority candidates runs counter to a Constitution that is supposed to be colorblind. In other words, there may be no such thing as a "good gerrymander."

Yet there is no doubt that the United States has a long history of discrimination against African American and Hispanic voters, especially in some southern states. The new districts resulted in the election of the first African American representatives from North Carolina in this century, and the first African American representative ever from Oklahoma (Julius Caesar "J.C." Watts). Significant gains in minority representation were made in other states as well. A policy that is so clearly effective in correcting past injustices should not be abandoned without careful consideration.

What does the future hold for race-based redistricting? In a 5 to 4 decision in 1995, the Supreme Court struck down the "race-based" redistricting plan in Cynthia McKinney's 260-mile long Eleventh District in Georgia.* Saying that this justice department-directed plan to create a third black majority district in the state violated the equal protection rights of white voters because it was based predominantly on race, the Court put similar plans throughout the nation (mainly in the South) in jeopardy by ruling that they must all be "narrowly tailored to achieve a compelling [state] interest." In other words, they must remedy specific instances of voting discrimination. However, since the Court on the same day left in force a redistricting plan in California which was based partly on race, it is not clear which race-based redistricting plans will be overturned and which will be upheld in the future. Likely future court challenges in Texas, Florida, Louisiana, and North Carolina will help refine this ruling.

*Miller v. Johnson, 132 L.Ed. 2d 762 (1995).

Source: Based on Abigail Thernstrom, "By Any Name, It's a Quota," New York Times, Dec. 7, 1994, p. A23.

electorate. They apparently wish to avoid Burke's fate: After hearing that Burke did not intend to follow their wishes, his constituency promptly ejected him from Parliament.

In practice, members of Congress combine the roles of delegate and trustee. They follow their constituency when voters have clear, strong preferences, but they vote their own best judgment when the electorate's desire is weak, mixed, or unclear. This approach to voting is called the *politico* role. Members of Congress frequently have to balance votes on issues of national importance against votes on issues that are important to their constituents.[14]

A particularly poignant example of the dilemma arose during the early civil rights era. Lawrence Brooks Hays, an Arkansas moderate from 1943 to 1959, was caught between his integrationist beliefs and his district's segregationist views. After he chose to act as a trustee in Congress, voting in favor of a civil rights bill, his constituents replaced him at the next election with someone closer to their own views. This case illustrates a problem all elected officials ultimately face. Do they do what is popular or what they believe is right?

The Incumbency Factor

Incumbents are individuals who currently hold public office. Since World War II, an average of 92 percent of House incumbents and 77 percent of Senate incumbents seeking reelection won those elections.[15] Despite the anti-incumbent sentiment of the 1994 election, over 90 percent of both the House and Senate incumbents who sought reelection still won. The advantage of incumbency is a relatively recent phenomenon. Before the Civil War, almost half of each new House session and one-third to one-quarter of each entering Senate class were composed of new members.

Incumbents enjoy a number of significant advantages in any election contest.[16] They often benefit from favorable redistricting during reapportionment. They nearly always enjoy greater name recognition than their challengers. They can hold press conferences for widespread publicity, participate in media events such as town meetings, and maintain offices back home that keep their names in the spotlight. Challengers must struggle for, and often fail to achieve, the kind of publicity and recognition that come automatically to an incumbent.

Incumbents can increase their visibility through use of the **franking privilege**—free mailing of newsletters and political brochures to their constituents. These mailings are used to solicit views and advice from constituents and serve to remind them of the incumbent's name and accomplishments. The use of franked mail has grown over the years. In 1994 each House member seeking reelection sent out well over a million pieces of mail.

Another advantage for incumbents is their staff, which helps them do favors for constituents. These services, known as **casework,** may involve arranging for the repair of potholes, expediting payment of social security benefits, or providing a tour of the Capitol. Casework is at the heart of the power of incumbents. Realizing that every voter remembers these little favors, members of Congress often have several full-time staff members who deal with cases involving individual constituents.[17]

Incumbents also have the advantage of legislative experience. They often sit on committees with jurisdiction over issues of particular importance to their constituents. Former rock star turned representative Sonny Bono of the Palm Springs District in Palm Springs, California, was made a member of the Judiciary Committee's Subcommittee on Courts and Intellectual Property because copyright issues are significant for the members of the record and motion picture industry in his district. This kind of experience allows incumbents campaigning for reelection to "point with pride" to favors done for their districts.

Perhaps the greatest advantage held by incumbents is financial. Parties, interest groups, and individuals tend to back the known candidates because they have the best chance of winning, while the relatively unknown challengers have great difficulty raising money. In 1994, House incumbents spent more than four times as much on their campaigns as their challengers did. House races frequently cost about $400,000, while Senate races average $3.7 million, with campaigns in large states costing as much as $43 million. Incumbents can raise that kind of money with little difficulty. Most challengers can't.[18] (Even those who can, do not always win, as in the case of California Republican Michael Huffington, who spent nearly $28 million of his own money on his losing Senate race.)

Seeking to change this pattern, many voters now favor some form of term limits. With polls in 1994 showing that 80 percent of the public wants term limits, twenty-two states have passed legislation limiting the length of time their senators and representatives can serve in Congress (usually a maximum of twelve years in each house). Underlying these measures is the growing public perception that incumbent legislators, feeling assured of reelection, have become either complacent or corrupt.

Although nine out of ten incumbents in the 1994 election were reelected, the actual turnover rate in Congress, due also to seats vacated because of deaths, retirements, and decisions to run for other offices, was 20 percent, the same as it has been for the last two decades. Since all but a handful of these seats were won by Republicans, the distribution of congressional power was changed. Congress failed to pass the Contract With America's promised term limits in early 1995, perhaps because incumbents no longer seemed invulnerable. Despite this failure, and the Supreme Court's 1995 invalidation of term limits for federal representatives, the growing term limits movements in the states make it unlikely that the issue will slip from view in the immediate future.

The Public's View of Congress

Congress is, and generally always has been, held in low regard by the public. Surveys conducted between 1966 and 1988 revealed a steady decline in the proportion of respondents rating Congress positively: from 49 percent to just 18 percent. By 1994, a *Washington Post*–ABC News poll showed that six out of ten respondents disapproved of the way Congress does its job. The same poll also showed that as people became more familiar with the workings of Congress their level of disapproval increased.[19] But if Americans are negative about Congress as an institution, most still feel a strong sense of loyalty to their individual senators and representatives. In the 1994 poll just mentioned, the same

The 1994 elections gave Republicans a clean sweep of the House and Senate. Instead of "reelecting nobody," voters showed their unhappiness with the Democratic incumbents and ushered in the new Republican majority, which, during the campaign, endorsed term limits for legislators (a part of their Contract With America). Once they became incumbents themselves, however, the Republicans' enthusiasm for term limits cooled considerably.

respondents who disapproved of Congress as an institution approved of the performance of their own senators and representatives. Similar results were obtained in a 1994 *New York Times*–CBS poll (see Figure 5.3).[20] No wonder most incumbents get reelected.

FIGURE 5.3 What the American Public Thinks

Source: Copyright © 1994 by The New York Times Company. Reprinted by permission.

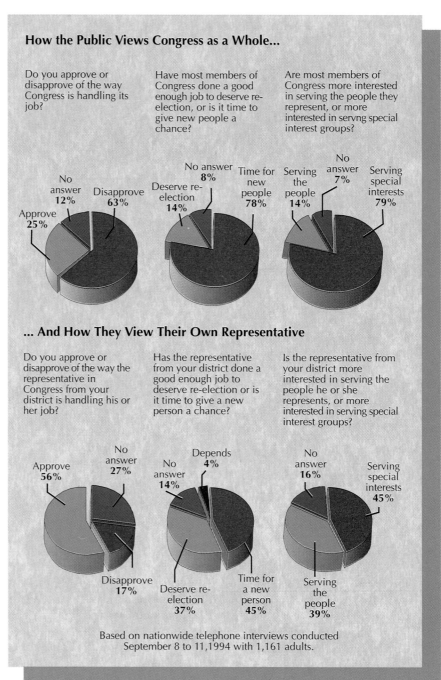

How the Public Views Congress as a Whole...

Do you approve or disapprove of the way Congress is handling its job?

No answer 12%
Approve 25%
Disapprove 63%

Have most members of Congress done a good enough job to deserve re-election, or is it time to give new people a chance?

No answer 8%
Deserve re-election 14%
Time for new people 78%

Are most members of Congress more interested in serving the people they represent, or more interested in servng special interest groups?

No answer 7%
Serving the people 14%
Serving special interests 79%

... And How They View Their Own Representative

Do you approve or disapprove of the way the representative in Congress from your district is handling his or her job?

Approve 56%
No answer 27%
Disapprove 17%

Has the representative from your district done a good enough job to deserve re-election or is it time to give a new person a chance?

Depends 4%
No answer 14%
Deserve re-election 37%
Time for a new person 45%

Is the representative from your district more interested in serving the people he or she represents, or more interested in serving special interest groups?

No answer 16%
Serving special interests 45%
Serving the people 39%

Based on nationwide telephone interviews conducted September 8 to 11,1994 with 1,161 adults.

This paradoxical view of Congress has long puzzled political observers. Of the various attempts to explain the phenomenon, one seems particularly solid. Incumbents have become very adept at running for office, but good campaigners don't necessarily make good legislators.[21]

Now that we have looked at the members of Congress, let's look at how a bill becomes law.

THE CONGRESSIONAL ODYSSEY: HOW A BILL BECOMES A LAW

Spread over several square blocks of Washington, D.C., are six buildings housing congressional offices. An underground subway carries members of Congress from their offices to the Capitol, a magnificent structure that includes the Senate and House chambers where the 535 elected senators and representatives work when Congress is in session.

As you know from the case study at the beginning of the chapter, transforming a bill into a law is a long and complicated process. To succeed, the bill must win 218 votes in the House, 51 votes in the Senate, and one presidential signature. In some cases, such as that of the 1995 bill that finally made Congress subject to the same laws it imposes on the rest of the nation, the process may take years. Conflicting policy goals, special interests, ideology, partisanship, and political ambitions often delay or obstruct the passage of legislation. Most bills never even reach the House or Senate floors for debate.[22] Yet some bills manage to make their way through the administrative and political maze. Let's see how that can happen.

THE CONGRESSIONAL AGENDA   When a member of Congress drafts and submits a piece of legislation dealing with a particular issue, that issue is said to be on the **congressional agenda.** Generally, an issue must gain widespread public attention to be viewed as important enough to require legislative action.[23] Often issues rise to prominence in response to a perceived national crisis. The AIDS epidemic and the growing crime rate are two examples. Other issues, such as health care or proposals for a balanced budget amendment build momentum slowly for years before reaching the level of national consciousness that ensures congressional action. Ideas for a bill can come to the attention of Congress from a number of sources, including the president, cabinet, research institutes, scholars, journalists, voters, and sometimes from **lobbyists** (people paid to further the aims of some interest group among members of Congress).[24] Any citizen can draft legislation and ask a representative or senator to submit it. Only members of Congress can introduce a bill.

CONGRESS CONSIDERS THE BILL   Once a bill has been introduced in Congress, it follows a formal process, or series of steps, on its way to becoming law (see Figure 5.4). In the House, every piece of legislation is introduced by a representative, who hands it to the clerk of the House or places it in a box called the *hopper.* In the Senate, a senator must be recognized by the presiding officer to announce the introduction of a bill. In either case, the bill is first *read* (printed in the *Congressional Record*) and referred to the appropriate committee (or committees if it is especially complex) by the Speaker of the House or the Senate majority leader.

FYI

According to the German leader Otto Von Bismarck, there are two things that one should never watch being made—sausage and legislation.

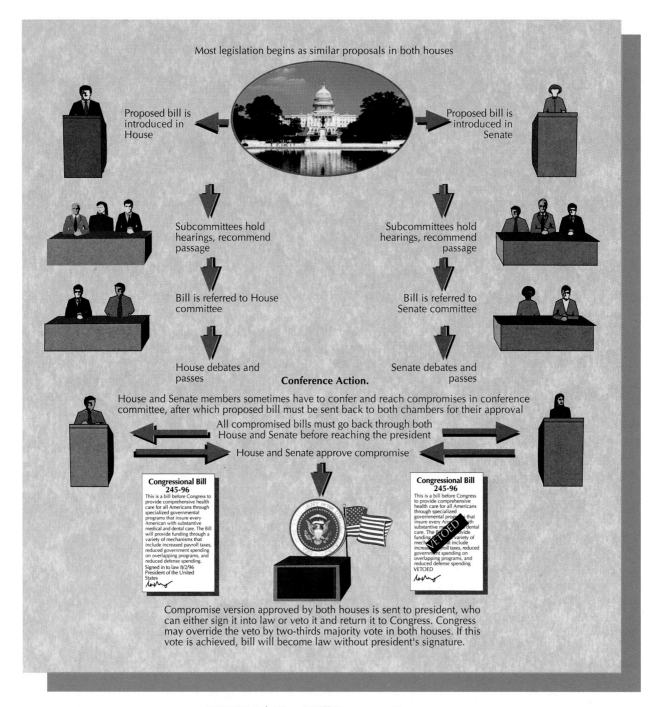

Most legislation begins as similar proposals in both houses

Proposed bill is introduced in House

Proposed bill is introduced in Senate

Subcommittees hold hearings, recommend passage

Subcommittees hold hearings, recommend passage

Bill is referred to House committee

Bill is referred to Senate committee

House debates and passes

Conference Action.

Senate debates and passes

House and Senate members sometimes have to confer and reach compromises in conference committee, after which proposed bill must be sent back to both chambers for their approval

All compromised bills must go back through both House and Senate before reaching the president

House and Senate approve compromise

Congressional Bill 245-96

This is a bill before Congress to provide comprehensive health care for all Americans through specialized governmental programs that insure every American with substantive medical and dental care. The Bill will provide funding through a variety of mechanisms that include increased payroll taxes, reduced government spending on overlapping programs, and reduced defense spending. Signed in to law 8/2/96 President of the United States

Congressional Bill 245-96

This is a bill before Congress to provide comprehensive health care for all Americans through specialized governmental programs that insure every American with substantive medical and dental care. The Bill will provide funding through a variety of mechanisms that include increased payroll taxes, reduced government spending on overlapping programs, and reduced defense spending VETOED

VETOED

Compromise version approved by both houses is sent to president, who can either sign it into law or veto it and return it to Congress. Congress may override the veto by two-thirds majority vote in both houses. If this vote is achieved, bill will become law without president's signature.

FIGURE 5.4 How a Bill Becomes a Law

After a bill has been assigned to a committee, the chair of that committee assigns it to a subcommittee. The subcommittee process usually begins with **hearings,** formal proceedings in which a range of people testify on the bill's pros and cons. Witnesses are usually experts on the subject matter of the bill;

sometimes they are citizens who have been or will be affected by the issue, including various administration officials and highly visible citizens such as movie stars. Subcommittee chairpersons can exercise great influence over the final content of a bill and its chances of passage simply by arranging for a preponderance of friendly (or hostile) witnesses or by planning for the type of testimony that will attract media attention.

After hearings, the subcommittee holds a **markup session** to revise the bill. (It was at this stage that the Americorps bill was trimmed to eliminate the language and provisions that stood in the way of its passage.) The subcommittee then sends the bill back to the full committee, where additional discussion, markup, and voting occur. Approval at that level enables the bill to be sent to the full House, but most bills must first move through the House Rules Committee, which schedules the timing and conditions under which bills are debated on the House floor. Acting like a traffic cop at a busy intersection, the Rules Committee decides which bills will move forward and when. Technically, it attaches a "rule" to each bill, setting a time limit for debate and indicating whether amendments will be allowed. Not until the full House has approved the Rules Committee's recommended rule can a bill be placed on the legislative calendar for floor debate.[25]

Once a bill reaches the House floor, its fate is still far from certain. Debate procedures are complex, and many votes are taken (usually on proposed amendments) before the bill secures final acceptance. Opponents have numerous opportunities at this stage to defeat the bill.

Being much smaller than the House, the Senate is an intimate body that operates with much less formality. Its procedures are fluid and open. The Senate needs no rules committee, for instance. After committee deliberation, bills are simply brought to the floor through informal agreements among Senate

Issues rise to prominence and reach the national agenda in many ways, but perhaps one of the most effective is through the use of symbols that create powerful images that stay with the public and lawmakers. Here organizers of a gun control demonstration assembled forty thousand pairs of shoes near the Capitol in September 1994 to symbolize and speak for the tens of thousands of Americans killed every year by gunfire. The bill they were supporting has since become law.

The House of Representatives uses an electronic voting system that posts each member's name on the wall of the chamber (shown on the left). Members insert a plastic card into a box attached to the chairs (shown on the right) to vote "yea," "nay," or "present." The results of the vote will then appear alongside each legislator's name. The electronic voting system has increased participation at roll calls. Watchdog groups have been known to keep a close eye on legislators who are frequently absent on important roll calls. In addition, legislators find the electronic system handy; it enables them to check how their colleagues are voting.

leaders. Individual senators can even bring bills directly to the floor, bypassing committees altogether. They do this by offering their bill as an amendment to whatever bill is then pending, even if the two are unrelated. These amendments have become known as **riders.** As you saw in the case study, Senator Jesse Helms of North Carolina tried unsuccessfully to add just such an unrelated amendment to the national-service program proposal.

But even if successful in the House and Senate, proposed legislation still faces hurdles. To become law, the bills passed in both houses of Congress must be worded identically. However, it is common for the two chambers to adopt similar but not identical bills. Sometimes the differences are resolved when one chamber adopts the language of the other. However, when the differences are not resolved (10 to 15 percent of the time), a conference committee composed of both House and Senate members forms to reconcile the differences in language and create a single version of the bill.[26] As noted in the case study, this occurred when the House and Senate passed different versions of the Americorps bill.

When the differences between versions of a bill have been ironed out, the final version is returned to both houses for approval. If it is then approved by both chambers, it becomes an **enrolled act,** or **resolution,** and is sent to the White House for the president's signature or veto. For measures that require spending, a separate **appropriation bill** must be passed to fund the measure. Thus, the Congress has two opportunities to debate a measure: first the measure itself, then the funding of it.

THE PRESIDENT CONSIDERS THE BILL   Once Congress has acted and sent a bill on to the president, four scenarios are possible. The president can sign the bill, and it becomes law. Or, the president can **veto** it; that is, return the bill to Congress with a statement of reasons for refusing to sign it. At that point, Congress can override the president's action only with a two-thirds vote in *both* the House and Senate. Congress can rarely muster this level of opposition to a sitting president, so vetoes are overridden less than 10 percent of the time.[27] President Bush, for example, successfully vetoed thirty-five consecutive pieces of legislation before Congress was finally able to muster the required votes to override his veto on cable TV regulation.

Two other outcomes are also possible. Once a bill reaches the president's desk, the president can simply do nothing, in which case the bill automatically becomes law after ten legislative days (not counting Sundays, and providing that Congress is still in session) in spite of remaining unsigned. The president can also refuse to sign a bill that Congress passes in the last ten days of its session. If Congress has adjourned, the unsigned bill automatically dies. This is called a **pocket veto.**

The mere threat of a veto can be a persuasive political lever that strengthens the president.[28] In 1985, for example, President Reagan borrowed from actor Clint Eastwood's movie character Dirty Harry and promised that any congressional tax increase would "make my day" and result in its immediate veto. No tax increase was passed. Sometimes, though, the veto threat can backfire. When Bill Clinton promised in 1994 to "take this pen and veto" any health-care bill that did not cover everyone, Congress chose, to Clinton's embarrassment, to pass nothing.

Now that we have an overview of how legislation is passed, let's explore the details of how Congress is organized.

HOW CONGRESS ORGANIZES ITSELF

Since the Constitution says very little about how each House of Congress should be organized, those structures have evolved over the decades. The result has been a tension between the centralizing influence of the congressional leadership and the decentralizing influence of the legislative subunits known as the committees and the subcommittees.

Congressional Leadership

LEADERSHIP IN THE HOUSE   The Constitution outlines only one presiding officer of the House, its most important figure, known as the **Speaker of the House.** Traditionally, this is the leader of the party with a majority of the seats. Currently, the Speaker is Republican Newt Gingrich of Georgia. One of the most powerful officeholders in the U.S. government, the Speaker would automatically become president in the event of the death or resignation of both the president and the vice president.

The Speaker's formal duties are to preside over the House when it is in session; to appoint all of the members to the Policy Committee, a representative body of the party conference that handles committee assignments and plans the legislative agenda; to appoint the party's legislative leaders and senior staff members; and to control the assignment of bills to committees.[29] When the majority party in the House is different from the president's party, the Speaker is often considered that party's national spokesperson.[30]

The power of the Speaker has varied over time. Around the turn of the twentieth century, Speakers Thomas Reed and Joseph Cannon were so powerful that they could personally appoint all committee chairs and determine committee membership, thus enabling them to personally block legislation and punish those who opposed them. Cannon's powers, though, were diluted by a House revolution in 1910. It was Speaker Sam Rayburn of Texas who exemplified from 1940 until his death in 1961 (with the exception of four years when the Republicans controlled the House) the use of all the formal and informal powers of the office. Rayburn's powers, however, were limited by the competing interests of entrenched conservative committee chairs.

A series of centralizing reforms in the 1970s made the speakership of Thomas ("Tip") O'Neill from 1977 to 1987 even more powerful. The Speaker was now able to dictate the selection of the committee chairs, committee members from the Speaker's party, and party members of the powerful Rules Committee. In addition, the office was given more power to refer bills to committees and dictate the order of the floor proceedings. Using these powers O'Neill became far more powerful than any Speaker since Cannon. The powers of the Speaker declined, though, when O'Neill's successor, James Wright of Texas, tried to use all of the office's powers for partisan goals, only to be forced to resign by a House revolt led by Georgia's Newt Gingrich. Ironically, it would be Gingrich who restored the Speaker's position to greater luster in 1995.

Little-known Fact

While the House Speaker has always been an elected member, the Constitution does not require it.

House Speaker Newt Gingrich receives the gavel from Democratic minority leader Richard Gephardt on the opening day of the 104th Congress (January 4, 1995). The gesture of passing the gavel symbolizes the transfer of power, in this case from Democrats to Republicans. Gingrich and Gephardt will lead their respective parties with help from colleagues in leadership positions.

House Speaker Newt Gingrich: A Man with a Vision

All Newton Leroy ("Newt") Gingrich ever wanted to be was Speaker of the U.S. House of Representatives. And all that stood in the way of this Republican history professor from West Georgia College (elected to Congress in 1978 from the Sixth District near Atlanta) was his party's 119-vote deficit in Congress, and the fact that no one outside of Atlanta had ever heard of him. But in the politics of the late twentieth century, a legislator's status and that of his or her party can change very quickly.

Raised in a military family, Gingrich had learned that life is a war won only by highly disciplined troops defending a clearly stated purpose. His clearly stated political purpose was to dismantle what he called the "corrupt liberal welfare state." So, unlike the freshmen representatives of days past, who served their early terms in silence, Gingrich began using C-SPAN (created in 1979) to give long televised speeches to a largely empty chamber. His goal: to energize a "grassroots" conservative constituency around the country.

Passing very little legislation, Gingrich sought instead to help his party achieve a working majority and make a name for himself. He became the "backbench" gadfly who waged guerilla warfare against Democratic Speaker Thomas P. ("Tip") O'Neill. He wrote books to share his views, founded the Conservative Opportunity Society, and took over a dying political action committee (called GOPAC, for Grand Old Party Action Committee), through which he could funnel campaign funds to conservative candidates. Slowly Gingrich began to tap into the growing national discontent with big government and politics as usual.

When Democrat James Wright became Speaker in 1987 it was Gingrich who goaded the media, the liberal Common Cause group, and eventually even Congress to probe for possible ethics violations relating to a book contract. Wright dismissed Gingrich as an "annoying gnat," but was soon forced to leave the House.

In 1989, Gingrich won the Republican post of minority whip by a mere two votes. But when the Republicans took over the House in 1995, it was partly because thirty-three of the seventy-three incoming freshmen had been recruited, trained, and financed by Gingrich and GOPAC. "Newt is like Moses," said congressional scholar Norman Ornstein. "He took them [the Republicans] out of captivity."

Since Minority Leader Robert Michel had just retired, as the former whip, Gingrich unanimously won election to the House as Speaker. In time, Gingrich may become the most powerful Speaker since the legendary Joe Cannon in the early twentieth century.

Sources: Based on Karen Tumulty, "Man with a Vision," *Time,* Jan. 9, 1995, p. 32; Howard Fineman, "The Warrior," *Newsweek,* Jan. 9, 1995, pp. 28–34; Adam Clymer, "Taking Power in the Age of Defiance," *New York Times,* Jan. 8, 1995, pp. E1, 3.

Next in line after the Speaker is the House **majority leader,** who in 1995 was Republican Richard Armey of Texas. The majority leader is elected by the party **caucus,** a conference of party members in Congress, and serves as the party's chief strategist and floor spokesperson. The majority leader also schedules bills and attempts to persuade members of the majority party to vote according to the party's official position on pending legislation.

The minority party is headed by the **minority leader,** in 1995 Democrat Richard Gephardt of Missouri. Should the minority party become the majority in Congress, the minority leader is likely to be a candidate for Speaker of the House.[31] Since the Republicans gained a majority in the House in 1994, and minority leader Robert Michel had retired, Newt Gingrich was able to make the dramatic move from his former whip position to his current one as Speaker.

Both the majority and minority party leaders work with the support of **whips,** who are charged with counting prospective votes on various issues and making certain that members have the information they need for floor action. The majority whip in 1995 is Thomas DeLay of Texas; the minority whip is David Bonior of Michigan. They are aided by a complex system of over 90 deputy whips, assistant regional whips and at-large whips.

LEADERSHIP IN THE SENATE   Other than making the vice president the **president of the Senate,** the Constitution does not specify a leadership structure for the Senate. However, the vice president presides over the Senate only on rare occasions—most commonly when a tie vote seems likely on a key piece of legislation. If a tie does ensue, the vice president can cast the deciding vote. Except for these rare moments and the occasional ceremonial event, the vice president rarely enters the Senate. To guide that body's day-to-day activities, the Constitution allows the election of a **president pro tempore.** This position is essentially honorary and goes by tradition to the majority party member with the longest continuous service. Strom Thurmond of South Carolina, first elected senator in 1954, currently holds the office. It is the president pro tempore who, in theory, presides over the Senate, although the position provides little political clout. The day-to-day task of the Senate presiding officer is usually farmed out to a wide range of senators, often junior ones who use the job to gain experience and "pay their dues."

The structure of party leadership in the Senate differs only slightly from its structure in the House. The majority party selects a Senate majority leader—currently Robert Dole of Kansas—whose functions are similar to those of the Speaker of the House.[32] The majority leader is responsible for scheduling legislation, directing committee assignments, and persuading members to vote along party lines. There is also a minority leader in the Senate—currently Tom Daschle of South Dakota—who works with the majority leader to establish the legislative agenda. As in the House, the majority and minority leaders are aided by whips, who help organize and count votes. The majority whip is Trent Lott of Mississippi; the minority whip is Wendell Ford of Kentucky.

The Senate majority leader is usually an influential politician. If the president is from the same party, the majority leader can be a valuable ally and spokesperson on Capitol Hill, as Democratic majority leader George Mitchell was for Bill Clinton during the 103rd Congress of 1993–94. But a majority leader who is a member of the opposing party can be among the president's toughest critics. Majority leader and Republican presidential aspirant Bob Dole used his position to stake out some clear differences between himself and the president he hoped to replace.

One of the most persuasive Senate majority leaders in recent history was Lyndon Baines Johnson of Texas, a Democrat who served as Senate leader from 1955 until he became vice president in 1961.[33] Nothing stood in Johnson's way. Once when Senator Hubert Humphrey of Minnesota was caught in a holding pattern flying over Washington and was needed for a key vote, Johnson ordered the air traffic controllers to clear the plane for immediate landing.

FYI

Whip is a fox-hunting term applied to the legislative process. During a fox hunt the whipper-in keeps the sniffing dogs from straying by whipping them back into the pack. Legislative whips are usually responsible for party discipline.

Senate majority leader Lyndon B. Johnson was known for administering the "Johnson treatment" to colleagues. Here he corners a fellow senator in search of a vote. A master at the art of political bargaining, Johnson had a talent for persuading members of the Senate to support him on key votes.

On another occasion, when Senator Alan Frear of Delaware opposed a bill, Johnson stood up on the floor of the Senate and yelled, "Change your goddamn vote!" Frear immediately complied.[34]

Modern congressional leaders, particularly in the Senate, are persuaders rather than dictators. They must be skilled at the give-and-take of bargaining and consensus building. The success of a Speaker or a Senate Majority Leader depends on how well they work with the leaders and members of the laboratories of Congress: the committees and subcommittees.

Congressional Committees: The Laboratories of Congress

Senator Nancy Kassebaum of Kansas, chair of the Senate Labor and Human Resources Committee, is the first woman to chair a major congressional committee. Here she conducts a committe meeting. Much like traffic lights at pedestrian crossings, the multicolored lights in front of her signal the amount of time committee members have for questions during hearings.

Some of Congress's most important work is done in committee and subcommittee. As Woodrow Wilson put it, "Congress on the floor is Congress on public exhibition; Congress in committee is Congress at work."[35]

There are four types of congressional committees: standing; select, or special; conference; and joint. Seats on all committees are allocated to each party in proportion to its representation in the entire House or Senate. Thus, the majority party in each house generally controls a corresponding majority in each committee. The assignment of members to committees is controlled by the party leadership. Figure 5.5 lists the key committees in Congress.

The most important committees in both houses of Congress are the **standing committees.** These permanent committees—seventeen in the Senate, eighteen in the House—determine whether proposed legislation should be sent to the entire chamber for consideration. Virtually all bills are considered by at least one standing committee and often by more than one. In 1994 five standing committees considered proposals for health-care reform: Ways and Means, Energy and Commerce, and Education and Labor in the House; Finance, and Labor and Human Resources in the Senate.

Select, or **special, committees** are established on a temporary basis to conduct investigations or study specific problems or crises. These committees

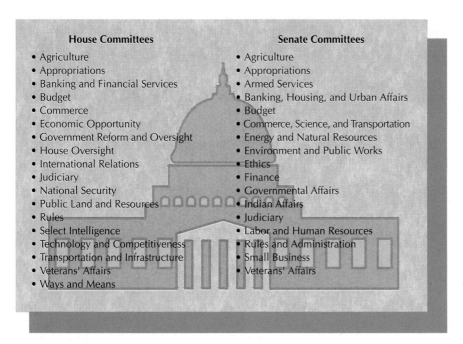

House Committees

- Agriculture
- Appropriations
- Banking and Financial Services
- Budget
- Commerce
- Economic Opportunity
- Government Reform and Oversight
- House Oversight
- International Relations
- Judiciary
- National Security
- Public Land and Resources
- Rules
- Select Intelligence
- Technology and Competitiveness
- Transportation and Infrastructure
- Veterans' Affairs
- Ways and Means

Senate Committees

- Agriculture
- Appropriations
- Armed Services
- Banking, Housing, and Urban Affairs
- Budget
- Commerce, Science, and Transportation
- Energy and Natural Resources
- Environment and Public Works
- Ethics
- Finance
- Governmental Affairs
- Indian Affairs
- Judiciary
- Labor and Human Resources
- Rules and Administration
- Small Business
- Veterans' Affairs

FIGURE 5.5 Key Committees in the House and Senate

possess no authority to propose bills and must be reauthorized by each new Congress. The creation and disbanding of these special committees mirror political forces in the nation at large. When a given issue is "hot" (e.g., concern about drug use, or hunger), pressures grow on Congress to act. Setting up special committees to investigate the matter may be one of Congress's responses. When the problem appears solved, the original pressure groups lose power, or interest in the issue dies away, the committee set up to deal with the problem also meets its end. On the other hand, if the original problem and the concerned constituency continue to grow, a new standing committee may be created, thus providing power and institutional permanence for those concerned with that issue.

Conference committees, as we have seen, are formed to reconcile differences between the versions of a bill passed by the House and the Senate. A conference committee can be very small, usually composed of the chairs of the relevant committees and subcommittees from each chamber.[36] On some major bills, however, as many as 250 representatives and senators may be involved. Conference committees rarely stay in existence for more than a few days.[37]

Since both houses jealously guard their independence and prerogatives, Congress establishes only a few **joint committees.** These groups, such as the Joint Economic Committee, consist of members from both chambers, and study broad areas that are of interest to Congress as a whole. More commonly, joint committees oversee congressional functioning and administration, such as the printing and distribution of federal government publications.

Why Does Congress Use Committees?

Committees enable Congress to do its work effectively by enabling members of Congress to consider several substantive matters at once. Each committee is concerned with a specific subject area, where members and staff develop

The select House and Senate committee investigating the Iran-Contra affair is shown here, in July 1987, as Lieutenant Colonel Oliver North takes the oath before testifying. The hearings were held in the historic Senate Caucus Room in the Russell Senate Office Building. Because they were televised, the hearings enabled millions of Americans to learn about the covert activities North pursued in the name of national security.

knowledge and expertise. Committees also provide a place for ideas to be transformed into policies on the basis of research and expert testimony. By providing multiple points of access for citizens and interest groups, committees serve as mini-legislative bodies representing the larger House or Senate.

Because committees play a major role in the operation of Congress, members actively seek seats on particular committees. In doing so, they have three goals in mind: to get reelected, to make good public policy, and to gain influence within the chamber.[38] The ideal committee helps them do all three. A seat on the House Rules Committee or the Ways and Means Committee, for instance, or on the Senate Appropriations Committee, ensures internal influence and authority.[39]

Other committees help members serve their districts directly. A representative from rural Illinois or California, both large agricultural states, might seek a seat on the agriculture committee. Membership on such a committee would increase the legislator's chances of influencing policies affecting constituents and thus be helpful at election time. As a former member who was on the Public Works Committee explains, "I could always go back to the district and say, 'Look at that road I got for you. See that beach erosion project over there? And those buildings? I got all those. I'm on Public Works.'"[40]

The committee system also provides opportunities for career advancement and public exposure. Consider the Senate Judiciary Committee, which holds confirmation hearings for Supreme Court nominees. A strong performance at these hearings can impress constituents, increase name recognition, and convey a positive, active image. But such visibility can also backfire. During the confirmation hearings for Judge Clarence Thomas, Senator Arlen Specter's reputation was damaged by the harsh manner in which he questioned a key witness, law professor Anita Hill, who had charged Thomas with sexual harassment. As a result, his appeal among women voters dropped sharply in his home state. He did manage to win reelection, but his margin of victory slipped from over half a million votes in 1986 to less than 140,000 in 1992.

The Rise of Subcommittees

Much of the legislative work of Congress is done in subcommittees, the smaller working groups that consider and draft legislation. In early 1995 the standing committees of the House included eighty-six subcommittees, while the Senate had forty-eight.[41] Subcommittees provide a further division of congressional labor. By narrowing the topic that members focus on, these groups allow for greater specialization. They also provide more opportunities for access to the legislative process. Subcommittees hold hearings to obtain a broad range of testimony from local administrators, group leaders, and individuals. Such hearings would be impossible for the whole House and difficult for a large committee, but are ideally suited to the smaller arena of the subcommittee.

Before 1970 congressional committees operated largely behind closed doors. The power of legislative decision making was concentrated in a few powerful chairs, traditionally appointed based on seniority, that were not representative of rank-and-file members. In the 1970s a revolution of sorts occurred. The younger rank-and-file members of Congress demanded and won more control over the policy agenda. In a crucial change, House Democrats made it technically possible to replace committee chairs by secret ballot of the entire caucus. They proceeded to underline that newly gained power by voting to replace three long-standing conservative chairs who were deemed to be seriously out of touch with the national party's moderate to liberal perspectives. Most Democratic chairs responded quickly to that lesson. They became remarkably open to rank-and-file concerns; only a handful got into trouble again while Democrats controlled the House.

Another crucial change adopted in the 1970s reform era brought a radical decentralization of power to the House. It is usually referred to as the *Subcommittee Bill of Rights* and involved the creation of additional subcommittees and seats on existing subcommittees.[42] Each House committee with more than twenty members had to create at least four standing subcommittees, and the committee chair could not easily tamper with subcommittee powers. Each subcommittee had its own chair, based largely on seniority (not political favoritism); it had the right to hire permanent staff people; and it could not be disbanded at the whim of the committee chair. All bills had to be referred to a subcommittee within two weeks of reaching the chair (thus preventing that person from killing bills by ignoring them). With this reform, subcommittee chairs became powerful, owing their position to no one person, heading groups that couldn't be easily dissolved, and commanding staff resources to support their work.

One additional fact ensured an extreme decentralization of power in the House. No one was allowed to head more than *one* of these many subcommittees. Thus, instead of the handful of powerful barons that ran Congress in the 1950s, a couple of hundred scattered knights held power of some kind or another in the 1980s: the heads at the time of the more than one hundred House and eighty Senate subcommittees. A recent reform reduced the number of subcommittees.

Congress on TV

Congress on TV? Well, yes. It may not stand very high in the ratings, but if you have cable television you can watch Congress in action. In 1979, for the first time, the House of Representatives voted to allow television cameras to record its proceedings. The cable television industry jumped in with both feet, creating the Cable-Satellite Public Affairs Network, or C-SPAN.

C-SPAN began with coverage of floor debate, open hearings, and other public business in the House. In 1986 the Senate too opened its doors to the cameras, and C-SPAN II was created to present continuous coverage of Senate debate and public hearings. Three years later C-SPAN offered American viewers a fascinating opportunity to compare their legislature with Britain's when it began airing excerpted broadcasts from the House of Commons.

The introduction of television cameras to Congress brought legislative politics into the homes of millions of people. It also provided a peculiar benefit to some legislators. Many of the young, conservative Republican representatives who rode into office on President Reagan's coattails in 1980 used the direct public access afforded by C-SPAN to attack their Democratic opponents after the business of the day had been completed and their colleagues had gone home. Standing in the empty House chamber, they delivered impassioned speeches that created the impression that they were tough enough to "take on" Congress. The Democrats responded by demanding that the cameras periodically show the empty chamber, revealing that no one was there to listen to these vigorous performances.

C-SPAN may bring Congress into the homes of Americans, but how much of Congress do viewers actually get to see? Actually, more than they used to. Prior to 1994 the televised coverage of the Senate and the House was directed solely to floor debates and votes, an arena more of rhetoric than action. In the 1994 election campaign, C-SPAN began covering the congressional races with news programming and commentary programs in such detail that public-opinion polls showed that C-SPAN viewers were more knowledgeable about Congress and thus more likely to participate in the political process. As a result, Republican incumbent candidates in the 1994 campaign began tailoring their speeches on the House floor to appeal to voters in the viewing audience. Realizing that the real work—the deliberations and hearings in committees—was never seen, the Republican-dominated 104th Congress made all open committee meetings available for televised and radio coverage.

While you might expect that the televised coverage of Congress's long-winded speeches and arcane parliamentary procedures would contribute to the public's generally negative view of Congress, in fact it may actually help to improve public confidence in Congress. Televised coverage of Congress provides at least some American viewers with an opportunity not available in most other nations: the chance to observe legislative activity at first hand. As a result of C-SPAN, the House and Senate are open not only to residents and tourists in Washington but to anyone interested enough to tune in.

This proliferation of subcommittees has had effects beyond decentralizing congressional power. For one thing, interest groups can now influence bills merely by supporting and persuading a handful of legislators—those legislators on a particular subcommittee. For another, it has made the legislative process more unwieldy, giving many individual members a veto over legislation. For example, thirty committees and seventy-seven subcommittees played a role in shaping the 1992 defense budget. Moreover, as the number of subcommittees has grown, so has the amount of time a legislator must devote to committee business. Many find it impossible even to read the bills, and so must rely on staff members and lobbyists to provide them with information about pending legislation.[43] As a result of these drawbacks, the decentralization of power represented by subcommittee government, once heralded as an important reform, came under strong attack by the Republican Congress of 1995.

Fully understanding how a bill becomes a law, and how that process has changed because of the evolution of Congress over the last several decades, leads us to explore the rules and norms that govern the body as whole, and the voting decisions of individual members.

CONGRESS IN SESSION

Together with the power and influence of congressional leaders and committee and subcommittee chairs, the rules and procedures of the House and Senate shape the outcomes of the legislative process.[44]

The Rules and Norms of Congress

The formal rules of Congress can be found in the Constitution, in the standing rules of each house, and in Thomas Jefferson's *Manual of Parliamentary Practice and Precedent.* Congressional rules, for example, dictate the timing, extent, and nature of floor debate. Imagine what might happen without rules. If, for example, each of the 435 members of the House tried to rise on the floor and speak for just one minute on just one bill, debate would last at least seven hours, not taking into account the time needed for amendments, procedural matters, and votes.

THE HOUSE RULES COMMITTEE   As noted earlier, the House Rules Committee plays a key role, directing the flow of bills through the legislative process. Except for revenue, budget, and appropriations bills, which are *privileged legislation* and go directly to the House floor from committee, bills that have been approved in a substantive committee are referred to the Rules Committee. The rules issued by the House Rules Committee determine which bills will be discussed, how long the debate will last, and which amendments will be allowed.[45] Rules can be either *open,* allowing members to freely suggest related amendments from the floor; *closed,* permitting no amendments except those offered by the sponsoring committee members; or *restrictive,* now the most commonly used procedure, which limits amendments to certain parts of a bill and dictates which members can offer such amendments. By refusing to attach a rule to a bill, the committee can delay the bill's consideration or even kill it.

During the 1950s the Rules Committee was dominated by conservative members who succeeded in blocking civil rights, education, and welfare legislation even though it was favored by a majority of House members.[46] Today, however, as a result of a series of democratizing reforms, such as empowering the Speaker to appoint all of the committee's members, the Rules Committee has become what Republican member Porter J. Goss calls "the handmaiden of the Speaker," directing the flow and nature of the legislative process according to the majority party's wishes.[47] If the Speaker wants a bill, the rule is passed; if not, the rule is denied; and if a long debate would prove embarrassing to the majority party, only a short debate under a closed rule will likely be allowed. Thus, contrary to earlier days when whole sessions of

Congress would pass without even a vote on a key issue, using his total control over the Rules Committee, Speaker Newt Gingrich directed the House to vote on each of the points of the Contract With America in the first one hundred days of the 104th Congress.

Because the Senate is smaller and more decentralized than the House, its rules for bringing a matter to the floor are much more relaxed. There is no rules committee; instead, while the majority leader has the formal power to do the scheduling, an informal agreement is usually made with the minority leader to accomplish this task. This scheduling is accomplished by the submission of *unanimous-consent agreements,* a waiver of the rules for consideration of a measure by a vote of all of the members. With no central traffic cop to control the flow of legislation, some bills are considered on the floor for weeks, even overlapping with the consideration of other measures, often at the expense of the substance of the measure.

AMENDMENTS TO A BILL A key procedural rule in the House requires that all discussion on the floor and all amendments to legislation must be germane, or relevant, to the bill being considered. The Senate, in contrast, places no limits on the addition of amendments to a bill.

The ability to attach unrelated *riders* to a bill can sometimes help a senator to secure the passage of a pet project by attaching it to a popular proposal. However, the use of riders can lead to problems. When budget bills are being considered, for example, members may add so many riders, each containing spending provisions desired by those individual members, that the result is known as a "Christmas tree bill" or a "budget buster." Because the president was required to either sign or veto a bill in its entirety, leading to spending bills that contained expensive pet projects inserted by legislators, Congress debited in 1995 a "line item veto" that would allow specific provisions to be vetoed independently of the rest of the bill, with Congress retaining the ability to override a veto. Whether this law, which could cut deeply into Congress's budgetary powers, will be passed and ruled constitutional in the inevitable Supreme Court challenge remains to be seen.

FILIBUSTERS AND CLOTURE There are few restrictions on debate in the Senate. It is possible to derail a bill by means of a **filibuster.** You will recall from the case study that Republican senators opposed to Americorps attempted to kill it with a filibuster. This technique allows a senator to speak against a bill, or talk about anything at all, just to "hold the floor" and prevent the Senate from moving forward with its business. He or she may yield to other like-minded senators, so that the marathon debate can continue for hours, or even days. The record for the longest individual filibuster belongs to Senator Strom Thurmond of South Carolina, who spoke against the Civil Rights Act of 1957 for an uninterrupted twenty-four hours and nineteen minutes.

Over time the Senate has made filibusters less strenuous, first by interrupting them when the Senate's workday ended, and then by allowing them to be interrupted by a vote to consider other work. In recent years, senators have begun using a scheduling rule called a "hold" on legislation, indicating that they would filibuster a bill if concessions were not offered by the bill's supporters.[48] Thus, several bills can be delayed at once.

Now the filibuster has become such a prevalent threat that any senator has the potential to derail any piece of legislation. Between 1940 and 1965 only nineteen filibusters were employed for major legislation, while between 1992 and 1994 the Republicans alone maintained twenty-eight filibusters. In fact, there were more filibusters in this period than in the previous sixty years.

How can the Senate get any work done under these conditions? In 1917 it adopted a procedure known as **cloture,** through which senators can vote to limit debate and stop a filibuster. Originally cloture required approval of two-thirds of the senators present and voting (sixty-seven members if all were present), but when such a vote proved too difficult to achieve, the required majority was reduced to three-fifths of the members, or sixty votes.

Although the majority required for a cloture vote can be difficult to muster, the number of successful cloture votes has increased in recent years.[49] Even if cloture has been voted, however, a postcloture filibuster can still continue for thirty more hours.[50] The reduction of the cloture requirement from two-thirds to 60 percent goes a long way toward explaining its increasing success as does a shift in attitudes in the Senate favoring greater efficiency.

Few congressional rules raise such interesting questions about Congress's ability to approach democracy as the Senate's filibuster and cloture devices. Does the ability to talk a bill to death, or to silence those seeking to do so, promote or hinder the democratic process? Liberals who objected to the use of filibusters to stall civil rights legislation took advantage of that same tactic to combat the conservative agenda of the Reagan administration. Some argue that the filibuster empowers minorities, while others claim that it is simply a stalling tactic that obstructs the will of the majority. The cloture rule can likewise be seen two ways.

To place the filibuster in perspective, remember that although it is abused on occasion, senators use it only on major issues where a large minority is intensely opposed to what the majority is trying to do. Unhappy minorities shouldn't necessarily win all they want, but neither can any political system remain healthy if it systematically neglects the demands of a large minority. Filibusters force the majority at least to hear the minority and perhaps respond to some minority demands. All in all, the benefits of the filibuster in giving voice to minorities probably outweigh the frustrations it creates for the majority.

INFORMAL RULES AND NORMS   In addition to the formal rules described above, Congress, like most large organizations, has informal, unwritten rules that facilitate its day-to-day operations. High among these is the rule of **seniority.** A member's rank in both House and Senate depends on how long he or she has served in that chamber. In the past the only way to become chair of a committee was by accumulating more years of continuous service on that committee than any other majority party member. Even membership on committees was tied to seniority. A companion to this norm once was the norm of *apprenticeship,* whereby younger members were expected to sit quietly and learn their legislative craft from their elders.

There has been some dilution of the seniority and apprenticeship norms over time, however. In the 104th Congress, Speaker of the House Newt Gingrich passed over several senior party colleagues in naming the chairs of three

Republican senator Jesse Helms of North Carolina, an ultra conservative and long-time senator (he has served for 22 years), heads the Senate Foreign Relations Committee. When Helms received the chairmanship, there was speculation that he would seek to cut foreign aid and contributions to the United Nations.

key House committees: Appropriations, Commerce, and Judiciary. This suggests that a new norm, *political loyalty,* might be replacing seniority, at least in the House.[51] In addition, the increased visibility of the junior members (over one-half of the freshmen in the 104th Congress made their maiden floor speech in the opening session), suggests a lessening of the apprenticeship norm.

The Senate is currently more traditional in its regard for seniority. In 1953, some dilution of seniority rights began when Senate Minority Leader Lyndon Johnson instituted what became known as the *Johnson rule,* which provided that no Democratic senator would receive more than one major committee assignment until everyone had one. Republicans adopted a similar rule in 1965. Thirty years later, however, when the Republicans once again controlled the Senate, Majority Leader Bob Dole decided instead to let seniority determine every committee chair, even though several Republican colleagues were uncomfortable with some of the results—most notably, archconservative Jesse Helms of North Carolina chairing the Foreign Relations Committee, and ninety-two-year-old Strom Thurmond of South Carolina chairing the Armed Services Committee.

Two norms used to push legislation through Congress are **specialization** and **reciprocity.** Legislators are expected to develop a certain expertise on one or more issues as a way to help the body in its lawmaking role. As a result, those members who lack expertise in a particular policy area defer to policy specialists with more knowledge, with the understanding that the favor will be reciprocated.

When reciprocity is applied to votes on key measures it results in a process called **logrolling,** which helps legislators cooperate effectively. The term comes from a competition in which two lumberjacks maintain their balance on a floating log by spinning it with their feet. In congressional logrolling, legislators seek the assistance of colleagues by offering to support legislation the colleagues both favor. For example, a Democratic senator from California might support a flood control project in Mississippi that has no relevance to West Coast voters, provided that the Republican senator from Mississippi promises to support a measure delaying the closing of an army base in California.[52]

In addition to formal and informal rules, Congress has a number of traditional norms that keep it running smoothly. One of those traditions is that of resolving the House or Senate into a *committee of the whole* in which all members gather together in the capacity of a committee rather than as a formal legislative body. Committee rules are looser and less formal than those that apply to the full House. For instance, only 100 House members need be present when the House is operating as the Committee of the Whole, whereas normally it takes 218 representatives on the floor to conduct business.

Another norm of Congress is designed to keep friction to a minimum. Debates on the floor and in committees are conducted with the utmost civility. One member never speaks directly to another; instead, members address the presiding officer, who may deflect damaging comments by ruling them out of order. Titles, not names, are used, as in "I would like to commend the senior senator from State X . . ." As you might expect, despite this norm, there are occasional breakdowns. As the two parties grow further apart and harden their ideological positions, angry and bitter words are, with ever-increasing frequency, being tossed back and forth on House and Senate floors.

Now we will look beyond the operations of the entire body to the actions of the individual legislator.

How Members Make Voting Decisions

Political scientists have long sought to understand why members of Congress vote as they do. Their research suggests seven major sources of influence.

PARTY AFFILIATION   A member's vote can be explained by his or her political party affiliation. The number of times that members of Congress vote based on party position has steadily increased from below 60 percent in 1970 to over 80 percent in the 1990s.[53] Sometimes, though, the members don't vote according to party. Democratic senator Sam Nunn of Georgia, for example, was more likely to support than oppose the initiatives of his supposed opponents, Republican presidents Reagan and Bush.[54] In the 104th Congress, two Democrats, Alabama senator Richard Shelby and Colorado senator Ben Nighthorse Campbell, found themselves voting so many times with the opposition party that they switched to the Republican party.

If the national party leadership or the president is committed to a particular vote, the chances of a vote along party lines are even greater. If the party's position runs counter to the member's personal views, however, it is less likely to influence the way he or she votes.[55]

CONSTITUENTS   Constituents have a significant influence on their representative's voting decisions.[56] No representative wants to lose touch with the district or appear to care more about national politics than about the people back home. This was why Oklahoma representative Mike Synar, a four-term liberal Democrat who supported gun control and the Family Leave Act while opposing a measure requiring parents to be notified if a teenaged daughter has an abortion, was defeated in a 1994 primary in his conservative district. Said a former supporter: "He's just lost touch." To avoid this, members regularly return to their districts to learn how constituents feel about issues on the congressional agenda.

THE PRESIDENT   Sometimes the president seeks to influence a member's vote by calling him or her to the White House for a consultation. The president may offer something in return (e.g., support for another piece of legislation or a spending project in the member's district) or threaten some kind of punishment for noncompliance. Sometimes the purpose of the consultation is simply to make the member look important to the voters back home—but even that serves as a political favor, inducing the member to look more kindly on presidential requests for legislative support.[57]

Presidential lobbying of undecided or politically exposed members can be a key factor in the outcome of a vote. First-term representative Marjorie Margolies-Mezvinsky of Pennsylvania learned this lesson in the summer of 1993, when her party's congressional leadership pressed for support of a deficit reduction bill that would raise taxes and offend her predominantly Republican constituents. On the day of the vote, Margolies-Mezvinsky decided to oppose the bill. However, when the vote was tied at 217 to 217 (which meant that the bill would fail), President Clinton implored her to back the bill for the good of the country and the party. After casting the deciding vote in favor of the bill, during the 1994 election she lost to the very same Republican she had beaten two years earlier.[58]

Senator Dianne Feinstein, one of the few Democrats to win reelection in the 1994 elections, worked hard to bring her message directly to constituents. Her challenger, Michael Huffington, broke all campaign-spending records, but Feinstein managed to get her message heard and retain her seat.

INTEREST GROUPS   Important interest groups and political action committees that have provided funds for past elections will try to influence a member's vote by lobbying intensely on key issues. In addition, lobbying organizations seek access to members of Congress through personal visits and calls.[59] Sometimes they apply pressure by generating "grassroots" campaigns among the general public, jamming members' phone lines and fax machines and filling their mail bags. In 1987 both liberal and conservative groups prevailed on followers to pressure the Senate concerning controversial judge Robert Bork's nomination for the Supreme Court. So many calls came in during this debate that some members' telephone switchboards literally broke down.

PERSONAL CONVICTIONS   The personal views of members of Congress can play a prominent role in their voting decisions. Recall, for example, Senator Harris Wofford's heartfelt plea to fellow Senator Bob Kerrey in the case study. When members care deeply about a policy matter, they usually vote their own preferences, sometimes risking their political careers in the process. Party leaders recognize the importance of personal convictions. "I have never asked a member to vote against his conscience," said former Speaker of the House John McCormack. "If he mentions his conscience—that's all. I don't press him any further."[60]

Sometimes such votes show the best aspects of congressional representation. In early 1995, Republican senator Mark Hatfield was so unwilling to provide his party with the winning vote to pass the balanced-budget amendment, saying that he opposed "tinkering with the Constitution," that he offered to resign instead. (Majority Leader Robert Dole declined the offer.)

CONGRESSIONAL STAFF   One of the functions of congressional staff members is to sort through the various sources of pressure and information. In so doing, they themselves become a source of pressure on members to vote in a particular way. Staff members organize hearings, conduct research, draft bill markups and amendments, prepare reports, assist committee chairs, interact with the press, and perform other liaison activities with lobbyists and constituents. In addition, as important players in the political game, they have their own preferences on many issues. With their expertise and political commitments, they can often convince members of Congress to vote for the bills they favor. However, since members of Congress will normally hire people whose political views reinforce their own, most often staff people simply help members of Congress be more efficient at what they want to do anyway: please their constituents, promote their party, and vote their convictions.[61]

Congressional staffs proliferated in the 1960s as the federal government grew in size and complexity. Members of both houses of Congress became increasingly dependent on staff for information about proposed legislation. Moreover, in an effort to stay closer to voters, members established district-based offices staffed by aides.[62] Today, more than twenty-five thousand staffers are employed by the House and the Senate. The number of staff members was cut nearly 30 percent by the new Republican leaders of Congress in 1995.

COLLEAGUES AND THE "CUE STRUCTURE"   What does a legislator do when all these influences—party leadership, president, personal convictions, voters, interest groups, and staff—are sending different messages about how to vote

Life of a Legislator

You might think of members of Congress as spending their days debating important issues and voting on major legislation, and their evenings attending receptions and fancy dinner parties. But in reality the life of a legislator is far from glamorous. Consider this story, told by former senator Daniel Evans: "My wife Nancy and I held a long-planned reception at our home for a former senator. It was a pleasant affair until the jarring sound of a dozen paging devices suddenly filled the room. Senators dashed to the door and headed to the chamber for a roll-call vote, leaving the remaining guests waiting. When we arrived at the Senate we learned that the vote was an inconsequential procedural matter, then we spent an hour arguing about whether another vote was required that evening."*

As this incident illustrates, members of Congress are never free from the demands of their jobs. Indeed, you may be surprised to discover just how hectic their lives really are. Debating and voting on legislation is just a small part of a member's job. On a typical day, the average member of Congress attends ten meetings, gives two or three interviews, makes an appearance at several receptions, conducts one or two congressional hearings, sees as many constituents and campaign contributors as can be fit into fifteen-minute blocks of time, and fills the remainder of the time answering mail, returning phone calls, and seeking money for reelection. The reward for a day's work is often a ten o'clock dinner at one's desk while the work continues. Legislators must also find time to visit their districts, attend to casework and pending legislation, and of course, campaign for reelection. All of these activities are carried out under the close scrutiny of reporters eager to publicize the slightest misstep.

The intense pace of the legislator's work leaves little time for personal life. Former senator Dan Quayle of Indiana found that the only time he could spend with his family was at picnics held on the Capitol Hill lawn between meetings and votes.† Former senator David Boren of Oklahoma tried to arrange a dinner at home with his wife, but found he could not do so for twenty-seven days.** Members whose families remain in their districts have to devise other arrangements. Some fly home for overnight visits despite the cost and frequent delays in air travel. Others live in Washington during the week and return home on weekends (but find those off days taken up with meetings with constituents). In addition, this dual-residence arrangement is expensive. To cut down on costs, four representatives chose to share a two-bedroom town house near the Capitol. Their "little den on D Street" is notorious for its unmade beds and empty refrigerator surrounded by counters littered with fast-food containers, and the roll-out couch bed occupied by the most junior member.†† In the 104th Congress some freshmen Republicans tried to save some money and indicate their dedication to the job of "citizen legislator" by actually living in their cramped Hill offices—sleeping on a futon next to their desk, eating in the Capitol building cafeteria, and showering in the House gymnasium.

It is clear that successful legislators need more than the political skills necessary to win public office. They must also be able to deal with all the daily personal and professional demands placed on them. (Senator Boren's method was to find a less demanding job; he became the president of the University of Oklahoma.) It is likely that the framers didn't anticipate the fast-paced lives led by their twentieth-century counterparts. Had they done so, they might have demanded "energy in the legislature" as well as in the executive.

*Daniel Evans, "Why I'm Quitting the Senate," *New York Times Magazine,* Apr. 17, 1988, pp. 48, 49.

†Tim Wirth, "Diary of a Dropout," *New York Times Magazine,* Aug. 9, 1992, pp. 25–36.

**David L. Boren, "Why I am Leaving the Senate," *New York Times,* May 13, 1994, p. A31.

††Todd S. Purdum, "For 4 Collegial Congressmen, Life Looks a Lot Like College," *New York Times,* May 30, 1994, pp. A1, 21.

on a particular bill? And what does a member do when there is not enough time to gather the necessary information about an issue before voting on it? To help them make quick decisions about how to vote, members develop a personal intelligence system that scholars label a *cue structure*. The cues can come from a number of sources: members of Congress who are experts, including members of a committee dealing with the bill; a knowledgeable member of the executive branch; key lobbyists; or media reports.[63] Sometimes the cues can come from special groups within Congress, such as the Black or Women's Caucuses, the Democratic Study Group, or the Republicans' Conservative Opportunity Society. Members also get cues from their particular "buddy system": other members whom they respect, who come from the same kinds of districts, and who have similar goals.[64]

Obstacles to Passage of a Bill

The backers of any bill must win support at each stage of all the lawmaking process: They must find majorities in each committee, they must find enthusiastic backers during each formal discussion, and so forth. Opponents of the bill have a much easier job. They can kill it at any step along the way. Sometimes they don't even need a majority—one unfriendly legislator in the right place may be sufficient.

To illustrate this point, imagine how you as a member of Congress could stop a bill you disliked. Here are some of the ways you could take action.

1. Lobby members of your party conference or caucus to stop, or at least slow down, consideration of the bill.

2. Convince the Speaker to stop, or slow down, consideration of the bill.

3. Lobby committee and subcommittee members to oppose the bill in committee hearings, deliberations, markups, and votes.

4. Lobby the Rules Committee to oppose giving the bill a rule, which dictates the timing and terms of a bill's debate.

5. Lobby colleagues on the House floor not to vote for the rule, thus preventing the bill from ever reaching floor discussion.

6. Speak against the bill on the House floor, get allies to speak against it, propose a series of amendments that weaken the bill or make it less attractive to potential supporters, vote against it at every opportunity.

7. If the bill does gain passage in the House, use the same tactics to stop it in the Senate, mustering opposition in committees and on the Senate floor.

8. Find senators who hate the bill and persuade them to "filibuster," or talk it to death in the Senate; or place a "hold" on it yourself.

9. If both House and Senate pass the bill, work against it in the conference committee, if one is needed.

10. If Congress passes the bill, seek allies in the White House who might persuade the president to veto it.

11. Once the bill becomes law, use similar steps to prevent Congress from funding the measure.

12. If the bill becomes law and is funded, work to rescind the law or to keep funding too low for it to be effective.

13. If all else fails, encourage some group to mount a constitutional challenge to the law, going all the way to the Supreme Court if necessary.

This array of blocking options favors those who oppose change. What you think of this system depends on how you like the status quo. A majority of congressional liberals in the 1960s often felt frustrated by the difficulty in working their agenda through an allied conservative minority of Republicans and Southern Democrats. Today, however, some of those same liberals find some value in these legislative obstacles.

The entire process works more or less as the framers intended. With the Constitution silent on all but a few rules of Congress, this complex legislative system slowly evolved to ensure that no idea can break through the maze of political roadblocks without securing wide general support of both the short- and long-term interests from many segments of society. Observes congressional scholar Ross Baker, "If James Madison were to come back and sit in the gallery of the House and Senate, he'd be pretty pleased with the way things are working."[65]

THE FUNCTIONS OF CONGRESS: OVERSIGHT AND BUDGET CONTROL

Aside from enacting legislation, two of the most important functions of Congress are oversight and budget control. Congressional **oversight** involves monitoring the effectiveness of laws passed by Congress. The Legislative Reorganization Act of 1946 specifically directs the committees of Congress to exercise "continuous watchfulness" over the agencies of the executive branch that actually carry out the laws and to supervise them to see that the laws are implemented as Congress intended. This oversight can be either *legislative* (in the form of pilot programs, special studies, or cost–benefit analysis) or *investigative* (in the form of hearings to examine possible legal or ethical infractions).[66] Examples of oversight investigations include the 1974 hearings on Watergate, the 1987 hearings on the Iran-Contra scandal, and the 1995 hearings on President and Mrs. Clinton's involvement in the Whitewater land development deal.[67]

Congress's budget-control powers are contained in the Constitution, which grants Congress the power to levy taxes, borrow money, coin money, regulate commerce among the states, and spend for the general welfare. All tax legislation (the raising of money) must originate in the House, but tax bills, along with appropriations bills (the spending of money), need approval from both House and Senate. This **power of the purse** is central to Congress's role. Through its influence on money matters, Congress can shape nearly every policy undertaken by the national government.[68]

In 1974 Congress passed the Congressional Budget and Impoundment Control Act. This legislation created the Congressional Budget Office (CBO), permanent budget committees in the House and Senate, and a new budget timetable. The act was intended to expand congressional control over the national budget at a time when the president usually dominated the process. The House and Senate budget committees review the president's annual budget as well as the projections made by the CBO. The CBO establishes budget totals and spending outlays, loan obligations, and deficit reduction strategies for the federal government.[69]

Formed in 1971, the Congressional Black Caucus has sought to actively promote the interests of African Americans. The caucus put strong pressure on the Clinton administration to do something during the crisis in Haiti. However, Republican ascendancy in both Houses of Congress meant lost eligibility for official funding for the Caucus and other legislative service organizations. Questions arose about just how much power and influence the Caucus would be able to wield as a result. Here, the head of the Black Caucus, Donald Payne, answers reporters' questions.

THE '94 ELECTIONS AND THE FUTURE OF CONGRESS

On January 4, 1995, the opening session of the 104th Congress, Republicans promised to use their 230-to-204-member advantage in the House to implement the party's "Contract with America." This pledge guaranteed that votes would be held in the House in the first hundred days on such popular issues as terms limits for Congress, a balanced-budget amendment, tax cuts for the middle class, changes in social security, crime bill changes, and welfare reform.

Seeking to speed this change, Speaker Gingrich moved to reduce the power of committee and subcommittee chairs, and disperse the increased power among the individual members. A six-year term limit was placed on the tenure of all committee and subcommittee chairs and members of the Budget Committee, reducing their long-term influence. In addition, Gingrich and his team of subordinates organized a series of planning meetings, issued a set of legislative schedules, and required legislative progress reports, to keep everyone focused on the mission at hand. Some would argue that Gingrich then increased the power of his own office, but in fact, he approached democracy by distributing more power to the individual members of Congress. With so much work to be done, committee and subcommittee chairs had no choice but to delegate important bill-drafting and -passing responsibilities to freshmen members. The changes in the institution were dramatic. "We have democratized the structure and the culture of our committees. Everybody matters," explained New York Republican Bill Paxon.[70] Seeking to mobilize the general public, Gingrich spent as much time on political spin as he did on the legislative flow, rivaling only President Clinton with his press and media attention. On April 7, 1995, Gingrich was even given network time to speak to the nation about Congress's achievements. By the end of the first hundred days of the 104th Congress, the House had held votes on all ten areas of promised legislation, passing all of them but term limits.

Despite these accomplishments, the House Republicans found the Senate acting as the "saucer that cooled" the House's tea. Gripped in "Byrdlock," the name given to the delaying tactics of Senator Robert Byrd of West Virginia, who displayed his mastery of the rules in launching a personal filibuster, the Senate took a full month just to consider the Balanced-Budget Amendment, before failing to pass it. Of the promised legislation in the "Contract with America," the Senate passed only the bills on congressional reforms, unfunded mandates, the line item veto, and paperwork reduction in the first 100 days.

Congress was working exactly as the framers intended, with the House providing an immediate response to public will and the Senate offering its evaluation more deliberatively. The voters will have to decide in 1996 how quickly they want government policy to follow.

CONGRESS AND APPROACHING DEMOCRACY

The complexity of the legislative process we've just explored was intended not to prevent the passage of legislation but to encourage a series of majority compromises on it along the way. The bicameral system, the committees, the complicated rules of Congress, the conference committee, the president's signature on legislation were all designed to allow differing views to be heard before legislation could be passed.

Although members of Congress are often sincere, honest, hard-working, and dedicated to doing a difficult job under trying circumstances, the institution in which they serve continually faces criticism. When Congress works in a deliberative fashion, as it was meant to, it is labeled as obstructionist; when it approves most of the president's programs, it is accused of being a rubber stamp. And if it takes strong actions on its own, it is accused of overreaching its powers.[71] Clearly the truth lies somewhere among these extremes. Above all, we need to recognize that Congress is a consensus-building institution in a nation where public preferences are frequently contradictory. For example, thinking back to the case study on Americorps, the Republican Congress sought in early 1995 to drastically cut the funding for the same program that had been passed two years before by the Democratic Congress.

Does Congress help America approach democracy? We have seen that as an institution Congress is criticized as being hopelessly inefficient, fragmented, and paralyzed by gridlock. Whether the actions of the Republican Congress under its "Contract with America" help to change that perception, or whether it positions the institution in an unaccustomed role as the leading generator of public policy, remains to be seen. What can be said is that the public in 1994 wanted change in government, and the House is certainly providing that appearance.

The strength of Congress, indeed its very constitutional purpose in American democracy, is its closeness to the people and its representational base. "To refine and enlarge public views" remains the principal responsibility of the national legislature and its most pressing challenge as Congress and America approach democracy and the twenty-first century.

SUMMARY

1. The Constitution established a bicameral Congress consisting of a House of Representatives whose members serve two-year terms and a Senate whose members serve six-year terms. Congress was given numerous major powers, including the power to collect taxes, declare war, and regulate commerce. The necessary and proper clause enables it to interpret these powers broadly.

2. A disproportionate number of Congress's members are rich white males drawn from the fields of law, banking, and big business. The ethnic diversity of Congress has increased in the twentieth century, but it still falls short of that of the population as a whole.

3. Today, each congressional district contains about 570,000 citizens. The number of representatives from each state is adjusted after each census (reapportionment). In states that gain or lose seats, district boundaries must be redrawn (redistricting). The term *gerrymander* is used to describe the often bizarre district boundaries that are drawn to favor the party in power.

4. Members of Congress sometimes find themselves torn between the role of delegate, in which they feel bound to follow the wishes of constituents, and the role of trustee, in which they use their best judgment regardless of the wishes of constituents. In practice, they tend to combine these roles.

5. Incumbents have several advantages over their challengers in an election, including greater name recognition, the franking privilege, the services of staff members, legislative experience, and greater financial backing. These advantages have led critics to call for legislation limiting the length of time members may serve in Congress.

6. A member of Congress places an issue on the congressional agenda by drafting a bill and submitting it to the House or Senate. The bill is then referred to the appropriate committee, whose chair assigns it to a subcommittee. After holding hearings on the proposed legislation, the subcommittee holds a markup session in which the language of the bill is revised. It then returns the bill to the full commit-

tee. If the committee approves the bill, it is then sent to the full House or Senate. If the two chambers pass different versions of a bill, it is sent to a conference committee, which reconciles the differences and creates a single bill. If the final version is approved by both chambers, it goes to the president to be signed or vetoed.

7. The presiding officer of the House is the leader of the majority party and is known as the Speaker of the House. Next in line is the House majority leader, who serves as the party's chief strategist. The minority party is headed by the minority leader, and both party leaders are assisted by whips. In the Senate, the majority party elects a president pro tempore, but this is essentially an honorary position. As in the House, there are majority and minority party leaders and whips.

8. There are four types of congressional committees: standing (permanent); select, or special (temporary); conference; and joint. Much of the legislative work of Congress is done in subcommittees. The power of the subcommittees since the 1970s has made the legislative process rather unwieldy, prompting calls for reform.

9. In the House, the Rules Committee determines what issues will be discussed, when, and under what conditions. In the Senate, scheduling is done by the majority leader in consultation with the minority leader. In the Senate there are no limits on floor debate. As a result, it is possible to derail a bill by means of a filibuster, in which a senator talks continuously to postpone or prevent a vote. Filibusters can be halted only by cloture, in which sixty or more senators vote to end the discussion.

10. The voting decisions of members of Congress are influenced by party affiliation, constituents, the president, interest groups, personal convictions, and congressional staff. Members also get cues about how to vote from their "buddy system" of other members whom they respect.

KEY TERMS

bicameral
elastic clause
reapportionment
gerrymander
delegates
trustees
incumbents
franking privilege
casework
lobbyists
congressional agenda
hearings
markup session

riders
enrolled act, or resolution
appropriation bill
veto
pocket veto
Speaker of the House
House majority leader
caucus
minority leader
whip
president of the Senate
president pro tempore
Senate majority leader

standing committees
select, or special, committees
conference committees
joint committees
filibuster
cloture
seniority
specialization
reciprocity
logrolling
oversight
power of the purse

SUGGESTED READINGS

- Barry, John N. *The Ambition and the Power: The Fall of Jim Wright—a True Story of Washington.* New York: Viking Press, 1989. An engagingly written account of the tenure of Democratic Speaker James Wright and his downfall in 1989, revealing how Congress really operates.

- Cwiklik, Robert. *House Rules: A Freshman Congressman's Initiation to the Backslapping, Backpedaling, and Backstabbing Ways of Washington.* New York: Villard Books, 1991. A window into the world of a member of Congress, tracking Nebraska Democrat Peter Hoagland's first year in office (1989).

- Davidson, Roger H. *The Postreform Congress.* New York: St. Martin's Press, 1992. Readings examining how Congress changed as a result of reforms in the 1970s.

- Davidson, Roger H., and Walter J. Oleszek. *Congress and Its Members.* 4th ed. Congressional Quarterly Press, 1994. A comprehensive text on the operations of Congress.

- Dodd, Lawrence C., and Bruce I. Oppenheimer. *Congress Reconsidered.* 4th ed. Washington, D.C.: Congressional Quarterly Press, 1989. A revealing series of articles on facets of Congress's operations.

- Fenno, Richard. *Congressmen in Committees.* Boston: Little, Brown, 1973. An analysis based on comprehensive interviews with members of Congress and their staff, describing how committees are staffed and organized, and how they operate.

- ———. *Home Style: House Members in Their Districts.* Boston: Little, Brown, 1973. A study showing how members of the House deal with their constituents.

- Fowler, Linda L., and Robert D. McClure. *Political Ambition.* New Haven, Conn.: Yale University Press, 1989. A wonderfully written account revealing how candidates for congressional seats are recruited.

- Martin, Janet M. *Lessons from the Hill: The Legislative Journey of an Education Program.* New York: St. Martin's Press, 1994. An account of how key education legislation was passed and reconsidered by later Congresses, written by a political science professor after working in two congressional offices.

- Simon, Paul. *Advice and Consent: Clarence Thomas, Robert Bork and the Intriguing History of the Supreme Court's Nomination Battles.* Washington, D.C.: National Press Books, 1992. An analysis of the changes in the Senate's confirmation power, together with suggested reforms, by a member of the Senate Judiciary Committee.

THE PRESIDENCY

CHAPTER OUTLINE

CASE STUDY: WATERGATE AND THE
PRESIDENCY
INTRODUCTION: THE PRESIDENCY AND
DEMOCRACY
THE CONSTITUTIONAL DESIGN
THE FUNCTIONAL ROLES OF THE
PRESIDENT
TWO VIEWS OF THE EXECUTIVE POWER

EXPANDING PRESIDENTIAL POWER:
MOVING BEYOND THE
CONSTITUTION
THE INSTITUTIONALIZED PRESIDENCY
THE CHALLENGES OF PRESIDENTIAL
LEADERSHIP
THE PRESIDENCY AND APPROACHING
DEMOCRACY

O n June 17, 1972, a presidential election year, five men were arrested while breaking into the Democratic National Committee headquarters in the Watergate complex.[1] The burglars wore business suits and surgical gloves and carried electronic eavesdropping equipment. They gave aliases at police headquarters, but one officer recognized Jim McCord, security chief at the Committee for the Re-election of the President, the organization formed to organize President Nixon's 1972 campaign. Later, a search of the burglars' Watergate Hotel room yielded thirty-five hundred dollars and an address book listing a White House telephone number next to the name "Howard Hunt (W-House)."

Watergate and the Presidency

What could this all mean? The security chief of the Republican party breaks into Democratic headquarters. The burglars are in possession of money that looks like some sort of payoff, and they have the private telephone number of a White House staff member (Hunt was a consultant to Charles Colson, President Nixon's special counsel). Did this mean that the burglars were not working alone? President Nixon's press secretary, Ron Zeigler, quickly described the break-in as a "third-rate burglary" and assured the public that the president had not been involved and that the White House would cooperate fully in efforts to uncover the facts. In reality, Nixon and his staff did the opposite, going so far as to tell FBI director L. Patrick Gray to call off his investigation and even offered a "national security" alibi involving the CIA. Thus began the Watergate coverup that eventually led to the resignation of President Richard M. Nixon on August 9, 1974.

Late in the investigation, Nixon's tapes of White House conversations were obtained; they revealed the president's involvement in a wide range of illegal activities both before Watergate and during the coverup that followed. Almost a year after the burglars were caught, Nixon oversaw the payment of $450,000 in "hush money" to them. To distance himself from Watergate, Nixon (a lawyer himself) advised his top aides to perjure themselves before the grand jury investigating the incident.

Why did Nixon go to such lengths to hide his connection with Watergate? The truth was that some members of his administration had also been involved, since 1970, in numerous covert intelligence operations aimed at discrediting Vietnam War protesters and political opponents. By July 1971, G. Gordon Liddy, a former FBI agent, began working for a secret White House investigation known as "the plumbers," who were assigned the task of finding and eliminating the source of national-security "leaks" from the government. The plumbers first focused on Daniel Ellsberg, a former Defense Department official, who had leaked the Pentagon Papers (an officially classified Defense Department history of Vietnam War decisions) to the New York Times. Obtaining disguises, aliases, and photographic equipment from the CIA, the plumbers first broke into Ellsberg's psychiatrist's office, hoping that Ellsberg might have disclosed secrets to his psychiatrist that could then be used to discredit Ellsberg. In September 1971 (well before the Watergate break-in), two members of the still-secret plumbers unit, Liddy and E. Howard Hunt, devised a plan to drop LSD into Ellsberg's soup prior to a speaking engagement, with the intent of making Ellsberg appear as a "burnt-out drug case." The plan involved bribing waiters, obtaining LSD-25 from the CIA, and also getting White House approval—which came too late from Charles Colson. Hunt and Liddy also decided to punish nationally syndicated columnist Jack Anderson because of his disclosures concerning secret CIA activities. Hunt favored using LSD but then learned how unreliable the LSD response could be. Liddy then proposed simply killing Anderson by arranging that Anderson become "a fatal victim of the notorious Washington street crime rate."

On January 27, 1972, Liddy walked into the office of the attorney general of the United States and, using an easel, colored paper, and a pointing rod, described to Attorney General John Mitchell his plans for "campaign intelligence" using the code name "Gemstone." Liddy proposed that one million dollars in campaign funds be used to pay for kidnapping and drugging hippie protesters at the August 1972 Republican convention to keep them out of sight until after Nixon's renomination. Mugging squads would be hired to disrupt the Democratic convention and cause bad press. Liddy and Hunt had already taken out an option on a houseboat (with money from the Committee for the Re-election of the President) equipped with a mirrored bedroom and other lush amenities, where trained call girls masquerading as rich women would lure prominent Democrats to be "bugged" in the act. Liddy also bought a blueprint of the Miami convention hall; he recommended that the commando team sabotage the Democratic convention by blowing up the air-conditioning system.

After hearing the presentation, the attorney general instructed Liddy to come back with something that cost less than one million dollars. On March 30, Liddy returned with a revised plan calling only for bugging the Democratic

National Committee offices—and he received Mitchell's "reluctant O.K." So on June 17, five men carrying out Liddy's revised plan were arrested at the Democratic headquarters in the Watergate complex.

So effective was the coverup that all of this and more was not known until almost two years after the burglars were caught. In fact, Nixon celebrated a landslide election victory on November 7, 1972, despite the appearance one month earlier of Washington Post reporters Carl Bernstein and Bob Woodward's first story revealing that the Watergate break-in was part of a massive campaign of political spying and sabotage directed by White House and reelection officials. Their work would later become an award-winning book and then a film—All the President's Men.[2]

With transcripts of the Watergate tapes as a backdrop, President Nixon announces that he would turn the transcripts over to the House Judiciary Committee's impeachment probe.

INTRODUCTION: THE PRESIDENCY AND DEMOCRACY

American government was set up to restrain the powerful. Its presidents may occasionally win dramatic victories, but they are all doomed by the rules of the system to suffer dramatic defeats. Only the most stable personality can accept the highs with equanimity, survive the lows with patience, and perform the job with integrity. As former senator Sam Ervin, chair of the Senate select committee investigating Watergate once observed: "One of the great advantages of the three separate branches of government is that it is difficult to corrupt all three at the same time."

Democracy was seriously strained during Watergate as the president used his powers to further his own political self-interests. He used the FBI, first, to investigate his political opponents and, later, to stop investigating Watergate. He also created an atmosphere that encouraged secrecy and illegality. Anonymous and largely unaccountable presidential assistants ran over and around the governing bodies of the country, frequently rationalizing their behavior in terms of the president's goals and their own narrow definition of the public interest. As Jeb Magruder, who served a prison term for his Watergate activities, said, "We convinced ourselves that wrong was right, and plunged ahead. There is no way to justify burglary, wiretapping, prying and all the other elements of the cover-up. In my own case, I think I was guilty of a tremendous insensitivity to the basic tenets of democracy."[3]

As incredible as the Watergate story may sound, it reveals much about the evolution of the American presidency as well as of the American political system. The issues raised by Watergate are as timeless as any in American politics. The framers appreciated the dangers of executive as well as legislative tyranny, and they went to great lengths to provide checks on the potential abuse of power. Yet by the time Richard Nixon became president in 1968 the powers of the office and the expectations of the American people had grown well beyond what the framers envisioned. The Constitution drafted by the framers was flexible enough to allow an Abraham Lincoln to save the Union and a Franklin Roosevelt to legislate the New Deal, but it could not prevent a president or his trusted lieutenants from violating the law, distorting the powers of the office, and, in effect, setting up a secret government alongside the constitutional one.

The presidency is an especially fascinating area of study today because we are still discussing how powerful a president should be within a constitutional system. This discussion is not about breaking laws but instead about the line item veto, war powers, balanced budgets, and appointments. The great paradox of the presidency is that nowhere in America is there an office that unites power as well as purpose to help Americans approach their democratic potential, yet also poses the most serious potential threats to democracy. Richard Nixon wasn't the first president to cross this line, but his case so clearly illustrates the dilemmas of democracy.

The office of president lies at the center of countless demands, many of them contradictory, some impossible to achieve under any conditions. The mere energy required to hold the position and carry out its duties puts it far beyond the

It is rare to find the current president and all of the living former presidents gathered in one place. Usually, only the dedication of a presidential library or a state funeral brings them together and provides a historical photo opportunity like this one. Here, the sitting president, his four living predecessors, and their wives pay their respects at Richard Nixon's funeral on April 27, 1994. From left: Bill Clinton and Hillary Rodham Clinton, George and Barbara Bush, Ronald and Nancy Reagan, Jimmy and Rosalyn Carter, and Gerald and Betty Ford.

average person's capacity. Several presidents have been broken by the office; many have been diminished by it. Even those who have risen to its challenge, whose records from the distance of history we admire, faced scathing criticism and fought determined foes throughout their tenure in the White House.

Still, some have thrived in the office, and a number of presidents have achieved greatness. It helps to have a tough skin, a strong character, a powerful intellect, diplomatic skills, leadership traits—and a good deal of luck. It is impossible to predict ahead of time who will or will not succeed at the job, but one thing is certain: The presidency lies at the core of the American democratic system. To understand how closely the American presidency can foster our approach to democracy, we must carefully examine this unique and powerful office.

THE CONSTITUTIONAL DESIGN

The creation of the presidency may be the framers' most original contribution. In a world of kings and emperors, most of whom left office feet first or on the wrong end of a bloody revolution, the president was to be unlike any other leader. In creating this unique position, the framers sought to avoid a monarchy like the one they had rebelled against, but they also wanted a strong, independent executive. They were appalled at the results of legislative omnipotence in the states, as had been the case under the Articles of Confederation.[4]

In creating a source of power independent of, and capable of balancing, the powers of Congress, the framers based the presidency on seven key principles. First, they set up a single presidency. To ensure its strength and energy, executive power was to center on one individual, not some group like a council or a cabinet. Second, the selection of president would be made neither by the Congress nor by the people. A president chosen by Congress could become its puppet. One chosen by the people could become a demagogue and tyrant. Creating an independent body of individual electors, themselves selected by the state legislatures (the electoral college) would instead make the president independent of the two branches.

Third, the president was given a fixed term of office. The genius of this idea lies in its assurance of both stability and constraint. Executives serve four years, period, and can't be forced from office by arbitrary "no-confidence" votes in Congress (votes that force the early resignation of entire governments in parliamentary systems). On the other hand, as our case study clearly demonstrates, no one can remain president without broad popular support. Those who put the president in office can just as well remove the president, thus reducing the likelihood that someone could permanently consolidate power in an arbitrary and unpopular way.

Fourth, the president would be eligible for more than one term of office, making the executive a continual source of potential power to balance or check congressional power. (This is no longer the case. The Twenty-second Amendment restricts the president to two terms.) If presidents remained popular and their policies successful, they could win reelection. Thus, Congress would always have to take the president into account.

Fifth, the president could be removed from office only by a cumbersome process of impeachment involving both houses of Congress; thus, a president would have to be continually reckoned with. On the other hand, the case study demonstrates that impeachment represents an ultimate check on arbitrary and excessive use of executive power.

Sixth, the president was given a veto power, enabling the executive to say no to Congress. This single provision makes the president a central player in the legislative process because a president's wishes must be taken into account as Congress goes about its work.

Finally, the president was not required to appoint an advisory council. Thus, presidents were allowed to act on their own, at least within their own constitutional realm of the executive arena.

The effect of this set of principles was to establish a strong but constrained executive, a single, symbolic head of the nation, possessed of serious means for exercising power, but operating under law and restricted in power by the countervailing institutions of Congress and the Supreme Court. Let's now look beyond these principles to the specifics in the Constitution.

Who Is Eligible to Be President?

The Constitution specifies only three requirements for becoming president. A president must be at least thirty-five years old, must have lived in the United States for at least fourteen years, and must be a natural-born citizen.

The framers set up the minimum-age requirement of thirty-five, which at that time represented "middle age," to guarantee that a president would be reasonably mature and experienced in politics. The fourteen-year-residence condition was set up to guard against the possibility of a president with divided loyalties between England and the United States—an obvious concern in the years following the American Revolution. For the same reason, the framers stipulated that presidents be natural-born citizens (born in the United States or to American citizens abroad), ruling out naturalized citizens, such as former secretary of state Henry Kissinger.

The Presidential Powers

What powers does the president possess to accomplish the office's broad range of responsibilities? The Constitution has remarkably little to say on this point. Only one-third of Article II is devoted to formal presidential powers. This brevity reflects the framers' uncertainty on the subject. Trusting that George Washington would almost certainly be the first president, the framers assumed that he would establish precedents for the office.

What the framers did write into the Constitution can be categorized in two ways. First, in clear, simple language they gave the president some very specific powers. Second, and more important, they also gave the executive some broad, even sweeping, powers written in vague language subject to individual interpretation. Let us now examine the specific, unambiguous powers allotted to American presidents by the U.S. Constitution.

THE VETO POWER   Perhaps the president's most potent legal weapon is the **veto,** a Latin word meaning "I forbid." The power to forbid or prevent an action of Congress gives the president a central role in the legislative process. When Congress passes a bill or joint resolution, the legislation goes to the White House for presidential action. The president then has four options. First, the

Although there are no gender specifications for the job of president, to date all American presidents have been men. But there have been women candidates for the office. Victoria Woodhull, shown here, a stockbroker and newspaper editor from New York, was the first woman presidential candidate. She ran for president in 1872 as a member of the Equal Rights party.

president can sign the bill, at which point it becomes law. Second, the president can do nothing, allowing the bill to become law without a signature in ten days. Third, if Congress adjourns before those ten days pass, by refusing to sign legislation the president can kill the bill by what is known as a **pocket veto.** Finally, the president can veto the bill, returning it to the House of origin with a message stating reasons for the veto. Congress then has the option to **override** the veto by a two-thirds vote in each house.

The framers saw the veto as a bulwark of executive independence, a basic building block in their efforts to separate and check power. Alexander Hamilton made this position clear in *Federalist* no. 73: "The primary inducement to conferring [the veto] power upon the executive is to enable him to defend himself; the second one is to increase the chances . . . against the passing of bad laws, through haste, inadvertence, or design."[5] The veto was thus conceived as a "negative" by which an executive could defend *against* legislative excesses.

Presidents can sometimes affect the wording or passage of a law by announcing ahead of time that they intend to veto a pending bill. In 1985 President Reagan dared Congress to raise taxes. Borrowing from Clint Eastwood, he said such actions would "make my day" and be met by a quick veto.

President Bush did not have a veto overridden until one month before the 1992 election, when Congress overrode a cable TV bill. Striking about the Bush vetoes is that he successfully vetoed bills with broad popular approval, such as parental leave and additional unemployment compensation.

President Clinton did not veto a single bill in his first two years of office, but he too gained attention with a veto threat. He warned Congress during a nationally televised State of the Union message: "If you send me legislation that does not guarantee every American private health insurance that can never be taken away, you will force me to take this pen [and] veto the legislation." Finally, in June 1995, President Clinton cast his first veto.

Table 6.1 shows the number of presidential vetoes from 1932 through 1994. Clearly, the veto remains a part of the president's arsenal of devices for influencing an always-recalcitrant Congress.

THE APPOINTMENT POWER   This is another specific and important power granted the president. The appointment power affects the president's ability to staff the executive branch with trusted allies. Article II, Section 2 of the Constitution gives the president, "by and with the consent of the Senate," the power to appoint ambassadors, public ministers, and consuls; judges of the federal courts; and other officers "of the United States whose appointments are not herein otherwise provided for, and which shall be established by law."

The power of appointment allows a president to recruit people who will help promote his policies. Without this power, presidents might be forced to work with congressional appointees or with entrenched bureaucrats who may not share his goals; such a scenario would limit a president's independence. Although appointment is an important administrative power of the president, over two thousand presidential appointments require Senate confirmation, which is sometimes difficult to obtain. President Clinton's controversial and unsuccessful nomination of Dr. Henry J. Foster to replace Joycelyn Elders as surgeon general, killed by a Senate filibuster is but one example of how politically divisive the appointment process can be.

Table 6.1
Presidential Vetoes 1932–94

PRESIDENT	VETOES*
Franklin D. Roosevelt	633
Harry S. Truman	250
Dwight D. Eisenhower	181
John F. Kennedy	21
Lyndon B. Johnson	30
Richard M. Nixon	43
Gerald R. Ford	66
Jimmy Carter	31
Ronald Reagan	78
George Bush	46
Bill Clinton	2

*Total includes vetoes and pocket vetoes.

Sources: Gary King and Lyn Ragsdale, *The Elusive Executive* (Washington, D.C.: Congressional Quarterly Press, 1988), p. 88; *Congressional Quarterly* and Office of Executive Clerk, the White House; and various newspaper compilations.

Perhaps the single-most important appointment presidents can make is the nomination of someone to fill a vacancy on the Supreme Court. The average president names only two justices during any four-year term of office, so it is a rare president who ends up naming a majority of Court members. Nevertheless, since the Court is usually split ideologically, even one or two appointments can affect the outcome of important constitutional cases. Presidents can use court nominations to bolster their own popularity or political philosophy, but they can also see their fortunes decline after an unwise choice. George Bush lost stature with the American people during the lengthy and embarrassing hearings on one of his candidates for the high bench, Clarence Thomas.

THE TREATY POWER   The Constitution also gives presidents the power to negotiate treaties with other nations. **Treaties** are formal international agreements between sovereign states. But the framers foresaw a system of consultation between the branches such that the executive's negotiation would involve the Senate's "advice and consent." When President George Washington went to Congress to solicit advice on an Indian treaty, however, he was made to stay several hours and answer questions that he believed had little bearing on the treaty. Irked by this experience, Washington resolved not to repeat it. Henceforth, while required to secure the consent of the Senate in ratifying treaties, he did not encourage senators to contribute their sometimes dubious "advice"—and later presidents have followed that model.

Since 1789, approximately 1,600 treaties have been submitted to the Senate for ratification. Over three-fourths have been approved with no modification.

The President versus the Court

During his first term as president, Franklin Delano Roosevelt was unable to make a single appointment to the Supreme Court. A liberal Democrat, Roosevelt faced a Court dominated by conservative justices who opposed virtually all government regulation of business—the philosophical foundation underlying Roosevelt's New Deal. During 1935 and 1936 Congress passed twelve New Deal bills, only to have them declared unconstitutional by the Court.

During his campaign for a second term Roosevelt vigorously attacked the Court's decisions; when he won the election with 60 percent of the popular vote, he was convinced that the American people favored the New Deal. He now faced a choice among three alternatives: He could bow to the will of the Court and stop introducing New Deal legislation into Congress, he could simply ignore the Court's rulings, or he could try to persuade Congress to pass legislation that would change the number of justices on the Court (thereby giving him an opportunity to appoint justices who shared his political philosophy). If you were president, what would you do?

Thinking Critically

What Happened

Two weeks after his inauguration Roosevelt proposed a controversial plan for judicial reorganization: For every justice who failed to resign from the Court within six months after reaching the age of seventy, the president would appoint a new justice, up to a total of six. (Because six of the nine sitting justices were over seventy, Roosevelt could conceivably have made six new appointments, thus increasing the number of justices to fifteen.)

Congress reacted negatively to Roosevelt's Court-packing scheme. Republicans saw it as a power grab by a president who had already taken over Congress to produce the most successful legislative record in U.S. history. Public-opinion polls revealed only lukewarm support for the idea. And almost no one over age seventy liked the plan, since it seemed to imply that seniority was tantamount to senility.

In March 1937, in a 5-to-4 vote often referred to as "the switch in time that saved nine," the Court reversed its earlier decision to strike down New York State's minimum wage for women. On April 12, it upheld the constitutionality of the National Labor Relations Act, and on May 24, the Social Security Act of 1935. Later that month Justice Van Devanter retired, giving Roosevelt an opportunity to appoint a new justice. His nominee, Hugo Black, was confirmed, and thereafter Roosevelt could count on a majority of the justices' votes on economic matters.

However, these numbers are misleading, since presidents withdrew 150 of the treaties when defeat seemed likely. Only 1 percent of all treaties submitted to the Senate have actually been defeated. Still, the possibility of treaty rejection gives the Senate a potential power, just as the possibility of a veto does for the president.

Treaty rejections do occur. The most dramatic example took place in 1919, when the Senate failed to ratify Woodrow Wilson's Treaty of Versailles ending World War I. The defeat of this treaty, which included membership in Wilson's coveted League of Nations, was seen as a direct slap in the president's face by a hostile Congress. It not only undermined Wilson's authority at home but helped doom the League—the predecessor of today's United Nations—to ineffectiveness abroad.[6]

Table 6.2
Treaties and Executive Agreements

YEARS	TREATIES	EXECUTIVE AGREEMENTS
1789–1839	60	27
1839–1889	215	238
1889–1939	524	917
1940–1970	310	5,653
1971–1977	110	2,062
1978–1983	114	1,999
1984–1988	65	1,890
1989–1993	84	1,606
Total	1,482	14,392

Sources: President and Congress: Louis Fisher, *Power and Policy,* p. 45. Copyright ©
1972 by The Free Press. Reprinted with permission of The Free Press, an imprint of Simon
and Schuster. Figures for 1971–93 provided by Department of State, Washington, D.C.

Treaty approval, then, is by no means a foregone conclusion, partly because it requires a two-thirds majority of senators present and voting. In addition, the Senate may attach amendments to treaties.

Treaties have declined as a potential congressional check on presidential
power because presidents have increasingly turned to another and more informal device for conducting foreign affairs. **Executive agreements,** diplomatic
contracts negotiated with other countries, allow presidents or their agents to
make important foreign-policy moves without Senate approval. These agreements appeal to harried presidents in their role as world leader. Unlike treaties,
which are well covered by the media, generate controversy, and take time to
ratify, executive agreements are usually negotiated in secret, making them a
particularly powerful foreign-policy tool. By executive agreement William
McKinley ended the Spanish–American War, Theodore Roosevelt restricted Japanese immigration to the United States, and Richard Nixon pledged continued
military support to Saigon.

Presidents may conclude an executive agreement on any subject within
their constitutional authority as long as the agreement is not inconsistent with
legislation enacted by Congress in the exercise of its constitutional authority.
Scholars agree that although not explicitly outlined in the Constitution, the
president's right to conduct foreign policy through executive agreement rests
on several sound constitutional bases. These include the president's authority
as chief executive to represent the nation in foreign affairs, the president's authority to receive ambassadors and other public ministers, the president's authority as commander in chief, and the president's authority to "take care that
the laws be faithfully executed."[7] Presidents are increasingly finding that executive agreements, unlike treaties, give them the flexibility they need to make
foreign policy in an increasingly complex and volatile world. Table 6.2 illustrates the increasing importance of this device.

OTHER CONSTITUTIONALLY DESIGNATED POWERS   The Constitution gives the president additional specific powers, such as the right to grant pardons (President Ford did pardon ex-president Nixon for any crimes he may have committed as president) and the right to convene Congress in extraordinary circumstances. Perhaps the most important specific power granted to the president by the Constitution is the power to be commander in chief of the armed forces. Presidents who use this power effectively can dramatically enhance their national and international stature. We examine the consequences of this power in detail later in the chapter.

Beyond specific grants of power, the Constitution gives the president a vague mandate to run the executive branch of government. Different presidents have interpreted that mandate in very different ways. We shall soon see that that vagueness in the Constitution has allowed presidents a good deal of leeway in expanding the powers of the chief executive during the two centuries since the framers wrote the Constitution. But first, we'll look at the various roles that define the job of chief executive.

THE FUNCTIONAL ROLES OF THE PRESIDENT

Presidential behavior depends only partly on laws that require action or prohibit it. Beyond formal legalities, all presidents are constrained and directed by informal or functional role expectations.[8] When leaders are *expected* to take an action, they do it—whether or not permission for the action is contained somewhere in a legal document. As leader of a vocal, democratic people the president stands at the center of a mass of such expectations. These presidential role expectations follow.

THE PRESIDENT AS CHIEF OF STATE   The president acts as a ceremonial chief of state, symbolizing the national government to people in this country and to other nations. At world gatherings the chief of state is put on the same high protocol rank as kings. Presidents greet foreign ambassadors, pin medals on heroes, hold barbecues on the White House lawn, and give state dinners. Virtually all of these opportunities help dramatize and personalize a presidency. From meeting astronauts to making an entrance to the tune "Hail to the Chief," presidents bask in the glory and often hide behind the pomp and circumstance of their office.

THE PRESIDENT AS COMMANDER IN CHIEF   Presidents have more than ceremonial duties, however. They hold awesome powers, particularly in their military leadership role. As commander in chief the president is charged with providing national security and defense. When necessary the president must defend American interests abroad by committing troops to war. George Bush did this in Iraq; so did Ronald Reagan in Grenada and Bill Clinton in Haiti. This military role is reinforced by the president's oath of office to "preserve, protect, and defend the Constitution of the United States." A president who fails to respond forcefully to a perceived threat is seen as weak or indecisive.

THE PRESIDENT AS CHIEF DIPLOMAT   Presidents must be international diplomats as well as warriors. Maintaining smooth relations with allies and a tough stance with potential or real enemies is expected of all presidents. For that rea-

FYI

The president travels in Air Force 1, a two-hundred-million-dollar Boeing 747 built in 1990. Air Force 1 is equipped with eighty-five telephones, nineteen televisions, and can travel seven thousand miles without refueling. It carries seventy passengers with a crew of twenty-three.

son most presidents spend a good deal of their time developing and overseeing American foreign policy. Even the Supreme Court has recognized the unique importance of foreign policy to the presidency.[9]

Indeed, so important is foreign policy that many presidents direct foreign relations from the Oval Office more than through the State Department. This reflects the significance of the president's role as world leader. President Kennedy once said, "The big difference [between domestic and foreign policy] is that between a bill being defeated and the country [being] wiped out."[10] Many presidents have found another reason for focusing on their diplomatic role. Domestically, their influence is constrained in a thousand ways. In foreign affairs they have traditionally been allowed far greater leeway to exercise power and affect policy.

THE PRESIDENT AS CHIEF LEGISLATOR   Despite numerous constraints, however, presidents do play a major role in domestic matters. Congress and the American public expect the president to send new legislative initiatives to Congress. Indeed, most legislation addressed by Congress originates in the executive branch. When President Dwight Eisenhower chose not to submit a program in 1953 (his first year in office), he was chided by a member of Congress: "Don't expect us to start from scratch. . . . That's not the way we do things here. You draft the bills and we work them over."[11]

The same criticism was lodged against Bill Clinton early in 1995, when he was willing to allow Republican Congressman Clay Shaw to draw up a welfare reform proposal instead of sending Congress one of his own. So deeply ingrained is the norm that presidents send major legislation to Congress that even a Congress controlled by a unified opposition party with an agenda of its own seems taken aback when a president fails to carry out this accustomed role.

Besides such involvement in the legislative process (proposing policies and lobbying for them), the president also has negative legislative power. As you've seen, presidents can thwart congressional attempts at legislation through the veto or by threats of a veto.

THE PRESIDENT AS CHIEF EXECUTIVE   Passing legislation is one matter, but implementing it is another altogether. As the nation's chief executive, the president signs the executive orders and presidential decrees setting the administrative direction and tone for the executive branch. As chief administrator or chief bureaucrat, the president oversees an army of officials, thousands of executive branch workers trying to carry out presidential policies effectively and quickly. And in this executive capacity, presidents do not act in a vacuum. They are closely monitored by interest groups throughout the country, all eager to see that the executive branch promotes policies and interprets laws to their liking.

THE PRESIDENT AS MORAL LEADER   The president is much more than a bureaucrat. The president must also set a high moral tone for the American people, even if it is folklore. George ("I cannot tell a lie") Washington and Abraham ("Honest Abe") Lincoln are the models a president is expected to emulate. Even though few citizens see politics as a fair and moral place, and even though no one can become president *except* through politics, Americans still seem to hold the president to higher standards than they do most politicians—or most citizens for that matter. Presidents are expected to be truthful, to deal openly with problems, to keep their word—and even to set high standards in their personal lives.

Richard Nixon's popular support melted away during the Watergate affair, and not just because of his specific illegal actions. Americans came to view his overall character as deceptive and untrustworthy. Many were shocked at his vulgar language, which they heard after large sections of the White House tapes were released to the public. His petty vulgarities rapidly undermined any claims he may once have had to moral leadership. Of course, many other presidents have gotten into trouble for perceived "character flaws" of one kind or another. Bill Clinton's standing with the public would surely have been more secure throughout his presidency had he not been continuously dogged by charges of womanizing, trying pot but not inhaling, and avoiding military service during the Vietnam War.

THE PRESIDENT AS PARTY LEADER   In almost direct contrast to the president's role as head of the nation (chief of state, moral leader), the president must carry out a more narrow set of duties. As long as presidents remain in office, they are the chief architects of their political party's fortunes. The Constitution makes no reference to party leadership—indeed, it makes no reference to parties at all—but today's presidents must never forget that their party put them in the Oval Office. A president's every action will either help or hurt that party, and its members will keep a close eye on the president to make sure that their party's ideas and fortunes are promoted. When President Clinton presented his own plan to balance the budget, many members of his party felt betrayed by their president's anti-party position.

Still, in campaigning and speaking for the party, the president must be careful. By playing that role too zealously, the president will come to be perceived as narrowly partisan and lose the image as leader of the entire nation. Since strong backers of the president's party rarely add up to even one-third of the electorate, presidents who act more like partisans than national leaders are asking for public disapproval.

THE PRESIDENT AS MANAGER OF PROSPERITY   On top of all these roles, the president must also serve as guardian of the nation's prosperity. The chief executive is, in a sense, the nation's chief economist. The political lessons of the Great Depression era are clear. No president can preside over hard times without being blamed for them. Herbert Hoover was soundly defeated after failing, in the public's eyes, to deal competently with the economic setbacks of that time. George Bush was sent into retirement because, in the words of political strategist James Carville, "it's the economy, stupid."[12] Democratic presidents have also suffered at the polls for the public's perception that they couldn't keep soaring inflation rates in check. Largely for that reason, Harry Truman lost his Democratic majority in Congress during the 1946 elections, and Jimmy Carter's fate might have been different if he could have averted the double-digit inflation of his last years in office.

The public expects the president to act as an economic superhero who will stave off both depression and inflation while keeping the economy at full employment. When presidents act in this capacity, they adopt the role that was described by political scientist Clinton Rossiter as "Manager of Prosperity."[13]

THE PRESIDENT AS JUGGLER OF ROLES   The president must play all of these roles—and others besides. Yet doing so, for all practical purposes, is an impossibility because the roles often conflict. How can one be both a partisan politician and a national unifier? For that matter, can one be a politician at all and still act as a moral guide to the nation? Can one be both a legislator and an administrator of laws? And how is it possible to reconcile the president's role in world affairs as both soldier and diplomat? In addition, in carrying out any of these roles, a major difficulty arises in speaking for a diverse and frequently fractious people. Just who does the president represent in any of these activities? How can a president seem fair and effective in the eyes of a multitude of constituencies? Finally, just finding the time and energy to carry out these expected tasks is surely beyond the capacity of any mortal.

The job of president, in short, is depressingly daunting. It is all the more so because the powers granted the person whom we expect to accomplish all of these roles fall far short of any imaginable capacity to carry them out. In fact, even though we expect herculean accomplishments of presidents, we hedge them with restrictions so that they look less like Captain Marvel and more like Gulliver, tied down by a thousand tiny ropes. We set up a perfect system for failure: a presidency with exaggerated expectations and a political/legal system of restraints. How then can anyone fill all the expected roles of the presidency? Let us examine two reactions to this system: presidents who accept the restraints and live within them and presidents who chafe at the restraints and invent ways to surpass or abolish them.

TWO VIEWS OF THE EXECUTIVE POWER

How strong should a president be? How much power does the office really possess? The Constitution is silent on this matter. Article II begins with the ambiguous sentence, "The executive Power shall be vested in a President of the United States of America." What did the framers mean by this elusive phrase "the executive Power?" Did it refer to a mere designation of office or did it imply a broad and sweeping mandate to rule? Scholars and politicians alike have long debated the question, but have come to no agreement. History has left it up to each president to determine the scope of executive powers, given a president's personality, philosophy, and the political circumstances of the time.

This executive power "wild card" has allowed many a president to go beyond what is narrowly prescribed in the Constitution when conditions call for extraordinary action—or when the president *thinks* such action is necessary. Activist presidents find ways to justify sweeping policy innovations even if no specific language in the Constitution allows for those policies. Franklin Roosevelt exemplified this approach in his inaugural address on March 4, 1933. With the country on the brink of economic collapse because of the Great Depression, Roosevelt declared in one of history's most memorable speeches, "Let me first assert my firm belief that the only thing we have to fear is fear itself—nameless, unreasoning, unjustified terror which paralyzes needed efforts to convert retreat into advance." Roosevelt then turned to the issue of means: "I shall ask the Congress for the one remaining instrument to meet the crisis—broad executive power to wage a war against the emergency, as great as the power that would be given to me if we were in fact invaded by a foreign foe."[14] Roosevelt then took a number of dramatic actions that included closing the banks by executive order, forbidding payments of gold, and restricting exports.

Not all presidents have made as sweeping claims to executive power as Franklin Roosevelt. Considering their different approaches to the use of power, we can categorize presidents in office as either stewards or constructionists.[15]

The **stewardship** approach to presidential power was articulated by Theodore Roosevelt and based on the presidencies of two of his predecessors, Abraham Lincoln and Andrew Jackson. Roosevelt believed that the president had a moral duty to serve popular interests. The president, in his eyes, was "a steward of the people bound actively and affirmatively to do all he could for the people." Roosevelt did not believe that the president needed specific authorization to take action.

> I did . . . many things not previously done by the President. . . . I did not usurp power, but I did greatly broaden the use of executive power. . . . I acted for the common well-being of all our people, . . . in whatever manner was necessary, unless prevented by direct constitutional or legislative prohibition.[16]

Roosevelt held an activist, expansionist view of presidential powers. In a classic example of the stewardship model, he ordered the U.S. seizure of Panama and the subsequent building of the Panama Canal. As he put it, "I took the [Panama] Canal Zone and let Congress debate, and while the debate goes on the canal does too."

Over the years, activist or steward presidents have used their powers broadly. Thomas Jefferson presided over the Louisiana Purchase in 1803, in which the American government bought a parcel of land larger than the remainder of the country at the time. Lincoln assumed enormous emergency powers during the Civil War, justifying them on the grounds of needing to take quick, decisive action during an extraordinary national crisis. Woodrow Wilson ran all facets of the government in World War I. He commandeered plants and mines, requisitioned supplies, fixed prices, seized and operated the nation's transportation and communication networks, and managed the production and distribution of foodstuffs.

Teddy Roosevelt (left), using the stewardship approach to presidential power, extended the reach and powers of the modern presidency. Articulating this approach, Roosevelt wrote, "I greatly enjoy the exercise of power. While President, I have been President, emphatically. I have used every ounce of power there was in the office." At the other end of the spectrum was William Howard Taft (right) who held a very restricted view of a president's powers. Unlike Roosevelt, Taft actually disliked politics.

In contrast to this stewardship view of executive power is the **constructionist** view espoused by William Howard Taft. Taft believed that the president could exercise no power unless it could be traced to or implied from an express grant in either the Constitution or an act of Congress. He scoffed at the idea of some "undefined residuum of power" that a president can exercise "because it seems to him to be in the public interest." The president, he believed, was limited by a strict reading of the Constitution. Unless that document gave the executive a specific power, that power was beyond the scope of legitimate presidential activity. Taft cringed in horror at Roosevelt's view that the president could "do anything that the needs of the nation demanded."[17]

Because of this restricted view of presidential power, Taft was a passive executive, reluctant to impose his will or the power of his office on the legislative process. He did not exert strong party leadership in Congress, nor did he embark on the ambitious and "extra-Constitutional" exercises of power typical of Teddy Roosevelt. Other presidents besides Taft have pursued this constructionist line, at least in certain situations. For example, Hoover was reluctant to exercise presidential powers to manipulate the economy during the Great

Little-known Fact

William Howard Taft was the only person to serve as both president of the United States and chief justice of the Supreme Court. At 321 pounds, he was also the country's largest president. Taft had an oversized bathtub specially constructed for the White House.

Great	*Average*
1. Lincoln	**18.** McKinley
2. F. Roosevelt	**19.** Taft
3. Washington	**20.** Van Buren
4. Jefferson	**21.** Hoover
	22. Hayes
Near Great	**23.** Arthur
5. T. Roosevelt	**24.** Ford
6. Wilson	**25.** Carter
7. Jackson	**26.** B. Harrison
8. Truman	
	Below Average
Above Average	**27.** Taylor
9. J. Adams	**28.** Tyler
10. L. Johnson	**29.** Fillmore
11. Eisenhower	**30.** Coolidge
12. Polk	**31.** Pierce
13. Kennedy	
14. Madison	*Failure*
15. Monroe	**32.** A. Johnson
16. J.Q. Adams	**33.** Buchanan
17. Cleveland	**34.** Nixon
	35. Grant
	36. Harding

FIGURE 6.1   Ranking Presidents

This is how a sample of 953 professors of American history responded when asked to rank American presidents. The poll was taken in 1982.

Source: Robert K. Murray and Tim H. Blessing, *Journal of American History*, December 1983.

Depression, appearing very much the constructionist—at least in economic policy. Indeed, it was this very reluctance that caused many voters to see him as indifferent to their economic plight.

On the whole, Americans have sided with an activist interpretation of the presidency. They expect dynamic leadership from the office. Almost none of the presidents regarded as "great" by either historians or the public (see Figure 6.1) has adopted a passive, constructionist approach to the job. The men who did much to create our idealized view of the presidency—Washington, Jefferson, Lincoln, the two Roosevelts—did not reach lofty status by minding their own business. They crossed and stretched constitutional boundaries in the name of the national interest. Their achievements stand as models, if not monuments. Current presidents invoke their names and strive to fill their shoes, while voters measure current occupants of the White House against these past giants. No one hopes that the next president will behave like William Howard Taft, and no one runs for that office promising "to govern in the spirit of Franklin Pierce."

At the end of the twentieth century, with the United States as the world's only superpower, presidents can hardly be anything but activist stewards of the nation. While we may not all agree with Woodrow Wilson that "the President has the right, in law and conscience, to be as big a man as he can be,"[18] the president can no longer be a passive actor in the political system. The trends of our time that make the president automatically and immensely powerful are many. It is time to give them a close examination.

EXPANDING PRESIDENTIAL POWER: MOVING BEYOND THE CONSTITUTION

Presidents have been gaining power for decades. The days are long gone when a passive president like Calvin Coolidge could identify his greatest accomplishment as "minding my own business." Yet we must account for the impact of personality, of presidential will, on behavior in the Oval Office. Even today, presidents cannot be powerful and activist unless they want to be. They must possess a character that leads them, in fact, to exercise those powers that have accrued, in theory, to their office.

Remember that the passive William Howard Taft *succeeded* the activist Teddy Roosevelt. Presumably, the powers of the American president changed little from 1908 (Roosevelt's last full year in office) to 1909 (Taft's first year). What changed was the personality of the president. The power of the president in our day derives not merely from an increase in the technical powers available to the office but in an increasing likelihood that occupants of the White House will be strong, activist individuals. Let us see why trends favor this type of president.

The Doctrine of Inherent Powers and Presidential Character

Activist presidents like Roosevelt have had to justify their broad interpretation of presidential powers. They have done so through a theory known as **inherent powers.** This theory holds that the Constitution grants authority to the executive, through the joining of in Article II, Section 1, "The Executive Power shall be vested in a President of the United States," with Article II, Section 3, that the president "take Care that the Laws be faithfully executed." Activist presidents argue that under certain emergency conditions, the executive may claim to possess extraordinary powers to act quickly, and without corresponding congressional action, to "save" the nation.[19]

The activist Thomas Jefferson was the first president to expound the theory of going beyond the law when necessary for national security. "A strict observation of the written laws is doubtless one of the higher duties of a good officer, but it is not the highest. The law of necessity, of self-preservation, of saving our country when in danger, are of higher obligation."[20] President Lincoln in 1864 reinforced this theory of inherent powers when he argued:

> My oath to preserve the Constitution to the best of my ability imposed upon me the duty of preserving, *by every indispensable means,* that government— that nation, of which that Constitution was the organic law. Was it possible to lose the nation, and yet preserve the Constitution? By general law life and limb must be protected. Yet often a limb must be amputated to save a life; but a life is never wisely given to save a limb. I felt that measures otherwise unconstitutional might become lawful by becoming indispensable to the preservation of the nation. Right or wrong, I assumed this ground, and now avow it. I could

Here, Richard Nixon, one of the presidents James David Barber categorizes as active-negative, checks his watch as he presses the flesh in Brussels in 1974. He is rushing to a high-powered diplomatic luncheon. Clearly, time constraints, the need for public appearances and personal diplomacy, and the wide array of day-to-day responsibilities, keep modern-day presidents forever caught up in a flurry of activity.

not feel that, to the best of my ability, I had even tried to preserve the Constitution, if, to save slavery . . . I should permit the wreck of government, country, and Constitution altogether.[21]

At the beginning of the Civil War Lincoln took such extraordinary actions as ordering the blockade of southern ports, enlarging the army and navy, spending treasury funds without congressional authorization, closing the mails to treasonable correspondence, suspending habeas corpus, and creating special military tribunals in areas where courts were operating. Lincoln justified his actions on a doctrine of necessity and his oath of office; not until after the crisis of war and Lincoln's assassination did the Supreme Court rule *some* of these measures unconstitutional.[22]

Although we often applaud the activist policies of strong presidents like Jefferson and Lincoln, the broad interpretation of executive powers in time of crisis can also be claimed for dubious goals. As we saw in the case study, President Nixon, another activist president, tried similar reasoning to justify wiretaps, break-ins, and domestic surveillance during the Watergate affair. The difference is that Nixon engaged in these activities for his personal political gain rather than for the good of the nation.

When are modern activist presidents likely to behave as Nixon did and misuse their enormous potential power? When are they likely to use their powers well? Political scientist James David Barber has offered a theory of presidential character that seeks to predict how presidents will behave based upon how they have already behaved. This theory uses another dimension of personality besides activism and passivity. Barber says that it's also important to learn whether or not our leaders *like* what they are doing.[23]

Some presidents have clearly been happy, exuberant characters who loved life, work, and politics. (Franklin Roosevelt, for instance, was always known as "the happy warrior.") Others have approached political activity with suspicion, distrust, and hostility. (Richard Nixon, known as "Tricky Dick," was famous for having developed an "enemies list.") Active presidents with a negative, cynical, suspicious bent to their character are more likely, Barber argues, to get into trouble. In their efforts to shore up and expand their powers, their resentment and fear of competitors lead them to step beyond any reasonable interpretation of the Constitution and move into shadowy areas that prove unacceptable to mass opinion or to other actors in the political system. *Active-negative presidents,* as Barber terms them, often rigidify their position when faced with opposition and collapse in ruins.

Active-positive presidents, on the other hand, possess character strengths that keep them from disaster. They are upbeat people with self-confidence and a firm grasp on reality. They are strong enough to admit making mistakes and are willing to alter policies that aren't working. Furthermore, active-positive presidents don't cut themselves off from potential allies or the public, so despite the inevitable setbacks that all presidents suffer, they remain close to the mainstream of public opinion and retain a level of support from other political actors.

Passive presidents, too, can be divided into two groups. *Passive-negative presidents* (like Calvin Coolidge) are something of an oddity. They don't invest much energy in the job, nor do they care much for it. *Passive-positive presidents* are not assertive or aggressive policymakers. Nevertheless, they enjoy political life, especially its friendships and the atmosphere of clubhouse joviality. Eager to please and gain acceptance, this type of leader is easily led (and sometimes misled). Warren Harding, for instance, was sickened when he learned that close friends whom he had placed in high positions abused their public trust and became involved in the Teapot Dome scandal.

Whether their character is positive or negative, presidents in our time, as we've seen, are much more likely than in the past to be active in office. Not only do they possess a tempting array of powers unavailable to previous presidents, and not only are they expected to use those powers (remember all the roles presidents must perform), but the circumstances by which politicians reach the White House make it more and more unlikely that a passive personality could achieve it. In this day of weak parties and candidate-centered campaigns, no one can become president by waiting for others to push them forward. Successful candidates must endure years of vigorous self-promotion and campaigning. These days a presidential nomination must be wrested away from others in a long, arduous competition.[24]

In addition to inherent powers and character, Congress has contributed to the expansion of presidential power.

Congress Delegates Power to the President

Presidents in our time have all gained the *potential* to exercise power far beyond that available to executives in the past. One major reason has been legislative acquiescence. Congress has willingly given over 470 emergency powers to the president. The most sweeping delegation of power came during the years 1933–39. With the approval of Congress, President Franklin Roosevelt set up one agency after another to help remedy the economic problems of the depression. These agencies—including the Civilian Conservation Corps (1933), the Public Works Administration (1933), the Farm Security Administration (1934), and the National Labor Relations Board (1935)—were given control over many important public-policy decisions. Although they were originally set up to deal with the "emergency" of the depression, many of these agencies and the policies associated with them continue to exist.[25]

In nonemergency situations, it is quite common for Congress to pass laws that give only general guidelines and then leave it to the executive to "fill in the details." For example, Congress may pass a bill requiring all companies to provide their employees with a "safe working environment." It is then the responsibility of an executive agency (in this case, the Occupational Safety and Health Administration, or OSHA) to set the specific standards for workplace safety. Since these executive agencies are usually run by presidential appointees, the president can exercise quite a bit of influence over the administration, regulation, and interpretation of laws. In many cases, by having direct control over the details, the agencies of the executive branch can actually shape the laws to fit the president's program.

The constitutionality of this congressional delegation of power has been challenged several times. With only a few exceptions, however, the Supreme Court has generally upheld the decision of Congress to give up some control over the administration of its laws. In the past, Congress has tried to reassert some of its administrative and legislative control through different measures.

One was the *legislative veto,* a statutory provision that allowed Congress to delay administrative actions for two or three months. During this time Congress could vote to approve or disapprove the administrative action altogether. Use of the legislative veto expanded rapidly during the Nixon–Ford–Carter years, but then died a swift death at the hands of the Supreme Court. In the case of *INS* v. *Chadha* (1983), the legislative veto was ruled unconstitutional on the grounds that it circumvented the president's own veto power.[26]

Congress still retains a variety of checks on the presidency. It can cut executive agencies, refuse to fund executive initiatives, oversee executive actions, and publicize executive incompetence or venality. Still, its support over the years for vague grants of power to the executive branch has undercut its own position and helped to ensure that presidents remain the central political force in American democracy.

THE LINE ITEM VETO   The 104th Congress seems determined to continue this trend of congressional grants of power to the president. In February 1995, barely a month after its first meeting, the House of Representatives adopted one more reform suggested in the Republican party's "Contract with America" by voting to provide presidents with a crucial power, the **line item veto** (sometimes known as the item veto). In March 1995, the Senate passed the Legislative Line Item Veto Act and President Clinton plans to sign it into law. This device would allow the president to eliminate specific parts of an appropriate bill without having to veto the entire legislation. The line item veto idea holds a superficial appeal. Most bills run scores of pages and may include hundreds of provisions. Some of these are small, objectionable, and costly items placed in the bill by self-interested legislators to aid some local pressure group. Why not give presidents the power to veto these expensive, unnecessary, and often irrelevant provisions, while still preserving the overall measure?

The answer is that no item is "costly, unnecessary, and irrelevant" to those who believe in it. Each separate item in a bill represents a *political* decision: to do X, to fund Y, to oversee Z. The issue is who gets the final say on these items: Congress or the president? Without a line item veto, presidents are often forced to take an entire bill rather than get nothing, even though they may dislike parts of it. That gives Congress power; savvy legislators can include items they want in bills that the president must sign. Even though Congress retains the ability to override a line item veto, the president has an enormous advantage, being able to go through an appropriations bill picking and choosing the parts he likes and crossing out the rest.

The real question then becomes: Should Congress lose some of its power? Should the president gain some? We cannot answer that question. Each citizen must individually grapple with the issue. We merely point out that congressional support for the line item veto stands in a long tradition of congressional delegations of power to the executive branch, a tradition that helps explain why the powers of the president have grown dramatically during this past century.[27]

Conducting Foreign Policy and Making War

Although the president's power has grown in domestic affairs, it is the role as head of the nation in an increasingly complex and dangerous world that has produced the greatest enlargement of executive branch powers.[28] At a time

Americans look to their president as the nation's guide in the arenas of foreign policy and national defense. President Bill Clinton, who avoided military service during the Vietnam War and participated in anti-war protests, has struggled somewhat with the role of military leader. He sought to bolster his commander-in-chief image by visiting victorious U.S. troops in Kuwait in 1994.

when key diplomatic and military decisions must often be made in hours, even minutes, presidents as single individuals with great authority have enormous advantages over a many-headed, continuously talking institution like Congress. At times national survival itself may require nothing less than rapid and unfettered presidential action. Congress, along with the rest of the nation, recognizes that reality. Even more clearly than in the domestic arena, it has delegated broad and sweeping powers that allow presidents to act in foreign affairs with few congressional restraints.

It is not Congress alone that defers to the president in foreign affairs. The executive's preeminence in this field has even been recognized and legitimated by the Supreme Court. Its position was enunciated in the 1936 case of *United States* v. *Curtiss-Wright*. Associate Justice Sutherland's opinion provides the rationale for an active presidential role by distinguishing between foreign and domestic affairs and the powers apportioned to each. While domestic power comes only from an express grant in the Constitution, he argued, in foreign affairs the president is sovereign. Sutherland concluded that the grant of foreign-policy power to the president did not depend on any constitutional provision but rather on the sovereignty of the national government. In sweeping language Sutherland stated: "In this vast external realm, with its important, complicated, delicate and manifold problems, the President alone has the power to speak or listen as a representative of the nation."[29]

PRESIDENTIAL WAR POWERS In philosophy, then, both Court and Congress see the president as the dominant force in foreign policy. This perspective is bolstered by the president's constitutionally delegated role as commander in chief of the American armed forces. Presidents have used this military role in a variety of ways to achieve their policy ends and expand the power of their office.

Some presidents have left the actual conduct of war to professional military personnel, while using their commander-in-chief role to set broad national and international policy. That policy often seemed far removed from urgent military matters. Abraham Lincoln, for instance, issued the Emancipation Proclamation "by the power in me vested as Commander-in-Chief of the Army" and "warranted by the Constitution upon military necessity." In short, Lincoln used his command over the military to abolish slavery. It was a worthy goal, but represents a broad interpretation of the commander-in-chief powers.[30]

In times of crisis, some presidents have gone even further than Lincoln. Following Japan's bombing of Pearl Harbor, Franklin Roosevelt ordered over 100,000 Japanese Americans living on the West Coast evacuated to interior places of internment, citing national security. He thus used his military powers to establish de facto concentration camps. Roosevelt also issued an ultimatum in a speech to Congress on September 7, 1942. Should legislators not repeal provisions within the Emergency Price Control Act, he stated that he would "accept the responsibility and act."[31] Roosevelt's claim here is impressive: that acting in his capacity as commander in chief, he could make domestic policy unrestrained by the wishes of Congress. Even more impressive, perhaps, is the fact that the American people strongly supported him on this matter.

The commander-in-chief role is also used by presidents to make war, and congressional delegation of power to the president has allowed for expansion of this role. Lyndon Johnson, for example, committed ground troops to Vietnam

The commander-in-chief role can be a difficult and burdensome one, as Lyndon Johnson discovered. Johnson's presidency, although marked by numerous successes on the domestic front, was destroyed by his escalation of the war in Vietnam. Johnson, in fact, decided against seeking another term as president because of the war and growing public opposition to it. This photo captures Johnson's personal anguish over Vietnam. He is shown reacting to a taped description of the war's progress sent from Vietnam by his son-in-law.

on the basis of a loosely worded congressional resolution of August 10, 1964. The Southeast Asia Resolution, remembered now as the Tonkin Gulf Resolution, stated that "the Congress approves and supports the determination of the President, as commander-in-chief, to take all necessary measures to repel any armed attack against the forces of the United States and to prevent further aggression." President Johnson later described the resolution as being like grandma's nightshirt—it covered everything!

Using his powers as commander in chief, Richard Nixon later ordered the Vietnam War expanded into Laos and Cambodia, neutral countries at the time. Hundreds of enemy sortie reports were falsified to justify the president's actions. Congress and the public were kept in the dark. The House Judiciary Committee considered but rejected a proposed article of impeachment against Nixon that cited his deliberate misleading of Congress "concerning the existence, scope, and nature" of the American operation in Cambodia. This article was dropped, however, suggesting just how reluctant Congress is to curb a president's powers, even those of an extremely unpopular one, as long as the president appears to be acting in the commander-in-chief capacity.

Still, military power does not make the president a dictator, and commanders in chief have at one time or another been restrained by both Congress and the Supreme Court. In a famous decision (*Youngstown Sheet and Tube Company* v. *Sawyer,* 1952), the Supreme Court struck down Harry Truman's seizure of the domestic steel industry. He had claimed that his powers as commander in chief in wartime (the Korean War) allowed him to seize and run the steel mills to ensure the ongoing efficacy of the war effort. The Court ruled that only a pressing national emergency, which in their opinion did not exist at the time, could justify such a sweeping action in the domestic sphere without approval of Congress.[32]

Congress too has challenged the president in military affairs. After all, the Constitution assigns Congress the power to declare war, order reprisals, raise and support armies, and provide for the common defense. Doesn't that give it the legal authority to commit American forces to combat and oversee their actions? Many legislators believed so and worked to assert Congress's constitutional prerogatives after the unpopular Vietnam War. The result was passage of the War Powers Resolution (1973) over President Nixon's veto.[33]

The resolution requires that the president "in every possible instance" report to Congress within forty-eight hours after committing U.S. troops to hostile action (if no state of war has been declared). If Congress disagrees with the action, the troops must be removed within ninety days. (Actually the troops must be withdrawn within sixty days unless the president requests thirty additional days to ensure their safety.) Since *INS* v. *Chadha* (discussed earlier), Congress can no longer stop the military commitment by concurrent resolution (a resolution passed by both houses in the same form).

The effectiveness of the resolution is debatable. This first test of the resolution occurred in May 1975, when President Gerald Ford quickly ordered the marines and navy to rescue the U.S. merchant ship *Mayaguez,* without any prior consultation with members of Congress. The ship, carrying both civilian and military cargo, was seized by Cambodian ships for being in Cambodia's territorial waters. In his report to Congress, which was submitted *after* the troops had been withdrawn, President Ford cited both his inherent executive power and his authority as commander in chief. According to Ford, "When a crisis breaks out, it is impossible to draw the Congress in with the decision-making process in an effective way."[34]

On October 25, 1983, President Reagan ordered nineteen hundred marine and army troops ashore in an invasion of Grenada. The Reagan administration did not comply with the prior-consultation requirements of the War Powers Resolution, and instead merely informed members of Congress that the invasion was taking place. Many other military actions by presidents have not been reported to Congress, in cases such as El Salvador, Honduras, Bolivia, Cyprus, and Zaire.

President Bush's action in the Persian Gulf was taken without consulting the full Congress. Before sending troops to Saudi Arabia in the summer of 1990, administration officials spoke to just one legislator: Senator Sam Nunn, chairman of the Armed Services Committee. Prior to the offensive operation of Desert Storm in January 1991, Bush relied on the support of the United Nations and a multinational coalition to commit U.S. troops in advance of congressional approval, but he did seek and receive a resolution of congressional approval.[35]

More recently, President Clinton (without congressional approval) took the initiative in 1994 to commit over twenty thousand American troops to the Caribbean island nation of Haiti to help restore democracy.

These examples illustrate that a congressional declaration of war is no longer needed for a president to send American troops into combat. While the Constitution grants Congress the power to "declare war," history, practice, precedent, and popular expectation have given the president authority to "make war." The history of war powers has been one of the presidents' making wars before Congress declares them. Congress is then left with few options but to support the action. Appropriations cutoffs expose legislators to charges of having stranded soldiers in the field. Perhaps these facts explain why presidents have committed troops abroad in dozens of combat situations, while Congress has actually declared war only five times.

Going Public

We have seen that the growing importance of America's role in the world has helped increase the president's power; an American president is a world leader. Another fact of modern life—electronic technology—has enhanced the stature of the presidency, elevating the executive to influence well beyond that conceived for it by the framers. Given the singular nature of the office, a President can use modern means of communication to curry public support for his policies. As individuals in an age of personality, they are in a position to manipulate the electronic media to enhance their reputation, which most members of Congress are unable to do.[36]

During the early years of the Republic, presidents promoted themselves through the prevailing means of communication: public speeches, pamphlets, and articles. Although nearly all of the early presidents had some experience in mass persuasion, that experience was by no means considered a vital component of the office.

Throughout the nineteenth century most presidents, with the conspicuous exception of Andrew Johnson, communicated to Congress in formal, written addresses. Public speeches were suspect, to be avoided as demagoguery.

Ronald Reagan was an expert at communicating with the American public. And no American president better understood how to make the best of a photo opportunity. The former movie actor was perfectly suited for television and the various communication techniques of the modern presidency.

president@white-house.gov

When Bill Clinton became president on January 20, 1993, he announced a "new beginning," thereby continuing the tradition in which every president, upon assuming office, declares that the new administration will be more "open" than its predecessor. Clinton and his staff, however, added a unique, high-tech twist to the promise of greater openness: They put the White House on line. Through electronic mail (E-mail), disgruntled taxpayers, loyal supporters, and political junkies can now access the White House directly to voice their complaints, express their support, or download the latest presidential speech or press release.

The electronic presidency actually began with Clinton's predecessor, George Bush. During the Bush administration the White House carried three commercial E-mail services, through which it received several thousand messages each week. But as one journalist pointed out, "It wasn't truly an electronic connection. The services collected messages on computer floppy disks, which they sent by mail or courier to the White House."

The Clinton administration's system established a direct link between the White House and the global electronic network known as the Internet. Anyone with a computer and a modem can leave a message for the president at his E-mail address: president@white-house.gov. There is a catch, however: As with any other correspondence addressed to 1600 Pennsylvania Avenue, E-mail directed to the president is not guaranteed to reach him. The president and vice president are given a sample of the messages that come in each day, but according to Lynda Rathbone, coordinator of the E-mail program, "It just depends on who has a lucky day that day and gets picked."

In theory, then, the fact that Americans can contact the president electronically can be seen as another step in approaching democracy. But in reality E-mail does little to remove the obstacles that prevent most Americans from participating in the political process. To begin with, not everyone owns a computer, and many of those who do are not linked to the Internet. Moreover, just as they rarely write letters to their elected officials, most Americans are unlikely to take the time to E-mail the president. And of course there's the fact that the president himself may not receive the message. It is safe to conclude, therefore, that E-mail has not made the White House more "open" than it was when people used a pen or a typewriter to write to the president.

Cutting Edge

Indeed, one of the impeachment charges against Johnson read that he "did . . . make and deliver with a loud voice certain intemperate, inflammatory, and scandalous harangues . . . particularly indecent and unbecoming in the chief Magistrate of the United States."[37] These charges seem laughable today when effective speechmaking has become a requirement of the presidency.

It was not until the twentieth-century presidency of Theodore Roosevelt, in fact, that presidents assumed the role of preachers in what Roosevelt called "the bully pulpit." Great American oratory—what there was of it—had always come from Congress, out of the mouths of speakers like Stephen Douglas, Daniel Webster, and Henry Clay. Roosevelt changed all that, at least for the duration of his term. He spoke loudly and often—but only when compared with presidents of his day, not presidents of ours.

Woodrow Wilson was the first twentieth-century president to use mass persuasion for a particular policy goal. Facing serious opposition in Congress after World War I, Wilson toured the country in search of support for the League of Nations. He was unsuccessful, but the presidency thereafter became a national

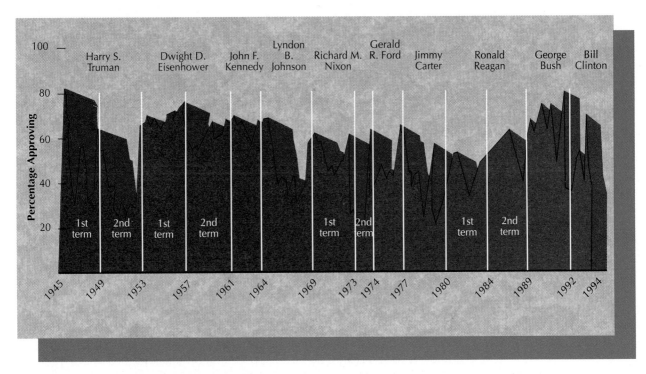

FIGURE 6.2   Presidential Approval Ratings

theater with the chief executive the most visible actor on the stage. That supreme thespian, Franklin D. Roosevelt, would soon be expertly using the presidency as a forum for mass persuasion.

A master of public communication, Roosevelt used that expertise to increase the power of the national government and in particular the president.
He did this in part by personalizing the office. People felt that they knew and
understood the president as a person, not just as a chief executive. What
Roosevelt began, other presidents continued. While varying widely in their skill
as communicators, no president since Roosevelt has attempted to govern without also attempting to create and maintain mass support.

Presidents see popular opinion as a source of power. Yet the need for public support is also a constraint: Presidents must now be *seen* to be governing
for people to believe that they *are* governing. Presidents must therefore be attentive to their approval ratings (see Figure 6.2) and dedicate increasing
amounts of time to the public side of their office. As a result, the office has
become increasingly more ceremonial and increasingly less deliberative than
the framers ever intended.

Nonetheless, presidents have long recognized the advantages of what political scientist Samuel Kernell calls **going public,** promoting themselves and
their policies to the American people.[38] The strategy includes televised press
conferences, prime-time addresses, White House ceremonies, and satellite
broadcasts.[39] Rather than bargain directly with Congress, presidents appeal to
the American public, hoping to generate popular pressure for their policy
aims. Presidents Reagan, Bush, and Clinton have all used this strategy. In one

nationally televised speech, for example, Reagan once appealed to the public to "contact your senators and congressmen. Tell them of your support for this bipartisan [tax] proposal." George Bush used to visit the districts of Republicans in Congress to generate support for himself and his policies. President Clinton has attempted to appeal to different national constituencies through appearances on popular television shows such as "Larry King Live" and on MTV. His televised New England–style "town meetings" also bring him into personal contact with some of his constituents.

Going public may appear to be an easier strategy than bargaining or negotiation, but it is a far riskier one. Members of Congress may feel themselves ill disposed toward a president who bypasses them and goes directly to the people. Going public thus carries risks for the often tenuous lines of communication between the White House and Capitol Hill. Generally, negotiators must be prepared to compromise, and bargaining proceeds best behind closed doors. By fixing a firm presidential position on an issue through public posturing, however, the strategy of going public may serve to rigidify a president's bargaining position and make later compromise with other politicians difficult.

Perhaps most dangerous of all considerations for a strategy of going public is the uncertain reaction it may produce in voters. Not all presidents are brilliant communicators. Not all presidents remain popular throughout their term. For an unpopular president, direct appeals to the public may actually backfire by underscoring a lack of popular support. Clinton's national health-care program was surely hurt by ineffective explanations of it to the American public.

Despite the risks of going public, that strategy along with inherent powers, presidential character, congressional delegation of power, and foreign-policy responsibilities has allowed for major expansion in the powers of the presidency.

THE INSTITUTIONALIZED PRESIDENCY

Although only one individual, the president is expected to manage a national government of some 2,700,000 employees. To describe this position is to define the problem. Presidents must effectively manage not only the national government but also their staffs, those hired to help them manage. The bureaucratic aspects of this job are daunting.

Before 1939 presidents relied on a few clerks for general staff assistance. One of President Washington's first decisions was to hire his nephew Lawrence Lewis as a clerical assistant. Lewis, the president's sole employee, was paid out of Washington's own pocket. That tradition continued for seventy years until Congress appropriated funds for the president's household staff in 1833.

Andrew Jackson was the first president to receive an allowance for a departmental clerk who was authorized only to sign land patents. For day-to-day functions such as writing letters or speeches, however, the president was still left to his own resources. Not until 1857 did Congress fund the first official household staff budget, including a private secretary ($2,000 a year), an executive mansion steward ($1,200), messengers ($900), and a contingency fund ($750).

Little had changed by 1937, when Franklin Roosevelt, who had a secretary, a press secretary, and a handful of aides, became overwhelmed by the administrative aspects of an expanded modern government and the proliferation of New

Deal agencies. Believing that expanded government requires management tools equal to the task, Roosevelt commissioned the Committee on Administrative Management, usually referred to as the *Brownlow Commission*. This group recommended that the president receive permanent staff for managing the executive branch. Its report began with a clarion call, "the President needs help," and recommended that the president receive both personal and institutional assistance.[40]

The Brownlow report displayed keen insight and sensitivity with regard to the potential dangers of installing unelected and anonymous staff into a White House office. It recognized that the effectiveness of presidential assistants could be directly proportional to their ability to discharge their functions with restraint. Therefore, they were to remain in the background, make no decisions, issue no orders, make no public statements, and never impose themselves between Cabinet officers and the president. These assistants were to have no independent power base and should "not attempt to exercise power on their own account." In the famous words of the Brownlow report, they were to have a "passion for anonymity." (Taken to excess by the Watergate plumbers.)

As presidential aides have multiplied, the Brownlow report's admirable goals have become difficult to maintain. Staff members have grown in power, along with the presidency, and in an open democracy few people with power can maintain anonymity for long. Many of them have come to hold important powers, despite being unmentioned in the Constitution, and the number of people working directly for the president has become so large that we need complex organizational charts merely to keep track of them. Let us look at a few of these institutions that compose the modern presidency.

The White House Office

Closest to the president are those who work in the White House, where the president both lives and works. Thus, White House staff are never far from their employer. The White House is located at 1600 Pennsylvania Avenue NW, Washington, D.C. The first family sleeps upstairs, while the president works downstairs in the West Wing Oval Office. Presidential staff also work downstairs in both the East and West wings.

The president's chief lieutenants operate nearby in the West Wing. Also located in the West Wing are the Situation Room, the Oval Office, the National Security Council staff, the vice president's office, assistants to the president, and the Cabinet Room. The East Wing houses the First Lady's office, congressional relations staff, and various social correspondence units.

All presidential assistants in the White House tread a thin line between the power they derive from being close to the president and their actual role as assistants and underlings. An office in the White House can transform the most sensible person into someone who cannot resist barking into a phone, "This is the White House calling." Jack Valenti, a special assistant to President Johnson from 1963 to 1966, explains the temptations:

> You sit next to the Sun King and you bask in his rays, and you have those three magic words, "the President wants." All of a sudden you have power unimagined by you before you got in that job. And if you don't watch out, you begin to believe that it is your splendid intellect, your charm and your insights into the human condition that give you all this power. . . . The arrogance sinks

From First Lady to First Woman

During the 1992 election campaign Hillary Rodham Clinton caught a lot of flak. She was attacked for her social and political ideas as well as for her fierce independence. The image she projected, a stark contrast to that of the traditional First Lady, was that of an established professional, a successful lawyer who brought with her a political agenda and a personal outlook formed long before she became involved in her husband's pursuit of the presidency. Many voters found her unfeminine and even threatening, a perception that was heightened by her statement that she was not interested in "staying home and baking cookies." The criticism continued after Bill Clinton took office and announced that the First Lady would head the task force assigned to formulate proposals for national health-care reform.

What the critics did not realize, or chose to ignore, was that Hillary Clinton was not the only First Lady with her own career, nor was she the first to serve as her husband's closest political adviser. She was the latest in a long line of influential First Ladies that stretches back to Abigail Adams and includes Nellie Taft, Florence Harding, Edith Wilson, Eleanor Roosevelt, and Rosalynn Carter.

The difference in Hillary Clinton's case is that she pursued her duties as "First Woman" with unprecedented vigor. Her appearances before congressional committees on behalf of the administration's health-care proposals were consummate performances in which she alternately charmed and finessed some of the toughest legislators in town. This unusual exercise of power drew volleys of criticism. Many observers felt that it went beyond the bounds of propriety and might even be unconstitutional. First Ladies, they felt, should be confined to social activities or figurehead roles such as leading campaigns to beautify America or combat drug abuse.

Here again, though, Rodham Clinton was not the first. As one observer has written, "Virtually every First Lady who has used her influence has been either ridiculed or vilified as deviating from women's proper role or has been feared as emasculating."* After the president's health-care reform proposals foundered in a divided and contentious Congress and the 1994 elections produced a shift in the balance of power in Washington, Rodham Clinton's public image suffered still further. For the time being, it appears that the nation is not yet ready to have a First Woman in the White House.

*Edith P. Mayo, "The Influence and Power of First Ladies," *Chronicle of Higher Education,* September 15, 1993, p. A52.

deeper into their veins than they think possible. What it does after a while is breed a kind of insularity that keeps you from being subject to the same fits of insecurity that most human beings have. Because you very seldom are ever turned down. You are seen in Washington. There are stories in *Newsweek* and *Time* about how important you are. I'm telling you this is like mainlining heroin. And while you are exercising it, it is so blinding and dazzling that you forget, literally forget, that it is borrowed and transitory power.[41]

These unelected, unconfirmed presidential assistants have taken on major administrative roles. Some of them gain almost as much power and fame as the presidents they serve. A few that come to mind are H. R. Haldeman and John Erlichman under Nixon, Hamilton Jordon under Carter, Jim Baker under Reagan, Sununu under Bush, and Leon Panetta under Clinton.

The size of the staff has increased with the growth of government. As presidents are expected to solve more and more problems, the number of specialists on the White House staff has come to look like "a veritable index of American society" (in political scientist Thomas Cronin's words).[42] These men and women come from every imaginable background. Because their loyalty is solely to the president and not an administrative agency, they seem more trustworthy to the president than Cabinet members or high-level officials from the civil service. The president therefore puts them to running the everyday operations of the presidency. White House staff members often end up usurping the policymaking power normally held by Cabinet secretaries, their staffs, and the staffs of various independent executive agencies.

THE CHIEF OF STAFF   The White House **chief of staff** is now the president's de facto top aide. Often earning a reputation as assistant president, this individual is responsible for the operation of the White House and acts as gatekeeper to the president. The chief of staff also plays a key role in policymaking. During the Eisenhower years, Chief of Staff Sherman Adams was so influential that the following joke became popular: "Wouldn't it be awful if Ike died, then we'd have Nixon as President?" Response: "But it would be even worse if Sherman Adams died. Then Eisenhower would be President." In like manner, H. R. Haldeman, Nixon's chief of staff, was once described as "an extension of the President."[43]

President Clinton's chief of staff Leon Panetta plays a multitude of roles. He heads the White House staff, serves as a public liaison, and acts as the president's chief of public relations. Panetta is a familiar face on television news programs where he explains and defends the administration's policies and goals. As chief of staff, he is perhaps the most influential of all nonconfirmed presidential assistants.

Leon Panetta, Clinton's chief of staff, has full authority over White House operations, but as with others who have held that position, his powers don't stop there. He played a major role, for instance, in forcing Cabinet members to cut their department budget proposals for the 1995 fiscal year. According to one observer, "He's got all the things you look for in a chief of staff—knowledge of the way Washington operates, broad acceptance on both sides of Capitol Hill. He's political. He's substantive. He understands where politics and substance merge." Since all presidents need help running the executive branch, they are likely to continue to install close, trusted advisers as chief of staff.

The Executive Office of the President

This title is somewhat misleading, since there is no single Executive Office building. Instead, the **Executive Office of the President (EOP)** consists of staff units that serve the president but are not located in the White House. Some of these units include the National Security Council, the Council of Economic Advisors, and the Office of Management and Budget, among others (see Figure 6.3).

THE NATIONAL SECURITY COUNCIL   The National Security Council (NSC) was established in 1947 and its formal membership consists of the president, vice-president, and secretaries of defense and state. The special assistant to the president for national security affairs is the council's principal supervisory officer. The NSC's job is to advise the president on all aspects of domestic, foreign, and military policy that relate to national security. During the Reagan years, the NSC went past advising and became involved in operational matters, as it did during the Iran-Contra affair. According to Reagan NSC head Admiral

FIGURE 6.3   **Executive Office of the President**

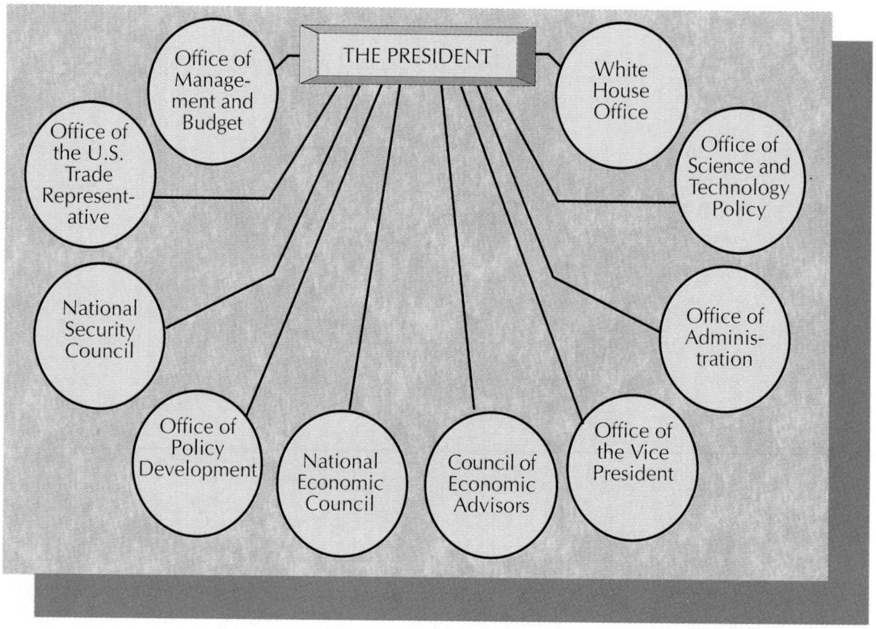

Poindexter, "In the very real world we live in, the NSC staff has got to be the catalyst that keeps the process moving forward, keeps the President's decisions moving along, and helps to make sure that they are implemented, and that often involves an operational role for the NSC staff. Their only loyalty is to the President."[44] During the first two years of the Clinton presidency the NSC has been headed by Anthony Lake, who has rejected the Poindexter model of operating.

THE COUNCIL OF ECONOMIC ADVISORS   The Council of Economic Advisors (CEA) was created by the Employment Act of 1946. The legislation was intended to give the president professional, institutionalized, economic staff resources. Today, the CEA is responsible for forecasting national economic trends, making economic analyses for the president, and helping to prepare the president's annual economic report to Congress. The CEA chairperson is appointed by the president with the advice and consent of Congress. The recently created National Economic Council is responsible for coordinating high-priority economic policy matters for the president.

Although the CEA is a valuable resource, the president actually gets most economic advice collectively, from a group referred to as the "troika"—a functional division of labor among the secretary of the treasury (revenue estimates), the CEA (the private economy), and the Office of Management and Budget (federal expenditures). When the chair of the Federal Reserve Board is included in the group, it is referred to as the "quadriad."

OFFICE OF MANAGEMENT AND THE BUDGET   Observers of American politics have long recognized the central role that the Office of Management and Budget (OMB) plays.[45] While the OMB's primary responsibility is to prepare and implement the budget, the office is also responsible for evaluating the performance of federal programs. As such, it reviews management processes within the executive branch, prepares executive orders and proclamations, plans the development of federal statistical services, and advises the president on the activities of all federal departments. The OMB also helps promote the president's legislative agenda with Congress. As the most highly developed coordinating and review unit in the Executive Office, the OMB is also the most powerful. It acts as the central institutional mechanism for imprinting (some would say inflicting) presidential will over the government.

The OMB began as the Bureau of the Budget (BOB) in 1921. It acted at first only as a super-accountant, keeping track of the executive branch's books. Over the years, BOB's powers continued to grow until, in 1970, a major executive office reorganization transformal BOB into OMB, with greatly expanded powers. Given its array of responsibilities and powers, OMB's influence now extends into every nook and cranny of the executive branch.

The Cabinet

Cabinet officers act as a link between the president and the rest of the American political system. Cabinet departments have been created by Congress, which has given them specific legal responsibilities and political mandates. Department heads are confirmed by the Senate and are frequently called to testify before congressional committees. As an institution the Cabinet itself is unusual. It is not mentioned in either the Constitution or in statutory law, yet it has

FYI

When a president delivers the State of the Union address, all but one cabinet member attends. The lone nonparticipant stays behind to represent the country should the Capitol be attacked.

FIGURE 6.4 Line of Succession to the Office of the Presidency of the United States

1. Vice president
2. Speaker of the House of Representatives
3. Senate president pro tempore
4. Secretary of State
5. Secretary of the Treasury
6. Secretary of Defense
7. Attorney General
8. Secretary of the Interior
9. Secretary of Agriculture
10. Secretary of Commerce
11. Secretary of Labor
12. Secretary of Health and Human Services
13. Secretary of Housing and Urban Development
14. Secretary of Transportation
15. Secretary of Energy
16. Secretary of Education
17. Secretary of Veterans Affairs

become a permanent part of the presidency. The framers considered but eventually rejected adding a council of any kind to the executive. Thus, "the cabinet" as such doesn't legally exist. Nevertheless, the idea of a cabinet surfaced early. Newspapers began using the term in the 1790s to describe the relationship between President Washington and his executive officers.

In its most formal meaning the **cabinet** refers to the secretaries of the major departments of the bureaucracy and any other officials the president designates (such as the OMB director). An informal distinction is often made between the inner and outer cabinet. Members of the *inner cabinet* are the most visible and enjoy more direct access to the president. Typically this inner cabinet is composed of the secretaries of state, defense, treasury, and justice. These being the most powerful positions, presidents tend to staff them with close political allies.[46]

Cabinet officers are responsible for running their departments as well as advising the president on matters of policy. Although many of its members have been quite distinguished, the cabinet has rarely served as a collective source of advice. John Kennedy, for instance, scoffed at calling full Cabinet meetings; he saw no reason to consult the postmaster general about matters of war and peace. Lincoln viewed his cabinet with something approaching disdain. On the occasion of signing the Emancipation Proclamation, he looked around his Cabinet table and said, "I have gathered you together to hear what I have written down. I do not wish your advice about the main matter. That I have determined for myself."

Presidents often say they will use the cabinet as a real policymaking group, but they rarely do. For instance, Harry Truman once promised that "the Cabinet is not merely a collection of executives administering different governmental functions. It is a body whose combined judgment the President uses to formulate the fundamental policies of the administration." Yet when North Korea attacked South Korea in 1950, Truman never once convened his cabinet on the matter of U.S. entry into war.

The president who took cabinet meetings most seriously was Dwight D. Eisenhower. Not only did his cabinet meet regularly with a set agenda, but Eisenhower also created the position of cabinet secretariat to serve as a liaison with the president. He also expanded the size of the official cabinet to include such important aides as U.S. ambassador to the United Nations, budget director, White House chief of staff, and a national security affairs assistant. Still, most presidents have followed a different pattern. Cabinet members end up as glorified bureaucrats, running their department and consulting with the president individually about their specialized activities.[47]

The Vice Presidency

The second-highest elected official in the United States, the **vice president,** has few significant constitutional responsibilities. Indeed, the only powers actually assigned to the vice president by the Constitution are to preside over the Senate (except in cases of impeachment) and cast a vote when the Senate is deadlocked. Even that job is one that most vice presidents shun. Few have wished to spend all day listening to senators talk. The vice president's most important job is the one Americans hope he never takes—succeeding to the presidency in case of death, resignation, or removal (Figure 6.4 outlines the line of succession to the presidency). As Woodrow Wilson once wrote, "There is very little to be said about the vice-president. . . . His importance consists in the fact that he may cease to be vice-president."

The actual work of the vice president ends up being whatever the president decides it will be. In recent years presidents have done more to bestow authority than to remove it. The growth in their own responsibilities has led them to turn to the vice president for help. For that reason the office of vice president, like that of the president, is becoming institutionalized. Between 1960 and 1980, vice presidential staff grew from twenty to more than seventy, and largely parallels the president's with domestic- and foreign-policy specialists, speech writers, congressional liaisons, and press secretaries.

Recent occupants of the office have been deeply involved in substantive matters of policy. Nelson Rockefeller chaired President Ford's Domestic Council. Walter Mondale served as a senior presidential advisor on matters of Carter administration policy. President Reagan appointed George Bush to lead the administration's crisis management team. Dan Quayle played an important role as chair of the Bush administration's Council on Competitiveness. Al Gore Jr. was placed in charge of President Clinton's ambitious program to "reinvent government" by downsizing the bureaucracy, streamlining procedures, updating systems, and eliminating some subsidies and programs. This mammoth endeavor was slated to save an estimated $108 billion by the year 2000 and involved the vice president in the fundamental workings of the entire federal government.

All in all, a new tradition seems to have been set up, making vice presidents an integral part of any current administration. While presidents in the past often ignored their vice presidents, such a relationship seems unlikely to occur in the future. The vice presidential office has come to play a major role in the modern presidency.

Vice President Mondale has been credited with rehabilitiating the role of the vice president. Here President Carter and Mondale meet in one of their regularly scheduled luncheons to discuss matters of national policy.

THE CHALLENGES OF PRESIDENTIAL LEADERSHIP

THE POWER TO PERSUADE   President Lyndon Baines Johnson once said in a moment of frustration, "Don't talk to me about power. The only power I have is nuclear, and I can't use that." Johnson's point was that the presidency is a democratic office in a democratic republic, not an authoritarian office in a dictatorship. Presidents may command, especially in their role as commander in chief, but most often they attempt to persuade. And persuasion is much more difficult and time-consuming than ordering, as every president discovers.

The thesis that leadership in a democracy depends on the practice of persuasion lies at the heart of political scientist Richard Neustadt's influential book *Presidential Power.*[48] In exercising power, Neustadt argues, a president has little real ability to command. Orders that are disliked can be gotten around, fudged, or even disobeyed. Precious energy can be wasted, and power resources depleted, trying to enforce unpopular commands. Many actors in the system (judges and justices, senators, state governors) simply can't be commanded. Persuasion remains a president's most common tool for getting what he wants. "Presidential power," says Neustadt, "is the power to persuade.

But how can the president persuade others to act? The secret is to convince them that it is in their own self-interest to do what the president suggests. It helps if the president can give them something they want. Neustadt admits that "the power to persuade is the power to bargain." Only by trading something of value can a president exert influence.

This power to persuade through bargaining lay at the heart of George Bush's success in building a world coalition against Saddam Hussein in Operation Desert Shield and Operation Desert Storm. He didn't (and couldn't) *order* allies and former enemies to back U.S. military efforts in the Gulf. Instead, he got on the telephone and *persuaded* world leaders "to do the right thing," as Harry Truman would have put it. When pure persuasion didn't work, he used promises and favors. Various countries judged that the prospect of trade concessions, military hardware, or diplomatic recognition was sufficient inducement to come to the support of American military policy. In this crisis President Bush used to his advantage abroad the classical repertory of tactical devices that American presidents have long found useful in dealing with Congress at home."

Some political scientists have argued that the president has more power to command policy than Neustadt envisions. An overwhelming number of decisions are routine bureaucratic ones that will be followed without question by lower staff and civil service members. Even securing compliance from top staff members may be easy; these assistants have longtime ties with the president and wish to continue their service. In addition, certain presidents have considerable charisma, which leads people to do what the White House wishes without the president even making a request. Other presidents can rely on a cadre of ideological allies eager to promote their programs. Still, the president needs considerable experience to recognize which decisions will be routinely implemented and which will need close personal attention.

PARTY WEAKNESS   Another challenge for presidential leadership skills derives from the weakness of American political parties. In many European countries, especially those with parliamentary systems, political parties provide the basis for organizing the national government. They propose and enact legislation, and they are collectively accountable for the results of that legislation. The weak American parties have generally been unable to run the country's fractured governing institutions.[49]

Party weakness has been both an advantage and a disadvantage for presidents. On the one hand, presidents' actions are relatively unrestrained by the political pressures of strong parties. They do not have to consult with their parties, nor are they really bound by the ideological preferences associated with strong parties. In other words, presidents have great flexibility and freedom of action compared with leaders of parliamentary systems.

On the other hand, presidents are also disadvantaged compared with prime ministers, for they must try to get their legislation enacted with considerably less partisan support in Congress. While presidents can generally count on most of the members of their parties to vote on their side of an issue, this is by no means guaranteed. Clinton's successes with both the North American Free Trade Agreement (NAFTA) and the 1994 crime bill were due largely to the support of many Republicans. If the president had counted simply on congressional Democrats, it is likely that neither bill would have passed. In like manner George Bush needed to convince some congressional Democrats, as well as his own Republicans, to support his aggressive military posture against Iraq. Presidents, then, must convince their partisans as well as their political opponents to vote for their measures. Since that is no easy task, the chances of failure at any given moment are high.

THE PERSONAL PRESIDENCY   To increase their likelihood of success in their dealings with Congress, presidents starting with Teddy Roosevelt, as we've seen, began to actively court the public to take their side. Modern presidents have made increasing use of this strategy. So prevalent are these attempts at mass persuasion that some scholars have coined a new term to describe them, the *rhetorical presidency*.[50] They point to a fundamental change in the development of the office: away from institutional leadership and toward personal leadership—a change that brings with it new challenges.

The president's ties with the public are deeply influenced by the mass media. As television has come to dominate national life, so the president dominates national news. This in turn has led to a focus on the president's personality rather than policies. Who the president is becomes more important than what the president does. This ever-increasing focus on personality also explains why the American public seems to care so much about the behavior and style of the president's spouse—indeed, the president's entire family.

The tendency to confuse policy success or failure with the president's personality, a key trend of our time, may ultimately weaken the executive branch. Political scientist Theodore Lowi has traced the development of a personal presidency from the founding period to the middle of the Reagan administration. He argues that modern presidents have become slaves to a level of public expectation they cannot hope to satisfy yet nonetheless encourage. They use their foreign-policy powers to become seemingly colossal figures on the world stage. They make an increasing number of bold promises to capture an ever-fragmenting electorate. Challengers to the office make even bolder claims, generating a spiral of promises and expectations about what a president can accomplish. As the public comes to see the presidency as powerful, it expects more from the office than the office can possibly deliver. Then, when expectations inevitably fail to be fulfilled, disillusionment sets in, and presidents take the blame. The result, says Lowi, is a series of broken promises, disenchanted electorates, and failed presidencies.

The chief characteristic of the personal presidency is that it derives power directly from the people without going through Congress or a political party. When presidents need help, they appeal to the people; when the people need assistance, they turn to the president. To maintain public support, presidents must make promises. If they keep these promises (not an easy task), they increase the level of public expectations for future performance. If they are unable to keep their promises (now almost a given, in Lowi's eyes), presidents are considered failures. The promises of past presidents set the standard by which others are judged, leading to the current perception of the president as "a combination of Jesus Christ and the Statue of Liberty." In this environment, presidential failure may become routine; no one can live up to the promises and expectations Americans hold for this office.[51]

Yet even in such a complex and daunting environment, some presidents have found ways to push their policies, work with Congress, avoid disasters, and maintain a reasonable level of public support. Dwight Eisenhower, John Kennedy, and Ronald Reagan come quickly to mind, and to a lesser extent

Throughout his presidency Franklin Roosevelt had an agreement with the press that he would not be photographed in his wheelchair or using crutches. That agreement was honored for the twelve years that Roosevelt was president. It is hard to imagine that such an agreement would be kept today, however, when virtually every aspect of a president's life is subject to media scrutiny.

In 1961, in a Congress far less diverse than today's, President John F. Kennedy delivers his State of the Union address. The nation's youngest elected president was a master orator who could inspire his audiences, whether they were fellow politicians or the general public.

Harry Truman and George Bush. The challenge of presidential leadership is how to govern in a system characterized by limited structural support, limited room for political maneuver, an emphasis on quick results and constant pressure for something new, a constant scrutiny of both the person and the politics of the president, and ever-escalating expectations of the office. In many ways, the president's job is an impossible one. The real surprise is that we have had relatively few clear failures in the office.

THE PRESIDENCY AND APPROACHING DEMOCRACY

Like the Constitution's designers, Americans have long been suspicious of power. We appear to believe, like Lord Acton, a British politician, that "power corrupts and absolute power corrupts absolutely." That belief has not changed much since the eighteenth century. What has changed, however, is the role government plays in American life. Americans have delegated increasing amounts of power to the national government and to the presidency; their expectations of both the government and the chief executive have risen proportionately. Yet the president remains embedded in a system designed to restrain power. This combination of high expectation and restraint on actual power produces contradictions, tensions, and challenges for presidents.

History has shown that some presidents were better qualified than others. Most were able to exercise their power within an acceptable range. In a few cases, notably that of Richard Nixon, the president abused both his power and the people's trust. Even then, American democracy worked as designed. Other institutions (Congress, the courts, a free press) came forward, exercising their own constitutional powers, to check and restrain an overarching president. If it were not for a free press, we might not have known about Watergate. Watergate also proved that we have a flexible Constitution. Through the use of our

own voices and laws we were able to "dethrone" a president without any bloodshed. The Constitution allowed for a peaceful and legitimate passage of power to another representative of the people. This should not be taken lightly; as daily news reports remind us, many countries in the world do not have this option.

The framers designed the presidency so that its potential for energy would be encouraged and its potential for tyranny would be minimized. Accomplishing both of those ends entailed the creation of a complicated separation and distribution of powers. But that distribution has been altered; presidents have gained power by formal grants of delegated power, Court-sanctioned assumptions of power, and popularly based expansions of power.

In our study of the presidency we have seen the dynamics of a democratic society at work. The Executive Office of the Presidency was created and expanded to help a twentieth-century president deal with managing a modern government of over two hundred million citizens. Yet despite this increase in the potential for power, presidents are seriously constrained by the context in which they are embedded. While great, their powers are far from absolute. Except in rare cases of clear emergencies, presidents do not act alone. They must seek and attain the approval of Congress, the courts, and the people. And those people have high expectations. No other office of government represents the elements of democracy to Americans more than the presidency. The president is perceived as the moral, political, economic, and military leader of the nation.

And even though the president's powers are limited by the Constitution, Americans expect the president to save them in a crisis, hold the president responsible for the good times and the bad, expect all presidential promises to be kept, and assume that the president is the guardian of America's ideals and hopes for the future.

Thus, some disenchantment with presidential performance in office seems almost inevitable, no matter who the president. Tensions between the promise and the limitations of this unique office are likely to continue to present the biggest challenges for this institution's approach to democracy.

SUMMARY

1. The framers designed the presidency to be independent of the legislature. This was achieved by creating a single executive who would be selected neither by Congress nor directly by the people. The president would serve a fixed term of office but be eligible to serve more than one term. The framers also made it very difficult to remove the president from office.

2. The veto power gives the president a central role in the legislative process. The president also has the power to appoint officials of the executive branch and nominate justices of the Supreme Court. Treaties with other nations are negotiated by the president but must be approved by a two-thirds majority of the Senate. To avoid seeking Senate approval, modern presidents have made increasing use of executive agreements.

3. The president performs a variety of roles, both formal and informal. Among these are chief of state, commander in chief, chief diplomat, chief legislator, chief executive, moral leader, and party leader. The president is also viewed as the manager of the nation's prosperity.

4. Activist presidents go beyond the powers prescribed in the Constitution when they feel that extraordinary action is required; this view of the presidency is referred to as stewardship. Constructionist presidents, in contrast, exercise no powers other than those that are expressly granted by the Constitution or an act of Congress. The theory of inherent powers holds that the Constitution grants broad authority to the executive during times of national emergency.

5. James David Barber has classified presidents according to their personality and character. Active-positive presidents interpret the powers of the presidency broadly and enjoy political activity; active-negative presidents also take an activist approach, but they view political activity with distrust and occasional hostility. Some earlier presidents were passive-positive or passive-negative, but few recent presidents have fallen into these categories.

6. Congressional grants of power to the president have greatly increased the power of the presidency. The greatest enlargement of executive branch powers has occurred in the areas of foreign and military policy. Bowing to the president's constitutionally delegated role as commander in chief of the armed forces, Congress has largely acquiesced to the president in matters related to war. In 1973, however, it passed the War Powers Resolution, which requires that the president report to Congress within forty-eight hours after committing U.S. troops to hostile action.

7. Advances in communications technology have increased the president's influence by enabling the president to reach ever-larger numbers of people more quickly. Modern presidents promote their policies to the people through televised press conferences, prime-time speeches, and the like.

8. In recent decades the president's staff has grown steadily, and staff members have come to hold important powers. The White House chief of staff is responsible for White House operations but also plays a key role in policymaking. The special assistant for national security affairs may also have considerable influence. The Office of Management and Budget plays a central role in executive policy because it is responsible for evaluating the performance of federal programs as well as budget formation.

9. The cabinet consists of the secretaries of the major departments of the federal bureaucracy and any other officials designated by the president. The inner cabinet consists of the secretaries of state, defense, treasury, and justice. Cabinet officials are responsible for running their Departments as well as advising the president on matters of policy.

10. In the event of the death, resignation, or removal of the president, the vice president succeeds to the presidency. In recent administrations vice presidents have become increasingly involved in substantive matters of policy.

11. One view of the presidency holds that the president's real power derives from the ability to persuade and bargain. Another view places more emphasis on the formal powers of the presidency but does not downplay the im-

portance of leadership skills. A key factor is the relative weakness of American political parties, which do not provide as much support in Congress as European political parties do in their legislatures. As a result, modern presidents often go public, that is, attempt to persuade the people to put pressure on their legislators in support of the president's policies.

KEY TERMS

veto
pocket veto
treaties
executive agreements
stewardship

constructionist
inherent powers
line item veto
going public

chief of staff
Executive Office of the President (EOP)
cabinet
vice president

SUGGESTED READINGS

- Barber, James David. *The Presidential Character: Predicting Performances in the White House.* Englewood Cliffs, N.J.: Prentice Hall, 1985. This provocative study postulates that from the pattern a person followed in political life, we can predict how that person will perform as president.

- Brace, Paul, and Barbara Hinkley. *Follow the Leader: Opinion Polls and the Modern Presidents.* New York: Basic Books, 1992. A systematic account of how presidents from Truman to Bush have been influenced by polls.

- Drew, Elizabeth. *On the Edge: The Clinton Presidency.* New York: Simon and Schuster, 1994. This is the first inside, full-spectrum assessment of the Clinton presidency's first two years.

- Edwards, George C., III, John H. Kessel, and Bert Rockman, eds. *Researching the Presidency.* Pittsburgh, Pa.: University of Pittsburgh Press, 1993. The most up-to-date evaluation of the major areas of current presidency scholarship. The book also offers new approaches to research on the presidency.

- Greenstein, Fred, ed. *Leadership in the Modern Presidency.* Cambridge, Mass.: Harvard University Press, 1988. This book provides detailed portraits of the leadership styles and organizational talents of presidents from Franklin D. Roosevelt through Ronald Reagan.

- Kernell, Samuel. *Going Public: New Strategies of Presidential Leadership.* Washington, D.C.: CQ Press, 1993. This important book examines presidential power in the context of political relations in Washington—particularly the strategy of bypassing bargaining on Capitol Hill and appealing directly to the American public.

- Lowi, Theodore J. *The Personal President: Power Invested, Promise Unfulfilled.* Ithaca, N.Y.: Cornell University Press, 1985. Lowi analyzes the effects of the "plebiscitary presidency"—the direct relationship between the president and the people.

- McDonald, Forrest. *The American Presidency: An Intellectual History.* Lawrence: University Press of Kansas, 1994. A fascinating examination of the roots of the American presidency. McDonald explores how and why the presidency has evolved into such a complex and powerful institution.

- Milkis, Sidney M. *The President and the Parties.* New York: Oxford University Press, 1993. This book shows how the growth of presidential power in the twentieth century has promoted the degradation of American democracy.

- Neustadt, Richard E. *Presidential Power and the Modern Presidents.* New York: Free Press, 1990. This classic study of presidential bargaining and influence has set the agenda for a generation of presidency scholars.

- Rossiter, Clinton. *The American Presidency.* Baltimore, Md.: Johns Hopkins University Press, 1987. Originally published in 1956 and reprinted with a new introduction by Michael Nelson, Rossiter examines the limits and evolution of presidential powers.

- Skowronek, Stephen. *The Politics Presidents Make: Leadership from John Adams to George Bush.* Cambridge, Mass.: Harvard University Press, 1993. This important and innovative book chronicles fifteen presidents and how they continually transformed the political landscape.

CHAPTER 7

THE JUDICIARY

EQUAL·JUSTICE·UNDER·LAW·

CHAPTER OUTLINE

CASE STUDY: THE COP AND THE BAR-
    TENDER
INTRODUCTION: THE COURTS AND
    DEMOCRACY
THE ORIGINS AND DEVELOPMENT OF
    JUDICIAL POWER
HOW THE AMERICAN COURT SYSTEM
    IS ORGANIZED

COURT APPOINTMENTS: THE PROCESS
    AND THE POLITICS
HOW THE SUPREME COURT OPERATES
ANALYZING SUPREME COURT DECISIONS
THE RESULTS OF SUPREME COURT DECI-
    SIONS
THE COURTS AND APPROACHING DE-
    MOCRACY

I t was 10:30 A.M. on July 5, 1982, and twenty-eight-year-old Michael Hardwick had worked the all-night shift at the gay nightclub known as The Cove.[1] Tired and thirsty, Hardwick was drinking a beer as he walked home, when officer Keith Torrick stopped him. As Torrick wrote out a ticket for drinking in public he said, "I'm counting on you to show up [in court]. If you don't, I'll take it that you're laughing in my face. And I will come find you. And I will lock you up."

The Cop and the Bartender

Torrick was a man of his word. Several hours after Hardwick failed to appear in court, Torrick went to Hardwick's house to serve the arrest warrant. Told by Hardwick's house guest that he was not there, Torrick said, "Tell him I will be back." As soon as Hardwick learned what had happened, he raced down to the court clerk's office, paid the fifty-dollar fine, and forgot about the incident.

Three weeks later, however, Officer Torrick came to the door once more with the arrest warrant. A house guest told Torrick to "look around" for the owner. So Torrick marched down the hall, found the back bedroom door slightly ajar, looked in, and saw Hardwick having sex with his male lover. Torrick then arrested Hardwick for violating Georgia Code Section 16-6-2, which outlaws sodomy.

"God bless the police officer," said John Sweet, an activist attorney with the American Civil Liberties Union (ACLU) in Atlanta, when he heard about the case. Officer Torrick had provided him with the perfect opportunity to challenge Georgia's anti-sodomy law, and similar laws in twenty-three other states, and show that such laws violate constitutional guarantees of privacy. The Supreme Court had established the privacy rights of married couples and unmarried heterosexual couples; the hope was that such precedents would be extended to homosexual couples. But Fulton County district attorney Lewis Slaton was not willing to give the ACLU this opportunity. He dropped the charges after the initial hearing on the case. Hardwick and the ACLU were not ready to give up, though, and filed a civil suit asking for a declaratory judgment, or a legal pronouncement that Georgia's law was an unconstitutional violation of the privacy rights safeguarded by the federal Constitution. What had begun as an encounter between a cop and a bartender was now a nationally prominent court case.

After Hardwick won in both the district court and the U.S. court of appeals, Georgia appealed to the Supreme Court. The case, Bowers v. Hardwick, was accepted by the Court for review because privacy rights for homosexuals was an important issue that it had never considered. As with many cases in the deeply divided Burger Court, the result hinged on the vote of centrist justice Lewis Powell. The initial vote was 5 to 4 to overturn the anti-sodomy law, with liberal justice Harry Blackmun assigned to write the opinion. The Blackmun majority viewed this as a privacy case, arguing that the nature of an individual's private, consensual sexual activity should be left to the individual, not to the government. The minority, led by Byron White, viewed this not as a case dealing with privacy but as one dealing with homosexual sodomy, which they argued was already banned as a criminal activity in twenty-four states. Powell had provided the fifth vote for overturning the law, saying he was troubled by the prospect of a twenty-year jail sentence for violation of this Georgia law. Several days later, though, Powell changed his vote. Reasoning that Hardwick's criminal case had been dropped and he was merely suing to test the anti-sodomy law, Powell believed it premature

217

to decide the issue. As a result, the votes swung to the conservatives, and White, now speaking for the majority, upheld Georgia's law, arguing that the Constitution does not confer a fundamental right of privacy to homosexuals engaging in sodomy. The four-justice dissent, led by Blackmun, responded that if the constitutional right to privacy means anything, it means that Georgia cannot prosecute its citizens for private consensual sexual activity.

The ruling on privacy rights puzzled many, with the New York Times *titling its account: "60 Years of Expansion Interrupted by Ruling." The gay community reacted to the decision with great distress. But several months later, Jeff Levi, executive director of the National Gay and Lesbian Task Force, noted that his organization was receiving an outpouring of public support and funds and said, "Five to ten years down the line, we may thank Byron White for writing that opinion."*[2] *✦*

INTRODUCTION: THE COURTS AND DEMOCRACY

Disputes brought to the Supreme Court by people like Michael Hardwick illustrate why we should be attentive to the workings of the American court system. All Michael Hardwick wanted was justice as he saw it. So did Steven Engel, Estelle Griswold, Jane Roe, Dolores Mapp, Ernesto Miranda, Linda Brown, and James E. Swann. These names may be unfamiliar to you now, but lawyers and scholars of the court immediately recognize their connection with some of the most important Supreme Court cases in the history of this country. (We cover these cases in greater detail in Chapters 14 and 15.)

> "We are very quiet . . . but it is the quiet of a storm center, as we all know."
>
> —Justice Oliver Wendell Holmes

The judicial decisions made in the cases of these individuals resulted in fundamental changes in U.S. society. Steven Engel's 1962 case resulted in the banning of prayer in public schools. Before Estelle Griswold's case in 1965, the only contraceptive devices available for sale in some states were found on the black market. Before Jane Roe's case in 1973, to have the abortion procedure performed women would often have to leave their state, or even the country, or violate the law. Dolores Mapp's and Ernesto Miranda's cases in the 1960's placed limits on police who search a residence, or question an individual about crimes. Linda Brown's case in 1954 outlawed segregation in public schools, while James Swann's case in 1971 made it possible to bus children to schools to achieve integration.

Whether or not you approve of these changes, they all resulted from decisions made by the Supreme Court. It falls to the Court to interpret definitively the Constitution. In the process, the Court can create new rights or expand, and even dramatically alter, existing ones.

One of the ironies in American democracy is that the Supreme Court, which interprets the Constitution, is the most undemocratic of the three branches of government. Operating in total secrecy, nine appointed, life-tenured jurists sit at the top of a complex legal structure designed to limit rather than encourage appeals and have almost total power to say what the law is. Michael Hardwick's case illustrates how those judgments sometimes hinge on the actions of just one justice. But as you will see, despite its undemocratic mode of operating, in the last sixty years the Court has actually helped to expand and protect the rights of Americans. As a result, the Court has helped America approach democracy.

Nearly all of the issues that make their way to the Supreme Court are raised initially in the lower federal courts or the state judicial systems. The prospect that state courts and federal courts can disagree with each other makes it necessary for a single Supreme Court to resolve those differences. In the Hardwick case, both the district court and the U.S. court of appeals had taken Hardwick's side, while twenty-three other states sided with Georgia.

In this chapter we examine the developing powers of the Supreme Court, the organization of the American court system, judicial appointments, and how cases are appealed to and then decided by the Supreme Court. We also look at how judges arrive at decisions and, perhaps most important, how those decisions affect both public policy and democracy.

THE ORIGINS AND DEVELOPMENT OF JUDICIAL POWER

Of the three branches of government created by the framers in the Constitution, the judiciary is the least defined both in its organization and the nature of its powers. Instead, it was left to the Court to define through its own rulings the nature of its power.

Creating the "Least Dangerous Branch"

The framers outlined the nature of the federal judicial branch in Article III of the Constitution, when they stated in the first sentence:

> The judicial power of the United States shall be vested in one Supreme Court, and in such inferior courts as Congress may from time to time ordain and establish.

As you can see from this sentence, the framers were vague about the structure of the courts and about how powerful they wanted the courts to be. And in establishing only a Supreme Court, they left it to Congress to design a lower federal court system.

The jurisdiction, or sphere of authority, of the federal courts was also left relatively undefined. Article III establishes that the Supreme Court, and the lower federal courts, shall decide all legal disputes of a federal nature or those arising under the Constitution, U.S. law, and treaties. In some cases, such as those involving disputes between or among states of the union, or involving foreign ambassadors, the Supreme Court will have **original jurisdiction,** or be the first court to hear the cases. For all other disputes, such as those involving the United States as a party, admiralty or maritime claims, disputes between citizens of two or more different states, and between a citizen and a state, the Court will hear cases on **appellate jurisdiction,** or after the matter has been argued in and decided by a lower federal or state court.

Although the full extent of the Supreme Court's powers was not specified, the framers designed the judiciary to be the least influential and weakest of the three branches of government. Some framers believed that in a representative government, the courts should not have much power because they do not have an explicitly political or representative role. Alexander Hamilton made this argument in the *Federalist* no. 78: "The judiciary . . . will always be the least dangerous to the political rights of the Constitution. . . . The judiciary . . . has no influence over either the sword or the purse . . . [and it] may be truly said to have neither FORCE nor WILL, but merely judgment."[3]

The framers left it to Congress to be more specific about the organization and jurisdiction of the judiciary. In the Judiciary Act of 1789, Congress established a three-tiered system of federal courts, consisting of district or trial courts, appellate courts, and one Supreme Court. The act also defined more fully the jurisdiction of the Supreme Court, granting it, among other things, the power to review state court rulings that reject federal claims.

Still, the Supreme Court remained weak, and often it had no cases to decide. Chief Justice John Jay (1789–95) was so distressed by the "intolerable" lack of prestige and power of his job that he quit to take a better one—as governor of New York. But the relative weakness of the Court changed in 1803 with the decision in *Marbury* v. *Madison.*[4]

Marbury v. Madison: The Source of Judicial Power

When the Federalist party lost the election of 1800, outgoing president John Adams tried to pack the federal courts with appointments from his own party by issuing a number of commissions the night before leaving office. When one of those commissions, the appointment of William Marbury as justice of the peace for the District of Columbia, was denied by the incoming Jefferson administration, Marbury sued for his post. The case became the landmark ***Marbury* v. *Madison.***

Chief Justice John Marshall (1801–35) guided the Supreme Court to many of the decisions that transformed America from a confederation of states into a nation. President John Adams, who appointed Marshall, would later say: "My gift of John Marshall to the People of the United States was the proudest act of my life." Not everyone was a fan, however; Marshall's distant cousin, Thomas Jefferson, once referred to him as "that gloomy malignity."

The issue in this case was whether the Supreme Court has the power to order federal officials to carry out their official duties, in this case to deliver a judicial commission. This power had been given to the Court by the Judiciary Act of 1789. Chief Justice John Marshall (1801–35), himself an Adams midnight appointee, wrote the Court's opinion. After conceding that the commissions were valid, he then proceeded to move beyond the issue to review the constitutionality of the Judiciary Act of 1789. Since no power to review the constitutionality of any law can be found in the Constitution, Marshall cleverly used this case to establish just such a power. He argued that since courts interpret law, and the Constitution is a form of law, then the Supreme Court can interpret the Constitution. Thus, Marshall created the power of **judicial review,** the power of the Supreme Court to overturn acts of the president, Congress, and the states if those acts violate the Constitution. In assuming the absolute and final power to say what the Constitution means, Marshall helped define the powers of the Court and placed it on an equal footing with the other branches. Marshall then used his new-found judicial-review power to deny Marbury his commission. As a result, there was no judicial order for the Jeffersonians to reject, so Marshall's establishment of judicial review stood unchallenged.

Few decisions in the early years of the nation had such a tremendous impact on America's approach to democracy. The Supreme Court now had the power in the system of checks and balances to negate potentially oppressive majority actions by the other political branches. Thus, minorities would have a place to go for relief. With the power of judicial review, the Supreme Court was also able to bring various state government actions, both political and judicial, into harmony with the national Constitution, thus altering the federal structure.

Judicial Review: The Court's Ultimate Power

Judicial review has been referred to as the Court's ultimate power because it is an awesome and absolute power. Professor Edward S. Corwin has called this power "American democracy's way of hedging its bet," meaning that wayward actions by the political branches can always be corrected by the Court.[5] Moreover, judicial review has allowed the Supreme Court to update the Constitution by continually reinterpreting its words to fit new situations.

Over the years, judicial review has become a feature of American government accepted by the political branches, the lower judiciary, and the general public. Since 1803, the Supreme Court has declared around 1,200 provisions of state laws and state constitutions to be unconstitutional, while exercising the same power with respect to 110 federal executive branch actions and the provisions of over 140 federal laws (of over 95,000 passed).[6]

Is judicial review a democratic power? While advocates of judicial review hold that someone has to have the final say over the meaning of the Constitution, others argue that this power is undemocratic because life-tenured, appointed justices can, by a simple one-vote majority, overrule the collective will of the elected branches. With only two mechanisms to countermand judicial review—constitutional amendment or Court reversal—that power is considerable. However, while it appears that judicial review provides the Court with unlimited power, as you will see later on, the political branches and the general public do possess considerable power to rein in the Court.

Other Powers of the Supreme Court

The Court has two other important powers in addition to the power of judicial review. Using its power of **statutory construction,** the Court can interpret or reinterpret a federal or state law. Since the wording of a law is not always clear, the justices must determine the law's true meaning and apply it to the facts in a specific case. This power is a considerable one. For instance, in 1957 the Supreme Court reviewed the case of fourteen officials of the American Communist party, who were convicted under the 1940 Smith Act, which made it illegal to advocate the violent overthrow of the government. Using statutory construction the Court overturned those convictions, interpreting the word *advocacy* in the law to mean advocacy of action, such as planning an actual overthrow, rather than as advocacy of an idea or "abstract doctrine."[7] With this ruling then, the

Democracy and Judicial Independence

In the United States, the concept of judicial independence means that judges are free to make decisions based on the law and do not feel compelled to comply with the wishes of powerful political leaders. But the degree of judicial independence varies from one nation to another.

As the accompanying map shows, there is a strong correlation between judicial independence and democratic government. In democratic countries judges are usually chosen on the basis of merit rather than politics and cannot be removed from office because of the nature of their decisions. In contrast, in authoritarian regimes judges are more likely to follow the dictates of political leaders and to be disciplined if they do not.

Global View

The link between stable, democratic government and full judicial independence can be seen in nations like Australia, Great Britain, Japan, and Scandinavia. The governments of many other nations, such as India, Argentina, Italy, and France, while democratic, are less stable, and their judicial systems have less independence.

The least independent judicial systems are found in countries with authoritarian governments, like China and many African nations. The limited court systems of these countries make few decisions, and the decisions they do make can be overruled by military and party leaders. Judges who make unpopular decisions risk being removed, jailed, or even killed.

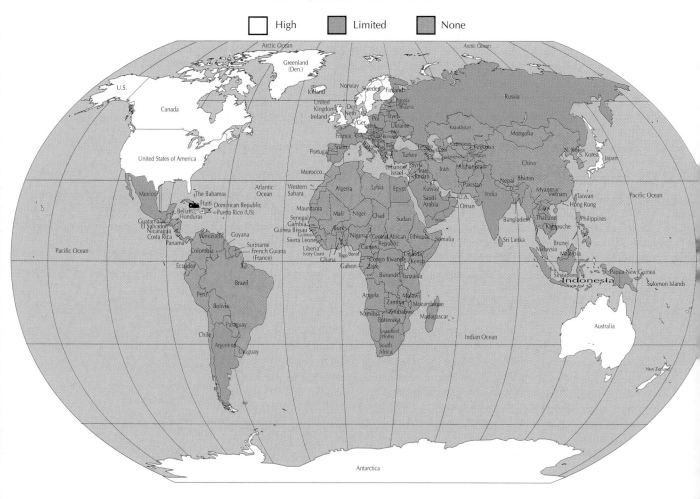

LEVELS OF JUDICIAL INDEPENDENCE

☐ High　　◼ Limited　　◼ None

Court rewrote the law and made it impossible to convict Communists unless it could be shown they were leading revolts rather than just talking about them.

The power used most frequently by the Supreme Court, though, is the power to do nothing by refusing to review a case, thus leaving a lower-court judgment in force. In refusing to hear cases, the Court can imply that it agrees with the lower-court ruling, that the issue presented is not significant enough to review, or that the Court is not yet ready to hear that issue. In using this power to do nothing, the Court can develop its constitutional doctrine incrementally and as it sees fit.

Independence of the Judiciary

The extent of a court's power depends on its independence, that is, to make decisions free of outside influences. The framers were aware of this and placed in the Constitution several provisions to help keep the Court free of pressures from the people, Congress, and the president. First, justices are appointed not elected; thus, they are not beholden to voters. Second, the power to appoint justices is shared by the president and the Senate; thus, the Court is not beholden to any one person or political party. Third, the justices are guaranteed their position for life, as long as they exhibit "good behavior." Even in cases of bad behavior, justices can be impeached only for "high crimes and misdemeanors," thus ensuring that the Court cannot be manipulated by the political branches.[8] Finally, the Constitution specifies that justices' salaries "shall not be diminished during their Continuance in Office," meaning that Congress cannot lower the Court's salary to punish it for its rulings.

But how much independence does the Court really possess? A great deal, although the Court is not completely shielded from outside influences. Presidents can change the direction of the Court with new appointments. Congress can attack the judiciary's independence through some or all of the following: abolishing all of the lower federal courts, refusing to raise salaries, using its power to remove certain classes of cases from the appellate docket (leaving the lower-court rulings in force), changing the number of justices on the Supreme Court, passing a law to reverse a Court decision, and attacking the Court in speeches. But only in a few rare instances has Congress attempted to use any of these methods to threaten the Court's independence. One effort came in 1957, when a Congress displeased with judicial limits placed on its investigative powers considered the Jenner–Butler Bill, which would have removed several classes of cases from the Supreme Court's docket. Only the efforts of the powerful Senate majority leader Lyndon Johnson prevented passage of the bill.

At times, mere threats to judicial independence can have an impact on Court decisions. Franklin Roosevelt's failed Court-packing plan still resulted in a change of direction among the justices in favor of New Deal programs. Although the Jenner–Butler Bill failed, Justices Felix Frankfurter (1939–62) and John Marshall Harlan (1955–71) changed their positions and began to uphold Congress's power to investigate.

In the end, the Court's greatest protection from political threats to its independence comes from the people, as long as justices are careful not to get too far ahead of public opinion in their decisions. An independent judiciary that secures the rights and liberties of citizens is a cherished part of the American political landscape, in which the rule of law is paramount. It is also one of the measures of true democracy, as you learned in Chapter 1.

HOW THE AMERICAN COURT SYSTEM IS ORGANIZED

The American judicial system consists of two separate and parallel court systems: an extensive system of state and local courts in which the vast majority of cases are decided, and a system of national or federal courts. Figure 7.1 illustrates how the American court system is structured. These two judicial systems operate independently of each other most of the time. State courts deal with state laws and constitutions, and federal courts deal with federal laws and the U.S. Constitution. But when the state courts handle issues touching on the federal Constitution or laws it is possible for a litigant to shift over to the federal system. The extensive lower-court system (all courts beneath the Supreme Court) functions as a gatekeeper, restricting the flow of appeals to the Supreme Court. Appeals come to the Supreme Court from both the highest courts in the fifty states and from the appellate court system.

Types of Courts

Federal and state courts are divided into trial and appellate courts. A **trial court,** also known as a *petit court,* is often the point of original entry in the legal system, with a single judge and at times a jury deciding matters both of fact and law in a case. Deciding issues of fact in a case involves determining what actually happened, while deciding issues of law involves applying

FIGURE 7.1 Structure of the American Court System

The dual system of federal and state courts consists of an extensive system of state and local courts where most cases are decided, as well as a system of national or federal courts. At the top of the system is the Supreme Court. Few cases make it this far, since the lower courts serve to restrict the flow of appeals to the highest court.

Sources: Administrative office of the U.S. Courts, *Federal Judicial Workload Statistics* (Washington, D.C.: Administrative Office of the U.S. Courts, Mar. 31, 1993); National Center for State Courts, *State Court Caseload Statistics: Annual Report 1990* (Williamsburg, Va.: National Center for State Courts, 1992); Henry J. Abraham, *The Judicial Process, An Introductory Analysis of the Courts of the United States, England, and France* (New York: Oxford University Press, 1993), pp. 143–53.

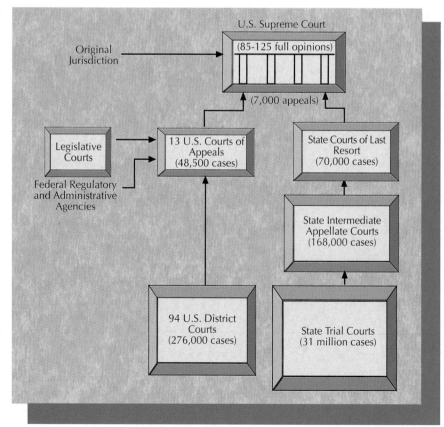

relevant statutes and constitutional provisions to the evidence and conduct of a trial. For instance, in a murder case, deciding a matter of fact would involve the jury's determining a defendant's guilt or innocence based on the evidence admitted into trial. Deciding a matter of law would involve the judge's determining whether certain pieces of evidence, such as a particular witness's testimony, should be admitted into the proceedings.

An **appellate court** reviews the proceedings of the trial court, often with a multijudge panel and without a jury. The appellate court considers only matters of law. Thus, in a murder case the appellate court would not be concerned with the jury's verdict of guilty or innocent; instead, it could reconsider the legality of the trial, such as whether the judge was correct in admitting some of the evidence into trial. An appellate court ruling could lead to a new trial if certain evidence is deemed inadmissible.

TYPES OF CASES   Trial and appeals courts hear both criminal and civil cases. In **criminal cases,** decisions are made regarding whether or not to punish individuals accused of violating the state or federal criminal (or penal) code. Murder, rape, robbery, and assault are covered by the criminal law, as are some nonviolent offenses such as embezzlement and tax fraud. The vast majority of criminal cases are dealt with at the state rather than the federal level, though the 1994 Crime Bill created new categories of federal crimes involving the use of firearms. More than 90 percent of criminal cases never come to trial but instead result in private conferences called **plea bargains,** in which the state agrees to press for either a reduced set of charges or a reduced sentence in return for a guilty plea. Plea bargains eliminate the need for a time-consuming trial, thus helping to keep the court system from becoming overloaded.[9]

In **civil cases,** courts resolve private disputes among individuals over finances, property, or personal well-being. Malpractice suits, libel suits, breach of contract suits, and personal injury suits are examples of civil cases. Judicial remedies in such cases can involve a judicial decree, requiring that some action be taken, or a monetary award. If a monetary award is involved it can require both *compensatory damages,* which reimburse a litigant for the harm done by another's actions, and *punitive damages,* which go beyond compensation, seeking to discourage such action in the future. In 1994, for example, a Chicago judge ordered a couple who lost a racial harassment suit to pay ten million dollars in compensatory and punitive damages; to prevent them from harassing anyone else they were also instructed to sell their home, and if they could not find a buyer within sixty days, to put it up for auction.[10]

Large groups of people affected by an action can unite in a **class action suit,** a single civil case in which the results are applicable to all participants. Often class action suits are used to compensate victims of large corporations. After the Exxon oil tanker *Valdez* spilled ten million gallons of oil into Prince William Sound, damaging the environment, Exxon faced a class action suit brought by 15,000 fishermen who had been harmed by the oil spill. A jury ordered Exxon to pay 287 million dollars in compensatory damages and five billion dollars in punitive damages, the largest punitive award ever against a U.S. corporation.[11] Class action suits have also been used by activist interest groups to accomplish public-policy aims. In this way, the ACLU ended the Chicago Police Department's practice of strip-searching people arrested for routine traffic violations.

The most famous and extensively discussed criminal case of this century—perhaps ever—has been the O. J. Simpson murder trial, which got underway in January 1995, in Los Angeles, California. Shown here is the court in session, with Judge Lance Ito presiding. Although the case served as entertainment for many, the constant media attention also focused a "microscope" on the American system of justice. Americans were exposed—some for the first time—to the specifics of criminal law and to how criminal courts, lawyers, judges, juries, and other participants function.

As with criminal cases, a great many class action suits and civil cases generally never come to trial because they are settled out of court.

Organization of the Federal Courts

As you've seen, the federal judiciary is organized in three tiers—the U.S. district courts at the bottom, the courts of appeals, and, at the top, the Supreme Court. These are all **constitutional courts,** so called because they are mentioned in Article III of the Constitution, the judicial article. All federal constitutional courts are staffed by life-tenured judges or justices.

The **U.S. district courts** are the trial courts serving as the original point of entry for almost all federal cases. There are ninety-four district courts, with at least one in every state, staffed in 1994 by 645 judges. These courts serve as the workhorses of the federal judicial system.[12] Over 275,000 civil and criminal cases are filed here every year. District courts hear cases arising under federal law, national treaties, and the federal Constitution, and they review the actions of various federal agencies and departments. In roughly half of the cases, juries are used. Since appealing cases to the next level is expensive and time-consuming, for roughly eighty-five percent of the cases decided at the district court level the judgment is final.

The next rung on the federal judicial ladder is the **U.S. courts of appeals,** consisting in 1994 of 167 judges in thirteen courts. Twelve of these appeals courts are geographically based, with eleven of them in multistate geographic regions called *circuits* (see Figure 7.2), so named because Supreme Court justices once literally "rode the circuit" to hear cases. The U.S. Court of Appeals for the Second Circuit, for example, is located in New York and serves New York state, Connecticut, and Vermont. The twelfth geographically based circuit court is the U.S. Court of Appeals for the District of Columbia, which hears appeals from federal regulatory commissions and agencies. Because of the important nature of the cases arising from federal agencies and departments, the Court of Appeals in the District of Columbia is viewed by many as the second-most important federal court after the Supreme Court. The U.S. Court of Appeals for the Federal Circuit is the thirteenth appeals court. It specializes in appeals involving patents and contract claims against the national government.

Appeals courts usually hear cases in three-judge panels, although sometimes cases are decided in ***en banc*** proceedings, in which all of the appeals judges in a particular circuit serve as a tribunal.

The court of appeals receives over forty-eight thousand appeals in a year. For the remaining 225,000 cases, the district court's judgment is left in force.[13] Because so few cases proceed on to the Supreme Court, the court of appeals has been described by one prominent judicial scholar as a "mini Supreme Court in the vast majority of cases."[14]

In addition to these constitutional appeals courts, the federal judiciary includes legislative courts of appeal. **Legislative courts** are called Article I courts because they are established by Congress based on Article I, Section 8 of the Constitution. These courts are designed to provide technical expertise on specific subjects. Unlike judges on constitutional courts, who are appointed for life, legislative court judges serve for a fixed term. Legislative courts include the U.S. Court of Military Appeals, the U.S. Tax Court, the U.S. Court of Veterans

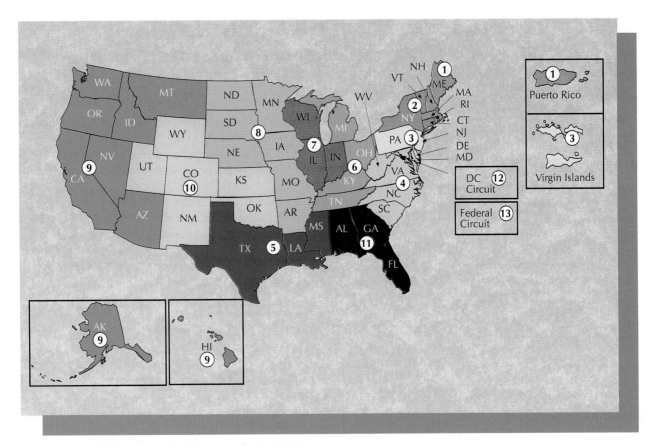

FIGURE 7.2 The Thirteen Federal Judicial Circuits
Source: Administrative Office of the United States Courts, Sept. 1991.

Appeals, and various territorial courts. Any decision by legislative courts can be appealed to the constitutional court system.

COURT APPOINTMENTS: THE PROCESS AND THE POLITICS

The process for appointing judges to the federal courts is stated clearly in Article II, Section 2 of the Constitution. There the president is charged with making the appointments and the Senate is charged with confirming those appointments by majority vote (its "advice and consent" role). While the framers wanted only the most "meritorious" candidates to be selected, politics plays an important part in the process and helps determine which judges end up on the federal bench.

The Supreme Court Appointment Process

At any given time there are about two dozen people who are qualified for a Supreme Court vacancy. How does an individual rise to the top and secure an appointment? While the process for appointing Supreme Court justices varies depending on the president and the candidate involved, in general it begins

On July 23, 1990, President George Bush interviewed Supreme Court nominee David Souter in Bush's private study at the White House. Souter, a court of appeals judge from Weare, New Hampshire was being considered for the vacancy resulting from William Brennan's retirement. Bush was undecided about the appointment and had another candidate secluded elsewhere in the White House waiting to be interviewed. Ultimately, however, Souter got the appointment.

with the collection and sifting through of names. When a vacancy occurs, suggestions for the new appointment come in to the White House and the Justice Department from politicians, senators, governors, friends of the candidates, the candidates themselves, and even sitting and retired federal judges. This list is then winnowed down to a few top names. A member of the attorney general's staff or the White House staff is then charged with gathering information on these top names. This information-gathering process involves a background check by the Federal Bureau of Investigation (FBI) to determine suitability of character and to uncover any potentially damaging information that might lead to problems with confirmation. A short list of candidates is then forwarded to the president for consideration.

A seat on the Court is the juiciest plum in the presidential patronage garden. It can go to a highly visible candidate or to someone close to a president. But an equally important consideration is partisanship. Presidents tend to be partisan in their choices, seeking both to reward members of their own party and to see their own political ideology mirrored on the Court. In addition, representativeness comes into play as do other players, such as the American Bar Association and the Senate.

THE ROLE OF PARTY   Well over 90 percent of the appointees to the Supreme Court have been from the president's own political party. In general, Democrats tend to appoint judges who are willing to extend constitutional and legal protections to the individual, while Republicans tend to appoint judges who are less attentive to individual rights and more willing to defer to the government. Republican George Bush appointed David Souter and Clarence Thomas to the Supreme Court, placing on the bench jurists with histories of upholding lower-court and regulatory agency decisions. Democrat Bill Clinton turned instead to Ruth Bader Ginsburg, a leader of the women's rights movement, and Stephen Breyer, a strong advocate of individual rights.

But even in trying to fill the Court with people of a similar mindset, presidents are sometimes unpleasantly surprised. What a person *was* can be a poor predictor of what he or she *will become* on the Supreme Court. While some scholars estimate that over 70 percent of the time presidents get exactly the sort of appointee they are expecting, miscalculations can happen.[15] Conservative president Dwight Eisenhower appointed Earl Warren (1953–69) and William Brennan (1956–90) to the Court on the assumption that they were conservatives. Warren's prior work as California governor and Brennan's as New Jersey State Supreme Court justice turned out to reveal little about how they might decide cases. They became two of the Court's great liberals. (When asked at the end of his career what he thought in retrospect about the Warren appointment, Eisenhower replied: "[I]t's one of the two biggest mistakes I made in my administration [the other, Ike indicated elsewhere, was Brennan's appointment].")

Essentially, the immense responsibilities of the office, the weight of the history of a Court seat, and interaction with new colleagues on the bench can all combine to create a very different kind of jurist than expected. In fact, two of the jurists in the Hardwick case are such examples: the conservative Byron White, who opposed privacy rights, was appointed by the liberal Democrat John F. Kennedy; while the liberal Harry Blackmun, who supported privacy rights, was an appointee of conservative Republican Richard Nixon.

Recently, presidents have tried to sharpen their ability to predict the ideology of their Supreme Court appointments by selecting candidates who are judges on the courts of appeals, where their prior judicial records might offer some clues regarding future decisions. This changes the kind of Court that is assembled. For instance, while the 1941–42 Roosevelt Court consisted of a Harvard law professor, two U.S. senators, a chairman of the Securities Exchange Commission, three former attorneys general, a solicitor general, and a U.S. attorney, the 1995 Court consists of a Justice Department official, a state judge, and seven court of appeals judges.

SEEKING A MORE REPRESENTATIVE COURT   Over the years the representative nature of the Court has become an issue, and a number of categories have emerged to guide presidents in selecting nominees. These include geography, religion, race, and gender. Presidents have used these factors to create a sort of "balanced" Court that keeps various constituencies satisfied.

An effort has always been made to have all geographical regions of the country represented on the Court. "Wiley, you have geography," Franklin Roosevelt told Iowan Wiley Rutledge (1943–49) when explaining his impending appointment to a Court whose only "non-Easterner," William O. Douglas (1939–75), had been raised in Yakima, Washington (although he actually lived on the East Coast since his law school years). Religion also plays a role. For over one hundred years there was a so-called Catholic seat on the Court, while the appointment of Louis Brandeis (1916–39) created a Jewish seat that remained until 1969 (and some believe was resumed in 1993). An African American seat was established by Thurgood Marshall's (1967–91) appointment. Clarence Thomas, also an African American, was appointed to fill that seat when Marshall retired. Sandra Day O'Connor's (1982–present) appointment seems to have established a female seat. There is now a growing movement within the Hispanic community for the establishment of a new seat for that ethnic group.

Judicial scholars continue to debate whether considering such representational factors is the proper way to staff the Court.[16] Many believe that merit should be the primary consideration. Some argue that given the small number of Court seats and the large number of interest groups, satisfying everyone is virtually impossible. It is believed that the recent appointments of Ruth Bader Ginsburg, the second woman on the Court, and Stephen Breyer, the Court's second Jewish member, were based on merit and that merit may be beginning once again to outweigh representational factors. Most appealing about Ginsburg were her accomplishments as a leading lawyer, as it so happens, in the women's movement. In Breyer's case, his background as an effective appeals court judge played a greater role than his religion. Still, political considerations are unavoidable in a democracy. Recent administrations have tried to appease their constituencies by mentioning during the initial winnowing-down process that candidates from various categories are "under consideration." But they then select other appointees based on other factors.

THE ROLE OF THE AMERICAN BAR ASSOCIATION   A short list of candidate names is often submitted to the American Bar Association, a national association for the legal profession, for an informal review by its Standing Committee on the Federal Judiciary. This review is performed by attorneys who canvas

FYI

Sandra Day O'Connor's favorite way of describing female Supreme Court justices before the appointment of Ruth Bader Ginsburg was "If you've seen one, you've seen 'em all."

Thurgood Marshall and the Fight for Integration

"When I was a youngster, a Pullman porter told me that . . . he had never been in any city in the United States where he had to put his hand up in front of his face to find out he was a Negro," Justice Thurgood Marshall remarked upon retiring from the Supreme Court in 1991. The porter's comment described the rigidly segregated society in which Marshall was born and raised. Before the 1960s, African Americans in the United States were required to ride in separate train cars and at the back of buses, and to drink from separate water fountains. When they traveled, it was hard for them to find a place to sleep or buy a meal. They could not hold the same jobs as whites; their children attended separate schools. Wherever they turned, they were told that they were not entitled to the same rights as white Americans.

Marshall dedicated his career to combating racial segregation and inequality. When his application to the University of Maryland law school was rejected because of his race, he went to the all-black Howard University Law School. There he was profoundly influenced by Charles Hamilton Houston, who urged his students to be "social engineers" rather than mere lawyers, to put their knowledge and abilities to work to change society. Marshall took Houston's words to heart. In one of his first legal victories, the University of Maryland law school was ordered to admit African American students.

In 1939 Marshall was named head of the Legal Defense and Education Fund of the National Association for the Advancement of Colored People (NAACP). It was in this position that he made perhaps his greatest contribution to the struggle for equality, spearheading the NAACP's strategy of promoting integration through court decisions. Over the next two decades he took thirty-two cases to the U.S. Supreme Court, winning twenty-nine of them. Perhaps the most famous of those cases was *Brown* v. *Board of Education* (1954), which ended the doctrine of "separate but equal" educational facilities and thus effectively ended segregation of public schools in twenty-one states.

In 1961 President Kennedy named Marshall to the U.S. Court of Appeals for the Second Circuit, and four years later President Johnson appointed him Solicitor

NAACP Legal Defense Fund attorneys (from left) George E. C. Hayes, Thurgood Marshall, and James M. Nabrit celebrate their historic victory in *Brown* v. *Board of Education* on May 17, 1954.

General of the United States, the first African American to hold that position. Then, in 1967, Johnson nominated him to become the first African American justice on the U.S. Supreme Court.

In more than two decades on the Court, Marshall served as a living reminder of the situation of minority groups in American society. He argued forcefully for integration, protection of the poor, elimination of the death penalty, and freedom of speech. When he retired in June 1991, however, he felt that the United States still had a long way to travel along the road to an integrated society. When asked if African Americans were "free at last," as Martin Luther King had said, he responded, "Well, I'm not free."

Thurgood Marshall died on January 25, 1993, revered as the man who had led the fight for desegregation through the legal system. "Without him," comments author Richard Kluger, "the whole civil rights movement and the legal enfranchisement of blacks might not have happened when it did. . . . That was the man's monument."*

The Struggle for Equality

---

*Quoted in Linda Greenhouse, "Thurgood Marshall, Civil Rights Hero and Former Justice Dies," *New York Times,* Jan. 25, 1993, p. B8.

judges and lawyers throughout the country regarding the nominees' qualifications. Based on these inquiries, ratings for nominees for the Supreme Court fall into the categories of "highly qualified," "not opposed," or "not qualified." Candidates for the lower courts are rated on a scale of "well qualified," "qualified," or "not qualified."[17] While the intent is to seek out information on the nominees' professional qualifications, personal and ideological considerations inevitably arise as well.[18]

In general, since there is no requirement to consult the ABA, if the president has settled on a nominee, a negative rating by this group will have little effect. For Clarence Thomas the ABA issued its worst rating ever. This did not prevent George Bush from calling Thomas the best-qualified lawyer in America and appointing him to the Court.

Court of appeals judge Robert Bork presents his case to the Senate Judiciary Committee during confirmation hearings for his nomination to the U. S. Supreme Court in 1987. When asked why he wanted to be on the Court, Bork answered that it would be an "intellectual feast." This reply was taken by liberal opponents to indicate that Bork, a highly conservative jurist, would not be active in preserving personal rights.

THE ROLE OF THE SENATE As we saw earlier, the Constitution charges the Senate with confirming Supreme Court appointments by majority vote. The Senate confirmation process begins with a Senate Judiciary Committee hearing designed to elicit views about a candidate. The committee then makes a recommendation for or against a candidate prior to a vote of the full Senate. Over the years, Senate confirmation has proven to be a significant hurdle, resulting in the rejection of over one in five presidential nominations.

In general, the president initially has the upper hand in the appointment process, but the Senate can oppose a nominee for a variety of reasons. Some rejections are due to unhappiness with the candidate's competence or political views. The Senate rejected G. Harrold Carswell in 1971, citing a lack of competence—but not before Nebraska senator Roman Hruska defended Carswell by saying: "Even if he is mediocre there are a lot of mediocre judges and people and lawyers. They are entitled to a little representation, aren't they?"[19] Other rejections have to do with partisan politics. A Democratic Senate may oppose the conservative candidate favored by a Republican president. In 1987, Republican president Ronald Reagan's appointee Robert Bork was confronted by a Senate Judiciary Committee controlled by the opposing Democratic party. After a massive media campaign by a coalition of liberal interest groups, vigorous questioning from the Judiciary Committee, and with the tide of public opinion turning against him, the intellectually qualified Bork was defeated because of his ultraconservative views, well documented in a trail of paper that spanned his entire career.[20] Some rejections may result from Senate opposition to the appointing president or may be intended to send a message of opposition to the current direction of the Court. In 1968, Senate conservatives opposed to the war in Vietnam and Democrat Lyndon Johnson's civil rights program, as well as to the revolutionary pro-rights Warren Court, rejected the nomination of Abe Fortas (1965–70) to become chief justice.[21]

Timing seems to be important in the success of a nomination. If a nomination comes early in a president's term or during a period of presidential popularity, the Senate is more likely to allow a nomination to succeed. Should it come late in the term or be made by a weak president, however, there is greater potential for a difficult confirmation. For instance, Bork's troubled nomination came in the next-to-last year of Reagan's presidency, while neither of Bill Clinton's nominations made in his first two years in office met with significant opposition.

Sometimes a nominee is challenged because of information uncovered in the Judiciary Committee investigation. When Clarence Thomas was nominated

Judicial Politics and the Media

In 1939, when William O. Douglas was nominated to the Supreme Court, the Senate's hearings on his nomination were closed to the press. Almost thirty years later, when Abe Fortas was nominated as chief justice, media coverage of the confirmation hearings was limited to newspaper reporters. Opponents of the nomination jumped at the opportunity to play to the press, stalling the proceedings and grilling witnesses. But the advent of television coverage in the 1980s introduced an entirely new dimension to senatorial confirmation hearings.

At first, television coverage of confirmation hearings was limited to brief items on evening news programs and cable news networks. But in 1987 the gloves came off with the nomination of Robert Bork. Bork's confirmation hearings were televised by the major networks with all the fanfare of a prime-time sporting event. The media delved into the details of the nominee's life, even obtaining a list of the videos rented by members of his family. Interest groups like People for the American Way presented their views in television commercials, often using well-known narrators like Gregory Peck.

Television cameras were not permitted within the Supreme Court building itself, but television correspondents began broadcasting live from outside the Courthouse when key rulings were issued. An amusing consequence of this trend was the sight of frantic reporters flipping through hundreds of pages of complex legal language in an attempt to instantaneously explain the Court's decision to the television audience.

It was the spectacle of Clarence Thomas's confirmation hearings in 1991 that demonstrated the potentially devastating effects of the combination of television and judicial politics. Millions of amazed viewers watched as an angry and embarrassed judge attempted to defend himself against charges that he had engaged in sexual harassment. The nomination was eventually confirmed, but the hearings unleashed a storm of controversy, with the result that sexual harassment became a subject of national debate and several other political leaders suffered damaged reputations.

In recent years the Senate has attempted to avoid such episodes by closing portions of confirmation hearings to the media. Recent judicial nominations have been noncontroversial enough to permit coverage by the cable channels, but it is not clear whether this practice will continue.

Also still to be decided is whether oral arguments before the Supreme Court may be televised. Chief Justices Burger and Rehnquist repeatedly denied requests to allow such coverage, even though lower-court trials and congressional debates are routinely televised. Those who favor televising Supreme Court proceedings argue that it would be a way of

---

by George Bush in 1991, charges were launched by law professor Anita Hill that she had been sexually harassed by Thomas while working for him in the Equal Employment Opportunity Commission (EEOC). The televised hearings were dramatic, with Senator Arlen Specter accusing Professor Hill of "flat-out perjury," and women's rights groups demanding that the nomination be defeated. In the end, Thomas was confirmed by a razor-thin 52-to-48 margin.[22]

In recent years, the Senate has sought greater influence in the confirmation process. After approving all Supreme Court candidates for nearly forty years, the Senate began to use its advice and consent role to such an extent that since 1968 it has turned down four nominees (Abe Fortas, G. Harrold Carswell, Clement Haynsworth, and Robert Bork), forced the withdrawal of another (Douglas

showing American democracy at work. Opponents, however, fear that it would turn the justices into television celebrities and thus destroy the anonym-ity that helps preserve the Court's independence from the other branches of government.

Court of appeals judge Clarence Thomas and University of Oklahoma Law Professor Anita Hill testify before the Senate Judiciary Committee in 1991. Thomas saw his appointment to the Supreme Court nearly derailed by Hill's testimony that he had sexually harassed her when both worked at the Equal Employment Opportunity Commission in the early 1980s. Thomas denied the charges and went on to receive a seat on the Court.

Ginsburg), and significantly attacked two other candidates (William Rehnquist for chief justice, and Clarence Thomas). The recent resurgence by the Senate has come about because of a heightened interest by the general public in Supreme Court confirmations since the Bork battle in 1987. Moreover, the televising of confirmation hearings and floor debates has made senators more conscious of the politics of the appointment process. Finally, the increased lobbying activity of interest groups, which now mount election-style media campaigns, has whipped up considerable public pressure on voting senators.

To counter this new-found willingness by the Senate to question seriously and even reject nominees, presidents have devised new appointment strategies. First, they have searched for "safe" candidates, ones lacking a large body of writings or decisions that are easy targets for attack. Seeking to avoid the problems faced by the highly visible and widely published legal scholar Bork, two years later President Bush appointed a little-known court of appeals judge from Weare, New Hampshire, David Souter. Because there was no paper trail to provide any inkling of Souter's leanings, he became known as the "stealth candidate." Presidents have also appointed friends and protégés of prominent senators, who they hope will lead the confirmation fight in the Senate. Clarence Thomas's nomination was greatly helped by his mentor, Democratic senator John Danforth of Missouri, while Stephen Breyer's nomination was helped along by the advocacy of fellow Massachusetts resident Senator Ted Kennedy. Finally, President Clinton has consulted with powerful members of the Senate, including opposing party members, *prior* to any appointment, seeking to eliminate any names that might cause difficulty. Thus, Secretary of the Interior Bruce Babbitt was dropped from the appointment list in 1994, when conservative Republican senator Orrin Hatch of Utah objected to his liberal philosophy.[23]

This search for "safe" candidates could have an impact on the nature of the Court. Highly qualified, but also highly controversial, legal scholars are now being passed over for appointment by presidents fearful of Senate rejection. In the past, controversial candidates such as Felix Frankfurter had a tremendous impact on the Court's direction. Some judicial scholars wonder whether this avoidance of talented but risky candidates will result in a Court unwilling to expand its decision-making role or make controversial decisions. This is impossible to predict, of course, because of the politics of appointment and the development of jurists once on the Court.

The Impact of Presidential Appointments on the Supreme Court

While every appointment to the Court is important, not every appointment changes the direction of the Court. Commonly a Supreme Court is named after its chief justice, such as the Rehnquist Court, but one would be better advised to categorize a Court according to the president who redirected it through judicial appointments.

In recent history, three presidents—Kennedy, Nixon, and Reagan—have dramatically changed the direction of the Court. In 1962, Democratic president John F. Kennedy shifted an ideologically-balanced moderate-conservative Court to a more liberal one by replacing the moderate-conservative justice Frankfurter with the more liberal Arthur Goldberg (1962–1965). In doing so, Kennedy assured a solid 5-to-4 vote in favor of civil rights and liberties cases. After Richard Nixon was elected on a "Law n' Order" platform in 1968, his four conservative appointments to the Supreme Court (William Rehnquist, Lewis Powell, Harry Blackmun, and Warren Burger) moved the Court in a more conservative direction, away from individual rights. After his election to the presidency in 1980, Ronald Reagan's four appointments—Sandra Day O'Connor, Antonin Scalia, Anthony Kennedy, and William Rehnquist as chief justice—created a Court able to reverse earlier rulings in such areas as defendants' rights. Thus, the rights of Americans can expand and contract as a result of their president's choices.

While presidents expect their legacy of Supreme Court appointments to live long after them (with the exception of William Howard Taft, who appointed sixty-six-year-old Edward White [1910–21] as chief justice, hoping that he would die shortly and leave the opening for Taft himself—which, in fact, did happen), fate sometimes dictates otherwise. The much-celebrated New Deal Court changed direction in late 1949 when liberals Frank Murphy (1940–49) and Wiley Rutledge died suddenly, to be replaced by moderate conservatives Tom Clark (1949–67) and Sherman Minton (1949–56). The current Rehnquist Court has been reshaped by two retirements—conservative Democrat Byron White and liberal Republican Harry Blackmun.

Thus far, Bill Clinton's appointments of moderate liberals Ruth Bader Ginsburg and Stephen Breyer have moved a conservative court toward the moderate center. Whether Clinton's hope of continuing to redirect the Court toward a more moderate, and perhaps even more liberal, direction is realized depends on how long he remains in office, how many more appointments he has the opportunity to make, and how well he can work with the confirmation power of a Republican-controlled Senate.

Staffing the Lower Federal Courts

The real impact of the presidential appointment power comes not so much at the Supreme Court level as at the lower federal court level. With hundreds of appointments of life-tenured judges, here, and 99.9 percent of all federal cases never reaching the Supreme Court, these appointments determine the direction of American law for many years to come. The legacy of a president's lower-court appointments will last for about two decades after the end of that president's term of office.[24]

The formal selection process for the lower federal courts is roughly the same as for the Supreme Court. Guided by officials in the Justice Department and White House, the president nominates candidates who have first been screened by the FBI and the ABA. The candidates' names are then sent to the Senate Judiciary Committee, beginning the confirmation proceedings. But there is one important difference in the selection process for lower-court judges. For federal district court appointments, presidents observe the practice of **senatorial courtesy** by submitting the names of nominees to senators from the same political party who are also from the nominee's home state. Failure to do so might lead to a senator declaring that a candidate is "personally obnoxious," dooming the appointment. Other senators, wishing to preserve the practice of senatorial courtesy for their own use in the future, will follow the first senator's lead and vote against the nomination. In these ways, senatorial courtesy has forced presidents to share their nomination power with the Senate.[25] In fact, in many cases the names of prospective candidates are forwarded to the White House by the senators from the president's party and the candidate's state (and sometimes even from powerful senators in the other party) *prior* to the nomination decision. These candidates often become the nominee.

The practice of senatorial courtesy is rarely used for appointments to the court of appeals and no longer applies to Supreme Court appointments, because the jurisdiction of judges in these courts extends beyond a particular senator's domain. Thus, a president could circumvent an objecting senator by making an appointment from another state.

A president's ability to use the appointment power to shape the lower federal court is determined by length of service in the White House, the number of vacancies that arise during that time, and whether the Senate confirms the nominees. There is also the possibility that Congress can expand the lower-court system, creating new seats to be filled. One-term President Jimmy Carter made 258 appointments, while two-term president Ronald Reagan made 368. When Republican George Bush's 185 appointments are combined with the holdovers from previous Republican administrations, we see that approximately 65 percent of the lower federal judiciary was appointed by the Republican party. Bush's judicial legacy could have been even greater, but he failed to fill 47 vacancies, and a democratically controlled Senate Judiciary Committee, still smarting from the Clarence Thomas confirmation battle, refused to confirm another 52 of his nominees. Thus, incoming president Bill Clinton had an opportunity to immediately begin reshaping the judiciary by filling 13 percent of its seats.

Recent presidents have clearly sought to leave their mark on the composition of the federal bench. President Jimmy Carter sought to make the court system more representative of the general population. After years of largely white male appointments, in 1976 Carter created merit-selection panels for choosing nominees to the appeals courts. Charged with searching for more diverse candidates as opposed to those that were just politically well-connected, these panels identified qualified female, African American, and Hispanic prospects. As a result, more than one-third of Carter's appointments were from these underrepresented groups.[26]

The Reagan administration abandoned the merit-selection process, seeking instead to correct a perceived ideological imbalance on the federal courts in favor of liberals. The President's Committee on Federal Judicial Selection was created to give the administration centralized ideological control over the selection process. In addition to the usual background checks, extensive written surveys and lengthy personal interviews were conducted to determine the nature and degree of the conservatism of the candidates. The result was, in the words of one judicial-selection expert, "the most consistent ideological or policy-orientation screening of judicial candidates since the first term of Franklin Roosevelt." And the change in the gender and ethnic composition of nominees was dramatic. Far fewer women, African Americans, and Hispanics were nominated (see Figure 7.3). The percentage of female and minority appointments for both the district and appeals courts dropped from 33 percent in the Carter administration to 13.6 percent in the Reagan administration.[27]

While the Bush administration ended the overt screening of candidates for conservatism, ideology remained as much a consideration as under the Reagan administration. Nonetheless, the Bush administration appointed more women to the federal bench than even Carter had (19.5 percent to 15.5 percent). Over 25 percent of Bush's appointments to the federal bench were women and minorities.

Clinton's appointments contrast starkly with those of his Republican predecessors. In his first two years of office, Clinton sought to make the courts even more representative and in the process made history because of the highly representative nature of his federal judicial appointments. More than 60 percent of his appointments were women and minorities, resulting in a federal judiciary in which more than one-quarter of the judges now come from these groups. While these percentages do not mirror the proportion of these groups

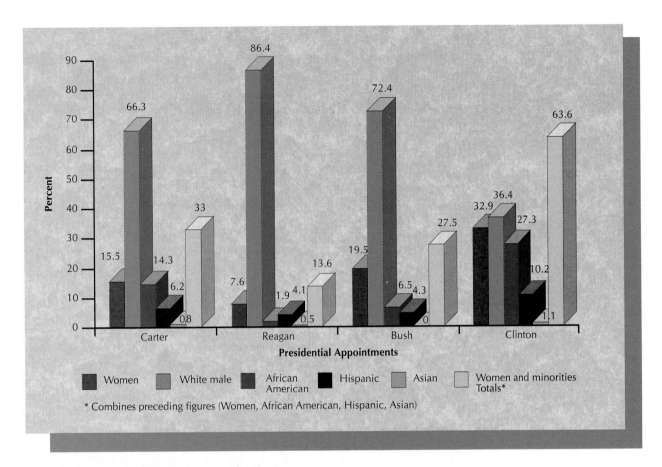

**FIGURE 7.3   Approaching Representative Democracy
on the Lower Federal Courts**
Prior to 1961 only two women, one African American, and one Hispanic held seats on
the federal bench. But times have changed, despite the fact that presidents have had
different opinions on the need for diversity on the courts. President Jimmy Carter sought
to make the court more representative of the general population by choosing qualified
female, African American, and Hispanic jurists. Ronald Reagan steered away from
choosing minorities when making appointments. George Bush, while allied ideologically with the Reagan administration, had a stronger record on gender appointments than
even Carter. But Clinton's appointments of minorities to the courts set him apart by sur-
passing those of any of his predecessors. The result, as this graph shows, is a much
more diverse lower federal court.
Source: Sheldon Goldman and Matthew D. Saronson, "Clinton's Nontraditional Judges: Creating a
More Representative Bench," *Judicature* 78, no. 2 (Sept.– Oct. 1994): 68–73.

in the total population, the percentage of women on the federal bench is now
much closer to the percentage of women in the legal profession, and the
percentage of African Americans on the bench is nearly three times the proportion of African Americans in that profession.[28]

Now that we've examined how federal judges get appointed, let's look at
how the highest federal court, the Supreme Court, does its job.

HOW THE SUPREME COURT OPERATES

How many times have you heard someone involved in a legal dispute proclaim defiantly, "If I lose this case I'm going to appeal it *all the way to the Supreme Court!*"? While Michael Hardwick had the opportunity to do this, the chances of someone following in his footsteps are less than that of being struck by lightning. In other words, a successful appeal to the Supreme Court is extremely rare. The reason, as you have already learned, has to do partly with the number of cases that are decided conclusively on their way to, and through, the intermediate appeals level. But it also has to do with the methods the Supreme Court uses to select the cases it will hear.

Each year the Supreme Court receives around seven thousand appeals. Of these, between 1 and 2 percent, or about one hundred cases, are placed on the Court's **docket,** or agenda, having been accepted for review. Nearly all of these cases are decided by a full written opinion. But a few will be decided *per curiam,* in a brief, unsigned, generally unanimous opinion by the Court. The lower-court judgment is left in effect for cases not accepted by the Court for review.

Nearly all of the Court's cases come from its *appellate jurisdiction,* cases that have already been reviewed and decided by one or more federal or state courts. About 90 percent of the appellate cases come from the lower federal courts, with most coming up the one step from the court of appeals. The 10 percent of cases coming from state courts must raise a federal question and have exhausted all possible state appeals to jump to the Supreme Court. This usually means that state cases come from the state court of last resort, though they need not do so. The second source of Court cases is its *original jurisdiction,* which as you learned earlier involves cases seeking to resolve disputes among states and cases affecting foreign ambassadors. The Court hears few original-jurisdiction cases today.

Selecting Cases

The rules for appealing a case to the Court have been established by congressional legislation. Appellate cases come to the Court through a formal writ called a **writ of certiorari,** a Latin term meaning "to be made more certain." Established in 1925, this discretionary writ enables the Court to accept cases for review only if there are "special and important reasons therefore." Essentially, the Court will consider accepting a case for review if it raises issues that impact on society or on the operation of government. You will recall that in the *Hardwick* case, the special reason for accepting the case for review was that the right of homosexual privacy had never been considered by the Court. Because of congressional-jurisdiction legislation passed in 1988, the Court now has virtually total discretion over the cases it will hear.

All of the justices (except John Paul Stevens, whose own clerks assist him) rely on a group of law clerks called a "cert pool" to do the initial screening of the appeals, summarize them in memo form, and then submit their recommendations to the justices.[29] While this might appear to make the law clerks into an intermediate court of review, in fact, the justices do form their own judgments about which cases are worthy of review. The justices then meet twice weekly to decide which appeals to accept. To speed up the decision process, appeals deemed worthy of consideration are placed on a "discuss list" by the chief justice. The remainder of the appeals are put on a "dead list," and unless at least one justice asks for further consideration, those appeals are denied by the Court without further discussion. The Court then votes on the cases on the discuss list. In what is known as the **rule of four,** a vote by at least four justices to hear the case will grant the petition for a writ of certiorari and put the case on the Court's docket.

Since the Court never explains why it accepts or rejects particular cases, political scientists have tried to discover what cues guide the Court's choices. One researcher found that during the period 1947–57 the Court tended to accept civil liberties cases, cases in which the national government was asking for a review of a lower federal court decision, and cases in which there was a difference of opinion among two or more lower federal courts.[30] Recently, though, Chief Justice Rehnquist (1972–present) reports, and political science research confirms, that if there is a set of conflicting rulings on an issue in the courts below, a misapplication of an earlier Supreme Court ruling by a lower court, or a request from certain interest groups that a case be heard, the justices will be inclined to consider seriously the appeal petition.[31]

Using its agenda-setting power to decide what cases to hear, the Court frequently waits for the ideal case or cases raising precisely the constitutional or legal issue it wants to rule on. For example, the Court ruled in the 1964 case *Escobedo* v. *Illinois*[32] that criminal suspects have the right to have an attorney present for police questioning if they ask for one. The Court then considered sixty-six cases before finding the ones with just the right facts for it to hold two years later in *Miranda* v. *Arizona*[33] that police would have to *inform* suspects of the right to an attorney before questioning.[34]

CASE SELECTION: RECENT TRENDS Since the late 1980s, the Supreme Court has been accepting and deciding fewer and fewer cases. While the number of appeals to the Court has increased by 85 percent in the last twenty-five years, the percentage of cases actually accepted by the justices has dropped dramatically. In the late 1970s and early 1980s, several hundred cases were decided yearly by either full opinions or unsigned orders. Of the 6,897 appeals coming to the Court in 1993, only 93 cases were decided by full opinion, while another 6 were decided per curiam, the lowest number since 1955.[35]

There are three possible explanations for the Court's shrinking docket. First, recent congressional legislation on federal jurisdiction eliminated nearly all categories of constitutional cases that the Court was once required to review. Second, the staffing of the vast majority of the lower federal courts with conservatives by the Reagan and Bush administrations has meant that a fairly conservative Supreme Court has had fewer lower-court opinions with which it disagrees. Finally, it is also possible that after the highly visible battles over abortion cases, and the bruising confirmation fights over Robert Bork and Clarence Thomas, the justices may be consciously trying to reduce the profile of the Court for a while by accepting fewer cases. Whether this is a long-term change or just a cyclical trend remains to be seen.

Drew Days, solicitor general in the Clinton Administration, at work in his Justice Department office. Days, a Yale law professor on leave, has had a distinguished career arguing civil rights cases. In 1994, however, he lost a chance to fill a vacant seat on the Supreme Court because of clashes with the White House over policy positions before the Court.

The Solicitor General: The "Tenth Justice"

One of the most important outside players influencing the Supreme Court's work, including its selection of cases, is the **solicitor general.** The third-ranking official in the Justice Department (after the attorney general and deputy attorney general), the solicitor general is appointed by the president and charged with representing the U.S. government before the Supreme Court. The solicitor general decides which federal cases to appeal from the lower courts, prepares those appeals, files briefs for accepted cases, and appears before the Court for oral argument. In cases that do not involve the national government as a party, the solicitor general may file **amicus curiae briefs,** or "friend of the court," briefs. Amicus briefs enable groups or individuals, including the national government, who are not parties to the litigation but have an interest in it, to attempt to influence the outcome of a case. All in all, the solicitor general is involved in about two-thirds of the cases before the Supreme Court.

The solicitor general has become so powerful and influential that the position is sometimes informally referred to as the "tenth justice."[36] The willingness of the solicitor general to become involved in a case alerts the justices to the need to hear that appeal. In this way, the solicitor general serves as eyes and ears for the Court and can play a role in setting the Court's agenda.

The solicitor general is often pulled in two directions. As a presidential appointee, he or she must be sensitive to the policy preferences and interests of the White House. At the same time, the solicitor general is an officer of the Court, representing the interests of both the judiciary and the entire national government. At times politics prevails. During the Reagan and Bush years the solicitor general's office took before the Court hardline conservative positions on controversial issues such as abortion favored by the administration . Sometimes the solicitor general's job is a tug of war. Clinton's solicitor general, Drew Days, has been trying as an officer of the Court to represent the position of the national government and judiciary. However, the White House has occasionally forced him to reverse his stance on certain issues for political reasons.[37]

The Process of Deciding Cases

Once a case is accepted for review it passes through a number of stages as it is being considered. Each of these stages is designed first to inform the jurists and then to give them a chance to organize a final decision. An overview of these stages appears in Figure 7.4.

THE FILING OF BRIEFS   When a case is accepted for argument, the attorneys for all sides are asked to submit **briefs.** These are hundreds of pages of written arguments outlining not only all of the facts and legal and constitutional issues in the case, but also answering all of the anticipated arguments of the opposing side.

These written arguments were once strictly legal in nature, but now it is common for attorneys to present extensive sociological, psychological, scientific, and historical arguments to bolster their legal documentation. In the case of *Brown* v. *Board of Education,*[38] which in 1954 raised the issue of desegregating public schools, the Court was presented with evidence from sociologist Kenneth Clark that African American youngsters were psychologically

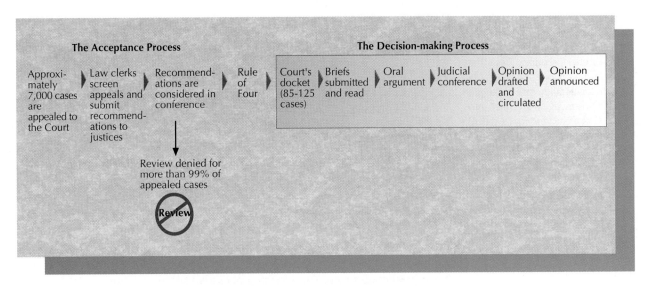

FIGURE 7.4 Supreme Court Acceptance and Decision of Cases: An Overview of the Process

harmed by segregated school systems.[39] As you will see in Chapter 15, it was primarily this evidence that contributed to the Court's decision to ignore legal precedents and rule that segregated schools are inherently unconstitutional.

ORAL ARGUMENT Once briefs are submitted, oral arguments follow. One of the most exciting and impressive events in Washington, D.C., is the public oral argument before the Supreme Court. Typically, the arguments are heard during the first three days of the first two weeks of each month from October through April. Lawyers from all sides, on occasion the solicitor general, and in the most important cases other interested parties including those who have submitted amicus curiae briefs are allowed to come before the justices and present their case. Each side is usually given only thirty minutes to speak, with time limits kept so carefully by the chief justice that during one Court session, a lawyer was interrupted in the middle of the word *if*.

Although lawyers come prepared with statements, they must stop to answer questions from the justices. Justices have very different questioning styles. Much as he did as a law professor, Antonin Scalia asks many rapid-fire questions. Ruth Bader Ginsburg asks carefully sculpted questions designed to keep counsel from avoiding issues, while Stephen Breyer usually waits until the end of counsel's time before asking one or two lengthy questions designed to crystallize the central issue in the case. By contrast, Clarence Thomas asked no questions during his first eighteen months on the bench.

What role does oral argument play in the decision-making process? For some justices, oral presentations help to crystallize in their minds the problems with the issue being raised by the written briefs and suggest possible avenues for decision. For others, written briefs are weighed more heavily. For this reason it is often difficult to predict how the Court will rule based on the nature of its questioning during oral argument.

The Supreme Court of the United States hears oral arguments in June 1932 with Chief Justice Charles Evans Hughes presiding. This is the only known photo of the Court in session. It was taken by a photographer who smuggled a camera into the Court's hearing room, where cameras are not allowed. The justices (from left) are Owen Roberts, Pierce Butler, Louis D. Brandeis, Willis Van Devanter, Hughes, George Sutherland, Harlan Fiske Stone, and Benjamin Cardozo.

THE DECISION-MAKING STAGE: THE CONFERENCE After the justices read the briefs and listen to oral arguments, the decision-making process begins in the judicial conference. These conferences take place on Wednesday afternoon for the cases argued on Monday, and all day Friday for the cases argued on Tuesday and Wednesday. At these meetings, the justices discuss both the cases under consideration and which appeals to grant in the future.

The meetings take place in total secrecy in an oak-paneled conference room, with only the justices present. Proceeding from the chief justice down to the most junior justice, the justices indicate both their views and how they will vote. Opinions expressed at this time constitute a preliminary vote.[40]

In recent years, the conference stage has changed dramatically. Harlan Fiske Stone (1925–46) conducted exhausting judicial conferences that went on for hours and often extended from Friday into Saturday. During these long meetings clerks recall hearing Felix Frankfurter and William O. Douglas screaming at each other so loudly that their voices carried down the hall. Recently, though, the conference stage has become briefer and less heated. "Not very much conferencing goes on," explains Justice Antonin Scalia. "In fact, to call our discussion of a case a conference is really something of a misnomer. It's much more a statement of the views of each of the nine justices, after which the totals are added and the case is assigned [for the drafting of the opinion]."[41]

ASSIGNMENT OF OPINIONS Once the discussion and voting are over, if the chief justice is in the majority he assigns one of the members voting in the majority to draft an **opinion,** the written version of the decision. Sometimes the chief justice will write the opinion in the hopes of expressing an even stronger view from the Court. If the chief is not in the majority, the senior justice in the majority makes the assignment or writes the opinion.

Assignments are made based on a number of factors. The expertise of certain members of the Court, their speed in drafting opinions, their ability to forge a consensus, and their current workload may be considered. At times, personal and symbolic considerations govern the choice. Earl Warren liked to give the most interesting opinions to his colleagues, while his successor, Warren Burger, was known to assign the least interesting opinions to the justices with whom he was unhappy.

The assignment of opinions is important because such choices determine the tone of Court opinions and how they are received by the public. A classic example of this tone-setting power was Chief Justice Harlan Fiske Stone's re-assignment of the *Smith* v. *Allwright*[42] opinion. That 1944 case barred all-white Democratic party primaries in Texas. After initially assigning the case to Felix Frankfurter, a political Independent from New England, Stone realized the potential for the opinion to arouse resentment in the Democratic party and in the South, where a white primary was considered a cherished right. So he reassigned the opinion to Stanley Reed (1938–57), an avowed Democrat from the border state of Kentucky. While the opinion was still controversial, it was more accepted as a result of Reed's role.[43]

Sometimes the voting lineup and thus the very decision in a case hinges on who is assigned the opinion. In 1992 five justices, including moderates David Souter, Sandra Day O'Connor, and Anthony Kennedy, seemed ready to overturn the *Roe* v. *Wade*[44] abortion decision in the case of *Planned Parenthood of Southeastern Pennsylvania* v. *Casey*.[45] When conservative chief justice Rehnquist assigned the opinion to himself because of the importance of the case, those three moderates decided instead, to everyone's amazement, to write a joint opinion upholding the precedent.[46]

Marshaling the Court: The Opinion-Drafting Process

After the judicial conference, the justice assigned to write the opinion takes weeks, and sometimes months, to develop a draft to circulate among the other justices. Special care is taken because conference votes are tentative, and justices will lobby to change their colleagues' positions. As Justice William Brennan used to say: "Five votes. Five votes can do anything around here."[47] And each side attempts to muster those five votes.

Years ago such lobbying took place through personal interaction. In recent years what little lobbying has taken place is usually done in writing. Despite such efforts, however, evidence suggests that votes change in less than 10 percent of the cases.[48] The *Hardwick* case provides an example of a justice changing his mind, when Justice Powell decided to change his vote and side with the conservatives.

Although actual votes rarely change, the language of opinions nearly always changes dramatically as a result of these lobbying efforts. Each opinion goes through multiple drafts, with justices negotiating with each other over changes on which votes may depend. And such negotiations take time. For this reason, opinions for major cases argued in the fall of a judicial term might not be issued until the spring of the following year. These negotiations come in the form of written comments on various opinion drafts, personal memos, and even personal lobbying. Justices have different styles in such lobbying efforts. Frankfurter used the "carrot" approach, often praising a justice for his brilliance (while saving less gracious comments for his personal diary). On the other hand, Justice James McReynolds (1914–41), sarcastically referred to as the Court's "Mr. Congeniality," used the "stick" approach, once writing on a colleague's draft, "This statement makes me sick."[49] At any point in this process, right up to the public announcement of the opinion, a justice can change a vote.

Sometimes the frustration of these unsuccessful negotiations is reflected in the final opinion. In one abortion case, Justice Antonin Scalia, by all accounts a charming man in person, described Justice Sandra Day O'Connor's opinion as "perverse," "irrational," and "not to be taken seriously."[50]

Little-known Fact

Until the late 1970s there was only one small photocopying machine in the entire Supreme Court building; thus, justices circulated eight typed carbon copies of opinions, called *flimsies*. It was only recently that the Court entered the computer age with PCs placed in nearly every office (David Souter's office remains computer-free, as he prefers it). Before the advent of modern-day office technology, justices wrote their opinions in longhand.

Only after there is an agreement by all the justices on the wording of the final opinion is it ready to be announced.

The Role of Law Clerks

Over the years, the Supreme Court, like the other two branches, has become more bureaucratic. Increasingly, justices use assistants known as *law clerks* to help get their work done. These are top graduates of prominent law schools with prior experience working as clerks on the lower federal courts. In the last fifty years the number of law clerks per justice has increased from one to four (with a fifth for the chief). Legal scholars have questioned whether law clerks now play a far greater role in the opinion-drafting process for the Court than is acknowledged.[51] For instance, during his first term on the Court, Clarence Thomas used Antonin Scalia's clerks from the previous year. Court observers noticed a remarkable similarity in the two justices' votes and opinions. While most if not all of the initial drafts of opinions are likely the work of law clerks, the final opinions always reflect the justices' votes and philosophical leanings.

The Announcement of Opinions

The vote on any case is final only when the decision or opinion is announced in open court. The Court's opinion not only states the facts of a case and announces the decision but since this will be the only public comment on the case, it contains supporting logic, precedents, and rationale to persuade the public of the merits of the judgment. In addition, the language used in an opinion is designed to then be used by lower courts, federal and state politicians, and the legal community to interpret similar cases in the future.

The Court makes its decision based on a majority (five votes of nine), called a **majority opinion,** which represents the agreed-upon compromise judgment of all the justices in the majority. This opinion is almost always signed only by its author. In cases where less than a majority agrees on the wording, a *plurality opinion* will be issued. This plurality opinion announces the opinion of the Court, but it does not have the same binding legal force as a majority opinion.

If a justice agrees with the majority decision of the Court but differs on the reasoning, a **concurring opinion** can be written. Justice Powell wrote a concurring opinion on the harshness of the possible sentence in the *Hardwick* case. A careful reading of the concurring opinions often reveals the true sentiments of the Court majority. In the landmark 1971 freedom of press case *New York Times Co.* v. *United States,*[52] the Court allowed several newspapers to publish the Pentagon Papers, a classified study of the decision-making process that led to America's involvement in Vietnam. However, the six concurring opinions revealed that if the government had sought to punish the *Times* editors *after* publication rather than prevent publication through prior censorship, a majority of the Court would have upheld it.

When a justice disagrees with the holding of the court, frequently he or she will write a **dissenting opinion,** speaking for that justice alone or a few of the members of the Court. From the stewardship of Chief Justice Marshall until the early 1920s, justices avoided dissents, fearing a diminution of the public authority of the Court. Now it is accepted that democracy is best served

Supreme Court justice Ruth Bader Ginsburg in her office, conferring with one of her law clerks. Law clerks are recent graduates of the top law schools who often serve first as clerks on the court of appeals and then serve as short-term clerks on the Court.

You Be the Judge

On January 11, 1983, twenty-five-year-old Nancy Cruzan lost control of her car on an icy road and the car overturned. By the time she was discovered by a state trooper, she had no pulse and was not breathing. She was revived after a lapse of some twelve to fourteen minutes, but during that time her brain had been deprived of oxygen and she had entered an irreversible coma. For several years she lay in a hospital bed in what physicians termed a "persistent vegetative state," unable to speak, move, or recognize her family.

Nancy's family insisted that she would not have wished to be kept alive under such conditions. However, hospital officials refused to detach the tubes that supplied her with food and water, saying that doctors and nurses had seen her look toward people who spoke to her. Besides, they pointed out, their duty is to protect and preserve life, not to end it. Nancy was not terminally ill. If the tubes were removed, she would starve.

The family went to court with their request that Nancy be allowed to die. They argued that she had no hope of recovery and that there was "clear and convincing evidence" that she would choose to end life support if given the chance. The lower court judge agreed with their claims and granted their request.

If you were the judge, how would you have ruled?

What Happened

The Cruzan case was appealed to the Missouri Supreme Court, which reversed the lower court's decision, saying that there was inadequate evidence that Nancy would wish to die rather than be maintained on life support. The court's ruling relied on the state's "strong policy favoring life" as embodied in its antiabortion law. The family appealed to the U.S. Supreme Court. It was the first time the issue of a "right to die" had come before the Court.

The family's attorney argued that every person has a right to be free of unwanted medical treatment and that family members are called upon to act in the best interests of a gravely ill relative. However, the justices were troubled by the fact that there is no means for determining the wishes of a comatose patient. In the words of Chief Justice Rehnquist, "Close family members may have a strong feeling . . . that they do not wish to witness the continuation of the life of a loved one which they regard as hopeless. . . . But there is no automatic assurance that the view of close family members will necessarily be the same as the patient's would have been." On June 25, 1990, the Court upheld the state's right to keep Nancy Cruzan alive.

Four of the justices voted against the decision, and in a dissenting opinion Justice Brennan argued that Nancy should not "remain a passive prisoner of medical technology." "No state interest," he claimed, "could outweigh the rights of an individual in Nancy Cruzan's position."

Nancy's family did not admit defeat. In a later hearing they brought in additional witnesses who could attest to her likely wishes in such a situation, and the judge granted their petition for termination of life support; this time the state supreme court approved the decision. Nancy died on December 26, 1990.

by the expression of differing views. In addition, the dissents of today can become the majority opinions of tomorrow with the change of a few members on the Court. Much of the current Court's restriction of defendant's rights was first expressed in solo dissents by William Rehnquist in the early 1970s.

The two most recent chief justices. Between them, they have served in that capacity for more than a quarter century. On the left is Warren Burger, chief justice from 1970 through 1986. On the right is his successor, the current chief justice, William Rehnquist.

The Chief Justice's Role

The chief justice is first among equals on the Supreme Court, with substantial powers to influence the Court's direction by assigning opinions, leading the judicial conference, and acting as the social and intellectual leader of the Court. In addition, as chief justice of the United States, he or she also heads, represents, and lobbies for the entire federal judiciary.

There has been much variation in the leadership styles of chief justices. Some have been more effective as leaders of the Supreme Court than others. The austere Charles Evans Hughes (1930–41) moved the Court along with military precision, while his replacement, the gregarious Harlan Fiske Stone (1941–46) lost control of the Court during judicial conferences. Fred Vinson (1946–53) was mismatched with the high-powered, egocentric Roosevelt appointees, leading to considerable rancor on the Court in those years. On the other hand, the relative harmony that followed came during the tenure of the politically skilled former governor of California, Earl Warren, (1953–70), known to his admiring colleagues as the "Super Chief." This period was in contrast to the sharply split Court under Warren Burger (1970–86), who was reputed to be an uninspiring leader.[53] Currently, the highly popular and respected William Rehnquist (1986–present) seems capable of forging and maintaining the Court's conservative coalition.[54]

Now that we've seen the official process used by the Court to arrive at a decision, let's look at the ingredients, both legal and personal, that lead individual justices, and the Court as a whole, to arrive at decisions.

ANALYZING SUPREME COURT DECISIONS

To analyze and understand any Supreme Court decision it helps to be aware of the following considerations: the Court's use of precedent and other legal factors, the mindset of the individual justices, the personalities of the justices, and the voting blocs on the Court at a particular time.

The Use of Precedent and Other Legal Factors

Judges throughout the entire legal system often decide cases on the basis of the doctrine of **stare decisis,** which means "to let the decision stand," or to adhere if at all possible to previously decided cases, or **precedents,** on the same issue. Federal and state courts, for example, are supposed to follow Supreme Court precedents in making their own decisions. The Supreme Court often rules based on its own precedents. By following the rulings of their predecessors, all courts, including the Supreme Court, seem to be nonpolitical, impartial arbiters, making incremental changes based on past decisions.

But following precedent is not as restrictive as it sounds. Since in practice precedents need interpretation, judges can argue about the meaning of an earlier case, or whether the facts of the current case differ substantially from those of past cases, thus requiring a different ruling. For instance, in the *Hardwick* case, both Justices Blackmun and White cited the same case of *Stanley* v. *Georgia,*[55] a privacy and pornography case, as a major precedent upholding their opposing positions. On some occasions, justices will give the appearance of upholding precedent when in fact they are deliberately ignoring it or consciously reinterpreting it to reach a different result.

Only in the most extreme cases is the Court willing to overturn an earlier decision, thus declaring it invalid. Precedents are usually overturned if they prove to be unworkable from a public-policy standpoint, outmoded, or just plain unwise. Sometimes though, the Court will overturn a precedent simply because of a change in personnel, thus changing the Court's direction, or because of a change in public opinion. For example, in 1991 the Court overruled two earlier Eighth Amendment capital punishment decisions barring the use of statements by victims in the penalty phase of a capital trial. The arrival of new conservative members made this possible but led frustrated liberal Thurgood Marshall to argue, "Power, not reason, is the new currency of this Court's decisionmaking."[56] In actuality, however, the Court rarely overrules its own precedents. Of the tens of thousands of decisions issued by the Court, it has overruled its own precedents in less than three hundred cases.[57]

A favorite technique for circumventing precedent without reversing a previous decision is to *distinguish* cases, that is, to claim that the earlier case and a more recent case are very different (even though they are in fact similar), thus requiring different decisions. The Court has been able to dilute the original ruling in the 1966 *Miranda* case using such a technique. That case established rules governing police conduct during the interrogation of witnesses. It has never been overruled, but the Court created so many exceptions to it when ruling in similar cases that the original ruling is almost entirely irrelevant.

Justices also look at a variety of factors beyond precedent to decide an issue, including the meaning of a law, the meaning of part of the Constitution, the lessons of history, and the possible impact on public policy. Justices may look carefully at the wording of a statute or a portion of the Constitution, using *strict construction,* interpreting the law as closely as possible to the literal meaning of the words in the text. When the wording is vague, these justices will then search for historical context, or for the so-called intent of the Framers, who wrote the law and the Constitution, to determine the true meaning of both. Proponents of the "original-intent" theory with respect to the Constitution, such as Judge Robert Bork, argue that it is the Court's duty to adhere solely to the original meaning of the framers to limit the power of Supreme Court justices. Others, however, argue that society has changed since the drafting of the Constitution and that the Court's decisions should thus reflect the needs of a continually changing society.

Sometimes justices examine the general history of an issue and the public-policy impact of their decision. In the *Hardwick* case, Justices Blackmun and White disagreed over both the history of anti-sodomy laws and the public-policy implications of protecting privacy rights in this area.

The Mindset of Individual Justices

Personal factors also need to be considered when analyzing judicial decisions. It is helpful to look at a judge's mindset—his or her political ideology, jurisprudential posture, and a combination of the two.

POLITICAL IDEOLOGY   Although some observers of the Court would prefer justices decide cases on the basis of neutral principles, the individuals sitting on

"Justice Douglas, you must remember one thing. At the constitutional level where we work, ninety percent of any decision is emotional. The rational part of us supplies the reasons for supporting our predilections."

—Chief Justice Charles Evans Hughes

The Supreme Court poses for its annual portrait in November 1994. Seated, from the left: Antonin Scalia, John Paul Stevens, Chief Justice William Rehnquist, Sandra Day O'Connor, and Anthony Kennedy. Standing, from left: Ruth Bader Ginsburg, David Souter, Clarence Thomas, and the Court's newest member, Stephen Breyer.

the Court are human beings influenced by their own biases.[58] A comprehensive study by two political scientists found a strong correlation between justices' votes on the Court and their ideological views as expressed in newspaper articles written during the appointment process.[59]

Like members of political parties, justices tend to be grouped ideologically as conservative, liberal, or moderate. Conservatives tend to support the government's position instead of the individual's, while liberals tend to defend and even expand the rights of the individual instead of the government. Moderates often flip back and forth between these two positions, depending on the issues. For example, Justice Lewis Powell, who in the *Hardwick* case shifted from a liberal to a conservative stance as he decided on his vote, was a conservative on defendant's rights and a liberal on freedom of religion cases.

Labeling jurists this way is helpful but in no way definitive. There are many varieties of liberals and conservatives and many legal issues that do not fit clearly into those groupings. Political ideology, then, is only a starting point for understanding a jurist's mindset. We must also consider the willingness of the justices to use their power.

JURISPRUDENTIAL POSTURE   Justices have a certain jurisprudential posture, meaning how willing they are to use their power on the Court. Some practice self-restraint, others are activists. Those justices who believe in **judicial restraint** see themselves as appointed rather than elected officials, who should defer to the elected legislature and uphold a law or political action if at all possible. "If the legislature wants to go to hell, I'm here to tell them they can do it," said Oliver Wendell Holmes. In deferring to the legislature, the Court can arrive at some unexpected rulings. In 1968, the Supreme Court upheld an amendment to the Selective Service Law banning the knowing destruction or mutilation of a draft card, despite the freedom of speech claim of the defendant, David Paul O'Brien, who had burned his card in a Vietnam War protest. In so doing, the Court allied itself with Congress and its clearly unconstitutional purpose of discouraging antiwar protests.[60]

Judicial activists believe that judges have a duty to reach out and decide issues, even to the point, some critics charge, of writing their own personal values into law. Judicial activists are more willing to strike down legislation, reject a presidential action, or create rights not specifically written in the Constitution. For example, the ruling in the case of *Griswold* v. *Connecticut*[61] created the right of privacy (eventually debated in the *Hardwick* case), even though such a right is not explicitly in the Constitution. The activist posture often leads to the charge by conservatives that the Court is acting as a "super-legislature," overruling duly elected bodies.[62]

"I don't follow precedents. I make 'em."

—Justice William O. Douglas

Activists come in many varieties and are given a number of labels. *Result-oriented* justices begin with the result they intend to reach in mind and simply announce that judgment, paying little attention to justifying their decision in the opinion. Another kind of activist, the *absolutist,* believes that the rights in the Constitution are paramount and no contrary interest of the state can be used to justify overruling them. Hugo Black (1937–1971), a New Deal justice, once typified the absolutist position in writing that when the First Amendment says that Congress shall make no law abridging freedom of speech, "no law means NO law!"[63]

Considering the jurisprudential posture of justices then will help you analyze Supreme Court cases. It provides you with a clue regarding whether or not the Court will insert itself into a public-policy issue. Generally speaking, activist jurists tend to get involved, while those who practice judicial restraint will try to duck an issue, preferring to let the other branches get involved.

THE FOUR-CELL METHOD FOR CLASSIFYING JUSTICES   It is often revealing to assess justices according to a four-cell categorization that takes into consideration both political ideology (whether a judge is liberal or conservative) and

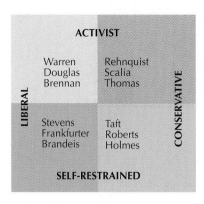

FIGURE 7.5 The Four-Cell Method for Classifying Justices
It is useful to assess justices by looking at their politics (whether they are liberal or conservative) *and* at their judicial philosophy (whether they are activist or self-restrained). We learn, as a result, that both types of self-restrained justices share an inclination to avoid innovation, while activists in the two camps can differ dramatically with regard to the goals of their activism.

jurisprudential posture (whether a judge is self-restrained or an activist). This scheme, illustrated in Figure 7.5, helps us better understand that self-restrained liberals and self-restrained conservatives on the Court have much in common because neither group will be inclined to break new ground. For instance, New Deal appointee Felix Frankfurter was frequently criticized by liberal colleagues because his self-restrained opinions upholding the letter of the law made him look too conservative. However, the activists on either side of the political spectrum can differ dramatically, as liberal activists are willing to reach beyond the law and write new individual rights into the Constitution, while conservative activists sometimes seek to create new governmental powers restricting individual rights. Thus, liberal activist Blackmun and conservative activist White disagreed vehemently with each other on the very nature of the issues in the *Hardwick* case. While Blackmun was ready to create a new privacy protection for homosexuals, White concerned himself only with state laws on sodomy.

But concentrating solely on the political and judicial views of a justice is not enough to understand decisions. Instead, in dealing with a life-tenured Court an additional angle needs to be considered: judicial character.

Judicial Character

The personalities of individual justices and how the justices interact with each other play a large role in the direction of the Court. Justice William Brennan explains: "In an institution this small, personalities play an important role. . . . How those people get along, how they relate, what ideas they have, how flexible or intractable they are, are all of enormous significance."[64] A justice can shade an opinion to secure the agreement of a colleague, or perhaps remain silent, rather than write a dissent, in the interest of interpersonal harmony. On the other hand, a justice can for personal or professional reasons simply chart a separate course, possibly creating friction on the Court.

Like any group, members of the Court can be divided into leaders, team players, and loners. The leader does not necessarily have to be the chief justice. One political scientist argued that on every Court there are "task leaders," who see that the work gets done, and "social leaders," who keep life on the Court harmonious.[65] Sometimes these two types of leaders can be rolled into one, as in the case of Justice Brennan, who during his tenure became known as a "playmaker," or the justice who unites a ruling majority on the Court. That role continued even during the highly conservative Rehnquist Court years, where the liberal Brennan's elfin, affectionate style enabled him to continue amassing five-person majorities. Then there are the team players, those justices usually willing to go along with the majority. On the present Court, there are three team players—O'Connor, Souter, and Kennedy—who have adopted a centrist position. In contrast are the loner justices who are willing to take a stand even if it means issuing frequent sole dissents and angering colleagues. Justice William O. Douglas and, in his early years, Justice Rehnquist adopted this role with such frequency that they were called "The Lone Rangers." Now conservative Justices Scalia and Thomas, and frequently liberal Justice Stevens, appear willing to adopt this role, especially on cases dealing with abortion and defendants' rights. While the conservatives now lack the kind of playmaker that the liberals had in Brennan, the present coalition of centrist justices may enable the Court to amass a consistently moderate-conservative majority.

Looking at the Whole Court and Voting Blocs

To analyze Court decisions, it helps to group the whole Court into blocs of like-minded jurists. Such blocs can be defined by ideology as conservative, liberal, and moderate (see Table 7.1). While justices sometimes shift over time within these blocs, more frequently change results from vacancies filled in a way that alters the balance of the Court. In the *Hardwick* case, for example, the Court was almost perfectly balanced—with four conservative justices (William Rehnquist, Warren Burger, Byron White, and Sandra Day O'Connor), four liberals (William Brennan, Thurgood Marshall, Harry Blackmun, and John Paul Stevens), and moderate justice Lewis Powell breaking the tie. These blocs are not absolute determinants of votes, however, since frequently the views of a justice, and thus the justice's position within a bloc, vary according to the issue under consideration.

Bloc analysis can be helpful in predicting which justices may become the "swing votes" that determine the outcome in a case. Law firms appearing before the Court make this kind of analysis so they can pitch their oral argument to one or two justices they deem to be critical to their case.

Replacing one of the members of a leading bloc of the Court with a member suited to the other bloc will sharply tip the balance of the Court. So while new Supreme Court appointments are always important, some of them take on greater importance because they have the potential to change the entire direction of the Court. That was why the prospect of replacing Warren Burger with Antonin Scalia in 1986—a conservative for a conservative—did not have nearly the impact and was not as controversial as the attempted replacement of the moderate Powell with the highly conservative activist Robert Bork a year later.

Limitations of Court Analysis

Although the preceding tools for analyzing Supreme Court decisions help us understand how the Court may have arrived at a decision, they have limitations as predictors of Court rulings. Because of the nature of the Court's independent role and the constantly evolving nature of the individuals on it, the Court does not always head in the direction that seems obvious or that the experts predict. Harry Blackmun and John Paul Stevens were expected to become conservatives on the Court, but instead they evolved into its most liberal members. Republican president George Bush's additions of conservatives David Souter and Clarence Thomas were expected to make the Court extremely conservative, but instead in the 1991–92 Court term Souter teamed up with two Reagan appointees, Anthony Kennedy and Sandra Day O'Connor, to create the controlling centrist bloc that frequently thwarts the conservatives (Thomas, as expected, has sided with the conservatives). Now it will be interesting to see whether the two Clinton appointees—Ruth Bader Ginsburg and Stephen Breyer—vote with the liberal John Paul Stevens, unite with the three centrists, or chart their own course.

THE RESULTS OF SUPREME COURT DECISIONS

Once the Supreme Court issues its ruling in a case, implementation of the decision is left to other political actors. Let's take a look at the process of implementation and see how public opinion figures into it.

FYI

The oldest justice ever to serve on the Court was Oliver Wendell Holmes, at age ninety, while the youngest to come to the Court was Joseph Story in the early 1800s, at age thirty-two. The longest-serving jurist on the Court was William O. Douglas (thirty-six years, seven months), while the shortest tenure was served by James F. Byrnes (fifteen months).

Table 7.1
Judicial Voting Blocs

	LIBERAL	MODERATE	CONSERVATIVE
Eisenhower Court (1961)	Warren Brennan Black Douglas	Whittaker Harlan	Frankfurter Stewart Clark
Kennedy Court (1963)	Warren Brennan Black Douglas Goldberg	Harlan	Stewart Clark White
Johnson Court (1969)	Warren Brennan Douglas Fortas Marshall	Harlan	Black* Stewart White
Nixon Court (1974)	Brennan Douglas Marshall	Powell Blackmun	Burger Rehnquist Stewart White
Ford Court (1976)	Brennan Marshall	Powell Blackmun Stevens	Burger Rehnquist Stewart White
Reagan Court (1989)	Brennan Blackmun† Marshall	Kennedy O'Connor Stevens	Rehnquist Scalia White
Bush Court (1993)	Blackmun Stevens	Kennedy Souter O'Connor	Rehnquist Scalia White Thomas
Clinton Court (1995)	Stevens	Kennedy Souter O'Connor Ginsburg Breyer	Rehnquist Scalia Thomas

*The liberal Hugo Black became a conservative after a stroke.

†It is interesting to note that when appointed in 1970, Blackmun was very conservative. By 1973, he had become a moderate, and later in his career he became a liberal.

Implementing Supreme Court Decisions

When the Supreme Court issues its judgments, in theory they become the law of the land, and one might expect compliance to be automatic. But that does not always happen. Some decisions are so controversial that they are ignored in many places. As a school board member in Deming, New Mexico, put it in defying the Court's ban on prayer in public schools: "Until those justices come down here and tell us to change, we'll do things our own way."[66]

Possessing neither "purse" nor "sword" the Supreme Court must maintain the support of political actors such as the president, the Congress, and the state and local governments that implement its decisions. This means that the Court, although an unelected body, cannot operate in a political vacuum when making its decisions.

THE PRESIDENT AND THE COURT   Compliance with a decision is influenced by whether the president is willing to lend the weight of his office to mobilize favorable public opinion. When state and local officials in Little Rock, Arkansas, resisted the *Brown* v. *Board of Education* school desegregation decision in 1957, President Eisenhower sent federal troops to help implement it.[67] It was Catholic president John F. Kennedy's support for the Court's 1962 decision outlawing school prayer that helped to build public support on behalf of that decision.[68]

While most often presidents have nothing to say about Court decisions, their occasional opposition can have an impact. The classic expression of this came in 1832 with a Supreme Court ruling in favor of the legal rights of the Cherokee Indians. The old frontier fighter president Andrew Jackson was reputed to have said: "Well, John Marshall has made his decision, now let him enforce it!"[69] Since the state of Georgia also opposed the rights of the Cherokee Indians, it would be left to the federal judiciary and Congress to safeguard their rights.

In the long run, however, presidents who do not support the direction of Court rulings can have a greater impact on the Court through appointments rather than through direct confrontation.

CONGRESS AND THE COURT   Frequently, Congress will say nothing about Court rulings, the majority of which interpret or define their laws. But if Congress disagrees with the Court's statutory ruling, it has four routes to convey its discontent: It can pass a new law or a revised version of an old law restating its original intentions, it can pass resolutions expressing disagreement with the Court, it can threaten to use one of its constitutional powers to attack the Court directly, or it can propose a constitutional amendment. Generally, Congress will choose to overturn statutory interpretations by passing another version of the law that has been struck down. For instance, in response to six anti–civil rights decisions by the Court in 1991, Congress passed new versions of the same laws guaranteeing those civil rights to citizens.

Less frequently, Congress attempts to reverse constitutional decisions by passing a new law limiting their effect. In 1993 Congress sought to use legislation to overturn a 1990 case that ruled that the state of Oregon could deny unemployment compensation to two Native Americans who, in smoking Peyote in a religious ritual, violated state antidrug laws.[70] When this ruling was then applied in more than sixty other cases to restrict free exercise of religion, Congress passed, and President Clinton signed into law, the Religious Freedom Restoration Act, which required the states to show a "compelling state interest," or a very high level of proof, before it could interfere with freedom of religion.[71] This and similar efforts to overturn a constitutional decision by the Court through legislative means risk review by the Court in the future. Should

Although the Supreme Court has banned prayer in the public schools, students pray or observe a moment of silence in many schools across the nation.

the Court choose to strike down the law, however, Congress retains the option of proposing a constitutional amendment.

While a lack of congressional support can weaken or undermine Supreme Court rulings, congressional displeasure with Court rulings is most often apparent during confirmation hearings for judicial vacancies.

THE IMPACT AT STATE AND LOCAL LEVELS The implementation of Supreme Court decisions, especially those that are controversial and complex, requires the cooperation of a large number of state and local officials. Often compliance is not immediate; it takes time for decisions to filter through the system and be made a workable part of everyday life.

Lower federal and state court judges play a role. They are empowered to apply Supreme Court rulings to new cases in their jurisdiction. Because Supreme Court decisions are sometimes couched in vague language, they are open to significant interpretation. Thus, lower courts have tremendous power to establish how a Supreme Court ruling will be applied.

Governors, state legislatures, local governments, and even school boards also play a role in the implementation of Supreme Court decisions. Even local law enforcement has considerable impact. Decisions limiting the power of the police to search for evidence will be implemented only if the police and prosecutors choose to observe them and state judges decide to enforce them. While the vast majority of decisions are implemented without question, a handful of highly controversial ones are not, illustrating the problems the Court faces when issuing decisions. More than four decades after the *Brown* desegregation ruling, many American school systems remain segregated, and three decades after the decision striking down prayer in public schools, students in many public schools participate in some form of devotional service. Although *Roe* v. *Wade* legalized abortion, state legislatures around the country have placed a wide variety of restrictions on that right.

Public Opinion and the Supreme Court

Finally, supportive public opinion plays an important part in implementation. While the Supreme Court is an unelected body and does not need to consult public opinion polls when making its rulings, the views of the American people do play a role in its decision making. Should the Court fail to capture the conscience of the public with the persuasiveness of its reasoning, the decision

The People's Court?

Judge Lance Ito? Sure, I know who he is. William Rehnquist? Who's he?

In a *Washington Post* opinion poll, only 9 percent of the respondents knew the name of the chief justice of the United States.* You can bet that today the same would not be true of Judge Ito. And that's not all. Less than one-third of the respondents could name even one Supreme Court justice. Only 3 percent could name five or more of the justices, and only two of the 1,005 people surveyed could name all nine. In fact, another survey found that only 23 percent of Americans know how many justices there are.† Although 80 percent of Americans know that one of the justices is a woman, only 59 percent know that the justices serve for life.

Why do Americans know so little about the Supreme Court? One reason is the secrecy of the Court proceedings—the closed conferences of the justices and the absence of television in the courtroom. Chief Justice Rehnquist is so little known that from time to time he has wandered through the halls of the Supreme Court building without being recognized. But even when the workings of the Court are publicized—as in Bob Woodward and Scott Armstrong's book *The Brethren,* a controversial "inside" account—the public's reaction is minimal.

Despite their lack of knowledge about the Court and their apparent lack of interest in its proceedings, Americans have strong opinions about its decisions. In such areas as abortion, the right to die, abused children, and the rights of women and racial minorities, more than half of survey respondents have strong views on how the Court should rule. Many

want the Court to take a more active role in the areas of privacy and racial and sex discrimination.

Also unaffected by Americans' rather hazy view of the Court is their trust in that institution. As can be seen in the accompanying chart, while the overall level of confidence in the Supreme Court has slipped in recent years, it remains relatively high—especially when compared with the public's trust in Congress.

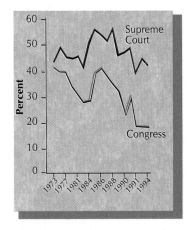

Rating America's Confidence in the Supreme Court and Congress, 1973–94
This graph indicates the percentage of Americans who said they have a "great deal" or "quite a lot" of confidence in the Court and in Congress.

---

*Richard Morin, "Wapner v. Rehnquist: No Contest," *Washington Post,* June 23, 1989, p. 19.

†Marcia Coyle, "How Americans View High Court," *The National Law Journal,* February 26, 1990, pp. 1, 36–7.

---

might never be fully implemented. The sharp public division over the abortion decision in *Roe* v. *Wade,* for example, has affected its level of acceptance.

Recent research has revealed the Court's general willingness to adhere to majority public sentiment in nearly 60 percent of its decisions.[72] In addition, when it makes bold innovative decisions public opinion is taken into account in that these decisions are often counterbalanced by a series of later, more conservative judgments to encourage acceptance. The Court is aware that if it gets too far out in front of public opinion, it risks losing support. Thus, the Court will change the law, and thereby public policy, incrementally to encourage implementation. After granting defendants the right to state-appointed attorneys in serious felony trials in the *Gideon* decision,[73] the Court was very slow to extend that right to other types of trials.

Should the Court lead or follow public opinion? The complete answer is that ideally it should do both. In general it is best to be attentive to the views of those implementing the decisions and to the general public, but at times the Court must lead when others in the political arena are unwilling to take the initiative. In this respect, the Court's independence is indispensable if it is to help America approach democracy.

THE COURTS AND APPROACHING DEMOCRACY

The Supreme Court, said political scientist (and later President) Woodrow Wilson, is "the balance wheel of our whole constitutional system."[74] Like the balancing middle wheel that keeps a machine running smoothly, the Supreme Court takes into consideration the demands of the president, Congress, the bureaucracy, the fifty states, and the American public, and attempts to arrive at decisions that bring them all into harmony.

The paradox here is that this vital role is being filled by one of the least democratic institutions in the world. In other countries, leaders who are unelected, hold their office for life, and rule in complete secrecy are either kings or dictators; in America they are Supreme Court justices. In theory, the justices can make any decisions that they like, but as you have seen, in reality, the judiciary is restrained by the possibility that its decisions will meet resistance or not be implemented at all.

What then is the role of an independent Supreme Court in the American system of democracy? Attempts to answer this question have led to a long-standing debate about whether the Court should actively make policy or whether it should practice judicial restraint. Should the Court adhere to the letter of the law and leave policymaking to the elected Congress and president? Should it be an architect of public policies that advance human rights? Or should the Court simply reflect the desires of the populace?

Many believe, along with liberal judicial activist Hugo Black that only an undemocratic institution such as the Court has the independence necessary to safeguard the rights of minorities: "Under our constitutional system courts stand against any winds that blow as havens of refuge for those who might otherwise suffer because they are helpless, weak, outnumbered, or because they are nonconforming victims of prejudice and public excitement."[75]

Others fear that too much judicial independence and activity will lead to an arrogant and aloof Court out of touch with the nation's problems. Self-restraint justice John Harlan argued throughout his career that the Court should not be making social policy: "[The] Constitution is not a panacea for every blot upon the public welfare, nor should this Court, ordained as a judicial body, be thought of as a general haven for reform movements."[76] Many opponents of Supreme Court power argue that by leaving judicial power undefined in the Constitution, the framers intentionally avoided creating an unchecked imperial force.[77]

Over the years, the willingness of the Supreme Court and the lower federal courts to use the full extent of their power has varied based on the nature of the legal issues, the number of cases heard, the political situation, and who the justices are. In recent years, the federal courts have been more willing to defer to Congress and the states. Will this continue, or will the courts staffed by Bill Clinton seek out a new direction and role? And where is the Supreme Court headed—will moderates or conservatives prevail? All this remains to be seen. But we can be assured that the actions of the judiciary in America's democracy will continue to have powerful implications for both government and individual rights.

SUMMARY

1. The federal courts decide all legal disputes arising under the Constitution, U.S. law, and treaties. In cases involving disputes between states or involving foreign ambassadors, the Supreme Court has original jurisdiction. For all other federal cases, it has appellate jurisdiction.

2. In the 1803 case of *Marbury* v. *Madison* Chief Justice Marshall argued that the Supreme Court has the power to interpret the Constitution. This power, known as judicial review, enables the Court to overturn actions of the executive and legislative branches and to reinterpret the Constitution to fit new situations. The power of statutory construction enables the Court to interpret a federal or state law.

3. The power to appoint justices to the Supreme Court is shared by the president and Congress. The justices are appointed for life and can be impeached only for "high crimes and misdemeanors." The president can influence the Court by appointing justices who support a particular philosophy. Congress can change the number of justices or pass a law to reverse a Court decision.

4. Most cases enter the judicial system through a trial court consisting of a single judge and, at times, a jury. The proceedings of the trial court are reviewed by an appellate court consisting of a multijudge panel but no jury. Criminal cases involve violations of state or federal criminal law; civil cases involve private disputes. Most criminal cases are resolved by plea bargains, in which the state agrees to reduce the charges or sentence in return for a guilty plea.

5. The federal judiciary is organized in three tiers. At the bottom are the ninety-four district courts, of which at least one is located in each state. At the next level are the courts of appeals, which hear cases from thirteen circuits, or regions, usually in three-judge panels. District and circuit courts are constitutional courts, but the federal judiciary also includes legislative courts, courts established by Congress.

6. Candidates for the Supreme Court are suggested by senators, governors, the candidates themselves and their friends, and federal judges and are screened by the FBI and the American Bar Association. Most nominees to the Court are members of the president's party and share the president's political philosophy.

7. The confirmation process begins with a hearing by the Senate Judiciary Committee, which makes a recommendation prior to a vote by the full Senate. These procedures can constitute major hurdles, resulting in the rejection of over one in five presidential nominations.

8. For nominations to district courts, the tradition of senatorial courtesy gives senators what amounts to a veto power. Often, however, candidates are suggested by senators who are members of the president's party. Recent presidents have attempted to make the federal judiciary more representative of the population as a whole.

9. The solicitor general decides which federal cases to appeal from the lower courts, prepares the appeals, and represents the United States before the Supreme Court. Appellate cases come to the Supreme Court through writs of certiorari. If at least four justices vote to hear a case, it is placed on the docket. In recent years the Court has decided fewer cases, even though the number of appeals reaching it has increased dramatically.

10. When the Court accepts a case, attorneys for all sides submit briefs, or written legal arguments. They then present oral arguments before the Court. The justices hold a conference to discuss and vote on the case, and one of the justices voting with the majority is assigned to draft the opinion, or written version of the decision. The opinion must be approved by at least five justices. A justice who agrees with the majority decision but differs on the reasoning may write a concurring opinion. When a justice disagrees with the Court's ruling, he or she may write a dissenting opinion.

11. Interpretation of a law or a portion of the Constitution as closely as possible to the literal meaning of the words is known as strict construction. When the wording is vague, some justices attempt to determine the original intent of the framers. In some cases, justices consider the effect a ruling would have on public policy. Some justices believe in judicial restraint, deferring to the other branches of government whenever possible. Others are

judicial activists, believing that judges have a duty to further certain causes.

12. Decisions of the Supreme Court become the law of the land. However, compliance with a decision is influenced

by the extent to which the president supports it. It may also be circumvented by Congress, which can pass a new law or propose a constitutional amendment restating its original intentions.

KEY TERMS

original jurisdiction
appellate jurisdiction
Marbury v. *Madison*
judicial review
statutory construction
trial court
appellate court
criminal cases
plea bargains
civil cases
class action suit

constitutional courts
U.S. district courts
U.S. courts of appeals
en banc
legislative courts
senatorial courtesy
docket
writ of certiorari
rule of four
solicitor general
amicus curiae briefs

briefs
opinion
majority opinion
concurring opinion
dissenting opinion
stare decisis
precedents
judicial restraint
judicial activism

SUGGESTED READINGS

- Abraham, Henry J. *Justices and Presidents: A Political History of Appointments to the Supreme Court.* 3d ed. New York: Oxford University Press, 1992. A complete history of presidential appointments to the Supreme Court and the decision making that resulted.

- ———. *The Judicial Process.* 6th ed. New York: Oxford University Press, 1993. An outstanding text on every facet of the judicial process. Includes a comparative perspective and is chock-full of interesting details and quotations.

- Bronner, Ethan. *Battle for Justice: How the Bork Nomination Shook America.* New York: Norton, 1989. An inside account of the Robert Bork nomination by a *Boston Globe* reporter, including the means used by liberal interest groups to defeat the nomination.

- Congressional Quarterly. *Guide to the U.S. Supreme Court.* Washington, D.C.: Congressional Quarterly, 1979. An encyclopedia of information on the Supreme Court, it is on the shelf of every court scholar.

- Howard, J. Woodford, Jr. *Courts of Appeals in the Federal Judicial System.* Princeton, N.J.: Princeton University Press, 1981. An excellent study on the workings of the U.S. courts of appeals.

- Jacob, Herbert. *Law and Politics in the United States.* 2d ed. New York: HarperCollins, 1994. An introductory textbook on the operations of the American legal system, showing the connections to the larger political system.

- Lewis, Anthony. *Gideon's Trumpet.* New York: Vintage Press, 1964. A study of the *Gideon* v. *Wainwright* case.

Still the best short, single volume on the progress of a case through the Supreme Court.

- Murphy, Bruce Allen. *Fortas: The Rise and Ruin of a Supreme Court Justice.* New York: Morrow, 1988. A political biography of the only justice ever to be forced to resign from the Supreme Court. Contains a complete account of both the 1968 confirmation battle and the 1969 investigation that ended Fortas's judicial career.

- O'Brien, David. *Storm Center: The Supreme Court in American Politics.* 3d ed. New York: Norton, 1993. A revealing text on the internal politics of the Supreme Court using sources from justices' papers in historical archives.

- Perry, H. W. *Deciding to Decide: Agenda Setting in the United States Supreme Court.* Cambridge, Mass.: Harvard University Press, 1991. A wonderful analysis of the process by which the Supreme Court accepts cases. Based on detailed interviews with sixty-four former law clerks and several Supreme Court justices.

- Phelps, Timothy, and Helen Winternitz. *Capitol Games: Clarence Thomas, Anita Hill, and the Story of a Supreme Court Nomination.* New York: Hyperion Books, 1992. A fascinating account of the Clarence Thomas confirmation battle by one of the reporters who broke the Anita Hill story. Reveals how the press can affect the confirmation process.

- Pritchett, C. Herman. *Constitutional Civil Liberties,* and its companion, *Constitutional Law of the Federal System.* Englewood Cliffs, N.J.: Prentice Hall, 1984. A complete account of how the Supreme Court's doctrine has developed.

- Savage, David. *Turning Right: The Making of the Rehnquist Supreme Court.* New York: Wiley, 1992. An inside account by the court reporter for the *Los Angeles Times* of the people who make up the Rehnquist Court and the ways their personal views and interactions shape public policy.

- Schwartz, Bernard. *Super Chief: Earl Warren and His Supreme Court—a Judicial Biography.* New York: New York University Press, 1983. A detailed case-by-case study of the internal workings of the Supreme Court under the chief justiceship of Earl Warren.

- Woodward, Bob, and Scott Armstrong. *The Brethren: Inside the Supreme Court.* New York: Avon Books, 1979. A highly controversial study of the inside workings of the Supreme Court from 1969 through 1975. Uses anonymous law clerk interviews and Court papers.

CHAPTER 8

THE BUREAUCRACY

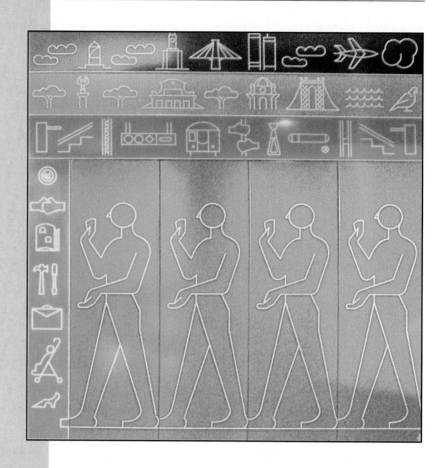

CHAPTER OUTLINE

CASE STUDY: ENGINEERING A DISASTER

INTRODUCTION: BUREAUCRACY AND DEMOCRACY

SOME BACKGROUND ON THE BUREAUCRACY

MEETING THE BUREAUCRACY

BUREAUCRATIC ACCOUNTABILITY

WHAT THE PUBLIC THINKS OF BUREAUCRACY

REFORMING THE BUREAUCRACY

BUREAUCRACY AND APPROACHING DEMOCRACY

Engineering a Disaster

The successful launch of the first space shuttle in April 1981 marked the beginning of a new era for the National Aeronautics and Space Administration (NASA), a long-established but somewhat neglected public bureaucracy. The shuttle was designed to cut the cost of delivering various hardware payloads, such as satellites, into space and to encourage public support for future research projects in space. The shuttle's first twenty-four missions went off almost flawlessly. Its success revived NASA's image and led to increased federal funding.

However, mission number twenty-five was to be different. Early on the morning of January 28, 1986, with temperatures well below freezing, NASA launched the space shuttle Challenger from the Kennedy Space Center in Florida. Seventy-three seconds after lift-off, Challenger exploded before millions of television viewers and stunned NASA officials. All seven astronauts on board died. One was Christa McAuliffe, a grade-school teacher whose training for the mission had been followed by schoolchildren all over the United States. It was the worst disaster in the history of the space program.

Americans were horrified by the tragedy and demanded to know what went wrong. President Ronald Reagan appointed a commission, headed by a former secretary of state, William Rogers, to investigate the disaster. The Rogers Commission concluded that most of the blame lay with NASA's bureaucratic culture. NASA's "can-do" atmosphere and its strict adherence to the principles of engineering had produced a string of historic accomplishments in aerospace exploration—the Apollo flights, the moon landings, and the first shuttle missions—but that

same culture sometimes led the agency to push too far too fast. In addition, the engineers' exclusive reliance on "hard" data and their reluctance to consider cautionary remarks expressed in less precise terms like "I feel" or "I expect" contributed to the breakdown of communications leading to the Challenger disaster. [1]

The Rogers Commission discovered that on the bitterly cold night before the fateful launch, officials from NASA and Morton Thiokol Industries (MTI), the designer of the shuttle's solid rocket booster system, debated the wisdom of launching Challenger. MTI engineers in Utah tried desperately to convince NASA officials in Florida and at the Johnson Space Center in Houston, Texas, to scrub the Challenger mission because the rocket booster system was not designed to withstand subfreezing temperatures. The O-ring seals that joined the sections of the fuel tanks had never been used below fifty-three degrees Fahrenheit. In laboratory experiments performed at freezing temperatures, the seals had disintegrated. One MTI executive said, "If we're wrong, and something goes wrong on this flight, I wouldn't want to have to be the person to stand up in front of a board of inquiry and say that I . . . told [NASA] to go ahead and fly this thing." According to the Rogers Commission published report, some NASA officials apparently did not hear this statement, and three top NASA people simply ignored it along with the other evidence. MTI's vice president and director of engineering recommended waiting for warmer weather to launch Challenger. Nonetheless, after hours of often heated debate, NASA officials decided the launch was safe and gave the go-ahead. Seconds after launch, the chilled O-ring seals failed. Escaping hot gases burned through and ignited the main fuel tank of liquid hydrogen and liquid oxygen, and the Challenger disintegrated in a burst of flame.

The Challenger disaster destroyed NASA's

decades-old reputation *"for diligent and systematic application of hard work and engineering principles."*[2] *The bureaucracy that had placed the first men on the moon in the 1960s now found itself facing a challenge to its very existence.*

Given the warnings from MTI officials, how could NASA have allowed the disaster to happen? The decision to ignore MTI's advice and launch Challenger *arose from a combination of problems within NASA that are all too common in large public bureaucracies. NASA officials were overconfident in light of the previous successes of the shuttle program. They worried about the public-image problems that might arise from a scrubbed mission and insinuations of technical failure. They wanted to guard against possible budget cutbacks if Congress concluded that technical flaws threatened the shuttle program. And they were concerned about costs. A postponed shuttle mission would be enormously expensive; the solid rocket fuel alone, which would have been lost in the event of a scrubbed launch,*

was valued at half a million dollars. Finally, decision makers were not sufficiently knowledgeable to assess the potential risk of the launch, and they chose to ignore the evidence of the engineers and other experts outside of NASA. ❖

The space shuttle *Challenger* exploding seventy-three seconds after lift-off on January 28, 1986.

INTRODUCTION: BUREAUCRACY AND DEMOCRACY

This case study on the *Challenger* disaster shows that something went very wrong within NASA. But this particular agency is also an enormously successful federal bureaucracy, one that since 1961 has engineered dramatic breakthroughs in space flight, allowing astronauts to orbit the earth, play golf on the moon, and repair previously inaccessible damaged satellites.

More than simply evidence of a bureaucratic breakdown, the *Challenger* disaster also serves as a dramatic illustration of a problem for all large government agencies. Americans usually measure the performance of bureaucratic agencies not by their routine successes but by the impact of their failures.[3] Most space shuttle missions have completed their specific tasks without difficulty, just as the overwhelming majority of letters sent through the U.S. Postal Service reach their destination without mishap. However, the bureaucracy commands the most attention when something goes wrong—when sacks of undelivered mail are discovered in some musty Chicago basement, or, as with the *Challenger* case study, when a string of successes is marred by a tragic disaster.

Part of the suspicion Americans feel about their bureaucracy comes from the realization that most government agencies function, most of the time, with little or no restraint from the American people. Indeed, the bureaucracy has been called the "fourth branch of government," as powerful as Congress, the president, and the Supreme Court, but operating without the regular elections that keep at least the first two institutions responsive to public opinion.

Despite their problems, bureaucracies are necessary and have come to characterize modern industrialized societies. Large-scale bureaucratic organizations allow for high levels of productivity and the coordination of government programs such as road building, air traffic control, environmental management, the postal system, and telecommunications. Nevertheless, bureaucracies can pose serious problems in terms of accountability and power. For example, how can organizations such as the Federal Bureau of Investigation (FBI) and the Central Intelligence Agency (CIA) have sufficient enforcement power to thwart terrorist attacks without compromising the rights of innocent citizens? In this chapter we will look at some of the contradictions that arise between bureaucratic necessity and democratic ideals.

What is the bureaucracy and how can it be held accountable? To answer these questions, we begin by defining *bureaucracy*. We then look at the growth and evolution of American bureaucracy, and meet the bureaucrats to see what they do and how the bureaucracy is structured to enable them to accomplish their tasks. We also explore how the bureaucracy works with the president and Congress. Finally we examine common criticisms of the federal bureaucracy and look at strategies for reforming it.

SOME BACKGROUND ON THE BUREAUCRACY

Bureaucracy Defined

A **bureaucracy** is a large and complex organizational system in which tasks, roles, and responsibilities are structured to achieve a goal. The term is rooted in the eighteenth-century French word for a woolen cloth *(burel)* used to cover a writing desk, or *bureau*. **Bureaucrats,** the people who work in a bureaucracy, include not only the obscure, faceless clerks normally disparaged by critics of government but also "street-level bureaucrats," such as police officers, social workers, and school teachers.[4]

German sociologist Max Weber (1865–1920) is considered the father of modern bureaucracy. He modeled his "ideal type" of bureaucratic organization on the Prussian government of the early twentieth century. He believed that the purpose of a bureaucracy was to improve efficiency, and that efficiency could be promoted in three ways—through specialization, hierarchy, and a system of formal rules.

The principle of **specialization** means that specific tasks should be delegated to individuals whose training and experience give them the expertise to execute them. As the responsibilities of government increase, so too does the need for more specialization, or more experts in various areas.

Bureaucratic organization also requires **hierarchy,** a clear chain of communication and command running from an executive director at the top down through all levels of workers, such as the mailroom clerks in the middle and janitors at the bottom. The hierarchy facilitates decision making and establishes clear lines of authority within a large, complex organization. Figure 8.1 illustrates the hierarchical organization within the FBI.

In addition to specialization and hierarchical authority, bureaucratic organizations use sets of **formal rules,** clearly defined procedures governing the

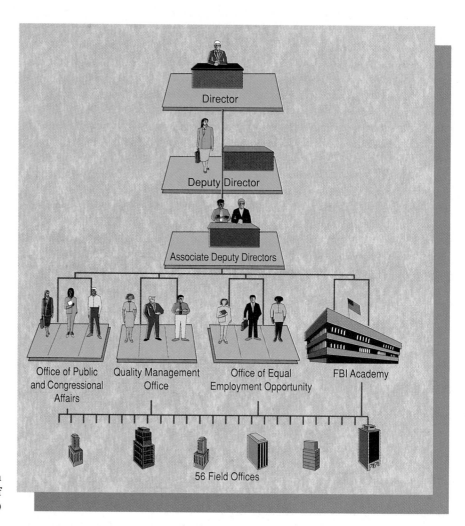

Director

Deputy Director

Associate Deputy Directors

Office of Public
and Congressional
Affairs

Quality Management
Office

Office of Equal
Employment Opportunity

FBI Academy

56 Field Offices

**FIGURE 8.1   Organization
Chart: The Federal Bureau of
Investigation (FBI)**

execution of all tasks within the jurisdiction of a given agency. Sometimes
called standard operating procedures (SOPs), these rules simplify and routinize
complex procedures, curtail favoritism, and improve the decision-making process by allowing bureaucrats to respond to a broad array of situations with a
minimum of delay and confusion. Such formal rules also apply to the professional lives of bureaucrats. There are clearly defined steps for job advancement, specific descriptions of job duties, and specific qualifications for salary
increases.

PROBLEMS INHERENT IN THE BUREAUCRATIC FORM   Specialization, hierarchy, and formal rules are all designed to improve the performance of bureaucracy. Usually this structure works. Consider the case study of the *Challenger,*
which illustrates a *rare* failure in the performance record of the huge, complex
organization that is NASA. Despite the enormous technical and organizational
demands of the space program, most of NASA's missions have been successful.
Likewise, although we sometimes hear horror stories about mail going

undelivered, the U.S. Post Office remains one of the most efficient public bureaucracies in the world. And for all of our moaning and groaning about taxes and the Internal Revenue Service (IRS), most of us receive our tax returns from the IRS promptly—and through the U.S. Mail.

Nevertheless, there are bureaucratic breakdowns, often the result of rigid adherence to one or more of the three organization principles just outlined. One of the failures of the *Challenger* mission was the inability of the various engineers and administrators, each specializing in a relatively narrow area, to communicate clearly with other specialists about the launch.

Indeed, the very nature of specialization within a bureaucracy can sometimes impede rather than improve performance, rendering an agency relatively efficient in some tasks but inflexible in others. Weber warned that bureaucratic organization might turn workers into "specialists without spirit," motivated only by narrowly defined tasks and unable to adapt to changing circumstances.

Such a situation led to the deaths of passengers on American Eagle Flight 4184 in 1994. Congress has charged the Federal Aviation Administration (FAA) with responsibility for approving the use of passenger airplanes and the weather conditions under which they can fly in the United States. One weather pattern that particularly worries pilots is freezing drizzle, which can form a layer of ice on an aircraft's wings and cause planes to spin out of control. But there were problems with the FAA's procedures. For example, the FAA relied on the optimistic performance evaluations of the ATR-72 turboprop, a popular short-distance passenger plane, made by specialists on the staffs of the airplane's manufacturers. In addition, the FAA's standards for planes were outdated, having been established based on a series of tests it conducted in the late 1940s.

Despite warnings of pilots about twenty incidents in which the plane had faltered, the FAA certified the aircraft for all-weather flight. In a chilly drizzle on October 31, 1994, the pilots of American Eagle Flight 4184 lost control of their ATR-72 turboprop. It slammed into a soybean field near Roselawn, Indiana, killing all sixty-eight aboard. Finally, the FAA grounded the plane.

What went wrong is obvious. The FAA relied on outdated SOPs, then ignored the pilots and showed an inappropriate level of deference to the manufacturers' testing specialists. One safety expert commented that the episode was an all-too-common example of the FAA's refusal to acknowledge a problem "until the blood gets deep enough."[5] Clearly, adaptability and flexibility are as important as specialization, hierarchy, and formal rules to the operation of a successful bureaucracy.

To understand the challenges facing the federal bureaucracy and better appreciate the successes typical of most agencies, it helps to look at how the federal bureaucracy has grown.

Growth of the Federal Bureaucracy

America's early bureaucracy hardly resembled today's Leviathan. George Washington's budget for the entire bureaucracy in 1790 was just under $1.5 million per year, and the money funded just three departments—State, War, and Treasury. The largest of these, the Department of the Treasury, employed just 70 workers in 1790, minuscule by modern standards.

The Treasury Department now employs 155,000 people. All told, nearly 5 million civilians and members of the armed forces work for the federal

FYI

Former Alabama governor and presidential candidate George Wallace, never a fan of the bureaucracy, once commented, "Send me to Washington and I will push those pointy-headed bureaucrats off their bicycles and throw their briefcases in the Potomac River."

One of the federal agencies least likely to win a popularity contest is the enormously powerful Internal Revenue Service (IRS) which is responsible for collecting taxes from Americans. The IRS is a vast organization (this photo shows just one branch office) constituting just one part of an immense federal bureaucracy that many Americans view as too large and inhabited by faceless bureaucrats.

FYI

How large is the bureaucracy? President Carter tried to find out, but after three months of searching, a White House official told him, "We were unable to obtain any single document containing a complete and current listing of government units which are part of the federal government." *The United States Government Organization Manual,* which runs to more than eight hundred pages, scarcely begins to convey the size and complexity of the U.S. government.

government. This huge force is spread among eighteen hundred departments, agencies, commissions, and government corporations in four hundred thousand government-owned buildings throughout the United States and the world. Today the federal government spends as much in thirty-three seconds as President Washington's three departments spent in a year. More specifically, with an annual budget of $1.5 *trillion,* the federal government spends about $2.7 million per minute.

The federal government's rapid growth began in the late nineteenth century. At that time, industrial expansion was increasing the size and complexity of the economy and was destabilizing American social life. As corporations became more powerful, the popular call for increased regulation of business and a larger role for government in protecting the welfare of its citizens intensified. Those calling for change were known as the Progressives, and they became successful advocates for increased popular participation in government, administrative reform at the local level, and changes in the federal government's hiring practices. The Progressives called on government to assume broad regulatory powers over corporations and began the modern trend toward viewing government involvement in a positive light. The belief in limited government that had prevailed through the nineteenth century began to yield to the idea of "an active government that would be without limitation, with power to pursue social and economic justice."[6]

This new faith in the power of government peaked during the thirty-year period in which government mobilized the nation's resources to fight the Great Depression, wage World War II, and combat domestic poverty and racial discrimination. The public's commitment to activist government paved the way for the astonishing growth of the federal bureaucracy in the twentieth century. The greatest growth is evident in the 1930s and 1940s, during what has become known as the emergence of the "welfare state."

THE WELFARE STATE Franklin D. Roosevelt's New Deal (1933–45) brought the government into everyday economic affairs and increased dramatically the size of the government's workforce and the scope and power of federal responsibilities. The New Deal was devised in response to the Great Depression, which brought massive unemployment—at times as much as a quarter of America's labor force was out of work—and a growing awareness of the need to provide more security for American citizens, both on the job and after retirement. The New Deal consisted of a series of legislative acts, executive orders, and proclamations creating large-scale federal programs that sought to provide retirement insurance, health care, economic security, and poverty relief of Americans.

New Deal programs aimed to create jobs and jump-start a stagnant economy. They also laid the legislative foundation for liberal Democratic policies. The Civilian Conservation Corps (CCC) granted millions of dollars to the states to pay young people to work at forestry, irrigation, and land projects. By 1935 over five hundred thousand youths were at work under the auspices of the CCC. The Tennessee Valley Authority (TVA) provided funds to build dams and reservoirs, creating thousands of jobs and bringing electricity to new areas. The Wagner Act established the National Labor Relations Board (NLRB) and gave workers the right to unionize and bargain collectively. The Social Security Act established a federally funded financial safety net for the elderly, infirm, and unemployed.

At the center of the debate about the welfare state is the fate of poor children. Nearly one child in four lives in poverty in America. While many Americans favor welfare reform, many are concerned about what such reform would mean for the children who constitute two-thirds of the fourteen million recipients of the main federal welfare program, Aid for Families with Dependent Children.

Roosevelt also used the power of the government to increase regulation of finance and commerce. Responding to a wave of bank failures and lost deposits, Roosevelt's administration established the Federal Deposit Insurance Corporation (FDIC) to insure most bank deposits. Roosevelt's administration also created the Securities and Exchange Commission (SEC), the Federal National Mortgage Association (FNMA, or "Fannie Mae"), and the Federal Communications Commission (FCC), to regulate the stock exchanges, the interstate mortgage market, and the public airwaves, respectively.

The New Deal programs became the core of the modern **welfare state.** Although designed as temporary emergency programs to relieve the suffering of the depression, most New Deal agencies became a permanent part of a dramatically enlarged federal bureaucracy. In addition to expanding the bureaucracy, the New Deal era led to a growing dependence upon that bureaucracy to administer and regulate many of the essential functions of modern American life.

Similarly during World War II, the federal government hired hundreds of thousands of temporary employees to plan and coordinate the vast assembly of personnel and machinery used to defeat the Axis Powers. After World War II, many of these "temporary" employees remained to work in government and were absorbed by agencies that redefined their civilian missions more broadly. But neither the growth of the bureaucracy nor the dependence upon it by increasing numbers of Americans stopped with the end of the Great Depression and World War II.

THE GREAT SOCIETY AND BEYOND   As you can see from Table 8.1, the real expansion in federal employment took place between the early twentieth century and the end of World War II. Since then the size of the federal bureaucracy has been relatively stable, although hardly stagnant.

The slight growth in the 1960s was the result of President Johnson's Great Society, an ambitious assault on racial injustice and poverty, which created scores of new government agencies. At the request of the president, Congress enacted programs to provide medical care, job opportunities, and business loans to the poor, and to improve the quality and availability of education at all levels. In addition, Congress enacted programs to conserve water, air, and natural resources.

Table 8.1
The Growing Federal Bureaucracy, 1816–present

YEAR	NUMBER OF EMPLOYEES
1816	4,837
1851	26,274
1871	51,020
1901	239,476
1921	561,142
1931	609,746
1941	1,437,682
1945	3,816,310
1946	2,696,529
1951	2,482,666
1961	2,435,804
1966	2,759,019
1971	2,860,000
1976	2,842,000
1981	2,865,000
1985	3,021,000
1995 (estimate)	2,887,221

Note: These figures do not include the nearly two million men and women serving in the armed forces.

Source: 1790–1970: *Historical Statistics, Colonial Times to 1970* (Washington, D.C.: Census Bureau, 1976); 1971 to 1985: *Statistical Abstract of the United States* (Washington, D.C.: Census Bureau, 1986); 1995: Estimate from *Budget of the U.S. Government: Analytical Perspectives, Fiscal Year 1995* (Washington, D.C.: U. S. Government Printing Office, 1994).

During the 1970s, growing citizen awareness of the problems of consumer safety and environmental degradation led to creation of the Consumer Product Safety Commission (CPSC) and the Environmental Protection Agency (EPA), and, thus, more bureaucratic growth. In the wake of the OPEC oil embargo, the old Office of Emergency Preparedness was systematically expanded. First it became the Federal Energy Office (FEO), then the Federal Energy Administration (FEA), and finally the cabinet-level Department of Energy (DOE). Mounting concern over safety in the workplace, coupled with evidence that corporations were not willing to adopt appropriate safety measures without government prodding, led to the creation of the Occupational Safety and Health Administration (OSHA).

Expansion of the responsibilities of government during the 1960s and 1970s brought major increases in the federal budget, largely because of increases in *transfer payments,* that is, money paid to individuals in the form of social-security benefits, welfare payments, and the like, thereby "transferring" money from one segment of society to another. Interestingly, the bureaucracy that administered this budget did not grow substantially. By allowing some

"H.U.D. called the F.A.A. The F.A.A. called the S.E.C. The S.E.C. called G.S.A. G.S.A. called O.M.B. O.M.B. called Y-O-U."

Drawing by Vietor, © 1981. The New York Magazine, Inc.

agencies to shrink from natural attrition and by transferring people from established agencies to new ones, presidents were able to keep actual bureaucratic growth to modest levels, with the exception of 1985, when there was an influx of regulatory bureaucracies under the Reagan administration as well as large increases in Pentagon spending.

DOWNSIZING GOVERNMENT: A LOSING BATTLE?   One of the key campaign promises made by conservative Republican presidential candidate Ronald Reagan when he ran against incumbent president Jimmy Carter in 1980 was that he would reduce the size and scope of the federal government. Throughout the campaign, Reagan attacked big government. Once in office, the Reagan administration attempted to reduce the number of federal workers through attrition and layoffs. Reagan also attempted to take over the bureaucracy. One of his key strategies involved appointing people hostile to the mission of agencies to run them.

Nevertheless, Reagan was unable to reduce the size or even the scope of bureaucratic power. One Reagan appointee, Secretary of Education William Bennett, a conservative ideologue and relentless opponent of bureaucracy, was unable to rein in a department whose employees disregarded their boss's sentiments and continued to perform the tasks he despised—promoting bilingual education, drawing up busing plans, and devising lesson plans for sex education programs.[7]

Reagan's failure to curtail the bureaucracy says more about bureaucracy than it does about the former president. Reagan encountered something presidents throughout American history have had to accept: The bureaucracy is a constantly evolving, growing, largely independent realm of government.

Evolution of the Bureaucracy: Creating a Civil Service

As you've seen, since the early days of the republic, the federal bureaucracy has grown enormously. There has also been a corresponding change in its character. Prior to the presidential election of Andrew Jackson in 1828, a small,

Drawing by D. Reilly, © 1995. The New Yorker Magazine, Inc.

elite group of wealthy, well-educated white males dominated the bureaucracy. Jackson, a Populist, was determined to make the federal workforce more representative by opening up jobs to the masses. He instituted a new system based on the declaration of his friend, Senator William Marcy: "To the victor go the spoils."

The emergence of this **spoils system** meant that Jackson and his subordinates would award top-level government jobs and contracts on the basis of party loyalty rather than social or economic status or relevant experience. Jackson's opponents in the Whig party recognized the advantages of using government jobs for patronage purposes and, when the parties traded elected offices, the bureaucracy was restaffed by those loyal to the Whigs. Later on, as the government grew, supporters of the spoils system found that if a thousand patronage jobs were beneficial, ten thousand or twenty thousand would be even more welcome.[8] The spoils system was used until the end of the nineteenth century, when with the advent of the Progressive era, the tide of public opinion turned against it and its potential for corruption and abuse.

Following the assassination of President James Garfield by Charles Guiteau in 1881, who was bitter about his inability to find a job in Garfield's administration, Congress passed the Pendleton Act of 1883. The act created a **civil service,** a system of hiring and promoting employees based on professional merit, not party loyalty. Such a system was designed to protect government employees from political threats to their job security. The act also created the three-person Civil Service Commission to oversee the implementation of the merit principle throughout the federal workforce. The Civil Service Commission evaluated job applicants on the basis of their performance on civil service examinations. Employees achieved permanent status after a probationary period, and they were promoted only with strong performance evaluations from supervisors. The Civil Service Commission functioned until 1978, when, under the Civil

Service Reform Act, it was replaced by two agencies. One, the Office of Personnel Management, administers civil service recruitment and promotion procedures, and the other, the independent Merit Systems Protection Board, conducts studies of the merit system and holds grievance and disciplinary hearings for federal employees.

Today, merit-based hiring and advancement have eliminated much of the corruption and cronyism of the old patronage system.[9] The civil service system encourages the hiring of people with high levels of skill and expertise and provides procedures for evaluating the qualifications and job performance of federal workers.

There is, however, a down side to the civil service. For one thing, it insulates federal employees from many of the pressures of a competitive private-sector job market. For example, the process for disciplining a federal employee is long and complicated, making it difficult to dismiss or demote a civil servant. The employee must receive written notice at least thirty days in advance, detailing the reasons for, and specific examples of, the conduct prompting the action. The employee may then appeal the action to the Merit Systems Protection Board (MSPB), which must grant a hearing, at which point the employee has the right to legal counsel. If the MSPB rejects the appeal, the employee may take the case to the U.S. Court of Appeals. The process has become so burdensome that, rather than attempt to fire unproductive employees, supervisors have learned to live with them. Employees who decide to kick back their feet and open a newspaper an hour before quitting time know that they do so with relative impunity.

Civil service guidelines not only insulate the federal workforce; they also tend to instill in some agencies a sense that they are "untouchable," whatever the periodic changes in the political climate of the country. One common remark associated with career civil servants when they are asked about a changing presidential administration is that while presidents are temporary employees, the careerists in the bureaucracy stay for life. Research has shown that most civil servants tend to conform to the policy directives of administrations as they come and go, but determined resistance to presidential initiatives can hamper a president's agenda considerably. To make the bureaucracy more responsive to the policy directives of changing presidential administrations and to move it in the direction of greater politically neutrality, Congress passed the Hatch Act in 1939.

THE HATCH ACT   The **Hatch Act**—named for its author, Senator Carl Hatch of New Mexico—is a list of political do's and don't's for federal employees. The act was designed to prevent federal civil servants from using their power or position to influence elections, thereby creating a nonpartisan, nonpolitical, professionalized bureaucracy. Under the Hatch Act, bureaucrats may express opinions about issues and candidates and contribute money to political organizations, but they cannot distribute campaign information, nor can they campaign actively for or against a candidate. A federal employee may register and vote in an election but cannot run as a candidate for public office.

Although the authors of the Hatch Act believed it necessary to restrict the political liberties of government employees to preserve the neutrality of the growing maze of federal agencies and programs, these restrictions illustrate one area where bureaucracy clashes with democratic ideals. Nearly three million American civilians who work for the federal government have their rights to full participation in the nation's political process sharply curtailed. Among those citizens are many who, because of their intimate contact with policy matters, could elevate the quality of public debate during election campaigns. Although many civil servants and constitutional scholars have denounced the Hatch Act as unconstitutional, the Supreme Court has disagreed with them.

Critics of the law have found some sympathy in Congress. In 1993 it amended the act to allow federal employees to participate more actively in partisan politics, with several restrictions. They cannot be candidates for public office in partisan elections, use official authority to influence or interfere with elections, or solicit funds from or discourage the political activity of any person undergoing an audit, investigation, or enforcement action. However, federal workers can register and vote as they choose, assist in voter registration, participate in campaigns when off duty, and seek and hold positions in political parties or other political organizations.

All of these changes in the Hatch Act are intended to allow federal workers to exercise more of the rights and privileges of political participation open to other American citizens. But as federal employees are granted more freedom to participate in politics, there is the potential for the reappearance of the kinds of partisanship that prompted the passage of the Pendleton and Hatch acts in the first place.

MEETING THE BUREAUCRACY

Now that we have seen how the bureaucracy has grown and evolved, let's look at what bureaucrats do and how the bureaucracy is organized to do its job.

What does the federal workforce look like? Among the nearly three million civilians employed by the federal government there are over 15,000 official categories of employees, ranging from electricians to paperhangers, from foreign-service officers to postal service workers. There are nearly 100,000 regulators; 150,000 engineers; hundreds of thousands of analysts, clerks, and secretarial staff; 15,000 foresters; 2,300 veterinarians; 3,000 photographers; and 500 chaplains. Surprisingly, nearly 90 percent of federal employees work outside Washington, D.C. California alone has almost as many federal employees as does the nation's capital.[10]

What the Bureaucracy Does

Americans today share a tradition as old as their government, an animosity toward "those damn faceless bureaucrats" in Washington, the state capitol, or city hall. Yet these bureaucrats perform many essential functions that we take for granted. Whenever a letter is delivered on time, an application for financial aid is processed, or a highway is repaired, the bureaucracy has done its job. The bureaucracy performs three key governmental tasks: implementation, administration, and regulation...

IMPLEMENTATION   One of the primary tasks of the bureaucracy is to implement the policies established by Congress and the executive. **Implementation** means to provide the organization and expertise required to put into action any

Bureaucrats perform important tasks such as directing the flow of air traffic, patrolling U.S. borders to control the flow of people and drugs, and delivering the mail. Civil servants, like those you see here, are typical working Americans whose jobs, although hardly glamorous, are important to the smooth functioning of society.

policy that has become law. When Congress passed legislation establishing the Head Start program of early-childhood care and education in the 1960s, a new agency was established to "flesh out" the guidelines of the program, hire and train employees, and disperse the federal monies appropriated to the program.

Implementation can involve a considerable amount of bureaucratic autonomy. In implementing legislation, administrators are able to exercise **administrative discretion,** which refers to the latitude that an agency, or even a single bureaucrat, has in interpreting and applying a law. When passing legislation, Congress often does little more than declare policy goals, assign their implementation to an agency, and make money available. This lack of statutory specificity may be necessary to get a bill over the hurdles of the legislative process, but it makes for poorly defined policy directives. After a bill is passed, bureaucratic managers must step in, and exercising administrative discretion, draft detailed guidelines for all the various procedures required to turn policies into workable programs.

Even when Congress and the bureaucracy are well intentioned, there are many points at which implementation can go awry. Frequently, interest groups at state and local levels resist new policies or raise questions—for example, about clean-air and -water laws—that make the implementation of such policies difficult if not impossible. In 1994–95, citizens in Maine, Pennsylvania, and Texas protested the implementation of strict auto emissions tests ordered by the Environmental Protection Administration (EPA). As a result, legislatures in

Diversity in the Federal Bureaucracy

The federal workforce is extraordinarily diverse. Over 40 percent of federal government employees are women, and over 25 percent are members of minority groups. Thus, the "fourth branch of government" is far more representative of the overall population than the other branches are. Only 11 percent of the members of Congress are women, and only 13 percent are members of ethnic or racial minorities. And all of the nation's presidents and vice presidents have been white males.

The diversity of the federal bureaucracy is significant from the standpoint of the struggle for equality. A workforce that reflects the diversity of the American people is more likely to make decisions that represent the will of the people and therefore is an important step in approaching democracy. But if one looks more closely one finds that those who make the decisions—those who hold the upper-level civil service jobs—are far less representative of the population as a whole than are those in the lower-level clerical and service jobs.

Most federal government jobs are classified according to the General Schedule, a grading system that assigns ranks based on levels of skills, training, experience, responsibility, and performance. Clerical workers are in the lowest four grades (GS-1 through GS-14). Grades 5 through 9 are professional entry-level grades (college graduates normally enter at grade 5). Federal employees move up the scale through promotions until they reach middle-management positions in grades 13 through 15. Above those levels is the Senior Executive Service, equivalent to grades 16 through 18.

As can be seen in the table on the facing page, there are striking differences in the diversity of the workforce at the top and the bottom levels of the General Schedule. While 38.9 percent of employees at the lowest level are African American, only 4.3 percent of those in GS-15 positions are African American. When one compares these figures to the percentage of African Americans in the population as a whole—12.6 percent—it is obvious that African Americans are significantly overrepresented at the lowest level and underrepresented at the top. The same comparisons can be made for women and Hispanics.

Women and minorities in the federal bureaucracy (as well as in private-sector jobs) seem to run into a "glass ceiling"—an invisible barrier that prevents them from entering the upper levels of the civil service. In addition, a recent study by the Office of Management and Budget found that 52 percent of federal workers who were involuntarily dismissed during the 1992 fiscal year were members of minority groups.* Despite these discouraging statistics, however, there are some encouraging trends. The number of women in GS grades 13-15

*Karen de Witt, "Blacks Prone to Dismissal by the U.S.," *New York Times*, Apr. 20, 1995, p. A19.

---

all three states suspended the programs, preferring the wrath of the EPA to the wrath of their constituents.

Another problem arises when Congress's instructions to the agency in charge of implementing a specific piece of legislation are legally questionable. How should a bureaucracy proceed? The National Endowment for the Arts (NEA) faced just such a dilemma in 1990, resulting in difficulties for the agency. Bowing to pressure from conservative legislators who were upset at several art exhibits funded by the NEA, Congress inserted a clause in the agency's reauthorizing legislation that prohibited the NEA from funding "indecent" art. John Frohnmayer,

doubled between 1974 and 1984, and by 1991 it had doubled again. Similar increases have occurred in minority employment at the upper levels. Thus, while there is still some distance to go, the federal bureaucracy is becoming more representative of the American people at all levels.

Federal Employment by General Schedule Level, Ethnic Group, and Gender

GENERAL SCHEDULE AND STARTING SALARY LEVEL	BLACK	HISPANIC	WOMEN
GS-1 $12,271	38.9%	11.1%	75.8%
GS-2 $13,796	35.0	11.2	71.0
GS-3 $15,054	29.5	7.8	71.3
GS-4 $16,900	27.7	6.7	74.9
GS-5 $18,907	23.6	6.4	73.8
GS-6 $21,075	24.8	5.6	77.1
GS-7 $23,419	20.5	5.9	68.7
GS-8 $25,936	24.3	4.5	60.9
GS-9 $28,648	14.2	6.2	52.8
GS-10 $31,549	13.3	6.2	53.4
GS-11 $34,662	11.5	5.0	38.1
GS-12 $41,543	10.0	3.8	30.8
GS-13 $49,401	7.9	3.1	23.1
GS-14 $58,377	5.9	2.4	18.1
GS-15 $68,667	4.3	2.3	14.2

Note: Percentage figures are from 1991 data. Salaries were effective January 1, 1994.

Sources: U.S. Office of Personnel Management. Figures reported in Harold W. Stanley and Richard G. Niemi, *Vital Statistics on American Politics,* 4th ed. (Washington, D.C.: Congressional Quarterly Press 1994), p. 406; George J. Gordon and Michael E. Milakovich, *Public Administration in America,* 5th ed. (New York: St. Martin's Press, 1995), p. 278.

a lawyer and chairman of the NEA, was caught between Congress and the arts community. He believed the legislation's language violated the First Amendment. Yet, as director of the NEA, he declared that the agency would implement and enforce the law and allow the courts to determine its constitutionality.

Frohnmayer's decision to implement what he considered to be a legally questionable policy came out of his respect for Congress, his allegiance to President Bush, who had nominated him, and his understanding that the NEA's role was to implement rather than make policy. His decision was met with an outpouring of criticism from the arts community that the NEA serves; during the

In 1990, the government expanded the Endangered Species Act by declaring the northern spotted owl a threatened species. But this effort to save a nearly extinct animal, which overjoyed environmentalists, was not well received by the timber industry, whose livelihood was at stake. Saving the owl meant that logging would be restricted on tens of millions of acres of forest in the Pacific Northwest. In response, the timber industry initiated a lawsuit against the government, revealing that in many instances the bureaucracy's efforts to implement the law are met with controversy and strong resistance.

rest of his tenure at the agency, Frohnmayer never fully recovered its cooperation and respect.

ADMINISTRATION   Another bureaucratic task is **administration,** which involves performing the routine tasks associated with a specific policy goal; bureaucrats exercise a lot less administrative discretion at this stage. For example, the Immigration and Naturalization Service (INS) controls the influx of people into the country through various routine tasks, such as issuing applications for permits (known as "green cards") that allow nonresidents to legally obtain employment in the United States, giving citizenship examinations to those who wish to become naturalized citizens, and deporting undesirable aliens. On the whole, the INS and other agencies perform their administrative duties effectively. On occasion, however, embarrassing problems come to the attention of the public. The INS, for example, is supposed to collect a six-dollar-per-person fee charged by all commercial airlines for each international passenger arriving in the United States. However, a 1994 Justice Department investigation revealed that the INS had failed to collect the fees from twenty-two airlines and six cruise lines, a loss to the agency—and a corresponding windfall to the travel industry—of more than twenty million dollars. When asked why the INS had failed to collect the fees, one agency official responded: "There are only two people down there [at the INS] monitoring this."[11]

REGULATION   Another important bureaucratic task is regulation. **Regulation** involves the making of rules, their enforcement, and the adjudication of disputes about them. In many areas of American life, the bureaucracy establishes and enforces guidelines regulating behavior and enforcing punishments for violation of those guidelines.

Administrative regulation is pervasive in America. Americans wake up in the morning and eat breakfast food whose quality is regulated by the U.S. Agriculture Department. When Americans get into their cars, they buckle their seat belts because it is the law, and it is the law because the Federal Highway Administration withholds federal funds from states that do not require seat belt use. Americans also drive to work in autos that do minimal harm to the air because of the catalytic converters mandated by the Environmental Protection Administration. At work, Americans conform to the antidiscrimination guidelines established by the Equal Employment Opportunity Commission. After a hard day, Americans may decide to flip on the television to watch programming whose content must fall within guidelines established by the Federal Communications Commission. Finally, at the end of the day, Americans crawl into bed and snuggle under blankets certified as fire resistant by the Consumer Product Safety Commission.

Whether regulating, implementing, or administrating, bureaucrats exercise a great deal of autonomy and have power over our lives. Given the complex demands made upon the bureaucracy, such power is inevitable. But some ask, whose interests do the bureaucrats serve? Are they responsive to the needs of the public? In fact, many bureaucrats do heed the voices of ordinary citizens and seek to stay in the good graces of the two government institutions most responsive to public opinion: Congress and the presidency.

Let's now look at how the federal bureaucracy is structured.

The Structure of the Federal Bureaucracy

The institutions that constitute the federal bureaucracy are part of the executive branch. There are four such government institutions: cabinet departments, independent agencies, independent regulatory commissions, and government corporations.

CABINET DEPARTMENTS   Cabinet departments are major administrative units responsible for conducting a broad range of government operations. Originally, the heads of these departments—usually called secretaries—were the president's closest advisors, though today, it is the president's personal staff in the White House that is more likely to command the president's attention. There are fourteen cabinet departments in the federal government. Each is subdivided into large agencies called bureaus, and then into smaller units called divisions, sections, agencies, and offices. The current cabinet departments are State, Treasury, Defense, Interior, Justice, Agriculture, Commerce, Labor, Health and Human Services, Housing and Urban Development, Transportation, Energy, Education, and Veterans Affairs. Although each of the departments has jurisdiction over a specific policy area, sometimes their responsibilities overlap, as when State and Defense address the diplomatic and strategic aspects of U.S. foreign policy.

INDEPENDENT AGENCIES   Independent agencies are usually smaller than cabinet departments and have a narrower set of responsibilities. Generally, they exist to perform a service. Congress may establish an independent agency so that it can keep particularly tight control over that agency's functions. For example, an independent agency may be established in response to demands from interest groups that wish to see a government function performed with care and attention rather than by some indifferent department. Among the major independent agencies are the Central Intelligence Agency (CIA), the Environmental Protection Agency (EPA), the General Services Administration (GSA—which manages federal property), the National Aeronautics and Space Administration, (NASA), the Small Business Administration (SBA), and the Peace Corps.

INDEPENDENT REGULATORY COMMISSIONS   Independent regulatory commissions are agencies established to regulate a sector of the nation's economy in the public interest. For example, an independent regulatory commission might guard against unfair business practices or unsafe products. They are generally run by a board whose members have set terms, although some of the newer regulatory bodies are headed by a single individual—making the label *commission* something of a misnomer. These bodies establish rules, enforce those rules, and adjudicate disputes about them. In so doing they perform all of the traditional functions of government—legislative, executive, and judicial. These agencies develop a great deal of expertise in a particular policy area, although sometimes they become too closely identified with the businesses they are charged with regulating. Congress and the courts rely on their expertise and are usually loath to overrule them. Among the more important independent regulatory commissions are the Federal Communications Commission (FCC), which regulates radio and television; the Federal Reserve Board (FED), whose

Secretary of the Interior Bruce Babbitt (at right) has a reputation for being a good listener and compromise maker. Both skills serve him well in his job, which requires addressing the conflicting demands of those seeking to protect the land and wildlife, and farmers and industry seeking access to federal land for grazing and logging.

members function as a central bank for the United States; the Federal Trade Commission (FTC), which regulates advertising and labeling; the National Labor Relations Board (NLRB), which enforces the laws governing labor–management disputes; and the Securities and Exchange Commission (SEC), which regulates trade in stocks and bonds.

GOVERNMENT CORPORATIONS   A **government corporation** is a semi-independent government agency that administers a business enterprise and takes the form of a business corporation. Congress creates such agencies on the assumption that they will serve the public interest, and gives them more independence and latitude for innovation than it gives other government agencies. A government corporation can raise its own capital and devise its own personnel system; it can determine, within the limits of the charter Congress gives it, the kind of services it provides; and when the occasion seems favorable, it may develop new services. The Tennessee Valley Authority (TVA), a government corporation originally set up to provide electricity to the area within the Tennessee River watershed, now manages the artificial lakes it created for recreational purposes, runs economic development programs, experiments with alternative energy development, and manages flood control in its vicinity.[12]

In addition to possessing much of the flexibility of a private company, a government corporation also has the authority of government. It can take land, levy fees, and make rules that govern the public. Though these agencies have more leeway in establishing the nature and cost of the services they provide, they generally remain subject to more regulation than private corporations do. Besides the TVA, other major government corporations include the Postal Service, the Corporation for Public Broadcasting, the Federal Deposit Insurance Corporation, the Export–Import Bank, and Amtrak. Currently there is talk in Washington of converting the Federal Aviation Administration—whose responsibilities include both regulation of airplane safety and operation of the nation's air traffic control system—into a government corporation. Doing so would allow the FAA to raise the enormous amount of capital necessary to adopt new, more reliable air traffic control measures.

Now that we have seen how the bureaucracy functions, let's consider some of the factors that impede its ability to do its job as well as it might.

Constraints on the Bureaucracy and Bureaucratic Culture

The bureaucracy faces three major constraints that shape its behavior. Bureaucratic agencies do not control revenue, decisions about how to deliver goods and services must be made according to rules established elsewhere, and goals are mandated by other institutions. Because of these constraints, bureaucrats and bureaucracies behave differently from employees and companies in the private sector. Certain norms, or unwritten rules of behavior, have developed, creating a unique bureaucratic culture.

First, Congress does not allow agencies to keep money left over when the fiscal year ends. Furthermore, an agency that ends the year with a surplus demonstrates to Congress that it can get by on less than the current year's budget.

As a consequence of these financial arrangements, bureaucrats have no incentive to conserve funds. In fact, there is every incentive to spend with abandon as the fiscal year draws to a close on September 30, in hopes of showing Congress that there is no surplus and that, in fact, more money is needed for the next year.

In addition, since bureaucrats are not supposed to profit from their dealings with government, they focus on other nonmonetary incentives such as prestige. The bigger the budget and the larger the agency, the more prestige a bureaucrat acquires, providing managers with another reason to put political pressure on Congress to allow their agencies to grow.

Second, to ensure fairness, efficiency, and comprehensive coverage of a program, decisions about hiring, purchasing, contracting, and budgeting must be made according to rules established by Congress and the president. Since the end of World War II Congress has passed an array of such rules, for example, the Administrative Procedure Act of 1946, a comprehensive set of regulations governing the way an agency makes rules, publicizes its operations, and settles disputes; the Freedom of Information Act of 1966, assuring that most agency records are available to interested citizens on demand; the National Environmental Policy Act of 1969, requiring federal agencies to prepare environmental impact statements for all actions that significantly affect the environment; the Privacy Act of 1974, a law that limits the circumstances in which information about individuals can be released to other agencies and to the public; and the Government in the Sunshine Act of 1976, mandating open meetings of most regulatory decision-making bodies. Such a system breeds rule-following managers, not managers who take initiative. It is no wonder that, surrounded by such a thicket of regulations and laws, bureaucratic managers worry more about violating procedure than about marching boldly ahead to promote the public good. After all, managers can always explain poor outcomes by claiming that they were just following the rules.

Finally, bureaucratic agencies do not control their own goals, which are set by Congress and the president. Congress has told the U.S. Postal Service that it must charge one rate to deliver a first-class letter no matter where the letter goes. Furthermore, the Postal Service must deliver newspapers, magazines, and junk mail below cost, and it must keep small post offices open even though they may not be economical to operate. Cost-conscious, practical business decisions that might be made in the private sector—by officers of Federal Express or United Parcel Service, for example—are not possible at the Postal Service. Postal Service managers may regret their lack of control over goals and stare wistfully at the accomplishments of their counterparts in the private sector; all the while, their own administrative imaginations are likely to atrophy.

Despite the constraints imposed by the unique character of public service, some administrative institutions flourish. A determined leader can install a sense of mission even in employees of an organization whose offices are scattered across the nation. The Social Security Administration is such a mission-driven agency. Its personnel officers recruit potential employees who show an orientation to customer satisfaction, and managers constantly invoke an ethic of service when they talk to employees. Bureaucrats who work for the Social Security Administration take pride in theirs jobs and do them well.[13]

FYI

Senator Dale Bumpers of Arkansas described the bureaucracy as "a 700 pound marshmallow. You can kick it, scream at it, and cuss it, but it is very reluctant to move."

Bureaucratic Doublespeak

During the Persian Gulf War, an American pilot returning from a bombing attack reported that he had "sanitized the area." When Congress voted itself a $23,200 pay increase, Senator Ted Stevens of Alaska described the raise as "a pay equalization concept." Car salespeople are "product consultants"; pizza deliverers are "delivery ambassadors"; telephone line workers are "outside aerial technicians."

These are just a few examples of *doublespeak,* which can be simply defined as language that doesn't call a spade a spade. The term blends two concepts introduced by George Orwell in his famous and frightening book *1984:* doublethink and newspeak. Although doublespeak occurs in all areas of social life, it is most frequently used—or abused—for political purposes. As Orwell explained in his 1945 essay "Politics and the English Language":

> Political speech and writing are largely the defense of the indefensible. Things like the continuance of British rule in India, the Russian purges and deportations, the dropping of the atom bombs on Japan, can indeed be defended, but only by arguments which are too brutal for most people to face, and which do not square with the professed aims of political parties. Thus political language has to consist largely of euphemism, question-begging, and sheer cloudy vagueness. Defenseless villages are bombarded from the air, the inhabitants driven out into the countryside, the cattle machine-gunned, the huts set on fire with incendiary bullets: this is called *pacification.* . . . People are imprisoned for years without trial, or shot in the back of the neck or sent to die of scurvy in Arctic lumber camps: this is called *elimination of unreliable elements.*

Such phraseology is needed if one wants to name the things without calling up mental pictures of them."[*]

The language used by the military in reporting on its operations in the Persian Gulf raised doublespeak to new heights. The war was referred to as an "armed situation," and warplanes were described as "visiting a site." Bombing was "disruption," destruction as a result of bombing was "attrition," buildings and human beings were "hard" and "soft" targets, respectively. A marine general told reporters, "We're prosecuting any target that's out there."

Doublespeak is not confined to the military, however. It pervades bureaucracies of all kinds, both public and private. Read the memos and directives issued by any government agency or corporate headquarters and you will find numerous examples of language designed to disguise reality. To illustrate: In recent years many corporations have undertaken programs of "rightsizing" or "streamlining" to achieve a "positive budget variance" (i.e., save money). How have they achieved this? By offering their workers "involuntary severance," "career assignment and relocation," "vocational relocation," or "voluntary termination." In other words, you're fired!

---

[*]George Orwell, "Politics and the English Language," in *Shooting an Elephant and Other Essays* (Orlando, Fla.: Harcourt Brace Jovanovich, 1945.)

Source: Richard Lederer, "Desert Storm Doublespeak Would Have Made Orwell Shudder," *Maine Sunday Telegram,* Dec. 8, 1991, p. C2.

BUREAUCRATIC ACCOUNTABILITY

Who controls the bureaucracy? Can anyone control it? Should the bureaucracy answer to the president, who is, after all, the chief executive, or should it be responsive to Congress, the policymaking body of the national government? Should we expect the bureaucracy to follow public opinion or to follow the advice of its experts? We have already discussed the growth and complexity of the federal bureaucracy. As the bureaucracy grew, so too did the concern that it was too remote, too large and unaccountable, too preoccupied with its own survival to serve a democratic political system. The story of late-twentieth-century American politics is in large part the story of attempts by the White House and Congress to control the powerful federal bureaucracy and make it more accountable.

Presidential Control

One of the most common complaints a president makes is that aligning the objectives of the federal bureaucracy with the priorities of the administration is terribly difficult. President Harry Truman once complained, "I thought I was the president, but when it comes to these bureaucrats, I can't do a damn thing." Truman may have been exaggerating, but presidential control of the bureaucracy is not as easy as most incoming chief executives either thought or hoped.

As the federal bureaucracy has grown, so too has the amount of energy expended by presidents to rein in the agencies that oppose their objectives. After a grueling election, the president enters with a policy agenda that was presumably supported by at least a plurality of the American people. To pursue that policy agenda, the president must try to convince not only Congress but the various agencies of the federal government to cooperate with the White House. There are four main strategies a president can use: the appointment power, reorganization, the budget, and the power of persuasion.

THE APPOINTMENT POWER   The president must be clear about the goals of the policy agenda. And to advance that agenda, the president can use a powerful weapon, the **appointment power.** The president can nominate some three thousand agency officials, of whom about seven hundred are in policymaking positions, such as cabinet and subcabinet officials and bureau chiefs. The rest are lower-level appointees who can provide the president with valuable information and a source of political patronage hearkening back to the old "spoils system."[14] A president who can secure loyalty from these appointed bureaucrats has overcome a major obstacle in pursuing the White House policy agenda.

Much can be learned from the experiences of recent presidents in their use of the appointment power and their respective influence on the bureaucracy. When Jimmy Carter became president, he was determined to use the power of government to protect Americans from irresponsible and potentially harmful business practices. He believed that the Occupational Safety and Health Administration and the Environmental Protection Agency had been influenced by the very industries they were supposed to regulate. He appointed pro-regulation advocates to turn these agencies around, then he consistently and actively supported his appointees in their attempts to expand their regulatory power.

Ronald Reagan, in contrast, campaigned on a promise to reduce the size, scope, and power of the federal government so that business could thrive. He used his appointment power to rein in bureaucratic agencies. Relying more than virtually any previous president on ideological criteria, Reagan sent a remarkable number of conservatives into federal agencies, where they devoted their efforts to reducing rather than protecting the scope and authority of the offices they ran. The Reagan appointees enjoyed mixed levels of success, but

"The federal bureaucratic monster who would slay private enterprise is learning a new command. It's called—heel."

—Ronald Reagan

Attorney General Janet Reno is a Clinton appointee. As attorney general, she oversees U.S. attorneys, the FBI, federal marshals, and the team of lawyers who represent the government in federal court. Here she meets with staff members (the solicitor general, Drew Days, is at the far right).

they did wipe scores of rules regulating trade, automobile manufacture, occupational safety, consumer protection, and the environment off the books.

More recently, Bill Clinton has used his appointment power to make the bureaucracy more diverse and representative of American society. The number of women he has appointed to critical executive positions in the Justice Department is striking. Among the top officials Clinton appointed were Attorney General Janet Reno; Deputy Attorney General Jamie S. Gorelick; Jo Ann Harris, head of the Criminal Division; and Anne K. Bingaman, head of the Antitrust Division. In all, Clinton's Justice Department included women in seven of the eleven top policymaking positions.[15]

But when using the appointment power to control the bureaucracy, the president must know what is going on within it. One of the presidents who did just that was Franklin Roosevelt. He filled federal agencies with people who were more loyal to him than to each other. Although his appointees battled each other over policy questions, they ultimately referred their disagreements to the president, who resolved them and in doing so exercised effective control over bureaucratic policymaking. Roosevelt's administration funneled information and decision-making authority to the top, and because Roosevelt had the intellectual capacity to understand the arguments of the specialists, he was able to settle their disputes with dispatch.[16] This is impossible today, given the size of government.

Other presidents have attempted to emulate Roosevelt's style. President Clinton has shown an extraordinary level of understanding of bureaucratic disputes, but he has been short on the decisiveness needed to make his administration work well.

REORGANIZATION   Having the power to move some programs around within specific agencies, presidents can also influence the bureaucracy through reorganization. For example, a president opposed to pesticide regulation might shift that program from the EPA, which favors regulation, to the Department of Agriculture, where pro-agriculture forces would tend to limit such regulation.[17]

A president may also choose to elevate an agency to cabinet level, thereby expanding its scope and power. In 1979, President Carter elevated one of the offices of the Department of Health, Education and Welfare to cabinet level, creating the Department of Education. He hoped that this reorganization would improve the prestige and status of the office and underscore the importance of education as a national priority.

Conversely, a president can remove an agency's cabinet status and thus, potentially, reduce its power and prestige. Upon succeeding Carter, Reagan sought several ways to reduce the power of the Department of Education, including an unsuccessful attempt to demote the agency from the cabinet level. The Reagan administration saw the department as wasteful and inefficient, and as an inappropriate extension of federal government into state and local realms. But the department dug in its heels and outlasted Reagan.

THE OFFICE OF MANAGEMENT AND BUDGET   One formidable tool for presidential control of the bureaucracy is the **Office of Management and Budget** (OMB). Established in 1921, transferred to the newly created Executive Office in 1939, and renamed OMB as part of the major Executive Office reorganization in 1970, the OMB's main responsibilities are to prepare and administer the president's annual budget. It is through the budget process that a president and the OMB can shape policy, since the process determines which departments and agencies grow, get cut, or remain the same as the year before. During the budget-preparation cycle, officers from OMB, all specially trained to assess government projects and spending requests, are in constant touch with government agencies to make sure that the agencies are adhering to the president's policies. Because the budget has a profound effect on an agency's ability to function and survive, it is rare for an administrator to defy the OMB.

Recently, the Clinton administration used the budget process to reinvigorate the Department of Education. While seeking cuts in several other federal agencies to help trim the size and cost of government, Clinton presided over the hiring of five hundred additional employees at the department. He also initiated Americorps, a national-service program that enables students to do public service in return for credit toward their college tuition.

THE POWER OF PERSUASION   Lastly, presidents can use the power to persuade in an attempt to control the bureaucracy. Some presidents, such as John F. Kennedy, inspired the bureaucracy with a vision of public service as a noble activity. Even though he was frequently thwarted by and frustrated with bureaucratic procedures, Kennedy saw the bureaucracy as capable of accomplishing innovation. Kennedy was able to reorganize the space program and convince its employees that despite the string of failures in attempting to launch unmanned rockets, NASA would put a man on the moon before the decade was out.

Presidents, then, have the capabilities to control the federal bureaucracy. A president who uses the power to appoint, to reorganize, to oversee the budget, and to persuade can work effectively with the bureaucracy and even achieve great things. Presidents, though, do not always wield these powers to their full potential; they often have other things on their minds.

Congressional Oversight

Congress is responsible for much of the oversight that keeps bureaucratic power in check (also see Chapter 5). To perform this task, Congress has several mechanisms at its disposal. Most important is the "power of the purse." Congress appropriates all funding for each federal agency. If there are problems, Congress can, and occasionally does, curb funds or even eliminate entire projects. One classic example of assertion of control over a runaway program is Congress's treatment of the Department of Energy's (DOE) superconducting supercollider project. Projected in 1982 to cost taxpayers $4.4 billion, the total budget for the huge particle accelerator, designed to allow scientists to learn more about atomic structure, ballooned to more than $11 billion by 1993. When the DOE carried out its own investigation of the Texas-based project, officials discovered a history of free-spending waste, including an expense of $56,000 for potted plants to adorn the project's offices. Finally, in late 1993, and after the expenditure of $2 billion, Congress canceled the entire program.[18]

Congress also has the power of *administrative oversight,* the practice of holding hearings and conducting investigations into bureaucratic activity. As a consequence of these hearings Congress can rewrite the guidelines for an agency to expand or narrow the scope of an agency's responsibilities. Finally, through its "advice and consent" role, the Senate can shape the direction of federal agencies by confirming or rejecting presidential nominees for top positions in the bureaucracy.

Although Congress has many tools to fulfill its oversight functions, it often chooses not to use them. Why would Congress not want to keep the bureaucracy under close control? One answer can be found by examining the mutually beneficial political relationship between federal agencies and members of Congress.

Legislators have the ability to keep federal agencies alive and funded. Those agencies provide goods and services—such as contracts, exemptions, and assistance—that members of Congress use to please their constituents. Legislators from agricultural states, for example, can work hard to keep crop subsidies in the federal budget, thus ensuring a future for the Department of Agriculture and its employees. In turn, the department can give special consideration to the crops grown in a member's district, thus helping to ensure a member's reelection.

These relationships have been characterized as iron triangles. An **iron triangle** is a strong interdependent relationship among three crucial actors in policymaking: legislators, particularly those on the relevant subcommittees with jurisdiction over the policy in question; lobbyists for specific interests affected by the policy; and bureaucrats at the agencies with jurisdiction over the implementation and administration of relevant policies.

Iron triangles are resistant to democratic accountability. The interlocking interests of its parts are so strong that few presidents and few members of Congress who are not a part of the triangles ever try to bring them under control.

Similar to but broader than iron triangles are **issue networks**, which are composed of political actors in a particular policy area. These networks usually include bureaucrats, congressional staffers, interest groups, think-tank researchers or academic experts, and media participants who all interact regularly on an issue. Issue networks dominate the policymaking process, and different issue networks exist for different policy areas.

The National-Security Bureaucracy

The national-security bureaucracy has been resistant to efforts to bring it under the control of Congress and the president. The agencies that form this bloc include the Central Intelligence Agency (CIA), the Federal Bureau of Investigation (FBI), the Defense Intelligence Agency (DIA), and the National Security Agency (NSA). In this agency alphabet soup we should also include the Bureau of Alcohol, Tobacco, and Firearms (ATF), the Drug Enforcement Administration (DEA), and even the Immigration and Naturalization Service (INS).

The sheer size of the national-security bureaucracy is daunting and makes control and accountability difficult. A comprehensive examination of the entire national security bureaucracy is nearly impossible. Much of the statistical data about expenditures and various activities are unavailable; they are kept secret and off budget purportedly to protect national security.

Yet it is difficult to imagine a nation as large as the United States, in a world as unstable as that of the last half century, maintaining the security of its borders and its internal stability without such a bureaucracy. Nevertheless, its growth and complexity have created some embarrassing moments for the federal government and resulted in some genuine concern about the security of the civil liberties of American citizens. Two agencies whose transgressions have garnered particular public attention are the FBI and the CIA.

The FBI was created in 1924 under the directorship of twenty-nine-year-old J. Edgar Hoover. The bureau soon developed a reputation as the nation's toughest crime-fighting agency. Much of this prestige was directly orchestrated by Hoover, who publicized the arrests of prominent criminals such as John Dillinger in 1930 and cooperated extensively in a series of Hollywood motion pictures celebrating the bureau's tough, efficient, crime-busting image, which was realistic.

By the 1950s Hoover had gained such power—largely as a result of using the bureau to assemble files on most of the prominent political figures of the day—that he could turn the FBI's scrutiny virtually wherever he pleased. Hoover deployed agents and government resources to investigate a seemingly endless labyrinth of communist "cells," many of which were established by FBI agents themselves, to lure potential "subversives." As vigorous a racist as he was an anticommunist, Hoover also used the FBI to infiltrate or attack every African American organization during the 1960s, and he mounted a personal attack on the reputation of civil rights leader Dr. Martin Luther King, Jr.

Aldrich Ames, formerly a CIA agent and now a federal prisoner, was responsible for the most devastating case of betrayal in the history of the CIA. Ames admitted to spying for the former Soviet Union, leading to the deaths of ten Soviet and Eastern European agents and the exposure of more than one hundred U.S. and allied intelligence operations. A Senate report on the case revealed that Ames, a drunken bumbler, was able to elude capture for nine years because of systemic failure at the CIA. The agency was aware of problems with Ames, but ignored them, was unable to investigate itself, and refused to cooperate with spycatchers in the FBI.

During the 1980s the FBI dramatically expanded its undercover operations. The subjects included Washington legislators caught taking bribes by undercover FBI agents as well as labor leaders and students. In the wake of the April 1995 bombing of a federal building in Oklahoma City, a public debate ensued about whether the agency's investigative powers should be expanded even further to aid efforts to combat terrorism.

Problems within the CIA also surface from time to time. Created as part of the National Security Act of 1947 to coordinate international intelligence data, the CIA gradually assumed a shadowy life of its own as America's chief covert operations apparatus. With nearly twenty thousand employees and a budget of three billion dollars, the CIA has vast responsibilities. Since 1981, when Ronald Reagan signed an executive order empowering it to do so, the CIA has used its large array of intelligence-gathering and counterespionage resources to scrutinize American citizens within the borders of the United States. With many of its expenditures "off budget" and its agents buried in false identities around the world, the CIA is among the most difficult of federal agencies to keep track of.

The French Bureaucracy

While American citizens are constantly complaining about excessive red tape and believe that civil servants are both too numerous and too lazy, the French regard their bureaucrats as competent, efficient, and highly ethical.* This is particularly striking in light of the inflexible and autocratic nature of the French bureaucracy.

Part of the explanation for this difference can be found in French culture, which assumes that the answer to every particular question can be found by deduction from general principles (as opposed to experimentation with different solutions). A French bureaucrat decides each individual case by reasoning deductively from a legal premise.† When the deduction is done properly, the citizen has no basis for disagreement with the decision. Pleading individual circumstances to bend the rules is simply not done.

The French bureaucracy is less attentive to public opinion than its American counterpart. Civil servants are recruited from the families of the political elite and educated in national schools of public administration, called *grandes écoles*. They tend to develop a sense of superiority that occasionally translates into contempt for the masses.** On some occasions they have deliberately made life difficult for citizens on the theory that it is good for citizens to spend time in the *marais,* or swamp. An American bureaucrat who showed such disrespect for citizens would stand a good chance of receiving an irate call from a congressional office.

Despite its elitist quality, French citizens hold their civil service in high esteem. One reason for this is the bureaucracy's long history of success in providing benefits to the public. France has had medical and dental insurance and retirement benefits for generations. During the Napoleonic era the French civil service built a national highway system radiating from Paris to every major provincial city; the United States did not even plan such a system until the 1950s. Furthermore, throughout almost two centuries of weak monarchies and confused republics that proved incapable of governing, the civil service has always managed to carry on the day-to-day operations of government.

Underlying the average French citizen's respect for civil servants is a long bureaucratic tradition. Whereas the American bureaucracy did not achieve its considerable size and power until the New Deal and World War II era, France has had strong bureaucratic institutions since the early nineteenth century. For the better part of two centuries, then, the bureaucracy has been an important part of the lives of French citizens. Today the French bureaucracy is regarded as among the most competent and efficient in the world. It thus should not be surprising that French bureaucrats enjoy a level of social prestige that is rare among their American counterparts.

---

*William Safran, *The French Polity,* 4th ed. (White Plains, N.Y.: Longman, 1995), pp. 243–44.

†B. Guy Peters, *The Politics of Bureaucracy,* 4th ed. (White Plains, N.Y.: Longman, 1995), pp. 49–50.

**Frank L. Wilson, *European Politics Today,* 2d ed. (Englewood Cliffs, N.J.: Prentice Hall, 1994), pp. 152–53.

Recently, however, there has been a tide of government and public opinion in favor of reforming the CIA. Its director, John Deutch, appointed by President Clinton in 1995, has vowed to make the CIA a leaner organization that operates more effectively in the post–Cold War world.

WHAT THE PUBLIC THINKS OF THE BUREAUCRACY

As you learned earlier, Americans do not like the administrative state. Only 14 percent of Americans trust government "most of the time," and nearly half of all Americans regard government as the "greatest threat to the country in the future."[19]

Politicians exploit the public's distrust of government. A few years ago members of Congress made headlines with stories about Defense Department purchases of $435 hammers and $91 screws. The stories, though exaggerated, confirmed long-held suspicions about government waste.[20] In 1994 Republicans capitalized on the public's souring on the bureaucracy and swept into control of both houses of Congress for the first time in forty years. Their message was that government is the problem, not the solution, and Americans were receptive to that idea.

Many Americans feel that government is expensive and wasteful. Each year the government spends $1.5 trillion, and a good deal of the money is spent unwisely. Highly publicized examples of government waste include how under the guise of saving family farms the Department of Agriculture sends subsidy checks to wealthy recipients in Beverly Hills, Chicago, and Manhattan.[21] Retired federal employees have been found to live at a level of luxury far beyond that of the ordinary taxpayer because the government guarantees them cost-of-living adjustments pegged to exaggerated calculations of the rate of inflation. And while the Commerce Department helps tobacco growers market their products, the Surgeon General works toward the goal of a smoke-free society by the year 2000. As a consequence of such stories, Americans have exaggerated the extent of government waste and have concluded that government wastes 42 cents of every dollar it spends.[22]

Americans also think the bureaucracy cannot accomplish the goals set for it. It is true that some agencies are ineffective. Congress gave the Federal Equal Employment Opportunity Commission the responsibility for investigating complaints of sexual, racial, and age discrimination in employment. But how effective can the agency be if it waits a full year before beginning an investigation, and then pursues the investigation slowly? As time passes, aggrieved employees are unable to seek redress; they move on to other jobs, witnesses' recollections fade, and cases disintegrate.[23] And government's reputation for ineptitude has important consequences for public policy. The public rejected President Clinton's proposal for a national health-insurance program largely because the prevailing opinion was that government could do nothing right.

One of the most common complaints is that government is not responsive to citizens. In implementing policies agencies should be attentive to the needs and circumstances of individual taxpayers. But too often, red tape prevents such flexibility. **Red tape** refers to the excessive number of rules and regulations that government employees must follow. While many employees chafe under the burden of these regulations, others welcome them. Rigid adherence to the rules relieves bureaucrats of the burden of thinking about individual cases and shelters employees from being criticized by their supervisors for making the wrong decision. One consequence of the proliferation of red tape in government is that citizens with unusual circumstances encounter delays while their cases are bumped up to higher levels for official rulings.[24]

Businesses complain that the bureaucracy hobbles them with unnecessary regulations and paperwork. Every time a company wants to expand its operations or use a new method for manufacturing its products, it must apply for permission from a host of government agencies and fill out a great many forms.

Many Americans complain that federal bureaucrats take advantage of their employers, the taxpayers. Some bureaucrats stretch their lunch breaks and knock off early at the end of the workday. Abuse of sick leave allowance is

"I agree with you, but I don't know if the government will."

—John Kennedy

The Equal Employment Opportunity Commission (EEOC) was created by Congress to stop discrimination in the workplace. But this agency has been mired in paper and unresolved cases, leading to a reputation for ineffectiveness. About one in seven workers who file complaints with the agency have their cases resolved favorably, although usually after long delays. These two workers, who filed accusations of sexual harassment against an employer, can count themselves among the lucky few who got unusually quick relief from the EEOC.

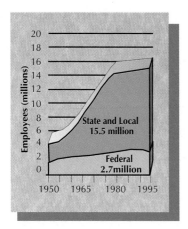

FIGURE 8.2 The Number of Civilian Government Employees

The bureaucracy serves a multitude of Americans. Learning-disabled students, for example, benefit from the provisions of the Individuals with Disabilities Act, or IDEA, a program that provides such students with the extra help and encouragement they need to succeed in college courses. Many critics of the federal bureaucracy, however, believe that such programs lead to dependency on the government and are simply too expensive in an age of fiscal belt-tightening.

rampant in some agencies. Employees of the Postal Service, whose motto is, "Neither snow nor rain nor heat nor gloom of night shall stay these carriers from their appointed rounds," took 5,752,180 sick days, worth $702,921,000, in 1992.[25]

Finally, many Americans think that the growth of the bureaucracy is simply out of control. In 1950, there were 6.8 million government employees in the United States. Over the next forty-five years government employment outpaced population growth. By 1995, there were nearly 19 million bureaucrats in the country. But despite this growth in total government employment, the number of federal civilian employees remained at around 3 million. In the meantime, state and local offices were expanding rapidly, until today they are teeming with nearly 16 million employees (see Figure 8.2).[26]

Are the Criticisms Justified?

The bureaucracy is a modern-day inevitability. And despite the criticisms, many Americans have come to rely on the goods and services that the bureaucracy provides. Although many of the criticisms are valid, there are two sides to every story about an institution as large as the federal government. Although bureaucratic waste is real, it is less prevalent than the public believes (the real extent of government waste is considerably less than 42 cents of every dollar spent). And it is important to keep in mind that government expenditures exist for reasons that many Americans would support. For example, most citizens want to ensure that no official awards a contract on the basis of personal friendship or bribery, so agencies are required to use costly bidding procedures on federal contracts. Most citizens would support programs that train people who lack skills to find jobs in the public sector. Such policies add to the cost of government, but ultimately, many citizens agree with the rationale for the expenditures.

While some agencies never accomplish the tasks given to them by Congress, the Social Security Administration has sustained a remarkable record for competence. It assigns a number to, and maintains a lifetime earnings record for, each taxpayer in the country, then mails a benefit check for everyone who becomes eligible for social security.[27]

Although businesses are dismayed by government rules and regulations, those guidelines almost always serve an important purpose. Automobile manufacturers complain about the hundred million dollars added to production costs by the government's requirement that cars have rear-window brake lights, but that requirement prevents nine hundred million dollars in property damage and a great deal of human suffering.[28] Furthermore, though chemical manufacturers may not like to fill out government forms specifying where they dump hazardous materials, no doubt most citizens would be reassured by the fact that manufacturers have to comply with that particular annoyance.[29]

While some civil servants use red tape to shield themselves from the public, some organizations, such as the Department of Energy and the Justice Department, have developed a reputation for flexibility and responsiveness.[30] And, do all federal bureaucrats take advantage of taxpayers? In contrast with the U.S. Postal Service, employees of the Peace Corps almost never miss a day's work.[31] Finally, although at some levels, government growth may be out of control, at the federal level, employment actually *decreased* between 1993 and 1995.[32]

In 1995, with House Speaker Newt Gingrich (right) at the helm, the Republican majority in Congress sought to drastically cut back the size of the welfare state created under the presidency of Franklin Roosevelt. Those opposed to such cuts note that many of the people who disapprove of big government are in a position to do so only because they or their parents or grandparents were its main beneficiaries. These opponents point out that Roosevelt's New Deal programs helped many Americans move into the middle class and created a model of government activism aimed at protecting people and workers. Those in favor of the cuts note that the challenges facing the United States in the late twentieth century and beyond call for less government and a new relationship between government and citizens.

In response to the various complaints, and in an effort to make the bureaucracy more effective and accountable, numerous efforts at and proposals for reforming the federal bureaucracy have been made. We will now look at some of them.

REFORMING THE BUREAUCRACY

There is no shortage of ideas on how to reform the federal bureaucracy. And judging from the criticisms of the bureaucracy and the results of the 1994 elections, the public seems ready for some changes.

Some advocates of reform have called for a partial return to the patronage system used up until the passage of the Pendleton Act in 1883. These political observers argue, just as Andrew Jackson did over a century ago, that patronage appointments will improve efficiency and democratic accountability by translating popular support for the objectives of an incoming president into actual policy. But, as the Progressive reformers who abolished patronage in the 1880s pointed out, patronage leads to widespread corruption, disorganization, and underqualified personnel in the bureaucracy.

Other reforms seek to address charges of an inert, unproductive workforce in federal agencies. One effort to improve innovation and productivity was the passage of the Civil Service Reform Act in 1978. One of its most important

Cutting Government Spending

The federal government spends more than a trillion dollars a year—an astronomical sum by any measure, and one that is the subject of a rising tide of criticism from both taxpayers and members of Congress. Of course, most of the money spent by government is allocated to programs that the majority of Americans consider worthwhile: defense, highway construction, social security, salaries of government employees, and so on. In addition, a whopping 20 percent of federal outlays go to pay interest on the public debt—more, in fact, than is spent on national defense. The interest payments cannot be reduced, and any efforts to cut back on "worthwhile" programs would meet with widespread public disapproval. Thus, the task of reducing government spending is a difficult one; some would say impossible. Nevertheless, political candidates and elected officials are continually promising to cut back on the government's expenditures.

Proposals to reduce government spending focus on two broad areas: unnecessary and wasteful spending, and spending on social programs like Aid to Families with Dependent Children (AFDC, popularly known as "welfare"). Reductions in the first area are generally approved; cutbacks in the second generate intense political conflict.

At first glance it would seem obvious that the way to reduce the overall level of government spending is to cut back on wasteful and unnecessary expenditures. Many examples of such expenditures can be cited. There was the $375,000 that the navy spent to test the flight characteristics of frisbees and the $46,000 spent by the National Science Foundation to study how the sight of scantily clad women affected men's driving. The Defense Department produced not one but twelve films on "How to Brush Your Teeth." The Postal Service sent 375,000 letters to employees warning them not to stick pencils in their ears or let their toenails grow to excessive lengths. A safety pamphlet sent to farmers at a cost of $500,000 warned of the dangers of stepping in wet manure (one might suffer "a bad fall").

The problem with attacking these kinds of waste is that one never knows where they will crop up next; there is no category in the federal budget la-

provisions was the creation of a Senior Executive Service (SES), a group of upper-management bureaucrats with access to private-sector incentives, such as bonuses, but who would also be subject to measurable job performance evaluations. Those who failed to achieve high ratings could be fired. The idea was that the senior bureaucrats would respond positively to productivity incentives, and that they would become more responsive to presidential policy leadership. The effects of the program have been uneven. While innovation has occurred, some career officers find exposure to political pressure uncomfortable. Few members of the SES have been fired, but many have left their jobs with a bad taste in their mouths.[33]

Another reform aimed at making the bureaucracy more effective and accountable is the Whistle Blower Act, passed by Congress in 1989. This Act encourages civil servants to report instances of bureaucratic mismanagement, financial impropriety, corruption, and inefficiency. It also protects civil servants from retaliation (from being fired, demoted, or relocated, for example). The Act has been effective in helping to identify and root out problems in the bureaucracy.

A proposed reform aimed at increasing the productivity of the federal bureaucracy involves imposing term limits on bureaucrats. As with the term

beled "Wasteful and Unnecessary Spending." Legislators wielding the budget-cutting knife therefore turn to specific programs like AFDC.

Today, 14.5 million Americans are enrolled in AFDC, which costs the federal government $13.8 billion annually. Critics of the program (primarily Republicans) charge that many welfare recipients are freeloaders and that the program creates a "culture" of lifelong dependency. Supporters (primarily Democrats) point out that welfare recipients are constantly seeking jobs but that the available jobs rarely pay enough to raise them above the poverty line. Both Republicans and Democrats agree that the present welfare system is flawed, but they disagree on the specific reforms needed.

If you were asked to vote on a bill that would reduce federal spending on AFDC, what would you do?

What Would Happen

At this writing, Congress is considering proposals that would limit the length of time a person can receive welfare benefits, sharply cut back on funding for the AFDC program, and turn over the administration of the program to the states. Cutting back on welfare spending would reduce the federal deficit, but it could have a number of serious social consequences. Limiting the length of time they can spend on welfare would force recipients to find other ways to make a living. However, many recipients are unable to work—two-thirds are children, and many others are permanently disabled. Welfare benefits have already been cut to the bone: In 1965 average AFDC benefits for a family amounted to 49.6 percent of the federally calculated poverty level; by 1995 they had shrunk to 28.6 percent of that level.[*] Further cuts would force those who are unable to work even deeper into poverty.

Cutbacks in welfare spending would have other results as well. Pregnant women living in poverty would be more likely to seek abortions rather than give birth to another child whom they would be unable to support. And reduced funding for the administration of AFDC would mean that there would be fewer social workers available to help welfare recipients find employment. Increases in rates of crime and homelessness are among the likely results.

---

[*]David E. Rosenbaum, "Welfare: Who Gets It? How Much Does It Cost?" *New York Times,* Mar. 23, 1995, p. A23.

---

limits proposal for members of Congress, the tenure of bureaucrats would be limited to a fixed appointment. The idea is that entrenched, nonproductive "lifers" would be replaced by an enthusiastic and driven group of bureaucrats who would achieve their goals and then move on. Critics of such a reform proposal charge that limiting the tenures of experienced bureaucrats could trigger a "brain drain" of qualified specialists, resulting in a crucial loss of expertise in federal agencies. Proponents maintain that the incentives for bureaucrats to perform well will far outweigh the disadvantages.

Some have proposed drastically reducing or even eliminating the bureaucracy altogether through privatization. **Privatization** involves turning over public responsibilities for regulation and for providing goods and services to privately owned and operated enterprises. Some economists argue that private enterprises could do a superior and less costly job of administering, implementing, and regulating government programs. Advocates of privatization point to the success of United Parcel Service and Federal Express, and compare these two companies with the more costly and less efficient U.S. Postal Service. They view this comparison as evidence that shifting services from governmental to private hands will greatly improve both quality and cost-effectiveness. But

Vice President Al Gore Jr., uses the airwaves to promote his campaign to "reinvent government." Here he tests an ashtray, purchased by the government, on the David Letterman Show. Gore's campaign, known in White House shorthand as REGO, involves cutting back to the basics—eliminating duplicated agencies and outdated subsidy programs and addressing the ever-growing number of government regulations.

"It's time we had a new customer service contract with the American people."

—Vice President Al Gore, on reinventing government

defenders of the Postal Service argue that such comparisons are unfair, since private companies, unlike the Postal Service, are not limited by costly congressional policy mandates.

Some degree of privatization has been advocated by the Clinton administration and, to a much greater extent, by the Republican majority in Congress. House Speaker Newt Gingrich is among those calling for the elimination of entire agencies and programs, bans on new regulations, and contracting programs out to the private sector whenever possible.

Like many of the administrations that preceded it, the Clinton administration, under the leadership of Vice President Al Gore, has attempted to reform the bureaucracy. With the publication of his National Performance Review (NPR)—an evaluation of the executive branch's effectiveness and a prescription for reform—Gore sought to rally support for a comprehensive program to "reinvent government." His program involved reorganizing and shrinking agencies, simplifying the bewildering 450 job-level classification system, reducing budgets, and otherwise overhauling an inefficient and sprawling bureaucracy.[34] Ultimately, these proposed reforms sought to eliminate a quarter of a million federal jobs and save taxpayers some $108 billion over five years.

Each of these proposed reforms has merit. But attempts at reform will always encounter a serious obstacle: the fact that the very people who have grown comfortable with the status quo—relevant legislators and the bureaucrats themselves—are responsible for developing, implementing, and administering the programs that would improve bureaucratic performance, democratize the bureaucracy, and enhance accountability. For this reason more than any other, attempts to dramatically reform the bureaucracy have encountered bristling opposition and have met with only partial success.

Opposition to the Clinton/Gore reform plan did not surprise senior White House officials. "I don't think the public doubts the sincerity of the president," remarked White House pollster Stan Greenberg. "It's that they're not sure Congress and the bureaucracy can be moved to reinvent government." Indeed, popular support for Gore's initiatives was widespread. Among the almost one in five Americans who had voted for Ross Perot in 1992, a majority cited excessive waste and inertia in the federal government as their chief concerns. And public-opinion polls regularly reveal a majority of Americans expressing similar sentiments.

BUREAUCRACY AND APPROACHING DEMOCRACY

Bureaucratic organizations are inherently undemocratic. Democracy requires plurality; traditional bureaucracy requires unity. Democratic society is organized around the principle of equality, while bureaucratic organization is hierarchical. A fundamental element in any democracy is openness, but bureaucratic operations often demand secrecy. A democratic political system ensures equal access to participation in politics, but bureaucratic participation depends on institutional authority. Finally, democracy assumes the election, and subsequent public accountability, of all officials, while bureaucrats are appointed and thus not subject to public accountability.[35]

Still, American bureaucracy has made major strides toward democratic accountability. Today, few bureaucracies operate outside the law as the FBI did under J. Edgar Hoover. Today's administrators, influenced by modern management techniques, spend as much time listening to their employees—and to the public—as they do giving orders. Even the CIA director, John Deutch, held a town meeting to discuss reform.

Although few administrative rules are made according to a democratic voting process, the policymaking process has opened up to include a variety of perspectives in recent years. Rule-making agencies take care to notify not only businesses subject to regulation about upcoming hearings but also invite consumer and civil rights groups to testify.

On secrecy, the picture is less clear. While the Administrative Procedure Act, the Freedom of Information Act, and the Government in the Sunshine Act have opened up routine administrative decisions to public scrutiny, the national-security establishment continues to operate behind closed doors.

Because bureaucrats have been facing pressure from private competitors, they have found it in their interest to be more attentive to public opinion and more open to useful suggestions from within the organization. This has occurred in spite of the fact that their institutional authority is based on professional expertise, and that most bureaucratic specialists feel—often rightly—that they know more than other bureaucrats and more than the general public, about an issue.

Finally, though bureaucrats are appointed rather than elected, the evidence shows that they are surprisingly similar to the public in terms not only of demographic characteristics but even in terms of their general values.[36] Those allegedly "faceless bureaucrats," then, look very much like the United States they serve.

Though the bureaucracy is an institution that is often scorned for its enormous size and lack of responsiveness or accountability, this "fourth branch" of government is charged with an important function that makes it indispensable: carrying forth the work of the federal government in America's approach to democracy.

SUMMARY

1. A bureaucracy is a large and complex organizational system in which tasks, roles, and responsibilities are structured to achieve a goal. Bureaucracies are characterized by specialization, hierarchy, and a system of formal rules. Bureaucratic failures often result from too-rigid adherence to one or more of these characteristics.

2. The federal bureaucracy began growing rapidly in the late nineteenth century, spurred by industrial expansion. The size of the bureaucracy has increased dramatically during the twentieth century, largely as a result of efforts to create a welfare state. Recent growth has resulted from legislation to address racial injustice, environmental degradation, and other problems in American society.

3. Before 1828 the federal bureaucracy was dominated by a small elite of wealthy, well-educated white males. Under the "spoils system" instituted by President Andrew Jackson, government jobs were awarded on the basis of party loyalty. In 1883 Congress passed the Pendleton Act, which created a civil service—a system that hires and promotes employees on the basis of professional merit and protects them from political threats to their job security.

4. The Hatch Act of 1939 established standards for federal employees. The political liberties of government employees were restricted to preserve the neutrality of federal agencies. Recent amendments allow federal employees to participate more actively in partisan politics, although they cannot run for office.

5. One of the primary tasks of the bureaucracy is to implement the policies established by Congress and the president. Administrators have considerable discretion in implementing legislation. As a result, the actual impact of a policy may be quite different from what was intended.

6. The administration of a policy involves the performance of routine tasks associated with a specific policy goal. Another task of bureaucratic agencies, regulation, consists of making rules, enforcing them, and adjudicating any disputes that arise as a result.

7. Cabinet departments are major administrative units responsible for conducting a broad range of government operations. Each department has jurisdiction over a specific policy area and is headed by a secretary who is also a member of the president's cabinet.

8. Independent agencies are smaller than cabinet departments and have a narrower set of responsibilities; they generally exist to perform a service such as space exploration or intelligence gathering. Independent regulatory commissions are established to regulate a sector of the nation's economy in the public interest and are generally run by a board whose members have set terms.

9. A government corporation is a semi-independent government agency that administers a business enterprise. It takes the form of a business corporation but possesses the authority of government.

10. Agencies of the federal bureaucracy are subject to three major constraints. They lack control over their revenues, over decisions about how to deliver goods and services, and over the goals they must attempt to achieve.

11. Presidents attempt to control the bureaucracy through the appointment power, which enables them to appoint agency officials who will support their policies. Reorganization is another tool available to presidents seeking to control the bureaucracy. The Office of Management and Budget, which administers the federal budget, can be used to control government agencies. Presidents can also seek to influence the bureaucracy through persuasion.

12. Congressional oversight of the bureaucracy occurs largely through the power of the purse, which gives Congress the power to appropriate all funding for federal agencies. Congress also has the power of administrative oversight, and the Senate can confirm or reject presidential nominees for top positions in the bureaucracy.

13. The term *iron triangle* is used to refer to a strong interdependent relationship among legislators, lobbyists, and bureaucrats concerned with a particular area of public policy. Iron triangles are resistant to democratic accountability.

14. The American public has a negative view of the bureaucracy, believing that government is expensive and wasteful and that the bureaucracy is incapable of achieving its goals. It is widely believed that the bureaucracy hobbles businesses with unnecessary regulations, that government is not responsive to citizens, that federal bureaucrats take advantage of the taxpayer, and that the growth of the bureaucracy is out of control.

15. Efforts to reform the bureaucracy led to the creation of the Senior Executive Service, which was intended to increase innovation and productivity in the federal workforce. Another proposed reform is privatization, or turning over certain governmental responsibilities to private enterprises. Current reform efforts focus on reorganizing and shrinking agencies, reducing budgets, and making the bureaucracy more efficient.

KEY TERMS

bureaucracy
bureaucrats
specialization
hierarchy
formal rules
welfare state
spoils system
civil service

Hatch Act
implementation
administrative discretion
administration
regulation
cabinet departments
independent agencies
independent regulatory commissions

government corporation
appointment power
Office of Management and Budget
iron triangle
issue networks
red tape
privatization

SUGGESTED READINGS

- Downs, Anthony. *Inside Bureaucracy*. Prospect Heights, Ill.: Waveland Press, 1994. This book is full of interesting theories and insights into bureaucratic decision making.

- Frohnmayer, John. *Leaving Town Alive: Confessions of an Arts Warrior*. Boston, Mass.: Houghton Mifflin, 1993. The head of the National Endowment for the Arts is caught between a solidly conventional Congress and an avant-garde arts community.

- Goodsell, Charles T. *The Case for Bureaucracy: A Public Administration Polemic*. 3d ed. Chatham, N.J.: Chatham House Publishers, 1993. Goodsell discusses a number of myths about the bureaucracy and shows that it usually does a better job than we give it credit for.

- Osborne, David, and Ted Gaebler. *Reinventing Government: How the Entrepreneurial Spirit Is Transforming the Public Sector*. Reading, Mass.: Addison-Wesley, 1992. A series of inspirational tales about lethargic government agencies that transform themselves into innovative organizations capable of competing with the private sector.

- Rohr, John A. *Ethics for Bureaucrats: An Essay on Law and Values*. 2d ed. New York: Marcel Dekker, 1989. This refreshing book argues that bureaucrats who encounter ethical dilemmas should solve them by abiding by American values rather than by slavishly following their agency's procedures manual.

- Summers, Anthony. *Official and Confidential: The Secret Life of J. Edgar Hoover*. New York: Putnam's, 1993. Tells the story of the bizarre life of the autocratic FBI chief who held on to his post despite the wishes of presidents and members of Congress.

- Trice, Harrison M. and Janice M. Beyer. *The Cultures of Work Organizations*. Englewood Cliffs, N.J.: Prentice Hall, 1993. A richly detailed picture of the development of cultures within organizations.

- Wilson, James Q. *Bureaucracy: What Government Agencies Do and Why They Do It*. New York: Basic Books, 1989. Wilson presents a lively, "bottom-up" view of bureaucracy and explains why some agencies work well, while others fail.

PUBLIC
OPINION

CHAPTER 9

CHAPTER OUTLINE

CASE STUDY: LANDON DEFEATS
    ROOSEVELT?
INTRODUCTION: PUBLIC OPINION
    AND DEMOCRACY
WHAT IS PUBLIC OPINION?
MEASURING PUBLIC OPINION
POLITICAL SOCIALIZATION
SOCIAL VARIABLES THAT INFLUENCE
    OPINION FORMATION

AMERICAN POLITICAL CULTURE
THE STATE OF AMERICAN PUBLIC
    OPINION
STABILITY AND CHANGE IN PUBLIC
    OPINION
FROM PUBLIC OPINION TO PUBLIC
    POLICY
PUBLIC OPINION AND APPROACHING
    DEMOCRACY

One of the most important elections in the twentieth-century United States occurred in 1936. The reelection landslide of President Franklin D. Roosevelt that year confirmed public support for the New Deal. Americans sent Washington a clear message. They expected the national government to play a key role in managing the economy to ensure security and even prosperity for the American people. Ever since, that role has been taken for granted in American politics. The election of 1936, then, signaled the beginning of a new era.

Landon Defeats Roosevelt?

Today we take it for granted that the New Deal was wildly popular, that Roosevelt's policies were widely supported, that Roosevelt himself was beloved by millions. Nothing is easier than hindsight. At the time, before the advent of sophisticated polling techniques, it was entirely unclear to most political observers what the outcome of the 1936 election would be. Indeed, the most respected polling outfit of the day predicted Roosevelt's sound thrashing by his Republican opponent, Kansas governor Alfred Landon.

Now if Alf Landon doesn't immediately strike you as a household name, you are correct. Landon suffered perhaps the worst election defeat in American history and promptly faded into obscurity, while Roosevelt then went on to win two more presidential elections in the next eight years. With such convincing evidence of public support for the president and the New Deal, how could anyone have imagined, in the fall of 1936, that Americans would back a little-known midwestern governor and a return to the Republican policies widely viewed as responsible for bringing on the depression?

The story of that mistake is instructive. It illustrates not only the difficulty of gauging public opinion but also the problem of relating that opinion to actual governmental policies. In other words, how can we know what people actually want, and how can we be sure that government will actually do what they want?

Beginning about 1916, the magazine Literary Digest made what was then the most sophisticated use of polling for political data. The magazine mailed surveys asking for opinions on a host of important issues to a large number of Americans. Using this data, the magazine claimed a high degree of accuracy in predicting election outcomes. Indeed, the Literary Digest poll of 1932 came within 1 percent of the actual vote in predicting Roosevelt's victory. So impressive was this predictive ability that Democratic National Chairman James Farley proclaimed just prior to the election: "I consider [the poll results] conclusive evidence as to the desire of the people of this country for a change in the national government. The Literary Digest poll is an achievement of no little magnitude."[1] This was high praise for a magazine whose editorial policy and readership were decidedly sympathetic to the Republican party.

But a major mistake made by Literary Digest in 1936 changed everything. Prior to the election that year, the Literary Digest reader poll predicted a landslide win for Landon, the Republican challenger. It claimed Roosevelt would gain only 41 percent of the vote to Landon's 55 percent, with 4 percent going to third-party candidate William Lemke. A disgusted James Farley, who had praised the Digest only four years earlier, now discounted entirely the poll results, predicting instead a Roosevelt sweep of all but eight electoral votes. His prediction was exactly right, and the rest is history. Landon suffered the landslide defeat, carrying only two states, while FDR garnered 61 percent of the popular vote. How, in light of over two million responses, could Literary Digest have been so wrong?

The problem was simple. The Digest had

worked with a biased sample. As with its earlier polls, the magazine in 1936 sent out millions of informal surveys, known as straw vote ballots, to people whose names had been culled from automobile registration lists and telephone books. (Altogether 10 million ballots were sent out, and nearly 2.4 million were returned—large numbers, but a response rate of under 25 percent.) Obviously, these respondents would not be representative of the total American public. They were wealthier, for one thing. After all, in a period of grinding economic depression they could still afford the luxury of an automobile and a telephone. They were also better educated than average. These two factors ensured a built-in bias against Roosevelt, since wealth and education have long correlated with support for Republicans.

In addition to these problems, participants in the poll were self-selected. They were picked not at random but simply on the basis of whether they chose to return the questionnaire. Since the individuals most motivated to respond to a political survey are almost never representative of the wider population, the results from such a self-selected survey are not very reliable.

Finally, the survey had no way to measure which of these respondents were likely to vote on election day. Consequently, when Literary Digest predicted a Landon victory, it was doing so based on preferences expressed by a largely wealthy, educated, and Republican segment of the population. Many people in this group were motivated to return their ballots because they badly wanted to get rid of Roosevelt. Despite their large numbers, they were hardly typical of the American public as a whole.

The editors of the Literary Digest openly confessed their chagrin in the postelection issue and vowed to rethink their methodology in subsequent polling efforts. Being contrite, however, did them little good. Their magazine was already a luxury during the depression. Under the further weight of this highly publicized embarrassment, the Digest went broke within a year. This incident marked an end to the era of the "legitimate" straw poll and pushed survey researchers to fine-tune their methods. It opened the door to today's much more sophisticated —and reliable—survey models. ✣

President Franklin D. Roosevelt during inauguration ceremonies, January 20, 1937.

INTRODUCTION: PUBLIC OPINION AND DEMOCRACY

For any system to be democratic its leaders must hear and respond to "the voice of the people." This leader–follower connection is central to democratic theory. Citizens in a democracy express their preferences through informed political activity, and leaders listen with a keen interest to those expressed preferences. If the masses are inactive or if the leaders ignore mass desires, democracy falters. To gauge the strength of democracy in America, we need to know what citizens desire, how well they communicate those desires through political activity, and how well political leaders respond to those desires.

At first glance, one is struck by a significant gap between what Americans say they want and what their leaders have been doing. The United States would be quite a different place if public opinion set public policy. Polls taken over the years have shown consistent support for proposals that American political leaders do little to implement. For instance, the following policies would all have been in force for some time if American public opinion were easily translated into the law of the land:

- Individuals would have the "right to die"
- The government would have a balanced budget
- Members of Congress would be limited to twelve years in office, and term limits would be placed on most other political offices as well
- Strict limits would be imposed on campaign spending
- The death penalty would be consistently imposed for murder
- Prayer would be permitted in public schools
- Interracial marriages would be limited
- Financial aid to other nations would be severely curtailed

Why hasn't American public policy reflected these majority preferences? For one thing, the simple mechanics of discovering the public will is far from easy. Then translating that will into public policy within a complex framework of divided powers takes time—often a good deal of time. Further slowing down the entire process is the persistent view of many Americans that the "common will" of the people does not always stand for the "common good" of society. Is asking leaders to immediately carry out the whims of the masses the best way to run a society? Those who are dubious use the complex governmental system to thwart the immediate implementation of mass desires.

How democratic, then, *is* the American system of government? We are hardly arguing that public opinion plays no role in America's national policy-making; rather, its role is complex and indirect. To begin to understand its impact, we will examine how public opinion is measured, where opinions on political issues come from, and the nature of public opinion in America. Let's begin by looking closely at the meaning of the term *public opinion*.

WHAT IS PUBLIC OPINION?

Public opinion is the collective expression of attitudes about the prominent issues and actors of the day. The concept of a "public" holding "opinions," or beliefs, on the various issues of the day is almost as old as politics itself. Plato, for instance, saw public opinion as a danger if it meant the free expression of individual desires by the mass of citizens. According to Plato, popular opinions were good only when they reflected the will of the state and its rulers. A very different view was expressed centuries later by John Stuart Mill, who in his essay *On Liberty* (1859) argued in favor of a populace free to express its diverse political views. Only by giving all individuals the maximum liberty to state their opinions, said Mill, could a society ever arrive at the "truth." Where Plato wanted to shape and control opinions, Mill advocated free rein to their expression.

James Madison took something of a middle stance between Plato and Mill. In *Federalist* no. 10, Madison acknowledged the inevitable diversity of opinion

Americans will always have different opinions on the important issues of the day. It helped President Bush that an overwhelming majority of the public supported U.S. participation in the Persian Gulf War. Victory in that war also helped change much of the lingering negative opinion about deployment of U.S. forces abroad—a sentiment resulting from the Vietnam War. On the left, supporters cheer soldiers who just returned from the Persian Gulf. On the right, some of the Americans opposed to the war in the Gulf aired their sentiments. The opinions of such protesters were in the minority of American public opinion at the time, however.

In democratic republics . . . tyranny . . . leaves the body alone and goes straight for the soul. The master no longer says: "Think like me or you die." He does say: "You are free not to think as I do; you can keep your life and property and all; but from this day you are a stranger among us. You can keep your privileges in the township, but they will be useless to you, for if you solicit your fellow citizens' votes, they will not give them to you, and if you only ask for their esteem, they will make excuses for refusing that."

—Alexis de Tocqueville, *Democracy in America*

that would develop in a free society but feared that competing opinions could lead to hostile factions that would divide rather than unify or improve society.

> A zeal for different opinions . . . [has] divided mankind into parties, inflamed them with mutual animosity, and rendered them . . . disposed to vex and oppress each other.[2]

Like most of the framers, Madison was concerned that an overzealous majority might inflict its irrational, prejudiced, or uninformed wishes on a political minority. Hence, the Founders made sure to install constitutional safeguards (such as the electoral college, the Senate, and the Supreme Court) against the too-easy implementation of public passions. On the other hand, they also allowed many outlets for the expression of public opinion—via voting, a free press, the right of assembly, and other forms of political participation.

How deeply public opinion should be taken into account, then, has long been the subject of intense political debate. But in this age, there are clear parameters for this debate. No longer can a legitimate public figure (like Plato) argue that the public should be ignored (or manipulated) in political decision making. The only real argument is whether the public's will should prevail "all of the time," "most of the time," or "some of the time." The public, in short, is a key player in the democratic game of politics. For that reason, discovering and publicizing the public's opinion has become a key political activity in modern democracies.

While the notion of public opinion has been with us for centuries, we have only recently developed reliable ways to measure it.

MEASURING PUBLIC OPINION

The first attempts at measuring public opinion began in the mid 1800s, with a variety of **straw polls.** A straw poll is a nonscientific method of measuring public opinion. It springs from the farmer's method of throwing straw in the air to gauge the strength and direction of the prevailing breeze. In a straw poll, one wishes to measure which way and how strong the political breezes are blowing.

As we saw in the case study, straw polls have inherent flaws that make them inappropriate as scientific indicators of public opinion. Their main problem is that they fail to obtain a **representative sample** of the public. A valid sample must be representative: It must include all the significant characteristics of the total population. A sample of Americans that included no women, for instance, would obviously be invalid. A nonrepresentative sample, like the infamous *Literary Digest* poll of 1936, which underrepresented poor and average-income people, is worthless.

After the 1936 fiasco, professional pollsters began a determined effort to make their work more scientific. George Gallup and Elmo Roper, among others, helped meet the growing demand for information about public attitudes. Applying modern statistical techniques, they found it possible through interviews with small but representative samples of voters to predict the behavior of the overall voting population.

To obtain that representative sample, some requirements need to be met. First, the number of people in the sample should number at least several hundred. Second, the people to be polled must be chosen through a technique known as random sampling. In addition, pollsters must guard against sampling bias.

SAMPLE SIZE AND RANDOM SAMPLING   When taking a survey, most national polling organizations seek between fifteen hundred and two thousand participants. Using statistical methods, pollsters have determined that information from that small a sample can be projected onto the entire population. The method does work. Most pollsters produce results of high reliability: Their findings are accurate at least 95 percent of the time within a **margin of error** of about 3 percent. A 3 percent margin of error means that if a poll shows Candidate A likely to win 57 percent of the vote, in the actual election Candidate A will win somewhere between 54 percent and 60 percent. In other words, the number for the *entire population* of voters will fall within a range of plus or minus three points of the number obtained for the small but representative sample of voters.

The second requirement for a good poll, random sampling, is harder to achieve. In a **random sample,** every member of the population must have an equal chance of appearing in the sample. To pick five people randomly from a group of a hundred, for instance, you might write each person's name on a three-by-five-inch card, mix all the cards thoroughly in a hat, then reach in blindfolded and withdraw five cards. In this way, each person in the group of one hundred has an equal chance of being chosen.

GUARDING AGAINST SAMPLING BIAS   Pollsters make every effort to guard against **sampling bias.** They try to ensure that no particular set of people in

A U.S. census taker interviews a U.S. citizen as part of the 1990 census, thus helping to accumulate an array of statistical information about Americans as required by the Constitution every ten years. Most polling outfits, including the Census Bureau, find that middle-aged female poll takers who appear nonthreatening and pleasant in appearance are most effective at obtaining access to respondents and securing honest and straightforward answers to questions.

the population at large—rich or poor, black or white, northerner or southerner—is any more or less likely to appear in the final sample than any other set of people. Recall that the major flaw in the *Literary Digest* poll of 1936 was the disproportionately high percentage of respondents who were relatively wealthy and well educated, which led to biased results.

Little room is left to interviewer discretion. Most polling organizations divide the population of the United States into categories based on the location and size of the city in which they live. Certain areas or blocks are then randomly selected and interviewers sent into the neighborhood, instructed to pick every nth house. Using another technique, pollsters carry out a survey using computer-generated lists of telephone numbers. Because they are selected completely at random, these lists will reflect an approximation of the entire nation. The result is that polls today come relatively close to meeting the crucial requirement that every American have an equal chance of appearing in any given pollster's sample.

Problems still occur, however. The reliance on telephones, while convenient and inexpensive, does introduce a modest degree of sampling bias. For example, 1990 census figures indicated that 20 percent of Native American households lack telephone service of any kind, as do 15 percent of black and Hispanic households; by contrast, only about 5 percent of white households have no telephone. Altogether, nearly five million of America's ninety-two million housing units lack telephones. Since a strong statistical correlation exists between poverty and lack of telephone facilities, it would appear that the most "phoneless" housing units are in areas of urban poverty. Polls done by telephone are therefore likely to underrepresent the urban, ethnic poor.

Pollsters confront a number of additional problems as they set out to conduct their polls. Interviewers must be carefully trained, for instance, to avoid interviewer bias. They must be courteous, businesslike, and neutral so as to elicit responses from the public that are open and honest. Interviewers must also be persistent. Some people are rarely home; others may hesitate to answer questions. Interviewers must make every effort to contact potential respondents and draw them out; they must learn how to extract truthful answers from shy, hostile, or simply bewildered members of the voting public. The questions themselves must be carefully worded, to avoid "leading" respondents to particular answers. Biased questions ("Shouldn't President Clinton be impeached?") produce unreliable results.

THE IMPORTANCE OF POLLS   Public-opinion polls have emerged as an integral part of American politics. Accurate polls are one of the most important sources of information used by political leaders in the decision-making process. Polls today that are conducted by reputable national polling organizations do provide a reasonably accurate picture of the beliefs and desires of the American public. Without polls, an understanding of what the public thinks and wants would be difficult to achieve.

The Washington Post–ABC News, NBC–Wall Street Journal, and CBS–New York Times organizations all have their own respected pollsters. Many public officials, the president included, now keep professional pollsters on their staff, always prepared to check the pulse of the people. Lobby groups are constantly releasing the results of polls they have commissioned to "prove" that the public supports their particular policy preferences.

The Presidential Pollster

No modern presidential candidate would dare to run a campaign without the advice of a political pollster—someone who can keep a finger on the pulse of the public and help design effective campaign strategies. When he sought the presidency in 1992, Democrat Bill Clinton chose political scientist and professional pollster Stanley Greenberg for this job.

Greenberg was no stranger to the world of presidential politics. His first political-polling experience came while he was a graduate student at Harvard, working on a forecasting model that was used in Robert F. Kennedy's bid for the 1968 presidential nomination. A lifelong Democrat, Greenberg also worked for George McGovern in 1972.

Beginning in 1985 Greenberg turned his attention to the growing disaffection of blue-collar workers, who were fleeing the Democratic party in droves during the Reagan years. His analyses suggested that the only way Democrats could regain the White House was to recapture the support of middle-class voters. He was also convinced that the "trickle-down" economic policies of the Reagan administration were losing their popular luster.

Greenberg's analysis, together with his reputation as a skilled pollster and a loyal Democrat, attracted Clinton's attention. "Clinton had a powerful critique of trickle-down economics," Greenberg says, "but he also had a critique of Democratic failure and was reaching out to [middle-class] voters." With Greenberg's help, the Clinton campaign appealed directly to the middle class, a strategy that paid off in a spectacular victory.

Since 1992 Greenberg has continued to take the pulse of the public, focusing on the unraveling of American party politics and the discontent among middle-class voters that revealed itself so dramatically in the 1994 congressional elections. In his recent book *Middle Class Dreams* he examines a political environment in which "voters are poised to shoot first and ask questions later." In his view, American politics has taken on a radical new shape, with many voters loyal to neither party and suspicious of both.

Greenberg has also continued to advise the president in the position of White House pollster. The job has turned out to be a tough one, as Clinton's public image has become increasingly tarnished. Once a week Greenberg meets with Clinton for fifteen minutes, during which time he must report on current levels of presidential approval and help plot strategies to boost presidential ratings. "In order to play my role," says Greenberg, "I have to be as honest as I can be and as confidential as I can be." With the president under attack on all sides and another presidential contest on the horizon, that role becomes more difficult every day.

Source: Stanley Greenberg, *Middle Class Dreams: The Politics and Power of the New American Majority.* New York: Times Books, 1985.

As a significant factor in determining public policy, the polling enterprise has helped advance American society toward the democratic ideal. Polls have made the voice of the people a powerful force in the never-ending debates among political leaders. The Republican "Contract with America" strikingly illustrates this power. Newt Gingrich included in the Contract only those proposals that had been shown by national polls to be strongly supported by the American public, especially legal reform. Thus, the Republican takeover of Congress in 1994, along with the subsequent radical upheaval of the national public agenda, owes much to the power of the modern, scientific public-opinion poll.

Increasingly sophisticated polling methods have given us a huge amount of data on public opinion. Later in this chapter we'll look at what these data actually tell us about the political attitudes of the American people. But first, we'll examine the origins of our political opinions.

POLITICAL SOCIALIZATION

Where do our ideas about politics come from? **Political socialization** refers to the process by which we learn about the world of politics and develop our political beliefs. Learning about politics begins early in childhood. Political thinkers have long observed that parent–child and sibling relationships shape the social and political outlook of future citizens. In this era, other institutions—schools, peer groups, mass media—also serve as agents of socialization.[3]

The Role of Family

Family influence is especially powerful in the development of political knowledge, understanding, and participation. Whether one grows up poor or rich, for instance, shapes one's view of the world and bears heavily on one's likelihood of developing an interest in politics. Other family traits—education level, race, even geographic location—deeply affect one's perspectives on the political world.

Around the age of ten, children begin to form their worldview, based significantly on family views toward politics. The role of family in political socialization is mostly informal. Parents rarely sit children down and inform them that they are Democrats, supply-siders, or isolationists. In this sense, the family unit has a unique advantage for influence. Children absorb the casually dropped remarks of their parents and, over time, unthinkingly adopt those views as their own.

The influence of family derives also from the strong emotional bonds forged by the family connection. Children *want* to adopt the views of their beloved mentors. Close-knit families produce offspring whose views differ little from those of the parents. The "power structure" of the family provides an additional key to the early political socialization of children. Strong parental-authority figures have an enormous impact on a child's values and attitudes. Many scholars believe, for instance, that harsh, punitive parents produce children who are more authoritarian, intolerant, and ultraconservative than the average American.

Because many variables affect political attitudes, it is difficult to trace the precise effects of family on the political opinions of adult Americans. In one area, however, parental impact seems clear and pronounced. Children tend to adopt the party loyalty of their parents. That's significant, because partisan identification helps people make sense of the political world and predicts their behavior within it. Interestingly, when each parent identifies with a different political party, children generally embrace the partisan affiliation of their mother. We are not certain why this is, but one possible explanation, which would certainly reinforce the importance of family socialization, is that children feel closer to their mother, from whom they received much early nurturing and affection.

Children, however, must adjust their values so they can adapt to a changing world. The concept of a "generation gap" describes the potential de-

Generational Change in Israel

Generational change is a familiar idea to Americans. Americans are used to the notion that every twenty years or so a new generation reaches adulthood, shaped by a unique set of experiences that produce a different set of attitudes from that of their elders. As adults, members of this new generation will take control of society's institutions, including political structures, and impose their own particular values on them. Americans have already seen the post–World War II generation, formed in depression and war, slowly give way to baby-boomers, symbolized by Bill Clinton and Newt Gingrich. Waiting in the wings to take power are young people in their twenties, members of the next age group: the so-called Generation X. And so it goes.

Generational transitions occur in other societies as well. A remarkable set of changes is now under way in Israel. These changes are revealed when young Israelis are contrasted with an older generation whose formative experiences included deeply etched memories of the Holocaust, a war for independence, and a series of wars and skirmishes with hostile Arab neighbors. These events produced a militant ideology stressing Israeli nationalism, admiration for military prowess, a stress on unity and discipline, and a willingness to sacrifice individual goals for the good of a people. The younger generation in Israel today views the world quite differently.

Young Israelis have been shaped by a very different set of circumstances from those faced by their parents and grandparents. They live with a growing sense of security, developed as Israel and its neighbors slowly learn to live together. The outbreak of peace has lowered respect for military values—including the idea of discipline and sacrifice. Many members of the under forty-five generation have begun to chafe against the tough military obligations expected of all Israelis. A rapid increase in well-being is also undermining older values. Materialist perspectives are taking hold, spurred by the commercial messages of increasingly powerful electronic media. Attitudes stressing individualism and consumerism are growing. Young people are becoming eager to pursue their own economic advancement, and resist postponing opportunities while working collectively to build a strong and secure Israel.

This new stress on personal fulfillment has produced a series of political consequences. One sees, for instance, growing criticism of Israel's high taxes, taxes that in the past represented people's willingness to sacrifice for common ends. One also sees a growing gap between rich and poor, as Israelis place more stress on individual economic advancement and less on the idea that the plight of all Israelis depends on dedication to a common, collective struggle. Finally, the decline of collectivist thinking seems to be moving Israeli politics in a direction that Americans are familiar with: toward a vigorous individualism that undermines old party loyalties.

This trend is symbolized by the recent independent actions of a relatively young Israeli politician, Haim Ramon. In 1994, at the age of forty-four, Ramon resigned from a cabinet post, walked away from a position of power high inside the ruling Labor party, and formed a political group of his own that proceeded to shock political observers by winning control of a key set of powerful trade unions. Playing to the younger generation of Israelis who, as he says, "are interested in the good life," Ramon, is already given a good chance of reaching the post of prime minister some day. The rapid ascent of this iconoclast tells much about changing generational attitudes in Israel.

In a fast-moving world, societies no longer reproduce themselves in predictable, timeless fashion. To understand the politics of any nation, we must explore more than just the age-old values of its culture. We must also learn about the experiences and outlook of the younger generations that are moving along the social pipeline toward power.

Source: Clyde Haberman, "New Israeli Generation: 'Me' Replaces Myths," *New York Times,* Jan. 12, 1995, pp. A1, A10.

In school, children learn to express devotion to the United States. Nationalism is reinforced by patriotic activities such as reciting the Pledge of Allegiance.

cline in family influence over children's values. It postulates that when children reach adulthood, they break away and may condemn their parents' political beliefs. The rebellious 1960s made this theory seem particularly apt. However, follow-up studies during the 1970s suggest that as the children of the 1960s grew older, many of them adopted some of their parents' political beliefs. What accounts for this transition? Among other things, we know that as people age, they settle down and grow slightly more conservative. The day-to-day responsibilities of a job, a family, and a home move individuals in the direction of preserving the status quo of society and politics. One cannot, after all, remain a rebellious youth forever.

Still, no generation simply mimics the views of its parents. Analysts have observed a strong **generational effect** in the socialization patterns of the American public. The generation of adults who grew up during the 1960s does appear to have its own outlook, differentiating itself from the previous age. Its views are characterized by weaker ties to political institutions, weaker partisan identification, and a higher incidence of political "independence" or "nonpartisanship." This pattern results from a host of factors, including the social dislocation of the 1960s, the Vietnam War, and Watergate, all of which have made Americans more critical of their political system.

Schooling

Outside the family, the most powerful institutional influence on political socialization is education. In schools children first learn the formal rules of social interaction and come face-to-face with institutional authority: teachers, staff, and principals. More specifically, they learn to develop positive attitudes toward citizenship through history and civics courses. Early primary education leads children to recognize the name and image of the president. Most children are taught to look at the president as a benevolent symbol of government and politics.

This early socialization carries over strongly into adult life. Even after Richard Nixon's resignation from office in the midst of the Watergate scandal, most American adults still placed enormous faith in the office of the presidency and believed in the notion of a strong political leader in the White House. But studies found stark discrepancies between Caucasian and African American children.[4]

Since schools are central to the socialization process, they have become the center of political controversy as those from different sides of the political spectrum struggle for control of what schools teach. The issue of prayer in the public schools, for example, sharply divides the American public and has led to heated debate. This clash fits into a larger debate between educational conservatives and liberals on the role of schools in modern American society. Both sides wish to use schools to socialize students to the perspectives they hold dear. Conservative critics charge that schools are failing to provide students with the traditions and norms of American culture. Liberal critics fault the schools for perpetuating class, race, and gender divisions and for failing to teach about "diversity" and "multiculturalism." As these arguments suggest, Americans live in a complex and increasingly divided society. Debate about the way schools should socialize young Americans is therefore likely to continue for some time.

University training also represents a key element in the process of socialization. Most people believe that the experience of attending a university somehow "makes people more liberal." The assumption is that young adults, exposed to the ideas of liberal professors, are impressionable enough to be "converted" to liberal political thinking.

In fact, recent years have witnessed an increase in the number of self-identified conservatives among university students. And historically, university students were every bit as likely to be Republicans as Democrats. Indeed, those who obtain both a university education and high socioeconomic status tend to be moderate or conservative, not liberal.

Peers

A child's peers make up another important source of political socialization. We all absorb the ideas and outlook of our contemporaries, especially close friends. However, studies have found that although on matters of taste, dress, and style, teenaged peer groups exert a significant impact, they do little more than reinforce parental and community values, at least when it comes to politics. Peer groups also appear to affect political attitudes on the rare public issues of special relevance to young people.[5] One's decision to resist the draft or to enlist in the 1960s, for example, would have been influenced by one's peer group.

In recent decades, many observers have described the emergence of a "youth culture." Urie Bronfenbrenner, for instance, has argued that children's peers (and television) are much more influential in American culture than they were in the past, due in large part to the breakdown of the family and decrease in its traditional influence.[6] The youth culture, he fears, stresses immature, violent, and commercialized perspectives on life, shielded as it is from the more responsible perspectives of an adult world and deeply influenced by images on the television screen. A whole generation has now come of age heavily influenced by youth culture norms. A landmark study by Robert Putnam suggests the consequences.[7] Americans today are less prone to engage in civic activities, less trusting of others, and more cynical about the institutions of American society than they were in previous generations. The values propagated in the peer groups of young adults may have a role in this trend.

Television

Perhaps more than anything else in American culture, television has emerged to dominate the social and political landscape. The language, habits, values, and norms of American society seem to derive as much from exposure to the imagery of television as from any other socializing force.

Despite a considerable literature devoted to the effects of television on political attitudes and behavior, no consensus exists regarding just how and to what degree television affects Americans. Television has come under severe scrutiny because of its ubiquity; its demonstrated power to absorb viewer time for several hours a day; and its unique blend of immediacy, proximity, and audiovisual appeal. Perhaps the major criticism of television focuses on its power to divert our attention from the serious to the trivial.

Since the vast majority of television shows are devoted to amusement rather than information, and most people watch television for entertainment, its effect in shaping political attitudes must be indirect. One study concludes that "politically relevant issues are now raised in virtually all types of programming."[8]

Television dominates the social and political landscape of the United States, and for most of 1994 and a good deal of 1995, the murder trial of O.J. Simpson, as well as the story of his life, his marriage, and so forth, dominated the media, and television in particular. The tawdry and gory tale became a fixture in American culture. Everyone seemed to have an opinion on the case and to know all of the details about all of those involved. Many observers wondered what the obsession with O.J. Simpson and with celebrity suggests about television's impact. They also wondered what it reveals about American values and behavior.

The values conveyed by television—commercialism, a tolerance for sex and violence, encouragement of an extreme form of rugged individualism—become, in other words, an unthinking part of the general culture. Viewers absorb these values and subconsciously draw on them when thinking about politics.

Despite all the criticism of television, however, many studies reveal a surprise. Although children watch an average of twenty-seven hours of television per week—close to the amount they spend in class—a significant amount of viewing actually increases exposure to and knowledge of politics and government. So while Americans are undoubtedly bombarded with huge daily doses of advertising, sports, and entertainment, television watching does at least expose viewers to a considerable amount of political information as well.

Political Socialization: A Lifelong Experience

Political socialization never ends. Adult attitudes and beliefs aren't merely the sum of childhood experiences. Socialization begins early in life, and early learning is often the most deeply ingrained. Yet human beings are flexible; we continue to learn at every age. Furthermore, we live adult lives amid constant change. Major events, such as a depression or war, can produce significant change in our opinion of government. As adults, we may shed our parents' heritage—or at least some of it—by switching party affiliation or changing our political outlook, the better to reflect our own experiences and ideals. We never stop learning about politics. The more we participate in it, the better we learn and the closer we come to approaching the democratic ideal of equal political involvement by all.

SOCIAL VARIABLES THAT INFLUENCE OPINION FORMATION

In learning about politics, we are all subject to influences from the same general forces that shape the mindset of our society. We learn in families a common set of norms and values; we live together through major political and economic events; we all go to school and are bound together by the unifying force of television. Still, even within the same culture people differ from each other in a number of ways. Different social circumstances—class and income, race and ethnicity, religion, region, and gender—produce very different life experiences that are bound to be reflected in differing political opinions.

Class and Income

Our relative standing in society shapes many of our social and political values. Class, or social status, rests high on every social scientist's list of the forces that mold behavior. Unfortunately, class is a complex and difficult variable to measure; no two analysts and no two citizens agree on its precise definition. Hence, we often resort to examining income, a key element in the concept of class and one that is far easier to define and study. As with class, people in different income groups often see the political world in very different ways.

As a general rule, the less money one makes, the more inclined one is to favor liberal economic policies that provide benefits to the less well off in society (see Figure 9.1). These policies include a social-security system, a system of progressive taxation, minimum-wage laws, generous unemployment benefits, and welfare payments to the disadvantaged. The more money one makes, the more one is likely to oppose such policies. Both positions reflect a degree of economic self-interest. Lower-income groups benefit from liberal economic policies, while the money to pay for these policies comes from higher-income groups.

Nevertheless, these tendencies are only that: tendencies. Many individuals in each income category take positions opposite to what we would expect. Some millionaires are liberals; some at the lower end of the economic spectrum are conservatives.

Income level strongly influences voting patterns in the United States. Roughly stated, poor people vote for Democrats (the more liberal party on economic policy); rich people vote for Republicans (the more conservative party); and middle-income people split their votes, depending on circumstance. To illustrate, if voting in 1992 had been restricted to people living in households with an annual income level of more than fifty thousand dollars, Republican George Bush would have been handily reelected to a second term, instead of running a poor second to Democrat Bill Clinton. In 1984, when Ronald Reagan won a landslide reelection victory, the poorest voters in the country actually gave a majority of their votes to the loser, Democrat Walter Mondale. Income level, then, clearly affects one's perspective on the political process.

Race and Ethnicity

Income is but one of many social influences that produce different perspectives on politics. In addition, one's racial and ethnic background strongly affects the attitudes one is likely to develop. Imagine how different your life experiences would have been, and how different the political attitudes you would have developed, had you been born into this world with a different skin color or a different ethnic heritage.

In most cultures, minorities are discriminated against. Hence, they can grow up feeling distrustful of and alienated from their society and its public authorities. These attitudes are expressed in politics in a number of ways.

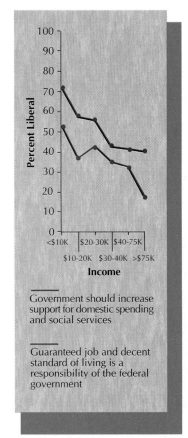

FIGURE 9.1 Social-Welfare Opinion by Family Income (Whites Only)

This figure shows that support for liberal economic policies by the federal government increases as one moves from high-income to low-income groups. To show the effects of income on opinion, independent of race, only whites were examined when this data was compiled.

Sources: Davis et al., 1993; and Miller et al., 1992. See full citation on p. 312, Table 9.1.

In the United States, for instance, blacks are clearly more alienated from the political process than whites are. As a result, they vote less frequently in elections and participate at a lower level in other areas of the political process. When they do vote, African Americans vote in large numbers for the party most associated with economic benefits for minorities and the less well off, that is, the Democrats. Indeed race, America's most enduring social cleavage, produces the clearest of all social delineations between the two major political parties. The vast majority of blacks consider themselves Democrats, whereas white voters are more closely divided in party identification.

Hispanics, too, such as Mexican Americans, tend to take a liberal position on economic issues and vote heavily for the Democratic party. However, the different groups within this population are not as unified on issues as African Americans tend to be. Cuban Americans, for example, are wealthier than average and are among the more conservative of American voting blocs.

As a general rule, ethnic groups become conservative as they rise in social status. Asian Americans, whose income levels have risen significantly in recent decades, are now among the most conservative groups in the nation. The same is true for so-called white ethnic voters, people whose ancestors immigrated from Ireland, Italy, or Poland. This group was heavily Democratic for decades, but as members rose into the middle class, they developed more conservative outlooks. We will explore the political consequences of race and ethnicity in Chapter 11, when we examine voting patterns.

Religion

In all countries religious differences produce serious political differences. Three general principles help explain the effect of religion on political attitudes. First, the less religious you are, the more liberal or "left" you are likely to be. In the United States, people with few religious connections are likely to take liberal stands on most social and economic questions and to vote Democratic. This pattern is not numerically significant, however, because most Americans profess religious belief of one kind or another.

More important for its political ramifications is the second principle: Members of any country's dominant religion tend to be more conservative. This stand makes sense: They have more investment in the status quo. By comparison, minority religious groups, especially the more oppressed ones, tend to favor liberal perspectives. This pattern can be seen clearly in the United States. Protestantism has long been the majority religion. Catholicism and Judaism were generally the religions of smaller minority groups who were discriminated against when they first immigrated to this country. As we would expect, over the years Protestants have been the most conservative religious group, while Catholics and Jews have been more liberal (and thus more likely to support Democrats).

These are, of course, broad generalizations; many individuals within each category deviate significantly from the pattern. Furthermore, changing social circumstances are changing this pattern. Many Catholics have entered America's mainstream and have become conservatives. But Catholics who still belong to minority ethnic groups are still more liberal and more likely to support Democrats than are Protestants, or other Catholics, for that matter. Jews remain the most liberal of all religious groups, but even they have moved modestly in a conservative direction, with the improvement of their economic situation in recent decades.

A final principle helps further explain the effect of religion on political outlook. Generally, the more religious one is, the more conservative one is likely to be. Thus, ardent churchgoers and committed believers take a conservative outlook on life; in politics they gravitate toward the right side of the political spectrum. This tendency helps explain a key trend of this age: White evangelical Protestants along with right-to-life supporters, have moved in significant numbers toward the Republican party.

Region

The political outlook people develop has been deeply influenced by the place in which they grew up and by the area in which they now live. In the United States certain sections of the country have deeply conservative traditions; other areas are more liberal. These local traditions touch area residents deeply. Those from conservative areas are likely to be conservative, and those from liberal areas liberal.

The South has always been America's most conservative region. Strongest among the many reasons for this pattern was that disheartened southern whites after the Civil War rejected all "Northern" values, including industrial-age liberalism. A firm stress on tradition, on order and hierarchy, and of course on religious fundamentalism have all helped keep the South a bastion of social—and now political—conservatism, especially for white residents of that area. By a quirk, however, the South remained Democratic for decades, a reaction to the Republicanism of Abraham Lincoln and the victorious North. In recent decades, the South has moved increasingly into the Republican camp, a trend especially strong during presidential elections and among white Protestant fundamentalists.

From a more general perspective, rural areas everywhere tend toward social and political conservatism. The reasons for this are complex; it may have something to do with the traditionalism associated with longtime, stable communities, along with a sense, developed from years of working on the land, that permanence and stability are the most desirable patterns of life. For whatever reason, conservatives and Republicans are stronger than average in smaller communities, in rural areas, and increasingly in the South (except among minorities). In contrast, one is much more likely to find liberal voters and Democrats in the urban areas of America, especially outside the South. In suburban areas, the two parties are closely matched and compete intensely for the moderate, middle-class vote.

Gender

Few forces shape one's world outlook as powerfully as gender. It should surprise no one that men and women differ in the way they see the world. That difference carries over into politics. Of all the trends in American public opinion, few are more striking than the consistent differences that pollsters find in the political opinions of men and women. In a pattern that has come to be known as the **gender gap,** women have consistently been more supportive of

"THIS POLL SHOWS THAT 50% OF AMERICANS ARE IN A BAD MOOD."

Table 9.1
The Gender Gap: Issue Differences between Men and Women

	MEN	WOMEN
Opposed to the death penalty	17%	27%
Favor stricter gun control laws	61	77
Would allow gays in the military	47	68
Support increased spending for government services	46	63
Favor more spending on Social Security	42	50
Support the use of government to reduce income differences among various groups in society	51	66

Sources: Davis, James A., and Tom W. Smith. GENERAL SOCIAL SURVEYS, 1972–1993: [CUMULATIVE FILE] [Computer file]. Chicago, IL: National Opinion Research Center [producer], 1993. Ann Arbor, MI: Inter-university Consortium for Political and Social Research [distributor], 1994; and Miller, Warren E., Donald R. Kinder, Steven J. Rosenstone, and the National Election Studies. AMERICAN NATIONAL ELECTION STUDY, 1992: PRE- AND POST-ELECTION SURVEY [ENHANCED WITH 1990 AND 1991 DATA] [Computer file]. Conducted by University of Michigan, Center for Political Studies. ICPSR ed. Ann Arbor, MI: University of Michigan, Center for Political Studies/Inter-university Consortium for Political and Social Research [producers], 1993. Ann Arbor, MI: Inter-university Consortium for Political and Social Research [distributor], 1993.

so-called compassion issues like integration and social-welfare programs than have men. Compared with men, women "are more supportive of arms control and peaceful foreign relations; they are more likely to oppose weapons build-ups or the use of force. They much more frequently favor gun control and oppose capital punishment."[9] Men, in contrast, are more likely than women to support military, police, and other sources of government force. In most cases, men take the tougher, more conservative stands. For instance, men are more likely than women to oppose environmental and consumer protection; busing and other forms of desegregation; and most programs to aid the sick, the unemployed, the poor, and ethnic minorities. Table 9.1 shows how the opinions of men and women vary significantly on certain issues.

The ultimate difference between men and women shows up at election time. Where candidates or parties show clear differences on these salient issues of force and compassion, women vote, on average, from four to eight percentage points further "left," that is, for the more liberal position, candidate, or party (usually the Democrats). Thus, in the 1980 election between President Jimmy Carter and challenger Ronald Reagan, men voted strongly for Reagan, whereas women split their vote almost evenly. Indeed, the perception that Reagan was wildly popular is based largely on his enthusiastic backing by one key group in American society: white men. Women were frequently divided in their feelings about Reagan, and black men were clearly hostile. This gender gap continues to show itself in presidential elections: About 45 percent of women supported Bill Clinton in 1992, for instance, compared with 40 percent of male voters.

On some issues, however, men and women hold similar views. One finds *almost* no difference at all in their views on abortion. Interestingly, where male and female opinions do begin to converge, the direction of change follows the prevailing opinion preferences of *women* rather than men. This has been the case on issues ranging from environmental protection to defense spending. For various reasons, men have become more supportive of what had historically been a "female" position. These findings may point to women's increasing political clout.

Now that we have explored where our opinions come from, let us look at what some of those opinions are.

AMERICAN POLITICAL CULTURE

Scholars have pored over a huge amount of data on public opinion and built up a picture of the American public's perspectives, or its political culture. They have discovered that American political culture is shaped by three key variables: core values, political ideology, and culture and lifestyle.

Core Values

At the deepest level, Americans are remarkably homogeneous. Surveys reveal a broad consensus on the core issues and ideals of government: individual liberty, political equality, and the rule of law. These values ensure the stability of the political system. Support for them is rock solid, in sharp contrast to the vacillating winds of change evident on everyday political issues. The genius of the Constitution rests in its embodiment of these core ideals. The founders, recognizing that the Constitution must elicit strong support, wrote these central values into the framework of that document. Those three basic principles and the presence of republican government have been held in high esteem by generations of Americans who sought to approach the democratic ideal.

Perhaps the leading American value is liberty. Central to the function of American government is the protection of basic individual rights that ensure freedom. Americans can, in theory, speak and act as they wish. These rights are legally guaranteed by the constitutional clauses stressing freedom of speech, assembly, and religion. Liberty is also central to the American economic system. Americans overwhelmingly support the concept of a free enterprise, capitalistic economy.

The American belief in equality represents another key American value. Americans place enormous stress on the ideas of *political* equality and formal political rights, seeking to guarantee equal access to the political system, universal voting rights, and equality under the law. Americans do not particularly support economic equality, however, especially if defined as a guarantee of equal economic outcomes. They do, however, support equality of another kind, namely, *equality of opportunity*. Americans are even willing to use government toward this goal—to level the playing field, so to speak. Americans want government to guarantee the existence of economic opportunities and to ensure that economic activity is free from coercion. They definitely do not want government to guarantee that economic outcomes will be the same for all.

Public support for the Constitution and the democratic institutions it created represents another core American value, although support for this ideal may be weakening. Part of this decrease in confidence derives from a paradox of this era: Americans expect government to provide increasing services in an age of decreasing resources. Americans want lower taxes, and blame government for their high tax bills—while still complaining about poor government

The Ku Klux Klan, or KKK, is a racist white-supremacist group with a long history in the United States, consisting largely of terrorism against minorities (African Americans in particular). Lynchings and cross-burnings are the hallmark of the KKK, along with white robes and hoods. Often, entire families, including the youngest members, attend Klan rallies. The Klan illustrates an extreme form of intolerance in the United States, and a majority of Americans reject its views.

service. The one government agency insulated from the public's increasing political negativism is the least democratic of all American institutions: the U.S. Supreme Court. Continued respect for that institution may illustrate the value we place on the concept of rule of law.

AMERICANS AND INTOLERANCE   Is tolerance a core American value? Many Americans believe it is, yet the evidence regarding how open Americans are to a wide range of political viewpoints is mixed. As far back as 1835, Tocqueville was writing, "I know of no country in which there is so little independence of mind and real freedom of discussion as in America."[10] Since before the Revolution, American political thinkers, and European counterparts like Tocqueville, feared the "tyranny of the majority." They worried that the "inflamed passions" of the majority might sweep away the opinions—and so the fragile liberty—of the minority, thus threatening the very core of American democracy.

How valid were the fears of the framers? Public-opinion data on intolerance give some credence to anxieties about majority tyranny. Statistically, Americans remain among the least tolerant of all people now living in industrialized democratic societies; that is, many Americans are still reluctant to allow the same liberties and opportunities that they enjoy—and that are protected by government institutions—to be enjoyed by those with whom they disagree or whom they simply do not like. Racism, homophobia, gender discrimination, and fear of foreigners are still powerful forces in American culture. And many Americans still feel reluctant or even afraid to speak out against prevailing majority opinion. How dangerous is this pattern of conformity and intolerance?

Political scientists studying the consequences of cultural conformity argue that intolerance in America constrains "the freedom available to ordinary citizens."[11] Studies have found, for instance, that blacks are much more likely to feel "unfree" than are whites. Compared with Americans as a whole, African Americans feel less comfortable expressing unpopular opinions and more worried about the power of government, including the police.[12]

Similar studies also reveal a "spiral of silence" and a "spiral of intolerance" in America. Individuals sensing the prevailing opinions of those around them echo those opinions to avoid social ostracism.[13] Their silence has a reinforcing effect. An initial reluctance to express opinions counter to the majority continues in an ever-tightening spiral, with the result that many Americans are pressured into conforming to dominant opinion, whether they agree with it or not. Public opinion thus becomes a form of social control.

Intolerance does constitute a serious problem, but it need not remain an inevitable feature of American society. Studies show that as socioeconomic status and level of education increase, so does tolerance for conflicting points of view and alternative lifestyles. Perhaps a "spiral of tolerance" will develop in which family, peers, community, and institutions reinforce rather than suppress tolerance. Over the years, programs such as school busing to break down segregation and affirmative action to ameliorate its negative impact have been employed to allow for the kind of socioeconomic and educational improvement that might, in time, reverse the spiral of intolerance. Teaching about "diversity" and "multiculturalism" (different perspectives and different ways of life) represents another attempt to combat intolerance.

Political Ideology

A second set of deep-seated public attitudes makes up our ideology. Technically, we may describe **political ideology** as a coherent way of viewing politics and government. Ideological perspectives include beliefs about the military, the role of government, the proper relation between government and the economy, the value of social-welfare programs, and the relative importance for society of liberty versus order.

Ideologies of every kind abound. Each one offers a coherent and unified body of ideas that explain the political process and the goals sought by participants within that process. The most common ideologies among politically aware Americans are *liberalism* and *conservatism*. Although these two outlooks alone capture only a part of the diversity of political attitudes of the American public, they do serve to categorize most people in the mainstream; they also offer a useful introduction to political differences at the national level.

These terms are often associated with political party affiliations—Democrats with liberalism, and Republicans with conservatism—but they go well beyond party allegiance. They express a political philosophy, one's view of human nature and the proper role of government in society. On the whole, **liberals** support government intervention to minimize economic inequality (they support progressive taxes, minimum wage laws) but oppose government actions that restrict cultural and social freedoms (they oppose censorship, prayer in school, restrictions on abortion). **Conservatives** take precisely the opposite positions. Some of the primary policy differences between modern American liberals and conservatives are outlined in Table 9.2.

Political observers have long debated whether Americans are becoming more conservative. Many saw the success of Ronald Reagan in 1980 and 1984

Table 9.2
How Liberals and Conservatives Differ on Policy Issues

ISSUE	LIBERAL	CONSERVATIVE
Military spending	Spend less	Spend more
United Nations	Viewed as a positive institution	Viewed with suspicion
Abortion	Support freedom of choice	Support right to life
School prayer	Opposed	Favor
Affirmative action	Favor	Opposed
Government role in the economy	Government should regulate in the public's interest	Free market should prevail
Taxes	Favor progressive tax that seeks more from the wealthiest	Minimize taxes
Social services	Favor government intervention to assist those in need of help	Minimize government services; rely on individual achievement
Crime	Crime is a social problem that emanates from poor education and lack of social services	Those who commit crimes should be severely punished for violating society's rules

The Political Spectrum: Left, Right, and Center

Consider these political terms: *liberal, rightist, moderate, leftist, conservative, centrist.* Do you know what they mean? Which apply to Republicans? To Democrats? To you?

If you can answer these questions, you are among a minority of adult Americans. Although these terms are among the most common in the lexicon of politics, their frequent use by professional politicians and political analysts often leaves average citizens bewildered. They are a kind of insider jargon. Each word represents shorthand or code, standing for a complex set of ideas about political preferences. Because they are central to the political discourse of our time, you must have a clear idea of what these words mean to follow ongoing policy debates.

The original left–right distinction grew out of the French Revolution. After Louis XVI called the Estates General, the moribund French parliament, back into session in 1789, representatives began meeting in a semicircular hall, facing the presiding officer, who stood at an elevated central podium. The more radical or revolutionary delegates began sitting together at the speaker's left-hand side and soon became known as "leftists." Those most opposed to this group (conservatives who wished to preserve the existing order) sat as far from them as possible—on the speaker's right-hand side—and thus became labeled "rightists." That arrangement left moderates to occupy center seats, where they became aptly named "centrists."

These terms retain much of their original meaning. The more radically you wish to change the existing system of power—the more you wish to take power and wealth from the haves and redistribute them to the have-nots—the more "left" you are considered. Rightists prefer to maintain the status quo; the more firmly you want to hold on to it, the more "right" you are. Extreme rightists (reactionaries) wish to go beyond just maintaining the status quo. They hope to roll back any gains previously made by the Left, so that they can reinstate the status quo of an earlier day. Centrists are content with the existing system, though willing to make modest reforms to deal with the specific problems that arise.

American culture has traditionally emphasized a centrist or moderate orientation toward politics. Citizens and politicians alike have been relatively satisfied with the existing state of affairs. Rather than seek radical change, Americans prefer tinker-

as a clear signal that the nation had turned to the right. Scholars have questioned this claim, however, by pointing out that while Reagan enjoyed high personal popularity (he left office with 67 percent approval rating), the policies and ideas that he advocated throughout his presidency met with only limited success and modest public backing. His attempts to cut government, balance the budget, and implement school prayer all failed. On the day Reagan left office, polls showed that while the president remained enormously popular, more and more Americans favored a decrease in military spending and diverting that money to social programs. This outlook directly opposed the one held by Reagan.

Still, Reagan's legacy of tax cuts and reforms, a strong military, and a reinvigoration of support for the presidency stands in contrast to his failures. Some see renewed support for Reagan's conservative ideals in the wave of Republican political victories in the fall of 1994. Ultimately, it is still uncertain whether Americans are turning conservative. Analysis of twenty years of polling data shows that conservatives do (modestly) outnumber liberals in American society, but that the percentages in each category have scarcely changed

ing with social problems in a pragmatic way to produce minor improvements. Americans are suspicious of proposals that would deviate dramatically from the status quo, such as a wholesale redistribution of wealth (a far-left idea) or the elimination of taxes and regulations on big business (a far-right idea).

Still, political activists in the two major American political parties deviate from the centrist position significantly more than does the population as a whole. The Democratic party has generally been associated with liberal stands, indicating support for a moderate redistribution of power. Thus, Democrats usually prefer higher taxes on business and on the wealthy than do Republicans, while advocating that governments use that tax money on an array of programs to help the less advantaged members of society. In contrast, Republicans stand for a more conservative set of ideas, preferring a system that maintains the existing distribution of money, power, and status. They thus oppose government programs (especially taxes and business regulations) that restrict what the economically better off can do with their money and power.

The accompanying figure shows how these common political terms relate to each other on a left–right spectrum of ideological positions. It also shows where core groups within the Democratic and Republican parties can usually be found on the continuum. Bear in mind that this simple diagram represents a rough approximation of reality. Many Democrats are moderate or conservative; many Republicans are moderate or liberal. Furthermore, this left–right spectrum is most useful for understanding positions on *economic* policy. It becomes much more difficult to categorize people and parties on this two-dimensional chart when we include a more complex set of issues relating to social and lifestyle matters.

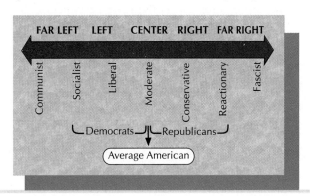

from 1972 to 1992. Furthermore, "middle-of-the-roaders" always constitute the largest set of respondents in any poll.[14] Finally, the very terms *liberal* and *conservative* don't mean a great deal to many Americans, so their voting decisions may not reflect an ideological preference. Indeed, some scholars argue that the real trend of this age is alienation and a general withdrawal from politics.[15]

The terms *liberal* and *conservative,* then, may have little more than symbolic meaning to most Americans. At the political leadership level, these terms work well to define people, but average citizens adopt a variety of political stands from all points on the political spectrum. How does one categorize, for instance, an individual who favors "conservative" positions such as deregulation of business and cuts in the capital gains tax, but who also supports the "liberal" stand of a woman's right to choose an abortion? Many Americans defy easy classification. How can we accurately describe public opinion, then, if ideology proves a weak guide?

Through an examination of culture and lifestyle, recent analyses have tried to explain Americans' seemingly contradictory preferences.

Most Americans are neither extremely liberal nor extremely conservative, but when scores on Senate votes are tabulated, Senator Ted Kennedy, a Massachussets Democrat, emerges as a symbol of liberalism. He wears the label proudly and has urged fellow Democrats not to mimic Republicans, but rather to follow his lead by sticking to the core values of the Democratic party.

Culture and Lifestyle

Culture theory argues that individual preferences "emerge from social interaction in defending or opposing different ways of life."[16] A "way of life" designates a social orientation, a *framework of attitudes* within which individuals develop preferences on the basis of how they relate to others and how they relate to the institutions of power. Recall the discussion of intolerance. Blacks tend to trust government less than whites do and to feel less free to express different opinions. That orientation cannot be explained by reference to "liberal" or "conservative" ideological positions. But in light of the disproportionately high number of African Americans who are arrested and imprisoned, the tendency to distrust and even fear government authority seems hardly surprising. This orientation is neither liberal nor conservative; rather, it reflects an "outlook on life" that might be characterized as suspicion of the law enforcement system and alienation from government in general. This explanation of political attitudes is cultural rather than ideological.

To some political scientists, George Bush's victory over Michael Dukakis in the 1988 presidential election signaled the rise to prominence of "cultural issues and images" as the basis of voter decisions.[17] Americans formulated their voting preferences on the basis of issues such as race, gender, religion, and "cultural lifestyle." In the absence of traditional ideological issues, the Bush campaign successfully captured the patriotic high ground by stressing family values and the sacred nature of the American flag. It also exploited simmering racial intolerance and anxieties about rising crime rates with an effective but much-criticized advertisement chastising Governor Dukakis for furloughing Willie Horton, a dangerous criminal who happened to be African American. Study after study has shown that orientation toward racial issues plays a large role in determining one's likely level of support for Democrats or Republicans. Such lifestyle orientations explain more about the way Americans will behave in politics than do data on ideological preferences.

THE STATE OF AMERICAN PUBLIC OPINION

We now have some idea of what lies at the heart of the average American's perspective on political life. But how interested are citizens in politics? How much do they know about politics and how likely are they to participate? And how do Americans form their opinions on political issues? By turning back to polling data, we can provide answers to these and other questions about the current state of American public opinion.

Political Awareness and Involvement

Knowledgeable insiders have often been appalled at the average citizen's grasp of public affairs. The respected journalist Walter Lippmann once wrote that the average American "does not know for certain what is going on, or who is doing it, or where he is being carried. . . . He lives in a world which he cannot see, does not understand and is unable to direct."[18] And scholar Joseph Schumpeter's view of citizens was even more caustic: "The typical citizen drops down to a lower level of mental performance as soon as he enters the political field. He

Source: © Tom Tomorrow.

argues and analyzes in a way he would readily recognize as infantile within the sphere of his real interests. He becomes a primitive again."[19] Lippmann and Schumpeter join a host of social scientists who have portrayed American voters as apathetic and poorly informed, their opinions unstable or even irrational.

To many, Americans do not seem terribly interested in or well informed about their own government, economy, and history. Polling research from the 1940s and 1950s revealed that Americans did not know very much about important issues and that they tended to confuse the issue positions of various candidates during campaigns. At the height of the Cold War, for instance, many Americans believed that the Soviet Union—the United States' foremost ideological enemy—was in fact part of the North Atlantic Treaty Organization (NATO), the military alliance to which the United States and its allies belonged. In 1984 more than half of Americans, according to one poll, could not make a single correct statement about either major political party, despite both parties having been at the core of American history for over one hundred years.[20] Typically, most Americans cannot even identify their own representatives and senators.

These data show that the American public falls short of the ideal advocated by democratic theorists: a well-informed citizenry. But it should not surprise us that citizens know little about politics. Their interest in politics is minimal as well. No more than a third of the electorate ever claims to be seriously active in electoral politics. Even smaller percentages take part in the political activities that influence those in power: writing an elected official, joining a political group, attending a political rally. And as we'll see in Chapter 11, few vote.

In addition, members of the general public seem to show little interest in the issues most hotly debated by politicians.[21] Over time, such issues as abortion rights, crime and violence, AIDS, racism, the environment, and arms control have dominated the political agenda of elected officials, party leaders, and interest group activists. During the same period, none of these issues was ever ranked by more than 5 percent of the general public as "the most important problem" facing the nation. Even when issues do catch the public's attention,

Recent surveys have found that today's college freshmen are less interested in politics and participate less than any group of freshmen in the last three decades. One of the great paradoxes of democracy is that the information age has produced a relatively indifferent and apathetic group of young people.

citizens don't always perceive them with the same gravity and commitment as do political activists. For example, America's concern with drugs, while not insignificant, skyrocketed briefly after President Bush's declaration of a "war on drugs," only to drop to relatively low levels within a matter of months. The public's interest in economic issues such as the deficit, unemployment, and the general health of the economy is similarly unstable, mirroring the ebbs and flows of the business cycle.

Some scholars counter this image of the ignorant, apathetic citizen by asserting that the American people *are* generally well informed and that their opinions are as sensible as those of their leaders. These scholars see the public as more rational than many observers are willing to concede, arguing that, while many Americans may not know all of the names of the people and places of politics, or the intricate details of every issue of the day, they do recognize and rationally distinguish between the alternatives presented to them, especially when they step into the voting booth.[22] Indeed, surveys show that when presented with a list of names, rather than having to rely on their own recall, most Americans can accurately identify their regional and national leaders.

Nonetheless, scholars continue to debate whether average citizens are politically informed and involved enough to make democracy work. We cannot supply a definitive answer here. Certainly few Americans live up to the ideal image of the citizen who is fully informed, ever alert, and deeply involved in the political process. Still, most citizens may be informed enough to make simple decisions on the small number of options presented to them on election day. Besides, the American system has a number of built-in safeguards in case citizens, for lack of information or other reasons, do not make the best decision. If people elect someone or some party they come to dislike, they can turn the miscreants out at the next election. And no matter who is elected, no position within the U.S. government carries overwhelming power, and all positions are checked by a number of other positions and institutions. Given this system of multiple checks and frequent elections, the American public may well be sufficiently informed to keep the system working and reasonably democratic.

How Are Political Opinions Formed?

If people know little about politics and have little interest in it, how is it that they develop seemingly strong opinions on a variety of political issues? How do they know who to vote for on election day? The answer is surprising. Average citizens develop broad orientations toward their world, including ways of thinking about politics, based on their entire set of life experiences. They then use these broad intellectual frameworks as shortcuts for processing new information.

These intellectual frameworks for evaluating the world, often called **schemas,** act as efficient filters or cues. When people encounter new issues or ideas, they often do not have the time or energy to study them in detail. It is simpler just to fit them into a preexisting perspective. Studies show, for instance, that Americans know nothing about the actual level of spending for foreign aid, nor do they have any idea which countries receive most U.S. foreign aid; nevertheless, they are still convinced that the United States spends too much abroad. That's because they have already developed a general orientation (opposition to government spending and fear or distrust of non-Americans, perhaps) that allows them to take a stand on foreign aid while knowing almost nothing about the subject.

As this example suggests, the facts are often irrelevant in the development of an opinion. Changing a deeply ingrained set of beliefs is psychologically painful. That's why people often avoid facts and resort to preexisting schemas. These schemas allow individuals to sift and categorize new information, so that it can be made "safe"—that is, congruent with an existing framework of attitudes. People ignore or explain away evidence that would undermine their carefully constructed worldviews.

PARTY IDENTIFICATION AS A SCHEMA Among the strongest psychological filters or schemas is political partisanship. When uncertain about the specifics of an issue or the qualifications of a candidate, Americans typically fall back on their identification with one of the two major political parties and follow the "party line" in formulating their opinion. For example, on foreign-policy issues, where Americans are usually not well informed, individuals often express opinions in line with the public stands of their party leaders.

These party ties represent one of the most enduring of all political attitudes held by Americans. However, even this apparently stable indicator of opinion can change over the course of time or under the impact of dramatic events. A broad-based change in partisanship is known as **realignment.** In a period of realignment, large groups of people shift allegiance from one party to another.[23] This occurred in the 1932 election, when many people took their support—and their votes—from the Republican to the Democratic party and Franklin Roosevelt's New Deal programs. The resulting "New Deal coalition" was a strong electoral force that kept Democrats the majority party for decades.

Many Americans hold deeply in-grained beliefs about political is-sues. In some cases, there is no room for compromise, and op-posing camps are unlikely to change the minds of those with whom they disagree. Perhaps the single most emotional issue in American politics is abortion. Those who are prochoice see the issue as one of women's rights and feel strongly about their posi-tion; those who oppose abortion feel strongly as well, viewing abortion as murder. Few issues in American politics are as divisive, although American public opin-ion is still largely prochoice.

It was not until the presidency of Ronald Reagan (1981–89) that Republi-cans began to attract former Democrats as well as independents. This trend was especially pronounced among southern white males. It is often called a "secu-lar" realignment, since it was largely limited to one area of the country.

Partisan identification and general political orientation can also change across generations. Several studies revealed a sharp decline of support for and trust in the institutions and actors of government following the war in Vietnam and the Watergate scandal. It was at this time that pollsters began to track a decline in partisan identification, the rise of political **independents**—people declaring no allegiance to either party—and a growing suspicion of govern-ment in general.

Other studies reveal that children born in the late 1960s were more likely to identify themselves as independent than were their parents. By the time Ronald Reagan left office in 1989, yet another generational trend had surfaced: a strong Republican identification among young Americans. Polls revealed that over half of Americans between the ages of thirteen and seventeen considered themselves Republicans, perhaps a response to the popularity of Reagan, since many of them rejected George Bush in 1992.

Even with periodic realignments and generational change, political parti-sanship remains the most stable indicator of political preference. It is not, of course, the only schema to affect people's political thinking. Others include ideology, ethnic consciousness, and regional identification. And people occasionally change their minds or ignore "the party line" when it comes to specific issues, events, and actors. Nevertheless, to understand how any citizen feels about a host of political matters, begin by learning that individual's parti-san allegiance.

STABILITY AND CHANGE IN PUBLIC OPINION

Though many of our opinions remain stable over long periods of time, others do change. Many scholars believe that people are flighty and changeable; others point to the deep-seated, longlasting nature of our opinions. To understand this difference in perspective, it helps to look at three factors: the intensity of the held opinion, whether or not the opinion is latent, and how salient the issue is.

INTENSITY   Consider the fact that opinions are not all equal. People feel some things more intensely than others, and that affects the strength and durability of opinions. **Intensity** is a measure of the depth of feeling associated with a given opinion. It affects the way people organize their beliefs and express their opinions on a wide variety of issues. For some, the issue of a woman's right to choose an abortion elicits an intense reaction; others are less interested. Still others express their most intense political sentiments for or against gun control. Try visiting a local senior center and suggest cutting social security benefits. On the other hand, try getting just about anyone to consider the propriety of soy-bean subsidies. Some issues elicit more intense reaction than others do.

Issues that provoke intense feelings are often called "hot-button" issues, since they strike a nerve, a "hot button," that can elicit strong reactions and af-fect voting choices. The more intensely an opinion is felt, the more likely it is to endure and to influence policy decisions. Thus, we can assume that attitudes about race (a subject most Americans have intense opinions about) will not change much over the next decade or two. Attitudes about U.S. foreign policy toward Belize, on the other hand, could prove extremely volatile. Few Americans hold intense feelings about Belize, so short-term events (a communist takeover) or the sudden pronouncements of respected American leaders ("Let's help Belize, our democratic neighbor to the south") could dramatically affect how Americans feel about that nation.

LATENCY   Public opinion is not always explicit. **Latent** feelings are "hidden" or unspoken, suggesting the potential for an attitude or behavior, but only when the right circumstances occur. Ross Perot's surprise bid for the presidency in 1992 unleashed an avalanche of latent antigovernment feeling. The American public's longstanding but often dormant distrust of government and politicians—and its admiration for successful entrepreneurs—leapt to the fore following a series of scandals, a sagging economy, and the burgeoning federal budget deficit. Those latent opinions gave Perot the highest third-party vote since Theodore Roosevelt in 1912, even though he withdrew and then re-entered the race.

Latent opinion may also have accounted for the rejection of Democrats in the 1994 congressional elections. Having captured the White House in 1992 while expanding their majorities in the House and Senate, the Democrats bore the brunt of public disaffection over the next two years. They were viewed as the governing party and the party of big government, neither of which was popular by 1994.

Latent attitudes do not always come to the fore, of course. Often they remain unseen and untapped. In 1988, for instance, Americans' latent hostility toward politicians played little role in the presidential race. The two major options represented consummate insiders: Vice President Bush and Governor Dukakis. Neither could easily claim the mantle of "populist outsider," so voters' choices that year rested on attitudes other than their latent antigovernment tendencies.

SALIENCE   Opinions can be intense, latent, or even nonexistent, usually depending on whether a given issue touches one directly or not. **Salience** is the extent to which people see an issue as having a clear impact on their lives. Salient issues stir up interest and participation. With the end of the Cold War, the Bush administration (and later the Clinton administration) began to reevaluate the strategic need for an extensive network of military bases at home and abroad. Consequently, the issue of base closures became prominent in discussions of the federal budget and national security. But this issue does not touch all Americans in the same way. It is most salient to the thousands of military and civilian employees who may lose their livelihood when installations close.

The issue of base closings is also more salient to residents of certain states, such as California, where the local, regional, and state economies rely on the proximity of military bases or lucrative contracts for the production of military hardware. Politicians decrying base closures might get a strong following in California but be ignored in New York City, where the issue lacks salience. To understand public opinion, then, and how that opinion will affect citizen actions, one must know how salient a given issue is to a given population.

HOW CHANGEABLE IS PUBLIC OPINION? Early research findings have suggested that individual political opinions are not firmly held.[24] When respondents are asked the same questions again and again over relatively brief time periods, their responses tend to vary and even to contradict earlier responses. Is this evidence that we tend to offer random, meaningless answers when asked our opinions?

Many scholars see this pattern as proving the "irrationality" of the American voter. However, much of the apparent "irrationality" may actually stem from faulty polling methods. When the same question is asked differently, or when questions are worded vaguely, respondents are more likely to change their answers. This is not so much evidence of "irrationality" as an indication that people are trying to make the best sense of what they are asked, even when the questions are difficult to understand. On the other hand, when researchers phrase questions so that they contain the information necessary to formulate firm opinions, results show that individuals actually do have stable, "rational" opinions. While Americans may not be particularly intimate with political specifics, they nonetheless harbor enduring and meaningful political beliefs. It is up to the pollster to find the best way to elicit these opinions.

Yet we do know that people's opinions sometimes change. As incomes rise, so does support for shorter work weeks, higher minimum wages, and increasing expenditure for workplace safety and environmental protection.[25] As more women have joined the workforce, there have been more calls for women's rights. And awareness of rising crime produces a demand for tougher laws and more police officers in the street. Changing circumstances trigger corresponding change in public opinion. Sudden events can also cause a change in opinions. In time of war Americans are likely to feel more "patriotic," to "rally around the flag" and the president; they are also likely to lower their levels of criticism of the government and national leadership.

The media's portrayal of events and actors can significantly influence public opinion. One foreign-policy analyst remarked that the media may not tell people what to think, but they do tell them what to think about.[26] In other words, the media sets the political agenda. When people see repeated references to specific events or personalities, these events become more important to their lives—more salient—and people begin to formulate specific opinions about them.[27]

The case of Somalia illustrates these points well. The United States sent troops to that country in December 1992, after television screens bombarded viewers with heart-rendering images of starving children. The United States withdrew those same troops a few months later after scenes of American soldiers' deaths and the brutal desecration of one soldier's corpse. In both cases, it would seem, dramatic television images molded public opinion and caused it to produce an almost instant foreign-policy reaction.

Although it appears that Americans respond in an almost knee-jerk fashion to appeals from popular figures or to images presented in the media, the malleability of public opinion should not be overestimated. On many issues Americans maintain a deep-seated set of attitudes that they don't particularly want to change, making them a "tough sell" when leaders solicit approval for actions that are not supported by the public.

Despite heart-rending scenes of suffering and destruction in Sarajevo, the American public opposed getting directly involved in the brutal conflict in what was formerly Yugoslavia. While most Americans are sympathetic to human suffering and to the sort of mounting death tolls that require converting sports arenas into cemeteries (the cemetery shown here is near the old Olympic Stadium in Sarajevo), it remains extremely difficult to garner overwhelming public-opinion majorities in favor of military intervention.

FROM PUBLIC OPINION TO PUBLIC POLICY

Public opinion is a crucial element in the political process. It can dramatically affect both the policies of government and government's legitimacy in the mind of the people. After all, the ultimate test for a democracy comes down to this: Do government actions, over the long run, reflect what citizens want?

How well has the U.S. government reflected its people's will over the last few decades? Has the United States approached democracy in the sense that government is doing what Americans want it to be doing? There are no easy answers to these questions. Clearly, American government policy does not always reflect popular desires—as we suggested early in this chapter. But a perfect reflection of public desires surely lies beyond the capability of any government. Some aspects of the public will are simply unrealistic ("more services, lower taxes!"). Others contradict the spirit of the Constitution and are opposed by most political actors; for example, a constitutional amendment allowing school prayer in public schools has been widely popular but until recently opposed by most decision makers.

To illustrate the degree to which government policy reflects the public will, see Table 9.3, which shows that a majority of the populace wants spending on all but one of these various social programs to stay the same or increase—and that is exactly what happens. Over the years, the programs listed here have remained in place, and many have seen their funding increased. On the other hand, the one program that the public is eager to cut (welfare) is in fact being cut. It is also being reformed in a number of ways at both federal and state levels. In other words, government is responding, in democratic fashion, to the popular will.

On any number of issues we also find government policies reasonably close to the general direction of public opinion. The United States has been an activist world power *with,* not in opposition to, the will of the American

The working of the popular will . . . has always called for explanation . . . what Sir Robert Peel called "that great compound of folly, weakness, prejudice, wrong feeling, right feeling, obstinacy and newspaper paragraphs which is called public opinion." Others have concluded that since out of drift and incoherence, settled aims do appear, there must be a mysterious contrivance at work somewhere over and above the inhabitants of a nation. They invoke a collective soul, a national mind, a spirit of the age which imposes order upon random opinion.

—Walter Lippmann,
Public Opinion, 1922

Only when AIDS activists made their voices heard by publicizing the AIDS crisis did the American public begin to recognize that something needed to be done. As a result, the government began funding research for a cure. But the battle in the public-opinion arena has hardly been won. Until a broad segment of Americans comes to see the AIDS crisis as a broad public-health issue, not just a problem for the gay community, research funding is likely to lag behind that for other health issues.

people. Laws and policies designed to ensure gender equality have gradually been implemented. as public attitudes shifted to favor them. Tough crime laws have increased in response to growing demands on government officials to "do something" about alarming crime rates. But as with school prayer, public desires are thwarted on occasion.

Keep in mind, too, that it takes time for an emerging public opinion to become government policy. On the whole, however, if a significant majority of the American people indicate over time that they believe government should act in a particular manner, the chances are good to excellent that government will accede to those wishes. For that reason, Americans remain loyal to their democratic political system

PUBLIC OPINION AND APPROACHING DEMOCRACY

Public opinion is the keystone of democracy. No government can claim to be the legitimate voice of a people, unless public opinion plays an integral role in the choice of political leaders and the development of public policy. Thus, the gathering of information about public opinion becomes a vital task for a democracy. Using sophisticated polling techniques, survey analysts are able to provide a relatively accurate snapshot of what Americans think and feel about specific issues, events, and candidates.

What conclusions can we draw about our "snapshot" of American public opinion? Recent evidence reveals some disturbing trends. During 1992 the Gallup organization conducted a series of polls to find out how Americans felt about the economy, race relations, and the American system. In the first week of January 1992, only 12 percent of surveyed Americans felt that the economy was in "good" condition; 46 percent thought it was only "fair," while 41 percent thought it was "poor."[28]

In the meantime the percentage of Americans expressing satisfaction with "the way democracy is working in this country" dropped from 48 to 36 percent, while nearly six in ten Americans said they were *dissatisfied* with American democracy. More significantly, nearly three out of every four *nonwhite* Americans felt dissatisfied with American democracy, compared with under 60 percent of white Americans. And for those who made less money—as measured by annual income—dissatisfaction with American democracy increased; while only about half of Americans making more than fifty thousand dollars annually felt dissatisfied, nearly seven in ten Americans making less than twenty thousand dollars expressed similar dissatisfaction.[29]

Of course, these attitudes, reflecting the economic downturn of the early 1990s, are not cause for serious alarm if, as one expects, the national economy strengthens. Americans' optimism and faith in the system have always increased during good times. For instance, by October 1994, the percentage of Americans claiming to be "satisfied with the way democracy is working in this country" had rebounded to 50 percent, just slightly more than the 48 percent who consider themselves "dissatisfied."[30] A healthy economy, it would appear, breeds contentment with the basic institutions of government.

A more disturbing trend for the political future may lie in the continued polarization over the issue of race. In a typical poll finding, a June 1991 survey revealed that only 29 percent of white Americans believed that "the quality of

Table 9.3
Opinions on Selected Federal Welfare Programs, 1992–93

SHOULD SPENDING INCREASE, DECREASE, OR STAY THE SAME FOR	INCREASE	STAY THE SAME	DECREASE
Social Security	46%	46%	8%
Improving and protecting health	74	18	8
Improving educational system	69	25	6
Welfare	17	26	57
Assistance to the poor	65	23	12
Protecting the environment	59	32	9
Food stamps	17	53	30
Aid to college students	61	31	8
Aid to homeless	73	21	6
Research on AIDS	62	30	7

Sources: Davis, James A., and Tom W. Smith. GENERAL SOCIAL SURVEYS, 1972–1993: [CUMULATIVE FILE] [Computer file]. Chicago, IL: National Opinion Research Center [producer], 1993. Ann Arbor, MI: Inter-university Consortium for Political and Social Research [distributor], 1994; and Miller, Warren E., Donald R. Kinder, Steven J. Rosenstone, and the National Election Studies. AMERICAN NATIONAL ELECTION STUDY, 1992: PRE- AND POST-ELECTION SURVEY [ENHANCED WITH 1990 AND 1991 DATA] [Computer file]. Conducted by University of Michigan, Center for Political Studies. ICPSR ed. Ann Arbor, MI: University of Michigan, Center for Political Studies/Inter-university Consortium for Political and Social Research [producers], 1993. Ann Arbor, MI: Inter-university Consortium for Political and Social Research [distributor], 1993.

life of blacks" had actually gotten worse over the preceding ten years; in stark contrast, nearly six in ten blacks felt that the quality of life for blacks was getting worse. Indeed, only 15 percent of black respondents felt that things had improved, compared with 37 percent of white Americans. In the same survey, while 55 percent of white respondents said they believed that "most white people want to see blacks get a better break," fewer than a third of black respondents agreed. Indeed, a strong minority of blacks (23 percent) believed that white Americans wanted to keep blacks from advancing. Only about one in ten white Americans said they believed this.

Despite evidence of this sort, we prefer to end on a note of cautious optimism. One must, after all, see the American public, not in terms of some impossible-to-achieve ideal, but in perspective within the real world. Political scientists Sidney Verba and Norman Nie point out that "levels of political activity in the United States (with the exception of voter turnout) are quite high when compared with rates in other industrial societies."[31] And unlike any other people, Americans have struggled for two hundred years to operate free institutions that allow for widespread public input into the policymaking process.

While not all Americans are politically active and informed, all have the *opportunity* to be, and millions do take advantage of that opportunity. Leaders are continually made aware of what citizens are thinking through any number of devices ranging from the telephone and the public meeting through the fax machine and E-mail, but they are particularly well informed about voter desires through a constant barrage of scientific public-opinion polls and a never-ending series of popular elections. Knowledgeable about what citizens want, leaders are likely to heed the public's wishes, a result that is central to any idea of democracy.

Americans, then, may not represent the ideal public, but they do at least represent an *adequate* public. They are sufficiently informed and participatory to keep leaders in touch with their desires, sufficiently open and tolerant to live together peacefully within a diverse and complex culture. We should never be satisfied with the current state of public opinion, but neither should we be blind to the American public's achievement in forging and maintaining the model for the world's mass democracies.

SUMMARY

1. Public opinion is the collective expression of attitudes about the prominent issues and actors of the day. Discovering and publicizing the public's opinion has become a key political activity in modern democracies.

2. Political polling began in the mid 1800s with informal straw polls. These failed to obtain a representative sample of the population, which must be chosen through random sampling. In a random sample, every member of the population must have an equal chance of appearing in the sample. Efforts must be made to avoid sampling bias, in which particular subsets of the population are over- or underrepresented in the sample.

3. Political socialization refers to the process by which we learn about the world of politics and develop our political beliefs. It begins early in childhood, starting with the family. Children tend to adopt their parents' party loyalties and, to some extent, their political ideology. Political socialization continues in school, where children learn about citizenship, and in college, where students may modify their political ideology. Other important sources of political socialization are peers and the mass media.

4. Numerous social variables influence the formation of opinions. They include social class as represented by income and educational level, race and ethnicity, religious differences, region and place of residence, and gender.

5. The leading core values of Americans are liberty and equality. Although Americans generally are not troubled by economic inequality, they do support equality of opportunity. Another important value is rule by law. Americans are much less tolerant than citizens of other industrialized democratic societies; intolerance is ex-

pressed in the form of racism, homophobia, gender discrimination, and fear of foreigners.

6. The most common ideologies among politically aware Americans are liberalism and conservatism. In general, liberals support government intervention to minimize economic inequality but oppose government actions that restrict cultural and social freedoms; conservatives take the opposite positions.

7. Culture theory argues that culture and lifestyle create a framework of attitudes within which individuals develop preferences. Lifestyle orientations explain more about political behavior than do ideological preferences.

8. Political opinions appear to be based on schemas—broad orientations toward the world based on previous life experiences. Schemas serve as cues for judging new issues or ideas. Among the strongest schemas is political partisanship. Even with periodic realignments and generational change, political partisanship remains the most stable indicator of political preference.

9. Intensity is a measure of the depth of feeling associated with a given opinion; issues that provoke intense feeling are often called "hot-button" issues. In contrast, latent feelings are unspoken, suggesting the potential for an attitude under the right circumstances. Whether an opinion is intense, latent, or nonexistent depends on the salience of the issue, that is, the extent to which people see it as having a clear impact on their lives.

10. The media's portrayal of events and actors can significantly influence public opinion. The media set the political agenda and influence opinions about who is to blame for various political events.

KEY TERMS

public opinion
straw poll
representative sample
margin of error
random sample
sampling bias
political socialization

generational effect
gender gap
political ideology
liberal
conservative
culture theory
schemas

realignment
independent
intensity
latency
salience

SUGGESTED READINGS

- Asher, Herbert. *Polling and the Public*. Washington, D.C.: Congressional Quarterly Press, 1988. Using contemporary example, this book helps make sense of the meaning and methods of public-opinion research.

- Brehm, John. *The Phantom Respondents: Opinion Surveys and Political Representation*. Ann Arbor: University of Michigan Press, 1993. A study of groups who do not participate in public-opinion surveys and the impact this can have on the results of polls.

- Erikson, Robert S., Norman R. Luttbeg, and Kent L. Tedin. *American Public Opinion: Its Origins, Content, and Impact*, 4th ed. New York: Macmillan, 1991. A comprehensive overview of the major aspects of American public opinion, including opinion formation, opinion distribution within society, and the influence of public opinion on public policy.

- Ginsberg, Benjamin. *The Captive Public: How Mass Opinion Promotes State Power*. New York: Basic Books, 1986.

An examination of the thesis that as it becomes a more prominent force in American politics, public opinion actually enhances the power of American government over its citizens.

- Rubenstein, Sondra Miller. *Surveying Public Opinion*. Students who wish to explore the topic of public opinion in depth might begin with this excellent introductory text.

- Page, Benjamin I., and Robert Y. Shapiro. *The Rational Public: Fifty Years of Trends in America's Policy Preferences*. Chicago: University of Chicago Press, 1992. Challenges the assumption that American public opinion is "irrational" by analyzing data revealing relatively steady public preferences over time, changing only under logical circumstances.

- Stimson, James A. *Public Opinion in America*. Boulder: Westview Press, 1991. A major study of public-opinion research and its link with major issues in American politics.

POLITICAL PARTIES

CHAPTER OUTLINE

CASE STUDY: THE FREEDOM
   DEMOCRATS
INTRODUCTION: POLITICAL PARTIES
   AND DEMOCRACY
DEFINING PARTY BY FUNCTION
A BRIEF HISTORY OF THE AMERICAN
   PARTY SYSTEM
WHY A TWO-PARTY SYSTEM?

MINOR PARTIES
PARTY ORGANIZATION
NOMINATING A PRESIDENT: PARTIES
   AND ELECTIONS
THE PARTY IN GOVERNMENT
POLITICAL PARTIES AND APPROACHING
   DEMOCRACY

The 1964 Democratic National Convention nominated incumbent president Lyndon Johnson as its presidential candidate, and he went on to win in a landslide election against Republican Barry Goldwater. Yet all was not calm in the months prior to the convention. Ten days before that meeting, five southern governors met to discuss what they saw as an urgent crisis, the imminent appearance at the convention of sixty-eight delegates from the Mississippi Freedom Democratic party. Considered "radicals," these delegates struck fear into the hearts of party elders hoping for a calm, unifying convention.

The Freedom Democrats

The Freedom Democrats, an organization of blacks and white civil rights workers, had been forged in the violence, drama, and hope of the long summer of 1964. In those months white and black volunteers from around the nation converged on the South to assist local civil rights workers in registering black Americans at the polls and helping them stand up for their legal rights—often against the staunch resistance of local authorities. It was the culmination of a decade of civil rights struggle inaugurated in 1954 with Brown v. Board of Education. The Freedom Democratic party, which grew out of this searing experience, demanded recognition as the official delegation from Mississippi to the Democratic Convention and denounced as illegitimate the official slate of delegates—white, conservative party regulars elected under rules excluding most blacks.[1]

The demands of the Freedom Democrats posed a serious political dilemma for the national Democratic party. To refuse the Freedom Democrats a place at the convention was to make a symbolic mockery of the historic progression of civil rights and racial justice that were supposedly hallmarks of American society. That decision would also cost the Democrats in practical terms, since the post–New Deal party depended heavily on strong support at the ballot box from African Americans. Still, to seat this illegal delegation could set an unhealthy precedent, one that might destroy stability and order within the party. It could open the door to threats and blackmail from a range of extralegal groups, all operating under the banner of some high-blown moral cause. Better take a stand for tradition and legality, no matter how worthy the Freedom Democrats' case, thought many Democratic leaders.

This conflict between outsiders and insiders would continue to wrack the Democratic party for years. But a short-term compromise in 1964 allowed two of the Freedom Democrats to sit as "delegates at large." It also required that the regular (white-only) Mississippi delegation sit only if it "pledged allegiance" to the Johnson/Humphrey ticket, that is, one committed to a strong civil rights program. Democratic party leaders declared that no delegations could be seated at subsequent conventions if they came from states where the party-nominating process "deprived citizens of the right to vote by reason of their race or color."

But this compromise merely forestalled the inevitable. In 1968, the fires of democracy ignited by the Freedom Democrats virtually consumed the Democratic convention in Chicago. Democratic party members battled each other with words on the convention floor, while thousands of activists clashed physically with police on the streets. As in 1964, the main lines of disagreement concerned both policies and procedure. Old-line party regulars stood for the moderate status quo on social issues and supported their Democratic president's policies in Vietnam.

Liberals and radicals in the party sought to push harder on civil rights and opposed the war in Vietnam. Procedurally, the liberal wing of the party saw itself shut out of power through outmoded, nondemocratic rules of an earlier era, rules favoring control by a conservative leadership—the much-hated "party bosses." Hence, they fought to open up the party, to "democratize" it. Naturally, the older, conservative factions fought just as hard to maintain the procedures that had led them to longtime party dominance.

Eventually, liberal activists carried the day. In the next decade, the party underwent a wave of democratization that transformed it, and the political landscape, forever. The party's long-established pattern of control by a conservative leadership of party bosses was shattered and replaced with reforms that produced a more egalitarian party.

Similar reforms would spread to the Republican party as well. Their combined effect was to broaden the base of opportunity for average citizens to participate in the democratic process. The era of party reform, begun in 1964 with the demands of the Freedom Democrats, allowed ordi-nary Americans to accelerate their approach to the democratic ideal. Party politics in the United States would never be the same again. [1] ✠

"If the Freedom Democratic Party is not seated now, I question America," proclaimed Fannie Lou Hamer. The epic convention battle over the seating of the all-white Mississippi delegation helped open the door to a more diverse set of nominating rules for the Democratic Party in its approach to democracy.

INTRODUCTION: POLITICAL PARTIES AND DEMOCRACY

Political parties lie at the heart of democracy, representing the crucial link between what citizens want and what government does.[2] That's why parties are trying continually to change, adapt, and adjust to the popular forces of their time. They want to stay in touch with the voters—those people from whom they derive support and power—so that they can gain control of government and the policymaking process.

The experience of the Freedom Democrats illustrates the pluralistic nature and adaptability of American parties. Although previously excluded from politics, this group worked through the party system to enter politics, make their voices heard, and gain some of their ends without resorting to the violent measures characteristic of groups who have no legal chance to participate freely and promote their aims. These attempts to open up the party gave the Freedom Democrats and those who followed access to power. Competitive and democratic political parties allow the peaceful entry into politics of a wide range of groups that might otherwise have to turn to illegitimate measures to gain their ends.

Political parties are a relatively new phenomenon, nonexistent up until two or three hundred years ago. There were no parties in Napoleon's day. Parties didn't vie for power under Henry VIII. Charlemagne needed no party nomination before heading the Holy Roman Empire. The reason why parties played little role in history is simple. The general public played little role in the political process. For most of human history politics was a game for elites. It consisted of struggles for power among a small inner circle of leaders, people who were trying to become rulers or seeking to curry favor with whoever did. The need for broad-based political parties arose with attempts to implement *political equality* in the eighteenth century, leading to an expansion in the number of people participating in the governing process. Parties became helpful in organizing the large number of participants then organized in legislative factions and helped to make effective their attempts to seek power and influence.

Political parties, then, are nongovernmental institutions that organize and give direction to mass political desires. They bring people together—people who think alike or who have common interests—and help them work toward common goals. The clearest goal of any political group is power, power to control government and thus bring about one's policy preferences. In an age of mass participation, power goes to those elites who can connect with the mass. Today, the Democratic and Republican parties are having trouble making that connection. Ross Perot's United We Stand America has tried to fill the void by making the two major political parties more responsive. Political parties are massive, complex institutions, incorporating large numbers of citizens into the political process; by their very nature, parties are forces of democratization.

In this chapter we'll look more closely at party functions as well as at the history, development, role, and future of American political parties.

"I have no personal agenda. My goal is to get them to do it, to educate voters and hope both parties repent and be reborn. But getting reborn takes a little time. They've got to deliver."

—Ross Perot

DEFINING PARTY BY FUNCTION

The governing institutions of the United States were designed to fragment and decentralize power, and they have succeeded very well at that task. The only institutions that work to pull people together—that exert a coherent, unified perspective on public affairs, that attempt to govern in a reasonably cohesive manner—are the United States' two major political parties.[3] The functions they perform within American society are many, varied, and crucial for the health of a democracy.

PARTIES ORGANIZE THE ELECTION PROCESS   A party's most basic role is to nominate candidates and win elections.[4] True, citizens need not belong to a political party to run for office, but to win high elective office, one must, with few exceptions, belong to one of the two major American political parties. Each president since 1853 has been either a Democrat or a Republican. All 100 senators in 1995 belonged to one of those two parties, as did 434 of 435 representatives and 49 of 50 governors. The stability of this pattern is impressive. For more than a century, the rule for any ambitious politician has been simple: To build a serious career in public life, first join either the Democratic or the Republican party. When dissatisfied, however, an elected politician can always switch parties, as several prominent Democratic members of Congress did in 1995.

Since winning office is crucial to party fortunes, party members spend much time and energy on the election process. Parties select candidates; provide money to local, state and national races; and arrange administrative support at all levels of electoral competition. They begin this work with the vital function of **recruitment.** Parties are continually looking for effective, popular candidates to help them win votes and offices. The search for good candidates never ends. Both major political parties would love to have Colin Powell join their ranks. Moreover, the Democrats will have to find a way to replace such popular senators as Bill Bradley of New Jersey.

In trying to find successful campaigners, parties perform another key function: representation. To win free, democratic elections, they follow a crucial axiom: Find out what voters want and promise to give it to them. No matter who is elected, the winners will attempt to remain committed to the popular programs on which they campaigned.

Following from this logic, parties must act responsibly and legislate the policies they promised. Parties elected under pledges to carry out a specific set of policies can, at the next election, be judged by voters on their achievements. Did they do what they promised? If not, voters can (and often do) reject them from office in favor of their rivals. Knowing punishment of this sort can occur, parties are under serious pressure when writing their platform. Backing away from or even flipflopping on a public commitment may often produce a devastating backlash.

In the long run, this open competition for power serves the desires of the voting public. By recruiting good candidates, representing voter wishes, and being held responsible for their actions in office, the two parties help Americans approach the democratic ideal of government.[5]

PARTIES REPRESENT GROUP INTERESTS   In their struggle for power, parties also speak for and unite different groups and their varied interests. Parties find that it pays to discover what groups want, then work with and through those groups to meet their desires. Thus, Republicans often work closely with business groups to articulate pro-business positions; Democrats do the same with labor union leaders. But parties must do more than speak for one narrow interest if they wish to gain the majorities needed to win public office; they must appeal to a wide range of social groups. In so doing, they learn to meld individual group interests into a larger whole with a coherent philosophy of the policy process.[6]

The need to combine a complex set of interests forces parties to become broad political coalitions. Republicans, for instance, must find a rationale for uniting under their banner the interests of multinational corporations and small businesses, rural evangelical Protestants and prolife Catholics. Democrats too must unite a diverse set of factions that include small-town white southerners, urban black workers, and ethnic white suburbanites. In the process of building a coalition from social subgroups, both parties perform another democratic function: Various groups are integrated into public life and the democratic process. Parties thus help mute the conflicts that might arise if each group had its own separate party and fought the others at every election.

PARTIES SIMPLIFY POLITICAL CHOICE   By bringing together a wide range of groups and creating a coherent platform for voters at election time, parties simplify political choices for voters. Most voters don't study every issue in depth, nor do they know where each candidate stands on every issue. How, then, can they make rational decisions at the ballot box? Parties help by melding a series of complex issues into a broad, general perspective and explaining that perspective in simple, direct ways. By election day, most voters have been educated. They know that their choices are not merely between two individual personalities but between two broadly differing philosophies of governance. Consider what the alternative would be: a ballot listing only a long series of names unconnected to any party and without any hint about what candidates stand for.

PARTIES ORGANIZE GOVERNMENT AND POLICYMAKING   Once elections are over, parties help organize the country's political institutions for governing. Public officials work together as organized members of the winning party. They try to carry out that party's aims and election pledges. The Republican takeover of Congress after the 1994 elections, for example, resulted in a very different set of policies than existed before that election, when Democrats were in the majority. Policy decisions in the United States result from party leaders attempting to govern in the spirit of their party's philosophy. To ensure continued success in these governance efforts, activists and leaders in both parties are always examining current policy options and developing new policy

In the process of building a coalition from different groups, both parties help integrate those groups into public life and the democratic process. In this scene from the Democratic Convention in 1992, women celebrate their accomplishments in the party.

proposals. This work is in both parties' interest. After all, the party that solves political problems wins mass support at the next election.

Now that we know what parties do, let's look at the history of American parties to see how the development of democracy is inextricably tied to the activity of political parties.

A BRIEF HISTORY OF THE AMERICAN PARTY SYSTEM

Many of the framers, beginning with George Washington, feared the development of a political party system. James Madison himself, the strongest influence on the Constitution's final shape, shared this hostility to parties, seeing them as a direct threat to the common good of society because their promotion of specialized interests would subvert the general welfare.

> "If I could not go to heaven but with a party, I would not go there at all."
>
> —Thomas Jefferson

Despite the framers' fears, political parties in the United States developed quickly. By 1800, they were already playing a major role in elections and governance. A party system began to emerge in the United States during a divisive and continuing debate between President Washington's secretary of the treasury, Alexander Hamilton, and his secretary of state, Thomas Jefferson. Hamilton, a supporter of a strong federal government, argued for the development of an industrialized society that would allow the United States to become a wealthy and self-sufficient trading partner in the world economy. The federal government would have a national bank with sufficient power to borrow and spend money, develop international agreements, and control the domestic economy. Conversely, Jefferson wished to see a United States that remained largely rural. He envisioned a nation that retained its republican roots built upon the base of a large working, agrarian class. These two visions for the country divided other leaders and the general public into factions—or "the spirit of party"—that the framers had feared.

In the first few years of the republic, many of the framers denounced party divisions. Hamilton, for instance, declared that a "faction" dominated by Madison and Jefferson was "decidedly hostile to me and my administration, . . . and dangerous to the union, peace and happiness of the country."[7] George Washington warned "in the most solemn manner against the harmful effects of the spirit of party." This spirit, he asserted, demands "uniform vigilance to prevent its bursting into a flame."[8] Washington's cautionary remarks about political parties may seem extreme by today's standards, but he was surely correct when he said that the "spirit of party" was indeed "a fire not to be quenched." While the party system in the United States has undergone a number of changes, the presence of political partisanship has been continuous from his day to ours.

Scholars have identified five different historical eras in which party influence, allegiance, and control have changed. These eras always begin with a **party realignment,** in which significant historical events or national crises cause a shift in fundamental party identification and loyalty. Realignments are the result of a change in public attitudes about the political system and the ability of each party to deliver favorable candidates and policies. They usher in new eras, which tend to be stable and lengthy in duration.[9] Let us examine these major periods in American political life.

The First Party System (1790s–1820s)

The Federalists, followers of Hamilton, and the Republicans, led by Jefferson (also called the Jeffersonian Republicans and later the Democratic Republicans), represented two competing groups. As such, they constituted America's first parties. Today's Democratic party is the direct descendant of Jefferson's party and is the oldest political party in the world. This party originally sided with rural and small-town forces in the previously noted struggle between agrarians and nonagrarians. Its followers resisted the trend toward nationalization of power, industrialization, and the development of urban capitalism. They promoted Jefferson's belief that a nation of small property owners represents the best society, one likely to be virtuous and egalitarian. Since the forces of modern industrial capitalism that undermined the power of small-town America were still weak at that time, Jeffersonian Democrats became the dominant power of the day.

The elections of 1789 and 1792 took place smoothly, since parties had yet to be formally established. On the first Wednesday of February in 1789, the newly established electoral college by unanimous balloting chose George Washington, who belonged to no party, as the nation's first president. Washington was easily reelected in 1792. With his departure from the political scene after his second term, however, the clash of organized political parties began.

The Federalist John Adams, and the Democratic Republican Thomas Jefferson opposed each other in the closely contested elections of 1796 and 1800. Adams barely won the initial contest, while Jefferson triumphed in the rematch and went on to win reelection in 1804. With Jeffersonians clearly dominating, Federalist support rapidly declined and the party soon disappeared altogether. In fact, during the presidencies of James Madison (1809–17) and James Monroe (1817–25), distinctions between the two parties disappeared. This so-called Era of Good Feelings was characterized by a lack of divisive issues and the rapid growth of the American economy.

The election of 1824 was the first in which popular votes were counted and the last to be settled by the House of Representatives. Four regional candidates could produce no electoral college winner (see Table 10.1). To become president, it is not sufficient to win more electoral college votes than anyone else—as Andrew Jackson clearly did in this election. According to the U.S.

Table 10.1
Results of the Presidential Election of 1824

CANDIDATE	POPULAR VOTES		ELECTORAL COLLEGE VOTES	
	NUMBER	**%**	**NUMBER**	**%**
Jackson	155,872	42.2	99	37.9
Adams	105,321	31.9	84	32.2
Crawford	44,282	12.9	41	15.7
Clay	46,587	13.0	37	14.2

Constitution's Twelfth Amendment, a candidate must win a *majority* of those electoral college votes, otherwise the U.S. House of Representatives is delegated to choose from among the top three contenders. The winner (and eventual president) must receive a majority of state delegations, that is, twenty-six out of fifty states in our time, and thirteen of twenty-four states in Jackson's day. Since Jackson won only 37.9 percent of the electoral college vote (more than anyone else, but short of a majority), the election was thrown into the House of Representatives for resolution.

Unpopular in Congress, where he was viewed as a political outsider and demagogue, Jackson's popularity with the public did not help him. Henry Clay, his weakest rival in the election but a power in the House, where he served as Speaker, threw his support behind the second-place candidate, John Quincy Adams. Clay's influence gave Adams his barely needed thirteen states, making him president by the slimmest of margins. In return, Adams named Clay secretary of state. This "deal" came to be widely resented in the nation at large, a fact Jackson exploited as he continued to campaign for president over the next four years. Furthermore, Adams soon proved an unpopular leader. A National Republican who favored major increases in the power of the national government to encourage domestic economic development, he met tremendous opposition in Congress and thereby generated the rebirth of the two-party system.[10]

The Second Party System (1820s–1850s)

Outraged and galvanized by having the election of 1824 "stolen" from them, followers of Jackson organized to take power in the next election. Their grassroots activism, under the energetic leadership of Jackson himself, reenergized the old Jeffersonian party and sent it forth in a modern format, that of the populist Jacksonian Democrats. Formalized by Jackson's presidential victory in 1828, the Jacksonian Democrats sought to revive Jeffersonian principles and return the United States to a more democratic, egalitarian society. The party consisted of an alliance of urban workers, westerners, and southern nonslave holders.

To symbolize this new democratic spirit, Jackson was chosen as a presidential candidate at a *national party convention* in which delegates, chosen by local party members throughout the country, selected a candidate, adopted a statement of party principles, and generated party spirit. This differed from the old system of nomination by *caucus* (also known as King Caucus), a small group of national legislative leaders.

When Jackson sought to dismantle the national bank, business interests joined with slaveholding southerners to form the Whig party. Much like the Hamiltonian Federalists, Whigs supported an active federal government. Their ranks in-cluded senators Henry Clay and Daniel Webster and Illinois lawyer Abraham Lincoln. This was an era of real two-party competition, with each party capturing a significant portion of political offices. The Whigs were particularly successful in winning congressional elections. Between 1836 and 1860 Democrats Martin Van Buren, James K. Polk, Franklin Pierce, and James Buchanan were victorious in presidential elections; however, Whigs William H. Harrison and Zachary Taylor also won, keeping the Whigs competitive. Ultimately, the Civil War and the issues of slavery and the nature of the union would lead to the disintegration of this second party system.

The Third Party System (1850s–1890s)

Slavery was the dominant political issue of the 1850s, and it splintered American society. Supreme Court decisions denying African Americans the rights of citizenship added fuel to the fire, as did congressional debates concerning the spread of slavery into the new western territories. The new Republican party emerged in 1854 as a party devoted to abolishing slavery. Northerners, progressive whites, and many of those settling in the West, along with activists from minor parties like the Liberty and Free Soil parties, came together to form the Republican party.

Lincoln, elected president in 1860 as part of this new political alignment, came to the Republican party from the Whigs. He and other Republican leaders developed policy platforms that stressed issues of moral conscience more than did previous political parties. The Whigs dropped from sight, while the Democratic party, weakened by its connection to the losing Confederate cause, kept a base in the South and Midwest, primarily among agricultural, rural voters. The Republican party dominated national politics until the 1890s by winning six consecutive presidential elections (1860–84). Grover Cleveland, in the very close elections of 1884 and 1892, was the lone Democrat to capture presidential office in this period.

The Fourth Party System (1896–1932)

The era of the late nineteenth and twentieth centuries is frequently characterized as one of party government. During this time, the Democratic and Republican parties became highly developed, well organized, and successful in attracting a loyal body of voters. The nation's huge influx of immigrants helped change the shape of domestic politics, leading to the growth of urban party "machines" and creating long-term alliances between various ethnic groups and political parties.

The election of 1896 did not dramatically change the domination enjoyed by Republicans in capturing the presidency or controlling the House of Representatives. It did, however, result in a long-term realignment of those voters identifying with each party. Republicans consolidated their control of the North and West, while Democrats continued to control the South. In 1893, a depression occurred under Democrat Grover Cleveland. Already the stronger party, Republicans gained even more voters in 1896, benefiting from the discredited economic policies of the Democrats. Hence, the 1896 election in which Republican William McKinley defeated Democrat William Jennings Bryan produced a fundamental shift in each party's constituency.

Only one Democrat, Woodrow Wilson, who served from 1913 to 1921, held the office of president between 1896 and 1932. Economic expansion, industrialization, immigration, and the emerging status of the United States as a world power brought with it great prosperity in the early decades of the twentieth century. However, Republican domination ended abruptly in 1932, as the Great Depression brought the next realignment in party identification and power.[11]

William Jennings Bryan, "the boy orator of the Platte," sought the presidency three times, in 1896, 1900, and 1908. His loss to William McKinley in 1896 ushered in a new period of Republican control of the White House.

The Major American Parties

In the last two hundred years, there have been only five political parties that have achieved and held a position in American politics for any amount of time. Of these five, only the Democrats and the Republicans hold such a position today.

1. *The Federalists.* This was the first American political party, named after its leaders' outspoken defense of the federal Constitution during the ratification process. It had the support of merchants, landowners, and those of wealth and status in the Northeast and the Atlantic states. But it was limited by this narrow base, and fell away before the successes of the next party, the Jeffersonians.

2. *The Jeffersonians.* This was a party of the small farmers, workers, and less wealthy citizens who were opposed to the nationalism of the Federalists and preferred the authority of the states. Its founder was Thomas Jefferson, and like him it espoused many of the ideals of the French Revolution, such as the idea of direct popular self-government. (At times this party was also called the Anti-Federalists, the Republicans, and the Democratic-Republicans.)

3. *The Democrats.* This was the first really broad-based, popular party in the United States. It represented less privileged voters, welcomed new immigrants, and stood up to nativist opposition to immigration; it also opposed national banking and high tariffs. The Democrats grew from the Jacksonian wing of the Jeffersonian party.

4. *The Whigs.* This party had a short life, during which it was the representative of many interests, among them nativism, property, and business and commerce. It had its roots in the old Federalist party,

and was formed in opposition to the strong presidency of Andrew Jackson.

5. *The Republicans.* This party grew out of Northern opposition to slavery and came to power as the Civil War approached. It was the party of the Union, Lincoln, and the freeing of the slaves. From the Whigs it also took on a concern for business and propertied interests.

The figure below shows where each of these parties falls on a historical continuum from 1788 to 1900.

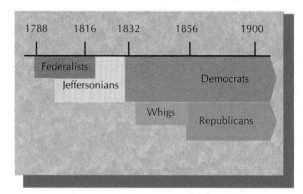

The Five Major American Political Parties
Five political parties have achieved a successful and competitive role in American politics. The Democrats and the Republicans have succeeded in the last century and a half where others have failed.

Source: From Congressional Quarterly, *Guide to Elections,* 2d ed. (Washington, D.C.: Congressional Quarterly, 1985), p. 224.

The Fifth Party System (1932–present)

By the summer of 1932, the Great Depression had left millions without work or economic relief. The incumbent president, Republican Herbert Hoover, did his best to assure a frightened American citizenry that prosperity was forthcoming; people just had to trust his leadership. Hoover clung relentlessly to faith in the gold standard and the need for a balanced budget; there would be no government dole. Meanwhile, New York governor Franklin Delano Roosevelt accepted the Democratic party's nomination for president claiming: "I pledge you, I pledge myself, to a new deal for the American people."

On November 8, 1932, Governor Roosevelt defeated President Hoover. "A frightened people," wrote James David Barber, "given the choice between two touters of confidence, pushed aside the one they knew let them down and went for the one they prayed might not."[12] No Democrat had been elected president since Woodrow Wilson. In carrying forty-two of the forty-eight states, Roosevelt amassed a 472-to-459 electoral college majority and a popular vote margin of 22,809,638 to 15,758,901. To gain this massive victory, he brought together an alliance of Americans that came to be known as the **New Deal coalition.** The key components of this successful amalgam consisted of the urban working class, most members of the newer ethnic groups (especially Irish, Poles, and Italians), African Americans, the bulk of American Catholics and Jews, the poor, southerners, and liberal intellectuals. This broad-based coalition allowed Roosevelt to forge scores of new government programs that increased government assistance and brought him immense popular support. It also brought about a new set of beliefs and attitudes toward government.

Riding a wave of enthusiasm for the New Deal, Democrats went on to dominate national politics between 1932 and 1968. The nation chose only one Republican president during this period: Dwight Eisenhower. Beyond giving Roosevelt four victories, voters also backed Democrats Harry S Truman, John F. Kennedy, and Lyndon B. Johnson in their bids for the White House. Each of Roosevelt's Democratic successors kept the New Deal coalition alive. Johnson (1963–69), in particular, gave renewed impetus to New Deal philosophy by expanding government economic-assistance programs with his "Great Society."[13]

A Sixth Party System?

Since 1968, the Republican party has won five of the last seven presidential elections, yet until 1995 scholars have been reluctant to describe the post-1968 period as another realignment. Although Republican presidents Richard Nixon, Gerald Ford, Ronald Reagan, and George Bush won the presidency, all were unsuccessful in dismantling the New Deal and Great Society programs, which have proven broadly popular. But Democrats retained majority control of the U.S. House of Representatives during a forty-year period: from January 1955 to January 1995. In past realignments, the emerging dominant party has swept to broad election victories in both Congress and the presidency—and in the majority of American states as well. Republicans remained the minority party in the American states throughout the post-1960s era.

There are many signs, however, that partisan strengths are shifting. Something is changing in the American electorate. For example, the percentage of self-identified "slightly conservative" and "conservative" Americans has gradually increased since the early 1970s, rising from about 25 percent in 1973 to 30 percent in 1980 and 35 percent in 1988.[14] Another striking trend over the last twenty years has been the steady increase in the number of young conservatives entering the electorate, a potential boon to Republicans. Furthermore, the number of Democratic voters has been slowly falling for several years, while the

Realignment versus Dealignment

"I'm a New Yorker, a worker, a Catholic, and a Democrat."

"I'm a Kansan, a farmer, a Methodist, and a Republican."

For most of us, our attachment to a political party helps define who we are. It is an emotional attachment that results from personal experiences that induce warm feelings and favorable impressions. Referred to as *party identification,* this attachment may be derived from family traditions, from the party's record of providing benefits to one's community, from approval of the party's policies. It creates a feeling of being close to one party and distant from another.

Once it has been formed, *your* party identification changes slowly. It therefore is the single best predictor of how an individual will vote in the next election. Although voters consider other factors, such as candidates' personalities and the issues of the day, their attachment to a particular party colors their interpretations of political events. Haven't you noticed how the candidates of *your* party are almost always brighter and more articulate than those of the other party? And how similar your party's policy positions are to your own?

This strong party allegiance ensures political stability—most of the time. Year in and year out, people vote roughly the same way, and there are no wild swings of power from one election to the next. But party attachments are not set in concrete. They change in response to changing political circumstances. Usually the change is gradual, but occasionally an especially significant political event results in a major redistribution of party loyalties. The Civil War and the Great Depression were two powerful developments that affected party identification. They produced major *realignments* of party forces. As you've already seen, during the depression the Democrats surged ahead and established a dominant position that would endure for more than four decades.

Trends in Party Identification (%)*

	1988	1989	1990	1991	1992	1993	1994
Republicans	27	33	32	31	28	27	29
Democrats	30	33	33	32	34	34	33
Independents	38	34	30	33	34	34	35

Today, many observers argue that a different and broader phenomenon, *dealignment,* is taking place. As the accompanying table shows, there has been a steady increase in the number of Americans who see themselves as nonaligned, that is, emotionally unattached to either party. Support for the Democrats has been dropping, but voters have not been flocking to the Republican ranks. Instead, growing numbers identify themselves as independent—40 percent in 1992, compared with 22 percent in 1960.

There can be little doubt that the major parties are becoming less firmly anchored in the sentiments of the American people. This decline of party attachment explains the trend toward split-ticket voting, in which an individual votes for candidates of more than one party. Obviously, voters are using other criteria besides a candidate's party affiliation in making their choices.

An interesting implication of these trends is the possibility that independent voters can be mobilized into a "third force." In 1992 Ross Perot showed that an independent candidate can make a serious run for the White House. If the number of independents continues to grow, someone, or some group, may come up with a formula, issue, or platform that will unite enough of these voters to give the other two parties serious competition.

Source: Adapted from Paul R. Abramson, John H. Aldrich, and David W. Rohde, *Change and Continuity in the 1992 Elections,* rev. ed. (Washington, D.C.: Congressional Quarterly Press, 1995). *The table is from The Times Mirror Center for the People and the Press, *The New Political Landscape*, October, 1994, p. 43.

number of independents is rising. A number of prominent Democrats have switched to the Republican party; several others, like New Jersey Senator Bill Bradley, have announced that they will not seek reelection and may even run as a third-party candidate. Ross Perot's United We Stand has grown in size and stature and threatens the security of Democratic and Republican candidates alike. Indeed, polls taken in 1995 show the number of independents rising steadily, with Republicans and Democrats losing traditional supporters.[15] Some kind of realignment is taking place; it seems that the United States has entered an era in which Democrats are no longer the dominant political party.

WHY A TWO-PARTY SYSTEM?

Throughout American history, two parties have been the rule rather than the exception. Yet most democratic nations are characterized by a **multi-party system** in which five to ten, and sometimes even more, parties regularly compete in elections, win seats, and have some chance of gaining power. Why is it that only two parties flourish in the United States? Attempts to answer this question draw on several factors.[16]

Institutional Factors

The most frequent explanation for the emergence and survival of the two-party system is the way the United States elects public officials. Known as the *single-member district electoral system,* it is widely believed to inhibit the development of third parties. In other democratic nations, districts are often, but not always large enough to contain many representatives, and each party elects about as many representatives as its proportion of the vote in that large district. In a ten-member district, for instance, a party obtaining 10 percent of the vote gets one elected legislator. If that party averages 10 percent of the vote across the country, it will end up with 10 percent of the members of the national legislature. Then if it maneuvers sensibly, it may be asked to form part of a governing coalition. The upshot of such a multimember district, or **proportional representation system,** is that small parties can gain seats and power, so there is an incentive for minor parties to form and contest elections.

In the United States, the incentives all favor the two large parties. The entire country is divided into **single-member districts,** and each district seat is awarded to the candidate with the most votes. Small parties, say one that wins 10 percent in every district across the nation, do not get a single seat in the legislature. With that performance, they would lose in each district to one of the two big parties, sure to get more than 10 percent of the vote. Hence, after every election, small parties end up with no seats and no power, and they gradually fade away as supporters grow discouraged. Potential supporters for a third party will simply join one of the two big parties and promote their policy aims within a successful political grouping where those aims have some chance of being implemented.[17]

This system not only prevents the creation of third parties but also inhibits breakaway factions of the two major parties from setting up shop on their own. Disgruntled party subgroups have no incentive to leave and form their own parties, because doing so will lead to political impotence.

"The system is now saying that something must be done, that neither political party is being responsive or is viewed as responsible. . . . The best analogy I can give you is a remote control device: people are clicking off politicians, the president, the speaker, the majority leader. . . . The next channel we may turn to is an independent channel."

—Kenneth M. Duberstein, former chief of staff to President Reagan

Table 10.2
1992 Presidential Election Results: Ohio

CANDIDATE	POPULAR VOTES	% OF TOTAL VOTES
Bill Clinton	1,984,942	40.4
George Bush	1,894,310	38.5
Ross Perot	1,036,426	21.1

Another institutional element favoring two-party competition is the **electoral college.** By its very design, the electoral college puts smaller parties at a disadvantage. The system produces, in effect, fifty-one "winner-take-all" state (plus District of Columbia) contests.[18] Each state is allotted a certain number of electoral college votes, depending on its representation in Congress. Votes for president are then counted by state, and in all but two small states (Maine and Nebraska), whichever candidate comes in first in that state gains *all* of that state's electoral votes—no matter how close the contest and even if the winning candidate falls short of a majority of the ballots cast (for example, see Table 10.2, which shows the 1992 presidential election results in Ohio). Despite Clinton's narrow margin over Bush and despite the fact that he polled barely two-fifths of Ohio voters, he still won all of Ohio's important twenty-one electoral votes, a victory that helped him enormously on his way to the White House.

As these results make clear, there is no consolation prize for finishing second, much less third or fourth, in American politics. A candidate comes in first or gets nothing. For that reason, many voters are reluctant to "throw their vote away" on a candidate outside the mainstream. They tend, in the end, to align with one of the two major parties.

Occasionally, most recently in the case of Ross Perot, a significant portion of the electorate will cast off such inhibitions and risk supporting a "third-party" candidate. But consider the result of Perot's 1992 campaign. Although he captured some twenty million votes—about 19 percent of the total—he did not receive a single vote in the electoral college. And remember that citizen votes do not make a president; only electoral college votes do. It is hardly surprising, then, that Perot-style candidacies have been the exception rather than the rule.

Cultural Factors

Some scholars believe that the American two-party system is built in to prevailing cultural norms and values. They point to the United States' supposed traditions of moderation, deliberation, and compromise. Whereas the French or Italian political cultures—out of which have sprung vigorous multiparty democracies—are often described as volatile and fragmented, American culture is supposedly centrist: devoid of the ideological extremes, class divisions, and group hatreds that produce political fragmentation elsewhere. This theory suggests that with citizens clustering at the center of the spectrum, the United States has no room for a variety of parties. These conditions produce a natural setting for just two parties, each vying for the large constituency of moderate voters.

This cultural explanation remained satisfying for decades, but in recent years scholars have begun to question it.[19] Particularly since the 1960s, American political culture appears to have become fragmented. Bitter struggles over civil rights, Vietnam, women's rights, and abortion have shattered the country's veneer of consensus and may help explain what many see as a weakening in the pattern of stable two-party dominance. In recent years, some of the most volatile issues tearing at the fabric of the two-party system and its stability have been essentially cultural: race, gender, sexuality, and family values.

Party Identification

Another attempt to explain the United States' two-party system centers on electorate psychology. Explanations of this type stress the deep-seated, enduring nature of party attachments. Many voters develop lasting loyalty to a political party, often because that party served their needs on some crucial issue. Thus, Republicans gained the loyalty of millions in the 1860s by standing for national unity and the abolition of slavery. Democrats gained lifelong supporters in the 1930s with their attempts to mitigate the worst aspects of the depression. Furthermore, voters have long memories. They stay faithful to their party for years, even for life, often passing these loyalties on to their children.

This psychological orientation, this long-term propensity to think positively of and vote regularly for a political party, is what political scientists call **party identification.** It does not explain the origins of the United States' two-party system, but it does help explain its persistence. The intense psychological ties that keep party voters faithful ensure both parties of long-term support. These old attachments hamper any new party trying to break through the status quo to gain followers.[20] Figure 10.1 indicates the characteristics of those who identify with each of the major parties. Those with the highest scores hold the most allegiance to the party. Note, however, the clustering of demographic characteristics around the middle.

Ultimately, the explanation for why the United States has only two parties must also include a discussion of the system by which the country finances political campaigns. This is done in Chapter 11. Besides this aspect, two parties are likely to arise because of the centrist tendencies of American political culture, combined with the single-member-district system of voting and the winner-take-all nature of electoral college balloting. Once two parties become dominant, party identification ensures their continued strength among voters. Adaptability to new forces by party activists keeps the parties open to change, so that they co-opt, rather than compete against, potential new rivals. Despite these plausible explanations, however, the complexity of the question, Why two parties?, keeps it a matter of open debate among political experts.

"I belong to no organized party—I am a Democrat."

—Will Rogers

MINOR PARTIES

Despite the power of the two major American parties, **minor** or **third parties** have made their appearance in every decade of American history. Why do they appear, how have they performed, and what do they accomplish? [21]

WHY MINOR PARTIES APPEAR   With most Americans clustering in the middle range of the ideological spectrum, the two major parties take relatively

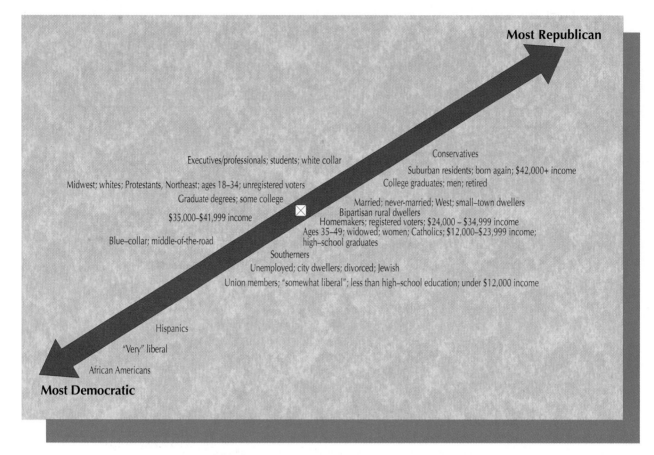

FIGURE 10.1 Party ID

The relationship between party identification and the demographic composition of the electorate is changing. Here, in 1988, Southerners and blue collar workers identified themselves as Democratic. During the 1980s, in particular during the Reagan years, their affiliation with the Democratic party weakened considerably. In 1980 and 1984, Ronald Reagan captured a significant proportion of these weak Democrats who later became known as the "Reagan Democrats."

moderate positions on most controversial policies. Any clear ideological stand far to the right or left of the average voter would alienate a large portion of the potential electorate. Since the major parties aim at winning votes and gaining office, they cast their nets as widely as possible and aim for broad inclusiveness. Both major parties end up focusing on the same central segment of the electorate, but do not necessarily give equal emphasis to the same issues.

In like fashion, the major parties can't aim their appeals too obviously at just one subgroup of the population, be it farmers, union members, gun owners. Since by definition any one social group represents a minority of Americans, any party that becomes identified as that group's champion risks alienating other segments of the population and becoming pigeonholed.

Of course, differences do exist between the parties, but everything is relative. From the point of view of a strong ideologue, a zealous group identifier, or

Go, Italy!

In the spring of 1994 Italian voters shocked themselves and the world by handing power to a flamboyant multimillionaire with no political experience. His name was Silvio Berlusconi, and his message included, among other promises, a pledge to stimulate the economy, provide jobs, cut taxes, and bring honesty to the national government. Sound familiar?

Berlusconi's message was remarkably similar to that of Texas billionaire Ross Perot. The two candidates appealed to the same kinds of voters, and they won similar percentages of the total vote: The Texan received 19 percent of the American vote, while the Italians gave Berlusconi 21 percent.

Despite the similarities, however, there were some dramatic differences. The clearest difference is that Berlusconi had the foresight and aptitude to create his own party and link it to two others in a successful political coalition. He gave his organization the colorful name "Forza Italia," the rallying cry of his soccer team, which translates as "Go, Italy!"

A second major difference lay in the situation faced by the two candidates. Although popular support for the major parties in the United States has been declining, they remain the picture of health compared with the traditional parties in Italy. By the early 1990s a weak economy and rampant political corruption had left most Italian parties with little mass support. The final blow was a series of scandals that erupted in 1992. Over one-third of Italy's national legislators were indicted or jailed, with the result that any support the traditional parties retained was decimated. Berlusconi and other new political forces thus faced little significant opposition.

Why did Berlusconi win while Perot came in third? Structural features of the Italian parliamentary system allowed Berlusconi to parlay 21 percent of the vote into a prime ministership. In a two-party system, a third party needs at least one-third of the vote, and usually a good deal more, to have any chance of winning political office. In a multiparty system like that of Italy, which includes a dozen or more parties, any party that musters even 10 percent of the vote can count on gaining some power, and a 20 percent performance automatically puts the party among the top two or three political forces in the country.

As it turned out, Berlusconi's party topped all the other parties in the 1994 parliamentary election. The number-two party received 20.4 percent of the vote. Thus, Berlusconi rose to the top in his first election because the mathematics of a multiparty system offer a big payoff for even modest electoral success.

To achieve power in a multiparty system, one must have the ability to form alliances and lead coalitions. In this regard Berlusconi's magnetic personality and forceful leadership skills allowed him to gain far more power than his fifth of the vote would indicate. He conducted his campaign not merely as the head of his own party but as the leader of a conservative coalition that included two other large parties. Indeed, his allies turned out to be the third and fourth most successful groups in the election, bringing the coalition a clear parliamentary majority.

Berlusconi and Perot are both independent mavericks who have difficulty working within traditional political patterns. This trait showed itself in 1992 in Perot's inability to join and work within either major party. Berlusconi's wild independence can be seen in his inability to work for long with the leadership of the Italian political elite. Less than a year after his miraculous victory at the polls, his coalition in the Italian parliament collapsed and he was rejected from his job as prime minister.

a single-issue promoter, both parties seem compromised by their willingness to move toward the center and to take a range of perspectives into account as they formulate broad policy positions designed to appeal to a majority of Americans.

This lack of ideological purity and the absence of narrow group promotion directly affects the character and formation of the minor American parties. Third parties are formed when an issue arises of such intensity to some Americans that they just can't be satisfied by the relatively moderate stands on that issue taken by both Democrats and Republicans. They are also formed when some group feels totally ignored and left out of the mainstream political process. The third parties that result from the organization of these interests almost always remain minor. Who today remembers much about the Liberty party, the Greenback party, the Populist party, the Socialist party, or the Progressive party?

MINOR-PARTY PERFORMANCE   Third parties do, on occasion, make waves, usually when an issue or set of issues become joined to a popular or charismatic leader. Under these conditions, some minor-party efforts have done remarkably well. Theodore Roosevelt, a former president, turned in the best performance of any minor party candidate. In 1912, he ran on the Progressive ticket and garnered 27 percent of the popular vote, along with 88 electoral votes (out of 531). Most remarkable about his achievement was placing second in the balloting—ahead of an incumbent president (William Howard Taft).

Another significant minor-party candidacy occurred in 1968, when Alabama's segregationist governor George Wallace, a Southern Democrat, ran as an American Independent. Wallace captured 14 percent of the popular vote and 46 electoral votes. In 1980 a former Republican and member of the House of Representatives, John Anderson, ran as an independent candidate, receiving 7 percent of the popular vote and no electoral votes. Texas billionaire H. Ross Perot stunned many observers when he ran in 1992, without any party affiliation, and, after dropping out and later reentering the race, still won 19 percent of the popular vote. His organization, United We Stand, however, was little more than a label attached to a group of amateur enthusiasts; at that time it was nothing like an organized party. In 1995, Perot's organization held a three-day national convention of independent voters which, once again, raised the possibility of a third part in 1996. Perot supporters are frequently identified as a new "radicalized center" in American politics whom Democratic and Republican party leaders cannot afford to ignore.

Despite these modest successes, third-party candidates have rarely been a significant force in American national elections. They face, as we have seen, the major psychological hurdle of party identification. Since most voters already feel an emotional link to one of the two major parties, voters are rarely eager to wrench themselves away from their traditional voting habits to support a new, little-known group with no governing track record.

Beyond psychology, candidates outside the two-party mainstream face serious procedural obstacles. To be listed on local and state ballots, minor-party candidates must obtain a certain number of signatures that demonstrate a minimal level of support. With few activists and little public recognition, minor parties frequently can't even get on the ballot. At the national level they have enormous difficulty meeting eligibility requirements for federal election campaign funds. They also face a key difficulty in simply making people aware of who they are and what they stand for. To capture national attention, candidates

In 1992, independent candidate and millionaire H. Ross Perot got 19 percent of the popular vote. Members of United We Stand America saw Perot as a straight-talking, no-nonsense, no politics-as-usual candidate who offered a refreshing alternative to the two major parties.

Chapter 10 Political Parties **349**

with little more than local or regional notoriety must court a national press often intent on following only the major candidates. Overall, the barriers to the creation of a successful third party are enormous.[22] United We Stand America is not yet a political party; it is a grass roots public interest group whose goal is to make both political parties more responsive to the American people.

FUNCTIONS OF MINOR PARTIES   Although minor parties rarely attain power in the United States, they do perform important functions in a democracy. In a way, they act as warning beacons to the two major parties. If enough dissatisfaction exists to fuel a third-party movement, both Democrats and Republicans quickly pay close attention. Almost always one and often both parties adopt enough of the third-party's proposals to defuse the grievances the third party represents— and incidentally deflate the chances of that third party ever gaining power.

A prime illustration of this process can be seen in the "radical" platform that Socialist Eugene Debs endorsed in his 1904 campaign for the presidency. It included such "subversive" promises as support for women's right to vote, an eight-hour day for factory workers, and an end to child labor practices. All of these ideas, of course, and many others from the Socialist program of that era, have long since become mainstream concepts, accepted by both major parties and most of the American electorate.

By being the first to champion original ideas that may later become widely endorsed, minor parties perform a major service for the democratic process. But even if their ideas never get adopted, they at least bring open discussion of new proposals, force mainstream groups to rethink and justify the status quo, and give life to key democratic norms, such as free speech and the right of all citizens to organize to promote their interests.

PARTY ORGANIZATION

Despite recent trends toward a strengthening of national party organizations, political parties are still relatively decentralized institutions. The flow of power moves upward—from local to state organizations, and from there to the national committees and conventions. Let's take a brief look at the central elements of party structure.

Parties at the Grassroots

Parties at the grassroots consist of local and state organizations. Party operations begin at the local level. The **local party organization** provides the initial point of entry for those seeking involvement in politics as volunteers, organizers, or candidates. Yet each local party is highly dependent on the level of interest demonstrated by the community. In some places awareness and interest are high. Party faithful eagerly fill slots as precinct chairs and election organizers, volunteer for administrative posts, and even run for slots to participate in state conventions. Where interest is low, party structures remain skeletal, with many posts going unfilled or a few party faithful keeping the organization going.

While linked to the national apparatus, local and state political parties have a great deal of independent power, often more than the national party. Local parties enjoy significantly higher personal interaction with members, are able to base their platforms on significant local issues, and can perform their duties

During the nomination stage, candidates depend on party organization and the efforts of campaign workers who distribute literature and other campaign materials. A well-organized campaign, spearheaded by energetic supporters, is a hallmark of successful party organization.

without seeking huge monetary donations. It is also easier for citizens to become involved at the local level in such activities as donating money or working for a campaign.

Political activists are vital in a democracy; they have an important influence on the party platform and on political decision-makers. Party activists are different from the population at large in that they tend to be wealthier and have higher levels of education. As a result of reforms in the methods the Democratic party uses to select delegates, the party has also encouraged increased activism on the part of women, minorities, and youth. And the Republican party has also opened its doors to these newer activists.[23] So while party activists have different characteristics from the population at large, party reform has resulted in a more demographically representative group.

The fifty **state party organizations** have very different systems. Through their two key roles as organizers of elections and providers of the electoral college votes needed to win the presidency, state party organizations play a critical part in American national politics. They also play a significant role in state politics. The leaders in each state party's *central committee* supervise the various functions vital to state parties, such as raising funds, identifying potential candidates, providing election services, offering advice on reapportionment matters, and developing campaign strategies. State parties also act in conjunction with state governments to conduct the primary elections or caucuses that are used by most states to register preferences for presidential candidates.

Party structure varies dramatically from state to state. Some party organizations, like that of Pennsylvania, now have a permanent headquarters, a regular calendar of events, frequent meetings with local officials, and a central committee staffed with professional administrators, strategists, and fundraisers. Parties in other states are less impressive. California is known to have weak political parties and so follows a common political rule: Where parties are weak, interest groups are strong. Candidates, after all, need volunteers and large sums of money to run for office. If parties cannot help them, interest groups will be only too happy to step in.

THE PARTY MACHINE   The local parties for many years constituted the main avenue for political party activity. From the final decades of the nineteenth century to the early or middle part of this century, an organizational style called **machine politics** flourished in New York, Chicago, Philadelphia, Kansas City, and elsewhere.

At the heart of the system lay an ingenious scheme of reciprocal influence. Party leaders (bosses) traded jobs, money, and favors for votes and campaign support. Party workers would help bosses win office, receiving patronage jobs in return. The party bosses, once in office, had jobs to distribute. (The civil service had yet to be invented; once established, its scope grew only slowly.) As for voters, those who supported the winning party could be assured of good local service, the occasional handout, the odd favor. The bosses, able to reach into the public till for party funds and personal enrichment, could use some of the purloined cash to keep voters and party workers happy.[24]

The system worked, for a time, to ensure strong, organized parties. It was based largely on an urban landscape of impoverished workers, often recent immigrants, who were more concerned with immediate benefits and simple economic survival than with the idealistic goals of good and honest government. Urban dwellers who were poor, hungry, and uneducated found that support of the party boss and the machine could ensure them a job or at least an economic safety net in tough times. The party machine acted as a combination employment agency, social-work outfit, and welfare state. Naturally, the machine and the party bosses didn't undertake these tasks merely for humanitarian reasons. They sought power, wealth, and privilege—primarily through the public coffers—and eventually their venality and corrupt behavior produced a backlash that swept them into oblivion.

The boss and the machine fell to several modernizing forces of the twentieth century.

To begin with, the increasing wealth and education of Americans produced a citizenry supportive of a government that serves people's interests and is less inclined to accept corrupt machine behavior. Candidates who ran against party bosses started getting elected in ever-larger numbers. Furthermore, in an increasingly wealthy society, people needed fewer of the favors that the bosses typically had at their disposal.

Four additional developments doomed the old machine system. First, the invention of the civil service robbed the party machine of those tangible and valued rewards for potential followers: government jobs. Second, the creation of the modern welfare state provided a social safety net for the poorest citizens, meaning that bosses were no longer needed to serve that purpose. Third, the proliferation of *primary elections* removed decision making about candidates and nominations from the hands of party bosses and gave it to a mass electorate. With little power to control the struggle for high office and few rewards to dole out to anyone, the influence of party bosses crumbled and nearly all of the traditional machines ground to a halt. Finally, the secret ballot helped speed the decline of party bosses' ability to intimidate voters.

Still, good organizations know how to adapt to changing circumstances. As the 1992 campaign revealed, party machines have not been dismantled but streamlined. Amid all the attention focused on candidates Bush, Clinton, and Perot, few noticed the veritable army of precinct workers—some carrying on a partisan family tradition handed down over generations—"pounding the pavement." They roamed up and down the streets of Chicago, New York, and Detroit knocking on doors, cajoling, joking, and fast-talking stubborn voters to get out to vote and to vote the "straight ticket" of the party. The "downsized" machines, then, continue to crank out voter loyalty, often quite successfully.

National Party Organization

The strength of the national party organization is most apparent during presidential elections. Even with the increasing "democratization" of the nominating process and the proliferation of interest groups and political action committees, the **national party organization** remains a crucial source of coordination and consensus building for both Republicans and Democrats.

Ostensibly, the national organization holds the highest authority for each political party, but in fact, it has always been weak. For decades, the national organization's primary task was to organize the national **party convention**

Haley Barbour, Chair of the Republican National Committee, helped oversee the electoral tidal wave of November 1994. The Chair's tasks include providing resources to candidates at the grass roots level as well as being the national spokesperson for the party.

Table 10.3
Party Platforms Reflect Party Differences

ISSUE	DEMOCRATIC POSITION	REPUBLICAN POSITION
Health care	Would enact health-care reform to guarantee universal health care for all Americans	Responsibility for health care should remain in the private sector
Abortion	Guarantees all women the right to a safe, legal abortion (support a national law protecting that right)	Support passing a constitutional amendment banning most abortions
Gay rights	Supports civil rights protection for gays and accept the presence of gays in the military	Oppose gay rights and would ban gays from the military
Gun control	Supports a "reasonable" waiting period before permitting handgun purchases and would ban most deadly assault weapons	Oppose all efforts at gun control
Minimum wage	Would raise the minimum wage	Would abolish the minimum wage
The economy	Maintains that the American dream of expanding opportunity has faded as the middle class struggles but falls behind	Maintains that this is an era of amazing growth and prosperity, with millions of new jobs, low inflation, low interest rates, and high productivity
The environment	Would protect the environment, including forests, wetlands, and critical habitats	Environmental progress must be tied to economic progress

In 1995, Senator Christopher Dodd replaced David Wilhelm as Chair of the Democratic National Committee. Dodd's most immediate challenge is to formulate a party strategy for the 1996 campaign and to raise money on behalf of Democratic candidates.

once every four years. The convention symbolizes the party's existence as a national institution. At this festive affair, party delegates from around the country come together to select presidential and vice-presidential candidates for the coming election and to write the party's platform. At no other time is the national party much in evidence to the American public.[25]

A **party platform** is a statement of principles and policies, the goals that a party pledges to carry out if voters give it control of government. It includes positions on prominent issues of the day, such as gun control, abortion, taxation, and social spending. The platform is also important as a way of setting the tone for each party and distinguishing one party from another. As we learned in Chapter 9, Democrats and Republicans differ from each other ideologically. These differences show up clearly in platform statements. Table 10.3 shows the very different stands the two parties take on some of the key issues of our time. It is based on the platforms adopted by the Democrats and Republicans at their 1992 conventions. Although many people assume that party platforms mean little to the actual performance of the party in government, we know this is not the case. For example, when the platform of a president's party is analyzed, platform positions tend to mirror subsequent government expenditures quite closely.

The day-to-day operations of the national party fall to the *national chair*. Each chair, selected by the presidential nominee of the party, is a true administrator. The chair is responsible for personnel, fundraising, scheduling, and the daily activities of the party. Modern fundraising techniques, such as computer-derived mailing lists and direct mail, have made both state and national party units more effective in recent years. Each party's ability to target specific voters—based on geography, demographics, previous financial support, and precinct location—becomes more sophisticated with each election. Given the administrative bias of the national chair's job, officeholders tend to be relatively unknown rather than popular national political figures (although the Democrats' appointment of Senator Christopher Dodd in 1995 is an exception).

PARTY SIMILARITIES AND DIFFERENCES   While a great deal of the organizational structure is similar for both parties, each bases that structure on different goals. The Republican party stresses *organization* by emphasizing the creation and maintenance of effective administrative structures (especially at the national level), which can supply assistance and raise funds for candidates. As a result, Republicans tend to be more bureaucratically oriented than Democrats, but also benefit from less ideological discord.

Conversely, the Democrats stress representation by promoting voter mobilization, activism, and debate. Because it encourages pluralistic participation, the Democratic party ensures acrimonious argument regarding policy and the selection of candidates. The Republican party seems more effective—especially when fundraising. In a typical election year, Republicans raise and distribute to candidates about 250 percent more money than Democrats do.[26]

> "The political debate has settled into two familiar ruts. The Republicans are infatuated with the 'magic' of the market and reflexively criticize government as the enemy of freedom, and the Democrats distrust the market, preach government as the answer to our problems, and prefer the bureaucrat they know to the consumer they can't control."
>
> —Senator Bill Bradley

NOMINATING A PRESIDENT: PARTIES AND ELECTIONS

Before a party can run government and make public policy, it must win control of the top political offices. In the United States, that means in particular the presidency. Let us examine the process by which a Democrat or a Republican becomes a candidate for president of the United States.

Nominating Candidates

Before candidates can be elected to public office, they must first be **nominated.** This can be thought of as the candidate's "sponsorship" by a political party. Party endorsement carries legal weight. Only one person can appear on any ballot with the word *Democrat* after his or her name; likewise, only one person on any ballot can legally claim to represent the Republican party. Since all other names on a ballot have next to no chance of getting elected, how the parties organize the nomination process matters a great deal. In the past, a small group of party leaders controlled nominations. That process has now been democratized, with major political consequences.

In the current American system, to gain a party's nomination for president, a candidate must win a majority of delegates at the party's quadrennial convention. Both parties hold these conventions in the summer before the November election. By tradition, the party currently holding the White House holds the later convention, usually in August. The challenging party holds its convention a month or so earlier, usually in July—perhaps on the theory that their candidate needs a running start to retake the presidency.

Delegates in the past were often *uncommitted,* or under the control of party leaders who frequently withheld any commitments until a politically opportune moment at the convention itself. Even on the convention's opening day, the race might remain wide open, with several candidates plausibly claiming likely victory. Today, however, nearly all delegates are *committed* long before the convention actually meets. In fact, it is usually clear to all who the nominee will be long before delegates convene, and the convention acts primarily as a formal ratifier

The first test of a presidential aspirant is met in the Iowa precinct caucuses, a grass roots meeting of party loyalists. Here, in Norwoodville, Iowa, neighbors assemble for what may be their most direct and unmediated experience with the workings of democracy.

of the obvious. Convention activities are now aimed less at choosing a candidate than at unifying the party faithful and gearing up for the fall election struggle.

Presidential candidates and delegates are chosen either in caucuses or, more commonly, in primaries.

CAUCUSES   **Caucuses** are meetings of party adherents who gather in precinct halls or even private homes to discuss and deliberate, and finally throw their support toward a candidate for president. They then select delegates who will represent their choices at higher-level state party meetings; eventually, their votes are reflected at the national convention itself. Candidates or their representatives often attend caucuses to discuss issues and make appeals. Caucus meetings are often all-day affairs that require a heavy investment of time. For that reason they are generally attended only by the most active and devoted party members. Any member of the party is by law allowed to attend, but this system makes it difficult for average citizens to play a role. It limits power to the more intense members of the voting public—usually people who are better-off economically and well educated. For that reason, as American society approaches democracy it has preferred to downplay caucuses, which appear elitist, in favor of primary elections, which are more inclusive and democratic in nature.

PRIMARIES   Primary elections date from the beginning of the twentieth century, in large part a response to pressure from that era's reformers, the Progressives, who tired of seeing their candidates pushed aside by political bosses and party machines. The Progressives argued that it was undemocratic to allow elites within the party to choose the party's candidate. Under pressure, party leaders buckled, and the primary system slowly developed. A **primary election** is essentially a preelection, allowing all members of a party, not just its leadership, to select the party's candidate for the general election in the fall.

The acceptance of the primary system is widespread. Today, political parties in about three-quarters of the states employ primaries to select candidates for national elections. Voters in presidential primaries vote for a specific candidate, and these votes are converted into delegates for that candidate. The delegates then attend the party's national convention, where they vote for the candidate they represent.

States that use primaries have employed various systems for parceling out delegates. Republicans allow greater variation in this than do Democrats. In some places they use a **winner-take-all system** for the entire state; the winner of the primary gets all of the state's convention delegates. In other states they distribute delegates by congressional district using a winner-take-all system for each district. Thus, a state could split its delegates among several candidates, if several of those candidates win at least one district. Finally, in some states Republicans use various systems of proportional representation to distribute delegates. Candidates who win, say, 20 percent of the statewide vote in the party primary will win about that same proportion of the state's delegates to the national convention. In contrast to Republicans, Democrats employ a mandatory system of proportional representation to distribute delegates. Any candidate who wins at least 15 percent of the vote in any statewide primary must be allocated delegates to the national convention, and those delegates must reflect the exact percentage of primary votes received. These generalizations about the delegate selection process only suggest the complexity of rules governing the winning of delegates. The arcane nature of the rules makes them comprehensible only to political insiders and specialists in the party organizations.[27]

There are different kinds of primaries. The **closed primary** is used by most states. In closed primaries only citizens registered as members of a political party may participate in that party's primary. A registered Republican, for instance, cannot cast a ballot in the Democratic primary. Conversely, **open primaries** allow all registered voters to vote in whichever party's primary they choose. Cross-party voting is thus possible. One reason why few states—seven at last count—use open primaries is that this system allows voters from one party to help decide who their rival party's nominee might be. An organized effort could bring crossover votes that select the opposition party's weakest candidate. Two states, Washington and Alaska, have *blanket primaries*, which allow voters to choose either party on an office-by-office basis.

For nearly half a century the New Hampshire primary has been the first big test of a candidate's legitimacy. Indeed, in ten straight presidential elections (from 1952 through 1988), nobody became president without first winning his party's presidential primary in New Hampshire. Why should this small and atypical American state assume a dominant role in the presidential selection process? Much of New Hampshire's influence stems from a simple fact: It

Little-known Fact

Although primaries have been around since 1901, when Florida adopted the concept, they played a relatively minor role in presidential selection until the 1960s. Only a handful of states allowed presidential primaries before 1968, and candidates who entered those primaries did so less to win the few available delegates than to demonstrate to party bosses their electability. John Kennedy's 1960 decision to enter the West Virginia primary (against Hubert Humphrey) was a calculated gamble to show that a Catholic could do well in a predominantly Protestant state.

The culminating event of every national party convention is the moment when the candidates on the ticket and their families take the podium and a celebration ensues. The party makes every effort to leave a positive image in the minds of the television audience, so these moments tend to be spectacularly orchestrated.

always holds the first primary of each presidential election year. Being first has a powerful effect on voter and media perceptions.

The traditional importance of New Hampshire is diminishing, however. Many states, including some of the large ones, came to resent its power in selecting the nominee. To give themselves more political clout, they changed the dates of their own primaries. More than half of both parties' convention delegates are now chosen in a time frame from one to six weeks after New Hampshire's primary, a process known as **frontloading.** Thus, ambitious candidates must campaign in a number of states, in addition to New Hampshire, to have any chance of gaining their party's nomination. They can't count on putting all their effort into winning New Hampshire and having a month or more, as they once did, to bask in that limelight and build national support. Indeed, in 1992 over twenty states held caucuses or primaries within three weeks of New Hampshire, allowing Bill Clinton to recover quickly from his loss there and go on to ultimate victory. This development favors candidates who already have a national reputation and can raise large sums of money early. It also makes it harder for a dark horse to come out of nowhere, do well in New Hampshire, and go on to win a major party's nomination, as George McGovern did in 1972.

After the long caucus and primary season (February to June), prospective nominees have several weeks before the party meets for its national party convention. If the race is still close, candidates use that time to keep pushing their nomination prospects. They seek to keep their committed delegates in line and to convince uncommitted delegates to declare for them. Negotiation, conciliation, and planning characterize this period.

In 1984 the Democratic party revised its rules to bring elected and party officials back in to the nominating process. They did this by creating a certain number of "independent" delegate spots (14 percent of the total) and allowing party and elected officials to attend the convention as unpledged **superdelegates.** The idea was that the presence of these superdelegates would get more media attention and give a display of party unity, and, because these delegates were not bound by primary elections, a candidate would still need the support of national party leaders to get the nomination.

Reforming the Nominating Process

Democratic convention politics were at one time conducted in what has often been derided as a "smoke-filled room." Critics saw nominations being made by middle-aged, cigar-chewing white men, wheeling and dealing around some back-room table. In fact, this scenario did occur with some frequency.

Since 1968 the presidential selection process has been radically altered. The Democrats' disastrously divisive convention in Chicago that year, which you read about in the chapter-opening case, fueled the impetus for change. There, holders of opposing perspectives clashed dramatically during several hot summer days in Chicago, at the height of the Vietnam War era. The party leaders who practiced old-style machine politics were led by the godfather of bosses himself, Chicago mayor Richard Daley. They still retained enough leverage to give the party's nomination to their candidate, Vice President, Hubert Humphrey, a man who had entered no primaries at all. But they were unable to contain the rising force of the next generation of political activists who demanded "democratization" and more opportunity to participate; clashes broke out in the convention hall itself and more forcefully on the streets outside to create disarray and acrimony throughout the party.[28]

The Chicago convention proved a watershed in American politics. Its most important accomplishment was to create widespread agreement that future party nominees had to depend on a deeper base of support than just the party hierarchy. In essence, the era of the primary began with that realization. Candidates at all levels in American politics have since then increasingly had to pass muster with the party rank and file in primaries before gaining the right to wear the party label in a general election.

Before the Chicago convention adjourned, activists succeeded in passing a resolution requiring that by 1972 all state parties "give all Democrats a full, meaningful, and timely opportunity to participate" in the selection of delegates. To create guidelines for compliance, the Democratic National Committee created the Commission on Party Structure and Delegate Selection. Usually called the **McGovern–Fraser Commission** (after its chairman, Senator George McGovern of South Dakota, and its vice chairman, Representative Donald Fraser of Minnesota), this group had far-reaching effects on the character of American politics. Its recommendations, largely adopted by the party, opened up meetings and votes to a large variety of party activists, made primaries rather than caucuses the common means of choosing convention delegates, weakened the power of party leaders, and set up rules to ensure that a wide range of party members—especially women, young people, and minority group representatives—could participate fully in all party operations.

Although Republicans did not adopt these reforms in all the details, they did follow Democrats on the essential point. Most of their delegates to the national convention, as well as their nominees for most lower-level offices, are now also chosen through the process of a party primary. No longer can a handful of leaders in either party dictate who the party will nominate for any office or what the party will stand for in an upcoming election.[29]

THE RESULTS OF REFORM   It is often said that every reform creates a series of unintended consequences, some of which may prove even less popular than the system the reform was designed to improve. Many observers feel this way about the post-1968 party reforms; they level particularly harsh criticism against the current dominance of primaries in the party nomination process.

The winds of reform that swept through the presidential nomination system touched party processes at every level in both parties. In essence, anyone who now wishes to run for office in a partisan election anywhere in the United States must first win a party primary, one likely to be contested by other ambitious party figures. In the past one gained party nominations by working within the party hierarchy, rising through party ranks, and demonstrating party loyalty to the inner circle of leaders. The implications of this change are enormous: Politicians stopped working within the party to please a small group of leaders and now work outside party structures to please a large mass of relatively uninformed voters.

As a result of this shift in focus from party elites to party masses, money became increasingly important in American politics. This was an unexpected and unintended consequence of the democratization of candidate selection. Yet it stands to reason that it costs more to sway a large number of people than a small number. Those in the past who desired party nominations sought to influence a few people who had a say in the decision. These would be at most a few hundred, more typically a few dozen, and in many cases a handful or even one (Mayor Daley, for example). Now decision makers (that is, registered party voters) number in the thousands or even millions. To reach them, a prospective candidate needs to hire a team of campaign specialists, conduct polls, create and mail out an impressive array of literature, and, most important, buy time on television.

In addition, the electronic media took on a new and important role in American politics. To impress the large mass of the electorate that votes in primaries, one must break through to their consciousness by appearing on the dominant media of the age. The centrality of television in modern political campaigns raises campaign costs and also changes politicians' behavior. Success on television doesn't always go to those who can craft clever soundbites and look attractive, but people with these skills are surely at an advantage in the struggle for power over those who lack them.

And increasingly, interest groups have become powerful and influential. Candidates need workers, support services, and money. They have found those resources in the variety of strong interest groups that have recently sprung up to promote specialized causes. Symbolic of this development is the growing influence of **political action committees,** or PACs, which promote specific interest groups' agendas. Those who won elections in the past owed much to the traditional party hierarchy. Now they owe much to their numerous interest group backers. The House Republican freshman class of 1995 received 45 percent of the money they raised in the first six months of 1995 from PACs. We shall examine the importance of this phenomenon in Chapter 12.

Finally, with the destruction of the old party leadership that once provided some continuity and cohesion for the party, politicians who win high office now do so on their own and see themselves as independent of the discipline of party structures. The result is a decline in party cohesiveness. In particular, the Democratic party in recent years has appeared to many observers like an uneasy coalition of squabbling individualists rather than a unified group of like-minded team players. It remains to be seen whether the recent unity displayed by Republicans, especially in the U.S. House of Representatives during the famous "first 100 days" of the 104th Congress in 1995, represents a new development or stands as an exception to the fragmentation of American party politics characteristic of the post-Vietnam era.

Despite these trends toward what many observers have called *candidate-centered politics* (as opposed to party-centered politics), we must not suppose that parties mean nothing once candidates gain power. Which party gains control of government still matters a great deal. Parties determine policy outcomes in the United States, and there can be little doubt that the most important thing parties do in American society is govern.

> "Television has changed the nominating conventions from deliberative, if volatile, bodies to orchestrated showcases."
>
> —George Comstock, "Television in America"

THE PARTY IN GOVERNMENT

Although not a word can be found in the Constitution about political parties, and the framers hoped that parties would play no role in the emerging republic, today, government institutions at all levels are organized via the party system. Party leaders run administrations at the state and national levels; many act as city or town mayors or hold other executive offices in a variety of political settings. Members of Congress and legislators in each state hold party caucuses practically every day. These meetings help them decide the direction of party policy and the best tactics to gain their ends. In Congress and in most state legislatures, the leadership of the chamber, the committee chairs, and committee membership rolls all result from partisan votes. Party is simply the first and dominant force in all of the upper-level institutions of American political life.

Among other things, party significantly influences the behavior of individual politicians. It proves to be, for instance, the single-most powerful variable for predicting how American legislators will vote. The number of times that members of Congress vote based on party affiliation has steadily increased from below 60 percent in 1970 to over 80 percent in the 1990s.[30] Simply put, party ideology matters; Democrats don't vote the same way as Republicans do.

The Importance of Party Ideology

It often surprises outsiders to learn just how much party matters in governance. Yet why should one be surprised? We already know that Democrats and Republicans hold different ideologies and represent different segments of society. Given the reasonably clear party differences, we should logically expect the parties to create different public policies when they control government. That has indeed been the case. What government does changes sharply when power clearly shifts from one party to the other. Democrats create liberal policies, Republicans build conservative ones.

An excellent way to illustrate party difference is to compare the voting records of Republicans and Democrats. For this purpose, we can make use of a device called an *interest group rating scheme*. Many interest groups routinely rank members of Congress on a scale from 0 to 100, as a way of publicizing each member's level of support for the group's aims. (The closer to 100, the higher the level of support.) The best-known of these groups, and indeed the one that started this practice back in the 1940s, is the liberal Americans for Democratic Action. The ADA, as it is known, each year gives each member of Congress a rating that represents the percentage of times that the member voted as the ADA desired on the thirty or forty most important bills taken up by Congress that year. The resulting number provides a rough idea of how "liberal" a member of Congress is. Ratings of 60 or higher indicate a clear liberal. Ratings of 40 or lower suggest a conservative. Middle numbers delineate moderates.

No scheme of this sort can be perfectly precise. A difference of 5 or 10 points between two legislators may reflect little more than a vote or two missed because of illness. Still, major differences over time clearly indicate different voting patterns and different philosophies. Year after year, Democrats score between 60 and 80 on the ADA scale, while Republicans rank in the 10 to 20 range. There can be little question about the basic pattern. Although some moderates can be found in both parties, the bulk of Republicans are conservative while the bulk of Democrats are liberal. No Democrat, for example, signed onto the Republicans' "Contract With America."

If this is the case, it really matters which party gains control of government.

"The evidence is now overwhelming that government without parties does not work."

—David Broder, American journalist

Three hundred and sixty-seven Republicans signed the Contract With America. One of their leaders was Congressman Richard Armey of Texas, who later became the House Majority Leader. The Contract promised to bring fundamental change to the way government did its business.

Table 10.4
Party Makes A Difference

HOUSE COMMITTEE	1995 CHAIR (REPUBLICAN)	ADA SCORE	1994 CHAIR (DEMOCRAT)	ADA SCORE
Agriculture	Roberts	5	de la Garza	53
Appropriation	Livingstone	5	Obey	95
Banking	Leach	58	Gonzalez	80
Budget	Kasich	8	Sabo	100
Commerce	Bliley	10	Dingell	80
Economic Opportunity	Goodling	10	Ford	95
Government Oversight	Clinger	8	Conyers	85
House Oversight	Thomas	10	Rose	83
International Relations	Gilman	65	Hamilton	63
Judiciary	Hyde	13	Brooks	68
National Security	Spence	10	Dellums	98
Public Lands	Young	20	Miller	93
Rules	Solomon	15	Moakley	83
Intelligence	Combest	8	Glickman	73
Technology	Walker	8	Brown	93
Transportation	Shuster	8	Mineta	90
Veterans Affairs	Stump	0	Montgomery	30
Ways and Means	Archer	3	Gibbons	70
Mean		15		80
Median		9		83

Note: ADA scores represent an average for two years, 1992 and 1993.

Table 10.4 provides a dramatic illustration of the point. It shows how a key group of powerful congressional leaders differ from each other. Committee chairs in Congress have a large impact on policy outcomes. They shepherd bills they like through the legislature and find ways to kill those they don't. The ultimate policies that emerge from government depend a good deal on what these key individuals do. With that in mind, notice the significant power shift that occurred when Republicans took over the House in 1995 and were able to name committee chairs. Table 10.3 shows clearly that when Republicans govern, conservative policies can be expected. When Democrats govern, liberal policies will occur. Despite the forces of fragmentation feared by many ob-servers as a result of the party reforms previously discussed, party ideological cohesion at the elite level still seems fairly intact.[31]

POLITICAL PARTIES AND APPROACHING DEMOCRACY

Several years ago, David Broder, a leading American journalist, wrote a grim analysis of America's party system entitled *The Party's Over*.[32] He claimed that American political parties were disintegrating, that they had lost their traditional stabilizing power over the electoral and governmental processes and were be-ing replaced by a proliferation of special-interest groups and the imagery of television.

Is the party really over? Many argue that declining rates of party identification, voter apathy, and the lack of any formal constraints to ensure party allegiance all indicate that American political parties are headed toward extinction. Optimists, however, see hope for the future of parties and even a role for them in the revival of a more participatory and stronger democracy. They argue that parties have re-sponded reasonably well to the many sources of change over the past three de-cades. After all, despite social upheavals, new forms of technology and communications, changing attitudes toward politics, institutional reforms in gov-ernment, generational shifts in support for politics, and major crises in government, parties have stayed afloat and even maintained their hold over a large percentage of the American electorate. Could dying institutions have such staying power?

Political parties are crucial democratic structures that link the popular will to governmental outcomes. Yet many reform proposals would take the parties back in time to a period before primaries, when small groups of party support-ers chose candidates at caucuses and when the party machine was strong. These retrogressive policy proposals seem unlikely to be implemented and would hardly be understood by a public that values citizen participation, not "rule by the few."

Every year millions of citizens take part in a wide range of party primaries at local, state, and national levels. Candidates who emerge from this process represent the people and their interests more than party-machine candidates in the past ever did. Surely the current party system of open caucuses and prima-ries comes closer to the democratic ideal than did the former narrow, elitist sys-tem of party machines. Activists like the Mississippi Freedom Democrats are no longer simply shut out of the process. The millions of Americans who identify with Ross Perot's United We Stand are full-fledged participants in the spirit of democratic involvement and party activism. In 1995 polls showed that more than half of all voters believed that the creation of a third party might be ben-eficial to the democratic processes of this country. As the United States ap-proaches democracy, power has shifted from the few to the many. Recent changes in the way parties operate are merely part of that ongoing process of democratization that is central to the current pattern of American political development.

Supporters of the re-election of President Bush and Dan Quayle gathered in Houston, Texas for their party convention in 1992. While not everyone was attired in an elephant nose and painted face, virtually all of those attend-ing the convention were dedi-cated and highly loyal party members.

SUMMARY

1. Political parties organize the election process by recruiting candidates for public office, hoping to represent the desires of voters, and attempting to ensure that their candidates carry out specific policies once in office. They also speak for and unite different groups and their varied interests through the formation of political coalitions. Other important functions of parties are to simplify political choices and organize government and policymaking.

2. Political parties have played a role in American democracy since 1790. The first party system pitted Federalists (led by Hamilton) against Democratic-Republicans (led by Jefferson) and was so unstable that it disappeared between 1808 and 1824. The second party system began with the formation of the Jacksonian Democrats, actually an outgrowth of the Jeffersonian party. Seeking to make the electoral process more democratic, the Jacksonian Democrats replaced the system of nomination by caucus with a national party convention. Opposition coalesced around a new party, the Whigs.

3. The third party system arose during the 1850s out of conflict over the issue of slavery. The new Republican party was devoted to abolishing slavery, while the Democratic party supported the Confederate cause; the Whigs dropped from sight. The fourth party system began with a realignment in party constituencies in the 1890s and lasted until 1932. During this period the Democratic and Republican parties became highly developed and well organized.

4. The fifth party system began in 1932 with the realignment in party identification known as the New Deal coalition. This broad-based coalition supported the Democratic party and enabled it to dominate national politics until 1968. Although Republicans have won five out of seven presidential elections since then, it is unclear whether another realignment is taking place.

5. The single-member-district system inhibits the development of third parties and thus produces and maintains a two-party system. In nations with systems of proportional representation, in which more than one member of the legislature can come from the same district, small parties can gain legislative seats and a multiparty system results. The electoral college favors a two-party system because the candidate who wins the most popular votes in a state receives all of that state's electoral votes.

6. Other explanations of the U.S. two-party system include cultural factors—some believe that the two-party system is built into prevailing cultural norms and values; the tendency toward party identification leads voters to deep-seated, enduring affinity for the major parties.

7. Although minor or third parties usually have no hope of gaining real power, such parties occasionally arise when an issue is not adequately addressed by the major parties. When a minor party has a popular or charismatic leader, it can affect the outcome of elections and force the major parties to adopt some of its proposals.

8. The local party provides the point of entry for those seeking involvement in politics. At the next level is the state party organization, which acts in conjunction with the state government to conduct primary elections. The national party organization is most active during presidential elections.

9. From the end of the nineteenth century to the middle of the twentieth, local parties often engaged in machine politics, in which party bosses traded jobs, money, and favors for votes and campaign support. Machine politics declined as a result of the creation of the civil service and the modern welfare state, and the proliferation of primary elections.

10. At the national party conventions delegates from the state parties meet to select presidential and vice-presidential candidates and write the party's platform, a statement of principles and policies that it will carry out if its candidates are elected.

11. Some state party organizations select candidates for presidential elections at a caucus, or meeting of party adherents. Other state parties hold primary elections that allow all of the party's members to vote for a candidate. In a closed primary, only citizens who are registered as members of a political party may participate in that party's primary. Open primaries allow registered voters to vote in whichever primary they choose, thus permitting cross-party voting.

12. Since 1968 the presidential selection process has been radically altered as a result of demands for "democratization." Reforms adopted by the Democratic party included selecting candidates by means of primaries rather than caucuses and increasing the diversity of delegates to national conventions. Some of these reforms were also adopted by the Republican party.

13. The greater power of rank-and-file party members has reduced the power of party bosses, increased the cost of conducting a campaign, reinforced the dominance of the electronic media in American politics, increased the power of interest groups and political action committees, and brought about a decline in party cohesiveness. The result is a trend toward candidate-centered, rather than party-centered, politics.

14. Although political parties are not mentioned in the Constitution, government institutions at all levels are organized via the party system. Party membership influences the behavior of individual politicians and leads to the creation of different public policies depending on which party is in control of the government.

KEY TERMS

political parties	minor or third parties	primary election
recruitment	local party organization	winner-take-all system
party realignment	state party organization	closed primary
New Deal coalition	machine politics	open primary
multiparty system	national party organization	frontloading
proportional representation system	party convention	superdelegate
single-member districts	party platform	McGovern–Fraser Commission
electoral college	nomination	political action committees
party identification	caucus	

SUGGESTED READINGS

- Kayden, Xandra, and Eddie Mahe, Jr. *The Party Goes On: The Persistence of the Two Party System in the United States.* New York: Basic Books, 1985. The first full-scale assessment of the strength of political parties and their impact on national political life.

- Key, V. O. *Southern Politics.* New York: Knopf, 1949. A classic account of one-party politics in the South.

- Polsby, Nelson. *Consequences of Party Reform.* New York: Oxford University Press, 1983. An excellent account of changes in party rules and the impact of those changes on party roles in government.

- Ranney, Austin. *Curing the Mischief of Faction: Party Reform in America.* Berkeley: University of California Press, 1975. A detailed account of the effect of party reforms on politics, with a special focus on the 1972 changes. Should be read with the following:

- Shafer, Byron E. *Quiet Revolution: The Struggle for the Democratic Party and the Shaping of Post-Reform Politics.* Washington, D.C.: Brookings, 1983. The story of party reform from 1968 to 1972 that produced a new era in national politics. The changes altered the very character of presidential politics, from campaign organization to grassroots participation.

- Sundquist, James L. *Dynamics of the Party System: Alignment and Realignment of Political Parties in the United States.* Washington, D.C.: Brookings, 1973. An analysis of the party system and the meaning of realignments in American history.

- Wattenberg, Martin. *The Decline of American Political Parties.* Cambridge, Mass.: Harvard University Press, 1989. A scholarly analysis of the declines in party identification, the rise in ticket splitting, and the challenges facing American political parties today.

CHAPTER 11

PARTICIPATION, VOTING, AND ELECTIONS

CHAPTER OUTLINE

CASE STUDY: THE MOTOR-VOTER LAW

INTRODUCTION: POLITICAL
    PARTICIPATION AND DEMOCRACY

WHO PARTICIPATES

VOTING

EXAMINING VOTING CHOICE

OTHER FORMS OF POLITICAL
    PARTICIPATION

ELECTIONS AND CAMPAIGNS

PARTICIPATION, VOTING,
    ELECTIONS, AND APPROACHING
    DEMOCRACY

I n September 1995 Attorney General Janet
Reno proudly announced that five million
Americans had already taken advantage of
the National Voter Registration Act, known as the
motor-voter law, by registering to vote at the Department of Motor Vehicles while renewing their
driver's licenses. The law, signed by President
Clinton in 1993, went into
effect on January 1, 1995,
and had an immediate im-
pact. According to the New
York Times, "if the surge
generated by the new law
continues, at least four of ev-
ery five adult Americans will be registered to vote,
compared with about three of every five now."[1]

The motor-voter law is designed to encourage voter registration by simplifying the registration process and thus, increase voter
turnout for elections. No American can vote
without being registered, but the registration
process in most states is cumbersome, time-consuming, and unpublicized. As a result, many
citizens lose their right to vote by failing to get
their names on the voting list. On election day,
when they suddenly decide that they want to
vote, it is too late. (In all but a few states, Americans must register several weeks before an
election if they wish to vote in it.) Under the
new law, states are required to allow mail-in
registration and provide registration forms at
motor vehicle departments, social-service agencies, and military recruitment offices.

Not everyone was in favor of the motor-voter
law. President George Bush vetoed a similar bill
in 1992. Democratic presidential candidate Bill
Clinton called the veto "nothing less than a slap
in the face to American democracy." His attack
was echoed by independent challenger H. Ross
Perot: "The only reason to veto this bill is to try to
keep people away from the polls this fall."

Within weeks after Clinton took office the
motor-voter bill was reintroduced in the House,
where it passed easily. In the Senate, however, it
was threatened by a Republican filibuster. Opponents of the law claimed that it would impose excessive expenses on financially strapped state
governments and that it would increase opportunities for voter fraud. Underlying the opposition was the belief that the law would benefit
Democrats more than Republicans by making it
easier for more inner-city and lower-income
people to register.

For years the Democrats have felt that tough
registration laws put them at a disadvantage.
Citizens who support Democratic candidates on
the average, have less education and have lower
incomes than those who support Republican
candidates. They are thus more likely to be deterred by complex and costly registration procedures. As a result, Democrats have long favored
easier methods of registering voters, while Republicans have resisted such methods.

With only fifty-seven members in the Senate,
the Democrats lacked the necessary sixty votes to
stop a filibuster. To win over enough Republican
support to pass the bill they needed to make some
concessions, including new language that tried
to ensure that recipients of public benefits were
not pressured by welfare agency employees into
registering to vote or registering for a particular
party.

Opposition continued after the law was
passed, with some states challenging the constitutionality of the new law. Republican governor
Pete Wilson of California refused to implement
the act, claiming that it would cost his state more
than thirty-five million dollars and that states
should not have to pay for "unfunded mandates" issued by the federal government. Wilson
also claimed that the law would increase voter
fraud by encouraging ineligible voters, such as
undocumented immigrants, to vote. The Justice
Department responded by filing lawsuits against

365

California and two other states to force compliance with the law.

Despite the arguments about which party will benefit most from the motor-voter law, its political ramifications remain unclear. The largest percentage of new voters do not identify with either party, instead considering themselves to be independents. One thing is certain, however. The increased ease of the registration process will advance the democratic ideal of political participation by all citizens. "It's hard to think of another law that has yielded so much for so little," said Attorney General Reno. "The law truly has strengthened our democratic process. It is one-stop shopping." Human Serve, a national voter registration organization, estimates that as many as twenty million voting-age Americans who are not registered will be by November 1996. By the turn of the century it is predicted that at least forty million new registrations will take place under the motor-voter law. Thus, passage of the motor-voter bill represents an important, if widely debated, step in America's approach to democracy.[2] ❖❖

MV-44 (11/94) NEW YORK STATE VOTER REGISTRATION APPLICATION INFORMATION
(Please read before you complete application on back.)

OFFICE USE ONLY

You Can Use This Form To:
- register to vote in New York State
- change your name and/or address, if there is a change since you voted
- enroll in a political party or change your enrollment

Información en español: si le interesa obtener este formulario en español, llame al 1-800-367-8683

中文資料:如果你有興趣索取本中文資料
表格，請電 1 - 800 - 367-8683

To Register You Must:
- be a U.S. citizen
- be 18 years old by December 31 of the year in which you file this form (*note: you must be 18 years old by the date of the general, primary or other election in which you want to vote.*)
- live at your present address at least 30 days before an election
- not be in jail or on parole for a felony conviction
- not claim the right to vote elsewhere

If you would like help in filling out the voter registration application form, we will help you. The decision whether to seek or accept help is yours. You may fill out the application form in private.

If you believe that someone has interfered with your right to register or decline to register to vote, your right to privacy in deciding whether to register or in applying to register to vote, or your right to choose your own political party or other political preference, you may file a complaint with the NYS Board of Elections, 6 Empire State Plaza, Suite 201, Albany NY 12223-1650, Phone 1-800-469-6872.

If you have any questions about registering to vote, you should call your County Board of Elections or call 1-800-FOR-VOTE. Hearing Impaired people with TDD may call 1-800-533-8683.

INTRODUCTION: POLITICAL PARTICIPATION AND DEMOCRACY

The motor-voter bill goes to the heart of the democratic ideal. Democracy simply cannot work without mass political involvement, or **participation.** Democracy is a system in which the people govern themselves—or, at the very least, play a major role in the governing process. In modern, representative democratic systems, the core of popular participation is the vote. If all citizens can easily register to vote and then exercise that right, then those candidates whom citizens choose will be representatives of the populace. If elected officials are "hired" by the mass of the nation's citizens, then they will need to take those citizens' wishes closely into account as they formulate public policy. Conversely, if most citizens do not have a chance to vote, then leaders will ignore them, leading to mass discontent and long-term disaffection from the political system.

Democratic involvement through voting and other acts of participation most often produces political stability. Citizens who have a say in the national decision-making process show greater levels of contentment with the political system as a whole. The very act of participation makes them feel a part of the system; in addition, citizens are gratified when they see that policy decisions,

"Nobody will ever deprive the American people of the right to vote, except the American people themselves—and the only way they could do that is by not voting."

—Franklin D. Roosevelt

over the long run, reflect their desires. Although mass participation produces high political tension, as many participants argue their various interests, in the long run it leads to democratic outcomes and mass acceptance of the system.

The motor-voter bill was one of a long series of efforts to extend democratic participation to average American citizens. The extension of citizenship rights to greater numbers of people has been a constant theme of American history. Thus, this bill takes its place alongside constitutional amendments extending voting rights to African Americans, women, and eighteen- to twenty-year-olds; and the various legal challenges end efforts to restrict suffrage.

One may well ask, of course, as did opponents of the motor-voter bill, just why this legislation was necessary. Americans already have the right to vote. In a sense they do, but voting is not always easy in the United States. As we shall see, both institutional and psychological barriers to voting still exist. This bill changed no one's rights, but it did make exercising them easier.

Since the ancient Greek theorists first debated various types of government, political thinkers have held that a citizen's informed participation represents the highest form of political expression within democracy. Indeed, the Greek word *idiot* originally described someone who did not participate in politics, a definition showing how much importance the ancient Greeks placed on democratic involvement. In Athens, citizens not only discussed politics but served in government as well. They held no elections as such; instead, everyone eligible regularly drew lots to serve in the legislature and fill other posts.

In a nation as large as the United States, this kind of direct democracy is considered logistically impossible. Instead, the United States has evolved a representative form of government, in which all eligible citizens may participate in electing officeholders who will represent their opinions in government. And Americans have the opportunity to go to the polls frequently. The United States has more elections than any nation in the world, with over five hundred thousand offices filled in any four-year election cycle. The standards of self-governance assume most citizens participate in some form of political activity, and that they base their participation upon a reasoned analysis of ideas, options, and choices. This link between widespread and informed participation, voting, elections, and public policy constitutes the fundamental component of democracy. Voting is but one form of political behavior essential to a democracy. Indeed, the right to choose not to vote is also essential to the workings of a successful democracy.[3] In this chapter we shall explore the degree to which the health of the democratic ideal is being met—or whether it is even possible to achieve.

WHO PARTICIPATES

The ancient Greeks assumed that being a participant in a democratic society was a full-time job for males who had full citizenship and owned property. Citizens would spend a good deal of time familiarizing themselves with the issues of the day, then make policy decisions based on informed reason and factual knowledge. This ideal is clearly difficult to achieve in a modern, large-scale mass democracy, where citizens must spend much of their time earning a living. For another, individuals' interests vary, and it is unrealistic to expect that

Table 11.1

The Varied Levels of Political Participation among Adults in the United States

CITIZEN TYPE	TYPICAL POLITICAL ACTIVITY	PERCENTAGE OF POPULATION
Unclassifiable	Unknown	7
Inactives	Not politically active	22
Voting specialists	Vote, but little more	21
Parochials	Contact officials concerning individual problems, but little more	4
Communalists	Work in voluntary groups, contact officials on a variety of issues, vote, but avoid campaign work	20
Campaigners	Vote, work actively in political campaigns and elections	15
Complete activists	Get involved in all aspects of political life	11

Adapted from Sidney Verba and Norman H. Nie, *Participation in America: Political Democracy and Social Equality* (New York: Harper and Row, 1972), pp. 118–119, Table 7-1.

Seniors are an influential voting block in the electorate. They tend to be well organized, highly motivated, politically attentive—and they vote!

in their spare time all citizens will participate in political activity. On the other hand, not all Americans are apathetic and uninvolved. A large number do come close to the ideal of full-time political involvement, and many others meet some of the criteria for democratic citizenship. Simple generalizations about the activity level of the American people do not take us very far.

A classic study of political participation levels painted a complex portrait of the American electorate.[4] Sidney Verba and Norman Nie found that citizens fall along a continuum of political engagement, ranging from those who are totally uninvolved in politics to those who engage in it as a full-time occupation. Table 11.1 summarizes their data. It shows that political participation is a many-sided activity in which citizens may choose to invest minimal or large blocs of time and effort. At the upper levels of effort we see that about a tenth of the population is deeply involved in the political process (the "complete activists"), but nearly half of American citizens engage in political activities of which the ancient Greeks would have approved. That is, if we add to the complete-activist group the number of those who are "campaigners," working for candidates or issues at election time, and those who are "communalists," working in groups to support social issues, we arrive at 46 percent of the population engaged in some kind of serious, politically oriented activity. In addition, another quarter of the population votes or contacts public officials for one purpose or another, leaving only about a fifth of American citizens completely inactive in the political process. One can debate whether this record could be improved upon, but still it does not appear as lamentable a performance as many social commentators make it appear.

The disturbing element to the variation in participation rates concerns the different types of people likely to be found in each category. Generally speaking, as one goes up the continuum from low to high levels of political activism, one finds fewer low-income people and minority group members. The group of complete activists, for instance, is dominated by well-educated, middle-income and well-to-do white voters, while "inactives" are disproportionately poorly educated, low-income African Americans or Hispanics. This is not to say that all active citizens are rich and white, or that all inactive ones are poor and black. The issue here is one of *tendency*.

These findings, reproduced in study after study, lead many observers to wonder how well American society is approaching the democratic ideal of equal political participation by all. The dominant social groups clearly can help solidify their dominance through political activity designed to promote their interests. The less well off groups hurt their interests by avoiding politics. These findings explain why the motor-voter bill generated intense political debate. Republicans, who benefit from the support of the groups most likely to vote, naturally found reasons to oppose an expansion of voting opportunities to groups unlikely to favor their party. Democrats, who typically gain the support of less well off Americans when those Americans do get to the polls, naturally figured that by expanding the voting rolls, the motor-voter bill would help them get elected to office. As this debate indicates, nothing in political life is simple. Even proposals to encourage democracy by facilitating the ability to vote can engender a storm of lively political debate.[5]

VOTING

As we have seen, participation in politics may take many forms, but the most central act in a democracy is the citizen's decision to vote. All other political acts cost more, in terms of time, effort, and money, and none produces such a level of equality as the vote: Each citizen is truly equal to all others in the privacy of the ballot box; there each person has one vote and all votes are counted the same. And votes in an election constitute the core political decision: who rules. Voting, then, is key to an understanding of the political process in a democracy, and we must therefore examine in some detail this vital political activity.

"Let us never forget that government is ourself and not an alien power over us. The ultimate rulers of our democracy are not a President and Senators and Congressmen and government officials, but the voters of this country."

—John F. Kennedy

A Brief History of the Vote in the United States

Historically, American politics have been notable for the steady erosion of barriers to democratic participation. Voting in particular, and other avenues of participation more generally, were closed for many years to minorities, women, and young people. Today, many barriers to participation have been broken.

Politics in the United States began as an activity reserved for white, property-holding, tax-paying, middle- and upper-class males. Perhaps a quarter of the American adult population met those criteria. Thus, poor whites and women were also disenfranchised. Slaves remained "property," retaining none of the citizenship rights that whites enjoyed. In fact, slaves were not even considered whole human beings. A compromise forged during the Constitutional Convention resulted in each slave being counted as three-fifths of a person for purposes of representation in the U.S. House and for assessing state taxes.

Property requirements for voting were gradually relaxed over the decades, disappearing by the middle of the nineteenth century, when virtually all white males were enfranchised. The Fifteenth Amendment, passed in 1870 as part of the Civil War Amendments, guaranteed that "the right of citizens of the United States to vote shall not be denied or abridged by the United States or by any State on account of race, color, or previous condition of servitude." The amendment's aim was to extend voting privileges to former slaves—and to African Americans in general. Though it seemed to pave the way for broader political participation, the spirit underlying the Fifteenth Amendment gave way, by the end of the nineteenth century, to the narrow perspective of southern state and local interests intent on keeping African Americans from voting.

Racism led government officials in the South to devise a number of techniques that kept African Americans from the polls. First and foremost was the simple tactic of intimidation. Local African Americans were victims of threats, beatings, home burnings, or in many cases were lynched by anonymous mobs. Naturally, when people are living under the constant fear of violence, an unsubtle "suggestion" that they not exercise their right to vote will be enough to deter all but the bravest of them.

Southern officials also devised formal ways to keep the African American vote down. First, they required payment of a **poll tax,** a fee that had to be paid before one could vote. In several states, an unpaid fee continued to accrue from one election to the next until it became a sum beyond the means of poor African Americans. Southern election officials also made selective use of the **literacy test,** a requirement that voting applicants demonstrate some ability to read and write. African American college graduates might be asked to read and explain complex passages of the Constitution, while white citizens were given simple grade-school paragraphs to read. A third device was the **good-character test,** requiring those wishing to vote to get two or more registered voters to vouch for their integrity. Since African Americans found it difficult to register, they also found it difficult to find registered friends to vouch for them, and registered whites were unwilling to come to their aid. Southern states used a variety of other devices as well to limit African American political power.[6]

These prohibitions were extremely successful. Since most African Americans lived in the South until well into the 1950s, southern interference with African American political rights effectively disenfranchised the vast majority of African Americans for decades. For the first half of the twentieth century, African Americans rarely participated in politics, few held public office, and less than 10 percent voted regularly.

Change came as the civil rights movement gained momentum in the 1950s and 1960s. The Voting Rights Act of 1965, providing protection to African Americans wishing to vote, and the Twenty-fourth Amendment (1964), outlawing the poll tax in federal elections, helped seal a new national commitment to equal opportunity in the political arena. The U.S. Supreme Court erased many barriers to African American participation, striking down state poll tax laws in 1966, for instance.

Women too were long denied political rights. The movement for women's political equality has a lengthy history, beginning with the first women's rights convention at Seneca Falls, New York, in 1848. After decades of pressuring for suffrage and other legal rights, women finally won the right to vote with passage of the Nineteenth Amendment in 1920. It guaranteed that "the right of citizens of the United States to vote shall not be denied or abridged by the United States or by any State on account of sex."

FYI

One wrong answer on Alabama's literacy test was enough to disqualify a voting applicant, and the most difficult questions were typically reserved for African Americans. Can you answer the following questions? Would you have qualified to vote under Alabama law?

1. Appropriation of money for the armed services can be only for a period limited to how many years?
2. If a state is a party to a case, the Constitution provides that original jurisdiction be in . . . ?
3. The Constitution limits the size of the District of Columbia to . . . ?

Further expansion of political participation came with ratification of the Twenty-sixth Amendment in 1971, giving the right to vote to all citizens of the United States eighteen years of age or older. Extending suffrage rights is a key step toward approaching the democratic ideal of equal political participation by all. It may be that the latest phase of this movement toward full and equal citizen involvement in public affairs began with passage of the motor-voter bill. As we shall see, the idea underlying that bill has generated numerous other proposals for facilitating the right to vote—a right deeply embedded in the sweep of American history.

Voter Turnout

Since voting is the sole political act that many citizens undertake from one year to the next, many observers of politics define the health of a representative democracy by the degree to which its citizens participate in elections. **Voter turnout** is often used as an indicator of a democratic system's health. This measure expresses the percentage of eligible voters who actually show up and vote on election day. Thus, a turnout rate of 80 percent for a given election means that 80 percent of all citizens legally able to vote actually did vote in that election. In the ideal democratic society, this turnout rate would stand in the high nineties or even hit 100 percent. Given that American citizens have both the opportunity and the obligation to vote, how does the United States stack up against this ideal?

Scholars have traced voter turnout in the United States over the years. Since 1860, voter turnout in presidential elections has shown a long, fairly steady decline (see Figure 11.1). In 1860, those who voted in the presidential election constituted over 82 percent of the eligible adult population; in 1992 only 55 percent voted.

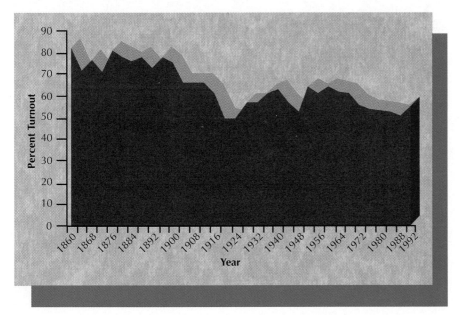

FIGURE 11.1 Voter Turnout
Levels of voter turnout as a percentage of the eligible voting population have experienced an overall decline since the 1960s. The exception to this trend occurred in 1992. With independent candidate Ross Perot and as a result of considerable effort to get out the vote in the 1992 election, voter turnout increased by 4% to 55% in 1992 (the highest level since 1972).

Source: Historical Statistics of the United States, Colonial Times to 1970; Statistical Abstract of the United States, 1980–1992.

These numbers do not tell the whole story, as we shall soon see, but for some they paint a dismal picture of the trend in American voting. The trend since 1968 is particularly troubling to many political scholars. The six elections between 1972 and 1992 mark the first time in the history of presidential elections that fewer than 60 percent of eligible voters went to the polls in six consecutive elections. The slight rise in turnout in 1992 may be an encouraging sign, and that trend continued in the 1994 election for members of Congress, but it is still far below the figures for most of the late nineteenth and early twentieth centuries.

Turnout is even lower when Americans elect members of Congress in non-presidential, **midterm elections.** For these races, voter turnout averages between 35 percent and 40 percent of the eligible adult population. Turnout sinks still lower in many state and local elections.

How can we explain these low turnout rates in the world's oldest democracy?[7] The level of voter turnout in the United States is lower than that of almost every other democratic country. Nations such as Italy, the Netherlands, Belgium, Sweden, Australia, Germany, and Norway boast an average turnout of over 80 percent in national elections. Some experts argue, however, that these figures are deceptive. Turnout data are not comparable from one nation to the next. Many nations such as Belgium make voting compulsory, for example, and fine people who don't vote. Naturally, their turnout will be higher than in nations where voting is voluntary. Furthermore, many foreign nations report turnout as a percentage of *registered* voters, whereas turnout rates in the United States (as shown in Figure 11.2) are usually given as a percentage of *all* adult citizens who are eligible to vote. This skews U.S. voting rates so that they appear lower, since only about 70 percent of Americans are actually registered. When the U.S. numbers are made comparable to data from other countries, by reporting turnout as a

The most visible and valuable expression of democracy is the vote. In South Africa, blacks had long been denied that vote, until April 1994 when these historic elections were held as a result of the abolition of apartheid.

percentage of registered voters, American turnout rates (at least for presidential elections) appear perfectly respectable. Nearly seven-eighths of registered voters do in fact vote, a record better than many democratic nations.

Still, many observers remain disappointed with American voting levels. Despite the reasonably good voting rates of registered voters, the fact remains that nearly one-third of Americans are not registered. Registration is crucial, since no American can vote in any election without being registered, that is, having one's name on the official voting list of one's city or town. Since American citizens who are registered to vote turn out in impressive numbers, it would appear that non-registration might be the key to low turnout rates in the United States.

The question then becomes not why many Americans fail to vote but why many Americans fail to *register* to vote. Political scientists have offered two general explanations for this phenomenon; one stresses institutional factors, and the other focuses on psychological issues. A complete explanation of registering nonvoting needs to take both perspectives into account.

WHY VOTER REGISTRATION AND TURNOUT ARE SO LOW To begin to explain nonvoting, start with a simple axiom: Nothing in this life is free. Even the simplest political action has costs. Consider what it takes to exercise the right to vote in America. First, a citizen must register to vote. Unlike the residents of other democracies, Americans have decided that registration is the individual's responsibility, requiring a conscious decision, and then the expenditure of time and energy.

And as you learned in the case study, registering is cumbersome. It usually means taking time to contact some government agency during business hours. Although reregistration is not required for every subsequent election, a voter must reregister when he or she moves to a new address. Thus, with every move, citizens lose the right to vote unless they make another conscious decision to get back on the voting list in their new community. One explanation for low voter turnout may be that the average American moves often—about every five years—and registering to vote is not usually the first thing on the mind of someone moving into a new home and adapting to a new community.

Registration laws in most states seem designed to depress election turnout rates. As you learned in the case study, in all but a few states citizens must register several weeks before the day of the actual election. Since many people don't pay much heed to an election until the campaign is in high gear two or three weeks before voting day, many of them lose the right to vote because by the time it occurs to them to register, it is too late.[8]

As one would expect, the states that do allow same-day registration and voting (such as Maine, Minnesota, and Wisconsin) have much higher turnout rates. But well over 90 percent of Americans live in the other forty-five states, where registering to vote must be done well in advance of the election. Motor-voter laws, of course, ease the registration process.

Even registered voters, however, don't always get to the polls. Most detrimental to election turnout in the United States is the traditional day of voting: Tuesday. While most states keep their polls open from 8:00 A.M. to at least 7:00 P.M., busy citizens with jobs, families, and errands to run often have difficulty finding the time to vote.

In recent years most states have taken steps to minimize the costs of registering and voting. Registration can be done closer to election day than in the

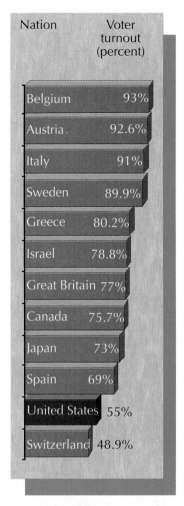

Nation	Voter turnout (percent)
Belgium	93%
Austria	92.6%
Italy	91%
Sweden	89.9%
Greece	80.2%
Israel	78.8%
Great Britain	77%
Canada	75.7%
Japan	73%
Spain	69%
United States	55%
Switzerland	48.9%

FIGURE 11.2 Voter Turnout in Selected Democracies, 1986–1992
Sources: David Glass et al., "Voter Turnout: An International Comparison," *Public Opinion,* December/January 1984, p. 52; Richard Flickinger and Donley Studlar, "The Disappearing Voter?" *West European Politics* 15 (April 1992), pp. 1–16.

Source: Kirk Anderson, St. Paul
Pioneer Press.

past, and polls stay open longer than in the past. In some states, such as California, employers are required to give employees paid time-off to go vote. Frequently civic groups target universities and colleges, grocery stores, shopping malls, and other crowded areas to register people. Other creative suggestions have been put forth by a variety of citizen groups: keeping polls open for twenty-four or forty-eight hours, same-day registration processes in all states, making election day a national holiday, and holding elections on weekends. All in all, registering and voting still involve some costs, but the costs have been declining. To understand nonvoting, then, institutional factors are not sufficient. We must also look at subjective, psychological explanations.

People have numerous reasons for failing to vote, and one is the possibility that they are simply satisfied with the way things are going and see no particular purpose to becoming involved politically. In this light, nonvoting may be "a reflection of stability in the system."[9] Today's nonvoters may, after all, become tomorrow's voters. Many may do so when a public controversy sears their conscience and forces them to act, as former Supreme Court justice Felix Frankfurter once argued.[10] Thus, nonvoters may start showing up on election day if they become unhappy enough with the choices of those citizens who do vote. This ability of nonvoters to vote, some argue, also keeps politicians honest. They know that truly unpopular actions could bring out a horde of formerly silent citizens eager to vote them out at the next election. Thus, from this perspective, nonvoting does not threaten the survival of democratic processes in America, it simply maintains the status quo.

Another school takes issue with this perspective. It claims that nonvoting, and nonparticipation in general, undermines the health of democratic politics. Citizens who remain outside the political process may come to feel little connection with the laws of the land and the government that administers those laws. They feel alienated—that their vote doesn't make a difference, that the process of voting is too difficult, and that the parties do not offer true alternatives. These people may turn to extremist groups advocating antigovernment actions that would undermine public confidence in democracy as a whole. (The Oklahoma City bombing and the existence of various militia groups in the United States come to mind.) From this perspective, nonvoting may be a symptom of social disconnectedness, itself an indication of social instability. A question gnawing at political observers in recent years is whether the number of American citizens who are disaffected from politics is growing, and if so, whether that trend bodes ill for the health of America's democratic system.

This view of nonvoting, however, seems too negative. Although isolation from the political system may undermine the health of the democratic process, the majority of Americans do participate fairly regularly. Furthermore, the people who are most alienated also tend to be the least likely to take political action. Most know little about politics, care little for it, and lead a life entirely divorced from political activity. It might be better for society if these social isolates were brought into the mainstream of public life, but it is doubtful that such nonparticipants could bring the solid foundations of American government tumbling to the ground.[11]

Who Votes?

The answer to the question Who votes? is crucial for understanding the political process, since it is natural for political leaders to pay more attention to voters (who determine politicians' fates) than to nonvoters (who play only a potential role in making or breaking governments). Many variables affect who votes. Education, according to every study, stands out as the leading influence. The more years of schooling one has, the more likely it is that one will consistently vote. Schooling increases one's ability for understanding subjects like politics. In turn, the ability to understand public affairs helps one see the benefit of taking political action, like voting, to enhance one's interests.

Social status is another crucial variable that determines one's likelihood of voting. Simply stated, the higher one's socioeconomic level, the more likely one is to participate in politics, especially to vote. Better-off people see themselves as having more of a stake in political outcomes. They also have the resources (money, connections, education) that allow them to understand the link between politics and their interests and then take effective political action to promote those interests.

Education and income quite frequently go together, of course, since it is becoming more difficult in modern society to gain economic success without an education. Those people who have both education and income possess two very strong motivators of political activity. Table 11.2 illustrates that the result of income and education is a high level of political involvement.

Social connections in general make political participation more likely. The more ties citizens have to their community, for instance, the more reason they see for getting involved in politics. They can work to keep their property taxes low, help support a new school for their children, or work for their next-door neighbor's city council campaign. Thus, it turns out that older people are more likely to vote than younger people, and long-time community residents are more likely to vote than newcomers. Similarly, married people are more likely to vote than those who are single.

These variables describe tendencies, of course, not iron laws. Not all young people are uninvolved in politics. But as a group the pattern is clear:

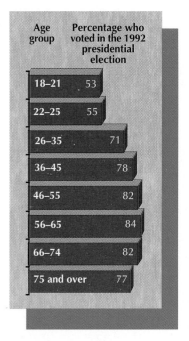

Age group	Percentage who voted in the 1992 presidential election
18–21	53
22–25	55
26–35	71
36–45	78
46–55	82
56–65	84
66–74	82
75 and over	77

FIGURE 11.3 Voting Tendencies and Age

In the 1992 presidential election, as in most modern American elections, there was a linear relationship between voter turnout and age—the older the potential voters, the more likely they were to vote. *Source:* Adapted from William H. Flanigan and Nancy Z. Zingale, *Political Behavior of the American Electorate*, 8th ed. (Washington, D.C.: Congressional Quarterly Press, 1994), p. 39, figure 2-4.

Table 11.2
The Effect of Education and Income on Political Activity

	HIGH POLITICAL INTEREST	CONTRIBUTED MONEY	ATTENDED POLITICAL ACTIVITY
Education			
College graduate plus advanced training	49%	16%	13%
College graduate	42	9	12
Some college	35	6	11
High school graduate	27	2	6
Less than high school	26	1	3
Income			
$50,000 or more	37%	11%	8%
$35,000–$49,999	36	6	7
$25,000–$34,999	32	7	9
$20,000–$24,999	34	4	10
$15,000–$19,999	27	3	8
$10,000–$14,999	29	2	7
under $10,000	29	1	7

Source: Center for Political Studies, University of Michigan, 1984 election surveys. "Warren E. Miller, and National Elections Studies/Center for Political Studies. AMERICAN NATIONAL ELECTION STUDY, 1984 [Compact file]. Conducted by University of Michigan, Center for Political Studies, 2/e, [CPSR Ed.] Ann Arbor, MI: Inter-University Consortium for Political and Social Research [Producer and Distributor], 1986.

eighteen- to twenty-year-olds vote less than any age group, followed by twenty-one- to twenty-five-year-olds, then twenty-six- to thirty-year-olds, and so on. People in their sixties, seventies, and even eighties, though they vote slightly less than middle-aged people do, are still far more likely to vote than people in their early twenties, as Figure 11.3 clearly indicates. This helps explain the powerful influence of the senior-citizen lobby and its chief representative, the American Association of Retired Persons (AARP).

Finally, we need to consider partisanship as a factor in determining who votes. For many years, political scientists argued that Republicans, by virtue of the demographic characteristics of those identifying with the party (higher education and socioeconomic status than Democrats), voted more frequently than Democrats. But recent studies have demonstrated that the partisan difference between voters and nonvoters is relatively small, and varies by issue and candidate.[12]

The continuing modest level of voting rates in the United States presents something of a puzzle to social observers. For four or five decades, Americans have been getting richer, older, and more educated. These demographic trends would suggest a pattern of increasing political participation and voting that has not materialized. Those dissatisfied with American voting levels continue to explore creative ways to encourage voters to get to the polls.

A Voting Trend: Direct Democracy

In recent years there has been increasing support for the use of initiatives and referenda. **Initiatives** are policy proposals placed on the ballot for voter consideration at the instigation of a group of citizens. Often they are ideas that have not met with success in a state's legislature or even contradict the law. Issues such as the lack of term limits for public officials or high property taxes and insurance rates have raised voter ire in recent years, leading to popular initiatives in the states. The initiative was designed to allow the public to take matters into its own hands. To qualify for the ballot, the initiative process requires that a proposal obtain a number of signatures—usually representing 10 percent of all registered voters—that can be verified by the secretary of state. Once verified, the initiative is placed on the ballot and put to a popular vote.

Referenda are submitted by the legislature to the public for a popular vote and focus on whether a state should spend money in a certain way. For example, in California the legislature often places bond issues before the voters, asking them to approve the sale of state bonds to finance various activities, such as education and prisons. At other times, the legislature seeks to determine the public's sentiment on an issue, so will place a referendum on the ballot.

These two methods of determining an issue, like the primary system that you read about in Chapter 10, grew out of attempts to broaden political participation and decrease the influence of special interests. They enable voters to directly determine the fate of political agendas and issues. Many people see these options as ways to approach direct democracy.

But initiatives and referenda have met with mixed success, and in recent years, there has been criticism of both methods. Some critics find that issues end up on the ballot even though they are too complex for simple yes or no decisions. Both methods have become costly, requiring expensive television campaigns, and are therefore subject to the influence of big business and concerned interest groups. Lastly, by involving the people so directly, these methods bypass the considered deliberations of American political institutions.

Although the idea of direct democracy remains appealing to many voters who seek to determine the direction of public policy, studies have shown that even when given the opportunity to vote via initiative or referenda, voter turnout does not dramatically increase. The most famous of all initiatives, California's Proposition 13 in 1978, called for a reduction in state property taxes. There was a tremendous amount of debate over Proposition 13, and the stakes were high. Passage would reduce property owner's rapidly escalating taxes, which were associated with the dramatic increase in home values throughout California in the 1970s. But passage would also curtail State revenue and fundamentally alter the delivery of government services. Voter turnout in that election was 58 percent.

Is direct democracy, then, an answer to the problems of voter turnout? Many have predicted that the United States will turn to using initiatives and referenda at the national level. And with the advent of more sophisticated telecommunications and computer technology, scholars and journalists now argue whether the United States should develop voting techniques that allow citizens

Town meetings such as this one offer a popular avenue for the expression of political opinions. In this photo, citizens of Pittman, N.J. air their concerns about a waste site to their elected city council members.

to hear a discussion or debate over an issue and then immediately vote. Such possibilities will not fade away; they go to the heart of one's conception of democracy and will remain at the center of political debate for some time.

EXAMINING VOTING CHOICE

Although not everyone votes in every election, tens of millions of Americans do vote with some regularity. When voters show up at the polls to make political choices, what determines their actual vote? Political scientists have long been studying the electoral process and the reasons why citizens vote as they do at the ballot box. We now have a good idea of the key influences on American voters: party, candidate appeal, policies and issues, and the campaign.

Party

More than five decades of study of the American electorate has shown that there is one overwhelming influence on voting decisions: party. Other things being equal, voters show up on election day and vote for candidates from the party to which they feel most connected. This idea of connection has been termed "party identification," a concept we explored in Chapter 10. **Party identification** is a psychological phenomenon. It's a deep-seated feeling that a particular party best represents one's interests or best symbolizes one's lifestyle. Once party attachments develop, especially if they develop early, they tend to remain in place for a lifetime, since it is psychologically painful to change party allegiance.[13]

Not all voters have strong party ties. Some are independents, and others are weak party identifiers. For these voters, other considerations enter the voting decision, and frequently they may cast **split-ticket ballots,** meaning that they vote for candidates from more than one party. Those with strong party connections, however—still 25 percent to 30 percent of the electorate—can be counted on to go to the polls and vote for only one party, known as a **straight-party ticket.** Only in exceptional circumstances (a friend is running on the other party's label, one's own party's candidate is particularly weak, a key issue of the day turns voters temporarily away from their party) do party loyalists break their longstanding decision to support their own party in an election.

But party is far from being the only determinant of voter choice. For one thing, some elections (usually local) are nonpartisan, so voters choose among candidates whose party is usually unknown to them. Other elections involve primary contests. In a party primary, all candidates on the ballot belong to the same party and vie to represent that party in the general election. Hence, party primary voters must often choose from among a number of candidates without party to guide their decisions. Finally, many elections—for example, referenda questions—involve votes on issues. Party positions on these policy matters are not indicated on the ballot, and often parties take no clear position during the campaign. Hence, party cues are missing in these elections as well. For a full understanding of how voters make electoral decisions, we must go beyond the useful but still limited variable of party preference.

Candidate Appeal

Personality has always played a major role in the United States' individualist culture. The American political system has been deeply touched by key personalities of the day: George Washington, Thomas Jefferson, Andrew Jackson, Abraham Lincoln, Theodore Roosevelt, Woodrow Wilson, Franklin Roosevelt, and Ronald Reagan, to name just a few. Colorful, authoritative, or charismatic individuals at the local, state, or national level have often won office by encouraging voters to change their longstanding party loyalties and by picking up the bulk of the independent vote as well. Republican Dwight Eisenhower, for instance, traded on his status as war hero to gain the votes of many Democratic loyalists in the 1950s. Ronald Reagan's movie star charisma and boyish charm, combined with a clear message of change, helped sway many traditionally Democratic voters into the Republican camp in 1980 and 1984. Colin Powell may be the new "hero" of 1996.

Strong or popular personalities have a major advantage in any political campaign. Through force of personality they can grab a voter's attention, and even support, at the ballot box. After all, most voters know little about the specifics of political life, except their own party preferences, the top issues of the day, and the names of just a few of the top political leaders of the time. Thus, in a typical election, whatever the office being contested, neither candidate is likely to make much of an impact on average voters, who simply vote their usual party allegiances. Becoming known to voters, gaining name recognition, means that candidates have a strong chance of picking up support.

What are the attributes that help a candidate become attractive to the voting public? Likability is surely important to Americans. A next-door-neighbor friendliness and a casual informality go a long way toward pleasing the American voter. It also helps to exude self-confidence, and especially to show a calm assurance when speaking in public. It does not hurt, of course, to be attractive. Studies show that while people vigorously deny it, they are clearly influenced to think better of individuals whose looks are well above average. This finding may explain why celebrities, who are well known at least in part because of their good looks, often have an advantage if they choose to run for office. Think of Ronald Reagan, or the one-time basketball star Bill Bradley, currently a senator from New Jersey.

Another important attribute is the candidate's message. No matter how attractive the candidate, or how folksy or self-assured, if he or she does not take policy positions that are popular with the electorate, the battle for office will be uphill, to say the least. No election for public office is a simple popularity contest. Candidates cannot get through a campaign without stating where they stand on the issues or explaining what they will do once elected.

Policies and Issues

Ultimately, elections are about what government is going to do: the policies it will undertake, or those it has already enacted. Despite cynicism on the part of many observers about voters choosing candidates on the basis of their teeth or hairstyle, the electorate does make decisions quite regularly on the basis of policy issues. Issue voting is a central part of the political process, although that is not always clear because issue voting is a complex matter.[14]

Let's say a voter feels strongly about ten issues. He or she then looks for a candidate who takes the "right" stand on those issues. It may turn out, however, that one of the two leading candidates for the contested office takes the voter's favored position on just five of those issues, while the other candidate takes the preferred stand on the other five. This situation leaves the issue-oriented voter without much direction on how to vote, and he or she may then consider other factors (like party or personality) to make a voting choice.

Other factors make pure issue voting difficult. What if both candidates take convoluted or ambiguous stands on all ten issues, leaving no clear idea of what they would do on these matters once in office? Or what if both candidates take the same position on all ten issues? Or what if both candidates do a poor job of campaigning, or the media do a poor job of reporting, so that in either case the voter fails to understand where the candidates stand on these ten issues? Or what if candidate A supports the two issues the voter cares most about, but candidate B supports the eight others? Do two favorable stands on the intensely held policy convictions outweigh eight favorable stands on the less intensely held ones?

For issue voting to occur, then, a number of factors must exist at the same time and in the same election:

1. The voter must care intensely enough about one or more issues to become informed about which positions each candidate takes on these issues.

2. Issue differences on these specific policy matters must exist between the leading candidates for the office.

3. These issue differences must be communicated clearly to all voters.

4. The voter's preferred positions on issues must not be split between the candidates but rather should fall mostly toward one candidate and away from the other.

5. Other factors, such as party and personality, should not detract from the voter's focus on issues.

Since in many elections all these elements do not come together, observers often conclude that issues are irrelevant to average voters. In fact, issues are often relevant to voters, but as we have seen, the structure of the voting situation may make issue voting difficult.

Those who criticize the American electorate for failing to take issues into account when voting may be missing another key point. Party voting itself, the key determinant of voting, is closely wrapped up with policy preferences and issue voting. Parties take issue positions on dozens, even hundreds, of current policy questions. A party vote is a vote to support those positions. Party-line voters may not agree with everything their party stands for, but studies show that by and large party identifiers agree much more often with their own party on the key issues of the day than with the other party. Thus, a party vote is in many ways an issues vote.

A particularly powerful form of issue voting occurs when voters look back over the last term or two to judge how well an incumbent or the "in party" has performed in office. This is known as **retrospective voting.**[15] If things have gone well (in the voters' eyes), if policy problems have been solved, if one's personal economic situation is good, if foreign or domestic crises have been skillfully addressed, then voters will reward the incumbents by returning them (or their party successors) to office. Ronald Reagan's reelection in 1984 and George Bush's victory in 1988 can be attributed to positive retrospective voting. The majority of those voting liked the way government was being run in the 1980s and rewarded the incumbents accordingly. Conversely, Gerald Ford's defeat in 1976, and Jimmy Carter's in 1980 and George Bush's in 1992 represent negative voter evaluations. The 1994 midterm elections marked a major party change in the control of Congress. Voters in these elections were unhappy with government policies for many reasons, and they showed their unhappiness by punishing these incumbents.

Campaigns

A final influence on voting choice is the campaign itself. At least one-third, and sometimes as much as one-half, of the electorate makes up its mind during political campaigns. With fewer Americans holding deeply rooted attachments to parties, campaigns can take on special significance. Many voters can be swayed by factors during the traditional two-month campaign. Issues and personalities of the day can move uncommitted voters in one direction or another with relative speed.

Campaigns also take on special significance for their ability to arouse voters' interest and get them to the polls. In fact, the candidate or party that inspires its supporters to vote on election day is the most likely to win. And citizens are most likely to turn out to vote after a well-organized and stimulating campaign. For these reasons, the last two decades have seen the rise of "campaign specialists"—public-relations people, media consultants, and fundraising experts. With the decline of the old party machine, a new world of political entrepreneurs (referred to by some as "Campaigns 'R Us") has arisen to provide advice and direction to any candidate with the money and will to hire them.[16]

We should not conclude, however, that money and a strong public-relations campaign alone can make a winning candidate. Remember that party and issues play key roles in voter decisions. There is not enough money in existence to catapult into office a minor party candidate taking unpopular positions on key issues. That assumes, of course, that such a candidate's opponent is reasonably competent and does not through scandal or incompetence "self-destruct." Finding a way to package a message cleverly and present oneself attractively are surely important. But the content of that message and the substance of a candidate's personality are even more important. If those don't impress voters, one's chances of winning, despite all the slick packaging imaginable, are slim.

OTHER FORMS OF POLITICAL PARTICIPATION

Voting in elections is the most common form of participation, but not the only form. There are many avenues for participation in the United States, including campaign work, information seeking, protest, civil disobedience, and even violence. In Chapter 12 we discuss participation through interest groups, but now we'll examine the other ways in which individuals can become involved in the political process.

Campaign and Election Activities

Unlike the pattern in most countries, Americans do not expect to join political parties and become dues-paying members who regularly attend monthly meetings. Still, some Americans volunteer time to work for their party in electoral campaigns, although the work is hard, the hours long, and the material benefits negligible. Even with the increasing use of sophisticated electronic media, the backbone of most campaigns is still people. Successful campaigns require volunteers to answer telephones, handle mail, canvass the electoral district, distribute candidate or party literature, and discuss the candidates and issues with people in the neighborhood. Why do people volunteer? They likely believe in what they are doing, they feel an obligation to participate actively in the political process, or they just plain enjoy the game of politics.

Interested citizens find still other ways to be actively involved during campaigns. Some participate by displaying signs or bumper stickers, or handing out literature of a favored party or candidate, hoping to induce others to echo such support at the polls. Others work as party volunteers in voter registration drives.

When all is said and done, the number of people who become involved in campaign activities is small. The percentage of people who claimed to work for a party or candidate in presidential or congressional elections never exceeded 7 percent in the seventeen election years between 1956 and 1988 (and never fell below 3 percent).[17] In recent years the number of people who wear a campaign button or put a bumper sticker on their car always falls below 10 percent of the adult population, as does the number of people who claim to have attended a political meeting in the last year.

We should not let these small percentages mislead us, however. After all, 5 percent of the voting-age population is close to ten million people. Thus, millions of Americans regularly approach the democratic ideal by working at election time to influence other voters and elect policymakers.

Information Seeking

Political knowledge is important. No one can exercise an effective citizenship role without being well informed. For that reason, the simple act of gaining knowledge about public affairs constitutes a form of political activity. Certainly, one who attends a meeting of public officials or the local government is participating in politics. In addition, every time a person reads a newspaper or news magazine, watches a news broadcast or political program, or enrolls in a political science class, he or she is actively seeking information that will assist in formulating political preferences and opinions. By just learning about politics, a citizen contributes to the overall "knowledge base" of the American political system. And each time a person discusses the prominent political events and issues of the day with friends and family or writes a letter to the editor to express an opinion on those events and issues, that person is participating in the continuous process of politics.

Acknowledging the importance of information to the workings of a democracy, Thomas Jefferson once remarked that, given the choice between a government without newspapers and newspapers without government, he would without hesitation choose the latter. The most recent innovation in the continuing development of outlets for political information is the myriad television stations and programs that focus on political affairs, such as C-SPAN, Court-TV, and cable television channels that air state legislature sessions and city council meetings. Another innovation is the development of an interactive computer

Participation via E-mail

Demonstrations and protests have long been the favored form of political participation for activists on college campuses. But now the job of organizing a protest is much easier than it used to be. The reason: electronic mail. "Electronic mail is a means to really have a participatory democracy," says a University of Virginia student. "Everyone can have their voices heard." Students throughout the country are linked together by the Internet, which enables them to join E-mail discussion groups and communicate with like-minded students on other campuses as well as their own.

In early 1995 campus organizers put the network to use in planning a day of demonstrations against the Republican party's legislative agenda, the Contract with America. They used E-mail to reach a broad coalition of student groups, who staged a variety of protest marches, sit-ins, and other demonstrations on campuses in several states. The speed and ease with which the campaign was carried out show how profoundly computer networking has changed the way students communicate.

Planning for the event was coordinated by the University Conversion Project/Center for Campus Organizing, based in Cambridge, Massachusetts. The idea was circulated by computer to several E-mail discussion groups; the result was a draft of a Call to Action, which was circulated to campus groups along with suggestions about how to mobilize support and plan protest events. Campus organizers then began exchanging ideas electronically. "Electronic mail has totally changed the way students do political activism," comments a former student protester who now works at the University Conversion Project.

There are some drawbacks to relying on electronic communication to plan student protests. One is that some colleges, especially community colleges, are not yet connected to the Internet; students there may never learn of a protest organized solely by computer. Another drawback is the impersonal nature of E-mail. According to Mark Naison, a former leader of Students for a Democratic Society and now a professor of history at Fordham University, "There is no substitute for the face-to-face interactions that build political commitments."

Nonetheless, more and more students arrive on campus already skilled at participatory democracy on-line.

Source: David M. Herszenhorn, "Students Turn to Internet for Nationwide Protest Planning," *New York Times,* Mar. 29, 1995, p. A20.

---

link with the White House, enabling interested individuals to obtain complete texts of presidential speeches and position papers. One can even leave personal messages for the president. The American political system derives much of its vitality from the free publication and expression of information.

Protest, Civil Disobedience, and Violence

When governments produce public policy, groups, institutions, and individuals in society invariably respond. This response may be simple support, such as

Peaceful civil disobedience as a form of protest has long been a hallmark of U.S. participation. The right to picket, to protest, to peacefully resist government policy is a political right cherished by Americans. In this photo, citizens protest budget cuts at their university.

acceptance of and participation in government-sponsored programs, voting in elections, paying taxes, or compliance with new laws. But sometimes the actions of the government may provoke expressions of dissatisfaction.

Occasionally, these expressions take the form of organized protests and acts of civil disobedience, either against existing policies or conditions or as a response to actual or threatened change in the status quo. **Protest** may take the form of demonstrations, letters to newspapers and public officials, or simple "opting out" of the system by failing to vote or participate in any other way. **Civil disobedience** is a more specific form of protest, in which disaffected citizens openly but nonviolently defy existing laws that they deem to be unjust.

Civil disobedience was commonly used in the 1960s by citizens seeking to protest the United States' continued involvement in the Vietnam War. Some draftees burned their Selective Service cards, and students organized boycotts of classes and "die-ins." Even disgruntled veterans' organizations marched on the Pentagon and the 1968 Republican and Democratic National Conventions to call attention to their opposition to the war.

Struggles for civil rights in the 1950s and 1960s were often carried out through the active violation of existing laws, on the basis that these laws were unjust, exclusionary, and racist. Civil disobedience was the principal means through which Martin Luther King, Jr., sought to bring equal justice to the political system. This civil disobedience included incidents in which African Americans would demand service at "whites-only" lunch counters, knowing that doing so would provoke a reaction by violating what they believed to be— and what were ultimately abolished as—morally unjust laws.

Demonstrations have been organized to protest the continued development of nuclear weapons and nuclear power, including the "blockade" of the Lawrence Livermore Laboratories in Palo Alto, California, in 1987, in which antinuclear protesters blocked traffic at the installation, provoking arrest and drawing media attention to their cause. More recently, opponents of legalized abortion, such as Operation Rescue, have organized similar blockades of clinics where abortions are performed. While these activities appear unorthodox when compared with involvement through voting, campaigning, information seeking, and talking about politics, protest and civil disobedience are commonly used and often effective methods of political participation.

Seldom discussed in the context of political participation is the phenomenon of political violence. **Political violence** is violent action motivated primarily by political aims and intended to have a political impact. When radical opponents of abortion bomb abortion clinics or shoot clinic workers, they claim that their actions are aimed at stopping the "murder of unborn citizens." But is often difficult to tell the true motives behind supposedly political acts of violence. The intermittent rise of white-supremacist and neo-Nazi movements is certainly, in part, a response to social conditions. We know that violent intolerance follows in the wake of sustained economic downturns, when competition for jobs and scarce governmental resources is most obvious.

When the residents of south-central Los Angeles rioted in the summer of 1992 after the Rodney King verdict, not all of them were simple looters and vandals. Some people were seeking an outlet for genuine frustration over the apparent failure of the system to mete out appropriate justice, not only in the King case but with regard to American minorities and the poor in general. It seems that most political violence is triggered by a combination of economic problems and political events.

The American political system is affected to varying degrees by each of the forms of participation just discussed. But the majority of Americans who participate do so through decidedly orthodox, institutional means. In addition, the vast majority of Americans strongly condemn unconventional actions that are criminal—those involving property damage and physical violence, for instance.

Since the most common type of participation is voting in periodic elections, we now turn our attention to elections and campaigns.

ELECTIONS AND CAMPAIGNS

Elections throughout the United States are organized at the state and local levels. While the federal government does regulate and administer campaigns through the Federal Election Commission (FEC), it does not play a significant role in organizing ballots, paying for and staffing election employees, or counting votes. Instead, the secretary of state in most states has these responsibilities. In addition, the secretary of state interprets state law to certify which candidates qualify to be on the ballot, determines the order in which candidates' names appear on the ballot, oversees printing and distribution of ballots, and releases the final tallies.

"Democracy's ceremonial, its feast, its great function, is the election."

—H.G. Wells

With the exception of the electoral college, which is used for electing a president, the United States employs a **single-member district plurality** electoral system for election to state legislatures, the U.S. House of Representatives, and the U.S. Senate. As you will recall from Chapter 10, the system works as follows. Each state is divided into geographical districts equal in population, and voters within each district elect one official to represent them. Since each district elects only one legislator, coming in second, even a close second, means nothing. The name of the game is "winner-take-all." In a hypothetical congressional election for a specific congressional district, if candidate X wins 52 percent of the vote and candidate Y wins 48 percent, candidate X and her party receive the seat, while candidate Y gains nothing.

Note that winning a **majority** (more than 50 percent of the vote) is unnecessary in most American elections. Candidate X would still win the election contest even if a third-party candidate had been in the race and candidate X won 44 percent of the vote; candidate Y, 41 percent; and candidate Z, 15 percent. With 56 percent of the district voting against her, Candidate X wins because she gained a **plurality** of the vote, that is, more votes than anyone else in the race.

A few states do require majority winners in certain elections, most frequently in primaries. But the vast majority of elective American political offices require nothing more than a plurality, no matter how few voters support the top candidate.

The one American institution that always requires a majority victory is the electoral college. To become president, a candidate must win a majority of electors. Winning even 49.9 percent of electors would not make one president.

As you learned in Chapter 10, the American electoral system differs greatly from those in many European democracies, in which there are **plural-member districts.** In these systems, legislative districts are large and receive several seats. Rarely does any one party receive all of a district's seats. Instead, seats are divided according to the percentage of votes a party receives in that district. This system rewards multiple parties more readily than does that of the United States, since it gives *proportional representation* in accord with a party's strength in each district. Plural-member districts can be found in the United States in many local races, especially in nonpartisan elections, but they rarely occur at the state or national levels.

We will now look at the two key elections at the national level: congressional and presidential elections. We will also look at presidential campaigns, the role of voters in presidential elections, and the role of money.

Congressional Elections

Under the Constitution, elections for the House and Senate are held every two years. Each of the 435 House members is up for reelection every two years, while just one-third of the senators (who serve six-year terms) are. Most candidates for Congress are not nationally known; they may not even be widely known within their own state or district. Although the current U.S. Senate includes an astronaut, a former movie actor, and a former NBA forward, most national legislators come from somewhat less conspicuous, if equally wealthy, backgrounds. For that and other reasons, many constituents may have little information about who their elected representatives are, what they stand for, or even what sort of work they actually do "on the Hill."[18]

Congressional elections do not generally receive the national media attention or voter turnout of the national contest for the presidency. In off-year, or midterm elections, when there is no presidential contest to galvanize press and voter attention, the usual voter turnout hovers around one-third of registered voters, far below even the relatively modest 50 to 55 percent turnout in recent presidential election years. Because of this, and because congressional elections are not federally subsidized like presidential elections, the race for House and Senate seats takes on a form decidedly different from a presidential campaign. These races tend to focus more on state and local issues and on local personalities than on national issues or disputes. And often the key factor in these races is incumbency. For decades 90 percent or more of sitting members of Congress who choose to run for reelection have won their races. In the 1994 midterm elections, Republican strategists identified their Contract With America as a plan to introduce major changes in government.

RIDING PRESIDENTIAL COATTAILS   Over the years, an interesting pattern has emerged in congressional elections. Typically in presidential election years, the party of the winning presidential candidate also gains power in the legislature; conversely, in off-year elections, members of the incumbent president's party often find reelection prospects diminished. This phenomenon varies somewhat over time, depending on the fortunes of the president, the state of the economy, and the possible flare-up of controversy or scandal. President Kennedy's Democrats lost relatively few seats in the midterm elections of 1962, while the opposite happened to Democrats in 1994.

When representatives or senators of a successful presidential candidate's party unseat incumbents, they are said to ride the president's coattails into office. Sometimes this **coattails effect** can be quite dramatic. For example, in

The race for president almost always begins in New Hampshire. In this photo, Senator Robert Dole, Republican candidate for president, begins his first day of campaigning for the presidency—an election that is still 18 months off.

1980, when Ronald Reagan defeated Democratic president Jimmy Carter, he brought enough Republican senators into office on his coattails to wrest control of the Senate away from Democrats for the first time since 1955. But usually the coattails effect is not so dramatic. Despite Republican George Bush's presidential victory in 1988, Democrats retained control of both House and Senate. The same result occurred in the 1968 and 1972 presidential victories of Republican Richard Nixon. Thus, the coattail effect is not an absolute guarantee in American politics, and many scholars believe its effect is waning as voters become more unpredictable, less tied to party, and more willing to vote a split ticket.

During off-year elections, with voter turnout low and the public able to look back on two years of presidential performance with a skeptical eye, the sitting president's party typically loses seats in the House and Senate. The 1994 midterm election offered a dramatic example of that pattern, as the Democratic party saw itself ejected from its longtime control of Congress by an electorate motivated, at least in part, by unhappiness over a widespread perception of incompetence on Democratic president Clinton's part.

Presidential Elections

Following the national party conventions, which take place every four years, usually in August, Americans spend their time enjoying the last days of summer. But once Labor Day is past, the nation's attention turns to the presidential election. The pack of presidential contenders has usually been narrowed to two, although occasionally a serious third candidate competes.

The rules of the game at this stage are quite different from those of the nomination phase (see Chapter 10 for more on the nomination process). The timetable is compressed from two years to two months, and the fight is now Democrat against Republican (and possibly, in 1996, a candidate representing United We Stand America). Candidates who previously spent all their efforts wooing the party faithful to gain the nomination must now broaden their sights to the mass of less committed party voters and independents who will determine the election outcome. The fall campaign involves juggling a number of balls successfully. Candidates must use federal funds strategically, define a clear campaign theme, anticipate any last-minute "October surprises" by opponents, avoid self-inflicted gaffes, attack opponents without seeming to mudsling, monitor the pulse of the nation, and manage a successful media campaign. All of these activities and more form part of every candidate's strategy for winning the all-important majority of electoral college votes that ensure victory.

THE ELECTORAL COLLEGE: THE FRAMERS' INTENTION   Many voters forget that it is not they but the electoral college that actually chooses the president. How did this little-understood institution come into being? The design for the electoral college was written into the Constitution from the beginning. The framers wanted to ensure that exactly the right type of person was chosen for the job, and they sought to clone the best aspects of the first role model— George Washington. Rather than getting ambitious demagogues who cater only to the whims of the electorate or act as the mouthpiece of Congress, the framers wanted to ensure the selection of a *statesman,* someone wise enough to unify the people behind a program that was in their best interest, even if they

The Drive for Congressional Term Limits

During the 1994 election Republican candidates placed term limits high on their list of promises to the American people. They were responding to polls showing that almost 80 percent of Americans approve of the idea of limiting the length of time a person may serve in the legislature. The voters swept the Republicans to victory.

After the election, however, the picture changed. While the public and congressional leaders continued to call for term limits, the House rejected four proposals for a constitutional amendment that would have limited the number of terms its members could serve. The votes came after a spirited debate between advocates of the idea of "citizen legislators," who must leave office before they lose touch with their home districts, and supporters of the notion of "career politicans," who bring the benefits of maturity and experience to their legislative decisions.

The public's opposition to career politicians stems from the belief that they become unresponsive to the needs of their constituents. "They get out of touch, . . . they get to be more a part of the Washington culture than the culture that elected them," comments Representative Dick Zimmer (R-N.J.).* There is also a sense of unfairness in that incumbents have many advantages over challengers in congressional campaigns. Experienced legislators argue, however, that there is no substitute for the knowledge gained through

many years of service in Congress. As Representative Henry J. Hyde (R-Ill.) explains:

To do your job around here you've got to know something about environmental issues, health care, banking and finance and tax policy, the farm problems, weapons systems, Bosnia-Herzegovina, North Korea, foreign policy, the administration of justice, crime and punishment, education, welfare, budgeting in the trillions of dollars, immigration. The list is endless, and we need our best people to deal with these issues.*

Underlying this debate is a more fundamental issue: voter choice. On the face of it, term limits would give voters more choices because an incumbent would not be permitted to run for reelection after a specified number of terms. But it can also be argued that term limits restrict voter choice because voters are barred from reelecting a legislator who has served them well for many years. Such a restriction goes against a fundamental principle of representative democracy, "that the people should choose whom they please to govern them."[†]

House Speaker Newt Gingrich believes that term limits are inevitable because Americans are "sick of professional politicians." Apparently agreeing with him, voters in twenty-two states voted to impose limits on the length of time their members could serve in Congress. However, the drive for congressional term limits received a severe setback in May 1995,

did not recognize it at the time. For this reason, after considerable discussion, the framers chose not to have Congress select the president, fearing that the president would then become dependent on that body. They also decided not to let the people choose the executive, hoping thus to insulate that office from what they considered the popular passions and transitory fancies of the electorate.

Instead, they designed a system unlike any in the world, the **electoral college,** which provided an indirect election method. Legislators from each state would choose individuals known as electors, the number to be chosen based on the state's representation in Congress. (A state with two senators and five representatives, for instance, would be allotted seven electors to the electoral college.) The electors of one state were not to meet the electors of another state. Instead, the electors would meet on the same day in their respective state capitals and cast votes for two persons for president, at least one of whom was not to be from their own state. The list of votes was then sent to the nation's

when the U.S. Supreme Court overturned an Arkansas term limits law. The Court ruled, in a narrow 5-to-4 decision, that it was unconstitutional for any state to impose term limits on members of Congress.

The majority reasoned that the Constitution specifies the qualifications for membership in Congress and that any additional qualification (or disqualification, such as having already served a certain number of terms) could result only from an amendment to the Constitution. Thus, individual states could not change the terms of the federal Constitution by merely changing their individual state laws. The

The fellow has it wrong. The framers opposed term limits, but that's all right. He represents the views of a large majority of U.S. citizens.

Court minority argued that since the Constitution does not specifically forbid the use of term limits laws, individual states are free to impose them on their own members of Congress if they wish.

The closeness of this decision shows the power of the term limits idea. Many states have already adopted term limits laws for members of state legislatures, and a drive to amend the U.S. Constitution will undoubtedly gather strength, now that the High Court has ruled that that is the only way to ensure term limits at the national level. Still, it is entirely possible that this reform proposal will fall by the wayside, since voters at the national level are already reaping the benefits of what term limits are supposed to ensure: rapid changeover of personnel and policy innovations. In 1995, for example, over half the members of the U.S. House had not been sitting members of that body in 1990, and power in the House and Senate had shifted from Democrats to Republicans, with drastic policy changes resulting. As Representative Bill Richardson (D-N.M.) put it during the house term limits debate, "We've already got term limits. They're called elections."

Source: Katharine O. Seelye, "House Turns Back Measures to Limit Terms in Congress," *New York Times,* Mar. 30, 1995, p. A20.

*Quoted in ibid.

†Alexander Hamilton, quoted in ibid.

capital, where the president of the Senate would count the votes at a joint session of Congress. The framers expected that electors would be individuals with experience and foresight who would meet, discuss in a calm, rational manner the attributes of those candidates who were best suited for the presidency, and then vote for the best figure to fill that post. Thus, presidents would be chosen by an elite group of state leaders in a sedate atmosphere unencumbered by political debts and considerations.

In practice, the electoral college has never worked as the framers had planned because the framers had not anticipated the emergence of political parties. Originally, the electors had near-absolute independence. They had two votes to cast and could vote for any two candidates, as long as one of their two votes went for someone from outside their state. (Today, this requirement ensures that the president and vice president cannot both be residents of the same state.) Until 1804 electors did not indicate specifically which of their two votes went for president and which for vice president. After the balloting the individual finishing first became president; the person finishing second became vice president.

The framers expected that under this system, most electors would cast one of their votes for the most popular person in their individual states but settle on the most worthy of the candidates for their second vote. Thus, the second choice of the majority of the electoral college delegates would emerge as the top vote getter.

This odd system worked well only in the first two presidential elections, when victories by George Washington were foregone conclusions. After his departure, the beginnings of the first party system had, by 1796, ensured that electors were not, in fact, disinterested elder statesmen. They were instead factional loyalists committed to one of the two leading competitors of the day, John Adams or Thomas Jefferson. Thus, in a straight-line vote after the 1796 election, the electoral college chose Adams for president by a scant three votes over Jefferson. This made Adams president but Jefferson, his chief rival, vice president. A modern-day equivalent of this would be George Bush, who came in second to Bill Clinton in the electoral voting of 1992, serving under him as vice president.

Things worsened in the election of 1800. By then, strong political parties with devoted loyal followers had arrived to stay, ensuring that members of the electoral college would vote the party line. Jefferson and Adams opposed each other again, but this time both chose running mates to avoid the anomaly of another Adams–Jefferson presidency. Jefferson's vice-presidential selection was Aaron Burr, and their ticket combined to win more electoral votes than either Adams or James Pinckney (Adams's running mate). However, all of Jefferson's supporters in the electoral college had been instructed by party leaders to cast their ballots for Jefferson and Burr, and when they did, the two men ended up in a tie vote for the presidency. This result threw the choice of president into the House of Representatives. It took a good deal of intrigue in the House before Jefferson finally emerged the winner and was named president.

The absurdity of these two elections brought cries for reform. The Twelfth Amendment was quickly proposed and ratified, directing the electoral college to cast separate ballots for president and vice president. Under this system the party that wins a majority of electors can first elect the party's nominee for president, then go on to choose the party's nominee for vice president. No longer can a president from one party and a vice president from another be elected, nor can there be tie votes between two candidates from the same party. In a way this early reform preserved the electoral college system, since in nearly all subsequent American elections it has worked, giving Americans the president that the majority indicated they wanted. To this day, the electoral college remains a central part of the American political system.

HOW THE ELECTORAL COLLEGE WORKS TODAY   When Americans go to the polls in a presidential election, most believe they are casting their ballots for an individual candidate. In fact, they are voting for a slate of electors, individuals selected by state party leaders, who are expected to cast ballots for their respective state's popular vote winner.

In theory, these electors can vote for whomever they choose, despite their pledges, and produce a totally unexpected outcome. That never happens, since electors are party loyalists and zealously back their organization's candidate. Still, electoral college votes produce the occasional **faithless elector,** who casts his

Little-known Fact

Throughout American history, only three candidates have received the largest popular vote and not won the presidency. They are Samuel J. Tilden (1876), Grover Cleveland (1888), and Andrew Jackson (1824).

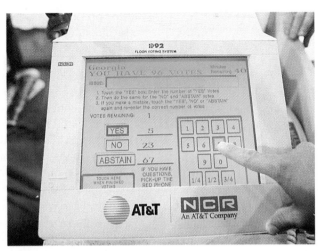

From Johannesburg, South Africa, to Greenwich Village, New York City, the process of voting and standing in line is very much the same. Here, voters in New York City take time from their busy day to vote in the 1992 election. Voting in many states is no longer pulling a lever, it is computerized. This speeds up the results.

or her electoral vote for someone other than the state's popular-vote winner. In 1988, for example, one of the electoral delegates from West Virginia cast a vote for Republican Robert Dole rather than for the party's nominee, George Bush.

Electors in some states are legally bound to vote for the popular-vote winner, but it is questionable whether state laws requiring electors to vote for a given candidate would be upheld in a constitutional challenge. After all, the Constitution provides the legal authority for the electoral college, but it mentions nothing about binding electors to vote a certain way. Indeed, it is clear that the framers expected electors to vote for president on the basis of their considered judgment, not party dictates or loyalties.

The electors selected in the presidential election meet in their respective state capitals on the first Monday after the second Wednesday in December. The term *electoral college* is deceptive, since the 538 electors never actually assemble en masse to cast their votes for president. Title 3, Chapter 1 of the U.S. Code provides that on the sixth day of January after every meeting of the electors—usually referred to as *Certification Day*—the electoral vote (which had been sent by registered mail to Washington) will be announced by the vice president before both houses of Congress. Not until that moment are the election results considered official (although the whole world has of course unofficially known these results for several weeks).

To become president, the winning candidate needs to receive a majority, or 270, of the 538 electoral votes. (The 538 votes are made up of 1 vote for each of the 435 members of the U.S. House of Representatives, plus 1 vote for each of the 100 senators, plus 3 votes for the District of Columbia.)

If no candidate receives the required majority in the electoral college, a contingency election is held in the House. Under the guidelines for a **contingency election**, the House chooses among the top three candidates, with each of the fifty states casting a single vote. This situation has occurred only twice in American history, after the elections of 1800 and 1824. If no candidate for vice president gets a majority of the electoral college votes, then the new vice president is chosen by the Senate from the top two vote-getters.

SHOULD THE ELECTORAL COLLEGE BE ABOLISHED?   Although the electoral college system has been stable and worked well over the years, many proposals have been put forth to reform it. So far none has gained the level of national support needed to secure the constitutional amendment that is required for any change to the system.

The most favored alternative to the electoral college is the *direct-vote plan* for election of the president. Scholars echo the sentiments of many when they write, "The choice of the chief executive must be the people's, and it should rest with none other than them."[19] Four American presidents—Johnson, Nixon, Ford, and Carter—have endorsed a constitutional amendment that would replace the electoral college with direct election. A November 1980 Gallup poll found that 67 percent of the American public favored direct election of the president, 19 percent opposed it, and 14 percent were undecided. Polls in 1977 and 1967 had similar results.

The direct-vote plan has its critics. What would happen, for instance, if four or five candidates ran for president, and someone with, say, 31 percent of the vote came in first? Would Americans accept as their legitimate leader someone for whom less than a third of the electorate had voted? To remedy that problem, most direct-election proposals would require 40 percent of the vote to win. If no candidate won 40 percent, a run-off election between the top two candidates would be held.

Critics then argue that such rules would encourage many candidates to enter the race, some representing single-issue parties, hoping to come in first or second, even with a relatively small percentage of the votes. The winner of a run-off election would, in this case, still have gained a very low level of national support on the first ballot. And it is possible for that person to emerge as president, even after coming in second on the first ballot. The adverse consequences for political legitimacy and perhaps even political stability would be quite significant in a nation that is unaccustomed to the idea of a runner-up winning the presidency.

Proposals to reform the electoral college ultimately founder for two reasons. First, every proposal for change carries with it new problems of its own, as we have seen, so that it is far from clear that the change would make a dramatic improvement in the status quo. And second, that status quo has so far not done such obvious damage to the nation that there is a need for dramatic institutional change. After all, in every election for a hundred years, the electoral college has done what Americans expect it to do: ratify the election of the candidate with the largest number of popular votes.

For an institution designed to rein in the expression of the popular will, the electoral college has adapted surprisingly well to the democratization of American political life. If it ever ceases to do its job, Americans will no doubt undertake the complex task of amending the U.S. Constitution to change the way presidents are elected. In the meantime, the attitude of many voters who bother to think about this issue at all seems to be, "If it ain't broke, don't fix it."

Campaigning for President

Presidential campaigns are shaped by the rules governing the operations of the electoral college. Since the name of the game is winning 270 electoral votes to become president, parties need to campaign in such a way as to improve their chances of winning those votes. That leads to a simple strategy: Go where the votes are. Thus, the "big" electoral states are at the heart of a presidential contest.

GOING WHERE THE VOTES ARE   The strategy of "going where the votes are" is crucial because of a voting system that gives the large states extraordinary influence in presidential elections. In all but two small states (Nebraska and Maine) electors are chosen on a "winner-take-all" basis. Whichever candidate wins the highest number of popular votes wins all of a state's electors. The consequences can be dramatic. A 54 percent to 46 percent victory, for example, in a large state like Ohio would give a candidate all of Ohio's important twenty-one electoral votes and hence a 21-to-0 lead over an opponent. If electors were allocated by proportional representation, with this same popular vote outcome, a candidate would hold a minuscule one-vote (11-to-10) electoral college lead over a rival.

Most states long ago decided to adopt this winner-take-all system to bolster their political importance. Naturally, candidates will take a state and its interests more seriously if that state can give candidates a large number of votes. If its vote totals were to be split, they would represent very little advantage to the winner. Most states settled on this winner-take-all method of distributing electors before 1832, so it has become ingrained in American political habits and seems unlikely to change (barring national consensus on a new way to elect presidents). The result is to exaggerate the power of the large states, where all rational candidates will end up spending most of their campaign time, effort, and money.

The eleven most populous states (determined by the 1990 census) produce the 270 electoral votes needed to become president. Indeed, the seven biggest states—California, New York, Texas, Florida, Pennsylvania, Illinois, and Ohio—produce over three-quarters of the total needed. Presidential candidates naturally campaign in these places, ignoring the smaller states like Delaware, Vermont, and Wyoming, that can't help them very much. After all, a candidate could win the thirty-nine smallest states plus the District of Columbia and still lose the election.

The weight given to the more populated states dramatically influences the way the presidential election game is played. For much of this century, especially from the 1930s through the 1960s, the states with the largest number of citizens tended to be urban, northeastern and north-central industrial states with many blue-collar workers, union members, and white-ethnic minority groups. These states provided precisely the kind of voters that made up the core of the Democratic party's liberal elements. To carry New York State, for instance, a candidate would have to pay close attention to the desires of its urban Jewish, Italian, and Irish unionized working class.

A Democratic candidate with a liberal message would naturally try to appeal to this audience. Republican candidates who hoped to win large chunks of electoral college votes would have to "move left" in this situation by taking a more liberal line than party regulars would normally adopt. The result was a series of elections in which either liberal Democrats became president (Franklin Roosevelt, Harry Truman, John F. Kennedy, Lyndon Johnson) or in which Republicans won the White House, but under the banner of a relatively moderate candidate (Dwight Eisenhower).

This system began to change in the 1960s for several reasons. Most important, Americans began moving south and west, so that states in the more conservative sections of the nation began gaining in power as liberal states lost numbers.

The growth of southern and southwestern political power in the past three or four decades has been dramatic. For example, the eleven southern states of the old Confederacy, along with New Mexico, Arizona, and California, supplied only 31.3 percent of the electoral college vote in the 1960 election, but 39.8 percent of it in 1992. The large Sunbelt states of California, Texas, and Florida together produced 66 electoral college votes in John F. Kennedy's election year, but 111 votes in Bill Clinton's. Conversely, the power of the old industrial northeastern states has declined. In thirty years New York dropped from 45 to 33 electoral votes, Pennsylvania from 32 to 23, and Illinois from 27 to 22.

Clearly, population changes have altered the political power equation in the United States and correspondingly changed the nature of presidential election campaigns. Liberals and Democrats are no longer advantaged by the system. Indeed, before Clinton's 1992 victory, many observers were already talking of a Republican "lock" on the electoral college. That's because a candidate can now become president through an entirely different strategy than was typically used in previous decades. This new strategy focuses on gathering the needed 270 electoral votes by winning the most conservative and moderate states of the South, Southwest, and Rocky Mountain Region.

Short of disaster, it would appear that Republicans begin every presidential race with the election in hand, and it is theirs to lose. To win, Democrats must take practically every state in the northeastern and north-central sections of the nation, along with California, and still find thirty or forty additional electoral votes. Their task is daunting.

Bill Clinton's victory proved that a Democratic presidential victory is not impossible, but it also showed just how hard it is to achieve. In an election during which nearly two-thirds of Americans were rejecting the incumbent president, Clinton managed to persuade a mere 43 percent of the electorate to give him their support, but he was able to win New York and California and put together a coalition of large electoral states. Further illustrating current Democratic difficulties in White House races, the previous Democratic president, Jimmy Carter, won office by the closest of margins (50 percent to 49 percent), after a closely contested 1976 race against incumbent president Jerry Ford. The last Democrat to win a presidential election by a large margin (61 percent to 39 percent) was Lyndon Johnson in 1964.

These data suggest that a conservative or moderate strategy is the only way at present to reach the White House. The situation now seems the reverse of New Deal–era circumstances, when liberal Democrats were advantaged and Republicans had to move to the left to have any hope of taking the White House. Now conservative Republicans are advantaged, and Democrats must move to the right to have any chance of gaining the presidency. This situation helps explain why the last two Democratic presidents, Jimmy Carter and Bill Clinton, were generally regarded as moderates within their liberal political party when compared with most of the rivals they beat out for their party's nomination.

FOCUSING ON SWING STATES   Beyond the general points just outlined, the electoral college system really operates like fifty-one separate electoral contests. Candidates go hunting for the magic 270 electoral votes in these fifty-one potential battlegrounds, but in doing so, they usually downplay states they are certain to win or lose, focusing on "swing" states, those that are highly competitive. Thus, Democrats need not spend much time campaigning in Massachusetts or Rhode Island, states solidly in their camp. Nor do Republicans spend much effort on Alaska, Utah, or Kansas, all Republican strongholds. Party strategists reason that if a party is in such bad shape that its candidate needs to pay close attention to these normally "safe" states, then all is probably lost anyway.

The serious battles for electoral votes occur in states like California, Ohio, Texas, Indiana, Missouri, Georgia, Washington, and New Jersey: states with enough electoral votes to be taken seriously and also with a tradition of closely contested races between the two parties—at least for the presidency. The large number of relatively moderate voters in these states is one more in the long list of factors indicating that the pattern of American politics has moved toward the center of the political spectrum. Neither party wishes to nominate a candidate seen as representing a marginal position, for fear of losing the support of voters in these politically crucial states.

Voters and Presidential Elections

The day after the election, virtually every politically interested citizen, including the president-elect, asks the same question: What message did voters send to their new (or reelected) leaders? The answer to that question is usually unclear.[20]

Election outcomes are notoriously difficult to interpret. For one thing, never in United States history has a president been elected with a majority of those eligible to vote. As we know, only 50 percent to 55 percent of the electorate turn out to vote for president. Nearly every one of them would have to vote for the same candidate for that person to gather a majority of adult Americans as supporters. Naturally, this has never happened in a free society and never will. Indeed, more citizens choose "none of the above" (by staying at home on election day) than vote for the winning presidential candidate.

Given low voter turnout, we cannot say for certain after any given election that the winner was even the preferred candidate of the majority of the nation's citizens. That is all the more true in most other elections to political office in the United States, since we know that turnout rates are even lower in races for offices other than the presidency. Many local elections occur with 20 percent to 30 percent turnout, meaning that many local officeholders will be elected with the support of just a tiny fraction of their fellow citizens.

Given this pattern, we could say that Americans tend to elect "plurality" presidents. That is true in two senses. First, as we have just seen, presidents never win office with the support of a majority of American citizens. But beyond this, candidates often end up winning the White House without capturing even a majority of those who actually bothered to vote. The most recent "plurality" president is Democrat Bill Clinton, who in 1992 edged out incumbent

Approaching Democracy in Mexico

There were delays in the opening of many polling stations. Many people were unable to vote because of a shortage of ballots. Some voters were coerced by members of the governing party, and in one state there were a few attempts at ballot stuffing. But the irregularities were not large enough to affect the results.

The occasion was Mexico's first truly free election since 1929. A record 70 percent of voters turned out in 1994 to elect a new president and federal legislature as well as many local officials. Photo credentials and computerized registration lists were used to identify voters, and each voter's thumb was marked with indelible ink to prevent fraud.

International and Mexican election observers agreed that the election was generally fair and clean, although the results were tarnished by irregularities in several areas. In view of Mexico's long history of electoral fraud, the 1994 election could be considered a historic advance along the road to democracy. But some question whether real progress is being made toward this goal. The ruling party, the Institutional Revolutionary party (PRI), has built up a political machine that vastly outspends opposition

Global View

parties and commands the loyalty of millions of voters. Its candidate for the presidency, Ernesto Zedillo Ponce de Leon, had little political experience; he had been selected only five months before the election to replace a candidate who was assassinated. Campaigning in a nation in turmoil, against an opposition clamoring for radical change, Zedillo nevertheless won easily, benefiting from the PRI's immense strength. "Even the dogs have 'Zedillo' written all over them," one voter complained. "They don't let the other parties compete. Is that democracy?"*

Despite the flaws in the electoral system, there is a growing commitment to democratic processes among the Mexican people, a commitment that can be seen in the large turnout for the 1994 election. "We have an obligation to elect a government that truly represents the people," noted one voter, who had stood on line for an hour and a half waiting his turn to vote. "That's a democracy, no?"**

*Quoted in Tim Golden, "Mexicans Cast Votes in Large Numbers," *New York Times,* Aug. 22, 1994, p. A6.

**Quoted in Anthony DePalma, "In Little Places, Democracy's Big Test," *New York Times,* Aug. 22, 1994, p. A6.

George Bush 43 percent to 38 percent, with approximately 19 percent going to independent challenger Ross Perot. Under such circumstances, it is difficult to say just what a presidential election means in terms of the general public's policy preferences.

In an attempt to make more sense of presidential contests, political scientists use party realignment theory to classify elections as maintaining, deviating, or realigning (or critical) elections. **Maintaining elections** were the most common type throughout much of the last fifty years (1936, 1940, 1944, 1948, 1960, 1964, and 1976). In this pattern the majority party of the day wins both Congress and the White House, maintaining its longstanding control of government. More recently, however, deviating elections have become common. In **deviating elections** the minority party captures the White House because of short-term intervening forces, and the country experiences a deviation from the expectation that power will remain in the hands of the dominant party. Deviating elections took place in 1952, 1956, 1968, 1972, 1980, 1984, and 1988. **Realigning elections** are characterized by massive shifts in partisan identification, as in 1932 with the New Deal coalition.[25]

The size of Reagan's 1984 electoral victory led many to speculate that it too represented a realignment that changed the electoral landscape. This interpretation was weakened, however, with the Democratic congressional victories of 1986, 1988, and 1992, and with Bill Clinton's triumph in the presidential race of 1992. The realignment thesis has been revived with the dramatic takeover of the House and Senate by the Republicans following the 1994 midterm elections. Analysts will need a few more years to assess the true nature of the voting changes occurring within the American electorate, but most do agree on one thing: regional realignment has undoubtedly occurred in the South, particularly among white males. That group, formerly a bastion of support for the Democratic party, can now be safely categorized as solidly Republican.

As we learned in Chapter 10, some political scientists characterize the current era by the term ***dealignment***—the moving away from partisanship. This term helps describe an increase in the number of self-styled independents, as well as the weakening of party ties among the many voters who still claim allegiance to one of the two major parties. This growing disaffection from the parties helps explain some recent electoral events, such as the elections of 1984 and 1988, when strong Republican wins at the level of the presidency failed to produce comparable victories for the party in Congress. Instead, voters showed their growing independence of party by ticket splitting: voting for a Republican president while continuing to back Democrats for Congress.

Money and Elections

It is often said that money is the mother's milk of politics. Candidates need large sums of money to have any hope of winning a contested political office.[21] For the most part, a simple rule holds: Spend more money than your opponent, and you are likely to win the election. Candidates therefore spend a good deal of time and effort raising campaign dollars. Over the years, laws governing this activity have been few, weak, and notoriously ill enforced. A series of reforms was enacted in the 1970s, but except for presidential elections, most campaigns are poorly supervised, and campaign money is not strictly regulated.

Presidential elections are conducted under the guidelines of the Federal Election Campaign Act of 1971. Before this campaign finance law was enacted, candidates could raise as much money as possible, with no limits on the size of individual contributions. Most of the money came from the large contributions of very wealthy individuals, corporations, and organized labor. For example, in the 1952 presidential contest, at least two-thirds of all the money raised and spent at the national level came from contributions of five hundred dollars or more (equivalent to two thousand dollars in 1996 dollars). This was the era of the political "fat cat," the wealthy capitalists who—along with rapidly growing labor unions—contributed most of the money and exerted most of the influence during campaigns.

The aftermath of the Watergate scandal led to the most significant election reform in history. The Federal Election Campaign Act of 1974 (amending the 1971 law) created the Federal Election Commission (FEC), limited individual contributions, and instituted a new system of public financing through an income tax checkoff. The 1974 amendments were immediately challenged, leading to an important judicial ruling.

FYI

The presidental candidate winning the highest popular vote ever was Ronald Reagan in 1984 with 54,455,075 votes.

On January 30, 1976, in the case *Buckley* v. *Valeo*[22] the Supreme Court struck down the limits on personal expenditures during campaigns for political office. The Court ruled that the First Amendment gives each citizen the right to spend his or her money, no matter how much, in any lawful way, as a matter of freedom of speech. In a later ruling the Court also struck down legal limits on the amount of money an interest group can spend on behalf of a candidate (as long as the group spends its money independently of the candidate's campaign organization). Despite these rulings, however, the fundamentals of the act remained intact.

The Court did back reformers on some crucial issues. It upheld contribution limits, disclosure rules, and public financing. Thus, individuals can give only modest amounts of money to campaigns, limiting the political power of the wealthy, in theory. Furthermore, all who give money to any campaign will be placed on public record through the disclosure provisions, meaning that under-the-table "buying" of political candidates seems unlikely to occur given the certainty of publicity. These reforms, along with the public financing of presidential campaigns, have led many to observe that American elections are approaching closer to the democratic ideal than in the days when a few wealthy groups and individuals surreptitiously paid for most of the candidates' expenses.

FEDERAL MATCHING FUNDS   During the long road to the nomination before the convention, almost all presidential candidates opt for **federal matching funds.** That is, once they raise a certain amount of money in the required way, they apply for and are given a matching sum of money from the federal government. The rules that govern qualifying for these funds are relatively simple. A candidate must raise $100,000 in individual contributions of $250 or less, with at least $5,000 collected in twenty states. Once this is accomplished, the federal government will match all individual contributions of $250 or less, dollar for dollar. Individual contributions over the $250 limit are not matched. This stipulation has led candidates to concentrate on raising $250 from as many contributors as possible. The result is an increase in small contributors ("kittens"), compared with the large contributors ("fat cats") who had previously dominated campaign financing.

In return for federal funds, candidates must accept a total preconvention spending limit plus a percentage limit on fundraising, as well as spending limits in each state. A state's spending limit is calculated at sixteen cents for each resident of voting age, plus an adjustment for inflation. In the forty states holding primaries in 1992 the overall state spending limit was around one-half million dollars in the less populated states, to over ten million dollars in California, the most populated. Thus, candidates who accepted matching funds had to develop careful strategies for where and when to spend.

Not all candidates accept matching funds. In 1980 John Connally refused to accept the limitations on spending and therefore did not request federal funds. But this did not mean that Connally was free of all financial restrictions. Although he was legally permitted to spend as much as he wanted of his own money in each state and had no overall spending limit, he was prohibited by federal law from accepting donations higher than $1,000 from individuals and $5,000 from political action committees (PACs).

Matching funds are cut off if a candidate does not receive 10 percent of the vote in two consecutive primaries. To requalify for funds, a candidate must receive 20 percent of the vote in another primary. The FEC requires twenty-five-days advance notification that a candidate is not participating in a particular primary. Candidates who run unopposed in the primaries, as Ronald Reagan did in 1984, are allowed to spend the legal limit anyway.

During the general election, candidates from each major political party are eligible for public funds for presidential elections. The money source is a three dollar income tax check-off to the Treasury's Presidential Campaign Fund. The percentage of taxpayers designating money was less than twenty percent in 1992. The taxpayer contribution was raised from one dollar to three dollars in 1994 in order to cover the next election in 1996.

EFFECTS OF CAMPAIGN FINANCE REFORM   Some observers believe that the thousand-dollar contribution limit has hurt long-shot candidates. Because campaigns are expensive, these candidates need big money early, to break through the pack of candidates in the early contests. Yet they are precisely the ones handicapped by finance limits. Money from many small contributors does not roll in to unknowns. If these candidates could persuade a few wealthy backers to give them millions, they might be able to get a serious campaign under way, but this is no longer an option. The result, some conclude, is less competition in elections because fewer challengers can afford to run.

Perhaps the major loophole in the campaign finance law involves **independent expenditures,** funds that are dispersed independently by a group or person in the name of a cause, and not coordinated by a candidate. Thus, a group or even an individual can spend unlimited sums of money promoting policies favored by a particular candidate. Naturally, these actions will help that candidate's chance of success in the ongoing political campaign, but they are entirely legal as long as the group and the candidate maintain separate organizations. The Supreme Court has ruled that in such cases, there can be no restrictions on individual or interest group spending. The rise of Political Action Committees or PACs should be understood in this context. PAC spending for candidates is unrestricted as long as it forms no part of the candidates' own campaign operations. Yet PACs naturally find it in their interest to have a president beholden to them, so they will surely spend large sums of money (unrestricted, after all) to back their favored candidates.

Another loophole in the law allows both political parties to raise *soft money,* contributions that are used by state and local party organizations for "party-building" activities. These include party mailings, voter registration work, get-out-the-vote efforts, recruitment of supporters at the grassroots level, and so forth. This money is considered "soft" because it does not go directly to boost a specific candidate's campaign. Therefore, it does not count toward the legal limits imposed on every presidential candidate who accepts federal matching funds. This provision allows candidates to get around legal spending limits, since the money, while intended to strengthen state and local parties, ends up (more than coincidentally) helping the party's national ticket as well.[23] Table 11.3 indicates the top soft-money donors to both parties in 1992.

While the new campaign finance laws have produced a broadening in the base of contributors, the fact remains that contributions still come from the

Table 11.3
Major Soft-Money Donors, 1992

CORPORATION	DEMOCRATIC NATIONAL COMMITTEE	REPUBLICAN NATIONAL COMMITTEE
Philip Morris	$152,000	$406,250
RJR Nabisco	145,800	362,650
Atlantic Richfield	171,573	304,641
Merrill Lynch	109,300	155,200
Revlon Group	139,200	100,000
Sony Corp. of America	130,650	100,000
Archer Daniels Midland	135,000	77,000
Bechtel Group	114,450	87,027
Occidental Petroleum	87,950	112,400
Pacific Telesis Group	81,300	111,727
Anheuser–Busch	105,000	66,727
Morgan Stanley	79,250	41,977
Bank of America	83,800	33,727

Source: Federal Election Commission and Common Cause. Reprinted with the permission of the *New York Times.*

wealthiest individuals and corporations. By far the highest percentages of individual contributions come from Americans who are university educated, professional or managerial types, with annual incomes in excess of thirty thousand dollars. Furthermore, campaign contributors were overwhelmingly white. And as with the pre-reform trend, the dominant sources of campaign revenue remain corporations, the engines from which many of the former "fat cats" derived their power and influence. By comparison, more "broad-based" labor PACs remain a much smaller source of PAC dollars. Figure 11.4 shows how corporate PACs outnumber other types of PACs.

PARTICIPATION, VOTING, ELECTIONS, AND APPROACHING DEMOCRACY

Active citizen participation can move the United States closer to the ideal of a democratic political system. Through voting and other forms of political participation such as campaigning, gathering information, joining groups, and protesting, Americans have sought to involve themselves in the democratic process. Closed to the vast majority in the framers' day, American government has become an accessible set of institutions, open to the input of millions, representing every conceivable point of view. Dozens of outlets for effective

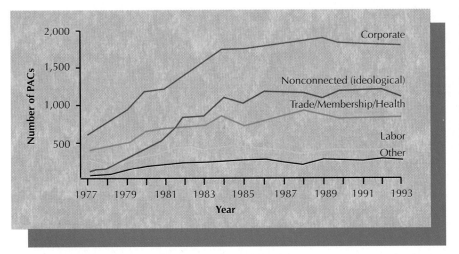

FIGURE 11.4 Growth of PACs
The passage of the Federal Election Campaign Act in 1971 and the 1974 amendments to the Act had an enormous impact on growth in the numbers of PACs registered and contributing to political campaigns. Designed to regulate and publicize the political fundraising process so as to prevent undue financial influence on legislative activity, the FECA also elevated the importance and expanded the numbers of the fundraising arm of interest groups, the PAC.
Source: Federal Election Commission.

political participation are available to any citizen who cares to make even a marginal effort to get involved.[24]

Some observers have expressed fear that democratization can reach excessive levels. The framers, among others, took this perspective. They believed, for instance, that the people should not be involved directly in selecting the president, much less in determining the composition of slates in a general election, as the primary process now allows them to do. As we have seen, recent trends in American politics have increased the chances for popular input in a variety of ways, including campaign finance reforms that encourage small contributions from a large number of donors.

For the framers, republican government represented a balance between popular input and deliberative statesmanship. Government officials would be elected by and ultimately be accountable to the people. On the other hand, they would be somewhat removed from the immediate expression of popular will through such devices as the electoral college. Hence, they could use discretion and deliberation in making public policy. Since the framers' day, the spirit of democratic equality has gained ascendancy over the more conservative view that officials should be removed from the immediate winds of public opinion. This development has not been a revolutionary one, evolving, often with painful slowness, over the entire course of American history, so that today it is fully ingrained in American political life. And the American people have evolved with it.

It is true that even today millions of Americans forgo their democratic rights by failing to take advantage of the many opportunities to participate in the politics of their free society. Nevertheless, it is also true that tens of millions of Americans, regardless of class, race, gender, or ethnic background, do express their political viewpoints and engage in civic activity to protect their interests. The American system presents no legal barriers to full participation by all; it also goes a long way toward minimizing the economic and psychological barriers that still hamper involvement for some. The people's relatively unrestricted ability to participate in political life stands as the best possible evidence that Americans have made enormous progress toward the ideal of a truly democratic society.

SUMMARY

1. About one-tenth of American citizens are deeply involved in the political process, but nearly half engage in political activities such as campaigning for candidates or working in groups to support social issues. Another 20 percent vote but do not participate in other ways.

2. Today all citizens who are eighteen years of age or older are eligible to vote. Over the years many barriers to voting have been removed, including property requirements, poll taxes, literacy and good-character tests, and prohibitions based on gender and age.

3. Voter turnout rates for presidential elections have been declining since the mid nineteenth century and are now below 60 percent. However, nearly seven-eighths of *registered* voters do in fact vote.

4. One reason for low voter turnout is that citizens must register to vote each time they move to a new address, and they must do so several weeks before the election. Another reason is that elections are held on Tuesdays, when most people are at work. Some experts see nonvoting as a sign of social disconnectedness on the part of many citizens.

5. Education is the leading influence on whether people vote, followed by social status; people with more education and income are more likely to vote. Social connections in general increase rates of political participation; thus, older people, married people, and people with ties to their community are more likely to vote.

6. In recent years there has been increasing support at the state level for the use of initiatives and referenda as ways to return to direct democracy. Initiatives are proposals by the public that are placed on the ballot for a popular vote; referenda are submitted by the legislature to the public for a popular vote.

7. The most important factor in voters' choices is identification with a political party. Voters who do not identify strongly with a party may cast split-ticket ballots, but those with strong party loyalty usually vote a straight-party ticket.

8. Other influences on voters' choices are the candidates' attractiveness, personality, and positions on key issues. Issue voting is likely to take the form of retrospective voting, in which voters judge how well the incumbent performed during the previous term. The skill with which the campaign is conducted also influences voter choice.

9. Many Americans volunteer time and energy to work on electoral campaigns: They answer telephones, handle mail, pass out candidate or party literature, and the like. Others make an effort to gain knowledge about public affairs, a process that has become easier with the advent of new media and communication technologies. Those who are dissatisfied with the actions of government may engage in protests or civil disobedience; a few engage in political violence.

10. In the United States, elections are organized at the state and local levels. The electoral college system is used for electing the president, but a single-member district plurality system is employed in electing state and federal legislators. (In Europe there are plural-member districts, resulting in proportional representation according to a party's strength in each district.)

11. In presidential election years, the party of the winning presidential candidate often also gains power in the legislature; this is known as riding on the president's coattails. In off-year elections, the president's party tends to experience some losses.

12. In a presidential election voters cast their ballots for a slate of electors who are expected to cast their ballots for the candidate who wins the most popular votes in their state. On rare occasions a "faithless elector" casts his or her electoral vote for a different candidate.

13. To become president, the winning candidate must receive a majority of the 538 electoral votes (1 for each member of Congress, plus 3 for the District of Columbia). If no candidate receives a majority, a contingency election is held in the House of Representatives, in which each state casts a single vote.

14. Under the winner-take-all system, all of a state's electoral votes go to the candidate who wins the most popular votes in that state. Presidential campaigns therefore focus on the states with the largest numbers of electoral college votes. Population changes have altered the electoral strength of various states, and campaign strategies have changed as a result.

15. In a maintaining election, the party currently in control wins both Congress and the White House. In a deviating election, the minority party captures the White House. Realigning or critical elections are characterized by massive shifts in party identification. Some political scientists believe that there is a trend toward dealignment, or a movement away from partisanship.

16. Presidential elections are conducted under the guidelines of the Federal Election Campaign Acts of 1971 and 1974, which place limits on the amounts that may be contributed to candidates by individuals and interest groups. The act also provides for federal matching funds for candidates who raise $100,000 in individual contributions of $250 or less; those who accept the funds must limit their spending in each state.

KEY TERMS

participation
poll tax
literacy test
good-character test
voter turnout
midterm elections
initiatives
referenda
party identification
split-ticket ballots

straight-party ticket
retrospective voting
protest
civil disobedience
political violence
single-member district plurality
majority
plurality
plural-member districts
coattails effect

electoral college
faithless elector
contingency election
maintaining election
deviating election
realigning election
dealignment
federal matching funds
independent expenditures

SUGGESTED READINGS

- Berns, Walter, ed. *After the People Vote: A Guide to the Electoral College.* Lanham, Md.: University Press of America, 1992. An exceptionally useful guide to the operations of the electoral college.

- Burnham, Walter Dean. *Critical Elections and the Mainsprings of American Politics.* New York: Norton, 1970. An important contribution to the understanding of American politics, electoral cycles, and elections.

- Campbell, Angus, Philip E. Converse, Warren E. Miller, and Donald Stokes. *The American Voter.* New York: Wiley, 1960. The classic study of voting, which even today should be the starting point for approaching the study of elections and politics.

- Crotty, William, ed. *America's Choice: The Election of 1992* (Guilford, Conn.: Dushkin, 1993. A valuable collection of articles on the 1992 elections.

- Nie, Norman H., Sidney Verba, and John R. Petrocik. *The Changing American Voter.* Cambridge, Mass.: Harvard University Press, 1976. An important study offering a fresh look at the classic 1960 study of the American voter.

- Piven, Frances Fox, and Richard Cloward. *Why Americans Don't Vote.* New York: Pantheon, 1988. This book is a starting point for understanding the problems associated with the decline in voting in America.

- Polsby, Nelson, and Aaron Wildavsky. *Presidential Elections.* New York: Scribner's Sons, 1992. An important book that provides a history and analysis of elections and American politics.

- Sabato, Larry. *PAC Power: Inside the World of Political Action Committees.* New York: Norton, 1984. A sympathetic and extremely valuable analysis of the role of political action committees. Especially strong on the issue of campaign contributions.

- Sorauf, Frank J. *Inside Campaign Finance: Myths and Realities.* New Haven, Conn.: Yale University Press, 1992; Sorauf, Frank J. *Money in American Elections.* New York: HarperCollins, 1988. These two books provide an exceptionally strong analysis of the role of money in politics and the many proposals for reform.

- Teixeira, Ray A. *The Disappearing American Voter.* Washington, D.C.: Brookings Institution, 1992. The reasons Americans don't vote and the effects of nonvoting on political life.

- Wolfinger, Raymond E., and Steven J. Rosenstone. *Who Votes.* New Haven, Conn.: Yale University Press, 1980. An important empirical analysis of voting, the results of which are then unified into a theory of voting behavior.

CHAPTER 12

INTEREST GROUPS

CHAPTER OUTLINE

CASE STUDY: REFORMING HEALTH
CARE?
INTRODUCTION: INTEREST GROUPS
AND DEMOCRACY
INTEREST GROUPS: A TRADITION IN
AMERICAN POLITICS
TYPES OF INTEREST GROUPS
CHARACTERISTICS OF INTEREST
GROUPS

INTEREST GROUP STRATEGY
POLITICAL ACTION COMMITTEES
REGULATION OF INTEREST GROUPS
ASSESSING THE IMPACT OF INTEREST
GROUPS
INTEREST GROUPS AND APPROACHING
DEMOCRACY

"Tonight we come together to write a new chapter in the American story. This health care system is badly broken, and we need to fix it," said President Bill Clinton as he stood before a joint session of Congress on September 22, 1993. With health-care industries constituting one-seventh of the American economy, the president's plan to provide guaranteed health care for every American would have been the largest new government program since social security was launched in the 1930s. For the 37 million people not covered by health insurance, Clinton's promise was a potential lifesaver. For the nation's business and health-industry interest groups, it was nothing short of a declaration of war.

Reforming Health Care?

Shortly after his inauguration in January 1993 the president had appointed his wife, Hillary Rodham Clinton, to head a task force of 500 people organized into fifteen "cluster groups" assigned to such issues as cost control, coverage, benefits, long-term care, and ethics. These groups held hearings throughout the country to gather information for use in drafting the bill. The plan eventually proposed by the task force was complex. It called for a "health-security system" in which every person would receive a "health-security card" that would guarantee a comprehensive package of benefits that could never be taken away. The benefits would be offered by different insurance systems rather than by a single federal bureaucracy, but the federal government would guarantee coverage by requiring all health-insurance providers to include the comprehensive package in their plans and to conform to new regulations designed to maintain health security.

Although large businesses had been paying for their employees' health care for decades, they reacted negatively to the complexity of the Clinton plan and to the expansion of federal authority it would involve. In February 1994 the Business Roundtable, which represents about two hundred of the nation's largest companies, withdrew its support from the Clinton plan. Then, at a town meeting in Kansas City, Herman Cain, the president of Godfather's Pizza, asked President Clinton what he could say to the workers in his restaurants who would be laid off as a result of the health-care plan. His question, according to one Senate aid, "was the lightning rod" for the nation's small businesses. Led by the National Federation of Independent Businesses (NFIB), they joined ranks to block the president's proposal to require smaller firms to offer health insurance to their employees.

The strongest opposition, however, came from the Health Insurance Association of America, which primarily represents the interests of doctors and health-insurance companies. Not content with traditional lobbying efforts, it attempted to influence lawmakers by changing the climate of public opinion through television advertising. Its series of ads featuring two "average Americans," Harry and Louise, ridiculed the Clinton plan as costly and unnecessary. (Louise: "This plan forces us to buy our insurance through these new mandatory government health alliances." Harry: "Run by tens of thousands of new bureaucrats." Louise: "Another billion-dollar bureaucracy.") Other interest groups followed suit, placing ads designed to scare the public in newspapers and other media. Typical was the one claiming that every American would have to carry a wallet-sized card with a microcomputer chip containing private medical facts, information that the government could use to "control every aspect of YOUR life."

Despite the support of equally powerful and well organized interest groups like the AFL–CIO, the American Academy of Pediatrics, the Catholic Health Association, and the American Association *of Retired Persons, the White House was unable to beat back the attacks on the health-care plan. In his State of the Union address on January 25, 1994, the president threatened to "take this pen and veto" any health-care reform plan that did not provide universal coverage. A few months later he was willing to compromise, but few members of Congress were willing to listen, much less offer a plan to refine. By the time the refined plan came before the Senate in August, Senator Phil Gramm, a Texas Republican, was already calling it a "dead body."*

In all, the interest groups opposed to the plan spent three hundred million dollars to defeat it—more than both political parties had spent on the presidential election campaigns of 1988 and 1992 combined. But they got value for their money. Although five congressional committees considered the plan and proposed several revisions, nothing was passed before the 1994 election. That election produced a massive change in the composition of both houses of Congress, ensuring conservative majorities against the Clinton plan. Health-care reform, if it occurred at all, would take a very different shape from that proposed by President Clinton.

The biggest opportunity to make social policy since the Great Society legislation of the 1960s

had evaporated. Why? Representative Benjamin Cardin (D-Maryland) summed it up: "The issue got away from everybody. . . . I don't think anybody anticipated the amount of resources that would be marshaled against it."[1] ✦

The "Harry and Louise" commercials were a classic example of an attempt by interest groups to target and influence public opinion on a specific policy issue—universal health insurance. This commercial identified its sponsor as "Citizens for a Sound Economy"—in actuality a group of corporate insurance sponsors organized by the Health Insurance Association of America (HIAA).

INTRODUCTION: INTEREST GROUPS AND DEMOCRACY

Few organizations are viewed with more suspicion than interest groups. Most Americans see them as sinister, selfish, high-pressure outfits that use illegitimate means to promote narrow ends at the expense of the public interest. Indeed, at a historic debate between President Bill Clinton and Speaker of the House Newt Gingrich in a small New Hampshire town on June 11, 1995, the very first citizen to speak denounced interest groups and asked what these two national leaders were going to do to curb the power of lobbyists. "Special interest groups are running the country," Frank McConnell declared, echoing the feelings of millions of his fellow citizens.

The defeat of health-care reform confirmed for many Americans the power of interest groups and their noxious effects on the body politic. In the view of these Americans, the government had proposed a sensible and much-needed health-reform package, one desired by a majority of citizens, yet a narrow set of established interests led by doctors and insurance companies that stood to lose financially by the changes banded together to crush the proposal, undermining the popular will as expressed by a popularly elected government (although the 43 percent popular vote for Clinton in 1992 is hardly a mandate).

However, many political analysts resist this perspective. The defeat of health-care reform, they argue, was not a question of "the people" versus parochial, selfish interests. Health care is a complex national issue, with no clear consensus on how to restructure the system. Millions of Americans can be found both for and against the administration's reform plan; the nation debated that plan openly and at length; and finally, Americans, through their political institutions, made the decision that the status quo in health care was, for the moment, preferable to the proposed changes advocated by the Clinton administration.

In addition, interest groups of all types could be found on both sides of the issue. If it turned out that some interest groups "won" (by blocking health-care reform), it was also true that a good number of interest groups "lost" (those supporting health-care reform). Thus, if interest groups do run the country, that would be news to, say, the American Association of Retired People (AARP) and the many other groups that supported the Clinton health-care plan, since they certainly didn't get the result they wanted.

Interest groups as a whole, then, don't run anything; they struggle against each other for influence with those who do run things. Each group wins some of the time and loses some of the time. Naturally, after every political decision some groups end up winners, but the statement that "some interest groups get some of what they want some of the time," while much more accurate than the overgeneralization that "special interests run this country," doesn't stir the emotional juices in the same way.

We also need to be suspicious of such generalizations when made by those who have lost a political battle. Many of the groups that found themselves on the losing side of health-care reform, like the politically powerful AARP, do get what they want on a number of issues. In those cases, their supporters presumably don't complain that "interest groups are running the country." Rather, they are inclined to believe that truth, justice, and the majority will prevail.

American animosity toward interest groups is especially curious, given the evidence that they are a natural and inevitable presence in free societies. Interest groups are here to stay, and they play a key role in American politics. In fact, interest groups are crucial to democratic society. They provide an easy means for average citizens to participate in the political process, thereby allowing all Americans to approach the democratic ideal. We need to look closely at interest groups to see how they broaden the possibilities for political participation. In doing so, we also need to learn why these agents for democratic influence are often accused of distorting and even undermining the democratic system.

INTEREST GROUPS: A TRADITION IN AMERICAN POLITICS

Foreign and domestic observers alike have long noted the propensity of Americans to form and join groups. "Americans of all ages, all stations in life, and all types of disposition," wrote Tocqueville in 1831, "are forever forming associations."[2] This tendency has been attributed to causes ranging from middle-class mores to the need for community cohesion imposed by the rugged conditions of the country's early history. For whatever reasons, the desire to come together in social groups for common ends has been deeply embedded in American culture.

This value is enshrined politically in the First Amendment's "freedom-of-association" clause:

> Congress shall make no law respecting . . . the right of the people peaceably to assemble, and to petition the government for a redress of grievances.

These simple words provide the legal framework for all citizen-based political activity in the United States. They ensure the existence of a vast array of interest groups, since government can literally do nothing ("Congress shall make no law") to interfere with people joining together ("peaceably to assemble") to try to influence government policies ("petition government for a redress of grievances").

Deeply ingrained in American culture, then, as well as in an entire body of legal expectations, is the norm that citizens may form any kind of group they please and try to influence government, as long as their activity is undertaken "peaceably." To help Americans in their effort to influence government, the Constitution gives them, in the very same sentence granting the rights of assembly and petition, the right to say what they want (freedom of speech) and to publish what they want (freedom of the press). And Americans have not been shy about using these rights. From the earliest days of the republic, they have formed groups of every type and description to defend common interests and obtain favorable government policies.

The result has been a complex array of competing and cooperating interests that practically defines modern democracy. After all, if you can find a political regime today that does not allow competing interest groups, you will also have found a political system that is not democratic.

What Is an Interest Group?

If interest groups are central to the democratic process, what precisely are they? In the broadest sense, **interest groups** are formal organizations of people who share a common outlook or social circumstance and who band together in the hope of influencing government policy.[3] Groups can take a wide variety of forms. One example is a labor union such as the United Auto Workers (UAW), an interest group formed in 1935 to secure improvements in wages and working conditions for automobile factory workers. Another example is the National Rifle Association (NRA), a large affiliation of firearms owners who have organized a powerful lobby for the Second Amendment right to "keep and bear arms." Groups can vary from large organizations with diffuse goals (the AARP, with its thirty five million members and its broad aim of promoting the interests of the elderly) to small outfits with very specific goals, such as the American Women's Society of Certified Public Accountants.

Some political scientists have found it useful to distinguish between actual and potential interest groups. **Actual groups** have already been formed; they have a headquarters, an organizational structure, paid employees, membership lists, and the like. **Potential groups** are interests that could come into being under the right circumstances. As yet, they have no substantive form and may never have one. Still, they cannot be discounted by political participants. Whenever substantial numbers of people share a common outlook or socioeconomic condition, they might well decide to join together to promote their

Interest group members use their first amendment rights "peaceably to assemble" in an effort to advocate, publicize, and influence government policy regarding their own particular issue agenda.

mutual interests. Politicians who ignore potential groups for long may in fact be encouraging their formation.

Often it takes little more than one or a few dynamic leaders, called **policy entrepreneurs,** to create the conditions whereby a potential group becomes an actual interest group. Ralph Nader stands as a classic example of a policy entrepreneur. Largely due to his untiring efforts, a number of consumer-oriented interest groups, such as Public Citizen Litigation Group and the Health Research Group, as well as various other Public Interest Research Groups (PIRGs), came into being in the 1970s, with a major impact on legislation at both the national and the state levels. A classic example of a potential interest group becoming an actual group can be seen in the establishment of Mothers against Drunk Drivers (MADD). For decades children have been killed or maimed by intoxicated motorists, creating the potential for bringing the parents of those children together into a group that would push for stricter laws to prevent and punish drunk driving. Yet no such group appeared until one woman, Candy Lightner, who lost a child to a drunk driver, decided to form such a group and devote her life to this work.

In a free society actual groups may form and even become powerful on very short notice. United We Stand America, an interest group, formed to support Ross Perot's 1992 presidential candidacy, went from nonexistence to the status of major player in national politics in the space of a few short months. Thus, politicians and observers of politics must always be aware of potential groups "out there" in the public. In taking any action, politicians must remember that their decisions may impinge on the interests of some currently amorphous set of people who would soon see their shared interest and organize in opposition. And these groups may form and gain power quickly if agitated enough by governmental actions or trends in society.

Of course, not every potential group will become a full-fledged power in politics. As we will see, some groups are more likely to form and to gain political clout than others. In making policy, politicians consider numerous factors without constantly trying to imagine whether an action they decide to take today could cause the formation of a group that will punish them tomorrow. Still, that possibility can never be wholly ignored and must play at least a modest role in the policymaking process.

A Long History of Association

From the very beginning of the republic, national leaders have wrestled with the idea of interest groups. In *Federalist* no. 10, James Madison wrote, "Liberty is to faction as air is to fire." To put it in modern terms, he saw that the development and proliferation of interest groups was inevitable in a free society. But Madison also saw a basic flaw in democratic politics when it came to interests. He worried that one set of interests (one "faction"), whether a majority or a minority of the population, might gain control of the levers of power and rule society for its own aims, to the detriment of the collective good.

Concerned as he was about the negative potential of factions, Madison worked to control their effects (while warning against any effort to eliminate factions altogether—an action that he knew would undermine Americans' precious liberties). He reasoned that the power of factions could be moderated by diffusing their influence. This diffusion would occur in two ways. First, the very act of joining the individual states into a large and diverse country undercut the power of any one faction. What group could successfully unite the industrial interests of the Northeast and the plantation interests of the South, small independent farmers, indentured servants, urban workers, artisans and merchants, sharecroppers, and all of the other groups in America at that time? The very size and complexity of the new nation would guard against the likelihood of any one faction controlling government.

Madison's second hedge against the triumph of any given faction was to make government complex. By dividing political power among several institutions representing different interests chosen at different times by different elements of the population, he strove to ensure that no one faction could ever gain control of all the key levers of power. As we know, Madison and the other framers were hugely successful at their task. Indeed, one of the major criticisms of the American political system is that the framers were too successful. America's national government is so hedged with restrictions on its powers and so open to the input of every imaginable faction or interest group that it can rarely develop a coherent set of national policies, as seen in the case study that introduced this chapter.[4]

Madison, then, strove to mitigate the worst effects of faction rather than eliminate the causes of faction altogether. As he saw it, the causes of faction are "sown into the nature of man." Given the human tendency toward disagreement and disharmony, factional differences will always exist. Thus, one can never eliminate the *causes* of faction, one can only eliminate or suppress faction itself. But governmental suppression of faction would destroy liberty, thus making the cure worse than the disease. Rather than try to suppress faction, Madison and the framers chose to allow a diversity of factions within a complex system of political and social pluralism, ensuring that all interests could be heard, while making it difficult for any one interest to gain tyrannical control of power.

From a modern perspective, Madison's view of faction was both wise and prescient. Tens of thousands of interest groups have formed and thrived since the early days of the republic, allowing widespread input into the policy process from millions of average citizens, yet no one group has ever gained full control of all the levers of political and social power. Setting group against group in relatively peaceful competition within a complex system of divided powers seems to have been a successful vision of the way to deal with the fissures and stresses that are inevitable in a free society.

Parties formed in the very early years of the republic, and groups of every type and description began to flourish soon thereafter. Revivalist religious groups, social-reform groups, peace groups, women's rights groups, abolitionist groups, temperance groups—these and hundreds of others that sprang up in the early years of the nineteenth century bore witness to Madison's expectation that the air of liberty would do nothing but nourish a swarm of factional organizations. It is hardly surprising that American political history is in many ways a history of diverse and competing interest groups.

The organizational ease with which groups are formed in the United States is often attributed to its democratic culture. Americans, who often see themselves as equals, generally find it easy to work together in groups toward common ends. Tocqueville wrote that "in no other country of the world has the principle of association been more successfully used, or more unsparingly applied to a multitude of different objects, than in America."[5] While all modern democracies exhibit interest group activity, few have achieved the level of vibrant nongovernmental group life apparent in the American system.

INTEREST GROUPS: RECENT TRENDS   Even though interest groups have been central to American political history, the number of groups trying to pressure government has grown dramatically in the last three decades. The reasons for this development are complex. For one, government policies since the 1960s have resulted in greater regulation of society. Responding to demands that it "do something" about the problems of civil rights, the environment, education, conditions in the workplace, health, women's rights, and so forth, the national government has developed policies that affect all sectors of society. Government regulations now touch all Americans. Naturally, people whose livelihoods and values are affected by government actions find it expedient to work together to influence those actions. Thus, as government's power to affect society grows, so too will the number of groups that aim to influence and pressure government.

Another explanation for the growth of interest groups stems from the success that liberal interest groups experienced starting in the 1950s. In the past, conservative groups rarely relied upon group activity to advance their aims because conservatives were already active in civic affairs, being on average wealthier, more educated, and more likely to participate in politics than average citizens. Thus, they were already well represented in government and believed that it adequately responded to their needs. Conversely, those groups most underrepresented in political institutions were most likely to use interest groups to pursue policy goals. These groups tended to promote the liberal aims of civil rights groups, environmentalists, the poor, and women.

By the 1970s, these liberal groups had gained many victories through the pressure they exerted on Congress, the executive branch, and the courts. Manufacturing and business leaders, along with ideological conservatives of every type, responded by forming their own interest groups. Moreover, the federal government actually sponsored citizen group involvement by reimbursing participants in agency proceedings with seed money or outright grants. Federal domestic legislation included provisions for citizen participation, which spurred group action such as environmental action councils, legal defense coalitions, health care organizations, and senior citizen groups.[6] These conservative groups developed their own dynamism in reaction to the social-policy gains previously made by liberals. While Planned Parenthood, the ACLU, and other groups considered liberal fought battles to gain abortion and privacy rights, political conservatives countered in the late 1970s and 1980s with groups such as Operation Rescue and the Moral Majority. Thus, the success of liberal interest groups led to the rise of conservative counterpart groups.

A major impetus toward increasing group involvement in politics came in the early 1970s with campaign finance reform. Two bills (one in 1971 and its amendments in 1974) changed the nature of money in American politics. As you saw in Chapter 11, these bills limited the role of individual "fat cats" and expanded the power of political action committees (PACs). Rather than seeking

Strongly held policy preferences are essential for interest group formation. Interest groups provide individuals that hold strong policy preferences with a way to disseminate information to legislators, make their preferences known, and work within the system to influence legislation.

large donations from a small number of very wealthy individuals, money would now be raised from large numbers of contributors through organized group efforts. The system, in short, supplies a strong incentive to group activity.

Finally, increasing income and education levels have led to increased levels of political activity in the United States over the past fifty to sixty years. The United States now possesses a large middle class and upper middle class of educated, affluent voters who are vitally aware of the political process and how it affects them. Many of these people have become deeply involved in politics—especially in groups that promote their interests and concerns. No theory seeking to explain the rise in the number and power of American interest groups can fail to take into account this important social development.

Interest Group Functions

Interest groups provide people with the opportunity to band together to influence public policy and are therefore central to the operations of democracy. They also provide policymakers with information; indeed, members of Congress have come to depend on the expertise and information provided by interest groups as part of their deliberative process.

INTEREST GROUPS ALLOW FOR COLLECTIVE ACTION People form and join interest groups because **collective action** (the action of many) is stronger, more credible, and more likely to influence policy outcomes than the isolated actions of individuals.[7] Imagine, for example, the modest influence you would have if you alone wrote a letter to your university president protesting next year's tuition increase. You would probably receive a letter written by a staff member of the president expressing concern about the cost of attending school, but a single letter will not change policy. But what if you joined a group whose goal was to persuade five thousand students to write and complain about tuition? Collective action of that sort would surely be taken more seriously than the actions of one or a few individuals. What if your group went on to pressure the student council and faculty members to set up a day-long protest? And if these actions failed, what if your group then encouraged five thousand students to march on the administration building? You may or may not win the battle over tuition, but you would surely stand a much better chance of broadcasting your aims as part of a group effort. In the early 1970s, students your age temporarily shut down many colleges across the nation as part of their protest of the Vietnam War.

Group action is also more effective in democratic politics, where the power of numbers carries special weight. Thus, interest groups serve a number of important functions in the American political system. They allow citizens to promote their specialized concerns. Through interest group activity, people can join with like-minded others rather than have to blend in with huge numbers of people under the common umbrella of a large political institution like a political party. In representing specific points of view in society, interest groups can project precise citizen demands into politics, bringing both government and the political parties closer to the people, thereby democratizing the national agenda. It was through interest group activity that the perspectives of the abolitionist movement (which sought to end slavery in the nineteenth century) came to be absorbed into the political outlook of the pre–Civil War Republican party, just as the perspective of the civil rights movement of the next century was largely absorbed by the post–New Deal Democrats.

INTEREST GROUPS PROVIDE INFORMATION   Interest groups possess the expertise needed to provide relevant information about policy goals to party leaders, public officials, and bureaucrats who would otherwise not have these facts at their disposal. Through this function, interest groups once again provide an important inroad for broader participation in the actual policymaking process.

Interest groups can provide government officials with a constant, regular source of information about popular sentiment. They thereby serve as a vital indicator of the system's responsiveness to citizen demands. The more that public officials hear the varied voices of the people, the more likely they are to take those voices into account in formulating government policies.

While interest groups are an important element in American democratic life, many observers fear that their effects are not all positive. Because interest groups focus on their own cause, they are said to downplay or ignore the public good. Furthermore, by creating a proliferation of competing demands and divisive rhetoric, the vast array of interest groups may drown out moderate voices of compromise and cooperation. The "information" supplied by interest groups can be biased, leaving officials and the public with just one perspective on an issue. Furthermore, interest groups are not all equal; the powerful groups tend to be those already in control of the major resources in society, especially money and property. Large corporations tend to dominate the sphere of interest group activity and are often willing to sacrifice consumer safety, workers' welfare, and environmental protection.[8]

Interest groups thus represent a peculiar irony of democracy: While stimulating citizen action and political involvement, they can also create confrontation instead of cooperation, diatribe in place of reasoned debate. While allowing a role for average citizens to promote their democratic goals, interest groups can also skew the political process to favor those who are already powerful and well off. The "factions" that so concerned Madison are now powerful, well-financed organizations. Can a modern democratic system preserve liberty (allowing groups free rein to promote their goals) without sacrificing the very essence of the democratic ideal, widespread access to power for all citizens? That is one of the central questions that American society continually confronts as it struggles to approach democracy.

TYPES OF INTEREST GROUPS

Nearly twenty thousand organized groups of every imaginable kind regularly seek to influence the policies of the American government. These groups take a wide variety of forms, but for simplicity we can divide them into a few major types: Economic, public interest, government, ideological, religious, civil rights, single issue, state, and local interest groups. Some of these groups are listed in Table 12.1.

The National Rifle Association is famous for the sheer size of its lobbying tactics. It has been known to generate millions of telegrams in a few days, also tying up Capitol Hill with so many phone calls that members cannot make outgoing calls.

Table 12.1
Selected Interest Groups

Economic

   Chamber of Commerce

   AFL–CIO

   American Farm Bureau Federation

   American Federation of State, County and Municipal Employees

   American Medical Association

   National Association of Manufacturers

Public Interest

   Common Cause

   League of Women Voters

   Consumers Union of the United States

   Public Citizen

Ideological

   Americans for Democratic Action

   American Conservative Union

   People for the American Way

   National Committee for the Effectiveness of Congress

Religious

   National Council of Churches

   B'nai B'rith

   Council of Catholic Bishops

   Mennonite Central Committee

Civil Rights

   American Indian Movement

   National Association for the Advancement of Colored People

   Congress of Racial Equality

   National Organization for Women

   Mexican-American Legal Defense and Educational Fund

Single-Issue

   Environmental Defense Fund

   National Right to Life Committee

   National Abortion Rights Action League

   National Rifle Association

   National Coalition to Ban Handguns

State and Local

   American Automobile Association

Economic Interest Groups

On a day-in, day-out basis most observers would rate the power of economic interests as dominant in politics. The old saying, "Most people vote their pocketbooks" applies to group activity as well: Most people take political action to protect or enhance their economic well-being. Thus, groups whose main aim is to help their members make money or keep their money will always play a central role in the political process of any democracy. Economic interest groups include big business, organized labor, and other groups.

BIG BUSINESS   Corporations have long dominated interest group activity in American politics. That pattern is hardly surprising in an environment of entrepreneurial capitalism. Calvin Coolidge made the point concisely: "The business of America is business." The United States' political process seems almost designed to illustrate Coolidge's saying. Over half the lobbies operating in Washington today represent corporate and industrial interests.[9]

Heading the list of business-oriented interest groups is the U.S. Chamber of Commerce, which represents 225,000 businesses across the nation, including manufacturers, retailers, construction firms, and financial, insurance, and real-estate companies. With an annual budget of over sixty-five million dollars and a full-time staff of fourteen hundred, the chamber carries considerable political clout. Other major big-business interest groups include the National Association of Manufacturers (NAM) and the Business Roundtable. These were the groups that battled over health care. In addition to belonging to these umbrella groups, many large and medium-sized companies, numbering some five hundred in Washington alone, such as IBM, Ford, General Motors, Exxon, and Xerox, maintain their own lobbyists to ensure that their voices are heard.

ORGANIZED LABOR   Despite its power, business is not the only voice of organized economic interest. Labor traditionally has played a major role in American politics. Indeed, the influential economist John Kenneth Galbraith once called labor unions an important "countervailing power" that could stand up to

Corporate executives from the U.S. tobacco industry testified that smoking does not cause cancer. Later internal documents proved that their own research has indicated that smoking causes cancer as well as other serious physical maladies such as emphysema and heart disease.

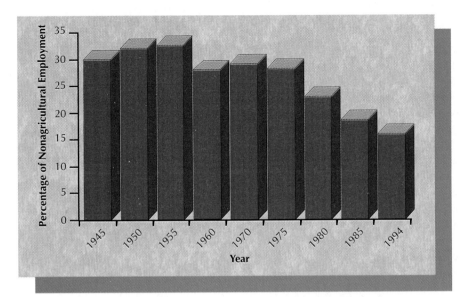

FIGURE 12.1
By 1994, union membership had declined significantly, representing only 15.1 percent of the workforce. This is explained in large part by the decrease in the proportion of blue-collar jobs in the workforce, a traditional source for union representation. Union expansion into the representation of public employees has not stopped the decline of union membership as a percentage of nonagricultural employment.

Source: Leo Troy and Neil Sheflin, *U. S. Union Sourcebook* (West Orange, N.J.: Industrial Relations Data and Information Services, 1985); and Bureau of Labor Statistics.

and dilute the power of big business.[10] Historically, labor groups have been among the most influential of organized interests in the twentieth century, but their power has declined in recent years (see Figure 12.1). Unionized workers, who once represented nearly 40 percent of the workforce now account for something closer to 15 percent of it. Still, the AFL–CIO, labor's umbrella organization, continues to represent millions of workers and puts intense pressure on politicians for better wages, improved working conditions, job protection, social programs, and health insurance. Other major labor groups include the United Auto Workers, the United Mine Workers, and the Teamsters (a union representing workers in the transportation industry).

Although it often appears that business and labor are always at odds, they occasionally join forces. For instance, when the Chrysler Corporation was seeking government loans in 1981, one of the most ardent backers of the loan program was the United Auto Workers, which hoped to preserve the tens of thousands of jobs its workers held in Chrysler plants.

OTHER ECONOMIC INTEREST GROUPS   It is probably no exaggeration to say that an interest group exists to protect and promote the interests of every group of people who make their living in the United States. Beyond workers and businesspeople, groups exist to advance the interests of lawyers (the American Bar Association), doctors (the American Medical Association), teachers (the National Education Association), and so forth.

Farmers were once among the most powerful of groups in the United States and are still solidly represented by such organizations as the American Farm Bureau Federation, the National Corn Growers Association, and the National Farmers Union. The power of agricultural interests has inevitably diminished as the number of farmers has steadily declined, mirroring a pattern in all industrial nations. People who make more than half of their income through farming now represent less than 2 percent of the United States workforce. Still,

The Case of Japanese Rice Farmers

Interest groups play a major role in democratic politics everywhere. If allowed to compete freely, small, highly organized, strategically placed groups can wield influence well beyond their numbers. The case of rice farmers in Japan perfectly illustrates this point.

The power of the Japanese farm lobby has long impressed, even astounded observers. Rice farmers in particular have been influential, in part because the crop they produce has long been a staple in the Japanese diet. The group constitutes, by the most generous definition, less than one percent of the Japanese population; the actual number of "full-time" rice farmers stands at fewer than a million people in a nation of more than 120 million inhabitants. Yet the Japanese government goes to great lengths to provide rice farmers with economic assistance. They are paid *not* to plant rice on much of their land, they receive massive government subsidies, and they are shielded from international competition by rigid import barriers. The Japanese people pay dearly for these policies.

The most conservative analysts agree that government rice policy costs Japanese taxpayers at least twenty billion dollars a year. Some estimates put the figure much higher: up to sixty billion dollars a year. Costs are incurred in several ways. Most dramatically, Japanese consumers pay *eight to nine times* as much as the rest of the world for the rice they buy every day. These high prices reflect the scarcity induced by government policies. Dropping these policies would bring a glut of rice onto Japanese markets, dropping the price drastically, and saving Japanese citizens large sums of money.

Japan's policy toward rice farmers has other serious consequences. By paying farmers to do nothing with their land, the government is preventing more efficient use of it. In a nation where land is already scarce, making millions of acres unavailable keeps the price of all the nation's land astronomically high. Allowing the market to decide how idling rice land should be used would save consumers money and enhance their welfare. One estimate holds that if currently unavailable farm land in Tokyo were allowed to go onto the free market, an additional one million residences could be built to house the tightly packed citizens of that crowded capital city.

Why are such obvious market irrationalities allowed to continue? The answer is simple. Japanese rice farmers, like American tobacco farmers, have long been a powerful pressure group. Like any successful interest, they have a lot going for them.

---

given the importance of this segment of the population, which provides food for Americans and many others around the world, it is safe to say that farm groups will continue to wield major political power for some time to come.

Public Interest Groups

Economic self-interest, though a powerful force, represents just one of the reasons that people come together in groups to secure collective action from government. One of the most interesting developments in American government since the 1960s is the dramatic increase in public interest groups. These groups represent the interests of average citizens as consumers, as holders of individual rights, as proponents of various causes, and as the nonwealthy. Public interest groups focus not on the immediate economic livelihood of their members but on achieving a broad set of goals that represent their members' vision of the collective good. Their members and leaders seek substantive policy as their goal ("clean air"), not specific increments of economic well-being ("twenty cents more an hour for minimum-wage workers").

They are well organized, they are well funded, they produce a vital and valued commodity for society, and they have a broad range of sympathy in the populace at large. (For many Japanese, rice has almost religious significance, and Japanese rice is held to be much better than any other country's rice.) But perhaps most important in explaining the success of Japanese rice farmers is their strategic political position.

Because legislative districts are badly apportioned in Japan, the average vote in a farming district counts five times as much as the average vote in a white-collar, urban area. This situation magnifies the power of rural interests, including rice farmers. In addition, rice farmers are politically concentrated and powerfully connected. They constitute a central pillar of support for the rurally based Liberal Democrats who ruled Japan from 1955 to 1993. Rice farmers gave Liberal Democrats money and strategically vital votes, and in return the party, when in power, showered rice farmers with favorable government policies.

This neat system is breaking down however. International pressures and poor rice harvests have forced the government to loosen its import restrictions on rice. As Japanese citizens have become aware of the huge costs they bear for government rice policies, their support for these policies has diminished. (This decline in support is strongest among younger Japanese, who have adopted Western eating habits and no longer view rice as sacred.) Furthermore, there are fewer rice farmers, the group has weakened with age, and the farmers are increasingly divided about what policies to press on the government. Finally, the power wielders they must influence have changed. Liberal Democrats lost their monopoly on power in the election of 1993, so the tight connections between rice farmers and politicians have diminished.

No interest group in a democracy gets all it wants all of the time. Eventually its interests collide with those of other segments of the population, and it must learn to live with less power and fewer benefits. But for several decades Japanese rice farmers seemed oblivious to this basic rule of politics. They stand as a model of the power a social interest can wield under the right political circumstances.

Sources: Peter Jegi Gordon, "Rice Policy of Japan's LDP: Domestic Trends toward Agreement," *Asian Survey* 30 (Oct. 1990): 943–58: Mayumi Itoh, "*Kome Kaikoku* and Japanese Internationalization," *Asian Survey* 34 (Nov. 1994): 991–1001.

Some of the best-known public interest groups include Citizens for Tax Justice, the Nature Conservancy, the Natural Resources Defense Council, the National Taxpayers Union, the National Organization for Women, the League of Women Voters, and Common Cause. Seeing their goal as the achievement of policy favorable to all citizens, public interest groups recruit widely and welcome the support of the general public.

Ralph Nader is one of the best-known public interest group advocates in the nation. A Harvard-trained lawyer, he became famous in the 1960s when he challenged General Motors and its Corvair automobile, which he considered unsafe. In 1965 he published *Unsafe at Any Speed* and later created the group Public Citizen, which is devoted to making the legal system more responsive to the public. In addition, in many states, Nader's Public Interest Research Groups (PIRGs) are popular with students. They provide oversight on auto safety, consumer issues, health issues, and the environment. Today there are more than two hundred of these groups, and they claim among their victories nonsmoking rules on airlines, nutrition labels, and laws requiring smoke detectors in apartment buildings.

Public interest groups like Ralph Nader's Public Citizen, Inc., began to proliferate in the 1970s due to a growing skepticism regarding the government's willingness to respond to the majority sentiment. In addition to popular support, the government itself sponsored and encouraged the formation of citizen groups by requiring citizen participation in federal domestic legislation.

Perhaps the best-known public interest group is Common Cause, which promotes campaign reform, the abolition of political action committees (PACs), the elimination of unneeded bureaucratic institutions, and other reforms for the achievement of "good" government. Common Cause has more than 250,000 members and an eleven-million-dollar annual budget. Its central target has been the abuse of money and PACS in the political process.[11]

Common Cause has been especially outraged by the cozy relationship between interest group contributions and political influence. It points, for instance, to the fact that the NRA can contribute money to members of the Senate Judiciary Committee, which has the job of reviewing firearms legislation, and that the American Medical Association (AMA) and American Dental Association (ADA) can contribute millions to members of Congress who serve on committees that consider regulations that affect business practices in these professions. Pointing out that PAC expenditures on congressional races are at an all-time high, Common Cause recently sought to organize "People vs. PACS," a campaign designed to clean up the financing of congressional elections. Common Cause's longtime efforts to reduce or eliminate the influence of money in politics has so far borne little fruit, but that may change, especially if something comes of the informal agreement between President Clinton and House Speaker Newt Gingrich in June 1995 to set up a blue-ribbon commission to investigate the problem.

Government Interest Groups

A recent addition to the interest group mix has been government itself. Today, the National Conference of Mayors, the National League of Cities, the National Governors' Association, and other organizations composed of government officials compete alongside traditional interest groups for funding, policies, and attention.

Although questions have been raised about whether government interest groups should be competing for scarce resources, these groups are well funded, very influential, and easily able to gain access to the halls of Congress. Their right to act as interest groups was affirmed in an important 1985 Supreme Court case, *Garcia* v. *San Antonio Metropolitan Transit Authority,* 469 US. 528 (1985). The opinion's author, Justice Harry Blackmun, refused to grant authority to the states to set their own compensation rates for municipal employees. States, he said, like private employers, would have to abide by the regulations governing wages established in the federal Fair Labor Standards Act. Blackmun argued that states were inherently well represented in Congress—through automatic representation in the Senate and secondary representation in the House—and were responsible for petitioning Congress to make laws in accordance with their wishes. Immediately following the decision, a number of government interest groups successfully lobbied Congress to grant exemptions from the Fair Labor Standards Act to public employees, thereby strengthening the concept of federalism. Thus, government agencies and officials are under no constitutional restraints when it comes to forming their own interest groups to place pressure on other agencies and officials of our government.

Other Interest Groups

Groups come in such a wide variety of forms that it is not always easy to categorize them. Following are several other kinds of interest groups that political observers have described at one time or another. Although these types may legitimately be seen as a variant of the public interest group, each is sufficiently distinct to be worthy of an individual examination.

IDEOLOGICAL INTEREST GROUPS   Some people get into politics to promote deep-seated ideological beliefs. They don't just want a subsidy or a bridge, or even a middle-range goal like term limits. They want nothing less than to transform society and the political process along the lines of some broad philosophical perspective. Such people form ideological interest groups. The best-known such group is the Americans for Democratic Action (ADA). Founded in 1947 by such strong liberals of the day as Hubert Humphrey, John Kenneth Galbraith, and Eleanor Roosevelt, it has been pushing ever since for an entire set of policy proposals that would create a coherently liberal society. To counter ADA efforts, a group known as the American Conservative Union (the ACU) sprang up a few years later to promote a conservative agenda.

Other ideologically oriented groups include People for the American Way (liberal) and the Concord Coalition (conservative). In keeping with American culture's tendency toward pragmatism, ideological interest groups have always been few in number and consist primarily of a small number of dedicated activists. Still, because these activists are energetic, well educated, well connected, and adept at raising money, ideological interest groups frequently wield a good deal more clout than one would expect from numbers alone.

RELIGIOUS INTEREST GROUPS   A variant of the ideological interest group is the group that wishes to transform society along the lines of its religious beliefs. As one would expect in a society where most people take religion seriously, groups seeking to bring religious values into the political arena have at one time or another had powerful effects on American politics. Perhaps the most famous example of religion's impact was the Prohibitionist movement, which early in this century sought to ban the sale and consumption of alcohol. The movement was driven by church and religious groups throughout the nation. Among the more powerful religious groups of the present are the National Council of Churches (representing mainstream Protestantism), B'nai B'rith (representing Judaism), Anti-Defamation League, and the Council of Catholic Bishops. In recent years groups representing conservative Protestant perspectives, such as the Moral Majority and the Christian Coalition, have gained a significant following.

CIVIL RIGHTS INTEREST GROUPS   Similar to ideological interest groups are those groups that seek to promote the legal rights of minorities and other people who have suffered discrimination. All of these groups seek to transform society to ensure legal equality and social justice for their members. They focus on creating an egalitarian society in which their members are treated equally, given equal opportunities for advancement, and are accepted into mainstream society without denigration. One of the best known of these groups is the National Association for the Advancement of Colored People (NAACP), which for decades was the driving force behind the black civil rights movement. Other well-known groups of this sort include the National Organization for Women (NOW), the American Indian Movement (AIM), the Mexican-American Legal Defense and Education Fund (MALDEF), and various organizations that protect and seek to advance the rights of gay Americans.[12]

SINGLE-ISSUE INTEREST GROUPS   As the name implies, single-issue interest groups are organizations that represent citizens who are primarily concerned with one particular policy matter or social problem. For many participants in such interest groups, the one issue that drives them to political activity looms so large in their value scheme that all other issues seem insignificant by comparison. Hence, group members are both intense and uncompromising in promoting their aims. Groups of this type that are currently powerful in American politics include the National Rifle Association (NRA), the National Coalition to Ban Handguns, the National Right to Life Committee, the National Abortion Rights Action League, NARAL, and the Environmental Defense Fund (EDF).

Given their uncompromising beliefs, single-issue activists present a prickly problem for politicians whose usual job consists of balancing competing demands and reaching judicious compromise solutions. Single-issue groups don't look kindly upon compromise. Their supporters often take a bipolar view of the world. If you're not with them, you're against them—an enemy to be crushed and defeated. Inevitably, single-issue groups raise political temperatures and exacerbate conflict whenever they get seriously involved in politics. Many politicians shudder at the prospect of having to deal with them.

CHARACTERISTICS OF INTEREST GROUPS

Although each interest group is unique, most share characteristics that distinguish them from other organizations in society. For instance, interest groups, unlike political parties, rarely try to get their leaders elected to major political positions, but they do target elected officials who are unsympathetic to their interests. Interest groups want to influence government, not *be* the government, but they do seek a government of policymakers who support their goals.

In addition, interest groups do not have as their main aim business, trade, or the making of money. They may promote business interests, and they may incidentally make money in one way or another (through the sale of books, maps, insurance policies, or other items for members), but profit is not their main focus. Interest groups are quintessentially government-influencing institutions. Their goal of pressuring government decision makers sets them apart from the other major structures of American society: government itself, political parties, business enterprises, and run-of-the-mill social groups that do not undertake political activities (such as the Lions Club or the Girl and Boy Scouts).

Let us now look at interest group membership and other characteristics such as group resources and leadership.

Interest Group Membership

Interest groups need members to survive and prosper, and in a democratic society, the more members a group has, the more political clout it will wield. Scholars have long sought to learn why some interest groups are more successful than others in attracting members. Closely related to that question is another: Why do some groups form and prosper while others never get started, or if they do, falter and disappear? These issues are worth examining in some detail.

MAINTAINING INTEREST GROUP MEMBERSHIP   An interest group forms when some citizens, be they few or many, perceive that the political arena is failing to provide the policy outcomes they prefer, or when some citizens have been adversely affected by technological change or by government policies. Many other factors influence the development of a particular interest group: the presence of strong, dynamic leaders, the financial and educational resources of the group, the geographic concentration of the group. (It's easier to unite workers in one large factory than people who clean individual homes across a large city.) All these factors and more help determine the likelihood that a group will become cognizant of itself as a collectivity and band together in a formal organization to promote a common interest.

Perhaps the central question about why people form and join interest groups follows from our earlier discussion about the likelihood of a potential group becoming an actual group. Just because people with a common interest exist, it doesn't follow automatically that they will form a group and become active in promoting its aims. No one is obliged to become an interest group member. As with all life choices, people must decide that the expenditure of time, money, and effort on interest group activity is worthwhile.

Since people don't automatically support a group even if it does "objectively" represent their interests, group leaders must devote a major portion of their time to **group maintenance;** that is, they must constantly canvass for new members and provide benefits (both psychological and material) for current members. Although the advancement of favorable policies is the initial impetus for forming the interest group, policy efforts soon become just one part of the equation when the group considers how best to use its resources. The Sierra Club, for example, has to devote a good deal of time, money, and energy to pleasing current members and recruiting new ones. The club organizes singles vacations to scenic areas and family package cruises, and offers discounts of many types for purchases of environmentally conscious products and subscriptions to its magazine.

THE FREE-RIDER PROBLEM   The need to keep current and potential group members happy stems from an issue known as the *free-rider problem*. Mancur Olson, a leading social theorist, has identified and described this issue.[13] To achieve a collective good, any group calls upon its members for resources, time, expertise, and so forth. But if everyone benefits anyway, why should one individual put in any time or money? Members who do not invest but still share in the collective benefits of group action are known as **free riders.** Some union members, for instance, may reason that there's no point in going to interminable union meetings, since they will end up getting the same pay hikes and improved working conditions as the members who put in all those hours of work attending meetings. The problem, of course, is that if everyone in the union thinks that way, management will realize that the union is ineffectual and will reduce, not increase, employee benefits. As a result of too many free riders, all members of a group may gain nothing, undermining the group's very reason for being.

If the benefits of a policy achieved by the group extend to nonmembers, an additional free-rider problem exists. The Sierra Club, for instance, has over a half million members, and its work to preserve the national parks benefits all Americans. But why should you join the club if you're guaranteed to benefit from its work anyway? Free riders receive benefits similar to those obtained by the Sierra Club's actual members. Similarly, union members pay dues and attend meetings, but many nonunion workers benefit from the improvement in working conditions and wage increases obtained through union activity. All citizens will benefit if the National Taxpayers Union succeeds in persuading Congress to lower tax rates. Why, then, put in the time and money to join the National Taxpayers Union?

However, the free-rider problem may be exaggerated. It rests heavily on the argument that most people join groups for material gain. In fact, people undertake voluntary group activity for any number of reasons, and most don't engage in economic calculations before deciding whether their involvement in a group is "worth it." Many Americans are induced by feelings of moral obligation to contribute to a group cause or get involved in a group's activity. And when people commit themselves intensely to political action, it is more likely that the rewards they gain are psychological rather than material. Thus, dedicated group activists may be motivated by a variety of psychological incentives, including the desire to make social contacts, the wish to advance political career chances, the opportunity to participate in a fascinating game (politics), and the urge to help improve the quality of government policy decisions. Most groups, then, can gain both supporters and active members without neccessarily offering them a material reward for their participation.[14]

Other Characteristics of Interest Groups

Interest groups differ from each other in many ways. These differences help to explain why some groups will be more effective than others, be more or less inclined to use a grassroots strategy, or be likely to operate at the state rather than the national level. One key difference centers on resources. Naturally, groups with money, connections, social prestige, and access to political elites will be greatly advantaged in the struggle to influence government. On the other hand, zeal and numbers can go a long way toward overcoming financial deficiencies. Any group that can get a large number of people writing letters, calling political leaders, and even marching in the street can have a serious impact on the policymaking process.

Whether a group is concentrated or diffuse matters. A neighborhood association trying to block construction of a nearby prison will have a greater chance of success than a broad potential group like the set of people who have recently lost jobs due to American free-trade policies. The level of government on which a group needs to exert pressure is also crucial. It's easier to get results at the local level than at the national level.

The leadership skill of group officers is also crucial. Naturally, the more forceful and persuasive the group leader, the more successfully that person can advance the group's cause and keep it in the public eye. Ralph Nader has been similarly effective as a leader for consumer interests. Whether a skilled, dynamic leader will emerge for any given group is, of course, subject to circumstance. One wonders, for instance, whether the American civil rights movement could have been as successful as it was if Martin Luther King, Jr., had never lived.

INTEREST GROUP STRATEGY

It is not always apparent how an interest group can best achieve its goals. A group must constantly make decisions about strategy: where it should focus its energies, what issues to push, with whom it should align, and so forth. Should the group target a House subcommittee, the Senate majority leader, the president, a deputy undersecretary in the administration, or key governors and mayors? Issues cut across political arenas at the local, state, and national levels, so the best place to apply pressure is frequently unclear. Groups must also consider whether to push at the grassroots, trying to create a populist groundswell for their ideas, or whether to pursue an inside strategy by going directly to powerful public officials. Let us examine the major strategic devices that interest groups have found effective over the years.

Lobbying

Lobbying represents the most common and effective way to influence public policy. **Lobbying** is the formal, organized attempt to influence legislation, usually through direct contact with legislators or their staff. The political use of the term *lobby* in the United States was first recorded in the annals of the Tenth Congress. In 1829 the term *lobby-agents* was used to describe favor seekers. During the period of President Ulysses S. Grant (1869–77), the president frequently walked from the White House to the Willard Hotel on Pennsylvania Avenue. When relaxing with legislators in the Willard's comfortable lobby, individuals seeking jobs or favors would visit the lobby—hence the term *lobbyists*.[15]

Lobbyists have never ranked high in the eyes of the public. However, the distasteful caricature of a fat-cat special-interest lobbyist who buys a vote by bribing a legislator is a gross distortion of what most lobbyists do. Outright bribery is rare; so too are other illegal attempts to gain the favor of political officials. The reason is simple. The rewards for corrupt behavior rarely outweigh the risks. After all, money leaves a trail that investigators can follow. Besides, people talk (especially those in politics), so keeping a political secret is no easy task. Astute reporters, of whom there are hundreds hoping to expose some juicy scandal, can ultimately uncover most bribery episodes. Furthermore, bribery is illegal, so not only are reporters hoping to uncover corruption, but so are state and federal legal officers.

Scandals in American electoral politics have not been a rare occurrence. The Abscam scandal in the early 1980s is a representative example. Created as an FBI "sting" operation, Abscam involved FBI agents who posed as Sheikh Kambir Abdul Rahman and his agents from the Middle East, representing their firm, "Abdul Enterprises Ltd." This group attempted to exchange large sums of cash for

Most lobbyists prefer to describe their work as "government relations" or "public affairs" due to the unsavory connotations that the term "lobbyist" invokes. Their work includes attendance at hearings, meetings with committee staff, attendance at receptions and fundraisers, keeping current on legislation, presenting testimony at Congressional hearings, and distributing information to members of Congress and their staff.

immigration, business, and legislative favors from congressional representatives. The FBI was able to film lawmakers accepting tens of thousands of dollars in cash on videotape in Washington hotel rooms. Between 1980 and 1981 one U.S. Senator and six U.S. Representatives were found guilty of corruption and sentenced to prison. State and local officials in both Pennsylvania and New Jersey were also tried, found guilty, and convicted.

Thus, national political leaders with a stake in maintaining their careers tend to avoid illegal behavior, as does most of the Washington community. How, then, do lobbyists work with politicians to achieve their aims? The relationship between lobbyists and politicians is one of the least understood in politics. Most lobbyists neither bribe nor threaten politicians. Both tactics are self-defeating. What they do instead is inform, persuade, and pressure. And since most people dislike pressure, the smart lobbyist does as little of that as possible and only as a last resort.

Lobbying Tactics

The tactic of persuasion is the key to successful lobbying. And persuasion starts (and often ends) with information, a lobbyist's most valuable resource. Legislators, whose staffs are small and usually stretched thin, often cannot get the vital information they need to make decisions about the possible impact of pending legislation. A good lobbyist gains access by providing this information. Naturally, the information will be skewed to favor the lobbyist's point of view. Still, it must never be an outright lie, or the interest group loses all credibility for future lobbying efforts. And even if lobbyists don't provide legislators with a well-rounded perspective on the issue, the information they do provide can be helpful. At a minimum it lets politicians know how key groups feel about the way pending legislation will affect their interests. And sensible politicians listen to a variety of groups and take a range of information into account before putting the final package of a given bill together.

Lobbyists are key players in the game of politics. Some are prominent Washington figures and major powerbrokers. Many are former government officials who have discovered that their expertise, access, influence, and good name are valuable assets, particularly to major industries. More than one public official has learned that it pays much better to be a lobbyist trying to influence policy from the outside than to be a public servant making policy on the inside. Former members of Congress are especially valued by interest groups working to recruit effective lobbyists, given their knowledge of government operations and their many contacts with the politically powerful. They can also command salaries well above what they were making in Congress, although ex-members are barred from lobbying Congress for a year after leaving that institution.

In 1961 there were 365 lobbyists registered in Washington. Today there are over 23,000. "Everybody in America has a lobby," declared former House Speaker Tip O'Neill. The leading lobby registrants are businesses and corporations, trade associations, state and local governments, citizen groups, and labor unions. Even foreign governments are actively involved in lobbying. Japanese companies and the Japanese government spend over $100 million to hire hundreds of lobbyists in Washington.[16]

A lobby exists to get results, and most Washington-based lobbies seek to influence policy in similar ways. To begin, the interests represented by the lobby will make campaign contributions to members of Congress. They hope thereby to elect representatives who see the world as they do and who will vote for the issues they support. Failing that, they hope that campaign contributions will at least buy them access: time to present their case to the members whose campaigns they supported. That explains why many large interests donate money to both parties. By hedging their bets, they hope to gain an audience with whatever group ends up controlling Congress.

Access is crucial; lobbyists can't influence people if they can't grab their attention. Lobbyists are salespeople. If they can make their case one on one, they will be effective. Good lobbyists get to know the members of Congress and their key staff people so that they can talk to influential politicians when the need arises. In some cases lobbyists and legislators work together so closely that lobbyists actually draft the legislation and submit it to Congress through their legislative contacts.

Beyond pushing their legislative aims in Congress, lobbyists spend a good deal of time presenting their case formally and publicly. They put out reports, pamphlets, brochures, and press releases, all aimed at presenting arguments and evidence to support their group's policy goals. They also give speeches; appear on television and radio, and at other public forums; and provide interviews, all in the hope that their message will be noticed and viewed favorably by those who have power or by those who can influence power holders. Among their many activities, lobbyists often testify before congressional committees about the value of the policies they hope to persuade Congress to adopt and write amicus curiae briefs to the Supreme Court. Interest groups have also successfully used the lower courts to sue government and private industry and have had an impact on public policy in this way, especially in the environmental arena. For an overview of lobbyists' activities, see Table 12.2.

Grassroots Activity

Rallying group members, as well as the public, behind their cause is a central element in most lobbyists' work, a strategy known as **grassroots activity.**[17] As we see in Table 12.2, 80 percent of lobbyists engage in this activity. The reason is simple. Just as nations with no army play little role in world affairs, lobby groups with no popular support play little role in a democracy. Those who make the laws gain office in a mass democratic election, so they pay particularly close attention to any matters that the mass of the people in their electoral districts seem to care about. A lobbyist is just one person, but a lobbyist with the backing of hundreds or thousands of voters in a legislative district is a power to be reckoned with. Thus, the most effective lobbyists are those who can clearly show an ability to rally grassroots support for their proposals.

Grassroots pressure "greases the wheels" of the policymaking process. Lobbyists can create this pressure by rousing constituents "back home" in a variety of ways: through political advertisements in newspapers and on radio and television, through speeches in local and national forums, by mobilizing interest group members to organize rallies or letter-writing campaigns. The aim of these activities is to influence policymakers. They are meant to let politicians know that a large number of voters agree with the lobbyist, so that the politicians will come to believe that supporting the lobby group's goal is the only

> "Our democracy has been the object of a hostile takeover. Government has become a Stop and Shop for every conceivable greedy and narrow interest."
>
> —Edmund G. Brown, Jr.

Table 12.2
What Lobbyists Do

ACTIVITY	% WHO USE TECHNIQUE
Testify at hearings	99
Have formal contact with public officials	98
Have informal contact with public officials	95
Present research information	92
Send letters to group members to update them on group activities	92
Enter into coalitions with other organizations	90
Attempt to shape the implementation of policy	89
Talk with the media	86
Consult with public officials to devise legislative strategy	85
Help to draft legislation	85
Sponsor letter writing campaigns	84
Help shape the government's agenda by calling attention to problems	84
Mount grassroots lobbying efforts	80
Have influential group members contact legislative offices	80
Help to draft regulations, rules, and guidelines	78
Serve on advisory commissions and boards	76
Alert legislators to the effects legislation will have on their districts	75
File suit or otherwise engage in litigation	72
Make financial contributions to campaigns	58
Assist officials by doing favors for them	56
Attempt to influence appointments to public office	53
Publicize candidates' voting records	44
Engage in direct-mail fundraising for the interest group	44
Use media advertisements to publicize the group's position on an issue	31
Contribute work, personnel, or services to electoral campaigns	24
Publicly endorse candidates for office	22
Engage in protests or demonstrations	20

Source: Kay Lehman Schlozman and John T. Tierney, *Organized Interests and American Democracy* (New York: Harper Collins, 1986), p. 150. Reprinted with permission.

Women's groups have gained prominence in the political arena. From NOW (National Organization for Women) to the conservative antifeminist women's group "Concerned Women for America," women have been making their policy positions on issues known and in so doing influencing legislation. In addition, two women's group PACs have been increasingly important in funding female candidacies—EMILY (Early Money Is Like Yeast–it makes the dough rise) for Democrats, and WISH (Women in the Senate and House) for Republicans.

sensible and expedient action. Certain groups are especially adept at grassroots activism. Surely the best example is the National Rifle Association and its battle to limit the inclusion of assault weapons in the Brady Bill. But the "Harry and Louise" ads that helped doom the Clinton health-care proposal also rank as one of the more effective grassroots campaigns of recent years.

An interest group using the grassroots strategy appeals directly to group members—or potential members—for support and action. A group using a letter-writing campaign appeals to its group members to "write your representative" and express support for the group's position on a given issue. (Congressional offices are periodically inundated by the cards, letters, telegrams, e-mail, and faxes of concerned group members and sympathizers, testimony to the effectiveness of this tactic.) The group may use *direct-mail* campaigns to barrage targeted citizens with mailings describing the group's cause, presenting its arguments, and requesting support or even money. An important political function of the direct-mail campaign is that it provides valuable information to the recipients of mailings, although most mailings are decidedly skewed toward the group's avowed position. The group often provides voting cues by giving voters a checklist to take with them into the voting booth. Another grassroots technique is to stage various events such as free concerts, speaking engagements, or even demonstrations. These events are often effective at raising both funds and citizens' consciousness of the group's cause, and they have the added advantage of attracting attention through news coverage.

From Grassroots to Astroturf

Interest groups are using a new weapon in their campaigns to influence politicians. It's called astroturf.

Astroturf refers to "synthetic" grassroots movements. Instead of encouraging citizens to write or call their representative in Congress about a particular piece of legislation, interest groups seek to affect the general climate of opinion. The idea is to convince members of Congress that there is a groundswell of public opinion in favor of or opposed to a policy. The primary tool used for this purpose is television advertising.

Interest groups have always engaged in advocacy advertising in newspapers, and they have always tried to shape news coverage—and, hence, public opinion. What is new is their extensive use of television advertising, which one expert describes as "a surrogate form of lobbying."* In 1994 the insurance industry used this approach in its series of ads featuring "Harry and Louise," a couple worrying about the impact of the Clinton health-care plan. Other groups followed suit. The Republican National Committee ran commercials asking viewers to support the balanced-budget amend-

Cutting Edge

ment; U.S. Term Limits ran ads calling for legislation to limit the tenure of federal lawmakers.

Most advocacy advertising appears on local stations; the networks generally do not accept such ads, preferring that debates over public policy be handled by their news departments so that both sides of an issue can be presented. Nevertheless, the amount of advertising focusing on public policy is growing.

One reason interest groups are turning to television is that it is a powerful tool for shaping opinion. Viewers become absorbed in the ads and identify with the "just plain folks" who seem to be speaking directly to them. Take the ad in which a nice older man describes the legal system as a circus controlled by lawyers and plaintiffs looking for easy money. "I tell you, the system is out of whack," he says, and suggests that viewers ask their representative to do something about it. Few viewers realize that the legislation in question is designed to discourage lawsuits by shareholders and consumers.

Adding to the effectiveness of "astroturf" campaigns is the fact that the sponsor of the advertising is not immediately apparent. The sponsor is not identified until the end of the commercial, and even then it may be disguised. Viewers of the "Harry and Louise" ads did not know that the ads were sponsored by the insurance industry; the issue was presented in terms of consumer choice. And the ads calling for reform of the legal system were sponsored by the innocuous-sounding Citizens for a Sound Economy, a front group for several large corporations.

Some question whether advocacy ads are as effective as their sponsors claim they are. It is not clear that such ads actually bring about a shift in public opinion. However, many politicians believe that they do. In this sense, therefore, the ads have their intended effect: They influence the beliefs, and hence the actions, of politicians.

Unlike traditional demonstrations, which only make it to the airwaves if there are thousands of participants, made-for-TV ads have a distinct and influential advantage in that they can simultaneously reach the grassroots, create a popular groundswell for ideas, and get directly to powerful public officials. However, the majority of such ads are sponsored by powerful corporations rather than public interests.

---

*Kathleen Hall Jamieson, quoted in Elizabeth Kolbert, "Special Interests' Special Weapon," *New York Times,* Mar. 26, 1995.

Some of the most effective interest group activity has grown out of attempts to take the group's message straight to the people in the hope of developing large, broad-based support for the group's cause. When grassroots activists Paul Gann and Howard Jarvis attempted to persuade the California legislature to cut property taxes in the late 1970s, they were unsuccessful. As a result, they turned to the kind of grassroots strategies just discussed. Their campaign included massive direct mailings, radio, newspaper, and television advertising, and various fundraising activities. The result was a voter-sponsored initiative, Proposition 13, that fundamentally altered both the property tax structure and government services in California and spread to other states.

Using the Courts and the Executive Branch

While grassroots strategies can often ignite large-scale popular support, interest groups must still directly reach the institutions of government to meet their objectives. Even large-scale grassroots movements sometimes fail to impress policymakers. They may simply disagree with the group's goals, the constituents who voted them into office may not support the group's goals, and the policymakers may be influenced by other powerful groups with opposing aims. When all is said and done, most grassroots campaigns fail to persuade Congress to produce the desired legislation. Consider, for example, these few recent failures: the campaign to limit congressional terms of office, the campaign to declare abortion illegal, the campaign to declare a freeze on the production of nuclear weapons, and the campaign to reform the national health-care system.

Despite the inevitability of setbacks, interest group leaders rarely give up easily. Groups unsuccessful in obtaining their goals from one institution often turn to another. The civil rights movement of the 1950s and 1960s is perhaps the best example of such group persistence. Unable to persuade either Congress or southern state legislatures to eliminate discriminatory laws and practices, civil rights groups turned for aid to the courts and to the executive branch, where they achieved a wide degree of success. It was the Supreme Court, after all, not Congress, that finally declared school segregation unconstitutional, and it was a series of presidents who were willing to use federal troops to enforce that decision. These judicial and executive actions, pushed along by interest group pressures, finally forced states to dismantle their segregated school systems and eliminate other legal forms of racial discrimination.

Today, conservative interest groups such as Operation Rescue, which seeks to restrict abortion, use the courts nearly as frequently as liberal groups of the past, a strategy that makes sense given the growing conservative inclination of the courts. Operation Rescue has combined traditional grassroots strategies with more aggressive tactics such as blockades of abortion clinics and the intimidation of clinic workers and patients. But a third, and quite effective, strategy of this group has been the continued appeal to state and federal courts in the attempt to eliminate all laws permitting abortion. Coupled with the publicity garnered from their grassroots and "aggression" tactics, Operation Rescue has become a political force that even the supposedly "nonpolitical" courts can no longer ignore. The federal judiciary, then, has once again become a key target for interest group activity.[18]

FYI

Did you know that there is a "Christian Left"? One such group, called Bread for the World, was founded in 1973 by Arthur Simon, a Lutheran pastor and brother of U.S. Senator Paul Simon. BFW has approximately 40,000 members, from mainly Catholic, Methodist, and Lutheran churches, and focuses on traditionally liberal issues, such as resolving hunger problems.

POLITICAL ACTION COMMITTEES

Of all the trends related to interest groups, the most dramatic new development has been the proliferation of **political action committees (PACs),** groups whose main aim is to financially promote the political goals of particular interest groups. The first PAC was created as early as 1948, when the AFL–CIO founded its Committee on Political Education (COPE) to channel union funds to prolabor candidates. In 1963 business created its first PAC, the Business–Industry Political Action Committee (BIPAC). But because campaign contributions were relatively unlimited until the 1970s, and recipients of large contributions were not required to report either the names of donors or the amount of money donated, most large industries and corporations simply funneled the money from corporate coffers directly to the campaigns of their chosen candidates or causes.

Things changed dramatically by the mid 1970s with passage of the Federal Election Campaign Act (FECA) of 1971, which placed a one-thousand-dollar limit on donations that individuals could make to any single campaign. The act did, however, allow labor unions, corporations, and other entities to create PACs that could donate up to five thousand dollars to any single campaign. The newly formed Federal Elections Commission (FEC) provided regulation and oversight. By 1976, the FEC had granted authority for universities, museums, trade associations, cooperatives, and eventually for private citizens to form PACs. It was at this time that a virtual explosion in PAC formation and activity occurred. Over four thousand PACs have since been registered with the FEC.

PACs have taken the traditional lobbying role of interest groups and added a new way to gain access and influence: donating tremendous amounts of money in relatively small increments to congressional election campaigns. For the 1992 elections, for example, the American Medical Association's PAC donated over $3.2 million to various congressional candidates. Table 12.3 indicates just how much PACs have contributed to House and Senate campaigns over the years and how that amount has been growing. Table 12.4 lists the top-ten PAC contributors in 1991–1992.

Table 12.3
PAC Contributions to Winning House and Senate Campaigns, 1975–90

ELECTION CYCLE	SENATE CAMPAIGNS		HOUSE CAMPAIGNS	
	AMOUNT (MILLIONS OF DOLLARS)	% OF TOTAL RECEIPTS	AMOUNT (MILLIONS OF DOLLARS)	% OF TOTAL RECEIPTS
1975–76	3.1	14.8	10.9	25.6
1977–78	6.0	14.0	17.0	28.3
1979–80	10.2	24.5	27.0	31.4
1981–82	15.6	22.0	42.7	34.7
1983–84	20.0	19.8	59.5	41.1
1985–86	28.4	26.6	72.8	42.2
1987–88	31.8	26.1	86.1	45.1
1989–90	31.1	25.6	91.6	46.4

Source: Federal Election Commission.

Table 12.4
Top Ten PACs, by Spending, 1991–1992

RANK	ORGANIZATION	DOLLARS
1.	Democratic Republican Independent Voter Education Committee (DRIVE-PAC)—the Teamsters Union	$11,825,340
2.	American Medical Association PAC—doctors	6,263,921
3.	National Education Association PAC—teachers union	5,817,975
4.	National Rifle Association Political Victory Fund	5,700,114
5.	Realtors PAC	4,939,014
6.	Association of Trial Lawyers of America PAC	4,392,462
7.	American Federation of State, County and Municipal Employees—PEOPLE PAC	4,281,395
8.	United Auto Workers PAC—labor union	4,257,166
9.	National Congressional Club—conservative causes	3,864,389
10.	National Abortion Rights Action League (NARAL)	3,881,321

Source: Harold W. Stanley and Richard G. Niemi, *Vital Statistics on American Politics,* 5th ed. (Washington, D.C.: CQ Press, 1995), p. 180.

Because PACs can legally donate more money than individuals, campaign fundraising has shifted away from seeking individual citizens' support to seeking money from PACs. In turn, the power of interest groups has increased, while the power of political parties has weakened. Politicians seeking elective office now turn to PAC groups for support rather than to party organizations. A Michigan Democrat running for the U.S. Senate, for instance, will be equally concerned with gaining the backing of state party officials than with soliciting support from the political action committees of the various unions that are powerful in that state, beginning with the United Auto Workers. With PACs helping to decide which candidates to support, they end up usurping one of the traditional roles reserved for parties: the recruitment and selection of candidates for office.

This growth of PAC influence in the candidate selection process has created problems for American politics.[19] Most PACs focus on a narrow range of issues or even on single issues. Candidates seeking scarce political resources for increasingly expensive campaigns often court the favors of influential PAC groups with their narrow agendas, while giving short shrift to the moderating perspective, broad-based public agenda, and amorphous ideology of political parties.

"Alarming. Outrageous. Downright outrageous. That's the only way to describe the threat posed by the torrents of special interest campaign cash being offered to our Representatives and Senators by the special interests. ... This democracy-threatening trend must be stopped."

—Fred Wertheimer, former president of Common Cause, an influential public interest lobby group

"Excuse me, but this campaign to kill [special interests] . . . is snobbish, elitist, antidemocratic, and un-American. . . . Destroy the PACs and you constrict the voice of small business, and restrict the political access of the millions who support them—enhancing the clout of Big Media, Big Business, Big Labor, and their ilk who can afford to maintain permanent lobbying representation in Washington."

—Patrick J. Buchanan

The result, as we saw in Chapter 10, is the "candidate-centered" campaign, the subsequent weakening of traditional party power, and a growing number of elected officials with narrow viewpoints and confrontational operating styles.

Political observers and insiders alike worry about the growth of PAC influence. Each session of Congress sees a flurry of activity surrounding legislative proposals that would reduce the amount of money PACs can donate to campaigns, limit the influence of PACS, or outlaw them altogether. Not surprisingly, such reform legislation is quickly defeated by those in office, who most benefit from the existence of PACs. In addition, in this age of sophisticated politics, conducted through direct mail, public-opinion polls, and interest groups, Madison's admonition—that removing the causes of faction reduces liberty—still rings strong. PACS have a basic right to participate in the system, and they fight, with all the considerable power they can muster, against attempts to restrict their activities.

REGULATION OF INTEREST GROUPS

Since interest group activity is protected by the First Amendment, politicians have been cautious about proposals to regulate these groups and their lobbyists. But the poor image many citizens have of "special interests" has brought periodic attempts at regulation. Some of these efforts have borne fruit and produced the occasional law aimed at reducing the scope of interest group influence. For the most part, however, these laws have been few and weak, leaving interest groups relatively unfettered.

The 1946 Federal Regulation of Lobbying Act stipulated that lobbyists seeking to influence congressional legislation must list all contributions, expenditures, and the names of anyone who received or contributed five hundred dollars or more. When the act was challenged on First Amendment grounds, the Supreme Court upheld the legislation (*U.S.* v. *Harriss,* 347 U.S. 612 (1954)), but interpreted the registration requirement to apply only to groups whose "primary purpose" was to influence legislation. Many large outfits such as the National Association of Manufacturers use this argument to avoid registering altogether. They claim no need to register as lobbyists, since influencing legislation is not their principal reason for existing as a group. For that reason and others, the 1946 act turned out to be virtually useless. It also lacked enforcement powers and did not apply to lobbying the executive branch, to grassroots organizing, or to indirect lobbying.

The 1971 and 1974 Federal Campaign Finance laws have been much more effective in their efforts to regulate, as we have seen, but also primarily ensured an increase in the power and proliferation of PACs, which represent many citizens, and thereby reducing the power of individual "fat cat" financiers. Another congressional action that has had some effect on lobbying behavior was the 1978 Ethics in Government Act, which codified rules governing conflict of interests. A key section of this law was meant to prevent the kind of "revolving-door" activity in which government officials leave their posts and immediately use their insider knowledge and contacts to lobby the very people for whom they had just been working. The law prohibited former government employees from lobbying their former agency for a period of one year after leaving office. It also prohibited them for two years from lobbying any department on an issue for which they clearly had direct responsibility.

In 1987 Michael Deaver, the former White House Deputy Chief of Staff, was found guilty of violating the Ethics in Government Act. Deaver left the White House in May 1985 and immediately started work for foreign governments. He was paid $105,000 by Canada, $250,000 by Rockwell International, $250,000 by Daewoo (a steel company in South Korea), and a large still undisclosed amount by Puerto Rico. None of this would have been illegal, but for one problem. Only two months after leaving office, Deaver spoke with National Security Advisor Robert McFarlane about Puerto Rico's objections to possible tax law revisions that would eliminate tax advantages for American businesses investing in that island. Deaver's conviction may have sent a message to other potential lobbyists that this particular law governing interest group activity must be taken seriously.[20]

ASSESSING THE IMPACT OF INTEREST GROUPS

The growth of interest groups presents new challenges and problems for the United States' political system. As more interest groups participate in the political arena, do they open or close opportunities for individual influence? As groups continue to increase in number, will they become the only legitimate channel for political expression?[21]

Scholars have devoted much effort to understanding the role groups play in American politics. Nearly a century ago political scientist Arthur Bentley argued that groups lie at the very heart of the political process.[22] Indeed, in his eyes all political phenomena can be understood in terms of group activity. He saw politics as a perpetual struggle for power: Groups compete endlessly for public goods and services, and only the fittest prosper and survive. Government is simply the agency that sorts out which groups are winning or losing at any given time. From this perspective, interest group activity is synonymous with politics itself.

Another leading interest group scholar, political scientist David Truman, argued in 1951 that groups play a stabilizing role in American politics.[23] Echoing both Madison and Bentley, Truman wrote that politics is best understood as a complex network of groups, each striving for access to government. In response to critics who felt that powerful economic interests have an advantage, Truman countered with two responses. First, most Americans have overlapping group memberships and are likely to belong to at least one group that benefits from government policies. Second, he pointed to the idea of potential groups. Certain issues could arise and galvanize unorganized citizens into cohesive groups. Formerly disadvantaged people would thus be represented in the halls of power, and these new groups would provide a vital balancing mechanism to counter the influence of groups already representing the wealthier elements of society.

These early scholars of group activity tended to theorize that the emergence of groups was a natural feature of the American political system. Groups occur almost automatically in a "nation of joiners." This perspective, often dubbed "pluralism," saw politics as an open marketplace of activity, with groups periodically emerging to represent people disturbed by some recent crisis, disorder, or turmoil.

This optimistic portrait obscures the complexity of group development and maintenance. It assumes that group formation is a foregone conclusion. This perspective was vigorously challenged in 1965 by economist Mancur Olson. In place of Truman's pluralist society and "nation of joiners," Olson saw interest groups representing a narrow range of socioeconomic forces. He pointed out that many large groups, such as the poor and the unemployed, cannot organize easily into effective groups and are thus left to "suffer in silence." He also noted the disproportionate power held by smaller groups, usually corporate or industrial interests, rather than groups established to protect the public good.

In yet another critique of the pluralist vision of group activity, political scientist Theodore Lowi maintained that contemporary group politics has fundamentally altered how the United States functions.[24] Lowi described a new political system, which he called **interest group liberalism.** In this system, interest groups have proliferated, expanding their control of legislative politics as the national bureaucracy has grown. Real policymaking stems neither from voter preference nor from Congress. Instead, it flows from a set of tight connections between the bureaucracy, selected members of Congress (especially subcommittee chairs), and special-interest groups representing the upper stratum of American society. Lowi and others have used the term *iron triangle* to characterize the typical cozy relationship among congressional elites, lobbyists, and bureaucrats.

Lowi believed that while Madison, Bentley, and Truman expected government to mediate and regulate conflict among groups, the opposite was now happening. Organized interests had come to dominate the government. Lowi dismissed Truman's argument that potential groups would organize if their interests were undermined. Instead, he perceived a permanent, unorganized class of lower-income, less-educated, and often minority citizens who were neglected and falling behind those with the resources to organize. An ironic consequence of increasing interest group activity, according to Lowi, is the narrowing of individual access to government. Groups have corrupted democratic government, in his view, helping powerful organized interests rather than average citizens.

Lowi and Olson also warned of the dangers of **hyperpluralism.** They believed that the rapid proliferation of interest groups, all competing for influence over policy, could place excessive and conflicting demands on public officials. In the face of massive political pressure, government might grind to a halt or continue to implement the status quo, as all efforts at change or reform are stymied by the many competing claims of powerful interest groups. Thus, hyperpluralism produces **gridlock,** a condition in which major government initiatives are impossible because existing groups can veto any effort at change and will do so, for fear of losing their own already-established connections and privileges.

Such pessimism is not universally accepted by interest group specialists. More optimistic scholars raise several points of objection. First, they claim that gridlock may derive less from the proliferation of interest groups than from American society's lack of consensus about which direction government policy should take. That lack of consensus has been a standard condition in American history, just as one would expect in a diverse and complex culture. But when Americans do reach consensus on political aims, government can take dramatic action with amazing speed, despite all the talk about interest groups causing hyperpluralist stagnation. That situation occurred in 1933 with the rapid approval of a vast range of New Deal programs, in 1941–42 with the United States' entry into World War II, in 1965 with passage of the Great Society programs, and in 1995 with the acceptance of many Republican "Contract with America" proposals. Group pressures did little to prevent those dramatic changes in national public policy. Perhaps interest groups don't create gridlock, but merely take advantage of its existence in a complex and diverse society.

The "iron-triangle" idea in like fashion has been much criticized. As early as 1978 political scientist Hugh Heclo pointed to the rise of a range of issue experts who forced legislators, bureaucrats, and lobbyists to pay attention to additional information and actors, thus undermining their cozy triangular relationship.[25] As a result, **policy networks** have formed. These networks are characterized by discussion of a wide range of options in the effort to resolve issues, conveying a more inclusive and less conspiratorial image of the policy process than "iron triangles" do.[26]

Other scholars have noted the vast array of new groups that have in recent years entered the political arena. This influx of groups has created conditions of uncertainty and unpredictability, helping to break up established connections between the principal actors of the old triangles. Hyperpluralism, then, does have one important element going for it. As the number of groups and interests operating in American society has dramatically expanded, political life has become more complex, making any generalization about how policies get made more and more difficult to substantiate.

Finally, we must remember that many of the new groups represent public interest activists, political participants who stand up for those segments of society not usually represented in the ongoing group struggles for power. Public interest lobbyists may be middle-class, but their aims, at least in theory, would benefit all citizens, particularly those at the lower ends of the socioeconomic spectrum. Thus, the argument that the less well off are disadvantaged by interest group activity, while retaining a strong kernel of truth, is less accurate today than it might have been two or three decades ago.

A "participation revolution" has been taking place in this country: while levels of voter participation have decreased, increasing numbers of citizens have become involved in interest group politics, joining protest groups, public interest groups, and single-issue interest groups.

INTEREST GROUPS AND APPROACHING DEMOCRACY

Interest groups provide a vital link between citizens and public officials. They convey substantive information and public sentiment to policymakers, and they provide knowledge about government programs to citizens and assist them in gaining access to these programs. Interest groups even provide the inspiration necessary to stimulate citizen involvement in politics. It remains true that the most powerful, most influential, and most resourceful interests have advantages. Politics is rarely played on a level field. Business and corporate interests far outweigh public interest groups in most power struggles. And small but powerful interests often gain their ends from government, seemingly at the expense of the public good.

Still, interest group activity is not the villain. Franklin Roosevelt once said that the only cure for the problems of democracy is more democracy. Along these lines, the only cure for the undue influence of some interests is for those currently unhappy with policy outcomes to organize and take advantage of their own right to become a powerful interest group. We have learned that

Societies rot from the top down. They reconstruct from the bottom up. Democracies are not just good for the economy. They are good for peace and tranquility, for character and local initiative, for justice and the pursuit of happiness.

Ralph Nader, consumer advocate

potential groups don't always form and lobby government, but over time countervailing forces often do arise to give the system some degree of balance (if not perfect justice). The growth of public interest groups has helped give the voiceless and the powerless some modest victories, in the form of government policies that work to their advantage rather than to the benefit of those with money and status. Such groups help America approach democracy.

Clearly, Americans have some way to go before interest group activity reflects the ideals of a democratic, participatory society, but all the elements are in place to make this possible. Americans have the right to organize, to lobby government, and to present their group's perspective to the nation. When Americans decide to take advantage of their many opportunities for influencing public policy, they will find few legal barriers that prevent them from forming groups for that purpose.

SUMMARY

1. Interest groups are formal organizations of people who share a common outlook or social circumstance and who band together in the hope of influencing government policy. Actual groups have a headquarters, an organizational structure, paid employees, and so forth; potential groups are interest groups that could come into being under the right circumstances. Those circumstances are often created by dynamic leaders known as policy entrepreneurs.

2. While all modern democracies exhibit interest group activity, few have achieved the level of nongovernmental group life found in the United States. The number of groups trying to pressure government has grown dramatically in recent years, partly owing to the growth and increased activity of the government and partly owing to other social trends such as higher average levels of education.

3. People form interest groups because collective action is stronger, more credible, and more likely to influence policy outcomes than the isolated actions of separate individuals are. However, because interest groups focus on their own cause, they are said to downplay or ignore the public good.

4. Economic interest groups include those representing big business, organized labor, farmers, and other economic interests. Public interest groups represent the interests of average citizens; they focus on achieving a broad set of goals that represent their members' vision of the collective good. Government interest groups compete alongside traditional interest groups for funding, policy goals, and attention. Other interest groups include ideological groups, religious groups, civil rights groups, and single-issue groups.

5. Interest groups are most likely to form when some citizens have been adversely affected by technological change or by government policies. Other factors, such as dynamic leaders and geographic concentration, also influence the development of an interest group.

6. Group leaders must devote much of their time to group maintenance—canvassing for new members and providing benefits for current members. In doing so they face the so-called free-rider problem, the tendency of individuals to share in the collective benefits of group action even if they do not themselves contribute to the group.

7. Lobbying is the formal, organized attempt to influence legislation, usually through direct contact with legislators or their staff. Lobbyists provide legislators with needed information and attempt to persuade, and sometimes pressure, them to support the interest group's goals. They also publicize the group's cause to the general public through published materials, speeches, television appearances, and the like.

8. A key aim of lobbying is to rally group members, as well as the public, to the cause—that is, to gain grassroots support for the group's proposals. An often-used tactic is the direct-mail campaign, in which targeted citizens receive mailings describing the group's cause and requesting their support.

9. An important trend is the proliferation of political action committees, groups whose main aim is to promote the political goals of particular interest groups. PACs donate large amounts of money to political campaigns, thereby undermining the role of political parties in recruiting and selecting candidates for office.

10. There are few legal restrictions on interest groups. Lobbyists must list their contributions and expenditures, but only if their "primary purpose" is to influence legislation. The Ethics in Government Act bars former government employees from lobbying their former agency for a year after leaving office and for two years on specific policy issues.

11. Some political scientists believe that policymaking stems from the connections among the bureaucracy, selected members of Congress, and interest groups—so-called iron triangles. The rapid proliferation of interest groups has led to hyperpluralism. Policy networks, which are more broad-based than iron triangles, now characterize the process. There can be no doubt that the number of groups and interests now operating in American society has dramatically expanded, adding to the complexity of political life.

KEY TERMS

interest groups
actual groups
potential groups
policy entrepreneurs
collective action

public interest groups
group maintenance
free riders
lobbying
grassroots activity

political action committees (PACs)
interest group liberalism
hyperpluralism
gridlock
policy networks

SUGGESTED READINGS

- Cigler, Allan J., and Burdett A. Loomis, eds. *Interest Group Politics*. 4th ed. Washington, D.C.: Congressional Quarterly Press, 1995. An excellent collection of readings on American interest groups.

- Dye, Thomas R. *Who's Running America: The Clinton Years*. 6th ed. Englewood Cliffs, N.J.: Prentice Hall, 1995. Dye describes the dominant political institutions of our time and the individuals who control them.

- Heinz, John P., Edward Q. Laumann, Robert L. Nelson, and Robert H. Salisbury. *The Hollow Core: Private Interests in National Policy Making*. Cambridge, Mass.: Harvard University Press, 1993. A scholarly examination of connections between interest groups, members of Congress, and bureaucrats. Sheds doubt on the theory of iron triangles.

- Kingdon, John W. *Agendas, Alternatives, and Public Policies*. Boston: Little, Brown, 1984. Provides a good analysis of the complexity of the political process within which interest groups must operate to gain their ends.

- Lowi, Theodore J. *The End of Liberalism: The Second Republic of the United States*. 2d ed. New York: Norton, 1979. Offers a provocative perspective on American government, arguing that the tight connections between interest groups and government officials have created a new kind of American political system.

- Olson, Mancur, Jr. *The Logic of Collective Action*. Cambridge, Mass.: Harvard University Press, 1965. An influential work, it argues that rational citizens have few incentives to join groups, and consequently the interests of nonjoiners are poorly represented in politics.

- Petracca, Mark P., ed. *The Politics of Interests: Interest Groups Transformed*. Boulder, Colo.: Westview Press, 1992. Another good collection of scholarly articles on interest groups.

- Rauch, Jonathan. *Demosclerosis: The Silent Killer of American Government*. New York: Random House/Times Books, 1994. A popularization of the Lowi–Olson thesis that interest groups dominate American politics and create a government of institutionalized gridlock.

- Rosenthal, Alan. *The Third House: Lobbyists and Lobbying in the States*. Washington, D.C.: Congressional Quarterly Press, 1993. What lobbyists look like and how they operate at the state level.

- Truman, David B. *The Governmental Process*. New York: Knopf, 1951. A classic book, presenting the pluralist vision of how interest groups operate in American politics.

- Walker, Jack L., Jr. *Mobilizing Interest Groups in America: Patrons, Professions, and Social Movements*. Ann Arbor: University of Michigan Press, 1991. An excellent and wide-ranging discussion of interest groups in modern American political life.

CHAPTER 13

THE MEDIA

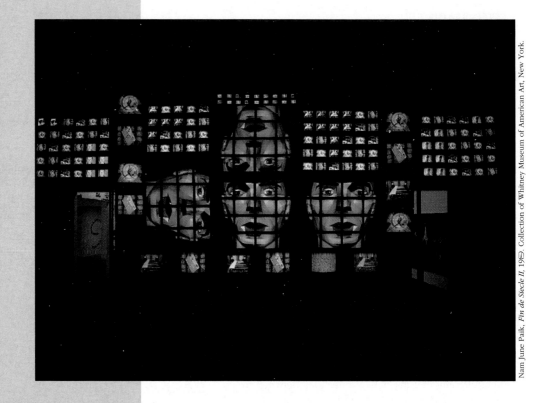

Nam June Paik, *Fin de Siecle II*, 1989. Collection of Whitney Museum of American Art, New York.

CHAPTER OUTLINE

CASE STUDY: "THE VOICE OF
  BAGHDAD"
INTRODUCTION: THE MEDIA AND
  DEMOCRACY
THE EMERGENCE OF THE MEDIA
FUNCTIONS OF THE MEDIA

LIMITS ON MEDIA FREEDOM
IDEOLOGICAL BIAS AND MEDIA
  CONTROL
THE MEDIA AND ELECTIONS
THE MEDIA AND APPROACHING
  DEMOCRACY

T he 1991 Persian Gulf War presented the Pentagon, the press, and the public with a peculiar situation. While most Western reporters fled the Iraqi capital of Baghdad, a handful remained behind, the most controversial of whom was Cable News Network's (CNN) Peter Arnett. The veteran journalist—his war correspondent experience extending back to the early days of Vietnam—reached an agreement with the Iraqi government allowing him to broadcast "live" from Baghdad. The nature of that agreement created an interesting dilemma.

CASE STUDY

"The Voice of Baghdad"

Every evening Arnett would slip into his favorite leather jacket—with one hundred thousand dollars sewn into the lining "just in case"—bring a satellite telephone uplink into the courtyard of the exclusive Al Rashid hotel in downtown Baghdad, and broadcast his analysis of events "on the scene." The controversy arose over the nature of Arnett's coverage, which he broadcast only after his script had first cleared Baghdad's official censors. In other words, the only "news" Arnett could describe had to be approved by the representatives of a government with which the United States was at war.

Arnett insists that he did the best, most objective job he could under the circumstances. Often his reports were punctuated by the sound of bursting shells only a few hundred yards away. He was constantly under observation by a crew of Iraqi "minders." "The censorship was fairly tough," he says, "but we tried to circumvent it." For example, a CNN anchor would ask about traffic on the road to the city of Basra; Arnett would mention that the traffic was heavy, but would add the subtle qualification that few civil-ians were on the road, implying heavy movement of Iraqi military forces.

Reaction to Arnett's coverage was sharply divided. A coalition of "patriotic" organizations, calling themselves the "Victory Committee," cried foul over Arnett's presence in Baghdad. The group, which included some of the estimated thirty thousand members of the conservative media watchdog Accuracy in Media (AIM), called Arnett "the U.S. voice of Baghdad," insisting that he was helping to "spread Saddam Hussein's propaganda in America." They demanded that CNN stop Arnett's broadcasts and "pull the plug on the voice of Baghdad." Conservative columnist William F. Buckley, Jr., wrote in the National Review that Arnett was "retailing Iraqi lies" about casualties among Iraq's civilian population and the destruction of an alleged biological-weapons plant, which Iraq insisted was a factory for baby formula. Republican senator Alan Simpson called Arnett an "Iraqi sympathizer," and verbally attacked even the journalist's family. In a letter to CNN, a group of thirty-nine U.S. representatives accused CNN of being a propaganda pawn of Saddam Hussein's regime. A small but vocal number of individual citizens also called CNN and various sponsors of the Gulf War coverage to express their displeasure with Arnett's "treason."

Among those defending Arnett were popular call-in show host Larry King and CNN's owner Ted Turner. King claimed that Arnett was doing only what any good journalist would do: broadcasting what he could of an important story in the best way he could manage, providing valuable insight that would otherwise be unavailable to the American public as well as the millions of viewers in the 105 countries served by CNN. Turner insisted that "at no time has [CNN] misrepresented the conditions under which the news in that country is gathered and reported.

We remain in Baghdad to do our best to report that side of the story." One reason Turner and many of his sponsors may not have "pulled the plug" on Arnett was the dramatic upward spike in ratings during the Gulf War—the estimated average twenty-four-hour CNN audience increased almost three times from its level a year earlier.

Ultimately, the plug was not pulled on Arnett. The hue and cry raised by groups like the Victory Committee gradually ebbed to a disgruntled murmur. Senator Simpson apologized publicly to Arnett and his family. When Arnett paid his first postwar visit to the United States in March 1991, he caused relatively little stir among those who had opposed his coverage.[1] ❧

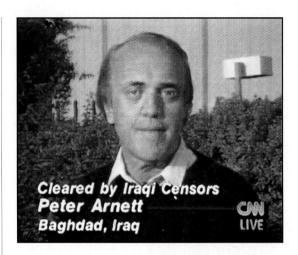

Peter Arnett of CNN broadcasts live from Baghdad, providing the world with its only news of military operations within Iraq during the Persian Gulf War.

FYI

Reporters covering the war in Vietnam used to refer to the official five o'clock military press briefings as the "five o'clock follies," since much of the information given out by American officials was so far removed from the actual battlefield experiences of the reporters.

INTRODUCTION: THE MEDIA AND DEMOCRACY

Although it yielded an unusual perspective on modern warfare, including a much-maligned exclusive interview with Hussein himself, Arnett's coverage during the Gulf War violated the established relationship between the press and the military. Senior military officials, mindful of the strategic and political disaster of allowing journalists relatively free rein during the Vietnam War, had imposed tight restrictions on press coverage of Desert Storm.[2] Historically, the U.S. government, like its counterparts throughout the world, has censored reporting of military operations, usually with little public outcry.

To foster unity and purpose at home, reporters were not permitted to interview troops or observe field operations unless military personnel accompanied them. And these opportunities were limited further by the imposition of "press pool" coverage monitored by a military attaché. A press pool is a selected group of journalists who travel with military personnel to observe various operations and then return to share their information with other reporters in addition to filing their own stories. Furthermore, the military imposed a "security review," a requirement that journalists in the press pools submit their material to military censors for clearance before *any* information could be passed on to other reporters or to the public. "Officials remember Vietnam," NBC anchor Tom Brokaw recalled. "And, in fairness to them, some got burned. Understandably [they don't want the press] to cause the same damage again." *New York Times* managing editor Joseph Lelyveld did not object to such strict rules. "The First Amendment gives us the right to publish just about anything," he commented. "It does not give us the right to go just about anywhere."[3]

Most citizens in our democratic society draw their conclusions about politics from the pictures given them by the media. During the Persian Gulf War, however, the media were permitted to present only pictures that the government wanted shown. There is also evidence that Pentagon spokespersons deliberately misled the media with regard to battlefield reports. Members of the media eventually spoke of "we" to describe coalition military action. "We knocked one of their Scuds out of the sky," observed the venerable Walter Cronkite of CBS. ABC anchor Peter Jennings extolled "the brilliance of laser-guided bombs," but the next evening condemned the Iraqui missile as "a horrifying killer." With the Iraqi and U.S. government controlling the images of war, and television anchors serving as cheerleaders for government policy, the average citizen was hardly in a position to evaluate questions about the strategic goals of military intervention and political objectives.

The tension between freedom of the press and government restrictions on that freedom is one of several key issues related to the role of the mass media—particularly broadcast media and the press—in a democratic society. Another issue is the extent to which the media themselves regulate the amount and nature of information conveyed to the public. At a minimum, democracy requires that citizens receive objective information so they can make informed decisions about candidates, policies, and government actions. Yet the media responsible for transmitting that information are often characterized by bias, distortion, and sensationalism. The job of the media entails simplifying complex and detailed realities into symbols and images. Thus, the information reaching the citizen consists primarily of soundbites and pictures, greatly simplifying the definition of political reality for millions of Americans. Indeed, it is not exaggeration to say that for most people politics has little reality apart from its media version.[4]

Perhaps no other chapter in this text raises issues that deal so directly with democracy. President Kennedy once said that

> the flow of ideas, the capacity to make informed choices, the ability to criticize, all of the assumptions on which political democracy rests, depend largely on communications.[5]

Democracy requires an informed citizenry, and the communication of political information is an essential prerequisite for political participation. A free press stands as one of the defining features of a democratic political system. On the other hand, elites both inside and outside government recognize that they have a major stake in how the media report political information. The **spin** of the news—the interpretation placed on it by those presenting it—is often more important than the news itself. (The term *spin* derives from such sports as soccer, pool, and basketball, in which by giving the ball the correct spin the players can make it go where they want it to.) Many experts believe that the effect of spin is to "erode the central requirement of a democracy that those who are governed give not only their consent, but their informed consent."[6]

In this chapter we examine the evolution of media technologies and electronic telecommunications, then take a close look at the media's coverage of politics. We also explore the process by which members of the media determine what is newsworthy and the ways in which government officials manipulate the media. Throughout the chapter it will be evident that freedom of the press and other media is of fundamental importance in approaching democracy.

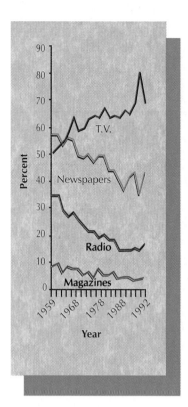

FIGURE 13.1 Where Americans Get the News

Source: Surveys by the Roper Organization for the Television Information Office, 1959–92. Note: Numbers do not equal 100 percent due to multiple responses.

THE EMERGENCE OF THE MEDIA

A medium is a means of transferring or conveying something. By **mass media** we mean the various means—newspapers, magazines, radio, television—through which information is transferred from its sources to large numbers of people. Perhaps more than any other nation, the United States has become a mass media society. Today more than forty percent of all adult Americans report that they read daily newspapers; slightly more than one in five regularly watches television's Cable News Network; and well over half make regular use of the nation's cable television systems (see Figure 13.1).

For most of the past two hundred years, the mass communication of political information has been dominated by newspapers and television; radio and magazines have been less influential, yet they have also played a role in the development of Americans' political attitudes. With the media occupying such a central place in political affairs today, it is important to understand how the media evolved over the course of American history. In this section we trace the evolution of the mass media in American society and note the impact of new technologies such as satellite transmission, cable television and the worldwide web internet.

Newspapers

The importance of the press in American politics dates from the revolutionary period when newspapers served as effective tools for mobilizing public opinion. They were also the primary vehicle for the debate over ratification of the Constitution. The *Federalist Papers* of Alexander Hamilton, James Madison, and John Jay were originally published as articles in the New York *Independent Journal*.

Early political leaders saw the press as the key to educating the public about the political system. Thomas Jefferson believed that the success of a participatory democracy depends on preventing citizens from making unwise decisions: "Give them full information of their affairs through the channel of the public papers, and . . . contrive that those papers should penetrate the whole mass of the people." In an address to Congress, President George Washington stressed the "importance of facilitating the circulation of political intelligence and information" through the press.[7]

In the period following revolution and independence, political leaders sought allies among newspaper publishers. As secretary of the treasury, Hamilton encouraged a staunch Federalist, John Fenno, to establish a newspaper that would espouse the administration's partisan positions. In return, Fenno was guaranteed financial assistance and printing jobs. Fenno moved from Boston to Washington and published the *Gazette of the United States*.

Not to be outdone, Jefferson and other Democratic-Republicans urged Philip Freneau to publish a Democratic-Republican newspaper, the *National Gazette*. While neither paper was a financial success, a relationship was forged between editors and their benefactors. As late as 1860, the superintendent of the census classified 80 percent of the nation's periodicals, including all 373 daily newspapers, as "political in their character."[8]

The mass media revolution can be said to have begun with the September 3, 1833, issue of the *New York Sun,* which was sold on the streets for one cent,

Should the Whole World Watch?

The signing of the Declaration of Independence is probably the single-most important event in American history, yet few people knew about it until much later. The Declaration was drafted over the course of several weeks during the summer of 1776 by delegates from twelve of the thirteen colonies (all except Rhode Island). The proceedings were held entirely in secret so that the public would not be aware of their revolutionary nature and opponents would have no opportunity to object. Numerous precautions were taken to prevent "leaks."

The Declaration was signed on July 4, but most of the colonists did not hear about it for several days, and in some cases weeks. It took twenty-nine days for news of the signing to travel from Philadelphia to Charleston, South Carolina. What might have happened if the Declaration had been drafted and signed today?

What Might Have Happened

If it had happened today, the event would be preceded by a news leak from "informed sources" telling us that at 3:30 P.M. eastern time Thomas Jefferson and his fellow revolutionaries planned to sign the Declaration. All the major networks would carry the signing live; CNN would broadcast the news around the world, and that evening on *Night Line* Ted Koppel would interview Jefferson and, via satellite, King George of England. The next morning Jefferson, John Hancock, Ben Franklin, and others would appear on talk shows to put their spin on the Declaration and the Revolution. The King's ministers would put a different spin on the event.

Within a week or two after the signing, *People* magazine would feature a story and pictures of Jefferson, but reporters from the *National Enquirer* would also be interviewing his slaves and raising questions about his private life and his suitability for public office. Jefferson might very well suffer a credibility gap unless he hired a "handler" or press secretary to organize and orchestrate his dealings with the mass media. He might also appear with his wife on "60 Minutes," although his mistress might appear on "A Current Affair," or "Hard Copy." The American people would then have to sort it all out themselves or get help from Phil, Oprah, or Geraldo.

Clearly, it is extremely difficult for any public figure to escape the eye of the media; this is especially true for presidents, who are followed from morning to night by reporters and camera crews. While the secrecy that surrounded the drafting of the Declaration of Independence probably could not be maintained today, some types of government activity are carried out in secret. For reasons of national security, many of the operations of the military, the State Department, and the CIA are treated as "classified," or secret. The deliberations of the Supreme Court are also conducted in secret. Despite the principles of freedom of the press and the "right to know," one could argue that secrecy is justified in these instances.

---

thereby earning the name "penny press." The paper was targeted at the masses and offered news of local events along with human interest stories and entertainment. Mass circulation was achieved through the low price (most newspapers at the time cost six cents) and making the paper available on virtually every street corner.

In the period from 1850 to 1900 the number of daily papers multiplied from 254 to 2,226. Total circulation increased nearly sevenfold, from 758,000 to over 15 million. As we will see shortly, the development of newspapers as mass communicators influenced the way in which news was presented and even the definition of what constituted "news."

Table 13.1
Top Ten Newspapers in Circulation, 1993

1.	*Wall Street Journal*	1,818,652
2.	*USA Today*	1,494,929
3.	*New York Times*	1,141,366
4.	*Los Angeles Times*	1,089,690
5.	*Washington Post*	813,908
6.	*New York Daily News*	764,070
7.	*Newsday*	747,890
8.	*Chicago Tribune*	690,842
9.	*Detroit Free Press*	566,116
10.	*San Francisco Chronicle*	544,253

Note: Total Monday-through-Saturday circulation for six-month period ending September 30, 1993.

Source: USA Today research, Dec. 6, 1993.

Today there are about 1,700 daily newspapers in the United States, with a total circulation of over 63 million. The top ten newspapers in circulation are listed in Table 13.1. The vast majority of daily papers are in the business of information and entertainment rather than politics. About 60 percent of a typical newspaper's space is taken up by advertising; human interest stories, sports, reviews, and recipes, and other features account for most of the remainder. The portion devoted to news and editorial coverage amounts to about 4 percent of the total.

MUCKRAKING AND YELLOW JOURNALISM   During the nineteenth century the style of journalism changed significantly—both in the way stories were reported and in the events that were considered newsworthy. The mass journalism that developed during that period included much less political and foreign-affairs reporting and more local news and sensationalism. In particular, newspapers began to feature coverage of dramatic court cases and criminal activity, along with a strong dose of sex or violence, or both. The new journalism also spawned two trends whose effects are still felt today: muckraking and yellow journalism.

The term **muckraking** is derived from the Man with the Muckrake, a character in John Bunyan's *Pilgrim's Progress* who could look only downward and rake the filth on the floor. The word is used to describe a style of reporting that was the precursor of what is now called investigative journalism. Muckraking journalists like Lincoln Steffens, Will Erwin, and cartoonist Thomas H. Nast came to prominence during the early 1900s, a period characterized by reform movements and populist politics known as the Progressive Era. They attempted to expose the power and corruption of the rich while championing the cause of workers and the poor. Their stories of political fat cats, machine politics, evil slumlords, and heartless millionaire industrialists enraged the political and social elite. Although these exposés inevitably suffered from subjectivity, not to mention bias, the muckrakers pulled newspaper reporting in a less elite direction and set a trend that continues today. Perhaps the most famous investigative journalists of recent years are Bob Woodward and Carl Bernstein, who attacked the Watergate conspiracy with the same zeal shown by Steffens and his contemporaries in attacking the abuses of their day.[9]

The darker side of the new journalist drew less on social conscience and more on the profit motive. **Yellow journalism**—named after the controversial "Yellow Kid" comic strip—is usually associated with the big-city daily newspapers of Joseph Pulitzer and William Randolph Hearst. Pulitzer and Hearst transformed the staid, rather dull publications of their predecessors into brash, colorful, well-illustrated, often lurid and sensationalized organs of half-truth, innuendo, and sometimes outright lies. The writing style became more casual and colloquial and the stories more dramatic, with the emphasis on sex and violence. Facts became less important than impact; if a story wasn't true, yellow journalists often left the onus on those most damaged by its publication, having little to fear from the ineffective libel and slander laws of the time.

The legacy of yellow journalism can be seen in many of today's daily papers. Partly in response to the competition of television, newspapers such as *USA Today* feature much of the splash, color, and excitement of the early yellow papers. However, the truthfulness of the stories is considerably greater than in the days of Pulitzer and Hearst.

Magazines

Although they are less prominent than newspapers as a source of political information, magazines enjoy wide circulation, attentive readership, and an important place in the political education of Americans. Of all the major mass media, magazines offer the widest variety of subject matter and ideological opinion. This is because successful magazines tend to target certain groups of readers on the basis of socioeconomic status, education, political views, or consumer habits. The proliferation of specialized magazines covering everything from aerobics to zoology is evidence of this strategy.

Of the major news magazines, the most widely read is *Time*. Originally, *Time* was the flagship of the publishing empire founded by Harry Luce. The son of a Presbyterian minister, Luce brought to the magazine his strident faith in the "American Century" and the exalted place of Western culture. According to journalist David Halberstam, Luce "was one of the first true *national* propagandists; he spoke to the whole nation on national issues, one man with one magazine speaking with one voice, and reaching an entire country."[10] Luce's domineering editorial stance reveals that the potential for ideological extremes is much greater for magazines than for the other mass media. For decades Luce's control of *Time* made him one of the most important and influential political forces in America.

Luce's impact on mass-readership magazines extended beyond politics. In addition to *Time*, his growing company published *Look, Life, Fortune,* and *Sports Illustrated*. But *Time* created an explosive popular appetite for news coverage. Luce's formula for the "modern" news magazine featured dramatic photographs, information, analysis, and opinion on the dominant issues of the day. *Time*'s success soon produced a host of competitors, including *Newsweek* and *U.S. News & World Report*. These and similar publications continue to serve as "sources of record" for elected officials, corporate executives, and informed citizens who pay close attention to political affairs.

Besides the news magazines, there are several magazines of political opinion. The most widely read of these are the conservative *National Review,* the moderate *New Republic,* and the liberal *Nation.* The ideological differences among these publications testifies both to the targeting of readership and to the breadth of political opinion among magazine readers.

Radio

Radio enjoyed a brief but important heyday as a significant source of political information for the American public. Developed in the late nineteenth century, radio technology underwent a revolution during World War I. From the 1930s until after World War II, radio was the dominant popular medium. Today's three major television networks—NBC, ABC, and CBS—began as radio networks.

Unlike printed media, radio broadcasts could report events as they were happening. This quality of immediacy produced some of the most dramatic "live" reporting in history, including the horrifying account of the explosion of the German zeppelin *Hindenburg* in 1937 and the CNN "voice of Baghdad" broadcasts described at the beginning of the chapter. The degree to which radio had become a trusted medium was revealed in October 1938, when Orson Welles and his Mercury Theater of the Air broadcast "War of the Worlds," a fictionalized invasion of the earth by Martians. So convincing were the dramatization's "live" news reports that many Americans believed that the invasion was real.

Radio journalism picked up where print journalism left off. Many of radio's early news reporters had begun as newspaper or magazine reporters. The most successful of them combined the journalistic skills of print reporters with the effective speaking voice required by a medium that "spoke" the news. One of radio's premier news reporters, Edward R. Murrow, established standards of integrity and reportorial skill that continue to this day. He combined the investigative traditions of the early muckrakers with concise writing and a compelling speaking voice. Murrow's career would outlast the peak of radio's popularity; he enjoyed equal fame as a television journalist.

Probably the most successful use of radio by a politician was the famous series of "fireside chats" by President Franklin Roosevelt. An impressive public speaker, Roosevelt used these brief broadcasts to bolster American confidence—and his own popularity—as he pushed for major legislative reforms to combat the depression. The immediacy of radio was also exploited by demagogues like the archconservative Reverend Charles Coughlin of Michigan. While Coughlin never ran for public office, his broadcast "sermons" included strident attacks on communists and Jews, even implying support for the Nazi regime at a time when the United States was seriously contemplating entering the war against Germany.

Radio's popularity began to ebb after World War II. Its chief competition came not from newspapers and magazines but from a new, even more immediate and compelling medium: television. By 1948 four networks were broadcasting regular programming on television. But radio has not been entirely eclipsed. In recent years radio talk shows like the Rush Limbaugh show have become an important source of news for the listening public. Many commuters tune in to such programs while traveling to and from work.

President Franklin D. Roosevelt is shown here during a radio broadcast in 1938. To build support for the New Deal, Roosevelt used radio, the predominant means of communicating with the public before television, to explain to the nation his policies and goals. During World War II he used radio to calm the nation's fears. Radio enabled Roosevelt to build a bond with the American people. Millions of Americans came to love their president on account of his extremely personal radio broadcasts known as "fireside chats."

Talk Radio

It's powerful. Extremely powerful. The medium that was supposed to have faded away with the advent of television has become a potent political force. It's talk radio.

Radio talk shows are believed to have significantly influenced the results of the 1994 congressional elections. With their call-in format and no-holds-barred commentary, they provided an outlet where Americans dissatisfied with the Clinton administration and a Congress controlled by Democrats could vent their frustration.

The most successful of the talk show hosts, Rush Limbaugh, is broadcast over 659 radio stations. Calling the press "willing accomplices to the liberal power base in Washington," Limbaugh and other hosts (70 percent of whom call themselves conservative) led the movement to transform Congress into a Republican stronghold. Listeners turned out to vote in droves: Polls showed that more than half of the voters surveyed at polling places said they listened to talk radio, and the frequent listeners voted Republican by a 3-to-1 ratio. Other surveys have found that while dedicated listeners make up only about 10 percent of the population, they have the highest level of voter registration.

What explains the effectiveness of talk radio? It appears that a major factor is public discontent. According to Andrew Kohut, director of the Times Mirror Center for the People and the Press, listeners "tune into a community of similar attitudes and discontent, and they reinforce one another's views about how bad things are in Washington."* Steve Wagner of Luntz Research, a Republican polling organization, adds that talk radio "flourishes best on the fundamental sense that things are not going well."†

There is more to it than that, however. Some analysts believe talk radio may be performing a function that was formerly the domain of political parties, unions, and civic groups: giving people a feeling of connection with the political process. With a simple phone call they obtain an opportunity to express their views to a wide audience. Talk radio is, in short, a forum for political discussion. Often, however, the discussion is one-sided, and opposing views are not presented.

Talk show hosts themselves insist that they do not create or change opinions. According to Michael Harrison, editor of *Talkers Magazine,* "Talk radio hosts really reflect and amplify more than they influence."** Perhaps, but the new Republican members of Congress would not agree—they made Limbaugh an honorary member of the Republican freshman class and gave him a pin with the words "Majority Maker."

Rush Limbaugh, the conservative talk show impresario, has helped transform talk radio into a popular forum for political discussion. Twenty million listeners are believed to tune in to his show each week.

---

*Quoted in Robin Toner, "Election Jitters in Limbaughland," *New York Times,* Nov. 3, 1994, p. A29.

†Quoted in Timothy Egan, "Triumph Leaves Talk Radio Pondering Its Next Targets," *New York Times,* Jan. 1, 1995, p. 22.

**Quoted in Toner, "Election Jitters in Limbaughland," p. A29.

Television is also a powerful and influential tool in Russia, so much so, that politicians in Russia have been known to be even more obsessed with its power than those in the United States. For this reason, when communism fell and the Soviet Union ceased to exist, control of television did not immediately give way to the forces of pluralism and democracy. Only in the last few years has the government's strict control of the airwaves been weakened by the emergence of privately owned and largely independent networks that offer the Russian people high-quality television news and more choice in programming than ever before.

Television

Unlike newspapers, magazines, and radio, television developed primarily as a commercial medium, designed not so much to provide information or opinion but to entertain and stimulate mass consumerism. Thus, most Americans tend to think of television as a low-cost leisure activity rather than as a source of political information.

Television is more pervasive and effective than any other form of mass communication in the United States. Advances in broadcast technology have made possible virtually instantaneous transmission of information and greatly expanded the range of programs for viewers to choose from. As a result, according to political scientist Richard Neustadt, television is "at once the primary news source for most Americans, the vehicle for national political competition, a crucial means to sell consumer goods, and an almost universal source of entertainment."[11]

The television viewing audience has also expanded. Ninety-eight percent of American residences now have televisions (often two or more sets), and at least 125 million Americans—half the population—typically tune in to the networks' prime-time (eight to eleven in the evening) shows. On the average, Americans watch twenty-nine hours of television every week, and over 70 percent watch network television news regularly. A large proportion of Americans believe that television gives them the most complete news coverage.[12]

Although most Americans see television as an entertainment medium, no public official or political candidate can afford to ignore its power as a means of communicating with the public. In fact, as we will see in the final section of this chapter, television plays a central role in elections, especially presidential campaigns.[13]

New Media Technologies

During President Ronald Reagan's vacations at his ranch in Santa Barbara, California, CBS News assigned two technicians to sit in a truck parked on a hilltop three miles away for the sole purpose of monitoring a TV screen. The screen was wired to a camera with a lens three feet long and weighing over four hundred pounds, custom-made for photographing the president when he appeared outdoors. "I'm going to fake a heart attack and tumble off this horse to see how quickly they get down the mountain with the news," Reagan joked.[14]

High-tech cameras are just one of many innovations that have greatly changed the nature of television reporting. Since the early 1970s many of the limitations on television reporting have been removed by technological advances such as battery power supplies and video recorders with sound capability. In 1962, the taping of "A Tour of the White House with Mrs. John F. Kennedy" required nine tons of lights, cameras, and cables put into place by fifty-four technicians. In contrast, the 1990 NBC special "A Day in the Life of the White House" was produced by a handful of technicians. It was filmed on a Monday, edited on a Tuesday, and broadcast that Wednesday.

SATELLITES   An especially significant technological advance is the satellite. As a result of satellite technology, television has become an instantaneous means of worldwide communication. One effect has been an expansion in coverage of the president's activities, both in Washington and abroad. In the early 1980s the number of local news stations with Washington bureaus grew from fifteen to more than fifty. The cost of satellite relay links between the East and West

Coasts of the United States dropped from four thousand dollars in the late 1970s to less than four hundred today, and the cost of transmission links to formerly remote areas in the Far East and Middle East has been reduced by half.

In the 1970s, fewer than half of all television news stories were shown on the day they occurred. Today, as a result of satellite technology, it is rare for any news story other than special features to be more than a day old. Satellites have also affected the political process. Senators and members of the administration, as well as candidates for office, are making increasing use of direct satellite links to bypass network news and appear on local television newscasts.

CABLE TV   Community antenna, or "cable," television was developed in the 1950s to bring television programming to remote areas that could not be reached by normal VHF and UHF broadcast signals. By transmitting television signals through coaxial cable to individual receivers, cable television avoided the environmental and atmospheric disturbances that often plagued regular broadcast signals. Since the 1980s cable TV has become almost universal throughout the United States. Cable systems are more popular than regular broadcasting because they provide superior signal definition and a wider variety of programming choices than any single broadcast market could provide. Cable channels like C-SPAN Ted Turner's Cable News Network, and CNN Headline News, as well as specialty channels for sports, feature films, and cultural programming, compete vigorously with the established broadcast networks for viewers' attention.

Cable TV has dramatically altered the ways in which citizens receive their news and entertainment. Fifty-eight percent of all households—fifty-four million—pay for cable television.

NARROWCASTING   Technological advances such as satellites, cable TV, low-power television broadcast stations, VCRs, and remote control all make possible lower costs and increased usage. Collectively, these advances have resulted in what media expert Austin Ranney terms *narrowcasting*. Network television is based on a broadcasting system in which television signals are transmitted over the air, aimed at huge, heterogeneous audiences, and transmitted to wireless receivers in viewers' homes. Narrowcasting, in contrast, is a mass communications system "in which television signals are transmitted either by air or by direct wires to people's homes and are aimed at smaller, more narrowly defined, and more homogeneous audiences."[15]

Narrowcasting involves more than a move toward greater programming efficiency; it has developed largely as a way to boost profits in an increasingly competitive media market. It is based on the idea that a more carefully targeted viewing audience is also a more homogeneous buying audience. Among the most successful experiments in narrowcasting are CNN (twenty-four-hour programming devoted exclusively to news and information), ESPN (twenty-four-hour sports programming), Nickelodeon (programming for children), and MTV (twenty-four-hour music and entertainment).

FUNCTIONS OF THE MEDIA

Social scientists are in general agreement that the mass media perform three basic functions: (1) surveillance of world events, (2) interpretation of events, and (3) socialization of individuals into cultural settings. "The manner in which

The nightly news anchors at the three major networks, Peter Jennings of ABC (shown here), Dan Rather of CBS, and Tom Brokaw of NBC, are highly respected reporters, popular television personalities, and institutions in their field. On a nightly basis, they convey the news headlines, helping to define what is newsworthy. They also serve an important role as soothers of the American psyche in times of crisis. Americans trust these familiar anchors and turn to them to get information and reassurance, as they did during the Persian Gulf War and after the bombing of the federal building in Oklahoma City.

these . . . functions are performed," writes political scientist Doris Graber, "affects the political fate of individuals, groups, and social organizations, as well as the course of domestic and international politics."[16]

Surveillance

In their surveillance role, the media function, as Marshall McLuhan observed, as "sense extensions" for people who do not participate directly in events.[17] From the media we learn about world conditions, cultural events, sports, weather, and much else. In many respects, the mass media have helped transform the world into a global community. Citizens of the now-united Germany watched the dismantling of the Berlin Wall at the same time as citizens of the United States did. When President Reagan underwent surgery to remove cancerous growths in his colon, the networks brought in medical experts to explain the exact nature of Reagan's medical problem and prognosis. Millions of viewers watched the confirmation hearings of Clarence Thomas and the trial of O. J. Simpson.

Every afternoon, television news anchors and their staffs sift through the myriad stories, tapes, and bits of information that have been funneled to them during the day. They do so to identify the most important information and events; these will be relayed to the public in evening news broadcasts. Thus, the news anchors actually define what is newsworthy.

The ability of the media to decide what constitutes news is a controversial aspect of their surveillance role. The media not only bring certain matters to public attention but also doom certain others to obscurity. During election campaigns, for example, the press is the "great mentioner," repeating the names of certain individuals, such as Jesse Jackson or Colin Powell who are being mentioned as possible candidates, or applying labels such as "dark horse" or "long shot." "At any given time in this country," wrote journalist David Broder, "there are several hundred persons who are potential candidates for nomination. . . . Who is it that winnows this field down to manageable size? The press—and particularly that small segment of the press called the national political reporters."[18] (Later in the chapter we will see how candidates fight to secure media attention in the struggle to stay in contention.)

There are few checks on the media's surveillance role. "The power of the media to set the civic agenda," writes Doris Graber, "is a matter of concern because it is not controlled by a system of formal checks and balances as is power at various levels of government. It is not subject to periodic review through the electoral process. If media emphases or claims are incorrect, remedies are few."[19]

Surveillance can occur at the private as well as public level. Local television newscasts offer monetary rewards to citizens who bring in videotapes that can be used on the evening news. An amateur's videotape of Los Angeles police officers beating motorist Rodney King, was aired on the evening news and became crucial evidence in the trial of four officers indicted on charges of violating King's civil rights.

Interpretation

The media do much more than provide public and private surveillance of events. They also *interpret* those events by giving them meaning and context, and in the process often shape opinions. Psychologist Hadley Cantril illustrates this point with the following example:

> Three umpires describe their job of calling balls and strikes in a baseball game. First umpire: "Some's balls and some's strikes and I calls 'em as they is." Second umpire: "Some's balls and some's strikes and I calls 'em as I sees 'em." Third umpire: "Some's balls and some's strikes but they ain't nothin' till I calls 'em."[20]

According to Cantril, very few journalists are like the first umpire, believing that the "balls and strikes" they count represent what is happening in the real world. Some journalists may admit to the second method of umpiring, using their judgment to "call them as they see them." The third umpire's style is the most controversial when applied to mass media coverage of significant events. For if, like the third umpire, journalists in print and television actually make the decisions regarding which actors or events are in or out of the "strike zone" or even determine their own "strike zone" or context for news, the potential power of media becomes immense, and assertions of media "objectivity" sound rather hollow.

Actually, the process of gathering, evaluating, editing, producing, and presenting "news" involves each of the three umpiring styles. Some reporters may pursue a case against a prominent public figure or institution in the belief that their article will finally expose the "reality" of corruption, scandal, or other wrongdoing. And every journalist—from reporters on the street to editors behind desks—exercises some judgment over which events are really "news" and which elements of a story are most "newsworthy"; an event is neither a curve ball in the dirt nor a fastball on the outside corner until some journalistic "umpire" makes the decision to cover it.

Political scientist Shanto Iyengar has developed a theory of media "framing effects" that is particularly relevant to television news coverage. In a series of carefully controlled experiments, Iyengar and his colleagues found that the way television portrays events and actors has a significant influence on the opinions of those who watch the coverage.[21] For example, coverage of terrorism that emphasizes the violence and brutality of a terrorist act without attempting to explain the motivations behind it is likely to influence viewers to consider all such actions brutal and violent, regardless of the motivations or historical explanations. This is an important point. Since the constraints of time tend to dictate relatively brief, often superficial coverage of important news, viewers are likely to form equally superficial opinions.

INVESTIGATIVE JOURNALISM   Journalism may have changed since the days of the muckrakers as the technology and political culture of America have changed, but the spirit of the muckraker can still be seen in the practice of **investigative journalism.** Investigative journalism differs from standard press coverage in the depth of coverage sought, the time spent researching the subject, and the shocking findings that often result from such reporting. Like their muckraking predecessors, today's investigative journalists turn their reportorial skills to the uncovering of corruption, scandal, conspiracy, and abuses of power in government and business. The most familiar example of such reporting occurred during the Watergate scandal of the 1970s, and developed out of extensive interviewing and analysis by two reporters for the *Washington Post,* Carl Bernstein and Bob Woodward. The editor of the *Post,* Ben Bradlee, risked his professional reputation and the reputation of his paper by running a series of investigative articles on the Watergate break-in and its connection to the

White House. Although the *Post* articles did not affect the outcome of the 1972 election, the resulting scandal eventually led to the resignation of President Richard Nixon.

Like the print media, television has also developed a tradition of investigative journalism, drawing on the early work of Edward R. Murrow, whose most famous piece may have been his 1952 exposé of the brutal practices of Senator Joseph McCarthy. Today, such programs as "60 Minutes" continue this tradition. Sometimes such televised "watchdog" journalism gets out of hand, however, as was the case when NBC's weekly television news magazine "Dateline" ran a report on the "exploding gas tanks" in older General Motors pickup trucks. Attempting to provide graphic video evidence of GM malfeasance in the construction and positioning of the gas tanks, a "Dateline" crew set up two collision tests in the hope that one or the other would yield a dramatic video of the pickup's gas tank exploding on collision. Not only did the gas tanks fail to rupture, but NBC later admitted that the testers had installed incendiary devices to the underside of the trucks to ignite any gas that might pour from a ruptured tank. The case reveals the lengths to which journalists will go in search of a "scoop," even manipulating the "facts" on occasion. It also demonstrates how the media's public service role can be distorted, turning the "watch dog" into an "attack dog."

Socialization

The media play an important role in **socialization,** the process by which people learn to conform to their society's norms and values. As we noted in Chapter 9, most of the information that children acquire about their world comes from the mass media, either directly or indirectly through the media's influence on parents, teachers, or friends. The mass media can also provide information that enables young people to develop their own opinions. During the 1992 presidential election, MTV provided a forum that enabled young people to learn about politics, issues, and candidates.

Studies of the effects of exposure to mass media have found that higher reliance on television as the primary source of information seems to correlate with a greater fear of crime and random violence, even when controlling for the socioeconomic status, education, and living conditions of the individual. While such findings are tentative and subject to interpretation, they indicate that the medium on which most Americans rely for most of their information about the rest of the world—television—may contribute to a growing sense of unease about current and future social, economic, and political conditions.

Much of the impact of mass media seems to involve reinforcing prevailing norms and values rather than creating new ones. Until the dissolution of the former Soviet Union in 1990, most commentary on socialism, communism, Eastern Europe, and the USSR simply reinforced the Cold War perspective in support of "free-market" capitalism and against communism; public opinion surveys indicate that this message was clearly received. Now that the Soviet Union is no more, most coverage of Eastern Europe and the newly formed Commonwealth of Independent Nations tends to emphasize these countries' "transition" to democracy and capitalism, and opinion polls seem to indicate that Americans are no longer as concerned about the potential "menace" of communism.[22]

The power of the media as a socializing agent is reflected in public concern about media violence, particularly in children's television programming. While analysts remain sharply divided about the actual impact of violent programming, efforts have been made to regulate the frequency and intensity of violent and sexually explicit media content. For example, in the wake of the assassinations of Robert Kennedy and Martin Luther King, Jr., television programmers suddenly canceled a number of popular but violent shows or changed the programs to reflect less explicit violence.[23] Televised screenings of feature films containing explicit violence or sexual content have adopted the motion picture precedent of rating these programs and including viewer discretion warnings, even when the theater versions are edited for television. Cable stations that air such films "uncut" also provide the original film rating and generally restrict the airing of such programming to the late evening, when children are more likely to be asleep. While such attempts to regulate the socializing influence of mass media are controversial, they demonstrate widespread agreement that freedom of expression must sometimes be limited to avert the threat of social harm.

LIMITS ON MEDIA FREEDOM

The First Amendment to the Constitution states that "Congress shall make no law . . . abridging the freedom of the press." Ideally, the media would investigate, report, provide information, and analyze political events without being subject to government-imposed restrictions. Such restrictions are commonplace in many other nations, where the media are subject to various degrees of restraint, prohibition, or censorship. Americans take pride in the tradition of a free press, yet as we will see in this section, that freedom is not absolute. Not only are there laws against libel, slander, and obscenity, but the media are regulated by a government agency, the Federal Communications Commission, and are subject to certain limitations imposed by the judiciary. The nature of media ownership also plays a role in limiting media freedom.

Regulating the Media

Regulation of the media began after World War I, in the heyday of radio. During that period large consortiums like the Radio Corporation of America (RCA) established networks to broadcast news, information, and entertainment, and millions of amateur "radio hams" were buying or building simple broadcast receivers and sending their own gossip, sermons, monologues, and conversations over the increasingly congested airwaves. In 1927 the federal government stepped in to clean up the chaotic radio waves. Congress created the five-member Federal Radio Commission (FRC) to allocate frequencies and regulate broadcasting procedures. Essentially, the objective of the FRC was to organize radio broadcasting and rationalize the growing broadcast radio industry to prevent monopolization and other unfair practices.

In 1934 Congress passed the Federal Communications Act, in which the jurisdiction of the FRC was expanded to include telephone and telegraph communications, the panel was enlarged to seven members (eventually reduced again to five in 1982), and the agency was renamed the **Federal Communications Commission (FCC).** As broadcast and cable (CATV) television

Rupert Murdoch, global-media mogul, holds interests in publishing, broadcasting, movies, and the new electronic media. He has a reputation for shattering conventions of the media business, leaving regulators—here and abroad—struggling to keep up. In the United States, he has often found himself embroiled in sticky legal disputes with federal regulators in his role as chairman of the independent Fox network. He won a recent battle with the FCC when it ruled that his network benefited the public and could therefore be granted a waiver for violating rules limiting the foreign ownership of American television stations (Murdoch is a native Australian).

developed, they too came under the scrutiny and jurisdiction of the FCC. The most recent communications innovations, multipoint distribution service (MDS), direct broadcast satellites (DBS), and satellite master antenna television (SMATV), have also come under the umbrella of FCC regulation.

The electronic media are regulated by four sets of guidelines:

1. rules limiting the number of stations owned or controlled by a single organization
2. examinations of the goals and performances of stations as part of periodic licensing
3. rules mandating public-service and local-interest programs
4. rules guaranteeing fair treatment to individuals and protecting their rights

Regulation of the electronic media has been consistently upheld by the Supreme Court under the **scarcity doctrine:** While there is no limit on the number of newspapers that can be published in a given area, two radio or television stations cannot broadcast signals at the same time and at the same frequency without jamming each other. Thus, it is clearly in the public interest that government allocate frequencies to broadcasters.[24] Broadcasting is viewed as a public resource, much like a national park, and the government establishes regulations designed to promote "the public convenience, interest, or necessity."

The scarcity doctrine, with its implications for the public interest, is the basis for the FCC's regulation of the political content of radio and television broadcasts. This regulation takes the form of three rules of the airwaves: the equal opportunities rule, the fairness doctrine, and the right to rebuttal.

THE EQUAL TIME RULE   Although a station is not required to give or sell air time to one candidate seeking a specific office, whenever it provides time to one candidate—whether for a price or for free—it must give equal time to all of the candidates running for the same office. This **equal time rule** holds whether there are two or two hundred candidates for office; each is entitled to equal time. Section 315 (a) of the Federal Communications Act stipulates: "If any licensee shall permit any person who is a legally qualified candidate for any public office to use a broadcasting station, he shall afford equal opportunities to all other such candidates for that office in the use of such broadcasting station."

The equal time rule has become important in recent presidential campaigns. When Ross Perot bought large blocks of time for his "infomercials" on various campaign issues, the networks involved were required to make similar blocks of time available to George Bush and Bill Clinton. However, the rule does not require that the candidates actually take advantage of the available time, only that they have the opportunity to purchase it on an equal basis with all other candidates.

THE FAIRNESS DOCTRINE   The **fairness doctrine,** now abandoned, required radio and television stations to provide a reasonable percentage of time for programs dealing with issues of public interest. Stations were also required to provide for those who wished to express opposition to any highly controversial public issue aired or discussed on the station. Defining what is controversial has traditionally been left to the administrative courts, but the FCC has ruled that "two viewpoints" satisfies the licensee's obligation. The fairness doctrine was upheld by the Supreme Court in 1969 in *Red Lion Broadcasting* v. *FCC.*[25] A federal court of appeals later ruled that the doctrine was not law and could be repealed without congressional approval. Congress then passed a bill that would have made the fairness doctrine permanent. President Reagan vetoed the bill, observing that "in any other medium besides broadcasting, such federal policing of the editorial judgment of journalists would be unthinkable." Following the veto, the FCC negated the doctrine.

THE RIGHT OF REBUTTAL   When the honesty, integrity, or morality of persons or groups is attacked on a station, they have the **right of rebuttal,** the right to refute the allegations, free of charge, within a reasonable time. The FCC operates under the assumption that a maligned person deserves a chance to reply, and the public has a right to hear that response. The rule does not apply to attacks on foreign groups or leaders, to personal attacks made by legally qualified candidates or their representatives, or to live, on-the-spot broadcasts.

Prior Restraint versus the Right to Know

In 1971 former government employee Daniel Ellsberg gave to the *New York Times* copies of classified documents on the Vietnam War. The documents had been prepared in 1968, during the presidency of Lyndon Johnson, and revealed the concerns of senior Defense Department officials during the Kennedy and Johnson years. The government sought to suppress the publication of the documents by obtaining a judicial restraining order, an action known as **prior restraint.** President Nixon maintained that publication of the papers would threaten the lives of servicemen and servicewomen, intelligence officers, and military plans that were still in operation in Vietnam.

The case eventually reached the Supreme Court, which decided in favor of the *Times.* In his concurring opinion on the case, Justice Hugo Black offered a strong argument for absolute freedom of the press:

> Paramount among the responsibilities of a free press is the duty to prevent any part of the Government from deceiving the people and sending them off to distant lands to die of foreign fever and foreign shot and shell. . . . The *New York Times* and the *Washington Post* and other newspapers should be commended for serving the purpose that the Founding Fathers saw so clearly. In revealing the workings of government that led to the Vietnam War, the newspapers nobly did precisely that which the Founders hoped and trusted they would do.[26]

A more recent case, however, shows that a more conservative Supreme Court may be willing to restrict publication of controversial material. When CNN broadcast recorded phone conversations involving Panamanian general Manuel Noriega as he awaited trial in Miami, in 1990, the Supreme Court refused to block a lower court's injunction banning all future broadcasts that CNN planned to air. The controversy raised important constitutional questions: At issue were Noriega's right to a fair trial as well as freedom of the press. What made the issue more intriguing was that the Court decided to suppress publication despite the fact that the U.S. government was responsible for the taping of the phone conversations in the first place.

Other cases have been concerned with the media's right to cover a trial and whether that coverage would threaten the fairness of the trial. The case of *Miami Herald Publishing Co.* vs. *Tornillo* (1974) brought up the issue of whether statutory guidelines implemented by Florida state law require newspapers to publish specific *replies* from political candidates attacked in their columns rather than merely publishing *retractions*. The Court ruled against the "right to reply" law, stating that it "turns afoul the elementary First Amendment proposition that government may not force a newspaper to print copy which, in the journalistic discretion, it chooses to leave on the newspaper floor." That is, even when accused of publicly defaming a political figure, newspapers could not be required by law to print the responses of the defamed figure, since this was to "force a newspaper to print copy" in violation of the constitutional guarantee of a free press. As Chief Justice Warren E. Burger noted, "A responsible press is an undoubtedly desirable goal, but press responsibility is not mandated by the Constitution, and like many other virtues, it cannot be legislated."[27]

Even with a relatively broad guarantee of freedom, there are laws restricting just how the press may cover news. Journalists are allowed wide latitude in levying charges against whomever they choose, and may even print facts or accusations that subsequently prove untrue, as long as they do not *knowingly* publish untruths or print intentionally damaging statements known as *libel.* Anyone attempting to sue a newspaper for libel must also prove that the publication in question actually caused damage. As you will see in Chapter 14, libel is very difficult to prove, especially for public figures whose reputation may be affected by any number of things besides a single journalistic "hit piece" and who have an opportunity to make a reply. In general, as long as journalists do not set out to attack a public figure *with malice,* they are free of prevailing laws against libel.

IDEOLOGICAL BIAS AND MEDIA CONTROL

Many observers believe that the mass media display ideological bias in the way they select and present news. According to research surveys, 55 percent of journalists consider themselves liberal, compared with about 23 percent of the population as a whole. And on a number of issues, such as government regulation, abortion, and school prayer, the media's liberal attitudes are pervasive (see Table 13.2). Do these attitudes affect news coverage?

In a recent *Times Mirror* survey of more than 250 members of the press, a substantial majority (55 percent) of American journalists who followed the 1992 presidential campaign believed that George Bush was harmed by press coverage. "Only 11% felt that Bill Clinton's campaign was harmed by press coverage. Moreover, one out of three journalists (36%) think that the media helped Arkansian Clinton win the presidency while a mere 3% believed that the press coverage helped the Bush effort."[28] During the waning days of the campaign President Bush frequently waved a red bumper sticker that stated, "Annoy the Media: Reelect Bush." The evidence is that Bush did indeed get more negative evening news coverage on CBS, ABC, and NBC than did Clinton and Perot.

An inherent problem with these studies is that there is no formal definition to "negative coverage." But researchers try to reduce the subjectivity of the results by coding the coverage on the basis of key words and phrases—*beleaguered*

Table 13.2
Journalist Opinion and Public Opinion

	JOURNALISTS	THE PUBLIC
Self-described ideology:		
Liberal	55%	23%
Conservative	17	29
Favor government regulation of business	49	22
U.S. should withdraw investments from South Africa	62	31
Allow women to have abortions	82	49
Allow prayer in public schools	25	74
Favor "affirmative action"	81	56
Favor death penalty for murder	47	75
Want stricter controls on handguns	78	50
Increase defense budget	15	38
Favor hiring homosexuals	89	55

Sources: Los Angeles Times poll of about three thousand citizens and two thousand, seven hundred journalists nationwide, as reported in William Schneider and I. A. Lewis, "Views on the News," *Public Opinion* (Aug.–Sept. 1985): 7. Reprinted with permission of American Enterprise Institute for Public Policy Research.

and *out of touch* registered as negative; *experienced* and *articulate* as positive.

The Center for Media and Public Affairs, a nonpartisan group with a conservative bent, found that Bush was consistently portrayed negatively. Between Labor Day and election day, the center took every evaluation of the candidates on the network news shows by a voter, a party official, or a policy expert and coded it as positive or negative. Only 31 percent were positive about Bush; 69 percent were negative. For Clinton, the results were not much better: 37 percent were positive. For Perot, 46 percent were positive, proving that good coverage doesn't guarantee election.

All of these findings are interesting, but they do not make a conclusive case for significant liberal or conservative media bias in news coverage. For a number of reasons, such findings are difficult to prove. We will now take a close look at some of those reasons.

Media Pluralism

First of all, we must recall that the word *media* is plural. There are differences among the various communications media that make lumping them all together impossible. For example, print media tend to offer considerably more breadth of opinion than television. While newspapers and magazines can boast a number of popular conservative and liberal publications—such as the conservative *National Review* and the liberal *Nation*—television tends to offer a much more homogeneous, mainstream view. There is, however, some diversity within the relatively narrow ideological parameters of television, particularly on the cable stations. CNN's "Crossfire" regularly features both a mainstream liberal and a

Sunday morning news shows, such as "This Week with David Brinkley," bring together a varied group of journalists and politicians to share their views on important issues with the American public. Here, the cast of "This Week with David Brinkley," including (from left) the moderate Cokie Roberts, the liberal Sam Donaldson, the conservative George Will, and Brinkley, the host, discuss their thoughts on the topics covered during that day's program. Because of different political perspectives elicited, such discussions are almost always interesting and lively.

mainstream conservative as co-hosts in a program of lively debates on topical issues. "Firing Line," hosted by conservative William F. Buckley, Jr., appears regularly on PBS stations, one of the few current-events programs regularly hosted by an avowed political conservative. But for the most part television represents a mainstream, status quo perspective.

What many critics fail to mention in their attacks on "liberal" media is the almost total absence of an outlet for "far-Left" opinion, especially in television. While socialist and even communist magazines, newspapers, and newsletters have come and gone, leftist viewpoints have been almost invisible on television. Throughout the history of network television, no program featuring a socialist or social democratic point of view—the equivalent of the political mainstream in a country like Sweden—has ever appeared as a regular part of television programming. The absence of "far-Left" programming becomes more striking when we realize that the success of the "religious Right" in capturing much of the Republican social agenda during the 1980s owes much to the power of television. Popular televangelists like Jerry Falwell, Jimmy Swaggart, and one-time Republican presidential candidate Pat Robertson garnered most of their political following from regularly scheduled religious broadcasting.

A Liberal "Media Elite"?

While the majority of reporters in both print and electronic media are fairly liberal, their bosses—the magazine and newspaper publishers and network executives—tend to be more conservative, sometimes decidedly so. Most of the statistical evidence supporting conservative claims of a liberally biased "media elite" does not clearly differentiate between the reporters, the editors, and the publishers and owners of media outlets; sometimes the only analysis is of the reporters, a peculiarly well-educated, well-paid, and liberal cohort of the American public. In the often-cited studies of Robert Lichter, Linda Lichter, and Stanley Rothman, for example, the "media elite" includes reporters, editors, and executives, but only as an aggregate population with no distinctions regarding the differences that might exist within this elite.[29] Simply establishing the liberal leanings of reporters does not prove liberal press bias.

Media Ownership and Control

Another reason to avoid making too much of the evidence of media "bias" concerns the economics of mass communication: specifically, the ownership and control of mass media outlets. Many recent analyses suggest that the overwhelming bias of mass media is neither liberal nor conservative but corporate. Media scholar Ben Bagdikian has written extensively on the development of what he calls a "private ministry of information" created by the formation of a "media monopoly." Bagdikian's studies reveal that most of America's daily newspapers, magazines, television, books, and motion pictures are controlled by only twenty-three corporations. As control of media slips into fewer and fewer hands, Bagdikian argues, the content of those media become increasingly similar. He claims this is because the overall interests of corporate executives tend to coincide, especially since many of them sit on the boards of directors of the same companies.[30] The result is a disturbingly homogeneous version of "reality," tempered by the priorities of large corporations who own and advertise through major media outlets. This includes a reluctance by media to attack their own corporate masters. An example is the refusal of NBC's "Today" show to include in its story on national boycotts of large corporations one of the largest—General Electric—which happens to own NBC.

Media–Government Symbiosis

A final problem with establishing a basis for ideological bias involves the symbiotic, or interdependent, relationship between the press and government. Just as the media have close ties with the largest American—and some international—corporations, so are they closely tied to the very government they are so often accused of attacking or treating unfairly. Reporters in all media rely overwhelmingly on "official sources"—usually well-placed public officials—when reporting government events. And journalist Philip Weiss has observed that, even when such "official" sources are consulted, a common practice among reporters is to allow these sources to exercise considerable approval over the way their statements are used in stories.[31] Certainly the practice of "quote approval" is not restricted to government officials alone, and it may be an attempt to ensure journalistic "objectivity" by allowing interviewees to verify the intentions as well as the language behind what they express in interviews. But practices like quote approval can draw reporters into an uncomfortably intimate relationship with the very individuals about whom they are supposed to be unbiased.

A classic example of the symbiotic relationship between media and the government is illustrated in the case study at the beginning of the chapter. Almost all that Americans learned about the Gulf War via media reporting came not from individual soldiers in the field, Iraqi citizens affected by the devastation, or opponents of U.S. intervention but from official representatives of the armed forces, the Pentagon, and the State Department. Only rarely are strong opponents of a government's foreign and domestic policy ever granted significant coverage in the mass media.

Table 13.3
Focus of Media Coverage in Election Campaigns

COVERAGE	TELEVISION NEWS	NEWSPAPERS	MAGAZINES
Horse race and hoopla	58%	56%	54%
Issue and policy	29	28	32
Other	13	12	14

Source: Adapted from W. Russell Neuman, *The Paradox of Mass Politics* (Cambridge, Mass.: Harvard University Press, 1986), p. 140.

Conclusions about the degree of ideological bias in the media are difficult to draw, but there is evidence of a relatively limited ideological bias in most mass media reporting. While the reporters themselves may be more liberal than the general public, the impact of media ownership and control and the symbiotic relationship between media and the government seem to keep most press coverage well within the political mainstream.

THE MEDIA AND ELECTIONS

No discussion of the media and politics would be complete without an examination of the uses of mass communication in elections. It is important here to distinguish between two types of media use in elections: coverage of the campaign by the media; and exploitation of media by candidates, in the form of political advertising and infomercials.

Press Coverage

The amount of media coverage can influence the outcome of an election campaign. By focusing on particular candidates or issues, the media often ignore others. Indeed, the media have been accused of focusing on the "horse race" nature of politics. As Table 13.3 shows, more than half of the coverage in any given campaign is devoted to the race itself rather than to the policies and issues around which the race revolves. As primary campaigns unfold, the press often gets caught up in reporting candidates' standing in the race. Coverage tends to be limited to the front-runners, thereby delivering the message that only the front-runners are worthy of public attention.[32]

Polling

Over the last fifteen years, media use of opinion polls has expanded dramatically. Not only are newspapers and television networks using more polls from the larger survey organizations like Gallup, Harris, and Roper; increasingly, major media outlets are conducting their own surveys. Large-circulation newspapers and magazines like the *New York Times, USA Today,* and *Newsweek,* as well as CNN and the major broadcast television networks, are constantly conducting public-

President Bill Clinton has often struggled with fairly low public-opinion-poll ratings. In hopes of boosting those ratings and staying in touch with the public, Clinton, like his predecessors, accommodates a press contingent that dutifully follows him around to record his every word and move for a public eager to know what their president is up to and how he is performing. Meetings with the press, like the one shown here, are always well choreographed to enhance the president's image. Note that Air Force One, a potent symbol of the presidency, is the backdrop for this session with the press.

opinion surveys on a variety of national issues. Much subsequent news coverage is based on these "in-house" polls. How significant is the impact of such coverage?

There is no solid evidence to suggest that media polling significantly affects public opinion; that is, such polling does not appear to change opinions. However, published accounts of consistently high or low public responses or sudden shifts of opinion can affect the political process. If candidates do not do well in published polls, they have much more trouble raising the contributions necessary to run expensive campaigns. And elected legislators, ever watchful for trends within their constituencies, obviously pay close attention to published opinion data concerning their states or districts. If we consider that polling techniques can sometimes distort public opinion simply by the way questions are worded, we are faced with the possibility that campaign contributors and legislators may sometimes be taking their cues from data that do not accurately reflect public preferences.[33]

There has also been growing controversy regarding published results of early exit polls taken of people who have just voted during the national elections and aired before the polls close. Many of Jimmy Carter's supporters complained that network broadcasting of early exit polls, which projected an easy victory for Ronald Reagan, actually discouraged Carter's supporters on the West Coast from voting.

Some scholars express concern about the reliance on polls, fearing serious consequences for democracy. Benjamin Ginsberg suggests that reliance on published polling data as a gauge of public opinion has actually distanced the people from their elected representatives. Instead of monitoring a diversity of expressed opinion and actual behavior—letters to the editor, voting patterns, and so on—public officials may actually be reading only a superficial image of what the people really think. The more the process of gathering even such

Media Masters

At least since the 1980s, political success at the national level has depended on the skillful use of the mass media, especially television. Consider the examples of Ronald Reagan, Ross Perot, and Newt Gingrich.

Perhaps more than any other president, Reagan understood television. A former movie actor, Reagan had hosted television's "G.E. Theater" in the 1950s and had served as public-relations spokesperson for General Electric. Thus, he was well versed not only in the technical aspects of television production but also in the ways in which television could be used for massive public-relations campaigns. He used the same principles to "sell" first his candidacy and then his presidency.

Reagan and his advisors clearly understood that television is overwhelmingly an entertainment medium, one that is heavily dependent on pictures rather than words to convey meaning. As Michael Deaver, Reagan's media advisor, put it, "We thought of ourselves as producers. We tried to create the most entertaining, visually attractive scene to fill that box [television], so that the networks would have to use it."* Reagan's public-relations staff produced an unending stream of images designed to warm the hearts of the viewing public: Reagan having a beer with working people in a Boston pub, Reagan working out in the White House gym (and arm wrestling with a well-known weight lifter), Reagan waving good-bye to his wife as he left the White House to go horseback riding. Throughout his presidency, all of Reagan's public appearances were scripted in advance, with the scripts based on a sophisticated understanding of the power of images in the television age.

In his 1992 presidential campaign, Texas billionaire H. Ross Perot also made effective use of television, though in a quite different fashion. Perot pioneered the use of the political infomercial, purchasing thirty-minute blocks of television time in which he delivered lectures about major issues such as the federal budget deficit and governmental reform. The infomercials—which also introduced candidate Perot to the American public—attracted a surprisingly large audience share and are credited with making him a serious contender for the presidency.

For sheer media savvy, perhaps no one currently on the political scene can equal House Speaker Newt Gingrich. Gingrich has built his congressional career by capitalizing on the media—notably C-Span, the cable channel that covers floor debate in Congress. He began a decade ago by making speeches denouncing the Democrats in front of C-Span's cameras, which did not show that the House chamber was empty and his opponents could not respond. More recently, he has taken advantage of every opportunity to get the attention of reporters and television camera crews.

A compelling public speaker, Gingrich understands the value of symbolism in communicating to a mass public. During the 1994 congressional election campaign he used emotionally charged symbolic language to convince the public that Congress was corrupt and in need of a complete overhaul—under his leadership. His strategy was overwhelmingly successful; not only did he win his own campaign, but he led a political revolution that transformed Congress. There can be little doubt that the most effective political leaders of the future will be those, like Gingrich, who have mastered the media.

---

*Michael K. Deaver with Mickey Herskowitz, *Behind the Scenes* (New York: William Morrow and Company, Inc., 1987).

dubious information is distanced from actual participation, the weaker the foundations of participatory democracy become. So while the media's use of in-house polls may not actually change opinion, it certainly may distort it.[34]

Talk Shows

The proliferation of call-in radio and television talk shows presents an interesting bridge between press coverage of campaigns and media utilization by the candidates. Today there are more than ten thousand radio stations and eleven hundred commercial television stations. Ninety-nine percent of all households have a radio; 95 percent of all cars have a radio; and 57 percent of all adult Americans have a radio at work. Talk radio has a large following.

During the 1992 election, talk shows emerged as a new platform in political campaigns and as the primary mode of discourse between candidates. Independent candidate H. Ross Perot decided to bypass journalists and appeal directly to the people on "Larry King Live." By the end of the 1992 campaign, candidates had appeared on MTV, Arsenio Hall's show, the three network morning shows, Nashville Network, ESPN, and radio talk shows.

During the 1994 congressional election, talk shows took on even greater importance. Conservative talk show hosts fanned the flames of anti-incumbent—particularly anti-Clinton—sentiment. Rush Limbaugh's show alone was carried by 659 radio stations with a weekly audience of twenty million. Along with Republican radio hosts in cities throughout the nation, Limbaugh mounted a barrage of criticism of President Clinton and led the campaign for revolutionary changes in Congress. When these hosts were in turn criticized for the obvious bias in their commentary, they countered that they were simply balancing what they consider to be a liberal bias in mainstream media coverage.

Television and Presidential Elections

While radio talk shows were the dominant medium during the 1994 congressional elections, television takes center stage in presidential elections. The acronym *ADI,* meaning "area of dominant influence," is part of the everyday

Just after a presidential election, the press is eager to satisfy the public's overwhelming desire to know every minute detail about their new president and the first family. They will go to any extreme to get a picture. Here, in a scene that can only be described as bordering on the outrageous, photographers (who staked out the governor's mansion where the Clintons lived) mob Chelsea Clinton's cat Socks.

Cartoon by Mike Luckovitch. *Newsweek,* September 19, 1988. © 1988 by Mike Luckovitch. Reprinted with permission of Mike Luckovitch and Creators Syndicate.

lexicon of the media strategists who have replaced party members as campaign organizers. The United States is divided into approximately sixty ADIs, which are further subdivided into *DMAs,* "local designated marketing areas." Every presidential campaign is geared to capturing this TV market. Candidates travel from one ADI to another, where "the old-fashioned political advance man now provides not only the proper crowds, but also the proper pictorial sites to silhouette his candidate's personality or proposal."[35] Days before the candidate arrives, advance staff are checking acoustics, traffic patterns, photo opportunities—even the location of the sun at various times of the day.

In 1992 the Clinton campaign used a sophisticated data-mapping operation in which media markets were superimposed on a map of the United States.

> Week by week, each media market was ranked in terms of the number of persuadable voters in the market weighted by the Electoral College votes and the perceived strategic importance of the states reached in that market. The resulting map, in which the media markets were arranged on an eight-point, color-coded scale, quickly revealed where the campaign needed to place its emphasis in travel, field organization, and media buys.[36]

The use of television by presidential candidates is geared toward one major goal: making the candidate look good for about ten seconds on the evening news. This is accomplished through a variety of techniques, of which the most effective is the soundbite. A **soundbite** is a very brief statement, usually a snippet from a speech, that conveys the essence of a longer statement and can be inserted into a news story. Lines such as "You're no Jack Kennedy," uttered by Lloyd Bentsen during the 1988 vice-presidential debate with Dan Quayle, and

"Are you better off now than you were four years ago?" asked by Ronald Reagan in his 1980 debate against Jimmy Carter, have become part of political lore because of their effectiveness in targeting a specific issue or sentiment. Today candidates come to debates prepared with one-liners they hope will be turned into soundbites and reported in the next day's news.

Over the years soundbites have become progressively shorter. In 1968 a presidential candidate averaged 43 seconds of uninterrupted speech on the evening news. The average soundbite during the 1984 presidential campaign was only 14.79 seconds. By 1988 the average was down to 9 seconds. A voter rarely hears a potential president utter a complete paragraph on the evening news.[37]

How much useful information about a policy or issue can a candidate relay to the viewer in a 9-second soundbite? Not much, according to NBC News anchor Tom Brokaw, who has described soundbites as a cancer. Alternative news broadcasts such as the PBS show "The McNeil/Lehrer Report" often devote up to 30 minutes of coverage to a single issue, but this show is watched by a very small number of viewers.

Political Advertising

Along with the horse race emphasis of press coverage and the political commentary of radio talk shows, the use of soundbites on television news contributes to the increasing focus on the candidates themselves at the expense of major issues facing the nation. This tendency is carried over into political advertising, which may refer to the issues but is geared primarily to depicting the positive qualities of the candidate and the negative—even sinister—characteristics of opposing candidates.

In political advertising, everything hinges on image, and the image maker's playground is the TV commercial, or "spot."[38] Among the most memorable, and infamous, images of recent campaigns have been the work of image makers. In 1964, for example, an anti-Goldwater spot was produced in which a little girl counted daisy petals. When she finished counting the frame froze, a nuclear device was detonated, and a giant mushroom cloud dominated the TV screen, with a voice-over: "These are the stakes, to make a world in which all God's children can live, or to go into the darkness. Either we must love each other or we must die." The ad was aired only once, but that was more than enough. The impression had been established that Goldwater was a danger to the future. In another spot, a little girl was shown eating an ice cream cone. The voice-over explained that strontium 90, a radioactive isotope present in fallout from nuclear explosions, is found in milk and that Goldwater had voted against the nuclear test ban treaty.

Such gripping, even terrifying, imagery is risky. Usually, therefore, media consultants try to establish some balance between their "negative" and "positive" political spots. Thus, not all political spots are as intensely negative as those just described. The 1960 presidential campaign featured a number of spots showing Kennedy sailing his yacht, riding horses, and frolicking with his family to demonstrate his "common" appeal, despite his uncommon wealth and social position. President Carter made use of similar spots in 1976 and 1980; they showed him helping his daughter Amy with her homework and toiling away in shirtsleeves behind his desk in the Oval Office. Even the normally stiff, formal Richard Nixon tried to infuse his image with more warmth by allowing a film crew to capture him

FYI

Peggy Noonan, former speech writer and image maker for Ronald Reagan and George Bush (she wrote Bush's famous "thousand points of light" speech), made the following observation about television's power over Americans:

Our sophistication means nothing; for all our knowledge of TV, it still fools us. We are like people who go to a magic show knowing it's all strings and mirrors and still being thrilled when the lady gets sawed in half.

casually strolling along a California beach. The effect became unintentionally hilarious when reporters noticed that Nixon was wearing dress shoes.

Some of the most compelling positive advertising appeared in 1984, when incumbent Ronald Reagan ran under the theme "Morning in America." Hiring the same advertising agency that had produced a successful series of Coca Cola commercials, Reagan's image management team crafted a series of spots showing smiling small-town men and women going about their daily business secure in the knowledge that America was "back." That America had had to "return" from some worse place, constituted a hint of negative advertising within an otherwise positive spot. These elegantly filmed, carefully designed spots are generally conceded to have played a major part in reinforcing Reagan's already formidable public support.

The expected result of positive ads is that undecided voters will watch the warm, homey images of these potential national leaders and embrace them not as abstract political ideas but as people. As often as not, however, media consultants employ more combative imagery. Negative advertising usually involves a harsh attack on a political opponent, implying that the opponent is dishonest, corrupt, ignorant, or worse. This kind of political mudslinging is as old as American politics itself. Research shows that voters are more willing to believe negative information about public officials than positive information. Negative ads are also more memorable than positive messages.[39]

The 1972 election was characterized by negative campaigning on both sides. A spot for George McGovern showed a napalmed baby in the arms of her mother, with dead skin falling from the baby's body. The voice-over was of a five-year-old saying, "Does a president know that planes drop bombs? Vote McGovern." A Nixon spot portrayed McGovern's face on both sides of a weather vane, shifting position in the wind. The most memorable negative spot showed a row of tiny tin soldiers with this voice-over: "The McGovern defense plan. He would cut the Marines by one-third. The Air Force by one-third. He'd cut Navy personnel by one-quarter." As a hand knocked down the toy soldiers, the voice-over said, "President Nixon doesn't believe we should play games with our national security."

Perhaps the most damaging negative ad in recent elections was aired in 1988 by the Bush campaign. It portrayed Willie Horton, a convicted rapist who had committed murder while on parole, and implied that opposing candidate Michael Dukakis was so soft on crime and criminals that the public safety was endangered. Later, however, Bush himself fell victim to negative advertising. During the 1992 Republican primaries Patrick Buchanan used scenes from the federally-funded documentary about homosexuals, "Tongues Untied," in an effort to portray President Bush as supporting funding for sadomasochistic homosexual behavior. "The specter of Willie Horton has returned," observed Marlon T. Riggs, the film's director.[40]

COUNTERING NEGATIVE ADVERTISING   When confronted with a negative ad, the candidate under attack has four options: (1) to defend against the charges, (2) to counterattack on the issue or another one that voters care about even more deeply, (3) to attack the credibility of the opponent, or (4) to ignore the attack.

Michael Dukakis's 1988 campaign illustrates the cost of taking the high road. Under attack from George Bush for releasing dangerous criminals, failing to clean up Boston Harbor, being ignorant about foreign policy, and vetoing a bill requiring Massachusetts schoolchildren to salute the flag, Dukakis responded by offering a variety of economic prescriptions. His seventeen-point lead in the polls disappeared, and he was trounced by Bush on election day.

In 1992 the Democrats decided that they would respond immediately to any negative ad about Bill Clinton. "A charge left unrefuted is a charge the public will believe," observed political scientist Chris Arterton. Thus began what came to be known as the fax attack: The Clinton response team faxed to the press immediate rebuttals to all charges made by opposing candidates. The goal was to prevent the charge from remaining unanswered through more than one news cycle.[41]

Infomercials

A recent trend in television advertising is the use of **infomercials,** which combine commercial advertising with "informational" discussions. Infomercials are used to advertise products ranging from home gymnasiums to psychic advisers. A typical infomercial includes a host, a few guests who offer testimonials for or demonstrations of the product being marketed, and a "studio audience" that cheers on the hucksters as they hawk their wares. The final ingredient of a successful infomercial is, of course, a sizable audience of television viewers.

Recent political campaigns have made increasing use of the infomercial format. Presidential candidates buy large blocks of television time—typically half an hour—during which they sit before the camera in a carefully contrived setting and hold forth on their agenda for the future, thereby also marketing themselves to the electorate. Opposing candidates may also use this format. During the 1992 campaign, for example, Ross Perot used half-hour spots to lecture allegedly apathetic and ignorant Americans about the federal budget deficit and other crucial issues, employing flip charts rather than slick computer graphics to illustrate his discussions. Despite the relatively crude presentation and Perot's sometimes pedantic delivery, the spots appeared to stimulate increased voter awareness and interest in the campaign. Indeed, Perot's political infomercials may have been one of the reasons that he garnered nearly one in five votes in the general election.

Ross Perot used thirty minute infomercials to help explain his programs and ideas to the American public during the 1992 presidential campaign. With the aid of charts, a pointer, straight talk, and a folksy sense of humor, Perot presented shows that were watched by large numbers of viewers. Here, he offers solutions to the nation's fiscal woes—a plan to balance the federal budget.

THE MEDIA AND APPROACHING DEMOCRACY

In the United States, information about politics is routinely transmitted to the public through the electronic and print media as well as through other means of communication such as faxes and electronic mail. Americans can read local, regional, national, and international newspapers; and twenty-four-hour news stations and coverage of local, state, and national public officials on television provide a firsthand look at the political process. But in a democratic polity the media must do more than bring political information to a broad audience. They must report events accurately and truthfully, free from control or censorship by government agencies. Freedom of press (and other media) is essential in a free society.

No other nation in the world, even among the industrialized democracies, enjoys the degree of media freedom found in the United States. Yet as we have seen in this chapter, there are a variety of limits on the independence of the media. These range from government-imposed restrictions, both foreign and domestic, as illustrated in the case of "the Voice of Baghdad" at the beginning of the chapter, to more subtle forms of censorship resulting from the symbiosis between reporters and "official sources" within the government. Thus, while media freedom in the United States represents a closer approach to democracy than has been achieved in any other nation, it is far from absolute.

SUMMARY

1. The mass media consist of the various means, such as newspapers, radio, and television, through which information is transferred from its source to large numbers of people.

2. Early political leaders saw newspapers as the key to educating the public about political affairs and gaining support for their parties' positions. Mass-circulation newspapers first appeared in the 1830s. The desire for dramatic stories led to muckraking, which attempted to expose the power and corruption of the rich, and yellow journalism, which sought to entertain the masses with little regard for the truth.

3. Of all the mass media, magazines offer the widest variety of subject matter and political opinion. The most successful news magazine is *Time;* there are also several magazines of political opinion.

4. Radio was very popular between the two world wars, largely because events could be described as they were happening. Politicians and public officials soon learned the value of speaking directly to the American people in radio broadcasts.

5. Television is more persuasive and effective than any other form of mass communication. It is an almost universal source of entertainment and the primary source of news for most Americans. New technologies such as satellites have expanded television coverage to permit instantaneous reporting of events throughout the world. Cable television has made possible a much wider range of programming choices, including entire channels aimed at specially targeted audiences.

6. One function of the mass media is surveillance of events throughout the world. This means that the media decide what events are newsworthy. The media also interpret events by giving them meaning and context, and thereby shape opinions. The third major function of the media is socialization, in which the members of a society learn to conform to society's norms and values. In general, the media serve to reinforce existing values rather than create new ones.

7. The electronic media are regulated by the Federal Communications Commission, which establishes regulations designed to protect the public interest. The FCC's rules of the air include the equal opportunities rule (for political candidates), the fairness doctrine (now abandoned), and the right of rebuttal.

8. On occasion the government has attempted to prevent the publication of information on the ground that doing so would pose a threat to national security. This is done through a judicial restraining order, an action known as prior restraint. The media are also restricted by laws against libel and slander.

9. It is often said that the media have a liberal bias. However, there are numerous conservative publications, and many radio and television commentators, as well as publishers and network executives, are distinctly conservative. Corporate control of the media tends to produce middle-of-the-road coverage tempered by the concerns of advertisers. Another factor is the symbiosis between reporters and "official sources" within the government.

10. Media coverage of campaigns can influence the outcome of elections. The media are often accused of focusing on the "horse race" aspect of campaigns, implying that only the front-runners are worthy of coverage. The increasing use of data from opinion polls can also affect the political process.

11. In recent campaigns radio talk shows have taken on increasing importance. This was especially true in 1994, when conservative talk show hosts led the movement to replace many Democrats in Congress with Republicans.

12. Television takes center stage in presidential elections. Candidates travel from one ADI—area of dominant influence—to another, giving speeches in settings designed to make them look good on the evening news. The news broadcasts usually contain only snippets of candidates' speeches, known as soundbites.

13. Political advertising takes the form of commercials designed by image makers. The right image can have a tremendous impact on the voting public. Media consultants try to achieve a balance between positive and negative images, but because negative advertising appears to be more effective there is a growing trend toward the use of such advertising. A recent variant on the commercial is the infomercial, which combines commercial advertising with an informational discussion.

KEY TERMS

spin
mass media
muckraking
yellow journalism
investigative journalism
socialization

Federal Communications Commission
  (FCC)
scarcity doctrine
equal time rule
fairness doctrine
right of rebuttal

prior restraint
libel
soundbite
infomercial

SUGGESTED READINGS

- Arnett, Peter. *Live from the Battlefield: From Vietnam to Baghdad.* New York: Simon & Schuster, 1994. The memoir of one correspondent's thirty-five years of news reporting from the war zones of the world, including his controversial television reports from Baghdad during the Gulf War.

- Bagdikian, Ben H. *The Media Monopoly.* 4th ed. Boston: Beacon Press, 1994. A fascinating analysis of the continuing concentration of ownership of mass media outlets into fewer hands.

- Barnouw, Eric. *Tube of Plenty: The Evolution of American Television.* New York: Oxford University Press, 1982. A comprehensive and lively history of the development of television and its impact on American culture.

- Halberstam, David. *The Powers That Be.* New York: Dell, 1979. A classic account of the rise of major media figures in America, written by one of America's foremost political journalists.

- Iyengar, Shanto. *Is Anyone Responsible? How Television Frames Political Issues.* Chicago: University of Chicago Press, 1991. A scholarly analysis of the power of television to "frame" political issues and influence the way viewers respond to and think about those issues.

- Kurtz, Howard. *Media Circus: The Trouble with America's Newspapers.* New York: Time Books, 1994. A critical analysis of the sometimes unimpressive press coverage of politics and scandal, written by the media critic of the *Washington Post.*

- McGinniss, Joe. *The Selling of the President, 1968.* New York: Pocket Books, 1970. A fascinating, sometimes startling account of the use of television to successfully "sell" the presidential candidacy of Richard Nixon in 1968.

CHAPTER 14

CIVIL LIBERTIES

CENSORSHIP IS UNAMERICAN

CHAPTER OUTLINE

CASE STUDY: FLAG BURNING AND THE FIRST AMENDMENT

INTRODUCTION: CIVIL LIBERTIES AND DEMOCRACY

A HISTORY OF THE APPLICATION OF CIVIL LIBERTIES TO THE STATES

FREEDOM OF RELIGION

FREEDOM OF SPEECH

FREEDOM OF THE PRESS

THE RIGHTS OF DEFENDANTS

IMPLIED RIGHTS

CIVIL LIBERTIES AND APPROACHING DEMOCRACY

Flag Burning and the First Amendment

All Gregory Johnson was looking for was a little attention. It was the summer of 1984, and the Republican National Convention was being held in Dallas. Members of the Revolutionary Communist Youth Brigade decided that it was an opportune time to protest the Reagan administration's policies in Central America. They staged a demonstration in which they marched through the business district, spray-painted slogans on buildings, and removed an American flag from a corporate headquarters. When the protesters arrived at City Hall they staged a "die-in" to protest the threat of nuclear war. But no one paid any attention to them.

Frustrated by the lack of reaction, Gregory Lee Johnson unfurled the stolen American flag, doused it with kerosene, and held a match to it. As the flag burned, he and his comrades chanted "America, the red, the white and the blue, we spit on you." The Dallas police arrested Johnson and charged him with desecration of the flag. He was sentenced to a year in jail and fined two thousand dollars.

Five years later, after numerous appeals, Johnson's case came before the Supreme Court. Was the Texas law barring desecration of the flag a violation of the freedom-of-speech provision of the First Amendment? The state of Texas claimed that Johnson had been arrested because of the potential for violent action by the observing crowd. It also claimed to have a duty to preserve the integrity of the flag as a symbol of the nation.

It was widely expected that the Court would rule in the state's favor. However, on June 21, 1989, it upheld Johnson's right to burn the flag.

"If there is a bedrock principle underlying the First Amendment," wrote Justice William Brennan, "it is that the government may not prohibit the expression of an idea simply because society finds the idea itself offensive or disagreeable." Didn't it seem likely, he added, that the state was punishing Johnson more for his ideas, however offensive they might be to some, than for the alleged potential for public disturbance? Moreover, where does one draw the line on government symbols which must be protected? What about the presidential seal? State flags? Copies of the Constitution? But for the majority of the Court, the biggest problem was a simple one: What power did a state have to preserve the integrity of the United States flag? Brennan noted that the duty to preserve the national flag belonged to the federal government and not to the states.[1]

Many Americans were outraged by the decision. President Bush stated that "flag burning is wrong—dead wrong" and called for a constitutional amendment to "overrule" the Supreme Court's decision. Senator Robert Dole of Kansas convinced the Senate to pass an amendment that would, in essence, ban flag burning, thereby denying First Amendment protection to this particular form of "speech." Both the Senate and the House also passed resolutions expressing disappointment in the Supreme Court's decision. Even liberal senator Joseph Biden of Delaware proposed a law that would make it illegal to mutilate, deface, burn, display on the ground, or trample an American flag. (The idea here was to outlaw the physical act of desecration, without crossing the boundary of the Court in attacking the motives of the protesters.)

Eventually the tide turned. Senator Bob Kerrey of Nebraska, who had lost a leg in the Vietnam War, made an impassioned speech in

473

defense of the flag but added that he believed it would be unwise to ban certain kinds of speech. Later that year Congress passed the Federal Flag Protection Act, which empowered the federal government to arrest anyone who "knowingly mutilates, defaces, physically defiles, burns, maintains on the floor or ground, or tramples upon the flag of the United States." President Bush, who would have preferred a constitutional amendment and feared that the law was not strong enough, allowed the measure to become law without his signature.

Within a few weeks a small group of protesters, including Gregory Johnson, decided to test the new law by burning a flag on the steps of the Capitol; three of the protesters were arrested, but Johnson could not convince the police that he should be arrested a second time. The new case came to the Supreme Court in 1990 as United States *v.* Eichman.[2] *Many expected that the Court would bow to political pressure, the will of Congress as expressed in the new statute, and uphold the law. However, once again the Court struck down the new statute, saying that like the Texas law, "it suppresses expression out of concern for its likely communicative impact" and therefore was unconstitutional.* ❧

Gregory Lee Johnson, whose conviction for burning a U.S. flag was overturned by the Supreme Court, poses with the flag in June 1989, after the Court ruled in his favor.

INTRODUCTION: CIVIL LIBERTIES AND DEMOCRACY

The case of Gregory Johnson illustrates the difficulty of defining and interpreting civil liberties. The quality of a democracy can be measured by the degree to which it protects the rights of all of its citizens, including those who, or whose expressed views, are unpopular. Frequently, this task is left to the Supreme Court of the United States, which may find itself safeguarding the rights of individuals charged with heinous crimes or with engaging in socially disvalued acts. In a democracy, the fundamental rights of such individuals are given the same protection as those of any other citizen.

The fundamental rights of U.S. citizens are set forth in the Bill of Rights, the first ten amendments to the Constitution, and we often speak of the "protection" provided by that document. However, individual rights are always in jeopardy if they are not zealously safeguarded by all the institutions of society. When public-school officials tell teachers that they may not begin the school day with a prayer, freedom of religion is at issue. When a security official stops you in the mall "for a chat," freedom of association is at issue. When a police officer asks to search the trunk of your car, the Fourth Amendment search-and-seizure provision is at issue. All of these situations and hundreds more are governed by the Bill of Rights.

In this chapter we will explore the historical development of civil liberties. We will begin with the framers' version of the Bill of Rights, which was much less protective of individual freedoms than you might realize. We will then explore the gradual expansion of civil liberties to the states over the course of the nation's history. We will also analyze how civil liberties have been defined, and how they have expanded and contracted over the last sixty years. These topics provide a dramatic demonstration of how the United States has approached democracy in the area of individual rights.

Civil Liberties and Civil Rights

Although the terms *civil liberties* and *civil rights* are often used interchangeably, they are not synonymous. **Civil liberties** are the individual freedoms and rights that are guaranteed to every citizen by the Bill of Rights and the due process clause of the Fourteenth Amendment. They include the most fundamental rights of Americans, such as freedom of speech and religion. **Civil rights** are concerned with protection of citizens against discrimination because of characteristics such as gender, race, ethnicity, or disability; they are derived largely from the equal-protection clause of the Fourteenth Amendment.

One way to distinguish between civil liberties and civil rights is to view them in terms of governmental action. Civil liberties are best understood as *freedom from* any government interference with, or violation of, individual rights. This is a "negative" freedom in the sense that people are understood to have a right to certain liberties, such as freedom of speech, which can be exercised without government interference. For this reason, the First Amendment begins with the words, "Congress shall make no law . . . " In contrast, civil rights may be understood as *freedom to* exercise certain rights that are guaranteed to all U.S. citizens under the Constitution and cannot be removed by the government. This is a "positive" freedom in that the government is expected to provide the conditions under which certain rights can be exercised. Examples include the right to vote, the right to equal job or living opportunities, and the right to equal education. We'll look more closely at civil rights in Chapter 15. In this chapter, we focus on civil liberties.

One reason the terms *civil liberties* and *civil rights* have become almost interchangeable in popular speech is that many issues involve aspects of both positive and negative freedom.[3] For example, consider the right to privacy, the central issue in the case of Michael Hardwick, which was described at the beginning of Chapter 7. This case involved civil liberties in the form of the issue of the policeman's entry into the bedroom. But it also involved civil rights in that Hardwick claimed the right to pursue an alternative sexual lifestyle.

Studying Civil Liberties

As the Johnson case shows, cases involving civil liberties nearly always come down to a conflict between the individual, seeking to exercise a certain right in a democracy, and the state, seeking to control the exercise of that right so as to

The conflicts between an individual's rights and the state's need to exercise control to promote safety and preserve the rights of others in a democracy is evident in many walks of life. High school students are no doubt familiar with scenes of dogs sniffing their lockers for contraband drugs—an example of state control that has been validated by some state courts and the Supreme Court. The Supreme Court has ruled that the constitutional rights of high-school students can be limited to allow authorities to justify school searches of carried belongings based only on "reasonable suspicion." Here, a police dog is being used to establish "reasonable suspicion."

preserve the rights of others. The judiciary is charged with drawing the lines between acceptable individual actions and permissible governmental controls.

But how are those lines drawn? You will recall from Chapter 7 that "activist" jurists tend to uphold the rights of individuals over those of the state, while "self-restraint" jurists tend to defer to the state. The great majority of jurists fall in neither camp and are called "balancers" because they look for the point at which the rights of the individual are overridden by the rights of society. We can use the "wings of the Supreme Court" scheme presented in Chapter 7 to better understand the subject of civil liberties. If the Court is dominated by a "self-restraint" wing of jurists, control by national and state governments will be upheld. If, on the other hand, the Court is dominated by an "activist" wing of jurists, citizens' rights will likely be expanded and new rights will be created.

Since the United States' "approach to democracy" in the area of civil liberties is relatively recent, we will focus on how these rights were created and expanded by the Warren Court (1954–69), partially cut back by the Burger Court (1970–86), and finally placed under full attack by the Rehnquist Court (1986–present) First, however, we will explore the history of the development of civil liberties and their application to the states as well as to the national government.

A HISTORY OF THE APPLICATION OF CIVIL LIBERTIES TO THE STATES

The history of civil liberties is one of gradual expansion of the protection of personal rights guaranteed by the Bill of Rights. This evolution occurred through a series of Supreme Court decisions that applied portions of the first ten amendments to the states, thereby protecting citizens from state action in relation to specific individual rights. This evolutionary process, summarized in Table 14.1, illustrates that it did not begin until 1897; and, surprisingly to most, the process did not really take hold until the 1960s.

In the early years of the nation's history the Bill of Rights provided far less protection for individual rights than is the case today. For example, the guarantee of freedom of speech did not prevent the Federalist party from passing the Alien and Sedition Act in 1798, which jailed opponents of John Adams's administration for simply expressing their political views.[4] And the right to counsel guaranteed by the Sixth Amendment did not prevent the passage of the Federal Crimes Act of 1790, which instructed courts to provide defendants with counsel only for capital offenses.

But as narrow as these protections were individually, in the 1833 case of *Barron* v. *Baltimore,*[5] the Supreme Court severely limited their collective impact. Silt unearthed by excavation and construction undertaken on behalf of the city of Baltimore was washed by rains and swollen rivers into Baltimore harbor, rendering a wharf owned by John Barron unusable. Barron claimed that he was entitled to money damages under the Fifth Amendment's "eminent domain" clause, which guarantees that the taking of property by government will result in "just compensation" from the state.

Although the nationalist-oriented Chief Justice John Marshall would normally be expected to extend the protections of the Bill of Rights to the states, instead he denied Barron's claim. The Bill of Rights, he ruled, "contain no expression indicating an intention to apply them to the state governments [so] this

Court cannot so apply them." The First Amendment, by stating that "*Congress shall make no law . . .* " indicates that the Bill of Rights applies only to the national government. Unable to use the Fifth Amendment to sustain his claim, Barron had no case. The entire Bill of Rights would not be applied to the states for another century. During that time civil liberties varied from state to state, even to the point of not existing at all in some states.

The Fourteenth Amendment

With the passage of the Fourteenth Amendment in 1868, the issue of state responsibility relative to civil liberties was raised once again. The Fourteenth Amendment was one of the so-called Civil War Amendments, which were designed to free the slaves and protect their rights as citizens. It reads: "No State shall make or enforce any law which shall abridge the privileges or immunities of citizens of the United States; nor shall any State deprive any person of life, liberty, or property, without due process of law; nor deny to any person . . . the equal protection of the laws."

Since the Fourteenth Amendment began with the words "No State shall make or enforce any law . . . ," some believed that it was intended to reverse the *Barron* ruling and extend the Bill of Rights to the states. Initially, the Supreme Court was asked to rule on whether the "privileges and immunities" clause of the amendment would accomplish this aim. However, the Court ruled that this language did not protect state rights of citizenship, such as property rights, but only national rights of citizenship, such as petitioning Congress for a redress of grievances and being protected from piracy on the high seas.[6]

In later cases the Court was asked whether some or all of the Bill of Rights could be *defined* as "due process" of law and thus be extended to the states under the language of the Fourteenth Amendment. This approach, in which the Bill of Rights would be absorbed into the due process clause by the simple act of redefinition, was called the **incorporation** of the Bill of Rights (see Figure 14.1). The argument was that under the Fourteenth Amendment the states must

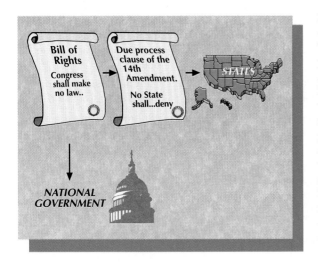

FIGURE 14.1   The Incorporation of the Bill of Rights

The Supreme Court has used the due process clause of the Fourteenth Amendment to apply portions of the Bill of Rights to the states (note the wording of the Amendment: "No state shall . . . deny"). In this way the due process clause acts like a paint roller, soaking up the colors of portions of the Bill of Rights and painting the states (all provisions of the Bill of Rights apply to the national government). The result is that the rights of citizens in different states are protected and those rights are more uniform.

Table 14.1
The Nationalization of the Bill of Rights

CASE	ISSUE	INCORPORATED
Chicago, Burlington and Quincy Railway Co. v. *Chicago* (1897)	Taking of property by the state without just compensation	5th Amendment guarantee of eminent domain
Gitlow v. *New York* (1925)	Arrest for speech threatening the state government	1st Amendment guarantee of free speech
Near v. *Minnesota* (1931)	Prior restraint (censorship) of press	1st Amendment guarantee of free press
Powell v. *Alabama* (1932)	Right to counsel in capital crimes. This was the famous *Scottsboro* case, in which seven minor black males were accused and convicted without the aid of counsel of raping two white females	6th Amendment guarantee of right to counsel in capital cases which were unfair
Hamilton v. *Regents of the University of California* (1934)	Challenged public institution's mandatory military drills on basis of religious objections	1st Amendment guarantee of freedom of religion
De Jonge v. *Oregon* (1937)	Peaceful assembly of Communist party members in Oregon	1st Amendment guarantees of free assembly and of right to petition the government for a redress of grievances
Palko v. *Connecticut* (1937)	Twice being tried for same offense. In this case, Justice Cardozo devised his famous "honor roll of superior rights"	None, but it was Cardozo's insistence that superior rights should be incorporated that begins "selective incorporation"
Cantwell v. *Conn.* (1940)	Whether religious groups (Jehovah's Witnesses) should have to be licensed to promote their religion	1st Amendment guarantee of free exercise of religion
Everson v. *Board of Education of Ewing Township* (1947)	State aid to bus children to parochial schools.	1st Amendment requirement that church and state be separate
In re Oliver (1948)	Can a judge act in secret simultaneously as a grand jury and a trial judge to find a defendant guilty without a proper trial	6th Amendment guarantee to a public trial
Wolf v. *Colorado* (1949)	Whether patient names from an appointment book of suspected abortionist gained by illegal search of doctor's office can be used in trial	The "core" of the 4th Amendment, defined as "arbitrary invasions of privacy by the police"
N.A.A.C.P. v. *Alabama* (1958)	Whether groups must register with the state and file membership names and addresses	1st Amendment guarantee of freedom of association
Mapp v. *Ohio* (1961)	Use of the fruits of an illegal search and seizure without a proper search warrant in trial	4th Amendment prohibition on unreasonable search or seizure, and its exclusionary rule
Robinson v. *California* (1962)	A California statute providing a mandatory 90-day jail sentence for conviction of addiction to narcotics without any evidence of drug use	8th Amendment guarantee against the infliction of cruel or unusual punishment

Table 14.1

The Nationalization of the Bill of Rights (Continued)

CASE	ISSUE	INCORPORATED
Gideon v. *Wainwright* (1963)	Legal counsel availability when someone is on trial for a misdemeanor, noncapital offense	6th Amendment guarantee of counsel was expanded to include all felony-level criminal cases
Malloy v. *Hogan* and *Murphy* v. *Waterfront Commission of New York* (1964)	Whether investigation into gambling offenses after serving a jail sentence for the crime resulted in self-incrimination	5th Amendment prohibition against self-incrimination
Pointer v. *Texas* (1965)	Whether the accused has the right to confront witnesses against him instead of a transcript of their earlier testimony during a trial	6th Amendment guarantee that the accused shall be confronted by the witnesses against him
Griswold v. *Connecticut* (1965)	Legality of use and counseling on the use of birth control by married couples	1st, 3rd, 4th, 5th, and 9th Amendments (and their penumbras) right of privacy
Parker v. *Gladden* (1966)	Whether bailiff statements rendered the jury unable to produce an impartial verdict	6th Amendment guarantee that the accused shall be judged by an impartial jury
Klopfer v. *North Carolina* (1967)	Whether a state can place a live case on inactive status only to take the case up again when it has more time and resources	6th Amendment guarantee of a speedy trial
Washington v. *Texas* (1967)	Whether a defendant can compel witnesses in his favor to appear in trial	6th amendment right to compulsory process for obtaining witnesses
Duncan v. *Louisiana* (1968)	Whether state must offer trial by jury in non capital cases	6th Amendment guarantee of a trial by jury in all criminal cases above the petty level
Benton v. *Maryland* (1969)	Whether a state must provide a guarantee against two trials for the same crime	5th Amendment guarantee against double jeopardy

protect due process, and since some or all of the Bill of Rights could be defined as due process, the states must also protect those portions of the Bill of Rights. However, in the late 1800s and early 1900s the Court was dominated by conservative jurists who were more concerned with protecting property rights than with extending personal civil rights by making this definitional leap. Did California's practice of using a list of evidence called a bill of information to indict people rather than the grand jury proceeding promised in the Fifth Amendment violate due process of law? No, said the Court, ruling that the "new" procedure can be just as fair as the "old" grand jury guarantee.[7] Did New Jersey's practice of allowing a judge to comment on a defendant's unwillingness to take the stand in his own defense, which a jury might interpret as an indication of guilt, violate the Fifth Amendment's guarantee that no person shall be "compelled . . . to be a witness against himself"? No, ruled the Court, because this was not a "fundamental" right that must be applied to the states.[8]

"The most stringent protection of free speech would not protect a man in falsely shouting fire in a theatre and causing a panic."

—Oliver Wendell Holmes, *Schenck v. United States*

The Court's position became known as **"no incorporation,"** since it was unwilling to define the Bill of Rights as part of the Fourteenth Amendment and thus to apply its amendments to the states. The states would be bound only by the dictates of due process contained in the Fourteenth Amendment. The only exception came in an 1897 case involving a railroad company's right of eminent domain under the Fifth Amendment, which because it protected property rights was extended to the states.[9] Opposing the majority was Justice John Harlan, who in arguing that the protections in the Bill of Rights were so fundamental that *all* of them should be applied to the states, created the position known as **"total incorporation."**

The "Clear and Present Danger" Test

The battle over the application of the Bill of Rights to the states was resumed during World War I, when the government was anxious to restrict certain individual liberties. In 1919, concern with wartime treason, spying, and obstruction of the military draft led to the first important case involving freedom of speech. Charles T. Schenck had been convicted of circulating pamphlets against the draft. In upholding the conviction, Justice Oliver Wendell Holmes argued that the state could restrict speech when "the words used are of such a nature as to create a *clear and present danger* that they will bring about the substantive evils that Congress has a right to prevent." In short, in some cases, such as falsely shouting "Fire!" in a crowded theater, the *circumstances and nature* of speech, or its effect, may justify restriction of this liberty. In ignoring the fact that there was no evidence showing that Schenck's "speech" had affected the draft, Holmes was saying that a wartime crisis was sufficient cause for restrictions on freedom of speech.[10]

Jacob Abrams (on the right), of the landmark Supreme Court case *Abrams* v. *United States,* is shown with fellow anarchists (from left to right) Samuel Lipman, Hyman Lachowsky, and Mollie Steimer. The four were arrested in 1918 for passing out leaflets encouraging American workers to go on strike in support of Russian workers. They appear here, in 1921, shortly before being deported to Russia at their own expense, having served two years in a federal prison. A fifth colleague, Jacob Schwartz, died in prison, quite possibly as a result of a brutal beating by police during questioning.

Two subsequent cases that also came to the Supreme Court in 1919 revealed the problems with the clear and present danger test. When a man named Jacob Frohwerk was convicted because of scholarly articles on the constitutionality and merits of the draft he wrote for a German-language newspaper in Missouri, the Court upheld the conviction.[11] And when labor activist Eugene Debs gave a prosocialism speech in St. Louis after signing an "Anti-war Proclamation and Program" attacking the draft, even that conviction was upheld by the Court as impeding the war effort.[12] Thus, the Court had convicted one man for writing for a tiny minority and another for the thoughts he *might* have held while speaking, neither of whom had any demonstrable effect on the draft.

Seeing the censoring effect of his test, Holmes changed his views. In the fall of 1919, when an anarchist named Jacob Abrams appealed his conviction for circulating pamphlets imploring American workers to go on strike in sympathy with Russian workers hurt by the revolution there, seven members of the Court upheld his conviction because his actions posed a "clear and present danger" to the war effort. However, Holmes, the inventor of the test, together with Louis D. Brandeis, dissented. They argued that Abrams was nothing more than a "poor and puny anonymity" whose "silly leaflet" represented no clear and present danger to the state.[13] Thus America's approach to freedom of speech had begun, but it still had a long way to go.

The Beginnings of Incorporation

Unlike the federal government, which passed laws against certain actions resulting from speech and thus did not attempt to control speech directly, some states, including New York, chose to outlaw the words themselves. In 1925 a radical named Benjamin Gitlow was convicted of advocating the overthrow of government under New York's Criminal Anarchy Act. In the *Gitlow* v. *New York*[14] case the Supreme Court ruled for the first time that the First Amendment guarantee of freedom of speech could be applied to the states; however, it upheld Gitlow's conviction, deferring to the state of New York's belief that certain speech had a "bad tendency."

Why would the Court be willing to apply the free-speech guarantee to the states but not use it to protect Gitlow himself? Because it had learned that the right of free speech could be used to protect businesses; for example, when a business refuses to give reasons for firing an employee. The Court was therefore setting a precedent that could be used to protect the status quo without actually condoning speech aimed against these very same interests.

In the early 1930s the Court applied three other parts of the Bill of Rights to the states. In 1931, when the Minnesota legislature passed a law censoring the *Saturday Press* (also called the *"Minnesota Rag"*), a muckraking tabloid printed by Jay Near, the Court incorporated the guarantee of freedom of the press into the Fourteenth Amendment, thus applying it to the states, and overturned the Minnesota law.[15]

A year later the Court was called upon to rule in the case of the "Scottsboro Boys," in which a group of black youths had been unjustly accused of raping two white women on a train and had been convicted in a trial in which, instead of assigning a defense attorney, the judge asked "the entire bar of the county" to defend them (in other words, they had no defense). In its decision the Court incorporated and applied to the states the notion of a "fair hearing" implied in the Sixth Amendment, thus guaranteeing the right to counsel, but only for capital crimes.[16]

Finally, in 1934 when the University of California required that courses in military training be taken by everyone on its campus, including religious pacifists, the Court incorporated the freedom of religion provision and applied it to the states while still leaving the program intact.[17] Thus, the Court made clear in all of these cases that extending rights to the states did not necessarily mean increased rights for individuals—states were still free to punish the press *after,* rather than before, publication; to deny the right to counsel in noncapital criminal cases; and to require even pacifist students to take courses in military training. Thus, the question remained whether a more general rule applying the Bill of Rights in a meaningful way to the states could be established.

Selective Incorporation of the Bill of Rights

It was not until 1937, in the landmark case of *Palko* v. *Connecticut*,[18] that the first step was taken toward establishing such a rule. Frank Jacob Palko had been convicted of the second-degree murder of two police officers and he objected to the state's plan to retry him because of procedural errors in the earlier trial for first-degree murder, which carried the death penalty. Palko claimed that a retrial would deny him the Fifth Amendment's protection against "double jeopardy," that is, the guarantee that one may not be tried twice for the same crime. However, the Supreme Court had not yet applied this right to the states. The Court ruled that only rights that were "implicit in the concept of ordered liberty" would be applied to the states. According to Justice Benjamin Cardozo, those rights were fundamental freedoms such as freedom of speech, the right to fair trial, and freedom of thought; the double-jeopardy protection was not one. Palko lost his appeal and, with no double-jeopardy right to worry about, the state retried him, convicted him, and put him to death. It was surely little comfort to him that his name was now associated with a new incorporation standard, **selective incorporation,** in which some portions of the Bill of Rights, but not all, were now part of the Fourteenth Amendment's due process clause and thus guaranteed against invasion by the states.

Gradually over the next forty-five years all but a handful of the provisions contained in the Bill of Rights were applied to the states via the Fourteenth Amendment. This judicial redefinition of civil liberties, particularly during the 1960s, was the greatest expansion of the power of the national government in the federal structure since the decisions in the 1930s that extended the interstate commerce power to the states.

Several amendments or portions thereof—including the Second, Third, and Seventh, the grand jury provision of the Fifth, and the excessive bails and fines provision of the Eighth—have not been, and probably will not be, incorporated. Since other rights that are not contained in the Bill of Rights, such as the right to privacy, have also been applied to the states, the best characterization of the approach now used by the Court might be "selective incorporation plus."

Once a provision of the Bill of Rights was applied to the states, additional questions such as exactly what the provision meant and thus how much protection it extended to the individual needed to be resolved. In the case of freedom of religion, for example, are religious practices protected if they violate other laws, such as the ban on polygamy? In the case of freedom of speech, is only actual speech protected, or is symbolic speech, such as flag burning, protected as well? In the next few sections of the chapter we examine these questions in relation to several key provisions of the Bill of Rights.

FREEDOM OF RELIGION

Few issues were closer to the framers' hearts than those involving religion. Many of the nation's earliest European settlers were religious zealots seeking independence from the state-run Anglican Church of England. Accordingly, they either established state religions of their own or supported various religions without giving preference to any of them. Since the potential for fragmentation of the new nation into different religious communities was too dangerous to be ignored, the guarantee of freedom of religion was placed first in the Bill of Rights.

For the framers, religion was a matter of personal choice and conscience, not an area for governmental control. However, by restricting government's "establishment" of religion while simultaneously guaranteeing the "free exercise" of religion, the framers created contradictory goals.[19] For example, if the

Does the separation of church and state in the freedom-of-religion clause of the First Amendment allow localities to erect religious displays, like this crèche, on public land? The answer is, it depends. If the display includes other nonreligious symbols of Christmas, such as a Santa, it is constitutional. However, if the display is strictly religious in nature, then the Court has ruled it unconstitutional.

government provides tax-exempt status for religious organizations, as it does for other charitable institutions, thus promoting "free exercise of religion," does this constitute an "establishment of religion"? On the other hand, if it fails to grant such tax relief, would this result in the closing of some churches and thus restrict "free exercise of religion" for some people?[20] Because of questions like these, the Supreme Court has chosen to focus more on the establishment clause rather than on the free-exercise clause.

Establishment of Religion

In deciding whether particular governmental practices would have the effect of "establishing" a religion, the Court has searched for the proper balance between two opposing views of the relationship between government and religion. These are known as the "government accommodation" position and the "high wall of separation" position. The high wall of separation position originated with the authors of this constitutional provision, Thomas Jefferson and James Madison, who were reacting to the fact that half of the colonies had adopted laws that provided support for religious institutions and practices.[21] Fearing that such laws could lead to religious persecution, they called for strict separation between church and state. However, there were too many incidental, and some would say beneficial, connections between church and state to bar them all. In the government accommodation view, the government would be allowed to assist religion, but only if the aid was indirect, available to all other groups, and religiously neutral.

The government accommodation position was first articulated in 1947 in the case of *Everson* v. *Board of Education of Ewing Township*.[22] A local school board, spurred by the desire to aid Catholic parochial schools, had provided funds to enable children to travel to those schools on city buses. The Court ruled that the state's policy did not violate the establishment clause because it was the *children,* not the *church,* who received the benefit. According to Justice Hugo Black, the transportation assistance was similar to other basic services, such as police and fire protection. Black deliberately ignored the fact that such assistance made it possible for children to attend the church schools, thereby indirectly aiding religion.

The high wall of separation doctrine was best described in 1962 in the case of *Engel* v. *Vitale*,[23] in which the Court ruled that a brief nondenominational prayer led by a teacher in a public school was unconstitutional. For the Court, the mere chance that a student might feel compelled to worship a God that he or she did not believe in was precisely the kind of establishment of religion that the framers had sought to avoid.

Partly because of the public outcry after the *Engel* decision, the Court began to search for a middle ground between "separation" and "accommodation." It took a step in this direction one year later in the case of *Abington School District* v. *Schempp*.[24] In ruling on this case, which involved the reading of selections from the Bible in Pennsylvania public schools, the Court adopted a "strict governmental neutrality" rule, under which a state was barred from doing anything that either advanced or inhibited religion. Since school-directed Bible reading clearly advanced religion, the practice was ruled unconstitutional.

During the 1960s the Court continued to search for the proper test for judging cases involving state aid to religious schools. If bus money could be provided to parochial school students, what about books? Since the books were loaned, the Court found this practice constitutional. Could the same be said for state aid to parochial-school teachers teaching nonreligious subjects? This question was raised by the 1971 case of *Lemon* v. *Kurtzman*.[25] In deciding that case the Court created a new test for determining the permissible level of state aid for church agencies. For such aid to be considered constitutional, the state had to prove that (1) the law had a secular purpose, (2) the primary purpose and effect of the law was neither to advance nor to inhibit religion, *and* (3) the law did not foster an "excessive governmental entanglement with religion." Since the aid in this case was for teachers of nonreligious subjects, the first two conditions were met. However, the only way the state could judge whether the funded teachers were aiding religion would be to monitor their classes; the law therefore violated the "excessive entanglement" provision of the test.

During the past two decades this three-pronged test, known as the **Lemon test,** has been applied in all cases involving establishment of religion. However, its application has varied over the years depending on the composition of the Court. During the early years of the Burger Court, the justices were sharply divided on the question of state aid to religious schools. States could supply standardized tests to parochial schools[26] and provide grants to all colleges, even church-related ones.[27] But they could not offer tuition reimbursement to students,[28] reimburse students for taking the New York State Regents exams,[29] or provide auxiliary services, such as counseling and speech therapy, to parochial-school students.[30]

In the early 1980s changes in the makeup of the Court produced a shift toward a more accommodationist position. The parents of parochial-school students in Minnesota were permitted to take an income tax deduction for the costs of tuition, textbooks, and transportation,[31] a chaplain could open the daily proceedings of the Nebraska legislature,[32] and a crèche could be placed in a public park in Pawtucket, Rhode Island, as part of a larger Christmas display.[33] On the other hand, certain practices were disallowed: The state of Kentucky was barred from posting the Ten Commandments in school classrooms,[34] the state of Alabama was barred from requiring a moment of silent meditation in public schools,[35] public-school teachers could not be sent to parochial schools to teach secular subjects,[36] and the state of Louisiana could not require the teaching of creationism as a way of providing a different perspective from Darwinian evolution.[37]

During the Rehnquist Court some of these positions were modified or reversed. The crèche that had been acceptable in Pawtucket five years earlier was now unacceptable on the grand staircase of the Allegheny County Courthouse in Pittsburgh. On the other hand, the placing of a menorah next to a Christmas tree and a sign saluting liberty just outside the City–County Building in the same city *was* acceptable.[38] A nondenominational prayer at a Rhode Island graduation was ruled to be unconstitutional because some students might refuse to attend their graduation for religious reasons.[39] The Court has yet to rule on student-led prayers held around the flagpole before school begins.

The continued viability of the *Lemon* test will depend on the views of the new justices appointed by President Clinton. While five members of the current

Does Freedom of Religion Include the Right to Pray in School?

The establishment clause of the First Amendment bars the state from preferring one religion over others, or any religion over no religion at all. The Supreme Court has ruled that public schools may not include prayer in their school activities, even if the prayer is nondenominational and voluntary. Case closed, right? Wrong!

Throughout the nation, but especially in the southern states, prayer and Bible reading can be found in public elementary and high schools. Led by religious clubs, prayer groups, and proprayer students, the movement to make prayer part of the school day is supported by a large percentage of the American public. Lunchtime prayer sessions are commonplace, and prayers are often included in opening ceremonies at football games and graduations.

To a large extent, this activity is private and voluntary, even though it occurs on public property. Some, however, goes beyond the guidelines established by the Court. Particularly in the South, the line between constitutional and unconstitutional activity is often blurred. But since more than 60 percent of Americans respond favorably to the idea of prayer in school, many communities are content to look the other way. Only occasionally is the practice challenged, as in the case of a Mississippi school district that allows prayers over the school intercom.

Critics believe that the increase in organized prayer in schools is a dangerous trend because it erodes the separation of church and state. In their view, permitting prayer in public schools is a step toward the establishment of religion. They point out that the establishment clause was included in the Bill of Rights to protect Americans from the religious persecution that drove many of their forebears to flee from European nations.

Those who favor school prayer believe that it can help counteract what they perceive as a general decline in moral values. This position is supported by many of the nation's current political leaders, including Speaker of the House Newt Gingrich, who has called for a constitutional amendment to allow school prayer. According to one high-school principal, "Although voluntary prayer is not going to cure the ills of society, it may be a step in the right direction."*

---

*Quoted in Peter Applebome, "Prayer in Public Schools? It's Nothing New for Many," *New York Times,* Nov. 22, 1994, p. A21.

Court have expressed some reservations about the test, seeing it as too "separationist" in its impact, it remains to be seen whether they can agree on a more accommodationist test.

In 1995, the Court signaled that it may be willing to further lower the barriers separating church and state, although the future relationship between the two institutions is uncertain. In a 5 to 4 decision, the Court ruled that the University of Virginia violated the First Amendment's Establishment of Religion clause by failing to fund a religious student magazine written by a Fundamentalist Christian student group, while funding similar magazines published by 118 other student groups, some of which were also religiously-based. While Justice Anthony Kennedy argued that the Court was only trying to achieve religious neutrality here, the importance of this decision was highlighted by the dissent of Justice David Souter, who wrote: "The Court today, for the first time, approves direct funding of core religious activities by an arm of the state."[40]

Free Exercise of Religion

Issues involving the free exercise of religion are particularly vexing. One look at some of the practices of government—the "In God We Trust" motto on its currency, the phrase "one nation under God" in the Pledge of Allegiance, the opening of Congress by a chaplain, and even the admonition "God save this honorable Court" that opens each session of the Supreme Court—tells us that religion is pervasive in American politics. But do these practices place limits on the free exercise of religion?

Free-exercise cases usually involve a law that applies to everyone but is perceived as imposing a hardship on a particular religious group. For example, can laws against mail fraud be used to prosecute religious groups that make dubious claims in letters to potential donors? In such cases the Court will not inquire into the nature of the religion, but it will examine whether the *actions* that result from that belief contravene the law. This so-called **secular regulation rule** holds that there is no constitutional right to exemption, on free-exercise grounds, from laws dealing with nonreligious matters. This rule was applied in 1878 in a case involving the practice of polygamy (taking multiple wives) by Mormons in the Utah Territory. The Court ruled that religious beliefs did not provide immunity from the law, in this case the law enforcing monogamy.[41]

Subsequently, it became clear that the secular regulation rule did impose undue hardship on religious groups in some instances. For example, the "blue laws," under which all businesses were required to close on Sunday, put business owners who observed the Sabbath on a different day at a competitive disadvantage because their businesses were closed on that day as well. Accordingly, the Court invented a new test—the **least-restrictive-means test**—in which the state was asked to find another way, perhaps through exemptions, to enforce its regulations while still protecting all other religions.[42]

This "live and let live" position on issues of free exercise prevailed until 1991, when the Rehnquist Court decided a case in which two Native Americans working as unemployment counselors in Oregon were held to have violated the state's antidrug laws by smoking peyote, a hallucinogenic drug, as part of a religious observance. The Court felt that it was more important to defer to the state's efforts to control drug use than to protect the free exercise of religion in this instance.[43] While the Court refused to use this precedent to allow the state of Florida to ban religious sacrifices of animals, this decision has been used by government authorities to justify even greater incursions into religious behavior: Autopsies have been ordered contrary to religious beliefs, and an FBI agent who refused a work assignment for religious reasons was fired.[44] (As noted in Chapter 7, this ruling was reversed by Congress in the Freedom of Religion Restoration Act.)

In sum, while the principle of freedom of religion appears straightforward on the surface, in practice it raises a variety of complex issues that have been resolved in various ways over the course of the nation's history. It appears not to be possible to erect a "high wall of separation" between church and state, but the degree of accommodation of government practices involving religious organizations may vary, depending on the composition of the Court and the specific test applied in each instance. The same is true in the area of free

Just how tolerant must a democratic society be of hate speech that may provoke violence? Such questions arose in the wake of the April 1995 bombing of a federal building in Oklahoma City, when it was discovered that the accused bomber had ties to U.S.-based paramilitary groups. Many of these groups oppose the federal government; some even advocate armed resistance against the government, its agents (federal workers, the FBI, judges), and law enforcement. A number of these paramilitary organizations have also been known to spread messages of hate against particular people and groups. Recently, intense national attention focused on these groups' sentiments, which are spread at conventions, on the radio, through various publications, and on the Internet. Shown here are two members of one of these groups, the Michigan Militia.

exercise, where the composition of the Court determines the degree of freedom afforded to religious groups against state regulations. In recent years, however, the Court has generally been willing to support religious freedom.

FREEDOM OF SPEECH

One of the hallmarks of a democratic state is the guarantee of freedom of speech. But just where does the state draw the line between a person's right to speak and other rights, such as the speech rights of others, that may be affected? Over the years the Supreme Court has taken two different approaches in attempting to solve this dilemma. One approach was suggested by Alexander Meiklejohn, a legal theorist who argued that while *public,* or *political, speech* on matters of public interest must be absolutely protected to preserve a democratic society, *private speech,* or speech intended for one's own purposes, can be restricted to protect the interests of other members of society.[45] On the other hand, Justice Oliver Wendell Holmes argued that democracy requires a "free marketplace of ideas" in which any view may be expressed, allowing the audience to decide what to believe. For Holmes, limits on freedom of speech were justified only when the consequences of speech endangered the state.[46]

Caught between these "absolutist" and "balancing" approaches, the Court has ruled in ways that protect certain kinds of speech but not others. All speech is afforded First Amendment protection unless it is offensive or obscene or poses a threat to national security. Since such utterances either convey no worthwhile ideas or do more harm to society than good, they are not deemed worthy of protection. Despite these guidelines, however, the degree of protection afforded to particular forms of speech has varied considerably, as we will see.

Political Speech

Where does the government draw the line between promoting full political discussion and protecting the government's right to exist? The Court faced this challenge in the early 1950s, when the tensions of the Cold War led to fears that Communist party members in the United States were actively seeking to overthrow the government. No longer were these "poor and puny anonymities," the government argued in prosecuting twelve Communist party leaders, but members of a worldwide organization calling for full-scale revolution.

In *Dennis* v. *United States*[47] the Court reviewed the convictions of the party leaders under the Smith Act, which made it a crime to teach or advocate overthrow of the government or to organize and conspire with those who do so. Did these actions pose a "clear and present danger" to the nation? In view of the tiny and disorganized nature of the American Communist party, the Court was unable to conclude that its actions created such a danger. However, the Court was anxious to uphold the convictions and therefore invented a new "sliding-scale" test in which the state needed to prove less about the probable results of speech if the potential threat involved was significant enough. In this case, since the Communists' goal was to overthrow the government, all that was needed to convict them was the presence of their names on a list of the party membership and possession of a copy of the *Communist Manifesto*.

Not until 1957 did the Court become willing to protect the speech of Communists as long as they were not actively plotting to overthrow the government.[48] By 1967 the Court had made it virtually impossible to deny First Amendment rights to someone just for being a Communist.[49] And by the end of the Warren Court in 1969, the Court had moved a considerable distance toward absolutism in protecting political speech. For example, when the leader of the Ku Klux Klan in Ohio was convicted for advocating unlawful methods of terrorism because he had appeared with a gun at a cross-burning rally that was filmed on television, the Court invented a new test: It would uphold convictions only for speech that incited "imminent lawless action" and was "likely to produce such action." On this basis, the conviction was reversed.[50]

Public Speech

States have passed many laws to protect those who might be offended or threatened by certain kinds of speech. Disturbing the peace, disorderly conduct, inciting to riot, terroristic threats, and fighting-word statutes are designed to preserve public order and safety. The main problem with such statutes is that sometimes they are crafted, or selectively enforced, specifically to exclude certain ideas or groups.

Laws involving public speech place the Supreme Court in the position of weighing the right of the speaker to say what he or she wishes against the right of the state to maintain law and order. Over the years the Court has developed three standards in this area. First, it asked whether a particular form of speech comes under the protective umbrella of the First Amendment. Thus, while controlled protests in public places such as the state library and state capitol are protected, calling a police officer "a goddamned racketeer" and "a damned fascist" is not; such expressions are considered **"fighting words."**[51] The Court looked next at the nature of the statute itself. Is the law overbroad, including some protected forms of speech among the proscribed ones; or is it underinclusive, failing to regulate some speech that should also be barred? For instance, a "disturbing the peace" law was used to arrest an anti-Semitic priest for making an inflammatory speech. The conviction was overturned because the law was used to punish speech that merely "invited dispute" or created "a condition of unrest"; it did not actually cause a riot.[52] The same standard is used today in determining the degree of protection that may be given to "hate speech" or speech and symbolic actions, such as cross-burning, that are laced with negative views toward certain groups of people. In two cases the Court ruled that government cannot selectively ban such speech based on its content, but it can increase punishment for those who physically assault minorities.[53]

Finally, assuming that a particular form of speech is protected and the statute is precisely and narrowly drawn, the Court will examine the facts of the case to see if the state's interests override those of the speaker. Can the state demonstrate that the dangers posed by the speech were significant enough to override the free-speech interests involved (meaning that the regulation would be upheld)? Or did the police make arrests because of their objection to the speech itself rather than the resulting action (meaning that the arrest would be overturned)? Thus, picketing on the state-owned jailhouse grounds, which risked causing a riot inside the jail, would constitute trespassing, and the arrests of the picketers would be upheld.[54] But arresting a civil rights leader the day after he had made a protest speech in front of a courthouse, claiming that he *might* have caused a riot, would not be allowed.[55]

Symbolic Speech

Not all speech involves words. Some actions, such as burning the American flag, take the place of speech and are commonly called **symbolic speech.** In a 1971 case, *Cohen* v. *California,*[56] the Court expanded its protection to these types of protests. Paul Cohen had appeared in a courthouse while wearing a leather jacket bearing the words "F--K THE DRAFT. STOP THE WAR." The Court might have argued that these were "fighting words," controllable actions, or obscenity forced upon a captive audience, but instead it ruled that because the offensive speech was meant to convey a larger symbolic meaning, the behavior was protected under the First Amendment. It was this protective view of symbolic speech that led the Court to uphold Gregory Johnson's right to burn the American flag even though many people found the action objectionable.

FREEDOM OF THE PRESS

Decisions in cases involving freedom of the press must establish a balance between the public's right to know and either (1) the government's right to secrecy, (2) an individual's right to personal reputation and/or privacy, (3) a defendant's right to a fair trial, or (4) an individual's personal and moral sensibilities. To illustrate this point, ask yourself whether the public's "right to know" about a controversial criminal trial like that of O. J. Simpson overrides both the defendant's right to receive a fair trial *and* society's right to maintain law and order. Similarly, some see the press as a critical "fourth branch," keeping a watchful eye on the government. But what if the revelation of certain government activities could be damaging to national security?

Often the balance between these two sets of rights depends on the kinds of laws used to restrict the press. **Prior-restraint,** or censorship, laws would prevent the press from revealing information before publication of that information by the government. Prior-restraint cases generally involve issues of national security, but they may also involve "gag orders" intended to preserve the right to a fair trial. In contrast, **subsequent-punishment** laws would punish writers and editors *after* the publication of certain information. Such laws are used to ban libel and obscenity because they are harmful to reputations or public sensibilities. The framers were more concerned with prior restraint than with subsequent punishment, believing that a trial by a jury of peers could deal with the latter, but in reality both can be equally harmful. A significant enough punishment threatened *after* publication can lead the press to censor itself *prior* to publication.

Prior Restraint

Probably the most significant case involving prior restraint was the 1971 Pentagon Papers case.[57] A Defense Department contractor named Daniel Ellsberg, who had worked on a study called "A History of the United States Decision Making Process on Vietnam Policy"—the so-called Pentagon Papers—had leaked almost all of the forty-seven-volume report to the *New York Times* and the *Washington Post*. When the newspapers planned to publish excerpts from the study, the government took the extraordinary step of seeking a court injunction to prevent their publication, claiming that it would be damaging to national security. Because of its controversial nature, the case went through the federal courts and reached the Supreme Court in the extraordinarily brief time of fifteen days. The Court ruled against prior restraint. In a concurring opinion, Justice Potter Stewart argued that prior censorship can be justified only when publication "will surely result in direct, immediate, and irreparable damage to our Nation or its people." Since the Pentagon Papers were strictly historical documents, Stewart failed to see the potential for such harm.

However, a closer analysis of the four concurring and three dissenting opinions reveals that the decision was not as great a victory for the press as it seemed. Five of the justices implied that if the government had tried to punish the press *after* publication, using laws barring the release of secret documents, the convictions would have been upheld. Accordingly, later administrations passed and enforced a series of administrative regulations and laws to prevent the divulging of secret information.

Another area in which the press is subject to restraints is its coverage of criminal proceedings. Judges sometimes issue "gag orders" barring the media from publishing information about an ongoing criminal case. In the early 1970s such orders were issued with great frequency to protect defendants against adverse pretrial publicity. However, in 1976 the Court ruled that a gag order issued by a Nebraska court in the pretrial hearing of a multiple-murder case was a prior restraint of the press and hence violated the First Amendment.[58] Because the Court extended its ruling in 1980 to open criminal trials to the press and public "absent an overriding interest to the contrary," gag orders are far less common today.[59]

Libel

In a democracy, the free flow of ideas must sometimes be prevented or limited when they are untruthful, malicious, or damaging to a person's reputation or good name. Speech that has these effects is termed **slander;** if it appears in written form, it is termed **libel.** The Supreme Court has ruled that slander and libel are not protected by the First Amendment. But how does one determine whether a published statement is libelous? Some published statements may be intended to defame a person's reputation, but in some instances defamation is a result of *negligence,* or failure to take reasonable care in verifying information before publication. Do the latter instances also constitute libel?

The Court addressed this question in 1964, when the *New York Times* printed an advertisement that was critical of the racial views of unnamed public officials in Alabama. An elected commissioner in Montgomery, Alabama, L. B. Sullivan, filed suit in an Alabama court, claiming that the ad libeled him personally; he won the case under an Alabama law requiring newspapers to establish the truth of material before publishing it. The *New York Times* appealed the case to the Supreme Court. Seeking to balance the newspaper's right to publish against Sullivan's right to maintain his reputation, the Court took careful notice of Sullivan's status as a public official. Unlike private individuals, public officials have opportunities to respond to published statements through such means as press conferences. On the other hand, if the press were prevented from publishing statements that are critical of political figures, it would be unable to fulfill its role as a watchdog of government. So the Court ruled that convictions in cases involving libel against public officials, expanded in later cases to public figures, could be upheld only if the defamatory article had been printed with "knowledge that it was false or reckless disregard whether it was false or not." In short, the untrue and defamatory piece would have to be printed without any effort to check the facts.[60] This is how supermarket tabloids are able to print untruthful articles about movie stars and public figures generally without fear of retribution.

Seeking to restrict the press, the Burger and Rehnquist Courts launched a two-pronged attack against the *Sullivan* standard. The class of people defined as "public figures" was narrowed,[61] and the press was instructed to turn over materials indicating its "state of mind" when publishing an article that was claimed to be libelous.[62] These changes had the effect of increasing the burden on the press to prove that it had not been negligent or malicious in publishing a statement that was challenged as being libelous.

Obscenity

Although the publication of obscene material is not protected by the First Amendment guarantee of freedom of the press, it is difficult to establish a definition of obscenity and, thus, to judge whether a particular publication is obscene. In a 1957 case, *Roth* v. *United States,* the Supreme Court stated that

The limits of the freedom-of-speech provision of the First Amendment were tested in Cincinnati in 1990, when an exhibit that included shocking and sexually explicit photographs by the acclaimed photographer Robert Mapplethorpe came to town. Many people were disturbed and outraged by the photographs—some of children in allegedly lewd poses. As a result, the directors of the Cincinnati Contemporary Arts Center faced charges of obscenity, and the exhibit was shut down. In court, however, a jury found that under the *Miller* v. *California* test the photos had sufficient artistic merit. The exhibit then opened again to throngs of art lovers and supporters of free expression.

material could be judged to be obscene if "the average person, applying contemporary community standards, [determines that] the dominant theme of the material, taken as a whole, appeals to the prurient interest."[63] Thus, a book like *Lady Chatterley's Lover* or *Peyton Place* could not be declared obscene because of a few scattered passages that might be offensive to a few highly susceptible people. In 1966 the Court added to the *Roth* standard the requirement that a work could be banned only if it was "utterly without redeeming social value."[64]

During the 1960s the Warren Court developed a "variable obscenity test" in which the definition of obscenity changed according to the circumstances of the material's use or sale. Material was judged to be obscene if it was thrust upon a "captive audience"—for example, a pornographic outdoor drive-in movie that was visible from the street—or sold to unsuspecting customers, such as children. In addition, material that was geared specifically toward customers with alternative sexual lifestyles could be banned.[65]

Because of the confusion and uncertainty resulting from this variable standard, the Burger Court tried to create a clearer standard in the 1973 case of *Miller* v. *California*. Henceforth, the definition of material as obscene would depend on "whether the average person applying contemporary community standards would find the work taken as a whole, appeals to the prurient interest; whether the work depicts or describes, *in a patently offensive way,* sexual conduct specifically defined by the applicable state law; and whether the work taken as a whole *lacks serious literary, artistic, political, or scientific value.*"[66] In contrast to the *Roth* standard, the *Miller* standard considered local tastes. But this did not solve the problem of defining obscenity. Each locality now had its own standard and applied it in varying ways to nationally distributed work. For example, the movie *Carnal Knowledge,* which did not depict sexual activity but contained a great deal of dialogue on the subject, was judged to be obscene in Georgia, but not elsewhere.[67]

The Rehnquist Court has made little progress toward establishing a clear definition of obscenity. The only clarity has come in the area of child pornography, for which the Court has so little tolerance that it has permitted convictions even for the possession of obscene videos of clothed children.[68] Thus, for the most part the question of how to determine whether a particular book or other published material is obscene, and thus to prevent or punish the publication of such material, remains unanswered.

THE RIGHTS OF DEFENDANTS

To the framers, fearful of the kinds of abuses that had prevailed under British rule, protection of the rights of defendants was vital. The Bill of Rights therefore contains several safeguards against government oppression, including the right to be left alone in one's home (in the Fourth Amendment), the right to remain silent (in the Fifth Amendment), and the right to be represented by counsel (in the Sixth Amendment). Remarkably, despite many changes in the technology of police work, these guarantees remain as vital today as they were two hundred years ago. Whether searches involve ransacking one's belongings under a writ of assistance or, two hundred years later, using technology to monitor one's computer or one's conversations, the balance is still

Inconsistencies in the Death Penalty

In Union, South Carolina, Susan Smith faced execution for drowning her two young sons. In Los Angeles, California, O. J. Simpson, accused of viciously stabbing to death his former wife and a friend, does not face the death penalty.

Both Connecticut and Texas have the death penalty, but there have been no executions in Connecticut since 1976, when the Supreme Court ruled that capital punishment is constitutional under certain circumstances. In stark contrast, Texas leads the nation in number of people executed, accounting for 92 out of the total of 266.

Even within a state with the death penalty there are wide variations in its application. Much depends on where the crime took place. More than one-third of those executed in Texas were from the Houston area, while in Dallas only five people have been executed.

There is no easy way to predict when prosecutors will seek the death penalty. "How do you figure out why lightning strikes one defendant and not another?" asks Cleveland law professor Victor Streib. "It's been studied for 20 years, and all I can say is, it's not a rational process."[*]

Prisoners on death row are disproportionately black, and almost all are male. Yet Simpson will not join them if he is convicted. Smith, on the other hand, faced the very real possibility that she would become the second woman to be executed since 1976. One could say that the difference has to do with wealth, and it is true that the death penalty is most often imposed on poor people who cannot pay for a skillful defense. But while Simpson is wealthy and Smith relatively poor, wealth alone does not explain the decisions of the prosecutors in these two cases.

According to legal experts, the key factor is the community in which the crime occurred.

The attitudes of members of the community vary with geography, among other factors. South Carolina is known as a law-and-order state, and public opinion there favored execution for Smith. In California, the death penalty is not normally sought when a defendant has no previous felony convictions. Moreover, prosecutors felt that putting a popular national figure like Simpson on trial for his life would alienate the public. According to legal experts, it is much easier to seek the death penalty for an obscure mill worker accused of drowning her babies than for a football hero. As Atlanta attorney Stephen Bright points out, "Simpson is like a member of the family, so much a part of American life. As a result, it is much more like having a friend or family member accused of a crime. Susan Smith is defined publicly only by the crime."[†]

Clearly, many factors interact to determine whether prosecutors will seek the death penalty. Not only the nature of the crime but also the geographic area in which it occurred, the opinions of members of the community, and various characteristics of the defendant play a role. Perhaps the most important factor, however, is whether prosecutors believe they can obtain a conviction in a particular case.

---

*Quoted in Tamar Lewin, "Who Decides Who Will Die? Even Within States, It Varies," *New York Times,* Feb. 23, 1995, p. A1.

†Quoted in Rick Bragg, "Two Crimes, Two Punishments," *New York Times,* Jan. 22, 1995, p. E1.

between the rights of the individual and the rights of society. However, as in many other areas involving civil liberties, this balance depends on the composition of the Supreme Court at any given time. No issue better illustrates this fact than the shifting nature of Fourth Amendment protection over the past three decades.

The Fourth Amendment

The Fourth Amendment tries to balance two rights: the individual's reasonable expectation of privacy and society's right to control crime and protect the public. Over the years the Supreme Court has devised different rules for establishing this balance. During the 1960s the so-called Warren Court revolution greatly expanded the protection provided by the expectation of privacy, but in subsequent decades the Burger and Rehnquist Courts shifted the balance back toward the state (i.e., the police). These shifts have had significant effects on both the nation's approach to, and recession from, democracy as expressed by the constrained and then increasing power of the state to investigate and imprison its people.

Many issues related to Fourth Amendment protections stem from the amendment's lack of an explicitly written *remedy*. What can a judge do if the police go too far in conducting a search? Can the evidence uncovered by such an illegal search be used in a trial? In other words, can the police break the law to uphold the law? As Justice Benjamin Cardozo put it, should "the criminal . . . go free because the constable had blundered"?[69] Debates over this issue center on the creation of an **exclusionary rule,** whereby evidence that was gathered by illegal means cannot be used in later trials. Under another doctrine, the "fruit of the poisonous tree," no other evidence gathered as a result of other searches or investigations based on this initially illegal search can be used either.

The exclusionary rule was created in 1914 in the case of *Weeks* v. *United States;*[70] it prevented federal courts from using illegally gathered evidence in a trial. This rule, it was argued, not only protected the privacy rights of the individual defendant but also deterred the authorities from conducting illegal searches in future cases. However, the rule gave rise to problems that were both legal and symbolic. In some cases it prevented the use of hard, observable evidence, thus possibly allowing guilty individuals to go free.[71]

Since the Fourth Amendment did not yet apply to the states, the exclusionary rule could be used only in federal cases. In ruling on the admissibility of illegally seized evidence in state cases the Supreme Court used the Fourteenth Amendment's due process clause. It held that only the results of searches that "shocked the conscience" of the justices could be barred from use in trials. The problem here was that different justices were "shocked" by different things. Justice Felix Frankfurter, the inventor of this test, was "shocked" by a case in which police officers broke into the office of a doctor suspected of performing abortions to find his patient book, which would then be used in making up a list of witnesses, and by a case in which a man's stomach was pumped to retrieve two morphine capsules,[72] but not by a case involving the taking of blood from an unconscious man to determine whether he was drunk.[73] Many of Frankfurter's fellow justices disagreed with his views. Not until after Frankfurter's retirement in 1962 did the Court begin to consider extending the exclusionary rule guarantee of the Fourth Amendment to defendants in state courts.

THE DUE PROCESS REVOLUTION   It was in the case of Dollree Mapp in 1961 that the Warren Court made its landmark ruling on the nature of the Fourth Amendment and its application to the states. The case began when the Cleveland police received a tip from a "reliable authority" that a "suspected bomber of a house porch and bookmaker" was in Mapp's home. When Mapp refused to let the police in, three officers broke into the house, waving a blank piece of paper in the air and claiming that it was a search warrant. After Mapp stuffed the "warrant" inside her blouse, the officers tried to retrieve it and handcuffed Mapp for resisting their search. The search through the house produced no bomber or bookmaker, but the officers arrested and the court convicted Mapp for possessing obscene materials.[74]

While all of this might have "shocked the conscience" of the justices in an earlier day, in this case the Court made the *Weeks* exclusionary rule a part of the Fourth Amendment and then incorporated it into the Fourteenth Amendment to apply it to the states. By this means the exclusionary rule was made uniform among the states and between the state and federal levels of government. Mapp's conviction was reversed and her case was sent back to the state court for a retrial, but with the pornographic materials now excluded from the new trial the state had no choice but to drop the charges.

LIMITING THE EXCLUSIONARY RULE   During the Burger Court years the justices were unhappy with the fact that under the exclusionary rule even the most minor of police violations resulted in the loss of *all* the evidence. So, the Court began to argue that the exclusionary rule should be restricted or eliminated, saying that it had little or no deterrent effect on police.[75] It began to question whether any possible deterrent effect of the rule outweighed the harm to society that might result from allowing guilty individuals to go free because of the exclusion from trial of improperly gathered evidence.

After limiting the use of the exclusionary rule in various criminal-justice proceedings, such as the grand jury[76] and habeas corpus proceedings in which convicted defendants were seeking a new trial,[77] the Court greatly reduced its application in the 1984 case of *United States* v. *Leon*.[78] Federal authorities had received a warrant to search some houses and cars for drugs on the basis of an unreliable informer's outdated tips. For the Warren Court this would have voided the search and excluded the use of its evidence, but the Burger Court ruled that since the police believed they had a valid search warrant, the resulting evidence could be used in a trial. This became known as the "good faith" exception to the Fourth Amendment. "Good faith" was not defined, but the watering-down effect on the exclusionary rule was clear. Now officers could justify the use of previously inadmissible evidence by saying the right words in court.

The Rehnquist Court appears to be willing to extend the "good faith" exception to cases in which no search warrant was issued. In *Illinois* v. *Rodriguez*,[79] for example, officers relied on the word of a woman who said that she had a right to enter her ex-boyfriend's apartment. Searching the apartment with her consent, they found illegal drugs. Despite the fact that the woman actually had no right to admit the police, the Court ruled that since the police had relied on her word in "good faith," the search was permissible. In early 1995, the Republican-dominated House of Representatives passed as part of a new crime bill a provision that would allow such "good faith" exceptions even in searches in which no warrant was used. These kinds of loopholes in the exclusionary rule seriously weaken the guarantee of privacy implied in the Fourth Amendment.[80]

Little-known Fact

The "reliable informant" in the *Mapp* case was Don King, later to become a boxing promoter and manager for heavyweight champion Mike Tyson. The "bombing suspect" King was calling about was former boxing champion Archie Moore.

FYI

According to the case *T.L.O.* v. *New Jersey,* for searches by school personnel in high schools the standard is not "probable cause" but "reasonable suspicion," which gives school authorities a wider leeway when searching.

WARRANTLESS SEARCHES. Another way in which the Court can affect Fourth Amendment rights is by broadening or contracting the nature of searches in which judges have not issued warrants, or warrantless searches. The Fourth Amendment defines a proper search as one in which a proper search warrant has been issued after the police have demonstrated to a neutral judge that there is **probable cause** that a crime has been or is about to be committed, and that evidence of such a crime can be found at a particular location. Only then will the judge issue a warrant stating specifically what can be searched for and where the police can search. But in some cases there isn't time to obtain a warrant. To cover these cases, the amendment adds that the people are protected against unreasonable searches. The question then becomes, What is a "reasonable search"?

Suppose a police officer stops a car, suspecting that it is carrying illegal weapons. Obviously, there is no time to get a warrant. If the officer can later demonstrate that the search was "reasonable," it will be allowed under a "movable automobile exception" to the Fourth Amendment.[81] The rationale in such a case is that the officer's safety might be in jeopardy and valuable evidence might be lost if the search is delayed until after the issue of a warrant, thus allowing the car and evidence to escape. On the other hand, what if a police officer enters a private house to speak with the occupant about a problem in the neighborhood and sees a Sidewinder missile hanging above the mantel? As long as the officer can give a valid reason for being there, what is in "plain view" can be seized as evidence even without a warrant.

In all Fourth Amendment cases, then, the central issue is whether a suspect's expectation of privacy is outweighed by the state's need to control crime by preserving evidence and ensuring the safety of police officers. On this basis many other exceptions to the Fourth Amendment have been created, including searches incident to a lawful arrest (on the person and within the person's reach), consent searches (if the suspect permits the search, the Fourth Amendment protection is waived), searches of fleeing suspects who might destroy evidence, and various kinds of administrative searches (for example, in airports and at national borders).[82]

The pattern of expanding and contracting Fourth Amendment rights can be seen in the evolution of the "stop-and-frisk" exception. A stop-and-frisk case is one in which the police detain a person and conduct a pat-down "search" of that person's outer clothing without a warrant or an arrest, basing their action on observed, potentially criminal conduct. The Warren Court first defined the constitutional limits of such searches in 1968 in *Terry* v. *Ohio,*[83] in which an experienced Ohio police officer had observed two men apparently planning one night to burglarize a store. The officer had approached the men, asked them some questions, and then patted down their clothing; the search revealed revolvers and bullets concealed under their jackets, and the officer thereupon arrested the men. The Court ruled that even though the officer did not have probable cause to arrest the suspects for the robbery until after he had conducted his full search, the initial frisk was legal because he could justify stopping the suspects in the first place.

During the Burger Court years certain limits were placed on such limited searches. In one case, a previously unreliable informant had told a police officer that a man sitting in a car at night in a high crime area was carrying a gun;

A common form of search and seizure under the Fourth Amendment takes place everyday as automobile drivers are tested with a breathalyzer machine for drunk driving.

```
                    WAIVER OF RIGHTS AND CONSENT TO SEARCH


_____                            _____
    TROOP-STATION                                  INCIDENT NUMBER

(1) PLACE(S), ITEM(S) OR VEHICLE(S) TO BE SEARCHED: _____

    _____

    ADDRESS OR LOCATION: _____

    _____

(2) ITEM(S) TO BE SEARCHED FOR AND SEIZED, IF FOUND: _____

    _____

(3) I, _____, HAVE BEEN REQUESTED BY _____
        (CONSENTOR SHALL PRINT FULL NAME)                      (PRINT NAME)
    OF THE _____ STATE POLICE TO GIVE MY CONSENT FOR POLICE OFFICERS TO SEARCH PLACE(S),
    ITEM(S) OR VEHICLE(S) DESCRIBED ABOVE FOR THE ITEMS DESCRIBED ABOVE. I HAVE BEEN TOLD THAT I
    DO NOT HAVE TO GIVE MY CONSENT. I UNDERSTAND THAT I HAVE THE RIGHT TO REFUSE THIS REQUEST,
    AND THAT THE POLICE MAY NOT BE ABLE TO CONDUCT THIS SEARCH WITHOUT A SEARCH WARRANT
    UNLESS I GIVE MY CONSENT. NONETHELESS, I VOLUNTARILY GIVE MY CONSENT TO THE POLICE TO
    CONDUCT THIS SEARCH.

(4) [ ] I am the owner of the place(s), item(s) or vehicle(s) to be searched.

    [ ] I rent or lease the place(s), item(s) or vehicle(s) to be searched from another person.

    [ ] With the permission of the owner, I have equal access and control over the place(s), item(s) or
        vehicle(s) to be searched.

(5) I also understand that in addition to the items described above, if the following is found it may also be seized:

    (1) any contraband, the fruits of a crime or things otherwise criminally possessed.

    (2) property which is or has been used as the means of committing a criminal offense.

    (3) property which constitutes evidence of the commission of a criminal offense.

(6) No one, including anyone from the_____ State Police or any other police officer, has threatened me in
    any way, nor has anything been promised to me in return for giving my consent to conduct this search.

            WITNESS(ES)                              CONSENTOR


_____              _____
(PRINT NAME)                              (PRINT NAME)


_____              _____
(SIGNATURE)                               (SIGNATURE)


_____              _____
(PRINT NAME)                              (ADDRESS)


_____              _____
(SIGNATURE)                               (CITY, STATE)


DATE:          TIME:            DATE:           TIME:
```

In some states, people asked to consent to a search would agree to waive the state version of their Fourth Amendment "search and seizure" rights by filling out and signing this form.

the officer reached through the car window and without further comment reached immediately under the suspect's jacket to grab the weapon. The suspect was arrested and searched, and the police found that he was carrying heroin. Although the initial search had been based on a tip and not on personal observation, the suspect had been doing nothing more suspicious than sitting in his car, and a full search under the clothing rather than a pat-down was conducted, the Court upheld the legality of the search, saying that the officer need only exercise "reasonable caution" in conducting the search.[84]

In 1991 the Rehnquist Court decided two cases involving stop-and-frisk searches. In the first, the Court ruled that police need only make a "show of authority" by ordering a person to halt; if the person runs away, the police have the right to "seize" the person and "search" his or her possessions.[85] In the second case, the Court allowed the practice of "working the buses," in which police officers board a bus carrying a person suspected of possessing drugs, announce that they are going to search the belongings of everyone aboard, and wait to see who tries to exit through the back door before searching them. According to Justice Sandra O'Connor, as long as each of the passengers feels free to decline the officers' request for a search "or otherwise terminate the encounter," such a search is legal.[86]

The Fifth and Sixth Amendments

The safeguards contained in the Fifth and Sixth Amendments were designed to prevent some of the worst practices of early English criminal law, such as secret interrogation and torture. In addition to guaranteeing the right not to be compelled to be a witness against oneself in a criminal trial, the Fifth Amendment provides the right to a grand jury, protection against double jeopardy (being tried twice for the same offense), and a guarantee against government taking one's property without just compensation, and requires due process of law. To the guarantee of a right to counsel in criminal cases the Sixth Amendment adds the rights to a speedy and public trial by an impartial jury, to be informed of the nature of the charges against oneself, to be confronted with the witnesses against oneself, and to compel the appearance of witnesses in one's defense. Such safeguards are vital to a democratic society and constitute a basic difference between democracies and totalitarian governments.

Like all the other civil liberties discussed in this chapter, the rights of accused persons have been subject to interpretation by the Supreme Court. Before the Fifth and Sixth Amendments were applied to the states, the Court used the due process clause of the Fourteenth Amendment in deciding cases involving police interrogations.[87] In such cases the justices examined the "totality of circumstances" of an interrogation to determine the "voluntariness" of a confession. If the "totality of circumstances" (e.g., the conditions under which the defendant had been questioned) indicated that a confession was not voluntary, it would not be allowed in a trial. If on the other hand, the suspect had done something like flagging down a police car or walking into a station house and starting to confess before a question could be asked, the confession would be considered voluntary. "Voluntariness" was an elusive concept, defying clear measurement, however. In one case a mentally challenged defendant was judged to have been compelled to confess because he had been refused the right to call his wife before talking to the police.[88]

After the protections of the Fifth and Sixth Amendments were extended to the states, the Court began to explore the question of whether a person could be compelled to confess simply by being confronted by the police. This question was the central issue in a 1964 case, *Escobedo* v. *Illinois*,[89] in which a man had been arrested for the murder of his brother-in-law and questioned by police without being allowed to see his attorney, who was then in the police station. The Supreme Court ruled that police questioning of suspects for the purpose of gaining a confession was just as important as the trial itself. Once the police had gone beyond the "general investigation" phase of their

The landmark 1963 Supreme Court case *Gideon* v. *Wainwright* extended the Sixth Amendment right to free legal counsel to all poor defendants accused of "serious crimes" in state courts. Shown here is Clarence Earl Gideon, who with a handwritten appeal from jail took his conviction for breaking and entering all the way to the Supreme Court. Gideon was acquitted of all charges after his case was retried in a Florida court with the assistance of counsel.

interrogation by seeking to secure a confession, they had shifted "from the investigatory to the accusatory" phase, and under the Sixth and Fourteenth Amendments the suspect had the right to have counsel present.

But should defendants be warned of their "right to silence," and just how far may the police go in their questioning? The answer came two years later in the case of *Miranda* v. *Arizona*.[90] If you watch movies or television you have surely seen police officers recite the so-called **Miranda warning** to a suspect before questioning: "You have the right to remain silent. Anything you say can and will be used against you. You have the right to an attorney. If you cannot afford an attorney, one will be provided for you. Do you understand these rights and are you willing to speak with us?" The requirement that suspects be informed of their rights stems from the *Miranda* case, in which a slightly psychotic suspect given to flights of fantasy had confessed to a kidnapping and rape after only two hours of questioning. The Court ruled that all police questioning was "inherently compulsory" and that confessions were therefore "inherently untrustworthy." Before questioning a suspect who had been taken into custody or "deprived of his freedom in any significant way," the police had to offer the warning just described. Otherwise, statements made by the accused could not be used in a trial or to gather related evidence.

This ruling was highly controversial. It looked as if the Court was legislating new rules that would make convicting known felons impossible. In reality, the Court was just applying to the states the practices that the Federal Bureau of Investigation had long used in interrogating suspects. Still, the outcry against the "criminal-coddling Warren Court" did serious damage to the Court's prestige and led some critics to demand that the decision be reversed.

Rather than overturning *Miranda* directly, the Burger and Rehnquist Courts chipped away at its underpinnings to such an extent that very little of it remains in force. The Burger Court increased the number of situations in which confessions could be used in a trial even if the suspect had not been read the Miranda warning, such as to impeach the credibility of a witness.[91] Police were also given more leeway to encourage a suspect to confess such as by making statements in his presence rather than questioning the suspect directly;[92] asking a suspect only where his or her weapon was located;[93] and questioning a suspect twice, reading him or her the warning after a "voluntary" confession had been secured.[94]

It was in the Rehnquist Court that a major step was taken toward possibly overturning *Miranda*. This occurred in the 1991 case of *Arizona* v. *Fulminante*.[95] A prisoner had confessed to the murder of his stepdaughter to a prison inmate who offered to protect him from harm but was in fact working as an informer with the F.B.I. After being released from jail, he again confessed to the crime, this time to the informer's wife. The Court ruled that such confessions, even this coerced one, could be used in trials, and defendants were put on notice that the absence of the Miranda warning would no longer result in the automatic overturning of a conviction.

In sum, while most of the basic rights of accused persons are protected in the Fourth, Fifth, and Sixth Amendments, the exact nature of those rights is subject to judicial interpretation. The Supreme Court is continually trying to balance the rights of suspects against the needs of the state, acting through the police. At times it has appeared to lean too far toward protecting criminals by disallowing evidence or confessions because of technical violations. At other

FYI

Ernesto Miranda was retried and convicted on the basis of his girlfriend's testimony. However, after his parole he was killed in a cardgame by an illegal alien who objected to his effort to raise the price of his autographed "Miranda cards" from one dollar to two dollars.

The Meaning of Silence

You do not have to say anything unless you wish to do so, but what you say may be given in evidence.

You do not have to say anything. But if you do not mention now something which you later use in your defense, the court may decide that your failure to mention it now strengthens the case against you.

These statements are the British equivalents of the Miranda warning. The first version is the one in current use; the second is a new version recently passed by Parliament as part of a major anticrime bill. Both versions give accused persons the right to remain silent, but the second version warns them that their silence might be used against them.

According to an official of the British government, the new version "is based on the proposition that, if an innocent person has an explanation to give, he can usually be expected to give it at the first opportunity, not store it up for use when the proceedings have developed as far as a trial."* In other words, "If someone hasn't got something to hide, let them speak." Under the new law, judges and juries will be allowed to draw inferences about defendants' refusal to answer questions or explain their actions—including the inference that the suspect was using silence to conceal guilt.

The new law has many critics, who feel that it flies in the face of the basic right of criminal suspects to be free from self-incrimination. Moreover, it tends to place the burden of proof on defendants rather than on the police—instead of being presumed innocent, an accused person must either explain his or her actions or face the possibility that silence will be construed as guilt. These views are supported by the Royal Commission on Criminal Justice, which recommended that the government do nothing to alter the right to silence because some innocent suspects might feel under pressure to explain themselves unnecessarily to the police, thereby increasing the risk of wrongful conviction.

Michael Howard, the home secretary, claims that the new version of the warning does not abolish the right to silence or curtail the presumption of innocence. Instead, it is intended to discourage professional criminals from exploiting the legal system. One study, for example, found that suspects with five or more convictions were 3.5 times more likely to exercise the right to remain silent than suspects without prior convictions.[†] Nevertheless, some lawyers believe that the change in wording will be challenged by the European Commission on Human Rights. In any case, it is certain that the new warning will continue to be a subject of intense debate between those who are alarmed by increasing rates of crime and those who fear that a basic civil liberty is threatened.

_____

*David Maclean, quoted in William E. Schmidt, "Silence May Speak Against the Accused in Britain," *New York Times,* Nov. 11, 1994, p. B20.

[†]Ibid.

---

times it has appeared to condone unreasonable police actions in the interest of protecting the public. This tension between the rights of the accused and the safety of the public makes the civil liberties of defendants a source of continuing debate.

IMPLIED RIGHTS

The *Bowers* case described in Chapter 7 illustrates an issue that is currently subject to considerable debate, both in the Supreme Court and in the general public. Are there rights beyond those set forth in the language of the Bill of Rights that should be safeguarded against governmental intrusion? If so, what are they and what are their limits? These are difficult questions that involve moral and ethical positions as well as legal and constitutional judgments.

Privacy

The right of privacy is not explicitly mentioned in the Constitution. Is this right implied in the Fourth Amendment's protection against "unreasonable searches and seizures"? Or did the framers intend it to be one of the "rights retained by the people" in the Ninth Amendment? Or was it so obvious and important that it did not need to be mentioned at all? And, assuming that such a right exists, what exactly does it encompass?

These issues were explored in a landmark 1965 case, *Griswold* v. *Connecticut*,[96] in which Estelle T. Griswold, the director of a New Haven birth control clinic opened by the Connecticut Planned Parenthood League, was charged with violating a state statute that prohibited the use, and medical counseling about the use, of birth control. This law had been passed in response to the concerns of its author, the entrepreneur P. T. Barnum, who wished to control the spread of adultery and unsavory diseases.[97] Private citizens, however, argued that the state had no business regulating personal conduct in the bedroom, especially the marital bedroom.

The Supreme Court ruled that the behavior of married people in their bedrooms is protected by the right of privacy. According to Justice William O. Douglas, such a right, while not explicitly stated, can be seen in the "penumbras, formed by emanations," or shadows of shadows, of the First, Third, Fourth, Fifth, and Ninth Amendments; these, he said, create several "zones of privacy." To dissenting justices and students of law, this statement was somewhat confusing in that the right of privacy could be glimpsed in several amendments but was not stated in any of them. Many felt that Douglas was inserting his own

> "We do not sit as a super-legislature to determine the wisdom, need and propriety of laws that touch economic problems, business affairs, or social conditions."
>
> William O. Douglas, in
> *Griswold* v. *Connecticut*

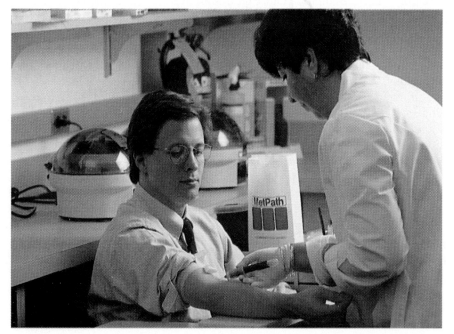

Can the government require that you be tested for AIDS or drug use? Although the courts have not yet ruled on AIDS testing, the issue of drug testing has been working its way through the courts. In a 1989 ruling the Supreme Court upheld that employees responsible for the public's safety—such as law enforcement and railroad employees—could be subject to drug tests without a search warrant. In 1995, the Court approved taking urine samples from high-school athletes to test for drugs, upholding the school's interest in education over students' privacy rights.

In response to religious and conservative groups seeking to ban abortion outright and have the *Roe* v. *Wade* case overturned, supporters of a woman's right to choose, like this protester, organize marches in Washington, D.C. to impress upon the Supreme Court and the country the merits of their position. In recent years, both sides in the abortion debate have made their presence felt in the nation's capital.

value preferences into the Constitution.[98] Three months after the decision, Griswold and Dr. Lee Buxton reopened their New Haven birth control clinic. The *Griswold* decision has stood as the basis for the expansion of privacy rights to the dismay of judicial conservatives and self-restraint advocates such as Robert Bork, who do not support such rights that are not explicitly written into the Constitution and its amendments.

Once privacy became an accepted part of constitutional interpretation, many additional rights could be created. It was not long before the right of privacy was extended to single, unmarried persons.[99] Eventually, this constitutional privacy right became a central element in debates over rights related to abortion, homosexuality, AIDS, drug testing, and euthanasia.

Abortion

If the constitutional right of privacy allows people to choose to *prevent* conception, does it allow them to terminate a pregnancy *after* conception? Before 1973 states were free to set restrictions on a woman's right to obtain an abortion, and many banned abortion entirely. As a result of differences in state laws, vast numbers of women went across state lines or out of the country to obtain abortions, and many others placed themselves in the hands of dangerous "back-alley" abortionists to terminate unwanted pregnancies.

In the 1973 case of *Roe* v. *Wade*[100] the Supreme Court reviewed a Texas law that limited a woman's right to obtain an abortion. The Court ruled that the right of privacy gave a woman the right to obtain an abortion. But as with all rights, limitations could be placed on the exercise of this right. Those limitations were dictated by the interests of others—in this case, the right of the state to protect the health of the mother and the rights of the unborn fetus.

The rights of the unborn fetus were the focal point in the *Roe* case. Some religious groups argue that the fetus is a living human being; for them, therefore, abortion constitutes murder. Other groups use the findings of medical science to argue that life begins when a fetus can be sustained by medical technology outside the mother's womb; this argument leads to a different set of limitations on the abortion procedure. Opposed to both of these arguments are those who claim that because the right of privacy gives a woman the right to control her own body, a woman has an unfettered right to choose to have an abortion.

In his majority opinion Justice Harry Blackmun attempted to strike a balance among these competing arguments by segmenting the term of the pregnancy into three trimesters. In the first three months, the woman has an absolute right to obtain an abortion, and the state has no legitimate interest in controlling a routine medical procedure. In the second trimester, the interests of the state become more important as the abortion procedure becomes more risky; thus, states may regulate abortions to ensure the woman's safety, but not to the extent of eliminating them. In the final three months, when the fetus has become viable and has interests that must be safeguarded, abortions can be banned completely.

Roe left open a number of questions. As medical technology advances and fetuses become viable earlier, can abortions be banned at an earlier stage of pregnancy? On the other hand, will the line move in the other direction as medical technology also makes abortions safer at later stages of pregnancy? And what will happen when new reproductive technologies make it possible for a fetus to develop outside of the womb?

Since the *Roe* decision some states, such as Louisiana, Utah, Ohio, and Pennsylvania, have limited and regulated abortions in various ways, including requiring notification of the parents of minors seeking abortions, establishing rules for determining which physicians and facilities are qualified to perform abortions, requiring notification of prospective fathers, and requiring a woman to follow a series of steps to inform herself about the nature of abortions before undergoing the procedure (see Figure 14.2).

At the federal level, the debate has centered on whether government medical assistance to the poor should cover the cost of abortions. Opponents of abortion argue that public funds should not be used to pay for a procedure that some taxpayers find objectionable. Since 1976 Congress has passed various measures limiting federal assistance for abortions except in cases of rape or incest and when the health of the mother is in jeopardy. Some states have followed suit. In 1980 the Supreme Court upheld these restrictions, essentially denying poor women their constitutional right to obtain an abortion.[101]

Initially, the Burger Court was inclined to strike down restrictions such as the requirement that a woman's husband, or her parents if she is a minor, be informed if she seeks an abortion.[102] In 1983, however, the Court reaffirmed the *Roe* decision in a case involving a number of regulations passed by the city

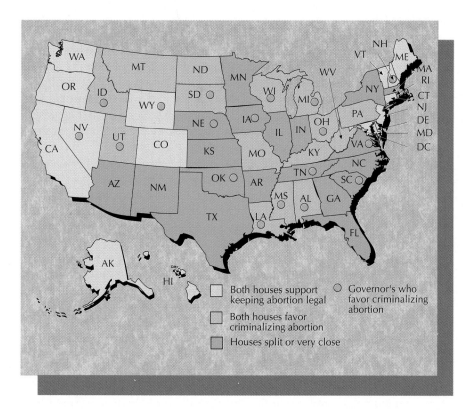

Both houses support keeping abortion legal

Both houses favor criminalizing abortion

Houses split or very close

Governor's who favor criminalizing abortion

FIGURE 14.2   The States and Abortion

This map gives you an idea of what states might do about criminalizing or legalizing abortion if the *Roe* v. *Wade* decision were to be overturned by the Supreme Court. Certain states such as Utah, Pennsylvania, and Missouri already use the discretion allowed by the Court to place restrictions on abortion, making it extremely difficult for women to have the procedure performed. Many of the current abortion test cases reaching the Supreme Court have come from these and other conservative states.

Source: Time, May 4, 1992. Data from NARAL.

"When this Court reexamines a prior holding, its judgment is customarily informed by a series of prudential and pragmatic considerations designed to test the consistency of overruling a prior decision with ideal of the rule of law, and to gauge the respective costs of reaffirming and overruling a prior case. . . . Although *Roe* has engendered opposition, it has in no sense proven 'unworkable,' representing as it does a simple limitation beyond which a state law is unenforceable."

—Justices O'Connor, Kennedy, and Souter, in *Planned Parenthood of Southeastern Pennsylvania,* v. *Casey* (1992)

of Akron, Ohio. The Court ruled that laws regulating abortion must be designed to protect the health of the mother. Justice Sandra Day O'Connor dissented, arguing that the Court should be concerned only with whether the law represents an "undue burden," or a severe obstacle, on the right to obtain an abortion.[103]

The Rehnquist Court has considered several cases involving abortion, beginning with the 1989 case of *Webster* v. *Reproductive Health Service.*[104] The state of Missouri had passed one of the most restrictive of all state abortion laws. Physicians performing abortions more than five months into the pregnancy were required to determine whether the fetus was viable, public employees or facilities could not be used to perform abortions, and public funds could not be spent to counsel women to seek abortions. The appointment of Justices Antonin Scalia and Anthony Kennedy had created an activist-conservative Court that seemed to have the votes to overturn the *Roe* decision; however, Justice O'Connor was still unwilling to do so. Thus, the Court upheld all the components of the Missouri law but allowed *Roe* to remain in force.

In 1993 the abortion issue again came before the Court, this time in a case dealing with a restrictive Pennsylvania statute.[105] In a surprising action three jurists, O'Connor, Kennedy, and David Souter, broke from their conservative colleagues and wrote a centrist opinion upholding *Roe* because of its long-standing value as a precedent. Shortly thereafter, two judges who seem to support abortion rights, Ruth Bader Ginsburg and Stephen Breyer, were appointed to the Court. For the moment, the right to obtain an abortion, though restricted in some instances, seems secure.

The Right to Die

As advances in medical technology allow people to live longer, questions arise about the quality of life experienced by those who are kept alive by artificial means. Should relatives and loved ones be allowed to turn off the life-support systems of critically ill patients? On another front, the efforts of a Detroit doctor, Jack Kevorkian, to assist the suicides of terminally ill patients raise the question of whether people have a right to conduct their own mercy killing. It was only a matter of time before these questions reached the courts.

During its 1989 term the Supreme Court heard arguments in the case of a Missouri woman, Nancy Cruzan, who had been in a coma for several years and was being kept alive by life-support equipment; because there was no hope that she would recover, her parents sought to have the life support removed. The Court ruled that because the state of Missouri requires clear and convincing evidence—such as a living will—that a person maintained on life support would not wish to be kept alive by such means, the life-support system could not be disconnected in the absence of such evidence. However, Chief Justice Rehnquist noted that "the principle that a competent person has a constitutionally protected liberty interest in refusing unwanted medical treatment may be inferred from our prior decisions."[106] (This case was described in more detail in Chapter 7.)

Are assisted suicides equivalent to murder, or do they simply represent the ultimate individual right stemming from the right of privacy? Issues involving the right to die, access to medical treatment and care, and the role medical personnel can or cannot play in terminating a patient's life can be expected to create continuing controversy in debates over the civil liberties of Americans.

CIVIL LIBERTIES AND APPROACHING DEMOCRACY

As we have seen throughout this chapter, while the civil liberties of Americans are guaranteed by the Bill of Rights, those individual rights tend to be dynamic, flexible, and even contradictory. One person's exercise of a constitutionally protected right may have the effect of infringing on another person's rights. Does everyone have the right to say and write what he or she wishes when it offends others or prevents them from expressing themselves? While a democracy guarantees that every person is entitled to due process of law, does letting an accused person go free on a technicality help the victims of a crime? And in resolving these dilemmas, is the purpose of the government to protect minorities or to express the will of the majority?

There can be little doubt that the individual rights of Americans are more fully protected today than they were during the framers' time. If he had burned the flag in 1800, Gregory Johnson surely would have been convicted of "seditious libel" under the 1798 Alien and Sedition Act. But because his action occurred almost two hundred years later, he is free as a result of a Supreme Court interpretation of the First Amendment. Parochial schools have been funded by the states in a way that would have been impossible under Madison and Jefferson's "high wall of separation" doctrine. The nature of defendants' rights is much more uniform among the states than it was in the 1800s and early 1900s. And the notions of privacy and personal autonomy are protected even though they are not even mentioned in the Bill of Rights.

As the composition of the Court has changed, so have the decisions of the justices and, hence, the nature of the protections and limitations on individual rights. Socialists and anarchists in the 1920s, Communists in the 1950s, protesters in the 1960s, and immigrants in the 1990s have sometimes found that their rights were not valued as highly as those of other Americans. Still, the fact that protections now exist for many of these groups tells us that progress has been made. In the area of civil liberties, the United States has traveled a considerable distance in approaching democracy, but with each new controversy we can see that it has a way yet to travel. Only the continued interest of the citizenry in their constitutional rights helps to ensure that the progress of the last two hundred years will continue.

SUMMARY

1. Although the terms *civil liberties* and *civil rights* are often used interchangeably, they are not synonymous. Civil liberties are the individual rights that are guaranteed to every citizen by the Bill of Rights and the due process clause of the Fourteenth Amendment. Civil rights are concerned with protecting citizens against discrimination resulting from characteristics such as race, gender, or disability and are derived largely from the equal-protection clause of the Fourteenth Amendment.

2. The history of civil liberties is one of gradual expansion of the degree of protection provided by the Bill of Rights. This evolution occurred initially through a series of Supreme Court decisions that applied portions of the first ten amendments to the states, thereby protecting citizens against state action in relation to specific individual rights. Those decisions centered on the question of "incorporation" of the Bill of Rights into the Fourteenth Amendment. Later cases then expanded the protection of these guarantees by judicial interpretation.

3. Issues involving freedom of religion are of two main types: those involving "establishment," or governmental preference for one religion over others, and those involving "free exercise," or individual religious practices. In deciding whether certain governmental actions would have the effect of "establishing" a religion, the Supreme Court has searched for the proper balance between complete

separation of church and state, known as the "high wall of separation" doctrine, and government accommodation, in which the government would be allowed to assist religious organizations indirectly and in a neutral manner. In deciding free-exercise cases, the Court's protection of religious freedom against state regulation has varied depending on changes in Court personnel.

4. In cases involving freedom of speech, the Court has ruled in ways that protect certain kinds of speech but not others. Political speech is protected if it is not likely to incite "imminent lawless action." Public speech is protected unless it consists of "fighting words" or can be shown to create a dangerous situation. Symbolic speech such as flag burning is also protected.

5. Issues involving freedom of the press hinge on the balance between the public's right to know and other rights, such as the government's right to secrecy or an individual's right to personal reputation. The Supreme Court has tended to rule against the state in cases of prior restraint, or censorship before publication, but not in cases of punishment *after* publication. In ruling on charges of libel, or the publication of statements that are untruthful and damaging to a person's reputation, the Court requires evidence of "actual malice" or "reckless disregard" for the truth. Cases involving obscenity have been most problematic because of the extreme difficulty of defining obscenity.

6. Many early debates over the Fourth Amendment's ban on unreasonable searches centered on the creation of an exclusionary rule whereby evidence gathered by illegal means cannot be used in later trials. Later, by defining "unreasonable searches" the Supreme Court has alternately expanded and limited the application of the Fourth Amendment; while generally protecting suspects against unreasonable searches, it has permitted a variety of exceptions that give the police some leeway in the methods used to obtain evidence.

7. The Fifth and Sixth Amendments contain several provisions designed to protect the rights of defendants. Of these, the most controversial have to do with the "right to silence" governing confessions resulting from police questioning. Since 1966 police officers have been required to read the so-called Miranda warning to suspects before questioning them; if they do not, statements made by the accused cannot be used in a trial. In recent years, however, the Court has increased the number of exceptions to this rule, and the absence of the Miranda warning will no longer result in the automatic overturning of a conviction.

8. The right of privacy is not explicitly mentioned in the Constitution, but the Supreme Court has ruled that such a right is implied by the wording of several provisions in the Bill of Rights. This right has been extended to cover a woman's right to obtain an abortion in the first three months of pregnancy. The Court has, however, allowed states to place certain restrictions on abortion. The right of privacy has also been extended to cover the right to die in cases involving patients kept alive by life-support equipment, provided that there is evidence that the patient would not have wished to be kept alive by such means.

KEY TERMS

civil liberties	*Lemon* test	subsequent punishment
civil rights	secular regulation rule	slander
incorporation	least-restrictive-means test	libel
no incorporation	fighting words	exclusionary rule
total incorporation	symbolic speech	probable cause
selective incorporation	prior restraint	Miranda warning

SUGGESTED READINGS

• Abraham, Henry J., and Barbara A. Perry. *Freedom and the Court: Civil Rights and Liberties in the United States.* 6th ed. New York: Oxford University Press, 1994. A comprehensive and highly readable survey of the Supreme Court's development of civil rights and liberties in the United States since the 1930s.

• Alderman, Ellen, and Caroline Kennedy. *In Our Defense: The Bill of Rights in Action.* New York: Avon Books, 1991. A timely journalistic account of the background and out-

come of several cases covered by the first ten amendments.

• Friendly, Fred W., and Martha J. H. Elliott. *The Constitution, That Delicate Balance: Landmark Cases That Shaped the Constitution.* New York: Random House, 1984. A fascinating account of sixteen major cases in civil liberties. Designed as a companion volume to the excellent videotape PBS series by the same name.

• Garrow, David J. *Liberty and Sexuality: The Right to Privacy and the Making of Roe v. Wade.* New York: Macmillan Press, 1994. A superb historical study of the Supreme Court's development of the right to privacy from *Griswold* v. *Connecticut* through *Roe* v. *Wade*.

- Lewis, Anthony. *Gideon's Trumpet*. New York: Vintage Press, 1966. Still the best one-volume account of a single Supreme Court case, in this instance the *Gideon* v. *Wainwright* case, which extended the right to counsel protections of the Sixth Amendment to state criminal defendants.

- ———. *Make No Law: The Sullivan Case and the First Amendment*. New York: Random House, 1991. An account of the development of the *New York Times* v. *Sullivan* case, in which the Supreme Court established the standards for libel by the press in cases involving public figures.

- O'Brien, David M. *Constitutional Law and Politics*. Volume 2: *Civil Rights and Civil Liberties*. New York: Norton, 1991. An excellent casebook containing cuttings of Supreme Court cases mixed with historical information and comprehensive charts showing the development of case law.

- Pritchett, C. Herman. *Constitutional Civil Liberties*. Englewood Cliffs, New Jersey: Prentice Hall, 1984. A complete survey of all of the case law in civil liberties broken down by amendment and subcategories within each amendment.

- Savage, David G. *Turning Right: The Making of the Rehnquist Supreme Court*. New York: Wiley, 1992. A well-researched journalistic behind-the-scenes account by the *Wall Street Journal's* Court reporter on the effort by the Rehnquist Court to shape legal doctrine in the civil rights and liberties area.

- Simon, James F. *The Center Holds: The Power Struggles Inside the Rehnquist Court*. New York: Simon & Schuster, 1995. An interesting account of the decision-making process of the current supreme court during the service of Chief Justice William Rehnquist.

- Weinreb, Lloyd L. *Leading Constitutional Cases on Criminal Justice*. Westbury, N.Y.: Foundation Press, 1995. A superb casebook on criminal-justice cases illustrating the development of legal doctrine in each of the amendments.

CHAPTER 15

CIVIL RIGHTS AND POLITICAL EQUALITY

CHAPTER OUTLINE

CASE STUDY: INTEGRATING YONKERS

INTRODUCTION: CIVIL RIGHTS AND DEMOCRACY

ESTABLISHING CONSTITUTIONAL EQUALITY

CREATING LEGAL SEGREGATION

ESTABLISHING LEGAL EQUALITY

THE CIVIL RIGHTS MOVEMENT

AFFIRMATIVE ACTION

WOMEN'S RIGHTS

CIVIL RIGHTS AND OTHER MINORITIES

CIVIL RIGHTS AND APPROACHING DEMOCRACY

I n August 1988 four members of the city council of Yonkers, New York, stood before a judge in a U.S. District Court. "I know of no parallel," the judge said, "for a court to say to an elected official, you are in contempt of court and subject to personal fines and may eventually be subject to personal imprisonment because of a

Integrating
Yonkers

manner in which you cast a vote. I find that extraordinary."

Yet that was what the judge was about to do. The Yonkers City Council had refused to put into effect a court-ordered plan to integrate housing in the city, and the judge was prepared to coerce them into doing so.

The struggle had begun in 1980, when the U.S. Department of Justice brought a desegregation suit against the city of Yonkers, charging that the city had discriminated against minorities in its housing policies and its school system. The U.S. Supreme Court had given federal judges broad powers to order remedies for such violations of civil rights. After a lengthy trial, federal district court judge Leonard B. Sand handed down a 277-page decision ruling that Yonkers was in violation of federal law and the Constitution. Judge Sand based his conclusion on the fact that the racial composition of the city's neighborhood schools was nearly identical to those of the surrounding communities, which were themselves segregated.

Judge Sand then ordered the city to prepare an acceptable plan for building public housing, which would have the effect of integrating the communities in which they were located. To desegregate the schools, the judge also ordered the creation of magnet schools (specialized schools to which students from many areas are bused). The city appealed the ruling, but without suc-

cess. By the end of September 1988 all but one of the city's schools were racially balanced, but since the surrounding communities were still segregated, there was much left to be done to achieve full integration.

When the judge indicated that such balance could only be achieved by changing the neighborhoods themselves, a new battle began. Claiming that Judge Sand had abused his authority as a federal judge, the Yonkers City Council indicated that it had no intention of complying with the court order to present a long-term housing plan. Previously, Judge Sand had persuaded the council to appoint an outside housing adviser who would identify sites for the required public housing, and the council had promised to build the housing on those sites. However, the reaction of community members was so hostile that the city council backed away from the plan, eventually notifying the judge that it was reneging on the deal.

Frustrated by the delays, the National Association for the Advancement of Colored People and the Department of Justice asked the court to prepare its own plan and order the city of Yonkers to carry it out. Judge Sand did so on June 13, 1988, only to have the city council declare a moratorium on all construction of public housing and all further legislative action on the matter. Judge Sand then ordered the city council to place the resolution regarding compliance with the housing order on its legislative agenda. Not surprisingly, when the resolution was placed on the agenda it was defeated. The judge then ruled that unless Yonkers passed an ordinance in favor of integrated public housing, the city would be fined and held in judicial contempt.

The city council considered the resolution again and this time defeated it by a vote of 4 to 3. Judge Sand responded:

There does have to come a moment of truth, a moment of reckoning, a moment when the City of Yonkers seeks not to become the national symbol of defiance to civil rights and to heap shame upon shame upon itself, but to recognize its obligation to conform to the laws of the land and not step by step, order by order, but in the way in which any responsible community concerned about the welfare of its citizens functions.

The four members of the city council who had voted against the resolution were held in contempt and fined.

The city appealed the court's order, charging that Judge Sand had exceeded his judicial authority in trying to force a legislator's vote. On September 1, 1988, the Supreme Court denied the city's application for a stay-of-contempt sanction, and one week later the Yonkers City Council voted to pass the housing ordinance. Finally, in May 1992, <u>twelve years</u> after the battle began, the first occupants began moving into the newly built, integrated public housing.[1]

Residents of Yonkers, New York, demonstrate outside the federal courthouse in 1988. Inside, members of their city council were being cited for contempt for opposing District Court Judge Sand's plan to create integrated public housing.

INTRODUCTION: CIVIL RIGHTS AND DEMOCRACY

When Rosa Parks refused to move from her seat on a bus in Montgomery, Alabama, she set off a boycott that eventually led to a federal court ruling that the city of Montgomery could not maintain its policy of segregated transportation. Despite the resolve and bravery of those involved in the boycott, however, the legal process took almost thirteen months before culminating in the decision that African Americans would be allowed to sit at the front of a bus. Nor did the story end there; in fact, it was only beginning.

Just as there was resistance to the Court's decree in Montgomery, in the Yonkers case study we see that nearly thirty years after the Supreme Court told the nation's public schools to desegregate "with all deliberate speed" in the landmark case of *Brown* v. *Board of Education* the goal seemed still to be out of reach. With such militant resistance to the decrees of Judge Sand in a northern and liberal city during the 1980s, is there any hope of approaching a democratic system of "equal rights for all" and "full participation by all" in the government? Often, the answer lies in our legal system. As you read this, legal battles for human rights are proceeding all around the country.

In this chapter we trace the history of civil rights in the United States, a history that did not really begin until the second half of the nineteenth century, when a nation recovering from a devastating civil war sought to establish equality of rights under the Constitution. But the real change did not come until nearly a century later. The period from 1896 to 1954 was spent debating the notion of legal equality, and from 1954 to 1968 the nation turned to the question of achieving actual equality. In the two decades that followed, debate centered on whether actual equality should be achieved, and if so, how.

Several groups within the U.S. population have suffered from discrimination at various periods in the nation's history, and many still do today. Although in much of this chapter we focus on the civil rights of African Americans and women, we also discuss the efforts of other groups, such as Hispanics and Native Americans, to obtain equal treatment. Not all of these groups are minorities. Women, for example, are not a numerical minority, but they have experienced discrimination throughout the nation's history and continue to encounter unequal treatment in the workplace and elsewhere.

Before discussing the history of civil rights, however, we need to clarify exactly what we mean by civil rights, equality, and discrimination.

Defining Civil Rights

Most people would agree that to truly approach democracy it is necessary to eliminate **discrimination,** that is, unequal treatment based on race, ethnicity, gender, and other distinctions. The primary means for achieving equal treatment is ensuring full protection of **civil rights,** the constitutionally guaranteed rights that may not be arbitrarily removed by the government. These rights are often referred to as natural, or inalienable, rights; they are believed to be granted by God or nature to all human beings. It was these rights that Thomas Jefferson had in mind when he wrote in the Declaration of Independence, "We hold these truths to be self-evident, that all men are created equal, that they are endowed by their Creator with certain unalienable Rights, that among these are Life, Liberty and the pursuit of Happiness."

Civil rights are closely linked with the ideal of equality. There are two basic forms of equality: equality before the law, or legal equality, and actual equality. Equality before the law, also called **de jure equality,** requires that there be no legally mandated obstacles to equal treatment, such as laws that prevent people from voting, living where they want to, or taking advantage of all the rights guaranteed to individuals by the laws of the federal, state, and local governments. Actual equality, also called **de facto equality,** looks at results: Do people live where they want to? Do they work under similar conditions? Do they have access to the same kinds of educational facilities? In a diverse and complex society like that of the United States it is often difficult to achieve de jure equality; it is even more difficult to create the conditions that will lead to de facto equality.

In the course of the nation's history there have been many turns along the road to equality, and while de jure equality has been achieved in some respects, de facto equality remains a distant objective. Let us look in more detail at the history of civil rights and the struggle for equality in the United States.

ESTABLISHING CONSTITUTIONAL EQUALITY

Although the Constitution was written to "secure the blessings of liberty to our-selves and our posterity," those blessings did not extend to African American slaves. This was not surprising; all references to slavery had been stricken from the Declaration of Independence, written eleven years before. Why did the constitutional framers ignore the plight of the slaves? And why did they choose to count "other persons"—that is, slaves—as only three-fifths of a person, with no rights at all? As we saw in Chapter 3, to create a constitution that would be ratified by a majority of the states the framers were forced to compromise. To preserve the economic position of the southern states, they allowed slavery to continue. But in doing so they also ensured that future battles would be fought over slavery.

Even for free African Americans, legal status varied in different regions of the country. By 1804 many northern states had either banned slavery or passed laws under which the children of slaves would be free. However, the right to vote was placed beyond the reach of most African Americans. In the South, measures were enacted that made the release of slaves extremely difficult.[2] At the federal level, Congress passed the Fugitive Slave Act, which allowed run-away slaves to be captured (even in parts of the nation where slavery was out-lawed) and returned to slave owners. African Americans were excluded by law from a procedure that enabled immigrants to become citizens (1790), from ser-vice in militias (1792), and from the right to carry the mail (1810).

In 1820, when the proposed introduction of Missouri as a slave state threat-ened to upset the equal division of slave and free states, the **Missouri Com-promise** was passed. Missouri was admitted along with the free state of Maine, and slavery was prohibited in the remainder of the Louisiana Purchase territory.

While some African Americans submitted to their condition, many others did not. Some withdrew psychologically; others committed suicide. Occasion-ally, they initiated violent uprisings, in which slave owners were killed. The most famous slave revolt occurred in August 1831, when Nat Turner led a re-bellion of about seventy slaves in Southhampton County, Virginia. In twelve hours of turmoil Turner's men killed dozens of whites. Eventually the insur-gents were defeated by hundreds of soldiers and militiamen, and Turner was executed along with scores of other slaves.

In the **Compromise of 1850,** which eliminated the slave trade and admit-ted California as a free state, the District of Columbia continued to permit sla-very, while the territories of New Mexico and Utah had no federal restrictions on slavery. In addition, Congress passed a stronger fugitive slave act, which provided for hundreds of additional federal officials to enforce it. The political prospects for equality seemed more remote than ever.

The Dred Scott Case

In 1856 the Supreme Court decided a case with far-reaching implications for the civil rights of African Americans. A slave named Dred Scott had been taken by his master from Missouri into the free state of Illinois and the free territory of Wisconsin. When his master died and Scott was returned to Missouri, he claimed that because he had lived in areas where slavery was illegal he was now a free man under the Missouri Compromise.

The case of *Dred Scott* v. *Sandford*[3] reached the Court at a time when the justices were seeking to settle the political differences between the North and the South. In a highly controversial decision, the Court ruled that Scott could not sue in federal court because no African American, free or enslaved, could ever become a citizen of the United States. According to Chief Justice Roger Taney, even if Scott was free he could not sue because African Americans were "not included, and were not intended to be included, under the word 'citizens' in the Constitution" and therefore had no rights under that document. Finally, the chief justice ruled that the Missouri Compromise was unconstitutional because Congress could not deprive people of their property rights, in this case slaves, under the due process clause of the Fifth Amendment.

The Civil War and Reconstruction

The *Dred Scott* case closed the door to judicial remedies for African Americans seeking legal protection. Political remedies were still open, however. By freeing the slaves in the Emancipation Proclamation of 1863, President Abraham Lincoln renewed the possibility of "equality for all." But for Lincoln's executive order to be implemented, Congress had to support it with legal authority. Thus, in the period following the Civil War Congress played a pivotal role in efforts to consider establishing equality for African Americans.

Congress drafted a series of constitutional amendments, known as the Civil War Amendments, that the defeated southern states had to ratify to rejoin the Union. The Thirteenth Amendment, which ensured that the slaves would remain free, was ratified in 1865 and reads as follows:

> Section 1.   Neither slavery nor involuntary servitude, except as a punishment for crime whereof the party shall have been duly convicted, shall exist within the United States, or in any place subject to their jurisdiction.

> Section 2.   Congress shall have power to enforce this article by appropriate legislation.

The Emancipation Proclamation now had constitutional authority, but what could be done to give African Americans legal protection against discrimination?

Led by a group of antidiscrimination members known as the Radical Republicans, Congress passed legislation allowing African Americans to testify against whites in federal courts (1864) and granting equal pay and benefits to all soldiers (1864). It also created the Freedmen's Bureau (1865), an agency of the War Department that was authorized to provide freed slaves with food, clothing, and sometimes land.

But the southern states were not yet ready to give up their traditional way of life. State legislatures passed laws, known as the *black codes,* that established labor practices designed to force the former slaves to remain on plantations. Congress did what it could to counteract these measures. Over President Andrew Johnson's vetoes, the Radical Republicans gave the Freedman's Bureau additional powers to settle labor disputes and nullify oppressive labor contracts. It also passed the Civil Rights Bill of 1866, which made African Americans U.S. citizens and empowered the federal government to protect their civil rights.

Since many members of Congress feared that the new law might not stand up in court, they drafted the Fourteenth Amendment to the Constitution, making African Americans citizens and giving them rights of that citizenship. Section I of the amendment states:

> All persons born or naturalized in the United States, and subject to the jurisdiction thereof, are citizens of the United States and of the State wherein they reside. No State shall make or enforce any law which shall abridge the privileges or immunities of citizens of the United States; nor shall any State deprive any person of life, liberty, or property, without due process of law; nor deny to any person within its jurisdiction the equal protection of the laws.

Section 5 of the amendment gave Congress the "power to enforce, by appropriate legislation, the provisions of this article." The new citizens were thus supposed to have the same rights as others, as well as be treated with fairness and equality under law.

Congress acted quickly. In 1867 it passed a law granting the newly freed African American citizens **suffrage,** or the right to vote. But it soon became evident that having the legal right to vote was not the same as having the actual ability to do so. Private groups like the Ku Klux Klan were formed with the goal of maintaining white supremacy by keeping African Americans from voting. The Klan attacked, beat, and sometimes killed African Americans who dared to stand up for their rights.

Realizing that more judicial power was needed, in 1870 Congress passed the Fifteenth Amendment, granting African Americans the right to vote. It reads: "The right of citizens of the United States to vote shall not be denied or abridged by the United States or any State on account of race, color, or previous condition of servitude." Again, Congress was given the power to "enforce this article by appropriate legislation." Because the Klan was a private organization, however, Congress also passed the Ku Klux Klan Act of 1871, making it a federal offense for two or more persons to conspire to deprive citizens of their equal protection and voting rights.

But the political branches of government could only create the tools for establishing legal equality. It remained to be seen whether the judicial branch would use those tools.

CREATING LEGAL SEGREGATION

In the post–Civil War period the Supreme Court showed little interest in enforcing the rights of African Americans. A prime example is the case of *United States* v. *Cruikshank* (1876).[4] In this case the Court considered the constitutionality of the Civil Rights Enforcement Laws of 1870, which made it a federal crime for private individuals to conspire to injure or oppress persons exercising their constitutional rights. William Cruikshank was part of a white mob that had murdered sixty African Americans in front of a courthouse. Since murder was not yet a federal offense and the state authorities had no intention of prosecuting anyone for the crime, the members of the mob were indicted for interfering with the murdered men's right to assemble. However, the Court ruled that under the Fourteenth Amendment only **state action,** or action by the state government under the color of law to deprive rights, was subject to decisions by the federal courts. In other words, the federal government could not prosecute *private individuals*. This ruling left the states free to ignore lynchings, assaults, and mob actions against African Americans within their borders.

Separate but Equal?

In the *Civil Rights Cases* (1883)[5] the Supreme Court applied its new "state-action" doctrine to overturn the Civil Rights Act of 1875, which prohibited racial segregation in transportation, inns, and theaters. The southern states thereupon passed a series of **Jim Crow** laws, which separated the races in public places such as trains, streetcars, schools, and cemeteries. This legal separation was challenged in the 1896 case of *Plessy* v. *Ferguson*.[6]

Homer Adolph Plessy, who was one-eighth African American, had sought to ride in a railroad car designated as "whites only" and had been arrested. The Supreme Court upheld the arrest, stating that the Fourteenth Amendment regulated only *legal* equality and not *social* equality. Therefore, the Court ruled that "separate but equal" facilities, or the notion that at least a superficial attempt to provide the same accommodations for different races in public places, did not violate the Fourteenth Amendment. According to Justice Henry Brown, any feelings of inferiority that African Americans might feel as a result of these conditions would be self-imposed and not a subject for judicial concern. The only dissenter to the Court's opinion was John Marshall Harlan, who argued that "our Constitution is color-blind, and neither knows nor tolerates classes among citizens." By that he meant that state laws should be absolutely neutral with respect to race.

The logical consequences of the *Plessy* ruling were revealed in *Cumming* v. *County Board of Education* (1899),[7] in which the Court approved "separate but equal" public schools in Kentucky. Though the facilities were not really "equal," by claiming they were, the Court could sanction segregation. It was not long before legally enforced segregation pervaded every other area of social life.

The Disenfranchisement of Black Voters

Seeking to disenfranchise African American voters, southern politicians invented loopholes in the voting laws, thus circumventing the Fifteenth Amendment. Since many freed slaves owned no land, property qualifications kept some of them off the voting rolls; literacy tests did the same for those who could not read. When these loopholes were found to exclude many poor whites, an "understanding clause" was used: People were permitted to vote only if they could properly interpret a portion of the state constitution. (Of course, there were different sections of the constitution and different standards for "proper interpretation" depending on the race of the test taker.)

Another loophole was the "grandfather clause," which exempted from property qualifications or literacy tests anyone whose relatives had voted before 1867, thus excluding the freed slaves. Some southern states also implemented a poll tax, that is, a fee for voting, which would exclude poor African Americans. Finally, since the Democratic party was, in effect, the only party in the South, states utilized whites-only primaries to select the Democratic candidate, making the votes of African Americans in the general election irrelevant.[8]

"Our Constitution is color-blind, and neither knows nor tolerates classes among citizens. In respect of civil rights, all citizens are equal before the law. The humblest is the peer of the most powerful. The law regards man as man, and takes no account of his surrounding or of his color when his civil rights as guaranteed by the supreme law of the land are involved."

—Justice John Harlan, 1896

For decades, the South was a racially divided society. Jim Crow laws helped to keep the races separate. These laws were based on the 1896 Supreme Court ruling in *Plessy* v. *Ferguson,* which upheld that all public facilities may be "separate but equal." This 1958 photo reveals two of the many practical applications of the ruling—separate drinking water and restroom facilities.

Thus, while African Americans were citizens of the United States, they were denied a voice in its government.

ESTABLISHING LEGAL EQUALITY

Around the turn of the century a movement sought to bring about greater equality in American society. In 1895 Booker T. Washington, a former slave who had founded Tuskegee University, argued that racism would eventually end if African Americans would accept their situation, work hard, and improve their education. On the other hand, W.E.B. DuBois, the first African American to earn a Ph.D. from Harvard, argued that all forms of racial segregation and discrimination should be aggressively attacked and eradicated.

In 1909 an interracial group called the National Association for the Advancement of Colored People (NAACP) was formed. Its primary strategy was to litigate on behalf of racial equality. In a series of cases decided between 1905 and 1914 the NAACP convinced the Court to use the Thirteenth Amendment to strike down **peonage,** in which employers advanced wages and then required workers to remain on their jobs, in effect enslaving them, until the debt was satisfied.

Encouraged by these successes, the NAACP supported a challenge to Oklahoma's voting grandfather clause. In *Guinn* v. *United States* (1915),[9] the Supreme Court struck down the provision as a violation of the Fifteenth Amendment.[10] Then, in 1927, the Court found that Texas's "white-primary" law violated the equal-protection clause of the Fourteenth Amendment.[11] Despite these successes, the southern states continued to disenfranchise blacks by reenacting the offending laws or inventing new loopholes. Clearly, a more general approach to protecting the civil rights of African Americans was needed.

The White House and Desegregation

During World War II the obvious inequity of expecting African Americans to fight for a country that did not afford them full protection of their civil rights gave rise to new efforts to achieve equality. This time the White House took the lead. President Franklin D. Roosevelt issued an order prohibiting discrimination in the defense business and creating a temporary wartime agency, the Fair Employment Practices Committee (FEPC), to investigate allegations of and provide compensation for such discrimination. In 1946, spurred by a spate of racial lynchings, President Harry Truman established a panel of citizens to examine the problem and recommend solutions.[12] He also issued an executive order making the FEPC a permanent executive branch agency.

But Truman's most significant action in relation to desegregation came in 1948, when he issued an executive order prohibiting segregation in the military and in federal employment. Truman also asked Congress to ban discrimination by private employers and labor unions, outlaw poll taxes, pass a federal antilynching law, create a permanent civil rights commission, and compel fair elections. However, these efforts were doomed by the opposition of conservative southerners who had split from the Democratic party under the leadership of South Carolina's Strom Thurmond to form the Dixiecrats. The struggle for equality now turned to the public-school system.

Achieving Racial Equality in South Africa

"They expect to be treated with dignity," commented an observer of the first fully democratic elections in South Africa. "Their status as a human being, as a South African, is nonnegotiable. Quite frankly, I feel that this election is more about honor and status than it is about houses and jobs."*

To a large extent, the struggle for dignity and status has been won. In recent years South African social and political life has been transformed as the system of racial segregation known as *apartheid* has been dismantled. Apartheid was a form of institutionalized racism that endured for almost five decades and left most black South Africans in a state of extreme poverty. Denied access to decent jobs, housing, and education, and rigidly separated from whites in all areas of daily life, many blacks were forced to perform menial work (*baaskop,* or work considered unfit for whites) and to live in backyard shacks or squatter camps. Today, their economic condition is improving very slowly, but they have achieved legal equality, and they are making full use of whatever opportunities are available to them.

In 1994, a policeman and a black woman celebrated the flourishing of democracy in South Africa as Nelson Mandela spoke at city hall in Cape Town. A historic first meeting of the new democratically elected Parliament had just named Mandela the country's first black president.

Besides voting, the most important area in which blacks are asserting their newly won rights is education. Schools are now open to children of all races, and black South Africans are enrolling their children in the best schools they can afford. Take the case of Henrietta Duma:

> Instead of enrolling her first-grade son in one of the battered, bookless local schools in Soweto, the black metropolis where she lives, she brought him to Suidheuwela Primary School, long a closed bastion of conservative, working-class white Afrikaners. . . . When she saw the books and toys and the broad green playing fields . . . , she did not begrudge the daily travel costs or the $190 in yearly fees that will come from her wages at the Pick 'N Pay supermarket.**

Although some feared that conflict and disruption would arise in the newly integrated schools, the children are getting along well. But not everyone can afford even the modest fees charged by semiprivate schools like Suidheuwela. There remains the problem of shifting teachers and funding to black schools—a problem similar to that faced by some large urban school districts in the United States.

It is clear that legal equality alone will not be enough to overcome the effects of decades of discrimination. But it is an all-important first step. Black South Africans realize that economic gains will come slowly. "They know the election doesn't mean then you are going to have a mansion," says one. In the meantime they are taking pride in what they have already achieved. This pride can be seen in the new "informal settlement" of Mandela Park, in which "the shacks are painted, numbered and customized—one even rises three stories on log pylons—and they are surrounded by flower beds, ornamental rock gardens, and lawns the size of throw rugs."[†]

---

*Quoted in Bill Keller, "Mandate for Human Dignity," *New York Times,* Apr. 27, 1994, p. A1.
**Bill Keller, "South Africa Opens Schools to All, and All's Well," *New York Times,* Jan. 14, 1994, p. 1.
[†]Keller, "Mandate for Human Dignity," p. A8.

Seeking Equality in the Schools

NAACP attorneys had long been planning a comprehensive legal attack on segregation in the public schools. Initially, their strategy was to work within the separate but equal standard, using a series of test cases to show that certain educational facilities were not in fact equal. In 1938 the NAACP challenged a Missouri statute that met the state's separate but equal requirement by offering tuition refunds to African Americans who attended an out-of-state law school. The Supreme Court overturned the law, stating that students who were required to go to out-of-state schools would be burdened by inconveniences and costs not imposed on students who attended law schools in their home state.[13]

In 1950, under the leadership of Thurgood Marshall, the NAACP challenged the University of Texas Law School's separate but equal plan, in which African American students were taught in the basement of an Austin office building rather than at the highly regarded state university. While the justices agreed that the two "separate" schools were not "equivalent" in any respect, for the first time the Court went beyond such physical differences to point out the constitutional importance of the intangible psychological differences represented by the differing academic environments, such as the differences in the prestige of the faculty, the students, and the law review.[14] On the same day, the Court ruled that Oklahoma could not satisfy its separate but equal requirement for graduate schools by forcing an African American student to sit in the doorway during class, study in a special section of the library, and eat at a table in the cafeteria labeled "For Colored Only."[15]

"Equal means getting the same thing, at the same time, and in the same place."

—Thurgood Marshall, during oral argument in *Brown* v. *Board of Education*

Now that the Court had ruled that psychologically "separate" facilities could not be considered equal in graduate education, Marshall and the NAACP were ready to take direct aim at overturning the separate but equal doctrine as applied to public schools. Suits were initiated to challenge the segregated school districts of four states (Kansas, Delaware, South Carolina, and Virginia) and the District of Columbia. The NAACP's strategy was to attack the *Plessy* decision by focusing on the "intangible" psychological effects of separate but equal public-school facilities.

Because all of the precedents supported *Plessy,* the only way to convince the Court to change its position was to present evidence from social-scientific research on the effects of segregation. An example was a series of studies by psychologist Kenneth Clark, who discovered that when African American schoolchildren were shown white and black dolls and asked which one they would prefer to be, they invariably chose the white doll. On the basis of such findings, Marshall argued that segregation had a devastating effect on African American children's self-esteem and that therefore the education received in separate educational facilities could never be equal.

In 1952 the Supreme Court decided to combine the four state cases and rule on them under *Brown* v. *Board of Education of Topeka, Kansas.*[16] Rather than handing down a decision, however, it called for reargument of the case. At about this time Chief Justice Fred Vinson died suddenly, leading Justice Felix Frankfurter, who realized the impact of this change for the *Brown* case, to say, "This is the first indication I have ever had that there is a God." The new chief justice, former California governor Earl Warren, was far more willing to use his political skills to persuade all of the justices, even Kentuckian Stanley Reed, to rule against segregation. On May 17, 1954, Warren announced the Court's unanimous decision that the separate but equal standard was henceforth unconstitutional. Warren argued that the importance of education in contemporary society was greater than it had been at the time of the *Plessy* ruling and stated that segregated schools put African American children at a disadvantage and thereby violated the equal-protection clause of the Fourteenth Amendment. On the same day, relying on the Fifth Amendment's due process clause to deal with schools under federal government supervision, the Court also struck down segregation in Washington D.C.'s public schools.[17]

A year later the Court issued a second statement on *Brown* v. *Board of Education* (commonly referred to as *Brown II*) dealing with implementation of the decision.[18] All of the cases were ordered back to the lower federal courts, which in turn would supervise plans for **desegregation,** or the elimination of laws and practices mandating segregation. The plans were to be implemented "with all deliberate speed." Missing from the Court's statement was a direct order to compel **integration,** efforts to balance the social composition of the schools. As is evident in the case of the Yonkers City Council, described at the beginning of the chapter, "deliberate speed" can be the pace of a snail or of a train, depending on the attitude of the decision makers.

Oliver Brown of Topeka, Kansas, was unhappy that his seven-year-old daughter Linda (front), could not attend the local all-white public school and instead had to travel across town to school. In 1950, Brown (shown with his family) decided to sue in federal court. His family's case became the lead case in Thurgood Marshall and the NAACP's legal challenge to "separate but equal" public schools. The case, *Brown* v. *Board of Education,* made its way to the Supreme Court. In 1954 the Court ruled in Brown's favor, upholding that segregated public schools are inherently unconstitutional.

State and Federal Responses

State governments responded to the *Brown* decision in a variety of ways. In Washington, D.C.; Kansas; and Delaware some progress toward desegregation was made. In the Deep South, however, violence directed against African American activists increased. In some places mobs gathered to block African Americans from attending previously segregated public schools and universities. State legislatures also took steps to fight the *Brown* decision. Some forbade state officials to enforce the decision, while others closed the public schools in some districts and paid the private-school tuitions of Caucasian children.[19] If any progress was to be made toward desegregation in the South, it would be up to the federal government.

Initially, with the exception of fifty-eight courageous federal district court judges in the South, the federal government was no more willing to take desegregation action than the states.[20] Southern politicians took President Eisenhower's ambivalence as a signal to continue their discriminatory practices without White House interference. Only reluctantly did the president decide to send federal troops to Little Rock, Arkansas, to help nine African American students desegregate the region's Central High School in the face of strong opposition (which included the deployment of state national guard units to prevent the students from entering the school).

Eisenhower also signed into law the Civil Rights Act of 1957, which created a Civil Rights Commission to recommend legislation and gave the Justice Department the power to initiate lawsuits on behalf of African Americans who were denied the right to vote. Then, in the Civil Rights Act of 1960, the Attorney General was authorized to call in federal officials to investigate voter registration in areas where discrimination may be occurring. Eisenhower also ended segregation in the military and federal government employment. While the Eisenhower administration did not use its new power vigorously, it did

On September 3, 1957, nine African American students asserted their rights under the *Brown* ruling, and attempted unsuccessfully to enroll at the public Central High School in Little Rock, Arkansas. Here, one of the students calmly walks by a jeering mob and a line of national guard troops sent by the state's governor to bar African American students from entering the school.

Three weeks later, President Eisenhower sent in federal troops to integrate the school. When the local school board resisted, the Supreme Court ruled in a rare unanimous opinion that the integration process must continue.

FYI

Perhaps the clearest view of the importance of the *Brown* case comes from Georgia representative John Lewis, an African American, who in 1994 commented on the impact of the case: "This country is a different country now. It is a better country. We have witnessed a nonviolent revolution."

demonstrate that the federal government could be effective, if it wished, in protecting civil rights. In the meantime, however, the struggle for equality was carried on by the people most affected—African Americans themselves.

THE CIVIL RIGHTS MOVEMENT

The modern civil rights protests began with Rosa Parks's refusal to give up her seat on a bus, which led to the bus boycott in Montgomery, Alabama, in 1957. Shortly afterward African American activists founded the Southern Christian Leadership Conference (SCLC), which was composed of civil rights advocates from throughout the South and headed by a charismatic leader, the Reverend Martin Luther King, Jr. Like Mahatma Gandhi of India, King preached the use of **civil disobedience,** that is, breaking the law in a nonviolent fashion and being willing to suffer the consequences, even to the point of going to jail, to publicly demonstrate that the law is unjust. To illustrate: A group, such as African Americans, denied access to the lending facilities of the town library might take books to that library and read them there, making it impossible for others to use the facilities, until the protesters are removed by law enforcement officers. Or, as in the Montgomery case, protesters might **boycott,** or refuse to patronize, a business that practices segregation. Another kind of demonstration is the **protest march,** in which people walk down a main street carrying signs, singing freedom songs, and chanting slogans. During the early years of the civil rights protests, counterprotesters frequently lined the streets to jeer at the marchers, and law enforcement officials, blaming the protesters for the disturbances in the audience, tried to break up the protest, using everything from clubs to firehoses.

The concept of civil disobedience was not confined to the SCLC. Inspired by the Montgomery boycott, in 1958 Oklahoma City's NAACP Youth Council decided to protest the segregation of lunch counters by sitting down on the stools and refusing to leave when they were not served. This protest technique became known as a **sit-in,** and it proved to be very effective. In 1960 four African American students used this technique, entering a Woolworth store in Greensboro, South Carolina, and sitting down at the segregated lunch counter. When they were refused service, they simply sat there and studied until the store closed. During the following days others, both African American and white, joined the protest, and soon more than a thousand people were sitting in at segregated eating establishments in Greensboro. The Greensboro protest gained national attention, and college students throughout the South began engaging in sit-ins. Many of the protesters were arrested, convicted, and jailed, thereby drawing further attention to the movement. The tide of public opinion turned, and eating establishments throughout the South began to desegregate.

Beginning in 1961, civil rights activists called **"freedom riders"** began traveling throughout the South on buses to test compliance with the Supreme Court's mandate to integrate bus terminals accommodating interstate travelers. In Anniston, Birmingham, and Montgomery, Alabama, the freedom riders were attacked by mobs while local police made themselves scarce. When a crowd threatened to burn down a church in which King was giving a speech to honor the freedom riders, Attorney General Robert Kennedy called in U.S. marshals to maintain order. However, the White House did not guarantee protection for protesters once they crossed state lines, and three hundred freedom riders were put in Mississippi jails.

During the same period the federal government worked with civil rights leaders to register African American voters in the hope of creating a legal revolution from within the system. With the aid of the Justice Department, the privately funded Voter Education Project began a campaign to enforce the voting rights provisions of the Civil Rights Act of 1957. As a result of these efforts, African American voter registration in the South rose from 26 to 40 percent between 1962 and 1964.[21]

Meanwhile the civil rights movement was encountering increasingly violent resistance. When extremists began harassing and even killing civil rights activists, the White House was forced to act. In 1962 federal troops were sent to Mississippi to protect an African American student, James Meredith, as he registered at the University of Mississippi. Then, in the spring of 1963, Martin Luther King decided to protest segregation in Birmingham with a series of demonstrations and marches designed to trigger a response by the segregationist police commissioner "Bull" Connor. The protest began with marches and sit-ins at segregated businesses, to which Connor responded by arresting protesters, including King himself, and obtaining a court injunction to prevent further demonstrations. Later, a thousand protesting children were put in jail. Finally, after Connor attacked nonviolent protesters with vicious police dogs and firehoses spewing water so forcefully that it stripped the bark off large trees, President John F. Kennedy sent Justice Department officials to Birmingham to work out a compromise, and business leaders agreed to desegregate their

Reverend Martin Luther King gained national attention for his leadership during the bus boycott in Alabama. Here he is shown being arrested in Montgomery, Alabama, in 1958 for "loitering" near a courthouse where one of his civil rights allies was being tried. King charged that he was beaten and choked by the arresting officers.

President Lyndon B. Johnson signs the 1964 Civil Rights Act into law as the crowd waits for commemorative signature pens. Note the pleased expression of the Reverend Martin Luther King (behind the president). Also note the unhappy expression of North Carolina senator Sam Ervin (at far left), one of the Southern conservative Dixiecrat Democrats. The Dixiecrats were very unhappy with the efforts of their fellow southerner, President Johnson, to expand the democratic rights of African Americans.

establishments. However, the night after the compromise was announced, bombs went off at the hotel where King was staying. Riots broke out, and peace was not restored until President Kennedy sent federal troops to a nearby fort and threatened to dispatch them to Birmingham if the violence continued.

The Civil Rights Acts

The civil rights movement had made great progress toward equality in the early 1960s, but there was still a long way to go. To succeed, it needed more effective legal tools. In 1963 President Lyndon Johnson urged Congress in the name of the assassinated President Kennedy to "enact a civil rights law so that we can move forward to eliminate from this nation every trace of discrimination and oppression that is based upon race or color." And Congress responded. The Twenty-fourth Amendment, which prohibited the use of poll taxes in federal elections, had been passed the in 1962. Then, after a fifty-seven-day filibuster led by southern senators but broken by the arm-twisting of President Johnson, Congress passed the Civil Rights Act of 1964.

The 1964 act was extremely comprehensive and greatly increased the federal government's ability to fight discrimination (its provisions are listed in Table 15.1). Because the government could withdraw funds from segregated schools and the attorney general was empowered to initiate school desegregation suits, African Americans would no longer have to rely on the slow case-by-case approach to ending school segregation. Moreover, by creating the Equal Employment Opportunity Commission (EEOC) and placing authority in the hands of the Commissioner of Education, the act put the power of the federal bureaucracy behind efforts to end discrimination.

The Voting Rights Act of 1965 was another step toward racial equality. Areas mostly in the south with long histories of discrimination where less than 50 percent of the population had been registered to vote or had voted in the 1964 presidential election, creating a presumption that blacks were being deprived of the right to vote, were automatically found to be in violation of the law. In those areas the use of literacy tests and similar devices was prohibited and no new voting qualifications could be required without the approval of the attorney general. The law also mandated that federal examiners be sent to those areas to assist in the registration of voters and to observe elections.

In addition to calling for this legislation, the president issued executive orders that brought the federal bureaucracy into the fight for civil rights. Among other things, Johnson instructed the Civil Service Commission to guarantee equal opportunity in federal employment, directed the secretary of labor to administer nondiscrimination policies in the awarding of government contracts, and ordered the attorney general to implement the section of the Civil Rights Act of 1964 that withdrew federal funds from any racially discriminatory programs.

By 1965 the federal government was clearly at the forefront of the struggle to end discrimination and guarantee the civil rights of all Americans. However, it remained to be seen whether the provisions of the new laws were constitutional.

Table 15.1
Major Provisions of the Civil Rights Act of 1964

Title I:	Banned any state actors from using different standards when registering people to vote, prohibited denying the right to vote because of an error in registration, and severely limited the use of literacy tests in federal elections.
Title II:	Prohibited discrimination by private businesses connected with interstate commerce. Combining its authority to regulate interstate commerce with its power to enforce the Fourteenth Amendment, Congress barred discrimination by restaurants, gas stations, hotels, theaters, and other businesses that could be shown to have any impact on interstate commerce. Both private citizens and the attorney general were given the power to begin lawsuits against businesses that violated the law.
Title III:	Gave the attorney general the power to initiate law suits contesting discriminatory practices in all public facilities except public schools.
Title IV:	Authorized the attorney general to begin a school desegregation suit if a complaint was filed. Also required the commissioner of education to assist local school boards that needed to develop desegregation plans.
Title V:	Gave the Civil Rights Commission the power to investigate all cases in which people claimed that they were deprived of equal protection.
Title VI:	Banned discrimination in any program that received federal funds and cut off funds from programs that continued to discriminate.
Title VII:	Prohibited discrimination in employment and created the Equal Employment Opportunity Commission (EEOC), a five-member body, which had the power to enforce the law.

The Supreme Court and Civil Rights

Less than six months after Congress passed the Civil Rights Act of 1964, two cases challenging its constitutionality reached the Supreme Court. In *Heart of Atlanta Motel* v. *United States*,[22] the proprietor of a motel claimed that as a private businessman and not a "state actor" he was not subject to Congress's power to enforce the Fourteenth Amendment. The Court ruled that since the motel was accessible to interstate travelers, and thus was engaging in interstate commerce, Congress could regulate it under the interstate commerce clause of Article I. In *Katzenbach* v. *McClung*,[23] the justices noted that while Ollie's Barbecue (in Birmingham, Alabama) had few interstate customers, it obtained supplies through interstate commerce; therefore, it too was subject to congressional regulation. After these decisions private businesses began voluntarily ending their discriminatory practices rather than risk losing costly lawsuits.

In 1966, in the case of *Harper* v. *Virginia Board of Elections,*[24] the Court held that all poll taxes, even those imposed by states, violated the equal-protection clause of the Fourteenth Amendment. By the end of the 1960s the number of African American voters in the Deep South had almost doubled.[25] This new voting bloc eventually defeated segregationist candidates, changed the views of politicians who had formerly favored segregation, and elected many African Americans to office at all levels of government. But while African Americans were gaining de jure equality, they were still far from de facto equality.

De Jure versus De Facto Discrimination

The "War on Poverty" declared by President Johnson in 1964 was in part an attempt to address the problem of racial inequality. But African American communities continued to be plagued by poverty, and it became evident to people throughout the nation that discrimination and its effects were not limited to the South. When civil rights groups began to concentrate on the discrimination that existed in the North, their arguments changed considerably. In the South, segregation had been de jure, or sanctioned by law. In the North, however, segregation was more likely to be de facto; that is, it had developed out of social, economic, and other nongovernmental factors. In the case of school segregation in Yonkers, for example, the problem was the de facto social discrimination resulting from patterns of housing in the city. That was why Judge Sand was concerned with the location of public housing. But how does one change the historical living patterns of a city or region?

As this problem was being considered, a major tragedy, the assassination of Martin Luther King, was turned into a dramatic achievement. Nine days after King's death on April 4, 1968, President Johnson signed into law the Civil Rights Act of 1968, which banned housing discrimination of all types. A few weeks later the Supreme Court upheld the government's power to regulate private housing, doing so by relying on the Civil Rights Act of 1866, which guaranteed all citizens the rights "to inherit, purchase, lease, sell, hold, and convey real and personal property."[26] Justice Potter Stewart linked this law to the Thirteenth Amendment's guarantee to eliminate "badges and incidents of slavery," saying that discrimination in housing "herds men into ghettos and makes the ability to buy property turn on the color of their skin." Now a home owner who wished to sell a house was required to sell it to any financially qualified buyer. In the future, the selling practices of home owners would not be permitted to create racially divided neighborhoods. But the question of what could be done about the racially divided neighborhoods that already existed, and about the segregated schools that resulted from those divisions, remained.

In 1969 the Supreme Court, tired of the continuing delay in school desegregation fifteen years after the *Brown* decision, ruled in *Alexander* v. *Holmes County Board of Education*[27] that every school district must "terminate dual school systems at once and . . . operate now and hereafter only unitary schools." In other words, they must desegregate immediately. School districts in the South complied within eight years, becoming the most integrated schools in the nation.[28] But in northern cities, where de facto segregation still existed, there was little progress.

Forty Years after Brown

In Topeka, Kansas, elementary schools were deliberately segregated before the Supreme Court's landmark ruling in 1954 in *Brown* v. *Board of Education of Topeka*. Today they are still segregated, only now the segregation is not deliberate. It is a result of segregation in housing patterns.

Like most other cities in the United States, Topeka has some neighborhoods that are predominantly white and some that are predominantly black. Children attend schools whose racial composition reflects that of the neighborhood in which they are located. Throughout the nation nearly 70 percent of black students attend schools where the majority of the students are black or Hispanic. These patterns are a result of a variety of social and economic trends that have left less affluent blacks and other minorities concentrated in inner-city neighborhoods while more affluent blacks and most whites moved to the suburbs.

In 1979 the American Civil Liberties Union reopened the *Brown* suit, charging that the existence of thirteen racially segregated schools in Topeka violated the Court's 1954 ruling. The case was not settled until 1993, when a federal court directed the Topeka school district to take actions that would increase integration. The district drew up plans to close several segregated schools, bus more students across neighborhood lines, and create magnet schools.

The Topeka case illustrates a problem that has proven extremely difficult to solve. In the decades since 1954, school districts have attempted to desegregate schools by means of busing programs that transport black children to predominantly white schools, magnet schools designed to attract white students from the suburbs, and school closings and consolidations designed to achieve racial balance.

But these efforts have not succeeded in eliminating school segregation.

The Civil Rights Act of 1968 was in part an attempt to correct this situation. It was hoped that giving members of minority groups the right to buy homes wherever they wished would lead to the creation of integrated neighborhoods and, hence, to integrated schools. But few minority buyers could afford homes in affluent suburban neighborhoods, and low-cost public housing was available almost exclusively in the inner cities. The problem was compounded by the unethical practices of biased real-estate agents and landlords.

Despite the many obstacles in the path of school integration (70 percent of African American children still attend segregated schools), there are some hopeful signs. In southern Florida, Palm Beach County called on developers to advertise to African American buyers with the aim of selling houses to a wider racial mix; some communities also altered their building codes to allow the construction of more modestly priced homes. Another innovative approach is the creation of workplace schools, such as the elementary school at Miami International Airport. The school is attended by children of the airport's white, black, Hispanic, and Asian employees. Similar schools are operated by the nation's sixteen military bases. The effectiveness of this approach can be seen in a remark by a woman whose daughters attend school at Fort Benning, Georgia: "When I talk to my children about their friends, I must admit the only way I know their color is when I see them. I'm kind of proud of that."*

---

*Quoted in William Celis III, "40 Years after Brown, Schools Still Struggle to End Segregation," *New York Times,* May 18, 1994, pp. A1, B7.

How far would a school district have to go to end segregation? Did the Court's command require that school districts undertake to *integrate* schools? Did it mean that schools would have to bus children of different races to schools outside their neighborhoods to achieve racial balance? In 1971 the

Few photographs depict more powerfully the divisions and resentment that arose from the struggle for civil rights than this one, taken in Boston in 1976. While the city was debating a federal district court judge's order to bus students to desegregate the public schools, a white protester marching toward the federal courthouse used a flagpole to attack an African American who was just in the wrong place at the wrong time.

Court considered these questions in the case of *Swann v. Charlotte-Mechlenburg Board of Education*.[29] It held that busing, racial quotas, and other techniques were constitutionally acceptable means of remedying past discrimination. Two years later, in *Keyes v. School District #1, Denver, Colorado,*[30] the Court ruled that even if there had previously been no law mandating segregation in the schools, school districts could be found to have discriminated if they had adopted other policies that led to segregation. Moreover, a finding of segregation in one part of a city could lead to a ruling that a citywide desegregation plan must be implemented even for parts of the city that were not segregated. This blurring of the distinction between de jure and de facto discrimination enabled Judge Sand to order the Yonkers city council to desegregate even though Yonkers had not engaged in de jure segregation.

In the early 1970s the political and legal climate changed, and the civil rights movement suffered a setback. After ruling unanimously in every racial case since *Brown,* the Supreme Court became increasingly divided. Encouraged by this division, people who felt that their neighborhood schools were threatened by busing and other integration programs made their views known, and political opposition to desegregation grew. In 1972 and 1974, congressional efforts to restrict the use of busing to remedy segregation were narrowly defeated. In 1976, however, opponents of busing managed to remove the power of the Department of Health, Education and Welfare (HEW) to cut off federal funds for school districts that refused to use busing as a remedy.

Amid the turmoil surrounding busing, the Supreme Court heard the case of *Milliken v. Bradley* (1974),[31] which asked whether the courts could go beyond the city limits of Detroit in requiring programs to remedy segregation. In Detroit as in many other cities, whites had left the inner city to live in the suburbs, and only a plan that bused suburban children to inner-city schools or inner-city children to suburban schools would achieve racial balance. However, arguing that the local operation of schools is a "deeply rooted" tradition, the Court ruled that since there had been no official acts of discrimination, the Detroit desegregation plan could not include the suburban school districts.

During the 1980s busing remained so controversial that the Justice Department turned instead to other measures, such as the creation of "magnet schools," or schools with special curricula designed to attract interested students from all parts of a city. (Recall that magnet schools were one of the devices used by Judge Sand in requiring the Yonkers school district to desegregate.) But the struggle for de facto equality was not limited to public schools. Discrimination in other areas of social life, such as employment and higher education, was coming under increased public scrutiny. Much of that scrutiny focused on efforts to make up for past discrimination through an approach known as affirmative action.

AFFIRMATIVE ACTION

In this section we turn to one of the most controversial aspects of the search for equality: programs that seek to increase equality but create temporary inequalities in the process. Such programs are collectively known as **affirmative action.** They attempt to improve the chances of minority applicants for jobs, housing, employment, government contracts, or graduate admissions by giving them a "boost" relative to white applicants with roughly the same qualifications. This is done, it is argued, because past discrimination has made it impossible for members of minority groups to achieve equality without such a boost. The problem, of course, is that such efforts appear to discriminate against white applicants. Affirmative action thus raises difficult questions about the nation's commitment to equality and the extent to which the civil rights of all citizens can be protected.

Seeking Full Equality: Opportunity or Result?

At the beginning of the chapter we distinguished between legal equality and actual equality. Much of the discussion so far has described the history of efforts to remove obstacles to legal equality. We have seen that removing legal obstacles does not automatically result in actual equality; often, doing so gives rise to a new set of questions. In particular, does "actual equality" mean equality of opportunity or equality of result?

Underlying the goal of **equality of opportunity** is the idea that "people should have equal rights and opportunities to develop their talents."[32] This implies that all people should begin at the same starting point in a race. But what if life's circumstances make that impossible, placing members of different groups at different starting points, some much farther behind others? For example, a person born into a poor minority family in which no one has ever graduated from high school is likely to be much less prepared for admission to college than a person born into a highly educated family. Because of such differences, many people feel that the nation should aim instead for **equality of result:** All forms of inequality, including economic disparities, should be completely eradicated. This may mean giving some people an advantage at the start so that everyone will complete the race at the same point.

Source: Reprinted by permission: Tribune Media Services.

To better understand this concept, consider an example. Imagine that a state's constitution has established that all persons within the state's boundaries possess "equal rights under the law." All persons thus have a right to an equal share of fishing rights in the state's only lake, which provides food for all. They now have full legal equality. However, immigrants from a neighboring state soon discover that the prime fishing areas are not available to them because the native-born citizens have established their residences on the lake shore and know the prime fishing spots and times. The immigrants have legal equality, but they do not have actual equality because while they can fish, their chances of getting a good catch are not very high. They have not achieved equality of result: Their nets contain far fewer fish than the nets of native-born citizens.

Some citizens argue that everyone has a legal opportunity to fish and that if the immigrants were better at it they would have better results. What these citizens do not acknowledge is the fear that if the immigrants were able to catch more fish, the number caught by the native-born citizens would decrease. Should the state reserve a special fishing opportunity for immigrants to create equality of result in terms of the number of fish caught?

As you can see, these two forms of equality—opportunity and result—are often in conflict. In a democracy, does providing rights or resources for one group take away rights from others? And if it does, would the action be undemocratic, or would it further approach democracy by improving the well-being of all? Judge Sand can order the Yonkers schools to integrate, but should he force the creation of integrated public housing and schools in an effort to seek actual equality? Even if he takes this action, he cannot personally change the attitudes of those who think that protecting the civil rights of others will diminish their own rights. This is the challenge facing those who argue that achieving equality of result sometimes means that equality of opportunity for some must be limited.

Affirmative action was a logical extension of the desegregation effort, but it raised the questions we have just discussed. Its proponents argued that in allowing minority candidates to compete on a more level playing field by first tilting the field in their favor, affirmative action would eventually produce equality. In some programs, called **quota programs,** the concept was taken a step further to guarantee a certain percentage of admissions, new hires, or promotions to members of minority groups. Opponents of affirmative action, however, labeled it "reverse discrimination" and argued that the provision of benefits solely on the basis of membership in a minority group would deny those benefits to other, more deserving candidates who had not themselves discriminated against minorities. In other words, equality of result for minorities took away equality of opportunity for majority applicants.

Affirmative action began with an executive order issued by President Johnson in 1965 requiring that federal contractors give a slight edge to minority applicants who were not quite equal to nonminority applicants. Between 1968 and 1971 the newly created Office of Federal Contract Compliance Programs (OFCCP) issued guidelines for federal contractors establishing certain "goals and timetables" if the percentages of African Americans and women they employed were lower than the percentages of those groups in the total workforce. Although the OFCCP's requirements dealt only with federal contractors, in 1972 Congress passed the Equal Employment Opportunity Act, which gave the Equal Employment Opportunity Commission the power to take employers to court if they did not eliminate discrimination in their hiring practices.

Those who supported affirmative action hailed these actions; they believed that discrimination that had nothing to do with job performance could be eliminated by these means. Those who opposed affirmative action believed that these "guidelines" and "goals" amounted to quotas that would exclude more-qualified white applicants. They argued that the Constitution was, and should be, "color-blind." Even the ultraliberal William O. Douglas expressed the opinion that the Fourteenth Amendment should be used "in a racially neutral way."[33]

The issue of affirmative action and quota programs reached the Supreme Court in 1978 in the case of *Regents of the University of California* v. *Bakke*.[34] At issue was a voluntary policy of the University of California Medical School at Davis, in which sixteen of the school's one hundred openings were set aside for minorities, who were given an advantage in admissions. Alan Bakke, a white male, claimed that the policy had deprived him of admission even though he was more qualified than some of the minority candidates who had been admitted. Four of the justices wanted to rule that the University of California's policy violated the Civil Rights Act of 1964 because the use of quotas discriminated on the basis of "race, color, religion, sex, or national origin." Four other justices wanted to uphold the university's policy of affirmative action as an appropriate remedy for the nationwide scarcity of African American doctors. The deciding vote was cast by Justice Louis Powell, who agreed in part with both groups. Powell argued that the university's admissions policy violated both the Civil Rights Act and the Fourteenth Amendment's equal-protection clause, because through its quota program it provided specific benefits for students solely on the basis of race. However, Powell also argued that since schools had "a substantial interest" in promoting a diverse student body, admission policies that took race, ethnicity, and social and economic factors into account, while not employing strict quotas, could be constitutional.

Confusion reigned after the *Bakke* decision, since many programs claimed not to use quotas yet accepted the same percentages of minority candidates

"The Equal Protection Clause commands the elimination of racial barriers, not their creation in order to satisfy our theory as to how society ought to be organized. The purpose of the University of Washington cannot be to produce black lawyers for blacks, Polish lawyers for Poles, Jewish lawyers for Jews, Irish lawyers for Irish. It should be to produce good lawyers for Americans."

—Justice William O. Douglas, 1974

Chipping Away at Affirmative Action

In 1992 the Center for Individual Rights persuaded the U.S. Court of Appeals for the District of Columbia to strike down a federal policy giving minorities preference in the awarding of radio licenses. In 1994 the Washington Legal Foundation won a ruling barring the University of Maryland from setting aside scholarships for African American students. The ruling was upheld by the Supreme Court a year later. Also in 1994, a federal district court judge ruled that the affirmative action admissions system at the University of Texas Law School was unconstitutional. And in 1995, the Supreme Court refused to uphold a federal affirmative action government contracts program.

These decisions reflect a trend that is gaining strength. Bolstered by a shift in public opinion, conservative public-interest law firms are going to court on behalf of clients who feel that they have been discriminated against by affirmative action—namely, whites, men, and property owners. But the attack on affirmative action is not limited to the courts. A conservative movement in California is seeking to bring affirmative action to a yes-or-no vote, probably in a state referendum to be held before the fall of 1996. A no vote would make California the first state to outlaw programs that extend special economic or educational privileges to individuals on the basis of their race or sex. The goal is to "restore true color-blind fairness in the United States," according to one of the movement's leaders.*

Opinions differ on whether there is continued need for affirmative action programs. The Glass Ceiling Commission, appointed by the federal government to conduct a study of barriers to promo-

tion, found that "many middle- and upper-level white male managers view the inclusion of minorities and women in management as a direct threat to their own chances for advancement"** and find numerous ways of stymieing the efforts of women and minorities to climb the corporate ladder. Other observers point to recent increases in the proportions of managerial positions held by women and minorities, claiming that these trends cannot be attributed to affirmative action but are due simply to greater equality of opportunity.

Efforts to eliminate or modify affirmative action draw support from the findings of public-opinion polls, which show that about two out of three Americans have serious doubts about the fairness of affirmative action, especially when it involves hiring quotas and contract set-asides. Even some longtime supporters of affirmative action believe that the approach has outlived its usefulness. Noting that affirmative action was never meant to be permanent, they recommend alternative approaches such as extending preferences on the basis of economic need. The debate is heating up, and the issue will no doubt occupy a prominent place in the 1996 presidential election campaign.

*Quoted in B. Drummond Ayres, Jr., "Conservatives Forge New Strategy to Challenge Affirmative Action," *New York Times,* Feb. 16, 1995, p. A1.

**Glass Ceiling Commission, "Good for Business: Making Full Use of the Nation's Human Capital," quoted in Peter T. Kilborn, "Women and Minorities Still Face 'Glass Ceiling,'" *New York Times,* Mar. 16, 1995, p. A22.

each year. The Court tried a year later to refine its mandate in a case involving the use of affirmative action in employment. In *United Steel Workers* v. *Weber*[35] it considered an affirmative action program designed to increase the numbers of African Americans employed in skilled jobs at the Kaiser Aluminum and Chemical Corporation. The company's training program guaranteed that half of the openings at its plant in Gramercy, Louisiana, would be filled by African Americans. The Court ruled that the Kaiser plan did not violate the Civil Rights Act, since the purpose of the act was to remedy the *effects* of past discrimination. In 1980 the Court reinforced this judgment in upholding a program in which 10 percent of the grants in the 1977 Public Works Employment Act were set aside for minority-owned businesses.[36]

Affirmative action remained controversial, however. Even those who might benefit from the policy opposed it, believing that it stigmatized individuals who wished to compete on their own merits. According to one critic, affirmative action programs "entail the assumption that people of color cannot at present compete on the same playing field with people who are white."[37] In other words, equality enforced through affirmative action is not the same as equality won by one's own merits. Nevertheless, proponents of affirmative action continued to argue that because of the effects of past discrimination, true equality could not be achieved until those effects are overcome by transition programs giving minorities a temporary advantage. Thus, in the area of affirmative action, the approach to democracy was hampered by lack of agreement not only over which *goal* is most democratic but also over which *means* represents the best approach.

Affirmative Action in the Reagan/Bush Era

Shortly after coming to office in 1981, President Ronald Reagan appointed officials who challenged many of the nation's civil rights policies. In reexamining affirmative action, the administration took the position that the various Civil Rights Acts prohibited *all* racial and sexual discrimination, including discrimination against white males. It further argued that *only* employers that had been found to have discriminated should be required to remedy their discriminatory practices, and that they should be required to hire or promote *only* individuals who could prove that they had been discriminated against.

A key issue was raised by programs in which recently hired minority employees were protected from "last-hired/first-fired" union layoff rules. White workers with more seniority who now faced layoffs argued that abrogation of those rules was a violation of *their* civil rights. In 1984 the administration persuaded the Supreme Court to overturn a ruling by a federal district court requiring a fire department to suspend seniority rules when laying off employees.[38]

In 1986 the Court overturned a program in which public-school teachers with more seniority in a district with no history of discrimination were laid off in favor of minority teachers.[39] However, it rejected the Reagan administration's position that race should *never* be a criterion for layoffs, ruling that such a plan may be justified in situations where it could be shown that there had been an intent to discriminate.[40]

Shortly thereafter in another case the Court accepted the use of a 29 percent hiring quota, which reflected the percentage of minorities in the local workforce in that case, because it was being used to remedy blatant past discrimination by the local sheet metal union.[41] And in a 1987 case involving state troopers in Alabama, where not a single African American had reached the rank of corporal,[42] the Court ruled that quotas could be used in promotion decisions when there had been blatant discrimination in the past.

In general, the Court was saying that affirmative action could be used in states and localities only in particular cases where there was demonstrable evidence of specific discrimination and the program was "narrowly tailored" to meet that offense. A similar pattern prevailed during the Bush administration, as can be seen in the Rehnquist Court's ruling on six cases:

1. In *Martin* v. *Wilks*[43] the Court held that even affirmative action programs that had been acceptable to employees and minority workers could later be challenged by nonminority workers.

2. In *City of Richmond* v. *Crosson*[44] the Court held that a state contract with a "set-aside" affirmative action plan could be designed only to remedy specific instances of past discrimination.

3. In *Patterson* v. *McLean Credit Union*[45] the Court held that once a private employment contract was made, federal law could not be used to deal with issues such as employer harassment, because such issues were subsequent to the "making" of that contract.

4. In *Lorance* v. *AT&T Technologies*[46] the Court reduced the amount of time available to plaintiffs wishing to bring employment discrimination suits.

5. In *Independent Federation of Flight Attendants* v. *Zipes*[47] the Court limited the right of recovery of attorneys' fees in employment discrimination cases.

6. In *Wards Cove Packing Co.* v. *Antonio*[48] the Court held that employees claiming employment discrimination had the burden of proving that employment qualifications were not necessary for the jobs they sought.

Seeing the pattern of these judicial decisions, civil rights leaders turned for help to Congress, which was dominated by a combination of liberal Democrats and southerners who depended on the African American vote for reelection. In February 1990 a bill was introduced that sought to overturn the Court's decisions in the six cases just described. Both houses of Congress passed the law, but President Bush vetoed it, claiming that it would support "quotas." However, after extensive negotiations, a few minor changes in wording, and passage of the new bill, the president agreed to sign it into law as the Civil Rights Act of 1991.

Whither Civil Rights?

The direction of the government's policy toward civil rights during the Clinton administration has been difficult to determine. While the initial rhetoric indicated a sensitivity toward further integrating American society, when the congressional Republicans' hostility toward affirmative action programs became clearer, the president placed all of these programs "under review," leading several women's groups to march in Washington shouting "No retreat! No retreat!" The president later pledged full support for such programs, perhaps with an eye toward the 1996 election. At the same time, in early 1995 the federal courts were sending mixed messages on racial equality. Faced with thirty-eight historically black publicly financed colleges in nineteen states which historically had segregated higher education systems, the federal court in Mississippi began to consider a case that has been termed the *Brown* v. *Board of Education* of higher education. Was the state's system of five historically white and three historically black universities constitutional? District court judge Neal B. Biggers, Jr., ruled the state's practice of historically different admission standards for the different schools to be unacceptable and ordered the state to spend more money to upgrade the black colleges. With similar legal challenges underway in states such as Alabama, Louisiana, and Tennessee, however, it was unclear how widespread the effect of this ruling would be.[49] At the same time, though, the Supreme Court let stand a lower federal court ruling that overturned the University of Maryland's program of blacks-only scholarships despite the school's admission that this program was designed to remedy its past discrimination. (One of those who had been discriminated against was Thurgood Marshall.) Once again, just what effect this ruling would have on similar programs in nearly half of the nation's other colleges is unclear.

Then, in a key 1995 decision involving a small business administration program giving a Hispanic-owned company an affirmative action advantage in bidding for a highway contract, the Supreme Court for the first time refused to uphold the federal program. Instead, the Court ruled that, like state and local affirmative action programs, federal programs must serve a compelling governmental interest and must be designed to remedy specific instances of past discrimination, rather than just overall societal discrimination. This test will make it much more difficult to uphold federal affirmative action programs. These rulings make clear that America's approach to democracy in the area of civil rights will continue to be debated year after year.[50]

WOMEN'S RIGHTS

In the early 1800s women in the United States were not permitted to vote, serve on juries, find profitable employment, attend institutions of higher education, or own land in their own name. Moreover, the English common-law notion of *coverture,* which held that upon marriage a woman lost her separate legal identity, had been adopted in the United States. As a consequence, married women could not sue in their own name, divorce an alcoholic or abusive spouse, own property independently, or enter into contracts.

When Elizabeth Cady Stanton and Lucretia Mott were not seated as duly elected delegates at the International Anti-Slavery Convention, held in London in 1840, they decided to take action. They organized a movement to attain full legal rights for women. At a convention held in Seneca Falls, New York, in 1848 the movement borrowed the language of the Declaration of Independence in issuing a Declaration of Sentiments concerning the "natural rights" of women. The document read in part as follows:

> When, in the course of human events, it becomes necessary for one portion of the family of man to assume among the people of the earth a position different from that which they have hitherto occupied, but one to which the laws of nature and of nature's God entitle them, a decent respect to the opinions of mankind requires that they should declare the causes that impel them to such a course.
>
> We hold these truths to be self-evident: that all men and women are created equal; that they are endowed by their Creator with certain inalienable rights; that among these are life, liberty, and the pursuit of happiness.[51]

The convention passed twelve resolutions calling for political and social rights for women.

In response to lobbying by women activists, the New York State legislature passed the Married Women's Property Act of 1848. The law gave women control over property they received through gifts and inheritance, even after

Susan B. Anthony and Elizabeth Cady Stanton were early leaders of the fight for women's rights and women's suffrage. As a result of their efforts, women got the vote in 1920 with ratification of the Nineteenth Amendment.

marriage. Encouraged by this success, Stanton, Susan B. Anthony, and other feminist leaders began to lobby for further reforms in New York and other states. Their efforts bore fruit in 1860, when New York passed a civil rights law that gave women control over their wages and inheritances, guaranteed them an inheritance of at least one-third of their husband's estate, granted them joint custody of their children, and allowed them to make contracts and sue in their own name.[52]

Two Steps Forward, One Step Back

The early successes of the women's rights movement were followed by some setbacks. In 1862 the New York State legislature rescinded and modified the earlier women's rights laws. Realizing that it was necessary to maintain constant pressure on legislators, Anthony and Stanton tried to link their cause with that of African Americans; they formed the Woman's National Loyal League to advocate a constitutional amendment to prohibit slavery. Soon thereafter they joined with supportive men to form an abolitionist alliance called the American Equal Rights Association.

The new group put aside its own goals to promote the Fourteenth Amendment. This proved to be a tactical error, as the amendment introduced the word *male* into the Constitution for the first time. When language giving women the vote was not included in the Fifteenth Amendment, Stanton and Anthony decided to form another organization designed to push solely for women's suffrage. In 1869 they formed the National Woman Suffrage Association and began a campaign for a constitutional amendment giving women the right to vote. Meanwhile, Lucy Stone, another longtime activist, formed an organization called the American Woman Suffrage Association, which sought to achieve suffrage on a state-by-state basis.

Just how far women had yet to go to achieve equality was made clear in

1873, when the first women's rights case reached the Supreme Court. In sustaining a law that barred women from the practice of law, Justice Joseph Bradley stated that "Man is, or should be, woman's protector and defender. The natural and proper timidity and delicacy which belongs to the female sex evidently unfits it for many of the occupations of civil life. . . . [The] paramount destiny and mission of women are to fulfill the noble and benign offices of wife and mother. This is the law of the Creator."[53] That "law" became the law of the land as well.

The Struggle for Suffrage

The question of whether the Fourteenth and Fifteenth Amendments were inclusive enough to permit women to vote still remained. In a test case that reached the Supreme Court in 1875, *Minor* v. *Happersett*,[54] Virginia Minor's husband (since women could still not sue in their own names) argued that the new "privileges and immunities" clause protected his wife's right to vote. However, the Court disagreed, arguing that this privilege was reserved only for men by the Constitution and the state laws.

Despite such setbacks at the federal level, gradual progress was being made at the state level. In 1869 and 1870 the Wyoming and Utah Territories granted full suffrage to women. Nebraska (1867) and Colorado (1876) gave women the right to vote in school elections. In 1890 Alice Stone Blackwell brought together the two rival suffrage organizations to form the National American Woman Suffrage Association, and lobbying for women's suffrage became more organized under its first president, Susan B. Anthony. By 1910, though, only four states (Colorado, Idaho, Utah, and Wyoming) had provided for full women's suffrage.

The new president of the National American Woman Suffrage Association, Carrie Chapman Catt, advocated the use of a coordinated **grassroots strategy,** that is, decentralized action by ordinary citizens, to seek suffrage. This strategy paid off, and by 1918 fifteen states, including New York and California, had given women the vote.

This progress was too slow for some. For five years Alice Paul had been running the Congressional Union (later to become the Woman's party) to fight for a constitutional amendment permitting women's suffrage. Arguing that the party in power should be held accountable for the continued disenfranchisement of women, the Congressional Union began picketing the White House and putting pressure on Congress to pass an amendment. But it was World War I that put the suffrage movement over the top. Women argued that their wartime service to the nation should be rewarded with the right of suffrage, and Congress agreed. The Nineteenth Amendment was passed in 1919.

The Road to Equality

Women successfully used their new electoral clout to secure congressional passage of the Married Women's Independent Citizenship Act of 1922, which granted women citizenship independent from their husbands. However, having achieved its main goal, the lobbying coalition fell apart, and actual equality for women would have to wait for decades.

Sex discrimination, also called **sexism,** could be seen in many areas of American society, but especially in education and employment. In 1961 the

FYI

To commemorate the seventy-fifth anniversary of women winning the right to vote, in 1995 the U.S. Postal Service issued a stamp portraying suffragette Alice Paul. The younger leaders of the women's rights movement had n ot even been born when the "elder" leaders—Anthony, Stanton, and Mott—began their fight.

Patricia Ireland has been a highly visible and outspoken president of the National Organization for Women (NOW). She has struggled to publicize issues that are important to women and families and to further women's rights. Here she speaks to reporters at a Washington, D.C., rally protesting violence against women.

uproar that resulted when President Kennedy appointed only two women to governmental positions spurred him to issue an executive order creating the President's Commission on the Status of Women, chaired by Eleanor Roosevelt. At the suggestion of the commission, Congress passed the Equal Pay Act of 1963, which required equal pay for equal work. Although this was a victory for women, the law's effectiveness was limited because employers were free to create different job classifications with varying rates of pay.

Surprisingly, it was the Civil Rights Act of 1964, originally intended to bring about equality for African Americans, that represented the greatest advance for women's rights. Ironically, the change came at the behest of a southern congressman, who proposed an amendment adding *sex* to the bill's language in the hope of diminishing support for the bill, only to see the measure passed with the language intact. The act thus barred discrimination against any person on the basis of "race, color, religion, *sex* or national origin."

Overburdened by an immense caseload, however, the EEOC was slow to enforce the provisions of the 1964 act. In 1966, outraged by the EEOC's inaction, several women organized the National Organization for Women (NOW). Borrowing techniques from the civil rights movement, NOW organized demonstrations and even picketed the *New York Times* because of its policy of printing a separate section advertising jobs for women. NOW also pressured the EEOC to hold hearings on regulations concerning sexual discrimination. Finally, in 1972 Congress amended the 1964 Civil Rights Act with Title V, under which federal funds could be denied to public and private programs that discriminated against women, and Title IX, which called for equal athletic opportunities for women in schools.

Leaders of the women's movement still hoped for a *constitutional* standard establishing equality for women. In 1967 NOW proposed the Equal Rights Amendment (ERA). Women's rights advocates entered the 1970s with the hope that the amendment would be passed and quickly ratified. However, as you learned in Chapter 3, despite congressional approval of the amendment in 1972 and the support of Presidents Nixon and Carter, the ERA fell three states short of the thirty-eight required for ratification. As a result, people are often surprised to learn that women are not specifically mentioned in, and thus not specifically protected by, the Constitution.

Seeking Equality through the Courts

The quest for equal rights now turned to the courts. The focus of this effort w: the Fourteenth Amendment, which states that "No state shall . . . deny to any person within its jurisdiction the equal protection of the laws." It seemed reasonable that a woman could be defined as a person and thus be included in the equal-protection clause. The key to this strategy would be the Supreme Court's interpretation of "equal protection," or treating people in different categories equally unless the state can demonstrate some constitutional reason for doing otherwise.

For many years sex discrimination cases had been decided by the **test of reasonableness,** or whether a reasonable person would agree that law had a "rational basis", thus making it constitutional. The burden was placed on the woman to prove that a law that discriminated by gender was arbitrary, capricious, and totally unjustifiable. Under this test, it was nearly impossible for women to win discrimination cases, because an acceptable rationale for the law could always be found, or invented, by the state. Thus, when the state of Michigan in the 1940s barred women from obtaining a bartender's license unless they were "the wife or daughter of the male owner," the Supreme Court accepted the state's rationale that it wanted to protect the sensibilities of women.[55] And when the state of Florida in the late 1950s declined to put women on jury lists unless they specifically asked to be included, the Court upheld the law because a "woman is still regarded as the center of home and family life" and had "special responsibilities" in this capacity.[56]

Women's rights advocates decided to seek a change in the legal standard by which the Court decided cases involving sex discrimination, one that shifted the burden of proof to the state, thus making it more possible for women to win their suits. Ruth Bader Ginsburg, a lawyer for the American Civil Liberties Union (ACLU), designed a campaign modeled on that led by Thurgood Marshall twenty years earlier for the NAACP to end racial segregation in the public schools. The idea was to move the Court incrementally, on a case-by-case basis, toward abandoning the reasonableness test and replacing it with a new test more favorable to the women's cause.

The first case, decided by the court in 1971, involved an Idaho law requiring that in naming the executor of a will a male must be chosen over equally qualified females. Under this law a divorced mother named Sally Reed had been prevented from supervising the will of her deceased son. It seemed likely that the law would be upheld under the reasonableness test. The state's "rational basis" for the law was that men know more than women about business and it was unnecessary for the courts to hold additional hearings to prove this fact.[57]

Ginsburg decided to use the *Reed* case to persuade the Supreme Court to use a different test, known as the **strict-scrutiny test,** in dealing with cases of sex discrimination. Under this test, laws that discriminate on the basis of a characteristic that is "immutable [or unchangeable] by birth," such as race or nationality, are considered "suspect." In cases involving such laws, the burden of proof shifts from the plaintiff to the state, which must demonstrate a "compelling state interest" to justify the discriminatory law. That is, the state must show that there was no other means of accomplishing a goal than to treat these classes of people unequally.

Because sex, like race and national origin, is "immutable by birth," Ginsburg hoped that the Court would add it to the list of "suspect categories." She was only partially successful. The Court still used the reasonableness test to decide the case, but for the first time it could not find an acceptable justification for the state's discriminatory policy. The law thus violated the equal-protection clause of the Fourteenth Amendment.

In 1973 the Court considered the case of Sharron Frontiero, a married Air Force lieutenant, who objected to a federal law that automatically provided benefits to dependents of married men in the armed forces while the husbands of women in the military received benefits only if they could prove that they were dependent on their wives. Four of the justices were now ready to expand the strict-scrutiny test to include women. However, just as he would do later for homosexual rights, the "swing justice," Lewis Powell, was not yet ready to do so, because the Equal Rights Amendment was then being considered for ratification. Thus, the less protective reasonableness test continued to be the standard, which became even more important when the ERA failed to be ratified.[58]

Former ACLU lawyer and current Supreme Court justice Ruth Bader Ginsburg makes a dramatic point during her confirmation hearings in 1993. Appointed to the Court by President Clinton because of her successful fight for women's legal rights in the 1970s, Ginsburg has been much more moderate in her women's rights decisions on the Court. However, in speeches off the bench, she remains a passionate defender of women's rights.

In an unusual turn of events, the next case in the series involved a man, Mel Kahn, who claimed to have been discriminated against on the basis of his sex by a Florida law that provided five hundred dollars more in property tax exemption for widows than for widowers.[59] Although the ACLU lost the case, it had made an important step forward. Rather than pressing for the strict-scrutiny test or accepting the reasonableness test, Ginsburg asked the Court to create an intermediate **"heightened-scrutiny" test.** Such a standard would force the state to prove more than just the "reasonableness" of the law, though not its "compelling" nature, to justify it. Thus, a law would now be upheld if the rights of the plaintiff were deemed on balance to be more important than the state's interests as represented in the law.

The present legal status of women was finally achieved in a 1976 case called *Craig* v. *Boren*[60] that on the face of it did not look like material for a landmark constitutional decision. An underaged fraternity boy and the Honk n' Holler convenience store had teamed up to challenge an Oklahoma statute under which eighteen-year-old girls could buy weak "3.2" beer, but boys could not do the same until they were twenty-one. The state justified the law on the basis of differential driving records for the two groups. According to Ginsburg, this was a "nonweighty interest pressed by thirsty boys," but it nonetheless led to a legal victory. In striking down the law as an unconstitutional violation of the equal-protection clause, the Supreme Court applied the heightened-scrutiny test. Under this test, laws that classify people according to their sex must now "serve *important governmental objectives* and must be *substantially related* to the achievement of those objectives." Women now had a realistic chance of gaining equal treatment through the legal system.

It remained to be seen how far the Supreme Court would go to advance the legal rights of women. In recent years the record has been mixed. For example, using the heightened-scrutiny test the Court upheld the Military Selective Service Act even though it requires only men to register for possible military service.[61] But in 1987 the Court ruled on an affirmative action case in which a white woman was given preference over a white man for a promotion to dispatcher in the Santa Clara Transportation Department. The Court upheld the constitutionality of the program, arguing that "sex is but one of several factors that may be taken into account in evaluating qualified applicants for a position."[62]

Much progress has been made toward equal rights for women in the United States, but it is clear that there is much progress yet to be made. Many of the gains have been evident in the political world. Hillary Clinton became the most effective first lady since Eleanor Roosevelt. In the past four presidential administrations seventeen cabinet heads have been women. With 56 congressional seats, nineteen thousand elective posts nationwide, 20 percent of the state legislative posts, and twenty-five hundred state and federal judicial posts (not to mention numerous college presidencies and state governorships) all being filled by women, the progress seems evident when measured against the days when Sandra Day O'Connor and Ruth Bader Ginsburg could not find fulfilling employment.[63]

Nevertheless, a recent commission discovered that the "glass ceiling" that prevents women from being promoted into higher-management jobs still exists. Despite the fact that women now constitute nearly 40 percent of the

FYI

In April 1995 a first occurred on the Supreme Court of the United States. Because both Chief Justice William Rehnquist and second in seniority John Paul Stevens were out of town, for the very first time a woman, Justice Sandra Day O'Connor, presided over the Supreme Court during a public session.

Spreading Hate

In their struggle for civil rights, minority groups often encounter opposition. Recently, the Internet and other modern technologies have provided those opposed to the advance of civil rights with a powerful means of spreading their word. It has become very easy to order racist publications or join a white-supremacy group via the Internet. Members of hate groups keep in touch on the Internet or on one of the seven national computer bulletin boards set up by such groups to exchange news and messages.

Computer networks are just one of the technologies being used by white-supremacy groups to spread their message of hate. There are numerous others, including desktop publishing, shortwave radio, fax networks, and private video production. The resulting communications network links together some 250 American and Canadian hate groups with a membership that has grown markedly in the past few years.

Among the most enterprising participants in this network is Resistance Inc., a Detroit-based company that promotes white separatism and anti-Semitism via video documentaries, records, rock bands, and a slick magazine, *Resistance,* that claims to have a circulation of over thirteen thousand. The company's founder, George Burdi, is credited with reawakening the neo-Nazi skinhead movement in the United States.

By far the most effective medium used by hate groups is the Internet. According to the operator of Stormfront, a white-supremacy bulletin board, "A third of households have computers and with the phenomenal growth of the Internet, tens of millions of people have access to our message if they wish. The access is anonymous and there is unlimited ability to communicate with others of a like mind."*

Civil rights leaders are deeply troubled by the ease with which modern technology can be used to communicate hate. Never before has the hate movement had access to such powerful communications technology, and its message is being spread far more effectively than before. While it is true that much of the content of hate speech is protected by the First Amendment, questions have been raised about its possible link with an increase in hate crimes, such as a triple murder committed by two skinheads who had attended concerts by bands sponsored by Resistance Inc.

In response to questions about this issue, Vice President Al Gore stated: "We have established principles in this country that define what is protected speech and what is not, and there are technological ways being developed to protect people from receiving provocative and hate speech over computer networks."** The nature of those technologies remains to be seen; in the meantime, the white-supremacy movement continues to recruit new supporters.

*Quoted in Keith Schneider, "Hate Groups Use Tools of the Electronic Trade," *New York Times,* Mar. 13, 1995, p. A12.
**Quoted in ibid.

workforce nationwide, they make up only 5 percent of the senior-management jobs in industries across the nation. This of course has dramatic implications for the earning capacity of women as well as their power in running those businesses.[64] Lacking an Equal Rights Amendment in the constitution, women still must rely on the courts to enforce their rights, making America's approach to democracy in this area a continual one.

CIVIL RIGHTS AND OTHER MINORITIES

Hispanic Americans

Immigrants to the United States from Mexico, Cuba, Puerto Rico, and other Spanish-speaking countries have experienced forms of discrimination similar to those faced by African Americans, though to different degrees. Mexican Americans have been robbed of their land, attacked by the Ku Klux Klan and rioting mobs, excluded from labor unions, and discriminated against in employment, housing, and education. Puerto Ricans and Cubans have also suffered from discrimination and de facto housing segregation.

During the 1950s Mexican Americans began a movement to gain more equal treatment in American society. They formed organizations that stressed electoral politics and attempted to reclaim lost lands in New Mexico. Perhaps the most famous aspect of the movement was the formation of a union of migrant Mexican American farmworkers under the leadership of Cesar Chavez. Through the use of strikes, boycotts, pickets, and political action, the United Farm Workers drew national attention to the conditions endured by migrant farmworkers.

In the late 1960s the Mexican American Legal Defense and Education Fund (MALDEF) was created. Through litigation and lobbying, MALDEF campaigned for integration, equal school financing, and full protection of voting rights, and against discrimination in employment. The success of MALDEF led to the creation of the Puerto Rican Legal Defense Fund. Other Hispanic American groups, such as the League of United American Citizens and the National Council of La Raza, have also fought for increased voter registration and electoral participation.

Along with African Americans, Hispanic Americans benefited from the Supreme Court's rulings on segregation, the Civil Rights Act of 1964, and the Voting Rights Act of 1965. In *Katzenbach* v. *Morgan*[65], for example, the Court upheld a portion of the Voting Rights Act of 1965 that outlawed the use of an English literacy test in New York. Through the actions of MALDEF and other groups, the Voting Rights Act was extended to Hispanic Americans, Native Americans, and Asian Americans.

The effort to achieve greater education equality suffered a setback in 1973 in the case of *San Antonio Independent School District* v. *Rodriguez*.[66] The Court was unwilling to overturn the use of property taxes to finance state school systems, despite the resulting inequality in educational resources between wealthy and poor communities. Despite this decision, several state supreme courts subsequently used their own state constitutions as a basis for requiring equal financing of education. The prospects for improved education for Hispanic American children increased in 1974, when the Court ordered that school districts that served a significant non-English-speaking population provide a bilingual program. Then, in 1982, the Court ordered that all children must be provided with schooling regardless of whether their parents were legal immigrants.[67]

Hispanic Americans continue to struggle against discrimination and poverty. Since it is predicted that early in the twenty-first century Hispanic Americans will make up nearly one-third of the U.S. population, achievement of legal and actual equality for this group deserves high priority.

Native Americans

The history of discrimination and segregation against Native Americans is well known. Native American tribes have been removed from their land, treaties have been broken, and Native Americans have been denied some of the basic rights of citizenship. In 1884 the Supreme Court ruled that Native Americans were not citizens of the United States and therefore were neither protected by the Fourteenth Amendment nor granted the right to vote. In the early 1900s Native Americans strove to attain both citizenship and tribal autonomy, while during the 1920s they struggled against attempts to establish reservations that could be exploited by miners. Finally, in 1924 Congress passed the Indian Citizenship Act, which gave Native Americans the right to vote.

Since then Native Americans have resisted various attempts to assimilate them into the mainstream culture of American society. In the 1940s, the National Congress of American Indians was formed to fight for education and legal aid. During the 1960s, Native Americans engaged in acts of civil disobedience such as delaying dam construction, occupying government offices, and holding sit-ins and other demonstrations to fight against discrimination. In 1969 a group of students occupied Alcatraz Island in California, which was formerly tribal land but was not then in use by the federal government. A group called the American Indian Movement (AIM) occupied buildings and staged demonstrations, and in 1973 AIM played a major part in the well-publicized occupation of Wounded Knee on the Pine Ridge Reservation.[68]

Protesting Native Americans face a challenge that most other minorities do not: They are divided into two movements with different aspirations. The *ethnic movement* shares the aspirations of other ethnic minorities to achieve equality in American society. In contrast, the separatist *tribal movement* seeks separate citizenship and a system of government based on the tribe. Whereas the ethnic movement wishes to participate in American democracy, the goal of the tribal movement is to create its own concept of democracy.

On December 28, 1990, a delegation of Native Americans commemorated the one hundredth anniversary of the massacre at Wounded Knee, South Dakota. On that site in 1890, the Seventh Cavalry caught and massacred two hundred Sioux who had gathered at Chief Sitting Bull's urging for a "Ghost Dance," seeking to bring back the Native American way of life. Descendants of the survivors are shown here marking that tragedy.

During the 1960s Native Americans made some progress with regard to tribal sovereignty and treaty rights, as well as changing public perceptions of "Indians." In recent years tribes in Rhode Island, Connecticut, and elsewhere have even used the exemption of their reservation lands from state laws to create gambling enterprises on their land, thus helping to raise money and create political clout. However, discrimination has not been eliminated, and equality is still an elusive goal as the Native American population in general remains among the poorest in the nation.

Americans with Disabilities

Unlike other minority groups, Americans with disabilities have been extremely successful in persuading Congress to pass legislation barring discrimination against them. In 1948 Congress passed a law prohibiting discrimination against the physically handicapped in the civil service. In 1968 it passed the Architectural Barriers Act, which required that all buildings constructed with federal money or leased by the federal government be accessible to the handicapped. Congress acted again in 1973, when it mandated that federal contractors and programs that received federal funds adopt policies of nondiscrimination and affirmative action for the disabled. When Congress passed the Civil Rights Restoration Act of 1988, it barred any institution that discriminated on the basis of race, sex, age, or *handicap* from receiving federal funds.

Despite the passage of these and other statutes that protected the rights of the disabled, Americans with disabilities continued to be deprived of many basic civil rights. For example, they still faced discrimination by private employers and establishments. Some progress was made in 1989, when Congress passed the Americans with Disabilities Act (ADA). Under the provisions of this act, firms with more than twenty-five employees are barred from discriminating against disabled individuals in making hiring or promotion decisions. In addition, companies are required to make "reasonable accommodations" for disabled employees, such as providing readers for blind workers or wider doors for those in wheelchairs. Recent studies have shown, however, that this law rarely helps the disabled seeking jobs; instead, in over one-third of the complaints it is being used to deal with such relatively minor problems as back pain, psychological stress, and substance abuse.[69]

Why has the struggle for equality been relatively easy for the disabled when compared with other minority groups? One reason is that laws requiring access to facilities are viewed as providing equality of opportunity, a goal on which most Americans agree. Another reason is that the experiences of the physically challenged are very close to all of us, including many politicians, such as Franklin D. Roosevelt and Robert Dole, who themselves are physically challenged or who have relatives with disabilities. The ADA demonstrates how far the United States can travel along the road to democracy when it is unified about the direction it wants to take.

CIVIL RIGHTS AND APPROACHING DEMOCRACY

After two hundred years of civil rights battles, how much farther do we need to go to achieve full equality for all Americans? Clearly, the struggle is not over. To make further progress, the nation must reach a consensus about the goals it seeks to achieve. The differences between Judge Sand and the Yonkers City Council illustrate this point. Can we pursue both equality of opportunity *and* equality of result? Few people oppose the idea of equal competition for resources, but when programs such as affirmative action try to guarantee equal results to make up for past discrimination, leading to diminished opportunity for others, the battles begin.

Another set of questions deals with just how inclusive society will be in approaching democracy. Inevitably, other minority groups will realize that they face discrimination and will demand greater equality. Two such groups are the elderly and homosexuals. With an ever-increasing percentage of Americans in the oldest age groups, there will be growing demands for protection of the civil rights of the elderly. While many of the elderly are covered by the ADA, new issues will undoubtedly arise. All of these will be pressed on the government by the thirty-million-member American Association of Retired Persons (AARP).

The challenge for the gay and lesbian community is unlike that faced by any other minority group in American society. A high percentage of the estimated twenty-five million to thirty million homosexual Americans live their lives in secret, undetected and unsuspected by a "straight" society that is prone to homophobia. While some states and localities attempt to protect the civil rights of homosexuals, the federal government and many states do not. It took a major battle concerning military policy over gays to reach a "don't ask, don't tell" policy during the Clinton administration. After the *Bowers* decision (see Chapter 7 case study), which some members of the gay community consider equivalent to the *Plessy* decision for African Americans, the fight for equal protection will be an uphill one. However, one wonders whether there will one day be a decision with the same impact as *Brown* for this community.

While the future is unknown, we can probably count on one thing: The struggle begun by a tired woman going home from work on a Montgomery bus will continue unabated. We have seen that at various times the protection of civil rights has fallen to the Supreme Court, at other times to Congress, and at still other times to the president. Throughout the struggle, the force behind the effort to achieve equal rights has been the "people power" of the civil rights movement, the women's movement, and others. Yet there is much left to be done. As Rosa Parks said in 1993, "I cannot say I'm completely satisfied with the condition we're in. As long as anybody's oppressed, and not free to get an education, and as long as we have so much crime among us, I can't say I'm really satisfied."[70] America will continue to approach democracy by guaranteeing legal and actual rights, but the road will not be a straight or smooth one.

> "We are a nation not of black and white alone, but one teeming with divergent communities. . . . Upon that basis, we are governed by one Constitution, providing a single guarantee of equal protection, one that extends equally to all citizens."
>
> —Justice Sandra Day O'Connor

SUMMARY

1. Discrimination is unequal treatment based on race, ethnicity, gender, and other distinctions. The primary means for achieving equal treatment is ensuring full protection of civil rights, the constitutionally guaranteed rights that may not be arbitrarily removed by the government.

2. Equality before the law, or de jure equality, requires that there be no legally mandated obstacles to equal treatment. Actual equality, or de facto equality, refers to results—the actual conditions of people's lives.

3. Although black slaves were freed during the Civil War, it took several decades to gain legal protection of the civil rights of African Americans. In the post–Civil War years the races were strictly segregated by Jim Crow laws, and in the *Plessy* v. *Ferguson* case the Supreme Court ruled that "separate but equal" facilities did not violate the Fourteenth Amendment. Although African Americans had been granted the right to vote, state voting laws contained many loopholes that effectively disenfranchised blacks. In the early

decades of the twentieth century the NAACP won several lawsuits that advanced the cause of racial equality.

4. During and after World War II the White House issued executive orders prohibiting discrimination in the defense business and the military. The battle for desegregation of the public schools was led by the NAACP and culminated in the historic *Brown* v. *Board of Education of Topeka* ruling that struck down the separate but equal doctrine.

5. Beginning with the Montgomery bus boycott in 1957, the civil rights movement employed techniques such as boycotts, protest marches, and sit-ins to publicly demonstrate the injustice of unequal treatment based on race. During the 1960s Congress passed several laws designed to eliminate discrimination, including the Civil Rights Act of 1964 (which focused on school segregation), the Voting Rights Act of 1965, and the Civil Rights Act of 1968 (which focused on discrimination in housing). Several cases decided by the Supreme Court during this period dealt with the specific means used to desegregate schools.

6. Affirmative action programs attempt to improve the chances of minority applicants for jobs, housing, employment, and graduate admissions by giving them a slight advantage over white applicants with similar qualifications. Such programs seek to increase equality but can create temporary inequalities in the process, and therefore are controversial. Underlying the controversy is a disagreement over the meaning of actual equality; some feel that the goal should be equality of opportunity, while others believe that the nation should strive for equality of result.

7. The Reagan administration challenged many of the nation's civil rights policies, claiming that the various Civil Rights Acts prohibited all racial and sexual discrimination, including discrimination against white males. In a series of cases the Supreme Court set specific limits on the use of affirmative action.

8. The movement for women's rights began with the Declaration of Sentiments drawn up at a convention held in Seneca Falls, New York, in 1848. Progress toward equality was slow and uneven throughout the next several decades; women gained control over their property but were unable to vote. It was not until 1919 that Congress passed the Nineteenth Amendment to the Constitution, which granted women the right of suffrage.

9. In response to complaints of sex discrimination in education and employment, Congress passed the Equal Pay Act of 1963, which required equal pay for equal work. The Civil Rights Act of 1964 also barred discrimination on the basis of sex. However, efforts to pass the Equal Rights Amendment to the Constitution, which would have given full protection to the civil rights of women, were unsuccessful.

10. In the 1970s efforts to gain equal protection for women's rights turned to the courts and focused on the standard used to determine whether a state law is constitutional. In a series of cases the Supreme Court gradually shifted from a "reasonableness" test, which upheld a law if the state could provide an acceptable rationale for the law, to a "heightened-scrutiny" test, in which laws that classify people according to their sex must serve important governmental objectives and be substantially related to the achievement of those objectives.

11. Hispanic Americans have made considerable progress toward equal treatment, particularly in the area of voting rights, but they continue to struggle against discrimination and poverty. Native Americans have also organized to demand the basic rights of citizenship and to fight against discrimination. In contrast to these and other minority groups, Americans with disabilities have been extremely successful in persuading Congress to pass legislation barring discrimination against them.

KEY TERMS

discrimination
civil rights
de jure equality
de facto equality
Missouri Compromise
Compromise of 1850
suffrage
state action
Jim Crow

peonage
desegregation
integration
civil disobedience
boycott
protest march
sit-in
freedom riders
affirmative action

equal opportunity
equality of result
quota programs
grassroots strategy
sexism
test of reasonableness
strict-scrutiny test
heightened-scrutiny test

SUGGESTED READINGS

- Abraham, Henry J., and Barbara A. Perry. *Freedom and the Court: Civil Rights and Liberties in the United States*. 6th ed. New York: Oxford University Press, 1994. An analysis of the development of American civil rights and liberties by the Supreme Court and the lower federal courts.

- Branch, Taylor. *Parting the Waters: America in the King Years, 1954–63*. New York: Simon and Schuster, 1988. A Pulitzer Prize winner, this is the first of two projected volumes of history of the development of the civil rights movement in the United States.

- Brown, Dee Alexander, *Bury My Heart at Wounded Knee: An Indian History of the American West,* (New York: Holt, Rinehart and Winston, 1971). A highly readable history of the sad treatment of Native Americans by the United States government and its people.

- Carter, Steven L. *Reflections of an Affirmative Action Baby*. New York: Basic Books, 1991. A learned critique of the affirmative action programs by an African American law professor from Yale who benefited from them.

- Garrow, David J. *Bearing the Cross: Martin Luther King, Jr., and the Southern Christian Leadership Conference*. New York: Morrow, 1986. A landmark biography of Martin Luther King; it won the Pulitzer Prize.

- Kluger, Richard. *Simple Justice*. New York: Knopf, 1976. The compelling story of the cases that made up the landmark *Brown* v. *Board of Education* case. Included is the remarkable story of the legendary NAACP attorney Thurgood Marshall.

- Mansbridge, Jane J. *Why We Lost the ERA*. Chicago: University of Chicago Press, 1986. An examination of the reasons for the failure of the Equal Rights Amendment.

- McGlen, Nancy E., and Karen O'Connor. *Women's Rights: The Struggle for Equality in the Nineteenth and Twentieth Centuries*. New York: Praeger, 1983. A useful history and analysis of the development of legal rights for women in America.

- Nieman, Donald G. *Promises to Keep: African-Americans and the Constitutional Order, 1776 to the Present*. New York: Oxford University Press, 1991. An informative history of the development of legal rights for African Americans.

- O'Brien, David M. *Constitutional Law and Politics*. Vol. 2: *Civil Rights and Civil Liberties*. New York: Norton, 1991. A comprehensive casebook of the development of civil rights by the Supreme Court.

- Peltason, Jack W. *Fifty-eight Lonely Men*. New York: Harcourt Brace Jovanovich, 1961. A study of the courageous southern federal district court judges charged with implementing the *Brown* v. *Board of Education* school desegregation decision.

- Pritchett, C. Herman. *Constitutional Civil Liberties*. Englewood Cliffs, N.J.: Prentice Hall, 1984. A comprehensive summary of the key decisions by the Supreme Court of the United States in the areas of civil rights and liberties.

- Stavans, Ilan, *The Hispanic Condition: Reflections on Culture and Identity in America,* (New York: Harper Collins, 1995). An up-to-date examination of the situation in America for the fastest-growing minority group in America.

- Verba, Sidney, and Gary R. Orren. *Equality in America: The View from the Top*. Cambridge, Mass.: Harvard University Press, 1985. An analysis of how close the United States has come to achieving true racial equality.

- Williams, Juan. *Eyes on the Prize: America's Civil Rights Years, 1954–1965*. New York: Penguin Books, 1987. The companion book to the PBS series on the history of the civil rights movement in the United States.

- Woodward, C. Vann. *The Strange Career of Jim Crow*. New York: Oxford University Press, 1957. An important history of the development of the segregated legal society in the United States by one of this nation's premier historians.

CHAPTER 16

PUBLIC POLICY: REGULATION AND SOCIAL WELFARE

Bearder, Romare, The Block, 1971. The Metropolitan Museum of Art, New York.

CHAPTER OUTLINE

CASE STUDY: AIDS AND THE
    GOVERNMENT
INTRODUCTION: PUBLIC POLICY AND
    DEMOCRACY
WHAT IS PUBLIC POLICY?
TYPES OF POLICIES

THE POLICYMAKING PROCESS
THE POLITICS OF POLICYMAKING
POLICYMAKING IN ACTION
PUBLIC POLICY AND APPROACHING
    DEMOCRACY

R EPRESENTATIVE HENRY WAXMAN (D–CALIF.): "I WOULD LIKE TO TAKE A FEW MORE MINUTES TO GO OVER WITH YOU THE RESPONSE OF OUR GOVERNMENT TO THE AIDS CRISIS. . . . THE CENTERS FOR DISEASE CONTROL HAS SPENT $4.5 MILLION LAST YEAR ON AIDS. . . . NOW, WHEN THE REAGAN ADMINISTRATION HAS SUBMITTED ITS BUDGET FOR 1984, THE REQUEST IS NOT FOR $4.5 MILLION OR MORE TO DEAL WITH AN ONGOING PUBLIC HEALTH CRISIS; THE REQUEST IS FOR ONLY $2 MILLION. A FEW MINUTES AGO, YOU SAID THAT THIS IS A COMPLEX MEDICAL PROBLEM; IT IS AN EPIDEMIC THAT WE MUST DEAL WITH; IT IS A PROBLEM THAT MUST BE SOLVED. YOUR RHETORIC WAS ONE OF RESOLVE. BUT THE ACTIONS OF THIS ADMINISTRATION ARE ONE OF NEGLECT. . . ."

EDWARD BRANDT, ASSISTANT SECRETARY OF HEALTH AND HUMAN SERVICES: "WELL, YOU KNOW OB-VIOUSLY ONE CAN ALWAYS GO BACK AND LOOK AT ONE'S ACTIONS EARLIER AND TRY TO DETERMINE WHETHER YOU WOULD HAVE DONE THINGS DIFFERENTLY, AND I THINK IN MOST INSTANCES EVERYTHING WOULD HAVE BEEN DONE. I THINK WE FOLLOWED LEADS AS THEY DEVELOPED, MR. CHAIRMAN." ∎

CASE STUDY
Politics and AIDS

B randt knew otherwise, and Waxman knew that he knew. What both men really knew was that the budget cutters in the Reagan administration were not inclined to allo-cate funds to fight a disease that they thought was affecting only drug users, Haitian immigrants, and the gay community. It was an opening shot in a battle by both men to try to move the AIDS epi-demic to a higher position on the government's poli-cymaking agenda.

In a memo to the assis-tant secretary of Manage-ment and Budget in the Department of Health and Human Services (HHS), Brandt wrote: "It has now reached the point where important AIDS work cannot be undertaken because of the lack of available resources." In May 1983, as a result of Brandt's efforts, $12 million was allo-cated to AIDS research by the Centers for Disease Control (CDC) and the National Institutes of Health (NIH). At the time, 1,450 Americans were infected with the human immunodeficien-cy virus (HIV), which causes AIDS, and 558 had died of the disease.

A month later Brandt convinced HHS secre-tary Margaret Heckler to give a speech on the need to fight the AIDS epidemic. Speaking before the U.S. Conference of Mayors in Denver, Heck-ler said: "Nothing I will say is more important than this: that the Department of Health and Human Services considers AIDS its number-one priority." This was not new to the mayors, who had asked for four times the amount of funding that the Reagan administration was proposing. In the last month alone, the death toll from AIDS had risen to 644, with 1,641 people infected by the HIV virus. Even more troubling was the CDC's prediction that the numbers would rise geometrically, doubling every six months.

By August 1983, Dr. Marcus Conant, an ex-pert on the disease, was telling Congress that "failure to respond to this epidemic now borders on a national scandal. . . . Congress, and in-deed the American people, have been misled about the response. We have been led to believe that the response has been timely and that the response has been appropriate, and I would sug-gest to you that that is not correct."

By May 1984 scientists were hard at work on a test that could identify AIDS-infected blood.

Source: This case is based on, and excerpts are quoted from, *And the Band Played On,* by Randy Shilts. ©1987 by Randy Shilts, St. Martin's Press, New York, NY. Printed by permission.

But the disease that was the "number-one priority" for HHS still was not getting the necessary funds. Brandt sent Heckler a memo arguing that $55 million in new funds would be needed to find a cure for AIDS.

Sympathetic members of Congress were now clamoring for more funding. However, Secretary Heckler declined Brandt's request for $55 million, telling him to redirect other funds for AIDS research. In the meantime another 600 Americans had died of AIDS, and 1,200 more were diagnosed as HIV positive. Brandt decided he had had enough and handed in his resignation.

But the fight had just begun. In November 1984 President Reagan was reelected. The number of people with HIV had now passed 7,000. By Christmas day the administration still had not decided whether to release the $8.4 million allocated by Congress to bring the HTLV-III antibody test to the nation's blood banks, and at the beginning of 1985 the administration called for a 10 percent cut in funding for AIDS research. While the administration and members of Congress fought over the level of funding, movie star Rock Hudson, a close personal friend of the president, died of AIDS in a Paris hospital. Suddenly the administration became acutely concerned about AIDS.

In October 1986 Surgeon General C. Everett Koop released a report that made AIDS the key item on the administration's agenda. By now 27,000 Americans had died or were dying of AIDS, and the disease had spread to every part of the globe. In May 1987 President Reagan announced that he would appoint a commission to study the epidemic. Movie stars like Elizabeth Taylor were now raising funds for research on AIDS, which was decimating the artistic community. Senators such as Ted Kennedy were calling for a billion dollars in new funding.

AIDS had now become the administration's top priority. But six years had passed since a scientist named Michael Gottlieb had published the first article about the mysterious new disease. One may well wonder how many lives could have been prolonged or saved if the government had been quicker to react to the need for massive funding of AIDS research.[1]

The AIDS quilt commemorates individuals who have died in what the Centers for Disease Control now term the AIDS pandemic.

INTRODUCTION: PUBLIC POLICY AND DEMOCRACY

The process by which an issue like AIDS rises from relative obscurity to a prominent place on the national policymaking agenda is the subject of this chapter.

The case of AIDS research shows that there are times when government policymakers fail to respond to a crisis, actually making it worse. What makes this example particularly poignant is the fact that the disease initially appeared to be limited to groups within the population that did not support the Reagan administration. The administration, in turn, chose to ignore the problem and hope that it would go away. But the failure to deal with the AIDS crisis in the early years involved more than the administration's reluctance to recognize the seriousness of the problem. It stemmed in part from a breakdown in communication within the federal bureaucracy, from the press's lack of adequate coverage, and from a lack of knowledge about AIDS on the part of both the public and the scientific community.

In recent years, as the public has learned that basketball star Magic Johnson and Olympic diver Greg Louganis are afflicted by the disease, and that tennis star Arthur Ashe died from it, press coverage and public awareness of AIDS have increased dramatically, as have activities of groups such as Act Up. As a result, AIDS has risen on the scale of legislative priorities for both Congress and the president.

In this chapter we begin by describing four types of public policies and outlining the policymaking process. We then consider the politics of policymaking, including such practices as "logrolling," "pork barrel politics," "iron triangles," and "issue networks." Finally, we explore recent trends in American public policy, showing that those policies are leading in an increasingly democratic direction.

WHAT IS PUBLIC POLICY?

Public policies are the decisions, actions, and commitments of government.[2] They are the means by which the government attempts to solve problems and to make life easier for its citizens. By looking more closely at public policies, we can better understand both *how* government operates and *how well* it does so.

Public policies enacted by the national government have four key aims:

1. *to regulate* key industries and aspects of American life, such as the savings and loan industry or the meat-packing industry, in the interests of public safety.

2. *to protect* Americans from actual or potential enemies at home and abroad by providing a powerful national defense.

3. *to encourage* the accomplishment of important social goals by providing such programs as Pell grants for college students and Head Start programs for low-income children.

4. *to assist* a wide range of American citizens, such as farmers (through grain subsidies), low-income families (through Aid to Families with Dependent Children, or AFDC), and state and local governments (through highway construction funds).[3]

TYPES OF POLICIES

As one examines the goals of policies, one begins to realize that they vary according to the types of programs being proposed. Public policies can be classified along four dimensions: substantive, symbolic, original, and incremental.[4] **Substantive policies** involve tangible rewards such as money, buildings, or jobs; in contrast, **symbolic policies** involve the use of symbols, assurances, and public values. The government may also choose to create an entirely new or **original policy,** or it may build on or add to an existing policy. Adding to an existing policy by small increments is called *incrementalism* or **incremental policy.**[5]

A policy may exhibit all of these characteristics at one time or another. As we saw in the case study, initially the government was willing to increase the funding for AIDS research only by small increments, despite calls by Assistant Secretary Brandt and members of the gay community for a fully funded original

The Federal Emergency Management Agency (FEMA) supervised the emergency response to the Los Angeles riots, which took place in 1992 following the acquittal of police officers involved in the Rodney King beating. FEMA is primarily responsible for the deployment of federal resources (primarily the President's Disaster Relief Fund) in response to disasters of catastrophic proportions. Created in 1979, FEMA consolidated all federal emergency programs and now works with state and local governments to train employees, create emergency management plans, and plan and administer multihazard responses.

program to deal with the crisis. Eventually Congress forced the administration to make some substantive efforts to increase the funding. But only after the death of his close friend, movie star Rock Hudson was President Reagan willing to make a speech in which he signified symbolically that the government was now committed to fighting the disease.

These dimensions of public policy can be combined in a variety of ways that have a significant effect on the nature of the resulting policies and programs. To better understand both the policymaking process and its outcomes, political scientists have developed *typologies,* or classification systems. A frequently used typology of public policy has four categories based on the dimensions just described. Reflexive policies are incremental and substantive; original policies are original and substantive; symbolic-reflexive policies are incremental and symbolic; and symbolic-original policies are original and symbolic.

The easiest way to understand these categories is to apply them to specific policy responses to an actual event. We will do so in the remainder of this section, using the example of policy responses to the riots in Los Angeles in 1992.

Reflexive Policies

In late April of 1992, following the controversial verdict in the case of the beating of an African American motorist, Rodney King, by Los Angeles police officers, the worst riot in the history of the United States broke out in South Central Los Angeles. More than forty people were killed, and estimates of the damage to buildings and property exceeded three billion dollars. The federal government used all four types of policy to meet the sudden crisis. President Bush declared Los Angeles a federal disaster area, and Congress acted on the president's declaration by appropriating five hundred million dollars in Small Business Administration loans and three hundred million dollars in assistance offered by the Federal Emergency Management Agency (FEMA) to help in rebuilding the burned and damaged areas of the city.

These policy responses were reflexive policies. **Reflexive policies** are incremental policies that build on past programs and policies; they "reflect back" on previous efforts and build on the assumption that the current or proposed policy will be modified over time.[6] In the case of the Los Angeles riots, the policies were an extension of what the federal government usually does in response to an emergency or disaster such as a hurricane, an earthquake, or an urban riot. Many, perhaps most, government policies are reflexive policies—they involve substantive rewards and are enacted in an incremental fashion.

Original Policies

The federal government also responded to the Los Angeles riots with **original policies,** that is, new substantive policies. President Bush called upon Congress to enact "weed-and-seed" programs to weed out urban crime and seed inner cities with more programs to improve urban living conditions. The program also called for "urban enterprise zones" with tax breaks for businesses willing to relocate to the inner cities.

It is important to note that while the president's urban aid package was new to the federal government when Bush proposed it, it was still, in a sense, incremental, since it was built on a proposal advanced three years earlier by

Jack Kemp, the secretary of Housing and Urban Development (HUD). Prior to his appointment as secretary of HUD, Kemp had attempted to secure passage of an urban enterprise zone program while serving as a member of Congress. Kemp's "original" idea, in turn, was a result of earlier experimentation with the concept of urban enterprise zones in England. "Original" policies thus are "original" to the federal government but usually have been tried out earlier, either in state or local programs or in other countries.

Symbolic-reflexive Policies

Symbolic-reflexive policies, which are both symbolic and incremental, were also adopted by the federal government after the Los Angeles riots. As political leaders traditionally do in such cases, President Bush visited the devastated neighborhoods of South Central Los Angeles. The visit was symbolic in that it demonstrated the president's concern and his commitment to restoring law and order, aiding the urban poor, and rebuilding the area. Unlike the six-billion-dollar urban aid package, the president's trip cost taxpayers very little. However, it was an important use of symbols by a president aware that the nation needed a highly visible sign that the crisis was over and that the underlying causes of the urban unrest would be addressed by policymakers in the national government.

Symbolic policies, sometimes called "symbolic reassurances," are frequently used by government officials to reassure American citizens that salient concerns are being addressed—that *something* is being done to solve the problem—even though the solution may take much longer to enact.[7] In this sense, symbolic policymaking is more affordable than alternative policies, since it involves the use of symbols, honors, or ceremonial gestures rather than the appropriation of large amounts of federal money. Symbolic-reflexive policy thus offers national policymakers a quick and relatively inexpensive way to reassure the American public that "help is on the way," that, in other words, the symbolic policy will soon be followed by more-substantive policy.

Symbolic-original Policies

President Bush also engaged in **symbolic-original policy.** During his visit to Los Angeles he gave a speech from the lectern of a church in the riot-torn neighborhood in which he urged that it was time to "bring the family together, the American family."[8] With this image the president was attempting to convey an original and symbolic reassurance that Los Angeles would be rebuilt and that the nation would heal the wounds and punish the lawbreakers.

While the image of the American family was not original with President Bush, very few other politicians had used it in such a context before. In this sense, the president's rhetoric is an example of symbolic-original policy. The reference to the family allowed Bush to connect the topic of the riots with a theme (the strength of the traditional family) that was central to his reelection campaign and implicitly criticize his Democratic rival, Arkansas governor Bill Clinton.

Many presidential candidates feel the need to underline the *newness* of their policy proposals. Election campaigns therefore often feature slogans incorporating symbolic-original policy proposals. For example, the 1992

The Clinton administration's attempt to fulfill its campaign promise of major health care reform was symbolized by a simple universal health coverage card. In actuality, the legislative solution was so complex that few Americans could understand it, a situation that engendered more fear than support.

presidential race included the following symbolic-original themes: "America First" (Pat Buchanan), a "New, New Deal" (Tom Harkin), and the "New American Mandate" (Paul Tsongas). Such sloganeering has a long history among candidates of both parties.[9] Consider, for example, the "New Birth of Freedom" of Abraham Lincoln, the "New Nationalism" of Theodore Roosevelt, the "New Freedom" of Woodrow Wilson, the "New Deal" of Franklin Roosevelt, the "Fair Deal" of Harry Truman, the "New America" of Adlai Stevenson, the "New Frontier" of John F. Kennedy, the "Great Society" of Lyndon Johnson, the "New American Revolution" and "New Federalism" of Richard Nixon, the "New Spirit" of Jimmy Carter, the "New Beginning" and "New Federalism" of Ronald Reagan, and finally, the "New World Order" of George Bush.

It would be tempting to dismiss symbolic-original policies and slogans as empty campaign rhetoric. The truth, however, goes much deeper than that. National leaders, particularly presidents, are expected to craft new policies, to chart new ground, and to distinguish themselves as much as possible from rivals and predecessors. The slogans and themes typical of symbolic-original policies are crucial components of presidential policymaking.

It is important to stress that policymaking is often far more complex than this policy typology suggests. Nevertheless, such typologies are useful because they can help us unravel some of the complexities of the policymaking process.

THE POLICYMAKING PROCESS

In addition to policy typologies, policy scholars have developed several *process models* that try to capture the flavor and substance of policymaking.[10] One such model views the policymaking process as a life cycle. This model is especially useful in analyzing how an issue like AIDS can be moved into the spotlight of the national agenda.[11]

The concepts of a public-policy agenda and a policy life cycle are part of a relatively new approach to studying public policy. This approach centers on the process by which the agenda of public policy is established. It seeks to discover how public conditions, events, or situations come to be viewed as political problems requiring a public-policy response from government. Stated differently, how do public policies arise? How are they "born"? How long do they live? Why do some have long "lives" while others "die" quick deaths? Why do some ideas never become policies at all, while others travel quickly through the early stages of the policy life cycle, only to be stopped later in the process? We will explore these questions as we describe each stage of the policy life cycle.

The policy life cycle consists of eleven steps or stages, each of which can be illustrated by recalling our opening case study. These stages are as follows:

1. Redefinition of a public or private "condition" as a public "problem." (In the case of the AIDS crisis, it took six years for the condition—a disease affecting certain subgroups of the population—to be defined as a problem to be addressed by public policy.)

2. Placement of the problem on the national policy agenda. (In the case of AIDS, this did not happen until Rock Hudson died of the disease.)

3. Emergence of the problem as a "public issue" requiring government action. (Only when Surgeon General C. Everett Koop announced that the problem was widespread did AIDS become a public issue.)

4. Formulation of a public-policy response; usually followed by a pledge of action. (With President Reagan's speech came the full-fledged willingness of the government to fund research on AIDS.)

5. One or more reformulations of the proposed policy. (Every year the question of how much funding would be provided for AIDS research led to a reformulation of the policy.)

6. Placement of the proposed policy on the formal agenda of government. (Despite the unwillingness of the Reagan administration to push for major funding for AIDS research, the public, the press, and Congress would not let the issue die.)

7. Enactment of part or all of the proposed policy. (President Reagan's announcement that he would appoint a committee to study the epidemic.)

8. Implementation of the policy. (Funding for AIDS research continued to grow to its present level of nearly $1 billion.)

9. Impacts caused by implementation of the policy. (Activist groups ranging from coalitions of celebrities to congressional members emerged to help raise funds.)

10. Evaluation of the impact(s) of the policy. (During the 1992 presidential election campaign, AIDS was one of the many issues used by challenger Bill Clinton to attack the Bush administration's policies.)

11. Termination or continued implementation and evaluation of the policy. (Although the government continues to fund AIDS research at high levels, the disease is now the primary cause of death for men between the ages of twenty-five and forty-five in cities throughout the United States.)

In the remainder of this section we will examine the policy life cycle in detail. We begin by exploring the question of why certain issues and not others become subjects for governmental action, that is, how they get onto the "agenda" of the political world.[12]

Getting onto the Public Agenda

Before it can enter the policymaking process, a potential subject of public policy must undergo a radical redefinition in the eyes of **policy elites**—members of Congress, the president, Supreme Court justices, cabinet officers, heads of key agencies and departments, leading editorial writers, and influential columnists and commentators—as well as the general public. Such a redefinition changes the way the topic is viewed and places it on the **public agenda,** the set of topics that are a source of concern for policy elites, the general public, or both.

The public agenda can be viewed as the informal agenda of government. It should not be confused with the **formal agenda,** that is, the policies that are actually scheduled for debate and potential adoption by Congress, the president, the Supreme Court, or executive departments and agencies. For example, pollution has been on the public agenda since the late 1960s, but it did not reach the formal agenda until 1970, when Congress debated and enacted the original Clean Air Act.

How do social concerns become translated or redefined into matters that are important enough to be placed on the public agenda? By being labeled as "problems." The difference between social conditions and social problems is

Immigrants and Public Policy

In recent years there has been an upsurge of anti-immigrant sentiment in the United States, and immigrants, both legal and illegal, are worried. They are afraid that many government programs that are now available to noncitizens will be eliminated. Already, California has passed Proposition 187, which makes illegal immigrants ineligible for nearly all government programs except emergency medical aid. And Congress is considering welfare legislation that would make legal immigrants ineligible for food stamps, Medicare, and other programs.

Among the programs most valued by immigrants is Supplemental Security Income (SSI), a welfare program for people over age sixty-five who have lived in the United States for more than three years and are not eligible for social security. Many older immigrants view SSI as a sort of retirement plan, since they have not worked long enough to earn social-security benefits and their children are unable or unwilling to support them. The welfare legislation under consideration in Congress would place limits on noncitizens' eligibility for SSI.

Immigrants who have spent most of their working lives in the United States are deeply troubled by the current political climate. "I'm afraid they are trying to take everything away from us," says Sirelio Flores, a Mexican who works as an appliance repairman in Houston. "I pay my taxes all the time. . . . Why are they coming after us?"* Immigrants, in short, are on the public agenda—and they would rather not be.

What Happened

Faced with the possibility of being denied access to basic social services such as education and health care, many immigrants have found a simple solution: Become a U.S. citizen. The number of applications for citizenship has doubled in the past year,

and the trend is accelerating. Immigrants who intended to remain citizens of their native land, and perhaps to retire there after spending their working lives in the United States, are changing their plans.

Several factors are contributing to the surge in applications for citizenship. One is the large pool of illegal immigrants who were granted amnesty under the 1986 Immigration Act and are now eligible for citizenship. Another is the switch to computer-compatible "green cards" for noncitizens residing in the United States. The Immigration and Naturalization Service requires all legal immigrants to apply for the new cards, which cost seventy-five dollars. Since an application for citizenship costs ninety-five dollars, many people are spending the extra twenty dollars and applying for citizenship.

Immigrants who have lived in the United States for five years with proper authorization and no criminal record are eligible to apply for citizenship. If they pass a test on basic facts about American history and government, they become U.S. citizens. Their immediate relatives are eligible to become citizens more quickly. With approximately ten million legal immigrants living in the United States, some demographers anticipate a vast increase in the number of applications for citizenship.

The large number of new citizens could have an impact extending well beyond eligibility for government programs. As one applicant put it, "I want to vote, I'll tell you that." Political leaders who call for the elimination of social services for immigrants might come to wish they had acknowledged this pool of potential voters.

---

*Quoted in Sam Howe Verhovek, "Legal Immigrants in Record Numbers Want Citizenship," *New York Times,* Apr. 2, 1995, p. 28.

---

more than a matter of semantics. Americans expect the government to solve social problems; they do not expect it to "solve" social conditions.[13] The distinction between "problems" and "conditions" is critical for understanding public policymaking. Citizens and policymakers are willing to live with various social conditions—pollution, high crime rates, low voter turnout, high rates of unemployment, or poverty rates—as long as those conditions do not come to be perceived as "problems." When a condition is redefined as a problem, however, the government is expected to do something about it.[14]

FROM "PROBLEMS" TO "ISSUES"   Problems are concerns that Americans believe the government should address and attempt to solve. For a "condition" to be redefined as a "problem," Americans must view the condition as a current or future problem with a possible governmental solution. Furthermore, the "problem" must eventually come to be framed as an "issue." Thus, during presidential election campaigns there is always a long list of issues, ranging from social issues such as abortion to domestic issues such as crime control and international issues such as the use of the military in foreign lands, that are matters of concern to the voting public. However, in 1992 Bill Clinton's campaign director, James Carville, kept a sign above his desk reading "It's the economy, Stupid!" By that he meant that the central issue of the campaign was whether the voters believed that the ongoing recession merited a change in leadership.

A potential policy reaches the **issue stage** when it is framed in terms of a yes-or-no policy option. For example, a yes-or-no policy option on fighting crime might include a variety of subissues: Should capital punishment be used against small-time drug dealers to deter drug use? and Should the federal government require a longer waiting period and check for a criminal record to make it more difficult to purchase handguns?

Because there is such a vast number of potential social issues and because Americans are often reluctant to pay additional tax dollars to fund proposed policies, many social conditions never become translated or redefined into social problems and therefore never manage to reach the public agenda. In turn, many policy problems succeed in making it onto the public agenda but fail to successfully emerge as policy issues.

There are two key ways in which existing social conditions become redefined as problems requiring governmental policy responses. First, a dramatic event may serve as a triggering mechanism. A **triggering mechanism** is "a critical development that converts a routine problem into a widely shared, negative public response."[15] It can transform a "condition" into a "problem" in the minds of the American public and political leadership alike. An earthquake, a tragic airplane accident, or an act of aggression such as the 1991 invasion of Kuwait by Iraq or the 1979 seizure of American hostages by Iran are examples of events that can quickly and sometimes dramatically affect public perceptions and place an issue on the public agenda.

As we have seen, despite all the lobbying for research funding both in and out of government, AIDS did not reach the public agenda until after the death of movie star Rock Hudson and the announcement that popular sports figures such as Magic Johnson and Arthur Ashe were infected with the disease. Prior to these triggering events, AIDS was not viewed as a major national problem demanding the attention of the public or its policymakers.

A potential policy can also reach the public agenda through the activities of **policy entrepreneurs,** individuals or groups who are instrumental in "selling" a program or policy to a policymaking body.[16] American political history is full of examples of policy entrepreneurs who succeeded in placing a potential policy issue on the public agenda. In the 1950s and 1960s Martin Luther

Homelessness has traditionally been accepted as a social condition rather than a targeted issue on the public policy agenda. Events have periodically managed to redefine homelessness as a social problem, but the absence of either a triggering mechanism or a determined policy entrepreneur has prevented large-scale governmental response to the situation.

King, Jr., the Congress on Racial Equality, the Southern Christian Leadership Conference, the Student Non-Violent Coordinating Council, and the National Association for the Advancement of Colored People used a series of lobbying and attention-getting, nonviolent tactics that successfully placed the issue of civil rights on both the public agenda and the formal agenda of the national government.[17]

As you saw in Chapter 15, in the case of the civil rights movement, the policy entrepreneurs used a variety of tactics. A series of lawsuits challenged the "separate but equal" doctrine in public education. Confrontational demonstrations such as the civil rights marches in Montgomery, Birmingham, Selma, and Washington, D.C., and rallies and speeches such as the famous "I have a dream" speech given on the steps of the Lincoln Memorial by Martin Luther King, Jr., made the civil rights movement more visible to the American public. The assassinations of President John F. Kennedy, Martin Luther King, Jr., and Robert Kennedy served as triggering mechanisms for the passage of additional Civil Rights Acts covering other areas of life. Thus, the efforts of a dedicated core of organizers and advocates stimulated actions and events that underscored existing problems in American society; the policy entrepreneurs then worked to promote specific solutions to those problems in the form of proposed policies.

Getting onto the Formal Agenda

As noted earlier, a policy reaches the formal agenda when it is actually scheduled for debate and potential adoption by policymaking bodies such as Congress. In the process, it is generally formulated and reformulated several times. In a formal sense, Congress actually *enacts* or passes legislation. But while only Congress actually passes laws, policy is "enacted"—constructed, designed, and put into effect—by all of the branches of the federal government. The president, for example, may submit bills to Congress or issue executive orders, as when President Lyndon Johnson ordered the federal government to take "affirmative action" to make the federal workforce more representative of the diversity of the American population in general.

Courts also formulate and reformulate public policy. Abortion is a case in point. In 1973 the Supreme Court adopted a policy position in the case of *Roe* v. *Wade,* arguing that women have an absolute right to choose an abortion in the first trimester of a pregnancy. More recently, in cases such as *Webster* v. *Reproductive Health Services* (1989), the Court has modified the earlier *Roe* policy in favor of a more restrictive policy on abortion.[18]

Policies are often formulated and reformulated in the committees and subcommittees of Congress, as well as during the process of debate and amendment on the floor of the House and Senate. Policy formulation also occurs in the government agencies that implement laws enacted by Congress. Those agencies often issue regulations explaining how the agency will enforce and interpret the new law. These regulations are issued in tentative form and subsequently modified as part of a regular hearing and appeal process. For example, the regulations issued by the Environmental Protection Agency to carry out the programs required by the amendments to the 1990 Clean Air Act were reformulated over a period of more than two years as the agency considered the requests and priorities of industry, environmentalists, the congressional sponsors of the legislation, and the Bush administration.

Implementing the Policy

Once a policy has been enacted, it must be implemented.[19] **Implementation** is the actual execution of a policy. Some policies are relatively easy to implement. For example, when Congress enacted a national highway speed limit of fifty-five miles per hour to conserve gasoline, the government quickly achieved full implementation of the policy by denying federal funds for highway construction to any state that did not enforce the new speed limit. Other policies, however, are more difficult to implement. An example is court-mandated school desegregation, which was first ordered by the Supreme Court in *Brown* v. *Board of Education,* 347 U.S. 483 (1954). Such desegregation was to occur "with all deliberate speed," in part to soften the blow for the conservative and historically segregationist southern states, which were powerfully represented in Congress. However, it soon became apparent that the ambiguous phrase "all deliberate speed" meant one thing to the justices of the Supreme Court and quite another to state and local officials who were reluctant to implement the policy. Ten years after the *Brown* decision, less than 2 percent of African American children in the South attended school with whites.[20] Thus, "all deliberate speed" turned out to mean a slow, sometimes painful process that has not achieved full implementation even in the 1990s.

Why are some federal policies easier to implement than others? The difficulty of implementing federal policies is a result of the "three Cs of implementation": *complexity, cooperation,* and *coordination.* Desegregating public schools is a far more complex process than changing the highway speed limit. Efforts to achieve full desegregation of public schools have had to confront the

Republican proposals designed to make cuts in federally funded school lunch programs for the poor met with vociferous resistance from those that the policies would affect. This resistance represents a larger and underlying philosophy that prevention is cheaper than later intervention. Programs designed to provide nutrition to school-age children from low-income families may have the effect of supporting their ability to function and learn with the other "better fed" students and in so doing prevent problems resulting from poor academic performance.

complexities presented by racial and ethnic hostilities in the American public, "white flight" to the suburban communities surrounding urban areas, and declining funds for public schools.

Another obstacle to implementation of the *Brown* decision was that the actual plans for desegregating the schools required the cooperation of local and state officials. More individuals and groups with the power to stop or delay a policy, such as officials of school districts and elected school boards, means more obstacles to full implementation of the policy. Some school districts, including those in Los Angeles and Boston, were actually turned over to "federal masters" appointed by federal courts to supervise desegregation in their areas.

As the difficulty of desegregating public schools increased, so did problems of coordination. In the cases of Los Angeles and Boston, coordination between the federal courts, the court-appointed "masters," the elected school boards, as well as the parents and students, presented one of the greatest implementation challenges ever faced by the federal government.

As the examples of highway speed limits and school desegregation illustrate, implementation of public policies is far from automatic. The probability of full implementation of any public policy is *inversely related* to the complexity, cooperation, and coordination required by the proposed policy. Complex policies requiring extensive cooperation and a great deal of coordination have much less chance of achieving full implementation than simpler policies.

Evaluating a Policy's Impact

All policies have an impact of some kind, though not all achieve the full impact intended by those who proposed and enacted them. It is difficult to generalize about which policies have greater impact and why, but scholars have been able to identify some characteristics that contribute to the effectiveness of public policies. They are (1) a clearly written law or policy statement, (2) strong presidential support for the policy, and (3) local cooperation in the implementation of the policy. Policies that combine all three of these basic ingredients have the greatest chance of achieving their full impact.

Most federal policies require a period of monitoring and analysis following implementation known as **policy evaluation.** Policy evaluation at the federal level is a mixture of scientific and political considerations. Trained policy analysts working in such agencies as the Congressional Budget Office, the General Accounting Office, or various legislative committees attempt to determine the costs and benefits associated with government policies. Sometimes policymakers are guided by such *cost–benefit analysis.* Other times, however, cost–benefit analysis is not helpful because the policy experts themselves disagree. For example, policy experts using the same data disagree on the effectiveness of such policies as capital punishment, gun control, spending for educational programs such as Head Start, busing to achieve school integration, and federal antipoverty programs.[21]

Despite the enormous resources for policy evaluation available to the federal government, policies are frequently "evaluated" in political terms. Head Start or the All-Volunteer Army, for example, are demonstrated policy successes, but funding and support for these and other key social programs have varied from one administration to the next, depending on the administration's political evaluation of these policies. For example, Reagan's initial reluctance to support funding for AIDS research resulted in part from his administration's political evaluation of such a policy direction: the appearance of sympathy for IV drug users and homosexuals and for potential alienation of key elements of Reagan's support, such as the religious right.

Terminating a Policy

Following evaluation, policies are either terminated or continued. If they are continued, they enter what social scientists call the "feedback loop." Information about the consequences of a policy can be "fed back" into the cycle to help in the formulation of new policies. The feedback may be positive, as is the case with Head Start, or negative, as was the case with the reduction in the speed limit on federal highways from sixty-five to fifty-five miles per hour. Unpopularity alone, however, is not enough to terminate most government policies. For example, the unpopularity of the lower speed limit was offset by other kinds of feedback, including a slight decrease in rates of highway accidents and fatalities and a slight increase in rates of energy conservation.

Termination of a policy is the end of the policy life cycle.[22] But policies must be strongly supported by policy entrepreneurs in the government and by interest groups outside the government to be enacted in the first place. These individuals and groups presumably benefit from the policy; as a result, public policies, once enacted, are rarely terminated. Thus, because of political

The Medicare program, implemented in 1965 and backed by a powerful and influential interest group, the American Association of Retired Persons (AARP), has proved to be difficult to cut back. On May 7, 1995, Speaker of the House Newt Gingrich appeared on "Meet the Press" (NBC) and spoke of "an unbelievable financial catastrophe" if Medicare reform fails. Even though advocating "painless cuts" in Medicare, Speaker Gingrich may have underestimated the power of the best-represented consumers of medical care—the elderly. This case is a good example of the "once enacted, rarely terminated" rule.

pressures, policies that have a difficult time being "born" have an even more difficult time "dying" or being terminated.

In the rare cases in which policies are terminated, it is usually because one of three scenarios takes place. First, the policy or program may come to be viewed as out of date and no longer important in light of new developments. An example is the nuclear-targeting policy of "mutual assured destruction (MAD)." MAD's targeting of civilian areas such as Moscow as part of a strategy to protect the nation against the threat of a nuclear strike by the Soviet Union was rendered obsolete after the breakup of the Soviet Union in 1990.

Second, the policy or program may fail to perform effectively, or an alternative policy may be viewed as performing better than the original policy. An example is court-ordered busing to achieve racial integration of public schools. Parents often resisted court-ordered busing of students, so the creation of magnet schools frequently proved more effective in attracting students from many neighborhoods and achieving integration than did the busing policies.

Policies may also be terminated when they lose the political support of the general public, the president, the Supreme Court, or members of Congress. President Bush, for example, responded to the Los Angeles riots of 1992 by proposing a two-billion-dollar emergency urban aid package. As noted at the beginning of the chapter, a central element of that proposal was a "weed-and-seed" program for increased law enforcement and social programs in poor, inner-city neighborhoods. Yet within two months the president withdrew his "weed-and-seed" proposal in favor of a less expensive urban aid proposal.[23]

Mature Policies: Continuation, Refinement, and Feedback

Some policies are implemented, evaluated over time, and refined or modified by key actors in the national policymaking process, such as the president, Congress, or the courts. Policies that survive the early stages of the policy life cycle and are actually implemented are still subject to periodic review and possible modification over time. For example, the basic mission of the National Aeronautics and Space Administration (NASA) has changed over time, from catching up with the Soviets (during the 1950s) to space exploration (1960–90) to analysis of the earth's weather and environmental patterns from space.[24]

Many policies survive because of political practices such as "logrolling" and arrangements such as "iron triangles" and "issue networks." Although we have described these practices in the chapters on Congress, the federal bureaucracy, and interest groups it is worthwhile to examine how they operate in the policymaking process. To do so, we must explore the politics of policymaking.

THE POLITICS OF POLICYMAKING

As noted earlier, policies often have a difficult time getting onto the agenda of the national government. Moreover, and somewhat ironically, once a policy has been enacted it is often difficult to terminate. Both of these facts can be explained by the politics of policymaking. Five aspects of American public policymaking—fragmentation, logrolling, pork barrel politics, iron triangles, and issue networks—act both separately and in combination to make policymaking a highly political process.

Federalism: Fragmentation and Multiple Actors

Because the nation's founders embraced *federalism,* separating the powers of the national and state governments, and because they also believed in *division of powers* and *checks and balances* at the national level, policymaking in the United States is often fragmented. This fragmentation is accompanied by the presence of multiple actors operating on multiple levels, all of which can affect the direction of policymaking. It is possible for policy in a particular area to involve the president; Congress; the governor and legislature of one or more states; the mayor and city council of one or more cities; and federal, state, and municipal courts and government agencies.

The Los Angeles riots of 1992 provide an excellent example of the role of fragmentation and multiple actors in American policymaking on social-welfare issues. At the federal level, President Bush engaged in both symbolic and substantive policy responses to the urban unrest. Congress enacted an urban aid bill in June 1992 in response to the riots. Federal agencies such as FEMA and the SBA allocated millions of dollars in disaster relief for residents of Los Angeles. At the state level, the governor of California declared South Central Los Angeles a disaster area, and the California legislature considered a riot-relief tax and other relief measures; and at the local level, the mayor of Los Angeles appointed a commission to oversee rebuilding efforts. The riot itself began after the verdict in the Rodney King case, which was heard in a state court. Add to these the successful efforts of the Los Angeles Police Commission to pressure the chief of police, Daryl Gates, into retirement and the awarding of two million dollars by the Ford Foundation to a civic organization to help rebuild the neighborhood destroyed by the riots, and one can begin to understand how multiple actors at multiple levels make policymaking in the United States a highly complex and political process.[25]

Logrolling and Pork Barrel Policies

Another factor that contributes to the political nature of American policymaking is **logrolling.** This term refers to a temporary political alliance between two policy actors who agree to support each other's policy goals. It is equivalent to saying "you scratch my back and I'll scratch yours."

Logrolling is often combined with **pork barrel legislation.** Pork barrel policies and programs are designed to create special benefits for a state or district, such as bridges, highways, dams, and military installations, all of which translate into jobs and money for the local economy. A prime example of "grade-A" pork is the annual Rivers and Harbors Bill, which often contains appropriations for bridges, dams, and water projects in numerous congressional districts. President Carter learned a difficult lesson in policymaking when he vetoed this bill soon after his inauguration in January 1977. Congress promptly overrode the veto, demonstrating the political strength of logrolling policy coalitions and pork barrel legislation.[26]

Iron Triangles and Issue Networks

Iron triangles are another factor contributing to the political nature of American national policymaking. Political scientists use terms such as *iron triangles,*

"As everyone in this room knows but few outside Washington understand, questions of public policy . . . are often decided by a trinity consisting of (1) representatives of an outside body, (2) middle level bureaucrats, and (3) selected members of Congress, particularly those concerned with appropriations. In a given field, these people may have collaborated for years. They have a durable alliance that cranks out legislation and appropriations on behalf of their special interests."

—John W. Gardner, Founder of Common Cause

subgovernments, and *cozy little triangles* to describe the informal three-way relationships that develop among key legislative committees, the executive agencies whose budgets are supervised by those committees, and interest groups with a vested interest in the policies created by those committees and agencies. These relationships have a major influence on the content of public policy and on how policies are carried out.

In his farewell address in 1960, President Dwight Eisenhower described one such iron triangle: the three-sided relationship between lobbyists for the defense industry, the defense appropriations committees in Congress, and the Department of Defense. Eisenhower complained that this "military–industrial complex" constituted a subgovernment strong enough to ward off attacks from competitors and rivals, even when one of those rivals was a former general and president of the United States. Such mutually supportive coalitions are considered to be strong as iron and tend to dominate the policy process by trading on information, influence, and money.[27]

Policymaking at the federal level often involves more than a three-sided relationship between three equally strong partners. The term **issue networks** has been used to describe a pattern of interaction that consists of numerous actors and levels and in which the actors move into and out of the lobbying and policy formation stages. While the boundaries of an issue network are less clearly drawn than those of an iron triangle—it may be more appropriate to describe it as a polygon—the network concept is a better description of most policy activity than the older iron-triangle concept.[28]

The idea of an issue network can be used to describe much policymaking activity in the national government today. Policymaking is often not only complex but chaotic. It usually involves numerous actors, including the president, members of Congress, cabinet officers, lobbyists, interest groups, and officials from various government agencies. Additional participants may include the professional staffs of congressional committees, executive agencies, and interest groups. Finally, scholars and advisers from such organizations as the Heritage Foundation, the Brookings Institution, the American Enterprise Institute, and the Joint Center for Political and Economic Studies have become increasingly visible in policy debates. All of these participants—who may number in the hundreds—take an active interest in policy formation and may testify before Congress and provide information to policymakers.[29] The case study offers just such an example of this kind of network that can spring up around an issue, and how this network can defy the rigidity of the iron triangle. Democratic legislators like Henry Waxman worked with Republican bureaucratic appointees like Edward Brandt, as well as with AMA and AIDS activists, in a much more open, dynamic process than one would expect in an iron triangle.

POLICYMAKING IN ACTION

Domestic policy can be divided into two major categories: regulatory policy and social-welfare policy. **Regulatory policy** involves the use of police powers by the federal government to supervise the conduct of individuals, businesses, and other governmental agencies. It is essentially a set of negative incentives put into place by government to prevent certain kinds of behavior.

For this reason, regulatory policy often focuses on social "villains"—industrial polluters, crooked savings and loan executives, or, in earlier times, unscrupulous railroad barons and meat packers.

In contrast to regulatory policy, **social-welfare policy** uses positive incentives (cash assistance, stipends, entitlements, grants, etc.) to promote or encourage basic social fairness. Longstanding American social-welfare objectives include aiding disadvantaged groups such as people living below the poverty line, older Americans, people of color, women, military veterans, and educationally, emotionally, or physically handicapped Americans.

In the remainder of the chapter we will explore both categories of policy, using case studies to illustrate policymaking in action.

Regulatory Policy

Regulatory policies are designed to regulate conduct and protect the health and welfare of all Americans. As political scientist Kenneth Meier has noted, "Regulation is any attempt by the government to control the behavior of citizens, corporations, or subgovernments."[30] The national government engages in six different kinds of regulatory activity. It may regulate (1) the *price* that can be charged for a good or service, (2) franchising or *licenses* granted to individuals or businesses, (3) performance of safety *standards,* or (4) *resources* (e.g., water or electricity from federal dams and hydroelectric projects) available to citizens or businesses. It may also (5) provide or withhold operating *subsidies* or (6) use regulatory *commissions* such as the Federal Trade Commission (FTC) or the Securities and Exchange Commission (SEC) to regulate vital industries and promote fair competition among individuals and businesses.[31]

THE RISE OF REGULATION   As Table 16.1 illustrates, regulatory activity by the federal government has increased gradually during the past century after being almost nonexistent during the first hundred years of the nation's history. The first significant regulation occurred in response to the political pressures of the granger and muckraker movements in the late 1800s and early 1900s. Another surge of regulatory activity occurred in the 1930s as a result of the problems created by the Great Depression. The highest levels of regulation were reached in the 1960s and 1970s in response to the consumer, civil rights, and environmental movements.

Beginning in the mid 1970s, regulatory activity by the federal government declined and a movement toward deregulation emerged. The government sold ("privatized") government-owned railroads to private investors and acted to deregulate the trucking, banking, and airline industries. Beginning in the late 1980s, however, there was a swing back toward increased regulation.

REGULATING THE ENVIRONMENT   Environmental policy provides a good illustration of regulatory policymaking. As Table 16.1 indicates, Americans became vitally interested in environmental issues in the 1960s and 1970s, and the federal government responded by enacting several key pieces of environmental legislation. The triggering mechanism for environmental policymaking at the federal level was the publication of *Silent Spring*, by Rachel Carson, in 1962. In

Table 16.1
Selected Highlights of the Federal Government's Regulatory Policies

DATE	POLICY	POLITICAL BACKGROUND
1887	Interstate Commerce Act	Granger movement
1890	Sherman Anti-Trust Act	Led to "trust-busting"
1906	Pure Food and Drug Act Meat Inspection Act	Upton Sinclair writes *The Jungle* (1906)
1933–38	Federal Deposit Insurance Corporation (FDIC), Security and Exchange Commission (SEC), Federal Communications Commission (FCC), National Labor Relations Board (NLRB), Federal Housing Administration (FHA), Tennessee Valley Authority (TVA), and the Agricultural Adjustment Administration (AAA) created	FDR and New Deal responses to the Great Depression
1958–60	Congress authorizes the Food & Drug Administration (FDA) to regulate chemical preservatives and artificial coloring in food. Federal Trade Commission (FTC) authorized to act against misleading advertisers. Warning labels on household products required	Beginnings of the consumer movement
1964	Civil Rights Act	
1965	Voting Rights Act	Civil rights movement
1966	Office of Civil Rights (OCR)	
1969	National Environmental Policy Act	Hallmark of federal environmental policy
1970	The Clean Air Act. Charged Department of Transportation to oversee reducing automobile emissions. Occupational Safety and Health Administration (OSHA) Environmental Protection Agency (EPA)	
1972	Water Pollution Control Act Federal Environmental Pesticide Control Act	Rachel Carson writes *Silent Spring* (1962); the environmental movement begins
1973	Endangered Species Act. Fish and Wildlife Service charged with preserving wilderness areas.	
1974	President Ford orders all regulatory agencies to consider the inflationary impact of regulatory decisions.	Deregulation movement begins
1978	Airline Deregulation Act. President Carter orders all regulatory agencies to consider alternative ways of achieving regulatory goals	
1979	Nuclear Regulatory Commission (NRC)	
1980	Rail Deregulation Act Motor Carrier Act Depository Institution Deregulation Act Superfund Clean-Up Law	Love Canal scandal
1981	President Reagan signs an Executive Order requiring that new federal regulations prove benefits	Deregulation movement continues

Table 16.1
Selected Highlights of the Federal Government's Regulatory Policies (Continued)

1982	Bus Deregulatory Reform Act Thrift Institutions Restructuring Act	
1988	Conrail sold to private investors	Deregulatory movement weakens
1989	Savings and loan bailout legislation	Savings and loan crisis spurs a reregulation movement
1990	Clean Air Act Amendments. Significantly increased controls on caps, oil refineries, chemical plants, utility plants	Reregulation movement continues Reauthorization of Clean Air Act
1991	Civil Rights Act of 1991	Womens' movement, civil rights movement, and reregulation movement continue
1993	Gays in military Abortion counseling	
1995	Attempts to dismantle environmental regulation	

this path-breaking book Carson argued that the widely used pesticide DDT was poisoning fields, streams, fish and wildlife, and ultimately the American consumer. The book spurred a scientific search to develop less hazardous pesticides, as well as a search by federal policymakers for environmentally sensitive policies and programs.[32]

In a landmark piece of legislation, the National Environmental Protection Act of 1969, Congress required that government agencies issue an *environmental-impact statement* listing the effects that proposed agency regulations would have on the environment. In 1970 Congress created the Environmental Protection Agency (EPA) to administer environmental programs and issue environmental regulations. It also enacted the Clean Air Act of 1970, which directed the EPA to monitor industrial air pollution and enforce compliance with existing pollution laws. The Department of Transportation was assigned the responsibility for monitoring and reducing pollution associated with automobile emissions.

In 1972, Congress passed the Water Pollution and Control Act, which was aimed at reducing pollution in the nation's rivers and lakes. In 1975, Congress added ocean dumping of wastes to the policy agenda with the Marine Protection Research Act, which was followed in 1976 by legislation regulating the dumping of hazardous waste. The 1976 legislation, the Resource Conservation and Recovery Act, not only regulated the disposal of hazardous waste but also sought to reduce the volume of waste by encouraging recycling, on-site disposal, incineration, and disposal of hazardous waste in safe landfills.

The enormous expense associated with cleaning up hazardous-waste sites led to the enactment in 1980 of the Superfund Law, which created a fund to pay for toxic-site cleanups and authorized the EPA to order polluters to clean

Lake Onondaga near Syracuse, New York, in April, 1993. One of the nation's most polluted lakes, it can be restored with existing cleanup plans costing more than $1 billion. Environmental regulation seeks to prevent the pollution that leads to these astounding cleanup costs through "negative incentives" that discourage polluting and encourage environmentally friendly technology. Even President George Bush, an unlikely advocate of environmental regulation, got into the act on behalf of the Bass Anglers Sportsman Society (BASS). Bush has been a life member since 1978 and through his membership became concerned about fisheries management and the water quality issues associated with fishing largemouth bass.

up sites where necessary. More recently, Congress enacted the Safe Water and Toxic Enforcement Act of 1986, regulating discharges into surface water and groundwater; the Toxic Substances Control Act of 1987, requiring the removal of carcinogenic material such as asbestos from buildings; and the Clean Air Act Amendments of 1990, which resolved a long-running conflict between coal-producing and auto-manufacturing states, such as West Virginia and Michigan, and states such as Maine and California, whose residents and local economies were more favorably inclined toward environmental protection.[33]

In coming decades environmental regulation must address three key sets of concerns. First, Congress will need to "clean up" the Clean Air Act of 1990. On the positive side, the 1990 legislation sets strict limitations on pollution from utilities and automobile emissions, mandates the use of less polluting fuels, and authorizes inspections of potential polluters ranging from automobiles to wood-burning stoves. In addition, the 1990 act authorizes the EPA to set standards for allowable pollutants by industries and limits emissions of sulfur dioxide, the primary cause of acid rain. On the negative side, there is no guarantee that cities or industries will meet the strict guidelines in the 1990 legislation. Many American cities do not yet meet the air quality standards established in the original Clean Air Act of 1970. Much will depend on the willingness of the EPA to issue the new regulations quickly and clearly and to enforce them aggressively.

A second set of concerns has to do with the fact that pollution and the need for environmental regulation spill over state and national borders into the arena of international politics. The first international conference on the environment was held in 1992 in Rio de Janiero, Brazil. The United States was the only major nation that would not sign the Rio Accords, which committed nations to environmental goals and required them to allocate a fixed percentage of their national budgets to take action on environmental concerns. The U.S. did not sign because probusiness conservative politicians did not like international entanglements that would cut into profits and had a general suspicion of multinational agreements like this one.

A third challenge facing environmental regulation is the increasing complexity of regulatory policy. *Offset policies* are a case in point. They allow a potential polluter to build a facility that otherwise would not be allowable by "offsetting" the increased pollution with lower pollution elsewhere. For example, the 1990 Clean Air Act created *pollution credits*. Industries and companies that fail to meet their emission standards can buy extra pollution "credits" sold by companies whose emissions are below the allowable level. While the overall level of pollution in a particular area must remain below the established limit, there can be significant differences among industries and businesses in the amounts of polluting substances they emit. How should such a market in pollution credits be regulated, and will it require further monitoring and regulation as it develops?

Off-site tradeoffs are another example of the complexity of environmental regulatory policy. Some states have recently allowed construction projects to go forward even though the environmental impact reports for those projects suggest that they will cause irreparable environmental damage. For example, in southern California a marina was built on an endangered marshland because the developers successfully proposed an off-site tradeoff. In this case, the construction corporation purchased a marshland in San Diego county to "replace" the one to be demolished and deeded it over to the county of San Diego. Given the complexity of regulatory offsets and off-site tradeoffs, and the dilemmas such choices present to environmental regulators, it is fair to say that environmental regulation will become increasingly difficult in coming years.

CASE STUDY: THE SAVINGS AND LOAN BAILOUT   The history of regulation and deregulation of savings and loan associations illustrates the complexities of regulatory policy. Until the 1960s, savings and loan associations, or S&Ls, were a highly regulated, locally owned alternative to commercial banks. They paid depositors 3 percent interest on savings accounts and made loans for home mortgages at 6 percent interest. The intent was to enable home buyers to secure low-cost, low-interest home mortgage loans. Depositors' savings were insured by the federal government.

Beginning in the 1960s, competition from commercial banks began to erode the market position of the S&Ls, or "thrifts" as they were called. Commercial banks were able to offer higher interest rates by creating certificates of deposit and money market accounts. Many S&L depositors shifted their accounts to banks. Congress came to the assistance of the S&Ls in the Depository Institution Deregulation and Monetary Control Act of 1980 and the Thrift Institutions Restructuring Act of 1982, allowing them to pay a higher rate of interest (which eventually reached 9 or 10 percent) on savings accounts. Since S&Ls had already tied up much of their assets in long-term (twenty-five- to thirty-year) home mortgages at the earlier 6 percent interest rate, S&Ls lost money at the new interest rates in their efforts to win back old customers and attract new ones. Congress therefore allowed them to invest in more risky ventures yielding (if successful) much higher returns. It also encouraged federal regulators to go easy on S&Ls' investment policies, and it increased the limit on deposit insurance from forty thousand dollars to one hundred thousand dollars per account.

Not having the money to pay high interest rates on savings, S&Ls began investing in highly speculative "junk-bond" and real-estate deals, many of which were unsuccessful. Beginning in the mid 1980s, hundreds of S&Ls went bankrupt. Since nearly all of the savings in depositors' accounts were insured by the Federal Deposit Insurance Corporation, the American taxpayer would have to pay for their mistakes.

Some effort was made to punish the managers of S&Ls for their irresponsible actions. In the most celebrated of the S&L prosecutions, Charles H. Keating, the former head of Lincoln Savings and Loan, was convicted of mismanagement and illegal investments. In another S&L-related scandal, the Senate Ethics Committee investigated five senators for their role in persuading federal regulators to go easy on the investment practices of shaky S&Ls. After a year of hearings, the Ethics Committee determined that all five senators had exercised poor judgment and that one, Senator Alan Cranston of California, may have acted improperly. Censured later in a vote by the full Senate, Cranston chose not to run for reelection when his Senate term expired in 1992.[34]

In 1989 Congress enacted legislation designed to strengthen federal oversight and regulation of existing S&Ls. It also set the cost of bailing out the failed thrifts at fifty billion dollars. However, the total cost of regulating, deregulating,

Deregulation of savings and loan institutions in this country resulted in investments in "junk bonds" and speculative real estate. The risky investments led to bankruptcy, prosecution, and conviction of some managers, a vote of censure for Senator Alan Cranston, and a bailout that is estimated to cost taxpayers $500 billion. But the hardest hit were the depositers in the banks that were closed. Shown here is the closing of the Freedom National Bank in New York City in 1990, where depositers wait for news about their savings.

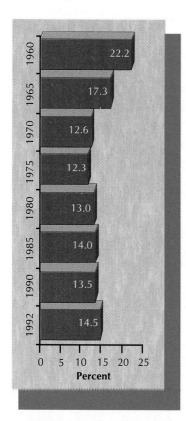

FIGURE 16.1 Percentage of U.S. Population below Poverty Level

The number of Americans who subsist below the poverty level has been growing slowly since its marked decline between 1960 and 1970. While Lyndon B. Johnson's "War on Poverty" during the 1960s seems to have at least partially achieved its goals, those achievements have begun to erode as the proportion of our population in poverty gradually increases.

Source: U.S. Bureau of the Census, *Current Population Reports, 1994.*

and *reregulating* S&Ls may eventually reach five hundred billion dollars, ten times the amount originally estimated by Congress. Reregulation will be supervised by the newly-created federal Resolution Trust Corporation (RTC), which is charged with selling over three hundred billion dollars in assets from failed thrifts—including not only junk bonds but also marinas, ski resorts, and over 35 percent of the city of Colorado Springs, Colorado—and bringing the remaining S&Ls back into line with citizen expectations and reasonable business practices.

Social-Welfare Policy

The second major category of public policy, social-welfare policy, is intended to alleviate the numerous problems associated with poverty in contemporary American society. While poverty has existed in the United States since the early colonial days, it first reached the public agenda in the early 1900s as a result of the writings of muckraking journalists (see Chapter 13). Two books, Lincoln Steffens's *Shame of the Cities* and Robert Hunter's *Poverty*, both published in 1904, were influential in elevating poverty to the status of a political issue. In his study of tenement dwellers in Boston and New York, Hunter shocked turn-of-the-century readers by estimating that between 12 percent and 25 percent of all Americans lived in poverty. As Figure 16.1 indicates, poverty persists today at approximately the same levels identified by Hunter.

The federal *poverty level*—the dollar amount of annual earnings below which a family is considered poor—is established by the Census Bureau and used to generate official government estimates of the number of Americans living in poverty. In 1992 that amount was $14,335 for a nonfarm family of four.

The official poverty level is a controversial figure. For one thing, it is not adjusted for differences in the cost of living in different regions of the country.[35] Housing, for example, is far more expensive in urban areas than in rural areas. In addition, many critics claim that the poverty level is an inadequate measure of real poverty in America. Conservatives argue that the official figure is actually too high because the dollar amount of in-kind assistance such as food stamps is not used in calculating total family income. Liberals insist that the figure is too low because it is based on an estimate of three times what an average family spent for food in the 1960s. At that time families spent one-third of their income on food, but today, mainly because of higher housing costs, they spend about one-fifth of their annual income on food. Liberals therefore argue that the poverty level should be increased to five times, rather than three times, the amount needed for food. If the government were to adopt this reasoning, the poverty figure would have to be raised by 67 percent. Since raising the poverty level would also increase the amount of welfare benefits paid to poor families, and because raising the poverty level would dramatically increase the estimate of the number of poor people in American society, policymakers can be expected to continue to argue about the definition of poverty and the precise number of people living in poverty.

Leaving aside the controversy over the official poverty level, three trends are apparent in the 1990s. First, poverty appears to be on the rise. In 1992, almost thirty-seven million Americans, or 14.5 percent of the population (up from 13.5 percent in 1990), were living in poverty. Second, in a trend often referred to as the "feminization of poverty," an increasing proportion of the poor

Inequality in an Egalitarian Society

Americans pride themselves on their society's two fundamental values: freedom and equality. But a look at comparative statistics on wealth and income reveals a wider gap between the rich and the poor in the United States than in any other industrial nation. Even in Great Britain, generally considered to be a class-based society, there is greater economic equality than in the United States. What's more, inequality is increasing at a faster rate in the United States than in the other industrial nations.

Consider a few representative facts:

- The richest 1 percent of American households (those worth at least $2.3 million) hold 40 percent of the nation's wealth; the comparable figure for Great Britain is 18 percent.

- The 20 percent of Americans with the lowest incomes earn only 5.7 percent of total after-tax income; in Finland, the lowest 20 percent earn 10.8 percent of after-tax income.

- In Japan, the chief executive of a manufacturing company earns about ten times the pay of workers in the company's factories; in the United States, chief executives are paid twenty-five times as much as the average worker.

Various explanations have been offered for the large and growing disparities of income and wealth in the United States. Among the possible causes are a decrease in real wages for unskilled workers, as well as a shortage of jobs for such workers as a result of automation. In addition, the minimum wage is relatively low. The rich, meanwhile, have benefited from low tax rates on their incomes during the 1980s, along with the rapid rise in the value of stocks and bonds during those years.

Social policy has also played a role. Other nations, such as Sweden, attempt to cushion the impact of income disparities through tax and social-welfare policies. In the United States, however, there is a strong drive to reduce federal welfare programs and further reduce taxes, which would have the effect of widening the gap between rich and poor Americans.

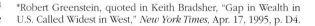

In the long run, economic disparities may have serious consequences for the nation as a whole as well as for poor individuals and families. In the words of one expert, "When you have a child poverty rate that is four times the average of Western European countries that are our principal industrial competitors, and when those children are a significant part of our future work force, you have to worry about the competitive effects as well as the social-fabric effects."*

---

*Robert Greenstein, quoted in Keith Bradsher, "Gap in Wealth in U.S. Called Widest in West," *New York Times,* Apr. 17, 1995, p. D4.

---

are single mothers. In 1992, 46 percent of all families with children headed by a single woman were living in poverty, compared with only 7 percent of families headed by a married couple. Third, the gap between the very poor and the very rich in American society is widening. A recent report by the Congressional Budget Office noted that between 1977 and 1989, 1 percent of the population—the wealthiest 660,000 families, each of which had an annual income of at least $310,000 a year for a household of four—earned 60 percent of all income in the United States. Meanwhile, middle-income Americans saw their income rise by only 4 percent, while the income of the poorest Americans actually decreased.[36]

In the 1990s the federal government faces vast challenges in the area of social-welfare policy. Not only must official policymakers agree on the definition and amount of poverty in American society; they also need to address the apparent rise in the number of poor families, the "feminization" of poverty, and the huge gap between the wealthy and the poor. To appreciate these challenges, it

Social Security as a general heading includes many different benefits programs from Old Age Survivors Disability Insurance and Medicare (both non–means-tested programs), to Supplementary Security Income, with means-tested benefits. Designed as a "safety net," the program has grown rapidly in recent years due to demographic changes (lower birthrates combined with increased longevity) resulting in the aging of the American population. The Social Security payroll tax has kept pace, growing from 6.05 percent in 1978 to 7.65 percent in 1991.

is necessary to understand the history of social-welfare policy in the twentieth century, beginning with the Social Security Act of 1935.[37]

THE SOCIAL SECURITY ACT The Social Security Act was the centerpiece of President Franklin D. Roosevelt's New Deal legislative program. Even today, social security—the largest single nondefense item in the federal budget—is at the heart of social-welfare policy in the United States. The Social Security Act established a "safety net" to catch those falling into poverty. It did so through a system of **entitlements**—government-sponsored benefits and cash payments—for which individuals might qualify by virtue of being poor, elderly, disabled, or a child living in poverty. The act created four major programs: social-security retirement benefits, unemployment compensation, a public assistance or welfare program, and a series of aid programs for blind, disabled, or otherwise ineligible senior citizens.

The key provision of the act was Old Age Survivors Disability Insurance (OASDI), which provided a *contributory* program of retirement and unemployment benefits. The payments were available to workers who retired at age sixty-two or later, or to their dependents in the event of death. The money to fund the program came from a payroll tax shared equally by employers and employees. In subsequent years the act was modified to include self-employed persons, some employees of state and local governments, agricultural workers, and other workers not protected under the original act. Each state administers a separate unemployment insurance system, with workers who lose their jobs eligible for twenty-six weeks of payments (although Congress has, on occasion, extended the eligibility period in times of high unemployment).

Congress has made several efforts to means-test social-security entitlements—that is, to link benefits to income and provide payments only to the "truly disadvantaged"—but such efforts have failed owing to successful lobbying by senior-citizen groups. Social-security benefits therefore remain non-means-tested entitlements; they are paid to any eligible recipient regardless of his or her income. As efforts to reduce the federal budget deficit continue, Congress will undoubtedly face increased pressure to means-test retirement benefits.

In addition to retirement benefits and unemployment insurance, a third program created by the 1935 act was a public-assistance program, Aid to Families with Dependent Children (AFDC). Commonly referred to as "welfare," this program has proved to be far less popular and more controversial than OASDI. AFDC, a noncontributory entitlement program, provides cash assistance to families below the official poverty line. Since the recipients are poor, they have been means-tested; that is, the government has found them to be eligible for benefits on the basis of their family income. Federal AFDC grants match state welfare and local general assistance expenditures up to specified amounts for individuals not already covered by old-age or social-security insurance. This results in widely varying welfare grants in different states, ranging from a high of $924 a month for a family of three in Alaska to a low of $120 a month in Mississippi.[38]

The fourth program created by the Social Security Act of 1935 is actually a series of programs, now known as Supplemental Security Income (SSI), that provide aid to senior citizens who have not contributed to social-security payroll taxes, as well as to blind or disabled citizens. Unlike the other programs just described, SSI is funded entirely by the federal government.

THE WAR ON POVERTY   Along with other New Deal legislation, the Social Security Act was spurred by the massive economic dislocation caused by the Great Depression; in other words, the Depression acted as a triggering mechanism to translate the economic "condition" of poverty into a political issue to be addressed by policymakers in the national government. Three decades later poverty again reached the public and formal agendas of national government. Influenced by the civil rights movement—in particular, by Martin Luther King, Jr.'s, call for civil rights *and jobs* for black Americans and Michael Harrington's description of the "invisible poor" in *The Other America*—President John F. Kennedy called for the creation of a "New Frontier" in which poverty would be attacked and overcome. Kennedy was assassinated before his program could be enacted, but his successor, President Lyndon Johnson, launched a "War on Poverty" with two major pieces of legislation: the Economic Opportunity Act (1964) and the Medicare Act (1965).

The Economic Opportunity Act created the Job Corps to train the long-term unemployed; the Neighborhood Youth Corps to train neighborhood and inner-city unemployed youth for jobs; literacy programs to help adults learn to read and prepare for the job market; Head Start preschool programs to help poor children gain the skills necessary to do well in school; and work-study programs for low-income college students. Unlike social security, these were community action programs (CAPs); they were designed to be run with the "maximum feasible participation" of people in poor neighborhoods. In other words, the poor themselves were to play a major role in the implementation of poverty programs in their communities.

"Maximum feasible participation" proved to be highly controversial. Many members of Congress believed they had too little control over vast sums of CAP money; mayors and other local officials believed they should control funds targeted for their cities; local community activists running CAP programs

On July 7, 1965, President Lyndon B. Johnson, shown here alongside ex-president Harry S. Truman, who first proposed the measure, signed the legislation that created Medicare as a part of his "War on Poverty." The legislation included compulsory hospital insurance, requiring premiums in the form of deductions from social security checks, and a voluntary insurance plan that was supported by monthly premiums paid by the recipient and covered physicians' fees for service and other related costs. Medicare is subsidized by the federal government via a workers' payroll tax amounting to 1.45 percent in 1991.

complained of insufficient funding and interference by local and federal officials. In the words of one key participant, Senator Daniel Patrick Moynihan of New York, maximum feasible participation quickly evolved into "maximum feasible misunderstanding."[39] Congress responded by passing the Hyde Amendment, which required that more control be given to local officials in deciding how CAP money would be spent.

The other major thrust of the War on Poverty was the Medicare Act, enacted in 1965, which added health insurance to the social-security program. Medicare provides basic health care and hospitalization coverage for people over sixty-five years old. A related program, Medicaid, provides health-care coverage for needy individuals under age sixty-five. The federal government pays a percentage of Medicaid costs, with state and local governments sharing the balance. Medicaid covers people who were not covered by Medicare, especially the blind, the disabled, and children living in poverty.[40]

THE POLITICS OF ENTITLEMENTS   In the 1970s and early 1980s no new major welfare programs were enacted, but there was a dramatic increase in entitlements under Presidents Nixon, Ford, and Carter, followed by an equally dramatic series of cuts under President Reagan. Entitlements, which now encompass nearly 50 percent of the federal budget, grew rapidly in the 1970–79 period. Social-security benefits were increased by 15 percent in 1970, 10 percent in 1971, and 20 percent in 1972. In 1974 social security was *indexed*, meaning that benefits were tied to changes in the consumer price index (CPI). As the CPI goes up due to inflation, so do social-security benefits. Eligibility for food stamps was expanded in 1974, and in 1979 the purchase requirement for food stamps was eliminated. In 1974 Medicare was expanded to provide more benefits and to extend coverage to disabled Americans.

FIGURE 16.2 Growing Commitments: America's Social-Welfare System

The increase in entitlement expenditures is due in large part to the nature of entitlement legislation. Ependitures are tied to the number of individuals who meet legislative thresholds, not limited to a specific appropriation amount. As the number of eligible individuals increases, so do federal expenditures. Importantly, AFDC and military retirement pay have remained stable, while Social Security and Medicare have experienced precipitous growth.
Source: Statistical Abstract, 1992, Nos. 135, 565, 567.

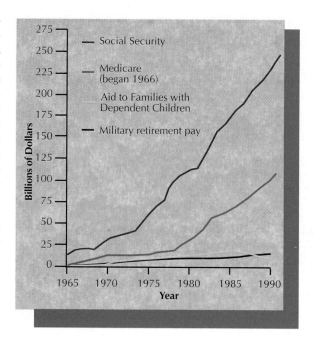

As a result of these changes, spending for entitlements grew rapidly, as did the number of people entitled to receive benefits. As political scientist Donald Kettl has pointed out, at the time, the rise in entitlements and the costs of indexation did not seem onerous, but "decision makers picked precisely the wrong time, from the budgetary point of view, to begin indexation. Shortly after the increase was passed, inflation quickly began mounting, which drove social security payments ever upward. As payments escalated, the number of recipients increased, and as the number and productivity of workers supporting the program declined, social-security deficits soared."[41] Figure 16.2 indicates how entitlement payments, in particular, Social Security, increased since the 1960s.

During the 1980s the entitlement roller coaster took a downward plunge. Shortly after his inauguration President Reagan announced his intention to attack the size of federal government in general and entitlements in particular. Reagan advocated the preservation of a basic "social safety net" but succeeded in achieving deep cuts in several social-welfare programs. Policy shifts that affected entitlements included calculating the worth of food stamps and housing assistance in determining eligibility for AFDC; eliminating 25 percent of food stamp recipients by holding the eligibility line at 130 percent above the poverty level; increasing deductibles for Medicare (i.e., the amounts that must be spent by the individual before receiving benefits); and reducing federal funding for Medicaid.

The Reagan administration also tried to decrease social-security benefits for individuals retiring before age sixty-five, to toughen eligibility requirements, and to reduce cost-of-living allowances (COLAs) for social-security recipients. The result was the worst political defeat of the Reagan years, because AARP launched a massive and successful lobbying effort, flooding Congress with letters and telephone calls. AARP has been very successful at increasing the percentage of the federal budget spent on the elderly, while America's young receive much less (see Figure 16.3).

In 1983 a commission investigating the social-security program succeeded in persuading Congress to make several changes in social security, including gradually increasing the retirement age to sixty-seven by the year 2007; extending social-security coverage to many employees who had not been covered previously; reducing COLAs; and significantly raising social-security payroll taxes for workers. Taken together, these changes helped place social security on a firm financial footing in a period when the number of retirees was growing while the workforce was shrinking.

THE FAMILY SUPPORT ACT OF 1988   In 1988, in the most fundamental revision of social-welfare policy since the 1960s, Congress enacted the Family Support Act. The act's chief legislative architect, Senator Daniel Patrick Moynihan of New York, described it as "a new social contract" between the poor, who agree to work in exchange for benefits, and society, which agrees to support the poor at a livable wage.

The Family Security Act attempted to address both the trend toward the "feminization" of poverty and the administration's desire for "workfare"—programs to assist welfare recipients in making the transition into the workforce. It provided for federal assistance in obtaining child support payments from absent fathers. It also created the JOBS program, which is designed to eventually replace AFDC with a program in which recipients (except mothers with children under three years old) must work in exchange for cash assistance.

The concept of "workfare" was legislatively driven by the Family Support Act of 1988. The act mandated nationwide programs that required work or job training in exchange for benefits. Job training, job searches, or work would have to be performed in order to receive AFDC assistance. Here, AFDC recipients are laying stones for a sidewalk in a workfare type of program implemented by Mayor Giuliani of New York City. The recipients of benefits in this program must either be enrolled in job training or complete a mandatory 70 hours of work per month.

FIGURE 16.3 Young and Old in the Federal Budget

There is a strong relationship between voting behavior, interest group power, and federal government budget outlays. The elderly vote in greater proportions than any other group and they are represented by the influential American Association of Retired People (AARP). As a result, expenditures on their behalf represent almost 40 percent of the entire federal budget. Younger Americans vote in the lowest proportions of any group, do not have effective interest group representation, and receive minimal federal expenditures.

Source: Budget of the United States Government, 1993.

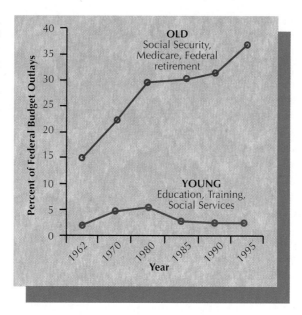

FYI

Reforming the welfare state is at the core of the Republicans' "Contract with America." According to House Speaker Newt Gingrich: "I believe we must remake government for reasons much larger than saving money or improving services. The fact is, no civilization can survive with 12-year-olds having babies, with 15-year-olds killing each other, with 17-year-olds dying of AIDS, with 18-year-olds getting diplomas they can't even read. Every night on every local news we see the human tragedies that have grown out of the current welfare state."

Recipients must be willing to engage in job training and job search activities as a condition for receiving benefits.

The JOBS program includes minimum participation requirements and penalties, educational requirements and assistance for young mothers, funding for child care, and training to help recipients gain self-sufficiency and job skills. States are required to shift a fixed percentage of their AFDC recipients to a JOBS-style program and encouraged to shift entirely to workfare approaches where feasible. Early studies indicate that the program, under consideration now in several states, has experienced measurable successes in helping recipients move from welfare to work and raising their self-esteem.[42]

CASE STUDY: REFORMING WELFARE   Despite the historic compromise represented by the Family Support Act of 1988, social-welfare policymakers and policy scholars remain divided into three camps. The first group, including Senator Moynihan and many other members of Congress, favors giving the Family Support Act several years to work, making incremental changes where appropriate as experience indicates. This middle-of-the-road policy coalition favors attempting to enforce child support and providing work skills training, job search assistance, and, where necessary, work and cash assistance to those in need.

A second, more conservative group favors tightening welfare requirements to address the issue of long-term dependence on welfare. They note that more than half of welfare recipients remain on the rolls for more than two years, and 45 percent receive benefits for more than four years (see Figure 16.4). Congressional sponsors of this approach, such as House Speaker Newt Gingrich, have called for limiting AFDC support for all recipients (except mothers with children under three years of age) to four years, during which recipients must work part-time or go to school. The plan would provide workfare-job assistance in place of traditional AFDC benefits, followed by a complete cutoff of governmental assistance at the end of the four-year period. Other conservative

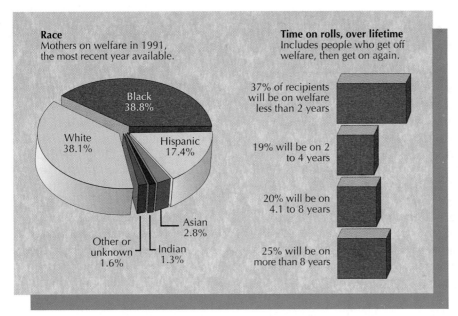

Race
Mothers on welfare in 1991, the most recent year available.

Black
38.8%

White
38.1%

Hispanic
17.4%

Asian
2.8%

Other or unknown
1.6%

Indian
1.3%

Time on rolls, over lifetime
Includes people who get off welfare, then get on again.

37% of recipients will be on welfare less than 2 years

19% will be on 2 to 4 years

20% will be on 4.1 to 8 years

25% will be on more than 8 years

FIGURE 16.4 Who's on Welfare, and for How Long
Currently, approximately 14.5 million individuals are receiving Aid to Families with Dependent Children. Mothers who are receiving welfare benefits are as likely to be white as they are to be black. More than half will exit the system within four years.
Source: LaDonna A. Pavetti, House Ways and Means Committee; Cited in Isabel Wilkerson, "An Intimate Look at Welfare: Women Who've Been There," *New York Times,* Feb. 17, 1995, p. A18.

proposals include eliminating the increase in AFDC benefits for additional children, reducing Medicaid services to the poor, and denying benefits to teenaged mothers who do not attend school.[43]

A third alternative, more liberal in orientation, concedes the desirability of shifting the focus of welfare to a workfare-style program. But advocates of this approach insist that the program needs to be open-ended, capable of supporting recipients longer than four years. In addition, it must be accompanied by programs to provide child health care, nutrition, education, adequate housing, and genuine racial integration if the central problems of joblessness, spiraling birthrates, and long-term welfare dependency are to be adequately addressed.[44]

The current social-welfare system cost Americans approximately $124 billion in 1994, yet the gap between rich and poor continues to widen, more women and children sink below the poverty line (however measured), and the consequences of poverty, especially crime and violence, continue to devastate American society. State and local governments are already hard-pressed to respond; indeed, a report by the 1994 U.S. Conference of Mayors revealed that several large cities, including St. Louis, St. Paul, Boston, Cleveland, Minneapolis, Nashville, Miami, Salt Lake City, San Francisco, Norfolk, New Orleans, Seattle, and Trenton, could no longer meet existing demands for emergency food and shelter. Whatever policies are ultimately adopted to respond to poverty, there is general agreement that current conditions have become "problems," and the issue of poverty has gained an increasingly prominent place on the national agenda.

PUBLIC POLICY AND APPROACHING DEMOCRACY

Like the programs that preceded it, the Family Security Act of 1988 will be altered and amended as policymakers continue to address the challenges presented by poverty in America. Which of these three paths to welfare reform national policymakers will choose is impossible to predict. Social-welfare

FYI

Does welfare need to be cut to balance the budget? According to groups opposed to the "Contract with America," such a claim is myth, and these are the facts: Aid for Families with Dependent Children equals $22 billion, or only 1 percent of total federal spending. In contrast, the federal savings and loan bailout cost $150 billion, and the U.S. military budget totaled $281 billion in 1994. These groups also note that huge deficits were not created until 1981, when military spending was doubled, and when the progressive taxation system was destroyed by the Phil Gramm/Warren Rudman tax bill.

Reforming Health Care

Almost all Americans agree on the need for health-care reform: Health-care costs, already high, are rising rapidly, and there seems to be no way of bringing them under control. A related problem is lack of universal coverage—more than thirty-five million Americans do not have health insurance and face financial ruin in the event of a serious illness requiring hospitalization or long-term care. The issue of health-care reform has had no trouble getting onto the public agenda and even the formal agenda of the national government. But it has been unable to make its way past the initial stages of the policymaking process.

Part of the difficulty stems from the sheer size of the problem. Total spending for health care in the United States rose from about $270 billion in 1970 to almost $878 billion in 1993 and now accounts for *one-seventh* of the American economy. The problem is also extremely complex, since much health care is covered by insurance that is paid for in part by businesses in the form of employee benefits. There are also numerous political obstacles to reform, especially in an era of intense partisanship and public distrust of government.

Efforts to gain some control over health-care costs go back to the early 1970s. At that time the concept of *health maintenance organizations,* or HMOs, was attracting attention because of its emphasis on preventing serious illnesses and other conditions that require hospitalization and surgery. HMOs are prepaid group practices that provide complete medical services to subscribers for a monthly fee. Since the fees are the HMO's only source of income, the HMO has a strong incentive to keep its members healthy through physical examinations, early detection and treatment, inoculations, and other forms of preventive medicine.

The Health Maintenance Act of 1973 provided funds for establishing new HMOs and gave employees the right to choose HMOs rather than group insurance plans. Enrollment in HMOs grew steadily throughout the 1980s; by 1990, however, total enrollment in HMOs was only a little over thirty-three million, and health-care costs were continuing to increase rapidly. Business, labor, and public policy analysts grew increasingly alarmed, and many believed that the health-care system was "in crisis."

During his 1992 campaign for the presidency, Bill Clinton promised voters that health-care reform would be a top priority of his administration. Shortly after taking office he took steps to carry out that promise, appointing his wife, Hillary Rodham Clinton, to head the Task Force on National Health Care Reform that would draft legislation to be submitted to Congress. After months of hearings and consultations, the Task Force devised a complex plan based on the concept of "managed competition," in which market forces, rather than government, act to hold down costs and expand access to health insurance.

On September 22, 1993, the president introduced the plan to a joint session of Congress, saying, "we must make this our most urgent priority: giving every American health security, health care that can never be taken away, health care that is always there." The plan had six basic components:

- *Security:* Comprehensive health benefits would be guaranteed to all Americans. Insurance companies would be barred from denying coverage to seriously ill people.
- *Simplicity:* All health-care plans would be required to provide a uniform package of benefits.
- *Savings:* The plan would create "health alliances" that could obtain lower prices for insurance coverage than consumers and small businesses could obtain on their own.
- *Quality:* The plan would provide for research on prevention and encourage training of primary-care physicians.
- *Choice:* Patients would be allowed to choose among several types of health-care plans.
- *Responsibility:* Drug companies would be expected to maintain reasonable prices; frivolous malpractice suits would be discouraged.

The Clinton plan soon ran into opposition. One of its most controversial aspects was the proposal to create regional health-care alliances that would combine the buying power of their members to reduce costs and share administrative expenses. The alliances would collect premiums from employers and pass them along to insurance providers. Critics claimed that the alliances would become huge bureaucracies with far too much power. The Business Roundtable, which represents many of the nation's largest companies, withdrew its support from the plan. Small businesses launched an intensive lobbying campaign to defeat the proposal, which would require them to provide health insurance for their employees. Insurance companies, doctors, hospitals, and drug companies formed political action committees to oppose the plan.

In his State of the Union Message in 1994, President Clinton threatened to veto any legislation that did not guarantee insurance coverage for all Americans. But the legislation became mired in five congressional committees whose members could not arrive at a consensus on how to achieve universal coverage. At this point several alternative plans were proposed. House Democratic leaders unveiled a plan that would require employers to pay 80 percent of the cost of insuring their workers, with subsidies for small companies, and would extend Medicare to provide coverage for the unemployed. Senate Democratic leaders introduced legislation to cover 95 percent

of Americans through voluntary measures and subsidies. A bipartisan group in the House introduced a bill offering billions of dollars to help the working poor buy health insurance without employer payments. These measures were stalled or sidelined, and when Congress recessed, it was clear that no health-care legislation could be passed in 1994.

The 1994 elections produced a shift of power from the Democrats to the Republicans. The Republican leadership places a high priority on balancing the federal budget without raising taxes, but this goal cannot be achieved without major cuts in spending on Medicare, the medical insurance that covers forty million elderly and disabled Americans. Spending for Medicare and Medicaid, the fastest-growing part of the federal budget, is projected to reach $349 billion by the year 1997 (see the accompanying figure). Thus, instead of overall health-care reform, the issue of spending on Medicare is now on the formal agenda of the national government. It is too early to predict the outcome, but there can be little doubt that health-care costs will remain on the public agenda for the foreseeable future.

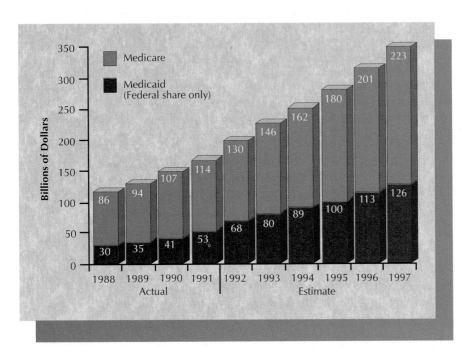

Rising Medicare and Medicaid Costs
The rapidly escalating costs of both Medicare and the federal portion of Medicaid are graphically represented in this figure. From 1988 to 1995 estimated Medicaid costs will have more than tripled and Medicare costs will have more than doubled. Skyrocketing health care costs have contributed to this growing problem.
Source: Congressional Quarterly (Jan. 2, 1993) p. 29. Reprinted with permission.

policymaking, like regulatory policymaking, has a long political history and faces tremendous challenges. As the debate swirls over the Contract with America's welfare reform proposals, there is no easy formula for providing equal resources for all, a fair chance for all to succeed, and the opportunity for all to flourish financially and personally. In May 1995 the House Republicans submitted a plan for a Better American Future, which was premised on "Doing the Right Thing," a program that would replace the Welfare State with an Opportunity Society. How well national policymakers respond to these challenges—and how democratic the policies are—will remain crucial questions as American government continues its task of approaching democracy.[45]

SUMMARY

1. Public policies are the decisions, actions, and commitments of government. They have four key aims: to regulate key industries and aspects of American life, to protect citizens from foreign powers and other potential enemies, to encourage the accomplishment of important social goals, and to assist citizens and state and local governments.

2. Substantive policies involve tangible rewards, while symbolic policies involve the use of symbols, assurances, and public values. An entirely new policy is known as an original policy. Adding to an existing policy by small increments produces an incremental policy. Policies may be classified as reflexive (incremental and substantive), original (original and substantive), symbolic-reflexive (incremental and symbolic), or symbolic-original (original and symbolic).

3. The policy life cycle consists of eleven stages: (a) redefinition of a condition as a public problem, (b) placement of the problem on the public agenda, (c) emergence of the problem as an issue requiring government action, (d) formulation of a public-policy response, (e) reformulation of the proposed policy, (f) placement of the policy on the formal agenda of government, (g) enactment of the policy, (h) implementation of the policy, (i) impacts caused by implementation of the policy, (j) evaluation of the impacts, and (k) termination or continued implementation and evaluation of the policy.

4. To reach the public agenda, a potential subject of public policy must undergo a radical redefinition in the eyes of policy elites; that is, it must be labeled as a problem to be solved by the government. A potential policy reaches the issue stage when it is framed in terms of a yes-or-no policy option. A dramatic event may serve as a triggering mechanism that causes a condition to be redefined as a problem, or an issue can reach the public agenda through the activities of policy entrepreneurs who "sell" it to a policymaking body. A policy reaches the formal agenda when it is actually scheduled for debate and potential adoption by a policymaking body.

5. Implementation is the execution of a policy. Some policies are difficult to implement because of their complexity, the cooperation required, and the need for coordination. Most federal policies require a period of monitoring and analysis known as policy evaluation. Following evaluation, policies are either terminated or continued.

6. Once a policy has been enacted, it is often difficult to terminate it. Several factors make public policymaking a highly political process. They include the fragmentation created by a federal system of government; temporary political alliances (logrolling), policies that benefit particular states or districts (pork barrel legislation); iron triangles, or informal relationships among legislative committees, executive agencies, and interest groups; and issue networks, in which large numbers of participants take an active interest in a particular policy.

7. Regulatory policy involves the use of police powers by the federal government to supervise the conduct of individuals, businesses, and other governmental agencies. The national government may regulate prices, franchising or licences, performance or safety standards, and resources available to citizens or businesses. It may also provide or withhold operating subsidies or use regulatory commissions to regulate vital industries and promote fair competition.

8. Regulatory activity by the federal government began in the late 1800s and increased during the Great Depression. The highest levels of regulation were reached in the 1960s and 1970s and were followed by a movement toward deregulation. Beginning in the late 1980s there was a swing back toward increased regulation.

9. Social-welfare policy uses positive incentives to promote or encourage basic social fairness. Much social-welfare policy is intended to alleviate the problems associated with poverty. The federal poverty level—the dollar amount of annual earnings below which a family is considered poor—is used to generate official government estimates of the number of Americans living in poverty.

10. The first major piece of social-welfare legislation was the Social Security Act of 1935, which created four major sets of entitlements: Old Age Survivors Disability Insurance, unemployment insurance, Aid to Families with Dependent Children, and Supplemental Security Income. Additional social-welfare legislation was enacted during the 1960s as part of the War on Poverty. During the 1970s and 1980s entitlements increased, only to be scaled back during the Reagan administration. The Family Support Act of 1988 introduced work requirements for recipients of welfare benefits, but many policymakers believe there is a need for further reform of social-welfare policy.

KEY TERMS

public policies
substantive policy
symbolic policy
original policy
incremental policy
reflexive policies
policy elite

public agenda
formal agenda
issue stage
triggering mechanism
policy entrepreneurs
implementation
policy evaluation

logrolling
pork barrel legislation
iron triangles
issue networks
regulatory policy
social-welfare policy
entitlements

SUGGESTED READING

- Glazer, Nathan. *The Limits of Social Policy*. Cambridge, Mass.: Harvard University Press, 1988. A critique of welfare that discusses the difficulty government has in solving social problems.

- Gore, Albert. *Earth in the Balance: Ecology and the Human Spirit*. Boston: Houghton Mifflin, 1992. The vice president presents a powerful argument for protecting the environment.

- Harrington, Michael. *The Other America*. New York: Macmillan, 1994. The most widely read essay about poverty in the United States.

- Jencks, Christopher. *Rethinking Social Policy: Race, Poverty, and the Underclass*. Cambridge, Mass.: Harvard University Press, 1992. A series of essays by a leading sociologist on social-welfare policy and poverty.

- Marmor, Theodore R. K., Jerry L. Mashaw, and Philip L. Harvey. *America's Misunderstood Welfare State*. New York: HarperCollins, 1990. This book examines myths about American social welfare.

- Murray, Charles. *Losing Ground: American Social Policy, 1950–1980*. New York: Basic Books, 1984. A popular and controversial book that addresses the idea that social-welfare programs for the poor have made things worse, not better.

CHAPTER 17

ECONOMIC POLICY

CHAPTER OUTLINE

CASE STUDY: THE 1994 BUDGET
INTRODUCTION: ECONOMIC-POLICY
    MAKING AND DEMOCRACY
THE GOALS OF ECONOMIC POLICY
THEORIES OF DOMESTIC ECONOMIC
    POLICY
THE POLITICS OF THE FEDERAL BUDGET
TAXATION

GOVERNMENT SPENDING
THE POLITICS OF INTERNATIONAL
    ECONOMIC POLICY
THE NEED FOR INTERNATIONAL POLICY
    COORDINATION
ECONOMIC POLICY AND
    APPROACHING DEMOCRACY

The 1994 Budget

It was late at night on Thursday, August 16, 1993. The Omnibus Budget Reconciliation Act of 1993, the first major legislation of the Clinton administration, was in trouble, the fledgling president along with it. The plan represented the president's blueprint for governmental action—his programmatic goals, the amount of money the programs would receive, ideas for raising the tax dollars needed to fund these programs, and the overall design for achieving a healthy economy. This should have been a moment for celebration. Earlier in the evening the House of Representatives had passed the act. But the frighteningly narrow margin of victory (218–216) and the fact that forty of Clinton's fellow Democrats defected from their president's plan was cause for concern. And the prospects for the next day's Senate vote looked even gloomier. The problem, despite all the campaign talk of "breaking gridlock," was not Republican opposition to the plan but the president's fellow Democrats, who were already worried about their next election.

Despite a relatively comfortable Democratic majority in the Senate (56–44), the bill was in trouble because several influential Democratic senators had already expressed their opposition. It seemed as though each day brought a new defection and threats of even more. Among those threatening to vote against the bill was Oklahoma's David Boren, who had publicly denounced one aspect of the president's program—a broad-based energy tax—as detrimental to the citizens of his oil-rich state. Arizona's Dennis DeConcini was also threatening to defect unless Clinton softened his stance on taxing elderly retirees. And earlier in the day, Bob Kerrey of Nebraska had called the White House to express his concern over the budget; Clinton's plan simply did not do enough for deficit reduction. Kerrey was now a no, and without his vote, the president's package would fail.

President Clinton was having problems convincing Republicans that his almost $1.5 trillion budget was worthwhile, and that was to be expected. After all, one of the main ingredients of the plan was a substantial tax hike for wealthy Americans, a prime constituency of the Republican coalition. Clinton's problems with his own party were a different story. Indeed, how could one plan so offend a president's own partisans?

The answer to this question illustrates the complex and highly political nature of the budgetary process; a process in which there are clear winners and losers, in which different theories about the role of government in the economy come into play, and in which differences in priorities necessitate bargaining and compromise before a final agreement can be reached. Each specific provision of the president's proposed budget plan had the potential to make at least one member of Congress angry, be it over tax rates, spending provisions, or program cuts. Thus, Senators Boren and DeConcini were willing to buck the president unless he changed his tax schemes, and Kerrey was causing trouble because too few programs were being cut to result in the overall economic impacts he thought were necessary.

In such a situation where the vote was close, and thus any senator could scuttle the plan, Clinton had to make deals, even with members of his own party. Thus, the president had to modify his plan at the last minute, offering Boren, DeConcini, Kerrey, and others at least some of what they wanted so he could ensure their votes and avoid an embarrassing defeat. The president had submitted a plan to Congress, but members of his own party were making him bargain parts of it away to lock in their votes.

Finally, the roll was called and the Senate passed the president's package, but only in the

*most dramatic fashion. Vice President Al Gore
had to exercise his constitutional authority as
president of the Senate to break a 50–50 tie. To
give Gore a chance to cast his vote, the president
had to agree to some additional compromises.
DeConcini forced him to ease up on new taxes
for wealthy social-security recipients, and Diane
Feinstein forced tax breaks for high-tech businesses in California. To get the votes of conservative Democrats, Clinton had to scale back
spending and even promise to submit further
program cuts to Congress in the future.*

*In the end, six of the president's own party
members defected to join a unified Republican
coalition against the plan, and several others,
including Boren, DeConcini, and Kerrey, had
to be wooed, sweet-talked, and cajoled at the last
minute to set the stage for Gore's dramatic vote.
Kerrey's price was particularly unprecedented:
the chance to criticize the president's economic
plan, and indeed the president's leadership abilities, in a prime-time speech before the Senate.
The budget plan passed, but the new president
was forced to contend with criticism even from
his fellow Democrats.*[1] ✣

During his first year in office, President Clinton called
on Congress to enact his plan to reduce the deficit by
$500 billion. Despite his claim that we were finally
putting our economic house in order, support from his
own Democratic party was not overwhelming. Even
with forced compromises and bargaining, Vice-President Gore had to exercise his privilege and position as
president of the Senate to cast the deciding vote.

INTRODUCTION: ECONOMIC POLICY MAKING AND DEMOCRACY

In this chapter we will examine a variety of political philosophies that guide
U.S. economic-policy making. We will look at federal policies that raise revenues (who pays and how much) and that allocate these revenues as goods and
services (who benefits and in what ways) through the construction of the federal budget. We will also examine some specific budgetary policies and some
of the institutions involved in the economic-policy process.[2]

One of the most crucial roles for modern government is the regulation of
the national economy. This is important not only for the multiple benefits it
yields to specific corporations and entrepreneurs but also because a stable,
growing economy—one in which levels of employment are high, prices are
reasonable, and families are afforded at least a modest degree of economic security—furnishes the environment for a stable, orderly, and democratically
healthy society.

The battle over President Clinton's first budget was guided fundamentally by
political questions that pitted members of Congress against their own president.
If they sense that their electoral fortunes are at stake, representatives and senators will side with their constituencies, as the price for giving up an important

program or tax break can be very dear indeed. When we look to the world of taxing and spending policy, we see very clearly that politics and economics are fundamentally intertwined. In studying American politics then, we need to understand how politics and economics are woven together to present opportunities and obstacles in the United States' continuing approach to democracy.[3]

Obviously, both Republicans and Democrats believe in a strong, healthy economy. Where they differ is on how best to achieve this goal. Within each party differences exist regarding broad goals and specific policies, differences that have important consequences for government's ability to make coherent budgetary policy, and for the lives of every American citizen.

The question of the desirability of government involvement in the private economy has long been debated in U.S. political culture, at least as far back as *The Federalist Papers,* the controversy over the First Bank of the United States, and Alexander Hamilton's *Report on Manufactures* to the first Congress (where he argued for government support of private industrial development). In today's world, some amount of government involvement in the economy is accepted, but the nature and extent of government influence remains hotly debated.[4]

The federal government influences the economy in many ways, both direct and indirect. We may organize government policies that affect the economy into three groups: fiscal policy, regulatory policy, and international economic policy. The clearest impacts occur through the *fiscal policy* decisions that are reflected in the budget. Government budgetary choices concerning when and how much to tax, spend, subsidize, and borrow affect the economic lives of all citizens. Government economic *regulatory policy* is also pervasive. Government regulates aspects of the workplace to achieve health, safety, and environmental goals. Finally, the government engages in an increasingly important number of *international economic policies* that influence economic relations with other countries through such avenues as exchange rates, trade negotiations, and international economic institutions like the World Bank, the International Monetary Fund (IMF), and the World Trade Organization (WTO) and its predecessor, the General Agreement on Tariffs and Trade (GATT).

Decisions about fiscal policy, regulatory policy, and international economic policy pose fundamental questions in the context of our theme of approaching democracy. We need to think about democracy not merely in political but also in economic terms. How fair is the tax system? How democratic is the process through which economic policy is created? Have the approaches taken to alleviate recent economic and budgetary crises eroded or strengthened the momentum of America's "approach to democracy"?

THE GOALS OF ECONOMIC POLICY

The goal of **economic policy** is to produce a vibrant, healthy, and growing economy. The federal government's role in making economic policy has increased during the post–World War II period. Conditioned by the experience of 25 percent unemployment rates during the Great Depression of the 1930s and the very high **inflation** rates (decline in value of money and corresponding increase in prices) and commodity shortages of the war years of the 1940s, Congress adopted the Employment Act of 1946, which formalized the federal government's responsibility to help guide the economy so as to achieve the three primary economic goals of stable prices (low or zero inflation rates), full employment (unemployment rate of four percent or less), and economic growth (substantial and sustained growth in the economy as measured by increases in the gross domestic product, for example).

The conditions necessary to achieve these three goals, as the postwar record shows, are difficult to achieve. The U.S. economy has experienced periods of high unemployment, periods of high inflation, and times of slow or even negative economic growth.

Economic policy to achieve these goals is difficult and complex, because actions that affect one goal also affect the others, often in undesirable ways. Policies that raise interest rates to push inflation down, for example, may discourage spending, which can raise unemployment rates, and may also reduce investment spending and the adoption of new technology, which can affect the rate of economic growth. Economic tradeoffs must thus be considered in addition to the political tradeoffs.

To make matters worse, it appears that to achieve the goals of stable prices, full employment, and economic growth, we also need to attain a secondary set of economic goals such as low and stable interest rates, stable exchange rates, and reduced federal budget deficits and balance-of-trade deficits. Progress toward these secondary economic goals seems necessary to achieve the rising living standards that are embodied in the principal economic goals that have been set for the nation.

In addition, economic policy suffers from the fact that there are many tools of economic policy, several competing theories of what policies should be adopted, and many actors involved in making it. It is also increasingly the case that economic policies adopted by one nation have international and even global effects on other nations through trade, finance, and exchange-rate impacts. Economic policy must thus consider foreign-policy effects and the nature of the United States' political and economic relations with other nations in addition to purely domestic political and economic impacts. The complex economics of fiscal, regulatory, and international economic policies, combined with their complicated politics, makes this an especially challenging and controversial area of government action.

Thus, when assessing the economy, policymakers must often make tradeoffs, decisions that influence the economic well-being of not just the national economy but the day-to-day lives of millions of Americans. It should not be surprising then that questions concerning how the nation's economy should be handled tend to dominate political discussion.

When there are tradeoffs among policy goals, it is necessary for policymakers to pursue one goal and sacrifice others. It used to be said, for example, that Democrats were willing to risk creating inflation to fight unemployment, while Republicans were willing to tolerate higher unemployment to keep inflation under control and economic growth on track. It was also said that Democrats raised economic growth through war and public spending, and Republicans lowered taxes and spending to help corporations and investors. Tradeoffs continue to exist today and choices still must be made, but these old stereotypes about Republicans and Democrats are no longer very accurate. Divisions on economic policy now often cut across party lines, as Clinton's 1994 budget showdown demonstrated, because of the combined impact of the politics of

In early 1992, this crowd of over 2,000 people arrived to fill out applications for just 500 jobs at a new Sheraton Hotel in Chicago. The job market for those with limited skills has been shrinking in this country. Tradeoffs are inherent in economic policy; lowering inflation in the 1980s came at the cost of higher unemployment.

The "Political Business Cycle"

Although in one sense the goal of economic policy is to produce a healthy and vibrant economy, we can evaluate goals for the economy in another, more political sense. Government intervention into the economy may be viewed as a way to manipulate voters. This theory suggests that there is a "political business cycle" in which those in control of government work to time economic upturns so that they coincide with elections—stimulating the economy in the short run to promote their reelection. Given what we know about voters, there is every reason to expect that politicians may indeed try such a strategy. Voters evaluate government performance in large part according to the state of the economy. If politicians can produce an expanding economy—rising employment, production, and incomes—at the right time, they are likely to be rewarded with a vote of confidence from the electorate.

Does the political business cycle exist? Political scientist Edward R. Tufte suggests that it might. In his analysis, Tufte found that from 1948 to 1976, unemployment was generally lower and disposable income higher in the months directly prior to presidential elections.[5] Tufte's evidence thus points to the possibility that politicians may be trying to influence the economy for reasons other than just the welfare of the nation and its citizens. Still, in the years since Tufte's study, the pattern has been more mixed, holding for 1984 and 1988 but not for 1980 and 1992.

Still, it is important to remember that manipulating the economy is a highly inexact science in which many things can go wrong and many others are beyond the control of politicians. The broader point is that economic issues do matter in electoral politics, and politicians will be rewarded or blamed for the state of the economy they manage. For evidence we need look no further than the 1992 presidential campaign, when a large number of voters expressed dissatisfaction with President Bush's leadership on economic issues. The now-famous response of the Clinton campaign team was to plaster the walls of their headquarters with the following four-word message designed to remind themselves of something Bush seemed to have forgotten: "It's the economy, stupid."

While overall economic conditions are important to voters, they are clearly not the only factor that voters consider. The U.S. economy had improved between 1992, when Clinton was elected, and 1994, the year of the midterm congressional elections. This seemed to favor the democratic legislators who supported Clinton's programs. Despite this favorable aspect of the political business cycle, the Republican party triumphed in the polls, gaining control of both the House and the Senate for the first time in forty years. This shows that voters are influenced by more than just the unemployment rate when they cast their ballots, factoring other economic variables as well as a broad range of noneconomic consideration into their calculations.

Although political decisions influence the economy, it also seems that the economic environment affects voting behavior. Economics and politics, then, become so intertwined that it is almost impossible to separate them.

constituent interests and the broader influence of disagreements regarding theoretical or philosophical issues. For example, both parties may oppose policies that seek to reduce inflation if these policies negatively impact their legislative district, and both may oppose policies that seek to reduce inflation if they believe the policies to be theoretically unsound or capable of producing detrimental long-run effects by, for example, increasing the budget deficit and the national debt.

Robert Rubin, the Secretary of the Treasury, nominated by the President and approved by the Senate, heads the Department of the Treasury—a cabinet level department responsible for formulating and proposing broad economic and monetary policy. Established in 1789, it is the largest and most complex department of the federal government, with twelve bureaus, including among them the Internal Revenue Service, the U.S. Secret Service, and the Bureau of Alcohol, Tobacco, and Firearms.

THEORIES OF DOMESTIC ECONOMIC POLICY

As noted earlier, the types of economic policies that members of Congress will favor depends on both the specific impacts of those policies on constituents and their more general effects on society and the economy. Various theories of economic policy have evolved over time, and their influence ebbs and flows. For our purposes, it is convenient to summarize these differences historically, tracing the evolution of views on economic policy from the laissez-faire ideas of Adam Smith through Keynesian economics, monetarism, and supply-side economics. All of these theories have influenced the thinking of today's policymakers, which is one reason why passing legislation that has broad economic (and political) effects is so difficult.

Laissez-faire Economics

Laissez-faire economics suggests that people should be allowed to "do as they please," to pursue their own economic self-interest in the market without the interference of government policies. As Adam Smith characterized them in *The Wealth of Nations* (1776), the forces of the market are quite powerful, acting as an "invisible hand" guiding production, employment, and prices in ways that benefit society as much as they benefit the self-interested individuals who constitute the market.

Advocates of laissez-faire economics policy believe that if the market is left alone, it will adjust itself over time, and thus the pursuit of individual interests will benefit society as a whole by resulting in a healthy economy. The proper role of government in such a system is minimal, serving only to safeguard the broad framework within which the market operates and to make sure that individuals are free to pursue their self-interest.

Smith's idea that the best government is the least government was based both on an appreciation of the market's efficiency and a belief that government policies create distortions, sometimes doing more harm than good. Smith's views are as powerful in the twentieth century as they were when *The Wealth of Nations* was first published.[6] Members of President Reagan's cabinet were known to wear neckties bearing Smith's image in homage to the contemporary validity of his ideas.

While laissez-faire economic theory generally favors free trade, low taxes, and constraints on government interference in the private economy, it is important to understand that some kinds of government activities are still considered desirable. Government is still needed, in this view, for national defense and foreign policy, to regulate the money supply, and to take limited actions to deal with health, poverty, and educational problems.

Keynesian Economics and Active Fiscal Policy

An important challenge to laissez-faire economic theory arose during the 1930s, when the entire world was drawn into deep recession, with high unemployment and great human suffering. Evolving during this period was a view of economic policy that suggested that government should play a far more active role in the economy: **Keynesian economics.**

A main component of laissez-faire economics is the belief that the market will correct itself. According to this theory, economic downturns, unemployment, and inflation are wrinkles in the fabric of a normally functioning economy that, if left alone, will smooth out over time. Just how much time this will take becomes an important political reality, however, for when people are out of work, prices are high, and businesses are failing, the public tends to want their government to act.

By the time of the Great Depression of the 1930s, many economists had come to disagree with the laissez-faire philosophy that government should do little about economic downturns and simply ride them out. Beginning with the writings of British economist John Maynard Keynes in *A General Theory of Employment, Interest, and Money* (1935), Keynesian economics argues that the economy can be manipulated to reverse periodic downturns in the capitalist business economy.

Keynesian economics stresses aggregate demand, which is spending by consumers, businesses, and government. According to the theory, economic downturns stem from too little demand for goods, which leads to a decline in production and increasing unemployment. When demand increases, factories produce more, and employment rises to meet this call for more goods and services. Thus, according to Keynesians, the primary way to stimulate demand and production is to stimulate spending.

The primary mechanism for stimulating spending is known as **fiscal policy,** government efforts to stabilize the economy through its power to tax and spend. According to Keynesian theory, governments can reduce unemployment by increasing government spending while cutting taxes—even to the

TOLES (1993) The Buffalo News. Reprinted with permission of *Universal Press Syndicate*.

extent of running budget deficits—so that citizens have money left after taxes and other obligations to spend on goods and services. Increased spending results in increased demands for goods and services, and thus increased employment to meet these demands. Similarly, fiscal policy can be used to slow an inflationary economy (when spending is too great, forcing prices to rise) by raising taxes and reducing spending, thereby giving people less money to spend and reducing demand.

From a political perspective Keynesian economics is important because it challenged the classical theory of the market's invisible hand, calling for *more* rather than *less* government intervention in the economy. Pushing aside the long-term view of classical laissez-faire economics, Keynes saw that the role and responsibility of government is to move the economy out of unemployment-producing downturns by undertaking policies designed to stimulate aggregate demand. Thus, with its clear call for an activist government in economic-policy making, Keynes's theory represented a revolution in economic thinking.[7]

Monetarism

While Keynes focused on the government's ability to stabilize the economy through the wise and active use of fiscal policy, other economic theorists took a different approach. **Monetarism** builds upon the ideas of laissez-faire economics and reacts to the abuses of Keynesian economic policies. Keynes saw fiscal policy as a tool to stabilize an otherwise unstable economic system. Monetarists, on the other hand, believe that the economy itself is the source of stability, while unwise economic policies are the cause of cycles of inflation, unemployment, and slow growth.

Monetarists, such as Milton Friedman, believe that the best way to control this problem is to minimize the use of destabilizing fiscal policies and to promote the smooth, stable growth of the economy by strictly controlling the growth of the money supply.[8] Monetarists thus call for a stable **monetary policy,** which is controlled by the Federal Reserve System, not directly by Congress or the president.

THE FEDERAL RESERVE SYSTEM   The **Federal Reserve System** (known as "the Fed") acts as the country's central bank and is the nation's principal overseer of monetary policy. Established in 1913 in response to recurring bank failures, the Fed is really a system of twelve banks run by an appointed board of governors and directed by a chair designated by the president. To keep the Fed independent of the president and Congress and free from political influences, the board of governors is appointed for staggered fourteen-year terms, while the chair serves a four-year term (with possible reappointments for other terms). The current chair of the Federal Reserve Board is Alan Greenspan, who was appointed by Ronald Reagan in 1987.

As the nation's primary agent of monetary policy, the Fed's most important role is to monitor and manage the supply of money. It does this in three ways, including buying and selling federal government securities (such as treasury notes and bonds), regulating the amount of money that member banks must have on deposit (the reserve requirement), and manipulating interest through changes in the rate that member banks have to pay when borrowing from a reserve bank (the discount rate).

Chairman of the Federal Reserve Board Alan Greenspan (left) heads an organization that controls the country's money supply, the amount that banks must keep in reserve, and the discount rate that banks must pay to borrow money from the "Fed." The Federal Reserve Board has relative freedom from the usual checks and balances. Its independence from Congress stems mainly from its self-financing status. Investments in income-earning securities allow the Fed to earn all the money it needs to run its operations.

Depending on the direction of these moves, the Fed's policies can have a strong tightening or loosening effect on the money supply, stimulating or contracting the economy. When inflation is not a perceived threat, as was the case throughout much of the early 1990s, the Fed can lower the reserve requirement, giving banks more money to lend; buy government securities from banks, giving banks more money to lend; and put more money into circulation or lower its discount rate, encouraging banks to lend more freely. All of these policies serve to stimulate the economy by encouraging borrowing and spending. If, however, inflation appears on the horizon, as was the case by 1993–94, the Fed can pull in the reins on a runaway economy by raising interest rates, selling securities, and increasing the reserve requirement.

There are two things that can disrupt the American economy. One is a war. The other is a meeting of the Federal Reserve Board.

—Will Rogers

These tools of monetary policy give the members of the Federal Reserve Board substantial power over Americans' economic lives. When interest rates are low, for example, home mortgages are easier to come by, meaning that those who could not previously afford a home might find it easier to do so. If it is true that one of the grandest aspects of the "American Dream" is buying a home, then the Fed can play an important role in making this dream come true.

Interestingly, it is not unusual to find the Fed working directly against the wishes of the president, especially when an election year is approaching and the president as a political candidate is calling for the Fed to stimulate the economy. Just such a situation occurred early in the Clinton presidency. As President Clinton was trying to push an economic-stimulus package through Congress—a combination of short-run fiscal policy spending measures—the Fed, worried about inflation, began raising interest rates to tighten the money supply and slow down the economy. Thus, as Clinton was trying to start his presidency by stimulating the economy, the Fed was trying to rein the economy in.[9]

Members of the Fed are, like the justices of the Supreme Court, nonelected policymakers. Indeed, it can even be argued that because the activities of the Federal Reserve Board are outside the direct control of Congress and the president, the chair of this institution is the most powerful single economic actor in the country today. While the Fed is not completely insulated from political forces, the fact that it operates as an independent agency, largely free from the political forces that affect Congress and the president, may mean that it is better able to make rational decisions about the country's economic destiny. Still, in the United States, some of the most powerful actors in one of the most important areas of our lives are largely untouched by the democratic process.[10]

Supply-side Economics and the Shrinking Role of Government

When Ronald Reagan took office in 1981 he brought with him what many hailed as a revolutionary new idea in economic policy, **supply-side economics,** an economic strategy emphasizing the stimulation of *supply* rather than *demand* to stabilize and reinvigorate the economy.[11] In many respects, supply-side economics can be thought of as a subspecies of monetarism. In addition to the monetarists' emphasis on stable monetary policy, however, supply-siders sought to stimulate growth in the economy through tax cuts, deregulation, and other policies.

Supply-side economics was a reaction to the economic problems of the 1970s and what many saw as the excessive influence of Keynesian fiscal policy ideas. Reagan took office during a period of **stagflation,** which from an

The Chairman of the House Budget Committee, Republican John Kasich (Ohio), sits before the ever-increasing national debt clock. Now over $4 trillion, the national debt represents accumulating annual deficits. Between 1981 and 1985 a large proportion of the deficits were financed by foreign capital. As a result, in 1985, for the first time since 1914, the United States became a debtor nation. The heritage for the next generation will be severe unless the debt and the onerous interest payments associated with it are reduced.

economic standpoint is the worst of both worlds: simultaneous high unemployment (10.5 percent) and high inflation (13.9 percent). Since Keynesian theory had suggested that rising inflation triggers reduced unemployment and vice versa, the existence of both conditions at the same time made many economists and politicians unenthusiastic about continuing to apply Keynesian theory. Keynesian theory did not anticipate, nor could it deal with, stagflation.

The key to supply-side economics is its focus on supply in the economy rather than on demand, as in Keynesian economics. Thus, rather than reducing demand for goods to reduce inflation, as Keynesian theory suggests, supply-side economics emphasizes that inflation can be lowered by increasing supply. In doing so, "supply-siders," as they have come to be called, emphasize the importance of the business sector. Creating incentives for business to invest and expand production—to stimulate supply—is, according to the theory, the key to reducing inflation and invigorating the economy. The way to do this is through tax cuts and decreased government regulation of business. The result of greater production will be large-scale corporate expansion, assuming that the beneficiaries of these economic policies turn significant percentages of their after-tax profits into new factories, new research and development, and new jobs, while boosting incomes for those already employed. All of this is supposed to increase government revenues by increasing the amount of taxable income, rather than by increasing the taxes themselves, more than enough to offset the tax cuts.

In its pure form, supply-side economics was a movement away from Keynesian theory and a return to the days of laissez faire and Adam Smith's invisible hand. It should not be surprising that political conservatives quickly embraced supply-side economics. For them, supply-side theory was the key to simultaneously reducing unemployment and inflation, while also decreasing government expenditures, resulting in balanced budgets. Most important, all of this could be achieved, they believed, through less rather than more government involvement in the economy, a basic conservative economic principle.

Supply-side economics may well have been one of the most interesting experiments in the history of U.S. economic-policy making, combining a laissez-faire, "hands-off" approach with a substantial tax cut to stimulate investment. Reagan made good on his promises to deregulate business and cut taxes, but he also dramatically increased government spending for the military, a policy that while consistent with his conservative and Republican leanings was contrary to supply-side theory, since it forced the government into heavy deficit spending.[12]

In the end, therefore, the results of the supply-side experiment were mixed. Initially, the tax cuts did stimulate productivity, and inflation dropped dramatically, from 13.9 percent in 1980 to 4.9 percent in 1988. But while inflation subsided, it did so initially at the cost of the highest unemployment levels since World War II, and after Reagan was succeeded by George Bush, unemployment continued to grow while the economy stalled. Likewise, the expected increases in the *rate of savings* never emerged, but the increase in the income gap between wealthy and poor Americans was constant and dramatic. Many economists also believe that the combination of corporate and wealthy tax cuts, combined with the largest peacetime military buildup in American

The good news is that a busload of supply-side economists plunged over a cliff. The bad news is that three seats were unoccupied at the time.

—Morris Udall

history, contributed to the economic recession after Reagan left office. Perhaps the most enduring legacy of Reaganomics may be the record national debt increase that more than tripled during the 1980s and the soaring budget deficits that continue to plague the U.S. Treasury and tie the hands of Congress and the president as they attempt to manage the economy.[13]

THE POLITICS OF THE FEDERAL BUDGET

> The final budget . . . Was a compromise in the sense that being bitten in half by a shark is a compromise with being swallowed whole. . . .
>
> —P. J. O'Rourke

There is perhaps no better place to observe how economic policy and political factors intertwine than the case of the federal budget. We have already discussed some of the ways government uses its power to tax and spend to influence the economy. Yet government also taxes and spends to provide services for its citizens. How policymakers attempt to provide these services—and more important, who pays for them and who receives them—gets to the very heart of the politics of the federal budget.[14]

Preparing the Budget: The President Proposes, Congress Disposes

Stated simply, the national budget is a document that proclaims how much the government will try to collect in taxes and how these revenues will be spent on various federal programs. Yet despite this seemingly simple definition, the preparation of the budget and its subsequent passage are both complex and profoundly political activities. The budget sets policy priorities by establishing the amount of money each program is slated to receive. Some programs are created, some receive more support than others, and still others are reduced or eliminated. The budget thus provides a policy blueprint for the nation, one in which there are real winners and losers among both elected officials and the American people.

Alice Rivlin, Director of the Office of Management and Budget, oversees the development of the budget that the President submits to Congress. In addition, the OMB provides economic forecasts regarding the state of the economy and thereby projects future changes in costs of federal programs.

How the Budget Is Prepared

Budgetary politics involves many actors, the most important being the president and Congress. While in a strict constitutional sense Congress has sole power to authorize spending of any federal monies, modern-day practice is for Congress to follow the lead of the president. The Budget and Accounting Act of 1921 conferred this responsibility upon the president, greatly enhancing the president's power in domestic affairs. First, the law requires government agencies to send their budget requests to the president for consideration. The president ultimately decides whether or not to include these requests in the budget plan. Second, the act created an executive budget office, the Bureau of the Budget (BOB), which became the **Office of Management and Budget (OMB)** under President Nixon. The director of the OMB has cabinet-level status and is one of the president's top advisers and policy strategists.

It is the OMB that analyzes the budgetary requests made by every government agency, after first providing each agency with instructions and guidelines reflecting presidential budgetary priorities. This process takes place during the spring and fall of the year, after which the OMB director goes to the president with a budget—a set of estimates for both revenues and expenditures. But this procedure is not simply a matter of adding up numbers. Agency heads submit

The 1994 election resulted in Republican majorities in both the House and the Senate, the first time Republicans have controlled the House since 1953. The policy goals of the 104th Congress are enumerated in their Contract With America. Many of their legislative proposals will inevitably conflict with those of a Democratic President. Freshman GOP representatives are shown here at an orientation session in December 1994. The United States, after a brief foray with a president from the same party as majorities in both the House and the Senate, is back to divided government.

budgetary figures that represent their goals, their ideologies, and even their own personal ambitions. This is an extremely political undertaking, with plenty of political maneuvering and overt lobbying geared toward protecting and enhancing each agency's share of the budgetary pie. Finally, in January, after adjustments by the president, the budget plan—the budget of the United States government—is submitted to Congress.

With the help of the OMB the president is able to submit to Congress a budget plan that outlines the national priorities, the president's vision for the policy agenda of the country. It is in this context that we see the workings of the old budgetary adage: "The president proposes and Congress disposes," for it is Congress that must approve the budget, turning the president's vision into tangible law. Congress uses its oversight authority to assess the performance of government agencies but also to check the president's power.

However, by 1973 it had become increasingly difficult for Congress to formulate a comprehensive, substantive alternative to the president's plan. Congress was often left with little control over the budget, making only incremental and marginal adjustments to what is clearly the president's blueprint for the nation. As we saw in Chapter 5, Congress is a highly decentralized and fragmented institution, one that allows its individual members to pursue their own personal policy and reelection goals. While the institutional setup of Congress works to the advantage of individual members, it is a detriment to Congress's ability to produce a collective vision of national priorities to balance that of the president.[15]

Partly in response to recurring budget battles with President Nixon and partly to reassert its ability to use the budget as an expression of its own policy vision, Congress passed the Budget and Impoundment Control Act of 1974. In essence, the act sought to provide Congress a procedure, independent of the president, to gain more control of the budget.[16] The goal of the act was to give Congress the ability to make comprehensive appropriations and spending decisions and thus provide a reasonable alternative to the president's budget. The act modified the budget process by allowing Congress to establish overall levels for taxing and spending, including breakdowns between areas such as national defense, foreign aid, health, infrastructure, and agriculture. Congress established the House and Senate budget committees to carry out these tasks and to hold hearings on the president's proposed budget. Finally, Congress set up the Congressional Budget Office (CBO), a staff of budgetary experts to provide both houses with their own source of budgetary data, enhancing their independence from the executive branch OMB. The House and Senate budget committees examine the president's budget. The committees send a budget to each chamber in the form of resolutions. A conference committee then hashes out a single congressional budget that can reward or punish different agencies.

The reform worked well for several years, increasing the congressional role in budget formation by allowing Congress to propose broad alternatives rather than make incremental modifications to the president's plans. For the most part recent budgets have reflected multiyear commitments to agencies and programs. At the same time budgets have been more sensitive to macroeconomic changes. By the mid 1980s a new problem was emerging, one that eventually led to further reform of the budgetary process. The combined tax cuts and increased military spending of the Reagan administration dramatically increased the existing budget deficits. In the same period, the percentage of the budget committed to entitlement programs (benefits to which people are entitled because they fall into a particular category, such as Medicaid or Medicare), rather than discretionary spending also grew, taking much of the budgetary flexibility away from both the White House and Congress.

Balancing the Budget

In response, Congress passed the Balanced Budget and Emergency Deficit Control Act of 1985, authored by Senators Phil Gramm (R-Tex.), Warren Rudman (R-N.H.), and Earnest Hollings (D-S.C.), and known more commonly as Gramm-Rudman. According to Senator Rudman, the goal of the act was to "force a discipline into this Congress and this administration and succeeding administrations that is totally lacking."[17]

In its original form, Gramm-Rudman called for Congress to reduce the annual budget deficit by thirty-six billion dollars in each of five consecutive years, with the budget finally being balanced by 1991. If Congress was unable to come within ten billion dollars of the required target, automatic budget cuts were to go into effect. These cuts were to come equally and across the board from defense and domestic categories. Several politically sensitive entitlement programs were excluded from the automatic budget ax, however, most notably social security, Aid to Families with Dependent Children (AFDC), food stamps, Medicaid, and veterans' benefits. The goal of Gramm-Rudman and its mechanism of automatic budget cuts was to reduce the deficit, even if the president and Congress lacked the political courage to do so.

This goal clearly has not been met, in large part because of the unwillingness of both Congress and the president to endure the political fallout of the automatic spending cuts. In 1987, for example, Gramm-Rudman was amended, postponing the balanced-budget deadline until 1992. And in 1990, with the possibility of budget cuts looming, President Bush and a Democratically

Balancing the Budget: Who Wins, Who Loses?

It's an annual battle. Each year Congress must decide on the national budget, setting limits on federal spending for everything from paper clips to space exploration. But in 1995 the battle turned into a war as Congress set out to balance the budget, that is, to reduce the vast federal deficit over a period of several years by making deep cuts in spending on many federally funded programs. Republicans, in control of both houses of Congress, proposed a budget that would reduce the deficit by nearly one trillion dollars within seven years. The Clinton administration proposed an alternative plan that would balance the budget within ten years while making less severe cuts in such areas as education and Medicare.

With both parties committed to balancing the budget, the question becomes who will pay the price and how much they will pay. Large portions of the federal budget are off limits to cuts; they include social-security benefits and interest payments on the national debt. Neither party is willing to make drastic cuts in military spending. The prime targets for cuts are social programs—Medicare, Medicaid, Aid to Families with Dependent Children (welfare), education, and the like. Not only are these programs likely to suffer drastic reductions in funding, but responsibility for some of them, such as public assistance, may be shifted from the national government to the states.

In the spring of 1995 both houses of Congress passed bills designed to balance the budget within seven years. As expected, the bills sought to reduce government spending on Medicare, Medicaid, welfare, agriculture, education, and other nonmilitary programs such as mass transit and national parks. Both houses also sought significant reductions in taxes, which of course would affect the amount of revenue available to the government and thus the difficulty of reducing the deficit.

Who would suffer most from these measures, and who would benefit?

Thinking Critically

What Would Happen

If the federal budget is balanced, many groups will be affected, some negatively but others positively. People who receive direct payments from the government will find those payments reduced or eliminated, but some will also benefit from tax cuts. In general, economists believe that most Americans will benefit indirectly from deficit reduction, which is expected to result in lower interest rates and faster growth in jobs and incomes. Among the groups most affected are the following:

- *The elderly.* Almost half the savings in the proposed budget will come from limits on spending for Medicare and Medicaid. This means that the elderly will have to pay a larger proportion of their health-care costs.

- *The young.* If the budget is not balanced, future generations will find themselves paying taxes at astronomical rates.

- *Government employees.* It is estimated that almost twelve thousand federal government jobs will be eliminated by the year 2003. In the words of one observer, this "qualifies as a neutron bomb—the kind that leaves buildings standing but eliminates people inside."*

- *The military.* Despite the fact that the nation is not at war, military spending will remain at high levels.

- *The poor.* People who depend on the government for cash payments, food stamps, housing assistance, and health care will suffer. On the other hand, there may be more job opportunities for unskilled workers.

- *The middle class.* The middle class is likely to gain the most from the economic effects of deficit reduction, such as lower interest rates and faster wage growth.

---

*Sylvia Nasar, "Doing Well in a Deficit-Free America. Or Not So Well," *New York Times,* May 21, 1995, p. E1.

controlled congress got together to suspend the automatic cuts until 1995, effectively gutting the original legislation. The result was a 1992 deficit of approximately $290 billion, well over ten times what the deficit was expected to be had the Gramm-Rudman automatic cuts gone into effect.[18]

The most recent attempt to impose budgetary discipline on Congress and the president came in the wake of the Republican capture of the House and Senate in 1994, in the form of a proposed amendment to the Constitution.[19] Part of the Republican "Contract with America," the Balanced Budget Amendment originally required a three-fifths supermajority for Congressional approval of all new taxation legislation (currently such laws are no different from any other regular legislation, requiring only a simple majority). The balanced budget amendment did not pass the Senate. By summer 1995 Congress and the president were moving decisively toward an agreement that would use spending cuts (combined with some tax cuts) to balance the budget by 2007. While there seems to be broad agreement concerning the overall goal of balancing the budget, however, it is apparent that there remain great differences over how, how much, and when to cut spending programs. These differences, as noted earlier, reflect both disagreements about what theory should guide economic policy as well as concerns about the retail political impact of spending cuts on districts and constituencies.

The latest battle over budget balancing may have been frustrating to all involved, but it did suggest that there is growing support for serious reform of the budgetary process. However, both within government and among the general public, there is still no overwhelming consensus regarding the best way to achieve this. For example, while an overwhelming majority of Americans (more than 70 percent) support some form of balanced-budget amendment, fewer than half are willing to support any proposal that allows for "plundering" the

The Contract With America has engendered strong feelings on both sides of the political spectrum. Republicans claim a conservative "revolution" and a clear mandate for conservative policies from a balanced budget amendment to dramatic cuts in welfare expenditures. However, the results in the 1994 elections were based on a voter turnout of just 39 percent of the electorate; the implications of these electoral outcomes will not be clear until the next presidential election.

social-security trust fund. And most Americans are reluctant to see government budgets balanced at the expense of those programs that benefit them most.

Taxing and Spending Policies

While all citizens want their fair share of the budgetary pie—whether for better highways or more powerful ICBMs—almost nobody wants to foot the bill for these services. Therein lies the strain in the politics of taxing and spending, a strain that is profoundly political. As we saw in the case study on the Clinton budget plan, his ideas about where government revenues should be spent and who should shoulder the burden of paying led to some serious battles, even among Clinton's fellow Democrats. Recall that Clinton's plan called for increased taxes on social security benefits for wealthy social-security recipients, a tax that Senator Dennis DeConcini from Arizona—a state with a substantial number of retirees—simply could not support. Thus, DeConcini felt pressure to side with his constituents rather than with his own president. DeConcini's reaction illustrates the highly political nature of taxing and spending policies: policy makers decide who will benefit from government programs and who will pay for them, and neither these benefits nor the burden of paying for them are distributed evenly across society.

TAXATION

Governments have never been able to meet public needs by relying on voluntary contributions alone. Indeed, this statement reveals a great deal about the relationship that a government has with its citizens. Most citizens want, and in fact, expect, government to provide us with certain things. From highly targeted benefits like subsidies for farmers, to broad, almost intangible things like national security, we look to our government as a provider. Yet when the government reaches into our pockets to pay for these services, we balk, we complain, some even risk stiff penalties by trying to evade paying their "fair share." Such is the relationship between a government and its people when taxes are concerned.[20]

Income taxes are today a significant source of tax dollars. It was not always so. In 1895 the Supreme Court ruled that any income tax was a "direct tax" and so was unconstitutional. Any imposition of a tax on income would require an amendment to the Constitution. And so in 1913, the Sixteenth Amendment to the Constitution was passed and subsequently allowed federal collection of income taxes.

This unwillingness to fork over hard-earned dollars is understandable. The idea of a free, democratic society is always challenged when governments demand and take private property, including portions of the profits of corporations and the much more modest wages of U.S. workers. Indeed, this concern has much to do with the fact that it was only early in this century that the federal government began to use its power to collect taxes from private corporations (1909) and individuals (1913). Prior to these new tax levies, money to run the government came primarily from tariffs, namely, taxes on goods imported into the country.

The power to tax has not always been easy to swallow for many U.S. citizens, leading to periodic "tax revolts." In 1978 the citizens of California staged one such revolt when they passed Proposition 13, a measure designed to permanently cap local property taxes. Antitax sentiment has appeared since then as well. Tax cuts were a central feature of the Reagan administration and led subsequently to George Bush's now infamous pledge of "no new taxes."

Coping with Taxes

Each year, as April 15 approaches, Americans respond with a chorus of moans. It's tax time again, time to give up some of their hard-earned dollars to pay for government services such as national defense and highway construction. Compared with taxpayers in Western Europe, however, they have it easy. Citizens of some Western European countries pay more than 45 percent of their income in taxes, and in many countries tax rates are going up.

Despite their high taxes, Europeans complain less about taxes than Americans do. But their taxes also pay for a wide array of social services that Americans' taxes don't, including free medical and nursing-home care, inexpensive college educations, generous pensions, and unemployment insurance. "As long as you have a job and pay your taxes, you are protected and don't have to worry about your future," comments Paul Breuer, a German book dealer whose tax rate is close to 60 percent.*

The importance of tax revenues in the economies of Western European nations is illustrated in the accompanying chart, which presents total tax revenues (including national, state, local, and social-security taxes) as a percentage of each nation's gross domestic product. These countries' leaders are reluctant to cut government spending because of the political risks of reducing the quality of life to which their citizens have grown accustomed. This leaves them little choice but to raise taxes. Sweden, for example, recently increased its highest income tax bracket from 51 percent to 56 percent.

In explaining their willingness to pay high taxes, Europeans often mention their countries' lower crime rates, cleaner streets, better mass transportation, and greater social stability compared with the United States. But there are some signs of discontent. Economists believe high taxes are stifling consumer spending. Some taxpayers admit that they are willing to cheat on taxes; and in some countries, particularly Italy, Greece, and Spain, there is growing resistance to higher taxes, manifested in increased tax evasion.

No one likes to pay taxes, even though it is generally agreed that taxes are necessary to fund government expenditures. But while voters in the United States openly rebel against candidates who even hint at raising taxes, most Europeans are philosophical

Still, while people don't like to be taxed, the power of government to raise revenues through taxation is generally accepted. Government needs money to function, and most of us realize it is our responsibility to provide part of it. Rather than the power to tax, the debate about taxation in this country revolves in general around who should be taxed, how much should be paid, and the degree of fairness in the tax structure.[21]

Sources of Tax Dollars

At least a partial answer to these questions comes from examining sources of federal revenues. As Figure 17.1 shows, the federal government relies to a significant degree on the personal income tax. Reliance on personal income has some important advantages. It puts the federal government in a position to benefit from the increases in personal income that accompany a healthy economy. The better the economy, the more revenues generated by the income tax. Interestingly, reliance on the income tax can also act as a buffer during economic downturns, in that the national pool of taxpayers means that economic

Government tax revenues as a percentage of gross domestic product in 1994

Denmark	58.6%
Sweden	56.2%
Norway	55.2%
Finland	54.0%
Netherlands	51.2%
Belgium	50.0%
France	49.6%
Austria	48.0%
Italy	46.3%
Germany	46.1%
Spain	39.5%
Britain	36.4%
United States	31.6%
Western Europe	45.5%

about their high taxes. Underlying this difference in attitude is a difference in perception. As one expert has put it, "If your system works correctly, there is a willingness to pay taxes as long as you see what you are getting for it."** Apparently, European taxpayers see their taxes producing tangible benefits, while American taxpayers, despite their lower tax burden, do not feel that they are getting enough benefits in exchange for their tax dollars.

*Quoted in Nathaniel C. Nash, "Europeans Shrug as Taxes Go Up," *New York Times,* Feb. 16, 1995, p. A10.
**Richard Reid, quoted in ibid.

Taxes in Western Europe are considerably higher than those of the United States when measured as a percentage of gross domestic product. Despite the relatively lighter tax burden, voters in the United States invariably support further tax reduction and will on occasion, as evidenced by the aftermath of George Bush's inability to keep his "Read My Lips—No New Taxes" promise, respond to tax increases by removing the incumbent from office.

Source: Nathaniel C. Nash, "Europeans Shrug As Taxes Go Up," *The New York Times*, February 16, 1995, p. A10.

slumps affecting some parts of the country are at least partially offset by greater prosperity in other parts. However, later we will see how this heavy reliance on individual taxpayers over large corporations can impose severe, some argue unfair, tax burdens, particularly for middle-class citizens.

When we evaluate the importance of income taxes, it is important to recognize that not all taxes are created equal—some taxes affect people differently than others. One way to judge income taxes, therefore, is according to who they affect and how much. **Progressive taxes,** which tax those who make more money at a higher rate, are often considered the fairest, as they place a larger burden on those people with the greatest ability to pay. In general, the greater the number of tax brackets—steps in which the percentage rate of tax increases—the more progressive the tax. **Regressive taxes,** on the other hand, tax all people by the same amount—thereby taking a higher fraction of the income of lower-income taxpayers, and thus are generally seen as less fair. The capital gains tax (tax on unearned income from rents, stocks, and interest) is an example of a progressive tax, since most of the revenue it gathers comes from a tiny portion of the wealthiest Americans. Meanwhile, taxes on consumer goods such

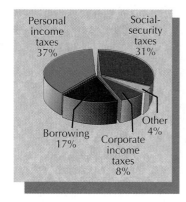

FIGURE 17.1
As a source of federal revenue, the government relies heavily upon the personal income tax (37 percent), especially when compared to the revenues it collects from corporations (8 percent). Many have argued that this imbalance, combined with the lack of progressivity in the current tax structure, has led to an unfair middle class tax burden.

Source: Budget of the U.S. Government.

Tax reform means don't tax you, don't tax me, tax that fellow behind the tree.

—Russell Long

The hardest thing in the world to understand is the income tax.

—Albert Einstein

as gasoline, cigarettes, and alcoholic beverages are generally regressive, since most of the consumption of these goods—hence most of the taxes paid—comes from the relatively larger group of middle- and lower-class Americans.

Tax Reform

Periodic attempts to reform the way government taxes are typically related to the issue of fairness. In 1986, after prolonged political battles over who would benefit and who would pay more, Congress passed major tax reform legislation: the Tax Reform Act of 1986. The purpose of the reform was to simplify an unwieldy tax structure and promote greater fairness. The first goal was advanced by reducing the number of tax rates from fifteen categories to three (including a zero rate for low-income individuals). The remaining brackets dropped the highest rate from 50 percent to 28 percent and the lowest rate to 15 percent. Thus, on the face of things, tax rates were actually lessened for higher-income individuals, suggesting that the tax structure actually became more regressive.

Yet the tax reform of 1986 included another important aspect, one that helped increase revenues and retain a degree of progressivity. In addition to changing tax rates, the reform also eliminated many tax deductions, or what are technically called tax expenditures. Tax expenditures are amounts taxpayers have spent for items that they are allowed to subtract from their income when filing their tax returns. The effect of these expenditures is to reduce the amount of income that is actually subject to taxes, resulting in losses of government revenue. Some of the most common tax expenditures are interest paid on home mortgages or business equipment, and business-related entertainment. Critics of such tax expenditures argue that they are a drain on the federal treasury and specifically benefit the relatively wealthy—after all, only those who can afford to buy a home can benefit from the mortgage interest reduction.

In the end, the 1986 reforms changed many of these deductions, eliminating deductions for state sales taxes, interest paid on credit card and other personal debt, and interest on mortgages on third or fourth homes, while reducing deductions for medical expenses and business entertainment, among others. The result was a simplified, more progressive tax code, in which many taxpayers now pay lower taxes and a greater burden was placed on upper-middle-income individuals. Critics argue, however, that the reform did not go far enough, and that as some deductions were eliminated, new deductions sprang up to take their place, effectively reducing the impact of any attempts to increase the degree of progressivity or fairness of the reforms.

Unfortunately for George Bush, these tax reforms had another effect: They did not bring in enough revenue to cover federal spending. The result was further increases in the annual budget deficit. Thus, in 1990, President Bush was forced to renege on his now well-known promise, "Read my lips, no new taxes," and enact a modest tax increase on wealthier Americans. Republicans who had supported Bush in 1988 were enraged by this, and it is likely that Bush paid a price for reneging on his pledge, as many Republicans voted for Ross Perot in 1992.[22]

In 1993, as newly elected president Bill Clinton prepared to submit his first budget, both Republicans and Democrats watched closely. With the ever-increasing budget deficit a major issue in the campaign, both sides expected changes in the tax structure as the first Democratic president in twelve years took office. Change is what they got.

Table 17.1
The Clinton Plan: Who Pays the Taxes?

INCOME	OVERALL TAX INCREASE (%)
Less than $10,000	-3
$10,000–$20,000	no change
$20,000–$30,000	+0.5
$30,000–$50,000	+2.9
$50,000–$75,000	+3.7
$75,000–$100,000	+3.4
$100,000–$200,000	+3.3
More than $200,000	+14

Includes social security, energy taxes, earned-income credits and others.

One major goal of Clinton's tax strategy was to make the tax structure more equitable, to make good on his campaign promise to make wealthier people "pay their fair share." With regard to the personal income tax, Clinton introduced a greater degree of progressivity by changing the tax structure. Individuals making over $115,000 saw their tax rates rise from 31 percent to 36 percent. Those making over $250,000 became subject to an additional boost, with a 10 percent surcharge making their tax-effective rate 39.6 percent. It is estimated that Clinton's plan will result in actual income tax increases for fewer than 2 percent of all taxpayers, with the greatest hit being taken by the wealthiest, and tax cuts going to the poorest Americans.

The next-largest source of federal revenue (31 percent) comes from social-security taxes paid by employers and their employees. While not raising the effective tax rate for these taxes, Clinton's plan does tax a larger percentage of social-security benefits from relatively wealthy recipients. Finally, Clinton's plan places a greater emphasis on a traditionally small part of federal revenue raised from excise taxes. Excise taxes are charges on the sale or manufacture of certain products, such as cigarettes, alcohol, or gasoline. Despite the concern of members of Congress from oil-producing states, Clinton won passage of an increased excise tax on gasoline.

Overall then, the Clinton plan raises taxes in several ways, but as we see from Table 17.1, when all taxes are combined and the earned-income tax credit for the poor is figured in, most Americans were subject to very modest tax increases. In keeping with his pledge, the Clinton tax reform places its emphasis on those Americans with the greatest ability to pay.

GOVERNMENT SPENDING

Just as deciding who pays taxes and how much is a profoundly political question, so is deciding where to spend those revenues. While most of us balk at picking up the bill, we are also quite ready to hold out our hands for our fair

Other Recent Tax Reform Alternatives

While the Clinton tax plan may have caused some consternation among wealthy Americans and certain senators, his policies were really quite mainstream: Raise the tax rates of wealthy individuals to make the tax system more progressive. Other recent proposals, however, have been much more controversial. One such proposal is that of a flat tax. Championed by Democratic presidential hopeful Jerry Brown in 1992, a flat tax has just one rate; everyone pays the same rate regardless of income level. Brown linked his flat-tax proposal to the removal of virtually all tax exemptions, thereby allowing for a lower overall rate (Brown proposed a rate of 13 percent) for everyone. Brown argued that a single, lower rate would promote economic growth. Opponents, on the other hand, base their arguments on tax equity: A flat tax is inherently regressive, thus distributing the burden of taxation unfairly.

House majority leader Dick Armey is the major proponent of the current flat tax proposal. It would consist of a 17 percent tax on all earned income, radically downsize the Internal Revenue Service, and eliminate tax deductions. There would be no tax on interest, inheritance, or stock dividends. The flat tax essentially ends the double taxation of investment which discourages savings and encourages consumption, and so is potentially capable of stimulating increased savings rates. To attempt to hedge the inherent regressivity of the flat tax, the first $33,000 of income for a family of four would be exempted. Tax code reform has received bipartisan Congressional support and tremendous popular support; however, the far-reaching and fundamental reform that the flat tax proposal represents may have to wait until a president who runs on that platform is elected.

Another recent reform idea has been proposed in the same vein. The value-added tax (VAT) is a form of sales tax that is levied on the value added to a product at each stage of production. While widely used in Europe, it has never caught on in the United States. Proponents argue that it raises a great deal of money and promotes savings over consumption, since it taxes spending and not income. Opponents, however, point to its strong regressivity, because it falls most heavily on low-income people, who would pay the same tax as the wealthy on necessities such as food and clothing.

Source: Based on Carolyn Lockhead, "Elimination of Tax Code Gaining Favor," _San Francisco Chronicle,_ July 24, 1995, p. A1; and Louis S. Richmond, "The Flat Tax," _Fortune,_ June 12, 1995, pgs. 36–46.

share (or more) of the federal treasury. Be it low-cost student loans, government-subsidized health care, or cleaning up the environment, everyone wants his or her program to receive funding, and the more funding the better.

In addition, the way federal tax revenues are spent is often taken as a sign of the government's programmatic priorities. Ronald Reagan, for example, sought to boost the prestige and visibility of the U.S. military and achieved this by dramatically increasing spending for national defense, with much of this money coming from cuts in social programs (and increase in the deficit). Of course, these priorities change, from year to year and administration to administration. Bill Clinton's first budget, for example, proposed a sharp drop of $112 billion in national defense, to be offset by spending increases in other areas such as education and training ($32 billion), and nutritional and educational programs for children ($32 billion). As these two examples show, where tax revenues end up depends at least in part on which political party voters put into office and the ability of the parties to put their programmatic vision into action.

The federal government raises roughly $1.2 trillion in revenue per year. Of this, estimates show that in 1993 the average American paid approximately $4,434 in federal income taxes. Figure 17.2 illustrates how these monies were spent. Direct payments to individuals via programs such as social security, Medicare, and AFDC account for the largest portions (46 percent) of the federal budget. Military spending accounted for roughly 18 percent. Finally, note that interest on the federal debt accounted for over 14 percent, more than was spent on education and training, transportation, agriculture, science and technology, veterans affairs, and the environment combined.

Another way to examine federal spending is in terms of controllable versus uncontrollable expenditures. Uncontrollable expenditures are those over which Congress and the president have little or no discretion, either because they are safeguarded by laws or are political "sacred cows," programs for which it is considered political suicide to even suggest paring down. Interest on the national debt is one example of an uncontrollable expenditure; the government is obligated to finance and so pay interest on the money it borrows.

Most other uncontrollable expenditures take the form of entitlement programs, such as social security, Medicare, Medicaid, public assistance, veterans benefits, and unemployment insurance, to which qualifying individuals feel entitled because they have been promised these benefits by politicians over the years. While not strictly uncontrollable in a technical sense—Congress could change the laws in these areas to modify benefits or the persons entitled to them—they are virtually uncontrollable in a political sense. To cut benefits or change eligibility standards would be to risk the wrath of interest groups, such as the American Association of Retired Persons (AARP), that have in some cases become extraordinarily politically active and powerful. When policymakers go after entitlements they tend to meet strong and vocal opposition. Clinton and others have encountered such opposition when suggesting that wealthy retirees should have their social security benefits taxed more, or even removed through "means tests." Members of Congress and presidents know this and show extreme caution when proposing any program that would attempt control of these "uncontrollable" expenditures. Unfortunately, uncontrollable expenditures account for a huge proportion of the federal budget—roughly two-thirds of all federal outlays.[23]

Controllable expenditures are those that Congress does have leeway to increase or decrease. Examples include spending on education, highways, science and technology, and the military, which at 18 percent in 1994 represents the largest controllable expenditure in the federal budget. Of course, how much money can actually be cut from the military is also a political question. Neither party wishes to be seen as willing to risk U.S. security by reducing defense spending. In the end then, even regarding controllable expenditures, political forces make it difficult to cut spending.

Balancing the Books: The Deficit and the National Debt

That such a large proportion of the federal budget is either technically or politically "uncontrollable" creates an even larger problem when we look at the federal deficit. One of the most important issues on the minds of voters in the 1992 election, the **federal budget deficit** is the annual shortfall between

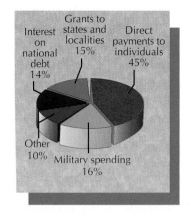

FIGURE 17.2

Direct payments to individuals in the form of social security, Medicare, and AFDC account for almost half of federal expenditures. Much of this is considered politically "uncontrollable" as a result of powerful and well-funded interest group organizations. While a major component of the Contract With America is the transfer of responsibility for programs to the state level, grants to all states and localities only represent about 14 percent of total expenditures. Defense expenditures still exceed grants to all states and localities.

Source: Budget of the U.S. Government. Expenditures in "other" category include education, transportation, science and technology, and the environment.

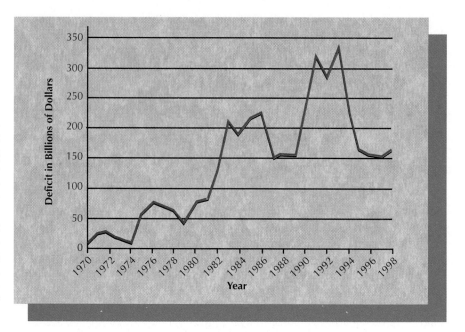

FIGURE 17.3
The amount that the United States has had to borrow each year just to meet its expenditures grew rapidly between 1979 and 1991. Continually increasing deficits have resulted in a soaring national debt, which has become a focal point for electoral politics. Projections for the future indicate that current economic policy may result in a strong decrease in deficit spending by 1996 and a leveling off for the two years following.

the monies that government takes in and what it spends. In this day and age, budget deficits are a routine occurrence. Indeed, the last time the federal government operated without an annual shortfall was 1951. The **national debt** is the cumulative unpaid total of all these annual budget deficits. Figure 17.3 and 17.4 show the growth of the budget deficit and total national debt over time and illustrate quite starkly why the deficit has become a major issue in U.S. politics. Both the deficit and the national debt together with its interest payment have grown to massive proportions and look to be running out of control.[24]

Just how big a threat are budget deficits? Many experts believe that as long as they are kept to a modest size, deficits are not a large threat at all. Recall that Keynesians call for moderate deficit spending to stimulate the economy. Yet many economists and policymakers fear that the extremely large deficits that have become commonplace represent a threat to the nation's economy, both domestically and in terms of its status with other countries. Domestically, huge deficits impede the ability of the government to engage in fiscal policy, meaning that policymakers attempting to regulate the economy are missing one of their most important tools. In addition, deficits increase interest rates because the government must cover its shortfall by borrowing. Because the funds available to borrow are limited, the increased competition from government borrowing pushes interest rates up, crowding out other borrowing and investments. Finally, the amount of money necessary to finance the debt (currently 14 percent of all government spending) takes away a large portion of the budget that could be used for other important programs.

In addition to tying the hands of policymakers here at home, large budget deficits also create problems for the United States as it deals with the global economy. To come up with the money to finance the debt, the United States must borrow from other countries. One result of this is that the United States

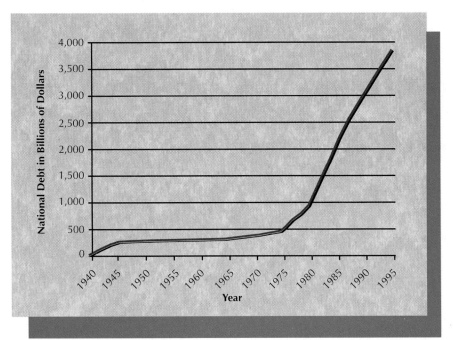

FIGURE 17.4
The accumulating debt more than tripled from 1980 to 1992. The United States has had to finance this debt by borrowing from other countries. Consequently, the United States has become the world's largest debtor nation, and interest payments on the debt represent over 14 percent of total expenditures each year. The inability to route these funds toward investment may, if it continues, result in a gradual erosion of the quality of life in this country.

is now the world's largest debtor nation, a status that makes it increasingly vulnerable to and dependent on international markets.[25]

Perhaps one of the most important questions to ask about the budget deficit and national debt is, Why the dramatic increase? The simple answer, of course, is that spending has far outstripped government revenues. More specifically, one of the main culprits was the supply-side policies of the Reagan administration. The 1981 and 1986 tax cuts did not produce the predicted increase in investment-driven revenues. Still, it is unfair to place all of the burden on the Reagan policies, as indeed, both the debt and annual deficit continued to increase during the Bush administration. President Clinton's administration is the first to decrease overall deficits since Eisenhower. For its first two years the deficit has gone from $290.4 to $234.8 billion. Thus, perhaps the most important reason for continued deficit spending lies in how the public views the role of government in their lives. Most of us want at least something from government, whether it be the ability to deduct the interest on our mortgages or a guarantee of income security when we retire. The reality of budgetary politics is that it is easier for politicians to offer these things to the public than it is to scale them back or to get the public to pay for them.

The budget deficit was an important issue in Bill Clinton's presidential campaign. Once in office, Americans wondered if he would make good on his promise to be a self-styled "new" Democrat who could reverse the trend of federal budget shortfalls. While it is too soon to gauge how successful he has been, history and a look at the president's economic plan tell us that the outlook is not rosy. Even under optimistic economic projections, the Clinton plan proposes to cut the deficit by a combined $473 billion by 1998. This is indeed a substantial reduction, if, unlike other recent presidents, Clinton can actually

Table 17.2
Promises, Promises: Cutting the Deficit

JIMMY CARTER			RONALD REAGAN			GEORGE BUSH		
1981 BUDGET	**GOAL**	**ACTUAL**	**1985 BUDGET**	**GOAL**	**ACTUAL**	**1993 BUDGET**	**GOAL**	**ACTUAL**
Spending	$575 billion	$678	Spending	$844 billion	$946	Spending	$1,284 billion	$1,475
Revenues	$584	$599	Revenues	$850	$734	Revenues	$1,287	$1,143
Balance	+ $ 9	–$ 79	Balance	+ $ 6	–$212	Balance	+ $ 3	–$ 332

Source: OMB.

pull it off (see Table 17.2). Still, even with tax increases and more modest cuts in spending, the deficit reduction is likely to be short-lived, with increases likely to begin again in 1998, as uncontrollable expenditures such as social security and Medicare are expected to take up an even larger share of the budget.

THE POLITICS OF INTERNATIONAL ECONOMIC POLICY

The political and economic problems of dealing with the federal budget deficit have increasingly tied Congress's hands in making fiscal policy. This has had two important effects. First has been to shift a good deal of the responsibility for making economic policy onto the shoulders of the Federal Reserve System. As noted earlier, the Federal Reserve is an independent agency, influenced by political factors, to be sure, but also insulated from them. This raises an important question about the nature and effect of democracy in the critical area of economic policy.

The second impact has been to shift attention somewhat from domestic economic policy toward international economic policy. Even though large deficits constrain Congress and the president at home, these actors still retain a variety of policy tools with which to influence international economic events. In fact, however, international economic policy would have become increasingly important in the United States even without the deficit dilemma. The global economy is becoming increasingly integrated, and nations are increasingly interdependent. To a greater extent than ever before, the United States must take account of global forces in making economic policy.

Many issues are involved in international economic policy. U.S. policies deal with issues affecting international trade, international monetary problems including exchange-rate policy, international finance and debt problems, and the actions of international economic institutions such as the World Bank, the IMF, and the WTO. Some economic issues are global in scope; others are multilateral, involving a group of nations; while still others are bilateral, between two nations. In the area of trade, for example, U.S. policy influences global trade policy through the GATT and the WTO, and regional trade policy through NAFTA. The U.S. also engages in bilateral trade negotiations with many nations, most notably Japan.

The United States, along with the rest of the world, is increasingly headed toward a globally interactive community where economic interchanges are coordinated multilaterally. The passage of both the GATT and NAFTA herald a new era of international cooperation and interdependence.

International economic policies, like their domestic cousins, are influenced both by political concerns and by broad philosophical and theoretical concerns. That is, when policymakers determine their support for international policies, they must consider both how their constituents will be affected and whether the policy is broadly beneficial, given their understanding of the way the international economy works. How these two sets of forces play against each other can be seen in the case of the politics of international trade in the early 1990s.

The GATT Uruguay Round

In 1994 Congress considered the GATT agreement, which derived from the Uruguay Round of multilateral trade negotiations. (GATT has since been superseded by the World Trade Organization as a forum for negotiating global trade agreements.) The Uruguay Round of GATT negotiations started under President Reagan in 1986, continued under President Bush, and concluded under President Clinton. The United States had sought in **GATT** to exchange further opening of its own markets to international goods and services for greater access to foreign markets, greater security for U.S. technology abroad, and more open access for U.S. service exports. The GATT agreements gave the United States some but not all that it sought in this regard.

In considering the GATT agreement, Congress weighed the laissez-faire argument that free trade is a global "invisible hand" that will benefit all nations against the argument that open markets are not in the national interest because of their impact on certain groups, especially low-wage manufacturing workers. Members of Congress understood that some individuals and businesses in their districts might be harmed by foreign competition but that other individuals and firms would gain from increased efficiency and exports. In the end, after some drama, the theory of free trade triumphed and the GATT treaty was ratified, but not without criticism of the international trade policymaking authority invested in the new WTO. Many fear that the WTO will overrule and thus weaken U.S. trade laws and undermine hard-won environmental protections.

The NAFTA Treaty

The politics of international trade were somewhat different in 1993, when Congress was asked to ratify the NAFTA agreement. **NAFTA**, the North American Free Trade Area, was begun under President Reagan as a trade agreement between the United States and Canada. Negotiations continued under President Bush were concluded under President Clinton, with Mexico being added to the three-nation free-trade zone. NAFTA goes beyond GATT in its ardor for regional free trade. When fully implemented in several years, GATT will make trade among the United States, Canada, and Mexico as free and easy as that among Ohio, Indiana, and Illinois.

The NAFTA vote was far more dramatic than the later GATT tally. Republican members of Congress voted as a block in favor of NAFTA for the most part because of its laissez-faire origins. For many of these representatives, NAFTA meant less government interference in international trade, which they favored. Many Democrats, however, opposed NAFTA, despite President Clinton's strong support of the measure. In many cases, opposition was based on a close calculation of local effects. NAFTA would create only a few jobs in each district, they figured, but it could produce great economic and political hard times in those sectors where the effect of competition with Canada or Mexico would be the greatest. The political entrepreneur Ross Perot appeared on "Larry King Live" national television to argue with Vice President Al Gore that NAFTA would produce the "giant sucking sound" of U.S. jobs heading south to Mexico. He argued that laissez-faire NAFTA was not in the national interest. Ironically, given all the controversy it raised, NAFTA was approved by a surprisingly large margin.

U.S.–Japanese Trade Negotiations

As noted above, Congress and the president decided strongly in favor of free trade in the case of GATT and more cautiously in favor of free trade in NAFTA. It is perhaps surprising, therefore, to consider how different the political response has been in U.S. bilateral trade negotiations with Japan.

The United States and Japan have engaged in trade negotiations for many years over a range of issues. U.S. policy in these negotiations has seldom been guided by the invisible hand of laissez-faire economic theory. Rather, the United States has consistently aimed to convince Japan to take actions that would benefit specific sectors of the U.S. economy. Retail politics, which weighs constituent gains against losses, has been a strong force in this case.

During the Reagan administration, for example, the United States convinced Japan to restrict its exports to the United States of such commodities as automobiles and computer chips. These export restraints went against Reagan's laissez-faire theories, but they benefited important industry groups. (It was also argued that the computer chip restraints were necessary to preserve U.S. competitiveness in the rapidly changing microelectronics industry.)

President Bush personally led a government–business delegation to Japan to demand that that nation purchase more U.S. auto parts and agricultural products. Recently, the Clinton administration threatened a 100 percent tariff against Japanese luxury automobiles if Japan did not agree to numeric quotas for increased purchases of U.S. auto parts. In taking these dramatic steps, Clinton and Bush (as Reagan before them) took positions on trade that were opposite their own free-trade stands on NAFTA and GATT.

This brief discussion of the politics of international economic policy illustrates that these types of decisions are based on some mix of economic theories and on local as well as national political concerns. In some cases, such as GATT, the issues are so large as to dwarf local political calculations. In the case of U.S.–Japan trade deals, however, the impact of trade on specific industries is potentially so large as to make economic philosophy almost irrelevant when weighed against local jobs and votes. On NAFTA, however, both political influences were quite strong, making the effect of this treaty unclear at this point.

THE NEED FOR INTERNATIONAL POLICY COORDINATION

The rapid globalization of economic activity also conditions the politics of international economic policy. Put simply, it is increasingly difficult for the United States to make economic policy when its economy is less distinctly national and more regional, part of the global web of commercial enterprises. Increasingly, the United States must take the policies of other nations into account when setting its own and attempt, when possible, to coordinate policies with Japan, the European Union, and other nations.

To see why policy coordination is more important now among nations, consider for a moment this simple analogy. Think of the economy as a bathtub. In previous years, each nation had its own small bathtub, which was connected to others in only a few ways. It was possible in this situation for governments to use monetary and fiscal policy like water faucets, to regulate the flow of water in their own bathtub/economy, without much regard to what other nations did. Domestic economic policy had great weight.

These days, however, the economy is increasingly global in scope. Markets span national borders through trade, finance, and telecommunications. People buy goods from around the world, invest money around the world, and participate in global culture. Globalization means that all the nations are, to a certain extent, now part of one big bathtub/economy. A large nation, like the United States, can have *some* effect on the flow of economic activity, but much less than before. It is difficult to get the water in its end of the bathtub to a higher level without raising the level for everyone else.

In these days of global bathtubs, individual nations have much less ability to alter their own economic fates through monetary and fiscal policies. The most effective way to change the economy is to coordinate economic policies with other nations. The need for coordinated actions among national governments, however, conflicts with the usual notion of the democratic process within nations. The effective economic policies of, say, the nation of France depend increasingly on the corresponding economic policies of Germany, Great Britain, and the United States.

The tension between domestic democratic processes and global economic forces was illustrated in 1995, when Mexico experienced sudden and unanticipated foreign-debt problems, which caused the peso's value to fall from about thirty to fifteen cents a peso over the course of a few days. Recognizing the interdependence of the U.S. and Mexican economies, especially after adoption of the NAFTA treaty, the Clinton administration quickly organized a plan to help finance some of Mexico's debt. The plan had to be withdrawn, however, when congressional leaders made it clear that they could not support this program because of negative voter sentiments. (California voters had approved a 1994 referendum restricting the rights of illegal aliens to receive public services, a vote that was widely seen as being aimed at Mexican immigrants, among others.)

The Clinton administration found itself faced with two facts. The market forces of global finance required that the United States do something to help finance Mexico's debt, at least in the short run. The democratic forces of U.S. voters, however, made this impossible. The Clinton administration solved the problem by shortcutting the democratic system. Assembling a somewhat smaller debt assistance plan that was implemented as a presidential executive order, the administration was able to avoid a vote in Congress.[26]

The fact of international economic interdependence has not destroyed the concept of domestic democracy, but it has changed it. On the critical matters of economic policy, the fundamental nature of the relationship among voters and elected officials, together with the policies they enact and the impact of those policies, has changed in subtle and important ways.

ECONOMIC POLICY AND APPROACHING DEMOCRACY

Economic-policy making is a vital arena of domestic governmental policymaking. The decisions made by elected and even unelected officials can influence the economic well-being of the nation as a whole, as well as each single individual, whether rich or poor, Republican or Democrat. Moreover, these decisions are often rooted in those officials' conception of the proper role of government in the lives of its citizens, and who should be taxed and how these revenues should be spent, and thus are likely to change as individuals representing different philosophies and political constituencies assume the reins of government. Whether you have a Keynesian, monetarist, supply-sider, or some other variation, managing the economy and deciding who to tax, how much those taxes will be, and who will benefit from these governmental revenues takes us to the very heart of the relationship between a government and its people. Voters know this, and they make their feelings known come election time.

The politics of economic policy have changed in recent years due to the rising importance of international economic policy. Here too, policy is conditioned by the interaction of broad theories of international economic effects and the local political issues of gaining or losing jobs and markets. As economic matters have become increasingly global, the very nature of democracy has changed with respect to international economic policies. These forces make the political analysis of international economics more and more complex even as they become more and more important in our daily lives.

Politicians know very well that they will be rewarded for good economic times and punished for economic downturns. Politics and economics are thus fundamentally intertwined, and it is this linkage, with all of its different variations, that provides the economic signposts on the road that America follows in its continuing approach to democracy.

SUMMARY

1. Government policies that affect the economy can be organized into three groups: fiscal policy (decisions to tax and spend), regulatory policy (policies designed to achieve health, safety, and environmental goals), and international economic policies (policies dealing with exchange rates, trade negotiations, and international economic institutions).

2. The three main goals of economic policy are stable prices, full employment, and economic growth. Achieving these goals involves achieving certain secondary goals as well, such as low and stable interest rates, stable exchange rates, and reduced federal budget deficits. Because of the complex interactions among these goals, economic-policy makers must often trade off one goal against another.

3. Laissez-faire economics holds that individuals should be free to pursue their own economic self-interest without the interference of government policies. Advocates of laissez-faire economic policies believe that, if left alone, the market will adjust itself over time.

4. Keynesian economics suggests that government should play an active role in the economy. It stresses aggregate demand, or spending by consumers, businesses, and government. The primary mechanism for stimulating spending is fiscal policy.

5. Monetarists believe that the best way to promote the smooth, stable growth of the economy is to strictly control the growth of the money supply. The Federal Reserve System controls the money supply by buying and selling federal government securities, regulating the amount of money member banks must have on deposit, and manipulating interest rates.

6. Supply-side economics emphasizes the stimulation of supply rather than demand. In this view, creating incentives for business to invest and expand production is the key to invigorating the economy. This can be done through tax cuts and decreased government regulation of business.

7. The federal budget is prepared by the Office of Management and Budget, which analyzes the budgetary requests made by every government agency. The president submits

the budget to Congress in January of each year. The budget committees in the two houses consider the president's proposals and establish overall levels for taxation and for various areas of government spending.

8. Numerous attempts to force Congress to balance the budget and reduce the federal budget deficit have been unsuccessful. Although there is growing support for serious reform of the budgetary process, most Americans are reluctant to see the federal budget balanced at the expense of the programs that benefit them most.

9. The federal personal income and capital gains taxes are progressive; that is, those who make more money are taxed at a higher rate. Taxes on consumer goods such as gasoline and cigarettes are regressive because they take a higher fraction of the income of lower-income taxpayers. Periodic attempts to reform the tax structure typically give rise to major political battles over who will benefit and who will pay more.

10. The largest proportion of federal spending consists of direct payments to individuals through programs such as social security. Military spending accounts for roughly 18 percent of government spending, while interest on the federal debt accounts for over 14 percent. Some areas of spending are "uncontrollable," either because they are safeguarded by laws or are highly politically sensitive. "Controllable" expenditures can be increased or decreased by Congress, but even these are difficult to cut because of political pressures.

11. The federal budget deficit is the annual shortfall between the monies that government takes in and what it spends. The national debt is the cumulative total of all these budget deficits. Both the deficit and the national debt have grown to massive proportions.

12. When policymakers consider international economic policies, they must consider both how their constituents will be affected and whether the policy is beneficial to the country as a whole. Thus, in considering the GATT agreement Congress weighed the potential benefits of free trade for all nations against the potential impact on certain groups, especially low-wage manufacturing workers. In considering the NAFTA treaty, it weighed the benefits of reduced government interference in international trade against the potential that large numbers of jobs would be moved to Mexico.

13. Increasingly, the United States must take the policies of other nations into account when making economic policy and must try to coordinate its policies with those of Japan, the European Union, and other nations.

KEY TERMS

inflation
economic policy
laissez-faire economics
Keynesian economics
fiscal policy
monetarism

monetary policy
Federal Reserve System
supply-side economics
stagflation
Office of Management and the Budget
  (OMB)

progressive taxes
regressive taxes
federal budget deficit
national debt
GATT
NAFTA

SUGGESTED READINGS

- Larry Berman, *The Office of Management and Budget and the Presidency, 1921–1979*. Princeton, N.J.: Princeton University Press, 1979. The first comprehensive study of the Office of Management and Budget's evolution as a presidential staff agency.

- William Greider, *Secrets of the Temple: How the Federal Reserve Runs the Country*. New York: Simon & Schuster, 1987. A fascinating account of how the Federal Reserve Board actually conducts its business.

- Robert Heilbroner and Peter Bernstein, *The Debt and the Deficit*. New York: Norton, 1989. Two economists explain what national debts and deficits are and what they are not. They downplay the theory that deficits are a burden to future generations, arguing instead that they are a potential means of financing economic growth.

- Donald F. Kettl, *Deficit Politics: Public Budgeting in Its Institutional and Historical Context*. New York: Macmillan, 1992. This book examines budgetary politics to explain why we suffer repeated annual deficits.

- Kevin Phillips, *The Politics of Rich and Poor: Wealth and the American Electorate in the Reagan Aftermath*. New York: Random House, 1990. The basic message of this book is that the 1980's represented a wealth shift to wealth accumulation by the richest Americans, while many others stagnated and declined.

- James Savage, *Balanced Budgets and American Politics*. Ithaca, N.Y.: Cornell University Press, 1988. A scholarly account of the history of how the political environment affects budgeting in the United States.

- Bob Woodward, *The Agenda: Inside the Clinton White House*. New York: Simon & Schuster, 1993. A valuable inside perspective of the first year of the Clinton presidency, focusing on the federal deficit, health care, welfare reform taxes, jobs, government spending, and interest rates.

CHAPTER 18

FOREIGN POLICY

CHAPTER OUTLINE

CASE STUDY: THE "JUST CAUSE"

INTRODUCTION: FOREIGN POLICY AND DEMOCRACY

A HISTORY OF AMERICAN FOREIGN POLICY

THE CONSTITUTION AND FOREIGN POLICY

THE PRESIDENT IN FOREIGN POLICY MAKING

CONGRESS AND THE FOREIGN-POLICY PROCESS

THE EXECUTIVE BUREAUCRACY IN FOREIGN POLICY MAKING

DEMOCRATIC CHECKS ON FOREIGN POLICY

FOREIGN POLICY AND APPROACHING DEMOCRACY

United States military personnel were not required to stop at Panamanian roadblocks. So it should have been no surprise when four American marines ran a roadblock set up by the Panamanian military on December 16, 1989. What was surprising was the reaction of the Panamanian "Machos del Monte" (macho men of the mountains), an elite combat squad trained by Cubans and fanatically loyal to Panamanian dictator General Manuel Noriega. The Machos shot at the marines' retreating Chevrolet Impala, killing twenty-four-year-old First Lieutenant Robert Paz.

The next morning, President George Bush read intelligence reports of the incident. "Enough is enough," Bush allegedly declared. Noriega had been taunting the U.S. for the last two years and this was the last straw. By that afternoon Bush called a secret meeting with his foreign-policy braintrust: chairman of the Joint Chiefs, General Colin Powell; National Security Adviser Brent Scowcroft; Defense Secretary Richard Cheney; Secretary of State James Baker III; White House spokesman Marlin Fitzwater; and Vice President Dan Quayle. This meeting laid the strategic groundwork for an American invasion of Panama, originally code-named "Blue Spoon," but rechristened "Just Cause" for rhetorical flair that would undoubtedly read better in the history books.

On Wednesday morning, just after one o'clock, twenty thousand U.S. troops swept into Panama City and surrounding areas, destroying Noriega's private command post and chasing the dictator into the sanctuary of the Catholic church. Ultimately, Noriega was delivered to American authorities and extradited to the United States to stand trial for his role in the Central American drug trade. But the "success" of "Just Cause" came at the cost of the lives of twenty-five Americans and perhaps one thousand Panamanians, and the destruction of $1.5 billion in property.

Bush's personal popularity jumped dramatically in the wake of Noriega's capture. On the surface, the invasion seemed consistent with Bush's rhetoric about a "war on drugs," as well as the need to defend American military and civilian lives in Panama. What Bush would rather not have explained, at least publicly, was that the invasion was the end of a long and stormy relationship with Noriega, punctuated by the Panamanian general's recent provocations and his implication in a host of crimes including money laundering, weapons deals, and illegal technology and drug trafficking. It was a relationship reaching back to the 1960s, when the young military cadet Manuel Antonio Noriega was recruited by the American CIA to ferret out communists and communist sympathizers. And it was a relationship that Bush had been made fully aware of as director of the CIA in 1976 and that he allowed to continue.

If Noriega was not a stranger to Bush, neither was the policy under which this unsavory character had been reluctantly embraced by the United States. Noriega was one of scores of dubious "assets" cultivated by the CIA and State Department as "foot soldiers" against communism during the Cold War. Particularly in the 1960s, both the United States and the Soviet Union had sought to capture "clients" among newly independent and already established Third World countries. Occasionally, this battle called for the United States to "look the other way" and ignore the illegal dealings of a Noriega. This represented a dilemma for U.S. policymakers, since it pitted the avowed American ideal of spreading liberal democratic values against the practice of supporting political leaders who were not only corrupt but who were often dictatorial. The *dilemma was rationalized as the price for "stabilizing" anticommunist regimes and containing Soviet expansion.[1]*

It was a price the United States had elected to pay often, not only with Noriega in Panama, but with Raphael Trujillo in the Dominican Republic, Fulgencio Batista in Cuba, Anastasio Samoza in Nicaragua, and a host of others not only in Latin America but around the world. And the "cause" was not always as "just" as anticommunism but sometimes as simple as ensuring favorable terms for American businesses in foreign countries or American access to valuable raw materials. The practice of propping up corrupt dictators involved not only President Bush but every modern American administration. It was Franklin Roosevelt who had once remarked of a troublesome American client in Latin America: "He may be a son-of-a-bitch but he's <u>our</u> son-of-a-bitch!" And it was another Roosevelt, Theodore, in 1903, who had dispatched American warships to dissuade Colombians from intervening in the "independence" of a newly forged American client-regime. Panama.

As of 1986, the United States knew or suspected that Manuel Noriega was working as a double agent for both the Central Intelligence Agency of the United States and Cuba's intelligence agency. He was also involved in drug trafficking and money laundering. After the December 1989 invasion of Panama, the United States prosecuted the former dictator of Panama on eight counts of cocaine trafficking, racketeering, and money laundering. He was found guilty in 1992, received a sentence of forty years in prison, and will be eligible for parole in 2002.

INTRODUCTION: FOREIGN POLICY AND DEMOCRACY

Foreign policy refers to actions taken by the U.S. government on behalf of U.S. national interests abroad. These actions are taken to ensure the security and well-being of Americans and the strength and competitiveness of the U.S. economy. The debate about foreign policy often focuses on the extent to which government should go to pursue those national interests abroad. Obviously, a secure citizenry requires protection of recognized national boundaries, a strong economy, and a stable, orderly society. Less obvious are the answers to questions such as these: Does the protection of U.S. strategic interests justify the illegal mining of Nicaraguan harbors, the bombing of Libya, or overt and covert funding of "anticommunist" leaders like Manuel Noriega? Did protection of American economic interests abroad justify the U.S. invasion of oil-rich Iraq in 1991? Do social stability and order justify random surveillance of citizens to detect subversives and terrorists?

Former secretary of state George Schultz listed some of the elements constituting U.S. national interests in a statement on February 20, 1987. This list essentially sums up the goals of American foreign policy:

1. to protect the safety of the United States against aggression and subversion;
2. to promote domestic prosperity;
3. to foster the values of freedom and democracy both at home and abroad;
4. to act in a manner consistent with the United States' humanitarian instincts;
5. to combat those activities that undermine the rule of law and domestic stability, particularly terrorism and narcotics trafficking.

This modest list also suggests the paradoxes of the concept of *national interest*.[2] Protection from "aggression and subversion" can work against "freedom and democracy" at home. Think, for example, of the anticommunist "witch hunts" in the early years of the Cold War. Promoting domestic prosperity can sometimes clash with the country's "humanitarian instincts," as when U.S. marines were deployed to seize control of the Dominican Republic in 1965 after a democratically elected but mildly socialist regime came to power but was perceived as a threat to U.S. strategic and economic interests in the Caribbean. And, as in the case of Panama, combating international activities that "violate the rule of law" can often clash with soliciting clients to help protect the United States from "aggression and subversion."

The dilemma in making foreign policy is that the U.S. government must try to reconcile such apparent contradictions in a changing and complex world. Particularly since the end of the Second World War, U.S. foreign policy has been a cautious, often clumsy, balancing act between American democratic ideals and U.S. military and economic interests. Increasing American globalism has placed incredible demands on the policymaking process. The end of the Cold War and the breakup of the Eastern bloc may have nearly eliminated the danger of global nuclear war, but it has perhaps also stimulated increasing hostility, violence, and warfare. For example, the massive U.S. deployment in the war with Iraq would have been almost unthinkable a decade earlier, when the Soviet Union was still a potential force to reckon with. In a different vein, the breakup of the former Yugoslavia triggered a genocidal war between various ethnic factions; the collapse of the Soviet Union set the stage for a violent showdown between Russian president Boris Yeltsin and his own Parliament. In each case, without the policy priority of anticommunism, the United States has had to weigh carefully both its own interests and its commitments to democracy and human rights before developing a policy response.

In this chapter we will look at American foreign policy, its history, how it is made, and by whom. We now turn to an examination of the history of U.S. foreign policy.

A HISTORY OF AMERICAN FOREIGN POLICY

It is possible to make a rough distinction between two eras in U.S. foreign policy. The first, from the founding of the republic until approximately the First World War, might be described as a period of isolationism from the empires of

Israeli Prime Minister Yitzhak Rabin and Palestine Liberation Organization Chairman Yasser Arafat sign a peace accord at the White House on September 13, 1993. Although the accord was a good beginning, the volatile history of the Middle East indicates that the real difficulty may lie not in the achievement of temporary agreements, but in keeping the peace.

Europe, along with vigorous expansion in the Western Hemisphere. The second, except for a brief attempt to return to relative isolation vis-à-vis Europe between the two world wars, extends from about 1898 to the present. This has been an era of increasing globalization of American interests and commitments, including two world wars, a "cold war" with the Soviet Union, and the current post–Cold War period.

Isolation and Regionalism

Once free of the domination of Great Britain, the United States was not eager to reestablish binding ties with European empires. However, the newly independent country was not about to commit economic suicide by cutting off lucrative ties with the great trading centers of Europe. A pattern of **isolationism** was gradually established in which the United States fostered economic relations with Europe without committing to strategic alliances that might draw the country into a European war. Initially, such a policy was easily pursued, since the United States had virtually no standing army and few military resources upon which European countries could call. The United States also enjoyed a peculiar geographic isolation, situated as it was between two vast oceans in a time of slow and dangerous sea travel.

The **Monroe Doctrine,** enunciated by President James Monroe in his December 2, 1823 State of the Union address reinforced the country's isolationism by proclaiming the North and South American continent to be in the United States' *sphere of influence,* hence out of bounds for European aspirations. The United States agreed in return not to become involved in European affairs. The

Monroe Doctrine also contributed to another crucial ideal of U.S. foreign policy, a vigorous territorial expansion within its own continental land mass that belied any absolute isolation of America.[3] Under the banner of "manifest destiny" U.S. foreign-policy makers invoked divine guidance to wrest control of former European possessions within what is now the continental United States. Then, the United States turned south, into Central America, the Caribbean, and South America. This began the transition from internal expansion to *regionalism* and an enhanced role for American foreign-policy making.

By the end of the nineteenth century, U.S. governmental and private agencies controlled vast oil fields in Mexico and plantations in the Dominican Republic and Cuba, and had taken the Philippines by force from the deteriorating Spanish empire. American businesses and diplomats were also turning toward the reluctantly opening door to China. Yet U.S. foreign policy was still regional, with a clear priority given to the resources and potential of the Western Hemisphere. Even as American power expanded within its own sphere of influence, the United States remained largely unencumbered by strategic obligations to the "Old World." All of this would change with the outbreak of the first "world war."

> "In the Western hemisphere the adherence of the United States to the Monroe Doctrine may force the United States, however reluctantly, in flagrant cases of wrongdoing or impotence, to the exercise of an international police power."
>
> —Theodore Roosevelt's corollary to the Monroe Doctrine, December 6, 1904

World War I

With the start of World War I in Europe in 1914, and the collapse of the Russian monarchy three years later, the United States began to position itself as a player of global rather than internal or regional stature. Despite strong isolationist and pacifist movements at home, and the country's policy of neutrality, the United States clearly favored Britain and provided escorts for British ocean liners and other American support. As long as trans-Atlantic shipping lanes were protected, the United States was reluctant to commit more than this indirect support. But in 1917 a German U-boat sunk the ocean liner *Lusitania,* and the death toll included American citizens. Many historians argue that the *Lusitania* was not really a "neutral" vessel, since evidence suggests that a large cache of munitions was in her hold. For U.S. policymakers, though, this act of aggression demonstrated the horrors of unrestricted German U-boat activity and the inability to contain the war to European shores. U.S. entry into World War I followed, and the country's departure from historic isolation was rationalized as a commitment to "make the world safe for democracy" while fighting a "war to end all wars." U.S. forces, while undoubtedly turning the tide against Germany, suffered over 120,000 casualties. Despite the rhetoric heralding U.S. entry into the war, neither antidemocratic nor warlike forces were completely vanquished in World War I.

With the end of hostilities in 1918, Americans were eager to put the horrors of world war behind them. President Wilson campaigned vigorously for the founding of an international organization of states to "outlaw" the sort of aggression that had triggered the war. While his efforts ultimately led to the founding of the League of Nations, Wilson was unable to get the U.S. Senate to approve U.S. entry into the League. The prevailing mood favored a return to the kind of isolationism the country had enjoyed before the war.

But the conditions leading to World War I and its consequences drew the

United States into inevitable conflict with another European country: the newly founded Soviet Union. In the midst of wartime chaos, a small but determined Bolshevik party had seized control of the Russian state. The Union of Soviet Socialists Republic (USSR) was founded in 1917, led by Vladimir Ulyanov, better known as Lenin. The USSR was the first large-scale attempt to form a modern socialist state and, since it was designed as an alternative to liberal capitalism, became an instant adversary of the United States. With little public knowledge, approximately ten thousand American troops were dispatched to aid in the disruption of the embryonic Soviet Union. This, along with repeated territorial disputes over what would become Alaska, contributed to a growing hostility between the United States and the USSR, a hostility that would not be fully apparent until after another world war.

World War II

Tensions between the United States and USSR were briefly tabled with the outbreak of World War II. As in World War I, the United States was initially reluctant to encumber itself with strategic alliances and pursued a policy of economic aid to the Allies. Even after Hitler invaded Poland in 1939, violating a nonaggression pact between Germany and the Soviet Union, President Roosevelt refused to commit American military might to help stop the German advance. Only in 1941, after Germany's Pacific ally, Japan, had bombed the U.S. naval base at Pearl Harbor, Hawaii, did the United States formally enter the war and send troops to Europe and the Pacific.

The December 7, 1941 Japanese bombing of Pearl Harbor galvanized the United States in outrage and subsequent willingness to enter World War II. The traditionally isolationist orientation of the United States had prevented any earlier intervention in the devastating and rapidly expanding international hostility. Here a motor launch is able to rescue a survivor from alongside the torpedo-damaged and sunken USS West Virginia.

Racial Harmony in the Military

At the beginning of World War II the nation's armed services were completely segregated. Black troops were not permitted to live in the same facilities with whites or to ride on the same buses or watch the same movies. Even the blood supply was segregated: Plasma from black donors was stored separately and marked "A" for "African." The 1.2 million blacks who served their country during the war were assigned to Negro units and for the most part limited to noncombat roles.

Although equality of opportunity and treatment became the official policy of the Defense Department in 1948 by order of President Truman, it would take several decades to integrate the armed forces. Strict segregation was abolished in the 1950s, but racial animosity remained rampant. In 1970 one army post in Korea averaged more than a hundred racial assaults a week.

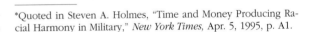

Today the picture is very different. The armed forces are perhaps the most integrated institutions in the country. Black, Hispanic, and white soldiers live and work together; the percentages of minorities have increased in both the enlisted ranks and the officer corps; and there are few incidents of racial bias or complaints of unequal treatment.

How has the military managed to transform itself so completely? The answer is that it developed a consistent policy and applied it consistently. It established tough standards for advancement while providing training and education to help candidates meet those standards. As President Clinton noted, there has been "an intense effort to develop the capacities of everybody who joins the military so they can fully participate and contribute as much as possible."*

Also contributing to racial harmony in the military is the increase in minority enlistment, particularly in the army. Blacks enlist in higher proportions than whites and are more likely to re-enlist. As a result, many black recruits are likely to have an immediate supervisor who is black. Moreover, the army sets affirmative action goals and takes diversity into account when granting promotions. The effects are most visible in the middle ranks, with the percentage of black majors increasing from 4.4 percent in 1980 to 12.5 percent in 1994.

Part of the explanation for these successes is the military tradition of discipline. Orders are followed, including orders to set specific goals and meet them. But more important is the fact that the armed services are committed to achieving racial harmony and have invested the necessary time, energy, and money to do so.

---

*Quoted in Steven A. Holmes, "Time and Money Producing Racial Harmony in Military," *New York Times,* Apr. 5, 1995, p. A1.

The wartime fates of the United States and the Soviet Union were strikingly different. For the United States, mired in the depth of economic depression, the expanded production and employment demanded by full wartime industrial mobilization actually helped to jump-start an economic boom. Beyond the initial destruction at Pearl Harbor, the country suffered no attacks on its own territory. By stark contrast, the Soviet Union was devastated. The Soviet Red Army had stopped the final advance of Germany, but at tremendous cost. Twenty million military personnel and civilians died, either from combat or through disease or starvation. As with most of battle-scarred Europe, the Soviet Union had the look of a defeated nation.

Given the striking differences between the United States and the Soviet Union at the end of World War II, it is surprising that they would both become the most powerful countries in the postwar world. So awesome would their dominance become that their very existence would inspire a new term: **superpower.** The term is intended to convey the disproportionate power—economic and military—that distinguished the United States and the Soviet Union from all other countries in the postwar era. And so pervasive was the superpower rivalry that relations between the United States and USSR would come to affect virtually every country in the world.

Globalism and the Cold War

Nothing in the international arena would be as it had been before the Second World War. The United States emerged from the war as the only major power with a completely intact infrastructure, booming industrial production, and a monopoly on the most revolutionary weaponry ever created: the atomic bomb. Two atomic bombs had been dropped on Japan at the end of World War II, not only to shock the Japanese into complete surrender but some believe to send a message to the Soviet Union that the United States not only possessed such military might but was prepared to use it.[4]

U.S. foreign policy after 1946 grew out of the doctrine of **containment,** a term coined by George Kennan, then a State Department Soviet expert. Kennan declared that the USSR's expansionist foreign policy "moves along the prescribed path, like a persistent toy automobile wound up and headed in a given direction, stopping only when it meets some unanswerable force." According to Kennan, that "unanswerable force" must be the United States, and Soviet "aggression" must be "contained by the adroit and vigilant application of counterforce at a series of constantly shifting geographical and political points." Somewhat prophetically, Kennan argued that if the United States could contain the Soviet Union without weakening itself politically or economically, the result would be "either the break-up or the gradual mellowing of Soviet power."[5]

But the ultimate "break-up" and "mellowing" of the Soviet Union was still decades away. Both the United States and the Soviet Union had joined the United Nations upon its creation in 1945, but the two countries remained adversaries. Soviet forces captured all of Eastern Europe, installing virtual puppet regimes behind an "iron curtain" of military might and political resolve. The United States applied the "counterforce" of billions of dollars in economic aid to Western Europe under the Marshall Plan of postwar reconstruction, as well as through numerous strategic treaties and agreements. In a historic address to Congress on March 12, 1947, President Harry Truman invoked the theory of containment in the *Truman Doctrine,* which pledged that the United States would halt the spread of communism in southeastern Europe. At home, the National Security Act of 1947 created the Central Intelligence Agency (CIA) and the National Security Council (NSC), signaling the United States' turn from regionalism to **globalism.** Now the American "sphere of influence" expanded beyond the Western Hemisphere to include virtually every corner of the globe where U.S. interests might be affected.

In 1949, the United States secured the commitment of eleven European nations to form the **North Atlantic Treaty Organization (NATO).** The

"The 1930s taught us a clear lesson. Aggressive conduct, if allowed to go unchecked and unchallenged, ultimately leads to war."

—John F. Kennedy on the Cuban Missile Crisis

NATO charter also signaled the end of American isolation and regionalism. Charter signatories agreed that an armed attack against one or more of them in Europe or North America would be interpreted as an attack against all. In the event of such attack, the treaty bound all members of NATO to assist the attacked country, employing "forthwith, individually and in concert with the other Parties, such action as it deems necessary, including the use of armed forces."[6]

Dramatic events continued through the remainder of the 1940s and into the 1950s. The U.S. monopoly of nuclear weapons ended in September 1949, when the Soviets detonated their first atomic bomb. In the same year, the American-backed regime in China collapsed and a communist state was created under the direction of party chairman Mao Zedong.

In April 1950 members of the NSC drafted what was to become the "blueprint" for waging the **Cold War** during the next twenty years: National Security Council Paper 68 (NSC-68). **NSC-68** outlined a sweeping mobilization of American economic and human resources in the struggle to contain Soviet communism. It was the first major document to acknowledge the new bipolar power struggle between the American and Soviet superpowers. In 1955 the Soviet Union and its Eastern European allies (called *satellites*) formed the Warsaw Pact, a military alliance which countered NATO. **Bipolarity** refers to the fundamental division of economic and military power between the poles of Western capitalism and Eastern communism. NSC-68 represented a hardline resistance to the Soviet Union. It recommended against negotiation with the Kremlin, advocated the development of a more powerful nuclear arsenal and rapid expansion of conventional military resources, and called for the full mobilization of American society within a "government-created 'consensus'" against the evils of communism.[7] The document also called for a dramatic American commitment to international strategic and economic alliances against the Eastern bloc, indicating yet another push away from isolation and regionalism toward globalism.

In June 1950, just months after the drafting of NSC-68, war in Korea became a major test of the country's Cold War containment policy. Ironically, the challenge here was posed not by the Soviet Union but by the new communist regime in China. Ultimately, the Korean conflict proved a political and military stalemate, and the decade came to a close with the declaration of a socialist revolution only ninety miles off the coast of Florida in Cuba and the ascension of Fidel Castro.

THE NUCLEAR WORLD   The nuclear age began with the atomic bombing of Hiroshima and Nagasaki in 1945. The exploding of a Soviet-made atomic device in 1949 triggered a superpower arms race with frightening global implications. Over the next forty years, both the United States and the Soviet Union poured billions of dollars into the development of more-powerful nuclear weapons, just as they devoted increasing intellectual resources to the development of foreign policies tailored to the new "nuclear world" that they had created.

The most dangerous nuclear confrontation of the Cold War occurred under the Kennedy administration in 1962.[8] Soviet premier Khrushchev had begun construction of missile bases in Cuba, an act seen by U.S. leaders as a direct

Little-known Fact

The term *cold war* was first used by Herbert Bayard Swope (1882–1958) in speeches he wrote for Bernard Baruch (1870–1965). After Baruch told the Senate War Investigating Committee on October 24, 1948, "Let us not be deceived—today we are in the midst of a cold war," the press picked up the phrase, and it became part of everyday speech.

Nuclear proliferation, unknown before World War II, became a fact of life afterward, resulting in a Cold War era mentality and approach to daily life that included routine nuclear bomb drills by grade school children across the country. Upon hearing the air raid siren, monitors made sure curtains were closed so that exploding glass would not injure students, and students scrambled to push their desks together, climb under, and then cover their eyes and the backs of their heads.

provocation, despite the fact that the United States had installed in Turkey similar missile bases aimed at the Soviet Union. After several tense days of secret debates within the U.S. national-security establishment, President Kennedy took the unprecedented step of going before the American people and announcing a naval blockade of Cuba aimed at keeping Soviet ships out. In a televised speech Kennedy demanded the immediate dismantling and removal of the bases. Ultimately Khrushchev backed down and the bases were dismantled. A "hot line," providing a communications link between the two leaders, was established in 1962, and the Limited Test Ban Treaty was negotiated in 1963. But the threat of a nuclear exchange continued.

> "We're eyeball to eyeball—and the other fellow just blinked."
>
> —Dean Rusk, Secretary of State during the Cuban Missile Crisis

MOUNTING AN ECONOMIC OFFENSIVE Cold War policymakers did not restrict their activity to military planning. U.S. foreign-aid commitments began to increase greatly during the Kennedy administration as a hedge against Soviet advances into less developed countries of the "Third World." One such U.S. effort was the founding of the Peace Corps, an organization of volunteers sent to all parts of the globe. Peace Corps volunteers were involved in everything from improving literacy and building roads and schools to starting immunization and other health-care programs. The Peace Corps remains the country's foremost experiment in fusing the aims of foreign policy with the resources of government and the initiative and expertise of private individuals.[9]

A second program initiated at this time, focusing on Latin America, was the Alliance for Progress. The policy really began in the last year of the Eisenhower administration with the formation of the Inter-American Development Bank, but it was popularized in 1961 under Kennedy. In exchange for a commitment of twenty billion dollars over ten years, the United States asked participating Latin American countries to liberalize their tax, land distribution, and social policies, which major players such as Argentina, Brazil, and Mexico were reluctant to do. In the end, the Alliance never lived up to its potential, either as a social and economic boon to Latin America or as a hedge against the blossoming of socialist and communist regimes in the region. By 1966 the Alliance had all but vanished. The U.S. commitment to foreign aid for the developing world continued, but not at the level envisioned by the Kennedy administration.

VIETNAM At the height of the Cold War, the United States entered into what would prove to be its most damaging military intervention. In the southeastern Asian country of Vietnam, nationalist forces from the north, led by Ho Chi Minh, had defeated French colonial forces at Dienbienphu in 1954. They then sought to unify the north with the south, a struggle that was opposed by both the regime in South Vietnam and by its primary patron, the United States. Beginning in the early months of the Kennedy administration, the United States began to commit first hundreds and then thousands of military "advisers" to South Vietnam. There was little public discussion of U.S. policy in Southeast Asia, and U.S. policymakers were left to pursue their own course, which proved to be a mounting commitment of military personnel and matériel.[10]

Within a few weeks of each other in November 1963, both South Vietnamese Prime Minister Diem and President Kennedy were assassinated. Lyndon Johnson assumed the presidency with public declarations of no desire to "widen" the war in Vietnam. Yet he convinced Congress to support a massive mil-

The Vietnam memorial was for many veterans a symbolic representation of a long-awaited public acknowledgment of their sacrifice in an "undeclared" war. It marked a beginning of the healing process for the nation's consciousness. Recently, furthering the effort to find closure regarding the war and America's subsequently strained relationship with Vietnam, President Clinton has opened trade between the two countries.

itary buildup in Southeast Asia. On August 2, 1964, the U.S. destroyer *Maddox* was returning from an electronic espionage mission when North Vietnamese torpedo boats fired on her. The attack was repulsed. Rather than withdrawing U.S. ships from this danger zone, the president ordered another destroyer, the *C. Turner Joy,* to join the *Maddox* in the Gulf of Tonkin. On August 4th both the *Maddox* and the *C. Turner Joy* reportedly came under attack by torpedo boats. Considerable doubt exists as to whether this second attack ever took place. While there is little doubt that North Vietnamese gunboats were operating in the area, weather conditions were so bad and tensions aboard ship so high that Johnson later quipped, "For all I know, our Navy was shooting at whales out there." But circumstantial evidence was all Johnson needed for ordering reprisals against the North. The Gulf of Tonkin Resolution, passed by Congress in August 1964, provided President Lyndon Johnson with broad legal authority to wage combat against North Vietnamese aggression.

In July 1965 Lyndon Johnson chose to Americanize the war in Vietnam by increasing U.S. combat strength in Vietnam from 75,000 to 125,000, with additional U.S. forces to be sent when requested by field commander General William Westmoreland. "Now," Johnson wrote in his memoirs, "we were committed to major combat in Vietnam. We had determined not to let that country fall under Communist rule as long as we could prevent it."[11]

By the early 1970s the American military was mired in the Asian jungles, at a cost of billions of dollars and tens of thousands of lives. The U.S. "national interest" in the region was no longer clear, and the antiwar movement grew until the country was hopelessly split on the issue. Finally, the United States negotiated a treaty with the North Vietnamese government that allowed the United States to withdraw in 1973.[12] Ultimately, the war in Vietnam not only ravaged a nation and a people but cost more than fifty-eight thousand American lives and helped destroy the credibility of much of the U.S. foreign-policy apparatus.

McNamara's War

In the early 1960s Americans living in Saigon went to sleep to the sound of mortar fire in the suburbs. The war between North and South Vietnam was heating up, and U.S. military advisers were becoming increasingly involved on the side of the South. In 1964 there were several terrorist attacks on Americans in Saigon, and in February 1965 all U.S. civilians were evacuated. The Vietnam War had begun.

Three decades later, the driving force behind the "Vietnam syndrome" is the desire not to repeat the mistakes that led to the tragedy of the Vietnam War. Those mistakes have recently been described in detail by, of all people, Robert McNamara, who served as secretary of defense from 1961 to 1968 and was one of the most vocal proponents of U.S. involvement in Vietnam—so much so that the war came to be known as "McNamara's War."

In his 1995 memoir titled *In Retrospect,* McNamara tells of the series of blunders that led to repeated escalations of the war and eventually to the deaths of more than fifty-eight thousand Americans. While he claims that the mistakes were "mostly honest," he is critical of the underlying assumptions on which U.S. policy was based—in particular, the "domino theory" that held that if South Vietnam were "lost to communism," Laos, Cambodia, Thailand, and Malaysia would fall like dominoes and communism would spread throughout Asia, encouraging the Russians and Chinese to extend their conquest and eventually provoke another world war.

The domino theory gave rise to further assumptions, notably that communism must be "contained," or prevented from spreading anywhere in the world. This was a central principle of U.S. foreign policy, and the United States responded by treating any uprising with a hint of communist involvement as a threat to American security. Thus U.S. policymakers misinterpreted Ho Chi Minh's drive to unite Vietnam as a movement to extend communist dominance in Southeast Asia.

Among other causes of the Vietnam War, according to McNamara, were misjudging the military capacity of North Vietnam, underrating the power of nationalism, failing to recognize the limitations of high-tech military equipment in the jungle, and failing to level with Congress and the American people. Most crucial, however, was the failure to question the "loose assumptions, unasked questions and thin analyses" underlying U.S. military strategy in Vietnam. "I deeply regret that I did not force a probing debate about whether it would ever be possible to forge a winning military effort on a foundation of political quicksand," he writes.

Asked whether the same mistakes could be repeated today, McNamara says, "Absolutely, not only can be but are being repeated." He believes that policymakers need to "think deeply and realistically about alternative courses of action and their consequences" to avoid being drawn into no-win situations like the Vietnam War.

Source: Robert McNamara, *In Retrospect: The Tragedy and Lessons of Vietnam* (New York: Random House, 1995).

DETENTE In the wake of the humiliating defeat in Southeast Asia, the American people became profoundly anti-international and antimilitary. "No more Vietnams" became the rallying cry for those opposed to military intervention in Africa and Central America. Richard Nixon, ironically as anticommunist a president as ever existed, began a policy of **detente,** an attempt to relax the tensions between the United States and USSR.[13] Each side began to discuss ways to reduce the nuclear threat. A series of strategic arms limitations talks culminated in the signing of the first Strategic Arms Limitation Treaty (SALT) in 1972 and a concern about reducing the worldwide threat of nuclear war. But the conflict between the two superpowers heated up with the Soviet invasion of Afghanistan in December 1979; the failure by both countries to ratify the SALT II agreements; and the continuation of the arms race, now more sophisticated, and involving weapons deployment in Europe.

Some argue that the end of detente came with President Ronald Reagan's announcement in 1983 of plans to devise a new satellite-based laser defense system, known as the Strategic Defense Initiative (SDI). Popularly known as "Star Wars," after the popular science fiction films of the era, SDI was a program that the Soviets could not manage financially or technologically. Many critics insisted that the program was a "pie-in-the-sky" scheme that even the Americans could not pull off.[14]

> "The SDI has been a singularly effective instrument for bringing the Soviets to the bargaining table."
>
> —Ronald Reagan, 1987

Beyond the technological challenges of SDI, both the United States and the Soviet Union had seriously undermined their own economies through decades of military buildup. By the end of the 1980s the USSR had bankrupted itself, and the United States was nearly a trillion dollars in debt.

The Post–Cold War Era and into the Future

1989 saw remarkable change in world politics and marked the beginning of the end of the Cold War. Eastern European communist regimes that had been in power at the start of the year were gone by the end. Then, between August and December 1991, the Soviet Union—the focal point of Cold War U.S. foreign policy—ceased to exist. With its demise, the Soviet threat to the United States disappeared, the Cold War came to an end, and the basic premise that drove U.S. foreign policy for almost fifty years—containment—ceased to be relevant. The threat of global nuclear war largely ceased to be a pressing issue (although there is a continuing threat of proliferation of nuclear weapons, and biological and chemical weapons). The end of the Cold War, however, has brought with it a dizzying array of complicated foreign-policy issues. Policymakers have no clear guideposts to determine the relative merits of these issues, and no clear formula for how to address them. Containment can no longer be the guiding principle of U.S. foreign policy, but a new point of reference has yet to be found.[15]

Even before the Cold War was over, the United States, through the United Nations and with the help of a broad international coalition of nations, embarked on a large-scale war against Iraq. In August 1990, Iraqi forces invaded Kuwait. The United States led the charge to make sure Iraq went no further (e.g., into Saudi Arabia) and to ultimately reverse the Iraqi move. In January 1991, the massive air war and follow-up hundred-hour ground war began. Iraq left Kuwait, and President George Bush heralded the beginning of a "new world order." This new era can be summed up, however, as being characterized more by debates than actual policies, as we will see.[16]

THE UNITED NATIONS AND THE NEW WORLD ORDER   The outlines of this "new world order" have never come clearly into focus, and the concept means different things to different people. At a minimum, President Bush seemed to have in mind the end of the bipolar order and the start of a new order involving the United Nations (UN) but actually led by the United States, the dominant military actor in the world. But just what the relationship between the United States and the UN should be, and whether there should be a relationship at all,

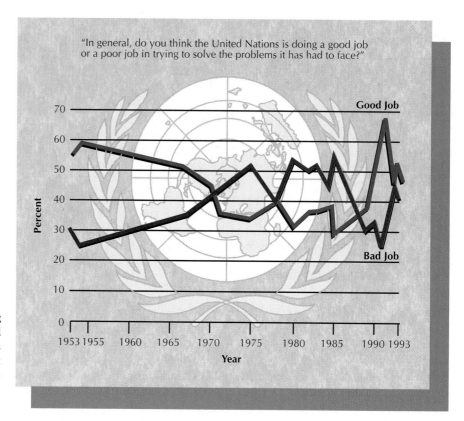

FIGURE 18.1 Changing Attitudes toward the United Nations

Source: All from Gallup Poll except 1989 and 1992 from the Roper organization and 1991 from Times/CBS News Poll.

continues to be debated, particularly in the light of controversial military operations in Somalia, Bosnia, and Haiti. Figure 18.1 shows how American attitudes toward the UN have changed over the years.

NATO The United Nations is not the only international organization that has been a point of debate for the United States in this new post–Cold War era; the future of NATO (the North Atlantic Treaty Organization) has also been debated. Many argue that with the collapse of the Soviet Union and end of the Cold War, NATO has ceased to have a purpose. Others stress the continuing relevance of a military–political alliance between the United States and Europe and yet argue over the extent to which NATO should expand to include new members. Poland, the Czech Republic, and Hungary seem likely new members, but this issue is far from settled.[17]

Favoring the continued existence of NATO, the Clinton administration has put forward the "Partnership for Peace" initiative, which would expand NATO. In short, the Partnership for Peace is a series of bilateral agreements between NATO and other states in Central Europe and the former Soviet Union seeking to provide a mechanism for increased military cooperation and integration as a first step toward NATO membership. However, such talk about NATO expansion is just "talk." The U.S. government and NATO have designated 1995 as a year for studying the feasibility of early entry for new NATO members. And 1996 is an election year in both the U.S. and Russia. Furthermore, any changes in NATO would require a two-thirds majority in the U.S. Senate for ratification.[18]

Free Trade versus Protectionism   Since the end of the Cold War, economic issues and concerns have risen in prominence. The economy has become increasingly globalized, and advances in technology continue to make the world even more interdependent. How the United States should respond to these economic challenges is a key question in this new era, especially in light of European economic integration and the astounding economic growth in Asia.[19]

One of the first foreign economic policy debates of this era was over the North American Free Trade Agreement (NAFTA), which was intended to ultimately create a North American economy by reducing and eventually eliminating all trade barriers between the United States, Canada, and Mexico. NAFTA sparked a heated debate and passed in the House and Senate only after much discussion. The evaluation of NAFTA's impact will be years away, but its significance as a policy debate can already be seen. NAFTA brought the issues of free trade versus protectionism to the fore by removing most tariffs and trade barriers among the three countries. These issues continue to be debated in the ratification battle over the latest round of the General Agreements on Tariffs and Trade (GATT), which moves the world economy toward a free-trade framework. No doubt, economic arrangements are likely to play at least as prominent a role in foreign-policy making as strategic military arrangements in this new era.[20]

A Policy of "Enlargement"   The Clinton administration has tried to respond to the new global economic environment by stressing the policy of "enlargement" (to replace the policy of containment). The idea behind enlargement is simply that the United States should support enlarging the sphere of market-oriented democracies on the assumption that more open, democratic, and open-market societies serve to further the interests of the United States. They are good for peace (based on the belief that democracies do not easily go to war with one another) and good for business (based on the belief that more market economies will expand the global market and global economic well-being).[21]

Exactly how to pursue a policy of enlargement is not self-evident, however. How the United States can help to encourage democratization will likely be a key question on the U.S. foreign-policy agenda in this new era.

Terrorism   While off the foreign policy front burner for a few years, the threat of terrorism returned in the 1990s. *Terrorism* can be defined as the use of force specifically targeted at civilians for the purpose of producing mass fear that will induce policy change. The February 26, 1993, bombing of the World Trade Center made the dangers of terrorism vivid for Americans. Combating terror and those who support it will continue to be high on the foreign-policy agenda. The fight against international terrorism may be aided by the various new forms of electronic surveillance that are being developed on the information superhighway.

Foreign Aid and Economic Sanctions   These two tools of foreign policy have also come under scrutiny and have been subject to debate in the post–Cold War world.

In 1995 the Republican-controlled Congress began to debate the future of U.S. foreign-aid programs. Historically, foreign aid has been used to help support U.S. allies and interests abroad. Making up a tiny portion of the total federal budget, foreign-aid programs (such as financial and other aid to Russia, Israel, Egypt, Africa, and Latin America) have come under fire and are likely to be curtailed. Those who favor these programs argue that eliminating them would have severe negative consequences for U.S. interests around the world.

Economic sanctions have also been the subject of debate. In an economically interdependent world, the use of economic sanctions is often seen as a useful tool of foreign policy. While sanctions logically seem appropriate to force policy change inside a targeted state, they are difficult tools to use. Sanctions may have helped force South Africa to eventually eliminate the system of apartheid and move in a more democratic direction, but their utility is limited. Sanctions against Iraq, Haiti, Bosnia and Serbia, and Cuba, for example, have not achieved their intended effect. While sanctions clearly hurt ordinary citizens by depriving them of goods or the opportunity to trade and earn a profit, the suffering is usually not endured by policymakers. Unless policymakers in a target state are moved by the suffering of their people to alter their course, or unless they are overthrown, sanctions often fail to have the desired result. The United States will continue to struggle with questions about the propriety and effectiveness of economic sanctions.[22]

THE USE OF FORCE   Paradoxically, the end of the Cold War has had the effect of making the use of force by the United States more likely. Cases in point include American military involvement in Panama, Bosnia, Somalia, and Haiti. Even while some talk of the "new" diplomacy based upon economics, the old diplomacy based upon the use of force is alive and well. Coming to terms with the strengths and shortcomings of the use of force in the new post–Cold War era will continue to be high on the U.S. foreign-policy agenda.

The use of "coercive diplomacy," or the effort to compel policy change on the part of a target state with tools such as economic sanctions and trade embargoes rather then the actual use of military force, will also continue to be examined, especially against so-called "rogue" states like Iran and North Korea.[23]

FOREIGN-POLICY INSTITUTIONS   Finally, the end of the Cold War has brought about the need to reexamine the institutions of U.S. foreign policy and national-security policymaking. Under examination include the structure of the State Department and the future of the Arms Control and Disarmament Agency, the U.S. Information Agency, and the U.S. Agency for International Development. Special commissions have been put in place to examine the roles and missions of both the Defense Department and the Intelligence Community. We'll look more closely at foreign-policy institutions later in this chapter.

THE CONSTITUTION AND FOREIGN POLICY

As you learned in Chapter 3, the Constitution designates certain formal powers that are especially significant for foreign policy to the president and Congress. The president was given four types of broad authority in foreign policy. As the commander in chief, the president has the power to commit troops to foreign lands. The president also has the power to negotiate treaties with other countries. It is the president who appoints United States ambassadors and the heads of all of the executive departments that make foreign policy. Finally, it is the president who decides whether or not to receive ambassadors, a decision that determines which nations the United States will formally recognize.

Congress also has significant foreign-policy powers, including the power to declare war, appropriate money, and make laws; thus, it has the power to decide whether to back presidential initiatives abroad. Congress also has the power to raise and support the armed forces. Through the advice and consent powers, the Senate has the power to ratify treaties and confirm presidential appointments.

This list of powers reveals how the framers envisioned the roles of these two branches of government in the foreign-policy arena. Realizing the problems of the committees in dealing with other countries under the Articles of Confederation, the president is given initiating power to deal with negotiations and use troops for foreign ventures. However, fearing the problem of a potential monarch in office, the Congress is given significant powers to check and balance presidential decisions.[24]

THE PRESIDENT IN FOREIGN POLICY MAKING

The president stands at the center of the foreign-policy process, empowered by the Constitution, judicial interpretation, the acquiescence of Congress, personal assertiveness, custom, organizational advantages, and tradition to formulate and carry out the nation's foreign policy.[25] The president plays a crucial role in determining the general direction of foreign policy, and once the direction has been chosen, it is the president's job to ensure the effective coordination and implementation of the policy by the bureaucracy. As the United States became a global power, the president emerged as an important figure both at home and abroad. Through two world wars; a continual political, economic, and ideological struggle against the Soviet Union; and into the post–Cold War era, the president has assumed a preeminent policymaking position. The use of emergency powers and executive agreements has helped contribute to the executive's preeminence.[26]

Source: John Branch/San Antonio Express-News.

Mexico's gratitude for the $20 bil-lion in loans that it received as a part of Clinton's peso bailout is clear in this headline exclaiming long life for Clinton. Clinton was able to bypass Congress and sup-port the Mexican economy with-out Senate approval through the use of an executive agreement, as opposed to a treaty process re-quiring ratification by a two-thirds majority. The executive agree-ment does not obligate future presidents but does retain all the legal power of a treaty.

EMERGENCY POWERS   In the event of a national emergency, the president has far-reaching authority to impose on the property and people of the United States a number of demands and restrictions that might, in the absence of a recognized condition of national emergency, be seen as unconstitutional. The word *emergency* does not appear in the Constitution. Yet emergencies have in-creased the president's preeminence over all governmental institutions. Presi-dential powers have expanded through the use of emergency enactments, some to meet very legitimate needs and others quite suspect. Once presidential authority has expanded, they have been reluctant to relinquish the legislative grants of temporary emergency powers.

EXECUTIVE AGREEMENTS   The Constitution gives the Senate the power to ratify, by a two-thirds majority, the treaties negotiated by the executive. But since the 1800s, presidents have often sought to avoid the inflexibility this im-posed on them by making use of the **executive agreement.** The executive agreement, as you learned in Chapter 6, is a government-to-government agree-ment with essentially the same legal force as a treaty. However, it may be con-cluded entirely without the approval, or even the knowledge, of the Senate. Unlike a treaty, an executive agreement cannot supersede existing law, nor does an agreement reached by one president bind subsequent presidents to comply. Otherwise, executive agreements carry the same force as formally rat-ified treaties.

The proliferation of executive agreements has been one of the most signif-icant changes in the character of foreign relations. For presidents since Franklin Roosevelt, these agreements have been by far the most favored form of inter-government agreement.

Generally, executive agreements are used to handle the mundane business of foreign affairs, such as supporting the various American diplomatic missions abroad. However, presidents also resort to executive agreements when the pre-vailing congressional or popular sentiment seems to oppose a presidential ini-tiative. Franklin Roosevelt used executive agreements to assist the British in their war against Nazi Germany at a time when isolationism was still predom-inant with Congress and the American people. Roosevelt and his successor, Harry Truman, also used secret executive agreements to reach postwar settle-ments with Russia and Britain at Yalta and Potsdam. Most recently, and with much controversy, in February 1995 President Clinton used his executive agreement authority to secure twenty billion dollars in loans to buttress the sag-ging Mexican economy.

CONGRESS AND THE FOREIGN-POLICY PROCESS

The president and the bureaucracy are not alone in the foreign-policy-making process. Congress is a powerful force. If the executive is the driving force be-hind U.S. foreign policy, Congress may act as the brakes on the president's initiatives. Through its constitutional powers to control the nation's purse strings, to ratify treaties and approve certain officials, and to make war, Con-gress may counterbalance the considerable power of the president, and thus has a very real impact on the direction of U.S. foreign policy. Much of this influence, however, depends upon the ever-changing willingness and ability of Congress to use its powers. Thus, Congress's influence in foreign policy has fluctuated greatly since World War II. We will now look at the constraints on Congress's ability to influence foreign policy and its impact through legislative oversight.

Constraints on Congress

The very nature of Congress limits its ability to influence foreign policy. Congress is a domestically oriented institution whose members are primarily interested in issues that directly influence their constituents. This orientation dampens interest in foreign policy and tends to warp policy to favor the narrow interests of individual districts. Furthermore, the size, procedures, and dispersed leadership of Congress make it difficult for Congress to act with the speed often necessary for foreign-policy decisions. The slow, deliberative procedures that characterize Congress mean that, on issues of urgency, it cannot compete with a president who is able to respond quickly and decisively to international events.

Finally, the president, as the head of the executive branch, enjoys access to the expertise of the executive bureaucracy, which coordinates and implements policy. Traditionally, Congress has felt inferior in this respect and has tended to defer to the executive on substantive foreign-policy matters. However, Congress has increased its access to foreign-policy information since the Vietnam War. The professional staff serving congressional committees has more than doubled since the early 1970s, now totaling about ten thousand. In addition to undertaking research, these staffers provide an important link between Congress and the foreign-policy bureaucracy. As such ties between Congress and the bureaucracy have strengthened, the view that foreign policy is the exclusive domain of the president has diminished. Although Congress is not and cannot be an expert on foreign policy, it has strengthened its oversight of presidential actions by passing specific legislation.

Congressional Oversight of Foreign Policy

Beyond Congress's constitutionally granted powers, which guarantee it a place in the foreign-policy-making process, Congress can have an impact through legislative oversight. It can hold hearings, pass laws, and dictate the appropriation of money in an attempt to influence or rein in a president's foreign-policy initiatives. Here are just three examples of the oversight process.

THE CASE-ZABLOCKI ACT Reacting to the common use of executive agreements, which Congress perceived as undermining its authority, Congress in 1972 passed the Case Act. Introduced by Senator Clifford Case (a New York Republican), this act requires the secretary of state to give Congress the text of any agreement between the United States and another country, other than a treaty, within sixty days of the time at which that agreement would go into effect. The Senate passed the Case Act by a vote of 81–0. Representative Clement Zablocki (a Wisconsin Democrat) introduced the same measure in the House. This act did not guarantee Congress a role in making such agreements, nor did it give Congress the right to alter such agreements once they were made. The

During a one-day visit, Senator Bob Dole met with former Prime Minister Margaret Thatcher, then-Foreign Secretary Douglas Hurd, and Prime Minister John Major to discuss the Bosnia situation. Despite an often local orientation, the slow nature of deliberations, and relatively limited access to expertise, Congress can marshall powerful counterbalancing resources in the area of foreign policy if the issue or plain politics inspire them to do so.

Congress passed the War Powers Act of 1973 in an attempt to restore the balance of power with the Executive Branch and prevent military involvement without Congressional approval. After passage of the legislation, a President could no longer commit troops for longer than sixty days without specific Congressional authorization. An optional thirty-day extension was included for issues involving troop safety. These provisions limited President Clinton's options with regard to human rights violations in Haiti.

act did, however, ensure that no agreement would remain hidden from Congress. This, combined with the more active role Congress has taken in the negotiation phases of many agreements, has given Congress a greater role in U.S. foreign policy.

THE WAR POWERS ACT One important legislative reaction to presidential excesses during the Vietnam War was the passage of the War Powers Act in 1973. Military involvement in Indochina escalated without the knowledge or approval of Congress and with steadily diminishing public support, leaving deep scars on the American political landscape. Among political elites and the general public the defeat in Vietnam spawned what has been described as the **Vietnam syndrome,** in which politicians and the public alike fear to commit militarily to the protection of any but the most obviously crucial and seriously threatened national interests.

The **War Powers Act** was a highly controversial measure, passed over President Nixon's veto. It stipulated that presidential commitments of U.S. military forces cannot extend beyond sixty days without specific congressional authorization. The sixty-day period can be extended an additional thirty days if the safety of American troops is at stake. The act also provides that any time American forces are engaged in hostilities without a specific congressional authorization, Congress can direct the president to disengage such troops by concurrent resolution of the two houses of Congress. The act also urges that the president consult Congress "in every possible instance" prior to committing U.S. forces to hostilities, or to situations likely to result in hostilities.[27]

In one respect this legislation sought to reverse the trend toward presidential domination of foreign affairs and fulfill the intent of the framers by ensuring "the collective judgment of the Congress and the President." But the act was also a response to the general expansion of presidential powers at the expense of legislative authority, an attempt to reassert congressional oversight over presidential actions and enhance the power of the legislature. The "success" of the War Powers Act is difficult to gauge. Presidents have generally ignored the reporting requirement of the act, seeing it as an unconstitutional infringement on the powers of the president as commander in chief. Still, presidents have generally found ways to inform Congress of the use of military force, often after the fact.

THE POWER OF MONEY: APPROPRIATIONS   Congress's control over federal spending gives it a powerful tool in foreign policy. Restrictions on foreign aid, military spending, and intelligence funding can severely restrict the executive branch's foreign-policy efforts. Congress uses each of these levers to varying degrees, depending on the electorate's mood and Congress's relationship with the president at the time.

Congress's ability to control foreign-aid appropriations is one example of its power in foreign affairs. Foreign aid in the form of cash, food, or other economic resources is one of the more benevolent policy options. Figure 18.2 shows the highs and lows of U.S. foreign aid since the end of World War II and indicates how that aid was allocated in 1994. The United States' annual foreign-aid commitment is generally less than one half of 1 percent of the federal budget, $14.8 billion in 1994, but such aid represents a large infusion of economic resources to the rest of the world. The popularity of foreign-aid programs has declined in the United States since the mid-1970s. Not surprisingly, they are a popular target today for budget cuts, in large part because such funding is typically of no concern to a legislator's constituency and thus provides a "painless" cut in the budget. Since the Republicans captured the House and Senate after the 1994 election, support for foreign aid has continued to evaporate. Upon assuming the chairmanship of the Senate Foreign Relations Committee, Jesse

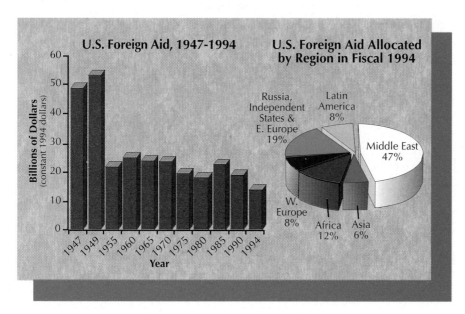

FIGURE 18.2 Foreign U.S. Aid
Contrary to popular perceptions, United States foreign aid is currently at its lowest level since 1947. Foreign aid consists of only about one half of 1 percent of the U.S. federal budget.

Source: Congressional Quarterly Weekly Report (Dec. 17, 1994); 3568. Data from Congressional Research Service and U.S. Agency for International Development.

Helms, a conservative Republican from North Carolina, with a long history of opposition to foreign aid, vowed to virtually abolish all U.S. direct foreign aid. While some support remains, growing debt and deficit problems, the current disposition of Congress, and prevailing popular sentiment suggest that foreign-aid outlays in the future will shrink.

Military-spending appropriations also give Congress an important role in the direction of United States foreign policy. On the whole, however, Congress has deviated little from the defense-funding requests of the executive branch. In the 1970s, congressional defense appropriations differed by an average of 5 percent from what was requested by the executive. This trend continued in the Reagan administration, which launched the most ambitious peacetime military buildup in United States history, proposing a 60 percent increase in military spending between 1982 and 1986. While this goal was trimmed somewhat, the buildup largely went forward as planned.

THE EXECUTIVE BUREAUCRACY IN FOREIGN POLICY MAKING

Assisting the president in foreign-policy development and implementation are some thirty-eight separate government departments and agencies. For our purposes, however, we will look at four core national-security areas and the organizations within each.

The first core national security area is foreign affairs, which is primarily the domain of the Department of State, with other related agencies playing supporting roles. These other agencies include the Agency for International Development, the Arms Control and Disarmament Agency, and the United States' Information Agency (which includes Radio Free Europe, Voice of America, and Radio Liberty).

The second core area is defense. National-security issues related to defense are dominated by the Department of Defense. In matters involving nuclear energy, the Department of Energy is also involved.

Intelligence is the third core area. While dominated by the Central Intelligence Agency (CIA), the intelligence community also includes the State Department's Bureau of Intelligence and Research, the Defense Department's Defense Intelligence Agency, the National Reconnaissance Office, the intelligence components of the individual military services, the Federal Bureau of Investigation (FBI), and the National Security Agency, a highly secret intelligence-gathering organization.

And finally, economic agencies constitute the fourth core national-security area. The United States faces fierce global economic competition. This situation has increased the importance and influence of the departments and agencies responsible for developing and implementing U.S. trade policies, negotiating tariffs with other governments, and representing the United States in various trade forums. Those most involved are the Department of the Treasury, the Departments of Commerce and Agriculture, and the Office of the United States Trade Representative.

We will now examine the organizations that are the key players in these four core foreign-policy areas: the Department of State, the Department of Defense, the National Security Council, the CIA, and the agencies behind economic policymaking.

The Department of State

The Department of State is the oldest and most preeminent department of the foreign-policy bureaucracy. It is responsible for managing foreign affairs on a daily basis, including pursuing diplomatic relations with other countries and international organizations, protecting American citizens and their interests abroad, and gathering and analyzing information bearing on U.S. foreign policy. The department's embassies, foreign-service officers, and representatives to international organizations make it the only department in the executive bureaucracy with a global view. Despite its important role, the Department of State, with twenty-five thousand employees, is fairly small.[28]

Critics of the State Department have found that its global perspective can lead it to focus more on what is happening abroad than at home, leading it to place the interests of other countries ahead of those of the United States. Foreign-service officers at U.S. embassies, for example, may try to please their constituents—that is, the local country's government. And, through what many critics consider acquiescence, the State Department lacks expertise in economic policy and defense issues, both intrinsic to foreign-policy development in today's world. This lack of expertise translates into diminished authority over departments such as Treasury, Commerce and Defense.

The State Department is headed by the secretary of state, who is responsible to both the president and the department. Often, a secretary must choose one at the risk of alienating the other. When the secretary chooses to follow the president's lead and oppose the career bureaucrats in the State Department, the department's morale suffers, and it can lose direction. Henry Kissinger's freewheeling diplomacy during his tenure as Richard Nixon's secretary of state was facilitated in part by his relative indifference to the advice and the priorities of his own department. Kissinger's independence tended to alienate the very bureaucrats who should have been his strongest supporters. Warren Christopher, on the other hand, has managed to be loyal to President Clinton while working closely with State Department employees.

The secretary of state not only heads the cabinet-level state department, but is the chief presidential advisor on foreign affairs, a member of the National Security Council, highest-ranking cabinet member, and fourth in line to the presidency. Here Secretary of State Warren Christopher walks with Japanese Foreign Minister Yohei Kono en route to lunch at the White House. It is reported that they discussed the possibility of support for light-water nuclear power reactors in North Korea.

The Department of Defense

The tense international political environment after World War II, in which military solutions were used to address diplomatic problems, put the Defense Department in the center of the foreign-policy making process. This huge department, located in the Pentagon building in Arlington, Virginia, commands a tremendous share of the federal budget, and with it a substantial amount of political influence. The Defense Department is responsible for the many military aspects of foreign policy, including the thousands of troops under its command at bases overseas.[29]

The Defense Department is composed of four service branches (army, navy, air force, and marines) that often compete with each other for influence, authority, and resources. Each branch of the service is headed by a chief of staff. Heading all four branches is the chairman of the Joint Chiefs of Staff, who acts as the voice of the military (as opposed to civilian) side of the Pentagon. The chairman of the Joint Chiefs is one of the president's principal military advisors.

Each of the four service branches also reports to a civilian secretary. Civilian agencies within the Defense Department handle functions such as logistics and communications. This combination of military and civilian personnel often results in overlapping duties and some confusion over the roles that each is supposed to play in the operation of the department.[30]

In many of the same areas where the State Department is weak, the Defense Department is exceptionally strong, making it a powerful force in foreign-policymaking. With nearly a million individuals employed by defense-related industries, the Defense Department has many people with a vested interest in its financial well-being. A cut in defense spending can mean the loss of a job for a welder in Lubbock, Texas, while a new air force base can turn a ghost town into a boom town. Thus, the Defense Department is an integral part of American social, political, and economic life. It has an impact in both the domestic and international spheres, which the State Department, with its exclusively global orientation, lacks. The Defense Department is much larger than the State Department, with around three million military and civilian employees.

The Defense Department's strongest influence in foreign policy has historically been the result of the close ties between the Pentagon and the corporations that dominate the U.S. weapons industry. Even as early as 1961, President Dwight Eisenhower, in his farewell address, warned of the growing power and influence resulting from the "conjunction of an immense military establishment and a large arms industry." Eisenhower called this phenomenon the **military–industrial complex**.[31] Its development meant that "the potential for the disastrous rise of misplaced power exists and will persist." With their seemingly insatiable appetite for more and better firepower, Pentagon officials are the defense industry's best—and sometimes only—customers. In turn, large corporations argue that their weapons production plants produce thousands of jobs and stimulate the economy at both the local and the national levels. Members of Congress are drawn into this relationship, either to protect local jobs by ensuring defense contracts or to appear sufficiently supportive of the military to satisfy their constituents back home. Together, the Pentagon, defense contractors, and key legislators form a strong lobby in support of sustained defense spending for the U.S. military and for export to other nations. However, since the collapse of the Soviet Union, the power of the military–industrial complex has begun to wane.

In these days of arms reductions and fiscal restraint, the Defense Department is finding its power lessened and its budgets cut. Since the 1990s, reductions in nuclear weapons arsenals have been negotiated by Russia and the United States, leading to the closing of many military bases and cuts in defense contracts.

The National Security Council

The National Security Council (NSC) was created in 1947 to provide the executive with advice on all domestic, foreign, and military policies relating to national security. Because of the need for immediate and accurate information

In May of 1995, Clinton was able to achieve partial concessions from Boris Yeltsin, the first popularly elected president in Russia's history, regarding Moscow's proposed sale of nuclear technology to Iran. He also convinced Yeltsin to formalize ties with NATO.

for policy planning, the president needed just such a foreign-policy advisory group. Members of the NSC include the president (as chair); the president's national-security adviser, who acts as the special assistant for national security; the vice president; and the secretaries of state and defense, with the director of the CIA and the chairman of the Joint Chiefs of Staff sitting in as advisers. Various other cabinet and agency heads, such as the secretary of the treasury, the attorney general, and the U.S. ambassador to the United Nations, participate as needed.

Through the NSC the president coordinates the different government agencies dealing with foreign or defense policy. The NSC became especially active under President Kennedy and Special Assistant for National Security McGeorge Bundy. The staff under Bundy became the president's key personal foreign-policy "team." What emerged was an informally structured organization for the formulation and implementation of foreign policy that has persisted to this day. Such an organization, however, works both for and against the executive branch, affording a base for quick and secretive executive-level responses to national-security problems, but allowing a sometimes dangerous policymaking latitude to unelected and relatively unaccountable decision makers. For example, it was in the NSC that the controversial Iran-Contra "arms-for-hostages" operation was conceived and run.[32]

By decreasing the president's reliance on the bureaucracy for information and advice the NSC adviser and staff can become a "screen" between the president and the rest of government, reducing the president's direct influence and personal leadership. This has led to serious rivalries between the national-security adviser, the secretaries of state and defense, the director of the CIA, and their staffs. The relative influence and access of each organization often depends upon the personal relationship between each department head and the president.

FYI

Henry Kissinger was both a National Security Advisor and Secretary of State.

The role of the national-security adviser has continued to change over the years, based on the personality of the appointee to the post, and as presidents have shaped the position to fit their personal management styles. On the whole, however, the national-security adviser is an extremely influential, although often anonymous, policymaker.

The CIA and Intelligence Gathering

The Central Intelligence Agency (CIA) is the dominant force in the intelligence community. It was established after World War II to be the president's nonpartisan resource for coordinated intelligence analysis. However, its mission quickly expanded to include covert operations such as espionage, psychological warfare, paramilitary maneuvers, and political and economic intervention.

The CIA's most important function, however, is information gathering. It is responsible for collecting information about the state of leadership in other countries, the political situation and stability, military capabilities, strengths and weaknesses, and possible intentions in the political, economic and military spheres. All of this information is analyzed and reported to policymakers to better enable them to make decisions on foreign-policy issues.

In addition to its international role, the CIA has expanded its activities on the domestic front, leading to concerns about the potential for abuse. Concerns about illegal activities against American citizens and dubious operations in foreign countries have led to more oversight by Congress. However, this oversight has proven to be less than effective. Under the Reagan administration, the CIA supported Nicaraguan insurgents and their mining of Nicaragua's harbors, activities that went unreported to Congress, despite legal requirements to keep Congress "fully and currently informed" of all intelligence activities. Congress could do little more than scold the CIA director for his disobedience. Faced with an inability to control the CIA, a member of the House Intelligence Committee at the time lamented, "We are like mushrooms. They keep us in the dark and feed us a lot of manure."[33]

Recently, as a direct result of the Aldrich Ames spy case, both Congress and President Clinton have sought to rein in the power of the CIA. Ames was both a CIA employee and spy who sold secrets about U.S. intelligence activities to the Soviets for years without being detected, although the signs of trouble were clearly evident. In response to this scandal, Congress in 1995 initiated hearings on CIA activities including covert operations. Signaling the most recent attempt by the president to bring intelligence gathering and covert operations more directly under the umbrella of executive branch authority, early in 1995 President Clinton signed a controversial executive order directing the CIA to follow a list of priorities when deploying its considerable intelligence-gathering resources around the world. Clinton also considered elevating the CIA director to cabinet-level status and appointed a commission to help prepare the intelligence community for the future.

Considering that the original purpose of the CIA was to insulate intelligence operations from the political pressures of Congress and the president, these recent moves may suggest potential changes in both the role and power of the CIA. However, most observers believe that the agency will retain much of its functional autonomy, despite ongoing attempts at restructuring.[34]

Patrolling the Information Superhighway

Sometimes the line between foreign and domestic policy becomes blurred, as the priorities of one overlap with the concerns of the other. During the early years of the Cold War, the rights of individual American citizens were often violated in governmental efforts to ferret out domestic communist "infiltration." In this case, the United States' commitment to a foreign policy of communist containment served as the rationale for the surveillance of American citizens and the reduction of individual privacy and freedom. This surveillance included illegal telephone taps and physical surveillance of private citizens. Even the bedroom of civil rights activist Martin Luther King, Jr., was bugged because of alleged—but false—communist associations and sympathies.

A similar phenomenon faces Americans at the end of the twentieth century, in the form of a tiny piece of microcircuitry and a battle against international "terrorism." Increasingly, economic transactions are being carried out through electronic computer networking. The use of credit cards, automated bank teller machines, personal computers, fiber optic digital telephone transmissions, and other avenues of the "information superhighway" makes American consumerism much more convenient than in the past. But these same kinds of innovations have stimulated the development of sophisticated technology to follow the electronic trail of any citizen who might attract the suspicion of the government.

The latest such innovation is the so-called "Clipper" computer chip. In early 1992 the supersecret National Security Agency (NSA) announced the development of a device that would electronically encrypt or "scramble" the communication of anyone using the Clipper to send and receive telephone or computer messages to another Clipper-enhanced device. The encoded messages would be more secure since they could not be decoded by anyone else. Anyone, that is, except for the NSA, which, along with the Federal Bureau of Investigation (FBI), retained sole possession of the two "keys" designed to "unlock" the encrypted messages. Since the primary jurisdiction of the NSA is the communications apparatus of the federal government (and the ever-expanding network of international communications), the use of the Clipper chip has some civil libertarians concerned that this enormous agency may be turning too much of its scrutiny on its own private citizens.

The Clinton administration and other advocates of the Clipper chip use a familiar rationale for such intrusions into individual privacy: an extension of a foreign-policy priority. Reminiscent of the anticommunist justifications of decades past, supporters of the chip cite the growing risk of international terrorism and espionage (both political and economic) as justification for granting the government exclusive surveillance access to all telecommunications transactions. Some use the example of the 1993 World Trade Center bombing as a case where such surveillance might assist authorities in tracking down suspected terrorists, even though the methods used to convict the four Islamic fundamentalists responsible for the bombing date back to the height of the Cold War.

The fight against terrorism around the world, like that against the expansion of communism during the Cold War, is not just a myth of foreign-policy makers. But whenever such foreign-policy priorities constrict the constitutionally guaranteed liberties of American citizens, America's approach to democracy is threatened.

Cutting Edge

The Agencies behind Economic Policy Making

Beginning in the 1960s the overwhelming economic superiority of the United States began to dwindle, caused in part by the economic dislocations triggered by financing the Vietnam War. But, more important, this period also witnessed

In February of 1995, Mickey Kantor, in his role as U.S. trade representative, played hardball with China, ordering 100 percent tariffs on imports from China totalling more than $1.08 billion. This punitive move was in response to evidence that China had stolen American computer software programs, movies, and music.

the first stirrings of real economic strength from the European and Asian economies that had been ravaged by World War II and rebuilt with considerable assistance from the United States. As the economies of Europe, and, in particular, Japan, expanded, the corresponding American share of world markets decreased. In addition, with the end of the Cold War, and in the absence of the ready reference point of communist "containment," the priorities of U.S. foreign policy changed. Such global economic shifts and political changes have led to similar shifts in the balance of influence among the U.S. government organizations involved in foreign policy. The power and influence of several departments not traditionally associated with foreign-policy decision-making have increased. Instead of a foreign-policy establishment dominated by the NSC, the State Department, and the Pentagon, U.S. policymaking now features actors such as the offices of Commerce and the Trade Representative in roles of unprecedented prominence. Economic power is the overriding issue for these agencies.

These departments and agencies play highly specialized roles in the foreign-policy-making process. The Department of Labor, for example, represents the United States in international negotiations on the General Agreement on Tariffs and Trade (GATT), the Organization for Economic Cooperation and Development (OECD), and the International Labor Organization (ILO). The Department of Agriculture has its own Foreign Agricultural Service, which is responsible for formulating, administering, and coordinating the department's programs overseas. The Department of Energy is responsible for conducting nuclear weapons research, as well as development, production, and surveillance operations.

The Departments of Treasury and Commerce, in particular, are central figures in the making of economic policy in the global arena. The Treasury Department is primarily concerned with the development of financial policy. It focuses on trade regulations, exchange rates, and the balance of payments. Unlike the State Department, which judges nations largely on the basis of their political systems, or Defense, which looks at military strength, the Treasury Department is concerned with a nation's economic system and how it affects the U.S. economy. For example, is a nation's exchange rate fair? Is its tariff structure conducive to U.S. exports? How do American exports to a particular nation compare with American imports from it? While the Treasury Department develops U.S. financial policy, the Commerce Department is responsible for expanding and protecting U.S. commerce abroad, which it does through the Foreign Commercial Service. Similar to the State Department's Foreign Service, the Foreign Commercial Service works through U.S. embassies and consulates, advising foreign businesses on their U.S.-related business activities. The Commerce Department also maintains nearly fifty offices in the United States to encourage U.S. firms to export their products.

The Agents behind Policy Making

Much of the actual foreign-policy making takes place within the nooks and crannies of the State Department, the Pentagon, and other agencies and departments, as career bureaucrats exercise their delegated and undelegated discretionary decision-making power to develop policy. These bureaucrats also have the expertise to analyze the immense volume of foreign-policy information. Thus, a president needs the support of the bureaucracy to be a successful foreign-policy president.

The bureaucracy also assists with the task of policy implementation. This task is a far-flung process in terms of geography (implementation is global) and in terms of the vast array of departments and agencies that must cooperate on a given issue. Officials in the field, for example, especially the State Department's Foreign Service Officers, tend to believe that those in Washington, D.C., far removed from the problems of their post, don't understand the realities of their situation.

At all but the lowest levels of the foreign-policy bureaucracy there are individuals who owe their jobs to the political process. These are the political appointees who form a large and powerful contingent within the foreign-policy bureaucracy; the deputy secretaries, undersecretaries, assistant secretaries, and office directors in the various departments and agencies involved in foreign-policy making. As a group, political appointees are ambitious people who want to have a hand in shaping U.S. foreign policy. Thus, they have to play the bureaucratic game in a way that will keep them involved in the action for as long as possible; they perform a delicate dance to maintain and expand their sphere of influence.

DEMOCRATIC CHECKS ON FOREIGN POLICY

In no other realm of government activity is the exercise of democratic control *less* apparent than in the making of foreign policy. Both the complex nature of global affairs and the crisis atmosphere that sometimes prevails over foreign-policy decision-making can lead the national-security establishment to ignore public opinion. Likewise, the increasing use of executive agreements and covert operations means that foreign-policy decisions often unfold out of public view and without any opportunity for public debate except after the fact.

Although the president is the primary initiator of foreign policy, there are important checks on presidential power to make foreign policy. We have already looked at how Congress can provide a mechanism to check presidential foreign-policy making, using its oversight power to force open the decision-making process.[35] We'll now look at how the press and public opinion can act as a check on foreign-policy outcomes.

THE PRESS   The press plays a very important role in the surveillance, investigation, criticism, and advocacy of the government's foreign-policy activities. In the process, the media provide American citizens with most of their knowledge of the rest of the world. While the media are ostensibly neutral and objective, they do project the foreign-policy agenda for the nation and typically mirror the opinions of the foreign-policy establishment.[36]

The media do sometimes offer competing perspectives on international affairs. On occasion, individual reporters have questioned or strongly opposed government policies, even in advance of public opposition. Early press criticism of the Johnson administration's direction of the Vietnam War, while not widespread, did serve to chip away at the "monopoly of information" enjoyed by the White House, challenging the government version of reality and stimulating public criticism of U.S. involvement in Southeast Asia.[37]

More commonly, though, the press serves as a conduit for the opinions of various actors involved in the policy process. The "leak," a calculated release of controversial information, is used by individuals at all levels of the bureaucracy for a variety of purposes. The right words at the right time can stir up Congress, the public, and foreign governments and put an end to a controversial foreign-policy initiative. Key players in the foreign-policy process also often release information to friendly reporters to test the waters of public response to policy options under consideration.

With very few exceptions, the American press is reluctant to strongly oppose the actions of the U.S. government, particularly where the deployment of American troops is involved. Throughout most of the Vietnam War, the press, like most of the general public, supported the U.S. presence in Southeast Asia, breaking with the official version of U.S. policy in Vietnam only when the inconsistencies and contradictions of that policy had become glaringly apparent. This supportive role was even more apparent during more recent foreign-policy actions, including the U.S. invasions of Grenada, Panama, and Iraq. In each case, most media analysts relied on government sources, accepted government explanations for the intervention in question, and focused predominantly on tactical and technical rather than ethical or moral analysis.

For example, mainstream press coverage of the Panama invasion and Noriega's capture tended to emphasize the size and power of the forces deployed, the peculiarities of Noriega's personal life, and the apparent effectiveness of the operation. Absent from most reports was the history of U.S. ties to the Panamanian dictator, the specific link between Noriega and Bush, or the fact that many of the casualties suffered by U.S. forces were the result of "friendly fire" from other U.S. military personnel. Since neither the White House nor the Pentagon wished to stress such negative details, the press reliance on government sources denied U.S. citizens access to the kind of information they needed to formulate a more balanced perspective on a complex policy. In such cases, the "watchdog" can become a "lapdog."

Nonetheless, the media can be credited with providing Americans with a wealth of information, thereby helping them to become better-informed citizens. And the constitutional guarantees of a free press and free speech afford American citizens a small but sometimes persistent and influential voice in the otherwise elite-dominated foreign-policy process.[38]

THE PUBLIC Often overlooked in analyses of foreign-policy decision-making is the role played by the public and public opinion. In some cases, the voice of public opinion can penetrate the carefully encrypted speech and muffled secrecy of foreign-policy making to have an impact. Some point to popular discontent with Vietnam as an example of the government abiding by public opinion to reverse a longstanding policy. The validity of this claim is open to argument, but the fact remains that typically the foreign-policy-making process is among the least democratic in the American system. Historically, U.S. citizens have had little significant influence on the foreign policy created by their government. From the end of World War II until quite recently, for example, the American defense budget had increased steadily, sometimes dramatically. Campaigning for the presidency in 1980, Ronald Reagan made much of the public demand for a "stronger" America, which he interpreted as a demand for a stronger American military. Once in office, even in the midst of a growing debt and deficit crisis, the Reagan administration continued the trend toward greater military spending despite the fact that the public "demand" had peaked by the end of 1981 and declined since then.

Why doesn't public opinion carry more weight? Generally, the majority of Americans know little about foreign affairs. The public is often poorly informed about the motivations behind government actions abroad and is unclear about the possible consequences in both the short and long term. Government reticence is partially to blame. In addition, the mainstream press tends to reinforce rather than challenge government actions and explanations. The public also tends to rally around the president in times of national crisis, such as war or international confrontation, reducing the likelihood of any sizable public opposition (see Table 18.1).

The greatest likelihood of any widespread, sustained public outcry against foreign policies occurs during prolonged and stalemated military actions when Americans watch their young men and women fight and die but see no tangible gains. The conflicts in Korea and Vietnam provide two examples of such opposition, while the relative public-opinion success of the invasions of Grenada, Panama, and Iraq suggests that public support will be strongest when the conflict in question is relatively brief, decisive, and victorious, and when information is carefully controlled by the military rather than left to the free-roaming inquiry of individual reporters.[39]

Table 18.1
Rallying around the President in Times of War and Crisis

PRESIDENT	YEAR	INCIDENT	PERCENTAGE CHANGES IN PRESIDENTS' APPROVAL RATINGS*
Johnson	1965	U.S. intervention in Dominican Republic	+ 7
Johnson	1965	U.S. ground troops enter Vietnam War	+ 6
Johnson	1968	North Korea seizes USS *Pueblo*	+ 7
Ford	1975	Cambodia seizes SS *Mayaquez*	+13
Carter	1980	Mission to rescue hostages in Iran fails	+10
Reagan	1983	U.S. invades Grenada	+ 4
Bush	1989	U.S. invades Panama	+ 9
Bush	1990	Iraq invades Kuwait	+14
Clinton	1993	U.S. bombs Iraq	+11

*Figures rounded to nearest percent.

Source: John T. Rourke, Ralph G. Carter, and Mark A. Boyer, *Making American Foreign Policy* (Guilford, CT: Dushkin, 1994), p. 187.

FOREIGN POLICY AND APPROACHING DEMOCRACY

Today the United States faces an impressive array of foreign-policy challenges. Policymakers and the public must cope with forces of change in politics, economics, technology, and demographics. The United States must assess not only its interests in world affairs but also its proper role. In this quickly changing world, questions about foreign policy abound. How will the United States lead in the post–Cold War era? What is the role of NATO, and how and at what pace should it expand? What is the proper relationship between the United States and the United Nations? What should be the future role of peacekeeping operations and U.S. foreign-aid programs? How will the United States balance economic and political interests when they collide? How will it balance economic and political interests against humanitarian and environmental concerns? Each historical era has posed serious challenges for the United States; this new era is no different.

As we have seen throughout this text, the United States must respond to these and other questions in the context of its ongoing experiment in self-government. Indeed, there are really two related challenges for U.S. foreign policy today. First, the United States must try to determine a foreign-policy course in a complicated and changing international environment, one that involves an appropriate balance of commitments and resources. Second, it must do so within the democratic limits established in the Constitution. Ultimately then, the paramount challenge is how to balance the interests of security and the requirements of democracy.

Understanding the link between foreign policy and democracy requires that we first recognize the dramatically altered world environment in the wake of the Cold War. The most distinctive characteristics of the post-Cold War era and the one that separates it from the recent past is the absence of outside threat as a central organizing principle. While controversy existed during the Cold War over the nature of the Soviet threat, the mere presence of an overarching strategic compass provided an anchor for U.S. foreign policy and imposed a set of priorities that (for better or worse) defined the parameters within which U.S. leaders acted in the world and resorted to force in the defense of national interests. The pre-1989 period seems far clearer in retrospect, but indisputably the Cold War provided a known and relatively predictable adversary, a familiar structure of conflict, and a set of important external constraints on U.S. action.[40]

Today, instead of a well-defined threat to anchor U.S. foreign policy, pervasive uncertainty faces the world's sole remaining superpower as it attempts to anticipate the future foreign-policy environment, establish a new psychological basis for engaging the nation in the world, and develop principles to guide the use of diplomatic, economic, and military tools abroad. For the United States, the post–Cold War world is characterized first and foremost by absence of a known and familiar adversary. Certainty about the enemy has been supplanted by questions about the identity of future adversaries, their goals and capabilities, and the time frame within which future challenges are likely to arise. Post–Cold War U.S. leaders face a set of novel, diffuse, and unfamiliar foreign-policy problems such as small peripheral states armed with weapons of mass destruction threatening regional and global security, and unconventional challenges posed by narco-terrorists, religious-fundamentalist movements, and ethnic and national violence. Of these, however, none are significant enough, even in the foreseeable future, to replace the strategic bell-whether that disappeared along with the Soviet Union.

Like Woodrow Wilson, President Clinton believes that democracy can be implanted in hostile soil, and this also underlies the strategy of enlargement.

U.S. leaders also confront problems of uncertainty regarding alliances. Who will be the country's future alliance and coalition partners? Is it more desirable to build on firm alliances or to rely on flexible partnerships, collective-security arrangements, or ad hoc coalitions? Absence of a hegemonic challenger has weakened the U.S. commitment to firm alliance arrangements such as NATO. Unconventional challenges, such as those posed by ethnic-nationalist violence, do not engender sufficient public concern or political resolve to answer these questions.

SUMMARY

1. *Foreign policy* refers to actions the government takes abroad to ensure the security and well-being of Americans and the strength and competitiveness of the U.S. economy. Foreign-policy making is often complex because of the need to balance democratic ideals against military and economic interests.

2. Before World War I, U.S. foreign policy was characterized by isolationism, in which the United States fostered economic relations with Europe without committing to strategic alliances. Despite its policy of neutrality, the United States clearly favored Britain during World War I and entered the war after the sinking of the *Lusitania*. After the war, however, isolationism again prevailed.

3. The United States was initially reluctant to enter World War II but did so after the bombing of Pearl Harbor. After the war its primary foreign-policy goal was the "containment" of communism, which placed it in direct opposition to the Soviet Union and created what came to be known as the Cold War.

4. After 1949 both the United States and the Soviet Union poured vast amounts of money into the development and deployment of nuclear weapons. During the same period U.S. foreign-aid commitments were increased in an effort to prevent Soviet advances in less developed countries.

5. During the 1960s the effort to contain communism gradually drew the United States into a full-scale war in Vietnam, a war that was a disaster both militarily and from the stand-

point of foreign policy. After the war the United States entered into a "detente" with the Soviet Union and began discussing ways to reduce the nuclear threat.

6. In 1991 the Soviet Union ceased to exist, thereby ending the Cold War and clearing the way for a new world order whose outlines remain unclear. The Clinton administration has espoused a policy of "enlargement," or supporting the expansion of market-oriented democracies.

7. The strategies of foreign policy are also changing. The use of foreign aid has come under fire, as has the use of economic sanctions as a means of forcing a target nation to change its policies. The temptation to find military solutions to political problems remains strong.

8. The Constitution gives the president the authority to commit troops to foreign lands, negotiate treaties, appoint ambassadors, and decide whether or not to receive ambassadors. Congress has the power to declare war, appropriate money, and make laws, thereby deciding whether to back presidential initiatives abroad. The Senate also has the power to ratify treaties and confirm presidential appointments.

9. The president determines the general direction of foreign policy and the effectiveness of its implementation by the bureaucracy. The president's influence has been increased by additional powers granted by Congress during emergencies. In addition, presidents have often entered into executive agreements with foreign governments, thereby avoiding the need for ratification by the Senate.

10. Congress tends to be oriented toward domestic policy and cannot respond quickly and decisively to international events. It has attempted to strengthen its oversight of foreign policy through legislation such as the Case Act, which requires the secretary of state to provide Congress with the text of any agreement with another country; and the War Powers Act, which stipulates that the president must receive congressional authorization for commitments of U.S. forces abroad beyond sixty days. Congress can also restrict the executive branch's foreign-policy efforts by limiting appropriations for foreign aid, military spending, and intelligence gathering.

11. Although the Department of State has primary responsibility for the development and implementation of foreign policy, the Department of Defense also plays an important role because it commands a large share of the federal budget and has considerable political clout. For information and policy planning, however, the president depends on the National Security Council, consisting of the president, the national security adviser, the vice president, and the secretaries of state and defense.

12. The Central Intelligence Agency, along with several other agencies, is responsible for gathering and analyzing intelligence about the activities of foreign governments. It also engages in covert operations such as espionage, psychological warfare, and paramilitary operations. Concern about possible abuses of power by the CIA has led to attempts to resturcture the agency and bring it under greater executive control.

13. Most of the detailed analysis and development of foreign policy is done by career bureaucrats in the State Department. At the higher levels are political appointees such as deputy secretaries and undersecretaries.

14. In addition to Congress, the Supreme Court may act to restrain foreign-policy making by the president. The press plays an important role in surveillance, investigation, criticism, and advocacy of foreign-policy activities, although it is usually reluctant to oppose the actions of the U.S. government overseas. Public opinion does not seem to have had a major influence on foreign policy.

KEY TERMS

foreign policy
isolationism
Monroe Doctrine
superpower
containment
globalism

North Atlantic Treaty Organization
(NATO)
Cold War
NSC-68
bipolarity
detente

executive agreement
Vietnam syndrome
War Powers Act
military–industrial complex

SUGGESTED READINGS

- Larry Berman and Emily O. Goldman, "Clinton's Foreign Policy at Midterm," in *The Clinton Presidency: First Appraisals,* edited by Colin Campbell and Bert Rockman. New Jersey: Chatham House Publisher, 1996. An analysis of the Clinton administration's struggle to delineate an overarching theme to the post-Cold War world.

- Laura D'Andrea Tyson, *Who's Bashing Whom? Trade Conflict in High Technology Industries.* Washington, D.C.: Institute for International Economics, 1992. The chair of the Economic Policy Council and former chair of the Council of Economic Advisers examines what trade policies the U.S. should adopt to support its high-technology industries.

- Henry Kissinger, *Diplomacy.* New York: Simon & Schuster, 1994. An insightful account by the former Sec-

retary of State of the ways in which the art of diplomacy and the balance of power have created the world we live in. Kissinger also analyzes the conduct of U.S. foreign policy and its idealistic foundation.

- Ariel E. Levite, Bruce W. Jentleson and Larry Berman, eds. *Foreign Military Intervention: The Dynamics of Protracted Conflict.* New York: Columbia University Press, 1992. Six case studies which examine the similarities and differences among nation-states that use military might to intervene in civil wars and otherwise reshape the domestic political order of weakened states.

- Robert McNamara, *In Retrospect: The Tragedy and Lessons of Vietnam.* New York: Random House 1995. In this controversial book, the former Secretary of Defense for Presidents Kennedy and Johnson, reveals how the U.S.

stumbled into the Vietnam War and why it was so difficult to withdraw. McNamara also reveals his own inner torment as the war became both frustrating and disastrous.

- Joseph S. Nye, Jr., *Bound to Lead: The Changing Nature of American Power.* New York: Basic Books, 1990. A leading scholar of international politics and former State Department official argues that the United States is still the dominant world power, with no challenger in sight.

APPENDICES

THE DECLARATION OF INDEPENDENCE

In Congress, July 4, 1776
The Unanimous Declaration of the Thirteen United States of America

When in the Course of human events, it becomes necessary for one people to dissolve the political bands which have connected them with another, and to assume among the Powers of the earth, the separate and equal station to which the Laws of Nature and of Nature's God entitle them, a decent respect to the opinions of mankind requires that they should declare the causes which impel them to the separation.

We hold these truths to be self-evident, that all men are created equal, that they are endowed by their Creator with certain unalienable Rights, that among these are Life, Liberty and the pursuit of Happiness. That to secure these rights, Governments are instituted among Men, deriving their just powers from the consent of the governed. That whenever any Form of Government becomes destructive of these ends, it is the Right of the People to alter or to abolish it, and to institute new Government, laying its foundation on such principles and organizing its powers in such form, as to them shall seem most likely to effect their Safety and Happiness. Prudence, indeed, will dictate that Governments long established should not be changed for light and transient causes; and accordingly all experience hath shown, that mankind are more disposed to suffer, while evils are sufferable, than to right themselves by abolishing the forms to which they are accustomed. But when a long train of abuses and usurpations, pursuing invariably the same Object evinces a design to reduce them under absolute Depotism, it is their right, it is their duty, to throw off such Government, and to provide new Guards for their future security.—Such has been the patient sufferance of these Colonies; and such is now the necessity which constrains them to alter their former Systems of Government. The history of the present King of Great Britain is a history of repeated injuries and usurpations, all having in direct object the establishment of an absolute Tyranny over these States. To prove this, let Facts be submitted to a candid world.

He has refused his Assent to Laws, the most wholesome and necessary for the public good.

He has forbidden his Governors to pass Laws of immediate and pressing importance, unless suspended in their operation till his Assent should be obtained; and when so suspended, he has utterly neglected to attend to them.

He has refused to pass other Laws for the accommodation of large districts of people, unless those people would relinquish the right of Representation in the Legislature, a right inestimable to them and formidable to tyrants only.

He has called together legislative bodies at places unusual, uncomfortable, and distant from the depository of their public Records, for the sole purpose of fatiguing them into compliance with his measures.

He has dissolved Representative Houses repeatedly for opposing with manly firmness his invasions on the rights of the people.

He has refused for a long time, after such dissolutions, to cause others to be elected; whereby the Legislative Powers, incapable of Annihilation, have returned to the People at large for their exercise; the State remaining in the mean time exposed to all the dangers of invasion from without, and convulsions within.

He has endeavoured to prevent the population of these States; for that purpose obstructing the Laws of Naturalization of Foreigners; refusing to pass others to encourage their migration higher, and raising the conditions of new Appropriations of Lands.

He has obstructed the Administration of Justice, by refusing his Assent to Laws for establishing Judiciary powers.

He has made Judges dependent on his Will alone, for the tenure of their offices, and the amount and payment of their salaries.

He has erected a multitude of New Offices, and sent hither swarms of Officers to harass our People, and eat out their substance.

He has kept among us in times of peace, Standing Armies without the Consent of our legislature.

He has affected to render the Military independent of and superior to the Civil power.

He has combined with others to subject us to a jurisdiction foreign to our constitution, and unacknowledged by our laws; giving his Assent to their acts of pretended Legislation.

For quartering large bodies of armed troops among us:

For protecting them, by a mock Trial, from punishment for any Murders which they should commit on the inhabitants of these States:

For cutting off our Trade with all parts of the world.

For imposing taxes on us without our Consent:

For depriving us in many cases, of the benefits of Trial by Jury:

For transporting us beyond Seas to be tried for pretended offences:

For abolishing the free System of English Laws in a neighbouring Province, establishing therein an Arbitrary government, and enlarging its Boundaries so as to render it at once an example and fit instrument for introducing the same absolute rule into these Colonies.

For taking away our Charters, abolishing our most valuable Laws, and altering fundamentally the Forms of our Governments:

For suspending our own Legislature, and declaring themselves invested with Power to legislate for us in all cases whatsoever.

He has abdicated Government here, by declaring us out of his Protection and waging War against us.

He has plundered our seas, ravaged our Coasts, burnt our towns, and destroyed the lives of our people.

He is at this time transporting large Armies of foreign Mercenaries to compleat the works of death, desolation and tyranny, already begun with circumstances of Cruelty & perfidy scarcely paralleled in the most barbarous ages, and totally unworthy the Head of a civilized nation.

He has constrained our fellow Citizens taken Captive on the high Seas to bear Arms against their Country, to become the executioners of their friends and Brethren, or to fall themselves by their Hands.

He has excited domestic insurrections amongst us, and has endeavoured to bring on the inhabitants of our frontiers, the merciless Indian Savages, whose known rule of warfare, is an undistinguished destruction of all ages, sexes and conditions.

In every stage of these Oppressions We have Petitioned for Redress in the most humble terms: Our repeated Petitions have been answered only by repeated injury. A Prince, whose character is thus marked by every act which may define a Tyrant, is unfit to be the ruler of a free People.

Nor have We been wanting in attention to our British brethren. We have warned them from time to time of attempts by their legislature to extend an unwarrantable jurisdiction over us. We have reminded them of the circumstances of our emigration and settlement here. We have appealed to their native justice and magnanimity, and we have conjured them by the ties of our common kindred to disavow these usurpations, which, would inevitably interrupt our connections and correspondence. They too have been deaf to the voice of justice and of consanguinity. We must, therefore, acquiesce in the necessity, which denounces our Separation, and hold them, as we hold the rest of mankind, Enemies in War, in Peace Friends.

We, therefore, the Representatives of the United States of America, in General Congress, Assembled, appealing to the Supreme Judge of the world for rectitude of our intentions, do, in the Name, and by Authority of the good People of these Colonies, solemnly publish and declare, That these United Colonies are, and of right ought to be Free and Independent States; that they are Absolved from all Allegiance to the British Crown, and that all political connection between them and the State of Great Britain, is and ought to be totally dissolved; and that as Free and Independent States, they have full Power to levy War, conclude Peace, contract Alliances, establish Commerce, and to do all other Acts and Things which Independent States may of right do. And for the support of this Declaration, with a firm reliance on the protection of Divine Providence, we mutually pledge to each other our Lives, our Fortunes and our sacred Honor.

John Hancock [President]
and fifty-five others

FEDERALIST NO. 10 [1787], JAMES MADISON

To the People of the State of New York: Among the numerous advantages promised by a well-constructed union, none deserves to be more accurately developed than its tendency to break and control the violence of faction. The friend of popular governments, never finds himself so much alarmed for their character and fate, as when he contemplates their propensity to this dangerous vice. He will not fail, therefore, to set a due value on any plan which, without violating the principles to which he is attached, provides a proper cure for it. The instability, injustice, and confusion introduced into the public councils, have, in truth, been the mortal diseases under which popular governments have everywhere perished; as they continue to be the favourite and fruitful topics from which the adversaries to liberty derive their most specious declamations. The valuable improvements made by the American constitutions on the popular models, both ancient and modern, cannot certainly be too much admired; but it would be an unwarrantable partiality, to contend that they have as effectually obviated the danger on this side, as was wished and expected. Complaints are everywhere heard from our most considerate and virtuous citizens, equally the friends of public and private faith, and of public and personal liberty, that our governments are too unstable; that the public good is disregarded in the conflicts of rival parties; and that measures are too often decided, not according to the rules of justice, and the rights of the minor party, but by the superior force of an interested and overbearing majority. However anxiously we may wish that these complaints had no foundation, the evidence of known facts will not permit us to deny that they are in some degree true. It will be found, indeed, on a candid review of our situation, that some of the distresses under which we labour have been erroneously charged on the operation of our governments; but it will be found, at the same time, that other causes will not alone account for many of our heaviest misfortunes; and, particularly, for that prevailing and increasing distrust of public engagements, and alarm for private rights, which are echoed from one end of the continent to the other. These must be chiefly, if not wholly, effects of the unsteadiness and injustice, with which a factious spirit has tainted our public administrations.

By a faction, I understand a number of citizens, whether amounting to a majority or minority of the whole, who are united and actuated by some common impulse of passion, or of interest, adverse to the rights of other citizens, or to the permanent and aggregate interests of the community.

There are two methods of curing the mischiefs of faction: The one, by removing its causes; the other, by controlling its effects.

There are again two methods of removing the causes of faction: The one, by destroying the liberty which is essential to its existence; the other, by giving to every citizen the same opinions, the same passions, and the same interests.

It could never be more truly said, than of the first remedy, that it was worse than the disease. Liberty is to faction what air is to fire, an aliment without which it instantly expires. But it could not be a less folly to abolish liberty, which is essential to political life, because it nourishes faction, than it would be to wish the annihilation of air, which is essential to animal life, because it imparts to fire its destructive agency.

The second expedient is as impracticable, as the first would be unwise. As long as the reason of man continues fallible, and he is at liberty to exercise it, different opinions will be formed. As long as the connection subsists between his reason and his self-love, his opinions and his passions will have a reciprocal influence on each other; and the former will be objects to which the latter will attach themselves. The diversity in the faculties of men, from which the rights of property originate, is not less an insuperable obstacle to a uniformity of interests. The protection of these faculties is the first object of government. From the protection of different and unequal faculties of acquiring property, the possession of different degrees and kinds of property immediately results; and from the influence of these on the sentiments and views of the respective proprietors, ensues a division of the society into different interests and parties.

The latent causes of action are thus sown in the nature of man; and we see them everywhere brought into different degrees of activity, according to the different circumstances of civil society. A zeal for different opinions concerning religion, concerning government, and many other points, as well as of speculation as of practice; an attachment to different leaders ambitiously contending for preeminence and power; or to persons of other descriptions whose fortunes have been interesting to the human passions, have, in turn, divided mankind into parties, inflamed them with mutual animosity, and rendered them much more disposed to vex and oppress each other, than to cooperate for their common good. So strong is this propensity of mankind, to fall into mutual animosities, that where no substantial occasion presents itself, the most frivolous and fanciful distinctions have been sufficient to kindle their unfriendly passions and excite their most violent conflicts. But the most common and durable source of factions, has been the various and unequal distribution of property. Those who hold, and those who are without property, have ever formed distinct interests in society. Those who are creditors, and those who are debtors, fall under a like discrimination. A landed interest, a manufacturing interest, a mercantile interest, a moneyed interest, with many lesser interests, grow up of necessity in civilized nations, and divide them into different classes, actuated by different sentiments and views. The regulation of these various and interfering interests forms the principal task of modern legislation, and involves the spirit of the party and faction in the necessary and ordinary operations of government.

No man is allowed to be a judge in his own cause; because his interest will certainly bias his judgment, and, not improbably, corrupt his integrity. With equal, nay, with greater reason, a body of men are unfit to be both judges and parties at the same time; yet what are many of the most important acts of legislation, but so many judicial determinations, not indeed concerning the right of single persons, but concerning the rights of large bodies of citizens? And what are the different classes of legislators, but advocates and parties to the causes which they determine? Is a law proposed concerning private debts? It is a question to which the creditors are parties on one side, and the debtors on the other. Justice ought to hold the balance between them. Yet the parties are, and must be, themselves the judges; and the most numerous party, or, in other words, the most powerful faction, must be expected to prevail. Shall domestic manufactures be encouraged, and in what degree, by restrictions on foreign manufactures? are questions which would be differently decided by the landed and the manufacturing classes; and probably by neither with a sole regard to justice and the public good. The apportionment of taxes, on the various descriptions of property, is an act which seems to require the most exact impartiality; yet there is, perhaps, no legislative act, in which greater opportunity and temptation are given to a predominant party to trample on the rules of justice. Every shilling, with which they overburden the inferior number, is a shilling saved to their own pockets.

It is in vain to say, that enlightened statesmen will be able to adjust these clashing interests, and render them all subservient to the public good. Enlightened statesmen will not always be at the helm: nor, in many cases, can such an adjustment be made at all, without taking into view indirect and remote considerations, which will rarely prevail over the immediate interest which one party may find in disregarding the rights of another, or the good of the whole.

The inference to which we are brought is, that the *causes* of faction cannot be removed; and that relief is only to be sought in the means of controlling its *effects*.

If a faction consists of less than a majority, relief is supplied by the republican principle, which enables the majority to defeat its sinister views, by regular vote. It may clog the administration, it may convulse the society; but it will be unable to execute and mask its violence under the forms of the Constitution. When a majority is included in a faction, the form of popular government, on the other hand, enables it to sacrifice to its ruling passion or interest, both the public good and the rights of other citizens. To secure the public good, and private rights, against the danger of such a faction, and at the same time to preserve the spirit and the form of popular government, is then the great object to which our inquiries are directed. Let me add, that it is the great desideratum, by which alone this form of government can be rescued from the opprobrium under which it has so long laboured, and be recommended to the esteem and adoption of mankind.

By what means is this object attainable? Evidently by one of two only. Either the existence of the same passion or interest in a majority, at the same time, must be prevented; or the majority, having such coexistent passion or interest, must be rendered, by their number and local situation, unable to concert and carry into effect schemes of oppression. If the impulse and the opportunity be suffered to coincide, we well know that neither moral nor religious motives can be relied on as an adequate control. They are not found to be such on the injustice and violence of individuals, and lose their efficacy in proportion to the number combined together; that is, in proportion as their efficacy becomes needful.

From this view of the subject, it may be concluded, that a pure democracy, by which I mean a society consisting of a small number of citizens, who assemble and administer the government in person, can admit of no cure for the mischiefs of faction. A common passion or interest will, in almost every case, be felt by a majority of the whole; a communication and concert, results from the form of government itself; and there

is nothing to check the inducements to sacrifice the weaker party, or an obnoxious individual. Hence, it is, that such democracies have ever been spectacles of turbulence and contention; have ever been found incompatible with personal security, or the rights of property; and have in general been as short in their lives, as they have been violent in their deaths. Theoretic politicians, who have patronized this species of government, have erroneously supposed, that by reducing mankind to a perfect equality in their political rights, they would, at the same time, be perfectly equalized and assimilated in their possessions, their opinions, and their passions.

A republic, by which I mean a government in which the scheme of representation takes place, opens a different prospect, and promises the cure for which we are seeking. Let us examine the points in which it varies from pure democracy, and we shall comprehend both the nature of the cure and the efficacy which it must derive from the union.

The two great points of difference, between a democracy and a republic, are, first, the delegation of the government, in the latter, to a small number of citizens, elected by the rest; secondly, the greatest number of citizens, and greater sphere of country, over which the latter may be extended.

The effect of the first difference is, on the one hand, to refine and enlarge the public views, by passing them through the medium of a chosen body of citizens, whose wisdom may best discern the true interest of their country, and whose patriotism and love of justice, will be least likely to sacrifice it to temporary or partial considerations. Under such a regulation, it may well happen, that the public voice, pronounced by the representatives of the people, will be more consonant to the public good, than if pronounced by the people themselves, convened for the purpose. On the other hand the effect may be inverted. Men of factious tempers, of local prejudices, or of sinister designs, may by intrigue, by corruption, or by other means, first obtain the suffrages, and then betray the interest of the people. The question resulting is, whether small or extensive republics are most favourable to the election of proper guardians of the public weal; and it is clearly decided in favour of the latter by two obvious considerations.

In the first place, it is to be remarked that, however small the republic may be, the representatives must be raised to a certain number, in order to guard against the cabals of a few; and that however large it may be, they must be limited to a certain number, in order to guard against the confusion of a multitude. Hence, the number of representatives in the two cases not being in proportion to that of the constituents, and being proportionally greatest in the small republic, it follows, that if the proportion of fit characters be not less in the large than in the small republic, the former will present a greater option, and consequently a greater probability of a fit choice.

In the next place, as each representative will be chosen by a greater number of citizens in the large than in the small republic, it will be more difficult for unworthy candidates to practise with success the vicious arts, by which elections are too often carried; and the suffrages of the people being more free, will be more likely to centre on men who possess the most attractive merit, and the most diffusive and established characters.

It must be confessed, that in this, as in most other cases, there is a mean, on both sides of which inconveniences will be found to lie. By enlarging too much the number of electors, you render the representative too little acquainted with all their local circumstances and lesser interests; as by reducing it too much, you render him unduly attached to these, and too little fit to comprehend and pursue great and national objects. The federal Constitution forms a happy combination in this respect; the great and aggregate interests being referred to the national, the local and particular, to the state legislatures.

The other point of difference is, the greater number of citizens, and extent of territory, which may be brought within the compass of republican, than of democratic government; and it is this circumstance principally which renders factious combinations less to be dreaded in the former, than in the latter. The smaller the society, the fewer probably will be the distinct parties and interests composing it; the fewer the distinct parties and interests, the more frequently will a majority be found of the same party; and the smaller the number of individuals composing a majority, and the smaller the compass within which they are placed, the more easily will they concert and execute their plans of oppression. Extend the sphere, and you take in a greater variety of parties and interests; you make it less probable that a majority of the whole will have a common motive to invade the rights of other citizens; or if such a common motive exists, it will be more difficult for all who feel it to discover their own strength, and to act in unison with each other. Besides other impediments, it may be remarked, that where there is a consciousness of unjust or dishonourable purposes, communication is always checked by distrust, in proportion to the number whose concurrence is necessary.

Hence, it clearly appears, that the same advantage, which a republic has over a democracy, in controlling the effects of faction, is enjoyed by a large over a small republic,— is enjoyed by the union over the states composing it. Does this advantage consist in the substitution of representatives, whose enlightened views and virtuous sentiments render them superior to local prejudices, and to schemes of injustice? It will not be denied that the representation of the union will be most likely to possess these requisite endowments. Does it consist in the greater security afforded by a greater variety of parties, against the event of any one party being able to outnumber and oppress the rest? In an equal degree does the increased variety of parties, comprised within the union, increase this security? Does it, in fine, consist in the greater obstacles opposed to the concert and accomplishment of the secret wishes of an unjust and interested majority? Here, again, the extent of the union gives it the most palpable advantage.

The influence of factious leaders may kindle a flame within their particular states, but will be unable to spread a general conflagration through the other states; a religious sect may degenerate into a political faction in a part of the confederacy; but the variety of sects dispersed over the entire face of it, must secure the national councils against any danger from that source: a rage for paper money, for an abolition of debts, for an equal division of property, or for any other improper or wicked project, will be less apt to pervade the whole body of the union than a particular member of it; in the same proportion as such a malady is more likely to taint a particular county or district, than an entire state.

In the extent and proper structure of the union, therefore, we behold a republican remedy for the diseases most incident to republican government. And according to the degree of pleasure and pride we feel in being republicans, ought to be our zeal in cherishing the spirit, and supporting the character of federalists.

FEDERALIST NO. 51 [1788], JAMES MADISON

To the People of the State of New York: To what expedient then shall we finally resort for maintaining in practice the necessary partition of power among the several departments, as laid down in the constitution? The only answer that can be given is, that as all these exterior provisions are found to be inadequate, the defect must be supplied, by so contriving the interior structure of the government, as that its several constituent parts may, by their mutual relations, be the means of keeping each other in their proper places. Without presuming to undertake a full development of this important idea, I will hazard a few general observations, which may perhaps place it in a clearer light, and enable us to form a more correct judgment of the principles and structure of the government planned by the convention.

In order to lay a due foundation for that separate and distinct exercise of the different powers of government, which to a certain extent, is admitted on all hands to be essential to the preservation of liberty, it is evident that each department should have a will of its own; and consequently should be constituted, that the members of each should have as little agency as possible in the appointment of the members of the others. Were this principle rigorously adhered to, it would require that all the appointments for the supreme executive, legislative, and judiciary magistracies, should be drawn from the same fountain of authority, the people, through channels, having no communication whatever with one another. Perhaps such a plan of constructing the several departments would be less difficult in practice than it may in contemplation appear. Some difficulties however, and some additional expense, would attend the execution of it. Some deviations therefore from the principle must be admitted. In the constitution of the judiciary department in particular, it might be inexpedient to insist rigorously on the principle; first, because peculiar qualifications being essential in the members, the primary consideration ought to be to select that mode of choice, which best secures these qualifications; secondly, because the permanent tenure by which the appointments are held in that department, must soon destroy all sense of dependence on the authority conferring them.

It is equally evident that the members of each department should be as little dependent as possible on those of the others, for the emoluments annexed to their offices. Were the executive magistrate, or the judges, not independent of the legislature in this particular, their independence in every other would be merely nominal.

But the great security against a gradual concentration of the several powers in the same department, consists in giving to those who administer each department, the necessary constitutional means, and personal motives, to resist encroachments of the others. The provision for defense must in this, as in all other cases, be made commensurate to the danger of attack. Ambition must be made to counteract ambition. The interest of the man must be connected with the constitutional rights of the place. It may be a reflection on human nature, that such devices should be necessary to control the abuses of government: But what is government itself but the greatest of all reflections on human nature? If men were angels, no government would be necessary. If angels were to govern men, neither external nor internal controls on government would be necessary. In framing a government which is to be administered by men over men, the great difficulty lies in this: You must first enable the government to control the governed; and in the next place, oblige it to control itself. A dependence on the people is no doubt the primary control on the government; but experience has taught mankind the necessity of auxiliary precautions.

This policy of supplying by opposite and rival interests, the defect of better motives, might be traced through the whole system of human affairs, private as well as public. We see it particularly displayed in all the subordinate distributions of power; where the constant aim is to divide and arrange the several offices in such a manner as that each may be a check on the other; that the private interest of every individual, may be a sentinel over the public rights. These inventions of prudence cannot be less requisite in the distribution of the supreme powers of the state.

But it is not possible to give to each department an equal power of self defense. In republican government the legislative authority, necessarily, predominates. The remedy for this inconveniency is, to divide the legislature into different branches; and to render them by different modes of election, and different principles of action, as little connected with each other, as the nature of their common functions, and their common dependence on the society, will admit. It may even be necessary to guard against dangerous encroachments by still further precautions. As the weight of the legislative authority requires that it should be thus divided, the weakness of the executive may require, on the other hand, that it should be fortified. An absolute negative, on the legislature, appears at first view to be the natural defense with which the executive magistrate should be armed. But perhaps it would be neither altogether safe, nor alone sufficient. On ordinary occasions, it might not be exerted with the requisite firmness; and on extraordinary occasions, it might be perfidiously abused. May not this defect of an absolute negative be supplied, by some qualified connection between this weaker department, and the weaker branch of the stronger department, by which the latter may be led to support the constitutional rights of the former, without being too much detached from the rights of its own department?

If the principles on which these observations are founded be just, as I persuade myself they are, and they be applied as a criterion, to the several state constitutions, and to the federal Constitution, it will be found, that if the latter does not perfectly correspond with them, the former are infinitely less able to bear such a test.

There are moreover two considerations particularly applicable to the federal system of America, which place that system in a very interesting point of view.

First. In a single republic, all the power surrendered by the people, is submitted to the administration of a single government; and usurpations are guarded against by a division of the government into distinct and separate departments. In the compound republic of America, the power surrendered by the people, is first divided between two distinct governments, and then the portion allotted to each, subdivided among distinct and separate departments. Hence a double security arises to the rights of the people. The different governments will control each other; at the same time that each will be controlled by itself.

Second. It is of great importance in a republic, not only to guard the society against the oppression of its rulers; but to guard one part of the society against the injustice of the other part. Different interests necessarily exist in different classes of citizens. If a majority be united by a common interest, the rights of the minority will be insecure. There are but two methods of providing against this evil: The one by creating a will in the community independent of the majority, that is, of the society itself; the other by comprehending in the society so many separate descriptions of citizens, as will render an unjust combination of a majority of the whole, very improbable, if not impracticable. The first method prevails in all governments possessing an hereditary or self appointed authority. This at best is but a precarious security; because a power independent of the society may as well espouse the unjust views of the major, as the rightful interests, of the minor party, and may possibly be turned against both parties. The second method will be exemplified in the federal republic of the United States. While all authority in it will be derived from and dependent on the society, the society itself will be broken into so many parts, interests and classes of citizens, that the rights of individuals or of the minority, will be in little danger from interested combinations of the majority. In a free government, the security for civil rights must be the same as that for religious rights. It consists in the one case in the multiplicity of interests, and in the other in the multiplicity of sects. The degree of security in both cases will depend on the number of interests and sects; and this may be presumed to depend on the extent of country and number of people comprehended under the same government. This view of the subject must particularly recommend a proper federal system to all the sincere and considerate friends of republican government: Since it shows that in exact proportion as the territory of the union may be formed into more circumscribed confederacies or states, oppressive combinations of a majority will be facilitated; the best security under the republican form, for the rights of every class of citizens, will be diminished; and consequently, the stability and independence of some member of the government, the only other security, must be proportionally increased. Justice is the end of government. It is the end of civil society. It ever has been, and ever will be pursued, until it be obtained, or until liberty be lost in the pursuit. In a society under the forms of which the stronger faction can readily unite and oppress the weaker, anarchy may as truly be said to reign, as in a state of nature where the weaker individual is not secured against the violence of the stronger: And as in the latter state even the stronger individuals are prompted by the uncertainty of their condition, to submit to a government which may protect the weak as well as themselves: So in the former state, will the more powerful factions or parties be gradually induced by a like motive, to wish for a government which will protect all parties, the weaker as well as the more powerful. It can be little doubted, that if the state of Rhode Island was separated from the confederacy, and left to itself, the insecurity of rights under the popular form of government within such narrow limits, would be displayed by such reiterated oppressions of factious majorities, that some power altogether independent of the people would soon be called for by the voice of the very factions whose misrule had proved the necessity of it. In the extended republic of the United States, and among the great variety of interests, parties and sects which it embraces, a coalition of a majority of the whole society could seldom take place on any other principles than those of justice and the general good; and there being thus less danger to a minor from the will of the major party, there must be less pretext also, to provide for the security of the former, by introducing into the government a will not dependent on the latter; or in other words, a will independent of the society itself. It is no less certain than it is important, notwithstanding the contrary opinions which have been entertained, that the larger the society, provided it lie within a practicable sphere, the more duly capable it will be of self government. And happily for the *republican cause,* the practicable sphere may be carried to a very great extent, by a judicious modification and mixture of the *federal principle.*

PRESIDENTS AND CONGRESSES, 1789–1995

TERM	PRESIDENT AND VICE PRESIDENT	PARTY OF PRESIDENT	CONGRESS	MAJORITY PARTY	
				HOUSE	SENATE
1789–97	**George Washington** John Adams	None	1st 2d 3d 4th	N/A N/A N/A N/A	N/A N/A N/A N/A
1797–1801	**John Adams** Thomas Jefferson	Fed	5th 6th	N/A Fed	N/A Fed
1801–09	**Thomas Jefferson** Aaron Burr (1801–5) George Clinton (1805–9)	Dem Rep	7th 8th 9th 10th	Dem Rep Dem Rep Dem Rep Dem Rep	Dem Rep Dem Rep Dem Rep Dem Rep
1809–17	**James Madison** George Clinton (1809–12)[1] Elbridge Gerry (1813–14)[1]	Dem Rep	11th 12th 13th 14th	Dem Rep Dem Rep Dem Rep Dem Rep	Dem Rep Dem Rep Dem Rep Dem Rep
1817–25	**James Monroe** Daniel D. Tompkins	Dem Rep	15th 16th 17th 18th	Dem Rep Dem Rep Dem Rep Dem Rep	Dem Rep Dem Rep Dem Rep Dem Rep
1825–29	**John Quincy Adams** John C. Calhoun	Nat'l Rep	19th 20th	Nat'l Rep Dem	Nat'l Rep Dem
1829–37	**Andrew Jackson** John C. Calhoun (1829–32)[2] Martin Van Buren (1833–37)	Dem	21st 22d 23d 24th	Dem Dem Dem Dem	Dem Dem Dem Dem
1837–41	**Martin Van Buren** Richard M. Johnson	Dem	25th 26th	Dem Dem	Dem Dem
1841	**William H. Harrison**[1] John Tyler (1841)	Whig			
1841–45	**John Tyler** (VP vacant)	Whig	27th 28th	Whig Dem	Whig Whig
1845–49	**James K. Polk** George M. Dallas	Dem	29th 30th	Dem Whig	Dem Dem
1849–50	**Zachary Taylor**[1] Millard Fillmore	Whig	31st	Dem	Dem
1850–53	**Millard Fillmore** (VP vacant)	Whig	32d	Dem	Dem
1853–57	**Franklin Pierce** William R. D. King (1853)[1]	Dem	33d 34th	Dem Rep	Dem Dem
1857–61	**James Buchanan** John C. Breckinridge	Dem	35th 36th	Dem Rep	Dem Dem
1861–65	**Abraham Lincoln**[1] Hannibal Hamlin (1861–65) Andrew Johnson (1865)	Rep	37th 38th 38th	Rep Rep Rep	Rep Rep Rep

				MAJORITY PARTY	
TERM	PRESIDENT AND VICE PRESIDENT	PARTY OF PRESIDENT	CONGRESS	HOUSE	SENATE
1865–69	**Andrew Johnson** (VP vacant)	Rep	39th 40th	Union Rep	Union Rep
1869–77	**Ulysses S. Grant** Schuyler Colfax (1869–73) Henry Wilson (1873–75)[1]	Rep	41st 42d 43d 44th	Rep Rep Rep Dem	Rep Rep Rep Rep
1877–81	**Rutherford B. Hayes** William A. Wheeler	Rep	45th 46th	Dem Dem	Rep Dem
1881	**James A. Garfield**[1] Chester A. Arthur	Rep	47th	Rep	Rep
1881–85	**Chester A. Arthur** (VP vacant)	Rep	48th	Dem	Rep
1885–89	**Grover Cleveland** Thomas A. Hendricks (1885)[1]	Dem	49th 50th	Dem Dem	Rep Rep
1889–93	**Benjamin Harrison** Levi P. Morton	Rep	51st 52d	Rep Dem	Rep Rep
1893–97	**Grover Cleveland** Adlai E. Stevenson	Dem	53d 54th	Dem Rep	Dem Rep
1897–1901	**William McKinley**[1] Garret A. Hobart (1897–99)[1] Theodore Roosevelt (1901)	Rep	55th 56th	Rep Rep	Rep Rep
1901–09	**Theodore Roosevelt** (VP vacant, 1901–5) Charles W. Fairbanks (1905–9)	Rep	57th 58th 59th 60th	Rep Rep Rep Rep	Rep Rep Rep Rep
1909–13	**William Howard Taft** James S. Sherman (1909–12)[1]	Rep	61st 62d	Rep Dem	Rep Rep
1913–21	**Woodrow Wilson** Thomas R. Marshall	Dem	63d 64th 65th 66th	Dem Dem Dem Rep	Dem Dem Dem Rep
1921–23	**Warren G. Harding**[1] Calvin Coolidge	Rep	67th	Rep	Rep
1923–29	**Calvin Coolidge** (VP vacant, 1923–25) Charles G. Dawes (1925–29)	Rep	68th 69th 70th	Rep Rep Rep	Rep Rep Rep
1929–33	**Herbert Hoover** Charles Curtis	Rep	71st 72d	Rep Dem	Rep Rep
1933–45	**Franklin D. Roosevelt**[1] John N. Garner (1933–41) Henry A. Wallace (1941–45) Harry S. Truman (1945)	Dem	73d 74th 75th 76th 77th 78th	Dem Dem Dem Dem Dem Dem	Dem Dem Dem Dem Dem Dem
1945–53	**Harry S. Truman** (VP vacant, 1945–49) Alben W. Barkley (1949–53)	Dem	79th 80th 81st 82d	Dem Rep Dem Dem	Dem Rep Dem Dem

| TERM | PRESIDENT AND VICE PRESIDENT | PARTY OF PRESIDENT | CONGRESS | MAJORITY PARTY | |
				HOUSE	SENATE
1953–61	**Dwight D. Eisenhower** Richard M. Nixon	Rep	83d 84th 85th 86th	Rep Dem Dem Dem	Rep Dem Dem Dem
1961–63	**John F. Kennedy**[1] Lyndon B. Johnson (1961–63)	Dem	87th	Dem	Dem
1963–69	**Lyndon B. Johnson** (VP vacant, 1963–65) Hubert H. Humphrey (1965–69)	Dem	88th 89th 90th	Dem Dem Dem	Dem Dem Dem
1969–74	**Richard M. Nixon**[3] Spiro T. Agnew (1969–73)[2] Gerald R. Ford (1973–74)[4]	Rep	91st 92d	Dem Dem	Dem Dem
1974–77	**Gerald R. Ford** Nelson A. Rockefeller[4]	Rep	93d 94th	Dem Dem	Dem Dem
1977–81	**Jimmy Carter** Walter Mondale	Dem	95th 96th	Dem Dem	Dem Dem
1981–89	**Ronald Reagan** George Bush	Rep	97th 98th 99th 100th	Dem Dem Dem Dem	Rep Rep Rep Dem
1989–93	**George Bush** J. Danforth Quayle	Rep	101st 102d	Dem Dem	Dem Dem
1993–	**William J. Clinton** Albert Gore, Jr.	Dem	103d 104th	Dem Rep	Dem Rep

[1]Died in office.
[2]Resigned from the vice presidency.
[3]Resigned from the presidency.
[4]Appointed vice president.

JUSTICES OF THE U.S. SUPREME COURT, 1789–1995

JUSTICE	APPOINTING PRESIDENT	YEARS OF SERVICE
John Jay	Washington	1789–95
John Rutledge	Washington	1789–91
William Cushing	Washington	1789–1810
James Wilson	Washington	1789–98
John Blair, Jr.	Washington	1789–96
James Iredell	Washington	1790–99
Thomas Johnson	Washington	1791–93
William Paterson	Washington	1793–1806
John Rutledge	Washington	1795
Samuel Chase	Washington	1796–1811
Oliver Ellsworth	Washington	1796–1800
Bushrod Washington	J. Adams	1798–1829
Alfred Moore	J. Adams	1799–1804
John Marshall	J. Adams	1801–35
William Johnson	Jefferson	1804–34
Henry B. Livingston	Jefferson	1806–23
Thomas Todd	Jefferson	1807–26
Gabriel Duval	Madison	1811–35
Joseph Story	Madison	1811–45
Smith Thompson	Monroe	1823–43
Robert Trimble	J. Q. Adams	1826–28
John McLean	Jackson	1829–61
Henry Baldwin	Jackson	1830–44
James M. Wayne	Jackson	1835–67
Roger B. Taney	Jackson	1836–64
Philip P. Barbour	Jackson	1836–41
John Catron	Van Buren	1837–65
John McKinley	Van Buren	1837–52
Peter V. Daniel	Van Buren	1841–60
Samuel Nelson	Tyler	1845–72
Levi Woodbury	Polk	1846–51
Robert C. Grier	Polk	1845–70
Benjamin R. Curtis	Fillmore	1851–57
John A. Campbell	Pierce	1853–61
Nathan Clifford	Buchanan	1858–81
Noah H. Swayne	Lincoln	1862–81
Samuel F. Miller	Lincoln	1862–90
David Davis	Lincoln	1862–77
Stephen J. Field	Lincoln	1863–97
Salmon P. Chase	Lincoln	1864–73
William Strong	Grant	1870–80
Joseph P. Bradley	Grant	1870–92
Ward Hunt	Grant	1872–82
Morrison R. Waite	Grant	1874–88
John M. Harlan	Hayes	1877–1911
William B. Woods	Hayes	1880–87

JUSTICE	APPOINTING PRESIDENT	YEARS OF SERVICE
Stanley Matthews	Garfield	1881–89
Horace Gray	Arthur	1881–1902
Samuel Blatchford	Arthur	1882–93
Lucius Q. C. Lamar	Cleveland	1888–93
Melville W. Fuller	Cleveland	1888–1910
David J. Brewer	Harrison	1889–1910
Henry B. Brown	Harrison	1890–1906
George Shiras, Jr.	Harrison	1892–1903
Howell E. Jackson	Harrison	1893–95
Edward D. White	Cleveland	1894–1910
Rufus W. Peckham	Cleveland	1895–1909
Joseph McKenna	McKinley	1898–1925
Oliver W. Holmes, Jr.	T. Roosevelt	1902–32
William R. Day	T. Roosevelt	1903–22
William H. Moody	T. Roosevelt	1906–10
Horace H. Lurton	Taft	1909–14
Charles E. Hughes	Taft	1910–16
Edward D. White	Taft	1910–21
Willis Van Devanter	Taft	1910–37
Joseph R. Lamar	Taft	1910–16
Mahlon Pitney	Taft	1912–22
James C. McReynolds	Wilson	1914–41
Louis D. Brandeis	Wilson	1916–39
John H. Clarke	Wilson	1916–22
William H. Taft	Harding	1921–30
George Sutherland	Harding	1922–38
Pierce Butler	Harding	1922–39
Edward T. Sanford	Harding	1923–30
Harlan F. Stone	Coolidge	1925–41
Charles E. Hughes	Hoover	1930–41
Owen J. Roberts	Hoover	1930–45
Benjamin N. Cardozo	Hoover	1932–38
Hugo Black	F. Roosevelt	1937–71
Stanley F. Reed	F. Roosevelt	1938–57
Felix Frankfurter	F. Roosevelt	1939–62
William O. Douglas	F. Roosevelt	1939–75
Frank Murphy	F. Roosevelt	1940–49
James F. Byrnes	F. Roosevelt	1941–42
Harlan F. Stone	F. Roosevelt	1941–46
Robert H. Jackson	F. Roosevelt	1941–54
Wiley B. Rutledge	F. Roosevelt	1943–49
Harold H. Burton	Truman	1945–58
Fred M. Vinson	Truman	1946–53
Tom C. Clark	Truman	1949–67
Sherman Minton	Truman	1949–56
Earl Warren	Eisenhower	1953–69
John M. Harlan	Eisenhower	1955–71
William J. Brennan, Jr.	Eisenhower	1956–90
Charles E. Whittaker	Eisenhower	1957–62

JUSTICE	APPOINTING PRESIDENT	YEARS OF SERVICE
Potter Stewart	Eisenhower	1958–81
Byron R. White	Kennedy	1962–93
Arthur J. Goldberg	Kennedy	1962–65
Abe Fortas	Johnson	1965–69
Thurgood Marshall	Johnson	1967–91
Warren E. Burger	Nixon	1969–86
Harry A. Blackmun	Nixon	1970–94
Lewis F. Powell, Jr.	Nixon	1972–87
William H. Rehnquist	Nixon	1972–86
John Paul Stevens	Ford	1975–
Sandra Day O'Connor	Reagan	1981–
William H. Rehnquist	Reagan	1986–
Antonin Scalia	Reagan	1986–
Anthony M. Kennedy	Reagan	1988–
David H. Souter	Bush	1990–
Clarence Thomas	Bush	1991–
Ruth Bader Ginsburg	Clinton	1993–
Stephen G. Breyer	Clinton	1994–

Bold type indicates chief justice.

actual groups Interest groups that have already been formed; they have headquarters, an organizational structure, paid employees, membership lists, and the like.

administration Performance of routine tasks associated with a specific policy goal; bureaucrats exercise a lot less administrative discretion at this stage.

administrative discretion The latitude that an agency, or even a single bureaucrat, has in interpreting and applying a law.

affirmative action Programs that attempt to improve the chances of minority applicants for jobs, housing, employment, or graduate admissions by giving them a "boost" relative to white applicants with roughly the same qualifications.

amicus curiae briefs Legal briefs that enable groups or individuals, including the national government, who are not parties to the litigation but have an interest in it, to attempt to influence the outcome of the case; literally, "friend of the court" briefs.

Anti-Federalists Strong states' rights advocates that organized in opposition to the ratification of the U.S. Constitution prior to its adoption.

appellate court The court that reviews an appeal of the proceedings of the trial court, often with a multijudge panel and without a jury; it considers only matters of law.

appellate jurisdiction The authority of a court to hear a case on appeal after it has been argued in and decided by a lower federal or state court.

appointment power The president's power to name some three thousand agency officials, of whom about seven hundred are in policymaking positions, such as cabinet and subcabinet officials and bureau chiefs.

appropriation bill A separate bill that must be passed by Congress to fund measures that require spending.

Articles of Confederation The first constitutional framework of the new United States of America. Approved in 1777 by the Second Continental Congress, it was later replaced by the current Constitution due to problems inherent in strong decentralization.

authoritarian regime An oppressive system of government in which citizens are deprived of their basic freedom to speak, write, associate, and participate in political life without fear of punishment.

bicameral legislature A legislative system consisting of two houses or chambers.

Bill of Rights The first ten amendments to the Constitution added in 1781.

bipolarity The fundamental division of economic and military power between the poles of western capitalism and eastern communism.

block grants A federal grant that provides money to states for general program funding with few strings attached.

Boston Massacre A 1770 incident in which British soldiers fired a volley of shots into a crowd of hecklers who had been throwing snowballs at the redcoats; five colonists were killed, including their leader, Crispus Attucks.

Boston Tea Party A 1773 act of civil disobedience in which colonists dressed as Native Americans dumped 342 chests of tea into Boston Harbor to protest increased taxes.

boycott Refusal to patronize any organization that practices policies that are perceived to be unfair for political, economic, or ideological reasons.

briefs Written arguments to the court outlining not only the facts and legal and constitutional issues in a court case, but also answering all of the anticipated arguments of the opposing side.

bureaucracy A large and complex organizational system in which tasks, roles, and responsibilities are structured to achieve a goal.

bureaucrats People who work in a bureaucracy, not only the obscure, faceless clerks normally disparaged by critics of government but also "street-level bureaucrats" such as police officers, social workers, and school teachers.

cabinet Group of presidential advisors including secretaries of the major departments of the bureaucracy and any other officials the president designates.

cabinet departments Major administrative units whose heads are presidential advisors appointed by the president and confirmed by the Senate. They are responsible for conducting a broad range of government operations.

casework Favors done as a service for constituents by those they have elected to Congress.

categorical grant The most common type of federal grant, given for specific purposes, usually with strict rules attached.

caucus Meeting of party adherents who gather to discuss, to deliberate, and finally to give their support to a candidate for president. They then select delegates who will represent their choices at higher-level party meetings; eventually, their votes get reflected at the national convention itself. Also means a conference of party members in Congress.

Central Intelligence Agency (CIA) The dominant force in the intelligence community. It was established after World War II to be the president's nonpartisan resource for coordinated intelligence analysis, but its mission quickly expanded to include covert operations such as espionage, psychological warfare, paramilitary maneuvers, and political and economic intervention.

checks and balances Systems that ensure that for every power in government there is an equal and opposite power placed in a separate branch to restrain that force.

chief of staff The president's top aide.

civil cases Non-criminal cases in which courts resolve disputes among individuals and parties to the case over finances, property, or personal well-being.

civil disobedience Breaking the law in a nonviolent fashion and being willing to suffer the consequences, even to the point of going to jail, in order to publicly demonstrate that the law is unjust.

civil government A type of government in which citizens agree to abide by the laws made by the leaders of their choosing.

civil liberties The individual rights that are guaranteed to every citizen in the Bill of Rights and the due process clause of the Fourteenth Amendment, including freedom of speech and religion.

civil rights The constitutionally guaranteed rights that may not be arbitrarily removed by the government. Among these rights are the right to vote and equal protection under the law.

civil service A system of hiring and promoting employees based on professional merit, not party loyalty.

class action suit A single civil case in which the plaintiff represents the whole class of individuals similarly situated and the Court's results apply to this entire class.

clear and present danger test Test that is applied to determine whether free speech may be protected. The Supreme Court's ruling that if speech creates a "clear and present danger," e.g., falsely shouting "Fire!" in a crowded theater, it is not protected.

closed primary A system of conducting primary elections in which only citizens registered as members of a particular political party may participate in that party's primary.

cloture A procedure through which a vote of 60 senators can vote to limit debate and stop a filibuster.

coattails effect "Riding the president's coattails into office"; occurs in an election when voters also elect representatives or senators of a successful presidential candidate's party.

Cold War The bipolar power struggle between the United States and the U.S.S.R. that began in the 1950s and ending in the 1990s.

collective action The political action of individuals who unite to influence policy.

Committees of Correspondence Formed in Boston in 1772, the first institutionalized mechanism for communication within and between the colonies and foreign countries.

Common Sense Thomas Paine's pamphlet of January 1776, which helped crystallize the idea of revolution for the colonists.

compact A type of agreement that legally binds two or more parties to enforceable rules.

Compromise of 1850 Group of acts passed in 1850 that allowed new territories to decide upon their own slave or free status. One of the issues that led to the Civil War.

concurrent powers Powers that are shared by both national and state levels of government.

concurring opinion A written opinion of a justice who agrees with the majority decision of the Court but differs on the reasoning.

confederation A league of sovereign states that delegates powers on selected issues to a central government.

conference committees Committees that reconcile differences between the versions of a bill passed by the House and the Senate.

congressional agenda A list of bills to be considered by Congress.

conservatives A person who opposes government intervention to minimize economic inequality, but supports government actions that restrict cultural and social freedoms. see Table 9.2, p. 315, for more detail.

constitutional courts Courts mentioned in Article III of the Constitution whose judges are life-tenured.

constructionist A view of presidential power espoused by William Howard Taft, who believed that the president could exercise no power unless it could be traced to or implied from an express grant in either the Constitution or an act of Congress.

containment A term coined in 1946 by George Kennan, who believed that Soviet "aggression" must be "contained by the adroit and vigilant application of counterforce" by the United States.

contingency election An election held in the House if no candidate receives the required majority in the Electoral College.

cooperative federalism A cooperative system in which solutions for various state and local problems are directed and sometimes funded by both the national and state governments. The administration of programs is characterized by shared power and shared responsibility.

council of revision A combined body of judges and members of the executive branch having a limited veto over national legislation and an absolute veto over state legislation.

creative federalism An initiative that expanded the concept of the partnership between the national government and the states under Lyndon Johnson in the 1960s.

criminal cases Cases in which decisions are made regarding whether or not to punish individuals accused of violating the state or federal criminal code.

culture theory A theory that individual preferences "emerge from social interaction in defending or opposing different ways of life."

de facto equality Equality of results which measure whether real world obstacles to equal treatment exist. Some examples are: Do people actually live where they want to? Do they work under similar conditions? etc.

de jure equality Equality before the law requiring that there be no legally mandated obstacles to equal treatment, such as laws that prevent people from voting, living where they want to, or taking advantage of all the rights guaranteed to individuals by the laws of the federal, state, and local governments.

dealignment The moving away from partisanship.

Declaration of Independence A formal proclamation declaring independence, approved and signed on July 4, 1775.

delegated powers Powers that are expressly granted or enumerated in the Constitution and limited in nature.

delegates Congress members who feel bound to follow the wishes of a majority of their constituents; they make frequent efforts to learn the opinions of voters in their state or district.

democracy A system of government in which the people rule, either directly or through elected representatives.

Democratic Party Growing out of the Jacksonian wing of the Jeffersonian party, this was initially Jackson's party and the first really broad-based, popular party in the United States.

desegregation The elimination of laws and practices mandating separation of the races.

detente An attempt to relax the tensions between the U.S. and the U.S.S.R. through limited cooperation.

deviating election Election in which the minority party captures the White House because of short-term intervening forces, and thus there is a deviation from the expectation that power will remain in the hands of the dominant party.

direct democracy A type of government in which people govern themselves, vote on policies and laws, and live by majority rule.

discrimination Unequal treatment based on race, ethnicity, gender, and other distinctions.

dissenting opinion A written opinion of a justice who disagrees with the holding of the Court.

docket The Supreme Court's agenda.

dual federalism A system in which each level of power remains supreme in its own jurisdiction, thus keeping the states separate and distinct from the national government.

economic policy Policy aimed at producing a vibrant, healthy, and growing economy.

elastic clause Clause of the Constitution which grants Congress the power to "make all laws which shall be necessary and proper" to carry out all other powers specified in Article I Section 8.

elections The institutions that give people the opportunity to participate in public life.

Electoral College The group of 538 electors who meet separately in each of their states and the District of Columbia on the first Monday following the second Wednesday in the December after a national presidential election. Their majority decision officially elects the President and Vice-President in the United States.

electoral college system Votes in the national presidential elections are actually indirect votes for a slate of presidential electors pledged to each party's candidate. Each state gets one elector for each of its representatives and Senators. The winning slate of electors cast their votes in their state's capital after the public election. Election of the president and vice-president in the United States is dependent upon receiving a majority (270) of the votes cast in the electoral college.

emergency powers Far-reaching authority to impose on the property and people of the United States a number of demands and restrictions that might, in the absence of a recognized condition of national emergency, be seen as unconstitutional.

en banc Proceedings in which all of the appeals judges in a particular circuit serve as a tribunal.

enrolled act (or resolution) The final version of a bill, approved by both chambers of Congress.

entitlements Government-sponsored benefits and cash payments to those who meet eligibility requirements.

equality A state in which all participants have equal access to the decision-making process, equal opportunity to influence the decisions made, and equal responsibility for those decisions.

equality of opportunity The idea that "people should have equal rights and opportunities to develop their talents," that all people should begin at the same starting point in a race.

equality of result The idea that all forms of inequality, including economic disparities, should be completely eradicated; this may mean giving some people an advantage at the start so that everyone will complete the race at the same point.

exclusionary rule Rule whereby evidence that was gathered by illegal means, and any other evidence gathered as a result, cannot be used in later trials.

executive agreement A government-to-government agreement with essentially the same legal force as a treaty. However, it may be concluded entirely without the knowledge and/or approval of the Senate.

executive branch The branch of the government that executes laws.

Executive Office of the President (EOP) Created in 1939, all of the staff units that serve to support the president in his administrative duties.

express powers Powers delegated specifically to the national government by the Constitution.

factions According to James Madison in Federalist Paper number 10 it is: "A number of citizens, whether amounting to a majority or a minority of the whole, who are united and actuated by some common impulse or passion or . . . interests."

faithless elector Member of the electoral college who casts his or her vote for someone other than the state's popular vote-winner.

federal budget deficit The annual shortfall between the monies that government takes in and spends.

Federal Communications Commission (FCC) A government commission formed to allocate radio and TV frequencies and regulate broadcasting procedures.

federal mandate National requirement that must be observed.

federal matching funds System under which presidential candidates who raise a certain amount of money in the required way are able to apply for and are given a matching sum of money from the federal government.

Federal Reserve System Created in 1913 it is the nation's principal overseer of monetary policy.

federalism The relationship between the centralized national government and the individual state governments.

Federalists Those in favor of the Constitution, many of whom were nationalists at the Convention.

Federalist Party The party of the new Constitution and strong national government, it was the first American political party.

fighting words Certain expressions, such as calling a police officer "a goddamned racketeer" and "A damned fascist" which are deemed to incite injury and are therefore not protected under the First Amendment.

filibuster A technique that allows a senator to speak against a bill, or talk about nothing at all, just to "hold the floor" and prevent the Senate from moving forward with a vote. He or she may yield to other like-minded senators, so that the marathon debate can continue for hours or even days.

First Continental Congress The meeting of fifty-six elected members (from provincial congresses or irregular conventions) that took place in Philadelphia's Carpenter's Hall in 1774. It resulted in a resolution to oppose acts of the British Parliament and a plan of association for the colonies.

fiscal policy Government efforts to stabilize the economy through the power to tax and spend.

flat tax Tax with just one rate; everyone pays the same rate regardless of income level.

foreign policy Policy adopted and actions taken by the U.S. government on behalf of U.S. national interests abroad. The president is this country's chief foreign policy maker.

formal agenda The policies that are actually scheduled for debate and potential adoption by Congress, the President, the Supreme Court, or executive departments and agencies.

formal rules In a bureaucracy, clearly defined procedures governing the execution of all tasks within the jurisdiction of a given agency.

formula grant A grant based on a prescribed legislative formula to determine how money will be distributed to eligible governmental units (states or big cities).

formula/project grant A grant in which competitive grants are awarded, but also restricted by use of a formula.

franking privilege The free mailing of newsletters and political brochures to constituents by members of Congress.

free press Media characterized by the open reporting of information without censorship by the government.

free riders Members who do not invest money or time in an interest group but still share in the collective benefits of group action.

freedom A value which suggests that no individual should be within the power or under the control of another.

freedom riders Civil rights activists who traveled throughout the South on buses to test compliance with the Supreme Court's mandate to integrate bus terminals and public facilities accommodating interstate travelers.

gender gap A difference in the political opinions of men and women; see Table 9.1, p. 316, for more detail.

General Agreement on Tariffs and Trade (GATT) Multinational trade agreements that seek to increase international trade by lowering barriers.

general revenue sharing (GRS) A system of the New Federalism program in which money is given to the states with no restrictions on how it can be spent.

generational effect Part of socialization patterns of the public in which a generation of adults who grew up during a certain decade or period appears to have its own outlook, differentiating itself from the previous age.

gerrymander A term used to describe any attempt during state redistricting of congressional voting boundaries, to create a "safe" seat for one party (a district in which the number of registered voters of one party is large enough to guarantee a victory for that party's candidate).

globalism View in which the U.S. "sphere of influence" has expanded beyond the western hemisphere to include virtually every corner of the globe where U.S. interests might be affected.

going public Actions taken by presidents to promote themselves and their policies to the American people.

good-character test A requirement that those wishing to vote get two or more registered voters to vouch for their integrity.

government corporation A semi-independent government agency that administers a business enterprise and takes the form of a business corporation.

grant-in-aid Money paid to states and localities to induce them to implement policies in accordance with federally-mandated guidelines.

grass-roots activity The rallying of group members, as well as the public, behind a lobby's cause.

grassroots strategy Decentralized lobbying action by ordinary citizens.

Great Compromise (also called the Connecticut Compromise) A plan presented at the Constitutional Convention that upheld the large-state position for the House, its membership based on proportional representation, balanced by the small-state posture of equal representation in the Senate, where each state would have two votes.

gridlock A condition in which major government initiatives are impossible because a closely balanced partisan division in the government structure (e.g., one party controls the White House and the other controls Congress, or the two parties are evenly balanced) accompanied by an unwillingness to work together toward compromise produces a stalemate.

Hatch Act Approved by Congress in 1939, and named for its author, Senator Carl Hatch of New Mexico, a list of political do's and don'ts for federal employees; designed to prevent federal civil servants from using their power or position to engage in political activities to influence elections, thereby creating a nonpartisan, nonpolitical, professionalized bureaucracy.

hearings Formal proceedings in which a range of people testify on a bill's pros and cons.

heightened scrutiny test A middle-level standard that would force the state to prove more than just the "reasonableness" of a law, though not its "compelling" nature, in order to justify it. For women's rights cases this means proving the importance of the law's goals and linking it to the wording of the law.

hierarchy A clear chain of communication and command running from an executive director at the top down through all levels of workers.

House majority leader The person elected by the majority party caucus who serves as the party's chief strategist and floor spokesperson.

hyper-pluralism The rapid proliferation of interest groups, all competing for influence over policy, in which excessive and conflicting demands could be made on public officials.

implementation The act of providing the organization and expertise required to put into action any policy that has become law. Also refers to the actual execution of a policy.

implied powers Powers not specifically stated in the Constitution but can be inferred from the delegated powers.

Impeachment Proceedings authorized by Article I of the Constitution that are designed to remove high officials including the president and vice-president from office for "treason, bribery, or other high crimes and misdemeanors." Initiated by the House of Representatives, the actual trial is conducted by the Senate.

Impoundment A decision by the executive branch to withhold funds that have already been appropriated by Congress. Prior to 1974, used as a form of an executive line-item veto. Congressional Budget and Impoundment Control Act of 1974 requires approval from Congress.

incorporation Most of the protections of the Bill of Rights have been found to apply to states and localities via the incorporation of those guarantees through the due process clause of the Fourteenth Amendment to the Constitution. The doctrine of incorporation successfully overcame the Supreme Court's previous position that the Bill of Rights applied only to federal laws.

incremental policy   A policy added to an existing policy in small increments.

incumbents   Individuals who currently hold public office.

independent   A person who declares no allegiance to a party.

independent agencies   Government agencies that are usually smaller and have a narrower set of responsibilities than cabinet departments.

independent expenditures   Loophole in the campaign finance law involving no limits to funds that are dispersed independently by a group or person in the name of a cause, and not coordinated by a candidate.

independent regulatory commissions   Agencies established to regulate a sector of the nation's economy in the public interest.

indirect democracy   A type of government in which voters designate a relatively small number of people to represent their interests; those people, or representatives, then meet in a legislative body and make decisions on behalf of the entire citizenry.

infomercial   A recent trend in television advertising combining commercial advertising with "informational" discussions, used to advertise products ranging from home gymnasiums to psychic advisers.

inherent powers   Powers which do not appear in the Constitution but are assumed because of the nature of government. Also refers to a theory that the Constitution grants authority to the executive, through the injunction in Article II, Section 3, that the president "take care that the Laws be faithfully executed."

initiatives   Legislative solutions to problems proposed by the public and voted upon during elections.

integration   Efforts to balance the racial composition of the schools.

intensity   In public opinion, a measure of the depth of feeling associated with a given opinion.

interest group liberalism   A system of politics in which interest groups have expanded their control of legislative politics as the national bureaucracy has grown.

interest groups   Formal organizations of people who share a common outlook or social circumstance and who band together in the hope of influencing government policy.

intergovernmental relations   An approach to the study of federalism that examines the pattern of interaction among the levels of government and government officials as a result of the aid sent from one level to another.

Intolerable Acts   A series of punitive measures passed by the British Parliament in the spring of 1774 as a response to the Boston Tea Party.

investigative journalism   The uncovering of corruption, scandal, conspiracy, and abuses of power in government and business; differs from standard press coverage in the depth of the coverage sought, the time spent researching the subject, and the shocking findings that often result from such reporting.

iron triangles   The informal three-way relationships that develop among key legislative committees, the bureaucracy whose budgets are supervised by those committees, and interest groups with a vested interest in the policies created by those committees and agencies.

isolationism   A pattern in which the United States fosters economic relations abroad without committing to strategic alliances that might draw the country into a war.

issue networks   Networks composed of political actors in a particular policy area, usually including bureaucrats, congressional staffers, interest groups, think-tank researchers or academic experts, and media participants, who all interact regularly on an issue.

issue stage   A stage reached by a potential policy when it is framed in terms of a yes-or-no policy option.

Jeffersonian Party   Opposed to the nationalism of the Federalists, a party of small farmers, workers, and less privileged citizens who preferred the authority of the states.

Jim Crow laws   Laws passed by Southern States that separated the races in public places such as railroads, streetcars, schools, and cemeteries.

joint committees   Groups of members from both chambers who study broad areas that are of interest to Congress as a whole.

judicial activism   An approach in which justices create new policy and decide issues, to the point, some critics charge, of writing their own personal values into law.

judicial restraint   An approach in which justices see themselves as appointed rather than elected officials, who should defer to the legislature and uphold a law or political action if at all possible.

judicial review   The power of the Supreme Court established in Marbury v. Madison to overturn acts of the president, Congress, and the states if those acts violate the Constitution. This power makes the Supreme Court the final interpreter of the Constitution.

judiciary   The branch of the government that interprets laws.

Keynesian economics   A view of economic policy that evolved during the 1930s and suggested that government had a far more active role to play in the economy.

laissez-faire economics   A school of thought suggesting that people should be allowed to "do as they please" and pursue their own economic self-interest in the market without the interference of government policies.

latency   In public opinion, feelings that are unspoken, suggesting the potential for an attitude or behavior, but only when the right circumstances occur.

least restrictive means test   A free exercise of religion test in which the state was asked to find another way, perhaps through exemptions, to enforce its regulations while still protecting all other religions.

legislative branch   The branch of the government that makes laws.

legislative courts   Courts designed to provide technical expertise on specific subjects based on Article I of the Constitution.

Lemon test   A test from the Supreme Court case *Lemon v. Kurtzman* in 1971 for determining the permissible level of state aid for church agencies by measuring whether the purpose of the state aid is non-religious in nature, whether it neither advances or inhibits religion, and whether it results in the excessive entanglement of the church and state.

libel   Published material which damages a person's reputation or good name in an untruthful and malicious way. As such it is not protected by the First Amendment.

liberal A person who supports government intervention to minimize economic inequality, but opposes government actions that restrict cultural and social freedoms. See Table 9.2, p. 315, for more detail.

limited government A type of government in which the powers of the government are clearly defined and bounded, so that governmental authority cannot intrude in the lives of private citizens.

line item veto A device that would allow the president to eliminate specific parts of an appropriation bill without having to veto the entire legislation.

literacy test A requirement that voting applicants had to demonstrate an understanding of national and state constitutions. Primarily used to prevent blacks from voting in the South.

lobbying The formal, organized attempt to influence legislation, usually through direct contact with legislators or their staff.

lobbyists People paid to pressure members of Congress to further the aims of some interest group.

local party organization The initial point of entry for those seeking involvement in politics as volunteers, organizers, or candidates.

logrolling A temporary political alliance between two policy actors who agree to support each other's policy goals.

machine politics An organizational style of local politics in which party bosses traded jobs, money, and favors for votes and campaign support.

maintaining election Election in which the majority party of the day wins both Congress and the White House, maintaining its control of government.

majority More than fifty percent of the vote.

majority opinion The decision of the Supreme Court which represents the agreed-upon compromise judgment of all the Supreme Court justices in the majority.

majority rule A decision-making process in which, when more than half of the voters agree on an issue, the entire group accepts the decision, even those in the minority who voted against it.

margin of error The measure of possible error in a survey, which means that the number for the *entire population* of voters will fall within a range of plus or minus several points of the number obtained from the small but representative sample of voters.

markup session A session held by a subcommittee to revise a bill.

mass media The various media—newspapers, magazines, radio, television—through which information is transferred from its sources to large numbers of people.

Mayflower Compact An agreement signed on November 21, 1620, by the forty-one adult males aboard the *Mayflower*.

McCarthyism Term referring to Senator Joseph R. McCarthy (1908–1957) and his anticommunism tactics.

McGovern-Fraser Commission Democratic Party commission that opened up meetings and votes to a large variety of party activists, made primaries rather than caucuses the common means of choosing convention delegates, weakened the power of party leaders, and set up rules to ensure that a wide range of party members could participate fully in all party operations.

mid-term elections Elections in which Americans elect members of Congress but not presidents; 1994 was a mid-term election.

military-industrial complex What President Eisenhower in 1961 called the growing power and influence resulting from the "conjunction of an immense military establishment and a large arms industry."

minor parties (or third parties) Parties in the American system other than the current duopoly, e.g., the Democrats or Republicans.

minority leader The leader of the minority party in Congress.

minority rights Rights given to those in the minority; based on the idea that tyranny of the majority is a danger to human rights.

Miranda warning A warning that must be recited by police officers to a suspect before questioning: "You have the right to remain silent; anything you say can and will be used against you. You have the right to an attorney. If you cannot afford an attorney, one will be provided for you. Do you understand these rights and are you willing to speak with us?" Established in *Miranda v. Arizona* 1966.

Missouri Compromise Passed in 1820, a compromise in which Missouri was admitted to the U.S. along with the free state of Maine, and dividing the remainder of the Louisiana Purchase territory into a free area in the North and slavery in the South.

monetarism Economic theory that the economy itself is the source of stability, while unwise economic policies are the cause of cycles of inflation, unemployment, and slow growth.

monetary policy Control of the growth of the money supply by the federal reserve system.

Monroe Doctrine A doctrine enunciated by President James Monroe in 1823 which proclaimed the North and South American continent to be in the United States sphere of influence, hence out of bounds for European aspirations. It reinforced growing isolationism by promising not to interfere in internal concerns of European states.

muckraking A word used to describe a style of reporting that was the precursor of what is now called investigative journalism.

multiparty system A characteristic of most democratic nations in which five to ten or more parties regularly compete in elections, win seats, and have some chance of gaining power. This is promoted by systems with proportional representation.

national debt The cumulative total of all budget deficits.

national party convention A gathering once every four years in which delegates from around the country come together to select presidential and vice-presidential candidates for the coming election and to write the party's platform.

national party organization An organization whose primary tasks include fundraising, distribution of information and recruitment.

National Security Council (NSC) Created in 1947 to provide the executive with advice on all domestic, foreign, and military policies relating to national security.

natural rights Rights derived from the natural state of human beings; they are rights that government cannot alter.

necessary and proper clause A clause in Article I, Section 8, Clause 18, of the Constitution stating that Congress can "make all Laws which shall be *necessary and proper* for carrying into Execution the foregoing Powers."

New Deal Franklin D. Roosevelt's domestic program that promoted the country's recovery from the Great Depression via the implementation of a legislative package including the Farm Credit

Association (FCA), the National Industrial Recovery Act (NIRA), the Social Security Act, and the Works Progress Administration (WPA) among others.

New Deal coalition   Brought together by Franklin Roosevelt in 1932, a broad electorate made up of the urban working class, most members of the newer ethnic groups, the bulk of American Catholics and Jews, the poor, the South, and liberal intellectuals.

New Federalism   A program under President Nixon that decentralized power as a response to New Deal centralization.

New Jersey Plan   A plan presented to the Constitutional Convention of 1787 designed to create a unicameral legislature with equal representation for all states. Its goal was to protect the interests of the smaller, less populous states.

no incorporation   An approach in which the states would be bound only by the dictates of due process contained in the Fourteenth Amendment.

nomination   A candidate's "sponsorship" by a political party.

North American Free Trade Area (NAFTA)   A trade agreement begun between the U.S. and Canada, with Mexico later being added to form a three-nation free-trade zone.

North Atlantic Treaty Organization (NATO)   Charter signed by the U.S., Canada, Turkey, and eleven European nations in 1949 agreeing that an armed attack against one or more of them in Europe or North America would be interpreted as an attack against all.

NSC-68   National Security Council paper outlining a sweeping mobilization of American economic and human resources in the struggle to contain Soviet communism.

nullification   A 19th Century theory which upholds that states faced with unacceptable national legislation can declare such laws null and void and refuse to observe them.

Office of Management and Budget (OMB)   The part of the Executive Office of the President whose main responsibilities are to prepare and administer the president's annual budget. It is through the budget process that a president and the OMB can shape policy, since the process determines which departments and agencies grow, get cut, or remain the same as the year before.

open primary   A system of conducting primary elections in which citizens vote in whichever party's primary they choose.

opinion   A written version of the decision of a court.

order   A condition in which the structures of a given society and the relationships thereby defined among individuals and classes comprising it are maintained and preserved by the rule of law and police power of the state.

original jurisdiction   The authority of a court to be the first to hear a case.

original policy   An entirely new policy.

override   A procedure by which Congress reverses a presidential veto by a two-thirds vote in each house.

oversight   Congressional function that involves monitoring the effectiveness of laws passed by examining the workings of the executive branch.

participation   Mass political involvement through voting campaign work, political protests, civil disobedience, among many others.

party identification   A psychological orientation, a long term propensity to think positively of and vote regularly for a particular political party.

party platform   The statement of principles and policies, the goals that a party pledges to carry out if voters give it control of the government.

party realignment   A shift in fundamental party identification and loyalty caused by significant historical events or national crises.

peonage   A system in which employers advance wages and then require workers to remain on their jobs, in effect enslaving them, until the debt is satisfied.

picket fence federalism   A portrayal of the federal system in which the horizontal crosspieces of the fence represent each level of the government—national, state, and local—and the vertical pickets of the fence represent a particular government policy area such as health, education, or transportation in which bureaucrats communicate across levels of government within their policy areas.

plea bargains   Agreements in which the state presses for either a reduced set of charges or a reduced sentence in return for a guilty plea.

pluralism   A system that occurs when those in the minority band together into groups based on particular interests and seek to influence policy by allying with other groups.

plurality   More votes than anyone else in the race, but not necessarily a majority of the total number of votes.

pocket veto   Presidential refusal to sign or veto a bill that Congress passes in the last ten days of its session; by not being signed, it automatically dies if Congress adjourns.

policy elites   Members of Congress, the President, Supreme Court justices, Cabinet officers, heads of key agencies and departments, leading editorial writers, and influential columnists and commentators.

policy entrepreneurs   Leaders who invest in and who create the conditions for a potential group to become an actual interest group. Ralph Nader stands as a classic example of a policy entrepreneur.

policy evaluation   A period of monitoring and analysis following implementation of a policy.

policy networks   Networks characterized by a wide-ranging discussion of options as issues are resolved, conveying a more inclusive and less conspiratorial image of the policy process than "iron triangles" do.

political action committees (PACs)   Committees formed as the fundraising and distribution arm of specific interest groups.

political ideology   A coherent way of viewing politics and government; ideological perspectives include beliefs about the military, the role of government, the proper relation between government and the economy, the value of social-welfare programs, and the relative importance for society of liberty and order.

political parties   The institution which exists to allow like-minded members of the population to group together and magnify their individual voices into a focus promoting individual candidates and government action.

political socialization   The process by which we learn about the world of politics and develop our political beliefs.

political violence Violent action motivated primarily by political aims and intended to have a political impact.

poll tax A fee that had to be paid before one could vote.

pork barrel legislation Policies and programs designed to create special benefits for a state or district, such as bridges, highways, dams, and military installations, all of which translate into jobs and money for the local economy and reelection for the incumbent.

potential groups Interest groups that could come into being under the right circumstances; as yet, they have no substantive form and may never have one, but they cannot be discounted by political participants.

poverty level The dollar amount of annual earnings below which a family of four is considered poor.

power of the purse Congress's power to levy taxes, borrow money, coin money, regulate commerce among the states, and spend for the general welfare.

precedents Previously decided court cases on an issue similar to the one being considered.

president pro tempore The majority party member with the longest continuous service in the Senate. Serves as the chief presiding officer in absence of Vice-president.

President of the Senate The Vice President of the United States.

primary election A pre-election that allows all members of a party, not just its leadership, to select the party's candidate for the general election in the fall.

prior restraint An action in which the government seeks to ban the publication of controversial material by the press before it is published; censorship.

privatization The turning over of public responsibilities to privately owned and operated enterprises for regulation and for providing goods and services.

probable cause A reasonable belief that a crime has been, is being, or is about to be committed. In cases of searches there must also be a belief that evidence of that crime may be located in a particular place. Police must establish this to a judge to secure a search warrant or retroactively justify a search which has already taken place.

progressive taxes System of taxation in which those who make more money are taxed at a higher rate. An example is the income tax.

project grant A grant not based on a formula, but distributed for specific purposes after a fairly competitive application and approval process.

proportional representation A system of representation popular in Europe whereby the number of seats in the legislature is based on the proportion of the vote received in the election.

proposal The first stage of the Constitutional amendment process, in which a change is proposed.

protest Expression of dissatisfaction; may take the form of demonstrations, letters to newspapers or public officials, or simple "opting out" of the system by failing to vote or participate in any other way.

protest march March in which people walk down a main street carrying signs, singing freedom songs, and chanting slogans.

public agenda The set of topics that are a source of concern for policy elites, the general public, or both.

public interest groups Groups that focus not on the immediate economic livelihood of their members, but on achieving a broad set of goals that represent their members' vision of the collective good. Examples include The National Taxpayers Union, The League of Women Voters, and Common Cause.

public opinion The collective expression of attitudes about the prominent issues and actors of the day.

public policies The decisions, actions, and commitments of government.

quota programs Programs that guarantee a certain percentage of admissions, new hires, or promotions to members of minority groups.

random sample The requirement for a good poll, which means that every member of the population has an equal chance of appearing in the sample.

ratify An act of approval of proposed Constitutional amendments by the states; the second step of the amendment process.

realigning election Election characterized by massive shifts in partisan identification, as in 1932 with the New Deal coalition.

realignment A broad-based change in partisanship in which large groups of people shift allegiance from one party to another.

reapportionment A process of redrawing voting district lines from time to time, and even adjusting the number of representatives allotted each state.

reciprocity A norm, used to push legislation through Congress, in which members defer to others with the understanding that the favor will be reciprocated.

recruitment The process through which parties look for effective, popular candidates to help them win votes and offices.

red tape The excessive number of rules and regulations that government employees must follow.

referendum A proposal submitted by a state legislature to the public for a popular vote; focuses on whether a state should spend money in a certain way.

reflexive policies Incremental policies that build on past programs and policies; they "reflect back" on previous efforts and build on the assumption that the current or proposed policy will be modified over time.

regressive taxes System of taxation in which taxes take a higher fraction of the income of lower income taxpayers. Examples are taxes on gasoline, cigarettes, and alcohol.

regulation The making of rules by an administrative body that must clarify and interpret legislation, their enforcement, and the adjudication of disputes about them.

regulatory policy Policy that involves the use of police powers by the federal government to supervise the conduct of individuals, businesses, and other governmental agencies.

representative democracy A system of government in which the voters select representatives to make decisions for them.

representative sample A sample that includes all the significant characteristics of the total population.

republic A system of government that allows indirect representation of the popular will.

Republican Party Born in 1854 as the great conflict of the Civil War approached, it was the party of northern opposition to slavery and its spread to the new territories. From the Whigs, it also inherited a concern for mercantile, business, and properties interests.

reserved powers Those powers not assigned by the Constitution to the national government but left with the states or to the people, according to the Tenth Amendment.

retrospective voting A particularly powerful form of issue voting in which voters look back over the last term or two to judge how well an incumbent or the "in party" has performed in office.

riders Amendments to bills which are often unrelated to the content of the bill.

right of rebuttal The right to refute the allegations presented on a radio or TV station, free of charge, within a reasonable time.

right to privacy The right to have the government stay out of the personal lives of its citizens.

rule of four A means of determining which cases will be heard by the Supreme Court; at least four justices must vote to hear a case and grant the petition for a writ of certiorari for the case to be put on the Court's docket.

salience In public opinion, the extent to which people see an issue as having a clear impact on their own lives.

sampling bias A bias in a survey that means that a particular set of people in the population at large is more or less likely to appear in the final sample than other sets of people.

schemas Intellectual frameworks for evaluating the world.

Second Continental Congress A meeting convened on May 10, 1775 with all thirteen colonies represented. The purpose of the Congress was to decide whether or not to sever bonds with England and declare independence.

secular regulation rule Rule that holds that there is no constitutional right to exemption, on free exercise grounds, from laws dealing with nonreligious matters.

select committees (or special committees) Temporary Congressional committees that conduct investigations or study specific problems or crises.

selective incorporation An incorporation standard in which some portions of the Bill of Rights, but not all, were made part of the Fourteenth Amendment's due process clause and thus guaranteed against invasion by the states.

Senate Majority Leader A senator selected by the majority party whose functions are similar to those of the speaker of the House.

senatorial courtesy A procedure in which a president submits the names of judicial nominees to senators from the same political party who are also from the nominee's home state for their approval prior to formal nomination.

seniority An informal, unwritten rule of Congress that more senior members (those who have served longer than others) are appointed to committees and as chairpersons of committees. This "rule" is being diluted in the House as other systems are developed for committee appointments.

separation of powers State in which the powers of the government are divided among the three branches: executive, legislative, and judicial.

sexism Prejudice against the female gender.

Shays's Rebellion A populist rebellion in western Massachusetts in 1786, led by Daniel Shays.

single-member districts Districts in which each seat goes to the candidate with the most votes. In this system, small parties, say one that wins 10 percent in every district across the nation, do not get a single seat in the legislature.

sit-in A protest technique in which protestors refuse to leave an area.

slander Speech that is untruthful, malicious, or damaging to a person's reputation or good name and thus not protected by the Free Speech Clause of the First Amendment.

social contract theorists A group of European philosophers who reasoned that the most effective way to create the best government was to understand human nature in a state prior to government.

social welfare policy Policy that uses positive incentives (cash assistance, stipends, entitlements, grants, etc.) to promote or encourage basic social and economic fairness.

socialization The process by which people learn to conform to their society's norms and values.

solicitor general The third-ranking official in the Justice Department, appointed by the president and charged with representing the U.S. government before the Supreme Court.

soundbite A very brief statement, usually a snippet from a speech, that conveys the essence of a longer statement and can be inserted into a news story.

sovereignty The independence and self-government of the unit being discussed.

Speaker of the House The only presiding officer of the House mentioned in the Constitution. The leader of the majority party in Congress and third in line for the Presidency.

special revenue sharing A system of the New Federalism program in which groups of categorical grants-in-aid in related policy areas such as crime control or health care are consolidated into a single block grant.

specialization A principle that in a bureaucracy, specific tasks should be delegated to individuals whose training and experience give them the expertise to execute them. Also refers to a norm used to push legislation through Congress in which members who lack expertise in a particular policy area defer to policy specialists with more knowledge.

spin The interpretation placed on the news by those presenting it.

split-ticket ballots Ballots on which people vote for candidates from more than one party.

spoils system A system in which government jobs and contracts are awarded on the basis of party loyalty rather than social or economic status or relevant experience.

stability A condition that is resistant to sudden change or overthrow.

stagflation Simultaneous high unemployment and high inflation.

Stamp Act A British act of 1765 that required that revenue stamps be placed on all printed matter and legal documents, making it felt in every aspect of commercial life in the colonies.

standing committees Permanent committees that determine whether proposed legislation should be sent to the entire chamber for consideration.

stare decisis A doctrine meaning "let the decision stand," or that judges deciding a case should adhere if at all possible to previously decided cases which are similar to the one under consideration; see precedents.

state party organizations Groups that organize elections and provide the electoral college votes needed to win the presidency; they supervise the various functions vital to state parties, such as fundraising, identifying potential candidates, providing election services, offering advice on reapportionment matters, and developing campaign strategies.

states' rights Those rights that have neither been granted to the national government nor forbidden to the states by the U.S. Constitution.

statutory construction The power of the Supreme Court to interpret or reinterpret a federal or state law.

stewardship An approach to presidential power that was articulated by Theodore Roosevelt and based on the presidencies of Lincoln and Jackson, who believed that the president had a moral duty to serve popular interests and did not need specific constitutional or legal authorization to take action.

straight-party ticket Ballots on which people vote for only one party.

straw poll A nonscientific method of measuring public opinion.

strict scrutiny test Test of laws which discriminate on the basis of a characteristic that is "immutable (or unchangeable) by birth," such as race or nationality; in such cases, the burden shifts from the plaintiff to the state forcing the government to show the compelling reasons for the law. That is, the state must show that no other possible way existed to accomplish this regulation.

subsequent punishment Laws that would punish someone for an action after it has taken place. For example, laws such as those banning libel and obscenity because they are harmful to reputations or public sensibilities punish writers, editors, and publishers after an item appears in print.

substantive policy Policy involving tangible rewards such as money, buildings, or jobs.

suffrage The right to vote.

Sugar Act A British act of 1764 that levied a three-penny-per-gallon tax on molasses and other goods imported into the colonies.

super-majority A majority vote required for Constitutional amendments; consists of more than a simple majority of 50 percent plus one.

superpower The disproportionate power—economic and military—that distinguished the United States and the Soviet Union from all other countries in the post-war era.

supply-side economics An economic strategy emphasizing the stimulating of supply rather than demand to stabilize and reinvigorate the economy.

supremacy clause A clause in Article IV of the Constitution holding that in any conflict between federal laws and treaties and state laws, the will of the national government always prevails.

symbolic policy Policy involving the use of governmental symbols, assurances, and public values.

symbolic speech Some actions, such as burning the American flag, that take the place of speech because they communicate a message.

terrorism The use of force specifically targeted at civilians for the purpose of producing mass fear that will induce policy changes.

test of reasonableness Test in court cases of what reasonable people would agree to be constitutional because the law has a rational basis for its existence.

three-fifths compromise A compromise which stated that the apportionment of representatives by state should be determined "by adding to the whole number of free persons . . . three-fifths of all other persons" (Article I, Section 2); meaning that it would take five slaves to equal three free people when counting the population for representation and taxation purposes.

total incorporation An approach arguing that the protections in the Bill of Rights were so fundamental that all of them should be applied to the states by absorbing them into the due process clause of the Fourteenth Amendment.

town meeting A form of governance dating back to the 1700s in which town business is transacted by the consent of a majority of eligible citizens, all of whom have an equal opportunity to express their views and cast their votes at an annual meeting.

Townshend Revenue Acts A series of taxes imposed by the British Parliament in 1767 on glass, lead, tea, and paper imported into the colonies.

treaties Formal international agreements between sovereign states.

triad of powers Three constitutional provisions—the interstate commerce clause, the general welfare clause, and the Tenth Amendment—that help to continually shift the balance of power between the national and state governments.

trial court The point of original entry in the legal system, with a single judge and at times a jury deciding matters of both fact and law in a case.

triggering mechanism A critical development that converts a routine problem into a widely shared, negative public response.

trustees Congress members who feel authorized to use their best judgment in considering legislation.

U.S. court of appeals The middle appeals level of judicial review beyond the district courts; in 1994, consisted of 167 judges in 13 courts, 12 of which are geographically based.

U.S. district courts The trial courts serving as the original point of entry for almost all federal cases.

universal suffrage The requirement that everyone must have the right to vote.

value added tax (VAT) A form of sales tax that is levied on the value added to a product at each stage of production.

veto Presidential power to forbid or prevent an action of Congress.

vice-president The second-highest elected official in the United States.

Vietnam syndrome Syndrome in which politicians and the public alike fear to commit militarily to the protection of any but the most crucial and seriously threatened national interests.

Virginia Plan A plan presented to the Constitutional Convention; favored by the delegates from the bigger states.

voter turnout The percent of eligible voters who actually show up and vote on election day.

War Powers Act A highly controversial measure, passed over President Nixon's veto, which stipulated that presidential commitments of U.S. military forces cannot extend beyond sixty days without specific congressional authorization.

welfare state A social system whereby the government assumes primary responsibility for the welfare of citizens.

Whig Party For its short life between 1836 and 1856, the Whig party was an unstable coalition of many interests, among them nativism, property owners, and business and commerce.

whip Congress members charged with counting prospective votes on various issues and making certain that members have the information they need for floor action.

winner-take-all system A system in which the winner of the primary or electoral college vote gets all of the state's convention or electoral college delegates.

writ of certiorari A Latin term meaning "to be made more certain"; this is a writ that enables the Court to accept cases for review only if there are "special and important reasons therefore."

yellow journalism Brash, colorful, well-illustrated, often lurid and sensationalized organs of half-truth, innuendo, and sometimes outright lies, usually associated with the big-city daily newspapers of Joseph Pulitzer and William Randolph Hearst.

REFERENCES

CHAPTER 1

1 Based on Taylor Branch, *Parting the Waters: America in the King Years, 1954–63* (New York: Simon & Schuster, 1988), pp. 124–42; David J. Garrow, *Bearing the Cross: Martin Luther King, Jr., and the Southern Christian Leadership Conference* (New York: Morrow, 1986), pp. 11–47.

2 See "Freedom Around the World, 1995," *Freedom Review*, 26, no. 1 (Jan.–Feb. 1995): .

3 See Alexis de Tocqueville, *Democracy in America* (first published 1835–40). Available in many editions.

4 See "The 2500 Anniversary of Democracy: Lessons of Athenian Democracy." PS (September 1993): 475–93.

5 See Thomas E. Cronin, *Direct Democracy: The Politics of Initiative, Referendum, and Recall* (Cambridge, Mass.: Harvard University Press, 1989).

6 E. E. Schattschneider, *Two Hundred Million Americans in Search of a Government* (Hillsdale, Ill.: Dryden Press, 1969), p. 27.

7 From a letter from John Adams to John Taylor of Caroline, 1814, cited in Richard Hofstadter, *The American Political Tradition and the Men Who Made It* (New York: Vintage Books, 1948), p. 13.

8 Sheldon Wolin, "Democracy: Electoral and Athenian," PS, (Sept. 1993): 475–76.

9 See J. Roland Pennock, *Democratic Political Theory* (Princeton, N.J.: Princeton University Press, 1979).

10 Isaiah Berlin, *Two Concepts of Liberty* (Oxford, England: Clarendon Press, 1958).

11 Sidney Verba and Gary R. Orren, *Equality in America: The View from the Top* (Cambridge, Mass.: Harvard University Press, 1985), p. 5.

12 See Robert Dahl, *Democracy and Its Critics* (New Haven, Conn.: Yale University Press, 1989).

13 From Friedrich A. Hayek, *The Constitution of Liberty* (Chicago: University of Chicago Press, 1960), pp. 103–17; Carole Pateman, *Participation and Democratic Theory* (Cambridge, Mass.: Cambridge University Press, 1970), pp. 22–44.

14 From Peter Jones, "Political Equality and Majority Rule," in D. Miller and L. Siedentop, eds., *The Nature of Political Theory* (Clarendon, England: Oxford University Press, 1983), pp. 155–82.

15 J.D. Richardson, ed., *Messages and Papers of the Presidents, 1789–1902,* 20 vols. (Washington, D.C., 1917, vol. I, pp. 309–12 *passim.*

16 From Joshua Cohen and Joel Rogers, *On Democracy* (Harmondsworth, Middlesex: Penguin Books, 1983), pp. 48–73.

17 Adam Michnick, "After the Revolution," *New Republic* (July 2, 1990): 28.

CHAPTER 2

1 Christopher Collier and James Lincoln Collier, *Decision in Philadelphia* (New York: Random House, 1986), p. 11.

2 See Robert A. Feer, *Shays's Rebellion* (New York: Garland, 1988), pp. 504–29; David Szatmary, *Shays's Rebellion* (Amhurst: University of Massachusetts Press, 1980), pp. 120–34.

3 See Gordon S. Wood, "The Origins of the Constitution," *This Constitution* 15 (Summer 1987): 4; Gordon S. Wood, "The Intellectual Origins of the American Constitution," *National Forum* 4 (Fall 1984): 5–8.

4 See George Brown Tindall, *America: A Narrative History* (New York: Norton, 1988), pp. 58–62; Alfred H. Kelly and Winfred A. Harbison, *The American Constitution: Its Origin and Development* (New York: Norton, 1976), pp. 7–16.

5 Alan Brinkley, *The Unfinished Nation* (New York: McGraw-Hill, 1993), p. 35.

6 Tindall, *America*, p. 63.

7 Tindall, *America*, p. 168; Ronald W. Clark, *Benjamin Franklin: A Biography* (New York: Random House, 1983), pp. 107–8.

8 See Kelly and Harbison, *American Constitution*, p. 69; Tindall, *America*, pp. 194–95. See also Philip B. Kurland and Ralph Lerner, *The Founders Constitution* (Chicago: University of Chicago Press, 1987).

9 Brinkley, *Unfinished Nation*, p. 108.

10 James MacGregor Burns, *The Vineyard of Liberty* (New York: Vintage Books, 1983), p. 83.

11 Tindall, *America*, pp. 206–7.

12 Ibid., pp. 207–8.

13 Brinkley, *Unfinished Nation*, p. 133.

14 Ibid., p. 255.

CHAPTER 3

1 "The Ark of America," *Time*, July 6, 1987, p. 30.

2 For an excellent and readable account of the Constitutional Convention, see Catherine Drinker Bowen, *The Miracle at Philadelphia: The Story of the Constitutional Convention, May to September 1787* (Boston: Little, Brown, 1966). Another highly readable version, incorporating new scholarship, can be found in Christopher Collier and James Lincoln Collier, *Decision in Philadelphia: The Constitutional Convention of 1787* (New York: Random House, 1986).

3 For more on the motivations of the framers, see Richard B. Bernstein, with Kym S. Rice, *Are We to Be a Nation? The Making of the Constitution* (Cambridge, Mass.: Harvard University Press, 1987), passim.

4 Bowen, *Miracle at Philadelphia,* p. 12.

5 The number of slaves at the time is taken from the notes of convention delegate Charles Cotesworth Pinckney, July 10, 1787, found in James H. Hutson, ed., *Supplement to Max Farrand's "The Records of the Federal Convention of 1787"* (New Haven, Conn.: Yale University Press, 1987), p. 160.

6 Collier and Collier, *Decision in Philadelphia*, p. 16.

7 For more on this possible motivation see John E. O'Connor, *William Paterson, Lawyer and Statesman, 1745–1806* (New Brunswick, N.J.: Rutgers University Press, 1979).

8 Everett S. Brown, ed., *William Plumer's Memorandum of Proceedings in the United States Senate, 1803–1807.* In Hutson, *Supplement to Farrand's "Records,"* p. 305.

9 Robert A. Goldwin, "Why Blacks, Women and Jews Are Not Mentioned in the Constitution," *Commentary*, May 1987, p. 29.

10 Bowen, *Miracle at Philadelphia,* p. 263.

11 George Washington, September 17, 1787. In Hutson, *Supplement to Farrand's "Records,"* p. 276.

12 Alexander Hamilton, James Madison, and John Jay, *Federalist Papers* (New York: New American Library, 1961), no. 51, p. 322.

13 *Youngstown Sheet and Tube v. Sawyer,* 343 U.S. 579 at p. 635 (1952).

14 Richard E. Neustadt, *Presidential Power: The Politics of Leadership from FDR to Carter* (New York: Wiley, 1980), p. 26.

15 Hamilton, Madison, and Jay, *Federalist Papers,* no. 10, p. 78.

16 Quoted in Charles L. Mee, Jr., *The Genius of the People* (New York: Harper and Row, 1987), p. 37.

17 Bowen, *Miracle at Philadelphia,* p. 310.

18 "The Ark of America," *Time,* July 6, 1987, p. 24.

19 *Dillon v. Gloss,* 256 U.S. 368 (1921). The Court refused to rule in 1939 in a case involving time limits contained in a child labor amendment, saying that it was a "political question," or a matter for the political bodies to decide (*Coleman v. Miller,* 307 U.S. 433 [1939]). Since 1939 the Supreme Court has refused to rule on such time limits.

20 The convention process was used because legislators in "dry" states were expected to be pressured by voters to vote against ratification. For more on the Eighteenth and Twenty-first amendments, and the entire amendment process, see Richard B. Bernstein, with Jerome Agel, *Amending America: If We Love the Constitution So Much, Why Do We Keep Trying to Change It?* (New York: Random House, Times Books, 1993), pp. 170–77, passim.

21 *Immigration and Naturalization Service v. Chadha,* 462 U.S. 919, at p. 978 (1982).

22 "The Ark of America," p. 29.

23 Anthony Lewis, "If Madison Were Here," *New York Times,* Dec. 13, 1991, sec. A.

CHAPTER 4

1 This was in fact the front page of the *Center Daily Times* in State College, Pennsylvania, on July 29, 1994. But it is very typical of the average day's news, as you will see from looking at your own newspaper after you read this chapter.

2 Alexander Hamilton, James Madison, and John Jay, *The Federalist Papers* (New York: New American Library, 1961), no. 10, p. 83.

3 Richard A. Knox, "Health Reform Fizzling in States," *Boston Globe,* July 17, 1994, pp. 1, 16.

4 *New State Ice Co. v. Liebmann,* 285 U.S. 262 (1932), p. 311.

5 *Heart of Atlanta Motel v. United States,* 379 U.S. 241 (1964); *Katzenbach v. McClung,* 379 U.S. 294 (1964).

6 In June 1987 the Supreme Court upheld the law, with Chief Justice Rehnquist ruling that Congress has the power to act "indirectly under its spending power to encourage uniformity in the States' drinking ages" (*South Dakota v. Dole,* 483 U.S. 203 [1987]).

7 See *Pennsylvania v. Nelson,* 350 U.S. 497 (1956).

8 *Gibbons v. Ogden,* 9 Wheaton 1 (1824), p. 195.

9 *United States v. E. C. Knight Co.,* 156 U.S. 1 (1895).

10 *Hammer v. Dagenhart,* 247 U. S. 251 (1919), p. 274.

11 *Schechter Poultry Corp. v. United States,* 295 U.S. 495 (1935); *Carter v. Carter Coal Co.,* 298 U.S. 238 (1936); *United States v. Butler,* 297 U.S. 1 (1936).

12 *National Labor Relations Board v. Jones and Laughlin Corp.,* 301 U.S. 1 (1937).

13 *United States v. Darby Lumber Co.,* 312 U.S. 100 (1941), p. 124.

14 Marshall E. Dimock, *Modern Politics and Administration: A Study of the Creative State* (New York: American Book, 1937), pp. 54–55.

15 In 1976, the Supreme Court signaled a possible return to dual federalism in the case of *National League of Cities v. Usery* (426 U.S. 833 [1976]), which dealt with extending national wages and hours legislation to state and municipal workers. Writing for a slim majority, Justice William Rehnquist banned national regulation of "core" state functions. Nine years later, however, the Court overturned *Usery* in the case of *Garcia v. San Antonio Metropolitan Transit Authority,* (469 U.S. 528 [1985]), which also dealt with wages and hours legislation. The Court shifted its position back to favoring national predominance, arguing that states must rely on Congress rather than the Court to decide which of their programs should be regulated by the national government. This ruling was reaffirmed by the Court in *South Carolina v. Baker* (485 U.S. 505 [1988]).

16 *Brown v. Board of Education,* 347 U.S. 483 (1954).

17 *Reynolds v. Sims,* 377 U.S. 533 (1964).

18 See *United States v. Butler,* 297 U.S. 1 (1936); *Wickard v. Filburn,* 317 U.S. 111 (1941); *Steward Machine Co. v. Davis,* 301 U.S. 548 (1937).

19 Advisory Commission on Intergovernmental Relations (ACIR), *Characteristics of Federal Grant-in-Aid Programs to State and Local Governments: Grants Funded FY 1993,* (Washington D.C.: ACIR), p. 1.

20 ACIR, *Federal Grant-in-Aid Programs,* p. 2.

21 ACIR, *Federal Grant-in-Aid Programs,* p. 2.

22 ACIR, *Federal Grant-in-Aid Programs,* pp. 22–42.

23 ACIR, *Federal Grant-in-Aid Programs,* p. 12.

24 ABC Nightly News, "American Agenda," Oct. 27, 1993.

25 David B. Walker, *Toward a Functioning Federalism* (Cambridge, Mass.: Winthrop, 1981), p. 68.

26 Walker, *Toward a Functioning Federalism,* p. 79.

27 John E. Schwarz, *America's Hidden Success: A Reassessment of Public Policy from Kennedy to Reagan* (New York: Norton, 1988), pp. 17–71.

28 Jeffrey Pressman and Aaron Wildavsky, *Implementation* (Berkeley: University of California Press, 1973).

29 See Schwarz, *America's Hidden Success;* Allen Matusow, *The Unraveling of America: A History of Liberalism in the 1960s* (New York: Harper and Row, 1984).

30 Terry Sanford, *Storm over the States* (New York: McGraw-Hill, 1967).

31 Ronald Reagan, inaugural speech of 1981, in Richard D. Heffner, ed., *A Documentary History of the United States* (New York: Mentor Books, 1991), pp. 398–401.

32 *Congressional Quarterly,* Feb. 21, 1981, p. 15ff.

33 Marshall Kaplan and Sue O'Brien, *The Governors and the New Federalism* (Westview Press, 1991), p. 2.

34 Michael de Courcy Hinds, "80's Leave States and Cities in Need," *New York Times,* Dec. 30, 1990, pp. 1, 16.

35 ACIR, *Federal Grant-in-Aid Programs,* p. 14.

36 Walker, *Toward a Functioning Federalism,* p. 114.

37 *U.S. Term Limits v. Thornton,* 63. *U.S. Law Week* 4413 (1995)

38 Joan Biskupic, "Ban on Guns Near Schools Is Rejected," *Washington Post,* April 27, 1995, p.1; Linda Greenhouse, "Justices Step In as Federalism's Referee," *New York Times,* Apr. 28, 1995, p.1; Nina Burleigh, "A Gun Ban Is Shot Down," *Newsweek,* May 8, 1995, p.85; and George Will, "Rethinking 1937," *Newsweek,* May 15, 1995, p.70.

39 "This Week with David Brinkley," A.B.C. Aug. 28, 1994.

CHAPTER 5

1 André Brown, Corporation for National and Community Service, interview with author, Jan. 17, 1995.

2 This case study is based on Steven Waldman, *The Bill: How the Adventures of Clinton's National Service Bill Reveal What Is Corrupt, Comic, Cynical—and Noble—about Washington* (New York: Viking Press, 1994).

3 Numbers are calculated from the *Commerce Clearing House Index,* 1993 and 1994 editions. These percentages are consistent with those of Congresses over the last thirty-five years. See Rozanne Barry, "Bills Introduced and Laws Enacted: Selected Legislative Statistics," *Congressional Research Service Report* (Jan. 15, 1993): 2; cited in Roger H. Davidson and Walter J. Oleszek, *Congress and Its Members,* 4th ed. (Washington, D.C.: Congressional Quarterly Press, 1994), p. 328.

4 See Morris P. Fiorina, *Congress: Keystone of the Washington Establishment* (New Haven, Conn.: Yale University Press, 1977).

5 On comparisons between the House and the Senate, see Ross K. Baker, *House and Senate* (New York: Norton, 1989).

6 See *How Congress Works* (Congressional Quarterly, 1994).

7 See Glenn R. Simpson, "Of the Rich, by the Rich, for the Rich: Will the Millionaires Turn Congress into a Plutocracy?" *Washington Post,* April 17, 1994, p. C4.

8 See in Hannah Fenichel Pitkin, *The Concept of Representation* (Berkeley: University of California Press, 1967).

9 Donna Cassata, "Freshman Class Boasts Resumes to Back Up 'Outsider' Image," *Congressional Quarterly* (Nov. 12, 1994): 9–12.

10 Gary C. Jacobson, *The Politics of Congressional Elections* (New York: Harper Collins, 1992), p. 11.

11 Elaine R. Jones, "In Peril: Black Lawmakers," *New York Times,* Sept. 11, 1994, p. E19; Ronald Smothers, "Fair Play or Racial Gerrymandering? Justices Study a 'Serpentine' District," *New York Times,* Apr. 16, 1993, p. B12.

12 See the extensive discussion of these ideas in John C. Wahlke, Heinz Eulau, William Buchanan, and LeRoy C. Ferguson, *The Legislative System* (New York: Wiley, 1962).

13 David C. Kozak, *Contexts of Congressional Decision Behavior* (Lanham, Md.: University Press of America, 1984); Thomas E. Cavanagh, "The Calculus of Representation: A Congressional Perspective," *Western Political Quarterly* 35 (Mar. 1982): 120–29.

14 Charles Clapp, *The Congressman: His Job as He Sees It* (Washington, D.C.: Brookings Institution, 1963); Roger H. Davidson, *The Role of the Congressman* (Indianapolis, Ind.: Bobbs-Merrill, 1969).

15 Davidson and Oleszek, *Congress and Its Members,* pp. 63–65; Cassata, "Freshman Class," 3237.

16 See David Mayhew, *Congress: The Electoral Connection* (New Haven, Conn.: Yale University Press, 1974).

17 For more on casework and Congress, see John R. Johannes, *To Serve the People: Congress and Constituency Review* (Lincoln: University of Nebraska Press, 1984); Morris P. Fiorina, *Congress: Keystone of the Washington Establishment,* 2d ed. (New Haven, Conn.: Yale University Press, 1989).

18 David B. Magleby and Candice J. Nelson, *The Money Chase* (Washington, D.C.: Brookings Institution, 1990), p. 71.

19 Richard Morin, "Six Out of Ten Disapprove of Way Hill Does Its Job," *Washington Post,* July 3, 1994, pp. 1, 5.

20 Richard L. Berke, "Democrats Glum about Prospects as Election Nears," *New York Times,* Sept. 4, 1994, p. A1.

21 See Glenn R. Parker and Roger H. Davidson, "Why do Americans Love Their Congressmen So Much More Than Their Congress?" *Legislative Studies Quarterly* 4 (Feb. 1979): 53–61.

22 Roughly ten thousand bills are introduced in each two-year session of Congress, and about six hundred laws are passed from that group. See Barry, "Bills Introduced and Laws Enacted," 2.

23 John W. Kingdon, *Agendas, Alternatives, and Public Policies* (Boston: Little, Brown, 1984).

24 See Paul Light, *Forging Legislation* (New York: Norton, 1992).

25 Stanley Bach and Steven Smith, *Managing Uncertainty in the House of Representatives: Adaptation and Innovation in Special Rules* (Washington, D.C.: Brookings Institution, 1988).

26 See Lawrence D. Longley and Walter J. Oleszek, *Bicameral Politics: Conference Committees in Congress* (New Haven, Conn.: Yale University Press).

27 Davidson and Oleszek, *Congress and Its Members,* p. 247.

28 See George C. Edwards III, *At the Margins: Presidential Leadership in Congress* (New Haven, Conn.: Yale University Press, 1989).

29 For the Democratic party, the names of these bodies are different: It is the Steering and Policy Committee that is chosen by the caucus.

30 Barbara Sinclair, *Majority Leadership in the U.S. House* (Baltimore, Md.: Johns Hopkins University Press, 1983).

31 For more on minority leaders, see Charles O. Jones, *Minority Party in Congress* (Boston: Little, Brown, 1970).

32 See Barbara Sinclair, *The Transformation of the U.S. Senate* (Baltimore, Md.: Johns Hopkins University Press, 1989).

33 Rowland Evans and Robert Novak, *Lyndon B. Johnson: The Exercise of Power* (New York: New American Library, 1966); Merle Miller, *Lyndon: An Oral Biography* (New York: Ballantine Books, 1980), chap. 2.

34 Harry McPherson, oral history, Lyndon Johnson Library, Austin Tex., pp. 78–88.

35 Woodrow Wilson, *Congressional Government* (New York: Meridian, 1967).

36 Davidson and Oleszek, *Congress and Its Members,* p. 349.

37 Longley and Oleszek, *Bicameral Politics, passim.*

38 Richard F. Fenno, Jr., *Congressmen in Committees* (New York: Little, Brown, 1973), p. 280.

39 The classic source on committees and the roles of members of Congress is Fenno, *Congressmen in Committees.* See also Steven Smith and Christopher Deering, *Committees in Congress,* 2d ed. (Washington, D.C.: Congressional Quarterly Press, 1990).

40 Quoted in James T. Murphy, "Political Parties and the Porkbarrel: Party Conflict and Cooperation in House Public Works Committee Decision Making," in Glen Parker, ed., *Studies in Congress* (Washington, D.C.: Congressional Quarterly Press, 1985), pp. 237–38.

41 These are numbers as of January 21, 1995, see *Congressional Quarterly Weekly Report,* January 21, 1995, pp. 217–40.

42 See Leroy N. Rieselbach, *Legislative Reform: The Policy Impact* (Lexington, Mass.: Lexington Books, 1978).

43 Thomas E. Mann and Norman J. Ornstein, eds., *Renewing Congress: A Second Report* (Washington, D.C.: American Enterprise Institute and The Brookings Institution, 1993), *passim.*

44 Walter J. Oleszek, *Congressional Procedures and the Policy Process* (Washington, D.C.: Congressional Quarterly Press, 1989).

45 Bach and Smith, *Managing Uncertainty in the House, passim.*

46 D. B. Hardeman and Donald C. Bacon, *Rayburn: A Biography* (Lanham, Md.: Madison Books, 1987).

47 David E. Rosenbaum, "Tax Bill Faces Fight, but First the Rules," *New York Times,* Apr. 2, 1995, p. 20.

48 See Steven S. Smith, *Call to Order: Floor Politics in the House and Senate* (Washington, D.C.: Brookings Institution, 1989).

49 See Fred R. Harris, *Deadlock on Decision: The U.S. Senate and the Rise of National Politics* (New York: Oxford University Press, 1993).

50 See ibid.

51 For more on the importance of seniority, apprenticeship, and political loyalty in Congress, see John R. Hibbing, *Congressional Careers: Contours of Life in the U.S. House of Representatives* (Chapel Hill: University of North Carolina Press, 1991), pp. 113–28; Donald Mathews, *U.S. Senators and Their World* (Chapel Hill: University of North Carolina Press, 1960), chap. 5.

52 John Ferejohn, "Logrolling in an Institutional Context: A Case of Food Stamp Legislation," in Gerald C. Wright, Jr., Leroy Rieselbach, and Lawrence C. Dodd, eds., *Congress and Policy Change* (New York: Agathon Press, 1986).

53 William R. Shaffer, *Party and Ideology in the*

United States Congress (Lanham, Md.: University Press of America, 1980); Norman Ornstein, Thomas E. Mann, and Michael Malbin, *Vital Statistics on Congress: 1993–94* (Washington, D.C.: Congressional Quarterly Press, 1994), p. 200.

54 Statistics taken from "Presidential Support and Opposition: Senate," *Congressional Quarterly,* for the years 1992, p. 3897; 1991, p. 3785; 1990, p. 4209; 1989, p. 3566; 1988, p. 3348; 1987, p. 3213; 1986, p. 2688; 1985, pp. 741–46; 1984, pp. 2802–8; 1983, p. 2781; and 1982, p. 2796.

55 David Rohde, *Parties and Leaders in the Post-Reform House* (Chicago: University of Chicago Press, 1991); Robert L. Peabody, *Leadership in Congress* (Boston: Little, Brown, 1976).

56 R. Douglas Arnold, *The Logic of Congressional Action* (New Haven, Conn.: Yale University Press, 1990), pp. 64–84; V. O. Key, Jr., *Public Opinion and American Democracy* (New York: Knopf, 1961), pp. 265–85.

57 Stephen Wayne and George Edwards III, *Presidential Influence in Congress* (San Francisco: Freeman, 1980); Stephen Wayne, *The Legislative Presidency* (New York: Harper and Row, 1978).

58 R. W. Apple, "In Pennsylvania, Feeling the Consequences of One Vote," *New York Times,* Sept. 27, 1994, p. A22.

59 See Jeffrey Birnbaum, *The Lobbyists* (New York: Times Books, 1992); Jeffrey Birnbaum and Alan S. Murray, *Showdown at Gucci Gulch* (New York: Vintage Press, 1987).

60 Quoted in Donald G. Tacheron and Morris K. Udall, *The Job of the Congressman,* 2d ed. (Indianapolis, Ind.: Bobbs-Merrill, 1970), p. 18.

61 See Harrison W. Fox, Jr., and Susan Webb Hammond, *Congressional Staffs: The Invisible Force in American Lawmaking* (New York: Free Press, 1977).

62 Richard Fenno, *Home Style: House Members in Their Districts* (New York: HarperCollins, 1987).

63 Donald R. Matthews and James A. Stimson, *Yeas and Nays* (New York: Wiley, 1975); David M. Kovenock, "Influence in the U.S. House of Representatives: A Statistical Study of Communications," *American Politics Quarterly* 1 (Oct. 1973): 456ff.

64 For more on congressional voting decisions, see John W. Kingdon, *Congressional Voting Decisions,* 3d ed. (Ann Arbor: University of Michigan Press, 1989); Aage R. Clausen, *How Congressman Decide* (New York: St. Martin's Press, 1973).

65 Ross Baker, quoted in Robin Toner, "Capitol Dynamic to Do the Framers Proud," *New York Times,* Feb. 26, 1995, p. 1.

66 Sinclair, *Transformation of the U.S. Senate.*

67 Joel D. Aberbach, *Keeping a Watchful Eye: The Politics of Congressional Oversight* (Washington, D.C.: Brookings Institution, 1990); James Q. Wilson, *Bureaucracy: What Government Agencies Do and Why They Do It* (New York: Basic Books, 1991).

68 See Richard F. Fenno, Jr., *The Power of the Purse* (Boston: Little, Brown, 1966).

69 Aaron Wildavsky, *The New Politics of the Budgetary Process* (Glenview, Ill.: Scott, Foresman/Little, Brown, 1988); Allen Schick, *The Capacity to Budget* (Washington, D.C.: Urban Institute, 1990).

70 See Richard E. Cohen, "The Transformers," *National Journal,* Mar. 4, 1995, p. 529.

71 See Fred R. Harris, *In Defense of Congress* (New York: St. Martin's Press, 1995).

CHAPTER 6

1 See Fred I. Greenstein, "A President Is Forced to Resign: Watergate, White House Organization, and Nixon's Personality," in Allan Sindler, ed., *America in the Seventies* (Boston: Little, Brown, 1977), pp. 50–102; *The Final Report of the Senate Select Committee on Presidential Activities,* chaired by Senator Sam Ervin; *Impeachment of Richard Nixon, President of the United States,* report of the Committee on Judiciary, House of Representatives. See also Michael Schudson, *Watergate in American Memory: How We Remember, Forget, and Reconstruct the Past* (Basic Books, 1992).

2 See Carl Bernstein and Bob Woodward, *All the President's Men* (New York: Simon and Schuster, 1974).

3 Jeb Stuart Magruder, *An American Life: One Man's View of Watergate* (New York: Atheneum, 1974).

4 See Sidney M. Milkis and Michael Nelson, *The American Presidency: Origins and Development, 1776–1990* (Washington, D.C.: CQ Press, 1990); Thomas E. Cronin, ed., *Inventing the Presidency* (Albany: State University of New York Press, 1988), p. 20.

5 See Robert J. Spitzer, *The Presidential Veto: Touchstone of the American Presidency* (Albany: State University of New York Press, 1988), p. 20.

6 See Alexander I. George and Juliette L. George, *Woodrow Wilson and Colonel House* (New York: John Day, 1956).

7 See Louis Fisher, *Constitutional Conflicts between Congress and the President* (Lawrence: University Press of Kansas, 1991).

8 See William Leuchtenburg, *In the Shadow of FDR,* rev. ed. (Ithaca, N.Y.: Cornell University Press, 1983).

9 See Edward S. Corwin, *The President: Office and Power, 1787–1984,* 5th rev. ed. (New York: New York University Press, 1984).

10 See Steven A. Shull, ed., *The Two Presidencies* (Chicago: Nelson-Hall, 1991).

11 Richard Neustadt, "Presidency and Legislation: Planning the President's Program," *American Political Science Review* 49 (Dec. 1955): 980–1021; and Richard Neustadt, "Presidency and Legislation: The

Growth of Central Clearance," *American Political Science Review* 48 (Sept. 1954): 641–71.

12 See John Frendreis and Raymond Tatolovich, *The Modern Presidency and Economic Policy* (Itasco, Ill.: F. E. Peacock Publishers, 1994), pp. 3–5.

13 Clinton Rossiter, *The American Presidency,* rev. ed. (Baltimore, Md.: Johns Hopkins University Press, 1987).

14 Cited in George Wolfskill, *Happy Days Are Here Again!* (Hinsdale, Ill.: Dryden, 1974), p. 189. See also James MacGregor Burns, *Roosevelt: The Lion and the Fox* (New York: Harcourt Brace Jovanovich, 1956), and *Roosevelt: The Soldier of Freedom, 1940–1945* (New York: Harcourt Brace Jovanovich, 1970); Frank Freidel, *Franklin D. Roosevelt,* 4 vols. (Boston: Little, Brown, 1952–53); Arthur Schlesinger, Jr., *The Age of Roosevelt,* 3 vols. (Boston: Houghton Mifflin, 1957–60).

15 See Stephen Skowronek, *The Politics Presidents Make* (Cambridge, Mass.: Harvard University Press, 1993).

16 Theodore Roosevelt, "The Stewardship Doctrine," in Harry Bailey, ed., *Classics of the American Presidency* (Oak Park, Ill.: Moore, 1980), pp. 35–36. See also *The Autobiography of Theodore Roosevelt* (New York: Scribner's, 1913), pp. 197–200.

17 William Howard Taft, *Our Chief Magistrate and His Powers* (New York: Columbia University Press, 1916), pp. 138–45.

18 See Bert A. Rockman, *The Leadership Question: The Presidency and the American System* (New York: Praeger, 1984), pp. 49–60.

19 See Inter-collegiate Debate Series, *Resolved: That the Powers of the Presidency Should Be Curtailed* (Congressional Research Service, 1974), document no. 93-273, pp. 62–79.

20 Jefferson to John Colvin, June 29, 1810. In Paul Ford, ed., *The Writings of Thomas Jefferson,* vol. 9 (New York: Putnam, 1899), vol. 9, p. 276.

21 See John Nicolay and John Hay, eds., *The Complete Works of Abraham Lincoln,* vol. 10 (New York: Francis Tandy, 1891), pp. 65–68.

22 Louis Fisher, *President and Congress* (New York: Free Press, 1972), pp. 29–41. See also Louis Fisher, *A Constitution between Friends* (New York: St. Martin's Press, 1978), pp. 7–46.

23 James David Barber, *The Presidential Character: Predicting Performance in the White House* (Englewood Cliffs, N.J.: Prentice Hall, 1985).

24 See Joseph A. Pika, Zelma Mosley, and Richard Watson, *The Presidential Contest* (Washington, D.C.: CQ Press, 1992).

25 See Harvey C. Mansfield, Jr., *Taming the Prince: The Ambivalence of Modern Executive Power* (Baltimore, Md.: Johns Hopkins University Press, 1993).

26 See *INS* v. *Chadha,* 103 S. Ct. 2764 (1983); Harold Relyea, "Executive Power and the *Chadha*

Case," *Presidential Studies Quarterly* 13 (Fall 1983): 651–53; Louis Fisher, "A Political Context for Legislative Vetoes," *Political Science Quarterly* 93 (Summer 1978): 241–54.

27 Judith A. Best, "The Item Veto: Would the Founders Approve?" *Presidential Studies Quarterly* (Spring 1984): 188.

28 28. See Arthur M. Schlesinger, Jr., *The Imperial Presidency* (Boston: Houghton Mifflin, 1973).

29 W. Taylor Reveley III, "Presidential War Making: Constitutional Prerogative or Usurpation?" *Virginia Law Review* 55 (Nov. 1969): 1243–1305; and W. Taylor Reveley III, *"Resolved: That the Powers of the Presidency Should Be Curtailed": A Collection of Excerpts and Bibliography Relating to the Intercollegiate Debate Topic, 1974–75* (Washington, D.C.: U.S. Government Printing Office, 1974), pp. 91–133; U.S. Congress, Senate, Committee on Foreign Relations, *Powers of the President to Send Armed Forces outside the United States,* 82d Cong., 1st sess., 1951; William Hardy, Jr., "A Tug of War: The War Powers Resolution and the Meaning of 'Hostilities,'" *Pacific Law Journal* 15 (Jan. 1984): 306–40.

30 See Phillip Shaw Paludan, *The Presidency of Abraham Lincoln* (Lawrence: University Press of Kansas, 1994).

31 See Forrest McDonald, *The American Presidency: An Intellectual History* (Lawrence: University Press of Kansas, 1994).

32 *Youngstown Sheet and Tube Co.* v. *Sawyer,* 343 U.S. 579 (1952). See Maeva Marcus, *Truman and the Steel Seizure Case* (New York: Columbia University Press, 1977); Alan Weston, *The Anatomy of a Constitutional Law Case* (New York: Macmillan, 1958).

33 See U.S. Congress, Senate, *Congressional Record,* 93d Cong., 1st sess., 1973, p. 119. See also U.S. Congress, Subcommittee on International Security and Scientific Affairs, *The War Powers Resolution: Relevant Documents, Correspondence, Reports,* 93d Cong., 3rd sess., June 1981; Hardy, "Tug of War," 306–40.

34 Gerald Ford, "The President and Political Leadership," in Kenneth Thompson, ed., *The Virginia Papers on the Presidency,* vol. 2 (Lanham, Md.: University Press of America, 1980), pp. 21–40. According to President Ford, "I never admitted that the war powers resolution, for example, was applicable to six instances where I committed U.S. military personnel: the evacuation of Da Nang, Saigon, Phnom Penh, the Mayaguez, and two evacuations from Lebanon in 1976. I strongly felt the enactment of the war power resolution was an enactment by the Legislative Branch on the prerogatives of the President."

35 Larry Berman and Bruce W. Jentleson, "Bush and the Post–Cold War World: New Challenges for American Leadership," in Colin Campbell and Bert A. Rockman, eds., *The Bush Presidency: First Appraisals* (Chatham, N.J.: Chatham House, 1991), pp. 93–94.

36 See Mary E. Stuckey, *The President as Interpreter-in-Chief* (Chatham, N.J.: Chatham House, 1991).

37 See Jeffrey K. Tulis, *The Rhetorical Presidency* (Princeton, N.J.: Princeton University Press, 1977), pp. 61–87.

38 Samuel Kernell, *Going Public: New Strategies of Presidential Leadership* (Washington, D.C.: CQ Press, 1993).

39 See Barbara Hinkley, *The Symbolic Presidency: How Presidents Portray Themselves* (New York: Routledge, 1990).

40 John Hart, *The Presidential Branch* (Chatham, N.J.: Chatham House, 1995), pp. 37–38; Peri Arnold, *Making the Managerial Presidency* (Princeton, N.J.: Princeton University Press, 1986).

41 Jack Valenti, "Life's Never the Same after the White House Power Trip," *Washington Post National Weekly Edition,* Mar. 19, 1984, p. 21.

42 See Thomas Cronin, "Everybody Believes in Democracy until He Gets to the White House: An Examination of White House–Departmental Relations," *Law and Contemporary Problems* 35 (Summer 1970): 573–625.

43 Fred I. Greenstein, *The Hidden-Hand Presidency: Eisenhower as Leader* (New York: Basic Books, 1982).

44 See Douglas Jeffrey, "The Iran-Contra Affair and the Real Crisis of American Government," *Claremont Review of Books* (Spring 1987): 3–8.

45 Larry Berman, *The Office of Management and Budget and the Presidency, 1921–1977* (Princeton, N.J.: Princeton University Press, 1977).

46 Jeffrey E. Cohen, *The Politics of the U.S. Cabinet* (Pittsburgh, Pa.: University of Pittsburgh Press, 1988).

47 See Bradley H. Patterson, Jr., *The Ring of Power* (New York: Basic Books, 1988).

48 Richard Neustadt, *Presidential Power and the Modern Presidents* (New York: Free Press, 1990).

49 Sydney M. Milkis, *The President and the Parties* (New York: Oxford University Press, 1993).

50 See Tulis, Rhetorical Presidency.

51 Theodore Lowi, *The Personal President: Power Invested, Promise Unfulfilled* (Ithaca, N.Y.: Cornell University Press, 1985).

CHAPTER 7

1 Account of facts from Art Harris, "The Unintended Battle of Michael Hardwick," *Washington Post,* Aug. 21, 1986, pp. C1, 4.

2 Lisa Leif, "Gay Cause Is Gaining Attention, Leaders Say," *Washington Post,* Aug. 26, 1986, p. 21. Sometimes the Court overturns one of its precedents because on reflection it believes that a mis-

take was made in the earlier decision. While the issue of homosexual privacy has not returned to the Court following the *Bowers* case described in our case study, after his retirement Justice Powell told an audience: "I think I probably made a mistake in that one. When I had the opportunity to reread the opinions . . . I thought the dissents had the better of the arguments." Since Powell provided the deciding vote in the case, it will be interesting to see what happens if this issue comes before the Court in the future. See John C. Jeffries, Jr., *Justice Lewis F. Powell, Jr.: A Biography* (New York: Charles Scribner's Sons, 1994), p. 530.

3 Alexander Hamilton, James Madison, John Jay, *The Federalist Papers* (New York: New American Library, 1961), no. 78, p. 465.

4 5 U.S. 137 (1803). The U.S. court of appeals was not established by congressional act until 1891. Before this time, the appellate courts were staffed by a panel of two district court judges and one circuit-riding Supreme Court justice.

5 Edward S. Corwin, review of Benjamin F. Wright's "Growth of American Constitutional Law," 56 *Harvard Law Review* 487 (1942).

6 Henry J. Abraham, *The Judicial Process,* 6th ed. (New York: Oxford University Press, 1993), p. 272. See also David O'Brien, *Constitutional Law and Politics, vol. 1, Struggles for Power and Governmental Accountability* (New York: Norton, 1991), p. 38.

7 See *Yates* v. *United States,* 354 U.S. 298 (1957). In 1951 a more conservative Vinson Court had upheld such convictions in *Dennis* v. *United States,* 339 U.S. 162 (1951).

8 For more here, see William H. Rehnquist, *Grand Inquests: The Historic Impeachments of Justice Samuel Chase and President Andrew Johnson* (New York: Morrow, 1992).

9 For more on this subject, see Milton Heumann, *Plea Bargaining: The Experiences of Prosecutors, Judges and Defense Attorneys* (Chicago: University of Chicago Press, 1977); John H. Langbein, "Torture and Plea Bargaining," *Public Interest* (Winter 1980): pp. 24–26.

10 Jon D. Hull, "Evict Thy Neighbor," *Time,* Nov. 21, 1994, p. 90.

11 "Verdicts: The Big Numbers of 1994," *The National Law Journal,* February 6, 1995, pp. C5–6.

12 Numbers of district court and court of appeals judges are as of October 1994 and rely on Sheldon Goldman and Matthew D. Saronson, "Clinton's Nontraditional Judges: Creating a More Representative Bench," *Judicature,* 78, no. 2 (Sept.–Oct. 1994): 69.

13 Abraham, *Judicial Process,* p. 163.

14 J. Woodford Howard, Jr., *Courts of Appeals in the Federal Judicial System* (Princeton, N.J.: Princeton University Press, 1981), p. 58.

15 See Laurence H. Tribe, *God Save This Honorable Court* (New York: Random House, 1985), pp.

50–77; William H. Rehnquist, *The Supreme Court: How It Was, How It Is* (New York: Morrow, 1987), pp. 235–53. And see John B. Gates and Jeffrey E. Cohen, "Presidents, Supreme Court Justices and Racial Equality Cases: 1954–1984," *Political Behavior,* Vol. 10, No. 1, pp. 22–36.

16 See Barbara Perry, *A "Representative" Supreme Court? The Impact of Race, Religion, and Gender on Appointments* (New York: Greenwood Press, 1991).

17 Until the Bush administration there used to be an "exceptionally well qualified" rating as well.

18 For more on the role of the ABA in the appointment process, see Joel Grossman, *Lawyers and Judges: The ABA and the Politics of Judicial Selection* (New York: Wiley, 1965).

19 Henry J. Abraham, *Justices and Presidents: A Political History of Appointments to the Supreme Court,* 3d ed. (New York: Oxford University Press, 1992), pp. 16–17.

20 For more on the Bork battle, see Ethan Bronner, *Battle for Justice: How the Bork Nomination Shook America* (New York: Norton, 1989).

21 For more on the Fortas nomination, see Bruce Allen Murphy, *Fortas: The Rise and Ruin of a Supreme Court Justice* (New York: Morrow, 1988); for more on the confirmation process generally, see John Massaro, *Supremely Political: The Role of Ideology and Presidential Management in Unsuccessful Supreme Court Nominations* (Albany: State University of New York Press, 1990).

22 For more on the Thomas confirmation battle, see Timothy M. Phelps and Helen Winternitz, *Capitol Games* (New York: Hyperion Books, 1991); Jane Mayer and Jill Abramson, *Strange Justice: The Selling of Clarence Thomas* (Boston, Mass.: Houghton Mifflin, 1994); John C. Danforth, *Resurrection: The Confirmation of Clarence Thomas* (New York: Viking Press, 1994).

23 Henry J. Reske, "The Safe Debate," *ABA Journal* (July 1994): 20.

24 Sheldon Goldman, "Bush's Judicial Legacy: The Final Imprint," *Judicature* 76, no. 6 (Apr.–May 1993): 295.

25 For more on the appointment process for district court judges, see Neil McFeeley, *Appointment of Judges: The Johnson Presidency* (Austin: University of Texas Press, 1987); Harold Chase, *Federal Judges: The Appointing Process* (Minneapolis, MN: University of Minnesota Press, 1972).

26 This information comes from Goldman and Saronson, "Clinton's Nontraditional Judges," 73. See also Goldman, "Bush's Final Legacy," *passim;* Goldman, "The Bush Imprint on the Judiciary: Carrying on a Tradition," *Judicature* 74, no. 6 (Apr.–May 1991): 294–306.

27 Sheldon Goldman, "Reagan's Second Term Judicial Appointments: The Battle at Midway," *Judicature* 70, no. 4 (Apr.–May 1987): 328–31.

28 Goldman and Saronson, "Clinton's Nontraditional Judges," 69.

29 David O'Brien, *Storm Center: The Supreme Court in American Politics,* 2d ed. (New York: Norton, 1990), pp. 165–66.

30 See Doris Marie Provine, *Case Selection in the United States Supreme Court* (Chicago: University of Chicago Press, 1980). This study also found that the Court gave special consideration to questions of federalism and organized labor issues. See also Joseph Tanenhaus, Marvin Schick, Matthew Muraskin, and Daniel Rosen, "The Supreme Court's Certiorari Jurisdiction: Cue Theory," in Glendon Schubert, ed., *Judicial Decision Making* (New York: Free Press, 1963), pp. 111–32.

31 Rehnquist, *Supreme Court,* p. 265. See also H. W. Perry, Jr., *Deciding to Decide: Agenda Setting in the United States Supreme Court* (Cambridge, Mass.: Harvard University Press, 1991); Gregory A. Caldeira and John R. Wright, "The Discuss List: Agenda Setting in the Supreme Court," *Law and Society Review* 24 (1990): 809–13.

32 378 U.S. 478 (1964).

33 384 U.S. 436 (1966). Besides the lead case, *Miranda,* the other appeals accepted were *Vignera* v. *New York, Westover* v. *United States,* and *California* v. *Stewart.* For the rest of the cases the Court had also decided there would be no "retroactivity," that is, the broad protections would not be extended back to previously decided cases (see *Linkletter* v. *Walker,* 381 U.S. 618 [1965]).

34 Liva Baker, *Miranda, Crime, Law, and Politics* (New York: Atheneum Press, 1983), p. 88.

35 Author interview with Toni House, Public Affairs Office, U.S. Supreme Court, 2/9/94.

36 For more, see Lincoln Caplan, *The Tenth Justice* (New York: Knopf, 1987).

37 Lincoln Caplan, "Uneasy Days in Court," *Newsweek,* Oct. 10, 1994, pp. 62–64; Linda Greenhouse, "Which Counts, Congress's Intent or Its Words," *New York Times,* Oct. 6, 1994, p. A18.

38 347 U.S. 483 (1954).

39 Richard Kluger, *Simple Justice* (New York: Knopf, 1975).

40 At one time, this was a two-stage process. The initial discussion of a case proceeded from the chief justice down the Court by seniority to the least senior justice. Then, to prevent pressure on junior justices in voting, the votes on a case would begin with the most junior justice and proceed up the Court by seniority to the chief justice. See letters from Robert Bradley, Chief Justice Rehnquist, and Henry J. Abraham in American Political Science Association, "Law, Courts and Judicial Process Section Newsletters," 6, no. 4 (Summer 1989): pp. 2–3; and 7, no. 1 (Fall 1989): Copy TK. See also Abraham, *Judicial Process,* p. 196.

41 Linda Greenhouse, "Ruling Fixed Opinions," *New York Times,* Feb. 22, 1988, p. A16.

42 321 U.S. 649 (1944).

43 Alpheus Thomas Mason, *Harlan Fiske Stone: Pillar of the Law* (New York: Viking Press, 1956). pp. 614–17.

44 410 U.S. 113 (1973).

45 112 S.Ct. 931 (1992).

46 David J. Garrow, "Justice Souter Emerges," *New York Times Magazine,* Sept. 25, 1994, pp. 36–42.

47 Nat Hentoff, "The Constitutionalist," *New Yorker,* Mar. 12, 1990, p. 60.

48 Harold Spaeth, *Studies in U.S. Supreme Court Behavior* (New York: Garland Press, 1990), *passim;* and Saul Brenner and Harold Spaeth, "Ideological Positions as a Variable in the Authoring of Dissenting Opinions," *American Politics Quarterly,* 16, (July 1988): 17–28.

49 Walter Murphy, *Elements of Judicial Strategy* (Chicago: University of Chicago Press, 1964), pp. 51–52.

50 *Webster* v. *Reproductive Health Services,* 106 L. Ed. 2d. 410 (1989), pp. 445–48. For the behind-the-scenes account of this battle, see also David Savage, *Turning Right: The Making of the Rehnquist Supreme Court* (New York: Wiley, 1992), pp. 209–14, 255–72, 288–98, especially pp. 292–93.

51 See Hentoff, "Constitutionalist," p. 60; O'Brien, *Storm Center,* pp. 156–70; and Perry, *Deciding to Decide, passim.*

52 403 U.S. 713 (1971).

53 Bernard Schwartz, *The Ascent of Pragmatism* (Reading, MA: Addison-Wesley, 1990), *passim;* and Bob Woodward and Scott Armstrong, *The Brethren* (New York: Avon Books, 1979), *passim.*

54 Savage, *Turning Right, passim.*

55 394 U.S. 557 (1969).

56 *Payne* v. *Tennessee,* 59 Law Week, 4823 (1991).

57 Abraham, *Judicial Process,* p. 325.

58 See Herbert Wechsler, *Principles, Politics, and Fundamental Law* (Cambridge, Mass.: Harvard University Press, 1961). See also Alexander M. Bickel, *The Least Dangerous Branch* (Indianapolis, Ind.: Bobbs-Merrill, 1962); Raoul Berger, *Government by Judiciary: The Transformation of the Fourteenth Amendment* (Cambridge, Mass.: Harvard University Press, 1977); Jesse H. Choper, *Judicial Review and the National Political Process* (Chicago: University of Chicago Press, 1980); John Hart Ely, *Democracy and Distrust: A Theory of Judicial Review* (Cambridge, Mass.: Harvard University Press, 1980).

59 Jeffrey Segal and Albert Cover, "Ideological Values and the Votes of U.S. Supreme Court Justices," *American Political Science Review,* Vol. 83 (No. 2, June 1989): 557–65.

60 Dean Alfange, Jr., "Free Speech and Symbolic Conduct: The Draft-Card Burning Case," Supreme Court Review (1968): 1–52.

61 381 U.S. 479 (1965).

62 For a fine example of this argument detailing the problems of the Court as a "superlegislature" see Robert Bork, *The Tempting of America: The Political Seduction of the Law* (New York: Free Press, 1990).

63 For more on Black's judicial philosophy, see Hugo Black, *A Constitutional Faith* (New York: Knopf, 1968); Roger K. Newman, *Hugo Black: A Biography* (New York: Pantheon Books, 1994), p. 512.

64 Jeffrey T. Leeds, "A Life on the Court," *New York Times Magazine*, Oct. 5, 1986, p. 74.

65 David J. Danelski, "The Influence of the Chief Justice in the Decisional Process of the Supreme Court," in Walter Murphy and Charles Herman Pritchett, eds., *Courts, Judges and Politics* (New York: Random House, 1986), p. 568.

66 Bob Cohn, "Supreme but Not Final," *Newsweek*, Oct. 12, 1992, p. 78–79.

67 Eisenhower was backing the decision by the Supreme Court to desegregate Central High School in Little Rock, Arkansas (*Cooper* v. *Aaron*, 358 U.S. 1 [1958]).

68 The decision banning school prayer is *Engel* v. *Vitale*, 370 U.S. 421 (1962).

69 Albert Beveridge, *Life of John Marshall*, vol. 4 (Boston: Houghton Mifflin, 1919), p. 551. The actual case is *Worcester* v. *Georgia*, 31 U.S. 515 (1832).

70 *Employment Division, Department of Human Resources of Oregon* v. *Smith*, 110 S.Ct. 1595 (1990).

71 David E. Anderson, "Signing of Religious Freedom Act Culminates Three-Year Push," *Washington Post*, Nov. 20, 1993, p. C6.

72 Thomas Marshall, *Public Opinion and the Supreme Court* (Boston: Unwin Hyman, 1989).

73 *Gideon* v. *Wainwright*, 372 U.S. 335 (1963).

74 Woodrow Wilson, *Constitutional Government in the United States* (New York: Columbia University Press, 1907), p. 142.

75 *Chambers* v. *Florida*, 309 U.S. 227 (1940), at 241.

76 *Reynolds* v. *Sims*, 377 U.S. 533 (1964), at 624.

77 See Bork, *The Tempting of America;* and Alexander Bickel, *Least Dangerous Branch: The Supreme Court at the Bar of Politics* (Indianapolis, IN: Bobbs-Merrill, 1962); and Berger, *Government by Judiciary*.

CHAPTER 8

1 James Q. Wilson, *Bureaucracy: What Government Agencies Do and Why They Do It* (New York: Basic Books, 1989), pp. 104–5.

2 Ibid, p. 104.

3 Gabriel A. Almond and Sidney Verba, *The Civic Culture* (Boston: Little, Brown, 1965), pp. 64–71.

4 See Max Weber, *Essays in Sociology,* trans. and ed. by H. H. Garth and C. W. Mills (New York: Oxford University Press, 1958), p. 232; Anthony Downs, Inside Bureaucracy (Boston: Little, Brown, 1967), pp. 24–25.

5 Stephen Engelberg and Adam Bryant, "Lost Chances in Making a Commuter Plane Safer," *New York Times*, Feb. 26, 1995, pp. 1, 24. See also Don Phillips, "How a Safety System Got Fogged In," *Washington Post National Weekly Edition*, Apr. 24–30, 1995, p. 29.

6 John Marini, *The Politics of Budget Control: Congress, the Presidency, and the Growth of the Administrative State.* (New York: Crane Russak, 1992), p. 191.

7 David Frum, *Dead Right* (New York: Basic Books, 1994), pp. 42–43.

8 William L. Riordon, *Plunkitt of Tammany Hall* (New York: Dutton, 1963), chap. 9.

9 Some pockets of cronyism remain. The Ramspect Act of 1985 allows former congressional staff members with three years of experience and certain qualifications to shift over to the civil service system without having to follow the same hiring procedures as other applicants (the justification for this is the congress member's experience). See Al Kamen, "No Invasion of Civil Service Yet: Few Hill Staffers Have Taken Advantage of a Law That Allows an Automatic Transfer," *Washington Post Weekly Edition*, Dec. 12–18, 1994, p. 17.

10 Kenneth J. Meier, *Politics and the Bureaucracy: Policymaking in the Fourth Branch of Government*, 4th ed. (Pacific Grove, Calif.: Brooks/Cole, 1993), p. 31, Hugh Heclo, *A Government of Strangers* (Washington, D.C. Brookings Institution, 1974).

11 Joel Brinkley, "Immigration Agency Pushes to Collect Travellers' Fees: Airlines Agree to Turn Over $5.6 Million," *New York Times*, Dec. 25, 1994, p. 9.

12 Erwin C. Hargrove, *Prisoners of Myth: The Leadership of the Tennessee Valley Authority, 1933–1990* (Princeton, N.J.: Princeton University Press, 1994).

13 Much of the argument in this section is based on Wilson, Bureaucracy, chap. 7. See also Guy Benveniste, Bureaucracy (San Francisco: Boyd and Frasier, 1977); Larry Hill, ed. The State of Public Bureaucracy (New York: M. E. Sharpe, 1992).

14 Meier, Politics and the Bureaucracy, p. 155.

15 Pierre Thomas, "Where Women Are in Charge: The Justice Department Boasts a Plethora of Female Lawyers in Senior Positions," *Washington Times Weekly Edition*, Aug. 8–14, 1994, p. 31.

16 Louis W. Koenig, The Chief Executive, 5th ed. (New York: Harcourt Brace Jovanovich, 1986), pp. 186–88.

17 Meier, *Politics and the Bureaucracy*, p. 159.

18 Michael D. Lemonick, "The $2 Billion Hole: Why Congress Finally Pulled the Plug on the World's Biggest and Most Expensive Physics Experiment," *Time*, Oct. 27, 1993, p. 69.

19 "Who Can Be Trusted?" *Gallup Poll Monthly*, Sept. 1992, p. 7, Larry B. Hill, "Refusing to Take Bureaucracy Seriously" (paper presented at the annual meeting of the Midwest Political Science Association, Chicago, 1993).

20 Though they did appear on Department of Defense invoices, the inflated prices were the product of accounting methods designed to save money. The real prices paid were closer to $20 for the hammers and 10 cents for the screws. See James Fairhall "The Case for the $435 Hammer," *Washington Monthly*, Jan. 1987, pp. 47–52.

21 Stephen Engelberg, "Farm Aid to Chicago? Miami? Study Hits an Inviting Target," *New York Times*, Mar. 15, 1995, p. 1.

22 Barry Sussman, "The Public Perceives a Stalemate in Reagan's War on Waste," *Washington Post National Weekly Edition*, Sept. 2, 1985, p. 37.

23 Peter T. Kilborn, "In Rare Move, Agency Acts Swiftly in a Sexual Harassment Case," *New York Times*, Jan. 10, 1995, p. A16; Stephen A. Holmes, "Programs Based on Sex and Race Are Under Attack," *New York Times*, Mar. 16, 1995, p. 1.

24 Anthony Downs, *Inside Bureaucracy* (Prospect Heights, Ill.: Waveland Press, 1994), pp. 100–1; Herbert Kaufman, *Red Tape: Its Uses and Abuses* (Washington, D.C. Brookings Institution, 1977).

25 "Sick Days," *Portland Press Herald*, Apr. 5, 1993, p. 1.

26 *Budget of the United States Government: Historical Tables, Fiscal Year 1995.* (Washington, D.C.: U.S. Government Printing Office, 1994), pp. 36–42.

27 Wilson, Bureaucracy, p. 160.

28 "Rats: What's for Dinner? Don't Ask." *New Yorker*, Mar. 6, 1995, pp. 7–8.

29 David Bullier and Joan Claybrook, "Regulations That Work," *Washington Monthly*, Apr. 1986, pp. 47–54.

30 Meier, *Politics and the Bureaucracy*, pp. 126–27.

31 "Sick Days," p. 1.

32 *Budget of the United States Government*, p. 42.

33 George J. Gordon and Michael E. Milakovitch, *Public Administration in America*, 5th ed. (New York: St. Martin's Press, 1995), pp. 294–97.

34 The concept comes from David Osborne and Ted Gaebler, *Reinventing Government: How the Entrepreneurial Spirit Is Transforming the Public Sector* (Reading, Mass.: Addison-Wesley, 1992). See also B. Wood and Richard W. Waterman, *Bureaucratic Dynamics: The Role of Bureaucracy in Democracy* (Boulder, Colo.: Westview Press, 1994).

35 David Nachimias and David H. Rosenbloom, *Bureaucratic Government: USA* (New York: St. Martin's Press, 1980).

36 Kenneth John Meier, "Representative Bureaucracy: An Empirical Analysis," *American Political Science Review 69* (June 1975): 526–42; James C. Garand, Catherine Parkhurst, and Russanne Jourdan Seoud, "Bureaucrats, Policy Attitudes, and Political Behavior: Extensions of the Bureau Voting Model of Government Growth," *Journal of Public Administration Research and Theory 1* (Apr. 1991): 177–212; Christopher Cornwell and J. Edward Kellough, "Women and Minorities in Government Agencies: Examining New Evidence from Panel Data," *Public Administration Review 54* (May–June 1994): 265–70.

CHAPTER 9

1 Quoted in Michael Wheeler, *Lies, Damn Lies, and Statistics: The Manipulation of Public Opinion in America* (New York: Dell, 1976). See also Albert Hadley Cantril, with Mildred Strunk, *Public Opinion, 1935–1946* (Princeton, N.J.: Princeton University Press, 1951), 151–55.

2 Alexander Hamilton, James Madison, and John Jay, *The Federalist Papers* (New York: New American Library, 1961), no. 10.

3 See Fred Greenstein, *Children and Politics* (New Haven, Conn.: Yale University Press, 1965).

4 Barbara Hinckley, *The Symbolic Presidency: How Presidents Portray Themselves* (New York: Routledge Press, 1990), pp. 10–11.

5 See the discussion in Robert S. Erikson and Kent L. Tedin, *American Public Opinion: Its Origins, Content, and Impact,* 5th ed. (Boston: Allyn and Bacon, 1995), pp. 128–30.

6 Urie Bronfenbrenner, *Two Worlds of Childhood: U.S. and U.S.S.R.* (New York: Simon & Schuster, 1970).

7 Robert D. Putnam, "Bowling Alone: America's Declining Social Capital," *Journal of Democracy 6* (1995): 65–78.

8 Todd Gitlin, *The Whole World Is Watching: Mass Media in the Making and Unmaking of the New Left* (Berkeley: University of California Press, 1980). See also Gitlin, *Watching Television: A Pantheon Guide to Popular Culture* (New York: Pantheon Books, 1986).

9 Benjamin I. Page and Robert Y. Shapiro, *The Rational Public* (Chicago: University of Chicago Press, 1992).

10 Alexis de Tocqueville, *Democracy in America* (New York: Harper and Row, 1966).

11 James Gibson, "The Political Consequences of Intolerance: Cultural Conformity and Political Freedom," *American Political Science Review,* 86 (June 1992): 338–56.

12 Ibid., 341.

13 Elizabeth Noelle-Neumann, *The Spiral of Silence* (Chicago: University of Chicago Press, 1984).

14 See William H. Flanigan and Nancy H. Zingale, *Political Behavior of the American Electorate,* 8th ed. (Washington, D.C.: Congressional Quarterly Press, 1994), p. 132 (Table 6-4).

15 See, for instance, Norman R. Luttbeg and Michael M. Gant, *American Electoral Behavior,* 1952–1992, 2d ed. (Itasca, Ill.: Peacock Publishers, 1995), esp. pp. 91–164.

16 Aaron Wildavsky, "Choosing Preferences by Constructing Institutions: A Cultural Theory of Preference Formation," *American Political Science Review* 81 (March 1987): 3–23.

17 See Gerald Pomper, ed., *The Election of 1988* (Chatham, N.J.: Chatham House, 1989).

18 Walter Lippmann, *The Phantom Public* (New York: The Macmillan Company, 1927), pp. 13–14.

19 Joseph Schumpeter, *Capitalism, Socialism and Democracy* (New York: Harper & Bros., 1950), p. 262.

20 Luttbeg and Gant, *American Electoral Behavior,* esp. chaps. 3–4, p. 67. See also Philip E. Converse, "Information Flow and the Stability of Partisan Attitudes," *Public Opinion Quarterly* 26, no. 4 (Winter 1962): 578–99.

21 See Michael Kagay, "In Judging Polls, What Counts Is When and How Who Is Asked What," *New York Times,* Sept. 12, 1988, p. A12. See also Michael Kagay, "As Candidates Hunt the Big Issue, Polls Can Give Them Clues," *New York Times,* Oct. 20, 1991, p. E3.

22 See Paul Brace and Barbara Hinckley, *Follow the Leader: Opinion Polls and Modern Presidents* (New York: Basic Books, 1992), pp. 97–115.

23 See Angus Campbell, Philip Converse, Warren Miller, and Donald Stokes, *The American Voter* (New York: Wiley, 1960).

24 See George Gallup, "Professor Gallup Describes a New Way of Measuring Public Opinion," *Independent Journal,* Nov. 15, 1935. See also Gallup, "The Quintamensional Plan of Question Design," *Public Opinion Quarterly* 11, no. 3 (Fall 1947): 385–93; "Polls and the Political Process: Past, Present and Future," *Public Opinion Quarterly* 29, no. 4 (Winter 1965–66): 544–49.

25 Page and Shapiro in Michael Mauser and Gary A. Margolis, eds., *Manipulating Public Opinion: Public Opinion as a Dependent Variable,* Pacific Grove, CA: Brooks/Cole Publishing Co., 1989.

26 Bernard Cohen, *The Public's Impact on Foreign Policy* (Boston: Little, Brown, 1972).

27 Shanto Iyengar and Donald R. Kinder, *News That Matters: Television and American Public Opinion* (Chicago: University of Chicago Press, 1987), esp. chap. 3.

28 George H. Gallup, *The Gallup Poll: Public Opinion 1992* (Wilmington, Del.: Scholarly Resources, 1993).

29 Ibid. See also George Gallup, Jr., *Gallup Poll* (Wilmington, Del.: Scholarly Resources, 1984, 1985, 1986).

30 See *Gallup Poll Monthly* (Nov., 1994), p. 39.

31 Sidney Verba and Norman H. Nie, *Participation in America: Political Democracy and Social Equality* (New York: Harper & Row, 1972), pp. 25–26

CHAPTER 10

1 See Theodore H. White, *The Making of the President, 1964* (New York: Atheneum, 1965), pp. 278–79.

2 See E. E. Schattschneider, *The Semi-sovereign People* (New York: Holt, 1960); V. O. Key, Jr., *Politics, Parties, and Pressure Groups* (New York: Crowell, 1964).

3 See Austin Ranney, *The Doctrine of Responsible Party Government: Its Origins and Present State* (Urbana: University of Illinois Press, 1962); Samuel J. Eldersvald, *Political Parties in American Society* (New York: Basic Books, 1982).

4 See L. Sandy Maisel, *Parties and Elections in America* (New York: McGraw Hill, 1992).

5 See John Aldrich, *Before the Convention: Strategies and Choices in Presidential Nomination Campaigns* (Chicago: University of Chicago Press, 1980).

6 See American Political Science Association, Committee on Political Parties, "Toward a More Responsible Two-Party System," *American Political Science Review* 64 (1950).

7 *National Party Conventions, 1831–1988* (Washington, D.C.: Congressional Quarterly Press, 1991), pp. 1–3. See also Michael Nelson, ed., *Guide to the Presidency* (Washington, D.C.: Congressional Quarterly Press, 1989), pp. 268–69.

8 See Noble E. Cunningham, *The Making of the American Party System, 1789 to 1809* (Englewood Cliffs, N.J.: Prentice Hall, 1965) and *The Jeffersonian Republicans* (Chapel Hill: University of North Carolina Press, 1957).

9 See Warren E. Miller, "Party Identification, Realignment, and Party Voting: Back to the Basics," *American Political Science Review* 85 (1991): p. 557.

10 See Ralph Ketcham, *Presidents above Party* (Chapel Hill: University of North Carolina Press, 1984).

11 See Frank Freidel, *Franklin D. Roosevelt: The Triumph* (Boston: Little, Brown, 1956), pp. 248–49.

12 James David Barber, *The Pulse of Politics* (New York: Norton, 1980), pp. 238–63.

13 See William Leuchtenburg, *In the Shadow of FDR* (Ithaca, N.Y.: Cornell University Press, 1983).

14 General Social Survey, National Opinion Research Center, University of Chicago.

15 Jonathan Alter, "Independents' Day," *Newsweek*, August 28, 1995: pp. 34–37; E. J. Dionne, jr., "Perot and Those Pandering Pols," *The Washington Post National Weekly Edition*, August 21–27, 1995: p. 29.

16 See Samuel Patterson, "The Etiology of Party Competition," *American Political Science Review* 78 (1984): 691.

17 The tendency of single-member district systems to be found in conjunction with two parties, while multimember districts correlate with a system of many parties, is often known as Duverger's Law. It is named for a well-known French political scientist, Maurice Duverger, who first enunciated this theory in his book *Political Parties* (London: Methuen, 1954).

18 Votes are cast in all fifty states and in the District of Columbia.

19 See Everett Carll Ladd, *American Political Parties: Social Change and Political Response* (New York: Norton, 1970); James L. Sundquist, *Dynamics of the Party System* (Washington, D.C.: Brookings Institution, 1973).

20 See Warren E. Miller, "Party Identification," in L. Sandy Maisel, ed., *Political Parties and Elections in the United States: An Encyclopedia* (New York: Garland, 1991).

21 See Frank Smallwood, *The Other Candidates: Third Parties in Presidential Elections* (Hanover, N.H.: University Press of New England, 1983); Steven J. Rosenstone, Roy L. Behr, and Edward H. Lazarus, *Third Parties in America: Citizen Response to Major Party Failure* (Princeton, N.J.: Princeton University Press, 1984).

22 See Byron Shafer, ed., *Beyond Realignment? Interpreting American Electoral Eras* (Madison: University of Wisconsin Press, 1991).

23 Edmond Constantini and Linda Ol Valenty, "The Motives-Ideology Connection among Political Party Activists," forthcoming article, and Peter B. Clark and James Q. Wilson, "Incentive Systems: A Theory of Organization," *Administrative Science Quarterly*, 6, 1961: 129–66.

24 See William L. Riordan, *Plunkitt of Tammany Hall* (New York: Knopf, 1905); Harold Gosnell, *Machine Politics* (Chicago: University of Chicago Press, 1939).

25 See Xandra Kayden and Eddie Mahe, Jr., *The Party Goes On* (New York: Basic Books, 1985).

26 See Howard Reiter, *Parties and Elections in Corporate America* (New York: Longman, 1973).

27 See Byron E. Shafer, *Quiet Revolution: The Struggle for the Democratic Party and the Shaping of Post-Reform Politics* (New York: Russell Sage Foundation, 1983).

28 See Theodore H. White, *The Making of the President, 1968* (New York: Atheneum, 1969).

29 See David E. Price, *Bringing Back the Parties* (Washington, D.C.: Congressional Quarterly Press, 1983).

30 William R. Shaffer, *Party and Ideology in the United States Congress* (Lanham, Md.: University Press of America, 1980); Norman Ornstein, Thomas E. Mann, and Michael Malbin, *Vital Statistics on Congress, 1993–94* (Washington, D.C.: Congressional Quarterly Press, 1994), p. 200.

31 See Larry S. Sabato, *The Party's Just Begun* (Boston: Scott Freeman, 1988); L. Sandy Maisel, ed., *The Parties Respond* (Boulder, Colo.: Westview Press, 1992).

32 David Broder, *The Party's Over* (New York: Harper and Row, 1971).

CHAPTER 11

1 See Ayres, B. Drummond, Jr., "Law to Ease Voter Registration Has Added 5 Million to the Polls," *The New York Times*, Sept. 3, 1995, p. A1; " 'Motor Voter' Bill Enacted after 5 Years," *CQ Almanac* XLIX (1993): pp. 199–201.

2 See Karen M. Arlington and William L. Taylor, eds., *Voting Rights in America: Continuing the Quest for Full Participation* (Lanham, Md.: University Press of America, 1992).

3 See Francis Fox Piven and Richard A. Cloward, *Why Americans Don't Vote* (New York: Pantheon, 1988); Raymond E. Wolfinger and Steven J. Rosenstone, *Who Votes* (New Haven, Conn.: Yale University Press, 1980).

4 Sidney Verba and Norman H. Nie, *Participation in America: Political Democracy and Social Equality* (New York: Harper and Row, 1972).

5 See Richard Sammon, "Senate Clears Filibuster Threat, Clears 'Motor Voter' Bill," *Congressional Quarterly Weekly Report* (May 15, 1993): 1221; Steven J. Rosenstone and Raymond E. Wolfinger, "The Effect of Registration Laws on Voter Turnout," *American Political Science Review* 72 (March 1978): pp. 25–30.

6 See August Meier and Elliot Rudwick, *From Plantation to Ghetto* (New York: Hill and Wang, 1966). On the grandfather clause, see *Guinn v. United States*, 238 U.S. 347 (1915); on white primary, see *Smith v Allwright*, 321 U.S. 649 (1944).

7 See Ray A. Teixeira, *The Disappearing American Voter* (Washington, D.C.: Brookings Institution, 1992); Paul Abrahamson and John H. Aldrich, "The Decline of Electoral Participation in America," *American Political Science Review* 76 (Sept. 1982): pp. 502–521. G. Bingham Powell, Jr., "American Voter Turnout in Comparative Perspective," *American Political Science Review* 80 (Mar. 1986): 17–44.

8 See Richard G. Niemi and Herbert F. Weisberg, eds., *Controversies in Voting Behavior*, 3d ed. (Washington, D.C.: Congressional Quarterly Press, 1993); Richard Morin, "The Dog Ate My Forms, and, Well, I Couldn't Find a Pen," *Washington Post National Weekly Edition*, Nov. 5–11, 1990, p. 38.

9 See George Will, "In Defense of Nonvoting," *Newsweek*, Oct. 10, 1983, p. 96.

10 Felix Frankfurter, dissenting in *Baker* v. *Carr*, 369 U.S. 186 (192), at 270.

11 See Michael M. Gant and William Lyons, "Democratic Theory, Nonvoting, and Public Policy: The 1972–1988 Presidential Elections," *American Politics Quarterly* 21 (April 1993): pp. 185–204; Priscilla L. Southwell, "*Alienation and Nonvoting* in the United States: A Refined Operationalization," *Western Political Quarterly* 38 (December 1985): pp. 663–675.

12 See Wolfinger and Rosenstone, *Who Votes*.

13 See Angus Campbell, Philip E. Converse, Warren E. Miller, and Donald Stokes, et al., *The American Voter* (New York: Wiley, 1960).

14 See Stanley Kelley, Jr., *Interpreting Elections* (Princeton, N.J.: Princeton University Press, 1983).

15 See Morris P. Fiorina, *Retrospective Voting in American National Elections* (New Haven, Conn.: Yale University Press, 1979).

16 See Nelson Polsby and Aaron Wildavsky, *Presidential Elections*, 9th ed. (New York: Free Press, 1995).

17 See M. Margaret Conway, *Political Participation in the United States* (Washington, D.C.: CQ Press, 1991), p. 8, Table 1–2.

18 See Gerald Pomper, ed., *The Election of 1992: Reports and Interpretations* (Chatham, N.J.: Chatham House, 1993).

19 See Neil Peirce and Lawrence D. Longley, *The Peoples' President* (New Haven, Conn.: Yale University Press, 1981; Martin Diamond, *The Electoral College and The American Idea of Democracy* (Washington, D.C.: American Enterprise Institute, 1977).

20 Verba and Nie, *Participation in America*, pp. 25–40.

21 See Elizabeth Drew, *Politics and Money: The New Road to Corruption* (New York: Macmillan, 1983).

22 See *Buckley* v. *Valeo*, 424 U.S. 1 (1976); *Federal Election Commission* v. *National Conservative Political Action Committee, et al.*, 450 U.S. 480 (1985); Larry Sabato, *The Party's Just Begun* (Glenview, Ill.: Scott, Foresman/Little, Brown, 1988), p. 125.

23 See Gary Jacobson, *Money in Congressional Elections* (New Haven, Conn., Yale University Press, 1980); Gary Jacobson, "The Effects of Campaign Spending in House Elections: New Evidence for Old Arguments," *American Political Science Review* 34 (May 1990): pp. 334–362.

24 See Conway, *Political Participation in the United States,* Chapter Two.

CHAPTER 12

1 See Adam Clymer, Robert Pear and Robin Toner, "For Health Care, Time Was A Killer." *New York Times,* August 29, 1994, p. A.1; Theodore R. Marmor, "The Politics of Universal Health Insurance: Lessons From Past Administrations?" *PS: Political Science and Politics,* vol. 27, 2 (June 1994), pp. 193-95; Catherine Manegold, "Health Care Bus: Lots of Miles, Not So Much Talk," *New York Times,* July 25, 1994, A. 7; Steve Waldman and Bob Cohn, "Health Care Reform: The Lost Chance," *Newsweek,* September 19, 1994, pp. 28–32.

2 Alexis de Tocqueville, *Democracy in America* (New York: Knopf, 1991 edition), p. 485.

3 See Jeffrey M. Berry, *The Interest Group Society* (Glenview, IL: Scott, Foreman/Little Brown 1989); Allan J. Cigler and Burdett A. Loomis, eds., *Interest Group Politics,* 4th edition (Washington, DC: Congressional Quarterly Press, 1995).

4 See Arthur F. Bentley, *The Process of Government* (Chicago: University of Chicago Press, 1906); David Truman, *The Governmental Process* (New York: Knopf, 1951); E.E. Schattschneider, *The Semi-Sovereign People* (New York: Holt, 1960).

5 Tocqueville, *Democracy in America,* p. 487.

6 See Burdett A. Loomis and Allan J. Cigler, "The Changing Nature of Interest Group Politics," in Loomis and Cigler, *Interest Group Politics,* pp. 1-31; Jack Walker, *Mobilizing Interest Groups In America* (Ann Arbor: University of Michigan Press, 1991).

7 See Mancur Olson, *The Logic of Collective Action* (Cambridge: Harvard University Press, 1965), pp. 5–52; Dennis Chong, *Collective Action and the Civil Rights Movement* (Chicago, University of Chicago Press, 1991).

8 See David Vogel, *Fluctuating Fortunes: The Political Power of Business in America* (New York: Basic Books, 1989); William Greider, *Who Will Tell The People?: The Betrayal of American Democracy* (New York: Simon & Schuster, 1992).

9 See Jeffrey H. Birnbaum and Alan S. Murray; *Showdown at Gucci Gulch* (New York: Vintage Books, 1988); Kay Lehman Schlozman and John T. Tierney, *Organized Interests and American Democracy* (New York: Harper and Row, 1986).

10 See the argument in John Kenneth Galbraith, *American Capitalism: The Concept of Countervailing Power* (Boston: Houghton Mifflin, 1952).

11 See Lawrence S. Rothenberg, *Linking Citizens to Government: Interest Group Politics at Common Cause* (New York: Cambridge University Press, 1992); Andrew S. McFarland, *Common Cause: Lobbying in the Public Interest* (Chatham, NJ: Chatham House, 1984).

12 See Karen O'Connor, *Women's Organizations' Use of the Courts* (Lexington, Mass.: Lexington Books, 1980); Mark P. Petracca, ed., *The Politics of Interests* (Boulder, Col.: Westview Press, 1992).

13 Mancur Olson, *The Logic of Collective Action;* See Robert H. Salisbury, "An Exchange Theory of Interest Groups." *Midwest Journal of Political Science,* (vol. 13, 1969) pp. 1-32.

14 For an extended discussion of the reasons why people decide to get involved in full-time political activity (including work within interest groups), see James L. Payne et al., *The Motivation of Politicians* (Chicago: Nelson-Hall, 1984).

15 See Jeffrey M. Berry, *Lobbying for the People* (Princeton, N.J.: Princeton University Press, 1977).

16 See Ronald J. Hrebenar and Clive S. Thomas, "The Japanese Lobby in Washington: How Different is it?" in Cigler and Loomis, *Interest Group Politics,* pp. 349-368; Pat Choate, *Agents of Influence: How Japan's Lobbyists in the United States Manipulate America's Political and Economic System* (New York: Knopf, 1990).

17 See Laura Woliver, *From Outrage to Action* (Urbana: University of Illinois Press, 1993).

18 James L. Guth, et al., "Onward Christian Soldiers: Religious Activist Groups in American Politics" in Cigler and Loomis, *Interest Group Politics* (1995).

19 See Frank J. Sorauf, "Adaptation and Innovation in Political Action Committees," in Cigler and Loomis, *Interest Group Politics,* pp. 175-192; Dan Clawson, Alan Neustadt and Denise Scott, *Money Talks: Corporate PACs and Political Influence* (New York: Basic Books, 1992).

20 See Bruce C. Wolpe, *Lobbying Congress: How the System Works* (Washington, D.C.: Congressional Quarterly Press, 1990).

21 Jonathan Rauch, *Demosclerosis: The Silent Killer of American Government* (New York: Random House, 1994).

22 Bentley, *The Process of Government,* 1908.

23 Truman, *The Governmental Process,* 1951.

24 Theodore Lowi, *The End of Liberalism* (New York: W. W. Norton, 1979). See Robert Dahl, *Preface to Democratic Theory* (Chicago: University of Chicago Press, 1956).

25 Hugh Heclo, "Issue Networks and the Executive Establishment," in Anthony King, ed., *The New American Political System* (Washington, D.C.: American Enterprise Institute, 1978).

26 John P. Heinz, Edward O. Lauman, Robert L. Nelson and Robert H. Salisbury, *The Hollow Core* (Cambridge: Harvard University Press, 1993).

CHAPTER 13

1 John Mueller, *Policy and Opinion in the Gulf War* (Chicago: University of Chicago Press, 1994); Philip M. Taylor, *War and the Media: Propaganda and Persuasion in the Gulf* (Manchester: Manchester University Press, 1992); W. Lance Bennett and David L. Paletz, eds., *Taken by Storm: The Media, Public Opinion, and U.S. Foreign Policy in the Gulf War* (Chicago: University of Chicago Press, 1994); Peter Arnett, *Live from the Battlefield: From Vietnam to Bagdad* (New York: Simon & Schuster, 1994).

2 Melvin Small, *Governing Dissent: The Media and the Anti-Vietnam War Movement* (New Brunswick, N.J.: Rutgers University Press, 1994); Daniel C. Hallen, *The "Uncensored War": The Media and Vietnam* (Berkeley: University of California Press, 1989).

3 Michael Parenti, *Inventing Reality: The Politics of the Mass Media* (New York: St. Martin's Press, 1993).

4 W. Russell Neuman, Marion R. Just, and Ann N. Crigler, *Common Knowledge: News and the Construction of Political Meaning* (Chicago: University of Chicago Press, 1992); Stephen Ansolabehere, Roy Behr, and Shanto Iyengar, *The Media Game: American Politics in the Television Age* (New York: Macmillan, 1993).

5 Harold W. Chase and Allen H. Lerman, *Kennedy and the Press* (New York: Crowell, 1965).

6 John Anthony Maltese, *Spin Control* (Berkeley: University of California Press, 1993); Robert M. Entman, *Democracy without Citizens: Media and the Decay of American Politics* (New York: Oxford University Press, 1989), pp. 8–9; Shanto Iyengar, *Is Anyone Responsible: How Television Frames Political Issues* (Chicago: University of Chicago Press, 1991); M. Russell Newman, *The Paradox of Mass Politics* (Cambridge: Harvard University Press, 1986).

7 Samuel Kernell, *Going Public* (Washington, D.C.: Congressional Quarterly Press, 1993); Jeffrey K. Tulis, *The Rhetorical Presidency* (Princeton, N.J.: Princeton University Press, 1987).

8 Ronald Berkman and Laura W. Kitch, *Politics in the Media* (New York: McGraw-Hill, 1986); Deane E. Alger, *The Media and Politics* (Englewood Cliffs, N.J.: Prentice Hall, 1989).

9 Carl Bernstein and Bob Woodward, *All the President's Men* (New York: Simon and Schuster, 1974).

10 David Halberstam, *The Powers That Be* (New York: Dell, 1979), p. 72.

11 Richard E. Neustadt, *Presidential Power and the Modern Presidents: The Politics of Leadership from Roosevelt to Reagan* (New York: Free Press, 1990), p. 260; Todd Gitlin, ed., *Watching Television* (New York: Pantheon, 1986).

12 Harold Stanley and Richard Neimi, "The Mass Media," *Vital Statistics on American Politics* (Washington, D.C.: Congressional Quarterly Press, 1992), p. 53.

13 See Thomas E. Patterson, *Out of Order* (New York: Knopf, 1993); Patterson, *The Mass Media Election: How Americans Choose Their President* (New York: Praeger, 1980); *1-800-President: The Report of the Twentieth-Century Fund Task Force on Television and the Campaign of 1992* (New York: Twentieth-Century Fund Press, 1993).

14 Sig Mickelson, *The Electric Mirror* (New York: Dodd, Mead, 1972), p. 154. See also Larry Speakes, *Speaking Out: The Reagan Presidency from Inside the White House* (New York: Scribner's 1988), p. 111.

15 Austin Ranney, *Channels of Power: The Impact of Television on American Politics* (New York: Basic Books, 1983).

16 Doris Graber, *Mass Media and American Politics* (Washington, DC: Congressional Quarterly Press, 1989), p. 12.

17 Marshall McLuhan, *Understanding Media: The Extensions of Man* (New York: McGraw-Hill, 1965).

18 See David Broder, *Behind the Front Page: A Candid Look at How News Is Made* (New York: Simon & Schuster, 1987). See also Jay Rosen and Paul Taylor, *The New News v. the Old News: The Press and Politics in the 1990s* (New York: Twentieth-Century Fund, 1992).

19 Graber, *Mass Media and American Politics,* p. 20.

20 Cited in Thomas Dye, Harmon Zeigler, and S. Robert Lichter, *American Politics in the Media Age* (Pacific Grove, Calif.: Brooks/Cole, 1992), p. 5.

21 Iyengar, *Is Anyone Responsible?* See also Douglas Kellner, *Television and the Crisis of Democracy* (Boulder, Colo.: Westview Press, 1990).

22 Thomas E. Skidmore, *Television, Politics, and the Transition to Democracy in Latin America* (Washington, D.C.: Woodrow Wilson Center Press, 1993).

23 Eric Barnouw, *Tube of Plenty: The Evolution of American Television* (New York: Oxford University Press, 1982), p. 415.

24 Ben Bagdikian, *The Media Monopoly* (Boston: Beacon Press, 1990).

25 395 U.S. 367 (1969).

26 *New York Times Co.* v. *United States* 403 U.S. 714 at 717 (1971).

27 Mark Cook and Jeff Cohen, "The Media Go to War: How Television Sold the Panama Invasion," *FAIR* 3, no. 2 (Jan.–Feb. 1991): 22–25.

28 Gerald Pomper, *The Election of 1992* (Chatham, N.J.: Chatham House Publishers, 1992).

29 Robert Lichter, Stanley Rothman, and Linda Lichter, *The Media Elite* (Alder and Alder, 1986).

30 Bagdikian, *Media Monopoly.*

31 Philip Weiss, "Who Gets Quote Approval?"

Columbia Journalism Review (May–June 1991): 52–54.

32 Howard Kurtz, "The Media Anoint Clinton: But How Do They Know That He's the Front-Runner?" *Washington Post Weekly,* Jan. 20–26, 1992, p. 13; Sidney Blumenthal, "The Anointed," *New Republic,* Feb. 3, 1992, pp. 24–27.

33 Richard Sobel, ed., *Public Opinion in U.S. Foreign Policy* (Latham, Md.: Rowan and Littlefield, 1993).

34 Richard Morin, "Maybe the Messenger Should Re-think the Message: Is the Media Polluting Our Politics?" *Washington Post Weekly,* Nov. 29–Dec. 5, 1993, p. 37.

35 Theodore White, *America in Search of Itself* (New York: Harper and Row, 1982), pp. 165–66. See also Roland Perry, *Hidden Power: The Programming of the President* (New York: Beaufort, 1984).

36 F. Christopher, "Campaign '92: Strategies and Tactics of the Candidates," in Pomper, *Election of 1992,* pp. 74–109.

37 Daniel Hallin, "Sound Bite News: Television Coverage of Elections, 1968–1988" (Media Studies Project Occasional Paper, Washington, D.C.: Woodrow Wilson International Center of Scholars, 1990). Mickey Kaus, "Sound-bitten," *New Republic,* 18 no. 207, Oct. 26, 1992: 16–18.; Kiku Adatto, "The Incredible Shrinking Sound Bite," *New Republic,* May 28, 1990, pp. 20–21.

38 Edwin Diamond and Stephen Bates, *The Spot: The Rise of Political Advertising on Television* (Cambridge, Mass.: MIT Press, 1992).

39 Kathleen Hall Jamieson, *Packaging the Presidency* (New York: Oxford University Press, 1984).

40 Patterson, *Out of Order,* chap. 5.

41 Tom Rosenthal, *Strange Bedfellows: How Television and the Presidential Candidates Changed American Politics, 1992* (New York: Hyperion, 1994).

CHAPTER 14

1 Case stud is based on *Texas* v. *Johnson,* 491 U.S. 397 (1989).

2 *United States* v. *Eichman,* 110 S.Ct. 2404 (1990).

3 For more on this argument, see Henry J. Abraham and Barbara A. Perry, *Freedom and the Court: Civil Rights and Liberties in the United States,* 6th ed. (New York: Oxford University Press, 1994), pp. 3–9.

4 See Leonard W. Levy, *Freedom of Speech and Press in Early American History: Legacy of Suppression* (New York: Harper and Row, 1963).

5 *Barron* v. *Baltimore,* 32 U.S. 243 (1833).

6 *The Slaughterhouse Cases,* 83 U.S. 36 (1873).

7 *Hurtado* v. *California,* 110 U.S. 516 (1884).

8 *Twining* v. *New Jersey,* 211 U.S. 78 (1908).

9 *Chicago, Burlington and Quincy Railway Co.* v. *Chicago,* 166 U.S. 226 (1897).

10 *Schenck* v. *United States,* 249 U.S. 47 (1919).

11 *Frohwerk* v. *United States,* 249 U.S. 204 (1919).

12 *Debs* v. *United States,* 249 U.S. 211 (1919).

13 *Abrams* v. *United States,* 250 U.S. 616 (1919).

14 *Gitlow* v. *New York,* 268 U.S. 652 (1925).

15 *Near* v. *Minnesota,* 283 U.S. 697 (1931).

16 *Powell* v. *Alabama,* 287 U.S. 45 (1932).

17 *Hamilton* v. *Board of Regents,* 293 U.S. 245 (1934).

18 *Palko* v. *Connecticut,* 302 U.S. 319 (1937).

19 For more, see Anson Phelps Stokes and Leo Pfeffer, *Church and State in the United States* (New York: Harper and Row, 1964).

20 *Walz* v. *Tax Commission,* 397 U.S. 664 (1970).

21 Abraham and Perry, *Freedom and the Court,* pp. 220–320.

22 *Everson* v. *Board of Education of Ewing Township,* 330 U.S. 1 (1947).

23 *Engel* v. *Vitale,* 370 U.S. 24 (1962).

24 *Abington School District* v. *Schempp,* 374 U.S. 203 (1963).

25 *Lemon* v. *Kurtzman,* 403 U.S. 602 (1971).

26 *Wolman* v. *Walter,* 433 U.S. 229 (1977).

27 *Roemer* v. *Board of Public Works of Maryland,* 426 U.S. 736 (1976).

28 *Committee for Public Education* v. *Nyquist,* 413 U.S. 756 (1973).

29 *Levitt* v. *Committee for Public Education and Religious Liberty,* 413 U.S. 472 (1973).

30 *Meek* v. *Pittenger,* 421 U.S. 349 (1975).

31 *Mueller* v. *Allen,* 463 U.S. 388 (1983).

32 *Marsh* v. *Chambers,* 463 U.S. 783 (1983).

33 *Lynch* v. *Donnelly,* 465 U.S. 668 (1984).

34 *Stone* v. *Graham,* 449 U.S. 39 (1980).

35 *Wallace* v. *Jaffree,* 472 U.S. 38 (1985).

36 *Grand Rapids School District* v. *Ball,* 473 U.S. 373 (1985).

37 *Edwards* v. *Aguillard,* 482 U.S. 578 (1987).

38 *County of Allegheny* v. *Greater Pittsburgh ACLU,* 497 U.S. 573 (1989).

39 *Lee* v. *Weisman,* 112 S.Ct. 2649 (1992).

40 *Rosenberger* v. *Rector and Visitors of University of Virginia,* 132 L.Ed.2d. 700 (1995).

41 *Reynolds* v. *United States,* 98 U.S. 145 (1879).

42 See *Braunfeld* v. *Brown,* 366 U.S. 599 (1961); *McGowan* v. *Maryland,* 366 U.S. 420 (1961); *Sherbert* v. *Verner,* 374 U.S. 398 (1963).

43 *Oregon Department of Human Resources* v. *Smith,* 294 U.S. 872 (1990).

44 Bob Cohn and David A. Kaplan, "A Chicken on Every Altar?" *Newsweek,* Nov. 9, 1992, p. 79.

45 See Alexander Meiklejohn, *Free Speech and Its Relation to Self-Government* (New York: Harper, 1948).

46 *Abrams* v. *United States,* 250 U.S. 187 (1919).

47 *Dennis* v. *United States,* 339 U.S. 494 (1951).

48 *Yates* v. *United States,* 356 U.S. 363 (1958).

49 See *Scales* v. *United States,* 367 U.S. 203 (1961); *United States* v. *Robel,* 389 U.S. 258 (1967).

50 *Brandenburg* v. *Ohio,* 385 U.S. 444 (1969).

51 See *Edwards* v. *South Carolina,* 372 U.S. 229 (1963); *Brown* v. *Louisiana,* 383 U.S. 131 (1966); *Chaplinsky* v. *New Hampshire,* 315 U.S. 568 (1942).

52 *Terminiello* v. *Chicago,* 337 U.S. 1 (1949).

53 *R.A.V.* v. *City of St. Paul,* 112 S.Ct. 2538 (1992); *Wisconsin* v. *Mitchell,* 113 S.Ct. 2194 (1993).

54 *Adderly* v. *Florida,* 385 U.S. 39 (1967).

55 *Cox* v. *Louisiana,* 379 U.S. 569 (1965).

56 *Cohen* v. *California,* 403 U.S. 15 (1971).

57 *New York Times Co.* v. *United States,* 403 U.S. 713 (1971).

58 *Nebraska Press Assn.* v. *Stuart,* 427 U.S. 539 (1976).

59 *Richmond Newspapers Inc.* v. *Virginia,* 448 U.S. 555 (1980).

60 See *New York Times* v. *Sullivan,* 376 U.S. 254 (1964); *Curtis Publishing Co.* v. *Butts,* 388 U.S. 130 (1967).

61 *Gertz* v. *Robert Welch Inc.,* 418 U.S. 323 (1974); *Rosenbloom* v. *Metromedia,* 403 U.S. 29 (1971).

62 *Herbert* v. *Lando,* 441 U.S. 153 (1979).

63 *Roth* v. *United States,* 354 U.S. 476 (1957).

64 *Memoirs* v. *Massachusetts,* 383 U.S. 413 (1966).

65 *Ginzburg* v. *United States,* 383 U.S. 463 (1966); *Ginsberg* v. *New York,* 390 U.S. 629 (1968); *Mishkin* v. *New York,* 383 U.S. 502 (1966); *Redrup* v. *New York,* 386 U.S. 767 (1967).

66 *Miller* v. *California,* 413 U.S. 15 (1973). (Italics added.)

67 *Jenkins* v. *Georgia,* 418 U.S. 153 (1974).

68 *Knox* v. *United States,* 114 S.Ct. 375. (1993).

69 *People of New York* v. *Defore,* 242 N.Y. 13, at 19–25.

70 *Weeks* v. *United States,* 232 U.S. 383 (1914).

71 For more, see David Fellman, *The Defendant's Rights Today* (Madison: University of Wisconsin Press, 1976), pp. 292–97.

72 *Wolf* v. *Colorado,* 338 U.S. 25 (1949); *Rochin* v. *California,* 342 U.S. 165 (1952).

73 *Breithaupt* v. *Abram,* 352 U.S. 432 (1957).

74 *Mapp* v. *Ohio,* 367 U.S. 643 (1961).

75 Dissent by Warren Burger, *Bivens* v. *Six Unknown Named Agents of Federal Bureau of Narcotics,* 403 U.S. 388 (1971).

76 *United States* v. *Calandra,* 414 U.S. 338 (1974).

77 *Stone* v. *Powell,* 428 U.S. 465 (1976).

78 *United States* v. *Leon,* 468 U.S. 902 (1984).

79 *Illinois* v. *Rodriguez,* 110 S.Ct. 2793 (1990).

80 See John Wesley Hall, Jr., "Privacy: Drug War Casualty," *National Law Journal* (Feb. 17, 1992): 19.

81 See *Carroll* v. *United States,* 267 U.S. 132 (1925); *United States* v. *Chadwick,* 433 U.S. 1 (1977); *Cady* v. *Dombroski,* 413 U.S. 433 (1973).

82 See *Chimel* v. *California,* 395 U.S. 752 (1969); *Coolidge* v. *New Hampshire,* 403 U.S. 443 (1971); *Schneckloth* v. *Bustamonte,* 412 U.S. 218 (1973); *United States* v. *Cortez,* 449 U.S. 411 (1981).

83 *Terry* v. *Ohio,* 391 U.S. 1 (1968).

84 *Adams* v. *Williams,* 407 U.S. 143 (1972).

85 *California* v. *Hodari D.,* 111 S.Ct. 1547 (1991).

86 *Florida* v. *Bostick,* 111 S.Ct. 2382 (1991).

87 *Brown* v. *Mississippi,* 297 U.S. 278 (1936).

88 *Haynes* v. *Washington,* 373 U.S. 503.

89 *Escobedo* v. *Illinois,* 378 U.S. 478 (1964).

90 *Miranda* v. *Arizona,* 384 U.S. 436 (1966).

91 *Harris* v. *New York,* 401 U.S. 222 (1971).

92 *Rhode Island* v. *Innis,* 446 U.S. 291 (1980).

93 *New York* v. *Quarles,* 467 U.S. 669 (1984).

94 *Oregon* v. *Elstad,* 470 U.S. 298 (1985).

95 *Arizona* v. *Fulminante,* 111 S.Ct. 1246 (1991).

96 *Griswold* v. *Connecticut,* 381 U.S. 479 (1965).

97 See David J. Garrow, *Liberty and Sexuality: The Right to Privacy and the Making of Roe v. Wade* (New York: Macmillan, 1994), pp. 16–195.

98 See Robert Bork, *The Tempting of America* (New York: Free Press, 1989); Ethan Bronner, *Battle for Justice: How the Bork Nomination Shook America* (New York: Norton, 1989).

99 *Eisenstadt* v. *Baird,* 405 U.S. 438 (1972); and *Doe* v. *Bolton,* 410 U.S. 179 (1973).

100 *Roe* v. *Wade,* 410 U.S. 113 (1973).

101 *Harris* v. *McRae,* 448 U.S. 297 (1980).

102 *Planned Parenthood of Central Missouri* v. *Danforth,* 428 U.S. 52 (1976).

103 *Akron* v. *Akron Center for Reproductive Health,* 462 U.S. 416 (1983).

104 *Webster* v. *Reproductive Health Services,* 492 U.S. 490 (1989).

105 *Planned Parenthood of Southeastern Pennsylvania* v. *Casey,* 112 S.Ct. 2791 (1992).

106 *Cruzan by Cruzan* v. *Director, Missouri Department of Health,* 110 S.Ct. 2841 (1990).

CHAPTER 15

1 This case study is based on Kenneth M. Mash, "The Limits of Judicial Power: Yonkers Revisited," Masters Thesis, Pennsylvania State University, 1991.

2 Donald G. Nieman, *Promises to Keep: African-Americans and the Constitutional Order, 1776 to the Present* (New York: Oxford University Press, 1991), pp. 3–5.

3 *Dred Scott* v. *Sandford,* 19 Howard 393 (1857).

4 *United States* v. *Cruikshank,* 92 U.S. 214 (1876).

5 *The Civil Rights Cases,* 109 U.S. 3 (1883).

6 *Plessy* v. *Ferguson,* 163 U.S. 537 (1896).

7 *Cumming* v. *County Board of Education,* 175 U.S. 528 (1899).

8 C. Vann Woodward, *Origins of the New South: 1877–1913,* 2d ed. (Baton Rouge, La.: Louisiana University Press, 1987) p. 331–38, 372–5.

9 *Guinn* v. *United States,* 238 U.S. 347 (1915).

10 Nieman, *Promises to Keep,* pp. 123–27.

11 *Nixon* v. *Herndon,* 273 U.S. 536 (1927).

12 Richard Kluger, *Simple Justice* (New York: Knopf, 1976), p. 250.

13 *Missouri ex rel. Gaines* v. *Canada,* 305 U.S. 337 (1938).

14 *Sweatt* v. *Painter,* 339 U.S. 629 (1950).

15 *McLaurin* v. *Oklahoma State of Regents,* 339 U.S. 637 (1950).

16 *Brown* v. *Board of Education of Topeka, Kansas,* 349 U.S. 294 (1955).

17 *Bolling* v. *Sharpe,* 347 U.S. 497 (1954).

18 *Brown* v. *Board of Education of Topeka, Kansas,* 349 U.S. 294 (1955).

19 Alfred H. Kelly and Winfred A. Harbinson, *The American Constitution: Origins and Development,* 4th ed. (New York: Norton, 1970), p. 940.

20 Jack W. Peltason, *Fifty-eight Lonely Men* (New York: Harcourt Brace Jovanovich, 1961).

21 Nieman, *Promises to Keep,* pp. 166–76.

22 *Heart of Atlanta Motel* v. *United States,* 379 U.S. 241 (1964).

23 *Katzenbach* v. *McClung,* 379 U.S. 294 (1964).

24 *Harper* v. *Virginia Board of Elections,* 383 U.S. 663 (1966).

25 Nieman, *Promises to Keep,* p. 180.

26 *Jones* v. *Alfred H. Mayer,* 329 U.S. 409 (1968).

27 *Alexander* v. *Holmes County Board of Elections,* 396 U.S. 19 (1969).

28 Nieman, *Promises to Keep,* p. 179.

29 *Swann* v. *Charlotte-Mecklenburg Board of Elections,* 402 U.S. 1 (1971).

30 *Keyes* v. *School District #1, Denver Colorado,* 413 U.S. 189 (1973).

31 *Milliken* v. *Bradley,* 418 U.S. 717 (1974).

32 Sidney Verba and Gary R. Orren, *Equality in America: The View from the Top* (Cambridge, Mass.: Harvard University Press, 1985), p. 5.

33 *DeFunis* v. *Odegaard,* 416 U.S. 312 (1974).

34 *Regents of the University of California* v. *Bakke,* 438 U.S. 265 (1978).

35 *United Steel Workers* v. *Weber,* 443 U.S. 193 (1979).

36 *Fullilove* v. *Klutznick,* 448 U.S. 448 (1980).

37 Steven L. Carter, *Reflections of an Affirmative Action Baby* (New York: Basic Books, 1991), p. 69.

38 *Firefighters Local Union No. 1784* v. *Stotts,* 467 U.S. 561 (1984).

39 *Wygant* v. *Jackson Board of Education,* 476 U.S. 267 (1986).

40 *Local Number 93, International Association of Firefighters* v. *City of Cleveland,* 478 U.S. 501 (1986).

41 *Local 28 of the Sheet Metal Workers' International Association* v. *EEOC,* 478 U.S. 421 (1986).

42 *U.S.* vs. *Paradise,* 480 U.S. 149 (1987).

43 *Martin* v. *Wilks,* 109 S.Ct. 2180 (1989).

44 *City of Richmond* v. *Crosson,* 488 U.S. 469 (1989).

45 *Patterson* v. *McLean Credit Union,* 109 S.Ct. 2363 (1989).

46 *Lorance* v. *AT&T Technologies,* 490 U.S. 900 (1989).

47 *Independent Federation of Flight Attendants* v. *Zipes,* 491 U.S. 754 (1989).

48 *Wards Cove Packing Co.* v. *Antonio,* 109 S.Ct. 2115 (1989).

49 Ronald Smothers, "Mississippi Mellows on Issue of Bias in State Universities," *New York Times,* Mar. 13, 1995, p. A14.

50 Charles Babington, "Supreme Court Lets Stand Ban on Blacks-only Scholarships," *Washington Post,* May 23, 1995, p. 1. The affirmative action case is *Adarand Constructors* v. *Pena,* 115 S.Ct. 2097 (1995).

51 Quoted in Nancy E. McGlen and Karen O'Connor, *Women's Rights: The Struggle for Equality in the Nineteenth and Twentieth Centuries* (New York: Praeger, 1983), pp. 389–91.

52 Ibid., pp. 272–74.

53 *Bradwell* v. *State of Illinois,* 83 U.S. 130 (1873).

54 *Minor* v. *Happersett,* 88 U.S. 162 (1875).

55 *Goesaert* v. *Cleary,* 335 U.S. 464 (1948).

56 *Hoyt* v. *Florida,* 368 U.S. 57 (1961).

57 *Reed* v. *Reed,* 404 U.S. 71 (1971).

58 *Frontiero* v. *Richardson,* 411 U.S. 677 (1973).

59 *Kahn* v. *Shevin,* 416 U.S. 351 (1974).

60 *Craig* v. *Boren,* 429 U.S. 190 (1976).

61 *Rostker* v. *Goldberg,* 453 U.S. 57 (1981).

62 *Johnson* v. *Transportation Agency, Santa Clara, California,* 480 U.S. 616 (1987).

63 Henry J. Abraham and Barbara A. Perry, *Freedom and the Court: Civil Rights and Liberties in the United States,* 6th ed. (New York: Oxford University Press, 1994), p. 421.

64 Frank Swoboda, "'Glass Ceiling' Firmly in Place, Panel Finds," *Washington Post,* Mar. 16, 1995, p.1.

65 *Katzenbach* v. *Morgan,* 384 U.S. 641 (1966).

66 *San Antonio Independent School District* v. *Rodriguez,* 411 U.S. 1 (1973).

67 *Plyler* v. *Doe,* 457 U.S. 202 (1982).

68 Dee Brown, *Bury My Heart at Wounded Knee: An Indian History of the American West* (New York: Holt, Rinehart and Winston, 1971).

69 Jay Mathews, "Landmark Law Failing to Achieve Workplace Goals," *Washington Post,* Apr. 16, 1995, p. 1.

70 Rosa Parks, quoted in *Center Daily Times,* February 8, 1993, p. 2A.

CHAPTER 16

1 The case is based on the excellent account in Randy Shilts, *And the Band Played On: Politics, People, and the Epidemic* (New York: St. Martins Press, 1987), p. 20.

2 Larry N. Gerston, *Making Public Policy: From Conflict to Resolution* (Boston: Little, Brown, 1983), p. 6. For the difficulties inherent in definitions of *public policy,* see the discussion in Thomas R. Dye, *Understanding Public Policy,* 6th ed. (Englewood Cliffs, N.J.: Prentice Hall, 1991).

3 For a recent argument that current national welfare policies are too conservative, see Charles Lockhart, *Gaining Ground* (Berkeley: University of California Press, 1973); Christopher Jencks, *Rethinking Social Policy: Rage, Poverty, and the Underclass* (Cambridge, Mass.: Harvard University Press, 1992). For an argument that current national welfare policies are too liberal, see Charles Murray, *Losing Ground: American Social Policy, 1950–1980* (New York: Basic Books, 1984); Lawrence Mead, *The New Politics of Poverty: The Non-Working Poor* (New York: Basic Books, 1992).

4 Murray Edleman, *The Symbolic Uses of Politics* (Urbana: University of Illinois Press, 1964); Edleman, *Constructing the Political Spectacle* (Chicago: University of Chicago Press, 1990).

5 For the origins of the "incremental" view of policymaking, see Charles Lindblom, *The Policymaking Process,* 2d ed. (Englewood Cliffs, N.J.: Prentice Hall, 1980); Lindblom, "The Science of Muddling Through," *Public Administration Review* 19 (Spring 1959): 79–88; Lindblom, "Policy Analysis," *American Economic Review* (June 1958): 298–312; Lindblom, "Still Muddling, Not Yet Through," *Public Administration Review* 39 (Nov.–Dec. 1979): 511–16; Lindblom, *Politics and Markets* (New York: Basic Books, 1977). See also Jeffrey L. Pressman and Aaron Wildavsky, *Implementation* (Berkeley: University of California Press, 1984, revised ed.).

6 The term *reflexive policy* is taken from Paul R. Schulman, *Large-Scale Policymaking* (New York: Elsevier, 1980).

7 Michael Lipsky, "Politics as a Political Resource," *American Political Science Review* 62 (Dec. 1968): 1155. See also Lipsky, *Protest in City Politics* (Chicago: Rand McNally, 1970).

8 Andrew Rosenthal, "Bush Finds 'Horror' on Los Angeles Tour: He Promises to Unite 'Family' of America," *New York Times,* May 8, 1992, p. 1.

9 Edwin Murray Hood, "When Presidential Slogans Meet the Realities of Government," *New York Times,* Apr. 12, 1992, p. 20E, letter to the editor.

10 Leading process models of policymaking include Randall Ripley and Grace Franklin, *Congress, the Bureaucracy, and Public Policy,* 5th ed. (Pacific Grove, Calif.: Brooks-Cole, 1991); Ripley and Franklin, *Policy Implementation in the United States,* 2d ed. (Homewood, Ill.: Dorsey Press, 1986); James E. Anderson, *Public Policymaking* (Boston: Houghton Mifflin, 1990). Leading policy typologies include Theodore Lowi, "Four Systems of Policy, Politics and Choice," *Public Administration Review* 32 (July–Aug. 1972): 298–310; Paul Peterson, *City Limits* (Chicago: University of Chicago Press, 1981); John W. Kingdon, Agendas, Alternatives, and Public Policies (Boston: Little, Brown, 1984).

11 Christopher Bosso (*Pesticides and Politics: The Life Cycle of a Public Issue* [Pittsburgh, Pa.: University of Pittsburgh Press, 1987]).

12 Leading scholars in the agenda-setting approach to understanding public policy include Roger Cobb and Charles Elder (*Participation in*

American Politics: The Dynamics of Agenda-Building, 2d ed. [Baltimore, Md.: Johns Hopkins University Press, 1983]), Bryan Jones (*Governing Urban America: A Policy Focus* [Boston: Little, Brown, 1982]), Barbara Nelson (*Making an Issue of Child Abuse* [Chicago: University of Chicago Press, 1984]), and, Robert Waste (*The Ecology of City Policymaking* [New York: Oxford University Press, 1989]).

13 Edward Banfield, *The Unheavenly City* (Boston: Little, Brown, 1970); Banfield, *The Unheavenly City, Revisited,* 2d ed. (Boston: Little, Brown, 1992).

14 John Kinsella, *Covering the Plague: AIDS and the American Press* (New Brunswick, N.J.: Rutgers University Press, 1989).

15 Gerston, *Making Public Policy,* p. 24.

16 For a discussion of policy entrepreneurs, see Eugene Lewis, *Public Entrepreneurship: Toward a Theory of Bureaucratic Political Power* (Bloomington: Indiana University Press, 1980). See also the discussion of policy entrepreneurs and "policy windows" in John Kingdon, *Policies, Politics, and Agendas,* 2d ed. (Chatham, N.J.: Chatham House, 1992). For an interesting account of policy entrepreneurs—some successful and some not—in the 1930's era Great Depression, see Alan Brinkley, *Voices of Protest: Huey Long, Father Coughlin, and the Great Depression* (New York: Knopf, 1982).

17 See Henry J. Abraham, *Freedom and the Court* (New York: Oxford University Press, 1988); Richard Klugar, *Simple Justice* (New York: Alfred A. Knopf, 1976).

18 See Gerald Rosenberg, *The Hollow Hope: Can Courts Bring About Social Change?* (Chicago: University of Chicago Press, 1992).

19 See Daniel Mazmanian and Paul Sabatier, *Implementation and Public Policy* (Glenview, Ill.: Scott, Foresman, 1984).

20 Jonathan Kozol, *Savage Inequalities: Children in America's Schools* (New York: Crown Publishers, 1991). See also Alex Kotlowitz, *There Are No Children Here* (New York: Doubleday, 1991); Tracy Kidder, *Among Schoolchildren* (New York: Avon, 1989). See also Thomas R. Dye, *Understanding Public Policy,* 7th ed. (Englewood Cliffs, N.J.: Prentice Hall, 1992), pp. 7–14, for an account of the celebrated Coleman Report.

21 Funding in fiscal year 1992 (FY92) for Head Start was two billion dollars. Funding for the B2 bomber program in FY92 included several bombers, each of which had a price tag of two billion dollars. Policy evaluations of the B2 bomber performance have demonstrated serious deficiencies with the new-generation deep-penetration bomber, while evaluations of Head Start have repeatedly established the positive cost–benefit ratio and performance levels of Head Start graduates. Funding for the two programs in the 1992 federal budget reflects both the scientific policy evaluation and the *political evaluation* and popularity of the two programs.

22 For a case in point that agencies, programs, and policies are extremely difficult to terminate, see Fred Bergerson, *The Army Gets an Air Force: The Tactics of Bureaucratic Insurgency* (Baltimore, Md.: Johns Hopkins Press, 1976), a prize-winning account of how policy entrepreneurs in the U.S. Army refused to accept the loss of air power to the U.S. Air Force and eventually emerged (behind the U.S. Air Force and the then Soviet Air Force) as the third-largest air power in the modern military world. This is a classic account of policy entrepreneurship, triggering activities, and the difficulty of terminating public policies.

23 This discussion of the demise of public policies draws heavily on the similar discussion of the reasons for the demise of public agencies in Anthony Downs, *Inside Bureaucracy* (Boston: Little, Brown, 1959).

24 For an excellent discussion of the life cycle of both NASA policies, and NASA as a bureaucratic organization, see Howard E. McCurdy, "Organizational Decline: NASA and the Life Cycle of Bureaus," *Public Administration Review* (July–Aug. 1991) 51: 308–15. See also McCurdy, *Space Station Decision: Incremental Politics and Technological Change* (Baltimore, MD: Johns Hopkins University Press, 1991); Arnold Levine, *Managing NASA in the Apollo Era* (Washington D.C.: NASA, SP-4102, 1982). Deborah A. Stone, *Policy Paradox and Political Reason* (Glenview, Ill.: Scott, Foresman, 1988).

25 One useful way to view policy formation is to depict public policymaking as a "game" with "players," "rules," "game strategies," and so on. See, for example, the account by Peter Navarro, *The Policy Game: How Special Interests and Ideologies Are Stealing America* (New York: John Wiley & Sons, Inc., 1984); and Sara Rimer, "Watts Organizer Feels Weight of Riots, History," *New York Times,* June 24, 1992, p. A9.

26 For an excellent account of pork barrel policymaking in Congress, see John Ferejohn, *Pork Barrel Politics: Rivers and Harbors Legislation, 1947–1968* (Stanford, Calif.: Stanford University Press, 1974). See also David Mayhew, *Congress: The Electoral Connection* (New Haven, Conn.: Yale University Press, 1974); Donald R. Matthews, *U.S. Senators and Their World* (New York: Vintage, 1960). For a discussion of coalitions attempting to secure "collective, material" goods, see Mancur Olson, *The Logic of Collective Action* (Cambridge, Mass.: Harvard University Press, 1965); and for a comparison of collective-goods (pork barrel) policy coalitions versus collective-bads (intrusive) policy coalitions, see Waste, *Ecology of City Policymaking.*

27 One of the weapons that Eisenhower had in mind when speaking of the strength of the iron triangle he labeled the military–industrial complex was a new-generation, strategic manned bomber first proposed as a replacement for the aging B-52's of the Strategic Air Command in the 1950s. One measure of the success of the bomber lobby was the eventual decision by Congress to fund the development and acquisition of not one but *two* bombers to replace the B-52's. For an excellent history of the long and troubled, but eventually successful, effort to build both the B-1 Strategic Bomber, and the B-2 (Stealth) Bomber, see Nick Kotz, *The Wild Blue Yonder* (New York: Pantheon, 1988).

28 For an earlier discussion of the policy triangle/policy polygon metaphor, see Waste, *Ecology of City Policymaking,* p. 28.

29 Hugh Heclo, "Issue Networks and Executive Establishment," in Anthony King, ed., *The New Political System* (Washington, D.C.: American Enterprise Institute, 1978), pp. 87–124. Robert Salisbury, John Heinz, Edward Laumann, and Robert Nelson, "Who Works with Whom? Interest Group Alliances and Opposition," *American Political Science Review* 81 (Dec. 1987): 1217–34.

30 Kenneth J. Meier, *Regulation: Politics, Bureaucracy, and Economics* (New York: St. Martin's Press, 1985), p. 1. See also Michael D. Reagan, *The Politics of Policy* (Boston: Little, Brown, 1987).

31 This discussion of the types of regulatory activity used by the federal government draws heavily upon the discussion of regulatory activity in Meier, *Regulation,* pp. 1–2.

32 See Rachel Carson, *Silent Spring* (Boston: Houghton Mifflin, 1962); Kent E. Portney, *Controversial Issues in Environmental Policy* (Newbury Park, Calif.: Sage Publications, 1992).

33 The best single account of environmental policymaking in this period is the agenda-setting study by Bosso, *Pesticides and Politics.* See also Thomas Dunlap, *DDT: Scientists,Citizens, and Public Policy* (Princeton, N.J.: Princeton University Press, 1981); Charles O. Jones, *Clean Air: The Policies and Politics of Pollution Control* (Pittsburgh, Pa.: University of Pittsburgh Press, 1975).

34 Nathaniel C. Nash, "Savings Unit Donation Criticized," *New York Times,* June 29, 1990, p. D4. See also John R. Cranford, "Decision in Keating Five Settles Little for Senate," *Congressional Quarterly Weekly Report* (Mar. 2, 1991): 517. Stephen Labaton, "The Bailout Agency Becomes a Highly Motivated Seller," *New York Times,* Mar. 31, 1991, p. E4.

35 See William Julius Wilson, *The Truly Disadvantaged* (Chicago: University of Chicago Press, 1987). For documentation that public opinion is strongly in favor of supporting programs in aid of the needy, see Theodore R. Marmor, Jerry L. Mashaw, and Philip L. Harvey, *America's Misunderstood Welfare State* (New York: Basic Books, 1990). See Herbert Gans, "The Dangers of the Underclass: It's Harmfulness as a Planning Concept," in *People, Plans and Policies* (New York: Columbia University Press, 1991), pp. 328–43; Christopher Jencks and Paul Peterson, *The Urban Underclass* (Washington, D.C.: Brookings Institution, 1991).

36 For a discussion of problems inherent in the

income figure used by the federal government to estimate the poverty rate, see Jason DeParle, "Poverty Rate Rose Sharply Last Year as Incomes Slipped," *New York Times,* Sept. 27, 1991, p. 1. See also John E. Schwartz and Thomas J. Volgy, "Social Support for Self-reliance: The Politics of Making Work Pay," *American Prospect* (Spring 1992): 77, which argues that the current income figure of 55 percent is too low and notes that "housing surveys from the late 1980's disclose that four-fifths of American households below 175 percent of the official poverty line had too little income to cover the costs of their shelter, even if they spent only the minimal amounts for the other necessities contained in the Department of Labor's 'low' budget" (p. 68).

37 Jonathan Marshall, "Beyond 'Murphy Brown': U.S. Battles Poverty of Single Parents," *San Francisco Chronicle,* June 11, 1992, p. 1. Erick Eckholm, "Young Mothers Try to Avoid a Lifetime on Welfare," *New York Times,* June 23, 1992, p. A6. Sylvia Nasar, "The 1980's: A Very Good Time for the Very Rich, Data Show the Top 1% Got 60% of Gain in Decade's Boom," *New York Times,* Mar. 3, 1992, p. 8.

38 While AFDC grants of $924 a month for a family of three in Alaska might sound extremely high and generous to a casual listener, the high cost of rent in states such as Alaska and California should be considered. As Laura Kurtzman noted of a recent study by the federal Department of Housing and Urban Development (HUD): "According to the HUD estimates, California is the second most expensive state, after Massachusetts. If a family of three paid the full cost of a one-bedroom unit, rent would consume 97 percent of their monthly check. Two bedrooms would consume 113 percent" ("State 17th in Welfare Study Says: Claims Housing Costs Pinch High Benefits," *Sacramento Bee,* June 11, 1992, p. B8).

39 Daniel Patrick Moynihan, *Maximum Feasible Misunderstanding: Community Action and the War on Poverty* (New York: Free Press, 1969).

40 Two dated but still excellent accounts of the policymaking battles surrounding the enactment of Medicare are Robert Alford, *Health Care Politics* (Chicago: University of Chicago Press, 1975); Theodore Marmor, *The Politics of Medicare* (Chicago: Aldine, 1973).

41 Office of Management and Budget, *FY 82 Budget Revisions,* (Mar. 1981): 8–9. Jason DeParle, "Moynihan, Welfare Dependency Signals New Ill," *New York Times,* Dec. 9, 1991, p. A8.

42 Donald F. Kettle, *Deficit Politics* (New York: Macmillan, 1992), p. 51.

43 Judith M. Gueron and Edward Pauly, *From Welfare to Work* (New York: Russell Sage Foundation, 1991).

44 John Leo, "Making Work the Norm: Riots and Jobs," *San Francisco Chronicle,* May 31, 1992, p. 5.

45 Adam Clymer, "G.O.P. Announces a Welfare Policy: House Leaders Offer Proposal as First of Several to Deal with Domestic Issues," *New York Times,* April 29, 1992, A14. See also Mickey Kaus, *The End of Equality* (New York: Basic Books, 1992).

CHAPTER 17

1 Bob Woodward, *The Agenda: Inside the Clinton White House* (New York: Simon & Schuster, 1994), Chapter 31. See Howard Fineman, Eleanor Clift, Bob Cohn, Ellen Ladowsky and Rich Thomas, "Whew!," *Newsweek,* August 16, 1993, p. 19.

2 See Harold Lasswell, *The Political Writings of Harold Laswell* (Glencoe, IL: Free Press, 1951).

3 See for example, Gerald H. Kramer, "Short-Term Fluctuations in U.S. Voting Behavior," *American Political Science Review* (1971), pp. 131–143; Edward R. Tufte, "Determinants of the Outcomes of Midterm Congressional Elections," *American Political Science Review,* (1975), pp. 812–826; Donald Kinder and D. Roderick Kiewiet, "Sociotropic Politics: The American Case," *British Journal of Political Science,* (1981), pp. 129–161.

4 Douglas Hibbs, "Political Parties and Macroeconomic Policy," *American Political Science Review* (1977), pp. 1467–1487; Nathanial Beck, "Parties, Administrations and American Macroeconomic Outcomes," *American Political Science Review* (1982), pp. 82–93.

5 Edward Tufte, *Political Control of the Economy* (Princeton: Princeton University Press, 1978).

6 Adam Smith, *An Inquiry into the Wealth of Nations* (1776; Reprinted in Bobs Merrill, 1961).

7 John Maynard Keynes, *The General Theory of Employment, Interest and Money* (1936).

8 Milton Friedman and Walter Heller, *Monetary versus Fiscal Policy* (New York: Norton, 1969).

9 See Denise E. Markovich and Ronald E. Pynn, *American Political Economy: Using Economics With Politics* (Brooks Cole, 1988), p. 214.

10 See John T. Woolley, *Monetary Politics: The Federal Reserve and the Politics of Monetary Policy* (London: Cambridge University Press, 1984).

11 See Larry Berman, ed., *Looking Back on the Reagan Presidency* (Baltimore: The Johns Hopkins University Press, 1990).

12 See Kevin Phillips, *The Politics of Rich and Poor* (New York: Harper Collins, 1990).

13 See Benjamin Friedman, *Day of Reckoning: The Consequences of American Economic Policy under Reagan and After* (New York: Random House, 1988); David S. Stockman, *The Triumph of Politics: Why the Reagan Revolution Failed* (New York: Harper, 1986).

14 James L. Gosling, *Budgetary Politics in American Governments* (Longman, 1992), pp. 73–74; Howard E. Shuman, *Politics and the Budget: The Struggle Between the President and the Congress* (Prentice Hall, 1988), p. 220.

15 See Aaron Wildavsky, *The New Politics of the Budgetary Process* (New York: Harper Collins, 1991).

16 See James Pfiffner, ed., *The President and Economic Policy* (Philadelphia: Institute for Human Issues, 1986).

17 Jackie Calmes, "Gramm-Rudman-Hollings: Has Its Time Passed?" *Congressional Quarterly Weekly Report* 47 41 (October 14, 1989), p. 2685.

18 See Donald F. Kettl, *Deficit Politics,* (New York: Macmillan, 1992); Robert Heilbronce and Peter Bernstein, *The Debt and Deficit* (New York: W.W. Norton, 1989).

19 James D. Savage, *Balanced Budgets and American Politics* (Ithaca, NY: Cornell University Press, 1988).

20 Jayne Bryant Quinn, "What's a Taxpayer to Do?" *Newsweek,* March 1, 1993, pp. 36–37; also see Robert Hall and Alvin Rabushka, *Low Tax, Simple Tax, Flat Tax* (New York: McGraw Hill, 1983).

21 See Richard Gephardt, "The 10% Solution." *The New York Times,* July 13, 1995, A15.

22 See Woodward, *The Agenda,* pp. 264–265.

23 See Kevin Phillips, *Boiling Point: Democrats, Republicans, and The Decline of Middle Class Prosperity* (New York: Random House, 1993).

24 See Herbert Stein, *Presidential Economics: The Maker of Economic Policy From Roosevelt to Reagan and Beyond,* 2nd ed., (Washington, D.C.: American Enterprise Institute, 1988).

25 See Alice Rivlin, *Reviving The American Dream* (Washington, D.C.: The Brookings Institute, 1992).

26 See Paul Quirk and Joseph Hinchfiffe, "Domestic Policy: The Trial of a Centrist Democrat," in *The Clinton Presidency: First Appraisals,* edited by Colin Campbell and Bert A. Rockman, (Chatham: Chatham House, 1996).

CHAPTER 18

1 Frederick Kempe, *Divorcing the Dictator: America's Bungled Affair with Noriega* (New York: G.P. Putnam's Sons, 1990).

2 See Hans Morgenthau, *Politics Among Nations: The Struggle for Power and Peace* (New York: Knopf, 1973); Robert C. Johansen, *The National Interest and the Human Interest: An Analysis of US Foreign Report* (Princeton: Princeton University Press, 1980).

3 See Ernest K. King, *The Making of the Monroe Doctrine* (Cambridge: Harvard University Press, 1975); David F. Ronfeldt, "Rethinking the Monroe Doctrine" *Orbis,* vol. 28, Winter 1985.

4 See Barton J. Bernstein, "Roosevelt, Truman, and the Atomic Bomb, 1941–1945," *Political Science Quarterly XC* (Spring 1975), p. 61.

5 George F. Kennan, "The Sources of Soviet Conduct" *Foreign Affairs,* vol. 25, July 1947, pp. 566–582.

6 From the NATO Charter, quoted in Walter LaFeber, *America, Russia, and the Cold War, 1945–1990* (New York: McGraw-Hill 1991) 6th ed., p. 82.

7 See LaFeber, *America, Russia, and the Cold War, 1945–1990,* especially pp 96–98.

8 See Graham Allison, *Essence of Decision: Explaining the Cuban Missile Crisis* (Boston: Little, Brown, 1971); See the account in Robert Kennedy *Thirteen Days* (New York: Signet Books, 1969), pp. 38–39; and James G. Blight, Joseph S. Nye, Jr., and David A. Welch, "The Cuban Missile Crisis Revisited," *Foreign Affairs,* vol. 66, Fall 1987, pp. 170–188.

9 See Gerald T. Rice, *The Bold Experiment: JFK's Peace Corps* (Notre Dame: University of Indiana Press, 1985).

10 See Larry Berman, *Planning A Tragedy: The Americanization of the War in Vietnam* (New York: W.W. Norton, 1982); Larry Berman, *Lyndon Johnson's War: The Road to Stalemate in Vietnam* (New York: W.W. Norton, 1989).

11 Lyndon Baines Johnson, *The Vantage Point: Perspectives on the Presidency, 1963–1969* (New York: Popular Library, 1971), p. 383.

12 See Arnold Issacs, *Without Honor: Defeat in Vietnam and Cambodia* (Baltimore: The Johns Hopkins University Press, 1984); Townsend Hoopes, *The Limits of Intervention* (New York: W.W. Norton, 1987).

13 See Raymond L. Garthoff, *Détente and Confrontation: American-soviet Relations From Nixon to Reagan* (Washington, DC: Brookings, 1985).

14 See McGeorge Bundy, George F. Kennan, Robert S. McNamara and Gerard Smith, "The President's Choice: Star Wars or Arms Control," *Foreign Affairs,* Winter 1984–1985.

15 See Larry Berman and Bruce W. Jentleson, "Bush and the Post-Cold War World: New Challenges for American Leadership," in *The Bush Presidency: First Appraisals,* Colin Campbell and Bert Rockman, eds. (Chatham: Chatham House, 1991), pp 93–94.

16 See Bruce W. Jentleson, *With Friends Like These* (New York: W.W. Norton 1994).

17 See, for example, Gary L. Geipel and Paul H. Nitze, "Symposium on the Future of NATO" *Insight,* December 5, 1994, pp. 18–22.

18 See Larry Berman and Emily O. Goldman, "Clinton's Foreign Policy at Midterm." in *The Clinton Presidency: First Appraisals,* Colin Campbell and Bert A. Rockman, eds., (Chatham: Chatham House, 1996), p. 324

19 See Laura D'Andrea Tyson, *Who's Bashing Whom? Trade Conflict in High-Technology Industries* (Washington, DC: Institute for International Economics, 1992); Henry R. Nau, *The Myth of America's Decline: Leading the World Economy into the 1990's* (New York: Oxford University Press, 1992).

20 See Donald M. Snow and Eugene Brown, *Puzzle Palaces and Foggy Bottom: U.S. Foreign and Defense Policy-Making in the 1990s* (New York: St. Martin's Press 1994); Donald M. Snow, *National Security* (New York: St. Martin's Press, 1995).

21 See the September 21, 1993 speech by National Security Advisor Anthony Lake at The Johns Hopkins University, "From Containment to Enlargement."

22 See David J. Richardson, "The Political Economy of Strategic Trade Policy," *International Organization,* vol. 44, Winter, 1990, pp. 101–135.

23 See Alexander L. George, *Forceful Persuasion* (Washington, DC: U.S. Institute of Peace Press, 1991); see also Alexander L. George and William E. Simmons, eds., *The Limits of Coercive Diplomacy.*

24 See Cecil V. Crabb, Jr. and Pat Holt, *Invitation to Strangle: Congress, the President and Foreign Policy* (Washington, DC: Congressional Quarterly, 1980); Louis Fisher, *Constitutional Conflicts Between Congress and the President* (Princeton: Princeton University Press, 1985).

25 Charles W. Kegley and Eugene R. Wittkopf, eds., *Perspectives on American Foreign Policy* (New York: St. Martin's Press 1983), p. 244.

26 See Arthur M. Schlesinger, Jr., *The Imperial Presidency* (Boston: Houghton Mifflin, 1973).

27 See Michael J. Glennon, "The War Powers Resolution Ten Years Later: More Politics Than Law," *American Journal of International Law,* vol. 78, July, 1984.

28 See Barry Rubin, *Secrets of State: The State Department and the Struggle Over US Foreign Policy* (New York: Oxford University Press, 1985).

29 See Barrett, Archie D. *Reappraising Defense Organization.* Washington, D.C.: National Defense University, 1988; Fallows, James. *National Defense.*

New York: Random House, 1981; Raymond, Jack. *Power at the Pentagon.* New York: Harper & Row, 1964.

30 See Bletzz, Donald. *The Role of the Military Professional in U.S. Foreign Policy.* New York: Praeger, 1972; Clark, Asa A., IV, and Peter W. Chiarelli, Jeffery S. McKitrick, and James W. Reed. *The Defense Reform Debate.* Baltimore: Johns Hopkins, 1984; Clotfelter, James. *The Military in American Politics.* New York: Harper & Row, 1973; Yarmolinsky, Adam. *The Military Establishment.* New York: Harper & Row, 1971.

31 See Robert J. Art, "Restructuring the Military-Industrial Complex: Arms Control in Institutional Perspective," *Public Policy,* vol. 22, Fall 1974.

32 See Theodore Draper, *A Very Thin Line: The Iran-Contra Affairs* (New York: Simon & Schuster, 1991).

33 Quoted in Charles W. Kegley and Eugene R. Wittkopf, eds., *Perspectives on American Foreign Policy* (New York: St. Martin's Press 1983), 4th ed., p. 383.

34 See Rhodri Jeffreys-Jones, *The CIA and American Democracy* (New Haven: Yale University Press, 1989); Loch K. Johnson, *America's Secret Power: The CIA in a Democratic Society* (New York: Oxford University Press, 1989); John Prados, *President's Secret Wars: CIA and Pentagon Covert Operations Since World War II* (New York: Morrow, 1986).

35 See James M. Lindsay, *Congress and the Politics of U.S. Foreign Policy* (Baltimore: The Johns Hopkins University Press, 1994).

36 Barbara J. Hinckley, *Less Than Meets the Eye* (Chicago: University of Chicago Press, 1994).

37 See Daniel C. Hallin, *The Uncensored War: The Media and Vietnam* (New York: Oxford University Press, 1986).

38 Philip M. Taylor, *War and the Media* (New York: Manchester University Press, 1992).

39 See John Mueller, *Policy and Opinion in the Gulf War* (Chicago, IL: University of Chicago Press, 1994).

40 See Berman and Golman, "Clinton's Foreign Policy at Mid-Term," pp. 318–19.

PHOTO CREDITS

Schumann/Saba Press Photos, Inc., 412 (right); John Duricka/AP/Wide World Photos, 416; AP/Wide World Photos, 420; Brad Markel/Gamma-Liaison, Inc., 426; Mark Wilson/AP/Wide World Photos, 429; Charles Tasnadi/AP/Wide World Photos, 430; Susan Steinkamp/Saba Press Photos, Inc., 437.

CHAPTER 13   Nam June Paik, *Fin de Siecle II*, 1989. 201 television sets with 4 laser discs. Sight: 480 X 60˝ (1219.2 X 426.7 X 152.4 cm.) Collection of Whitney Museum of American Art, Gift of Laila and Thurston Twigg-Smith, 93.139. Copyright © 1996: Whitney Museum of American Art, 404; CNN, Inc./Photoreporters, Inc., 442; UPI/Bettmann, 448; Kevin Horan/Outline Press, 449; Jeff Greenberg/DMRP/Photoedit, 450; E. Adams/Sygma, 452; Clark Jones/AP/Wide World Photos, 455; Terry Ashe/ABC, 460; Larry Downing/Sygma, 463; Mike Nelson/RS/GN/Agence France-Pressd, 465; AP/Wide World Photos, 469.

CHAPTER 14   Commissioned by Virgin Records, © 1996 Josh Gosfield, 472; UPI/Bettmann, 474; Jeff Atteberry-Indianapolis Star/Sipa Press, 475; Dr. Paul Avrich/Queens College, 480; Mike Malyszku, 482; Cynthia Howe/Sygma, 487; N. Tully/Sygma, 492; Frank Fisher/Gamma-Liaison, Inc., 496; Bettmann, 498; Seth Resnick/Gamma-Liaison, Inc., 501; Viviane Moos/Saba Press Photos, Inc., 502.

CHAPTER 15   Philip Evergood, *American Tragedy* (1936). Oil on canvas. 29 1/2 X 39 1/2˝/Terry Dintenfass Gallery, 508; RAIA/New York Newsday, 510; Fred Ward/Black Star, 516; Juda Ngweny/Reuter/Bettmann, 517; Carl Iwasaki/Life Magazine, Time Warner, Inc., 519; AP/Wide World Photos, 520; UPI/Bettmann, 521; Cecil Stoughton/LBJ Library Collection, 522; Stanley Forman, 526; The Schlesinger Library, Radcliffe College, 534; P. Scully/Gamma-Liaison, Inc., 536; Larry Downing/Sygma, 537; Michael Springer/Gamma-Liaison, Inc., 541.

CHAPTER 16   Bearden, Romare, *The Block*, 1971. Cut and pasted papers on masonite. Overall: 4 ft. X 18 ft., The Metropolitan Museum of Art, Gift of Mr. and Mrs. Samual Shore, 1978. (1978.61.1-.3). Courtesy Estate of Romare Bearden, 546; C. Niklas Hill/Gamma-Liaison, Inc., 548; Bob Riha/Gamma-Liaison, Inc., 550; Wally McNamee/Sygma, 552; Renato Rotolo/Gamma-Liaison, Inc., 555; Mark Wilson/AP/Wide World Photos, 557; Joe Marquette/AP/Wide World Photos, 559; Mike Okoniewski/AP/Wide World Photos, 566; Tony Savino/Sipa Press, 567; Randy Taylor/Sygma, 570; Yoichi R. Okamoto/LBJ Library Collection, 571; Stephen Ferry/Gamma-Liaison, Inc., 573.

CHAPTER 17   Andy Warhol, *Dollar Signs*, 1981. Synthetic polymer paint and silkscreen ink on canvas, 90 X 70 in. © 1995 The Andy Warhol Foundation, Inc., 580; Ron Edmonds/AP/Wide World Photos, 582; Ralf-Finn Hestoft/Saba Press Photos, Inc., 584; Larry Downing/Sygma, 586; Denis Paquin/AP/Wide World Photos, 589; Larry Downing/Sygma, 590; Jeffrey Markowitz/Sygma, 592; Maureen Keating/Roll Call, 593; Allan Tannenbaum/Sygma, 596; Angel Franco/NYT Pictures, 597; Jeffrey Aaronson/Network Aspen, 606.

CHAPTER 18   Ed McGowin, *Grown Men Playing with the Planet Earth*, 1991. Collection of Dain Bosworth Incorporated; photo courtesy of the artist, 612; Mark Peterson/Saba Press Photos, Inc., 614; Ron Edmonds/AP/Wide World Photos, 616; National Archives, 618; Bettmann, 621; Paul S. Conklin, 623; Sergio Dorantes/Sygma, 630; Lamarque/Reuter/Bettmann, 631; Michael Stravato/AP/Wide World Photos, 632; J. David Ake/Agence France-Pressd, 635; Alexander Zemlianichenko/AP/Wide World Photos, 637; Joe Marquette/AP/Wide World Photos, 640.

INDEX TO REFERENCES

Aberbach, Joel D., Ch. 5 n. 67
Abraham, Henry J., Ch. 7 n. 6, 13, 19, 40, 57;
    Ch. 14 n. 3, 21; Ch. 15 n. 63
Abramson, Jill, Ch. 7 n. 22
Adams, John, Ch. 1 n. 7
Adatto, Kiku, Ch. 13 n. 37
Agel, Jerome, Ch. 3 n. 20
Aldrich, John, Ch. 10 n. 5
Alfange, Dean Jr., Ch. 7 n. 60
Alford, Robert, Ch. 16 n. 41
Alger, Deane E., Ch. 13 n. 8
Allison, Graham, Ch. 18 n. 8
Almond, Gabriel A., Ch. 8 n. 3
Anderson, David E., Ch. 7 n. 72
Anderson, James E., Ch. 16 n. 12
Ansolabehere, Stephen, Ch. 13 n. 4
Apple, R.W., Ch. 5 n. 58
Arlington, Karen M., Ch. 11 n. 2
Armstrong, Scott, Ch. 7 n. 53
Arnett, Peter, Ch. 13 n. 1
Arnold, Peri, Ch. 6 n. 40
Arnold, R. Douglas, Ch. 5 n. 56
Art, Robert J., Ch. 18 n. 31

Babington, Charles, Ch. 15 n. 50
Bach, Stanley, Ch. 5 n. 25, 45
Bacon, Donald C., Ch. 5 n. 46
Bagdikian, Ben, Ch. 13 n. 24, 30
Baker, Liva, Ch. 7 n. 34
Baker, Ross, Ch. 5 n. 5; Ch. 6 n. 65
Banfield, Edward, Ch. 16 n. 14
Barber, James David, Ch. 6 n. 23; Ch. 10 n. 12
Barnouw, Eric, Ch. 13 n. 23
Barrett, Archie D., Ch. 18 n. 29
Barry, Rozanne, Ch. 5 n. 3, 22
Bates, Stephen, Ch. 13 n. 38
Beck, Nathaniel, Ch. 7 n. 4
Behr, Roy, Ch. 10 n. 21; Ch. 13 n. 4
Bennett, W. Lance, Ch. 13 n. 1
Bentley, Arthur F., Ch. 12 n. 4, 22
Beveniste, Guy, Ch. 8 n. 13
Berger, Raoul, Ch. 7 n. 58
Bergerson, Fred, Ch. 16 n. 23
Berke, Richard L., Ch. 5 n. 20
Berkman, Ronald, Ch. 13 n. 8
Berlin, Isaih, Ch. 1 n. 10
Berman, Larry, Ch. 6 n. 35, 45; Ch. 18 n. 10, 11, 15
Bernstein, Barton J., Ch. 18 n. 4
Bernstein, Carl, Ch. 6 n. 2; Ch. 13 n. 9
Bernstein, Peter, Ch. 17 Ch., 1
Bernstein, Richard B., Ch. 3 n. 3, 20
Berry, Jeffrey M., Ch. 12 n. 3, 15
Best, Judith, A., Ch. 6 n. 27
Beveridge, Albert, Ch. 7 n. 69
Bickel, Alexander M., Ch. 7 n. 58
Birnbaum, Jeffrey, Ch. 5 n. 50; Ch. 12 n. 9
Biskupic, Joan, Ch. 4 n. 38
Black, Hugo, Ch. 7 n. 63
Bletzz, Donald, Ch. 18 n. 30
Blight, James G., Ch. 18 n. 8
Blumenthal, Sidney, Ch. 13 n. 32
Bork, Robert, Ch. 7 n. 62, 77; Ch. 14 n. 98
Bosso, Christopher, Ch. 16 n. 13, 34
Bowen, Catherine Drinker, Ch. 3 n. 2, 4, 10, 17
Brace, Paul, Ch. 9 n. 22
Bradley, Robert, Ch. 7 n. 40
Branch, Taylor, Ch. 1 n. 1
Brenner, Saul, Ch. 7 n. 48

Brinkley, Alan, Ch. 2 n. 5, 9, 13, 14; Ch. 16 n. 17
Brinkley, Joel, Ch. 8 n. 11
Broder, David, Ch. 10 n. 32; Ch. 13 n. 18
Bronfenbrenner, Urie, Ch. 9 n. 6
Bronner, Ethan, Ch. 7 n. 20; Ch. 14 n. 98
Brown, Andre, Ch. 5 n. 1
Brown, Dee, Ch. 15 n. 68
Brown, Eugene, Ch. 18 n. 20
Brown, Everett S., Ch. 3 n. 8
Bryant, Adam, Ch. 8 n. 5
Buchanan, William, Ch. 5 n. 12
Bullier, David, Ch. 8 n. 29
Bundy, McGeorge, Ch. 18 n. 14
Burger, Warren, Ch. 14 n. 75
Burke, John, Ch. 18 n. 11
Burleigh, Nina, Ch. 4 n. 38
Burns, James MacGregor, Ch. 2 n. 10, Ch. 6 n. 14

Caldeira, Gregory, A., Ch. 7 n. 31
Calmes, Jackie, Ch. 17 n. 17
Campbell, Angus, Ch. 9 n. 23; Ch. 11 n. 13
Cantril, Albert Hadley, Ch. 9 n. 1
Caplan, Lincoln, Ch. 7 n. 36, 37
Carter, Steven L., Ch. 15 n. 37
Cassata, Donna, Ch. 5 n. 9
Cavanagh, Thomas E., Ch. 5 n. 13
Center Daily Times, Ch. 4 n. 1
Chase, Harold, Ch. 7 n. 25; Ch. 13 n. 5
Chiarelli, Peter W., Ch. 18 n. 30
Chong, Dennis, Ch. 12 n. 7
Choper, Jesse H., Ch. 7 n. 58
Christopher, F., Ch. 13 n. 36
Cigler, Allan J., Ch. 12 n. 6, 16, 19
Clapp, Charles, Ch. 5 n. 14
Clard, Asa A., Ch. 18 n. 30
Clausen, Aage R., Ch. 5 n. 64
Clawson, Dan, Ch. 12 n. 19
Claybrook, Joan, Ch. 8 n. 29
Clift, Eleanor, Ch. 17 n. 1
Clotfelter, James, Ch. 18 n. 30
Cloward, Richard A., Ch. 11 n. 3
Clymer, Adam, Ch. 12 n. 1, Ch. 16 n. 46
Cobb, Roger, Ch. 16 n. 13
Cohen, Bernard, Ch. 9 n. 26
Cohen, Jeffrey, Ch. 6 n. 46; Ch. 7 n. 15;
    Ch. 13 n. 27
Cohen, Joshua, Ch. 1 n. 16
Cohen, Richard E., Ch. 5 n. 70
Cohn, Bob, Ch. 12 n. 1; Ch. 14 n. 44; Ch.17 n. 1
Collier, Christopher, Ch. 2 Ch. 1; Ch. 3 n. 2, 6
Collier, James Lincoln, Ch. 2 Ch. 1; Ch. 3 n. 2, 6
Colvin, John, Ch. 6 n. 20
Congressional Quarterly, Ch. 5 n. 54
Converse, Philip E., Ch. 9 n. 20, 23; Ch. 11 n. 13
Conway, M. Margaret, Ch. 11 n. 17, 25
Cook, Mark, Ch. 13 n. 27
Cornwell, Christopher, Ch. 8 n. 36
Corwin, Edward S., Ch. 6 n. 9; Ch. 7 n. 5
Crabb, Cecil V. Jr., Ch. 18 n. 24
Cranford, John R., Ch. 16 n. 35
Crigler, Ann N., Ch. 13 n. 4
Cronin, Thomas E., Ch. 1 n. 5; Ch. 6 n. 42
Cunningham, Noble E., Ch. 10 n. 8

Dahl, Robert, Ch. 1 n. 12; Ch. 12 n. 24
Danelski, David J., Ch. 7 n. 65
Danforth, John C., Ch. 7 n. 22

Davidson, Roger H., Ch. 5 n. 3, 14, 15, 21, 27, 36
Deering, Christopher, Ch. 5 n. 39
DeParle, Jason, Ch. 16 n. 37, 42
Diamond, Edwin, Ch. 13 n. 38
Diamond, Martin, Ch. 11 n. 19
Dimock, Marshall E., Ch. 4 n. 14
Downs, Anthony, Ch. 8 n. 4, 24; Ch. 16 n. 24
Drew, Elizabeth, Ch. 11 n. 21
Dunlap, Thomas, Ch. 16 n. 34
Duverger, Maurice, Ch. 10 n. 17
Dye, Thomas, Ch. 13 n. 20; Ch. 16 n. 2, 21

Eckholm, Erick, Ch. 16 n. 38
Edleman, Murray, Ch. 16 n. 4
Edwards, George C. III, Ch. 5 n. 28, 57
Elder, Charles, Ch. 16 n. 13
Eldersvald, Samuel J., Ch. 10n. 3
Ely, John Hart, Ch. 7 n. 58
Engelberg, Stephen, Ch. 8 n. 5, 21
Entman, Robert M., Ch. 13 n. 6
Erikson, Robert S., Ch. 9 n. 5
Eulau, Heinz, Ch. 5 n. 12
Evans, Rowland, Ch. 5 n. 33

Fairhall, James, Ch. 8 n. 20
Fallows, James, Ch. 18 n. 29
Feer, Robert A., Ch. 2 n. 2
Fellman, David, Ch. 14 n.71
Fenno, Richard F. Jr., Ch. 5 n. 38, 39, 62, 68
Ferehohn, John, Ch. 5 n. 52
Ferguson, LeRoy C., Ch. 5 n. 12
Fineman, Howard, Ch. 17 n. 1
Fiorina, Morris P., Ch. 5 n. 4, 17; Ch. 11 n. 15
Fisher, Louis, Ch. 6 n. 26; Ch. 18 n. 24
Flanigan, William H., Ch. 9 n. 14
Ford, Gerald, Ch. 6 n. 34
Forejohn, John, Ch. 16 n. 27
Fox, Harrison W. Jr., Ch. 5 n. 61
Franklin, Grace, Ch. 16 n. 12
Freedom Review, Ch. 1 n. 2
Freidel, Frank, Ch. 6 n. 14; Ch. 10 n. 11
Frendreis, John, Ch. 6n. 12
Friedman, Benjamin, Ch. 17 n. 13
Friedman, Milton, Ch. 17 n. 8
Frum, David, Ch. 8 n. 7

Gaebler, Ted, Ch. 8 n. 34
Galbraith, John Kenneth, Ch. 12 n. 10
Gallup, George, Ch. 9 n. 24, 28, 29, 30
Gans, Herbert, Ch. 16 n. 36
Gant, Michael M., Ch. 9 n. 15, 20
Garand, James C., Ch. 8 n. 36
Garrow, David J., Ch. 1 n. 1; Ch. 7 n. 46;
    Ch. 14 n. 97
Garthoff, Raymond L., Ch. 18 n. 13
Gates, John B., Ch. 7 n. 15
Geipel, Gary L., Ch. 18 n. 17
George, Alexander I., Ch. 6 n. 6; Ch. 18 n. 23
George, Juliette L., Ch. 6 n. 6
Gephardt, Richard, Ch. 17 n. 21
Gerston, Larry N., Ch. 16 n. 2, 16
Gibson, James, Ch. 9 n. 11, 12
Gitlin, Todd, Ch. 9 n. 8
Glennon, Michael J., Ch. 18 n. 27
Goldman, Emily O., Ch. 18 n. 18
Goldman, Sheldon, Ch. 9 n. 12, 24, 26, 27, 28

Goldwin, Robert A., Ch. 3 n. 9
Gordon, George J., Ch. 8 n. 33
Gosling, James L., Ch. 17 n. 14
Gosnell, Harold, Ch. 10 n. 23
Graber, Doris, Ch. 13 n. 16, 19
Greenhouse, Linda, Ch. 4 n. 38; Ch. 7 n. 37, 41
Greenstein, Fred, Ch. 6 n. 1, 43; Ch. 9 Ch. 3; Ch. 18 n. 11
Greider, William, Ch. 12 n. 8
Grossman, Joel, Ch. 7 n. 18
Gueron, Judith, M. Ch. 16 n. 44
Guth, James L., Ch. 12 n. 18

Halberstam, David, Ch. 13 n. 10; Ch. 18 n. 36
Hallen, Daniel C., Ch. 13 n. 2, 37
Hall, John Wesley Jr., Ch. 14 n. 80
Hamilton, Alexander, Ch. 3 n. 12, 15; Ch. 4 n. 2; Ch. 7 n. 3; Ch. 9 n. 2
Hammond, Susasn Webb, Ch. 5 n. 61
Harbinson, Winfred A., Ch. 2 n. 4, 8; Ch. 15 n. 19
Hardemann, D. B., Ch. 5 n. 46
Hardy, William, Jr., Ch. 6 n. 29, 33
Hargrove, Edwin C., Ch. 8 n. 12
Harris, Art, Ch. 7 n. 1
Harris, Fred R., Ch. 5 n. 49, 50, 71
Hart, John, Ch. 6 n. 40
Harvey, Philip L, Ch. 16 n. 36
Hayek, Friedrich A., Ch. 1 n. 13
Hay, John, Ch. 6 n. 21
Heclo, Hugh, Ch. 8 n. 10; Ch. 12 n. 25; Ch. 16 n. 30
Heilbronce, Robert, Ch. 17 n. 18
Heinz, John P., Ch. 12 n. 26; Ch. 16 n. 30
Heller, Walter, Ch. 17 n. 8
Hentoff, Nat, Ch. 7 n. 47, 51
Heumann, Milton, Ch. 7 n. 9
Hibbing, John R., Ch. 5 n. 51
Hibbs, Douglas, Ch. 17 n. 4
Hill, Larry B., Ch. 8 n. 13, 19
Hinchfiffe, Joseph, Ch. 17 n. 26
Hinckley, Barbara, Ch. 9 n. 4, 22; Ch. 18 n. 34
Hinds, Michael de Courcy, Ch. 4 n. 34
Holmes, Stephen A., Ch. 8 n. 23
Holt, Pat, Ch. 18 n. 24
Hood, Edwin Murray, Ch. 16 n. 9, 10
Hoopes, Townsend, Ch. 18 n. 12
House, Toni, Ch. 7 n. 35
Howard, J. Woodford, Jr., Ch. 7, n. 14
Hrebenar, Ronald J., Ch. 12 n. 16
Hull, Jon D., Ch. 7 n. 10

Immerman, Richard, Ch. 18 n. 11
Issacs, Arnold, Ch. 18 n. 12
Iyengar, Shanto, Ch. 9 n. 27; Ch. 13 n. 4, 6, 21

Jacobson, Gary, Ch. 5 n. 10; Ch. 11 n. 23
Jamieson, Kathleen Hall, Ch. 13 n. 39
Jay, John, Ch. 3 n. 12, 15; Ch. 4 n. 2; Ch. 9 n. 2
Jefferson, Thomas, Ch. 6 n. 20
Jeffrey, Douglas, Ch. 6 n. 44
Jeffreys-Jones, Rhodri, Ch. 18 n. 33
Jencks, Christopher, Ch. 16 n. 3, 21, 36
Jentleson, Bruce, W., Ch. 6 n. 35; Ch. 18 n. 15, 16
Johannes, John R., Ch. 5 n. 17
Johansen, Robert C., Ch. 18 n. 2
Johnson, Loch K., Ch. 18 n. 33
Jones, Bryan, Ch. 16 n. 13
Jones, Charles O., Ch. 5 n. 31; Ch. 16 n. 34
Jones, Elaine R., Ch. 5 n. 11
Jones, Peter, Ch. 1 n. 14
Just, Marion R., Ch. 13 n. 4

Kagay, Michael, Ch. 9 n. 21
Kamen, Al, Ch. 8 n. 9
Kaplan, David A., Ch. 14 n. 44
Kaplan, Marshall, Ch. 4 n. 33
Kaufman, Herbert, Ch. 8 n. 24
Kaus, Mickey, Ch. 13 n. 37; Ch. 16 n. 46
Kayden, Xandra, Ch. 10 n. 24
Kelley, Stanley, Jr., Ch. 11 n. 14
Kellough, J. Edward, Ch. 8 n. 36
Kelly, Alfred H., Ch. 2 n. 4, 8; Ch. 15 n. 19
Kempe, Frederick, Ch. 18 n. 1
Kennan, George F., Ch. 18 n. 5, 14
Kennedy, Robert, Ch. 18 n. 8
Kernell, Samuel, Ch. 6 n. 38; Ch. 13 n. 7
Ketcham, Ralph, Ch. 10 n. 10
Kettl, Donald F., Ch. 16 n. 43; Ch. 17 n. 18
Keynes, John Maynard, Ch. 17 n. 7
Key, V. O., Jr., Ch. 5 n. 56; Ch. 10 n. 2
Kidder, Tracy, Ch. 16 n. 18
Kiewiet, D. Roderick, Ch. 17 n. 3
Kilborn, Peter T., Ch. 8 n. 23
Kinder, Donald, Ch. 9 n. 27; Ch. 17 n. 3
Kingdon, John W., Ch. 5 n. 23, 64; Ch. 16 n. 17
King, Ernest K., Ch. 18 n. 3
Kinsella, John, Ch. 16 n. 15
Kitch, Laura W., Ch. 13 n. 8
Kluger, Richard, Ch. 7 n. 39; Ch. 15 n. 12
Knox, Richard A., Ch. 4 n. 3
Koenig, Louis W., Ch. 8 n. 16
Koh, Harold H., Ch. 18 n. 35
Kotlowitz, Alex, Ch. 16 n. 18
Kotz, Nick, Ch. 16 n. 28
Kovenock, David M., Ch. 5 n. 63
Kozak, David C., Ch. 5 n. 13
Kozol, Jonathan, Ch. 16 n. 18
Kramer, Gerald H., Ch. 17 n. 3
Kurland, Philip B., Ch. 2 n. 8
Kurtz, Howard, Ch. 13 n. 32
Kurtzman, Laura, Ch. 16 n. 39

Labaton, Stephen, Ch. 16 n. 35
Ladd, Everett Carll, Ch. 10 n. 19
Ladowsky, Ellen, Ch. 17 n. 1
LaFeber, Walter, Ch. 18 n. 6, 7
Lake, Anthony, Ch. 19 n. 21
Langbein, John H., Ch. 7 n. 9
Langley, Lawrence D., Ch. 11 n. 19
Lasswell, Harold, Ch. 17 n. 2
Lauman, Edward O., Ch. 12 n. 26; Ch. 16 n. 30
Lazarus, Edward H., Ch. 10 n. 21
Leif, Lisa, Ch. 7 n. 2
Lemonick, Michael D., Ch. 8 n. 18
Leo, John, Ch. 16 n. 45
Lerman, Allen H., Ch. 13 n. 5
Lerner, Ralph, Ch. 2 n. 8
Leuchtenburg, William, Ch. 6 n. 8; Ch. 10 n. 13
Levine, Arnold, Ch. 16 n. 25
Levy, Leonard W., Ch. 14 n. 4
Lewis, Anthony, Ch. 3 n. 23
Lewis, Eugene, Ch. 16 n. 17
Lichter, Linda, Ch. 13 n. 29
Lichter, S. Robert, Ch. 13 n. 20, 29
Light, Paul, Ch. 5 n. 24
Lincoln, Abraham, Ch. 6 n. 22
Lindblom, Charles, Ch. 16 n. 5
Lindsay, James M., Ch. 18 n. 34
Lippmann, Walter, Ch. 9 n. 18; Ch. 18 n. 37
Lipsky, Michael, Ch. 16 n. 7
Lockhart, Charles, Ch. 16 n. 3, 21
Longley, Lawrence D., Ch. 5 n. 26
Loomis, Burdett A., Ch. 12 n. 6, 16, 19

Lowi, Theodore, Ch. 6 n. 51; Ch. 12 n. 24; Ch. 17 n. 11
Luttbeg, Norman R., Ch. 9 n. 15, 20

Madison, James, Ch. 3 n. 12, 15; Ch. 4 n. 2; Ch. 7 n. 3; Ch. 9 n. 2
Magleby, David B., Ch. 5 n. 18
Magruder, Jeb Stuart, Ch. 6 n. 3
Mahe, Eddie, Jr., Ch. 10 n. 24
Maisel, L. Sandy, Ch. 10 n. 4
Malbin, Michael, Ch. 5 n. 53
Maltese, John Anthony, Ch. 13 n. 6
Manegold, Catherine, Ch. 12 n. 1
Mann, Thomas E., Ch. 5 n. 53
Mansfield, Harvey C., Jr., Ch. 6 n. 25
Marcus, Maeva, Ch. 6 n. 32
Marini, John, Ch. 8 n. 6
Markovich, Denise E., Ch. 17 n. 9
Marmor, Theodore R., Ch. 12 n. 1; Ch. 16 n. 36, 41
Marshall, Jonathan, Ch. 16 n. 38
Marshall, Thomas, Ch. 7 n. 72
Mashaw, Jerry L., Ch. 16 n. 36
Mash, Kenneth M., Ch. 15 n. 1
Mason, Alpheus Thomas, Ch. 7 n. 43
Massaro, John, Ch. 7 n. 21
Mathews, Jay, Ch. 15 n. 69
Matthews, Donald R., Ch. 5 n. 63; Ch. 16 n. 27
Matusow, Allen, Ch. 4 n. 29
Mayer, Jane, Ch. 7 n. 22
Mayhew, David, Ch. 5 n. 16; Ch. 16 n. 27
Mazmanian, Daniel, Ch. 16 n. 20
McCurdy, Howard E., Ch. 16 n. 25
McDonald, Forrest, Ch. 6 n. 31
McFelley, Neil, Ch. 7 n. 25
McGlen, Nancy E., Ch. 15 n. 51, 52
McKitrick, Jeffrey S., Ch. 18 n. 30
McLuhan, Marshall, Ch. 13 n. 17
McNamara, Robert S., Ch. 18 n. 14
McPherson, Harry, Ch. 5 n. 34
Mead, Lawrence, Ch. 16 n. 3, 21
Mee, Charles L., Jr., Ch. 3 n. 16
Meier, August, Ch. 11 n. 6
Meier, Kenneth J., Ch. 8 n. 10, 14, 17, 30, 36; Ch. 16 n. 31, 32
Meiklejohn, Alexander, Ch. 14 n. 45
Michnick, Adam, Ch. 1 n. 17
Mickelson, Sig, Ch. 13 n. 14
Milakovitch, Michael E., Ch. 8 n. 33
Milkis, Sidney M., Ch. 6 n. 4, 49
Miller, Merle, Ch. 5 n. 33
Miller, Warren, Ch. 9 n. 23; Ch. 10 n. 9, 20; Ch. 11 n. 13
Morgenthau, Hans, Ch. 18 n. 2
Morin, Richard, Ch. 5 n. 19; Ch. 11 n. 8, Ch. 13 n. 34
Mosley, Zelma, Ch. 6 n. 24
Moynihan, Daniel Patrick, Ch. 16 n. 40
Mueller, John, Ch. 13 n. 1
Muraskin, Matthew, Ch. 7 n. 30
Murphy, Bruce Allen, Ch. 7 n. 21
Murphy, James R., Ch. 5 n. 40
Murphy, Walter, Ch. 7 n. 49
Murray, Alan S., Ch. 5 n. 59; Ch. 12 n. 9
Murray, Charles, Ch. 16 n. 3, 21
Muthews, Donald, Ch. 5 n. 51

Nachimias, David, Ch. 8 n. 35
Nasar, Sylvia, Ch. 16 n. 38
Nash, Nathaniel C., Ch. 16 n. 35
Nau, Henry R., Ch. 18 n. 19
Navarro, Peter, Ch. 16 n. 26

Neimi, Richard, Ch. 13 n. 12
Nelson, Barbara, Ch. 16 n. 13
Nelson, Candice J., Ch. 5 n. 18
Nelson, Michael, Ch. 6 n. 4
Nelson, Robert L., Ch. 12 n. 26; Ch. 16 n. 30
Neuman, W. Russell, Ch. 13 n. 4
Neustadt, Alan, Ch. 12 n. 19
Neustadt, Richard E., Ch. 3 n. 14, Ch. 6 n. 11, 48; Ch. 13 n. 11
Newman, M. Russell, Ch. 13 n. 6
Newman, Roger K., Ch. 7 n. 63
Newsweek, Ch. 4 n. 38
New York Times, Ch. 4 n. 38; Ch. 5 n. 20
Nicolay, John, Ch. 6 n. 21
Nieman, Donald G., Ch. 15 n. 2, 10, 21, 25, 28
Niems, Richard G., Ch. 11 n. 8
Nie, Norman H., Ch. 9 n. 31; Ch. 11 n. 4, 20
Noelle-Neumann, Elizabeth, Ch. 9 n. 13
Novak, Robert, Ch. 5 n. 33
Nye, Joseph Jr., Ch. 18 n. 8

O'Brien, David, Ch. 7 n. 29
O'Brien, Sue, Ch. 4 n. 33
O'Connor, John E., Ch. 3 n. 7
O'Connor, Karen, Ch. 10 n. 12; Ch. 15 n. 51, 52
Oleszek, Walter J., Ch. 5 n. 3, 15, 26, 27, 36, 44
Olson, Mancur, Ch. 12 n. 7, 13; Ch. 16 n. 27
Ornstein, Norman, Ch. 5 n. 53
Orren, Gary R., Ch. 1 n. 11; Ch. 15 n. 32
Osborne, David, Ch. 8 n. 34

Page, Benjamin I., Ch. 9 n. 9, 25; Ch. 16 n. 33
Paludan, Phillip Shaw, Ch. 6 n. 30
Parenti, Michael, Ch. 13 n. 3
Parker, Glenn R., Ch. 5 n. 21
Parkhurst, Catherine, Ch. 8 n. 36
Parks, Rosa, Ch. 15 n. 70
Pateman, Carole, Ch. 1 n. 13
Patterson, Bradley H., Jr., Ch. 6 n. 47
Patterson, Samuel, Ch. 10 n. 16
Patterson, Thomas E., Ch. 13 n. 13, 40
Pauly, Edward, Ch. 16 n. 44
Payne, James L., Ch. 12 n. 14
Peabody, Robert L., Ch. 5 n. 55
Pear, Robert, Ch. 12 n. 1
Peirce, Neil, Ch. 11 n. 19
Peltason, Jack W., Ch. 15 n. 20
Pennock, J. Ronald, Ch. 1 n. 9
Perry, Barbara, Ch. 7 n. 26; Ch. 14 n. 3, 21; Ch. 15 n. 63
Perry, H.W., Jr., Ch. 7 n. 31
Perry, Roland, Ch. 13 n. 35
Peterson, Paul, Ch. 16 n. 11, 36
Pfeffer, Leo, Ch. 14 Ch., 19
Phelps, Timothy M., Ch. 7 n. 22
Phillips, Don, Ch. 8 n. 5
Phillips, Kevin, Ch. 17 n. 12, 23
Pika, Joseph, A., Ch. 6 n. 24
Pinckney, Charles Cotesworth, Ch. 3 n. 5
Pitkin, Hannah Fenichel, Ch. 5 n. 8
Piven, Francis Fox, Ch. 11 n. 3
Polsby, Nelson, Ch. 11 n. 16
Pomper, Gerald, Ch. 9 n. 17; Ch. 11 n. 18; Ch. 13 n. 28
Powell, G. Bingham, Jr., Ch. 11 n. 11
Prados, John, Ch. 18 n. 33
Pressman, Jeffrey, Ch. 4 n. 28
Price, David E., Ch. 10 n. 29
Provine, Doris Marie, Ch. 7 n. 30
Putnam, Robert D., Ch. 9 n. 7
Pynn, Ronald E., Ch. 17 n. 9

Quinn, Jayne Bryant, Ch. 17 n. 20
Quirk, Paul, Ch. 17 n. 26

Ranney, Austin, Ch. 10 n. 3; Ch. 13 n. 15
Rauch, Jonathan, Ch. 12 n. 21
Raymond, Jack, Ch. 18 n. 29
Reagan, Michael D., Ch. 16 n. 31
Reagan, Ronald, Ch. 4 n. 31
Reed, James W., Ch. 18 n. 30
Rehnquist, William H., Ch. 7 n. 8, 15, 31, 40
Reiter, Howard, Ch. 10 n. 26
Relyea, Harold, Ch. 6 n. 26
Reske, Henry J., Ch. 7 n. 23
Reveley, W. Taylor, III, Ch. 6 n. 29
Rice, Gerald T., Ch. 18 n. 9
Rice, Kym S., Ch. 3 n. 3
Richardson, David J., Ch. 18 n. 22
Richardson, J. E., Ch. 1 n. 15
Rimer, Sara, Ch. 16 n. 26
Riordon, William L., Ch. 8 n. 8; Ch. 10 Ch., 23
Ripley, Randall, Ch. 16 n. 12
Riselbach, Leroy N., Ch. 5 n. 42
Rivlin, Alice, Ch. 17 n. 25
Rockman, Bert A., Ch. 6 n. 18
Rogers, Joel, Ch. 1 n. 16
Rohde, David, Ch. 5 n. 55
Ronfeldt, David F., Ch. 19 n. 3
Roosevelt, Theodore, Ch. 6 n. 16
Rosenbaum, David E., Ch. 5 n. 47
Rosenberg, Gerald, Ch. 16 n. 19
Rosenbloom, David H., Ch. 8 n. 35
Rosen, Daniel, Ch. 7 n. 30
Rosen, Jay, Ch. 13 n. 18
Rosenstone, Steven J., Ch. 10 n. 21; Ch. 11 n. 3, 12
Rosenthal, Andrew, Ch. 16 n. 8
Rosenthal, Tom, Ch. 13 n. 41
Rossiter, Clinton, Ch. 6 n. 13
Rothenberg, Lawrence S., Ch. 12 n. 11
Rothman, Stanley, Ch. 13 n. 29
Rubin, Barry, Ch. 18 n. 28
Rudwick, Elliot, Ch. 11 n. 6

Sabatier, Paul, Ch. 16 n. 20
Sabato, Larry, Ch. 10 n. 31; Ch. 11 n. 22
Salisbury, Robert H., Ch. 12 n. 13, 26; Ch. 16 n. 30
Sammon, Richard, Ch. 11 n. 5
Sanford, Terry, Ch. 4 n. 30
Saronson, Matthew D., Ch. 7 n. 12, 26, 28
Savage, David, Ch. 7 n. 50, 54
Savage, James D., Ch. 17 n. 19
Schattschneider, E. E., Ch. 1 n. 6; Ch. 10 n. 2; Ch. 12 n. 4
Schick, Allen, Ch. 5 n. 69
Schick, Marvin, Ch. 7 n. 30
Schlesinger, Arthur M. Jr., Ch. 6 n. 14, 28; Ch. 18 n. 26
Schlozman, Kay Lehman, Ch. 12 n. 9
Schudson, Michael, Ch. 6 n. 1
Schulman, Paul R., Ch. 16 n. 6
Schumpeter, Joseph, Ch. 9 n. 19
Schwartz, Bernard, Ch. 7 n. 53
Schwartz, John E., Ch. 4 n. 27, 29; Ch. 16 n. 37
Scott, Denise, Ch. 12 n. 19
Segal, Jeffrey, Ch. 7 n. 59
Seoud, Russanne Jourdan, Ch. 8 n. 36
Shafer, Byron, Ch. 10 n. 22, 27
Shaffer, William R., Ch. 5 n. 53
Shapiro, Robert Y., Ch. 9 n. 9, 25; Ch. 16 n. 33
Shilts, Randy, Ch. 16 n. 1
Shull, Steven, Ch. 6 n. 10
Shuman, Howard E., Ch. 17 n. 14

Simpson, Glenn R., Ch. 5 n. 7
Sinclair, Barbara, Ch. 5 n. 30, 32, 66
Skidmore, Thomas E., Ch. 13 n. 22
Skowronek, Stephen, Ch. 6 n. 15
Small, Melvin, Ch. 13 n. 2
Smallwood, Frank, Ch. 10 n. 21
Smith, Adam, Ch. 17 n. 6
Smith, Gerard, Ch. 18 n. 14
Smith, Steven, Ch. 5 n. 25, 39, 45, 48
Smothers, Ronald, Ch. 5 n. 11; Ch. 15 n. 49
Snow, Donald M., Ch. 18 n. 20
Sorauf, Frank J., Ch. 11 n. 24; Ch. 12 n. 19
Spaeth, Harold, Ch. 7 n. 48
Speakes, Larry, Ch. 13 n. 14
Spitzer, Robert J., Ch. 6 n. 5
Stanley, Harold, Ch. 13 n. 12
Stein, Herbert, Ch. 17 n. 24
Stimson, James A., Ch. 5 n. 63
Stockman, David S., Ch. 17 n. 13
Stokes, Anson Phelps, Ch. 14 n. 19
Stokes, Donald, Ch. 9 n. 23; Ch. 11 n. 13
Stone, Deborah, A., Ch. 16 n. 12, 25
Strunk, Mildred, Ch. 9 n. 1
Stuckey, Mary E., Ch. 6 n. 36
Sundquist, James L., Ch. 10 n. 19
Sussman, Barry, Ch. 8 n. 22
Swoboda, Frank, Ch. 15 n. 64
Szatmary, David, Ch. 2 n. 2

Tacheron, Donald G., Ch. 5 n. 60
Taft, William Howard, Ch. 6 n. 17
Tanenhaus, Joseph, Ch. 7 n. 30
Tatolovich, Raymond, Ch. 6 n. 12
Taylor, John, Ch. 1 n. 7
Taylor, Paul, Ch. 13 n. 18
Taylor, Philip M., Ch. 13 n. 1
Taylor, William L., Ch. 11 n. 2
Tedin, Kent T., Ch. 9 n. 5
Teixeira, Ray A., Ch. 11 n. 7
Thomas, Clive S., Ch. 12 n. 16
Thomas, Pierre, Ch. 8 n. 15
Thomas, Rich, Ch. 17 n. 1
Tierney, John T., Ch. 12 n. 9
Time, Ch. 3 n. 1, 18, 22
Tindall, George Brown, Ch. 2 n. 4, 6, 7, 11, 12
de Tocqueville, Alexis, Ch. 1 n. 3; Ch. 9 n. 10; Ch. 12 n. 2, 5
Toner, Robin, Ch. 12 n. 1
Tribe, Laurence H., Ch. 7 n. 15
Truman, David, Ch. 12 n. 4, 23
Tufte, Edward R., Ch. 17 n. 3, 5
Tulis, Jeffrey K., Ch. 6 n. 37, 50; Ch. 13 n. 7
Tyson, Laura D'Andrea, Ch. 18 n. 19

Udall, Morris K., Ch. 5 n. 60
Usowski, Peter S., Ch. 18 n. 8

Valenti, Jack, Ch. 6 n. 41
Verba, Sidney, Ch. 1 n. 11; Ch. 8 n. 3, 31; Ch. 11 n. 4, 20; Ch. 15 n. 32
Vogel, David, Ch. 12 n. 8
Volgy, Thomas J., Ch. 16 n. 37

Wahlke, John C., Ch. 5 n. 12
Waldman, Steven, Ch. 5 n. 2; Ch. 12 n. 1
Walker, David B., Ch. 4 n. 25, 26, 36
Walker, Jack, Ch. 12 n. 6
Washington, George, Ch. 3 n. 11
Waste, Robert, Ch. 16 n. 13, 27, 29
Waterman, Richard W., Ch. 8 n. 34

Watson, Richard, Ch. 6 n. 24
Wayne, Stephen, Ch. 5 n. 57
Weber, Max, Ch. 8 n. 4
Wechsler, Herbert, Ch. 7 n. 58
Weisberg, Herbert F., Ch. 11 n. 8
Weiss, Philip, Ch. 13 n. 31
Welch, David A., Ch. 18 n. 8
Weston, Alan, Ch. 6 n. 32
Wheeler, Michael, Ch. 9 n. 1
White, Theodore H., Ch. 10 n. 1, 28; Ch. 13 n. 35
Wildavsky, Aaron, Ch. 4 n. 28; Ch. 5 n. 69; Ch. 9 n. 16; Ch. 11 n. 16; Ch. 16 n. 5; Ch. 17 n. 15

Will, George, Ch. 4 n. 38; Ch. 11 n. 9
Wilson, James Q., Ch. 5 n. 67; Ch. 8 n. 1, 2, 20, 27; Ch. 16 n. 11
Wilson, William Julius, Ch. 16 n. 36
Wilson, Woodrow, Ch. 5 n. 35; Ch. 7 n. 74
Winternitz, Helen, Ch. 7 n. 22
Wolfinger, Raymond E., Ch. 11 n. 3, 12, 12
Wolfskill, George, Ch. 6 n. 14
Wolin, Sheldon, Ch. 1 n. 8
Woliver, Laura, Ch. 12 n. 17
Wolpe, Bruce C., Ch. 12 n. 20
Wood, B., Ch. 8 n. 34

Wood, Gordon S., Ch. 2 n. 3
Woodward, Bob, Ch. 6 n. 2; Ch. 7 n. 53; Ch. 13 n. 9; Ch. 17 n. 1, 22
Woodward, C. Vann, Ch. 15 n. 8
Woolley, John T., Ch. 17 n. 10
Wright, John R., Ch. 7 n. 31

Yarmolinsky, Adam, Ch. 18 n. 30

Zeigler, Harmon, Ch. 13 n. 20
Zingale, Nancy H., Ch. 9 n. 14

Abington School District v. *Schempp*, 483
Abortion issue, 255, 502-4
  government funding issue, 503
  opinions in, 322*i*
  Roe v. *Wade*, 502-3
  Webster decision, 504, 556
Abrams, Jacob, 480
Abrams v. *United States*, 480*i*
Accuracy in Media, 441
Acton, Lord, 212
Actual groups, interest groups, 408
Adams, Abigail, 51, 204
Adams, John, 42, 45-46, 51, 337, 388
  election to presidency, 337
Adams, John Quincy, election to president, 338
Adams, Samuel, 39, 42
Adams, Sherman, 205
Administration, and bureaucracy, 276
Administrative discretion, 273
Administrative Procedure Act, 279, 293
Advertising, political advertising, 467-69
Advocacy, meaning of, 221
Affirmative action, 527-33, 556
  and *Bakke* decision, 529-30
  in Clinton administration, 532-33
  creation of, 529
  purpose of, 527
  quota programs, 528-29
  in Reagan/Bush era, 531-32
  and reverse discrimination, 530
  seniority rules and layoffs, 531
AFL-CIO, 415, 416, 432
African Americans:
  affirmative action, 527-33
  in bureaucracy, 274-75
  colonial population of, 59
  in Congress, 141-42
  federal court appointments, 236-37, 237*i*
  and military, 516, 519, 619
  political opinion of, 310
  school desegregation, 518-20, 524-27
  segregation of, 515-19
  on Supreme Court, 229, 230
  voting rights, 370, 514, 515-16, 522, 524
  and white supremacy groups, 514
  See also Civil rights; Slavery
Agency for International Development, 634
Agricultural Adjustment Administration, 564
Agricultural interest groups, 417-18
Aid to Families with Dependent Children (AFDC),
  127, 290, 291, 570, 572, 575, 594
AIDS:
  activism, 326*i*
  government response to, 547-48, 555
  testing issue, 501*i*
Air Force One, 463*i*
Airline Deregulation Act, 564
Airlines, deregulation of, 564
Akaka, Daniel K., 141
Alaska, 618
Albany Plan, 35-36, 42
Alexander v. *Holmes County Board of*
  Education, 524
Alien and Sedition Act, 15, 476, 505
Alliance for Progress, 622
All-Volunteer Army, 558
Amendment process, 86-90
  Article V of Constitution, 78
  effectiveness of, 88

  stages of, 86-87
  time limits, 87
America First, 552
American Association of Retired Persons (AARP),
  124*i*, 376, 407, 543, 559
American Automobile Association, 415
American Bar Association, 417
  and Supreme Court appointment, 229, 231
American Civil Liberties Union, sex discrimination
  cases, 537, 538
American Conservative Union, 415, 421
American Dental Association, 420
American Enterprise Institute, 562
American Equal Rights Association, 534
American Farm Bureau Federation, 415, 417
American Federation of State, County and
  Municipal Employees, 415
  PAC contribution of, 433
American Independent Party, 348
American Indian Movement, 415, 422, 541
American Medical Association, 415, 417, 420, 432
  PAC donations of, 433
American Revolution, 41-49, 42-45, 47, 48
  end of, 47
  Lexington and Concord, 42-43, 47
Americans for Democratic Action, 359, 415, 421
Americans with Disabilities Act, 120, 121*i*, 542
American Women's Society of Certified Public
  Accountants, 408
Americorps, 283
  passing law for, 134-35
Ames, Aldrich, 285*i*, 638
Amicus curiae briefs, 240
Amtrak, 278
Anderson, Jack, 178
Anderson, John, 348
Anglican Church, 482
Annapolis Convention, 50
Ann, Paul, 431
Anthony, Susan B., 91, 535
Anti-Defamation League, 421
Antifederalists, 78-82, 340
  leader of, 80
  position of, 78, 80-82
  and ratification, 83
  writings of, 80
Antinationalists, at Constitutional Convention,
  61-62
Apartheid, 517
Appeals courts:
  circuit courts, 226, 227
  civil cases, 225
  criminal cases, 225
  en banc proceedings, 226
Appellate courts, 225
Appellate jurisdiction, Supreme Court, 220, 238
Appointment power, of president, 182-83
Appropriation bill, 154
Appropriations:
  foreign aid, 633
  military spending, 634
Arbella, 30
Architectural Barriers Act, 542
Area of dominant influence (ADI), 465-66
Aristide, Jean-Bertrand, 9*i*, 20
Arizona v. *Fulninante*, 499
Armey, Richard, 135, 156, 602
Arms Control and Disarmament Agency, 628, 634
Arnett, Peter, 441-42

Article I courts, 226
Articles of Confederation, 47-50, 57
  limitations of, 48-49
  provisions of, 48-49
Articles of Constitution, 75-78
  Article I, 75-76, 103, 104, 110
  Article II, 76
  Article III, 76-77, 219
  Article IV, 77-78
  Article V, 78
  Article VI, 78
  Article VII, 78
  provisions of, 48-49
Ashe, Arthur, 555
Asian-Americans:
  in Congress, 141, 142
  federal court appointments, 237
  political opinion of, 310
Association of Trial Lawyers of America, PAC
  contribution of, 433
Astroturf activities, 430
Atomic bomb, Japan, 621
Attorney general, role of, 282*i*
Attucks, Crispus, 39, 40*i*
Authoritarian regime, definition of, 6

Babbitt, Bruce, 234
Baby-boomers, 305
Baker, James III, 613
Baker, Jim, 205
Balanced-Budget Amendment, 87-88, 172, 596
Balanced Budget and Emergency Deficit Control
  Act, 594
  features of, 594
Baldwin, Abraham, 66, 67
Baltimore, Lord, 31
Banks, national-powers position, 111
Barbour, Haley, 351*i*
Barron, John, 476
Barron v. *Baltimore*, 476-77
Bass Anglers Sportsman Society (BASS), 566
Batista, Fulgencio, 614
Baucus, Max, 97
Bayh, Birch, 116
Bedford, Gunning, 67
Bennett, William, 269
Benton v. *Maryland*, 479
Bentsen, Lloyd, 466
Berlin Wall, dismantling of, 6*i*
Berlusconi, Silvio, 347
Bernstein, Carl, 178, 447, 453
Bicameral legislature, meaning of, 31, 63, 138
Biden, Joseph, 473
Biggers, Neal B., Jr., 532
Bill:
  amendments to, 164
  law-making process, 151-55
Bill of Rights, 85-86
  amendments of, 85
  application to states, 476-82
  and Fourteenth Amendment, 477, 479-80
  incorporation of, 115, 477, 479, 481
  nationalization of, 478-79
  no incorporation of, 480
  origins of, 82, 83
  selective incorporation, 481-82
  total incorporation of, 480
Bills of attainder, 110

Bingaman, Anne K., 282
Bipolarity, meaning of, 621
Black Caucus, 170
Black codes, 513
Black, Hugo, 249, 457
Blackmun, Harry, 228, 234, 235, 247, 251, 420, 502
Blackwell, Alice Stone, 535
Blanket primaries, 355
Block grants, 119
  nature of, 119
  types of, 119
Blue laws, 486
B'nai B'rith, 415, 421
Bonior, David, 157
Bono, Sonny, 148
Boren, David, 169, 581, 582
Bork, Robert, 168, 231, 231*i*, 232
Bosnia, 626, 628, 631*i*
Boston Massacre, 39, 40*i*
Boston Tea Party, 40, 41*i*, 42
Bowdoin, James, 26
Bowers v. *Hardwick*, 217-18, 246, 247, 249, 251, 500, 543
Boycott, meaning of, 520
Bradford, William, 29
Bradlee, Ben, 453
Bradley, Bill, 379
Bradley, Joseph, 535
Brady Bill, 429
Brandeis, Louis D., 101, 242*i*, 480
Brandt, Edward, 547-48, 562
Branstad, Terry, 99*i*
Brennan, William, 228, 228*i*, 250, 251, 473
Breyer, Stephen, 228, 229, 234, 241, 248*i*, 251, 504
Briefs, to Supreme Court, 240-41
Brinkley, David, 460*i*
Brokaw, Tom, 452*i*
Brookings Institution, 562
Brown, Henry, 515
Brown, Jerry, 602
Brown, Linda, 218
Brownlow Commission, 203
Brown, Oliver, 519*i*
Brown v. *Board of Education*, 102, 115, 230, 240, 253, 254, 510, 518-19, 525, 557
  Brown II, 519
Bryan, William Jennings, 339*i*
BuBois, W.E.B., 516
Buchanan, James, 338
Buchanan, Pat, 468, 552
Buckley v. *Valeo*, 398
Buckley, William F., Jr., 441
Budget and Accounting Act, 592
Budget buster, 164
Budget and Impoundment Control Act, 593
Budget. *See* Federal budget
Bundy, McGeorge, 637
Burdi, George, 539
Bureau of Alcohol, Tobacco, and Firearms, 285, 586
Bureau of the Budget, 207, 592
Bureaucracy:
  and administrative oversight, 284
  administrative task of, 276
  appointment power of president, 281-82
  benefits of, 288-89
  cabinet departments, 277
  civil service, 270-71
  and Congress, 278-79, 283-84
  constraints on, 278-79

definition of, 263
and democracy, 293
development of, 269-72
diversity in, 274
doublespeak of, 280
downsizing efforts, 269
features of, 263-64
government corporations, 278
and Great Society, 267-68
growth of, 265-69
and Hatch Act, 271-72
implementation task of, 272-76
independent agencies, 277
independent regulatory commission, 277-78
national-security bureaucracy, 284-85
and president, 281-83
problems of, 264-65
public opinion of, 286-88
red tape, 287
reform of, 289-93
regulatory task of, 276
and spoils system, 270
and welfare state, 267
Bureaucrat, role of, 263
Bureau of Intelligence and Research, 634
Burger, Warren, 234, 246, 246*i*, 251, 458
Burke, Edmund, 44, 146-47
Burns, James MacGregor, 41-42
Burr, Aaron, 59, 388
Burton, John, 145
Burton, Philip, 145
Bus Deregulation Reform Act, 564
Bush, George, 188, 209, 341, 381, 387, 552
  and affirmative action, 532
  and federal court system, 236
  federalism under, 128
  and New World Order, 625-26
  and Noriega capture, 613-14
  and Persian Gulf War, 199, 625
  and taxation, 600
  and veto, 182
Business-Industry Political Action Committee, 432
Business Loans program, 123
Business Roundtable, 405, 416
Busing, for school desegregation, 525, 526-27
Butler, Pierce, 242*i*
Byrdlock, 172
Byrd, Robert, 172

Cabinet, 107
  creation of, 207-8
  functions of, 208
Cabinet departments, 277
  current departments, 277
Cable News Network (CNN), 451, 461
Cable TV, 451
Cain, Herman, 405
Calhoun, John, 112
Cambodia, 198, 624
Cambridge Agreement of 1629, 30
Campaigns:
  campaign specialists, 381
  influence on voting, 381
  volunteer workers, 381-82
Campbell, Ben Nighthorse, 13, 143*i*, 167
Canada:
  Charlottetown Accord, 104
  Quebec as independent state, 105
Candidate-centered politics, 358, 434
Cannon, Joseph, 155, 156
Cantwell v. *Connecticut*, 478
Cape Cod, 29

Capitol, 151
Cardin, Benjamin, 406
Cardozo, Benjamin, 242*i*, 482, 494
Carrot-and-stick programs, 104-5
Carruthers, Garrey, 98
Carson, Rachel, 563, 565
Carswell, G. Harrold, 231, 232
Carter, Jimmy, 188, 282, 381, 552
  and bureaucracy, 281
  and federal court system, 236
  federalism under, 125
Carter, Rosalynn, 204
Carville, James, 555
Case Act, 631
Case, Clifford, 631
Casework, Congressional members, 148
Casey, William, 98
Castro, Fidel, 621-22
Categorical grants, 117-18
  increases in, 118
  nature of, 117-18
Catt, Carrie Chapman, 535
Caucus, 338
  definition of, 354
  presidential nomination, 354
Center for Media and Public Affairs, 459
Central High School, desegregation efforts, 519, 520
Central Intelligence Agency (CIA), 277, 285-86, 634
  and foreign policy, 638
  functions of, 638
  limiting power of, 638
  reform movement, 286
Certification Day, 391
Challenger disaster, 261-62
  and bureaucracy, 264-65
  investigation of, 261-62
Chamber of Commerce, 415, 416
Charles I, King of England, 30
Charlottetown Accord, 104
Chavez, Cesar, 540
Checks and balances, meaning of, 73
Cheney, Richard, 613
Chicago, Burlington and Quincy Railway Co. v. *Chicago*, 478
Chief justice, role of, 246
Chief of staff, 205-6
  functions of, 205-6
Chief of state, president as, 186
Chiles, Lawton, 78
Christian Coalition, 421
Christmas tree bill, 164
Christopher, Warren, 635*i*
Circuit courts, 226, 227
Citizenship rights:
  African Americans, 514
  for women, 535
Citizens for a Sound Economy, 430
Citizens for Tax Justice, 419
City of Richmond v. *Crosson*, 532
Civil cases, 225
  class action suits, 225-26
  damages in, 225
Civil disobedience:
  and civil rights movement, 384, 520
  examples of, 384
  as political participation, 384
Civil government, meaning of, 29
Civilian Conservation Corps, 195, 266
Civil liberties:
  defendants rights, 492-500
  definition of, 475

and democracy, 474-75, 505
extension of Bill of Rights protection, 476-77
freedom from approach to, 475
freedom of press, 489-92
freedom of religion, 482-87
freedom of speech, 487-89
privacy rights, 501-4
right to die, 504
and states, 477-82
Civil rights:
and Civil War Amendments, 513-14
Compromise of 1850, 512
definition of, 475, 511
and democracy, 510-11, 542-43
of disabled persons, 542
of Hispanic Americans, 540
and ideal of equality, 511
Missouri Compromise, 512, 513
of Native Americans, 541-42
of women, 533-36
Civil Rights Commission, 523
Civil rights interest groups, 415, 421
types of, 415, 422
Civil rights laws:
challenges to, 523-24
Civil Rights Act of 1875, 515
Civil Rights Act of 1957, 519, 521
Civil Rights Act of 1960, 519
Civil Rights Act of 1964, 55, 103, 522-23, 529, 536
Civil Rights Act of 1968, 524, 525, 565
Civil Rights Act of 1991, 532
Civil Rights Bill of 1866, 513, 524
Civil Rights Enforcement Laws, 514
Civil Rights Restoration Act, 542
Civil rights movement, 520-22
beginning of, 520
and civil disobedience, 384, 520
demonstration methods, 520-21
freedom riders, 521
National Association for the Advancement of Colored People (NAACP), 516
violence against, 521-22
Civil service, 270-71
Civil Service Commission, 270
Civil Service Reform Act, 270-71, 289
Civil War, 69
Civil War Amendments, 513-14
Clark, Kenneth, 518
Clark, Tom, 235
Class action suits, 225-26
Clay, Henry, 200, 338
Clayton, Eva, 142*i*
Clean Air Act of 1963, 120, 126, 553
Clean Air Act of 1970, 564, 565
Clean Air Act of 1990, 126, 556, 565, 566
Clear and present danger test, 480
Supreme Court decisions, 480
Cleveland, Grover, 339
Clinton, Bill, 99*i*, 463*i*
and affirmative action, 532-33
Americorps program, 134-35
and bureaucracy, 282, 292-93
crime bill, 210
and deficit reduction, 582*i*
and executive agreements, 630
and federal budget deficit decrease, 605
and federal court system, 236
federalism under, 128-29
foreign policy, 626-28
and Haiti, 199
health care reform, 101, 128-29, 405-6, 552*i*, 576-77

Mexico debt assistance, 609, 630, 630*i*
1994 election, 394, 395-96, 397
and North American Free Trade Agreement (NAFTA), 77*i*, 210, 607-8
and Omnibus Budget Reconciliation Act, 581-82
reputation of, 188
and Supreme Court, 235
and taxation, 600-601, 602
town meetings of, 202
and veto, 155, 182
and women in government, 228, 229, 282
Clinton, Hillary Rodham:
accomplishments as First Lady, 204, 538
criticisms of, 204
and health care reform, 204, 405, 576
Clipper computer chip, 639
Closed primary, 355
Cloture, 165
CNN Headline News, 451
Coattails effect, congressional elections, 386-87
Coercive Acts, 40
Coercive diplomacy, 628
Cohen, Paul, 489
Cohen v. *California*, 489
Cold War, 621-23
and bipolarity, 621
and containment policy, 620
Cuban missile crisis, 621-22
end of, 615, 625
Korean War, 621
and NSC-68, 621
Vietnam War, 622-23
Collective action:
and American political system, 413
and interest groups, 412-13
Colonial America:
Albany Plan, 35-36
American Revolution, 42-45, 47, 48
Annapolis Convention, 50
Articles of Confederation, 47-50
Boston Massacre, 39
Boston Tea Party, 40, 42
Committee of Correspondence, 39-40
Common Sense, 43-44
compact, government by, 27, 29
Declaration of Independence, 45-46
First Continental Congress, 42
governors in, 32
Intolerable Acts, 40-41
key events in, 47
Massachusetts Bay colony, 30
Mayflower Compact, 29
proprietary colonies, 30-32
Second Continental Congress, 45
social contract theorists, 32-35
Stamp Act congress, 37-38
Sugar and Stamp Acts, 36-37
thirteen colonies (map), 28
Townshend Revenue Acts, 38-39
Colson, Charles, 177
Commander in chief, president as, 186, 197-19
Commerce clause:
example of use, 103-4
Supreme Court interpretation (1994-95), 130
Committee of Correspondence, 39-40, 41
Committee on Political Education, 432
Committee of the whole, 166
Common Cause, 156, 415, 419, 420
issues of, 420
Common Sense, 43-44
Communism, Cold War, 621-23
Community action programs, 571-72
Compact:

definition of, 27-28
Mayflower Compact, 29
Compensatory damages, 225
Compromise of 1850, 512
Conant, Dr. Marcus, 547-48
Concerned Women for America, 429*i*
Concord Coalition, 421
Concurrent powers, nature of, 109-10
Concurring opinion, Supreme Court, 244
Confederate flag issue, 13
Confederation, meaning of, 35, 99
Conference committees, 159
Congress:
bicameralism, 31, 63, 138
and bureaucracy, 278-79, 283-84
committee of the whole, 166
debates, rules related to, 166
delegation of power to president, 195-96
and democracy, 136-37, 138, 172-73
and elastic clause, 140
and foreign-aid appropriations, 633-34
and foreign policy, 630-34
framer's conception of, 138-40
future view for, 172
law-making process, 151-55
limits on power, 140-41
main powers of, 139
oversight, 171
and party affiliation, 358-59, 360
and policy making, 556-57
power of, 137-38
power of purse, 171, 283-84
and president, 141
proportional representation, 62-63
public view of, 149-51
Republican of 1995, 120, 126, 129, 137, 149, 163, 168, 172, 289*i*
and Supreme Court, 253-54
term limits, 388-89
TV coverage, 162
and War Powers Act, 632-33
See also House of Representatives; Senate
Congressional agenda, 151
Congressional Budget and Impoundment Control Act, 171
Congressional Budget Office, 594
Congressional committees:
conference committees, 159
functions of, 159-61
joint committees, 159
select/special committees, 158-59
standing committees, 158
subcommittees, 161-63
Congressional districts, 143-45
gerrymandering, 144
race-based redistricting, 146-47
reapportionment, 143-44
redistricting process, elements of, 144-45
Congressional elections, 386-87
coattails effect, 386-87
voter turnout for, 386, 387
Congressional members:
apprenticeship of, 165-66
casework, 148
decision making, sources of influence, 167-70
as delegates, 145-46
demands of job, 169
diversity of members, 141-42
franking privilege, 148
incumbents, 148-49
profile of, 141-42
seniority of, 165-66
as trustees, 146-47

Congressional Record, 151
Congressional staff:
cutting of, 168
functions of, 168
and legislator's voting decision, 168
Congressional Union, 535
Congress of Racial Equality, 415, 556
Connally, John, 398
Connecticut Compromise. *See* Great Compromise
Connor, "Bull," 521
Conrail, 565
Conservative Opportunity Society, 156, 170
Conservatives, 315-18
conservatism as trend, 315-17, 341, 343
interest groups, 411, 431
compared to liberals, 315
and media, 449, 460
political stance of, 315
Constituents, and legislator's voting decision, 167
Constitution:
as adaptable instrument, 76, 86, 90-92
amendment process, 86-90
Articles of, 75-78
Bill of Rights, 85-86
Congress, creation of, 138-41
delegated and reserved powers, 75
and democratic ideals, 92, 94
federalism, 73, 102
Federalists versus Antifederalists, 78-83
and foreign policy, 628-29
horizontal and vertical powers, 74
and interest groups, 408
and judicial review, 90
and judiciary, 219-23
and presidency, 179, 180-86
ratification of, 82-84
and republican government, 71-72
separation of powers, 73, 74
supremacy clause, 106
and women, 79, 536
Constitutional Convention:
Great Compromise, 67
nationalists versus antinationalists, 60-62
New Jersey Plan, 64-65
participants at, 59-62
presidency issue, 69-70
purpose of, 58-59
setting for, 60-61
three-fifths compromise, 68-69
Virginia Plan, 62-64
See also Constitution
Constitutions, U.S. Constitution as model for, 93
Constructionist view, of president, 191-92
Consumer price index, and social security, 572
Consumer Product Safety Commission, 268, 276
Consumers Union of the United States, 415
Containment:
and Cold War, 620-21, 624
nature of, 620
Contingency election, 391-92
Contract with America, 120, 149, 164, 172, 303, 359, 437, 574i, 596
Conventions, and political parties, 351-52
Coolidge, Calvin, 193, 416
Cooperative federalism, 114-15
Corporation for Public Broadcasting, 278
Cost-benefit analysis, 558
Cost-of-living allowances (COLAs), 573
Coughlin, Charles, 448
Council of Catholic Bishops, 415, 421
Council on Competitiveness, 209
Council of Economic Advisors, 207
functions of, 207

Council of revision, 64
Court of Military Appeals, 226
Courts of appeal, 226
Court system:
appellate courts, 225
judges, appointment of, 235-37
legislative courts, 226
structure of, 224
trial courts, 224-25
U.S. courts of appeal, 226
U.S. district courts, 226
See also Supreme Court
Court of Veterans Appeals, 226
Craig v. *Boren*, 538
Cranston, Alan, 567
Creative federalism, 120-23, 125
Crime Bill of 1994, 225
Crime bill, 210
Criminal cases, 225
plea bargains, 225
Cronkite, Walter, 443
"Crossfire," 459
Cruzan, Nancy, 245, 504
C-SPAN, 451
Congressional coverage, 162, 464
Cuba:
Cuban missile crisis, 621-22
economic sanctions, 628
Cue structure, and legislator's voting decision, 168, 170
Culture theory, basis of, 318
Cumming v. *County Board of Education*, 515

Daewoo, 435
Daley, Richard, 356
D'Amato, Alfonse, 136
Danforth, John, 234
Daschle, Tom, 157
"Dateline," 454
Daughters of Liberty, 40
Davie, William R., 60
Dawes, William, 43
Days, Drew, 240i
Day, William R., 113
Dealignment, political parties, 342, 397
Death penalty, 493
Deaver, Michael, 435, 464
Debs, Eugene, 349, 480
Declaration of American Rights, 42
Declaration of Causes and Necessity of Taking Up Arms, 44
Declaration of Independence, 25, 45-46
philosophical foundation of, 33, 46
purpose of, 46
Declaration of Sentiments, 533
DeConcini, Dennis, 581-82, 597
De facto equality, 511
De facto segregation, 524
Defendants rights, 492-500
double jeopardy, protection against, 498
due process, 494-95
exclusionary rule, 494, 495
Fifth Amendment, 498-99
Fourth Amendment, 494-98
Miranda warning, 499
right to speedy trial, 498
search and seizure, 496-98
Sixth Amendment, 498-99
Defense Intelligence Agency, 285, 634
De Jonge v. *Oregon*, 478
De jure equality, 511
De jure segregation, 524

DeLay, Thomas, 157
Delegated powers, meaning of, 75
Delegates, Congressional members as, 145-46
Democracy:
Athenian model of, 9-10, 17, 27
and bureaucracy, 293
and civil liberties, 474-75, 505
and civil rights, 542-43
and Congress, 136-37, 138, 172-73
constrained models of, 3, 4
definition of, 6
direct democracy, 6, 7-8
and economic policy, 610
and equality, 12, 528
as evolutionary process, 3-6
and federalism, 130-32
and foreign policy, 615, 644-45
and freedom, 4, 10-12, 19
indirect democracy, 6, 8-9
and interest groups, 414, 437-38
and judicial review, 20
and judiciary, 222
and majority rule, 14-15
and media, 442-43
military in, 20
and order and stability, 13-14
and participation, 15-19
and political parties, 332-33, 361
and presidency, 212-14
and public policy, 548-49, 575, 578
compared to republican system, 72
and Supreme Court, 256-57
Democracy in America (Tocqueville), 6
Democratic Party:
approach to organization of, 353
development of, 81
historical view, 339, 340
and New Deal, 341
new versus old Democrat concept, 128
platform of, 352
Democratic Republican Independent Voter Education Committee, PAC contributions of, 433
Democratic-Republican Party, 81, 337
Democratic Study Group, 170
Dennis v. *United States*, 488
Department of Agriculture, and foreign policy making, 640
Department of Commerce, and foreign policy making, 640
Department of Defense:
and foreign policy, 635-36
heads of, 635-36
military-industrial complex, 636
power of, 636
Department of Education, creation of, 282-83
Department of Energy, 268, 284
and foreign policy making, 640
Department of Labor, and foreign policy making, 640
Department of State:
criticisms of, 635
and foreign policy, 635
head of, 635
Department of Treasury, 586i
and foreign policy making, 640
Depository Institution Deregulation and Monetary Control Act, 564, 567
Deregulation:
airlines, 564
savings and loans associations, 567-68
Desegregation:
meaning of, 519

in military, 516, 519
in schools, 518–20
Desert Shield, 210
Desert Storm, 199, 210
Detente, 624–25
    meaning of, 624
Deutch, John, 286, 293
Deviating elections, 396
Dickinson, John, 37, 39, 42, 59
Dienbienphu, 622
Dilinger, John, 285
Diplomatic relations, and president, 186–87
Direct broadcast satellites (DBS), 456
Direct democracy, 6, 7–8, 377–78
    definition of, 6
    forms of, 7
    initiatives, 377
    referenda, 377
Direct-mail campaigns, of lobbyists, 429
Disabled persons:
    and employment discrimination, 542
    laws related to, 542
    reasonable accommodations for, 542
Disaster relief, 550, 561
Discount rate, 588
Discrimination:
    definition of, 511
    Dred Scott decision, 513
    housing, 524
    in military, 516
    and Roosevelt, F.D., 516
    and Truman, 516
Dissenting opinion, Supreme Court, 244–45
District courts, 226
Dixiecrats, 516
Docket, of Supreme Court, 238
Dodd, Christopher, 352i, 353
Dole, Robert, 157, 166, 473, 542, 631i
Dominican Republic, 615
Domino theory, 624
Donaldson, Sam, 460i
Double jeopardy, protection against, 482, 498
Doublespeak, 280
Douglas, Stephen, 200
Douglas, William O., 229, 232, 242, 250, 501, 529
Dred Scott v. Sandford, 513
Drug Enforcement Administration, 285
Dual federalism, 112–13
    definition of, 112
    end of, 113
Due process, 115, 477, 494–95, 519
    and Bill of Rights, 479
Dukakis, Michael, 318, 468
    and political advertising, 468–69
Dulany, Daniel, 38
Duncan v. Louisiana, 479
Durenberger, David, 135

Eastern Europe:
    satellites, 621
    Soviet control of, 620
East India Company, 40
Economic interest groups, 415, 416–18
    agricultural groups, 417–18
    big business, 416
    examples of, 415, 416
    organized labor, 416–17
Economic Opportunity Act, 571
Economic policy:
    components of, 583
    and democracy, 582–83, 610
    federal budget, 592–97

fiscal policy, 583, 587–88
    goals of, 583–85
    government spending, 601–6
    international economic policy, 606–10
    Keynesian economics, 586–88
    laissez-faire economics, 586
    monetarism, 588–90
    and political cycles, 585
    supply-side economics, 590–92
    taxation, 597–601
    tradeoffs in, 584–85
Economic sanctions, 628
    usefulness of, 628
Economy:
    inflation, 583
    stagflation, 590–91
Educational level:
    and interest group involvement, 412
    and political opinion, 306–7
    and tolerance, 314
    and voting, 375, 376
Education Committee, 158
Eighteenth Amendment, 87, 88, 89
Eighth Amendment, 85
Eisenhower, Dwight, 187, 228, 341, 379
    and civil rights, 519–20
Elastic clause, 104, 110–11
    and Congress, 140
Elderly, and civil rights, 543
Elders, Joycelyn, 182
Elections:
    congressional elections, 386–87
    majority vote, 385
    midterm elections, 372
    plural-member districts, 385–86
    and political parties, 333–34
    presidential elections, 387–99
    purpose of, 18
    single-member district plurality system, 385
    volunteer activities, 381–82
Electoral college, 387–92
    and contingency election, 391–92
    faithless elector, 390–91
    and framers, 388–90
    operation of, 70, 390–92
    presidential election votes needed, 391
    reform issue, 392
    Twelfth Amendment reform, 388
    and two-party system, 344
Electronic mail:
    political organizing by, 383
    White House on Internet, 200
Elementary and Secondary Education Act, 122
Eleventh Amendment, 89
Ellsberg, Daniel, 177, 457, 490
Emancipation Proclamation, 197, 208, 513–14
Emergency powers, of president, 630
Emergency Price Control Act, 197
EMILY, 429i
Employment Act of 1946, 207, 583
Employment discrimination:
    and African Americans, 516, 522
    and disables, 542
    and women, 536–39
En banc proceedings, 226
Endangered Species Act, 276i, 564
Energy and Commerce Committee, 158
Engel, Steven, 218
Engel v. Vitale, 483
Enlargement policy, foreign relations, 627
Enrolled act, 154
Entitlements, 572–73
    functions of, 570

politics of, 572–73
    social security, 570
Environmental Defense Fund, 415, 422
Environmental-impact statement, 565
Environmental policy, 563, 565–67
    legislation related to, 126, 564–66
    offset policy, 566
    off-site tradeoffs, 566–67
    pollution reduction timetable, 126
Environmental Protection Agency (EPA), 268, 273, 276, 277, 556
    creation of, 565
    functions of, 126
Environment-related conferences, 566
Equal Employment Opportunity Act, 529
Equal Employment Opportunity Commission (EEOC), 276, 287, 529
    creation of, 522, 523
    inefficiency of, 287i
Equality:
    as American value, 313
    de facto equality, 511
    de jure equality, 511
    and democracy, 12, 528
    in direct democracy, 7
    equality of opportunity, 12, 313, 527–28
    equality of result, 12, 527–28
    and freedom, 12
    political equality, 313
Equal Pay Act, 55, 536
Equal protection clause, 516, 529, 536, 537
Equal Rights Amendment (ERA), 79, 87, 88
    defeat of, 536
    ratification issues, 55–56
Equal Rights Party, 181i
Equal time rule, media regulation, 455
Era of Good Feelings, 337
Erlichman, John, 205
Ervin, Sam, 178, 522
Erwin, Will, 446
Escobedo v. Illinois, 239, 498
ESPN, 451
Establishment of religion, 483–85
    Lemon test, 484–85
    school prayer issue, 485
Ethics in Government Act, 434, 435
Evans, Daniel, 169
Everson v. Board of Education of Ewing Township, 478, 483
Exclusionary rule, 494, 495
    limitation of, 495
    meaning of, 494
Executive agreements, 185
    and Case-Zablocki Act, 631–32
    nature of, 185, 630
    uses of, 630
Executive branch:
    Article II of Constitution, 76
    role of, 62, 74
Executive Office of the President, 206–7
    Council of Economic Advisors, 207
    National Security Council, 206–7
    Office of Management and Budget (OMB), 207
Export-Import Bank, 278
Express powers, nature of, 107
Exxon Valdez, 225

Factions, meaning of, 81
Fair Deal, 552
Fair Employment Practices Committee, 516
Fair Labor Standards Act, 420
Fairness doctrine, media regulation, 455–56

Faithless elector, 390-91
Falwell, Jerry, 460
Family, and political socialization, 304, 306
Family Leave Act, 167
Family Security Act, 573, 575
Family Support Act, 573, 574
Farley, James, 297
Farm Security Administration, 195
Faulkner, Shannon, 16*i*
Fax attack, 469
Federal Aviation Administration (FAA), 265, 278
Federal budget, 592-97
  and Balanced-Budget Amendment, 87-88, 172, 596
  balancing budget, 594-96
  and Congress, 593-94
  effects of balancing budget, 595
  and Office of Management and Budget (OMB), 592-94
  preparation of, 592-94
Federal budget deficit, 603-6
  decrease and Clinton administration, 605
  implications of, 604-5
  increase, reasons for, 605
  nature of, 603-4
Federal Bureau of Investigation (FBI), 228, 634
  expansion of powers, 285
  Hoover directorship, 285
  organization of, 264
Federal Communications Act, 455, 456
Federal Communications Commission (FCC), 267, 276, 277
  and media regulation, 455-56
Federal Contract Compliance Programs, 529
Federal Crimes Act of 1790, 476
Federal Deposit Insurance Corporation (FDIC), 267, 278, 564
Federal Election Campaign Act, 397, 432
Federal Election Commission, 397, 432
Federal Emergency Management Agency, 550, 561
Federal employment, law against discrimination in, 516, 522
Federal Energy Administration, 268
Federal Energy Office, 268
Federal Environmental Pesticide Control Act, 564
Federal Flag Protection Act, 474
Federal grants, 117-19
  block grants, 119
  categorical grants, 117-18
  federal mandates, 119-20
  formula grants, 118-19
  formula/project grant, 119
  grant-in-aid, 117
  project grant, 119
Federal Highway Administration, 276
Federal Housing Administration, 564
Federalism:
  advantages of, 101
  under Bush, 128
  under Carter, 125
  and Clinton administration, 128-29
  cooperative federalism, 114-15
  creative federalism, 120-23, 125
  definition of, 73, 99
  and democracy, 130-32
  development of, 110-17
  disadvantages of, 102
  dual federalism, 112-13
  federal grants, 117-19
  future view for, 130
  intergovernmental relations, 123-24
  under Johnson, 120-23
  metaphor for study of, 100

  and New Deal era, 113-15
  New Federalism, 124-25
  picket fence federalism, 123-24
  post-New Deal era, 115, 117
  and public policy, 561
  under Reagan, 125-28
  and triad of power, 102-6
Federalist no. 10 (Madison), 81, 99, 299-300, 409
Federalist no. 51 (Madison), 73, 81
Federalist no. 73 (Hamilton), 182
Federalist no. 78 (Hamilton), 220
Federalist Papers, 27, 79-80, 444, 583
  purpose of, 80
Federalists, 78-82, 81
  historical view, 337-38, 340
  leaders of, 80
  position of, 78, 80-82
  and ratification, 83
Federal mandates, 119-20
  nature of, 119-20
  shifting burden to states, 120
Federal matching funds, 398-99
Federal National Mortgage Association (FNMA), 267
Federal Radio Commission (FRC), 455
Federal Regulation of Lobbying Act, 434
Federal Reserve Board, 277
Federal Reserve System, 588-90
  establishment of, 588
  functions of, 588-90
Federal Trade Commission, 278, 563
  function of, 564
Feedback loop, 559
Feinstein, Dianne, 124*i*
Feminization of poverty, 568-69
Fenno, John, 444
Fifteenth Amendment, 18, 89, 370, 514
Fifth Amendment, 85, 477, 482, 492, 498-99, 519
Fighting words, freedom of speech, 489
Filibuster, 164-65
  method of, 164
  record for, 164
Finance Committee, 158
Fireside chats, 448
First Amendment, 85, 408, 442, 455, 475, 477
First Bank of United States, 583
First Continental Congress, 42
First Lady, Hillary Rodham Clinton as, 204
Fiscal policy, 583, 587-88
  meaning of, 583, 587-88
Fish and Wildlife Service, 564
Fitzwater, Marlin, 613
Flag burning, 473-74
Food and Drug Administration, role of, 564
Food stamps, 127, 572, 594
Ford, Gerald, 186, 341, 381
  and *Mayaguez*, 198-99
Ford, Wendell, 157
Foreign Agricultural Service, 640
Foreign aid, 627-28
  appropriations, 633-34
Foreign Commercial Service, 640
Foreign policy:
  agencies and foreign-policy making, 639-40
  and Central Intelligence Agency (CIA), 638
  coercive diplomacy, 628
  and Cold War, 621-23
  and Congress, 630-34
  and Constitution, 628-29
  containment, 620, 624
  definition of, 614
  and democracy, 615, 644-45
  and Department of Defense, 635-36

  and Department of State, 635
  detente, 624-25
  economic agencies, 634
  economic sanctions, 628
  end of Cold War, 625
  enlargement policy, 627
  foreign aid, 627-28
  foreign policy bureaucrats, 641
  free trade, 627
  globalism, 620-21
  goals of, 615
  institutions of, 628
  intelligence activities, 634
  isolationism, 616
  Monroe Doctrine, 616-17
  national security agencies, 634
  and National Security Council, 636-38
  North Atlantic Treaty Organization (NATO), 620-21, 626
  and president, 196-97, 629-30
  and press, 641-42
  and public opinion, 642-43
  terrorism, 627
  and United Nations (UN), 625-26
  and World War I, 617-18
  and World War II, 618-20
Foreign Service Officers, 641
Formal agenda, and policy making process, 553-54, 556-57
Formal rules, and bureaucracy, 263
Formula grants, 118-19
  nature of, 118-19
Formula/project grant, 119
  nature of, 119
Fortas, Abe, 231, 232
Fortune, 447
Foster, Dr. Henry J., 182
Fourteenth Amendment, 89, 92, 115, 514, 516, 529
  and Bill of Rights, 477, 479-80
  equal protection clause, 516, 529, 536, 537
  and state action, 514-15
Fourth Amendment, 85, 492, 493, 494-98
  exclusionary rule, 494-95
  search and seizure, 496-98
Fourth party system, 339-40
France, bureaucracy of, 286
Frankfurter, Felix, 223, 234, 242, 494, 518
Franking privilege, 148
Franklin, Benjamin, 35, 46, 61, 70, 83
Frear, Alan, 158
Freedmen's Bureau, 513
Freedom:
  and democracy, 4, 10-12
  and equality, 12
  meaning of, 10
  negative and positive, 11-12
Freedom Democrats, 331-32, 332
Freedom House, 4
Freedom of Information Act, 279, 293
Freedom of press, 19, 442, 469, 489-92
  libel, 491
  obscenity, 491-92
  prior restraint, 490-91
  subsequent-punishment, 490
Freedom of religion, 482-87
  establishment of religion, 483-85
  free exercise of religion, 486-87
Freedom riders, 521
Freedom of speech, 487-89
  clear and present danger test, 480
  fighting words, 489
  political speech, 488

private speech, 487
public speech, 487, 488-89
symbolic speech, 489
Free exercise of religion, 486-87
least-restrictive means test, 486
secular regulation rule, 486
Free-rider problem, interest groups, 423-24
Free Soil Party, 339
French and Indian War, 35, 36
Freneau, Philip, 444
Friedan, Betty, 55
Friedman, Milton, 588
Frohnmayer, John, 274-75
Frohwerk, Jacob, 480
Frontiero, Sharron, 537
Frontloading, 356
Fugitive Slave Act, 512
Fundamental Orders of Connecticut, 29, 35

Gage, Thomas, 40-41, 42-43
Gag orders, 490-91
Galbraith, John Kenneth, 421
Galloway, George, 42
Gallup, George, 301
Garcia v. *San Antonio Metropolitan Transit Authority*, 420
Garfield, James, 270
Gates, Daryl, 561
Gazette of the United States, 444
Gender, and political opinion, 311-13
Gender gap, 311-12
examples of issues, 312
General Agreement on Tariffs and Trade (GATT), 583, 607
criticisms of, 607
goal of, 627
U.S. goal in, 607
General Court, 30
General revenue sharing, 124
General Services Administration (GSA), 277
General Theory of Employment, Interest, and Money (Keynes), 587
General welfare clause, 104-6
uses of, 105-6
Generational effect, and political socialization, 306
Generation gap, 304
Generation X, 305
Genuine Information (Martin), 80
George III, King of England, 41, 44, 46
Gephardt, Richard, 155*i*, 156
Germany:
and World War I, 616
and World War II, 618
Gerry, Elbridge, 59, 144
Gerrymandering, 144
Gibbons, Thomas, 112
Gibbons v. *Ogden*, 111-12
Gideon, Clarence Earl, 498*i*
Gideon v. *Wainwright*, 479, 498*i*
Gingrich, Newt, 17*i*, 155, 155*i*, 164, 303, 388
actions in Congress, 172
biographical information, 156
on bureaucracy, 289*i*, 292
Medicare cuts, 559*i*
use of media, 464
welfare reform plan, 574
Ginsburg, Douglas, 232-33
Ginsburg, Ruth Bader, 92, 228, 229, 235, 241, 244*i*, 248*i*, 251, 504
and women's rights, 537
Gitlow v. *New York*, 478, 481
Glass ceiling, 530, 538-39

Glass Ceiling Commission, 530
Globalism, 620-21
meaning of, 620
Globalization, meaning of, 609
Going public, by president, 201-2
Goldberg, Arthur, 234
Goldwater, Barry, 331, 467
Good-character test, and voting, 370
Gore, Al, Jr., 209, 292-93, 292*i*, 608*i*
Gorelick, Jamie S., 282
Goss, Porter J., 163
Gottlieb, Michael, 548
Governmental branches:
checks and balances, 73
executive branch, 74
judiciary, 74
legislative branch, 74
separation of powers, 62, 73, 74
and Virginia Plan, 62
Governmental interest groups, 415, 420
types of, 415, 420
Governmental powers:
concurrent powers, 109-10
divisions of, 107
express powers, 107
and general welfare clause, 104-6
Gibbons v. *Ogden*, 111-12
implied powers, 107
inherent powers, 107-8
and interstate commerce clause, 103-4
McCulloch v. *Maryland*, 111
reserved powers, 108-9
and Tenth Amendment, 106
Government corporations, 278
example of, 278
Government securities, 588
Government spending, 601-6
controllable versus uncontrollable expenditures, 603
and federal budget deficit, 603-6
and national debt, 604-5
spending of tax revenues, 602-3
Governor, in colonies, 32
Gramm, Phil, 406, 594
Grand Old Party Action Committee, 156
Grant-in-aid, 117, 122
increases in, 117, 120
nature of, 117
Grant, Ulysses S., 425
Grassroots activity, 427, 429-31
astroturf activities, 430
effectiveness of, 431
grassroots strategy, meaning of, 535
meaning of, 427
tactics used, 429
Gray, L. Patrick, 177
Grayson, William, 59
Great Britain:
bicameral government, 31, 138
Magna Carta, 27
Great Compromise, 67
propositions of, 67
Great Depression:
and New Deal, 113-15, 131, 190, 266-67
and rise of regulation, 563
Great Society, 120-23, 131, 267-68, 341, 552
effectiveness of, 122-23
programs in, 122
Greeks, ancient, and democracy, 9-10, 17, 27
Greenberg, Stanley, 293, 303
Green card, 276, 554
Greenspan, Alan, 588, 589*i*
Grenada, 199, 642

Grenville, Lord George, 36, 38
Griswold, Estelle T., 218, 501
Griswold v. *Connecticut*, 249, 479, 501
Guinn v. *United States*, 516
Guiteau, Charles, 270
Gulf of Tonkin, 623
Gun control, 167

Haiti, 626, 628
Haldeman, H.R., 205
Hamilton, Alexander, 27, 50, 59, 79-80, 110, 220, 336, 337
Hamilton v. *Regents of the University of California*, 478
Hammer v. *Dagenhart*, 113
Hancock, John, 83
Hansen, James, 97
Harding, Warren, 195
Hardwick, Michael, 217, 475
Harkin, Tom, 552
Harlan, John Marshall, 223, 256, 515
Harper v. *Virginia Board of Education*, 524
Harris, Jo Ann, 282
Harrison, Michael, 449
Harrison, William H., 338
Hatch Act, 271-72
Hatch, Carl, 271
Hatch, Orrin, 234
Hatfield, Mark, 168
Havel, Vaclav, 3*i*, 92
Haynsworth, Clement, 232
Hays, Lawrence Brooks, 147
Head Start, 123, 558
Health care, grants-in-aid for, 117
Health care reform, 576-77
components of program, 576
failure of, 128-29, 552*i*
health-security system proposal, 405
and Hillary Rodham Clinton, 204, 405
opposition to, 405-6, 576-77
Health Insurance Association of America, 405
Health Maintenance Act, 576
Health maintenance organizations (HMOs), 576
Health Research Group, 409
Hearings, law-making process, 152-53
Hearst, William Randolph, 447
Heart of Atlanta Motel v. *United States*, 523
Heckler, Margaret, 547-48
Heflin, Howard, 13
Heightened-scrutiny test, 538
Helms, Jesse, 13, 136, 154, 166, 633-34
Henry, Patrick, 42, 50, 83
Heritage Foundation, 562
Hierarchy, and bureaucracy, 263
Hill, Anita, 160, 232, 233*i*
Hindenburg, 448
Hiroshima, 621
Hispanic Americans:
in bureaucracy, 274-75
civil rights of, 540
in Congress, 142
federal court appointments, 237
political opinion of, 310
Hitler, Adolf, 618
Hobbes, Thomas, 33
Ho Chi Minh, 622, 624
Hollings, Earnest, 594
Holmes, Oliver Wendell, 248, 480, 487
Homelessness, 555*i*
Homosexuals, and civil rights, 543
Hoover, Herbert, 188, 341
Hoover, J. Edgar, 285, 293

Hopper, 151
Horton, Willie, 318, 468
House of Burgesses, 37, 42
House of Commons, 138
House of Lords, 138
House of Representatives:
  committees of, 158-59
  decentralization of power in, 161
  districts and voting, 8
  framer's conception of, 138
  and law-making process, 151-54
  majority leader, 156
  minority leader, 156-57
  powers of, 140
  procedural rules, 163-64
  Rules Committee, 163-64
  compared to Senate, 140
  seniority in, 165-66
  Speaker of the House, 155
  subcommittees, increase in, 161
  voting system of, 153*i*
House Rules Committee, 153, 160
Housing discrimination, 524
Houston, Charles Hamilton, 230
Howard, James, 97
Hruska, Roman, 231
Hudson, Rock, 548, 550, 555
Hughes, Charles Evans, 242*i*, 246
Human Resources Committee, 158
Human Serve, 366
Humphrey, Hubert, 157, 356, 421
Hunt, E. Howard, 177, 178
Hunter, Robert, 568
Hurricane Andrew, 78
Hussein, Saddam, 210
Hyde, Henry J., 388
Hyperpluralism, 436

Ideological interest groups, 415, 421
  types of, 415, 421
Illinois v. *Rodriguez*, 495
Immigrants:
  elimination from government programs, 554
  green card, 554
  increase in, reasons for, 554
  and public policy, 554
Immigration Act of 1986, 554
Immigration and Naturalization Service (INS), 276, 285
Impeachment, of president, 180-81
Implementation:
  and bureaucracy, 272-76
  of public policy, 557-58
Implied powers, nature of, 107
Impounding, 76
Income:
  and political opinion, 309
  and voting, 375, 376
  and voting patterns, 309
Income inequality:
  facts about, 569
  and Reagan era, 591
Income tax, 598-99
Incorporation, of Bill of Rights, 115, 477, 479, 481
Incremental policy, 549
Incumbents, 148-49
  advantages to, 148-49
  and franking privilege, 148
  reelection of, 149
Independent agencies, 277
  types of, 277
Independent expenditures, presidential

campaigns, 399
Independent Federation of Flight Attendants v. *Zipes*, 532
Independent Journal, 444
Independent regulatory commission, 277-78
  types of, 277-78
Independents, meaning of, 322
Indian Citizenship Act, 541
Indirect democracy, 6, 8-9
  definition of, 6
  forms of, 8
Individuals with Disabilities Act, 288*i*
Inflation, meaning of, 583
Infomercials, in political campaigns, 464, 469
Information seeking, as political participation, 382-83
Inherent powers:
  nature of, 107-8, 193
  of president, 193-94
Initiatives, 377
Inouye, Daniel K., 141
In re Oliver, 478
INS v. *Chadha*, 196, 198
Integration, meaning of, 519
Intelligence activities, organizations for, 634
Intensity, of public opinion, 322-23
Inter-American Development Bank, 622
Interest group liberalism, 436
Interest group rating scheme, 359
Interest groups:
  actual groups, 408
  civil rights interest groups, 415, 421
  and collective action, 412-13
  concentrated versus diffuse groups, 424
  and Constitution, 408
  courts, use by, 431
  definition of, 408
  and democracy, 414, 437-38
  economic interest groups, 415, 416-18
  and framers, 409-10
  free-rider problem, 423-24
  governmental interest groups, 415, 420
  grassroots activity, 168, 427, 429-31
  growth of, 411-12
  ideological interest groups, 415, 421
  impact of, 435-37
  as information source, 413
  leadership, effects of, 425
  and legislator's voting decision, 168
  lobbying, 425-27
  maintenance of membership, 423
  and policy entrepreneurs, 409
  political action committees (PACs), 432-34
  and political process, 414
  potential groups, 408
  public interest groups, 415, 418-20
  purpose of, 19
  regulation of, 434-35
  religious interest groups, 415, 421
  single-issue interest groups, 415, 422
Interest rates, and Federal Reserve Board, 588, 589
Internal Revenue Service (IRS), 586*i*
International Anti-Slavery Convention, 533
International economic policy, 606-10
  functions of, 583
  General Agreement on Tariffs and Trade (GATT), 607
  issues in, 606
  North American Free Trade Area (NAFTA), 607-8
  policy coordination, importance of, 608-9
  U.S. and Japanese trade negotiations, 608
International Monetary Fund, 583
Internet:

White House on, 200
  white-supremacy groups on, 539
Interpretation function, media, 452-53
Interstate Commerce Act, 564
Interstate commerce clause, 103-4
  Court interpretation of, 112
Intolerable Acts, 40-41
Intolerance in America, 314
Investigative journalism, 453-54
Iran-Contra affair, 160*i*, 206, 637
Ireland, Patricia, 536*i*
Iron curtain, 620
Iron triangles, 436, 437, 560
  nature of, 284, 562
  and public policy, 561-62
Isolationism, nature of, 616
Issue networks, 560
  nature of, 284, 562
  and public policy, 562
Issue stage, policy making process, 555
Ito, Lance, 225*i*

Jackson, Andrew, 112, 190, 202, 269-70, 289
  election to presidency, 338
Jacksonian Democrats, historical view, 338-39
Jackson, Jesse, 452
Jackson, Robert, 73
Japan:
  atomic bombing of, 621
  farm lobby, 418-19
  and World War II, 618
Japanese Americans, internment of, 2, 197
Jars, Howard, 431
Jay, John, 26, 42, 79-80, 220
Jeffersonian Republicans, historical view, 337, 340
Jefferson, Thomas, 9, 15, 26, 41, 46, 76, 80, 81, 91, 111, 190, 336, 337, 444
  activist policy of, 193-94
  election to presidency, 337
Jenner-Butler Bill, 223
Jennings, Peter, 443, 452*i*
Jim Crow laws, 515, 516*i*
Job Corps, 571
JOBS program, 573-74
Johnson, Andrew, 199, 513
Johnson, Gregory, 473-74, 489, 505
Johnson, Lyndon, 115, 209, 341, 552
  civil rights laws, 522, 522*i*
  federalism under, 120-23
  Great Society, 120-23
  as Senate majority leader, 157-58, 158*i*, 166
  and Vietnam War, 197-98, 622-23
  War on Poverty, 115, 524, 568*i*, 571-72
Johnson, Magic, 555
Johnson rule, 166
Joint Center for Political and Economic Studies, 562
Joint Chiefs of Staff, 635-36, 637
Joint committees, 159
Jordon, Hamilton, 205
Journalism:
  investigative, 453-54
  watchdog, 454
  yellow, 447
  See also Media; Newspapers
Judges, appointment of, 235-37
  merit-selection process, 236
  and minorities, 236-37
  and president, 236
  senatorial courtesy, 235
  See also Supreme Court justices
Judicial activism, 249

Judicial restraint, 248
Judicial review, 20, 220-21
    and Constitution, 90
    establishment of, 220-21
    meaning of, 20, 73, 90, 220
    power of, 221
Judiciary:
    Article III of Constitution, 76-77
    and Constitution, 219-23
    and democracy, 222
    independence of, 223
    role of, 62, 74
    See also Court system; Supreme Court
Judiciary Act of 1789, 220
Judiciary Committee, 160, 231, 235
Jungle, The (Sinclair), 564
Junk bonds, and savings and loan scandal, 567
Just Cause, Noriega capture, 613-14

Kahn, Mel, 538
Kantor, Mickey, 640i
Kasich, John, 590
Kassebaum, Nancy, 135, 136, 158i
Katzenbach v. McClung, 523
Katzenbach v. Morgan, 540
Keating, Charles H., 567
Keating Owen Child Labor Act, 113
Kemp, Jack, 551
Kennan, George, 620
Kennedy, Anthony, 234, 248i, 250, 485, 504
Kennedy, John F., 208, 212i, 230, 341, 467, 552
    assassination of, 556, 622
    and bureaucracy, 283
    and Cuban missile crisis, 622
    and poverty, 571
    and Supreme Court, 234, 253
Kennedy, Robert, 455, 521
    assassination of, 556
Kennedy, Ted, 141, 234
Kerrey, Bob, 135, 168, 473, 581, 582
Kevorkian, Jack, 504
Keyes v. School District #1, Denver, Colorado, 526
Keynesian economics, 586-88
    elements of, 587-88
Keynes, John Maynard, 587
Khrushchev, Nikita, 621
King, Larry, 441
King, Martin Luther, Jr.:
    assassination of, 556
    and civil rights movement, 1-2, 51, 91, 425,
        455, 520, 521i, 522, 522i, 524, 556
King, Rodney, 109, 384-85, 452, 550
Kissinger, Henry, 635
Klopfer v. North Carolina, 479
Kohut, Andrew, 449
Kono, Yohei, 635i
Koop, C. Everett, 548
Korean War, 208, 621
Ku Klux Klan Act, 514
Ku Klux Klan (KKK), 314i, 488, 540
    activities of, 514

Labor Committee, 158
Lachowsky, Hyman, 480i
Laissez-faire economics, 586
    elements of, 586
Lake, Anthony, 207
Lake Erie pollution, 126
Landon, Alfred, 297-98
Laos, 198, 624
"Larry King Live," 465

Latency, and public opinion, 323
Latin America, and Alliance for Progress, 622
Law clerks, 244
Law-making process, 151-55
    appropriation bill, 154
    congressional agenda, 151
    filibuster, 164-65
    hearings, 152-53
    introduction of bill, 152-53
    legislators' decisions, sources of influence, 167-
        70
    lobbyists, role of, 151
    logrolling, 166
    markup session, 153
    obstacles to passage of bill, 170-71
    riders, 154, 164
    and specialization of legislators, 166
    veto, 154
    votes needed, 151
League of Nations, 200, 617
League of United American Citizens, 540
League of Women Voters, 415, 419
Least-restrictive means test, free exercise of
    religion, 486
Lee, Richard Henry, 45, 45i
Leftist politics:
    and media, 460
    roots of, 316
Legislative branch:
    Article I of Constitution, 75-76
    bicameralism, 31, 63, 138
    role of, 62, 74
    See also Congress; House of Representatives;
        Senate
Legislative courts, 226
Legislative Reorganization Act of 1946, 171
Legislative veto, 196
Lemon test, establishment of religion, 484-85
Lemon v. Kurtzman, 484
Letters of Brutus (Yates), 80
"Letters of a Pennsylvania Farmer," 38
Leviathan (Hobbes), 33
Lewis, Lawrence, 202
Libel, meaning of, 458, 491
Liberals, 315-18
    compared to conservatives, 315
    interest groups, 411
    and media, 460-61
    political stance of, 315
Liberty Party, 339
Lichter, Linda, 460
Lichter, Robert, 460
Liddy, G. Gordon, 177-78
Life, 447
Lifestyle, and political opinion, 318
Limbaugh, Rush, 448, 449, 465
Limited government, meaning of, 34
Limited Test Ban Treaty, 622
Lincoln, Abraham, 91, 190, 338, 552
    and abolition of slavery, 197, 513
    presidential power of, 190, 194
Lincoln, Benjamin, 25-26
Lindberg Law, 109
Line item veto, 164, 196
Line Item Veto Act, 196
Lipman, Samuel, 480i
Literacy test, and voting, 370, 515
Literary Digest, Roosevelt election poll, 297-98,
    301, 302
Lobbying, 425-27
    definition of, 425
    grassroots activity, 427, 429-31
    historical view, 424

and law-making, 151
    lobbyist activities, 428
    lobbyists, profile of, 426
    public opinion of, 425
    tactics used, 426-27
Local party organization, 349-50
Locke, John, 33-35, 39, 46
Logrolling, 166, 560
    definition of, 561
    and public policy, 561
Look, 447
Lorance v. AT&T Technologies, 532
Los Angeles riots, 550, 560, 561
Lott, Trent, 157
Louisiana Territory, 91, 190
Loyalists, 39-40
Luce, Harry, 447
Lusitania, 617

Machine politics, 350-51
    modernizing forces, 351
Madison, James, 10, 26, 27, 46, 60, 60-61, 62i, 65,
    79-80, 84, 138, 299-300, 336, 409-10
Magazines, 447-48
    historical view, 447-48
    most widely read, 447
Magna Carta, 27, 82
Magnet schools, 525, 527
Magruder, Jeb, 179
Maintaining elections, 396
Majority leader:
    House of Representatives, 156
    Senate, 157
Majority opinion, Supreme Court, 244
Majority rule:
    meaning of, 7
    and minority rights, 14-15
Majority vote, 385
Major, John, 631i
Malaysia, 624
Malloy v. Hogan and Murphy v. Waterfront
    Commission of New York, 479
Mandela, Nelson, 517
Manual of Parliamentary Practice and Precedent
    (Jefferson), 163
Mao Zedong, 621
Mapp, Dollree, 494-95
Mapp, Dolores, 218
Mapplethorpe, Robert, 492i
Mapp v. Ohio, 478
Marbury v. Madison, 77, 90, 220-21
Marcy, William, 270
Margin of error, and public opinion measures, 301
Margolies-Mezvinsky, Marjorie, 167
Marine Protection Research Act, 565
Markup session, law-making process, 153
Married Women's Independent Citizenship Act,
    535
Married Women's Property Act, 533-34
Marrou, Andre, 17
Marshall, John, 77, 90, 111, 220, 221, 244, 253,
    476
Marshall Plan, 620
Marshall, Thurgood, 86, 229, 251
    career of, 230
    and school desegregation, 518
Martin, Luther, 61, 66, 80
Martin v. Wilks, 532
Mason, George, 59
Massachusetts Bay colony, government of, 30
Massachusetts Bay Company, 30
"Massachusetts Circular Letter," 39

Mass media:
definition of, 444
See also Media
Matching funds, 398–99
Mayaguez, 198
Mayflower, 29
Mayflower Compact, 29, 35
McAuliff, Christa, 261
McCarthyism, 19*i*
McCarthy, Joseph, 19*i*, 454
McConnell, Frank, 406
McCord, Jim, 177
McCormack, John, 168
McCulloch v. *Maryland*, 111
McFarlane, Robert, 435
McGovern-Fraser Commission, 357
McGovern, George, 303, 357, 468
McKinley, William, 339
McKinney, Cynthia, 142*i*, 146, 147
McNamara, Robert, and Vietnam War, 624
Means tests, 603
Meat Inspection Act, 564
Media:
and democracy, 442–43, 469–70
and foreign policy, 641–42
framing effects concept, 453
interpretation function, 452–53
investigative journalism, 453–54
leak, 642
liberal media elite, 460–61
magazines, 447–48
media monopoly issue, 461
newspapers, 444–47
pluralism, 459–60
political programs, 382–83
radio, 448–50
regulation of. *See* Media regulation
and socialization, 454–55
spin of news story, 443
surveillance function, 452
symbiotic relationship with government,
461–62
television, 450–51
Media and elections:
area of dominant influence (ADI), 465–66
equal time rule, 456
infomercials, 469
political advertising, 467–69
polling, 462–64
press coverage, 462
talk shows, 465
television soundbites, 465–67
Media regulation, 455–58
equal time rule, 455
fairness doctrine, 455–56
and Federal Communications Commission
(FCC), 455–56
guidelines for, 456
historical view, 455
prior restraint, 457–58
right of rebuttal, 457
scarcity doctrine, 455
Medicaid, 126, 594
beginning of, 122
functions of, 572
rising costs, 577
Medicare, 571*i*
beginning of, 122
cuts to, 559*i*
rising costs, 577
Medicare Act, 571, 572
Meek, Carrie, 142*i*
Mennonite Central Committee, 415

Mercury Theater of the Air, 448
Meredith, James, 521
Merit Systems Protection Board, 271
Mexican American Legal Defense and Education
Fund, 415, 422, 540
Mexican Americans, and civil rights, 540
Mexico:
debt assistance to, 609, 630, 630*i*
democratic processes in, 396
Miami Herald Publishing Co. v. *Tornillo*, 458
Michel, Robert, 156, 157
Michnik, Adam, 18
Midterm elections, 372, 387
Military:
appropriations, 634
civilian control of, 20
desegregation of, 516, 519, 619
and Reagan administration, 634, 643
Military-industrial complex, 562
nature of, 636
Military Selective Service Act, 538
Miller v. *California*, 492, 492*i*
Milliken v. *Bradley*, 526
Mill, John Stuart, 6, 299
Minorities:
in bureaucracy, 274–75
in Congress, 141–42
federal court appointments, 236
glass ceiling, 530
and political opinion, 309–10
race-based redistricting, 144, 146–47
Minority leader:
House of Representatives, 156–57
Senate, 157
Minority rights, and majority rule, 14–15
Minor parties, 345–46, 348–49
functions of, 349
performance of, 348–49
reasons for emergence of, 345–46, 348
Minor v. *Happersett*, 535
Minor, Virginia, 535
Minton, Sherman, 235
Minutemen, 43, 48
Miranda, Ernesto, 218
Miranda v. *Arizona*, 239, 247, 499
Miranda warning, 499
Mississippi Freedom Democrats, 361
Missouri Compromise, 512, 513
Mitchell, George, 157
Mitchell, John, 178
Model Cities, 122
Mondale, Walter, 209
Monetarism, 588–90
elements of, 588
and monetary policy, 588
Money supply, and Federal Reserve, 588–90
Monroe Doctrine, 616–17
Monroe, James, 337, 616
Montesquieu, Charles de, 32
Moral leader, president as, 187–88
Moral Majority, 411, 421
Morning in America, 468
Morris, Gouverneur, 59
Morris, Robert, 59
Mosely-Braun, Carol, 13, 136, 141
Mothers Against Drunk Driving (MADD), 105, 409
Motor Carrier Act, 564
Motor-voter bill, 365–66, 367
Mott, Lucretia, 533, 534*i*
Moynihan, Daniel Patrick, 572, 573
MTV, 451, 454, 465
Muckraking, 446–47
Multi-party system, 343

Multipoint distribution service (MDS), 456
Murphy, Frank, 235
Murrow, Edward R., 448, 454
Mutual assured destruction (MAD), 560

N.A.A.C.P. v. *Alabama*, 478
Nadar, Ralph, 409, 419, 420*i*, 425
Nagasaki, 621
Narrowcasting, 451
examples of, 451
Nast, Thomas H., 446
Nation, 448, 459
National Abortion Rights Action League, 415, 422
PAC contribution of, 433
National Aeronautics and Space Administration
(NASA), 277
Challenger disaster, 261–62
goal changes over time, 560
National American Woman Suffrage Association,
535
National Association for the Advancement of
Colored People (NAACP), 230, 415, 422, 556
origins of, 516
and school desegregation, 518–19
National Association of Manufacturers, 415, 416,
434
National Coalition to Ban Handguns, 415, 422
National Committee for the Effectiveness of
Congress, 415
National and Community Service Trust Act, 136
National Conference of Mayors, 420
National Congress of American Indians, 541
National Congressional Club, PAC contribution of,
433
National Corn Growers Association, 417
National Council of Churches, 415, 421
National Council of La Raza, 540
National debt, 604–5
nature of, 604
National Economic Council, 207
National Education Association, 417
PAC contribution of, 433
National Endowment for the Arts, 274–75
National Environmental Policy Act, 279, 564
National Environmental Protection Act, 565
National Farmers Union, 417
National Federation of Independent Businesses,
405
National Gazette, 444
National Governors' Association, 420
Nationalists, at Constitutional Convention, 60–61
National Labor Relations Board (NLRB), 278, 564
creation of, 195, 266
National Labor Relations Board (NLRB) v. *Jones
and Laughlin Steel*, 114
National League of Cities, 420
National Organization for Women (NOW), 415,
419, 422, 429*i*
activities of, 536
National party organization, 351–53
national chair, 352
party platform, 352
National Performance Review, 292
National Reconnaissance Office, 634
National Recovery Administration (NRA), 113
National Review, 448, 459
National Rifle Association, 408, 414*i*, 415, 422, 429
PAC contribution of, 433
National Right to Life Committee, 415, 422
National Security Act, 285
National Security Agency, 285, 634
and Clipper computer chip, 639

National-security bureaucracy, 284-85
  agencies of, 285
National Security Council, 206-7, 620
  and foreign policy, 636-38
  functions of, 206-7, 637
  members of, 637
National Security Paper 68 (NSC-68), 621
National service program, 283
  passing law for, 134-35
National Taxpayers Union, 419, 424
National Voter Registration Act, 365-66
National Woman Suffrage Association, 534
National Women's Party, 55
National Women for Women (NOW), 55
Native Americans, 541-42
  civil rights activities of, 541
  in Congress, 142, 143*i*
  and Constitution, 59
  ethnic and tribal movements, 450
  extermination of, 2
  gambling enterprises of, 542
  peyote and religious rituals, 253, 486
Natural Resources Defense Council, 419
Natural rights, meaning of, 29
Nature Conservancy, 419
Near v. *Minnesota*, 478
Necessary and proper clause, and flexibility of
  Constitution, 76
Neighborhood Youth Corps, 571
Neo-Nazi movement, 539
New America, 552
New American Mandate, 552
New Beginning, 552
New Birth of Freedom, 552
New Deal, 131, 190, 223, 266-67, 289*i*
  cooperative federalism of, 113-15
  New Deal coalition, 341
  organizations created, 267
  programs of, 195, 266, 564
  and welfare state, 267
New Federalism, 124-25, 552
New Freedom, 552
New Frontier, 552, 571
New Hampshire primary, 355-56
New Jersey Plan, 64-65
  propositions of, 64
  compared to Virginia Plan, 65
New Nationalism, 552
New, New Deal, 552
New Republic, 448
Newspapers, 444-47
  historical view, 444-45
  muckraking, 446-47
  top ten in circulation, 446
  yellow journalism, 447
New Spirit, 552
Newsweek, 447, 462
New Voice, 552
New World Order, 552
New York Sun, 444-45
New York Times, 462
New York Times Co. v. *United States*, 244
New York Times v. *Sullivan*, 491
Nickelodeon, 451
Nineteenth Amendment, 18, 72, 89, 92, 370, 535
Ninth Amendment, 85
Nixon, Richard, 179*i*, 194*i*, 341, 467-68, 552
  and detente, 624-25
  pardon of, 186
  and Supreme Court, 234
  and Vietnam War, 198, 623
  Watergate, 177-78, 178*i*, 179, 188
No incorporation, of Bill of Rights, 480

Noriega, Manuel, 457, 613-14, 614*i*, 642
North American Free Trade Agreement (NAFTA),
  77*i*, 210, 607-8
  impact of, 627
  opposition to, 607-8
North Atlantic Treaty Organization (NATO),
  620-21, 626
  Partnership for Peace, 626
  terms of, 621
Northern spotted owl, 276*i*
North, Oliver, 160*i*
NSC-68 (National Security Council Paper 68, 621
Nuclear weapons:
  atomic bombing of Japan, 621
  Limited Test Ban Treaty, 622
  nuclear bomb drills, 621*i*
  protest against, 384
  Strategic Arms Limitation Treaty (SALT), 624-25
Nullification, 112
Nunn, Sam, 167, 199

Oath of a Free-man, 31
O'Brien, David Paul, 248
Obscenity, 491-92
Observations on the New Constitution...by a
  Columbian Patriot (Warren), 80
Occupational Safety and Health Administration,
  195, 268
O'Connor, Sandra Day, 146-47, 229, 234, 248*i*,
  250, 251, 498, 538
Office of Management and Budget (OMB), 207,
  283, 592-94
  and budget preparation, 592-94
  functions of, 207, 283
Office of Personnel Management, 271
Offset policy, 566
Off-site tradeoffs, 566-67
Ogden, Aaron, 112
Oklahoma City bombing, 285, 487*i*
Old Age Survivors Disability Insurance, 570
Olive Branch Petition, 44
Omnibus Budget Reconciliation Act, 125, 581-82
O'Neill, Thomas (Tip), 155, 156, 426
On Liberty (Mill), 299
Open primary, 355
Operation Rescue, 384, 411, 431
Opinion. *See* Political opinions; Public opinion
Opinion, Supreme Court, 242-45
  assignment of, 242-43
  concurring opinion, 244
  dissenting opinion, 244-45
  majority opinion, 244
  opinion-drafting process, 243-44
  plurality opinion, 244
Order, and democracy, 13-14
Oregon v. *Michell*, 116
Original jurisdiction, Supreme Court, 220, 238
Original policy, 549, 550-51
Ornstein, Norman, 156
Otis, James, 37-38, 39
Override, of veto, 182
Oversight:
  Congressional, 171, 284
  examples of hearings, 171

Paine, Thomas, 43
Palko v. *Connecticut*, 478, 481
Panama, 628, 642
  Noriega capture, 613-14, 642
Panama Canal, 190
Panetta, Leon, 205, 206

Pardon, by president, 186
Parker v. *Gladden*, 479
Parks, Rosa, 1-2, 2*i*, 3, 21, 91, 510, 520, 543
Participation:
  amendments related to, 18
  and democracy, 15-19
  universal suffrage, 15-16
  vehicles for, 18-19
Partisanship:
  and dealignment, 397
  realignment, 321-22, 342, 397
  and voting, 376
Partnership for Health Act of 1966, 119
Partnership for Peace, 626
Party identification:
  and demographic factors, 346
  origins of, 342
  and political opinions, 321-22
  psychological factors, 345, 378
  and realignment, 321-22
  trends in, 342
  and two-party system, 345
  and voting, 378
Party leader, president as, 188
Party platform, 352
  of Democrats, 352
  meaning of, 352
  of Republicans, 352
Party realignment:
  causes of, 336
  versus dealignment, 342
Paterson, William, 61, 64
Patterson v. *McLean Credit Union*, 532
Paul, Alice, 535
Paxon, Bill, 172
Paz, Robert, 613
Peace Corps, 277, 288, 622
  mission of, 622
Pearl Harbor, 197, 618*i*
Peers, and political socialization, 307
Pendleton Act, 270, 289
Pennsylvania Chronicle, 39
Pennsylvania Gazette, The, 35
Penny press, 445
Pentagon, 636, 640
Pentagon Papers, 244, 490
Peonage, definition of, 516
People for the American Way, 232, 415, 421
People vs. *PACS*, 420
Perot, H. Ross, 293, 333, 342, 343, 348*i*, 456, 469*i*
  as independent candidate, 344, 347, 348
  use of media, 455, 464, 465, 469
Persian Gulf War, 20, 199, 280
  events of, 625
  media coverage of, 441-43, 461
Persuasion, and president, 200-202, 209-10
Petit court, 224
Picket fence federalism, 123-24
Pierce, Franklin, 338
Pilgrims, Plymouth Colony settlement, 29
Pinckney, Charles, 69
Pinckney, James, 388
Pitt, William, 38
Planned Parenthood, 411
Plato, 299
Plea bargains, 225
Plessy, Adolph, 515
Plessy v. *Ferguson*, 1, 515, 516*i*, 518
Pluralism:
  meaning of, 15
  media, 459-60
Plurality of vote, 385
Plural-member districts, 385-86

Plymouth Colony, Mayflower Compact, 29
Pocket veto, 154, 182
Pointer v. *Texas*, 479
Police power, 109
    types of powers, 109
Policy Committee, 155
Policy elites, and policy making process, 553
Policy entrepreneurs:
    and interest groups, 409
    and policy making process, 555-56
    tactics of, 556
Policy evaluation, 558-59
Policy making process:
    continuation of policies, 560
    and formal agenda, 553-54, 556-57
    implementation of policy, 557-58
    issue stage, 555
    and policy elites, 553
    and policy entrepreneurs, 555-56
    policy evaluation, 558-59
    and public agenda, 553
    stages on, 552-53
    termination of policy, 559-60
    triggering mechanism in, 555, 556
    See also Public policy
Political action committees (PACs), 432-34
    campaign financing, 399-400
    contributions (1975-1990), 432
    functions of, 432
    growth of, 399, 401
    influence of, 358
    problems related to, 433-34
    top contributors, 433
Political advertising, 466-67
    examples of, 467-68
    image making in, 467-68
    negative advertising, countering of, 468-69
Political awareness, and public opinion, 318-21
Political ideology:
    conservatives, 315-18
    importance to political parties, 359-61
    left and right, roots of, 316
    liberals, 315-18
    meaning of, 315
    and political opinion, 315-18
Political opinion:
    and core values, 313-14
    and gender, 311-13
    and income, 309
    and lifestyle, 318
    and minorities, 309-10
    and party identification, 321-22
    and political ideology, 315-18
    and region, 311
    and religious affiliation, 310-11
    schemas in formation of, 321
    and social class, 309
Political participation:
    campaign/election activities, 381-82
    civil disobedience, 384
    and democracy, 400-401
    information seeking as, 382-83
    levels of, 368
    and political stability, 366-67
    political violence, 384-85
    protest, 384
    and socioeconomic status, 369
    voting, 369-81
Political parties:
    conventions, 351-52
    dealignment, 342, 397
    definition of, 333
    and democracy, 332-33, 361

and election process, 333-34
historical view, 336-43
and legislator's voting decision, 167
local party organization, 349-50
machine politics, 350-51
minor parties, 345-46, 348-49
multi-party system, 343
national party organization, 351-53
and organization of government, 335
party identification, 321-22, 342, 345
party platform, 352
party realignment, 336
and policy making, 335-36
and political choice, 335
political ideology, importance of, 359-61
presidential nomination, 353-58
purpose of, 19
realignment, 321-22, 342, 397
and representation of group interests, 334
state party organization, 350
two-party system, 343-45
Political socialization:
    definition of, 304
    family in, 304, 306
    generational effect, 306
    and peers, 307
    and school, 306-27
    and television, 307-8
Political speech, freedom of speech, 488
Political violence, 384-85
Politico role, meaning of, 147
Polk, James K., 338
Polls:
    flaws of, 205, 302
    importance of, 302-4
    media election polls, 462-64
    and sample size, 301
    straw polls, 301
Poll tax, 370, 524
Pollution credits, 566
Polygamy, and Mormons, 486
Populists, 270
Pork barrel legislation:
    nature of, 561
    and public policy, 561
Postal Service, 278, 279, 288, 291-92
Potential groups, interest groups, 408
Potsdam, 630
Poverty:
    feminization of, 568-69
    trends related to, 568-69
Poverty (Hunter), 568
Poverty level:
    controversy related to, 568
    figures for, 568
Powell, Colin, 20, 379, 452, 613
Powell, Lewis, 234, 248, 529, 537
Powell v. *Alabama*, 478
Prayer in schools, 254*i*
Precedents, Supreme Court decisions, 246-47
Prescott, Samuel, 43
Presidency:
    Brownlow report, 203
    Cabinet, 207-8
    and democracy, 212-14
    Executive Office of President, 206-7
    vice president, 208-9
    White House Office, 203-6
President:
    active versus passive presidents, 194-95
    and appointment of judges, 236
    appointment power, 182-83
    approval ratings, 201

and bureaucracy, 281-83
as chief diplomat, 186-87
as chief executive, 187
as chief legislator, 187
as chief of state, 186
as commander in chief, 186, 197-99
and Congress, 141
Congressional delegation of power to, 195-96
and Constitution, 69-70, 179, 180-86
constructionist view of, 191-92
eligibility requirements, 181
emergency powers, 630
executive agreements, 185, 630
and foreign policy, 629-30
impeachment, 180-81
inherent powers, 193-94
as juggler of roles, 189
and legislator's voting decision, 167
line of succession for, 208
as manager of prosperity, 188
as moral leader, 187-88
pardon power, 186
as party leader, 188
party weakness, effect of, 210-11
personal presidency concept, 211-12
power of persuasion of, 200-202, 209-10
powers of, 181-86
as public figure, 199-202
ranking of presidents, 192
stewardship view of, 190
and Supreme Court, 253
and Supreme Court appointments, 234-35
term of office, 180
treaty power, 183-85
veto power, 181-82
war powers of, 197-99
Presidential campaign, 392-95
    and electoral votes from states, 393-94
    polling, 303
    and population changes, 394
    swing states, 395
    themes of, 552
Presidential campaign finances, 397-400
    federal matching funds, 398-99
    independent expenditures, 399
    legislation related to, 397, 434
    and political action committees (PACs), 399
    reform, effects of, 399-400
    soft-money donors, 399, 400
Presidential candidates:
    personality factors, 379
    recruitment of, 334
Presidential election, 387-99
    campaign finances, 397-400
    deviating elections, 396
    direct vote plan, 392
    electoral college, 70
    and electoral college, 387-92
    maintaining elections, 396
    and media. *See* Media and elections
    nomination, 353-58
    plurality presidents, 395-96
    prediction of winner, 395
    presidential campaign, 392-95
    realigning elections, 396-97
Presidential nomination, 353-58
    caucuses, 354
    and political action committees (PACs), 358
    primaries, 355
    reform of process, 356-58
President pro tempore, Senate, 157
President's Commission on the Status of Women, 536

President's Committee on Federal Judicial
  Selection, 236
President of the Senate, 157
Press, freedom of. *See* Freedom of press
Preston, Levi, 48
Primaries, 355
  blanket primaries, 355
  closed primary, 355
  frontloading, 356
  New Hampshire primary, 355-56
  open primary, 355
  purpose of, 355
  superdelegates, 356
  winner-take-all system, 355
Prior restraint:
  freedom of press, 490-91
  media regulation, 457-58
  versus right to know, 457-58
Privacy Act, 279
Privacy rights, 19, 217-18, 501-4
  birth control issues, 501-2
  zones of privacy, 501
Private speech, freedom of speech, 487
Privatization, 291-92, 563
  meaning of, 291
  pros and cons of, 291-92
Probable cause, meaning of, 496
Progressive Era, 446
Progressives, 266, 270
Progressive taxes, 599
Prohibition:
  illegal activities during, 90*i*
  repeal of, 88, 90
Project grant, 119
  as discretionary grants, 119
  types of, 119
Property, women's rights, 533-34
Property ownership, and voting rights, 515
Proportional representation, 66, 386
  meaning of, 62-63
Proportional representation system, 343
Proposal, in amendment process, 86
Proposition 13, 377, 431, 597
Proposition 187, 7*i*
Proprietary colonies, government of, 30-32
Protest, as political participation, 384
Protest march, meaning of, 520
Public agenda, and policy making process, 553
Public Citizen, 415, 419, 420*i*
Public Citizen Litigation Group, 409
Public interest groups, 415, 418-20
  types of, 415, 419
Public Interest Research Group, 409, 419
Public opinion:
  of bureaucracy, 286-88
  changeability of, 324
  of Congress, 149-51
  and democracy, 326-28
  and foreign policy, 642-43
  and framers, 299-300
  influence on public policy, 325-26
  intensity of, 322-23
  versus journalists opinion, 459
  and latency, 323
  meaning of, 299
  and political awareness, 318-21
  and salience, 323
  of Supreme Court, 254-56
  on welfare programs, 327
  See also Political opinions
Public opinion measures:
  importance of, 302-4
  and margin of error, 301

problems of, 301, 302
random sample, 301
and representative sample, 301
and sampling bias, 301-2
straw polls, 301
Public policy:
  aims of, 549
  definition of, 549
  and democracy, 548-49, 575, 578
  and federalism, 561
  and immigrants, 554
  incremental policy, 549
  and iron triangles, 561-62
  and issue networks, 562
  and logrolling, 561
  original policy, 549, 550-51
  and political parties, 335-36
  and pork barrel legislation, 561
  public opinion, influence of, 325-26
  reflexive policies, 550
  regulatory policy, 562-68
  social welfare policy, 563, 568-75
  substantive policies, 549
  symbolic-original policies, 551-52
  symbolic policies, 549
  symbolic-reflexive policies, 551
  See also Policy making process
Public speech, freedom of speech, 487, 488-89
Public Works Administration, 195
Public Works Committee, 160
Publius, 79
Puerto Rican Legal Defense Fund, 540
Pulitzer, Joseph, 447
Punitive damages, 225
Pure Food and Drug Act, 564

Quayle, Dan, 169, 209, 466, 613
Quota programs, 528-29

Radical Republicans, 513
Radio, 448-50
  historical view, 448
  talk radio, 449, 465
Radio Corporation of America (RCA), 455
Radio Free Europe, 634
Radio Liberty, 634
Rahman, Sheikh Kambir Abdul, 425
Rail Deregulation Act, 564
Railroads, deregulation of, 564
Ramon, Haim, 305
Randolph, Edmund, 59, 62, 69, 84
Random sample, 301
Rankin, Jeannette, 142*i*
Rather, Dan, 452*i*
Ratification, in amendment process, 86
Ratification of Constitution:
  Article VII of Constitution, 78
  events of, 78-85
Rayburn, Sam, 155
Reagan, Ronald, 97, 341, 387
  and affirmative action, 531-32
  and AIDS crisis, 547-48, 550
  communication skills of, 199*i*, 464
  and conservative trend, 315-17
  and downsizing bureaucracy, 269, 281-82
  and federal court system, 236
  federalism under, 125-28
  Grenada invasion, 199
  military buildup, 634, 643
  personality appeal, 379
  Reaganomics, 591-92, 605

and Supreme Court, 234
and veto, 155, 182
Reaganomics, 591-92
Realigning elections, 396-97
Realignment, of partisanship, 321-22, 342, 397
Realtors PAC, contribution of, 433
Reapportionment, 143-45
  race-based redistricting, 144, 146-47
  time frame for, 144
Reapportionment Act of 1929, 143
Reasonableness test, 536-37
Reciprocity, of legislators, 166
Reconsideration rule, 60
Red Lion Broadcasting v. *FCC*, 457
Red tape, of bureaucracy, 287
Reed, Stanley, 518
Reed, Thomas, 155
Referenda, 377
Reflexive policies, 550
Regents of the University of California v. *Bakke*,
  529
Region, and political opinion, 311
Regressive taxes, 599-600
Regulation, and bureaucracy, 276
Regulatory policy, 562-68
  elements of, 562-63
  environmental policy, 563, 565-67
  key policies, listing of, 564-65
  rise of, 563
  savings and loans associations, 567-68
  types of policies, 563
Rehnquist, William, 233, 234, 245, 246, 246*i*, 248,
  248*i*, 250, 251, 504
Religion, freedom of. *See* Freedom of religion
Religious affiliation, and political opinion, 310-11
Religious Freedom Restoration Act, 253
Religious interest groups, 415, 421
  types of, 415, 421
Religious right, and media, 460
Reno, Janet, 282*i*, 365-66
Report on Manufactures (Hamilton), 583
Representative democracy, nature of, 8
Representative sample, and public opinion
  measures, 301
Republic, meaning of, 8, 27
Republican Party:
  approach to organization of, 353
  development of, 81
  historical view, 337, 339, 340
  platform of, 352
Republican system, 71-72
  function of, 71
  compared to pure democracy, 72
  shift to democracy over time, 72
Reserved powers:
  meaning of, 75, 108-9
  nature of, 108-9
Resistance, 539
Resolution, 154
Resolution Trust Corporation, 568
Resource Conservation and Recovery Act, 565
Retrospective voting, 380-81
Revenue sharing:
  general revenue sharing, 124
  special revenue sharing, 124
Revere, Paul, 40*i*, 42, 43
Reverse discrimination, 530
Revolutionary Communist Youth Brigade, 473
Revolutionary War. *See* American Revolution
Reynolds v. *Sims*, 115
Rhetorical presidency, 211
Riders, to bills, 154, 164
Right to die, 504

assisted suicide, 504
  life support maintenance, 504
Right of rebuttal, media regulation, 457
Rio Accords, 566
Riots:
  political violence, 384–85
  and Rodney King verdict, 550, 560, 561
Rivers and Harbors Bill, 561
Rivlin, Alice, 592*i*
Roberts, Barbara, 17
Roberts, Cokie, 460*i*
Roberts, Owen, 242*i*
Robinson v. *California*, 478
Rockefeller, Jay, 141
Rockefeller, Nelson, 209
Rockwell International, 435
Roe, Jane, 218
Roe v. *Wade*, 254, 255, 502–3, 556
Rogers Commission, 261–62
Rogers, William, 261–62
Rome, ancient, and republic, 27
Roosevelt, Eleanor, 204, 421, 536, 538
Roosevelt, Franklin D., 91, 202–3, 210, 542
  and bureaucracy, 282
  and discrimination, 516
  election of, 341
  and executive agreements, 630
  federalism under, 113–15
  fireside chats, 448
  and internment of Japanese Americans, 197
  Literary Digest election poll, 297–98, 301, 302
  New Deal, 113–15, 223, 289*i*
  presidential power, 190, 195
Roosevelt, Theodore, 191*i*, 552
  as minor party candidate, 348
Roper, Elmo, 301
Rothman, Stanley, 460
Roth v. *United States*, 491–92
Rubin, Robert, 586*i*
Rudman, Warren, 594
Rule of four, 239
Rules Committee, 163–64
Rush, Benjamin, 84–85
Russia, television in, 450*i*
Rutledge, John, 59
Rutledge, Wiley, 229, 235

Safe Streets Act of 1968, 119
Safe Water and Toxic Enforcement Act, 566
Salience, and public opinion, 323
Sample, and polling, 301–2
Sampling bias, 301–2
San Antonio Independent School District v.
  Rodriguez, 540
Sand, Leonard B., 509–10
Sarajevo, 325*i*
Satellites, Soviet, 621
Satellite technology:
  and broadcasting, 450–51
  satellite master antenna television (SMATV), 456
Saturday Press, 481
Savings and loan problem:
  bailout of S & Ls, 567–68
  cause of, 567
  reregulation, 565
Scalia, Antonin, 234, 241, 242, 244, 248*i*, 250, 251
Scarcity doctrine, media regulation, 455
Schemas, 321
Schenck, Charles T., 480
Schlafly, Phyllis, 55–56
School, and political socialization, 306–27
School desegregation, 518–20, 524–27

Brown II, 519
Brown v. *Board of Education*, 102, 115, 230,
  240, 253, 254, 518–19
  and busing, 525, 526–27
  and Central High School, 519, 520*i*
  and Civil Rights Act of 1964, 522, 523
  federal response to, 519–20
  implementation of, 519, 557
  magnet schools, 525, 527
  methods of, 525
  and segregation in housing patterns, 525
  state responses to, 519
School lunch programs, 557*i*
School prayer issue, 485
School segregation, Court approval of, 515
Schwartz, Jacob, 480*i*
Schwartzkopf, Norman, 20
Scott, Dred, 512–13
Scottsboro case, 115, 481
Scowcroft, Brent, 613
Search and seizure, 496–98
  consent agreement, 497
  Miranda warning, 499
  and probable cause, 496
  school searches, ruling on, 475*i*
  stop-and-frisk searches, 496
Second Amendment, 85
Second Continental Congress, 45
  Articles of Confederation, 47–50
  Declaration of Independence, 45–46
Second Treatise of Civil Government (Locke), 34
Secret Service, 586*i*
Secular regulation rule, free exercise of religion,
  486
Securities and Exchange Commission (SEC), 267,
  278, 563, 564
Segregation, 515–19
  de facto segregation, 524
  de jure segregation, 524
  Jim Crow laws, 515, 516*i*
  legal basis of, 515
  separate but equal concept, 515, 516*i*, 518
Selective incorporation, Bill of Rights, 481–82
Select/special committees, 158–59
Senate:
  cloture, 165
  committees of, 158–59
  framer's conception of, 138
  compared to House of Representatives, 140
  and law-making process, 151, 152, 153–54
  majority leader, 157
  minority leader, 157
  powers of, 140
  president of, 157
  president pro tempore, 157
  procedural rules, 164
  seniority in, 166
  and Supreme Court appointment, 231–34
  unanimous-consent agreements, 164
Senate Appropriations Committee, 160
Senate Ethics Committee, 567
Senatorial courtesy, 235
Seneca Falls convention, 533
Senior Executive Service, 290
Seniority, Congressional members, 165–66
Separate but equal concept, 515, 516*i*, 518
Separation of powers, 62, 73, 74
  meaning of, 62
Serbia, 628
Seventeenth Amendment, 18, 72, 89
Seventh Amendment, 85
Seven Years' War, 35
Sex discrimination, 536–39

heightened-scrutiny test, 538
  involving men, 538
  strict-scrutiny test, 537
  test of reasonableness, 536–37
Sexism, 535–36
Shallus, Jacob, 90
Shame of Cities (Steffens), 568
Shaw, Clay, 187
Shaw v. *Reno*, 144, 146
Shays, Daniel, 25–26, 26*i*
Shays's Rebellion, 25–26, 48, 49
  philosophical foundation of, 33
Shelby, Richard, 167
Sherman Anti-Trust Act, 564
Sherman, Roger, 59, 62
Sierra Club, 424
Silent Spring (Carson), 563, 564, 565
Simpson, Alan, 441
Simpson, O.J., 225*i*, 308*i*, 452, 490, 493
Sinclair, Upton, 564
Single-issue interest groups, 415, 422
Single-member district plurality system, 385
Single-member districts, 343
Sit-ins, meaning of, 521
Sixteenth Amendment, 89, 110, 597*i*
Sixth Amendment, 85, 115, 476, 492, 498–99
Sixth party system, 341, 343
"60 Minutes," 454
Slander, meaning of, 491
Slaton, Lewis, 217
Slavery:
  and Civil War Amendments, 513
  and Constitution, 68–69
  and *Dred Scott* v. *Sandford*, 513
  Emancipation Proclamation, 513–14
  and Fourteenth Amendment, 477
  origins of, 68
  slave auctions, 49*i*
  slave uprisings, 512
  three-fifths compromise, 68
Small Business Administration (SBA), 277
Smith Act of 1940, 221
Smith, Adam, 586
Social class, and political opinion, 309
Social contract:
  purpose of, 32–33
  theorists of, 32–35
Socialization, and media, 454–55
Social security, 570
  indexing of, 572
  taxation of benefits proposal, 603
  types of programs, 570
Social Security Act, 101, 266, 570
Social Security Administration, 279
Social welfare policy, 563, 568–75
  cost of, 575
  elements of, 563
  entitlements, 572–73
  family support programs, 573–74
  growth of, 573
  social security, 570
  War on Poverty programs, 571–72
  welfare reform, 574–75
Socioeconomic status:
  and interest group involvement, 412
  and political opinion, 309
  and political participation, 369
  and tolerance, 314
  and voting, 375
Solicitor general, 240
Somalia, 324, 626, 628
Sons of Liberty, 37*i*, 39
Soundbites, 465–67

examples of, 466
nature of, 466-67
Souter, David, 130, 228i, 234, 248i, 250, 251, 504
South Africa, racial equality, 517
Southeast Asia Resolution, 198, 623
Southern Christian Leadership Conference, 520, 556
Sovereignty, meaning of, 47
Soviet Union:
  and Cold War, 621-23
  and detente, 624-25
  expansionist policy of, 620
  and World War I, 617
  and World War II, 619-20
Speaker of the House, 155
  power of, 155
  role of, 155
Specialization:
  and bureaucracy, 263
  of legislators, 166
Special revenue sharing, 124
Specter, Arlen, 160-61, 232
Speech, freedom of. See Freedom of speech
Speed limit, lifting of national limit, 97-98
Sphere of influence, 616
Spin of news story, 443
Spirit of the Laws, The (Montesquieu), 32
Split-ticket ballots, 378
Spoils system, 270
Sports Illustrated, 447
Stability, and democracy, 13-14
Stagflation, meaning of, 590-91
Stamp Act, 36-37
Stamp Act congress, 37-38
Standing Committee on the Federal Judiciary, 229, 231
Standing committees, 158
Stanley v. Georgia, 246
Stanton, Elizabeth Cady, 91, 533, 534i
Stare decisis, 246
Star Wars, 625
State action:
  and Fourteenth Amendment, 514-15
  meaning of, 514
State party organization, 350
State power:
  concurrent powers, 109-10
  constitutional guarantees and limits on, 108-9, 110
  and dual federalism, 112-13
  nullification theory, 112
  reserved powers, 75, 108-9
  and supremacy clause, 75, 109-10
  and Tenth Amendment, 106, 114, 130
  types of, 107
States:
  Antifederalist position on, 80
  and Article IV of Constitution, 77-78
  and Article VI of Constitution, 78
  and civil liberties, 477-82
  and health care, 102
State's rights, meaning of, 98
Statutory construction, Supreme Court, 221, 223
Steffens, Lincoln, 446
Steimer, Mollie, 480i
Stevens, John Paul, 238, 248, 250, 251
Stevenson, Adlai, 552
Stevens, Ted, 280
Stewardship view, of president, 190
Stewart, Potter, 490, 524
Stone, Harlan Fiske, 242, 242i, 246
Stop-and-frisk searches, 496
Straight-party ticket, 378

Strategic Arms Limitation Treaty (SALT), 624-25
Strategic Arms Limitation Treaty II (SALT II), 625
Strategic Defense Initiative, 625
Straw polls, 301
Strict-scrutiny test, 537
Student Non-Violent Coordinating Council, 556
Subcommittee Bill of Rights, 161
Subcommittees, Congressional, 161-63
Subsequent-punishment, freedom of press, 490
Substantive policies, 549
Suffolk Resolves, 42
Suffrage:
  African Americans, 370, 514
  meaning of, 514
  women, 16i, 370, 534-35
Sugar Act, 36-37
Sullivan, L.B., 491
Sunshine Act, 279, 293
Sununu, John, 205
Superdelegates, 356
Superfund, 564, 565
Supermajority, and amendment process, 86
Superpowers, meaning of, 620
Supplemental Security Income (SSI), 554, 570
Supply-side economics, 590-92
  and budget deficit, 605
  elements of, 590-92
  results of, 591-92
Supremacy clause:
  function of, 65, 75, 106
  preemption of state power, 109-10, 111
Supreme Court:
  analysis of decisions, 251
  appellate jurisdiction, 220, 238
  and Congress, 253-54
  and democracy, 256-57
  docket, 238
  implementation of decisions, 254
  judicial review, 20, 73, 90, 220-21
  law clerks, 244
  original jurisdiction, 220, 238
  and policy making, 556
  public opinion of, 254-56
  solicitor general, 240
  statutory construction, 221, 223
  updating of Constitution, 90
Supreme Court appointment, 227-35
  and American Bar Association, 229, 231
  presidential influence on, 234-35
  and presidential political party, 228-29
  representational factors, 229
  and Senate, 231-34
Supreme Court cases:
  amicus curiae briefs, 240
  briefs, filing of, 240-41
  concurring opinion, 244
  dissenting opinion, 244-45
  majority opinion, 244
  opinion, assignment of, 242-43
  opinion-drafting process, 243-44
  oral argument, 241
  precedents, 246-47
  rule of four, 239
  selection of cases, 238-39
  stare decisis, 246
  trends related to, 239
Supreme Court justices:
  absolutists, 249
  appointment of. See Supreme Court appointment
  chief justice, role of, 246
  classification by four-cell method, 249-50

judicial activism, 249
  judicial character of, 250
  judicial restraint, 248
  liberals/moderates/conservatives, listing of, 252
  political ideology of, 247-48
  voting blocks, 251, 252
Surgeon General, 287
Surveillance function, media, 452
Sutherland, George, 197, 242i
Swaggart, Jimmy, 460
Swann, James E., 218
Swann v. Charlotte-Mecklenburg Board of Education, 526
Sweet, John, 217
Symbolic-original policies, 551-52
Symbolic policies, 549
Symbolic-reflexive policies, 551
Symbolic speech, freedom of, 489
Synar, Mike, 167

Taft, Nellie, 204
Taft, William Howard, 191i, 234, 348
  presidential power of, 191-92, 193
Talk shows, 465
  and presidential election, 465
  talk radio, 449, 465
Task Force on National Health Care Reform, 576
Taxation, 597-601
  and Clinton administration, 600-601, 602
  cross-cultural view, 598-99
  flat tax proposal, 602
  historical view, 597i
  income tax, 598-99
  progressive taxes, 599
  regressive taxes, 599-600
  spending of tax revenues, 602-3
  tax reform, 600-601
  tax revolts, 597
  value-added tax, 602
Tax Court, 226
Tax Reform Act of 1986, 600
Taylor, Zachary, 338
Teamsters, 417
Teapot Dome scandal, 195
Technology, and political participation, 17
Television, 450-51
  cable TV, 451
  narrowcasting, 451
  and political socialization, 307-8
  satellites, 450-51
  talk shows, 465
Tennessee Valley Authority, 266, 278, 564
Tenth Amendment, 85, 106, 108, 114, 130
Term limits, Congress, 388-89
Terrorism, 627
  definition of, 627
Terry v. Ohio, 496
Test of reasonableness, 536-37
Thailand, 624
Thatcher, Margaret, 631i
Third Amendment, 85
Third parties. See Minor parties
Third party system, 339
Third World, 622
Thirteenth Amendment, 2, 18, 89, 513
"This Week with David Brinkley," 460
Thomas, Clarence, 160, 228, 231, 233i, 234, 241, 244, 248i, 452
Thomas (on-line information system), 17
Three-fifths compromise, 68-69, 512
Thrift Institutions Restructuring Act, 564, 567
Thurmond, Strom, 13, 157, 164, 166, 516

Tiananmen Square, 3*i*, 4-5, 33
Time, 447
Title V, 536
Title IX, 103*i*, 536
Tocqueville, Alexis de, 6, 314, 407
Tonkin Gulf Resolution, 198
Torrick, Keith, 217
Total incorporation, of Bill of Rights, 480
Town meeting:
    Clinton's televised town meetings, 202
    definition of, 7
    electronic, 17
    representative town meetings, 8
Townshend Revenue Acts, 38-39
Toxic Substances Control Act, 566
Trade:
    free trade versus protectionism, 627
    General Agreement on Tariffs and Trade (GATT), 607
    North American Free Trade Area (NAFTA), 607-8
    U.S. and Japanese trade negotiations, 608
Transfer payments, 268-69
Treasury Department, 265-66
Treaty of Paris, 25, 48
Treaty power, of president, 183-85
Triad of powers, 102-6
    general welfare clause, 104-6
    interstate commerce clause, 103-4
    operation of, 106
    Tenth Amendment, 106
Trial courts, 224-25
    civil cases, 225
    criminal cases, 225
Triggering mechanism, in policy making process, 555, 556
Trujillo, Raphael, 614
Truman Doctrine, 620
Truman, Harry, 188, 341, 552, 620
    and discrimination, 516
    executive agreements, 630
    seizure of steel mills, 198
Trustees, Congressional members as, 146-47
Tsongas, Paul, 552
Turner, Nat, 512
Turner, Ted, 441
Tuskegee University, 516
Twelfth Amendment, 89, 388
Twentieth Amendment, 89
Twenty-fifth Amendment, 89
Twenty-first Amendment, 87, 88, 89, 90
Twenty-fourth Amendment, 18, 89, 370, 522
Twenty-second Amendment, 89
Twenty-seventh Amendment, 89
Twenty-sixth Amendment, 18, 72, 89, 116, 371
Twenty-third Amendment, 89
Two-party system, 343-45
    cultural aspects of, 344-45
    and electoral college, 344
    institutional aspects of, 343-44
    psychological factors, 345
Two Treatises on Government (Locke), 33-34

Ulyanov, Vladimir, 617
Unanimous-consent agreements, 164
Unions:
    decline in membership, 417
    as interest group, 416-17
    types of, 417
Unitary system, meaning of, 99
United Auto Workers, 408, 417
    PAC contribution of, 433
United Mine Workers, 417

United Nations (UN), 625-26
    and New World Order, 625-26
United States' Information Agency, 634
United States v. Cruikshank, 514, 514-15
United States v. Curtiss-Wright, 197
United States v. Darby, 114
United States v. E.C. Knight, 113
United States v. Eichman, 474
United States v. Leon, 495
United States v. Lopez, 130
United We Stand America, 333, 343, 348
Universal suffrage, definition of, 15-16
Urban enterprise zones, 550
Uruguay Round, General Agreement on Tariffs and Trade (GATT), 583, 607
U.S. Agency for International Development, 628
USA Today, 447, 462
U.S. Information Agency, 628
U.S. News & World Report, 447
U.S. v. Harris, 434

Valenti, Jack, 203
Value-added tax, 602
Values:
    and political opinion, 313-14
    types of American values, 313
Van Buren, Martin, 338
Van Devanter, Willis, 242*i*
Veto:
    of bill, 154
    legislative veto, 196
    line item veto, 164, 196
    override of, 182
    pocket veto, 154, 182
    as presidential power, 181-82
    presidential use of, 155, 182
Vice president, 208-9
    as president of the Senate, 157
    role of, 208-9
Vietnam memorial, 623*i*
Vietnam syndrome, 632
Vietnam War, 622-23
    and Johnson, 197-98
    and Nixon, 198
    protests, 33*i*, 248, 384
    Tonkin Gulf incident, 623
    Vietnamization, 623
Vinson, Fred, 246, 518
Violence, political violence, 384-85
Virginia Plan, 62-64
    basis of, 62-64
    compared to New Jersey Plan, 65
Voice of America, 634
Voter Education Project, 521
Voter turnout, 371-73
    for congressional elections, 386, 387
    cross-cultural view, 372
    historical view, 371-72
    as indicator, 371
    low rates, reasons for, 373-75
    and voter registration laws, 373
Vote Smart, 17
Voting, 369-81
    age and voting tendencies, 375
    and campaigns, 381
    and candidate appeal, 379
    direct democracy, 377-78
    and educational level, 375, 376
    historical view, 369-71
    and income, 375, 376
    initiatives, 377
    low voter registration, reasons for, 373-75

and partisanship, 376
    and party identification, 378
    and policies/issues, 379-81
    referenda, 377
    retrospective voting, 380-81
    and socioeconomic status, 375
    split-ticket ballots, 378
    straight-party ticket, 378
    voters, profile of, 375-76
    voter turnout, 371-73
Voting rights:
    African Americans, 370, 514, 515-16, 522, 524
    amendments related to, 18
    Hispanic Americans, 540
    and literacy tests, 370, 515
    Native Americans, 541
    universal suffrage concept, 15-16
    voting age, 116
    women, 534-35
Voting Rights Act, 370, 522, 540

Wagner Act, 266
Wallace, George, 102*i*, 348
Wards Cove Packing Co. v. Antonio, 532
War on Poverty, 115, 524, 568*i*
    programs of, 571-72
War powers, of president, 197-99
War Powers Act, 198, 199, 632-33
    aspects of, 632-33
    controversy related to, 632
    effectiveness of, 633
Warren, Earl, 228, 246, 518-19
Warren, Mercy Otis, 80
Warsaw Pact, 621
"War of the Worlds" broadcast, 448
Washington, Booker T., 516
Washington, George, 20, 26, 42, 44, 60, 66*i*, 70, 81, 202, 336, 388
    election as president, 337
    on political parties, 336
Washington Legal Foundation, 530
Washington Post, 453-54
Washington v. Texas, 479
Watergate, 177-78, 179, 212-13
    and election reform, 397
    and investigative journalism, 453-54
    and Nixon reputation, 188
Water Pollution Control Act, 126, 564, 565
Waxman, Henry, 547, 562
Ways and Means Committee, 158, 160
Wealth of Nations, The (Smith), 586
Weber, Max, 263
Webster, Daniel, 200, 338
Webster v. Reproductive Health Service, 504, 556
Weed-and-seed programs, 550, 560
Weeks v. United States, 494
Welfare:
    cost of, 575
    reform proposals, 574-75
Welfare programs, public opinion on, 327
Welfare state, and New Deal, 267
Welles, Orson, 448
Whig Party, 81, 270
    historical view, 339, 340
    political successes of, 338
Whistle Blower Act, 290
White, Byron, 91, 217, 228, 235, 251
White, Edward, 234-35
White House, working environment of, 203
White House Office, 203-6
    chief of staff, 205-6
White supremacy groups, 539

on Internet, 539
Ku Klux Klan (KKK), 314*i*, 488, 514, 540
Whitewater affair, 171
Wilhelm, David, 352*i*
Will, George, 460*i*
Wilson, Edith, 204
Wilson, James, 64, 67, 69, 83
Wilson, Pete, 365
Wilson, Woodrow, 158, 193, 256, 339, 552, 617
  persuasive powers of, 200-201
Winner-take-all system, 355, 385, 393
Winthrop, John, 30
WISH, 429*i*
Wofford, Harris, 136, 168
Wolf v. *Colorado*, 478
Woman's Party, 535
Women:
  in bureaucracy, 274-75
  Clinton appointees, 228, 229, 282
  in Congress, 141-42*i*
  and Constitution, 79, 536
  federal court appointments, 237
  feminization of poverty, 568-69
  gender gap, 311-12

glass ceiling, 530, 538-39
political opinion, 311-13
sex discrimination, 535-39
on Supreme Court, 228, 229
Title IX, 103*i*
voting patterns, 312
Women's Caucus, 170
Women's National Loyal League, 534
Women's rights:
  athletic opportunities in schools, 536
  citizenship rights, 535
  to equal pay, 536
  history of women's movement, 533-35
  and National Organization for Women (NOW), 536
  Seneca Falls convention, 533
  voting rights, 16*i*, 370, 534-35
Woodhull, Victoria, 181*i*
Woodward, Bob, 178, 447, 453
Workfare, 573*i*, 575
Workplace schools, 525
World Bank, 583, 606
World Trade Center bombings, 627
World Trade Organization, 583, 606

World War I, 617-18
  beginning of, 617
  and Soviet Union, 617
World War II, 618-20
  U.S. entry, 618
Wounded Knee, 541*i*
Wright, James, 155, 156
Writ of certiorari, 238

Yalta, 630
Yates, Robert, 80
Yellow journalism, 447
Yeltsin, Boris, 615, 637*i*
York, Duke of, 31
Youngstown Sheet and Tube Company v. *Sawyer*, 198
Yugoslavia, 615

Zeigler, Ron, 177
Zimmer, Dick, 388
Zoblocki, Clement, 631